Violence in the Model City

Violence in the Model City

The Cavanagh Administration,
Race Relations, and
the Detroit Riot of 1967

S IDNEY F INE

Michigan State University Press
East Lansing

∞ The paper used in this publication meets the minimum requirements of ANSI/NISO
Z39.48-1992 (R 1997) (Permanence of Paper).

 Michigan State University Press
East Lansing, Michigan 48823-5245

Printed and bound in the United States of America.

13 12 11 10 09 08 07   1 2 3 4 5 6 7 8 9 10

LIBRARY OF CONGRESS CATALOGING-IN-PUBLICATION DATA
Fine, Sidney, 1920–
Violence in the model city : the Cavanagh administration, race relations, and the Detroit riot of
1967 / [Sidney Fine].
p. cm.
Includes bibliographical references and index.
ISBN-13: 978-0-87013-815-7 (MSUP pbk. : alk. paper)
ISBN-10: 0-472-10104-8 (UMP original hardcover ed.)
1. Detroit (Mich.)—Race relations—History—20th century. 2. Riots—Michigan—Detroit—
History—20th century. 3. Violence—Michigan—Detroit—History—20th century. 4. African
Americans—Michigan—Detroit—History—20th century. 5. Cavanagh, Jerome P. 6. Detroit
(Mich.)—Social policy. I. Title.
F574.D49N4394 2007
977.4'3400496073—dc22
2007026119

Cover design by Heather Truelove Aiston

g green
press
INITIATIVE
Michigan State University Press is a member of the Green Press Initiative and
is committed to developing and encouraging ecologically responsible publishing
practices. For more information about the Green Press Initiative and the use of recycled paper
in book publishing, please visit www.greenpressinitiative.org.

Visit Michigan State University Press on the World Wide Web at www.msupress.msu.edu

To Daniel and Emily

From the Publisher

To mark the fortieth anniversary of the 1967 Detroit riot, Michigan State University Press is issuing a new paperback edition of Sidney Fine's masterful work *Violence in the Model City: The Cavanaugh Administration, Race Relations and the Detroit Riot of 1967*. Published originally in 1989, this book remains *the* definitive study of what followed a 23 July police raid on an illegal after-hours drinking establishment—a "blind pig"—in Detroit. In addition, *Violence in the Model City* is a comprehensive and detailed analysis of public policy during the years following the tragedy, as well as of the quarter century of political insensitivity, white racism, and poorly conceived urban planning that characterized Detroit between a 1943 riot and the bloody event in 1967. It is a chronicle of how a "model city" was transformed into an urban-American war zone.

In many ways, Detroit's 1967 riot was an event of "the Sixties," a part of the tableau of escalating violence that occurred in many cities at a time when the nation was obsessed with the Vietnam War. It also was a hostile reaction to neglect, mistreatment, and misplaced beliefs held by many northern whites that integration issues, "the civil rights struggle," and "racial prejudice" were artifacts of the Old South. The late 1960s and the Detroit riot demonstrated that segregation and racism were not confined to regions below of the Mason Dixon Line. Jim Crow was alive in the north; he just showed his face a bit differently there.

That summer of 1967, Detroit citizens, both black and white, took to the streets armed with guns and other weapons; buildings burned, business were looted; people were killed. The Detroit Police Department, the Michigan National Guard, and ultimately the U.S. Army intervened to restore order. In the process, authorities unleashed brutal counterattacks, some against innocent citizens—most of whom were black; at least forty-three people died. A "model American city" was transformed almost overnight into a symbol of all that was wrong with American urban life. This is a disturbing narrative that makes for arresting reading. Although Fine's book was out of print for a number of years, it remains a key point of departure for informed readers who seek to understand what happened to Detroit during the second half of the twentieth century. Forty years after the riot, *Violence in the Model City* provides us with an opportunity to revisit 1967 and to measure the distance we have come since that time. It should also inspire us to ask ourselves what, if anything, we have learned.

Preface

I have sought in this volume to place the great Detroit riot of 1967 in the context of race-relations developments in the city during the years 1962–69, when Jerome P. Cavanagh was Detroit's mayor. The Detroit riot of 1967 was the most destructive of the many urban riots of the 1960s. It came as a surprise to most observers, since Detroit during the first five-and-one-half years of the Cavanagh mayoralty was widely regarded as a model for the nation in the area of race relations. I have consequently sought in chapters 1 through 6 to trace the history of race relations in Detroit during the Cavanagh years preceding the riot, to explain why Detroit was regarded as a model city, and to judge whether that reputation was deserved.

The Detroit riot began on July 23, 1967, following a triggering event that was to a large degree the result of chance. The ebb and flow of the disturbance that followed were the product, in the main, of the interaction between the rioters and the forces of law and order, city, state, and national, that sought to control the disorder. I focus in chapters 7 through 15 on the behavior of the rioters, the reaction of the control forces and the criminal justice system, the identity of the rioters, and the meaning of their actions. The riot had important consequences for the city of Detroit, the state of Michigan, and the nation, consequences that are the subject of chapters 16 through 19. In the final chapter, I compare Detroit in the year of the riot with the city twenty years after that event.

I incurred a substantial number of scholarly obligations in the preparation of this book that I am pleased to acknowledge. My research was facilitated by a grant-in-aid from the Lyndon Baines Johnson Foundation. Dr. Elliot D. Luby permitted me to use the "Violence in the Model City" title that he had given to an unpublished manuscript on the riot whose preparation he had supervised. I am indebted to Kathleen McGauley for permission to examine the indispensable Jerome P. Cavanagh Papers; Chief William L. Hart, for permission to examine relevant files in the Detroit Police Department; Paul J. Scheips, for permission to examine documents pertaining to Task Force Detroit that he had brought together in the Center of Military History; George

Edwards, for permission to examine the George Edwards Papers; W. A. Anderson, for access to several record groups in the Office of the Adjutant General of the Department of the Army; and to Professors Joel D. Aberbach and Jack L. Walker, for permission to examine papers now deposited in the Michigan Historical Collections as the Institute for Public Policy Studies, Aberbach-Walker Riot Studies.

The following individuals generously made documents of one sort or another available to me: Dr. Nathan S. Caplan, Robert Conot, Dr. Lillian Gleiberman, Professor Harlan Hahn, Captain Michael H. Johnson, Professor Maurice Kelman, Professor Edward Lurie, Dr. Philip P. Mason, Professor Xavier Nicholas, Paul J. Scheips, Kae Resh, Jonathan Rose, Professor Peter H. Rossi, Stephen C. Schlesinger, Winston Wessels, and Albert Zack.

My research was skillfully assisted by Dr. Francis X. Blouin, Thomas E. Powers, Nancy Bartlett, and the staff of the Bentley Library of the Michigan Historical Collections; Dr. Philip P. Mason, Warner Pflug, and the staff of the Walter Reuther Library of the Archives of Labor History and Urban Affairs; Inspector Micheal J. Falvo and Lieutenant Donna Cotton of the Detroit Police Department; Mrs. Alice C. Dalligan and Joseph Oldenberg of the Burton Historical Collection; Betty W. Havlena of the *Detroit News*; LeRoy Barnett of the State Archives of the Michigan History Division; Lieutenant Ostrom of the State Police Department; Elizabeth Yakel of the Archives of the Archdiocese of Detroit; Harry Middleton, Tina Lawson, Gary Gallagher, Nancy Smith, and Linda Hanson of the Lyndon Baines Johnson Presidential Library; and David R. Kepley of the National Archives and Records Administration. Dale Austin prepared the maps for the book, and Pat Zacharias and Jeanette Bartz of the *Detroit News* assisted me in the selection of photographs.

My colleagues Professors Terrence McDonald and Bradford Perkins gave the manuscript a detailed reading and made numerous suggestions for its improvement. Christine Weideman assisted me on some of the interviews that I conducted and performed one or two research chores for me. Stephen Grossbart provided me with computer assistance. I owe thanks to Jeanette Diuble, Janet Rose, and Julia Routson for the typing of the manuscript. As in all my endeavors, my wife, Jean Fine, encouraged and assisted me in the preparation of this book.

I have received permission from the *Michigan Quarterly Review* and the *Wayne Law Review*, respectively, to use passages from my articles: "Chance and History: Some Aspects of the Detroit Riot of 1967," *Michigan Quarterly Review* 25 (Spring 1986): 403–23; and "Rioters and Judges: The Response of the Criminal Justice System to the Detroit Riot of 1967," *Wayne Law Review* 33, no. 5 (1987): 1723–64.

Contents

Maps

CHAPTER 1

"Phooie on Louie"

In an editorial of July 25, 1967, the *Washington Post* characterized the riot then raging in Detroit as "the greatest tragedy of all the long succession of Negro ghetto outbursts." "For years," the *Post* editorialized, "Detroit has been the American model of intelligence and courage applied to the governance of a huge industrial city." The *Post* was referring specifically to developments in Detroit that had followed the accession to the mayoralty in January 1962 of Jerome P. Cavanagh.[1]

What especially attracted favorable national attention to Detroit during the Cavanagh years was the reputed state of its race relations. The Cavanagh administration, however, was heir to a concern about race that had characterized leadership circles in Detroit since 1943. Detroit in that year had suffered through a terrible race riot, and some members of the city's establishment were determined that the experience not be repeated.[2]

Erupting on June 20, 1943, the 1943 riot was the ugly climax to an increasingly bitter racial conflict between whites and blacks in the wartime city over jobs and housing and clashes between the races in the schools, the parks, and on the city buses. The riot began in the black ghetto, in Paradise Valley on the city's lower east side, where blacks attacked whites and white-owned stores. It then spread to Woodward Avenue, the city's main artery, where gangs of whites attacked and beat blacks and burned black-owned automobiles. As Thurgood Marshall reported, Detroit's overwhelmingly white police force largely used "persuasion" to deter white rioters but "the ultimate in force" to subdue black rioters. Of the thirty-four deaths resulting from the riot, twenty-five were blacks, seventeen of them shot to death by the police. The riot, additionally, resulted in 675 injuries and 1,893 arrests.[3]

The Detroit riot was put down by federal troops, who were first deployed on the city's streets during the late evening of June 21. The mayor of Detroit, Edward J. Jeffries, Jr., later conceded that he had waited too long in asking Michigan's governor for additional manpower to put down the riot; and the subsequent arrival of federal troops was delayed for about twelve hours at the height of the riot because neither the state nor federal authorities who dealt with this matter knew what the proper procedure was for a state government to request federal aid in subduing domestic violence. Following the riot, the War Department provided its commands and state governors with a memorandum regarding the legal prerequisites for the use of federal troops in a civil disorder; and responding to the request of President Franklin D. Roosevelt, the secretary of war and the attorney general prepared a second memorandum specifically for the president that "succinctly" advised him of the law on the subject. No one in a responsible position in Washington or Lansing appeared to be aware of the existence of either of these memoranda when the need for federal troops became apparent during the Detroit riot of 1967.[4]

"The responsible authorities at all three levels of government, City, State, and Federal, were greenhorns . . . [regarding] race riots," Jeffries told the Common Council at the end of June, "but we are greenhorns no longer. We are veterans. I admit we made some mistakes, but we will not make the same ones again."[5] Jeffries proved to be a very poor prophet. When Detroit was once again the scene of a major riot in 1967, it turned out that city, state, and federal officials had learned next to nothing from the 1943 riot regarding the proper procedure for securing federal troops, riot control tactics, and the processing of riot arrestees. Institutional memory, as has so often been true in the nation's history, proved to be lamentably short.

Toward the end of 1943 Jeffries appointed an Interracial Peace Committee, which limited itself to studying the causes of the riot and making recommendations to prevent a recurrence. The mayor replaced this group in January 1944 with the Mayor's Interracial Committee, an eleven-member body that has been characterized as "the first regular city biracial agency." During the next several years the committee sought to monitor racial problems in Detroit and to deal with racial discrimination in housing, employment, and restaurants. It created the Coordinating Council on Human Relations in 1947, thereby linking the committee with a variety of community groups interested in civil rights. By the end of 1960 fifty-seven different agencies were affiliated with the council, which conducted leadership clinics concerned with such matters as education and housing and sought in its meetings to develop more enlightened public attitudes with regard to human relations.[6]

The Mayor's Interracial Committee gave way in 1953 to the Detroit Commission on Community Relations (CCR), created by the Common Council and authorized to "seek to correct situations" that it found "to be endangering the peace and welfare of the community or to be unjust and discriminatory." Lacking enforcement powers, the commission was to rely on "negotiation and education" to resolve "tensions, conflict and practices of discrimination or . . . activities of individuals or groups" that incited discord or disadvantaged "persons or groups because of race, color, origin or ancestry." As of 1962, the committee consisted of fifteen members appointed by the mayor and a secretary-director appointed by the commission subject to the mayor's approval.[7]

In the decade and a half following World War II Detroit experienced economic and population shifts that profoundly affected the well-being of its inhabitants and the character of its race relations. The loss of defense contracts held by the Big Three automobile manufacturers and the decentralization of their operations, the decline in employment at Chrysler Corporation, the shutdown of Packard and Hudson, the impact of the reduced demand for parts on auto supplier firms, and the flight of businesses to the suburbs drastically affected employment in Detroit in the 1950s. The city suffered through four recessions in the 1950s; its unemployment rate at the end of the decade was 10.2 percent overall and 18.2 percent for blacks. Unemployment was especially high among black youths. The Detroit Commission on Children and Youth reported that in July 1960, 76 percent of blacks between the ages of 16 and 19 were unemployed, 35 percent between 20 and 24, and 21 percent between 25 and 29.[8]

During the 1950s Detroit lost 23.4 percent of its white population, while the number of nonwhites, all but about five thousand of whom were black, increased from 303,000 to 487,000 and their percentage of the total population from 16 to 29.1. Since it was predominantly young white families that left the city for the suburbs, the whites who remained in Detroit were older on the average than the city's blacks. The median age of whites in the city in 1960 was 36.4 years, as compared with a median age of 26.4 years for blacks; and whereas 31.9 percent of the whites were 19 years of age or less, 42.8 percent of the blacks were in this younger age group.[9]

When blacks began arriving in Detroit in fairly large numbers after 1910, they lived primarily on the lower east side (east of Woodward and south of Gratiot) in the Black Bottom and the "notorious" Paradise Valley. Just after World War II blacks moved farther east to Mt. Elliott, north toward East Grand Boulevard, and south to the Detroit River. The construction of the Chrysler and Edsel Ford freeways and the Gratiot Redevelopment Project in the 1950s spelled the end of Paradise Valley and part of the lower east side ghetto and caused many blacks from the area to move across Woodward to the city's near northwest side, north of West Grand Boulevard and east of Grand River. They were soon joined by other migrants, displaced by the Lafayette Park development, a southern extension of the Gratiot Project; the denizens of Michigan Avenue's skid row, forced to relocate by the Central Business District Number One Development; and blacks moving north from the inner city south of West Grand Boulevard. Some blacks had occupied homes between the Lodge Freeway west of Woodward and Twelfth Street before World War II, but the heavy postwar black migration was to streets farther west, between Twelfth Street and Linwood (see maps 1 and 2).[10]

The transition from white to black on Detroit's near northwest side occurred at a remarkably rapid rate. The Twelfth Street area had been a Jewish neighborhood in the 1930s, but in a familiar pattern of neighborhood succession, as blacks moved in after World War II, the Jews moved out. The first black migrants to the area were middle-class persons seeking to escape the confines of Paradise Valley. They enjoyed about "five good years" in their new homes until underworld and seedier elements from Hastings Street and Paradise Valley, the poor and the indigent from the inner city, and winos and derelicts from skid row flowed into the area. Some of the commercial establishments on Twelfth Street gave way to pool halls, liquor stores, sleazy bars, pawn shops, and second-hand businesses. Already suffering from a housing shortage and a lack of open space, Twelfth Street became even more "densely packed" as apartments were subdivided and six to eight families began to live where two had resided before. The 21,376 persons per square mile in the area in 1960 were almost double the city's average. "The blight — human misery — was setting in," a black who lived in the area at the time recalled. "You could feel it in the air, smell it coming rancid out of the bars, watch it . . . on the faces of kids not 20 years old yet."[11]

The streets running east and west of Twelfth Street contained many decent-looking dwellings with well-kept lawns that surprised visitors expecting to find a typical big-city slum in the area. Twelfth Street's commercial strip, however, running north from West Grand Boulevard to Clairmount Avenue, was a congested, unkempt, "ugly neon scar," with "squalid apartments" above its first-story shops. It was "the nastiest street in town," "Sin Street," a jungle, where, it was said, you could get "anything, pot, horse, numbers, hookers, young girls, young boys."[12]

Blind pigs, that is, after-hours drinking establishments, and prostitution were two of the major industries of Twelfth Street. Prostitution was one Twelfth Street activity that involved racial mixing, the black prostitutes serving a predominantly white clientele whom they charged a reported $10 for ten minutes. What you could always see on Twelfth Street, a young man who lived there in the 1960s recalled, was "the hustlers, pimps, prostitutes and cops." The police, as he remembered it, "rode around . . . busting prostitutes, dope pushers, and just plain fucking with people." As Twelfth Street became "a city-wide attraction for those seeking the bizarre," its problems became even more acute.[13]

The "physical and social deterioration" on Twelfth Street and its immediate environs led to conflict between the home-owning, middle-class black residents and the rootless lower-class renters who had more recently moved into the area. Older residents began to complain that there were "too many residents from the eastside" in the neighborhood and that the neighborhood itself was starting "to look like the lower eastside." Troubled by the disorganization of family life, rising crime rates, loitering around commercial establishments, inadequate police protection, the failure of impecunious tenants and absentee landlords to maintain the rental property that predominated in the area, and the "cultural standard of living" of the newcomers, the homeowners in the late 1950s turned to the city government for help. Meeting with Mayor Louis C. Miriani on August 11, 1960, a coordinating committee representing five neighborhood associations pleaded for city assistance in improving the quality of life in the Twelfth Street area. Ten city departments thereupon sought "to eliminate unwholesome conditions" in the neighborhood, but without visible result.[14]

Whatever the problems of Twelfth Street, blacks in the area west of Woodward and north of West Grand Boulevard and in the neighborhoods surrounding Twelfth Street were, generally speaking, more affluent at the end of the 1950s than blacks in the inner city south of the boulevard. To speak of the black west side or of the Twelfth Street area as a whole, however, is to mask the fact that there were sizable differences in income even among census tracts adjoining one another. Some census tracts in the Twelfth Street area had median family incomes in 1959 well below the city average for nonwhites, while some were well above the average. Wherever they lived, however, Detroit blacks, collectively speaking, had considerably smaller incomes than Detroit whites. A detailed study by the CCR revealed that the median family income of whites in 1959 was $7,050, as compared to $4,370 for nonwhites.[15]

Detroit blacks at the end of the 1950s not only had less income than whites; they were also substantially less healthy. Comparing a nearly all-white and a nearly all-black area in the city, the Detroit Urban League (DUL) found that the TB rate was 2 per 100,000 for whites and 33.3 for blacks; the heart disease rate, 418.4 per 100,000 for whites and 649.1 for blacks; and the infant mortality rate, 10.1 per 1,000 live births for whites and 35.1 for blacks. There were also substantial differences in the family structure of whites and blacks. Whereas 6.9 percent of white families in the Detroit standard metropolitan statistical area were headed by females, 19.1 percent of black families had female heads. Nearly one-third of all black children under eighteen, as compared to 7.6 percent of white children, lived in broken homes.[16]

Reflecting the temper of the times, the growing number of blacks, and the development of "a significant middle class" in the black community, Detroit black organizations as the 1950s drew to a close seemed more inclined than they had been to confront the city government with their demands for equality of opportunity.[17] The "most important organization" representing the city's blacks at the time was the Detroit branch of the National Association for the Advancement of Colored People (NAACP). With its twenty-four thousand members, the Detroit unit was the largest NAACP affiliate in the nation.[18]

Unlike the Detroit NAACP, which had gained a reputation for militancy, the DUL had traditionally been "relatively inactive and conservative." It became somewhat more aggressive beginning in 1960, however, when Francis Kornegay replaced John Dancy as executive director. The Detroit chapter of the Congress of Racial Equality was more activist than the NAACP, but it had a rather small membership that included many whites. Detroit's black professionals and businessmen had their own organization, the Cotillion Club. Although it had originated toward the end of the 1940s as a social organization, the club, which had about 650 members, began to involve itself actively in civic and political affairs in the 1960s.[19]

The United Automobile Workers (UAW), more than any other organization, helped to organize Detroit's black community to play an active role in the city. Most of Detroit's seventy-five thousand black union members belonged to the UAW, and many blacks who became active in Democratic politics in Michigan gained their political experience as UAW stewards, committeemen, or rank-and-file members. Lacking a political organization of their own in nonpartisan Detroit, blacks, led by the UAW, became part of a political coalition—including labor, liberals, minority groups, and regular Democrats—that became increasingly important in the state following the gubernatorial victory of G. Mennen Williams in 1948. Black leaders in Detroit, the *Detroit News* reported in October 1962, thought that "the marriage of labor and politics" had been the single most important factor in assuring black "progress" during the preceding two decades. It was this "marriage" that contributed to the election of the city's first black councilman in 1957 and a black member of the city's Board of Education in 1955.[20]

Concerned about the lack of black representation in the highest councils of the UAW and trade union discrimination against black workers, UAW leaders Horace Sheffield, Nelson Jack Edwards, and Robert "Buddy" Battle joined other Detroit unionists in 1957 to form the Trade Union Leadership Council (TULC). Although it was initially concerned with the elimination of job discrimination against blacks, the TULC's interests soon broadened to the promotion of "community civil rights objectives" in general. By 1962 the TULC had a membership of nine to ten thousand black and white unionists, and it had become an important pressure group in the city.[21]

When the United States Commission on Civil Rights held hearings in Detroit on December 14 and 15, 1960, the city's civil rights leaders vented their concerns about discrimination against blacks in jobs, education, and housing and also about the recruitment procedures of the Detroit Police Department. These same concerns were to echo throughout the years leading to the 1967 riot.

The disparity in occupational status between whites and blacks in Detroit as of 1960 was striking. Whereas 49.3 percent of white workers were classified as white collar, 20.7 percent of black workers were so classified. Only 7.6 percent of the black workers but 19.9 percent of the white workers were classified as professional or managerial. Twice as many black as white workers proportionally (70.2 percent compared to 35.2 percent) were categorized as operatives (assemblers, polishers, truck drivers, etc.), laborers, service workers (janitors, waiters), or household workers.[22]

Although blacks found jobs in large numbers in the auto industry beginning in the 1940s, UAW president Walter Reuther told the Civil Rights Commission that his union had failed to persuade even one major auto manufacturer to agree to a fair employment clause in its contract with the UAW. He conceded that the union's Fair Practices and Anti-Discrimination Department had been ineffective in the area of hiring, as figures for the skilled trades in the Big Three's Detroit area plants unmistakably revealed. Although one quarter of the employees in Chrysler's Detroit area plants, for example, were black, there were only twenty-four blacks among the 7,425 skilled workers in these plants.[23]

The executive director of the Detroit Round Table of the National Conference of Christians and Jews told the Civil Rights Commission that employers, despite Michigan's Fair Employment Practices Act, discriminated against blacks in employment by "subtle and sophisticated devices." Two-thirds of the twelve hundred cases of discrimination filed with the state's Fair Employment Practices Commission between 1955 and 1960 originated in the greater Detroit area, and more than 90 percent of them involved race. In just under 50 percent of the cases, the commission found enough evidence of discrimination to warrant conciliation efforts.[24]

The DUL expressed its concern to the Civil Rights Commission about "inequities" in the hiring of young blacks. Less than 2 percent of the apprentices receiving training in the construction trades in the Detroit public schools, which served only apprentices already hired, were black. A similarly small percentage of blacks were enrolled in the cooperative educational program of the Detroit public schools, which combined classroom instruction and supervised employment.[25]

The Detroit public school system was a fiscally independent organization headed by a seven-member board of education elected at large on a nonpartisan basis. Citizen groups complained in the late 1940s and the 1950s that the board was insufficiently responsive to community concerns. This helps to explain why the school board, in seeking a new superintendent of schools in 1956, selected Samuel H. Brownell, a recognized advocate of citizen participation who had previously served as superintendent of schools in Grosse Pointe, Michigan, and as United States commissioner of education. In 1957 Brownell appointed a Citizens Advisory Committee on School Needs, headed by George Romney, then the president of American Motors. In its report eighteen months later, the committee made a series of recommendations regarding curriculum, personnel, school community relations, school plant, and school finance. After the report was submitted, the voters in April 1959 approved a substantial millage and bonding increase that enabled the school district to devote $90 million to a building program over the next five years. The school building program in the preceding ten years had centered in northeastern and northwestern Detroit, where the school population had been growing rapidly and inner-city building needs had largely been neglected. The 1959–64 school construction program, however, was primarily directed at the "old city."[26]

Blacks complained that the school administration was pursuing racially discriminatory policies that resulted in the segregation of both students and faculties. At the beginning of the 1960s, seventy-five of Detroit's public schools were all white, and eight were all black; thirty-one had at least a 90 percent white student enrollment, and seventy had at least a 90 percent black enrollment; only eighty-nine had a mixed enrollment (more than 10 percent of both races). White schools had white teachers, whereas black teachers, who made up 21.6 percent of the faculty, were concentrated in black schools.[27]

The school administration insisted that segregated student bodies resulted from segregated housing patterns and that black teachers taught in black schools because the schools were in the neighborhoods where the teachers lived and preferred to teach. But critics of school administration policies, including the black member of the Board of Education, charged that as blacks moved westward in the 1950s, school authorities redrew the boundaries of the system's nine administrative districts so as to maintain a pattern of segregation, a contention disputed by Brownell. Whatever the cause, as of 1961, a majority of the students in four districts were black, including 95 percent of the students in the center district, and three districts were almost entirely white.[28]

Arthur Johnson, executive secretary of the Detroit NAACP at the time, later characterized Brownell as "a very able man" but "one who didn't really want to come to terms with race." Brownell, Johnson remarked, knew the situation was "not all right" but could not "bring himself to really break with tradition." He was "cold," George Crockett, who took the school system to court, said of Brownell, "he wasn't any . . . loveboat for the blacks." Brownell and the school board, however, were by no means unresponsive to the changing composition of Detroit's school population. In December 1955 the board voted to require contractors to include a stipulation not to discriminate in their contracts with the school system. The next month the board adopted the provisions of the Michigan Fair Employment Practices Act as the official policy of the school system. In a successful effort to increase the number of black teachers, the board of education in 1956 created biracial teacher recruiting teams and biracial selection review committees. In 1959 the board began to eliminate the optional attendance areas in neighborhoods undergoing transition from white to black that permitted pupils in these areas to attend either one of two high schools and, in effect, enabled white pupils to escape attending predominantly black high schools.

After committing the school system in a 1959 bylaw not to "discriminate against any person or group because of race, color, creed, or national origin," the school board in December 1959 appointed a Citizens Advisory Committee on Equal Educational Opportunities. The committee over the next two years made a study of the school system that confirmed many of the integrationists' criticisms and led the school administration to modify some of its policies. In 1960 the board adopted an open schools policy that permitted parents, if the school their children would normally have attended was unable to provide them with "schooling essential" to them, to send the children to any school that had space, provided that the parents furnished the transportation. When the school board arranged in the fall of 1960 to transfer 311 black elementary school children from two overcrowded inner-city schools to two all-white schools and one almost entirely white school on the city's far northwest side, a parents' group in the area began to circulate petitions for the recall of the school board members, and parents kept about 60 percent of the school children from attending classes for three days.[29]

Seeking to cope with the growing problem of school dropouts, the Brownell administration introduced a job-upgrading program that was later hailed by the school superintendent as the "grandaddy" of federal programs to aid unemployed school dropouts. The Detroit program provided unemployed dropouts between the ages of sixteen and twenty-one with counseling, some classroom work, and subsidized work experience in city departments, social agencies, or nonprofit organizations.[30]

Brownell played a leading role in persuading educators to focus on the special needs of culturally deprived youngsters in urban school systems. With Brownell and the superintendent of schools in Chicago taking the lead, school systems in the nation's fourteen largest cities joined to create the Great Cities School Improvement Project, which made the "total education of . . . culturally different children" its special concern.

The school systems involved in the Great Cities Project turned to the Ford Foundation for support, but pending a decision from that source, the Detroit Board of Education initiated a pilot program in September 1959 in two elementary schools and one junior high school. When Ford Foundation funding became available in June 1960, Detroit extended the program to an additional four schools and a total of 10,400 students in the seven schools. The schools were each provided with a school community agent, who was supposed to "bridge the gap" between the school and the community, a visiting teacher or social worker whose special concern was the emotionally disturbed child, and a "coaching teacher" who was responsible for remedial education. The project also included staff orien-

tation training, field trips, after-school educational and recreational programs for students and adults, improvements in instructional equipment
and materials, and new methods of teaching. The program was eventually extended to additional schools with the federal government's
support.[31]

Housing, Richard V. Marks, the secretary-director of the CCR,
declared in 1960, was "the crucial area of intergroup conflict" in Detroit.
The housing concerns of Detroit's black leadership in the 1950s centered
about segregated public and private housing. In 1943 it became official
city policy to preserve the racial characteristics of neighborhoods in
locating public housing projects. This policy was rescinded in 1952, after
which one previously all-white project was integrated. That very little
had changed, however, became evident in June 1954 when a federal
district court enjoined the Detroit Housing Commission (DHC) from
maintaining racially segregated projects, leasing housing units on the
basis of color or race, and listing applicants for public housing separately
by race. On appeal, the DHC secured a delay in implementing the court
order so that it could develop "orderly procedures" to desegregate its
projects. Beginning slowly in April 1955, the process of integration culminated in March 1960, when the DHC implemented a strong policy
statement that pledged the commission to follow a policy of open occupancy in its projects.[32]

In testifying before the Civil Rights Commission in December 1960,
Marks bluntly but correctly stated that the "overall character of the
housing market" in Detroit was one of "racial restriction." Despite the
spatial expansion of black residences in the 1950s, "invisible walls" continued to separate whites and blacks. Blacks, indeed, were actually more
segregated in their housing in 1960 than they had been thirty years earlier. Between 1930 and 1960 the percentage of blacks living in areas 90
percent or more black increased from 15.8 to 23, and those living in areas
between 50 and 89 percent black, from 33 to 61.8. Slightly more than
half of Detroit's blacks lived in predominantly white areas (50–89.9 percent white) in 1930, but only 15.2 percent of the city's blacks lived in such
areas in 1960. According to the oft-cited study of urban residential segregation by Karl E. and Alma F. Taeuber, Detroit was somewhat less
segregated in 1960 than Philadelphia, Cleveland, and Chicago but more
segregated than New York, Newark, and Los Angeles.[33]

Although the Federal Housing Administration was partly responsible, the director-secretary of the DHC thought that the "root cause" for
residential segregation in Detroit was the practices of its realtors. Not
only were they disinclined to give blacks the opportunity to buy homes in
white areas, but lending institutions also refused to provide loans to
blacks desiring to purchase homes in such neighborhoods or to builders
planning to construct homes adjacent to white neighborhoods that would
be made available to blacks. Of the 330,000 new housing units built in

the Detroit metropolitan area between 1950 and 1960, only 3 percent were made available to blacks. Middle-class blacks had to compete for the "better moderately aged housing" that whites disposed of when they left for the suburbs, while poor blacks were "forced to forage in the aged, less insurable, housing trash piles" in the inner city. It is consequently not surprising that 72 percent of Detroit's blacks in 1960, as compared to only 17 percent of the whites, lived in the lowest-rated socioeconomic areas of the city. When blacks were able to move into a home in a white neighborhood, they were sometimes subjected to harassment by their white neighbors.[34]

Whereas 69.6 percent of Detroit's whites in 1960 lived in housing built before 1939, 91 percent of the nonwhites lived in such dwellings. The homes nonwhites lived in, moreover, were less valuable and less soundly built than white-owned homes. The median value of owner-occupied nonwhite homes in 1960 was $10,200, that of owner-occupied white homes, $12,600; and 27.9 percent of nonwhite homes, as compared to 9.8 percent of the white homes, were dilapidated or deteriorating. Unlike Detroit whites, 64.7 percent of whom owned their homes, 61.1 percent of the nonwhites lived in rental units. Although nonwhites lived in inferior dwellings as compared to whites, they nevertheless paid approximately the same rent as their white counterparts: $76 was the median rent per month for nonwhites, $77 for whites. Since they had lower incomes than whites, rent absorbed 29.2 percent of the income of nonwhite renters, as compared to 19.7 percent of the income of white renters.[35]

Of greater importance in terms of race relations in Detroit than education and housing and more directly related to the 1967 riot was the state of police-community relations. At the time of the 1943 riot, the Detroit Police Department was reportedly "one of the most bigoted" departments in the nation. During the next seventeen years the racial composition of the department changed but slightly and its reputation in the black community not at all. In a poll in the early 1950s, 42 percent of the black respondents, as compared to 12 percent of the white, thought the department "not good" or "definitely bad."[36]

Following a study in December 1958 of the procedures of the Police Department in recruitment, assignment, and promotion, the DUL concluded that the department was unwilling "to meet the problems of prejudice and discrimination" in its personnel policies. Blacks made up 23 percent of the city's population but only 3 percent of its police force, there were no black officers in six of the city's fifteen precincts, and 80 percent of the black officers were concentrated in the four precincts that had a large black population. Segregation was the rule in the department in walking beats, riding in scout cars, and partner assignments. Blacks were permitted to supervise only blacks and were permitted to patrol only in "certain clearly defined areas." Not only was it more difficult for blacks than whites to be assigned to scout cars, but whites were sometimes assigned to ride with blacks as a form of punishment.[37]

Although blacks applied for positions in the department in numbers at least proportional to their representation in the city's population, a far smaller percentage of black than white applicants met the qualifications prescribed for new police officers. Applicants had to be between twenty-one and twenty-six years of age, at least 5 feet 9½ inches in height, and weigh at least 152 pounds. Qualified applicants had to take a two-and-a-half hour written examination designed to test intellectual capacity, although it was not self-evident that the examination tested the ability of applicants to perform police duties. Those who passed the written examination were given a test of physical agility and a medical examination. They were then subjected to a character examination by four police officers. The final hurdle was an oral interview conducted by three police officers. That subjective factors could enter into the judgments made in the last two stages of the recruitment process is obvious.[38]

How difficult it was for blacks to meet the department's qualifications is illustrated by the selection of officers in 1959. Of the 1,566 applicants for positions in the department that year, 434 (27.7 percent) were black. Only one of the blacks, however, compared to 54 (4.7 percent) of the whites, met the department's qualifications and was hired.[39]

In May 1960 the Baptist Ministerial Alliance petitioned the Common Council to look into what the Alliance thought was "a pattern of discrimination" in the selection of police officers. The council assigned the task to the CCR, which decided to examine the manner in which the recruitment process had operated in 1959. What the CCR discovered was that the failure of black applicants was "consistently greater" than the failure of whites in all phases of the screening process. In reporting the CCR's findings to the mayor, a staff member asserted that there appeared to be "a highly refined series of *screens* through which the applicant must filter to get on the eligible list. Every one of these screens . . . ," the aide noted, "has a greater impact on the negro job applicant than on his white counterpart."[40]

Promotion procedures of the Police Department posed special problems for those blacks who managed to survive the recruitment process. For promotion to detective and sergeant, the required written examination was weighted 50 percent; the service rating, 40 percent; and seniority, 10 percent. For promotion to lieutenant, the weights were written examination, 40 percent; service rating, 30 percent; promotional evaluation, 20 percent; and seniority, 10 percent. The heavy weight assigned to service ratings and promotional evaluations gave superior officers considerable discretion in determining whom to promote. In 1958 only 8 percent of the blacks on the force, as compared to 20 percent of the whites, were in ranks above that of patrolman, and not a single black in the uniformed division had ever held a rank above that of sergeant.[41]

Unhappy as blacks were about the recruitment, promotion, and assignment of police officers, they were even more disturbed about the manner in which the department enforced the law. The executive secretary of the Detroit NAACP told the Civil Rights Commission that Detroit blacks were subjected to "unreasonable and illegal arrests, indiscriminate and open searching of their person on the public streets, disrespectful and profane language, derogatory references to their race and color, interference with personal associations . . . and violent, intimidating police reactions to their protests against improper treatment." The white deputy chief of the department later told a federal district court that "informal police rules" in the 1940s and 1950s called for the investigation of "all blacks west of Woodward Avenue after sundown . . . unless they were known to the police officer."[42]

A retired black policeman recalled in 1960 that the police in one precinct amused themselves in the 1950s by beating up blacks. The managing editor of the black newspaper, the *Michigan Chronicle*, a long-time observer of police behavior, asserted at the same time that brutality was "commonplace" in the department and that he had personally observed police officers, without apparent cause, beating up persons under arrest. The command personnel of the department, he charged, sanctioned a "planned policy of 'containment' and harassment of average Negro citizens."[43]

In 1946 the Police Department agreed to process complaints of police misbehavior submitted to it by the Detroit NAACP. Between January 1 and November 30, 1956, the NAACP received 244 complaints of police misconduct. After eliminating complaints that did not appear to be properly supported, the NAACP referred fifty-one brutality cases to the Police Department, which found wrongdoing in only four instances. The department, it should be noted, did not at that time assign complaints to investigators specially appointed for that purpose but rather entrusted the task to the commanding officer of the policeman involved.[44]

In January 1959 the Police Department adopted new procedures requiring an immediate investigation, whether or not a complaint had been submitted, whenever a police officer was required to use force or a policeman or citizen was injured in connection with a police incident. Of 264 such incidents in 1959, involving 149 blacks and 115 whites, the department found citizens at fault in 260 cases. The results were roughly similar during the first nine months of 1960. Not a single police trial board case during the years 1958–60 involved a charge of brutality.[45]

Acting on the CCR's advice, Mayor Louis C. Miriani in August 1958 appointed a prestigious thirteen-person Citizens Advisory Committee on Police Procedures that included five blacks.[46] Before the committee reported in March 1960, the Police Department had made some changes in its procedures. In February 1959, partly in response to the intercession with the mayor of a black leadership group, the department announced that scout cars would be integrated on a temporary basis. When this policy was made permanent, the response of white police officers was to stage a slowdown in the writing of tickets, the number soon dwindling to about 5 percent of the normal total. As of the middle of December 1960, only twenty-four of the department's 118 scout cars had been integrated. The commissioner stated that the policy had been "a terrific flop" since the "work production" of integrated crews was "far below normal."[47]

The Police Department also took some steps at this time to improve police-community relations. The police commissioner instructed the inspectors in each precinct to hold quarterly meetings with community groups and monthly meetings with his supervisory officers to review community relations and other matters.[48]

During their 375 hours of instruction in the Police Academy as of July 1960, police recruits received only ten hours of human relations training, the emphasis being on the necessity of enforcing the law impartially without regard to color considerations. In addition to academy training, every police officer was required to take eight hours of in-service training every three months that included some attention to human relations. It is doubtful, however, that the department's human relations training was particularly effective. The managing editor of the *Michigan Chronicle* informed the Civil Rights Commission that five black officers from three precincts had told him that a directive from the commissioner regarding the handling of civil rights complaints was read at roll call in a " 'disdainful, comic' fashion" and that one executive officer apologized for having to read the order.[49]

The Citizens Advisory Committee stated in its March 1960 report that the Detroit Police Department was "among the best in the nation." Although concluding that it was "in no position to pass judgment on the equitable and unbiased conduct of the department" with regard to recruitment, it nevertheless recommended some changes in recruitment procedures. Claiming quite erroneously that the scout-car integration order had "gone a long way toward creating confidence in this phase of department policy," the committee recommended the extension of this principle throughout the department. Although the committee reported that it had received more complaints about promotion policy than about any other matter, its only suggestion for improvement was that the department assure both the public and its own personnel that promotions would be based on performance without regard to race, creed, or nationality.

The committee observed that citizen complaints of police misconduct were a major and unresolved problem in the area of police-community relations. In addition to making some unexceptional suggestions as to how complaints should be processed and calling for "intensified" instruction on civil rights, the committee recommended that if departmental action did not produce "noticeable improvement," the mayor should create a citizens committee to whom complainants might appeal. The police commissioner rejected this suggestion out of hand, but in May 1961 he established a Community Relations Bureau in the department to investigate complaints of police misconduct as well as to represent the departments at community-relations meetings.[50]

Although there was no dissent from the committee's report, it is hard to believe that all committee members fully subscribed to the document's language. Perhaps the committee thought that the Police Department was moving in the right direction and that a gentle shove rather than a hard slap was the proper tactic to secure additional reforms. Arthur Johnson's comment that the report "whitewashed" police misconduct is, perhaps, an excessively harsh judgment on the rather cautious but well-intentioned report, but it is not all that far from the truth.[51]

It was crime and its association with blacks that triggered a major crisis in race relations in Detroit in December 1960. Four days after the Civil Rights Commission concluded its hearings in the city, the *Detroit News* noted in an editorial that although blacks constituted 26 percent of the city's population, they were responsible for almost 65 percent of its serious crimes. Asserting that the black community bore "a share of responsibility" for this fact, the *News* complained that the black leadership had "not pressed as hard" on this issue as it should have. "A wave of murders, rapes and purse snatchings," with blacks identified as the perpetrators, culminated that same month in the murder of a white nurse's aide, a twenty-eight-year-old mother of three.[52]

"We have got to take stronger measures," Mayor Miriani said in response to the "crime wave." Commissioner Herbert W. Hart placed the police on a six-day week and called on them to "make 'a supreme effort' " to drive crime from the streets. "This is a desperate situation requiring desperate measures," the commissioner stated. The "desperate measures" included not only stepped-up patrolling by police officers but a return to the unrestricted investigation arrests that Hart called the "old fashioned method of police patrol" and that police reforms adopted in March 1959 had substantially reduced. In the next forty-eight hours the police made six hundred arrests of allegedly suspicious persons. The police "crackdown" was concentrated in high crime areas, which were the areas where blacks lived. Some of the city's most prominent blacks were among those frisked and subjected to "humiliating questioning."[53]

At a "community problems" meeting at the end of December, the Detroit NAACP criticized the mayor, the police, and the press for their reaction to the recent unsolved murders and for the targeting of blacks as being guilty of "some sort of grand conspiracy." The president of the local branch of the American Civil Liberties Union charged that the police crackdown violated basic civil liberties. On February 9, 1961, a group of clergymen and labor and business leaders met with the mayor and requested action to ease the "serious tensions" between the police and black citizens. They urged the mayor to issue a statement calling for equal law enforcement and respect for the dignity of the individual. At a second meeting with the mayor on the same day, the NAACP asked for the replacement of Commissioner Hart by a board of police commissioners and the creation of a civilian review board. Miriani's unresponsiveness to these requests and his support of the police crackdown led the black leadership in Detroit to conclude that the city needed a new mayor.[54]

Miriani was challenged in the 1961 mayoral election by the relatively "unknown, untried, and uninhibited" Jerome Patrick Cavanagh, who became the beneficiary of the blacks' "Phooie on Louie" campaign. Born on June 16, 1928, the Roman Catholic Cavanagh received both his undergraduate and law degrees from the University of Detroit. Before filing for the mayoralty on July 29, 1961, he had served as chairman of the Wayne County Young Democrats, deputy sheriff, administrative assistant for the Michigan State Fair Authority, member of the Metropolitan Airport Board of Zoning Appeals, and as a lawyer with a "moderately lucrative practice." He was a bright, handsome, charming, and gregarious person with an engaging platform manner.[55]

Running his first-ever campaign for office on what an aide described as "nickels and Novenas," Cavanagh turned to the black community for support. He met with black leaders and told the president of the Cotillion Club and probably others that, if elected, he would name a police commissioner in whom the blacks would have confidence and that he would "do the right thing" by the city's blacks. The Cotillion Club thereupon gave Cavanagh its very first political endorsement. Although the city's entire power structure, including the UAW, supported Miriani, the TULC backed Cavanagh.[56]

Cavanagh survived the primary although trailing far behind Miriani,[57] but he defeated the mayor in the final election by a vote of 200,413 to 158,778. Although Cavanagh garnered an estimated 85 percent of the black vote, it appears that it was the white homeowners, upset at the level of the property tax and regarding Miriani as too partial to blacks, who actually defeated the mayor. Be that as it may, Detroit blacks saw the election results as "a startling victory" for the city's black community and a demonstration of their "political strength." After the election, Cavanagh promised black leaders that he would speed up integration and end the police excesses of Miriani's final year in office. Blacks looked forward to a new era in Detroit politics and race relations.[58] Their expectations were to be satisfied in some measure, but not entirely.

CHAPTER 2

The Model City

I

"Detroit in Decline" was the caption for a *Time* magazine story of October 26, 1961. The article noted the federal government's classification of Detroit as a place of "substantial and persistent unemployment," the exodus of the white middle class to the suburbs, and the blight that was "creeping like a fungus through many of Detroit's proud old neighborhoods." According to another periodical, Detroit as of 1961 was known for three things: "automobiles, bad race relations and civic sloth."[1] This was the city of which Jerome P. Cavanagh became mayor on January 2, 1962.

The Detroit city government was of the strong mayor, city council, nonpartisan type, its nine councilmen being elected at large. The city's economy was dominated by a single industry, and the union in that industry was the most important in Detroit. The Big Three automobile companies, their economies geared to a national market, traditionally played a small role in city government affairs. The United Automobile Workers (UAW), a major force on the liberal side in state politics, was a lesser influence in city politics because of Detroit's nonpartisan character and the conservatism on such issues as taxation of lower-middle-class homeowners, who predominated in the city.[2]

Facing a deficit of $19 million and a projected deficit of $28 million by the end of the fiscal year, Cavanagh announced in his inaugural address that Detroit's economic recovery would be his "first and greatest concern." He promised to use his "moral influence . . . not only as it relates to the problems of Negroes, but to all citizens of Detroit." In the months that followed, Detroit began a remarkable resurgence that attracted admiring attention to the mayor and drastically altered the city's unfavorable national image.[3]

Cavanagh met Detroit's fiscal problems by securing approval of an income tax of 1 percent on city residents and 0.5 percent on nonresidents who worked in the city. By the end of June 1963 Detroit's financial books were in balance. Seeing the need for federal aid as the city's tax base shrank, the Cavanagh administration turned to Washington for assistance. It enjoyed remarkable success in tapping federal coffers for Detroit's share of the funding for national programs and, indeed, was sometimes at least a coauthor of these programs. "We had a very receptive Administration in Washington, one that was looking for programs that would make them look good," Cavanagh remarked toward the end of his mayoralty. "Well, what we used to do is come up with an idea, take it to Washington, sell it to the Administration, and at the same time have a stack of applications ready on their desk for the moment the legislation was passed. The idea was to get there fastest with the mostest." Between July 1, 1962, and August 1, 1967, Detroit received $230,422,000 from the federal government for one program or another. Cavanagh, according to a *Detroit Free Press* reporter, was an admirer of "arithmetic," which, for him, was "essentially the process of perpetual subtraction from the federal government."[4]

Detroit's improving economic fortunes were attested to not only by the state of the city's budget but also by the new jobs provided by the auto industry, which enjoyed good years from 1962 into 1966. The Cavanagh administration also sought to create new employment opportunities by taking advantage of the federal government's Area Redevelopment Act of 1961 and the Accelerated Public Works Act of 1962. Detroit itself had "geared up" the latter statute and had helped to draft the regulations for its implementation. The city government provided $15.5 million and private industry $1.9 million to supplement the $14.5 million supplied by the federal government, using the money to improve public facilities and to build an addition to the Eastern Market. Loans under the Area Redevelopment Act were processed by the Detroit Metropolitan Industrial Development Corporation, a nonprofit organization that Cavanagh created to stimulate employment and that included business and labor leaders. The Cavanagh administration continued the redevelopment of the city's central business district initiated while Louis Miriani was mayor; it aided in the development of the city's cultural center in the Wayne State University area; and it pointed with pride to the first major construction downtown since the 1920s. The mayor brought labor peace to Cobo Hall, the city's convention center, and this helped to attract more convention business to Detroit.[5]

The most noteworthy accomplishment of the Cavanagh administration appeared to be in the area of race relations. As the city's controller, Cavanagh appointed Alfred Pelham, the first black to fill so important a position in Detroit's government. Blacks were also appointed to head the Mayor's Commission on Children and Youth and as secretary of the Department of Public Works; but the appointment most pleasing to blacks was that of a white, George Edwards, Jr., to serve as commissioner of police. The impeccably liberal Edwards had served as a UAW organizer and national director of its welfare department, director of the Detroit Housing

Commission, city councilman, and in several judicial posts leading up to the Michigan Supreme Court, from which he resigned to accept the commissionership. The then executive secretary of the Detroit branch of the National Association for the Advancement of Colored People (NAACP) recalled that the Edwards appointment was the equivalent for Detroit's blacks of President Lyndon B. Johnson's later appointment of Thurgood Marshall to the United States Supreme Court.[6]

As his first executive order, issued on February 22, 1962, Cavanagh specified that city employees were to be "recruited, appointed, trained, assigned, and promoted without regard to race, color, religion, national origin, or ancestry." A survey conducted in 1963 by the Civil Service Commission and the Commission on Community Relations (CCR), the two agencies the mayor designated to implement the executive order, revealed that 34.5 percent of 25,762 city employees were nonwhite—the city was 28.3 percent nonwhite at the time—and that blacks were employed in all city agencies except zoning appeals. Blacks, however, constituted only 22.5 percent of professional and managerial employees and tended to be concentrated in public works (63.9 percent), which employed many laborers, and in those departments that had lots of contacts with blacks, notably health (57 percent), housing (49 percent), and welfare (52 percent).[7]

The 1963 city employment census led the CCR to prod city agencies like the Detroit Street Railways, in which blacks held only lowly positions, to upgrade blacks in their employ. A supplementary census released in March 1966, when the city was 33.1 percent nonwhite, indicated that the percentage of nonwhites employed by the city had risen to 39.7 percent. Blacks were by then present in every city department, and there had been an increase since 1963 in the ratio of nonwhites to whites in all job categories except professional and technical, where there had been a slight decline. Blacks, however, were still disproportionately concentrated in certain agencies: eleven agencies employed 87.4 percent of all the blacks in the city's service.[8]

In October 1962 Cavanagh instructed the CCR to ensure that city contractors observed the nondiscriminatory practices required by Michigan's 1955 Fair Employment Practices Act. The CCR thereupon drew up contract compliance procedures requiring companies doing business with the city to specify the number of blacks and minority persons in each job category. In a few instances, the companies concerned began to hire blacks, and others at least initiated a review of their employment practices. Accepting the CCR's advice, the Common Council in 1966 enacted an ordinance requiring city contractors to adopt affirmative action procedures for the hiring of minority employees and providing for the cancellation of contracts on the CCR's recommendation. As of the time of the riot in July 1967, however, the city government had not canceled a single contract as the result of this ordinance.[9]

Meeting with the CCR in February 1962, Cavanagh stressed the central importance of the commission's work for the well-being of the community. Concerned almost entirely with matters involving blacks, the CCR sought in the Cavanagh years "to anticipate, diagnose, prevent, and/or resolve outcroppings of violence" and to foster "genuine community social change." It promoted open occupancy, equal employment opportunities, desegregated public education, and improved police-community relations.[10]

Although the CCR pursued its goal of improved race relations with seriousness and sincerity, there is a good deal of question about its effectiveness. The commission lacked enforcement powers, and its staff of twenty-one was too small to fulfill its responsibilities. For all his ability and commitment to racial justice, Richard V. Marks, the CCR's secretary-director, was a sometimes tactless person and reportedly had poor relations with the commission's staff. Most important of all, although the commission did a "credible job" of communicating with government officials and civic and business leaders, it appeared to be "out of touch with the community at a neighborhood level." A survey of a neighborhood that had experienced a miniriot in the summer of 1966 revealed that sixty of seventy-three respondents did not even know of the CCR's existence.[11]

The efforts of the CCR to create what Cavanagh called a "climate of decency" in Detroit were supplemented by the state's Civil Rights Commission (CRC) and, more importantly, by private groups. Created by the revision of the Michigan constitution that became effective in January 1964, the CRC was the first body of its kind in the nation to enjoy constitutional status. The eight-member bipartisan commission was authorized to "investigate alleged discrimination against any person because of religion, race, color or national origin in the enjoyment of civil rights guaranteed by law" or the state constitution, and it was given the necessary power to carry out its responsibilities. It set up a regional office on Detroit's west side and then, in April 1967, a second such office on the east side.

Unlike the CCR, the CRC had enforcement powers, but it was reluctant to exercise them. Although constantly concerned with police misconduct in Detroit and although it may have helped somewhat to restrain police misbehavior, it never, during the Cavanagh mayoralty, sought a court order against the Detroit department or any of its members, a point that some commission members found troubling.[12]

More important than the CRC insofar as Detroit was concerned was the Citizens Committee for Equal Opportunity (CCEO). In June 1963 Walter Reuther invited representatives of civic, religious, and liberal groups as well as business and labor to a meeting to consider "this great moral issue" of civil rights. Those attending assigned an ad hoc committee the responsibility of establishing the CCEO with the aim of mobilizing "the broadest possible support in the community" for the promotion of equal opportunity for all of Detroit's citizens and in the hope that the committee would serve as an example for the rest of the nation. The Episcopalian bishop, the redoubtable Richard S. Emrich, became the new organization's chairman, and Hubert Locke, pastor of the United Church of Christ of Conant Gardens and director of the Office of Religious Affairs of Wayne State University, was appointed its full-time executive secretary. The membership of eighty included the "top man" from several of Detroit's major companies, the president of the UAW, the president of the Detroit NAACP, leading clergymen, and other bellwethers of the Detroit establishment. Many members, it turned out, were singularly uninformed about the state of race relations in Detroit. When Locke attended an early meeting of the organization, he was "shocked" at the "naivete" of its white members. Locke himself was under no illusion about the magnitude of the problem with which the CCEO had to deal. "The problems and complexities of the racial situation," he wrote Emrich, "are so enormous as to be almost overwhelming."[13]

Initially, the CCEO appointed subcommittees to deal with housing, employment, education, and public accommodations. Before long, however, police-community relations became a central concern of the organization. Much of what the CCEO did, it did "quietly" in off-the-record sessions with the press, government officials, and civil rights groups and also by developing channels through which policies could be effected. It met with officials of the city's newspapers in an effort to secure more balanced press treatment of police-community relations and to avoid the use of "loaded terms such as 'brutality.' " It urged the presidents and vice presidents of Detroit's seven principal banks to provide equal employment opportunities, to offer credit on a nondiscriminatory basis, and to support open housing. It held several meetings with segments of the housing industry to secure their cooperation in achieving "complete mobility in the housing market" for all citizens. It sought in numerous ways to improve relations between the police and the city's black and white communities and to assist Police Department efforts to recruit more minority members.[14]

In June 1964 the CCEO sponsored a half-day seminar to consider with business, civic, education, government, and law enforcement leaders in southeast Michigan the role they could play in "preserving and enhancing a positive, progressive racial climate." It conducted a seminar on equal employment that same year and another on manpower development in 1966, and its Employment Sub-Committee prepared a filmstrip on job opportunities for black high school and college graduates. On May 23, 1967, the Employment Sub-Committee held a Jobs Now conference in the Twelfth Street area for youths aged sixteen to twenty-five in which nineteen companies participated and that resulted in the hiring of 92 young people and the referral to various agencies of an additional

1,305 youths. The CCEO also issued important public reports on such matters as housing, crime, and the police.[15]

The CCEO played a large role in seeking to influence the outcome of the Detroit councilmanic race in 1965. The city approached the September 14 primary election "against a background of heightened racial tension," partly because of the volatile issue of crime in the inner city.[16] Analysis of the primary vote appeared to indicate that black voters had cast their ballots for both black and white candidates, whereas the white electorate had voted almost entirely for white candidates, especially for white conservatives. Although four black candidates survived the primary, it seemed likely that all would be defeated in the final election, a point seized on by black nationalists, who urged blacks to vote only for blacks, and one that threatened to polarize the city along racial lines.[17]

Alarmed at the prospect of a racially divided city, the CCEO set up a special committee to acquaint white "moderate conservative[s]" with the crucial importance of the election for Detroit's racial image. The CCEO's principal objective was to increase the white vote for two of the black candidates, but it was also anxious to prevent a fall-off in the black vote for liberal white candidates. The CCEO importuned Detroit's clergy to bring "the serious moral issues" at stake in the election to the attention of their congregations. Seventy-five community leaders met to discuss ways to persuade white groups to invite black candidates to their affairs, CCEO members enlisted the assistance of the media, and the organization arranged for advertisements containing the names of prominent Detroiters who supported the CCEO's position in the election.[18]

The CCEO viewed the results of the November 2 election "with some satisfaction and certainly with great surprise." Instead of the all-white council dominated by ultraconservatives that it feared would be a "disaster" for the city's racial peace, the new council was to include one black, who supplanted a white incumbent judged to be particularly anti-black, and a majority of members in what the CCEO described as "the progressive liberal camp."[19]

The CCEO, unsurprisingly, claimed some of the credit for the preservation of racial peace in Detroit before the 1967 riot. Quite apart from any specific accomplishments, the organization provided evidence of concern for a racially integrated society on the part of the city's leadership, and it served as a forum where blacks could express their grievances to "an 'across-the-board' leadership group" and white leaders could gain a better understanding of the city's blacks.[20]

Like the CCEO, Detroit's religious establishment sought to supplement the activities of public authorities with its own efforts to achieve greater racial understanding and racial equality. The Detroit Archdiocese played the leading role in this regard, a not insignificant fact in a city in which about half of the religious identification was Catholic. The Catholic effort was directed by the Archbishop's Committee on Human Relations, which was organized in 1960 and became fully operative in 1962, when James T. Sheehan became its executive secretary. Its "most intensive area of operation" was "the parishes in changing and white neighborhoods," where it sought to combat "racial prejudice." This took the organizational form of Project Commitment, described as "an educational effort in the area of human relations." Developed in Detroit, Project Commitment became a model for Catholics in other cities. Detroit's Protestant Council of Churches cooperated with the project, using techniques of group dynamics in an effort to establish communication between the suburbs and inner-city blacks.[21]

Like the city government, the Archdiocese sought as part of Project Equality, initiated in May 1965, to limit its purchases to equal opportunity employers. A program of the National Catholic Conference for Racial Justice, Project Equality was "piloted" in Detroit and then spread throughout the nation. In Detroit, the Council of Churches urged its affiliates to align themselves with the archdiocese in this matter. Additionally, an Ad Hoc Committee of Clergymen Concerned with the Elimination of Discrimination in Employment, which appears to have begun functioning in 1964, cooperated with the CCR in its efforts to eliminate discrimination in firms doing business with the city.[22]

Although Father Sheehan expressed unhappiness in March 1967 about what the Archdiocese had been able to accomplish in the area of open housing, Detroit's religious establishment had devoted a good deal of attention to this matter. In January 1963 the archdiocese, the Detroit Council of Churches, and the Jewish Community Council of Metropolitan Detroit, in cooperation with the CCR, held a Metropolitan Conference on Open Occupancy and pledged themselves to do what they could "to *emancipate* the housing market" from "the unconscionable evils of discrimination for reasons of color, religion or national origin." The conference recommended that every church and synagogue seek to promote open occupancy and to become "a generating center of the forces of intergroup understanding." Attended by thirteen hundred persons, the conference added a moral dimension to the drive to secure open occupancy.

Following the conference, the group that had planned the event brought black leaders and the Greek Orthodox diocese into their organization. Taking the name Religion and Race, the organization held a series of conferences over the next several years in an effort to reduce interracial tensions by a "challenge to conscience" aimed primarily at the white middle class.[23]

At a meeting of March 1965, the CCEO executive board agreed that the organization must support "the responsible Negro leadership" lest the city's blacks take their cue from a "less responsible" black leadership, as had occurred elsewhere.[24] The CCEO was responding to the challenge to the established black organizations in the city that took one form or another throughout the Cavanagh years.

In criticizing the traditional black leadership, militant blacks were influenced by the civil rights movement of the 1960s and the heightened racial consciousness and racial pride, particularly among younger and northern-born blacks, that followed in its wake. What happened in the South, in places like Birmingham and Selma, caused northern blacks to become more sensitive to and more critical of racial injustice in their own communities. This led to demands for change that public authorities were often unprepared to meet. The result was mounting militant criticism of the black leadership, which, as the alleged spokesman for the black community, had failed to extract meaningful concessions from the relevant government officials. Detroit was no exception to these developments, and beneath a surface calm there was a good deal of unrest in the black community. The question, as Locke put it, was whether the city would move "fast enough to allay the frustrations, the unrest and the fears of its Negro citizens."[25]

To their critics in the black community, the traditional black leaders were "Uncle Toms" who played "the game" and told whites what they wanted to hear. These leaders had benefited from the civil rights movement and their association with the white leadership, but, the militants charged, they were out of touch with less fortunate blacks in the ghetto and unresponsive to their needs. "Our leaders . . . our so-called representatives . . . ," a Twelfth Street black declared, "they don't do no good for anybody. They don't ever push the things through."[26]

Many lower-class blacks resented the success of the black middle class, who appeared to ghetto blacks to be more concerned about their own status than about the needs of their less fortunate brethren. That successful blacks were aware of this resentment was poignantly revealed in a letter sent to Governor George Romney just after the 1967 riot. "I have been discriminated against and disadvantaged by racial bigotry like all Negroes," the writer noted. "In spite of this I believe that I have begun to make progress toward the good life. For the first time I have to fight not only against the acts and influence of white racist[s] and the indifference of white moderates; but also the extremists element within my race who are against Negroes who have attained any success."[27]

The militants were undoubtedly correct in their allegation that the established civil rights organizations like the NAACP had no real base in the ghetto. The implicit assumption behind that charge was that the militants were the true voice of the ghetto, but, strong as their rhetoric was, they were not. The sad fact was that no one really spoke for the ghetto, which was leaderless, lacked "a strong sense of community," and was without the kind of formal organization to which city authorities could relate. There were, to be sure, block clubs throughout the black neighborhoods, but they were made up mostly of homeowners, and their orientation was middle class. "The voice from the slum is never heard," a black community representative declared after the riot. No one in

Detroit, she lamented, either spoke for or understood the people of the ghetto.[28]

The most articulate spokesman among the black militants and the central figure in the development of a "strident" black nationalism in Detroit during the 1960s was the Reverend Albert Cleage, Jr. The son of a doctor and recipient of a B.A. from Wayne State University and a divinity degree from Oberlin, Cleage was pastor of the Central United Church of Christ on Linwood, just west of Twelfth Street. He was light-skinned, and his church until the late 1950s had apparently been a "white church" for light-skinned blacks. It was to take on quite a different character in the 1960s.[29]

By 1962 Cleage was denouncing Detroit's black leadership as the "flabbiest" in any big city in the nation. A "pervasive, unifying theme" of the *Illustrated News*, a Cleage family journal for all practical purposes, was the "betrayal" of black Detroit by "Uncle Toms as they lunch[ed] and confer[red] privately with white bosses." The established black organizations—the NAACP, the Detroit Urban League (DUL), and the Trade Union Leadership Council (TULC)—Cleage charged, did not have "the slightest understanding of the total situation nor of their proper role in the total struggle."

The two major themes stressed by Cleage were self-determination and black separatism. Only blacks, he claimed, could solve the problems that faced them because they were black; they must "commit their vitality to community reform by Negroes for Negroes." Rejecting integration, Cleage declared in 1964, "The most important thing that's happening in Detroit is the shifting emphasis in the FREEDOM STRUGGLE from 'integration' to 'Separation.'" Blacks, he said, had to "think black, vote black, and buy black" if they were to be "free."

Rhetorically at least, Cleage rejected the conventional approaches of the civil rights movement. Nonviolence, he declared in 1964, had failed, and so also, he claimed, had mass protest and what he dismissed as the "social work approach" of the NAACP and the DUL. He asserted that blacks must be prepared to defend themselves "against brutality by striking back when knocked down," and he talked about blacks seizing their rights.[30]

In March 1967 Cleage launched the Black Christian Nationalist Movement with the unveiling of an eighteen-foot oil painting of a Black Madonna in an arched canvas above the altar of his church. Cleage explained that "the contradictions inherent in the worship of a white Christ by black people oppressed by whites" had become "increasingly acute." He saw his church and himself as giving meaning to the role of Jesus as "the non-white leader of a non-white people struggling for national liberation against the rule of a white nation, Rome."[31]

Black nationalist and black power groups proliferated in Detroit in the 1960s, and the city became a center for militant black organizing and thinking. Although a keen observer of the Detroit racial scene thought that the "single theme" of these groups was "despair about the possibility of achieving an integrated society," some of them, in their militant way, continued to pursue integrationist goals. As was characteristic of the 1960s, the extremist rhetoric of the black power advocates received a good deal of attention, but the militants attracted few followers. Their most celebrated figure, the Reverend Cleage, ran for office four times in the 1960s and was badly defeated on each occasion.[32]

When Stokely Carmichael, the national chairman of the Student Non-violent Coordinating Committee (SNCC), spoke in Cobo Hall at the end of July 1966, he attracted an audience of only five to six hundred to an auditorium that seated twelve thousand. Attacking civil rights organizations as "buffers," he declared, "We are going to use any force that is necessary to take what is ours. America does not understand non-violence. America understands power." The previous month Martin Luther King, Jr., had preached nonviolence in the same auditorium to a standing-room-only crowd. Always stronger in the South than the North, SNCC attracted only a small following in Detroit. Echoing Carmichael, its Detroit coordinator defined black power in September 1966 as meaning that "Negroes must have power, even if they must resort to violence to get it. When they throw bricks everybody wants to help them."[33]

Cleage was one of the directors of the Group of Advanced Leadership (GOAL), organized early in 1962 and active until about March 1965. Its principal figure was Richard Henry, employed at the United States Army Tank Center. GOAL resorted to picketing to protest police brutality and in pursuit of integration, increased black employment, and the display by merchants of black products; and it sought to organize black workers in an effort to end discrimination in the skilled trades in Detroit. In July 1964 GOAL members organized the Medgar Evers Rifle Club, whose purpose, Henry later asserted, was "to serve as a deterrent to reckless whites who believe all Negroes are non-violent." In February 1965 Henry and a few others formed the Fox and Wolf Hunt Club, to which GOAL soon surrendered its office. The establishment of this new organization, which Henry claimed was "a sportsman type club," was consistent with the Henry view that every black family in Detroit should "own and know how to use a gun." If the members of the two gun clubs, which seem to have been little more than paper organizations, ever fired their weapons in anger, evidence appears to be lacking.[34]

Members of the Revolutionary Action Movement (RAM) were included in the small group that formed the Fox and Wolf Hunt Club. RAM had been founded in 1963 by followers of Robert F. Williams, an advocate of the use of "organized violence" by blacks to win their freedom. RAM appeared in Detroit in 1963 or 1964, but it never had more than a tiny following in the city. It was, however, to come to public notice in the form of the Black Guard just before the 1967 riot.[35]

Some of those associated with RAM, notably the Marxist theoreti-
cian James Boggs, who, along with his wife Grace, was close to Cleage,
met in Detroit on May 1, 1965, with black radicals from elsewhere in the
United States to form the Organization for Black Power. The manifesto
of the organization proclaimed that blacks had to replace the existing
"system," which exploited blacks, with "the right system" and had to
"struggle to control, to govern the cities." The organization's efforts do
not appear to have gone beyond inflammatory rhetoric.[36]

Like RAM, UHURU, which was formed in March 1963 by a group
of "militant black students" attending Wayne State University, rejected
nonviolence as a tactic in combating "the anti-Negro machine that is
America." Not until white society was "destroyed," declared UHURU's
young president, Luke Tripp, would blacks be able to obtain the freedom
to which UHURU (which means "freedom now" in Swahili) was
pledged.

UHURU achieved its principal notoriety in Detroit when some of its
members booed during the playing of the national anthem at a ceremony
on October 11, 1963, that was one of the events in Detroit's campaign to
be designated the site of the 1968 Olympics. Five UHURU members,
including Tripp, were charged with disturbing the peace, but all were
subsequently acquitted in a jury trial. Little was heard of UHURU following the Olympics ceremony, but its youthful adherents remained
active in the cause of black militancy in Detroit.[37]

Although indicative of a growing militancy in a segment of Detroit's
black population, GOAL, UHURU, SNCC, and RAM were flyspecks in
terms of posing a threat to the black leadership position occupied in
Detroit by the NAACP. It appeared, however, for a brief moment in
1963 that another black organization, the Detroit Council for Human
Rights (DCHR), might actually develop as a major rival of the NAACP.
Organized on May 17, 1963, at a meeting of eight hundred blacks mark-
ing the twentieth anniversary of the 1943 riot, the new group was headed
by the Reverend C. L. Franklin, pastor of the New Bethel Baptist
Church, and included Cleage on its board of directors. The DCHR's
founders thought that the black leadership in Detroit was losing contact
with "the Negro man-in-the-street" and was "too close" to the white
leadership.[38]

The great event in the short history of the DCHR was the leadership
position it assumed in organizing the remarkable Walk to Freedom of
June 23, 1963. The march down Woodward Avenue to Cobo Hall,
designed as a show of support for Martin Luther King's effort to desegregate Birmingham, Alabama, as well as to protest the unequal treatment
of blacks in Detroit, was to be headed by Dr. King. The Congress of
Racial Equality (CORE), the Cotillion Club, the TULC, and the UAW
all pledged their support for the march, but the NAACP, which had
played no part in planning the event, was slow to decide on its role. It

distrusted the blacks who had organized the event, and it was aware that King was not coming to Detroit to promote the NAACP. In the end, however, the NAACP concluded that it could not absent itself from the march. Its executive secretary then quietly arranged for hundreds of NAACP signs to be distributed to the marchers.[39]

A massive turnout of 125,000 persons, led by King and Cavanagh, marched in orderly fashion down Woodward Avenue on July 23. It was, as the *Detroit Free Press* reported, "the largest civil rights demonstration in the nation's history" to that time. A "cheering, stomping, screaming" overflow crowd of 25,000 packed the Cobo Hall convention area to hear King proclaim, "We want all our rights and we want them now." The impassioned rhetoric of King's Detroit address found its way into the better-known address that King delivered on August 28, 1963, climaxing the March on Washington.

Detroit blacks were exultant about the Walk to Freedom. "Negroes took over downtown Detroit . . .," a writer in the *Michigan Chronicle* asserted. "This was a long-awaited triumph." "You know Detroit will never be the same after this day," a DCHR official remarked. Continuing its attack on the NAACP, the DCHR insisted that the march placed it at the head of Detroit's black organizations. By the end of 1963, however, the DCHR, which proved to be an organization of leaders without followers, had begun to fade from the Detroit scene.[40]

The DCHR had planned a Regional Leadership Conference for November 1963 to form a Northern Christian Leadership Conference to parallel the similar organization in the South. When the Reverend Franklin made it clear, however, that he would not permit the conference to give any consideration to the all-black, proseparation Freedom Now party, which Cleage, Tripp, Henry, and others had formed on October 11, 1963, GOAL hastily arranged a rival Northern Negro Grassroots Leadership Conference. The GOAL conference was "dominated" by out-of-towners, including Malcolm X. "Welcome to the revolution!" proclaimed Henry to the one hundred or so persons attending the conference. Rejecting nonviolence, Cleage told the delegates that Christ had not taught the kind of nonviolence advocated by Martin Luther King. The conference agreed to the establishment of a new organization of which James Boggs became the chairman. It called for self-determination by blacks and announced a program of action that included a national school boycott to end discrimination against blacks, but it then disappeared from sight.[41]

Cleage resigned from the DCHR because of the opposition of the Regional Leadership Conference to the Freedom Now party. "Independent black political action" as well as "regional and national economic action by united Negro communities" now became the strategy advocated by Cleage. The Michigan Freedom Now party, which was linked to the national movement launched in Washington, D.C., in August 1963, was an essential element of the Cleage strategy. Cleage became the party's candidate for governor of Michigan in 1964, but he garnered only 4,767 votes.[42]

Young black militants in Detroit were conspicuously involved in the Northern Student Movement (NSM) and the Adult Community Movement for Equality (ACME). Founded at Yale in 1961 as an interracial organization to provide northern support for southern civil rights groups, the NSM began operating in Detroit in 1962. It devoted its principal efforts to the development of a civil rights organization among teenagers and young adults on Detroit's east side. In January 1965 the twenty-four-year-old Alvin Harrison arrived in Detroit from New York to serve as the NSM's field secretary. The NSM had aided in organizing ACME on the east side in 1964, and Harrison, an advocate of black nationalism, became its best-known figure. For all the attention that it received, ACME's membership probably never exceeded forty.[43]

In "Black Power Rallies" on July 23, 1966, on Twelfth Street and on the east side, Harrison denounced the city of Detroit as "Upper Mississippi." He told the Twelfth Street crowd to "get this white man off your backs" and commented that the white press treated "black power" as "something dangerous" and that, indeed, it was "dangerous" to whites. A Cavanagh aide advised the mayor that "certain elements" in ACME would "spill blood if necessary to gain its demands."[44]

The focus of ACME's concern and its chief antagonist was the Detroit Police Department, particularly the police of the Fifth Precinct, on the east side. A frequent picketer of the precinct station and committed to the wholesale reform of the department, ACME, with good reason, complained that it was the object of police harassment. A series of confrontations between the two culminated, as we shall see, in a miniriot in August 1966 on Detroit's east side.[45]

Some black militants became associated in 1966 with the so-called Forum Movement, which defined itself as "a large group of black brothers and sisters dedicated to the support of Black Nationalism throughout the world." Forum adherents met in biweekly sessions at the Dexter bookstore of Edward Vaughn, the first important black bookstore in the city. Those associated with Forum espoused black nationalism and talked of the need for black revolution. "Our rhetoric was pretty strong," Vaughn later remarked.[46]

Forum efforts and organizing led to the First Annual Black Arts Conference, held in Cleage's church in June 1966. It was sponsored by something called the Black Arts Confederation of Unity, self-described as "a nationwide organization for black organizations dedicated to the cause of Black Nationalism, unity, and self determination." Quotations from Malcolm X and SNCC's black power slogans predominated at the conference, which featured an exhibit of Afro-American art and history.[47]

The Second Annual Black Arts Conference, held in Cleage's church from June 29 to July 2, 1967, attracted some well-known black leaders from Detroit and elsewhere, including H. "Rap" Brown, who had succeeded Carmichael as chairman of SNCC. The convention program was dedicated to Malcolm X, who, the conference planners proclaimed, "taught us that freedom should be achieved by any means necessary." The "recurring theme" expressed at the conference was that blacks would "take the pressure off Whitey" only when whites learned that they could and would "bleed" as quickly as blacks and that a majority of blacks were willing to die for their rights. In his inflammatory speech, Rap Brown declared that the United States was on the brink of revolution. "Motown," he warned Detroit, "if you don't come around, we are going to burn you down."

An FBI source reported that there were comments during the conference that young blacks had Molotov cocktails available for use against "white credit stores on the Detroit west side" in a possible July 4 uprising. According to police intelligence, a member of a SNCC delegation to the conference from Cincinnati, where there had been a riot on June 11 and 12, said, "We already had our riot and we're here to show you how it's done." The Detroit riot began three weeks later on Detroit's west side.[48]

Of all the new militant Detroit organizations of the 1960s, the most effective was the West Central Organization (WCO). Whatever they may have revealed about the existence of a strain of radicalism in Detroit's black community, organizations like UHURU, RAM, and ACME were distinguished by their rhetoric, not by their accomplishments. The WCO, which was not racially oriented, was also long on rhetoric, but it enjoyed some success in a public policy sense as well. Organized in late June 1965, the WCO drew its inspiration from Saul Alinsky and his view that the way to move the poor to act was by "rubbing raw the sores of their discontent." Two of WCO's original staff members had worked in Alinsky's Chicago-based Industrial Areas Foundation, and Alinsky himself served as a consultant to the WCO. "Our job," declared the Reverend Richard Venus, the youthful white president of the WCO, "is to build power. It is to channel the discontent that exists in slums into constructive change." The WCO was prepared to be "a little nasty" and to use "unacceptable tactics" in drawing attention to its demands and pursuing its goals.

The WCO's base of operations was Detroit's lower west side, west of Woodward and south of Grand Boulevard. Mobilizing the block clubs, church groups, and school groups in this racially mixed area, it became Detroit's "largest active civil [rights] organization," representing a claimed sixty thousand persons.[49]

The major concern of the WCO was housing and urban renewal. Focusing on specific issues, it had both the "power" and "organizational skills" to compel the city administration to pay it heed. Despite the

WCO's ofttimes raucous behavior and its willingness "to go to the fringe of law-breaking," the Cavanagh administration, as we shall see, responded positively to its demands for low-cost housing and a modification of the city's urban renewal plans.[50]

Although present on the Detroit scene before the 1960s, the city's small CORE chapter had more in common with the new black power groups that appeared in that yeasty decade than with the mainstream civil rights organizations. In June 1964 CORE decided to devote its principal efforts to community organizing. Hoping to train ghetto dwellers to help themselves in dealing with their problems, it opened an office on Twelfth Street as a base of operations. As part of this effort, it began to organize tenants living in substandard and unsanitary housing.[51]

Unlike the nationalist organizations that so unremittingly attacked them, Detroit's traditional civil rights organizations were committed to the ideal of a racially integrated society and sought to work with the city's leadership to achieve that goal. Charged with being Uncle Toms and supine in their behavior, they were neither. They were, to be sure, more moderate in their rhetoric than their rivals, but they were nevertheless activist; and though they were middle class in their leadership and, to some degree, in their membership and were more in tune with older than younger blacks, they were by no means unconcerned about ghetto conditions and the fate of the black poor. Having access to the city government, they sought to bring to the attention of public officials the concerns of the black community regarding education, housing, employment, police-community relations, and other matters.

Insisting, incorrectly, that it was the "real and only voice" of the city's black community, Detroit's large NAACP chapter claimed in rebuttal to Cleage that it was "militant — just as militant" as it had to be. Because it believed that the white community tended to act on racial demands only when it was "pushed," it was willing, on occasion in the 1960s, to use the tactics of "direct action," to picket, boycott, march, and demonstrate, but not to use violence.[52]

Although the DUL in the 1960s continued to believe that the black and white leadership of the city could resolve racial problems "without a flaring of tempers," Kornegay let it be known in 1963 that his organization did not rule out black protests against conditions in the black community. Like the NAACP, the DUL pressed the city government to deal with such matters as housing, employment, and police-community relations even though it did not take to the streets. Characteristically, its executive director declared in 1966 that he believed in "greenback power," not black power.[53]

The TULC, for a few years, capitalized on its close relationship with the Cavanagh administration. The TULC lost influence after 1964, however, when its congressional candidate in the newly created and largely black First Congressional District, Richard Austin, was narrowly defeated by John Conyers, member of a faction that had broken away from the TULC. The UAW was probably also of declining influence in the black community in the second half of the 1960s, particularly among the unskilled auto workers. "As black demands mounted," J. David Greenstone succinctly stated in his study of labor and politics, "the capacity of the UAW in Detroit to control them declined."[54]

II

Whatever its racial problems, Detroit acquired a national reputation while Cavanagh was mayor as a model city in terms of its ability to cope with the problems that all big cities faced in the 1960s, especially racial problems. "Detroit," the *New York Times* editorialized when it became evident on July 23, 1967, that the city did not have a patent on racial peace, "probably had more going for it than any other major city in the North." Those who saw Detroit as a model city noted that it had a large and prosperous black middle class and that its blue collar workers had jobs in the auto industry that paid the unskilled wages that were 20 percent above the average for unskilled workers in the nation. Detroit as of 1967 drew attention as the only city to have two black congressmen — they made up half of the black representation in Congress. There was only one black on the Common Council, but there were three black judges in Detroit in 1965; two blacks served on the Board of Education in 1966; two of the five members of the Housing Commission in 1966 were black; and twelve Detroit blacks were members of the Michigan legislature in 1967. Detroit was lauded for its ability to secure federal funds, having one of the best per capita records in the nation in this respect. Most of the money Detroit received from Washington was directed to the inner city. "If the white middle-class knew how disproportionate our expenditures on the inner city were," a high-ranking city official declared during the 1967 riot, "we'd probably have a white revolt on our hands."[55]

Detroit's black housing left a great deal to be desired, but visitors from other cities thought that this housing was superior to what was available to blacks in their cities. Although "intolerable" in a few areas, housing was "not a terribly serious problem," an aide advised President Johnson in May 1967 after a visit to Detroit. The quality of black housing was, indeed, slightly above that of New York, Chicago, Cleveland, and Philadelphia. Although a racially segregated city, Detroit as of 1960 was somewhat less segregated than the mean for large cities in the nation. Detroit's school system before the riot was regarded by some as "noticeably better" than that of any other large midwestern city, and the *Washington Post* praised Detroit's inner-city schools as "one of the country's leading examples of forceful reform in education." Detroit's poverty program, the *Post* also noted, was "regularly cited as the most effective in the United States." Even more important, the Department of Justice's Office of Law Enforcement Assistance designated Detroit as the nation's "model for police-community relations."[56]

What especially attracted favorable attention to Detroit in the years immediately preceding the 1967 riot was the reputed state of its race relations. "Of all the accomplishments in the recent history of the city," a writer in *Fortune* asserted in 1965, "the most significant is the progress Detroit has made in race relations." Detroit, the head of the National Urban League stated the next year, was on the way to becoming a "demonstration city" in the area of race relations. Not only had the leading citizens of the community come together in the CCEO and in church organizations to improve race relations, but blacks reputedly had access to City Hall and saw themselves for the first time as "part of the city." Cavanagh estimated early in 1967 that he was spending three quarters of his long working day dealing with the problems of the inner city.[57]

Detroit, Judge Horace W. Gilmore, the head of the CCEO's Police-Community Relations Subcommittee, declared in 1965, was "the most sophisticated city in the country on the matter of intergroup relations." The black deputy director of the CRC did not delude himself that Detroit had solved or was even near solving its racial problems, but he nevertheless stated at the beginning of 1966 that Detroit's "good image" was "justly reflective of a degree of communication and cooperation between white and Negro" that was "unmatched anywhere else in the United States," with the possible exception of Atlanta. The same point was made even more strongly in May 1967 by Detroit's only black councilman. "With all of its problems," Nicholas Hood declared, "Detroit is far ahead of any major city in America because we have a city administration that will not only listen to the concerns brought to it but will set out to work on these concerns."[58]

Proud of Detroit's race-relations image, Cavanagh stated a few weeks before the July 1967 riot that, in Detroit, you did not "need to throw a brick to communicate with City Hall." It was, indeed, the fact that blacks were not throwing bricks at City Hall at a time when racially related riots were spreading across the land that made Detroit appear to be a national symbol of hope. Detroit, as we shall see, experienced a minidisturbance in the summer of 1966, but the city quelled it so easily and bloodlessly that what had occurred actually enhanced Detroit's model city image. The Cavanagh administration, understandably, was willing "to promote" that image and, to a degree, to believe in its validity. "It is no accident," Cavanagh declared a month before the July riot, "that Detroit has escaped any great amount of civic unrest." It was due rather, he said, to the city's responsiveness to the "needs in the streets."[59]

Social scientists visited Detroit in the Cavanagh years to learn how a city could deal successfully with its racial problems. Detroit and its mayor became the subjects of praise in the nation's magazines and newspapers, admiring articles appearing in such places as *Fortune*, *Newsweek*, *Harper's*, *U.S. News & World Report*, *Look*, the *Wall Street Journal*, the *Christian Science Monitor*, the *Los Angeles Times*, and the *Cleveland Plain Dealer*. The view of the city in the periodical press was echoed by the Department of Justice's Summer Project, which pointed to Detroit as "a racial model." In 1965 the American Institute of Architects gave Detroit and one other city its first awards for urban redevelopment plans that "successfully realized the objective of creating vital environments for the core of American cities." In March 1967 the National Municipal League and *Look* magazine designated Detroit an "All-America City" because of the development of its $250 million cultural center, thus reversing thirty years of "under-emphasis on culture," its urban renewal and redevelopment plans, and the manner in which it had reacted to its small 1966 disturbance.[60]

Jerry Cavanagh, an aide remarked, "not only got a great deal of press, he got brilliant press." The "best known" and most "glamorous" city mayor of the time, he was portrayed nationally as "The Dynamo in Detroit" who had pulled "a once dead industrial city out of its physical, economic and cultural doldrums" and as having gone further than other mayors in responding to slum problems. *Life* selected "the hot young mayor" as one of the one hundred members of the "Take Over Generation," and the United States Junior Chamber of Commerce named him one of the ten "outstanding young men" of the nation. Although Cavanagh had his enemies in Detroit, he was reported at the end of 1963 to be "the object of nearly constant worship" by the city's press and its civic, business, and labor leaders. Two years later a writer in *Fortune* described Cavanagh as the "image" of the city's new consensus, "the symbol of the city's aspirations." When someone said to the president of Michigan Bell that the unemployment rate among Detroit's black youth was disturbingly high, he replied, "One of these days Jerry Cavanagh will get a few people together and come up with a program."

When Cavanagh ran for reelection in 1965, he received a crushing 69 percent of the vote. The next year he became the first mayor simultaneously to head both the United States Conference of Mayors and the National League of Cities. His advice was sought by the White House, he came to be seen as a presidential possibility himself, and he relished the idea. "On a clear day," an aide said of Cavanagh, he could "see the White House." The mayor's favorite song was said to be "Impossible Dream," and he appeared for a time to be living it.[61]

Things began to turn sour for Cavanagh in 1966. Believing himself "politically hot," he decided to challenge former Michigan Governor G. Mennen Williams for the Democratic nomination for the United States Senate. The electoral problem for Cavanagh in what was certainly a political blunder was that Williams appealed to the same labor, liberal, and black constituency as the mayor, and Williams had endeared himself to those groups as governor before Cavanagh had appeared on the political scene. Williams defeated Cavanagh in the primary, swamping the mayor in Detroit's black precincts. Cavanagh's candidacy not only "alienated" some of his Detroit supporters, but it also dealt a blow to assumptions about his political invincibility and raised the ire of Democrats, who blamed the divisive primary for Williams's defeat in the final election. By that time, moreover, Cavanagh had come out against America's involvement in the war in Vietnam and had criticized federal spending for space exploration, positions that did not endear the mayor to President Johnson. Cavanagh soon "detected . . . somewhat of a chill around the White House" where he was concerned.[62]

Misfortune seemed to plague Cavanagh from 1966 onward. The Detroit TV and radio personality Lou Gordon, once an ardent supporter of the mayor, turned on Cavanagh, questioning his character and integrity and claiming that his senatorial candidacy had been a betrayal of a promise to serve out his second term as mayor. Councilwoman Mary Beck, seizing on the emotional crime issue, mounted a recall campaign against the mayor in the spring of 1967. A grand jury investigation of the Police Department spawned a crop of nasty rumors that involved the mayor. There were rumors also that the Catholic mayor was having marital difficulties, rumors that were confirmed when the mayor's wife and the mother of their eight children filed for separate maintenance on July 18, 1967. Fed information and misinformation by the mayor's Detroit foes, the nationally syndicated columnist Drew Pearson wrote a particularly venomous piece about Cavanagh in May 1967. On July 21, 1967, two days before the Detroit riot, a Cavanagh aide remarked, "You know, the only thing the poor guy has not had is a riot."[63]

It would be a mistake to assume that Cavanagh, despite a sea of troubles, saw his career at an end on the eve of the July 1967 riot or that his national image had dimmed to any significant degree. Whatever the view of him in Detroit — and an independent survey in June 1967 revealed that he was still solidly backed by the Detroit electorate — he remained an admired national personage. *Newsweek* in March 1967 not only hailed Cavanagh as "urban America's most articulate spokesman" but placed him and New York's John Lindsay at the top of any list of mayors who might have national political futures. Echoing *Newsweek*, the *Detroit News* reported just a few days before the Detroit riot began that the city and the nation were still looking closely at Jerry Cavanagh because of the reputation that he enjoyed across the land. As the national reaction to the Detroit riot made abundantly clear, the mayor's troubles, in any event, had not rubbed off on his city, which continued up to July 23, 1967, to enjoy a reputation as a model city.[64]

Did Detroit deserve its reputation as a model city, particularly in its race relations? That the city's reputation was grossly inflated in an absolute sense goes almost without saying. Detroit blacks during the

Cavanagh years before the 1967 riot complained with good reason about unemployment, job discrimination, and the quality of the housing and the public education available to them; and their relationship with the Police Department was one of mutual antagonism and constant strain. Detroit had its CCR, its CCEO, and its Archbishop's Committee on Human Relations; but it also had its white homeowners who adamantly opposed open housing, and almost 70 percent of the white respondents in a postriot survey indicated that they thought blacks had been "pushing too fast" for what they wanted.[65]

As a successful black businessman in the city stated just after the riot, Detroit offered considerable opportunity to "the enterprising Negro," but its numerous programs did not appear to be reaching the very poor and the hard-core unemployed. Putting the matter somewhat differently, a Cavanagh aide, in assessing the performance of the Cavanagh administration as of September 1966, concluded, "I would say that up to now we have played with heady ideas . . . [but] we still have to produce the major part of what we set out to do."[66]

For all of the publicity that it received about its open lines of communication to the black community, the Cavanagh administration was not really in close touch with the ghetto poor and the unemployed youngsters on the street corners. Cavanagh conceded the point after the riot. Hard as his administration had tried, he stated, it had failed to "get down to the streets" and did not really know what was going on there. There was actually a good deal of unrest in Detroit, but it was not apparent on the surface. Councilman Mel Ravitz compared Detroit in February 1966 to an iceberg, a city with "a bright, attractive, well-publicized face but [with] submerged dangers" that could not "readily be seen."[67]

Inadequate as were its efforts to deal with its problems in any absolute sense, Detroit, in a comparative sense, may nevertheless have deserved its preriot model city reputation. This was, indeed, the view of Detroit's first black councilman, William T. Patrick, Jr., who said just after the riot that although Detroit, "in a pure sense," had "many problems," relations between the races were good "in a relative sense compared with the rest of the nation." "Detroit," he remarked, "is damn good compared with other cities." When a *Detroit News* reporter compared Detroit with four other large midwestern cities in May 1967, he concluded that Detroit, although not "the ideal city" or "the perfect model," was responding more successfully to the urban problems of the day than the other cities were. However little progress it had made in the areas to which its programs were addressed, Detroit, Cavanagh correctly said during the riot, had done "more of the textbook things than any other city."[68]

The evidence is conflicting as to whether Detroit blacks thought that they were better off than blacks in other cities. A compilation of mean dissatisfaction scores for city services based on a survey of blacks aged 16 to 69 in fifteen major cities in early 1968, after the riot, revealed that Detroit blacks stood at about the midpoint in terms of their level of dissatisfaction with four city services: schools, parks, police, and garbage collection. Detroit blacks also did not differ appreciably from blacks in the other cities in their estimation of whether their mayor was trying as hard as he could or fairly hard to solve city problems. On the other hand, when the Detroit Urban League and the *Detroit Free Press* in a postriot random sample survey asked blacks in the principal Detroit riot areas to compare their lot with that of blacks in other northern cities, 45.5 percent responded that Detroit blacks had "better than average income," as compared to 8 percent who thought the opposite; 39 percent thought that they had better jobs, as compared to 8 percent who thought they had worse jobs; and 24.5 percent thought that they had received a "better than average education," as compared to 10 percent who thought the reverse.[69]

In the final analysis, how Detroit blacks compared their condition with that of blacks elsewhere may be of less significance in ascertaining the degree of their dissatisfaction than the comparison they made between themselves and Detroit's whites. "Black Detroiters," a black official at the time of the riot later stated, "didn't compare their lot in life to Black Wattsites, Black Harlemites or Black anywhere else. Black Detroiters compared their lot in life to white Detroiters." As we have seen, whites had more income, better homes, and better jobs, and suffered less unemployment than the city's blacks. Whites were also more satisfied than blacks with the quality of their schools and parks and the police protection they received, and Detroit blacks, no doubt, thought that there was good reason for this.[70]

That Detroit could be compared so favorably with other Northern cities in terms of its ability to cope with racial problems should be taken as less an indication of Detroit's success than of the even greater inadequacy of what was being done elsewhere. Cavanagh, indeed, conceded after the riot that the Detroit effort had been "like putting a bandaid on a severe wound."[71] It is easy enough to disparage the Detroit effort, but the problems of the black ghetto and poverty that Detroit and other big cities faced in the 1960s were not all that tractable, as the record of the years that have followed makes painfully evident.

The two faces presented by Detroit just before the riot, the city so proud of its accomplishments, so often under attack from inside for its shortcomings, was nicely illustrated when Detroit received its All-America City award in March 1967. Since the award was, in part, based on the city's urban rehabilitation and housing efforts in the WCO area of Detroit, the city government invited the WCO to attend the award ceremony. The organization's president responded that the award was nothing but "a big joke" and that the WCO did not want to be included in "such a hypocritical ceremony."[72]

CHAPTER 3

The "Divided City"

Following the riot, a Kerner Commission staffer reported that he had not found a single black in Detroit who was "happy" about conditions in the city.[1] Throughout the years of the Cavanagh mayoralty preceding the July 1967 riot, there was, indeed, a steady drumbeat of complaints by blacks regarding their general condition and the racial status quo in Detroit. Those conditions and the black perception of them do not in themselves fully explain why the riot occurred, when it occurred, and where in the city it occurred, but one can nevertheless assume that since it was blacks primarily who rioted, there was something about their circumstances that persuaded at least some of them to take to the streets and others to express support for the riotous behavior that resulted.

Black complaints centered about the segregated existence of the city's nonwhite population, mistreatment by merchants, the shortage of recreational facilities, the quality of education and housing available to blacks, the way the war on poverty operated in Detroit, and, most important of all, jobs and the behavior of the police. A series of incidents punctuated the racial calm in the city, but it was not until July 1967 that Detroit experienced a full-fledged riot.

As a 1966 survey of the adult population of the Detroit standard metropolitan statistical area revealed, the "interaction" between blacks and whites paralleled their "housing lines" in the city. The investigators concluded that Detroit was becoming "increasingly segregated in interaction as well as housing."[2] At the same time, Detroit in its public policy was moving in the direction of integration, but doing so at too slow a pace to satisfy the city's blacks.

In 1963 the Detroit branch of the National Association for the Advancement of Colored People (NAACP) referred twenty-eight violations of Michigan's stringent equal accommodations statute to the Police Department's Community Relations Bureau. There were additional complaints in 1964, but thanks to state and federal law, the Subcommittee on Public Accommodations of the Citizens Committee for Equal Opportunity (CCEO) was able to report in June 1965 that "perhaps the one area" in which equal opportunity had been largely achieved was access to places of public accommodation. The next year the CCEO decided that it no longer needed a subcommittee on public accommodations.[3]

Racial discrimination had long been a "serious problem" in the majority of Detroit's hospitals and in the health field in general. The efforts of the city government's civil rights organization beginning in 1952 to cope with this problem were supplemented in 1962 by a Community Coordinating Council composed of representatives of several black organizations that gathered data regarding bias in Detroit hospitals. Responding to the charges of discrimination, the Common Council in 1963 enacted a hospital ordinance that forbade discrimination in medical services, the use of facilities and bed assignments, the appointment of doctors, nurses, and other hospital employees, and in the nurse training program. The ordinance appeared to have little effect during the next several years, the state Civil Rights Commission (CRC) reporting in July 1966 that hospital bias remained a "serious" problem in Detroit. The report was a spur to action, the CRC noting in February 1967 that there was by then "little confirmed discrimination in hospital employment."[4] The health of blacks, however, judging from infant mortality rates, cases of tuberculosis, and examinations for venereal disease, continued to be much inferior to that of whites.[5]

In a postriot survey conducted at the beginning of 1968, 53 percent of the black Detroit respondents aged sixteen to sixty-nine indicated that they were "somewhat" or "very dissatisfied" with the parks and play-grounds available in their neighborhoods, and 48 percent expressed a similarly negative opinion about the available sports and recreation centers for teenagers. Blacks were more dissatisfied with their recreational facilities than whites, 38 percent of whom were dissatisfied with their neighborhood parks and playgrounds and 39 percent with their neighborhood recreation centers. Public recreational facilities were lacking in low-income neighborhoods and especially in the Twelfth Street–Dexter area, which became the principal center of the 1967 riot.

After the riot, the Mayor's Development Team described the Department of Parks and Recreation as "an ingrown agency" that was "viewed with hostility by large segments of the community." The team reported that the department had been inadequately responsive to demographic changes in the city in the preceding twenty-five years and that its program was geared to a middle-class constituency rather than to the needs of the inner city and the poor. The head of the department, however, attributed the inadequacy of recreational facilities in the inner city to the lack of available land and the refusal of the city government to provide necessary funding. Rejecting black complaints about city services, he revealingly stated after the riot that Detroit had been "leaning over backward for Negroes."[6]

The alleged exploitation of ghetto inhabitants by ghetto merchants was a long-standing grievance of the inner city and black residents. The

Trade Union Leadership Council (TULC), the Congress of Racial Equality (CORE), and the NAACP all took up this issue during the Cavanagh years, the TULC declaring war on ghetto merchants in March 1966. The common complaint in Detroit and other large cities was that ghetto merchants charged high prices for inferior merchandise, engaged in sharp and unethical credit practices, were discourteous if not "abusive" to their customers, and commonly took their profits to the suburbs. "They sell us garbage at high prices" was the way a black woman on the west side put it. When asked why ghetto merchants behaved as they did, another west sider responded, "because they can get away with it."[7]

In the Angus Campbell-Howard Schuman fifteen-city survey conducted for the Kerner Commission following the riot, 62 percent of the adult black respondents in Detroit claimed they had been unfairly overcharged by their neighborhood stores "often" (25 percent) or "sometimes" (37 percent); 44 percent indicated that they had been sold inferior goods "often" (13 percent) or "sometimes" (31 percent); and 20.5 percent asserted that the ghetto stores treated their customers disrespectfully "often" (2.5 percent) or "sometimes" (18 percent). This was somewhat above the figures for the fifteen cities as a whole, the corresponding percentages for the three categories of complaints being 56, 42, and 17. Judging from a probability sample survey of 452 blacks aged fifteen and over conducted by the *Detroit Free Press* in August and September 1968, dissatisfaction with merchandise practices was especially high in the riot areas of the city. Whereas 25 percent of blacks in Detroit as a whole in the Campbell-Schuman survey indicated that they had been "often" overcharged for goods, a whopping 55 percent of riot area blacks made this claim.[8]

That ghetto grocery stores charged higher prices than grocery stores elsewhere in the city and in the suburbs was confirmed in a study published in the *Free Press* just before the riot and, more impressively, in a 1968 survey conducted under the auspices of the Detroit Archdiocese that was reputedly the largest local shoppers' survey ever undertaken in the United States to that time. Because of the absence of competing stores and the small size of independents available to them, the very poor in the inner city paid about 20 percent more for grocery items than suburban shoppers did. This "racial class tax" was a matter of no small importance since the very poor reportedly spent from 35 to 40 percent of their income on food.[9]

Some of the price disparity between inner- and outer-city stores reflected sheer exploitation or what an archdiocesan official associated with the grocery survey said was "the complete lack of respect in these stores for poor blacks." There were, however, valid reasons for at least some of the price differences. Chain stores in the inner city were older and somewhat smaller than those located elsewhere in the metropolitan area, had lower volume, and were less able to adopt newer and more efficient merchandising methods. The owners of ghetto independent stores, which served 81 percent of Detroit's nonwhites, had higher overhead costs than independents elsewhere because they had to pay higher insurance rates, if insurance was available to them at all, and because they suffered disproportionately from vandalism, pilferage, and robbery and had to take extra precautions to protect their property. They charged more for credit than the average, but they were often dealing with bad credit risks who would have had a hard time even securing credit at stores outside the ghetto. "I'm not fair," an inner-city druggist conceded just after the riot. "I've never been fair. I'm not in a fair neighborhood. If you're looking for fairness," he said, "go to Grosse Pointe."[10]

Since white merchants with whom they dealt were among the few whites blacks encountered in the ghetto, it is understandable that black perceptions of black-white relations were influenced by the treatment white store owners accorded them. It is a mistake, however, to assume that the Detroit ghetto merchants were overwhelmingly white and, as has also been assumed, predominantly Jewish. In 1966, 38 percent of inner-city businesses were actually black-owned, but these stores tended to be small retail businesses of the "mom and pop" variety. At the time of the 1967 riot, Jews owned less than 15 percent of the stores in the principal riot area. Jewish merchants, however, owned many of the larger, more prosperous businesses on the west side. They tended to be older persons who had remained behind when the Jewish middle class moved out of the area in the 1950s. As they retired or gave up their businesses for one reason or another, they were often replaced by Chaldeans (Catholic immigrants from Iraq).[11]

The Detroit school system faced a serious problem in financing the education of a school population composed of increasingly large numbers of educationally disadvantaged and culturally deprived students. Between 1962 and 1966, while the city population was decreasing, the public school population increased from 283,811 to 294,653. The schools lost about twenty-seven thousand white students, mostly from middle- and upper-income families with relatively strong educational backgrounds, but added about thirty-eight thousand black students, mostly from families that were economically and educationally deprived. While the percentage of nonwhites in the city increased from 26.7 to 34.8, the percentage of nonwhites in the schools jumped from 45.8 to 56.7.[12]

The Detroit school system, unfortunately, had to finance its growing costs on a diminishing tax base. The valuation of the real property on which the school millage was based decreased from $5.672 billion in 1960–61 to $4.807 billion in 1966–67, which cost the schools a total of $58.2 million between the 1960–61 and 1967–68 school years. The operating tax rate for the schools remained the same for the period, the problem for the school district being to maintain that rate, the major portion of which had to be periodically approved by the voters, rather than to increase it. Millages were defeated in the spring of 1963 and 1966 but then approved by the voters in each instance in the fall. The opposition came primarily from white voters — not a single black precinct cast a negative vote in the six millage elections between 1957 and 1967. Whites were more apt than blacks to vote no in millage elections because a higher proportion of the whites were property owners, whites who remained in the city were likely to be older than blacks and without school-aged children, and middle-class whites were more likely than blacks to send their children to private schools.[13]

The increased cost of operating the Detroit public schools in the 1960s was met by increased state and federal aid. Michigan's share of the operating budget for the Detroit public schools increased from 33 percent in 1961–62 ($44 million of the $134.9 million total) to 41.3 percent in 1966–67 ($67.1 million of the $162.5 million total), the federal share from 1.3 percent ($1.8 million) to 9.2 percent ($15 million). The state allocated its aid not on the basis of need but rather on the basis of property valuation per pupil, which disadvantaged Detroit, with its rising number of students and its decreasing assessed property valuation. The state's allocation formula thus yielded Detroit $193 per pupil in 1966–67 and the remainder of the state $225 per pupil even though the Detroit Board of Education estimated that it cost twice as much to educate a ghetto child properly as to educate a suburban child.[14]

The increasing federal share of the operating budget of the Detroit schools was primarily the result of Title I of the Elementary and Secondary Education Act of 1965, which allocated funds to local school districts on the basis of the number of school children from low-income families. Of Detroit's 295,000 students at the beginning of the 1967–68 school year, 59 percent were eligible for this aid. This number included 84.5 percent of the black students in the district and 30 percent of the white students.[15]

As compared to the rest of Michigan, Detroit was short of both teachers and classrooms. Although state law set the maximum class size at thirty-five, classes in the inner city and in predominantly black areas often had forty or more students. Because of the shortage of teachers in the inner city, fifth and sixth graders were occasionally left in charge of kindergarten pupils. At the time of the riot, Detroit would have needed 1,650 teachers and one thousand additional classrooms to have the same ratio of teachers per thousand pupils as in the remainder of the state.[16]

The status of the Detroit public school system with regard to the central issue of education in the 1960s, that of segregation and integration, was made evident when the Citizens Advisory Committee on Equal Educational Opportunities issued its long-awaited report in March 1962. The committee found a "clear-cut pattern of racial discrimination in the assignment of teachers and principals to schools throughout the city," and it expressed dissatisfaction with the pace at which the school board was adjusting school attendance boundaries to combat racial and class segregation. It pointed to "grave discrimination in employment and training opportunities" in the apprenticeship program. It recommended that additional personnel and resources be devoted to the culturally deprived and that high school texts be aimed more at black students, and it urged school administrators to develop "a higher sensitivity to human and intergroup relations."[17]

The Detroit Board of Education, in short order, approved most of the Advisory Committee's recommendations. Since the school board, as already noted, had adopted a bylaw in 1959 banning discrimination in "all school operations and activities," Dr. Remus Robinson, the board's sole black member, charged that the Advisory Committee's report made it evident that there had been "obvious laxity" and even "insubordination" in the implementation of board policies.[18]

The school board was prodded to act not only by the Advisory Committee's report but also by the demands of both mainstream and militant black organizations, a lawsuit initiated by black parents, and the quiet pressure exerted by the Cavanagh administration through the Commission on Community Relations (CCR). There was "widespread concern" in the black community about the pace at which the school system was being desegregated, the size of classes, the quality of education black children received, and the attitude of white teachers toward their nonwhite students.[19]

Assuming that the school system would not "move on the major issues of racial discrimination without pressure," the Detroit NAACP announced in June 1963 that it was "prepared to take any steps necessary—legal or mass protest"—to achieve its educational objectives. The NAACP wanted the school board to adopt "a positive program of integration" rather than simply of "desegregation." It favored integration even if this meant busing, its executive secretary stating in 1963, "I know of no other way to prevent the Negro child from being short-changed in education in the years ahead." The NAACP also wanted the school administration to remove "any vestige of discriminatory practice" in the hiring, placement, and promotion of school personnel and to require all firms doing business with the schools to pursue affirmative action policies. It favored extension of the open schools policy as a tool to achieve integration, remedial programs in schools in economically and socially depressed areas of the city, and the setting of minimum achievement standards at each grade level.[20]

The integrationist efforts of the NAACP were supplemented in March 1965 by the formation of the Ad Hoc Committee Concerned with Equal Educational Opportunities. Headed by the Reverend William Ardrey, pastor of the St. Paul AME Zion Church, the seventy-member committee sought "specific action" from the school board "to end the isolation of the Negro from education in Detroit."[21]

Like the NAACP, militants such as the Reverend Cleage and those associated with the Group of Advanced Leadership (GOAL) initially favored "a positive policy of racial integration." They wanted this policy to be adopted immediately, and they were quite specific as to what this meant, including the immediate adjustment of school boundary lines to achieve integration, the immediate placement of at least one black teacher in each school, and the promotion of blacks to top administrative posts in the school system. They called for the withdrawal of social studies textbooks with a racial, nationality, or class bias and the removal from predominantly black schools of all "incompetent and racially prejudiced" teachers, principals, and administrators.[22]

Although Cleage initially appeared to be an advocate of school integration, he later declared, "I did not have a philosophical commitment to integration at any point." Whether or not this accurately represented Cleage's views at the outset of the Cavanagh administration, there is no doubt that he had abandoned integration as a goal by the time of the 1967 riot. In 1967 he became the chairman of the Inner City Parents Council, which presented the school board in June 1967 with the first formal demand it had received for "black schools for black children." The council wanted black schools to be manned by black administrators, black principals, and black teachers since, Cleage claimed, black children could not identify with white academic personnel who were often guilty of "a condescending attitude" toward black students and their parents. The board rejected the proposal for all-black schools, its two black members speaking out against the idea.[23]

The Inner City Parents Council was especially concerned about what it regarded as the inadequate education being received by inner-city children. This became for the militants a more important matter than whether the schools were segregated or integrated. The moderates were equally concerned about what went on in the schools, but they believed that a quality education must be an integrated education. There was, to be sure, plenty of reason for both militants and moderates to be concerned about the character of education received by ghetto children. Several teachers and counselors at Northwestern High, for example, described the school in 1962 as an "attendance school" where students remained for four years without learning anything and where teachers were pressured to pass students regardless of the quality of their academic performance.

A *Detroit Free Press* reporter who served as a substitute teacher for seven days in an inner-city junior high school in the fall of 1966 concluded that the chief educational problem in the inner-city school was the attitude of the teachers, many of whom, he judged, did not believe in what they were doing, did not believe themselves respected by either the students or their parents, and did not believe their students wanted to learn. "Most of these kids are just plain dumb," he reported as the view of one group of teachers. "You'll never teach them anything." He heard one teacher refer to some students as "ADC leeches" for failing to bring pencils to class.[24]

"The teachers don't teach a damn thing . . .," one rioter later declared. "They don't give a damn if you don't learn or nothing, you know. . . . Man I didn't learn shit till I hit the 12th grade." Often "scared to death of their students," many inner-city teachers thought their students uneducable, as many students came to realize. Ghetto parents and their children and even the black vice-president of the Detroit Federation of Teachers (DFT) increasingly saw the existing public school education as "almost an irrelevant factor in shaping and preparing young people." This was partly because the high school diplomas of inner-city students did not lead to decent jobs and higher incomes since employers heavily discounted the value of such diplomas as a measure of educational achievement. The Michigan Employment Security Commission reported in 1966 that only 6–7 percent of the prospective graduates from inner-city schools had good employment prospects as compared to 40 percent or more of graduates from schools on the city's periphery. An eighteen-year-old looter commented after the riot that when black high school graduates saw whites get jobs for which the blacks believed themselves qualified, it "make[s] you want to do something bad."[25]

The high dropout rate among students in predominantly black schools and their poor performance on standardized national achievement tests helped to convince concerned blacks that something was terribly wrong with inner-city schools. The number of students dropping out between the tenth and twelfth grades from predominantly black high schools at the time of the riot ranged from 50 to 62.5 percent, well above the 40 percent figure for the nation as a whole. The percentage dropping out of black high schools in any one year nearly equaled the percentage graduating, whereas in the city's white high schools the graduates exceeded the dropouts by anywhere from three to six to one.[26]

The academic achievement of students in Detroit's predominantly black schools, a Task Force on Quality Integrated Education reported in 1967, was one and one-half to three years behind that of white students in schools on the city's periphery. On the Iowa Test of Basic Skills given to eighth graders in October 1965, students in seven of the eight high school constellations in the city in which blacks made up at least 70 percent of the student body ranked about two years behind grade level and at or near the bottom of the city's twenty-one high school constellations.[27]

The mainstream answer to low academic achievement in black schools was compensatory education. The Inner City Parents Council, however, thought what was needed was stress on Afro-American history and culture and the development of the creative abilities of black children in writing, the arts, and the dance, all of which, it maintained, required black teachers and administrators in black schools.[28]

The black complaint about the allegedly discriminatory character of the school system took a legal turn with the filing of the Sherrill School bias suit in the United States District Court for the Eastern District of Michigan in January 1962. The Sherrill Elementary School had gone from white to black in the 1950s and by the beginning of 1962 was 95 percent black. It had been included in the western district, which was 93 percent white, but a boundary adjustment in 1958 placed it in the southwestern district, which was 58 percent white. At the same time, however, provision had been made for most Sherrill graduates to attend predominantly white McKenzie High. When the school administration, allegedly in order to relieve overcrowding, appeared to jeopardize this arrangement by ordering the transfer of 143 Sherrill eighth graders to an elementary school near a black high school, the Sherrill Parents Committee, of which Cleage was chairman, went to court to enjoin the action.

The Sherrill suit charged that school board policies confined black students to black schools, with the result that they received a "second-rate education" and suffered harmful "social and psychological effects." The suit charged the school board with "drawing, redrawing and gerrymandering" school district lines and with a variety of other discriminatory practices. The TULC underwrote the suit, which eventually attracted NAACP support as well.[29]

In an interim finding submitted in September 1964, Judge Fred W. Kaess instructed the school board to proceed "forthwith" to achieve the "substantial" integration of faculty and professional personnel in all schools and of students in junior and senior high schools by the beginning of the February 1965 term and to discontinue any apprenticeship program not integrated by that time. When attorneys for the plaintiff expressed dissatisfaction with the progress report Superintendent of Schools Samuel Brownell submitted to the court in March 1965, the court set a trial date for the suit. In the hope of avoiding the trial, the school board, to which a liberal majority had been elected in 1964, ordered Brownell to speed up the integration process, which led the plaintiff to agree to an indefinite adjournment of the case.[30]

In consenting to the adjournment of the Sherrill suit, attorneys for the plaintiff stated that the school system's action represented "substantial and significant progress" in the direction of integration. During the Cavanagh mayoralty, the school system, indeed, moved in the direction of greater integration of students, faculty, and supervisory staff and also sought to adjust instructional material and the curriculum to the changing racial composition of the city's schools. The integration of the student population, however, partly because of the increasing number of black students and decreasing number of white students, proceeded at a snail's pace. The number of schools without any blacks decreased from seventy-three in 1961 to twenty-two in October 1966, but the number of all-black schools increased from eight to fourteen during these same years. According to the calculations of a committee of the National Education Association (NEA), 67 percent of the Detroit schools were segregated in 1961 and 65 percent in 1965, hardly a significant change.[31]

Defending its policies, the school administration noted in March 1965 that all the black students in twenty-nine schools were there only because of the open schools policy. Some transfers under this plan, however, actually increased segregation because whites took advantage of the policy to transfer their children out of black schools. As a result, the school board in July 1966 decided to permit transfers in the future only if they contributed to school integration. In response to the Sherrill suit, the school administration in 1964 redrew district lines, placing two or three high school constellations in each district. The school board claimed that each district was now "highly integrated," with no district having "less than 27 percent student integration" or "less than 21 percent faculty integration." Individual high school constellations remained highly segregated, however, three of them approaching an almost 100 percent black enrollment. As a federal district court pointed out in 1971, had the school board drawn the boundary lines between school attendance areas in an east-west rather than the north-south direction actually followed, the result would have been "significant integration" of the schools.[32]

Detroit had been busing students for many years to relieve overcrowding, but in 1966 the school board decided that busing should thereafter be used not only for this purpose but also, if possible, to further integration. Despite this policy decision, school authorities bused black children from overcrowded black schools to other black schools that had space for them even if this meant busing them past white schools that could have accommodated the youngsters. What school authorities did not do during the next several years was to bus white children to predominantly black schools that had space for additional students. To be sure, given Detroit's residential patterns, there was not too much the school administration could have done to achieve meaningful school integration without massive busing, as a school staff report of 1967 made clear. This, however, was not an option that was seriously debated in Detroit before the riot.[33]

The school board's effort beginning in May 1962 to end the "grave discrimination" against blacks in the apprentice training program, for which the school system provided the instructors and the building but did not select the trainees, ran into the stubborn opposition of the building trades. In August 1963 the board informed employers and unions using the Training School for their apprentices that it would not cooperate in the program with any of them that practiced discrimination. In pursuance of this policy, the board in September 1963 temporarily suspended the training program for electrical workers, and it later sought the assistance of the CRC in seeking to determine whether or not a particular trade actually practiced discrimination when it was accused of doing so. The number of black construction trades apprentices in the school rose, but ever so slightly, from 11 of 1,113 trainees (1 percent) in July 1963, to 62 of 2,526 trainees (2.5 percent) in October 1966. In January 1967 the school board notified six construction trades that it would not provide new training classes for them until they increased the number of black trainees. Some of these classes remained closed at the time of the July 1967 riot.[34]

When Brownell discussed the assignment of teachers with the Citizens Advisory Committee, he advocated a "color-blind" approach to the problem. Several committee members, however, favored a "color-conscious" approach, urging the school board to assign at least one black teacher to each school as evidence of its good faith regarding faculty integration. Following the committee's report, the school board and the school administration began to shift teaching personnel to achieve more racially balanced staffs. In doing so, the administration faced the opposition of both the DFT and the Detroit Education Association, which wanted no tampering with the principle of seniority. The CCR, on the other hand, formed a Committee on Schools and sought to prod the school system to accelerate the process of integration.[35]

In an effort to increase faculty integration, the school board in June 1963 decided that new teachers would henceforth be assigned to the first school vacancy rather than being permitted to choose from a list of three schools. Also, teachers who had served more than three years in a school were to be reassigned to a different school, where they could then remain. In 1965 the board decided to follow assignment procedures that would result in students being exposed to teachers and administrators of different races, and service in an integrated school became a criterion for promotion. Neither the board nor the CCR, however, favored a quota policy in assignments.[36]

The number of black teachers in the Detroit school system increased from 2,275 or 21.6 percent of the total in February 1961 to 3,628 or 31.7 percent of the total in October 1966, a figure that corresponded closely with the percentage of blacks in the city. Forty-one schools had been without a single black teacher in October 1963, but there was only one such school in October 1966. Although believing that "much further progress" was required, the CCR's Richard Marks stated in the fall of 1965 that there was no longer any "spot" in the school system where race was "an obstacle to service"; and the school board by that time thought that it had reached its goal of balanced staffs. There had, to be sure, been progress in the area of faculty integration, but black teachers still tended to be assigned to black schools. In the 1965–66 school year, for example, two-thirds of the black elementary school teachers were working in schools that were 90–100 percent black.[37]

At the school administration level, the two most significant developments during the Cavanagh years were the appointment of a new superintendent and the creation of the post of deputy superintendent to head the Community Relations Division. When Brownell announced that he did not wish to continue as superintendent when his contract expired in 1966, the city's black newspaper editorialized that he had "performed admirably under most difficult and trying situations." The liberal group on the Board of Education, however, thought that he had been insufficiently "aggressive" in pushing integration, and the CCR was critical of what Marks described as the Brownell view that "nothing needs to be done other than to proceed 'without regard to race.' " Norman Drachler, who had been assistant superintendent in charge of School Relations and Special Services, was named acting superintendent and then became superintendent in March 1967. An "aggressive integrationist" and more committed to a color-conscious policy than his predecessor, Drachler had a more comfortable relationship with the black community than Brownell had enjoyed.[38]

The decision of the school board in 1966 to elevate the headship of the Community Relations Division to the level of deputy superintendent appears to have been the first time that a school system had raised a unit of this sort to so high a level. The first deputy superintendent was Arthur Johnson, the former executive secretary of the Detroit NAACP and deputy director of the CRC. Johnson's responsibilities included community use of the schools, intergroup relations, and affirmative action.[39]

Partly because of seniority considerations, there was a considerably smaller proportion of blacks among administrators in the Detroit school system than among the teaching staff. As of February 1967, about 6 percent of the principals (16 of 266), 9 percent of the assistant principals (30 of 337), and 9 percent of department heads (35 of 370) were black. These numbers were substantially above 1961 levels and continued to increase in the next two school years, but the NAACP saw the gains as reflecting "overt tokenism." But slow as progress in faculty and staff integration was, Detroit, as board member A. L. Zwerdling pointed out in 1967, had the highest percentage of black teachers and school administrators of any city in the nation.[40] How typical this was of Detroit's reputation as a model city in the 1960s: progressive as compared to other cities but rather far away from achieving genuine racial equality.

The school board's commitment to equal employment extended to contractors doing business with the school system. In January 1965 the board adopted an "affirmative action standard for contract performance," anticipating the action of the city government the next year. In 1966 the board required potential contractors to submit a statistical report of their employment practices that could be reviewed along with their bids.[41]

The Detroit school system led the nation in seeing to it that minorities, especially blacks, were fairly and accurately portrayed in textbooks and visual materials used in the schools. GOAL in particular was instrumental in persuading the school board to move in this direction. Detroit began work in 1962 on what became the Detroit City Schools Reader Series, the first primers in the nation depicting black and white youngsters and their families engaged in common activities. The school board informed publishers in 1963 that the school system would not purchase textbooks that did not provide fair treatment of minorities and their contribution to the nation. The Community Relations Division was given the responsibility of scrutinizing textbooks to ensure their compliance with this policy. The school administration also created a committee to preview visual aids to ensure that they depicted blacks in a nondiscriminatory manner—the committee rejected a film on Detroit that omitted blacks from its street scenes. In May 1967 the school board decided to provide publishers with illustrations reflecting the pluralistic nature of American society.[42]

Detroit, as noted, had pioneered with its Great Cities School Improvement Project in seeking to cope with the cultural disadvantages of inner-city children. Federal funding beginning in 1964 made it possible for the city to extend the program to a total of twenty-six schools and twenty-four thousand school children. Through the Great Cities Extended School Project, which also benefited from federal funding, Detroit was able to bring a roughly similar program to fifteen to twenty thousand additional students and their parents in fifty-one schools in culturally deprived neighborhoods.[43]

The Great Cities projects were among the numerous programs the Detroit public school system devised to compensate for the environmental inadequacies of inner-city children. The school administration developed a volunteer service that utilized more than four thousand adults in lower-income neighborhoods to tutor school children and assist teachers in other ways. The Shared Experiences Project the school system devised in 1965 enabled students attending schools of different racial composition to join together in a variety of extracurricular activities. More than twenty-three thousand students took part in such activities in the 1966–67 school year. In an effort to preserve integration in three school neighborhoods undergoing racial change, Detroit in 1965, with the aid of state funds, developed an early version of the magnet school idea by enriching the curriculum of three high school constellations (McKenzie, Mumford, and Pershing) and providing additional services for their fifty thousand students. Reacting negatively to the program, a black educator complained that money allocated for the project should have been used to benefit slum schools, not to subsidize whites to remain in Detroit. "Whites," he said, "have an option to move away. Blacks can only go back to the ghetto."[44] The formulation of educational policy was obviously no easy matter in a racially divided city.

A delegate agency in the city's war on poverty, the Detroit public schools provided a panoply of programs subsidized by the federal government that were designed to provide cultural enrichment and "academic remediation and development." These included, in addition to what has already been noted, Pre-School Child and Parent Education (for three-year-olds and their low-income parents), Head Start, Remedial Education for Adults (for illiterate and semiliterate adults), Continuing Education for Pregnant Girls, In-School Youth Work Training Program, Neighborhood Youth Corps, and the Intramural Physical Education Program. These and similar programs administered by the archdiocese, twenty-one programs in all, served ninety-five thousand children and adults as of June 1966.[45]

The director of the Detroit East Regional Office of the CRC and many school employees and parents thought that Detroit's compensatory education programs were of limited effect in the years just before the riot. They believed that this was because the school establishment, as an NEA committee put it, "operated largely in isolation from and insulation against the concerns of inner-city communities."[46] Although this was not an entirely accurate judgment, there is no disputing the charge of ineffectiveness. This was not, however, because Detroit had failed to address itself to the problem of the changing racial composition of its school population—it had made as determined an effort to do so as any large school system in the nation—but rather because of the immense difficulty of the problem itself, as the record of later years has demonstrated.

Black concern about the quality of education available to blacks in Detroit was brought to the fore in the year before the riot as the result of a student boycott of classes at Northern High. Northern High, on Woodward Avenue and Owen, was not all that different from other predominantly black high schools. More than 98 percent of its twenty-three hundred students as of 1966 were black, and most did not appear to be making very much academic progress. In a 1965–66 test of randomly selected ninth-grade students, 55.5 percent of Northern's ninth graders scored below the sixth-grade level in reading ability. On a February 1965 educational progress test given 10B and 12B students, 76 percent of the tested Northern students scored below average in math, 78 percent in science, and 79 percent in reading. Only about 20 percent of the class scheduled to graduate in June 1966 had actually achieved a twelfth-grade academic level. Familiar with the academic program at white high schools, some Northern students thought that their school "looked awful by comparison," and they attributed this to the color of their skins. As a former Northern student later remarked, "any time there is an all-black school, people just don't care, man, they just don't care whether you learn or not."[47]

There was a good deal of dissension among the Northern faculty reflecting differences between older and younger teachers and members of the DFT, the exclusive bargaining agency, and the rival Detroit Education Association. Some students claimed that the principal, Arthur J. Carty, who had been in the school system for forty years, "badgered" students and that the assistant principal, George Donaldson, was "rude" to students and parents alike. Students also complained about the rough treatment accorded them by Bonnie Lucas, the black policeman who had been assigned to the school in 1963 because a Northern teacher had been threatened by dope addicts.[48]

The immediate cause of the Northern boycott was the censorship of an editorial entitled "Educational Camouflage" written for the student newspaper toward the end of March 1966 by twelfth-grade honors student Charles Colding. The editorial criticized the social promotion policy of the school and its failure to prepare students for college. Noting that similar conditions prevailed in other black schools, Colding wondered if these schools were "being operated on the principle that Negroes aren't as capable of learning as whites, so why bother with them?" Just before the Easter break, the principal, who was leaving town, entrusted the decision of whether to publish the article to the chairman of the English department rather than to the student paper's faculty advisor, who favored publication. Claiming that the editorial was "inflammatory and full of unsupported charges," the chairman killed the piece.[49]

Three students, Colding, Judy Walker, and Michael Batchelor, began to organize Northern students for a demonstration on April 7, two days before the Easter vacation. They received some advice and help from the chairman of the Detroit chapter of CORE, but what happened was basically "a kid's movement." Brownell met with the students on April 6 and, recognizing the inevitable, gave permission for the walkout, reversed the censorship decision, and promised that the school board would address the academic problems the students had raised.[50]

About twenty-three hundred students and parents milled about outside Northern on April 7. Carty, who thought that "subversive elements," including some teachers, had instigated the action, claimed that he had received numerous calls from parents informing him that their children were being "intimidated" to join the walkout. At a meeting of about one thousand students and parents at nearby St. Joseph's Episcopal Church, whose rector, the Reverend David Gracie, the boycotters accepted as an "ally," the students agreed on a list of demands that were refined a few days later. The students called for the removal of Carty, without his being replaced by Donaldson—"the antipathy of the kids toward Carty borders on the paranoid," an observer noted; the replacement of Lucas by a Youth Bureau officer; permission for qualified teachers to remain at Northern despite the three-year rule; school board provision of "comparative information" about academic standards at Northern and other schools and a written "plan of action" to correct the situation; creation of a student-elected student-faculty council to study school problems; the appointment of a school community agent at Northern; and no reprisals against students. Deadlines were set for each of these demands, which were forwarded to Brownell on April 15. The students stated that they would not return to school on April 18, when classes were to resume after the Easter vacation, unless Carty and Lucas had been removed by then.[51]

The school administration had canceled classes at Northern on April 8, the day before the Easter break. By the time the students returned to Northern on April 18, the school board had agreed to permit students, faculty, and community leaders to air their complaints about Northern at an April 19 board meeting. The board had also announced the appointment of a study committee headed by the Reverend Gracie—he was later demoted to vice-chairman—to study "all aspects" of the situation at Northern; and, even more important and as a "direct response" to the complaints of Northern students and their parents about the quality of education in predominantly black schools, the board also announced the launching of a major study of all of Detroit's twenty-two high schools.[52]

Brownell advised the student leaders on April 15 that it was his understanding that Lucas was no longer assigned to Northern and that an assistant superintendent and a school field executive would be in charge when school resumed on April 18. Dissatisfied with what Brownell had told them as well as with the school board's actions, the Northern student leaders charged the Board of Education with "bad faith and procrastination" in responding to their demands.[53]

Northern reopened on April 18, with Carty remaining away for the time being, ostensibly to aid school administrators in the evaluation of Northern's problems. Brownell and the school board, however, decided to return Carty to Northern on April 20. Student anger at this action as well as their dissatisfaction with the character of the board hearing the night before provoked a boycott of classes by all but about two hundred students on April 20. A large group of student boycotters met at St. Joseph's Church, and lest it be thought that they were "playing hooky," they decided to set up a Freedom School. Colding contacted Wayne State University economics professor Karl Gregory, a Northern graduate, who agreed to serve as principal of the school and to help recruit a faculty. Within a few days, about 150 teachers, several of them Wayne State faculty members, had volunteered their services. The Freedom School opened at St. Joseph's Church on April 21, one of the first two lectures being delivered by Professor David Herreshof on "Civil Disobedience." To accommodate the large number of students wishing to attend, the Freedom School found space in two additional churches. In a few days the faculty was augmented by thirty-one Northern teachers, whom the Board of Education permitted to teach in the Freedom School.[54]

The first homework assignment of the Freedom School students was to write an essay on what was wrong at Northern. "I wasn't learning anything," wrote one student. "I want a better education and to be taught by teachers who care," was the comment of a second student. A third student observed, "They [teachers] say the black boys and girls don't want to learn, so therefore they don't put much in their jobs."[55]

The school board ordered the Northern students back to school on April 20, and Brownell warned parents two days later that school attendance was "a parental responsibility." As of Friday, April 22, the day of a sympathy demonstration at Eastern High, 964 students were attending classes at Northern, as compared to more than one thousand in forty classes of the Freedom School. Over the weekend the community began to polarize. Some civil rights groups urged the students to continue the boycott, and a group of students for whom Cleage served as spokesman began planning for a one-day walkout at other high schools on April 27. The NAACP and the white "establishment," however, advised the students to return to Northern, the NAACP chapter president saying that he was not sure that the level of education in the Freedom School was superior to that at Northern.[56]

Having been privately assured by the chairman of the Board of Education that Carty would not be at Northern when they returned to their classes and that they and their parents would participate in the investigation of the school, Northern students voted on April 26 to end the boycott. Conceding that the school could not resume "normal operations" under Carty, Brownell announced in July that Donaldson would be the new Northern principal. By that time, the Northern High School Study Committee had issued its Interim Report. Its summary of conditions at Northern, "*a dissatisfied student body, a divided teaching staff and an estranged community*," spoke for itself.[57]

The Northern boycott had far-reaching effects. It "focused" the community's attention on the Detroit educational system as never before and created sharp divisions in the city regarding educational policy. The boycott was "a central issue of every discussion with Detroit citizens," an NEA investigating committee that visited the city on May 10 reported. Many citizens, especially white citizens, and school administrators were outraged that Brownell had removed a principal because of student complaints and "threats" and was "letting the students run the schools." Critical mail to the school board, critical editorials in the newspapers and on TV, and expressions of concern in the white community were followed by a negative vote in the school millage election on May 9. The associate executive director of the CCEO thought that it was "a punitive vote" by whites that went "far beyond" hard-core voters opposed to a tax increase and revealed "a decided gap in attitude" between blacks, who voted for the millage, and whites.[58]

Black concern about the quality of education in black schools was heightened by the Northern boycott. An east side conference on "The Crisis in the Inner City Schools" sponsored by Congressman Charles C.

Diggs, Jr., and state legislators urged black parents to set up a "watch dog committee" to ensure that promises to close the "learning gap" between whites and blacks were carried out. For some blacks, the reason the school system failed to educate black children properly was racism. When the Michigan and Detroit Federation of Teachers sponsored a conference on "Racism in Education" in May, black nationalists dominated the proceedings. Their demand that black administrators should replace white administrators in ghetto schools "shot through the total community[,] raising a massive reaction," according to a report to the Department of Justice's Community Relations Service. A black grass roots worker told the *Michigan Chronicle* in May that the poor quality of education available to Detroit blacks would be the target of groups mobilizing to make the summer of 1967 "long and hot."[59]

That conditions at Northern were not unique was made painfully evident in the reports of the individual study commissions for other black high schools. The final report of the High School Study Commission, which included the chairmen of the twenty-two high school study groups, was not published until June 1968, after the riot. The report's appraisal of the Detroit high schools was devastating. Excepting some schools, the report drew a picture of "poor physical facilities, inadequate school administrations, teachers who perform poorly, an inequitable distribution of qualified teachers, questionable teacher assignment and reassignment policies, faculty uncertainty with respect to students' abilities and needs, programs and curricula which lead nowhere and have little relevance to future goals and employment opportunities." Seniors in fifteen of the schools, the report indicated, were at least three years behind grade level in reading, and every third student failed at least one course per term. "Our high schools," one of the two cochairmen of the commission declared, "are appallingly inadequate, a disgrace to the community and a tragedy for the thousands of young men and women whom we compel and cajole to sit in them."[60]

Bad as the situation was in Detroit high schools in general, it was worse in the predominantly black schools. Superintendent Drachler told the Kerner Commission in August 1967 that the reports of the individual high school study groups helped one to understand "a little better" why there had been a riot in Detroit. Although, judging from the fifteen-city survey, Detroit's blacks were no more dissatisfied with their schools than blacks in other big cities with their schools, they were more dissatisfied than whites in the city were with their schools: in the fifteen-city survey, 36 percent of the black respondents but only 22 percent of the whites indicated that they were "somewhat" or "very dissatisfied" with their neighborhood schools.[61]

One lesson young blacks, at least, may have learned from the Northern boycott was that direct action was what was required to move the white establishment to action. When the boycott ended, Karl Gregory told the Northern students that they had done more to improve inner-city education than all the citizens' committees of the preceding ten years. It was the boycott, after all, that had led to the removal of Carty, the establishment of the High School Study Commission, and efforts to improve the quality of education and student services at Northern itself. The Northern boycott was followed by disruptions and walkouts at other black schools, as young blacks developed a sense of themselves and pride in their identity.[62] This was not unrelated to the even more dramatic events that were to follow in the city.

Important as the issue of education was for Detroit blacks in the years just before the 1967 riot, housing was an even more important matter. The CRC's deputy director thought that housing was "the most pervasive of all discrimination problems"; the DUL judged it to be "the foremost problem" of Detroit's blacks; and the head of the CCEO called it "the greatest single problem in the greater Detroit area." In a riot retrospective, Mayor Cavanagh remarked that if there was one area in which his administration had not done enough, it was housing.[63]

As is so typical of Detroit's model city reputation, the housing of Detroit blacks could be and was compared favorably with that of blacks elsewhere in the nation. Between 1960 and 1967 the percentage of home ownership among black households in Detroit increased from 39 percent to 48 percent, the highest figure for blacks in the nation. Also, a much higher percentage of Detroit blacks lived in sound housing as of 1965 (74 percent compared to 55 percent of blacks elsewhere).[64]

If black housing in Detroit was "good" as compared to black housing elsewhere, it was, however, "very bad" compared to white housing in the city. Of the more than thirty-six thousand households in Detroit living in substandard housing in 1966, 29,600 (about 120,000 individuals) were black. They lived in housing that was overcrowded, rat infested, and had leaky roofs, holes in the walls, and defective plumbing. They were the victims of low incomes, absentee landlords, and poor code enforcement.[65]

The expanding black population in Detroit in the 1960s had to find living space in a diminishing housing market. Between 1960 and 1967, 25,927 dwellings were demolished in the city because of freeway construction, urban renewal, school and recreational use, or because they had been abandoned, and only 15,494 new housing units were built. The new units, moreover, were mainly for middle- or upper-income households. In 1964 the vacancy rate in Detroit was 6.2 percent, which constituted "a fair balance between supply and demand." In the spring of 1967, however, the Detroit rate was 1 percent, "probably the lowest of any big city market in the country." At the time of the riot, the Detroit area was simply "starved for housing."[66]

Just before the riot, Robert D. Knox, the director-secretary of the Detroit Housing Commission (DHC), stated that Detroit needed eighty thousand low-income housing units, 60 percent of them for blacks. Absent additional private construction, for which high construction costs and the scarcity and high price of land served as deterrents, Detroit might have made more housing available to blacks by providing additional public housing or by enlarging the housing market for blacks by an open occupancy policy.[67]

Knox, of course, was aware that no new public housing had been built in Detroit since 1952. In the words of a CCEO report, the 8,155 public housing units in the city, 60 percent of them occupied by blacks, were "a drop in the bucket" considering the "thousands of families in cramped quarters, living with relatives, in rooming houses, under threat of eviction, and in the throes of urban renewal." Seeking to increase the amount of public housing, Detroit in the months before the riot began the planning for 1,235 units for seniors and large families to be built in small concentrations in nine different locations. This effort laid bare the racial implications of public housing policy in Detroit. Most of the housing was to be built in white areas, which led whites to object that "forced integration by municipal action" was an improper function of the city government. Responding to the pressure of white homeowners, the Common Council rejected two of the proposed sites. As of the time of the riot, none of the units had actually been constructed.[68]

Since the demand for nonwhite housing was increasing at a time when the housing market was racially "closed," one seeming solution for Detroit's housing crisis was to open that market. The CCR, the CCEO, and church groups joined the NAACP and the Detroit Urban League (DUL) in making open housing a cause. Marks was later to characterize open housing as "the cornerstone of civil rights," contending that it increased the supply of housing, improved schools, and provided employment. The CCR urged the Common Council to act on the matter, it conferred with black realtors about ways to cope with the problem, and it distributed literature on the availability of repossessed homes. When blacks moved into white neighborhoods, the CCR tried to form human relations councils in the area to ease acceptance of the blacks. The CCEO understood the need to educate whites about open occupancy, and it sought to overcome the opposition of realtors. The efforts of the CCR and CCEO were abetted beginning in 1965 by the Greater Detroit Committee for Fair Housing Practice, which cooperated with suburban human relations councils to inform potential minority renters or home buyers about available housing in the suburbs.[69]

The opposition to open housing in Detroit was unyielding before the riot. Blacks moving into white areas continued to be harassed despite improved police protection. The threat of racial change in a neighborhood—the "tipping" point could be as low as 5 percent—led to "emotional fears, 'panic' selling, [and] improper real estate marketing practices." The forces opposed to open housing proved to be stronger before the riot than the forces supporting a racially free housing market. In the fifteen-city survey, 73 percent of Detroit's black respondents thought that there were "many" (40 percent) or "some" (33 percent) places where they could not buy or rent.[70]

Willing to restrain real estate brokers who exploited racial fears but unwilling to adopt an open occupancy ordinance, the Common Council in 1962 enacted a Fair Neighborhood Practice Ordinance. The ordinance, which the CCR was to enforce, restricted the number, location, and length of time that realty signs could be displayed and made it unlawful to refer to race in seeking property listings or in published or written realty advertising. In enforcing the ordinance, the CCR sought voluntary compliance, stressing education and negotiation. By July 1966, it had found 855 violations of the ordinance and had recommended twelve prosecutions, the defendants being convicted in seven instances.

Although the DUL thought that the ordinance had "aided slightly" in stabilizing neighborhoods, continuing complaints about realtor practices led the CCR to hold public hearings on the matter in February 1966. The hearings revealed that although the types of racial appeal proscribed by the ordinance had declined, realtors used "subtler forms of pressure" that contributed to racial segregation. Residents in changing neighborhoods were subjected to excessive solicitation of listings, houses in such neighborhoods were marketed only to blacks, who were rarely shown anything else, and white customers were diverted to other areas. CCR staff members concluded that the realtor argument that they were simply following the wishes of their customers rather than determining housing practices had been "blown to bits" in the hearings.[71]

The CCR's housing hearings led the Common Council in July 1966 to add an "equal service annex" to the Fair Neighborhood Practice Ordinance. The annex made it a misdemeanor for an agent to refuse to show a property listed for sale, rental, or lease or to refuse to forward an offer to the owner of a listed property because of the race, color, or national origin of the prospective buyer. In fourteen months of enforcing the annex, the CCR was unable in dealing with complaints to make it possible for a single black to purchase a home of his choice.[72]

Following the Metropolitan Conference on Open Occupancy in January 1963, the Common Council requested the CCR to draft an open housing ordinance. The proposed ordinance, which exempted only homeowners who rented space in a two-family or single-family dwelling in which the homeowner lived, was introduced on July 1, 1963, by William Patrick, Detroit's first black councilman, and Mel Ravitz. Claiming to represent forty homeowner organizations, the Greater Detroit Homeowners Council responded to the proposed ordinance by circulating petitions for a rival ordinance prohibiting any restrictions on the sale or rental of homes. Thomas L. Poindexter, the Homeowners cochairman, described the ordinance as "a 'free choice' ordinance, just the opposite of an open occupancy ordinance." Within four days, the Homeowners Council had gathered twice the number of signatures required to compel submission of the ordinance to the voters should the Common Council fail to act on it, which is precisely what happened.[73]

Faced with two rival housing ordinances and aware of the deep public interest in the matter, the Common Council scheduled a public hearing for September 17 that attracted two thousand people, about equally divided between whites and blacks. The president of the Detroit NAACP charged that Detroit was a "divided city" in which blacks did not enjoy "real" freedom since they could not buy homes where they pleased. Homeowners Council representatives sounded quite a different note, one of them maintaining that "the Negro is not suitable for the place in society which he is trying to push into," and another charging that a "secret government" was behind the open housing campaign.[74]

Before the Common Council could vote on the Patrick-Ravitz measure, a ruling by Michigan's attorney general, Frank Kelley, muddied the waters. Kelley announced in October 1963 that the new Michigan constitution, which was to go into effect on January 1, 1964, gave the CRC sole authority to enforce civil rights in housing and that the power of a local body like the CCR could extend to "education, counseling, conciliation or mediation" but not enforcement. Six days later, the Common Council defeated the Patrick-Ravitz ordinance by a 7 to 2 vote. "Detroit," declared the *Michigan Chronicle*, "was forced to lay bare its soul and observe the painful reality of the ruthless insistence by many of our fellow Detroiters that they have preserved their right to racially discriminate in the sale and rental of housing."[75]

The NAACP mounted a legal challenge to the placing of the Homeowners' ordinance on the city ballot. In a "scathing opinion," Wayne County Circuit Court Judge Joseph A. Moynihan ruled the ordinance unconstitutional, stating that "its real purpose" was to "advance the cause of racial bigotry in the field of housing." The Michigan Supreme Court, however, overruled Moynihan and stipulated that the ordinance must be submitted to the voters. In the September 1964 primary election, the electorate approved the ordinance by a vote of 136,671 to 111,994 and, in a further indication of its sentiments, took the first step leading to Poindexter's election to the council to replace Patrick, who had resigned. The ordinance did not go into effect, however, since the Wayne County Circuit Court ruled it unconstitutional in a second suit. Poindexter himself was defeated when he sought reelection in 1965.[76]

The major concern of the Detroit city government regarding housing was less segregated housing than it was the removal of blight in the city by adopting programs of urban renewal, neighborhood conservation, and code enforcement. Detroit officials estimated that 15 percent of the city, which included 18 percent of its structures, was in "some stage of

blight." The ideal approach to this problem as the DHC and Knox conceived it was slum clearance and urban renewal for the most blighted
areas, neighborhood conservation and spot clearance for "middle-aged
areas," and code enforcement in newer areas.[77]

Detroit was one of the nation's pioneers in the area of urban redevelopment or, as it later came to be known, urban renewal. Detroit initially
conceived of urban renewal as a way to arrest the exodus of business
from the central city, to convert slum property to better housing, and to
enlarge the city's tax base. In 1946 Detroit, as part of the Detroit Plan,
initiated the Gratiot Redevelopment Project on a 129-acre site on the
city's lower east side that included a portion of Hastings Street. The city's
plan for the area prefigured the substance of Title I of the Housing Act
of 1949, which provided federal funds for urban renewal. Under the
federal statute, local authorities were to draw up plans for urban redevelopment, acquire and clear the site, and sell the land to developers at
market prices. The federal government paid the city two-thirds of the
difference between the costs it incurred in purchasing and clearing the
site and the price paid by the developer for the bare land. The local
agency was to provide for the relocation of the displaced families by
making available " 'decent, safe, and sanitary dwellings' at reasonable
rents and reasonably accessible to places of employment."[78]

The Housing Act of 1954 authorized federal assistance to cities for
conservation and rehabilitation in addition to slum clearance. Cities were
required to submit a "Workable Program," which had to explain how
they proposed to deal with "urban decay" and had to make provision for
code enforcement and for citizen participation in the urban renewal
process. Relocation payments for the displaced of up to $25,000 for
businesses and $200 for families were authorized by the Housing Act of
1950. A 1964 housing amendment authorized not only "reasonable and
necessary moving expenses" for the displaced but also a "relocation
adjustment payment" of up to $500 per family. Whatever the federal
housing legislation stipulated, urban renewal, as Lawrence Friedman
noted, was not a program to build houses but "a program to remake the
cities in a physical sense." The concern was the urban slum, not the urban
slum dweller. Detroit was no exception to this generalization.[79]

The Common Council selected the DHC to administer the city's
urban renewal program. Subsequently assigned the task of providing
relocation services for the displaced, the DHC in 1957 established a
Relocation Advisory Committee, one of the first such agencies in the
nation. Detroit took advantage of the Housing Act of 1959 to secure
funding in June 1962 for the formulation of a comprehensive urban
renewal program, a task Cavanagh entrusted to the Mayor's Committee
for Community Renewal. The committee did not confine its investigations to the "traditional aspects of urban renewal" but rather placed
considerable emphasis on "the social and economic factors of blight."[80]

Detroit's renewal projects were almost entirely confined to the inner city south of Grand Boulevard. By March 1963 Detroit had ten urban renewal projects underway in addition to the Gratiot Project. More than ten thousand structures had been demolished or were scheduled for demolition, and 43,096 persons, 70 percent of them black, had been displaced or were to be displaced by the various projects. The projects aimed at the reconstruction of residential areas, the rebuilding of the central business district, industrial reuse, institutional and cultural development, and port rehabilitation. By the end of 1962 Detroit had become "a pilot city" for urban redevelopment and was being "watched nationally and internationally."[81]

Few issues appeared to be more troubling to blacks in the Cavanagh years than urban renewal. The displacement and relocation of people that urban renewal entailed involved mainly blacks, and the fate of the neighborhoods as the projects developed and the character of the housing that relocatees were able to obtain became matters of grave concern for those affected and the black community in general. One urban renewal problem was summed up by the phrase "blight by announcement." There was commonly a delay of several years between the time a neighborhood was designated for urban renewal and the actual taking of the property began, and in the interval the area deteriorated. There was no longer incentive for renters or property owners to improve their homes, and since the area was to be bulldozed, the city government became lax in providing services. Once the condemnation process started, the bulldozers moved in, and the residents began to leave, there was an increase in vandalism, and vacant homes became fire traps for unwary children. The transient nature of such an area also provided a "cover" for prostitution and other illicit activities.

After a renewal area was cleared, there was often an additional delay of several years until the city could find developers for the site and they in turn could obtain the necessary financing. After the city cleared the Gratiot site, for example, it could not find developers willing to build low- or moderate-cost housing there, and so the land remained vacant for several years, derisively referred to as "Ragweed Acres."[82]

The most troublesome problem associated with urban renewal, as with state government freeway construction, was the relocation of displaced families and individuals. The slum areas that were bulldozed were commonly converted in Detroit and elsewhere to commercial and nonresidential use or were replaced by housing priced beyond the means of the residents who had been on the site. As of 1968, Detroit's urban renewal projects had resulted in the razing of about eleven thousand homes, largely occupied by low-income blacks, and their replacement by 3,814 housing units, 2,797 of which were priced for middle- or high-income persons. "They tore down to put up new apartments we couldn't afford," declared a black woman after the riot. "This urban renewal," she said, "is for the birds." Urban renewal not only destroyed sometimes cohesive neighborhoods but also contributed to the city's growing housing shortage, which in turn led to an increase in rents and the price of homes.[83]

The most effective opponent of urban renewal in Detroit during the Cavanagh mayoralty was the West Central Organization (WCO). Given its lower west side location, the WCO's concern was the University City development, which involved the clearance of 304 acres in five phases to permit the expansion of Wayne State University and the construction of residential and commercial property. The first phase, which led to the demolition of housing that had accommodated more than three thousand persons so as to make way for a large physical education complex for Wayne State, began late in 1964, just before the WCO was organized. The WCO, in its raucous way, demanded that residents be fully involved in the planning of urban renewal projects and have a veto power over projects affecting them. They urged the construction of low-cost housing in the same general area for those to be displaced before their residences were demolished, elimination of the delay between the announcement of a project and clearance of the site, and use of urban renewal funds by the city, as permitted by federal law, to assist nonprofit groups to sponsor low-cost housing developments.

In pushing its urban renewal demands, the WCO, to be sure, also wanted to build its "image" as a defender of the poor. Claiming that the affected citizens, in violation of federal law, had had nothing to say about the "inhuman removal" that was taking place and that Cavanagh was "stalling" in meeting its demands, the WCO in November 1965 took its case to the midwest regional administrator of the United States Urban Renewal Administration and, in "two dramatic meetings," to Governor Romney the next month. When the federal official expressed "sympathy" for the WCO's concerns, a black WCO member retorted, "We've had 100 years of sympathy. We want action now." Romney criticized Detroit's urban renewal procedures and expressed support for greater citizen participation in both urban renewal and highway planning.[84]

It was DHC policy to survey each family and individual on the urban renewal site regarding their relocation needs and desires and to inform them about all aspects of the program. Those without relocation plans of their own were supposed to be referred to proper housing that they could afford. With each project, the DHC boasted of improved success in relocating the displaced, claiming in 1965, for example, that 99 percent of the families and individuals in its relocation workload for the first phase of the Elmwood Park Project, just east of the Gratiot site, had been relocated in decent and affordable housing. It rejected the WCO's charges, denying any violation of federal law and noting how often the mayor, his staff, the City Plan Commission, and the DHC had met with WCO representatives.[85]

The WCO was always willing to use unconventional tactics, to say the least, to attract attention and to achieve its goals. It brought a skunk to a meeting of the Board of Governors of Wayne State University to show its disgust with university policy regarding the University City Project; it camped on Knox's lawn; and despite the arrest of fourteen members and sympathizers, it forcibly moved a family into a vacant home near Wayne State to dramatize the hardships of relocation. In the end, the WCO was able to influence the city government to modify its urban renewal policy. After the Common Council in February 1966 approved the sale of forty-four acres of urban renewal land to Wayne State for athletic and recreational facilities, the aldermen pledged not to approve any further sale of urban renewal land until adequate housing had been provided for families forced to relocate. Wayne State and the city agreed to restudy the remaining phases of the University City Project so as to include low- and moderate-cost housing. Cavanagh also agreed to set up an advisory council of citizens on the lower west side to join with city officials in planning renewal and relocation projects.

After the state legislature in 1966 required the creation of citizens councils in areas where relocation was to occur, the DHC established such councils in three areas to give residents "a clearer voice" in the relocation process. The city also agreed to use city funds to assist the WCO and two other nonprofit groups to sponsor the construction of 540 units of low-cost housing. The state government finally agreed in 1965 to begin paying relocation costs for families displaced by highway construction and to involve citizens in the planning of the relocation required by such construction.[86]

Knox asserted in November 1965 that urban renewal was one of the city's "most satisfying programs." Not only had it added $7 million to the city's tax base, but, he claimed, most of the displaced had left substandard housing for "a better life." After the riot, he rejected the oft-heard assertion that urban renewal was "Negro removal" and said that blacks largely supported the program. Although Cavanagh's executive secretary asserted at the end of 1967 that Detroit's relocation efforts had been "uncoordinated and inadequate," Knox maintained that Detroit had the best relocation program in the nation. He conceded, however, "We are not doing the job we should be doing."[87]

Although the black leadership and others regularly complained about the harmful impact of urban renewal on the black community, the major pieces of evidence that we have with respect to the black relocatees themselves present a more mixed picture of the effect of urban renewal on those personally affected by the process. In 1964 interviewers talked with a sample of 152 household heads, 95 percent of them black, who had been forced to move from the Elmwood Park No. 1 and Medical Center No. 1 sites in the winter of 1961–62 and the summer of 1963. Stressing threats to both life and property, the interviewees "painted a rather frightening picture of neighborhood decay" once the city had acquired the two sites. Although they had a very favorable opinion of DHC personnel with whom they had come into contact, the "summary judgment" of 52 percent of the respondents was that the city had been of "no help" or "very little help" in the relocation process. Despite the fact that they preferred their old neighborhoods by a five to four ratio, 61 percent of the relocatees judged their new housing to be superior in quality to the old housing that they had been forced to abandon. As was true in other cities also, the housing costs of the Detroit relocatees had increased (16 percent) as a result of their move.

Fifty-two percent of the interviewees thought there was a "racial motive" to urban renewal. "Just pushing colored out so the white people can move down there" was how one relocatee characterized urban renewal. Although most thought that the physical effect of urban renewal was positive—it was "making the city look better," said one black—more than 70 percent of the interviewees "felt bad, sometimes to the point of serious depression," about the short-term impact of relocation on their lives. Those who expressed negative feelings of this sort were commonly concerned about the loss of "especially valued personal friendships and neighborhood relations." A few even feared that relocation "marked the end of their lives in any meaningful sense." Many of those who assessed the immediate impact of relocation in negative terms, however, had become reconciled to their lot by the time they were interviewed. It was thus the judgment of the interviewers that whereas 13 percent of the relocatees were "very bitter, hostile, angry" about urban renewal and 30 percent showed "some resentment, irritation," 25 percent were "somewhat positive, pleased," and 9 percent were "very satisfied, delighted."[88]

Interviews in 1964 with a sample survey of 216 households in Census Tract 515 on Detroit's lower east side, selected as an almost all-black area similar to neighborhoods that had undergone urban renewal and adjacent to an area selected for urban renewal, revealed that 64 percent of the respondents had a "positive attitude" regarding urban renewal and only 20 percent had a "negative attitude." On the other hand, 44 percent thought it was "very true" or "partly true" that urban renewal meant "Negro removal." Of the twenty-four among the 199 black Detroit respondents in the fifteen-city survey who had been forced to move or told they would have to move because of urban renewal, seventeen thought urban renewal "more fair" than "unfair."[89] These bits of data, although far from conclusive, suggest that opposition to urban renewal may have been somewhat less pronounced in the black community than the black leadership indicated, but the picture was certainly not as rosy as the DHC maintained.

As with urban renewal, Detroit pioneered in the field of neighborhood conservation. In 1953 Mayor Albert E. Cobo appointed the Mayor's Committee for Neighborhood Conservation and Improved Housing as part of an effort to improve neighborhoods and to prevent the spread of blight in both residential and commercial areas. The idea then found its way into the Housing Act of 1954, which provided two-thirds of the cost to cities that met federal standards regarding physical conservation. The Cavanagh administration supplemented the federal effort by introducing the concept of "non-assisted conservation."[90]

The Committee for Neighborhood Conservation and Improved Housing consisted in 1965 of ninety-one members, one-third of them city officials and the remainder private citizens appointed by the mayor. Its functions were to use public and private resources to "(1) preserve, maintain, protect and improve new and stable areas; (2) conserve and rejuvenate middle-aged areas facing decline; and (3) hold the line and reverse the trend in deteriorating areas." It worked through Detroit's thirteen hundred block clubs, community councils, and neighborhood organizations, many of which had been formed at the committee's initiative.[91]

Detroit had two federally assisted conservation projects, the first in the nation, one on the east side in a neighborhood that was two-thirds black, the other an all-black enclave on the west side. Both projects involved the demolition of severely blighted structures, the rehabilitation and upgrading of other structures, and various neighborhood improvements.[92] The Cavanagh administration developed eight nonassisted conservation projects in middle-aged parts of the city that were deteriorating but did not require complete clearance. The DHC supplied each project with a project manager who served as a liaison between the project area and the city government. The program for the projects normally involved efforts to persuade residents to renovate their homes and improve their neighborhoods. Although the program of nonassisted conservation was only a qualified success, it attracted national attention as a model for other cities.[93]

The block clubs and community organizations were located primarily in black areas or in neighborhoods undergoing racial change. They dealt with such matters as housing improvement, demolition of blighted structures, "dangerous open houses," code enforcement, zoning violations, fire insurance, garbage pick-up, untrimmed trees, traffic problems, recreational needs, prostitution, blind pigs, and police protection. A 1962 survey of block club members in the Tenth Precinct, where the 1967 riot centered, revealed that racial discrimination was not an important concern of the approximately 230 clubs in the precinct. Although the Cavanagh administration, which worked with the clubs, did not really know how representative they were, the membership appears to have been primarily middle-aged and middle class and out of touch with the unruly elements in their neighborhoods. The clubs nevertheless provided an element of social stability in neighborhoods beset with more than their share of problems. The designation of Detroit as an All-America city in

March 1967 was partly based on the rehabilitation efforts of three of the city's neighborhood organizations.[94]

Many block clubs belonged to large community councils. One of these, the West Grand Boulevard–Clairmount Improvement Association, included thirty block clubs in the area in which the riot centered. The neighborhood, a sixty-block area of about forty thousand people bounded by West Grand Boulevard, Clairmount, Woodrow Wilson, the Lodge Freeway, and Fourteenth, was designated in 1964 as the site for a nonassisted conservation project, taking the name Keifer-Ford. In 1966 the citizens of Keifer-Ford, concerned about the increase of crime and vice in the area, petitioned the Common Council to request a federal planning grant so that the city and the neighborhood could joir.tly plan the rehabilitation of the area. The council complied, and late in 1966, by which time Keifer-Ford had been renamed the Virginia Park Citizens Rehabilitation Committee, the federal government approved a survey and planning grant. The Virginia Park organization then formed the Virginia Park Service Corporation and successfully sought federal assistance for its rehabilitation.[95]

One of the concerns of the block clubs and neighborhood associations was the difficulty experienced by residents of black neighborhoods and neighborhoods undergoing racial change in obtaining insurance at reasonable rates, if at all. The state's insurance commissioner noted in 1963 that "timid" underwriters had "eliminated" entire neighborhoods in Detroit. Two years later the West Side Improvement Association called for a legislative investigation of the indiscriminate cancellation of fire insurance when property changed hands.

When the Common Council conducted an investigation into insurance practices in older and changing neighborhoods, it discovered that insurers did indeed "red-line" areas with a high concentration of blacks and that it was difficult to secure insurance at standard rates, if at all, in such "undesirable or high risk areas." This had compelled residents to forego insurance or to turn to "non-admitted" companies, not licensed in the state, which charged as much as ten times the normal rates.

As a result of the council inquiry and the efforts of the Mayor's Committee for Neighborhood Conservation and Improved Housing, the Michigan Insurance Bureau devised the Michigan Fire Insurance Inspection Plan for high-risk areas in Detroit. The plan, which became effective on January 1, 1966, provided for free inspection by the Michigan Inspection Bureau, a rating agency for the insurance companies, of any dwelling whose owner had either been refused coverage or offered insurance at exorbitant rates. If the dwelling met the requirements for minimum insurability, the companies had to provide coverage at standard rates. If the dwelling was below minimum standards, the owner could insure it temporarily at an increased rate while bringing the property up to standard. An owner who waived inspection or failed to meet the minimum standards could seek coverage from licensed companies at three times the standard rate, if available, or turn to the nonadmitted companies and pay whatever they charged. Of thirty-five hundred applicants for inspection in 1966, twenty-four hundred were accepted at the standard rate. Six thousand owners, two-thirds of them absentees, waived inspection and purchased high-risk insurance. That the plan was not a panacea for high-risk areas became evident during the 1967 riot.[96]

To eliminate blight in neighborhoods that were insufficiently deteriorated to be designated conservation areas, Detroit relied primarily on code enforcement. The state housing code that Detroit had adopted at the end of World War I was "outdated and irrelevant," it was poorly enforced, and the sanctions it provided for violations were meaningless. The deterioration of the housing stock in Detroit before the riot was partly due to ineffective code enforcement.

The enforcement of the Detroit housing code was the responsibility of the Department of Buildings and Safety Engineering, the Health Department, and the Fire Prevention Bureau of the Fire Department. The three agencies, according to the director-secretary of the DHC, did "an inadequate job," and all of them, according to a Kerner Commission staff member, were "very much subject to the political power (if not control) of the real estate firms in Detroit." There were actually too few inspectors in the three agencies for a city of 1.6 million people, and the coordination among them left much to be desired.[97]

The effort to enforce compliance once a code violation had been discovered was "slow and cumbersome." The law stipulated that emergency conditions were to be corrected in three days and other violations in thirty to forty days, but this standard was honored only in the breach. Although the Department of Buildings and Safety Engineering enjoyed a reputation as "probably the most effective code enforcement agency in the country," an Urban Housing Council study revealed that the average length of time between notice of violation by the department and compliance was four and one-half months and that some cases remained unresolved after two years. The average length of time between notice and compliance for health violations was more than eight months. The CCR discovered in a study of twenty-two inner-city multiple dwellings in 1967 that of twenty-five code violation notices issued since 1964, the owner had complied with only four.

From 5 to 10 percent of the code violation cases ended up in traffic and ordinance court. The judicial mill ground slowly, and the fines imposed were far too low to deter code violations. In twenty-two Buildings and Safety Engineering cases in 1965, the average fine was $28; and in the sixteen health cases that year, the largest fine was $20. According to Knox, the only person ever jailed for a code violation before the riot was a woman on public assistance who had failed to purchase a trash receptacle when ordered to do so![98]

The chief victims of the "erratic and generally sluggish" character of code enforcement, as well as of lax zoning enforcement, were occupants of multiple dwellings in the central city, most of whom were black. According to the Field Division of the CCR, there was "wide spread racial discrimination" in the enforcement of the housing code. A detailed report on twenty buildings in the key Virginia Park area at the end of 1966 noted the presence of rats and vermin, fire damage, leaky plumbing, damaged receptacles, broken steps, missing faucets, and poor flooring. Few laws protected tenant rights before the riot, and leases were rare except in public housing and in middle- and upper-income dwellings. It was not uncommon for landlords to evict tenants who complained about code violations.[99]

There was a rising tide of concern in Detroit in the 1960s regarding the rights of tenants and increased activism to redress their grievances. Following demonstrations against slum conditions on Twelfth Street, the city government, at the urging of the CCR and the DHC, began to withhold rent payments to landlords of welfare clients living in substandard apartments until the properties had been improved. The block clubs at the beginning of 1965 decided to make landlords who failed to maintain their property in black areas the principal block-club target for the year. After some tenants on Twelfth Street were evicted for refusing to pay rents for substandard apartments until improvements had been made, CORE began organizing Twelfth Street tenants into tenant action councils. The NAACP, which had been protesting racial discrimination in the fixing of rents, declared war on slum landlords in 1966 and announced that it too would organize tenant councils, a tactic also adopted by the city's poverty agency. In 1967 the DHC established a Tenant Review Board to review DHC decisions affecting public housing tenants and applicants that involved matters of judgment.[100]

After two children in September 1966 were bitten by rats and mice within twenty-four hours in a west side apartment owned by Goodman Brothers, a notorious slumlord, the enraged tenants initiated a rent strike and a lawsuit. There were additional rent strikes on the west side in the following months in a "continuing war against slum landlords." Landlords, who had often reacted to tenant actions to force repairs by raising rents, sometimes reacted to rent strikes by evicting the strikers. In the spring of 1967, however, Neighborhood Legal Service in Detroit won a lawsuit against Goodman Brothers involving the harassment and retaliatory eviction of complaining tenants.[101]

Whites had better housing than blacks, a young black looter declared just after the riot. "Most Negroes," he said, "they live in slums and houses with rats and roaches and all kinds of things in their homes." Housing was incontrovertibly a major grievance of Detroit blacks on the eve of the July 1967 riot. Judging from a postriot survey of a community sample of Detroit blacks, more blacks (38 percent) believed that they had experienced discrimination with regard to their housing than with regard to their schooling (27 percent). The housing problem was particularly acute in the Twelfth Street area, where overcrowding and lax code enforcement adversely affected living conditions.[102] The Detroit city government had been unable to meet an acknowledged need for low-cost housing, it was guilty of lax enforcement of the housing code, and its urban renewal program, whatever benefits it may have brought the city, had caused many black citizens a good deal of pain.

CHAPTER 4

Detroit's War on Poverty

Low incomes, unemployment, and the poverty that resulted were disproportionately the lot of blacks as compared to whites in the nation and in Detroit in the 1960s. President Lyndon B. Johnson declared war on poverty in his State of the Union address in January 1964, and Congress responded in August by passing the Economic Opportunity Act. Detroit by that time had launched its own war on poverty and was better able than other cities to seek its share of the funds federal law made available.

Blacks in Detroit gained markedly in income as compared to whites and as compared to blacks elsewhere in the nation between 1960 and 1965. Whereas the median family income in Detroit in 1960 was $4,366 for blacks and $6,769 for whites, the estimated nonwhite median family income had increased sharply by 1965 to $6,405, well above the national figure of $3,886 for nonwhites, while the estimated white family income of $6,846 was only slightly above the 1960 figure. The president of the Detroit branch of the National Association for the Advancement of Colored People (NAACP) observed in the summer of 1964 that blacks were "eating better" in Detroit than elsewhere in the nation.[1]

The improvement in black income in Detroit reflected the substantial decrease in unemployment in the city beginning in 1963. Detroit lost 165,000 jobs between 1955 and 1962, but, sparked by the auto industry, employment improved markedly beginning in 1963. Detroit's auto workers became increasingly black in the 1960s, as white workers moved to jobs in suburban auto plants. In 1961 white unemployment in Detroit was 7.1 percent of the labor force and black, 17.4 percent; but by 1965 the white unemployment rate had been reduced to a miniscule 1.6 percent and the black to 3.4 percent.

Despite the decline in their unemployment rate, blacks were concerned about the character of their jobs and job discrimination. A survey of the Detroit standard metropolitan statistical area in the summer of 1966 revealed that twice as large a proportion of blacks as whites held unskilled blue-collar jobs and that the proportion of whites in professional, technical, and kindred jobs exceeded the proportion of blacks in such jobs by seven to one. In the same survey, 28 percent of black

workers, as compared to 11 percent of white workers, expressed themselves as "fairly unsatisfied" or "very dissatisfied" with their jobs.[2]

In a postriot survey of Detroit blacks aged eighteen and over
selected primarily from a directory of addresses, 48 percent of the
respondents claimed they had experienced discrimination in "obtaining,
holding, or advancing in a job." In responding to a narrower definition
of job discrimination in the fifteen-city postriot survey, 28 percent of the
Detroit blacks claimed that they had been denied jobs because of their
skin color, which compared to 30 percent for blacks in the fifteen cities as
a whole.[3]

The black organizations in Detroit sought to deal with the issues of
black unemployment and job discrimination by negotiation and direct
action. The Trade Union Leadership Council (TULC) in 1963 marshaled
the support of numerous black organizations behind Operation Negro
Equality (ONE), which declared war on job discrimination in the building trades and negotiated with the Big Three automobile manufacturers
to provide more auto jobs for blacks. Cavanagh responded to ONE's
efforts by helping to persuade the Detroit Building Trades Council in
July 1963 to agree to take immediate steps to promote equal employment
opportunities for construction jobs. The Congress of Racial Equality
(CORE) boycotted Kroger, and black ministers conducted a boycott
campaign against A&P in what proved to be a successful effort to persuade both grocery chains to hire additional blacks. CORE reached a
similar agreement with Grinnell Brothers. The NAACP, CORE, the
Group of Advanced Leadership, Freedom Now, and other organizations
picketed the General Motors Building in May 1964 because of the
absence of black GM dealers.[4]

In the 1961 mayoral campaign Cavanagh promised to do more as
mayor to alleviate poverty than his predecessors had done. When the
mayor testified in favor of the Economic Opportunity Bill in April 1964,
he noted, "We [Detroit] have not merely been standing by awaiting the
declaration of the so-called war on poverty because we have been
engaged in some preliminary activity and achieved some degree of
success."[5]

In the fall of 1962 Cavanagh appointed a Committee on Community
Action for Detroit Youth (CADY) to study the needs of young people
aged sixteen to twenty-one in a small economically and culturally
deprived area in the inner city. Financed by a planning grant from the
President's Committee on Juvenile Delinquency, the study revealed that
84 percent of those interviewed needed job counseling as well as health
care. In its application for the planning grant, Detroit called attention to
the heavy unemployment among the city's youth—a drop of 60 percent in
the employment of sixteen and seventeen-year-olds since 1952—and
stated the city's intention to link public and private agencies in a program
of action to deal with juvenile delinquency in two east side areas.

The establishment of CADY was the modest beginning of Detroit's war on poverty. The program involved the formation of "community intervention teams" to work with juveniles from the time they were picked up by the police until they could be absorbed back into the community. Funded at the very modest level of $311,000, two-thirds of the sum coming from the federal government, CADY was, perforce, a very small-scale program. It did, however, provide Detroit with some information on the nature and degree of poverty in the inner city, information that it shared with Washington as the federal government sought to devise an antipoverty program. When Detroit launched its formal antipoverty program, CADY was absorbed into it.[6]

CADY and its exposure of substantial youth unemployment, which Cavanagh asserted at the end of 1963 was the city's most pressing problem, led Detroit to seek and secure Department of Labor funds in August 1963 for a Special Youth Employment Project (SYEP) that CADY oversaw. Inaugurated in 1964, SYEP was designed to train out-of-school youth aged sixteen to twenty-one, providing them with work experience in city job stations and supplementary training for half of their time in a youth employment center. Of the 512 persons trained by March 1965, 88 percent had been placed in jobs.[7]

Concerned about hard-core unemployment in the city, the Cavanagh administration arranged a conference of city, state, and federal officials in January 1964 to consider a proposal to make Detroit "a pilot area for a massive Federal assault on hard-core unemployment." Soon after the conference the mayor asked the Metropolitan Employment Opportunity Committee—a body formed at Cavanagh's request that included representatives of the business community, labor, the public school system, the churches, and state and local service agencies—to serve as an advisory group in developing a plan to attack the problem of poverty. The committee requested the Mayor's Committee for Community Renewal to draft a community action program and agreed to serve as the policy body for that program.[8]

Aided by personnel from other city agencies as well as private consultants, the Mayor's Committee for Community Renewal drew up a proposal for a community action program to combat poverty. The city's objective, the proposal stated, was to develop programs that would "assist people in becoming self-sufficient and socially responsible citizens, generate greater participation in community life and the problems of others, and build into the lives of the impoverished the skills and aspirations necessary for rewarding and useful lives." The attack on poverty, the proposal urged, had to be "comprehensive and coordinated," services to prevent distress had to be concentrated in the neighborhoods of the people for whom they were intended, jobs had to be found for the poor, and the poor had to be involved in planning the program.

The Community Renewal proposal pointed to four target areas to which Detroit's antipoverty program should be directed, two on the east side, two on the west side. The population of the four areas totaled 295,581 in 1960 (392,734 by 1965), of whom 68 percent were nonwhite. The blacks in the four areas constituted 87 percent of the city's black population as of 1965. Thirty-seven percent of the families, as compared to 16 percent for the rest of the city, had annual incomes below $3,000. Although the target areas contained 18 percent of the city's population in 1960, 28 percent of the city's unemployed resided there. The inhabitants were twice as likely as other Detroiters to be renters (60 percent compared to 30 percent), they were less well educated, they were considerably more likely to be receiving direct relief and other forms of public assistance, and they were less healthy.[9]

Believing that it needed additional information on the target area population, the city of Detroit contracted with Greenleigh Associates to undertake a home interview study of low-income families in Detroit. The study, conducted from June 1964 to January 1965 and based on a random probability sample of 2,081 low-income households living in blighted and substandard housing, was "the first . . . large-scale depth interview study of an active poverty population" designed to provide "first hand data" for both antipoverty and urban renewal planning.

Of the 2,081 households surveyed, 1,743 were living in severe poverty. Black households, which constituted 68 percent of the total, were more impoverished than white households, with a monthly per capita income of $68, as compared to $88 for whites. The poorest households had the most severe family, employment, health, school, and housing problems. The unemployment rate among black heads of households in the labor force was 33 percent, as compared to 22 percent among white household heads; and only one-fourth of the families whose heads were employed had annual incomes of $6,000 or more, the sum considered necessary in Detroit for "a modest but adequate budget." Almost all the private housing of those surveyed was blighted, 94 percent of the homes requiring major repairs. About one-third of the homes had problems with rats and vermin, and 20 percent had not had adequate heat the previous winter.

Only 35 percent of the households surveyed were composed of a mother, father, and their children. Among the black households with children, 35 percent were one-parent families, double the rate of white families with children. About 22 percent of the families, 84 percent of them black, were receiving public assistance.

Although the problems of the poor were "multiple and interrelated," the Greenleigh study noted that the various social agencies with which the poor came into contact offered only a single service. The "particularization of services, the lack of a comprehensive approach, the lack of a family-centered approach, the failure to provide follow-up service," the report concluded, "all tend to create a gap between the needs of those in poverty and the existing social structure."[10] It was this "gap" that Detroit's antipoverty program sought to fill.

In a companion study, Greenleigh Associates amplified their comments about the inadequacy of social services available in Detroit. Existing services, the study commented, did not provide "a full range of preventive, diagnostic, remedial and rehabilitative" programs, were not "closely meshed," were focused on middle-class and lower middle-class families, not poor families, and gave the poor "little voice" in the development of policy and programs. The Greenleigh criticisms, which Cavanagh viewed as a "devastating indictment of both the public and private social agencies" in the city, helped to influence the city government to develop the concept of a "multi-functional service center" for the poor that became the national pattern.[11]

In June 1964 the emerging Detroit poverty program was given the name Total Action against Poverty (TAP), with the committee of community leaders serving as its policy body. Responding to the mayor's request for assistance in planning, the Common Council named Mel Ravitz as its representative, and he chaired a series of "brainstorming" meetings with community leaders to discuss Detroit's war against poverty. By the time the Economic Opportunity Act was passed in August, Detroit, well ahead of most communities, had developed and was ready to submit its antipoverty plan to Washington for funding.[12]

Detroit had not only been in the vanguard among the nation's cities in fashioning an antipoverty program; it also influenced the shape of the Economic Opportunity Act. Cavanagh made "some input" while the federal statute was being drafted to ensure that "it wasn't structured outside of city government and outside the control of the mayor." He testified before the House of Representatives subcommittee that was considering the legislation, explained what Detroit was already doing, and emphasized that Detroit could not move ahead successfully in this effort without federal aid. Members of what became the TAP Policy Advisory Committee (PAC) also consulted with officials who were developing the federal program.[13]

The day after the Economic Opportunity Act was passed, Detroit, which was "virtually waiting on OEO's [Office of Economic Opportunity] doorstep," submitted its antipoverty proposal to the new federal agency. The $3.2 million the OEO granted Detroit in November was the largest per capita grant and the second largest initial sum awarded any city. By August 31, 1967, Detroit had received $47,725,000 from the OEO and the Department of Labor for programs to combat poverty. This sum was supplemented by local expenditures of about $5.5 million. Only Chicago and New York received more federal funding for the war on poverty.[14]

Detroit's community action agency was the TAP PAC. It consisted initially of thirty-one members, including the mayor. Each of the four target areas at the outset sent two representatives to the committee, whose selection the mayor could veto, and the remainder were appointed by the mayor to represent the community and the various agencies serving the poor. TAP differed from the community action agencies in most other cities in that it not only oversaw the funding and programs of delegate agencies but also operated its own programs. It carried out its programs through four Community Development Centers (eventually called Community Action Centers), one in each target area, and fifteen subcenters (Neighborhood Service Centers). The two major delegate agencies were the Detroit Public Schools and the Archdiocesan Opportunity Program (AOP). TAP became the Mayor's Committee for Human Resources Development (MCHRD) in March 1967. The name change reflected the broadening role of the war on poverty to include not just aid to the poverty-stricken but also the development of human resources and a relationship between the poverty agency and state and federal agencies not directly related to the war on poverty. The new name was also designed to avoid stigmatizing the clients of the poverty agency.[15]

One purpose of the national antipoverty program was to give the poor, particularly blacks, an effective voice in the decision-making process in the expectation that this would provide "institutional change in the interests of the poor." A community action program, the Economic Opportunity Act declared, was a program "developed, conducted, and administered with maximum feasible participation of residents." There were three different administrative levels at which residents of the poverty areas could have had an impact on Detroit's antipoverty program: the PAC, the Area Advisory Committees (AACs) in each target area, and community contacts at the grass roots developed by community and counselor aides.[16]

Cavanagh was intent from the start that the city government control Detroit's antipoverty program. Although about 80 percent of the community action agencies at the outset took the form of nonprofit corporations, Detroit did not go this route. Cavanagh explained that this was not a feasible alternative for Detroit since the city charter permitted only the city government to expend federal and city government funds. Inconsistently, the city also claimed that when in 1964 it canvassed the possibility of some arrangement other than city control, no other agency was prepared to commit itself to provide the 10 percent local share required for OEO grants. Whatever the validity of the reasons publicly advanced by the Cavanagh administration for city hall control, the mayor viewed the poverty program as too important to permit its direction to be in hands other than his own.[17]

Cavanagh appointed the director and deputy director of TAP, and the PAC operated out of the mayor's office. The mayor successfully resisted efforts to give target area representatives majority control of the

PAC. At a May 1965 meeting of the PAC, Julian Witherspoon, a fiery representative from the Area 4 AAC on the west side and the chief critic of city hall control of the antipoverty program, moved that the PAC include four representatives from each target area rather than two. Since the assumption at that time was that the number of target areas would soon be increased to six, Witherspoon's motion, which was greeted with "stunned silence," was designed to result ultimately in a PAC membership of forty-seven, twenty-four of whom would be from the target areas.[18]

When the majority-control motion was considered at a subsequent PAC meeting, area representatives who favored it insisted that if the cycle of poverty were to be broken, "the people on the bottom of society" had to have "control" over their "destiny." Cavanagh responded that only the city government could legally spend taxpayer money. One of the mayor's PAC appointees stated the matter more bluntly, declaring that "outside groups should not be able to out-vote the state." In the end, the PAC rejected Witherspoon's motion. Although the number of representatives from each target area was increased to four in order to increase the number of blacks on the PAC, no new target areas were added to the original four, leaving the sixteen target area representatives still short of a majority on the thirty-nine-member PAC. Although continuing to be a minority on the committee, the target area representatives were "no rubber stamps," according to an "Inspection report" of the agency. "They're active, vocal, militant," the report declared, "and they do their homework before taking the administrators of the program to task."[19]

Although resisting target area efforts to gain control of the PAC, Cavanagh did make some concessions to the AAC representatives on the committee. He appointed a Citizen Participation Sub-Committee to consider the role that the poor should play in the program, agreed that there should be at least one target area representative on each PAC subcommittee, agreed further that all programs be submitted to the AACs for review and ranking as to priority before the PAC took action on them, and eventually created a committee of Target Area Consultants to advise TAP's director of planning and program development and to appraise programs from the point of view of their clients. Since Cavanagh was anxious that a black be the director of the program, when Robert Roselle, TAP's first director, moved to the job of city controller, the mayor named Philip Rutledge, a black who had been serving as director of the Bureau of Health Education in the Health Department, to head the poverty agency.[20]

Detroit was hardly unique in denying the poor majority control of its poverty program. Cavanagh, indeed, claimed in October 1965 that the sixteen AAC representatives on the PAC constituted "the largest single bloc" of representatives of the poor on any community action agency. As of September 1966, the poor constituted 29 percent of the membership of the community action agencies in the nation, below the 34 percent figure for Detroit. Congress specified in the fall of 1966 that, as of March 1, 1967, only one-third of the members of a community action agency had to be elected representatives of the poor. As of the fall of 1967 the poor were in control only in San Francisco, Newark, and Syracuse. By the time Congress authorized city-government takeover of privately operated community action agencies late in 1967, the mayors had won the battle for control of the war on poverty at the municipal level.[21]

The AACs, "the basic unit[s] providing citizen's participation in policy making" in TAP, were supposed to "create and generate community programs, community action, and maximum participation of the residents" of their areas. The number of members of the individual AACs ranged from thirty-six to fifty-two. The TAP staff took the initiative in setting up a steering or advisory committee of community activists in each area to select the initial AAC membership. About one-half of the AAC membership came from the ranks of the unemployed and ADC mothers; the remainder were teachers, social workers, and others among the professionally or subprofessionally employed. Many of the original members had been spokespersons for their communities as leaders of block clubs, welfare rights organizations, or civil rights groups. The majority of the AAC members were women, over thirty years of age, and "relatively conservative." Little effort was apparently made in the target areas to involve individuals from the "less moderate organizations" or the "really hard core poor."[22]

AAC meetings tended to be poorly attended, the professionals being the most likely to appear. A member of the Citizen Participation Sub-Committee contended that target area representatives who did not come to meetings claimed that TAP had "nothing to offer," and so it was "a waste of time" for them to attend. More important was the fact that the poor found it difficult to play a meaningful role in the AACs. They generally lacked education and the knowledge and political skills to know "how to participate." They did not have the money to arrange for baby-sitters and, sometimes, even the fare needed to attend meetings. Some of them feared to speak lest others think they were speaking incorrectly. Some stopped coming to meetings when they discovered that they would not be paid for attending.[23]

The relationship between the AACs and TAP's professional staff, a large percentage of whom were black, was one of strain. The constant complaint of the more vocal AAC members was that they were not included in the program planning process and their programmatic demands were ignored. Unlike AAC members, the professionals, of course, had the staff, the time, and the knowledge to devise programs. Also, complainants were often not fully aware of the extent to which programs and program changes were determined not by the professional staff but by funding availability, OEO guidelines, and the city's acceptance of national programs designed in Washington. There is, at the same time, no question that some professional staffers viewed the poor on the AACs negatively, were condescending in their treatment of them, and became "defensive" rather than "constructive" when questioned. The relationship was that of "superordinate-subordinate rather than one of equality."[24]

After studying the operation of the AAC in Target Area 2, the Center for Urban Studies of the University of Chicago concluded that the committee did "very little" and was "torn by bitter, personal disputes." The AAC did not appear to the Chicago group to be a "mechanism for developing and planning new programs for the area," and "few positive suggestions of any sort" emanated from it.[25]

The Center for Urban Studies thought that it was not self-evident that the "professional representatives of the poor" who dominated the Detroit AACs were seeking anything more than jobs for the poor in the program. That AAC members were seeking jobs for the poor is clear, but this after all was one of the purposes of the program. It would be a mistake as a matter of fact to speak of the AACs only in negative terms. At the very least, they provided a "forum" where the poor could air their grievances. Also, when it was possible to make changes suggested by area residents, the staff and PAC, the Chicago study concluded, were "very often" supportive. However little the AACs had to say about the planning and staffing of programs, they were not entirely without influence.[26]

The lowest level personnel in the TAP program who might conceivably have encouraged participation by target area poor were the 234 community aides and 174 counselor aides. The community aides were supposed to spend their time in the field ascertaining the needs of target area residents and informing them of the services available to them. They were also the link to the community agencies in the area. The counselor aides, who worked in the Community Development Centers (CDCs) and the Neighborhood Service Centers, were supposed to help visitors to the centers define their needs and then to counsel them as to how to meet those needs. They also counseled Neighborhood Youth Corps (NYC) enrollees with personal and work-adjustment problems. Although apparently successful in meeting these responsibilities, they did not, generally speaking, make much of an effort to involve the poor more fully in the operation of the antipoverty program. The community aides, however, did help to establish or revivify some block clubs and did set up some tenants' councils.[27]

Unemployed area residents, eager for jobs in the poverty program, were dismayed to learn when the available positions were first announced that they were to be filled by persons meeting the civil service requirements. Elements of the community, Roselle informed the mayor, feared that civil service procedures would "operate against the Negro." There was additional concern that the use of the Civil Service Commission (CSC) as the program's recruitment agency would result in the employment of persons from outside the target areas who would be unfamiliar with their problems. Responsive to these concerns, Cavanagh prevailed upon the CSC to drop the requirement of a written test for community aides and to base their appointment primarily on an oral interview and also to reduce the weight of the written examination for counselor aides from 70 percent to 50 percent and to give greater emphasis to such factors as character and experience. Community aide positions were to be restricted to target area residents, who were also to be given priority for appointment as counselor aides. At least 75 percent of the community and counselor aides turned out to be target area residents. All in all, the poverty program employed an estimated three thousand target area residents, 88 percent of whom were black.[28]

The community and counselor aides did not have the status of regular city employees. They did not receive the fringe benefits of such employees, and their employment depended entirely on the availability of federal funds. The chief complaint of the AACs regarding the status of the two types of aides was their failure to move upward in the TAP hierarchy. Promotion depended on passing the required civil service tests, and despite a training program for subprofessionals, no more than 10 percent were able to qualify for better positions. Since the civil service tests for "lower skilled jobs" were widely viewed by target area residents as either "irrelevant or too demanding," this became a major grievance among the poor and their AAC representatives. Resentment was also expressed in the target areas that many jobs in the program were filled by career employees transferred from other city departments rather than by the unemployed. Some blacks also complained that too many of the top positions in TAP were held by whites and that it was they who ran the program.[29]

Rutledge conceded in June 1966 that the Detroit program had not reached the goal of maximum involvement of community people. Participation by the poor in policy making, as an outside evaluation of Detroit's community action agency concluded, was nevertheless "significantly greater" in Detroit than in "most community action programs." Sargent Shriver, the head of OEO, stated in 1966 that Detroit had "moved progressively to involve poor people more effectively than other cities"; and in their study of community participation in the war on poverty, J. David Greenstone and Paul Peterson concluded that "by comparison with other large cities," black leaders in Detroit had "substantially shaped the poverty program." What participation, however, had failed to any significant degree to achieve, in Detroit and elsewhere, was the community organizing and the institutional change that planners of the national war on poverty had seen as one of its purposes.[30]

In addition to their putative role as catalytic agents to achieve social change, the CDCs were supposed to coordinate the services available to the poor and to deliver services to them in new ways. Since poverty was believed to result from a combination of problems, the centers provided the multiple services supposedly needed to cope with the matter. Shriver thus accurately described the CDCs as "supermarkets for social services." The first of the Detroit centers, opened on the west side north of Grand Boulevard, was apparently "the first multi-purpose center" funded under the Economic Opportunity Act.[31]

There were three basic units in a Detroit CDC: interviewing and counseling, information and education, and community services. The range of services offered the poor included job placement, job counseling, and job training; medical and dental examinations; pediatric care; family counseling; vocational rehabilitation; legal advice; adult education; and home services (home management advisors to aid housewives with homemaking, decorating, budgeting, and child care; and homemakers to aid families requiring live-in adult assistance such as emergency prenatal care and to serve as "substitute mothers" when the mother of the house was ill or absent). The subcenters served mainly as "vehicles for outreach," employing resident aides who recruited clients and referred them to a CDC or other agency.[32]

The 130,000 CDC contacts with individuals in 1966 resulted in 26,000 job and training referrals, 66,342 referrals for medical or dental service, and 9,217 referrals for vocational rehabilitation, legal aid, homemaker services, or educational upgrading. There is no question that the CDCs and the subcenters provided necessary services for the poor that they could not afford to have purchased. The centers, an outside appraisal of TAP concluded in April 1967, were "alive with activity" and were "vital forces in community life." But since the city, presumably because of lack of funding, failed to create additional target areas, about 200,000 eligible Detroiters were left beyond walking distance from a CDC. Although CDC services were theoretically available to all of the city's poor, only 44 percent of Detroit's poverty families lived in the target areas.

There were also gaps in the services provided by the CDCs. The medical and dental clinics at the centers, for example, were plagued by lack of funds, equipment, and the facilities needed to provide proper services. This was a matter of considerable importance since more than 60 percent of the registrants at the CDCs had "untreated medical or dental problems." At the end of June 1967 the OEO granted Detroit $2.86 million to set up a neighborhood health care system to serve thirty-three thousand persons in the inner city. It was to be administered, however, not by the MCHRD but rather by a nonprofit Metropolitan Health Research and Service Fund. This decision no doubt reflected OEO's judgment about TAP-MCHRD's failures in the delivery of health care.[33]

In addition to the services offered by the CDCs, TAP and the delegate agencies provided a wide range of programs for the poor and the jobless. Many of these programs were concerned with job training and placement. Since Detroit reportedly had a shortage of trained manpower during these years, the assumption was that training of the unemployed would lead to remunerative employment.[34]

The Michigan Employment Security Commission (MESC) and the Detroit Skills Center were vital links in the implementation of the various programs in Detroit to train and find jobs for the unemployed. The MESC, the state's job placement agency, set up testing and placement mobile units in the CDCs. It concentrated its efforts on the young jobless, referring adults to the agency's branch offices in the city. The MESC staff, however, was too small to provide "full job placement services" for the disadvantaged, which explains why it was primarily concerned not with the hard-core unemployed but with those whom it was easier to place. Despite a lack of flexibility in its program, it reportedly had the highest rate of success in the nation among similar agencies in placing the unemployed. A black rioter later complained regarding the MESC, "Well, you go out to that Michigan employment office, it's really ridiculous, the things you go through." The MESC, however, did find him a job.[35]

Manpower experts hailed the Detroit Skills Center as one of the best operations of its kind in the entire world. Detroit acquired the site for the center in May 1964 to train workers under the Manpower Development and Training Act of 1962 and the Vocational Rehabilitation Act of 1963. The Department of Labor provided 90 percent of the funds for the operation of the center, which was staffed by the Detroit Public Schools and the MESC. Able to train 2,500 persons in three shifts at any one time, the center offered courses in the automotive, metal, and service trades. Its enrollment was almost entirely black.[36]

In January 1967 Henry Ford II helped to finance the establishment of the Career Development Center as a privately operated manpower development agency to train and retrain the unemployed and the underemployed of the inner city. The creation of the center probably reflected the fact that Detroit's major corporations had largely failed to develop training programs to prepare minority group youths for entry-level jobs.[37]

Of the various job training programs, the Adult and Youth Employment Program (AYEP) was peculiarly Detroit's own. Growing out of the SYEP and jointly funded by the OEO and the Department of Labor, the AYEP provided pre-entry and on-the-job training coupled with classroom instruction for target area adults and youths. The instructional phase of the program was subcontracted to the Detroit Board of Education, and the program operated through the Skills Center. The AYEP included as additional components a Higher Education Opportunities Program to recruit and train potential college enrollees; a pre–practical nurses program; Project Growth, designed to give inner-city youths work experience in an agricultural setting; and Project Exploration, a "combined job experience–classwork program" aimed at motivating potential high school dropouts. A program that attracted national attention, the AYEP had served 1,417 individuals as of February 1967 and had an 84 percent job placement rate.[38]

The NYC, funded by the Department of Labor, was a considerably larger program than the AYEP. A work experience program for young men and women between the ages of sixteen and twenty-one, it provided paid work for up to twenty-four hours a week for six months at $1.25 an hour and nonpaid counseling for sixteen hours for out-of-school youths and work for in-school youths for as few as seven hours per week. The MESC referred the youths to the NYC, from which they went on to jobs, the Skills Center, the Job Corps, the military, or school. The Detroit Public Schools administered the in-school program, TAP itself, the out-of-school program.

The combined out-of-school, in-school, and summer NYC programs had enrolled 12,500 youths by February 1967. Many of them were high school girls, an NYC official reporting that there was "a constant war" with the pimps in recruiting the young ladies. Although the program claimed a 70 percent "positive termination" rate, the Chicago Regional Council of federal agencies judged the job placement of NYC graduates to have been rather "haphazard." Placement in good jobs was a problem since enrollees generally lacked the resources to upgrade their skills significantly. "NYC helped me in lots of ways," declared one sixteen-year-old. "They gave me a chance." Dropouts, however, may have agreed with a rioter who said he had appreciated the NYC training but dismissed the $26 a week he had earned as "just bus fare to work."[39]

The On-the-Job Training (OJT) program launched in Detroit in 1965 was characterized by Cavanagh as "the cheapest, most easily expanded" program of its kind and the one with the "greatest potential for job creation and job training." OJT contracted with more than one hundred employers to engage and train target area residents for whom the employers received $30 per week for up to twenty-six weeks. Males so hired received an average of $2 per hour, females, $1.65 per hour. Those whom the MESC referred to the program were supposed to be individuals handicapped in gaining employment because of lack of education or skill, automation, or racial discrimination. More than one thousand target area residents had been assigned to the program by June 1967. OJT also operated a small Work Experience Project for welfare mothers.[40]

In the half year or so before the riot Detroit put two additional manpower training programs into effect: Specialized Training and Employment Placement Service (STEPS), initiated in late November 1966, and Urban Areas Employment Program (UAEP), beginning on June 1, 1967. STEPS was distinguished by "intensive and personal attention" to the disadvantaged, whom it counseled, trained, and sought to place in jobs and for whom it provided "supportive services." STEPS also conducted research in job market trends and, going beyond mere referral, worked with employers to create new subprofessional job categories. As part of the program, field service teams sought to match the unemployed with job openings. By April 25, 1967, the teams had met with more than five thousand job applicants and had placed 992 of them.[41]

UAEP or, as it came to be known, the Concentrated Employment Program, was focused entirely on a "special impact" slum area that included parts of the four target areas. The program provided counseling, public service training and employment, on-the-job training, child care, medical and dental examinations, and a variety of other services that supposedly contributed to employment. The program was just getting underway at the time of the July 1967 riot.[42]

There are a variety of estimates as to the number who received training and found employment as a result of the various manpower programs that operated in the city between 1962 and the 1967 riot. A study of seventy-seven census tracts in the inner city in the fall of 1966 revealed that 39 percent of the males and 28 percent of the females had received some kind of occupational training. The Kerner Commission reported that about 44 percent of the unemployed in the city as a whole had received job training in the first nine months of 1967. The CDCs, MESC, TAP, and the Skills Center claimed success rates ranging from 30 percent for the CDCs to 83 percent for the Skills Center, but the figures may well have been exaggerated.[43]

In a cost-benefit analysis of some of the manpower programs based on a survey of 72 percent of their graduates, Cavanagh in March 1967 argued that the benefits in the form of wages earned and taxes paid by the graduates far exceeded program costs. He contended, for example, that the NYC program had yielded $10.5 million in alumni wages and $1.75 million in taxes at a cost of $5.4 million and that the AYEP had cost $788,000 and that its trainees were earning $4 million a year and paying $650,000 in taxes. Robert Roselle stated later that he would not want to rely on the accuracy of these figures, put out to impress Congress and the public, but he nevertheless asserted that the programs were "doing something meaningful about the needs . . . and doing it in an efficient and effective way." This was also the verdict of the President's Committee on Manpower.[44]

Not everyone agreed with the favorable evaluations of the effect of the manpower programs in Detroit. The Chicago Regional Council concluded that these programs had failed to reach those in the target areas most needing counseling, training, and placement services. The University of Chicago's Center for Urban Studies thought that the manpower programs were more concerned with numbers than with training in depth, and there were charges in Detroit that some of the training was in skills that were obsolete.

One of the most damning indictments of the manpower programs came from Cavanagh's own Mayor's Development Team (MDT), set up after the riot. What the MDT found was "a multitude of training activities, related, unrelated, independent, interdependent and dependent . . . without coordination or apparent direction." The individual trainee requiring assistance, the MDT reported, was "required to shuttle in and through confusing and overlapping agencies." It was obvious to the MDT that those seeking employment had to be "highly motivated persons" to surmount the barriers of the " 'Manpower System' as a spring board into the middle class."[45]

Following the Watts riot in August 1965, Secretary of Labor Willard Wirtz created a task force to look into the matter of job training and employment opportunities for lower-income groups in the large cities. The secretary's hope was that the provision of "imaginative programs" would prevent future riots.[46] Detroit had one of the most imaginative of the nation's job training and placement programs, but it did not prevent the city from experiencing the most damaging of all the 1960s riots.

TAP administered a variety of programs other than those directly related to training and employment. Two, in particular, merit attention, Neighborhood Legal Service (NLS), because of the role it played in the riot, and the Small Business Development Center, because it was a harbinger of a policy that commanded a good deal of attention as a reaction to the riot.

The NLS program was initiated in September 1965 with a federal grant to the University of Detroit Law School for a legal research project and the establishment of a legal service clinic for the indigent, staffed by law students under the supervision of attorneys. A larger federal grant in 1966 provided for the setting up of three NLS Centers where the poor could receive legal assistance, a legal research division, misdemeanant representation, and a bail release project. By the end of 1966 the NLS program in Detroit had provided just over two thousand persons with legal assistance. The four Small Business Development Centers established in each of the target areas provided economic opportunity loans of up to $25,000, management training, and counseling in business methods to small businesses in the inner city. The program had aided 1,850 businesses by June 1967, 71 percent of them black-owned.[47]

Of the funding for the war on poverty that Detroit had received by the spring of 1967, 48 percent went to the city's two principal delegate agencies, the Detroit Public Schools (39 percent) and the Archdiocesan Opportunity Program (9 percent).[48] Among the numerous education programs administered by the public school system, the Great Cities School Improvement Project and Head Start were the most important. Initiated in the summer of 1965, repeated the next summer, and expanded in 1967,

Head Start in the summer of 1967 served sixty-three hundred children aged three to five, 85 percent of them black. They were taken on field trips and received medical examinations, nutritional supplements, psychological, speech, and language development assistance, audiovisual services, and social services if necessary. The Archdiocesan Opportunity Program (AOP) and the public schools ran a much smaller full-year Head Start program. TAP itself was the processing agent for a federal grant to thirteen institutions of higher education for a work-study program that paid students $1.50 per hour for up to fifteen hours of work per week. All in all, the OEO ranked the Detroit education programs as "the best" in the Great Lakes region.[49]

The Cavanagh administration decided to include the Detroit Archdiocese as a delegate agency as the best way of involving the city's Catholic parochial schools in the educational programs of the war on poverty. The thirty-one parochial schools in the target areas had an enrollment of fifteen thousand pupils, many of them not Catholic. The AOP itself was created at the initiative of the Michigan Catholic Conference following the passage of the Economic Opportunity Act of 1964. Although a TAP delegate agency, some of the AOP's funds came from sources other than the OEO, and the programs financed by these funds were not subject to TAP supervision.[50]

The AOP operated a variety of educational programs besides Head Start, most of them small scale: the School Retention and Education Stimulus Center, a retention program for elementary school children that involved remedial instruction and a diagnostic and counseling service for emotionally disturbed and educationally disadvantaged youngsters; the Reading Materials Distribution Program, which provided libraries, free reading material, speakers, art shows, volunteer tutors, and homemaking classes; and School Preparation, designed to provide social and educational stimulation for target area children aged three to five. The poverty-related educational programs of the AOP and the public schools were serving ninety-five thousand adults and children as of June 1966.

In addition to its education programs, the AOP administered many noneducational programs: NYC in-school and out-of-school programs; Freshstart, a job training, counseling, and job placement program for women who had served sentences in the Detroit House of Corrections; Project Return, a program to resocialize males who had served light prison sentences; Project Identity, a program of counseling and work preparation for juvenile offenders; Project Scope, a summer day camp program for children aged seven to twelve; Project Challenge, a special day camp program for retarded children; and three day-care centers for children between the ages of three and six whose parents were in a skill training program. As of May 1967 the AOP programs, funded at $3 million, were serving 21,800 persons. This figure, however, does not include the more than fifty-five thousand persons who took advantage of the AOP's distribution of free reading material, an "astonishingly good record" according to the Center for Urban Studies of the University of Chicago.[51]

Although the Chicago Regional Council reported that the AOP had isolated itself from "actual community life," the reverse appears to have been true. On the basis of "good, impressionistic evidence," the Center for Urban Studies concluded that the poor participated in "meaningful ways" in the AOP, and its interviews left no doubt that they placed greater trust in the AOP than in TAP-MCHRD. On a visit to Detroit in May 1966, a member of President Johnson's White House staff found that the persons to whom he spoke thought the AOP a more successful program than TAP because of "better leadership, greater community involvement, and better identification of problems."[52]

In November 1965 federal officials asked for a proposal from Detroit for the establishment of a demonstration city program to ascertain whether a federally supported "large scale attack on a wide range of municipal problems" could bring about "significant change." This concept, which took legislative form with the passage in November 1966 of the Demonstration Cities and Metropolitan Development Act, was something that Cavanagh had been discussing with federal officials for some time, particularly in his role in 1964 as a member of the President's Task Force on Urban and Metropolitan Problems. In his effort to make Detroit "Model City USA" for federally financed urban programs, Cavanagh had written President Johnson in September 1965 about the need to select certain cities differentiated by size and location to demonstrate how the implementation of a "whole range of federal programs" in these cities could achieve their physical and social rehabilitation. Cavanagh's concern was that the war on poverty, despite his praise of the Detroit program, would solve neither the problem of poverty nor the problems of the large city. He thus told a congressional committee in August 1966 that the vast array of OEO programs, some four hundred in all, seldom reached "the angry young man standing on a ghetto street." Whereas the problems of the city were "interrelated and interacting," the OEO, Cavanagh remarked, approached these problems in a fragmented way. The mayor thought that what was needed was a coordinated approach that channeled programs and services into the areas of greatest need.[53]

The Demonstration Cities statute provided grants to the cities in two stages, the first for planning a program and then, if the program was approved, a grant for the program itself. There was a good deal of merit to the Cavanagh concept of a model city program, but what emerged from Congress was "far more watered down" than the mayor anticipated, and the money was distributed among so many cities that the funds any one city received were too small to have much effect.[54]

Once the Demonstration Cities Act had been passed, Detroit created a task force to formulate its application for a planning grant. The area of Detroit selected as the model city was a nine-square-mile section of the inner city, "a city-within-a city," that was largely in Target Area 1 on the lower east side but also included a section of Target Area 2 on the lower west side. It had a population of 133,873, about 9 percent of the city's population, almost equally divided between white and black. It included about 20 percent of the city's poverty families, 28 percent of its welfare case load, 18 percent of its unemployment, and 51 percent of its substandard housing. Its infant mortality and crime rates were double those of the city as a whole, its death rate six times higher. Half of its sixth-grade students were two or more years below grade level. Seemingly untouched by the war on poverty, it was a victim of poor employment, poor education, poor health, and poor housing.

The city's plan for the neighborhood, submitted to the federal government in April 1967, contemplated the rehabilitation of all buildings not conforming to code, the elimination of blighted land use, the creation of parks and recreation areas, improved police protection, employment and health services, and a variety of other services provided through family centers. "It deals," the document stated, "with every aspect of urban life in Detroit, its problems, its needs and its future." It warned that the condition of the poor could lead to "demonstrations, riots, sprees of vandalism and crime."[55]

Although the Department of Housing and Urban Development, which was to administer the model cities program, provided no "specific guidelines" as to how cities were to prepare their proposals, it did expect citizen participation in the process. The Grass Roots Organization Workers (GROW), a community organization based on a black neighborhood on the east side, was particularly concerned about the role citizens would play in shaping the Detroit program. In an effort to secure "people participation" in the program, GROW helped organize various citizen groups into the Congress of Grass Roots Organizations (CONGRO). The plan GROW and the WCO drew up for citizen participation came to be known as the CONGRO document, and shortly before Detroit in November 1967 received approval for its planning grant proposal, Cavanagh approved the document. Since the grant was only one-fourth the sum Detroit had requested, the city had to submit a revised "work program," and it included the CONGRO document in that plan.[56]

Once Detroit received its initial model cities grant, it became evident that there was a difference of opinion in the city as to just who the "people" were. This clash of views came to the fore as members of the AACs and CONGRO battled each other over the choice of members for the model city governing board. It was a conflict, essentially, between the largely black AAC members on the east side and the "integrated militants" from the west side, but it also reflected the fears of the AACs that the model city would take funds from the poverty program. The battle for participation in what increasingly became a relatively unimportant program continued to the end of the Cavanagh administration.[57]

If it is easy to speak in largely negative terms about the model cities program in Detroit, it is difficult to appraise the impact of the war on poverty in the years leading up to the 1967 riot. Indeed, one criticism of Detroit's antipoverty effort was the city's failure to have developed a system to appraise the various programs that comprised its war on poverty. When the Common Council at the end of 1966 asked Rutledge to "show it some results" from the war on poverty, he promised a report in six months, but the report was not forthcoming.[58]

As Cavanagh explained to Congress, Detroit and other cities believed themselves handicapped in fighting the war on poverty by the constraints Washington imposed on their programs. The earmarking of funds for "single purpose projects," he noted, denied the cities a needed flexibility and made a mockery of citizen participation. He pointed out that year-to-year funding prevented cities from engaging in long-range planning and was both "a needless hardship and an expensive one." The mayor also complained that funding for the war on poverty was below what Shriver had said was "the irreducible minimum."[59]

Funding, to be sure, was a major limitation on Detroit's efforts to alleviate poverty. An OEO unit judged that nearly all of Detroit's programs were "grossly under-financed and understaffed" and were little more than "pilot studies of the approaches to the problems of poverty." Rutledge noted at the outset of the riot that had the city distributed its entire antipoverty budget as of that time among the city's poor, each would have received only $60.[60]

In the years preceding the 1967 riot, the Detroit antipoverty effort drew consistent praise from outside the city as one of the best programs in the nation. The Detroit program, according to a Washington appraisal in the spring of 1967, enjoyed "a national reputation as a well-administered program with highly developed services and methods" that were "used as models for other programs," and it was "one of the most frequently visited programs" in the nation. Sargent Shriver wrote Cavanagh at one point that an OEO evaluation had concluded that Pittsburgh and Detroit had "the best local programs" in the United States. Vice President Hubert H. Humphrey concurred, declaring in February 1966 that Detroit was "second to none" in the use it had made of antipoverty money.[61]

It would have been a cause for wonderment had not the Cavanagh administration joined in the praise of a program so much praised outside Detroit. Detroit's war on poverty was "the country's outstanding success story," the mayor stated in 1966. Less than two weeks before the start of the Detroit riot, Cavanagh lauded the program as "the best in America." Although he could have been expected to make remarks of this sort, Cavanagh did see the war on poverty as one of the great accomplishments of his service as mayor, and he took pride in the fact that so many of the national programs in that war had been "first launched in Detroit on a pilot basis."[62]

Detroit officials recognized that the city's antipoverty program might be arousing expectations among the poor that it could not satisfy. "The program is in great danger of oversell," Roselle remarked in November 1965. In congressional testimony in March 1967, Cavanagh expressed concern that not enough money was being spent on the antipoverty effort to satisfy the expectations it had stimulated, and he warned that this could lead to "extremely serious difficulty in these communities all across the face of this country."[63] The mayor was obviously using this argument to persuade Congress to fund the war on poverty at a higher level, but what he said was not without substance.

One proposed goal of a community action agency, as we have seen, was the coordination of services available to the poor. The OEO, the comptroller general of the United States, and the University of Chicago's Center for Urban Studies all found fault with the Detroit program in this respect. Detroit, the Chicago study noted, had created "something approaching a 'service system' " for the poor, but the system was poorly coordinated, and there was considerable service overlap. "We have so many programs," Cavanagh told a Senate subcommittee, "that I lose track of the names that we have given some of them."

Detroit made some effort to coordinate its programs, particularly in the manpower field, where it set up a Manpower Council that included representatives from the relevant agencies. Within TAP itself, program subcommittees were supposed to coordinate efforts in their respective jurisdictions. What Detroit failed to do, however, despite the creation of an Administrative Council for the purpose, was to coordinate the efforts of TAP-MCHRD, the Detroit Public Schools, and the AOP. It was this failure that led an OEO official to characterize Detroit's administrative structure for the war on poverty as a "three-headed monster." Detroit, however, was not unusual among the nation's cities in its failure to achieve effective coordination of services in the war on poverty: these services almost everywhere were "piecemeal and uncoordinated."[64]

Questions were also raised in Detroit and the Michigan legislature about the number of poor people the poverty programs actually served. A Michigan House of Representatives committee charged after the riot that so few of the poor had been served during the years 1964–67 and so little money had been left to aid them after salaries and overhead had been paid that the antipoverty program was actually a fraud. The MCHRD, however, successfully rebutted these allegations, which appear to have been inspired largely by personal and political considerations.[65]

When asked in the fifteen-city survey if anyone in their family had participated in the Detroit antipoverty program, 17 percent of the black respondents, drawn from the entire city, responded in the affirmative.

This percentage translates into about 100,000 blacks, a figure consonant with the total number of blacks living in poverty in the target areas. In a postriot survey of the riot areas, which were not coterminous with the target areas, the participation response for antipoverty programs was 55.5 percent (assuming that each affirmative response indicated participation in no more than one program, a point the survey leaves unclear). Cavanagh estimated in 1968 that the program had served 67 percent of those eligible. It is probably safe to assume that at least half of the target area residents participated in one or another of the numerous antipoverty programs.[66]

The real question, of course, is not how many were served but who was served and how effectively. The constant complaint was that the really poor were untouched by the programs. "The poor people in Detroit's inner city," a Kerner Commission field team leader concluded after the riot, "believe that they are untouched by federal programs." Thirty Twelfth Street youths wearing "do-rags" appeared at a Common Council meeting in January 1966 to charge that TAP was not reaching hard-core indigents. "If you are not reaching the people on 12th Street," the president of Twelfth Street's Community Youth Council declared, "you are not reaching the people who need to be reached."[67]

The Cavanagh administration and TAP officials responded ambiguously and inconsistently to charges that the antipoverty programs were not reaching the poor. Sometimes they simply rejected the allegation. Defending the antipoverty effort before Congress, Cavanagh testified that programs like the AYEP, NYC, and OJT had demonstrated "complete success in lifting people out of poverty." On other occasions, however, the mayor conceded that the programs had not reached the hard-core poor; and when he was about to leave office in December 1969, he stated that the war on poverty had "scarcely been able to touch the lives of many of the poor."[68]

Certainly the poor in the model city neighborhood do not appear to have benefited economically from the war on poverty. Whereas 44 percent of the families in the area had annual incomes below $3,000 in 1959, the number of such families had increased to 47 percent by 1967. The percentage of the total Detroit population in poverty, however, appears to have declined between 1965 and 1967. In 1965, the estimated percentage of Detroit households in poverty was 21 percent (18.9 percent of white households and 25.9 percent of black). This compared with a national figure of 13.3 percent for whites and 47.1 percent for nonwhites. The MCHRD director estimated the 1967 figure for the city as 16 percent, which almost certainly meant a reduction in the black poverty rate; and a state official advised Governor George Romney at the time of the riot that the poverty rate for blacks in Detroit had fallen to 19 percent, which was far below the national rate for blacks of 37.2 percent.[69] The extent to which the war on poverty, apart from general economic conditions, contributed to the decline in Detroit's poverty rate is difficult to determine.

It is also difficult to determine if manpower programs affected the unemployment rate in Detroit. The low rate of 1965 continued throughout 1966, but unemployment rose in 1967 and more so in July, the month of the riot. The monthly average unemployment rate in the Detroit area for the fiscal year July 1966 to June 1967 was 3.9 percent, but the June 1967 figure was 4.8 percent and the July figure, 6.2 percent, a five-year high. The number of unemployed in the Detroit area increased from 65,000 in May to 100,000 in July, partly the result of the changeover in automobile models. The black unemployment rate was about 8 percent in July, and the rate in what became the riot areas, 11 percent or more. The highest unemployment rate at the time of the riot, probably between 25 and 30 percent, was among black youths aged eighteen to twenty-four. This meant a large number of young blacks hanging around street corners with nothing to do, "looking for action," and susceptible to talk about reforming or changing the system. "People been telling me if you can't make it in Detroit, you can't make it nowhere else," an unemployed rioter declared. "That's bullshit man."[70]

More important from the perspective of the racial background of the riot than the actual effectiveness of Detroit's war on poverty was how the city's blacks appraised the program. Following the riot, the head of the Kerner Commission's field team in Detroit reported that no one in the black community praised the city's war on poverty except for Head Start and NLS. This was certainly hyperbole, but the fact remains that Detroit's war on poverty, for all its national acclaim, was less popular among the city's blacks than were the antipoverty efforts of other large cities among their blacks. Whereas 38 percent of the black respondents in the fifteen-city postriot survey thought that the antipoverty programs in their cities were "doing a good job," only 27 percent of Detroit blacks made the same judgment about Detroit's program. On Twelfth Street, according to a postriot modified probability sample survey of 270 black residents, 36 percent of the respondents approved of the program; the remainder disapproved (41 percent) or were undecided (23 percent). This compared with less than 12 percent of the black respondents in the Watts curfew area who had an unfavorable view of the war on poverty in their city. The less favorable opinion of the war on poverty among Detroit blacks probably resulted from the fact, as Cavanagh had feared, that the heralded Detroit program had aroused greater expectations of the benefits it would produce than was true of the effort in other cities. In Detroit, the head of the Kerner Commission's field team in the city asserted, the war on poverty was seen as "a tease or an empty promise."[71]

The Detroit war on poverty had certainly been oversold, but it cannot be dismissed as an "empty promise." It had improved the lives of many Detroit citizens, white and black, and it could point to "some solid achievements" in the areas of job training, employment, education, health, and, probably, family income. One positive result of Detroit's war on poverty was the "identifying and grooming" of a number of black leaders who gained recognition as spokesmen for the poor, blacks like Julian Witherspoon, Philip Rutledge, and Richard Simmons. On the other hand, the University of Chicago's Center for Urban Studies thought that the Detroit war on poverty might have gained a "certain subtle and informal authority over civil rights groups" by coopting their leadership. In support of this view, the center pointed to militant CORE members, the chairman of the Student Nonviolent Coordinating Committee in Detroit, and others who held jobs in the poverty program or were members of its committees.[72]

In March 1967 Cavanagh told a congressional subcommittee that Detroit had escaped the civil disorders that had afflicted other cities partly because of its implementation of programs made possible by the Economic Opportunity Act of 1964. Rutledge had stated a year earlier that Detroit's community action program would "reduce considerably the chances of a Watts-type outbreak" in Detroit. Quite apart from the supposed effect of the program as a mitigator of discontent, TAP-MCHRD personnel were trained to deal with conflict situations. They checked out rumors of possible trouble and "campaigned in the neighborhoods" to urge peaceful methods of settling disputes. When the war on poverty proved not to be a riot deterrent, the Detroit response was that, however damaging the city's riot, it would have been even worse had not Detroit combated poverty so aggressively. Rutledge and others pointed out that the rioters had not vented their wrath on a single antipoverty facility and that only three of the five thousand youths enrolled in the various antipoverty programs at the time had engaged in riotous acts more serious than curfew violation.[73]

That the Detroit riot would have been even more deadly had not the city waged a war on poverty is an argument not susceptible to proof. What can be asserted categorically, however, is that Detroit's war on poverty had far less to do with the way the riot began and how it unfolded than did the more explosive issue of police-community relations.

CHAPTER 5

"The Single Most Important Problem": Police-Community Relations

I

"Perhaps the major domestic conflict of the 1960s," Harlan Hahn and Joe R. Feagin have asserted, "was produced by the urban confrontation of predominantly white police forces and expanding black communities." The "black hostility toward the police," they noted, "became so common and so intense that the mere presence of a white policeman performing routine duties in the ghetto, when coupled with other conditions conducive to unrest, often was sufficient to ignite explosive violence." In Detroit it was a police action on Twelfth Street, "coupled with other conditions," that precipitated the great July 1967 riot. It is not surprising that the president of the Detroit branch of the National Association for the Advancement of Colored People (NAACP) regarded police-community relations as "the single most important problem in the city."[1]

The head of the Community Relations Division of the Michigan Civil Rights Commission (CRC), Burton Levy, concluded in 1965 that since 96 percent of the black community was law-abiding and 98 percent of the police had never been charged with brutality, the gulf between the black and white communities insofar as the police were concerned could be closed by human relations training for the police and greater professionalism. But after two years study of the matter and personal experience with the police in various parts of the country, particularly in Detroit, Levy concluded that it was the *police system*," not "a few 'bad eggs,' " that was at fault. The "police system," he wrote in 1968, "recruits a significant number of bigots, reinforces the bigotry through the department's value system and socialization with older officers, and then takes the worst of the officers and puts them on duty in the ghetto, where the opportunity to act out the prejudice is always available." A field survey conducted for the President's Commission on Law Enforcement and

Administration of Justice before the Detroit riot revealed that 45 percent
of police working in black neighborhoods were "extremely anti-Negro"
and an additional 34 percent were "prejudiced."[2]

Although police performance in the 1960s was almost certainly
superior to what it had been, blacks expressed greater resentment at
police behavior in that decade than in earlier years. This was almost
certainly a consequence of the civil rights movement and increased black
pride and self-consciousness. The televised police violence against civil
rights demonstrators in the South aroused black antagonism to police
everywhere and led blacks to become more active in protesting police
misconduct. Poorly educated for the most part, poorly trained, and
living in "relative isolation" from the rest of society, the police did not
understand and were not prepared to deal with the law-enforcement
problems stemming from the black revolt of the 1960s. Of the principal
institutions of American society, police departments proved to be "least
responsive to the demands of the black community."[3]

"The most important way" a mayor could affect police behavior was
through his selection of the head of the city's police department and "the
molding of the expectations that govern his role." Jerome Cavanagh, as
we shall see, selected liberal police commissioners attuned to the implications of the civil rights revolution, but the ability of the mayor and his
civilian police commissioner to influence police behavior was limited at
best. As Richard Marks, the secretary-director of Detroit's Commission
on Community Relations (CCR), noted, the long-standing view of the
Detroit police was, "we don't give a damn who's police commissioner.
He'll do things our way, or we'll break him." It was the "entrenched
bureaucracy," which, knowledgeable people in Detroit agreed, left
"much to be desired in the area of race relations," that ran the department and largely resisted the mayor and his liberal police commissioners.
The result was that the policies of the commissioner "never seemed to get
down to the street."[4]

John Nichols, deputy superintendent during the 1967 riot, and Ray
Girardin, the police commissioner at the time, both spoke ruefully in
later years about the difficulty of altering police behavior. Police departments "do not change," Nichols remarked. "You try to change a police
organization . . . and . . . it's like a rubber band, you go back there and
they're in the same shape again." Girardin commented, "It's a son of a
bitch to stop. These guys [police] are hard to handle, [and] they can
screw you in 90 ways." If at all possible, the commissioner had to back
his troops because otherwise, Girardin stated, "you've got no morale or
no police department."[5]

Detroit's police, overwhelmingly white, brought "a white working
class set of values" to their jobs. About two-thirds of the police at the
time of the riot were from blue-collar families, and about 80 percent had
held blue-collar jobs or served in the armed forces before becoming

police officers. According to in-depth interviews with 286 randomly selected officers just after the riot, white police held "predominantly negative views of the black community." Lower-echelon white officers saw Detroit's blacks as "a privileged minority . . . without real grievances, deficient in respect for law and order and ready to use violence to attain a still greater advantage vis-a-vis the white community." Sizable majorities among the patrolmen thought that blacks were treated the same as or better than whites with regard to education (99 percent), jobs (74 percent), housing (56 percent), law enforcement (91 percent), and in stores (83 percent). Slightly more than 80 percent of the white patrolmen thought that the more blacks received, the more they wanted and the more likely they were to resort to violence to satisfy their desires. Detectives, sergeants, lieutenants, and inspectors largely shared these views.[6]

The attitudes toward blacks expressed by Detroit police officers after the riot were quite similar to the attitudes of white police officers in other cities. Although the Detroit police were no doubt influenced by the riot itself, there is little reason to think that a preriot survey would have produced a much different result. Drawing on his two-year experience as Cavanagh's first police commissioner, George Edwards concluded that 90 percent of the police force were "bigoted." After an in-depth discussion with Girardin in September 1964, Cavanagh's executive secretary advised the mayor that some policemen spoke as one expected "racists to speak. Also they complain of your [liberal] administration," the aide noted. "When you talk to them about civil rights and community relations, they think you're *touched*," Girardin reported. The police view of the way to treat blacks, he said, was "to hit them on the side of the head."[7]

The way police viewed blacks was probably determined before they joined the department, and their experience with blacks after that time simply reinforced police prejudices. Blacks whom the police encountered while on duty were generally those "getting into trouble," and all too many police concluded that blacks were likely to be troublemakers. The reaction of a veteran policeman at the beginning of 1965 to the insistence of the head of the Detroit NAACP that the police had to change their view of blacks was, "Tell Negroes to stay the hell out of so much trouble." The officer noted that of 36,420 persons against whom the police had requested warrants in 1963, 23,094 were nonwhite. Showing a newsman a report on major crime in Detroit during a twenty-four-hour period in the preceding week, he said, "All Negroes. . . . It's like that every morning." A sociologist could have explained these figures, but the police were not sociologists.[8]

Many policemen saw themselves as belonging to "an economic and social sub-culture," poorly paid for their efforts and lacking in community support. In a study prepared by the Marketing and Research Department of Campbell-Ewald Company for the Greater Detroit Board of

Commerce shortly before the riot, the police expressed high regard for their department but reacted negatively to their personal status. Sixty-five percent thought that the department was one of the best in the nation, and an additional 28 percent that it was above average in quality; but only 24 percent believed that the public appreciated and understood police work, and only 32 percent believed that the media treated the police fairly. If they had to do it all over again, only 39 percent indicated that they would have become policemen, and only 24 percent wanted their sons to become policemen. Like police elsewhere, Detroit police had no doubt decided to become police officers because of the relative job security and fringe benefits such as retirement pay the position provided rather than because of the nature of the job itself.[9]

Responding to a questionnaire from the federal government just before the riot, the Police Department rated support for police in the ghetto as "very weak — if at all." Their isolation from the rest of society and the sense that they were "a distinct and often deprived group" lacking in the public respect they believed due them led to "a magnified sense of group solidarity" among the police in Detroit and elsewhere. "The police officer is always right," Cavanagh's first police commissioner noted, was "a familiar slogan in police precincts."[10]

Although the salaries of patrolmen after four years of service rose from $6,364 in 1962–63 to $8,335 in 1966–67, well above the median salary of $7,008 for police in large cities, 87 percent of the Detroit police, according to the Board of Commerce survey, believed themselves underpaid. The police also saw their department as "severely undermanned." Detroit's 4,268 police officers as of March 1967 had to police a city of 139 square miles. New York, with four times as many residents, had six times as many policemen as Detroit, and Philadelphia, with 300,000 more residents, had thirteen hundred more police. When asked in the Board of Commerce survey to list the biggest problem of the department, 38 percent of the respondents placed manpower strength first, more than double the percentage selecting any other problem. Girardin said after the riot that the size of the department had kept him "awake nights worrying about it."[11]

Detroit's patrolmen sought to press their demands for improved terms of employment through the Detroit Police Officers Association (DPOA). Formed in 1944, the DPOA was pretty much a company union until 1952, and primarily a social organization until 1965, when the state of Michigan authorized collective bargaining by public employees, although forbidding them to strike. The detectives, lieutenants, and sergeants had their own organization, and the few black policemen, at odds with the DPOA, established the Guardians in 1962 as their spokesman.[12]

As the only city officials present in the ghetto around the clock, the police, to the ghetto dweller, were the "most visible symbol" of white society, the "extended arm" of the city government that implemented the racial policies of the dominant white community. The result was that the police bore "the full brunt of the accumulated frustrations and hostility of the ghetto."[13]

Summarizing the black view of the police, the president of the Detroit NAACP declared in 1965, "The Negroes in Detroit feel they are part of an occupied country. The Negroes have no rights which the police have to respect. It would appear that the average policeman looks upon the Negro as being a criminal type." Blacks in Detroit, as in other large cities, complained, on the one hand, about police brutality and, on the other hand, about a lack of police protection. Police brutality has been defined by an academic expert on the subject as "the judgment [of individuals] that they have not been treated with the full rights and dignity owing citizens in a democratic society." As so defined, police brutality ranged from verbal abuse to the improper use of physical and, perhaps, fatal force.[14]

It was a common practice for Detroit police, like white police elsewhere, to talk down to blacks, calling adult males "boys" or addressing them in a discourteous or abusive manner. Police had "traditionally" engaged in this form of "status degradation" in dealing with minority or lower-class individuals, perhaps because of the discrepancy between the self-esteem of the police and their low public esteem. "They don't know how to talk to you like an adult," declared a black male in the riot area to whom the police had used "all kinds of foul language." "Those monkies have called me nigger," recalled a twenty-six-year-old Detroit black, just as others complained about "this boy business." Young blacks were resentful that police referred to them as "punks and swear and things like that." Black women complained that the police assumed that they were prostitutes or called them "Honey, Baby with no provocation." In the fifteen-city postriot survey, 40 percent of the black respondents in Detroit claimed that the police used disrespectful and insulting language in dealing with blacks in their neighborhood, and 17 percent indicated that this had happened to them.[15]

Brutality, a black official at the time of the riot recalled, was more "psychological than physical. What made people so mad was the idea you could be stopped and frisked in a humiliating manner for no other reason than the fact you were Black." You "can't walk down the street without being picked up," remarked a sixteen-year-old black, and another recalled being arrested for making a wrong vehicular turn and then being "searched, insulted, harassed." A black professional basketball player driving an expensive car was stopped by the police and taken to the precinct station to prove that the car was his. In the fifteen-city survey, 43 percent of the black respondents in Detroit thought that the police frisked fellow blacks without good reason, and 12 percent of the respondents claimed that this had happened to them.[16]

Another form of police harassment was to treat young blacks stand-

ing on street corners as suspicious persons, either arresting them or telling them to move on. "You can't stand around and talk to the fellows—
they tell you to move on," a black female reported. A seventeen-year-old
black stated just after the riot that he had been standing on a corner with
friends when a police car drove up and an officer said, "move along you
black niggers."[17]

The most obvious form of police brutality, of course, was the use of
excessive physical force. Police sometimes used excessive force against
their prisoners in the station house or against individuals in the ghetto,
where white policemen believed themselves both hated and in the presence of danger. The likelihood that misuse of force might occur was
increased by the fact that most police contacts with civilians were not
subject to close surveillance and the police could claim that they had
acted in self-defense or because the suspect had resisted arrest. The head
of the Detroit NAACP remarked in 1965 that at one time in Detroit
"every Negro arrested somehow fell down" and suffered a cracked skull.
Now, he declared, every black shot by the police seemed to be carrying a
knife. The Center for Research in Social Organization found that the
police were actually more apt to use excessive force against white suspects than black, but it was the brutality or alleged brutality against
blacks, involving both injuries and deaths, that became a police-
community issue of major proportions in preriot Detroit. The issue was
of such concern that the *Michigan Chronicle*, the city's black newspaper,
assigned a reporter specifically to cover this subject.[18]

The executive secretary of the Detroit NAACP during Cavanagh's
first term as mayor thought that police "intimidation" of blacks by
"physical abuse and then killing them" was the "most dehumanizing"
aspect of what he characterized as the "American system of racial
oppression." In the fifteen-city survey, 34 percent of the black Detroit
respondents believed the police roughed up people unnecessarily in making arrests in their neighborhoods, and 4 percent said that this had happened to them. When a *Chronicle* reporter in August 1964 talked to
twenty-five Twelfth Street blacks, most young and male, nearly all of
them complained about police harassment or brutality. "They rough you
up a lot," one of them declared. Of the 1,041 citizens injured in alterca-
tions with the police between May 1961 and February 1964, 617 were
black. Blacks in Detroit were far more likely than whites to be roughed
up, frisked, and subjected to verbal abuse by the police, but they were
much less apt to be the victims of police misbehavior than blacks in
Watts, judging from a survey of the Watts curfew area following the
1965 Watts riot.[19]

Some of the black concern about police brutality in Detroit focused
on the so-called Big Four police cruisers, which had "a gestapo-like
image" in the black community. The three plainclothesmen and the uniformed driver riding in these vehicles, none of them integrated before

1965, were armed with shotguns, machine guns, and tear gas. A black official later recalled that the Big Four personnel "slammed some heads up against the wall and kicked some rear ends" in an alley just west of Twelfth Street. Blacks "hated and feared" the cruisers.[20]

In Detroit and elsewhere, the other side of the coin insofar as black complaints against police behavior were concerned was the alleged lack of law enforcement in the ghetto. Late in May 1967 about two hundred black leaders in Detroit met to consider initiating a lawsuit against the Police Department not just because of alleged brutality but also because of failure to protect inner-city blacks. Blacks charged that the police were slow to respond to calls from the ghetto, were not particularly concerned about crimes that involved blacks alone, and were either tolerant of or associated with the vice that was so much a part of life in the ghetto. A black police inspector later explained delay in responding to calls from black neighborhoods as reflecting "the attitude of 'let them kill themselves and we will go pick up the pieces.' " Slightly more than 60 percent of Detroit's blacks, judging from the fifteen-city survey, thought that the police did not respond quickly to calls from black neighborhoods, and about 30 percent indicated that their answers were based on personal experience. "I feel if I call the policemen I wouldn't get any result," a black in the riot area declared just after the disturbance; and another remarked, "They just don't care what happen to colored people." Interestingly enough, about the same percentage of Detroit whites as blacks, according to the fifteen-city survey, complained that the police did not come quickly when called, but only 14 percent of the white respondents said that this had happened to them.[21]

Vice, organized crime, and the ghetto went "hand-in-hand," and many blacks believed the police were at least partly to blame. Some saw the police as "crooked" and running "a police racket" in the ghetto, and only one in twenty blacks in a postriot survey of Twelfth Street blacks thought the police were "always honest." "Too many of the bastards were so busy shaking people down that they didn't have time to give you any protection," declared a lower east side resident. Police Commissioner George Edwards told a Kerner Commission investigator that the police had "strong tie-ins" with organized crime.[22]

The biggest black complaint about vice in the ghetto concerned prostitution, which the black leadership saw as having a "debilitating effect" on the community and which led to "serious interracial incidents" that severely affected police-community relations. As younger and younger girls were recruited as street walkers and as the venereal disease rate mounted, the black leadership demanded that the police enforce the laws against "this growing and terrible problem." Blacks complained that the police did little more than administer "a slap on the wrist" to black prostitutes and did nothing at all to white johns who drove into the ghetto. The police responded that an order in 1964 to end "arrests for 'investigation as disorderly persons' " limited their ability to cope with prostitution. The police, however, became somewhat more aggressive in trying to limit prostitution just before the riot. In April 1967 the Police Department assigned four integrated police teams to patrol the Twelfth Street blocks between West Grand Boulevard and Clairmount, which became the epicenter of the riot three months later.[23]

When a black woman in the riot area was asked why she had said that the police treated blacks "kind of bad," she replied, "you're a Nigger[,] man." Whereas 80 percent of Detroit whites in a Market Opinion Research survey in 1965 thought the police enforced the law fairly with respect to all groups, only 32 percent of blacks shared this view. More than 80 percent of a sample of Twelfth Street adult blacks following the riot believed that the police did not treat people equally and that they treated young unemployed blacks, black teenagers, and black power advocates worst of all.[24]

Black criticism of law enforcement in Detroit was not confined to police behavior; it extended rather to the entire legal system. There was talk in Detroit, especially among black attorneys, of a "triple conspiracy" among the Police Department, the prosecutor's office, and the Detroit Recorder's Court that "severely unbalanced" the "scales of justice for Negroes." The fact that police headquarters and the office of the county prosecutor were in the same building and the Recorder's Court building was just behind the two appeared to provide physical evidence of the link among the "unholy trio" that blacks saw as "the enemy."[25]

Professor William Pierce of the University of Michigan Law School thought that the Wayne County prosecutor's office acted "too much as a legal mouthpiece of the police." Blacks maintained that Samuel Olsen, prosecutor during most of the Cavanagh administration, was "adept at white-washing policemen in the slaying of unarmed Negroes." They pointed out that of thirty-four whites killed by blacks between 1958 and 1961, the prosecutor had not once found the homicide to have been justifiable, but he had ruled the homicide justifiable in fifteen of the twenty-three slayings of blacks by whites, twelve of these by the police.

Both the Saul E. Levin Memorial Foundation and a task force panel of the President's Commission on Law Enforcement and Administration of Justice issued reports before the 1967 riot that were highly critical of the Recorder's Court, which had exclusive criminal jurisdiction in Detroit. The task force panel characterized the Recorder's Court as "unseemly, disreputable, inadequate and unfair" and as having "no regard for justice." The Legal Redress Committee of the Detroit NAACP charged that the court demonstrated an "attitude of disrespect toward the rights of the poor and especially the Negro," and George Edwards thought it tended to be "pro police." In the fifteen-city survey, 19 percent of the Detroit black respondents thought the Recorder's Court was harder on blacks than whites, as compared to 2 percent who thought the reverse.[26]

When Cavanagh assumed the office of mayor, racial tension stemming from the Miriani police "crackdown" was so great that the mayor and others thought Detroit was "the [nation's] most likely candidate for a major race riot." George Edwards, who agreed to become police commissioner on the condition he would be free to run the department without political interference, thought that "a 'river of hate' coursed through the city he loved," and he wanted "to build some bridges across that river." Cavanagh told Edwards that he wanted his police commissioner to provide both effective and equal law enforcement, and Edwards devoted himself to that task. He had a notice posted above the admitting desk of each precinct setting forth his objectives as commissioner: more vigorous law enforcement, equal protection and enforcement of the law, and citizen support for law enforcement. He hoped in this way "to move Detroit away from the possibility of serious racial strife and in the direction of a more united and a safer city."[27]

"My job," Edwards recalled, "was to teach the police they didn't have a constitutional right to beat up Negroes on arrest." He told the police that it was "their job . . . to serve the citizens, not to ride herd on them." In what he believed was a successful effort to see "due process on the street, rather than in the library," he ordered an end to the so-called "alley court," that is, the police practice of "exacting physical punishment on the street." He ordered that police prisoners be brought before a magistrate without delay and that misdemeanants be permitted to post bond at a police station to avoid spending the night or a weekend in jail. He also sought to curb the continuing practice of random arrests for investigative purposes. At night he sometimes rode along in a scout car to watch the police "deal with the human beings who are the raw material of our attempt to build a democratic civilization." Precinct inspectors explained the new policies to their officers, police were reminded of the policies at roll calls, and they were incorporated in the training at the Police Academy.[28]

The high command of the Police Department sought to frustrate Edwards's reform efforts, but in November 1962 both the superintendent and deputy superintendent resigned, perhaps influenced to do so by the commissioner, who had publicly criticized the superintendent's vote in a trial board ruling in favor of five officers accused of beating a black. The director of Michigan State University's School of Police Administration and Public Safety thought that Edwards's choice of Eugene Reuter and James Lupton as the new superintendent and deputy superintendent, respectively, was just right, "one [Reuter] being the rough and ready type and the other suave and smooth." A fellow police officer later noted, however, that Reuter, who had "not grown beyond being a sergeant" and did not "project very well," was not "the man for the times." John

Nichols, though an admirer of Reuter, nevertheless agreed that the superintendent was not "sensitized" to Detroit's changing racial climate, and a Police Community Task Force of prominent citizens urged the mayor in 1965 to place both the superintendent and deputy superintendent in positions where they would not be in "direct control of attitudes in the department." The black leadership was intensely dissatisfied with the new appointees, viewing them as "villains" biased against blacks and alleging that they subverted the commissioner's policies.[29]

Seeking community support for his department, Edwards explained his policy of "tough" but "fair" law enforcement to numerous meetings in black neighborhoods. After several months of effort, the commissioner claimed success for his reforms, noting particularly the increase in reported crimes in black neighborhoods. Blacks, he said in explanation, were now cooperating with the police and were willing to turn to them "in times of difficulty." Whereas not a single black received a citizen's award for helping the police at the first awards ceremony that Edwards attended, blacks were receiving 40–50 percent of the awards by the time Edwards left the commissionership. In 1962, also, the Detroit NAACP and the Cotillion Club, in what was seen as an unprecedented action, supported an increase in the police budget. At the end of his first year of service, Edwards confidently stated that the trend toward conflict in police-community relations had been reversed.[30]

Edwards assumed his position as commissioner just as the CCR had, in effect, confirmed black charges of discrimination in the recruitment of police officers. Edwards, who informed the CCR that he agreed with its recommendations concerning personnel selection, expressed his willingness to discuss any instance in which the commission believed a qualified applicant had been rejected by the department. "The most important single statistic" in the CCR report, Edwards stated, was that there were only thirty-six blacks on a force of forty-two hundred, and he intended, he said, to correct this imbalance.[31]

True to Edwards's word, the Police Department initiated a massive recruiting campaign in 1962 aimed particularly at blacks. Patrolman Avery Jackson, a black, was moved into the recruiting office and was the first person an applicant for the department encountered. The results of the campaign during Edwards's two years as commissioner were, however, very meager. Of a total of 457 police hired in 1962 and 1963, only 19 were black. The 144 blacks on the force as of October 1963 constituted 3.28 percent of the total complement, a very slight advance since 1958, when the 113 blacks made up 3 percent of the force. According to the department's personnel director, most blacks who had been rejected had failed to meet the required physical and educational standards. Although the department also attributed the poor result to the availability of better jobs for blacks outside the department, an expert analysis of the relevant labor market provided for a federal district court indicated that, absent discrimination, the department would have hired 125, not 19, blacks in 1962 and 1963.[32]

Edwards was able to point to some modest improvements in black assignments and promotions during his commissionership. By the time he left the position at the end of 1963, blacks had been assigned to all but two precincts, as compared to six in 1958; eight of the seventeen blacks above the rank of patrolman had been promoted since the beginning of 1962; sixteen blacks had been assigned to so-called preferred jobs; and the first black ever had been promoted to the rank of inspector. Although the Detroit Urban League (DUL) claimed that superiors were still assigning white officers to integrated scout cars as "a form of punishment," which the department denounced as an "absolute untruth," there appeared to have been real progress in the integration of the vehicles. Despite these gains, the executive secretary of the NAACP charged as Edwards left office that the Police Department was still "clearly a segregated institution" with "very little career promise for the Negro officer."[33]

Commissioner Herbert W. Hart, it will be recalled, had sought to improve police-community relations by arranging meetings between the police and the citizenry. Little preparation, however, had gone into these meetings, and police officers treated them as "a lot of baloney." Edwards followed up on the idea by holding meetings in the precincts at which "grass roots" blacks could air their grievances against the department and also by holding city-wide meetings that involved not only police and blacks but also, on occasion, educators, clergymen, and social workers. Edwards thought that the program worked "pretty well," but the meetings were apparently "a complete flop" since the police had "no conception of what the Commissioner was attempting to do."[34]

Following a review of the department's training program, Edwards increased the hours devoted to human relations in the Police Academy from ten or less to twenty-nine. In cooperation with the Detroit Round Table of the National Conference of Christians and Jews, the department in 1963 gave 704 policemen above the rank of sergeant additional instruction in police-community relations.[35]

Blacks with complaints about police behavior could take them to the department's Community Relations Bureau (CRB). In an effort to secure a more objective evaluation of complaints, Edwards transferred the investigatory function from line officers to staff officers. He took some satisfaction from the fact that whereas the CRB had received sixty-four complaints of discourtesy during the seven months of its existence in 1961, only twenty-one such complaints were submitted during the same months of 1962.[36]

In August 1962 the CRB reported that it had not received a single brutality complaint in six months. Eleven months later, however, the killing by a "notorious cop" of the "notorious" prostitute, Cynthia Scott, inflamed police-community relations and became a cause célèbre in the black community. Scott, sometimes known as "Saint Cynthia," was a six-foot tall, 193-pound prostitute who had been convicted eleven times for accosting and soliciting. On July 5, 1963, Theodore Spicher, a policeman with a poor reputation in the black community, and his scout-car partner, Robert Marshall, observed Scott, money in hand, walking with a black male. According to the police report, the two officers approached Scott and her companion to question her about the money since there had been "a lot of jack-rolling by prostitutes and pimps" in the area. Spicher told Scott, who was apparently drunk, that she was under arrest for larceny from a person and ordered her to enter the scout car. As she was about to do so, she turned on Spicher and cut him on the index finger. She started to run, and when Spicher tried to stop her, she slashed him again. He shot her twice in the back as she fled, and when she turned and allegedly sought to slash him a third time, he shot her in the stomach, and she fell. As Marshall then sought to disarm her, she cut him on the arm. A Homicide Bureau investigation produced some corroborative evidence, but there were allegations in the black community that the police had provoked the incident by trying to make an illegal arrest, that Scott was resisting a "police shakedown," that the money in her hand was change her companion had returned to her after she had sent him to buy some food, and that she did not have a knife or that Spicher had removed the knife from her person only after he had shot and killed her and had then used the knife to cut Marshall.[37]

Three days after the Scott shooting, Prosecutor Olsen ruled that Spicher had had a legal right to use fatal force to stop a fleeing felon. The killing, followed by Olsen's prompt exoneration of Spicher, ignited a fire storm in the black community. Seven hundred persons, many from UHURU and the Group of Advanced Leadership (GOAL), picketed police headquarters on July 13. UHURU followed this with a series of street rallies, and GOAL not only sought to bring Spicher to trial but also aided Scott's mother in initiating a $5 million suit against Spicher and the Police Department. The NAACP demanded that Reuter investigate the slaying and also appealed to Michigan's attorney general to review the case. Representatives from a wide spectrum of black and civil rights organizations set up an unofficial committee to investigate "alleged police brutality," and a UHURU-led group of fifteen staged a sit-in in Cavanagh's reception room, demanding appointment of a black police commissioner, disarming of the police, and the arrest of Olsen.

A citizens committee headed by Congressman John Conyers as well as the Metropolitan Detroit Branch of the American Civil Liberties Union criticized the prosecutor, and petitions were circulated for his recall. In a letter to Cavanagh, Congressman Charles Diggs, Jr., asserted that as a result of the Scott affair and also the police slaying in a car chase on July 12 of an eighteen-year-old youth driving a stolen car, the progress in police-community relations Edwards had achieved could be "seen going down the drain." In Barbara Tinker's 1970 novel, *When the Fire Reaches Us*, one of the characters remarks, "there is damned few black people around Detroit who has forgot" the killing of Cynthia Scott. "The cop didn't get so much as a slap on the wrist for killing her."[38]

Edwards had been out of the country when the Scott slaying occurred. When he returned to Detroit, he conducted his own investigation of the affair and concluded that Spicher had acted in self-defense. After the commissioner appeared on television to present his findings, the NAACP and other black organizations demanded and were granted equal time to reply. They used the occasion to call for a civilian review board for the Police Department.[39]

The Scott slaying persuaded Edwards not only to remove Spicher from scout-car duty but also to revise the department's procedures for dealing with incidents involving police use of fatal force. In such circumstances, the officer involved was to be relieved of duty without prejudice and with pay pending an investigation, the commissioner was to appoint a board of inquiry of three senior officers who were not part of the same unit as the suspended officer, and the board was to report within five to ten days unless there was good cause for delay.[40]

Although police-community relations took a turn for the better while Edwards was police commissioner, it is doubtful that the Police Department changed very much during his two years at the helm. His efforts at reform had been resisted from the start by the department's bureaucracy, and as a police official who headed a special squad at the time asserted, Edwards was commissioner for too short a time to have had any real impact at the "rank and file level." The Scott affair somewhat dimmed Edwards's luster in the black community, but it does not appear that the black leadership "ever left him." When Edwards resigned at the end of 1963 to move to the federal bench, the *Michigan Chronicle* editorialized that although "prejudice and brutality" had not been eliminated from the Police Department, the state of police-community relations was "markedly better" than it had been before Edwards became commissioner. Edwards's own optimistic appraisal was that Detroit in two years had been transformed from "the most explosive big city in the North over racial tensions to the least explosive."[41]

The symbol of improved police-community relations during the Edwards commissionership was the department's incident-free handling of the mammoth Walk to Freedom, just a few days before the Scott slaying. Voicing the feelings of Detroit's black leadership, James N. Garrett, the vice president of the Cotillion Club, hailed the police performance as "a MASTERPIECE in police-community relations." "For the first time," Garrett stated, "Negroes in Detroit looked with honor and pride on our police force." Martin Luther King wrote Edwards that the Police Department had demonstrated to the black community that it was "a genuine protector and friend" rather than "an enemy."[42]

As Edwards's successor, Cavanagh turned to his executive secretary for the preceding eighteen months, Ray Girardin. A Cavanagh loyalist, Girardin had become something of a legend as a crime reporter for the *Detroit Times* from 1930 to 1960 and had then served as the chief probation officer of the Recorder's Court before moving to the mayor's staff. Because of his long experience as a crime reporter, Girardin was well known to the police and was perceived by them as being more "knowledgeable" about the department's operations than his predecessor. He was a liberal but not the "crusader" that Edwards was. What distinguished Girardin physically was a face so wrinkled that one policeman remarked that "it could hold a three-day rainfall."[43]

The consensus in Detroit was that Girardin's heart was "in the right place" but that he was "too weak an administrator to press his views on the [police] force." He had a good relationship with the black community, which admired his decency and his humanity, but most black leaders thought he was weak and indecisive and no match for the department's bureaucracy, which they believed was "calling the shots" in the department. In the Board of Commerce survey released shortly before the riot, only 26 percent of the police and 27 percent of the citizens surveyed thought Girardin was a "very effective commissioner"; 60 percent of the police and 56 percent of the citizens thought that he was "somewhat effective."[44]

Girardin made recruitment of blacks one of his top priorities. With this in mind, he placed a black on the oral interview board and agreed to permit the DUL to observe how interviews were conducted. The department's recruiting efforts in 1964 and 1965, as Cavanagh conceded, were, however, "remarkably unsuccessful": of 314 police officers hired, only 22 were black.[45]

In the spring of 1966 Girardin asked his black administrative assistant what a reasonable departmental goal should be for the recruitment of blacks. The assistant's response was "something approaching" 33 percent, which corresponded to the percentage of blacks in Detroit's population. The two then agreed on a 25 percent figure for subsequent training classes. Following a miniriot on Detroit's east side some months thereafter, Girardin assigned two more black officers to the recruitment effort and also formed integrated recruiting teams to aid in attracting more blacks. The intensive recruitment effort, which enjoyed the support of the city's churches and synagogues, block clubs, and citizen groups, involved the distribution of literature door to door, the use of mobile units in shopping centers, a public-relations campaign run by the Greater Detroit Board of Commerce, and a state-wide drive in cooperation with various state agencies.

By May 1967 about half of the applicants for positions in the Police

Department were black. Between July 1966 and May 1967 the number of blacks in the department increased from 134 to 227. This still meant, however, that only about 5 percent of the police on the eve of the 1967 riot were black, about the same percentage as in New York but well below the number in Philadelphia (20 percent) and Chicago (17 percent) and slightly below the median for black sworn personnel in twenty-eight departments.[46]

Although an increasing number of blacks applied for positions in the Police Department, blacks attributed the department's failure to recruit more blacks partly to its "bad image" in the black community. Blacks regarded it as "a sort of betrayal" of the black community to join the department, and they also cited the alleged lack of opportunity for blacks to move ahead in the department as a deterrent. Black policemen may have discouraged some qualified blacks from applying. A black policeman later recalled that white officers did not react to him as man to man. Some white officers refused to show him how to prepare a report properly or how to correct his errors. When he rode in a scout car with a white officer, there was no conversation, and he remembered that it was "really tough." Kerner Commission staff members claimed that there was "enormous, if not unbearable, pressure within the ranks . . . exerted by white patrolmen to drive Negroes out of the force." Not one of the hundred policemen interviewed for the Board of Commerce survey of the department favored an affirmative action approach to recruiting as a means of increasing the number of blacks in the department.[47]

Black police privately complained that they were regularly passed over for promotion despite their seniority because their superiors would not give them good performance scores. Discrimination *"definitely exists,"* a black policeman told a Kerner Commission staffer, and the President's Commission on Law Enforcement and Administration of Justice agreed. As of April 1966, whereas about one in three whites held ranks above patrolman in the department, only about one in eight blacks were in such positions.[48] Seniority explains much but not all of this.

In addition to seeking to recruit more blacks, Girardin, despite opposition within the department, sought a greater integration of existing personnel. He succeeded without "fanfare" in integrating the Detective Bureau and in placing at least one black in every precinct; he placed a black in command of one of the precincts, the first time this had occurred in Detroit; and he added the first blacks ever to the Police Academy staff, the Accident Prevention Bureau, and the General Service Bureau. He increased the number of integrated scout cars from eighteen to thirty-one, about 18 percent of the total, and in 1965 the department began to integrate its Big Four cruiser crews.[49]

In April 1966 Hubert Locke, executive director of the Citizens Committee for Equal Opportunity (CCEO), was sworn in as Girardin's administrative assistant, the closest to the top that a black had ever come in the history of the department. A police relations specialist of the CRC reported to the commissioner in January 1967 that Locke was "respected throughout" the department and had achieved "a satisfactory identity" with the city's police. Locke, who could advise but not decide, did the best he could under difficult circumstances, but since he was identified with the black middle class, black militants disparaged him as a "do nothing or Uncle Tom."[50]

Quite apart from justice and fairness, the question remains whether the presence of more blacks on the police force would, in and of itself, have made a meaningful difference in the years leading up to the 1967 riot. After a trip to Detroit in February 1967, a federal investigator concluded that additional black police would have made no difference in terms of police-community relations because a black who was "anti-police" did "not see past the blue uniform." A black policeman with twenty-six years of service informed Governor George Romney during the riot that black police were so proud of their badge that their behavior was often worse than that of white officers. Insecure black officers in an overwhelmingly white department might very well have sought to prove themselves to their white colleagues by treating blacks with particular harshness. An authority on the subject contended in 1971 that black police, like white police, were "most likely to exercise force against members of their own race." Edwards, after leaving office, thought that it was necessary to "correct . . . [the] attitude" of black officers and to improve "their posture in the community." In the fifteen-city survey, only 8.5 percent of black Detroit respondents thought that they received better treatment from black than white police, 6 percent thought the reverse, and 75 percent indicated that the color of a policeman's skin made little difference in his behavior toward blacks. The fact that black police officers patrolling the black ghetto were better able than white officers to establish rapport with ghetto residents thus appeared to have only minimal effect on the reaction of blacks to police of their own race.

After 1973 an increasingly black police force in a city undergoing racial change under black leadership unquestionably helped to improve police-community relations. But to have increased the black component of the force from 5 to say 10 percent by 1967, which is about all that could reasonably have been expected judging by the analysis of the relevant labor market, would probably have made little difference in the way events unfolded in 1967. The Newark police force had a 10 percent nonwhite component in 1967, but Newark was not spared a major riot that year. Although blacks constituted 10.5 percent of the Detroit police force in 1970, the relationship between the black community and the Police Department continued to be one of pronounced hostility.[51]

Quite apart from integrating the police force in more than a token way, the department could conceivably have improved police-black relations by an effective police-community relations program. The Police

Task Force of the President's Commission on Law Enforcement and Administration of Justice regarded programs of this sort, which were essentially police–minority group relations programs, as "the best method of riot control available to the police." The Detroit Police Department sought to address this problem by training at the Police Academy, in-service training, the establishment of police-community relations committees in the precincts, special programs for youth, and improved procedures in dealing with civilian complaints.[52]

Girardin in August 1966 increased the number of hours devoted to human relations in the Police Academy from twenty-nine to fifty, about 14 percent of the number of hours recruits spent in the academy. There is every reason to believe, however, that this type of training in Detroit, as elsewhere, was next to useless. Indeed, a 1966 survey indicated that police officers were more prejudiced after such training than before! The head of the Detroit Round Table of the National Conference of Christians and Jews thought that no real effort was made in the academy to provide recruits with an understanding of the black community, and the CCEO characterized the human relations training as "lacking in depth and seriousness."[53]

Even had academy training been of better quality, its effectiveness would have been nullified as graduates became socialized in the department. Rookie cops in Detroit, as elsewhere, learned how to behave not in the academy but from veterans on the force; and what they heard from veteran police officers, according to a black policeman, was "not to pay any attention to that community relations crap." The way to do their job, they learned, was not by following human relations precepts but by instilling fear in potential lawbreakers, especially the young among them.[54]

Impressed with the possible value of police-community relations training, Total Action against Poverty (TAP) sought and received an Office of Economic Opportunity grant in 1965 to train eighteen hundred officers drawn mainly from the eight precincts where most low income and minority group individuals lived. The stated purpose of the grant was "to develop in police officers an appreciation of the civil rights of the public" and "the ability to meet, without undue militance, aggressiveness, hostility or prejudice, police situations involving minority groups."

The participants in the in-service training attended the sessions during their off-duty hours for five hours a week for four weeks and were paid at their regular hourly rate. Each class consisted of about 450 officers. The program's content was devised by the Police Department, TAP, and the CCR. Each of the two weekly two-and-a-half-hour sessions consisted of a lecture by a community-relations expert followed by discussion and then, in the second part of the session, small-group consideration of a "real life episode" supposedly typical of what police might encounter in the area of human relations.[55]

Although Girardin and Marks labeled the program "a tremendous success" after the first group completed its training, a less favorable verdict seems in order. One outside participant thought the questions police officers asked were "fairly idiotic." Judge Horace Gilmore, the chairman of the CCEO's Sub-Committee on Police-Community Relations, and Hubert Locke were "aghast" at their experience as lecturers in the program. One policeman who had been raised in Mississippi stood up to say, "If all Negroes were white they would still be Negroes." Both Gilmore and Locke concluded from their participation that most police officers had "absolutely no knowledge of the law" and were "totally unprepared both in background and training, to deal effectively with police responsibilities in a large urban community." They nevertheless thought that the program had some value since they believed that the opportunity it gave the police to vent their "aggressions" and to express "their contempt for Negroes" was "a first step in beginning to reach people."[56] Among the officers in the three classes held in 1965, 59 to 65 percent expressed disappointment in the program. The program was not repeated in 1966, but in June 1967 the Office of Law Enforcement Assistance funded a similar program for six hundred officers to begin in July.[57]

Going beyond his predecessors, Girardin sought to establish formal police-community relations committees in the precincts. In the Fifth Precinct, where there had been monthly meetings of some sort since the spring of 1963, Robert Frehse, the head of the Detroit Round Table, Inspector Paul Sheridan, and Joseph B. Sample, Jr., a school community agent, took the initiative in March 1965 in setting up a Citizen-Police Committee governed by an eighteen-member elected board of directors. The committee processed citizen complaints against the police and developed a program to consider "crowd tension" and "law and order vs. mob violence." It was credited with having played an effective peacemaking role when there was a miniriot in the precinct in August 1966, and its performance helped Detroit to win its All-America city award.[58]

In 1966 Girardin requested the Citizen Complaint Bureau (CCB), as the CRB had been renamed, to review existing police-community relations programs in Detroit and to gather information from around the country. When its study was completed, Girardin called in the precinct commanders and instructed them to establish citizen-police committees in their precincts. The committees were to meet once a month in the precincts with large minority group populations and bimonthly elsewhere. Guidelines for the committees made it clear that they were "not to supplant police power."[59]

When the CCB evaluated the Police Department's community-relations program in May 1967, it concluded that the precinct citizens committees were "one of the most valuable aspects" of the program. Its own evidence, however, indicated that the precinct program was functioning ineffectively. Despite the commissioner's order, five of the sixteen precincts had still not formed a citizens committee. Committee memberships, moreover, did not include "all segments of the total community," particularly "dissenting groups," young blacks, and the unemployed, all elements that might have caused trouble for the police. Ranking officers and career administrators did not fully support the program, resentful, an observer of the meetings noted, that they should be made "to answer for themselves." Not only did the rather rigid format of the meetings prevent "real two-way communication," but some precinct commanders apparently held meetings only so that they could say that they had done so. Rank-and-file policemen, whose racial stereotypes might have been altered by contact with law-abiding blacks, played no part in the program, ostensibly because they could not be spared from street duty.

As a high ranking police official later conceded, Detroit's precinct community-relations program turned out to be "cosmetic." Girardin, nevertheless, may not have been exaggerating when he told a Kerner Commission interviewer that Detroit was "way ahead of every other city in its police-community relations program." Only 38 percent of the cities with populations over 100,000 even had such programs, and most programs had failed to win the confidence of minority groups.[60]

Since young people were especially hostile to the police and committed a disproportionate number of crimes, an effective police-community relations program had to reach out to juveniles as well as adults. The Detroit police tried to do this through two programs, Active Community Teams (ACT) and the Youth Service Corps (YSC). ACT, a juvenile delinquency and crime-prevention program, was inaugurated in the summer of 1965. Directed by a nonprofit corporation and centering initially in an area of high juvenile crime in the Tenth Precinct and later also in a similar section in the Seventh Precinct, on the east side, the program was financed by the federal government until August 1966 and then continued with city funds. Two teams consisting of five members—a social worker, a lawyer, a teacher, a neighborhood resident, and a juvenile court worker—provided intensive counseling for juvenile offenders and their families in an effort to instill "pride" in the youngsters and forestall recidivism. The police referred the youngsters, mostly minor offenders, to the teams rather than to juvenile court. In the first six months of ACT, there were only four "repeaters" among the fifty-nine offenders in the Tenth Precinct whom the teams had counseled, as compared to the normal 67 percent repeat rate; and the juvenile crime rate in the area had declined by about 38 percent. The program served three hundred youngsters during its first fifteen months.[61]

Conceived by the CCEO, funded by United Community Services and the McGregor Fund, and initiated by the Neighborhood Service Organization and the Youth Bureau of the Police Department, the YSC began functioning in 1965 as a summer program in four inner-city precincts. The program, which was open to boys aged fourteen to sixteen, initially enrolled 156 youths, mostly black, who performed minor police assignments such as reporting abandoned cars or failed street lights and searching for lost children. They also received instruction regarding the duties of the police and the functioning of the Police Department. The hope was that the YSC experience would cause the youngsters to develop a positive image of the Police Department and to consider law enforcement as a career. Thanks to federal funding, the program was extended to seven precincts and 630 boys in the summer of 1966, to 503 youths in the same precincts in the summer of 1967, and to 220 youngsters on a year-round basis. Directed mainly at "the problem boy," the YSC enabled youngsters to earn some money—they were paid $1.25 an hour beginning in 1966—helped to curb juvenile delinquency, and, according to an attitude survey, encouraged enrollees to view the police more favorably.[62]

In the view of the CCR, "the most important single issue" in the area of police-community relations was the objective investigation of citizen complaints. Despite Edwards's efforts, the view in the black community as of 1964, and with good reason, was that the department's complaint unit was simply not doing its job. As Girardin later remarked, it was "not uncommon" for a black to come to a police station to enter a complaint only to "get the piss knocked out of him and get locked up." When he became commissioner, Girardin discovered that whites and blacks in the CRB "hated each other" and were not even on speaking terms. Confidential records would disappear from the unit and then turn up in the hands of black militants, and the records would indicate the opposite of what the commissioner had been told.[63]

The police view of the CRB as of 1964 was illustrated when the associate editor of the *Michigan Chronicle* phoned the head of the unit and heard the policeman assigned to the switchboard refer to the agency as "the nigger agitating division." The CRB simply lacked "status" within the department and was unable to demand cooperation from the precincts and other units, commanded by inspectors of equal rank with the head of the CRB.[64]

When Girardin met with the DUL in March 1964, he stated that the CRB would be more effective in the future since it would be working with the newly established CRC, which he claimed would serve, in effect, as a civilian review board. The CRC was soon complaining, however, about a lack of cooperation by the Police Department in processing complaints and of "delaying tactics and difficulties" in the department's dealings with CRC staff.[65]

Seeking to reconcile their differences, the CRC and the CRB agreed on procedures in September 1964 for the handling of civil rights complaints involving the police submitted to the two agencies. It became necessary, however, to supplement the agreement with additional agreements in December 1964 and April 1965 because the Police Department failed to live up to its commitments, such as providing personnel records and information. The CRC during the entire period leading up to the riot remained dissatisfied with the manner in which the Detroit department processed citizen complaints.[66]

In an effort to meet the criticisms of the CRB and to deflect mounting black demands for a civilian review board, Girardin in January 1965 revised the Police Department's complaint procedures. The CRB was renamed the Citizen Complaint Bureau, and its commanding officer was henceforth to report directly to the commissioner. The CCB was to be responsible not only for citizen complaints but also for initiating investigations of police misconduct as well as civil rights violations. Girardin subsequently moved the CCB from police headquarters to the downtown building of the YMCA, where, he said, "citizens would not have to walk into the lion's den to complain about the lions."[67]

As of April 1966, the CCB was composed of twelve officers, five of them black. Complaints were assigned to an investigator, who reported to the three supervisory personnel in the bureau, one of whom was black. After the three decided whether or not to sustain a complaint, they forwarded the file to the commissioner, who decided on the appropriate sanction if the complaint was sustained. No officer, however, could be suspended or dismissed without a hearing before the department's trial board, consisting of the commissioner, the superintendent, and the deputy superintendent or chief of detectives. Plaintiffs dissatisfied with the department's decision on a complaint could appeal to the CRC. Plaintiffs and interested organizations were permitted to review CCB case files.[68]

The police received 397 complaints between January 1, 1964, and July 23, 1967, the day the riot began. The number rose from an average of about 7 per month in 1964 to between 12 and 13 per month in the first seven months of 1967. The increase in the number of complaints did not disturb Girardin, who said, "I encourage complaints because it is a means of keeping people from harboring hostility for the Police Department." He contended, moreover, that the complaints in 1967 were less serious than those submitted in previous years, that there was a decrease in complaints just before the riot, and that, in any event, the number of complaints was small when one considered that the police had ten million contacts per year with the public. The number of complaints was indeed small, but according to one of the CCB's black investigators, this was because 80 percent of the city's blacks had never heard of the CCB, and those who had, mistrusted it as a part of the hated Police Department. The same considerations limited black complaints about police misbehavior everywhere in the nation.[69]

More complaints came to the Police Department from the CRC than from any other source. Ninety to 95 percent of the complaints were from blacks. Of the complaints submitted to the CCB and CRC in the years immediately preceding the riot, about half were for physical abuse. Other complaints were for verbal abuse, illegal search, illegal arrest, harassment, and lack of service. The Detroit department sustained or partially sustained 83 of the 397 complaints (21 percent) it received between January 1, 1964, and the beginning of the riot. Of 263 complaints the CRC reported for the periods January 1, 1965, to March 30, 1966, and January 1 to April 27, 1967, it found probable cause of civil rights violations in about half during the former period and about one-quarter during the latter.

When complaints were sustained—the Police Department was supposed to act on complaints sustained by the CRC—the officer involved was generally transferred, received a commissioner's hearing, an investigative conference, or a verbal or written reprimand, or was "reinstructed." Only five officers in the entire period from January 1, 1964, to July 23, 1967, went before the trial board, which presumably meant that the commissioner had recommended their suspension or discharge. Four were exonerated, but three of these officers were then transferred, and the fourth took medical retirement. For the entire period 1965–67, only one officer was dismissed because of a sustained complaint, and fewer than ten suffered any loss of pay, one of them for an entire year.[70]

The NAACP, the CRC, the League of Women Voters, and other organizations criticized the lightness of the penalties imposed on offending officers and the fact that the punishment assigned rarely appeared to be commensurate with the offense. The NAACP was also concerned about the slowness with which the Police Department processed cases and the tendency of the department and the prosecutor's office to respond to complaints of brutality by issuing warrants against complainants for resisting arrest or interfering with an officer in the performance of his duties. The CRC was distressed that violations involving civil rights did not receive "the same consideration" in the Police Department as other violations insofar as the disciplining of offenders was concerned.[71]

Noting after he left office that he could not have changed a "tradition-bound" department by snapping his fingers, Girardin insisted that to take a police officer before the trial board for mistreating a citizen was a bold step for the time. He pointed out, furthermore, that transferring an officer was a "rough" penalty because it cost him "points," which could affect his promotion. Girardin also observed that statistics regarding complaints did not take account of officers who resigned rather than face the trial board.

Girardin, of course, had to contend with the hard fact that the CCB, as its supervisors acknowledged, lacked the support of the department's personnel, many of whom regarded CCB members as "finks." Police reacted to the CCB just as they would have to a civilian review board, which meant that the "Blue Curtain" (defined as "an unofficial policy or

practice which prohibits a police officer from making an official statement that would . . . tend to adversely affect a fellow officer") fell in
front of the complaint unit. Feeling themselves "harassed" by the charges
against them and the questioning by the CCB and CRC, police
responded to complaints investigations with "hostility and suspicion."
They protested that they were compelled to provide statements lest they
face suspension whereas complainants did not have to supply affidavits
or swear to the truth of their charges.[72]

Two cases of brutality, one involving Barbara Jackson, the other,
Howard King, had a particularly chilling effect on police-community
relations and illustrated why blacks had so little faith in the willingness of
the Police Department to deal with the misconduct of its officers. Jackson, a black prostitute, was arrested in August 1964 after a white john
erroneously claimed that she had stolen money from him. Protesting that
she was "a whore but no thief," Jackson kicked the john. In the garage of
police headquarters, with her arms handcuffed behind her, she either fell
while trying to kick the john again, as the police claimed, or, as she
claimed, two police officers pushed her to the concrete floor and
slammed her face into it, breaking one of her teeth and loosening others,
kicked her, and smashed her face on a door frame, disfiguring her "hor-
ribly." The president of the Detroit NAACP and others took Jackson
directly to Girardin and then to Cavanagh, who promised to give the
matter his personal attention. Jackson was arrested again a few days
later and held incommunicado for several hours in a police effort to get
her to deny any police brutality. One of the two officers involved was
taken before the trial board and was reprimanded and transferred to a
less favorable assignment for failing to protect his prisoner.[73]

Howard King, a fifteen-year-old black, and several others were
arrested by Patrolman Jimmie D. Parker in September 1965 for allegedly
disturbing the peace. Parker struck the handcuffed King with a nightstick in the garage of the Second Precinct, gashing his head and breaking
a bone in his hand. Parker, who had been involved in seven previous
incidents in which police had injured citizens, claimed that he had acted
only after King had kneed him in the groin. The affair led to an investigation by both the CCB and the CRC. Six police officers, including Patrolman Kenneth Johnson, a black, had witnessed the basement incident,
but when the CCB asked them to file reports on the arrest, none referred
to Parker's beating of King. Johnson later claimed that he had not
wanted to "make the department look bad." Some time thereafter, probably after receiving a report from the CRC, Girardin asked Johnson for
a second report, and this time he told the truth. In what Locke claimed
was an unprecedented action, Girardin immediately suspended Parker
pending a trial board hearing. Following the hearing, Parker was suspended for six months.

Although Johnson's second report was supposedly confidential, it was leaked to the press, and Johnson became persona non grata in the Police Department. The tires of his car were punctured, "obscene and derogatory remarks" were scribbled alongside his name on assignment sheets and placed on the bulletin board, and he had a fist fight with one officer and confrontations with others. He was transferred to the Seventh Precinct, where he continued to be harassed and was made to walk a beat despite his seniority. At his request, he was again transferred, this time to the Tenth Precinct, but with the same result, and so he was assigned to the Records Bureau. Department administrators made no effort to halt the harassment of Johnson. To add insult to injury, after he testified against Parker before the trial board, Johnson received a commissioner's hearing because of the inconsistency of the two reports he had submitted about the incident. He was found guilty, required to forfeit fifteen days of pay, and received a written reprimand. Although all of the white police who had witnessed King's beating had filed false reports, none was disciplined, nor had any officer ever been disciplined before for giving the CCB false information.

Johnson took his case to the CRC, which more than a year after the riot ruled that Johnson's civil rights had been violated. Finding the Police Department guilty of "racial antagonism," the CRC ordered it to cease discriminating against Johnson, restore his lost pay, and remove the reprimand from his file.[74] No brutality case better explains why blacks viewed the Detroit Police Department with profound mistrust.

In addition to his efforts to improve the processing of complaints, Girardin took several other steps designed to achieve equal law enforcement and to reduce black hostility to the Police Department. By the spring of 1965 the department had instructed its personnel to address all persons with whom they came into contact by their last name and appropriate title (Mr., Miss); it had, at last, eliminated arrests for investigation; and it had discontinued the arrest of disorderly persons against whom it had no intention of bringing charges. The *Police Manual* was revised in the fall of 1965 to stipulate that detectives were to advise complainants in civil rights cases that they had the right to file their complaint with the CRC. A department bulletin of May 1966 instructed police that they were not to subject persons to unlawful arrests or searches and were not to show bias against persons of any race, religion, or group.[75]

The issue of crime and its identification with blacks complicated the problem of police-community relations in Detroit. This was an issue, to a degree, throughout the Cavanagh administration, but it assumed a particularly virulent form in the months just before the July 1967 riot. Complaining about "an appalling disregard for the facts" regarding crime and seeking to calm public fears about the matter, the CCEO insisted in a report to the community in the summer of 1965 that the crime rate was not increasing in Detroit. Conceding that there had been a

13 percent increase of "serious crimes" in 1964, it noted that crimes of all types had decreased by 8.1 percent since 1963 and that the crime rate was below the national average in every major category. The CCEO rejected as "untrue and unfair" the impression in some circles that whites believed in law and order but blacks did not. Its Special Sub-Committee on Police Community Relations had reported to the public in February 1965 that the relatively high crime rate among the city's blacks was explained not by race but by economic conditions, cultural deprivation, and a slum environment.[76]

Whatever the effect of the CCEO's two 1965 reports on crime, the sharp increase in reported crimes in 1965, 1966, and the first six months of 1967 kept the issue front and center in Detroit. The total number of offenses reported rose from 75,000 in 1964 to 76,397 in 1965, 101,773 in 1966, and 71,637 for the first six months of 1967. Homicides increased from 125 in 1964 to 214 in 1966, forcible rapes from 475 to 744, and robberies from 4,739 to 9,102, but the number of aggravated assaults fell from 7,804 to 7,493. The Kerner Commission's Research Office reported just after the riot that 96 percent of all cities with a population over 100,000 had lower crime rates in 1966 than Detroit and that crime had increased more rapidly in Detroit since 1961 than in all but 14 percent of the nation's largest cities. Felony warrants secured by the police in the first six months of 1967 were 40 percent above the number in the first six months of 1966. Crime statistics are, of course, notoriously unreliable, and the Cavanagh administration correctly explained that part of the statistical increase in crime in Detroit was a result of the city's adoption in May 1966 of the FBI system of reporting crime. Until then, each precinct had turned in its own crime report, and only about 50 to 75 percent of the calls to the precincts had been reported. Under the new system, however, 90 to 95 percent were reported.[77]

Reacting to the public alarm about crime, Cavanagh in the spring of 1965 obtained Common Council approval for the creation of the Tactical Mobile Unit (TMU) and PREP, the acronym for the personally equipped radio patrolman. The TMU was described as "a deterrent force which is highly visible and flexible." Originally a 60-man unit and later increased to 125 officers, the TMU received training in crime suppression and crowd control. It operated on a platoon basis in vehicles equipped with car-to-car radios, shotguns, gas devices and gas masks, and helmets that gave it not only a crime-control but a riot-control capacity. Hailed as "an original Detroit success story," the TMU was widely copied elsewhere. The PREP system, with its four hundred radios and a network of thirteen antennae located so that the radios could be used anywhere in the city, became the largest working walkie-talkie system in the nation. It served as a vital communications link in the 1967 riot.[78]

A few days after calling for the TMU and PREP and after four women had been raped in a twenty-four-hour period, Cavanagh placed five hundred police on overtime and called for a state law authorizing the police to stop and search citizens on reasonable suspicion. The "stop-and-frisk" issue remained quiescent until the fall of 1965, when the city administration, without properly preparing the ground, induced a storm of controversy by reviving the proposal. Girardin defended the idea as the way to stop a "build-up of crime," but black and civil rights leaders unanimously denounced the proposal and expressed fear that Cavanagh was taking the city back to the Miriani "crackdown." The CCEO, the Trade Union Leadership Council, and the Cotillion Club suggested as "an excellent alternative" that Cavanagh convene a crime conference involving every segment of the community, an idea that appealed to the mayor as a way of reassuring white conservatives, but without antagonizing blacks, that he was not soft on crime. By early 1966, the divisive stop-and-frisk proposal, seen by blacks as "yet another move to harass and oppress Negro citizens," was dead.[79]

As it turned out, the Mayor's Conference on Law Enforcement and Administration of Justice was not held until March 10–11, 1967. At the opening session, picketed by fifteen grocers in white aprons who complained that the mayor was soft on crime, Cavanagh asserted that a " 'get tough' policy" by the police was no solution to the crime problem. Experts at the conference opposed a stop-and-frisk law and called for greater cooperation between the police and the citizenry, youth programs, and higher police salaries. All in all, the conference was a rather tepid affair that attracted scant attention.[80]

An increase in homicides from forty-eight in the first six months of 1966 to fifty-eight in the first six months of 1967 and the widely publicized murder of two white children, allegedly by blacks, led to increased concern about crime in Detroit. Councilwoman Mary Beck seized on the issue, writing Cavanagh, "No man, woman or child in Detroit appears to be safe, either on the streets or in their home or any business place." She declared "a war on crime" and also on the mayor, whose recall she now sought. The recall campaign had strong racial overtones, its message being, as one of those circulating petitions stated, that no "white" person was "safe on the streets" as long as Cavanagh was mayor. To counter charges that he was not doing enough to fight crime, Cavanagh, among other things, called for "saturation patrolling" in high crime areas. City officials informed neighborhood groups in advance about the stepped-up police action, and Cavanagh avoided the code word "crackdown," but the heavy patrolling of the black ghetto by the predominantly white police force must have aroused resentment among blacks, as similar tactics did in other cities, and worsened police-community relations.[81]

Cavanagh appeared on TV on May 17, 1967, to defend his administration against Beck's charges. He explained the apparent increase in crime as a statistical aberration and called attention to the TMU and PREP as crime-fighting devices. Asserting that "the roots of crime overlap the roots of poverty," he pointed to all that Detroit had done to combat poverty. Detroit was "a tranquil city," he concluded, because its people wanted it that way, and he thought the city government deserved "a small part of the credit." The CCEO reinforced the mayor's remarks on the crime issue in another report to the community in which it deplored the racially divisive recall campaign. As it turned out, the recall campaign commanded scant support: in a June 1967 poll conducted by Marketing Strategy, Inc., 60 percent of the Detroit respondents agreed that Cavanagh was doing all that he could to combat crime.[82]

In his May 17 television address, Cavanagh referred to both the so-called Grecian Gardens affair and to police salaries. The "little black books" associated with the former and the "blue flu" episode soon triggered by the latter were both to reflect poorly on the police in the community and to impair police morale just as the Police Department had to face the sternest test in its history. The Grecian Gardens Restaurant affair goes back in a sense to August 31, 1965, when a one-man Wayne County grand jury conducted by Judge Edward Piggins began an investigation of a traffic-ticket scandal in Wayne County. On January 21, 1966, with Piggins and Vincent Piersante, the head of the Police Department's Criminal Intelligence Division, leading the way, Detroit police raided the Grecian Gardens Restaurant on the city's lower east side. In the process, they seized documents, which came to be known as the "little black books," that appeared to be a record of bribes paid police officers presumably to influence them to ignore gambling and liquor violations at the restaurant. The proprietors of the restaurant, Peter Vitale and Costa (Gust) Colacasides, alleged Mafia leaders, were arrested on a charge of bribing a police officer who had been acting with the knowledge of his superiors. The Piggins grand jury, its successor George E. Bowles one-man grand jury, and a Board of Inquiry convened by Girardin all probed the Grecian Gardens affair. Although the investigators were unable fully to resolve the question of whether the little black books actually provided a record of payoffs to the police, the Piggins grand jury indicted twenty-one officers for falsely stating that they had not received payoffs from west side bar owners, and Girardin suspended thirteen of these officers as well as five others, including the head of the CCB. The trial board exonerated one of these officers but found the other four guilty and fined them the loss of two weeks' pay. The charges against four of the thirteen officers suspended for non–Grecian Gardens causes were dismissed in court about the same time the Board of Inquiry released its report. In addition to the suspensions, Girardin ordered the transfer of all vice squad officers who appeared to be associated with the affair. The deputy superintendent and a district inspector, whose names appeared in the documents, resigned.[83]

The Grecian Gardens affair, as Locke later noted, was a major "internal calamity" for the Police Department, and it had "a pretty dramatic effect" on police morale. The bad publicity "rubbed off on every-one," individual officers were harassed in their neighborhoods, and even their children were "vilified." For those who already suspected that the Police Department was corrupt and on-the-take, the affair confirmed their suspicions. It "made people lose faith in their police department," declared a young black looter just after the riot.[84]

When Cavanagh appeared on TV on May 17, 1967, to laud the efforts of the Police Department in combating crime, police officers had just initiated a slowdown in ticket writing in an effort to force a pay increase. They had received a large $1,000 salary increase in 1966 that had raised their pay to $8,335 after four years of service, but they wanted this sum increased to $10,000; and the hold-the-line budget submitted by the mayor for the fiscal year 1967–68 made no provision for a salary increase. Recently authorized to engage in collective bargaining and "looking to show its muscle," the DPOA seized on the pay issue as the way of proving itself to its 2,200 members among the 2,668 patrolmen. Between May 16 and June 14 the police wrote 66.9 percent fewer tickets than in the preceding thirty days.[85]

When Cavanagh late in May ordered Girardin to take disciplinary action to end the ticket-writing slowdown, the police threatened "war" against the mayor. Girardin ordered the police to issue tickets at the normal rate, but they ignored the order. Girardin responded by transfer-ring to street patrol duty forty-five officers whose primary responsibility had been enforcement of the traffic laws. The reaction of the police, 84 percent of whom had recently agreed that police should not strike, was to begin calling in sick at an unusual rate, thus beginning the blue flu, the first police strike in the nation since 1919. This led the commissioner to increase the working day for officers to twelve hours, cancel leaves and furloughs, place police with desk jobs in scout cars, and alert the State Police and National Guard. The city also secured an injunction on June 15 from Wayne County Circuit Court Judge Thomas J. Foley requiring the DPOA to halt its "illegal and unauthorized work stoppage." Girardin then stated that all officers reporting sick would be examined by police doctors and would be suspended if found physically fit.

Between June 15 and June 20 Girardin suspended 186 officers. Judge Blair Moody, Jr., to whom the court case had been transferred since Foley had once been a DPOA attorney, continued the restraining order on June 17, which led the DPOA head to order all police who were not ill to return to work. On June 19 three thousand wives and children of police officers picketed the City-County Building and distributed peti-tions for the mayor's recall.

On June 19 the number of absent police reached 847, about 20 percent of the force. The Police Department dispatched patrol cars to transport some of the allegedly sick officers to headquarters for medical examinations. The DPOA initiated a court suit seeking $100,000 from the city for harassing patrolmen and $1 million additional in punitive damages, thus countering the city's suit against the DPOA for $1 million in damages and $50,000 a day while the strike lasted. The strike was becoming increasingly ugly, with Cavanagh threatening contempt proceedings against DPOA officers and individual policemen.[86]

Viewing the situation as "critical and deteriorating," the CCEO stepped in and negotiated a truce on June 20. The terms called for normal police operations to resume at once, for all suspensions to be lifted, and for the police to carry out their assignments in a normal manner. While the parties negotiated in the succeeding ten days to resolve issues in dispute, the department was to suspend all disciplinary actions except for flagrant cases. At the end of the ten days unresolved issues were to be referred to a panel of arbitrators acceptable to both the mayor and the DPOA.[87]

Negotiations between the city and the DPOA that began on June 23 nearly broke down when Cavanagh stated in an interview that pay would be withheld from suspended officers for the period of their suspension. An agreement, however, was concluded on July 11 and subsequently ratified. The agreement resolved the noneconomic issues but sent to arbitration the all-important pay issue as well as the question of whether the blue flu was subject to departmental discipline as an illegal strike. There was no longer to be a "norm" for the issuance of traffic tickets, fringe benefits for the police were improved, and police were no longer required to live in Detroit. The city also agreed to recognize the DPOA as the exclusive bargaining agency for patrolmen, making Detroit the first city in the nation to recognize a police union.[88]

"That was a bastard thing to go through," Girardin later said about the police strike. "I was practically helpless. I couldn't force them to work." Coming at the same time as the recall campaign and when many Detroiters were overwrought about crime in the city, the blue flu, as Cavanagh maintained, contributed to "a rather unsettling sort of climate in the city, political and otherwise." It strained relations between patrolmen and the police high command, as well as between patrolmen and the city's mayor. It was "a very bitter subject," recalled one of the police officers who became involved in the riot's most publicized incident.[89]

The Police Department had gone through a rather bad period since the beginning of 1966, the "worst" in their experience according to some veteran officers. More police quit the force than could be hired to replace them. "It was an already tense, undermanned, overtaxed department," Girardin's administrative assistant asserted, that had to cope with the July 1967 riot.[90]

As a Kerner Commission staff man noted just after the riot, there was apparently "a relatively low" crime rate during the strike in what became the principal riot area, and residents welcomed the reduced police presence. When the sick-in ended, the police appeared in force on

Twelfth Street and elsewhere, and there was an increasing number of petty arrests that undoubtedly added to the tension between the Police Department and the black community.[91] It could hardly have escaped the notice of black activists, moreover, that the enforcers of law and order were themselves willing to resort to direct action to attain their ends even if that meant violation of a state law and a court order.

II

The changes in Police Department behavior for which Edwards, Girardin, and the mayor were responsible between January 1, 1962, and July 23, 1967, were hardly as thoroughgoing as the black leadership would have liked. The department, however, believed that what had been done had definitely had a beneficial effect on police-community relations. Hubert Locke remarked in April 1967 that police-community relations were no longer the "volatile issue" they had been three years earlier. Some black leaders agreed with Girardin's administrative assistant. Damon Keith, the black cochairman of the CRC and a Detroiter, remarked in August 1966 that although there were some "brutal bigots" in the department, it was a "good" department compared to most others. Three months later the TULC's Horace Sheffield asserted that police-community relations in the city had taken a turn for the better, a view shared by the city's only black councilman.[92]

Some survey results suggest that many black Detroiters believed that the Police Department, although still leaving a good deal to be desired, had improved since Cavanagh had become mayor. In the Board of Commerce survey released in May 1967, 58 percent of the randomly selected cross section of blacks indicated that they thought the department had improved in the preceding five years; and 59 percent of the blacks, as compared to 52 percent of the whites, thought that the Detroit department was one of the best in the nation or, at least, was somewhat above average. By contrast, polls conducted by the National Opinion Research Center of the University of Chicago and National Analyst, Inc., following the municipal elections of 1965 and 1966 indicated a lower black approval rate for the police in 1966 (53 percent) than in 1965 (66 percent). The comparable percentages for whites were 79 and 74 respectively.[93]

The performance of the Police Department in the Cavanagh years preceding the riot did not detract from Detroit's reputation as a model city. In March 1967 Cavanagh stated that the Detroit police were "among the best paid, best trained, best equipped and best led in the entire nation." One might have expected Detroit's mayor to say something like this, but his words were echoed, at least to some degree, outside the city. At about the same time as Cavanagh appraised the Detroit department so favorably, for example, the Office of Law Enforcement Assistance of the Department of Justice was hailing Detroit as "the model for police community relations."[94]

In terms of police behavior as in so many other areas of Detroit life, Detroit's model city reputation rested on a comparison between Detroit and other large cities. There was insufficient understanding outside Detroit or, probably, even among the city's white leaders of the degree of disaffection among blacks with regard to police behavior any more than with regard to housing, education, employment, and other matters. The white leadership stressed the degree of communication between the black community and city hall, but, as Richard Marks pointed out in September 1964, Detroit could "no longer harbor the illusion that 'increasing interracial communication lines'" were "the magic key to good Police-Community Relations." There also had to be "action" to deal with the problems "communicated." He noted that other cities had experienced riots sparked by police incidents because they had failed to respond to "communicated police-community problems. It does not take a crystal ball," he warned, "to see this same situation developing in Detroit."[95]

CHAPTER 6

"The Riot That Didn't Happen"

I

"I feel," Ray Girardin declared in March 1967, "that police departments are as obliged to prevent civil unrest as they are to prevent crimes." This meant having not only an effective program of police-community relations but also a plan to prevent civil disorders from getting out of control. When Girardin, however, upon becoming police commissioner asked Superintendent Eugene Reuter for a copy of the department's riot plan, his response, as Girardin recalled it, was "What riot plans?" The Police Department, as a matter of fact, had a manual of procedures for dealing with crowd-control problems that had developed out of World War II civil defense plans, but the problems anticipated in this "extremely limited document" and the procedures outlined were not relevant to the kinds of riots that occurred in the 1960s. Although the department had a force dating from the 1943 riot to deal with crowd control—the commandos of the Motor Traffic Bureau—the dozen or so members of the unit were veteran officers well along in years. Girardin not only discovered that the department did not have an up-to-date riot plan but that the weaponry to deal with a disturbance consisted of a few shotguns and some obsolescent tear gas stored in the municipal garage and improperly secured. "I stayed awake all night getting that stuff fixed," Girardin remembered.[1]

In June 1965, after serious racial disorders had occurred in Cleveland, Harlem, Rochester, and Philadelphia, Girardin formed a special staff to appraise and to modernize the department's "plans, procedures and equipment" for dealing with a riot. The Police Department at that time began sending representatives to observe police operations in "involved cities" and to seek the advice of police departments that had experienced riots. A Committee on Means of Handling Civil Disturbances, headed by District Inspector John Nichols, later deputy superintendent, made a series of riot control recommendations to Girardin in August 1965 largely based on the committee's study of the Watts riot of that month. These recommendations became the principal element in the formulation of Detroit's riot plan.[2]

The Detroit plan[3] called for a central headquarters command post as an "imperative" but also for a field command post at the perimeter of the rioting. This arrangement derived from the conclusion of the Nichols committee that Watts had demonstrated that the usual police command structure "could not function during a riot." A basic principle of the Detroit plan was the essentiality of "a maximum initial response" to what appeared to be a major civil disorder by the immediate mobilization of the "full departmental resources of manpower and equipment." A strong show of force at the outset of a disturbance and readiness to use that force were recognized by planners of riot control strategy as the indispensable key to preventing a disorder from escalating.[4]

The "initial striking forces" in the Detroit riot plan, "the front line of defense" in a riot, were the Tactical Mobile Unit (TMU) and the commandos of the Motor Traffic Bureau. Like the TMU, the commandos received training in both crowd and riot control and were equipped with shotguns, bayonets, and helmets. The Mounted Bureau of the department, by 1966, had also been trained in crowd and riot control and was to be utilized with the other two units if needed. In addition, each precinct had a special support force of thirty men and three command officers to augment the three strike units. The TMU, the commandos, and the Mounted Bureau, if committed, were to be withdrawn from the immediate riot area and held in reserve as soon as adequate reinforcements could be made available from the precinct forces. Because of Detroit's geographical size and the possibility that disturbances would occur simultaneously in widely separated parts of the city, the Police Department thought it essential to have a mobile reserve force available in a riot, the role reserved for the strike units.

The Detroit riot plan called for containment of the affected area, dispersal of the rioters, and prevention of their regrouping. Tear gas was described in the plan as "an effective and humane method of riot control when a mass must be rendered physically ineffective for a limited period." The police were to provide a "rifle-shotgun guard" for firemen entering the riot area. They were to avoid "personality clashes" with rioters, maintain "a completely neutral attitude" at the scene of the disorder, ignore verbal abuse from rioters, and refrain from using "insulting terms and names" and "unnecessary or rough handling" of those involved. The police were instructed to remove their badges and take other precautions in self-defense before entering a riot zone.

Nichols reported that the Los Angeles police regarded as "a tactical error" their initial decision to withdraw from the riot area in the hope that the disturbance would subside if no police were on the scene. The Detroit riot plan permitted a "tactical withdrawal necessitated by great superiority of numbers" on the part of the rioters but "only . . . to gain time" to assemble the force needed to quell the disorder. The Nichols committee recommended against permitting "civic and minority group leaders" to enter the riot area as peacemakers since this tactic had proved unsuccessful in cities that had experienced riots. Only the commissioner, the Detroit plan specified, could authorize the withdrawal of the police from a riot zone to permit the entry of peacemakers.

The Nichols committee recommended that the Police Department make "a firm policy determination" regarding the "control of criminal looting" in a riot as well as the use of firearms for "other than self protection." The committee noted that the city government in Philadelphia had been much criticized for permitting "uncontrolled looting" and that Los Angeles had apparently followed a similar course in the Watts riot. Among the factors the department should consider in making a decision about looting, the committee listed the age and sex of the looters and the adverse public opinion that would result from "wanton killing." Inked in alongside the committee's recommendation for a policy regarding looting on the Police Department's copy of the committee document are the words "no shooting," but the riot plan itself simply referred police to departmental policy regarding the use of firearms. Girardin later claimed that, having studied the Philadelphia and Harlem riots, he had concluded that the use of excessive force in seeking to quell a riot did more harm than good.[5]

The Nichols committee recognized that a major riot would place considerable strain on Detroit's legal system. The committee favored a high bond policy for "major instigators" of the disturbance. Recognizing that existing prison space might be inadequate in a riot, it suggested the use of underground parking garages or the armories as temporary detention facilities. To avoid the commitment of manpower required for normal arrest procedures and "to maintain maximum effectiveness of units in the field," the committee called for the use of a "mobile jail" in the vicinity of the disorder.

The Nichols committee concluded that the Police Department was short of the equipment needed to contain a major riot. It recommended that the department acquire additional shotguns, carbines, helmets, gas guns, gas vests, and gas masks. It noted that the Los Angeles department believed that its "greatest need" in the Watts riot had been communications equipment even though its communications system was superior to Detroit's. It was undoubtedly this concern that led Detroit to expand its PREP system, which became fully functional early in 1966. The department, however, was short of both shotguns and gas equipment at the time of the July 1967 riot. It was allegedly reluctant to acquire too much police hardware lest this serve as an irritant to the community.[6]

Following the recommendations of the Nichols committee, the Police Department developed a riot training program that involved commando and riot-squad formations, the use of rifles, shotguns, and gas weapons, and "psychological" training. The principal tactic practiced was the use of small squads of about twelve men in a "tight military formation" to break up large crowds into smaller groups and then to disperse them. The three special riot control units regularly practiced appropriate crowd-control tactics, and the remainder of the department received riot training during a three-day period once a year. This was in addition to the twenty-four hours devoted to riot control that was part of the instructional program in the Police Academy.[7]

The Police Department claimed after the 1967 riot that it had focused in its riot training on crowd control and had not anticipated the looting, arson, and sniping that occurred. This is true, however, only in the extent to which these riot activities, particularly the first two, occurred. Although the emphasis in riot control training was on crowd control, the riot plan specified looting, firebombing, and sniping as riot tactics, made provision for protecting fire fighters and dealing with barricaded snipers, and recognized that the conventional riot pattern involving "the mass confrontation of police and mob" had "given way" to " 'guerilla' type activities." The weakness, of course, of all riot control plans, as Commissioner Herbert Hart had pointed out in 1961, is that "no two situations ever are identical, and . . . trying to give procedural steps is virtually impossible because tactics issued in one set of circumstances may not necessarily be proper in another."[8] Detroit learned this lesson, painfully, in July 1967.

Intelligence was to be an essential part of the operation of both the headquarters command post and the field command post, but gathering intelligence in the black community was an area of conspicuous police weakness. Although the department's Special Intelligence Bureau had a race-relations detail, the inspector in charge of intelligence at the time of the riot later recalled that "there was damn little intelligence and damn little effort to gather intelligence on black radicals." Girardin explained that the department "had a hell of a time" gathering intelligence in the black community because it did not know "who[m] to send to get it and where to go to get it." Although the department had some informants in the black community, it did not know if they could be relied on, Girardin claimed, because they had not yet proved themselves.[9] The information provided by informants before the July 1967 riot proved to be more misleading than helpful.

After evaluating after-action reports of cities that had experienced major civil disturbances, the Detroit Police Department concluded that its riot control plan must provide for "the immediate mobilization and commitment" of National Guard troops. Planning for liaison among the police, the Guard, and the State Police in the event of a major riot in Detroit went back to June 1963, when Governor George Romney directed state officials to meet with Detroit authorities to coordinate plans for a civil disturbance. The plan, developed in 1965, updated in

May 1967, and given the name Operation Sundown, specified the method by which the Detroit department was to alert the State Police and the Guard and the action the state units would take as a result. Operation Sundown provided for the establishment of command posts and assembly areas, command liaison, communications, and the issuance of necessary proclamations by the governor. At the request of the police commissioner, the Guard was immediately to form a task force that would assemble in unit areas properly equipped and prepared to move into action upon the receipt of orders to mobilize. It was assumed that the Guard would be employed in "control of arsonists, and guarding against snipers." The plan specified the conditions under which live ammunition and chemical agents were to be issued to and used by Guardsmen. Both the State Police and the Guard were to be under the "central direction" of the Detroit Police Department, but the assumption was that the Guard would be assigned duties within its military command structure, with at least one police officer serving with each Guard unit.[10]

Girardin had "quietly suggested" for some time before the 1967 riot that the quelling of large-scale urban riots should be the responsibility of the United States Army. The Police Department arranged in 1965 to effect liaison with the federal government in the event of a civil disturbance, with the United States attorney in Detroit serving as the federal coordinator. Detroit also made provision for notifying the FBI in the event of a riot, but it does not appear that Detroit or Lansing devoted much, if any, thought to the legal requirements for securing the assistance of the army if local forces were unable to cope with a disorder.[11]

II

Despite several racially inflammatory incidents, Detroit was spared significant racial trouble until August 1966, when a miniriot developed on the city's lower east side that the police quelled in a thoroughly professional manner. Detroit made elaborate preparations to avoid trouble in the summer of 1967, and yet it was caught unawares when a police incident, seemingly less serious than other incidents of a racial nature that had passed without real trouble, escalated into the most violent of all the urban riots of the 1960s.

Inspector Paul Sheridan told a reporter in the spring of 1963 that although "a few rabble-rousing Negroes" were attempting to stir up trouble, few blacks listened to them, and the racial climate was "generally good." Richard Marks was more troubled than Sheridan about the state of race relations in Detroit. What had happened in Birmingham, Alabama, that year, the secretary-director of the Commission on Community Relations (CCR) thought, had altered the perspective of blacks in Detroit and had caused them to reassess their position in the city. Marks was especially concerned that young, out-of-school, and unemployed blacks might turn to violence.[12]

The summer of 1963 passed in Detroit without school boycotts, as in New York, Boston, and Chicago, and without a "near riot" over housing integration, as in Philadelphia. What Detroit did experience was the Walk to Freedom, which Hubert Locke thought provided "a rather dignified and eloquent testimony" to the city's "apparently mature and responsible climate of race relations." Locke, however, warned the Citizens Committee for Equal Opportunity (CCEO) that although Detroit had "moved forward . . . dramatically on racial issues," it had "not moved fast enough to allay the frustrations, the unrest and the fears of its Negro citizens." He called attention to the "deep and growing conviction" among blacks that the white community took action on racial matters only when "pushed" and noted that this had led blacks to "the strategy of 'direct action' " as the way to effect social change. The new militant groups were gaining strength, he observed, because the civil rights movement had primarily benefited only "a very small segment" of the black community but had been of "negligible good to the low-income, educationally handicapped, culturally deprived, often un- or under-employed" blacks. This fact, he warned, made the city "ripe for trouble."[13]

According to the CCR, 1964, like 1963, was "a relatively good year" for Detroit in racial terms. It was not, however, a trouble-free year. There were several racial incidents in parks and recreational facilities that summer and some friction between black and white teenage groups. When twenty-five black youths were asked if the riots could spread to Detroit, those in better-off neighborhoods said no, but the young men on Twelfth Street thought "riots could erupt" in the city. If trouble started, their view was, it would be because of the police. "The young people are gonna start this thing and then the older ones will just join in," one of them prophetically declared. A riot did not "erupt" in Detroit that summer, but the CCR was sufficiently concerned about "malignant rumors" spreading in the city in the fall to develop "a communication network for rumor and incident control" in cooperation with the Department of Parks and Recreation, the Board of Education, and the Metropolitan Association of Community Councils.[14]

Detroit's racial peace was marred by several incidents in the late winter and spring of 1965. On March 1 Jacob Azzam, son of the proprietor of Azzam's Market on the near west side, killed a black customer, John Christian, following a fight over the theft of a small cake from the store during which Christian allegedly knifed Azzam and his aunt. The slaying attracted especially angry attention in the community because of the Azzams's allegedly abusive treatment of their customers and because Jacob's brother Abraham, while serving as a policeman in 1961, had shot a burglary suspect, leading to the amputation of one of his legs and the payment to him of $23,000 by the city. Residents of the community began picketing the market as well as the Azzam-owned Zam's Party Store across the street. The picketers were soon joined by members of the Congress of Racial Equality (CORE), the Northern Student Movement, and the Adult Community Movement for Equality (ACME), which sought to use the incident as a basis for "grassroots community" organizing. The prolonged picketing led the county prosecutor, who had ruled the slaying justifiable homicide, to recommend warrants for the arrest of seventeen picketers for engaging in a criminal conspiracy to drive the Azzams out of business. The Michigan Civil Rights Commission (CRC) and the CCR sought to compose the dispute, which became the subject of "inaccurate and inflammatory" TV editorials. The affair ended up in the courts.[15]

Twenty-five crosses were burned in Detroit in April 1965, many of them in front of black residences in integrated neighborhoods. This hateful action reflected increasing resentment by whites at what they regarded as the "molly coddling" of blacks by city authorities. Some television stations appeared to be exploiting white fears, implying that blacks were seeking gains for themselves at white expense.[16]

The cross burnings, the Azzam affair, and Councilman Thomas Poindexter's campaign to abolish the CCR led Congressman Charles Diggs, Jr., to urge the mayor to call a citizens meeting to discuss the possibility of racial conflict in the summer. Similarly concerned, Bishop Richard Emrich and the CCEO's executive committee met with the press, the police, public school officials, and the heads of community agencies asking them to do what they could to promote "racial peace and harmony" during "the tense summer months." The CCR, for its part, expanded its communication network for rumor and incident control to include contacts with the police, civil rights groups, and neighborhood organizations.[17]

As a result of CCEO prompting, the United Fund provided United Community Services of Detroit (UCS) with $50,000 for the Summer Week-End Evening Emergency Program (SWEEP). This "crash program" was designed to "reach and attract" inner-city "troubled and idle youth" aged fourteen to eighteen who were not being served by existing social agencies and who were not old enough to take advantage of services provided by the Economic Opportunity Act. The six agencies that participated in SWEEP in 1965 operated in ten inner-city neighborhoods, providing services particularly during the evenings and weekends of July and August. The UCS pronounced the program, which served about thirty-five hundred young people, an "unqualified success in terms of positive and wholesome effects on troubled youth" and as a preventer of racial trouble.[18]

SWEEP was but one of several programs offered by Detroit agencies to ease the city through "the long hot summer" in 1965. The Metropolitan Detroit Council of Churches developed a coordinated program of summer activities for youth in church facilities. The public schools kept 140 schools open during the day and evening that offered programs for young people and adults alike. The school system also enrolled twenty-two hundred youngsters in special summer projects as part of the In-School Work-Training Program. The Mayor's Commission on Children and Youth employed an additional one thousand youths in summer programs. Total Action against Poverty (TAP) offered an eight-week day-camp program for forty-two hundred children and six hundred mothers from the inner city. Detroit businesses answered President Johnson's appeal for summer jobs for young people by providing five thousand jobs. Detroit also launched its Youth Service Corps that summer.[19]

Despite the efforts of private and public agencies, the summer of 1965 was not free of volatile racial incidents. The worst trouble occurred in August against the backdrop of the Watts riot. On August 13 the shooting of a young black by a private guard on Twelfth and Philadelphia attracted a hostile crowd and led the president of the Detroit branch of the National Association for the Advancement of Colored People (NAACP) to say that this "could have been the spark that set off a riot." Two days later a white male, for no apparent reason, shot a black woman in Rouge Park. On the same day white youths stopped a car near Cass Park and assaulted its black passengers. The police, and especially the TMU, dealt with these incidents effectively before trouble could ensue.[20]

At a December 1, 1965, conference at Wayne State University on "The Future of Race Relations in Metropolitan Detroit," a panel of experts agreed that race relations in the city were relatively good but that there was much tension beneath the surface. Congressman John Conyers warned the city against taking any comfort from the fact that it had gone through the preceding summer without major incident. "That just means," he said, "that the wrong citizen and the wrong policeman didn't happen to get together."[21]

"The forces of good will and enlightenment are on the offensive in Detroit," Mayor Cavanagh declared at the beginning of 1966. In the spring the city's black leadership, more or less agreeing with the mayor, rejected the assertion of Floyd McKissick, the national CORE chairman, that Detroit was "a racial tinderbox." The Detroit Urban League's (DUL) Francis Kornegay, who thought Detroit was experiencing "the best [racial] climate in many years," did not believe the city was "heading for trouble." Although he did not view Detroit as "paradise," the executive secretary of the NAACP asserted, "We are not a Watts by any stretch of the imagination." Councilman Nicholas Hood, although rejecting the tinderbox analogy, nevertheless noted that the Northern High boycott showed that there was "serious unrest" that was not "apparent on the surface."[22]

As in 1965, public and private agencies in 1966 sought to devise programs to help keep the city racially peaceful during the troublesome summer months. The CCR worked with the SWEEP staff to identify twenty-eight areas of the city where SWEEP should concentrate its efforts. The selection of these areas was an essential part of the CCR's early warning system and its tension control efforts. When the CCR's Field Division staff detected "a hostile or unjust situation," it contacted the relevant community or social agency so that "early and peaceful resolution" of the problem could be achieved.[23]

Again operating with $50,000 provided by the United Fund, SWEEP served 898 persons in 1966, nearly all of them black. The program, which operated in twelve Detroit neighborhoods and one in nearby Oakland County, concentrated on actual and potential school dropouts. It helped them find jobs, referred them to job training, aided them in school-related and personal matters, and involved them in recreational activities. Although UCS contended that the program "kindled hope and promise of a better tomorrow" among black youths, the agencies concerned thought that a short-term program like SWEEP could have only a limited effect in terms of preventing racial disorder.[24]

The SWEEP effort was supplemented by a variety of church and secular organizations that joined in providing recreational opportunities for young people as part of a "Summer Program for Youth." Also in 1966 TAP made a major effort to engage young people in meaningful activities, find jobs for them, and help them to cope with the frustrations that, Cavanagh said, rose "with the temperature." TAP offered fifteen recreational, educational, and work programs, provided employment for almost seven thousand persons, and allegedly served more than two hundred thousand target area residents. In areas where the program operated, overall crime, as compared to previous years, dropped 30 percent and delinquency, 45 percent.[25]

There were numerous rumors about racial trouble in the summer of 1966, some ugly incidents on Belle Isle, and continued harassment of blacks moving into white areas.[26] The only trouble of consequence, however, occurred in the Kercheval-Pennsylvania area on the lower east side in August (see map 1). Locke had advised the CCEO that this area, which was in the Fifth Precinct, was one of the city's "danger spots," and it was one of twenty-eight neighborhoods identified by the CCR as a possible source of racial trouble. The CCR's Field Division characterized the area as one of low-income families, weak in parental support for children, lacking in facilities for youth, and marked by racial tension between its white residents, many of southern origin, and its blacks.

A *Detroit Free Press* reporter described the inhabitants of the census tract in which the Kercheval disturbance centered as "the poorest of the poor." In 1960 the median family income of the 1,836 nonwhite residents of the tract was $2,964, which compared with $4,366 for nonwhites in Detroit as a whole. It was a neighborhood that the city and private social agencies had largely neglected. The nearest TAP office was two miles away, and recreational facilities in the area were conspicuous by their absence. Unlike Twelfth Street, it was not a neighborhood of high-rise buildings but rather of "single and double dwellings." When sixty black residents were asked in a survey of the area following the disturbance what they regarded as the main problems facing them and their families, more mentioned police and housing than any other problems.[27]

There was a good deal of generational conflict within the black community in the Fifth Precinct and the Kercheval-Pennsylvania neighborhood. The older and better-established blacks and the homeowners and block-club members played key roles in the Fifth Precinct Citizen-Police Committee and were supportive of the police, urging them to rid the neighborhood of "hoodlums" and to arrest the loiterers. Young blacks, however, complained that the police were "continually harassing" them by telling them to "move on" even though they had no place to meet their friends other than on street corners. "The police have been f—ing the people too damn long," one black youth said. "We're just sick of it." Young blacks maintained that the police had abused their parents and grandparents, but, one of them defiantly stated, "it ain't like that anymore. We intend to stand up for what we believe in and fight him back."[28]

The Kercheval miniriot of August 1966 was the culminating event in a series of confrontations between the police and ACME and its Afro-American Unity Movement (AAUM) and Afro-American Youth Movement (AAYM) successors. As we have seen, ACME-AAUM, whose headquarters were on Kercheval, saw the police as its chief antagonist.[29] The police, in turn, had little use for the organization or its members. Late in November 1964 the police arrested forty-three ACME members and friends of members in a private home that the police claimed, and ACME denied, was a blind pig. The arrestees were held in the precinct station for ten hours and then released. Wilbert McClendon, ACME's cochairman, charged that this was just "the latest in a series of harassments" by the police, who, he claimed, were "trying to intimidate the organization."[30]

A more serious incident in May 1965 began with the arrest of ACME member Moses Wedlow for driving without a license. When other ACME members went to the precinct station to post bond for Wedlow, as regulations permitted, they were told that they could not do so. One ACME member then sought to make a phone call from a booth near the station's exit, but police officers dragged him from the booth and punched him. The police "manhandled" other ACME members inside the station and choked McClendon in the parking lot and hit him with brass knuckles. Seven ACME members were then booked for resisting arrest, and two were additionally charged with resisting a police officer in the performance of his duty. After the incident, ACME distributed questionnaires door-to-door on the east side in an effort to gather evidence of police "misconduct." One month before the miniriot AAUM, as was its wont, was picketing police headquarters, and Alvin Harrison, the youthful AAUM director, was charging that the Detroit police were "as bad as any in the country."[31]

There is some inconclusive evidence that AAUM was planning a disturbance on the east side and that the police, in turn, were seeking to crack down on the organization. During the disturbance the police arrested two juveniles, Molotov cocktails in hand, who claimed, without corroboration, that at an October 1965 ACME meeting Harrison exhorted those present not to "let the white brothers take over the community." He told them, the juveniles claimed, to "get black clothes and guns and fight the police," who were their "enemies." The director of Project Scope of the Archdiocesan Opportunity Program (AOP), also without corroboration, claimed that two or three weeks before the disturbance he had been taken blindfolded to what was presumably an AAUM meeting and told to remove day-camp children in the project from the area because there would be a small riot there two or three weeks later.[32]

At rallies on July 23, 1966, Harrison, as we have seen, urged his black listeners to "get the white man off your backs" and, according to police intelligence, to "go and take over" a grocery store and a liquor store in the Kercheval-Pennsylvania area. Two hours before the Kercheval disturbance began on August 9, Harrison, according to the same two juveniles who had reported the October 1965 ACME meeting, told his followers, "we've got to get our rights and we're going to get them even if we have to break car and store windows." Wedlow, the youths claimed, stood on a table and shouted, "Brothers, go home and get your guns. . . . We'll throw rocks to break the windows, and when the police arrive we'll shoot them." Although these remarks were not corroborated and may have constituted nothing more than juvenile reconstruction of events to please the police, ACME did express sympathy in its newsletter for violence by blacks to achieve their goals. Hubert Locke informed the CCEO just after the disturbance that the "evidence" was "overwhelming and clear cut" that the Kercheval affair was "a carefully planned albeit, not-too-well supervised conflagration" initiated by AAYM members.[33]

Three nights before the miniriot, Inspector Anthony Rozman of the Fifth Precinct asked the precinct's Citizen-Police Committee, "could you tell us what we can do about the trouble-making [Afro-American] group[?]." He said that he would like to rip the antiwhite posters off the walls of AAYM headquarters. Defending Rozman, the civilian head of the committee claimed that what the inspector had said was that he would like to "constrict" the AAYM if he could do so "within the law," and that he was saying this as a citizen, not as a police officer.[34]

The Kercheval incident began at 8:25 P.M. on August 9 when a Big Four cruiser, manned by an all-white crew, observed seven black males "loitering" and allegedly impeding traffic on Kercheval. When the officers, according to the police account, instructed the seven, all "known police characters," to move on, four did, but McClendon, who had received seven previous loitering tickets, Clarence Reed, and James Robertson did not. They became belligerent when one of the officers asked them for identification so that he could write up the tickets, one of them shouting, "We won't be moved. Whitey is going to kill us." The police called for assistance, and two TMU scout cars responded. When two officers tried to place Reed in one of the cars, he jumped one of them, and McClendon and Robertson began fighting with the other officers. "This is the start of a riot," McClendon hollered, and a crowd of about one hundred began to gather as McClendon called for help and urged bystanders not to "let them do this to us." The police subdued their prisoners, Reed and two officers suffering injuries in the process. The crowd became unruly, throwing bottles at passing motorists and breaking windows as Wedlow shouted "black power" and said that a riot had begun.[35]

Realizing that other police departments had failed to respond with sufficient force at the onset of disturbances in their communities, Detroit's police high command reacted to the Kercheval trouble by immediately ordering a "limited departmental mobilization." It was an ideal time for the department in terms of the availability of manpower, the force being at its maximum strength between 4:00 P.M. and midnight. The two commando squads of the Motor Traffic Bureau were available; one section of the TMU was in the area; and, as chance would have it, a second section was in the nearby downtown area that night to police an anti–Vietnam War rally. Since police shifts changed at midnight, it was possible for the department to hold the afternoon shift over in reserve when the midnight shift came on duty. The department was placed on twelve-hour shifts, and some of the police held in reserve and additional equipment were sent to the Fifth Precinct. Following Cavanagh's instructions "not to over-react," Girardin ordered the police "to avoid physical contact with the citizens."[36]

The 150 to 175 police quickly deployed in the Kercheval disturbance area outnumbered the one hundred or so rioters. Moving out from a field command post, helmeted TMU and commando squads, their bayonets fixed, swept the street and successfully dispersed the crowd. The police then cordoned the area. Police patrolled the area for the rest of the night in task force units composed of two cruisers and a patrol wagon containing a squad of police. The TMU, in six-car units, supplemented the patrolling force, but the commandos were withdrawn to a reserve status to be available should the disorder spread to other parts of the city. The mayor ordered the closing of bars and liquor stores in the Kercheval area, and Belle Isle, adjacent to the Fifth Precinct, was also closed.

The CCR, CCEO, and the Fifth Precinct Citizen-Police Committee all aided the police effort to contain and quell the Kercheval disturbance. Three members of the CCR's staff worked with police officers to ensure "proper policing" and with the mass media to prevent distortion of the news. Reinforcing the CCR's efforts, the CCEO arranged an emergency meeting with the media to urge them to use "extreme caution" in reporting the disturbance. The precinct committee launched a telephone campaign to advise citizens to remain at home and to keep their children off the street. The police, however, complained that the media, which magnified the affair, brought people into the streets.[37]

The rioting of August 9 stretched along a mile-long strip of Kercheval. It may have been stimulated to a degree by rumors that the police had killed a black man and another rumor that they had broken the arms of one or two black males, presumably during the initial arrests. The crowd stoned about three dozen police and civilian cars, there was some window breaking, a failed attempt at a firebombing, the shooting and wounding of a white male, but no looting. Other than the shooting, the ugliest incident occurred when a white motorist was beaten by some black youths after he left his car, which had been stoned, to inspect the damage it had incurred. The police made no arrests beyond the initial three in an effort to forestall the emergence of a "martyr or mob hero." This was consistent with the mayor's desire to have the Kercheval affair treated as an "incident," not a riot. Girardin similarly played down what had happened, calling it "a rampage, not a riot," and insisting that it was not a racial disturbance.[38]

At 1:30 A.M. on August 10 the police received information from the FBI that led them to follow four cars leaving AAUM headquarters on Kercheval. When they stopped and searched the vehicles, one of them occupied by General Gordon Baker, a militant black nationalist, and Glanton Dowdell, the painter of the Black Madonna in Cleage's church, they discovered a variety of guns, a bayonet, hatchets, a claw hammer, and bricks. Girardin informed the mayor that the arrest of the occupants of the vehicles and the seizure of the weaponry prevented "some known agitators and quantities of armaments" from reaching "potential rioters."[39]

Early in the morning of August 10 repair trucks of the Department of Public Works removed debris from streets in the disturbance area. At the request of the city government, businesses in the area remained open that day as an expression of confidence in the ability of the forces of law and order to control the situation. TAP opened a youth recreation center in the area and sent a team to recruit youngsters for the Neighborhood Youth Corps (NYC). CCR personnel met with AAYM leaders and other dissident elements in the area to get their views of what was happening, conducted interviews in the neighborhood, contacted black, civil rights, and community leaders to set forth the facts, and relayed to Cavanagh complaints from the community about "saturation policing." Clergymen in the area were anxious to do what they could to prevent further rioting, but it was evident that they were without influence on those involved.[40]

There was some rock throwing in the evening, a drugstore was fire-bombed, and white youths in a passing car shot a young black male in the shoulder. The police, perhaps two hundred in number, broke up and dispersed a small group of rioters, and made forty-three felony arrests. Some black clergy and block club leaders circulated in the area, urging those on the streets to return to their homes. The major ally of the police and the few peacemakers that night was a steady, drenching rain.[41]

On August 11 TAP sent forty employees into the disturbance area to promote Detroit's poverty program and to communicate the city government's concern about the needs of residents. At a meeting of about 150 community leaders in the area that was conducted under CCR auspices and that revealed "extensive support" for the police, the decision was reached to send "peace patrols" in groups of two into the streets to dispel the rumors that were circulating. Although there was some more fire-bombing and other damage that night and the police made a few arrests, the worst of the trouble was over. Agreeing at the CCR's urging to review the police approach to the disorder, Girardin that day replaced the four-man cruisers with two-man scout cars and removed the TMU from "general patrol" into reserve status. The commissioner thought that the peace patrols had played a key role in producing the relative calm of that night, but this was a misreading of what had taken place. Not only was the disturbance winding down by then, but, as Father James J. Sheehan reported, the peace patrollers had "fits" because they were "completely out of touch" with the young Kercheval activists and could no more communicate with them than the police could.[42]

The police maintained their augmented patrols on the night of August 12, and the peace patrols operated for a second night. There were only a few "isolated incidents" that night, and the next day the police began phasing out the Kercheval operation. During the miniriot, seventy-three police and civilian cars had been hit by rocks, forty-eight windows had been broken, and there had been a small amount of looting. No one had been killed, but ten police officers and eleven civilians had been injured. Although thirty-seven cases of arson or "preparing to burn" were reported, they involved mainly the possession of Molotov cocktails rather than actual fire damage. Window-breaking had been indiscriminate, affecting black and white merchants alike and including even two black storefront churches. On the other hand, all the automobiles that had been damaged had been driven by whites, cries of "Here comes Whitey" often preceding the stoning of a vehicle.[43]

Eighty-nine adults and ninety-three juveniles were arrested during the course of the Kercheval disturbance, including the principal figures of the AAUM and AAYM. The median age of the defendants was nineteen. The police were able to obtain warrants for only forty-three of the adult arrestees, including ten AAUM-AAYM militants, eight of whom were charged with felony offenses. Shortly after the arrests, Harrison met with black community leaders to arrange for bail and the legal defense of the arrestees. Twenty to twenty-five lawyers, mostly but not entirely black, agreed to handle the cases on a voluntary basis. Charges against eight defendants were dropped at the preliminary examinations, and of the twenty-seven brought to trial by the end of 1972, fourteen were convicted, including four AAUM-AAYM leaders. Three of the fourteen received jail sentences; the others were placed on probation. Baker and Dowdell, found guilty of carrying concealed weapons in a motor vehicle, were sentenced to five-years probation and $500 court costs.[44]

The AAUM-AAYM charged that the police had instigated the Kercheval affair. The miniriot that followed, Harrison asserted, was "a rebellion of the black community against an oppressive situation" that involved the police, slumlords, white merchants, and unresponsive politicians. Without condoning the violence, black leaders agreed that the police, who, it was said, had been "leaning on" the AAUM, had provoked the disturbance by their "over zealousness."[45]

The responsible black leadership was aware that it was out of touch with the militants who had been out on the streets. The Reverend Roy Allen reported that Harrison and his group dismissed "people on commissions and in the power structure" as "Uncle Toms." When Allen met with Harrison, the clergyman was "cussed out." "We haven't reached these young people down on Kercheval," the chairman of the Fifth Precinct Citizen-Police Committee remarked.[46]

An "interested group" of black and white community leaders met with the mayor on August 13 to express their concern about "the angry young men" whom the city's numerous programs had seemingly failed to reach. The leadership group was anxious to correct "the fundamental causes" of the Kercheval disturbance and to prevent a recurrence. They did not believe that a riot could be prevented by "an armed 'show of power'" by an all-white police force in a black neighborhood. Detroit, they thought, needed a police department more representative of the city's racial mix as well as improvement of employment and housing conditions in the inner city.[47]

An exclusively black leadership group calling itself the Ad Hoc Committee on Community Peace met two days later to consider what they might do in response to the Kercheval disturbance. "What we do as leadership people," Arthur Johnson optimistically declared, "can prevent the kind of violence in this community that has been experienced in other communities." Accompanied by Harrison, representatives of the committee presented Cavanagh on August 18 with a five-point program calling for an increase in the number and improvement in the quality of recreational facilities in the inner city, quality integrated education, the recruitment of one thousand black police officers, equal employment opportunities, and a "crash program" to deal with ghetto housing and slum conditions. The view of the black leadership that Detroit's blacks still "found themselves lock[ed] in as a result of poverty, ignorance, prejudice, discrimination and segregation" illustrated once again the wide gap between Detroit's reputation as a model city and how much more needed to be done, according to the black leadership and the CCR, which endorsed the black demands, to improve the condition of blacks and the state of race relations in the city.[48]

Girardin pointed with pride to the professional manner in which the Police Department had comported itself throughout the Kercheval mini-riot. It had quelled the disturbance without firing a single shot, without using tear gas, and without making mass arrests. Overlooking the few instances in which police officers had shouted "nigger" at blacks or had acted provocatively, Girardin praised his men for having refused to be "baited into hasty action" despite the missiles and insults rioters hurled at them. The department's riot plan had proved itself "sound and effective," and only slight modification of the plan appeared to be required.

The Police Department decided that it now knew how to cope with a riot, that it was "ready for any eventuality," but it should have recognized the uniqueness of the Kercheval affair rather than believing that history would repeat itself the next time the department faced a disturbance. When the July 1967 riot began, the police and the city administration should have recalled the time of night when the Kercheval trouble began, the availability of police manpower at that time, the number of officers on the scene as compared to the size of the crowd, the difference between Kercheval and the narrow and more congested Twelfth Street, and the fortuitous rain on the second night of the Kercheval affair. The department was misled, furthermore, by its inaccurate judgment that peace patrols had helped quiet the Kercheval disturbance and that the department's in-service training and its precinct police-citizen committee had proved their worth.[49] Detroit may have learned how to quell a miniriot like that of Kercheval, not any riot, and it might have coped more effectively with the July 1967 riot had it not allowed the Kercheval experience to serve as a guide to action.

Like the Police Department, the mayor's office saw the Kercheval incident, "the riot that didn't happen," as proof of the value of the city's social programs, its racial policies, and its "open channels of communication." As Cavanagh later admitted, the city government was "lulled" into "a false sense" of its ability to keep disturbances under control because of its Kercheval success. Like Girardin, Cavanagh saw Kercheval as the model to follow when the city had to deal with a very different disturbance on Twelfth Street the next year.[50]

Outside Detroit, what had happened confirmed Detroit's reputation as a model city in its race relations. The Community Relations Service of the United States Conference of Mayors issued a special report in June 1967 offering the Detroit approach of "prevention and preparation" as the model for other communities to follow in planning "to alleviate the threat of civil disturbances." Cavanagh recalled that people came to Detroit from all over the United States to learn how the city had dealt with the disturbance.[51]

III

In the spring of 1967 the CCR, the CCEO, and the mayor's office became apprehensive about an outbreak of racial violence during the coming summer. Unemployment, as we have seen, was mounting, especially among young blacks; it appeared that the federal government would not make funds available for the summer job and recreational programs Detroit had offered in 1966; the United Fund seemed disinclined to finance SWEEP for a third summer; and the city government, because of budget constraints, indicated that it would have to close forty-four playgrounds in the inner city and would be unable to provide new recreational programs for young people. With more youths in the streets and with neither summer jobs nor recreational programs available to them, the city's leadership feared that the young would resort to violence to vent their frustration and rage and would undo all those efforts that had gained Detroit its reputation as a model city in racial terms.

The appearance of posters in black areas urging blacks to join the "Black Guard," a "mystery group" later identified as synonymous with the Revolutionary Action Movement, and to "unite" and "defend themselves" or "perish," heightened concerns about "the long hot summer." The Reverend Albert Cleage was telling his flock that the Black Guard was "a good thing," that blacks should "arm" and "defend" themselves, and that it was time for them "to stop being 'House Niggers and slaves like Whitney Young and Roy Wilkins — and to stand and fight like Stokley [sic] Carmichael and Cassius Clay.' " The concurrent concern in Detroit about street crime, the effort to recall the mayor, and the blue flu affair did nothing to lessen the mood of apprehension.[52]

White House staffer James Gaither, who visited Detroit in May, informed President Johnson that "the favorite topic of discussion" among Detroiters was the possibility of "a long hot summer." Cavanagh declared on May 2 that he was "more fearful" about "possible civil unrest" than at any time since he had become mayor. "If there are a couple of serious crimes with a hint of racial overtones," he remarked, "the city could explode." Cavanagh no doubt believed what he said, but he was also crying wolf to pry loose the federal funds he was seeking for summer jobs and recreation. He apparently saw no inconsistency between his warning that Detroit could so easily explode and his remark soon thereafter that it was "no accident" that the city had not exploded.[53] The CCR echoed the mayor's words, although it asserted that the problem was not lack of money but rather Detroit's "pattern of segregation and discrimination."[54]

Cavanagh and the CCR came under attack in Detroit for their warnings about possible racial trouble in the summer. Many persons, Gaither told the president, thought that kind of talk put "new ideas into the minds of disenchanted young people" and also made the police "uneasy." Criticizing "the long hot summer riot mongers," black Councilman Nicholas Hood told the press, "you only hear white people talking about violence. Negroes aren't talking violence." Detroit had its problems, he said, but it was nevertheless "far ahead of any major city" in the state of its race relations. The Common Council "rebuked" the CCR for its predictions of racial trouble, Councilman Ed Carey declaring, "you are generating unrest where it does not now exist."[55]

The CCR, the CCEO, and the mayor's office joined in an effort to provide the city's restless black youths with jobs and recreational and other programs during the summer months. In largely off-the-record meetings, the CCEO urged the city's social agencies to continue SWEEP for another summer, sought to persuade the city's church leadership to fill some gaps in the planned summer programs, and prodded the Department of Parks and Recreation to channel funds into needed summer programs. As previously noted, the CCEO's Employment Sub-Committee held a Jobs Now Conference in the Twelfth Street area in May.[56]

Richard Marks thought that there was "a too-easy acceptance of the premise that if we have program services, we will avoid unrest or violence." Despite this view, the CCR staff, in an effort "to ring the bell," urged private agencies and voluntary groups to do what they could to provide jobs and services for young people during the summer to help relieve the anticipated tension. What was needed, CCR staffers thought, were activities that provided young people with "responsibility and dignity" and perhaps some money.[57]

Acting on the recommendation of the UCS, the United Fund, in the end, made $50,000 available for a third time so that SWEEP could continue in the summer of 1967. Five social agencies participated in the program this time, serving 1,462 young people. UCS optimistically concluded that it had been able to engage the youngsters in meaningful programs and had helped to solve their problems.[58]

The Council of Churches, through a Summer Opportunity Action Program, provided funds and personnel to make possible the staffing of the forty-four playgrounds that the city, in the end, decided to keep open. The primary focus of the churches' program was "job readiness; job application; [and] follow-up support while on the job" for lower-income older teenagers and young adults in the city's four poverty target areas. Since the total sum disbursed by the program was $2,760, it is doubtful that anything substantial was achieved.[59]

Cavanagh pleaded with Congress in March 1967 to provide the funding to make the summer "more acceptable." Federal funds belatedly made it possible for the Mayor's Committee for Human Resources Development (MCHRD), the AOP, and the public schools to provide a range of services similar to what the city had offered in 1966: day camps, the Youth Service Corps, NYC, employment programs for inner-city high school students, Head Start, Upward Bound, summer arts, and fitness and recreational activities. The various programs provided summer jobs for almost three thousand persons and services for an additional seventy thousand. Unfortunately, the delay in the authorization of the federal funds meant that most programs did not become fully operative until some time after July 10, too late to have much, if any effect, before July 23 and the beginning of the riot.[60]

In addition to programs made possible by federal funds, the Detroit public schools operated the largest summer program in the city's history. It enrolled one hundred thousand students that summer, compared to forty-nine thousand in 1966, and provided scholarships for ten thousand of them. At the end of June the city launched the largest recreational program in its history, Cavanagh telling program leaders that they were "the front-line troops" in seeking a "climate of decency" in Detroit. During the next ten weeks recreational leaders directed activities at 684 sites. In a further effort to provide jobs, education, and recreation for young people, Cavanagh late in June asked the employment committee of the Detroit Commission on Children and Youth to become the nucleus of a Mayor's Council on Youth Opportunities. The new council had barely begun to function by July 23, but it did undertake a jobs-for-kids program during the summer that provided "casual labor type jobs."[61]

As an additional means of forestalling serious racial trouble in the summer, the CCR sought to expand and perfect its "early warning system" for incident control. "We need to prevent small jitters, fear, and frustration from developing into serious trouble," a CCR staffer said. On the basis of its 1966 experience and a set of maps prepared by the Commission on Children and Youth that revealed concentrations of unemployment, police Youth Bureau contacts, high school dropouts, health problems, and welfare recipients, the CCR selected thirty areas for special attention as centers of possible tension and racial conflict. It established "contacts in depth" in these neighborhoods so as to get "continuing 'on-the-spot' analyses of community conditions and prompt information on critical developments." "The hope," Marks later explained, "was that we'd find an issue and that we would get leadership to it as fast as required to keep 'action and reaction' from developing."

He described the project to the *New York Times* as "a kind of human radar system to report possible racial trouble."[62]

The mayor's office could have utilized the CCR's early warning system as the city's mechanism for incident control. Marks, however, did not enjoy the mayor's confidence, and Cavanagh probably resented the secretary-director's remark that it was "discrimination" that characterized the status of blacks in Detroit. In any event, Cavanagh decided on May 5 to establish a rival early warning system, the Summer Task Force (STF), and to operate it out of the mayor's office. The STF, which became fully operational on June 5, was coordinated by Conrad Mallett, a former police officer and school teacher who had headed the Mayor's Youth Employment Program in 1964 and was serving at the time as assistant to the mayor. It was supervised by Malcolm G. Dade, Jr., the administrative assistant to the Commission on Children and Youth, and it was assisted by an Ad Hoc Committee composed of representatives from city, state, and private agencies.[63]

The STF served as the coordinating agency for the city's various summer programs, but its main function was incident control. It sought to do this, very much in the manner of the CCR's early warning system, through a neighborhood reporting system and mobile resource units. The neighborhood reporting system utilized a "network" of city employees, some of them allegedly in contact with hostile black groups and the so-called "no-win" crowd. The informants were to report incidents of neighborhood tension over telephone lines manned in a city information center from 8:30 A.M. to midnight seven days a week by STF personnel and city employees designated by each city department. The incidents reported were charted on a map in the belief that this would indicate areas needing attention. Information that the STF thought significant was transmitted to the appropriate city agency for action. When, for example, reports at the very beginning of the summer indicated that youngsters in some congested areas of the city were getting restless, the STF turned to the Police Department, which opened fire hydrants in those neighborhoods on hot days. "There is no telling if the service averted serious problems," Dade declared four days before the riot, "but little things—like street showers—mean a lot." That the STF did not hesitate to "think small" is evident. One can presume, on the other hand, that the CRC member of the Ad Hoc Committee, who headed the CRC's Tension Control Division, impressed upon the STF the critical importance of police behavior in any incident calling for police attention. Since many riots had been triggered by a contact between a white police officer and a black citizen, the CRC warned the state's mayors, police chiefs, and other city officials that the police "must do everything possible not to have their action serve as the spark of civil disorder."[64]

The mobile resource units, composed of personnel from key public agencies, were "the social service equivalents" of the TMU, available as "stand-by reserves" to be deployed if needed. If reports coming in from the field indicated that a neighborhood required one service or another, such as a medical service, a recreational program, or jobs for youth, a resource mobile unit was to move into the area to provide the service.[65]

The neighborhood reporting system yielded a grand total of only sixteen calls during the first three-and-a-half weeks of its operation and one or two per week in the two weeks preceding the riot. Most calls came in from city departments, especially the Police Department, rather than from individual contacts, and the reports failed to reveal any particular pattern. Some reports clearly involved racial incidents that might have escalated, such as the report of fifty to sixty black youths armed with bricks and clubs heading for a battle with white youths that the police averted. "No extraordinary events," however, were reported on July 22, 1967, on the very eve of the great riot.[66]

In a postriot evaluation, Dade contended that the neighborhood reporting system failed to achieve the purpose for which it had been designed because city employees in the field had not cooperated to the extent anticipated. The neighborhood reporters, it should be noted, were not trained in the collection of intelligence, and the STF did not provide them with guidelines regarding the types of incidents to report. Dade also stated that it had been difficult to implement the mobile resource unit concept since the departments involved claimed that they were already providing services where needed and to the extent their budgets permitted.[67]

On July 20, 1967, Mallett prepared a scenario of how a riot might develop in Detroit that apparently derived from an incident that had occurred three weeks earlier. He placed the simulated incident at Twelfth and Clairmount, eerily the starting point of the July 23 riot. The hypothetical episode began with an automobile accident that injured nineteen persons. Able to accommodate only one person, the ambulance called to the scene removed an injured white woman who was pregnant but left a bleeding black behind. A second ambulance could not get through the crowd that had gathered, a brick was thrown, the police arrived, looting began, and the riot was on. The members of the STF's Ad Hoc Committee were to consider what part their units would play in these circumstances. Before they could prepare their responses, they had to deal with a real riot, not a simulated one.[68]

Both the CCR's early warning system and the STF concept proved to be failures. Since the July 23 riot began in the early hours of the morning, the STF phone lines were not even manned at the time. The assumption of the mobile resource unit concept was that a riot would develop over a period of time following an incident, thus permitting time for remedial action to avert escalation of the original episode. The riots of the 1960s, however, developed immediately and spontaneously following a triggering event. The Detroit leadership, as a matter of fact, did not believe that a riot of the proportions of the disorder that began on July 23 could occur in Detroit, not in the model city. At worst, they thought that there would be another Kercheval-type disturbance, and they knew how to deal with affairs of that character and magnitude.[69]

The police, of course, were not solely dependent on the STF for their intelligence. They were aware of the inflammatory talk at Detroit's Second Black Arts Conference of late June and early July and the remark of the SNCC delegate from Cincinnati, "We already had our riot and we're here to show you how it's done." The department received a report on July 13 about caches of arms being put aside in Detroit for a riot during the second week of August and another report on July 17 about a riot scheduled for August 12. On July 21 the police received a report from an STF member and an MCHRD official that there would be a riot beginning August 1 in four areas of the city, including Twelfth Street. Locke stated in 1968 that the police had concluded five days before the July 23 riot that Detroit would experience a riot during the second week of August. "We were just wrong in time, not in the occurrence," he said. The smell of a riot was in the air in Detroit in July 1967.[70]

In view of the way the riot began, the police could hardly have been expected to predict its precise timing, but they might have handled the triggering incident more effectively had they focused their attention on an event that had occurred about six weeks before the riot started. On June 11 the police raided a blind pig located on Dunedin, just west of Twelfth Street, and, to their surprise, found the unusually large number of seventy-one persons inside. It took a considerable amount of time for the police to secure the necessary vehicles to transport the arrestees to the precinct station for booking, and in the meantime a crowd gathered at the scene, and its mood began to "turn ugly." Locke, who had accompanied the police on the raid, informed the superintendent that, to avoid trouble, it was essential for the police "to insure adequate transportation" for raids of this sort. The police, however, failed before July 23 "to work out the logistics" for dealing with this kind of problem.[71]

Three events—the harassing of an interracial couple who had moved into a white neighborhood in suburban Warren, the murder of Danny Thomas, and the slaying of Vivian Williams—added to the tension in the black community in the weeks immediately preceding the July 23 riot. The move of Carado Bailey and his white wife into a white neighborhood produced an angry reaction from their white neighbors. On June 12 a crowd of between eighty and one hundred persons surrounded the Bailey home shouting obscenities, and then someone threw a smoke bomb into the dwelling. This was the first of three nights of racial trouble that led to police intervention and the sealing off of a four-block area surrounding the Bailey home. The Detroit civil rights leadership claimed that the Warren police had incited the disturbance, and whether or not this was an accurate judgment, the affair served as a graphic reminder to Detroit blacks of their own troubles with white racism and with the police.[72]

The Danny Thomas slaying, according to the managing editor of the *Michigan Chronicle*, Albert J. Dunmore, was "the most serious" incident preceding the riot. It was, as a matter of fact, a more inflammatory incident than the event that triggered the riot, but it did not attract a hostile crowd to the scene as the July 23 incident did. The Thomas family lived on West Euclid, a few blocks from where the July 23 riot began, but the slaying itself occurred in Rouge Park, in a white neighborhood. Thomas, a Vietnam veteran and a Ford worker, and his pregnant wife went to the park with another couple on June 23. The phonograph the Thomases were playing attracted a crowd of whites, and a white bystander reportedly said, "Those boys should kill all niggers."

The Thomases drove the other couple home and then returned to the park after midnight. The mood of the whites had changed for the worse by then. Hearing the word "rape" and believing that some of the whites intended to assault Mrs. Thomas sexually, the couple decided to leave, but their car would not start since someone had tampered with the wires. Thomas asked the black caretaker in the park to call the police, and Thomas and his wife, while being pelted with rocks and bottles, sought refuge in the park's recreation building. Claiming that it was against his orders, the caretaker would not admit the couple into the building despite Mrs. Thomas's plea on bended knee. The Thomases then took refuge behind two pillars that flanked the structure, as the missile throwing continued, and there were shouts of "Niggers keep out of Rouge Park." When Danny Thomas stepped out from behind one of the pillars to plead with the whites, he was jumped. He broke free and ran, whereupon Mrs. Thomas heard three shots, and her husband fell. Mrs. Thomas, who, the *Michigan Chronicle* later reported, suffered a miscarriage, stated that fifteen to twenty whites had taken part in the assault and the killing of her husband. The police promptly charged Michael W. Palchlopek with the murder and also arrested five of his companions. Palchlopek was held without bond, but the five others were released almost immediately without being charged.[73]

As Barbara Tinker indicated in her novel, the Thomas murder "really set the pot boiling" in the black community. It became a major topic of conversation "because you see," one of the novel's characters said, "the same thing might a happened to any of us." Rumors stemming from the affair galvanized the STF into action. MCHRD workers were sent into the black community to deal with the rumors, and the CCR not only "worked directly" with the Thomas family to assure them that everything was being done to apprehend and punish the guilty but also to arrange for Mrs. Thomas's support.[74]

Quite apart from the horror of the Thomas murder, blacks were distressed about the police and press reaction to the affair. They were concerned that only one suspect was being held and claimed that the police would have acted quite differently had a black killed a white under similar circumstances. The police and the prosecutor's office actually considered charging some of Palchlopek's companions with conspiracy to rape or felonious assault, but Mrs. Thomas apparently could not identify those involved; and the police concluded that it would weaken the case against Palchlopek to couple it with a shaky conspiracy indictment. Blacks assumed Palchlopek would escape punishment since, they claimed, no white had ever been found guilty of killing a black in Detroit. Palchlopek was brought to trial, but a jury found him not guilty in December 1968.[75]

Blacks resented what they considered the downplaying of the Thomas murder by the city's daily newspapers. This, as a matter of fact, was not true of the *Detroit Free Press*, which gave the story front-page attention and included pictures of Mrs. Thomas and Palchlopek. The *Detroit News*, however, carried the story on page six under the headline, "Three Freed in Killing in Rouge Park." There was no reference in the story to the fact that the assailants were white and the victim black, and there were no pictures. The subdued and misleading treatment of the affair was allegedly designed to "cool" matters, but, if so, it "backfired." The *News*'s handling of the slaying infuriated its black reporter, Joseph Strickland, who had covered the story. He had wanted to include a photograph of Mrs. Thomas but was told, "We don't want to get involved in race issues." At a news media seminar after the riot, Strickland, capturing the black view of the Thomas slaying that a "Negro's life is worth nothing," reported as the white view, "We don't care if negroes kill negroes. We don't care if white people kill negroes, but you'd better not let one black man kill a white man, for any reason and under any circumstances."[76]

Vivian Williams, a young black prostitute who had been arrested twenty-two times for prostitution and three times for loitering, was killed on the night of July 1 at the corner of Twelfth and Hazelwood, three blocks from where the riot began three weeks later. The story regarding Williams in the black community was that a white policeman had been slashed in a failed attempt to arrest her on that corner on June 29—a policeman had been knifed attempting to make an arrest of a prostitute at that spot on that night—and that he had returned two nights later and killed Williams. The source for the story appears to have been another prostitute, who later, however, changed her story and was presumably protecting the real murderer. According to the Homicide Bureau investigation, Williams had been killed by a black male to whom she had denied her services, but Girardin claimed that she had been slain by a pimp. Whatever the truth of the matter, the Williams slaying "reactivated" the smoldering Cynthia Scott affair of 1963 and angered the black community in the Twelfth Street area. "I don't think anybody ever knew the right of it," Barbara Tinker has one of her characters say, but "there'd been so many times where policemen had hurt black people in one way or other that we believed just about anything you could tell us about their meanness."[77]

The harassment of the Baileys and the slayings of Danny Thomas and Vivian Williams did not lead inexorably to the July 23 riot, although they may have contributed to the mood that sustained it. The riot could very well have occurred without these events, just as it might not have occurred despite them. Because of the condition of blacks in Detroit, there was a good deal of combustible material lying around in the city's predominantly black areas, although probably somewhat less than in most large northern cities. Whether that material was to be ignited depended on the coming together of a particular set of circumstances at a particular time and at a particular place.

When the Detroit riot began at Twelfth and Clairmount, Tom Johnson, the head of the CRC's staff, conceded that he had had "no indication" that a riot was coming. He recalled, however, that in 1966 his office had pointed to Twelfth and Clairmount as "the most likely trouble spot in the city." The STF and the police commissioner had also anticipated that Twelfth Street would be the site if Detroit were to fall victim to the riot fever.[78]

Those who saw Twelfth Street as the likely location for a riot were undoubtedly referring to the poorest and most crime-ridden census tracts in the Twelfth Street environs rather than to the Virginia Park area as a whole or the more extensive area on the west side to which the riot actually spread. The available data—the best data we have are for the year 1965—make it evident that nonwhites living in the west side riot area were considerably better off than nonwhites south of the Boulevard in terms of median family income ($6,208 versus $3,640), home ownership (39.7 percent versus 26.1 percent), education (27.5 percent high school graduates among household heads versus 14.1 percent), and employment (2.6 percent unemployment versus 6.2 percent). They were slightly worse off than nonwhites in the city as a whole in median family income ($6,208 versus $6,405) and home ownership (39.7 percent versus 45.2 percent) but not in education (27.5 percent versus 22.1 percent high school graduates) or in employment (2.6 percent versus 3.4 percent unemployed). They were worse off than the city's whites in all four respects (white median family income was $6,846; 68.9 percent of the whites owned their homes; 29 percent of white household heads were high school graduates; and their unemployment rate was 1.6 percent).[79]

The center of the west side disorder area was the so-called Twelfth Street neighborhood as defined by the Mayor's Committee for Community Renewal; but, more narrowly, Target Area 4b, which was essentially the Virginia Park area plus two adjoining census tracts; and, more pre-

TABLE 1. Indices of Social Disruption

	Twelfth Street Area Rates[a]	Target Area 4B[b]	Model Neighborhood Area Rates	Total City Rates
Police data				
Crimes	64.9	74.9	112.5	48.8
Arrests	40.0	47.1	133.8	30.1
Youth Bureau contacts	26.2	31.0	40.9	17.0
Women's Division	4.5	5.6	7.0	3.2
Welfare data				
General Relief openings	2.7	6.3	5.7	1.8
General Relief closings	3.8	8.9	9.1	2.6
Food stamp openings	5.4	7.6	7.0	3.0
Food stamp closings	0.9	1.4	1.5	0.6
ADC openings	4.2	5.2	3.8	1.9
ADC applications denied[b]	1.3	1.8	1.5	0.7
ADC closings	4.7	4.1	3.6	1.9
ADCU openings	0.4	6.7	0.8	0.3
ADCU applications denied[b]	0.2	0.3	0.3	0.2
ADCU closings	0.9	1.3	1.6	0.6
State aid openings	2.3	5.9	6.6	1.9
State aid applications denied[b]	1.3	3.3	3.6	1.1
State aid closings	3.4	6.5	9.2	2.7
Welfare Registration Bureau	26.1	37.8	43.2	16.6
Legal Aid Bureau[c]	5.4	7.8	7.3	2.6
Health data				
Visiting Nurses	7.2	7.7	6.0	3.7
Venereal disease	6.4	8.5	6.2	2.4
Tuberculosis	0.8	1.3	1.6	0.6
Sanitation complaints	1.4	6.7	7.9	3.9
School data[d]				
Truancies	33.6	38.0	50.4	24.7
Dropouts	9.6	12.9	17.5	7.0

Sources: Harold Black and James D. Wiley, "Dissecting a Riot Neighborhood," *Nation's Cities* 6 (Sept. 1968): 19. Data for Target Area 4b from Social Data Bank tables, Area 4B, Box 345, George Romney Papers, MHC.

Note: 1965 population estimates based on the 1965 school census.

aThese rates are the number of occurrences per month per 10,000 persons total population 1965 for all categories except Youth Bureau contacts, truancies, and dropouts. The rates for these categories are the number of occurrences per month per 10,000 persons 5–19 years.

bThere are no application denied records for March 1965.

cThere are no Legal Aid Bureau records for May 1965.

dThere is no school data for the months of July and August.

cisely still, Census Tract 187. As table 1 indicates, the quality of life in the Twelfth Street area was vastly superior to that in the model city neighborhood inside the Boulevard, was somewhat better than that of Target Area 4b, but was decidedly inferior to that of the city as a whole. Census Tract 187 (bounded by Woodrow Wilson on the east, Fourteenth on the west, Euclid on the south, and Gladstone on the north) was the Twelfth Street neighborhood at its worst (see map 2). Here, where the population of 4,893 was 98 percent black, the median family income in 1965 was $4,000, and the unemployment rate was 10 percent, triple the nonwhite rate for the city and six times as high as the white rate. Only 17 percent of the dwellings in the tract were owner-occupied, far below the percentage for nonwhites and whites in the city as a whole. The population density of the Virginia Park area was twice that of the city as a whole, but the 137 persons per residential acre in Census Tract 187 was more than three times as high. Census Tract 187 was one of the most congested in the entire city, a fact of some importance in explaining the beginning of the riot.[80]

In a survey conducted between October 1966 and February 1967, 84 percent of the inhabitants of Census Tract 187 did not care for their neighborhood, and 92 percent wanted to move to another neighborhood. Seventy-two percent thought the neighborhood was "not too safe" or "not safe at all"; 91 percent said they were "somewhat or very likely" "to get robbed/beaten at night"; 80 percent were dissatisfied with the recreational facilities available in the area; and 33 percent were unhappy about the education their children were receiving. Whereas 48 percent of the blacks in a well-to-do census tract in 1965 indicated that the police would respond to a call about "housebreaking" in their neighborhood in ten minutes or less, only 22 percent in Census Tract 187 were of that opinion.[81]

Those referring to Twelfth Street as the scene of the Detroit riot were not always referring to the same place. When *New York Times* reporter J. Anthony Lukas stated that Twelfth Street and Detroit's near west side were "several notches up the pole" even by Detroit standards, he was not referring to the street itself, the "nastiest street in town," running from West Grand Boulevard to Clairmount, nor to Census Tract 187, but to a broadly defined Twelfth Street that included streets, with middle-class homes, running perpendicular to Twelfth Street (see map 2). When the Kerner Commission referred to Twelfth Street, it was referring to the worst part of the area, Census Tract 187. As the riot revealed, there were some blacks living in the neighborhood called Twelfth Street who felt they had "nothing to lose" by the riot but also others who wanted to protect what they had. There were those who made a determined effort to defend their homes, offering protection to firemen being pelted by the rioters, and there was the black who said, "Man, how can you call this place a home? This ain't no mother-fucking home. This is a prison. I'd just as soon burn down this damn place as any other."[82]

As survey data gathered in the main following the riot made clear, many blacks in the areas of the city where the riot centered were dissatisfied with the quality of their housing, the city's urban renewal program, the nature of code enforcement, the quality of the education provided by the public schools, the lack of recreational space in their neighborhoods, the character of their jobs, the practices of the merchants with whom they dealt, and above all, the behavior of the police. Influenced by the civil rights movement, rising black self-consciousness, and rioting elsewhere, they were less willing than blacks had been to put up with conditions that had long been their lot even though those conditions had improved and even though they were better off, on the average, than blacks elsewhere in the nation. Their grievances were no doubt accentuated by the rising unemployment that, as we have seen, reached 11 percent in the disorder area in July and perhaps 25 to 30 percent among the crucial eighteen to twenty-four-year-old group.[83]

Sixteen cities, according to the calculations of Bryan T. Downes, experienced racial disorders in 1964, twenty in 1965, and forty-four in 1966. In the first six months of 1967, according to a much broader definition of "disorder" used by the Kerner Commission, there were thirty-three disorders in the nation, three of them major. In July, when the racial turbulence reached its peak, there were 103 disorders, 5 of them major. Newark experienced a major riot between July 12 and July 17 that followed the arrest of a cab driver. Six days later the "worst civil disorder" experienced by an American city in the twentieth century began in Detroit following a police raid on a blind pig.[84]

CHAPTER 7

"A Little Trouble on Twelfth Street": July 23, 1967

The precipitating incident of the Detroit riot of 1967 was a police raid on a blind pig that began in an entirely routine manner. Blind pigs, after-hours drinking establishments, had served middle-class blacks in Detroit when they were effectively barred from downtown restaurants and bars. After 1948, when white facilities began to serve blacks, blind pigs, according to Hubert Locke, became "the haunts of off-duty prostitutes, pimps, narcotics peddlers, and out-of-towners looking for a little action." This may, indeed, have been the view of middle-class blacks, but it is doubtful that ghetto blacks saw blind pigs as dens of iniquity. When Errol Miller of the Justice Department visited Detroit in April 1967, he discovered that police raids on blind pigs were "one of the chief sources of complaints" among blacks with whom he discussed race relations. He concluded that the pigs were "an important part of life in Detroit's ghetto" and that police raids on them were "an unwise attempt by a white middle class to foist its morals on the lower class."[1] A police raid on a blind pig thus might very well have been seen by some ghetto blacks not as a simple problem of law enforcement but as an event with both racial and symbolic significance.

It has been said that there were more illegal pigs than legal bars in the Twelfth Street area. Although open earlier, they did their principal business after 2:00 A.M., when state law forbade the sale of liquor. They were often places for gambling as well as drinking. Middle-class blacks and bar owners, who had to buy liquor licenses to operate, complained to the police about the blind pigs in their neighborhoods, and there were allegations in the black community that the police, because of payoffs, tolerated the operation of pigs known to them.[2]

The blind pig that the police raided on July 23 was located at 9125 Twelfth Street, on the corner of Twelfth and Clairmount, in "a dingy second floor apartment" above a vacant print shop (see map 2). It had begun its existence in 1964 as the United Community League for Civic Action, allegedly a political organization, but it subsequently became a typical blind pig. The police had attempted to raid the pig nine times in the twelve months preceding July 23, 1967, and had succeeded in doing so twice, arresting ten persons on the first occasion and twenty-eight the second time, on June 30, 1967. The raid on July 23 resulted, according to the raiding party, from a complaint in the neighborhood, but one of the three owners of the pig claimed in a postriot interview that the police had harassed him for about a month before the raid because he had refused to make payoffs. In a postriot deposition, state Representative James Del Rio asserted that he had heard some of those apprehended in the raid say, "We got sick and tired of paying off the police and just told them to go to hell and we meant it." Corroboration of these allegations is lacking.[3]

July 22 was "an exceedingly hot, muggy" Saturday. Charles Henry and Joseph Brown, black plainclothesmen who were part of Sergeant Arthur Howison's clean-up crew or vice squad, vainly sought to gain entry into the pig at about 10:00 or 10:30 P.M., claiming that Brown was a basketball player from Cincinnati looking for some action. The two, however, were unable to get past the downstairs doorman until about 3:45 A.M. on July 23, when they mingled with three women entering the building. The practice of the clean-up crew under these circumstances was to wait for ten minutes and, if the plainclothesmen did not exit, to assume that they had made a buy – Henry had purchased a beer – and hence proved a violation. After waiting the allotted time, Howison, a member of his crew, and two policemen who had arrived at the scene broke the downstairs glass door with a sledgehammer and charged up the stairs. As soon as the upstairs doorman spotted them, he left his post. Since one of the blind pig owners was giving a party for two servicemen back from Vietnam and one likely to be sent there, there were eighty-five persons in the establishment, an unusually large number. This included some hiding in the kitchen and toilets but apparently not "some people" who jumped out of a back window even though it was a "long drop" to the ground.[4]

When Howison announced the raid, there was "complete chaos" inside the pig. Fights broke out, and the police were pushed into the hallway before they were able to subdue those present. Some gambling had been going on, perhaps only a dice game, but the police did not actually detect anyone gambling. It was operating procedure for the police at that time to arrest all those present in a blind pig, the owners for operating an illegal establishment and the others for loitering or frequenting. Howison, however, had the "option" of arresting the owners alone and simply taking the names of the customers or at least the women present. He considered doing so because of the large number of persons present, all of them black, about one-half of them female, but he decided against this procedure because some in the pig had resisted arrest and the police recognized or thought they recognized others wanted by

Map 1. Detroit. Lower East Side

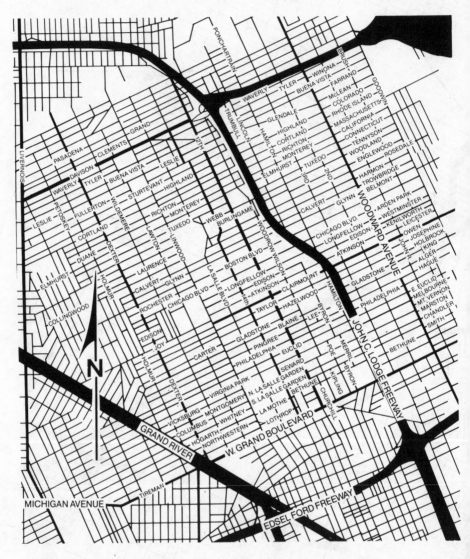

Map 2. West Side Riot Area

the police. Howison, on the other hand, might have considered the risks in terms of "crowd control" of arresting so many people in that particular neighborhood, the fears expressed by city officials and the police concerning racial trouble that summer, and the fact that Newark had just experienced a major riot growing out of an arrest. All of this, however, is probably clearer in retrospect than it must have appeared to Howison at the time, before the arrests turned out to be, in the words of the *Detroit Free Press*, "the most expensive pinch in history."[5]

Once the police decided to arrest all those found in the pig, normal procedure would have been to take the arrestees through the rear door of the pig to the alley behind the building rather than out the front to Twelfth Street, a main thoroughfare. A padlocked steel door, however, barred the rear exit, and the police could neither find a key nor break the door. Howison also noted in his report of the raid that, because the alley dead-ended immediately north of the blind pig, patrol wagons in the alley could have been cut off from the street by cars parked on Clairmount. After Girardin personally inspected the pig, he agreed that it would have been "the greatest mistake in the world" for Howison and his crew to have taken their prisoners out the back door. "You would have gotten your men killed in there," he told Howison.[6]

Howison had sent out a call for a Tenth Precinct wagon before entering the building, but a wagon was apparently unavailable at that moment. Since a wagon held a maximum of fourteen people, in the end Howison had to summon three other wagons from two precincts to accommodate the large number of arrestees. At least a full hour elapsed from the time the clean-up crew entered the blind pig until the last prisoner was loaded into a wagon. The delay was occasioned not only by the number of arrestees involved but also by the need to secure wagons from other precincts and by the fact that one wagon driver, unfamiliar with the area, got lost on a return trip from the Tenth Precinct station to pick up another load of prisoners.[7]

While the police were loading their prisoners into wagons, the crowd outside observing the proceedings grew from about ten or twenty persons to two hundred. In most neighborhoods it would have been unlikely for a large crowd to gather at 4:00 or 5:00 A.M. to witness an arrest, but Twelfth Street, the owner of a barbershop there later said, "was 24 hours." As Girardin remarked, you could "blow a whistle at three o'clock in the morning" on congested Twelfth Street and attract two thousand people. This was especially true on a sultry July morning when it was difficult to sleep in the overcrowded upstairs apartments on the street. What was critical in precipitating most 1960s riots was the assembling of a crowd at the scene of the triggering incident. In this instance, a series of chance events—an unusually large number of people in the blind pig, the decision to arrest them all, a steel door, the physical shape of the alley behind the pig, and a lost paddy wagon—all played a part in the assembling process.[8]

The crowd that gathered outside 9125 Twelfth Street in the early hours of July 23 was composed of "elements of the bar scene and the popular street scene." "There were some drunks and some drifters," prostitutes, and "petty gamblers," Cavanagh reported, but there were also some middle-class persons and factory workers on their way to work, a combination of the "least stable social elements" in the area and of ordinary citizens who happened to be up and about at that hour. Their mood was "jovial" at the outset, some of those present joking with the prisoners about their fate as they were brought out to the wagons.[9] The temper of the crowd soon began to change, however, almost certainly because some onlookers believed the police had roughed up their prisoners and because two young black males helped to channel the hostility toward the police undoubtedly already present among at least some of those assembled.

The people "got mad," a youngster who worked in a nearby shoe store remarked, "not because of busting the blind pig, but the way they [the police] were treating everybody." Eyewitnesses claimed that the police beat some of their prisoners, "pushed and kicked" a handcuffed man down the stairs and hit him with a gun butt, hit one prisoner with a nightstick when he failed to produce identification, and were "pushing, kicking and twisting" the arms of women prisoners. A youth at the scene alleged that he saw a policeman "drag this particular lady out. Her clothes was all pulled off. . . . [I]t was really horrible," he asserted. According to still another report, a woman arrestee stuck her head out of one of the wagons and shouted "brutality."[10]

The police later conducted an investigation of the brutality charges and found no evidence that the arresting officers had been "unduly rough or profane or impolite." Perhaps the onlookers interpreted rough treatment as brutality, but their belief that the police had abused their prisoners, which fit the mindset of Twelfth Street residents, is the essential fact in explaining their reaction, whatever the reality.[11]

Two black youths outside the blind pig summoned the crowd to action. According to the testimony of Patrolman Edward Zimmerman, who had been stationed at the entrance of the blind pig, one youth, who came to be known as Greensleeves because of the green shirt and pants he was wearing, shouted, "Black Power, don't let them take our people away; look what they are doing to our people. . . . Let's kill them whitey motherfuckers . . . let's get the bricks and bottles going." "Why do they [the police] come down here and do this to our neighborhood?" Greensleeves yelled. "If this happened in Grosse Pointe, they wouldn't be acting this way." He came up between one of the two policemen stationed at the downstairs entrance of the pig and said, "I'm going to baptize this motherfucker with a beer bottle," and a bottle then landed at the officer's feet. The crowd "started joining in and jeering and milling about and closing in toward the police," who had arrived on the scene in eight to ten scout cars. "Things were getting a little hairy" outside, one officer informed the clean-up crew still inside the pig. Some in the crowd began throwing bottles, beer cans, and rocks that hit the building or crashed in the street. It was "quite a torrent," a police officer testified. The police spotted Greensleeves at Twelfth and Hazelwood later that morning and claimed that he was shouting directions to looters.[12]

The second black male, according to his own account, was William Scott III, the son of one of the owners of the blind pig. Claiming that he "really got mad" when he saw police "dragging people down the stairs," including his father and sister, he began calling the officers "some beautiful names." The police ran after him but backed off when the crowd came toward Scott to protect him. "Are we going to let these peckerwood motherfuckers come down here any time they want and mess us around?" Scott reported himself as saying to the crowd, which was getting "pretty mad." Grabbing a bottle in a nearby playground, Scott threw it at a policeman in front of 9125 Twelfth Street and shouted to the crowd, "Get your god damn sticks and bottles and start hurtin baby." At some point before the raiding party left the area, the owner of a black restaurant in the neighborhood heard cries of "Let's have a riot."[13]

The police completed loading their wagons at about 4:40 A.M. As the police departed, a bottle broke the rear window of one of the cruisers. A few minutes later, apparently, the police in the cruisers and scout cars in the immediate vicinity of 9125 Twelfth Street were ordered to withdraw from the area. Just who gave the order is unclear,[14] but it was based on the presumption that the police presence in "an inflamed neighborhood" served as "a knitting factor" and, as one Twelfth Street resident quipped, "if they left, the crowd would leave too." The crowd, however, saw the departure of the police as a victory for themselves. "For the first time in our lives we felt free," young Scott recalled.

It may have been a tactical error for the police to pull out at that moment and to remove for a brief period whatever restraining force might have been available to check what soon happened. The Detroit Police Department knew that the Los Angeles police had concluded that their withdrawal from the Watts area at the outset of the Watts riot had been a mistake, and the tactic had failed in the June 1967 Tampa disturbance as well. An authority on control strategy has suggested that the proper tactic for police to pursue when heavily outnumbered by rioters is to ignore the disorder or use firearms. The Detroit police, however, adopted neither alternative. They quickly returned to the disturbance area, probably more outnumbered than when they had been ordered to withdraw, and then did not use firearms.[15]

The police took their eighty-five prisoners to the Tenth Precinct station, where the owners were booked for engaging in an illegal occupation, one arrestee was charged with probation violation, a few were held for traffic violations, and the remainder were released without being charged. After being released on bail, Billy O'Neal, one of the three owners, made his way to Highland Park, was shortly thereafter arrested on a charge of inciting to riot, and later sentenced to three to five years in prison. As for those released at the station, they could just as easily have been released at the scene of the arrest. As Girardin later remarked with some exaggeration, the police arrested them, then dismissed them all, and "got the whole city burned down."[16]

When Lieutenant Raymond Good, the officer in charge of the Tenth Precinct, received word about an unruly crowd outside 9125 Twelfth Street, he telephoned his wife and recalled saying, "Honey, I got a little trouble on 12th Street." As he drove out to the area with Sergeant Lawrence Mulvihill to investigate, he thought, "It's going to be a hot July day." Mulvihill testified that when Good and he approached Twelfth and Clairmount shortly after 5:00 A.M., several hundred people were milling about in the area. Greensleeves approached the police car, shouting, "There's the motherfuckin' cops now; let's run them out of here"; "The streets are ours." Good stepped out of the car to get a better view of what was happening and was promptly hit above the right ear by a piece of concrete, the first known injury of the riot. He got back into the scout car and told the driver to "get the hell out" of there. As the car raced down Twelfth Street, Good saw the crowd surging into the street. The clean-up crew's Joseph Brown, who had remained behind after the arrests, saw young people "running around, throwing 'unknown objects' and breaking windows." The Detroit riot had begun.[17]

On August 13 Patrolman Zimmerman arrested a young man on Twelfth Street in a familiar green attire whom the patrolman and Good identified as Greensleeves. The arrestee was Michael Lewis, a twenty-two year-old black who had lived in Detroit most of his life and worked at the Ford Motor Company. A high school dropout, he had been found guilty in January 1967 of carrying an unregistered gun and placed on probation. There was no indication of his involvement with any black extremist organization. Arraigned on charges of rioting and inciting to riot, Lewis pleaded innocent, claiming that he had not been in the vicinity of the blind pig on the morning of July 23. The prosecutor dismissed the charges against Lewis in April 1971 after two trials had resulted in hung juries. Young Scott was also arrested during the riot but not on an incitement-to-riot charge.[18]

The Detroit riot began very much as many other riots did in the 1960s. Riots of that era were normally preceded by rumors that a riot was coming. Although 53 percent of black Detroit respondents in one survey indicated that they had been surprised by the riot, residents of the disturbance areas stated in interviews that they had been hearing before July

23, 1967, that Detroit was "long overdue" for a riot and that it "would be next." They said that "you could just feel it coming" and that the word was that people were "tired of waiting" and wanted "revenge." Against this background, "the most important factor" in getting a riot started was the occurrence of an event that typified "the kinds of complaints and grievances" a community had, or, to put it differently, the occurrence of "some real or perceived act of violence upon blacks." It is not surprising, then, that six of the ten riots occurring between 1964 and 1966 that David Boesel examined and twelve of twenty-four riots in the summer of 1967 that the Kerner Commission looked at began with a police action, and "force or violence" was an element in the origin of ten or more of the Kerner sample. This precipitating police incident was often "simply the final link in a long chain of circumstances that actually were the true precipitants of the riot."

The crowd that gathered at the scene of the precipitating incident, an indispensable precondition for a riot, "served as a highly partisan chorus, interpreting the event in terms of a wider range of black experience." In Detroit, Greensleeves, Scott, and, no doubt, others helped to communicate "specific grievances throughout the forming crowd," which probably saw the blind pig raid in the context of long-standing grievances against the police and, more immediately, in the context of the slaying of Danny Thomas and Vivian Williams, which had "raised the community's level of anger to the boiling point." As a distinguished sociologist has written, a racial disturbance may result when a minority group believes that a particular organization, in this instance the police, has engaged in action "in keeping with its threatened character."[19]

This is not to say that a riot in Detroit was inevitable at that time. To be sure, had not the particular conjunction of events on the morning of July 23, 1967, triggered a riot, another set of events on another day might very well have done so. It is just as likely, however, that the necessary juxtaposition of events would not have occurred. The potential for a riot was certainly present in Detroit, as in every northern city with a substantial black population, but it was not inevitable that the potential become the actual. Worse conditions elsewhere did not, after all, lead to major riots in those cities.

Had the two plainclothesmen of Howison's crew been able to enter the blind pig at 10:30 P.M. on July 22 when they made their initial attempt, the police might very well have been able to control any ensuing trouble since the police force at that hour, as at the outset of the Kercheval disturbance, would have been at its maximum strength. As chance would have it, the force was at its lowest strength of the week when the disorder began. The four or five hours after 3:30 A.M. on Sunday were the time of the lowest incidence of crime in Detroit. At 5:00 A.M. on July 23, as the looting was about to begin, there were only thirty-three police officers on duty in the riot area. The riot-trained Tactical Mobile Unit

(TMU) and the commandos of the Motor Traffic Bureau (MTB) had gone off duty at 3:00 A.M., and Sunday was normally the day off for the Mounted Bureau, the department's third crowd-control unit. The riot was almost certainly unplanned, but, as Girardin later put it, "if the greatest strategists in the world had planned it," they could not have picked a better time for the riot to begin.[20]

When Deputy Superintendent John Nichols was informed of the disorder, he ordered Charles Gentry, the west side district inspector, to dispatch enough scout cars from other precincts to quell the disorder. There were only ninety-nine scout cars operating at that time, and only 193 patrolmen on the streets throughout the city. Reviewing the situation after he arrived at headquarters at about 6:00 A.M., Girardin, in accordance with the department's riot plan, ordered the mobilization of the department. The midnight platoon was held over when the day platoon came on duty, the police were placed on twelve-hour duty, and leaves were canceled.

Because it was a Sunday at the height of the summer, the police could not put their riot mobilization plan into effect as quickly as they might have at some other time. "Notorious sportsmen and outdoor people," many police officers were away from their homes or even away from the city. As a matter of fact, only about one in four officers could be reached immediately. Mobilization, as Girardin noted, is "inherently a time-consuming process no matter how efficient," and the timing of the disorder made it even more time-consuming. As the Mayor's Inspection Team wryly concluded, the rioters mobilized faster than the police did. Girardin, moreover, was reluctant to commit all the police available to the Twelfth Street area because he feared that the trouble there might be a diversion and that the real riot would develop on the east side of the city, where Chrysler Corporation, Parke Davis, Detroit Edison, and the city waterworks were located. Aware of a Revolutionary Action Movement scenario that called for seizing control of a city by controlling its vital industries and public utilities, Girardin instructed Superintendent Eugene Reuter to keep an adequate force on the east side.[21]

By 6:00 A.M. about thirty windows had been broken in the riot area, and the police had made their first looting arrest. At 7:00 A.M. the Police Department alerted the State Police, the Michigan National Guard, the Wayne County sheriff and prosecutor, and the FBI; and forty-five minutes later Girardin gave orders to seal off Belle Isle, where the 1943 riot had originated. As the riot control plan provided, the department began to set up a headquarters command post in police headquarters and a field command post in a section of the Herman Keifer Hospital in the riot area. Despite the riot plan, however, the department had not clearly demarcated the sphere of field responsibilities, and it lacked "properly trained Command Post personnel."[22]

As police arrived at the Tenth Precinct station, they were formed into units of three scout cars, four officers to a car, and sent to patrol Twelfth Street. The tactic was totally ineffective, the heavily outnumbered police being tied up by the crowd, which by 8:00 A.M. numbered about three thousand. The police did nothing to stop the window breaking and looting that was underway. Young Scott claimed that he broke the first window, throwing a litter basket through the window of Hardy's Drug Store, which was apparently the first store looted. Hardy's was black-owned and filled prescriptions on credit. "Why would Negroes want to tear up their own business places?" the owner asked.[23]

The initial hours of the riot, after the police first pulled out and then did almost nothing to restrain lawbreaking when they returned, were "just like a holiday," a young black male told a *New York Times* reporter. "All the kids wandered around saying, real amazed like, 'The fuzz is scared; they ain't goin' to do nothin.' " In the words of the Kerner Commission, "an epidemic of excitement . . . swept over persons on the street." A "carnival atmosphere" of this sort was a characteristic phenomenon at this stage of the 1960s riots, constituting "a giddy sense of release from the oppression of routine, white-dominated life in the ghetto," a relatively danger-free opportunity for ghetto residents to "exact revenge" against those whom they believed had for so long mistreated them. "The very pavement shook with the energy of their enchantment," Joyce Carol Oates wrote in her novel *Them.*

When the Reverend Robert Potts, pastor of Grace Episcopal Church in the Twelfth Street area, went out into the streets to see if he could calm the situation, he found "a gleefulness in throwing stuff and getting stuff out of the buildings." "I really enjoyed myself," a young black remarked about his riot activities that morning. Those simply watching what was going on, some of them still in their nightclothes, outnumbered the participants at this stage. Young militants, however, appear to have attempted to stimulate the spectators into action. A political scientist on Twelfth Street that morning claimed that the militants recruited the spectators with "talk of brotherhood and threats of physical retribution."[24]

At 7:50 A.M., as rock and bottle throwing became intense, the police decided to conduct a sweep of Twelfth Street, a standard control tactic that the department had successfully employed in the Kercheval disorder. By that time, about 1,000 police were on duty in the precincts and bureaus of the department, 360 in the riot area and perhaps 150 on the street. They were heavily outnumbered by the crowd, numbering at least three thousand, and the riot control plan specifically advised against using a sweep in squad formation under these circumstances. The Police Department's high command nevertheless believed that it could control the situation, informing the mayor's office that the riot was "going to break up." Had the department at this early stage of the disorder believed that its forces were inadequate to cope with the situation, it would presumably have sought the assistance of the State Police and the National Guard, as Operation Sundown provided, and it is doubtful that it would have ordered the sweep of Twelfth Street.

The assumption behind the sweep was that heavily armed squads of police would be able to disperse the riotous crowd with a show of force. The balance of forces, however, was not in favor of the police this time, as two squads of twelve men each, vainly trying to operate in a V formation, confronted a mob many times their number. As the police, probably a mixture of some of the commandos who had reported for duty and members of the precinct support force, moved forward, the crowd scattered into the numerous alleys perpendicular to Twelfth Street and then reformed behind the police. This is precisely what had happened in Watts, where the rioters ran behind the houses and curled back behind the police. It was "a show of weakness," so recognized by the rioters, and it emboldened them. The police had not only ignored the numbers involved and the physical character of Twelfth Street but also the principle that "too weak a display of force" could have a more harmful effect than not using any force at all.[25]

After the failure of the sweep, the police decided to isolate the rioters by sealing off Twelfth Street from Clairmount to West Grand Boulevard and for four to five blocks east and west of Twelfth Street. The plan was to let no one enter the area from the outside but to permit those inside the cordon to leave if they so desired. The hope was, as the mayor's executive secretary later put it, if "you just put a perimeter around it [the disturbance area], it would self-liquidate." The Police Department, however, did not have enough men on the scene or enough sawhorses to blockade the area effectively, nor did Twelfth Street lend itself readily to a control tactic of this sort. Concluding eventually that the area could not be completely sealed off, the department limited the containment effort to street blockades at key intersections, each guarded by helmeted police who might better have been used to deal with the situation inside the cordoned area.[26]

Between 8:00 A.M. and noon the crowd on Twelfth Street swelled to between eight and nine thousand, some attracted there by the sirens of police cars as officers raced from place to place in response to radio calls. The first fire occurred at 8:24 A.M. in a shoe store at Twelfth and Blaine, part of a three-story brick and frame structure that included eighteen apartments and five stores. Looters had been in the store for two hours when word was passed to them that the police were on their way. The store owner then heard someone say, "okay, set it," and the store was quickly set ablaze.[27]

The mood of the crowd on Twelfth Street was adversely affected by a report that the police had bayoneted a black man and left him either to bleed to death or to bleed for some time before removing him to a hospital. Accounts of the alleged event place it at different times, most commonly as having occurred during the police sweep of Twelfth Street. It was alleged that when a drunk did not move as ordered by the police, an officer pushed him to the ground and then bayoneted him in the side and back. Charles Colding claimed that he saw the bayoneting at about 7:00 A.M., took a photograph of the man, and watched him bleed for twenty minutes before aid came. Karl Gregory stated that he took pictures of the victim later that morning, pictures that he showed to a Kerner Commission interviewer and one of which, he alleged, was subsequently published in the *Michigan Chronicle*. The *Chronicle*, however, reported that the picture it displayed had been taken at 12:15 A.M. on July 24; and although it shows a man on the ground, it cannot be visually deduced that the individual had been bayoneted or even that the legs of the persons surrounding him in the picture are those of police officers. Gregory, however, insists that the picture in the *Chronicle* is the one he took, that he "saw the wound," and that the *Chronicle* simply misdated the picture.

Eighteen-year-old Norvell Harrington, then an investigator for Wayne County Suburban Legal Services, claimed that he saw the bayoneting, which he placed at 12:45 P.M. on July 23, several hours after the sweep. He told a Kerner Commission interviewer that although he did not know the fate of the individual, he later photographed a man lying on a front lawn with his intestines coming out of his mouth. The interviewer reported that this was apparently a picture that Gregory had displayed, but it is not the picture that appeared in the *Chronicle*.

Although there is a lack of hard evidence to confirm the Colding, Gregory, and Harrington stories, an Associated Press dispatch on July 24 told of a black man sprawled on the pavement, bleeding from cuts, and of a police officer standing nearby with a rifle and fixed bayonet. The police, who took the man to a hospital, claimed, however, that they had found him on the pavement and were not responsible for his condition. There are at least three additional accounts of a stabbing or something similar on July 23 that specifically relate what supposedly happened to other than police action. The individual stabbed or "kicked to death" in these accounts was a white male.

The police lists of the injuries and deaths resulting from the riot do not include either an injury or death corresponding to any of the accounts of the bayoneting or stabbing that allegedly took place on July 23. The injury list, however, is certainly incomplete, and many blacks believed that far more deaths resulted from the riot than were officially reported. Whatever the truth of the matter, word spread on Twelfth Street on July 23 that a bayoneting had occurred, and the effect on the crowd was dramatic. "I never did know whether there was any truth to that story," the narrator in Barbara Tinker's novel declares, "but whole lots of peoples believed it and the crowd was turning from being good-natured to being angry and downright ugly."[28] Rumors of one sort or another have, of course, played an important part in many riots, including Detroit's 1943 riot and 65 percent of the disorders studied by the Kerner Commission.[29]

The failure of the police to disperse the rioters by sweeping Twelfth Street and the ineffectiveness of the street blockade led Girardin to consent to a third riot control strategy, the entry of black peace patrollers into the disturbance area. By 9:30 A.M. or so the TMU, which was being held in reserve, had been partly mobilized, and the commandos of the MTB were lined up shoulder to shoulder on Twelfth Street. They were wearing helmets and plastic face shields, their rifles were upright, their bayonets unsheathed. As Gregory recalled it, the all-white commandos looked as though they were daring the crowd "to move toward them" and "seemed to be challenging the manhood of the people in the crowd." However provocative the commandos may have been — "too much visible force" sometimes served as an irritant in the 1960s riots — they were not to go into action but were rather to give way to the peace patrols.[30]

Individual black leaders had vainly sought from early in the morning of July 23 to discourage looting and to persuade the people in the streets to return to their homes. The Reverend Otis W. Saunders, pastor of the Trinity Community Church in the area, members of the Virginia Park Citizens Rehabilitation Committee, and Julian Witherspoon had all sought to prevent escalation of the disturbance; and block club leaders in the area had used the telephone for the same purpose.[31]

At about 10:00 A.M. Hubert Locke, Arthur Johnson, John Conyers, Damon Keith, clergymen and businessmen from the Twelfth Street area, and other black community leaders, about twenty persons in all, gathered in Grace Episcopal Church to decide on a course of action. There was talk among those present about the "provocative" character of the commandos, and fears were expressed that lives would be lost if the commandos were committed to action. Better to permit rioting, the consensus was, than to have people killed. The decision reached was for the leadership to go out in four cars through the "hard-core blocks" to tell people to get off the streets, but on the condition that the commandos first be withdrawn. Locke phoned Girardin, who gave his consent.

The police commissioner later claimed that he had agreed to the request for peace patrols even though he knew that they "would do no damn good in the world." It is more likely that Girardin believed that the tactic had helped ease the Kercheval disturbance, which is questionable, and might do so again. He overlooked the fact that "self-styled leaders" had failed to have a calming effect in Harlem in 1964, where Bayard Rustin had been shouted down; in Philadelphia in 1964; in Watts in 1965, where the black leadership had failed in repeated efforts to halt the riot and Dick Gregory had been shot in the leg while playing the role of peacemaker; and in Newark in July 1967. He also overlooked the fact that the framers of the Detroit riot plan had categorized the tactic as "ineffective" in a large-scale disturbance. The official view in Detroit, to be sure, was that the situation was under control, but individual policemen were telling reporters that the disturbance was "decidedly not under control" and was spreading. The Police Department started a disorder log at 10:45 A.M., and the entry for 10:50 was "large crowd, can't control, officer in trouble — getting attacked by mob." At about 11:00 A.M. four squads of police, including the commandos, were withdrawn from the disturbance area to the Herman Keifer Command Post to permit the entry of the peace patrols.[32]

There was a delay of about forty-five minutes while the peace patrollers waited for the bullhorns they had requested from the police to be delivered from Belle Isle, where they apparently were stored. When the black leaders went out into the streets at about 11:15 A.M., they were jeered or ignored. John Conyers, in a car driven by Arthur Johnson, had the roughest time. The two men encountered little or no trouble as they went down the side streets urging people on porches to stay out of trouble and reporting that the police were cooperating. The scene, however, turned ugly when Conyers and Johnson reached Twelfth and Hazelwood. What Johnson never forgot about the event was "the sound of things," of glass breaking, fires burning, and excited people, the sound of a riot. He had never heard that sound before, and it frightened him.

Conyers had been out in the streets earlier, before the police had been removed, and when he had told the crowd to go home, they had shouted, "Why should we go home? Tell the cops to go home. This is where we live." One person in the crowd had yelled, "I want to kill those — — —." Now, when Conyers got up on the hood of Johnson's car to tell the crowd that if they dispersed, he could get the police removed, he met with much hostility, especially from young blacks. When he said, "We're with you," the response was "We don't want to hear it," and he was asked why he was "defending the cops and the establishment." Bottles smashed on the curb, and a rock landed near Johnson's car. Later that day Conyers said, "You try to talk to those people and they'll knock you into the middle of next year." Girardin later commented that the black peace patrollers were "practically white when they came back."[33]

Locke, Johnson, and no doubt the other peace patrollers realized that the situation was now beyond the ability of the police to control and that Twelfth Street, as Locke told Girardin at noon, was "a lost cause." The Police Department had frittered away an hour between 11:00 A.M. and noon while the forces the department had trained to deal with a riot stood by and the riot escalated. "I think the time might have been better used," Nichols later remarked, and Reuter agreed. Paul Donley, the inspector in charge of the MTB commandos, was furious at what had occurred. When he retired from the department a few days later, he complained that he had been "hamstrung" by "politicians" in executing police tactics. Girardin said in a 1971 interview that the failure of the peace patrols meant that "force" had to be the answer, but that was not his initial reaction to the collapse of the peacemaking effort, even though the disorder at that point, as the FBI was being advised by its sources, was "spreading rapidly from the focal point."[34]

The "decisive turning point" for him, Girardin informed Cavanagh a few weeks after the riot, came at 1:00 P.M., when the crowd pelted firemen as they responded to alarms at four separate locations along Twelfth Street. This meant, Girardin reported, that police who could have been used to tighten the cordon now had to be assigned to protect firemen. If Girardin really viewed the "decisive turning point" as having come at 1:00 P.M., it is remarkable that shortly before 2:00 P.M. he advised Colonel Frederick Davids, director of the State Police, that the city did not require the assistance of state troopers. At 2:05 P.M., however, Girardin, although still not sure that he had a "full blown riot" on his hands, and Reuter requested the State Police to provide Detroit with "all assistance possible."[35]

Alerted to the disturbance at 7:15 A.M., the State Police assigned an observer to the Tenth Precinct soon thereafter. At 10:57 Davids ordered a mobilization alert of seven State Police districts because the information reaching the State Police from "good reliable" black informants on Twelfth Street did not accord with what the Detroit Police Department, which Davids believed was receiving "inadequate" and possibly "inaccurate information" from the streets, was reporting about the disturbance. Davids spoke to Girardin three times between 7:15 A.M. and 2:00 P.M. and was assured in each instance that State Police assistance was not required. Following Detroit's request for aid, the State Police, whose total strength was 1,459, dispatched 360 troopers from Lower Peninsula districts to the Detroit Artillery Armory, the marshalling point for Operation Sundown.[36]

Shortly before 3:30 P.M. the looting, burning, and rioting spread to Linwood, west of Twelfth Street, which led the police to give up their attempt to contain Twelfth Street. At 4:10 P.M. Cavanagh requested Governor Romney to authorize the use of the National Guard in Detroit. This was nine hours after the city had alerted the Guard to the trouble brewing on Twelfth Street. At 10:00 A.M., as Operation Sundown provided, Major General Clarence C. Schnipke, Michigan's adjutant general and director of the Michigan State Military Department, and Major General Cecil L. Simmons, commander of the 46th Infantry Division, dispatched Brigadier General Noble Moore, the assistant commander of the 46th Division, to Detroit to be available should the Guard be needed. At Romney's request, Robert J. Danhof, the governor's legal advisor, phoned Cavanagh at 10:45 A.M. to advise the mayor that state assistance was available and that 380 Guardsmen of the 156th Signal Battalion were already present in the Detroit Artillery Armory, where, by chance, they were involved in a "multiple unit training assembly." Although Cavanagh responded that "no help was needed," state authorities decided to keep the batallion in the armory in the event it would be needed rather than to release it in the afternoon, as scheduled.

Arriving in Detroit at 1:20 P.M., Moore went directly to the Tenth Precinct, where he was briefed. At about the same time Colonel Ralph Phillips, the military support plan officer of the adjutant general's office, set up a command post in the Artillery Armory. At 2:15 P.M. Moore met with Reuter and Nichols, and the three agreed that the Guard's assistance was required. Girardin and Cavanagh thought otherwise, however. At 4:00 P.M. Moore requested Schnipke to authorize the mobilization of the 156th Signal Battalion, but Schnipke responded that Cavanagh had to make the request. Acting on Moore's recommendation, Cavanagh did so at 4:10 P.M. Romney promptly acceded to the request. Additional units were mobilized during the next several hours.[37]

In view of the deteriorating situation on Twelfth Street and repeated statements by Cavanagh and Girardin that the Police Department lacked the manpower to quell the riot as it developed on July 23, why had the city administration delayed so long in seeking the outside assistance that, in hindsight at least, was so obviously required? As was true of local officials in other riot cities, in Watts and Newark, for example, the reluctance of Detroit officials to seek the entry of "higher levels of force" reflected the city government's desire to demonstrate, as it had in the Kercheval miniriot, that it could deal with a racial disturbance unaided.[38]

In all likelihood, Cavanagh would have been less reluctant to appeal to Michigan's governor for help had that individual been someone other than George Romney. The easy-going, Irish-American, Catholic Cavanagh and the self-righteous Mormon Romney were, as Roselle put it, "just two different people," and they had no liking for each other. Both were ambitious politicians, the mayor a nationally prominent Democrat who had not lost his taste for higher office despite the reverses he had lately suffered, the governor a prime candidate for the 1968 Republican presidential nomination. Cavanagh thought Romney "the creature of an overawed press" and a person who saw "plots in everything." Romney, for his part, did not fully trust Cavanagh—the governor recalled many years later that when both men had been seeking in 1963 to secure the summer Olympics for Detroit, Cavanagh had asked to see Romney's speech on the subject and then had used the speech himself.[39]

Cavanagh and Romney had clashed over Detroit's urban renewal and antipoverty programs. When Romney, responding to the West Central Organization's complaints about urban renewal, had scheduled a meeting with that group late in 1965, Cavanagh had spurned the governor's invitation to attend on the grounds that state issues were not involved. Viewing the mayor's declination as an insult, an angry Romney had retorted that city officials should not forget that the state government was "the source of their power" in the urban renewal area. The two men had also clashed when Romney temporarily held up a $7.3 million grant to Detroit for its war on poverty, and Cavanagh then campaigned to have Congress abolish the veto power over such grants that existing legislation gave governors. When Cyrus Vance came to Detroit during the riot to represent President Johnson, he was surprised at "the intensity of some of the feelings" between the mayor and the governor. It was, he agreed, "a bad mix."[40]

Quite apart from personality and political differences between Cavanagh and Romney, the mayor and his police commissioner had reservations about the use of the State Police and the National Guard in dealing with a riot. According to the recollection of Deputy Superintendent Nichols, the Detroit Police Department did not have a "cordial" relationship with the State Police, although there is no reason to think that the department questioned the professional competence of the troopers. Girardin and others did, however, have serious reservations about the effectiveness of the Guard as a riot control agency. As a reporter, Girardin had seen the Guardsmen in action on more than one occasion, and he was "scared stiff" that there "would be a slaughter if they came in." The city administration may also have been concerned that the State Police and the Guard were "all white."[41]

Detroit's reluctance to seek state aid is further explained by the commitment of the mayor and the police commissioner to a policy of restraint in dealing with the disturbance on Twelfth Street. Restraint, after all, had worked in the Kercheval disturbance and had gained Detroit national acclaim. Ignoring the fact that restraint had proved effective on that occasion because it was backed up by a massive police presence and police control of the streets, Girardin believed that the same "walk soft[ly]" strategy would be effective on Twelfth Street even though the police were heavily outnumbered by the rioters. Rather than relying on the inapplicable Kercheval precedent, Detroit should have looked to the more nearly analogous Watts riot, which the Detroit police had carefully studied, and the Newark riot, too recent for Detroit to have examined in detail, in both of which a policy of restraint had failed. "We'd have been a lot better off if we never had the Kercheval incident," a member of Girardin's staff ruefully remarked. "We'd have gone on Twelfth Street and cleaned it up fast."[42] Like generals who are always fighting the last war, the Detroit police were fighting an earlier riot on July 23.

Although it is hazardous to predict the outcome of different riot control strategies and although strategies that succeeded in one riot failed in another,[43] most students of riot control procedures have agreed, in the words of Neil Smelser, that "vacillation on the part of police authorities in deciding to utilize force tends to encourage the spread of disorder." As Ralph Conant explained in 1971, "the presence of police who do not exert control encourages the acceptance of deviant behavior [looting, burning] as normal," which is precisely what happened in Detroit. Following a study of riots occurring during the years 1964–68, David Boesel concluded that "there were no cases where the early use of massive force was followed by widespread violence."[44]

In the Kercheval disturbance, it will be recalled, the police did not fire a shot, did not use tear gas, and made relatively few arrests. During the critical hours on July 23 when the mob gained control of the streets, the Detroit police did not fire a shot, did not use tear gas, and made few arrests. When these tactics came under attack, the police commissioner and the mayor not only justified them by the Kercheval precedent but also claimed that the police could not have used other tactics safely because they were so heavily outnumbered. This was certainly true at 4:00 A.M., when the blind pig raid was underway, but by 11:00 A.M., with the situation still not fully out of control, there were 543 lieutenants, sergeants, and patrolmen on duty in the riot area, probably about two hundred of them on the street, and there were 1,177 police officers on duty throughout the city. James Bannon, the inspector in charge of intelligence at the time and later deputy chief of the department, rejected the numbers argument as the cause for restraint. "Oh, that's bullshit," he snapped in response. That explanation, he insisted, was a "subsequent rationalization of the decision that was made not to allow the police to do anything. . . . [I]t was a cover-up on all of our parts" for having "screwed up." As Bannon viewed the matter, the resources were available to the police by late Sunday morning for them to have gained control of the streets. Whether outnumbered or not, the then secretary-director of the city's civil rights agency declared, "you're not supposed to wait until the town's burning" to put down a riot even though that necessarily means hurting people. "Because there was no attempt to secure, if you will," the Detroit Urban League's (DUL) Roy Levy Williams later declared, "a lot more destruction was done."[45]

Whether or not Bannon and others who have made the same point are correct, the Cavanagh-Girardin defense of police inaction is vitiated by the fact that had numbers been the cause for police restraint, the city could have called in the State Police and the National Guard many hours before it took those steps. Girardin later admitted that he had made "a mistake in judgment" and that he should have called for the Guard at 7:00 A.M. He conceded that he had been hoping for a "miracle" that would enable the city to repeat its Kercheval success.

"If we had put more men in sooner," Davids told a Michigan Senate committee, "we could have controlled the situation." Schnipke agreed, contending that the situation had "bloomed too much" before Detroit sought the Guard's aid on July 23. It is possible that had the Guard arrived in force in the daytime, before the riot was fully out of control, the sheer number of law enforcement personnel on the streets would have overawed the rioters. "The solution for effective riot control," Schnipke correctly stated, "lies in getting sufficient strength at the scene before it gets out of control." As it turned out, the lateness of the Guard's arrival and the manner in which it was then used nullified the impact of numbers.[46] The way the Guardsmen behaved in the streets under these circumstances had an aggravating rather than a calming effect on the riot.

It is hard to know in assessing police behavior on July 23 and the city's delay in calling for state aid whether policy was determined by the mayor or his police commissioner or the two of them together. Most likely Girardin deferred to the mayor, whose reputation was at stake. Those familiar with the relationship of the two men were aware that Girardin, who had been the mayor's executive secretary, was "intensely loyal" to Cavanagh. Girardin "did everything the mayor wanted him to do," Richard Marks recalled. Too much can be made of this point, however. If Girardin was responsive to the mayor's wishes regarding the use of force on July 23, it was not because he subordinated his own judgment to Cavanagh's but because he agreed with the policy of restraint.[47]

No aspect of the "walk soft[ly]" strategy of July 23 became more a subject of contention than the failure of the police to use firearms against looters and other violators of the law. Although the Committee on Means of Handling Civil Disturbances had recommended in 1965, as we have seen, that the Police Department make "a firm policy determination" regarding the "control of criminal looting" in a riot as well as the use of firearms for "other than self protection," no such "firm policy" had been formulated. Police officers, to be sure, were authorized by state law and the *Police Manual* to use their firearms to prevent the escape of someone committing a felony like breaking and entering, and there were standing orders in the department permitting officers to use "all necessary force" to prevent looting and rioting and to protect life and property. Despite the massive lawbreaking on July 23, however, the first shooting and wounding of a looter by the police, according to the Headquarters Command Post Activity Log, did not occur until 10:15 P.M. on July 23.[48]

Although there were reports in Detroit that the mayor or the police commissioner had ordered the police not to use their firearms, neither had issued such an order. The decision was made by lieutenants, sergeants, and individual patrolmen on the street, but, as Girardin noted, "restraint" was "a basic part of the training and procedure" of Detroit police officers.[49]

Police at the scene of the riot on July 23 were under the impression that they were not to use firearms. They assumed that this was departmental policy, and they feared that they would have been charged with brutality had they used their weapons. On July 24 at 12:45 P.M. the chief inspector of the department notified police that they were to "use discretion" in shooting looters, the only instruction on the subject the police received during the riot. It is unlikely that such an instruction would have been issued had the police understood their role in this regard from the outset. In the Watts and Newark riots, as in Detroit, the police were confused at the outset as to how they were to respond to looting and rioting and interpreted the lack of clear direction from the top as tantamount to an order not to fire. It is safe to dismiss the allegation that, in acting as they did, the police were seeking to "retaliate" against and discredit a city administration that had refused to meet their salary demands before the riot and had suspended some of them during the blue flu episode.[50]

Had Girardin or the mayor disagreed with the no-use-of-firearms policy, they could, of course, have issued an order to the contrary. Cavanagh, who had arranged to receive half-hourly reports from a Neighborhood Conservation worker on Twelfth Street, praised the police for not having used their weapons, and as late as midnight on July 23 did not go beyond saying that the police could fire if their lives were endangered. Noting that the police had reacted to the Kercheval disorder without "going in there swinging" and that there were large numbers of women and children in the streets in the disturbance area on July 23, Girardin equated the shooting of looters with murder and contended that the police would have been "massacred" on the first day of the riot had they used firearms. "My men are police officers not public executioners," the commissioner stated. Quite apart from Girardin's conflation of vigorous law enforcement with the kind of brutality that might have invited retaliation and his fallacious assumption that shooting meant shooting to kill — the vast majority of those shot during the riot were not killed — it was not just numbers that explains the nonuse of firearms by the police on July 23. "It cannot be overstressed," Hubert Locke later wrote, that restraint was "a deliberate policy decision, dictated not only by the paucity of personnel but also by a desire not to respond in a manner that would subsequently subject the department to charges of inhumaneness or brutality." Just after the riot, however, Locke told the Michigan Commission on Crime, "There's just no gentle way to quell a riot; when you are at war people get hurt."[51]

The Police Department was as unwilling to authorize the use of tear gas as the use of firearms, even though "riot control authorities" viewed the use of nonlethal chemical agents such as tear gas as "the single most valuable and effective type of middle-range weapons in controlling civil disorders." The FBI riot manual characterized such weapons as not only "the most effective" but also "the most humane means of achieving temporary neutralization of a mob with a minimum of personal injury." Maryland's adjutant general informed the Kerner Commission that tear gas could "stop any looting." Police departments, however, were either unwilling or unprepared to use tear gas in riot situations: they resorted to its use in only four of the twenty-four disorders examined by the Kerner Commission.[52]

Detroit's riot plan provided for the use of gas, but the Police Department did not order its employment during the early morning hours of July 23 when the police were so badly outnumbered. Shortly before 2:00 P.M. the police on Twelfth Street requested permission to use gas, but the superintendent specifically forbade its employment. Girardin attributed the failure to use gas primarily to wind conditions and the population density of the Twelfth Street riot zone. He pointed particularly to wind conditions during the afternoon of July 23, noting that the wind velocity at that time would probably have dispersed "an even massive concentration" of gas. The most appropriate time for gas to have been used, however, would have been between 7:00 A.M. and noon, when the rioters were so much more numerous than the police. At 10:00 A.M., the wind velocity was 6.9 miles per hour, and at 1:00 P.M., just before the police on the street requested permission to use gas, the velocity had risen to 9.2 miles per hour, the average figure for the day as a whole. There were hours during the day, as at 4:00 P.M., when the use of tear gas would have been problematical, but during most of the day wind conditions should not have deterred its use.[53]

As an additional reason for not using tear gas, Girardin explained that the "massive doses" required to cover the affected area would have seeped into dwellings on densely packed Twelfth Street, bringing more people into the streets to challenge the police. Girardin also claimed that for tear gas to be effective there had to be a mass of people confronting the police, but that was precisely the state of affairs during the critical morning hours of July 23. Locke, by contrast, has maintained that tear gas had sometimes proved "useless" when employed to disperse large crowds. Police using gas would, of course, have had to wear gas masks, which would have limited their visibility, another reason offered by Girardin and Locke for the decision to forgo employment of the weapon.[54]

One suspects that the reasons the Police Department offered for not using tear gas, although not without some validity, were largely rationalizations after the fact. Bannon has suggested that the department's pre-riot experience with gas had "not been very favorable" and that this had led the police to discount its value even though it probably could have been used successfully on July 23. General Simmons contended that the police did not have enough gas masks to permit them to use gas. And a black police officer, who believed tear gas could have been effectively used, told the Kerner Commission that on at least one occasion the weapon was not employed because no lieutenant was on the scene to supervise its use, as regulations required.[55]

Once again following the Kercheval precedent, the police made very few arrests during the early hours of the riot. In the Tenth Precinct, where the riot centered on July 23, the police made fourteen arrests between 8:00 A.M. and noon and only an additional nine arrests between noon and 2:00 P.M. The police, a *Michigan Chronicle* columnist reported, apprehended only those who "flouted their goods in the cops' faces or taunted them." "Even the looters," the columnist reported, "asked each other, 'why aren't the police arresting us?' " Not until 7:00 P.M., by which time the riot was completely out of control, did the police begin making large-scale arrests. Locke attributed the limited number of arrests at the riot's outset to the small number of police on the street and to the need to avoid arrests that might have led to a "violent" reaction by onlookers or the arrestees themselves. Girardin remarked that, although he realized "you had to be tough," he thought selective arrests preferable to mass arrests as a riot control tactic.[56]

It cannot be proved that a firmer police response during the initial seven or eight hours of the riot would have suppressed the disorder or, at least, brought it to a close with fewer deaths, injuries, and property destruction than actually occurred. We cannot be certain how the police would have applied force had they been permitted to do so at the riot's outset, nor can we be absolutely sure how the rioters would have reacted to the early use of force. Some rioters undoubtedly would have been killed and others injured, but had the riot been halted by the early use of force, as other riots were, there would have been fewer deaths and injuries than resulted from the prolongation of the disturbance. What is certain is that the policy of restraint proved to be a conspicuous failure. As eye-witnesses and participants testified, to quote a Twelfth Street resident, "it started because the police just stood there when the looting started." He would have stopped, one looter said, if a policeman had "pulled a gun"; but the police, he thought, "seemed to be enjoying seeing 12th Street tore down." One arrestee later reported that he had carried a transistor radio so that he could learn if the presumed order not to shoot had been rescinded. When Richard L. Simmons, assistant director of the Mayor's Committee for Human Resources Development (MCHRD) and a member of the Summer Task Force (STF), walked on Twelfth Street at 7:30 A.M. on July 23, he thought the situation was under control. Then, however, he reported, word spread that the police were not shooting looters, and, hearing this, "the youngsters had a field day." Police restraint, a *Chronicle* columnist stated, made Detroit "a looter's paradise."

When the police pulled up to one store being looted, the looters started to flee, but an eleven-year-old youngster told them that they need have no fear. "They [police] won't shoot," he said. "The mayor said they aren't supposed to 'shoot.' " A looter emerging from a bar with a basket of liquor bottles told a policeman, "Watcha gonna do about it whitey pig?" and another looter said to the same officer, "You can't do anything to me white man. Black power." The mob realized that it was "in charge" on Twelfth Street and concluded that the police had accepted that fact. By failing at the outset to increase the "mobilization costs" of the rioters, to use the phrasing of Charles Tilly in the model he provides of collective action leading from mobilization to revolution, public authorities facilitated the looting and burning that they were eventually able to halt only by substantially raising the cost of such behavior.[57]

John Nichols and Richard Marks thought that Girardin had been unduly influenced by black leaders in urging a policy of police restraint. It is true that some prominent blacks, like state Senator Coleman Young, defended the police behavior on July 23. Most black leaders, however, the black middle class, and even many Twelfth Street residents criticized the police toleration of looting and arson. Girardin, indeed, recalled that black leaders who had regularly complained about police brutality now wanted force used against "those awful criminals." The executive secretary of the Detroit branch of the National Association for the Advancement of Colored People, Robert Tindal, expressed concern about the "restrained" police response to looting. The police should have used tear gas and gone in "with all the power that they could," remarked black councilman Nicholas Hood. "It Could Have Been Stopped," the city's black newspaper, the *Michigan Chronicle*, declared in a banner headline in its first issue after the beginning of the riot. "Did the police just write off 12th Street?" asked Longworth Quinn, the newspaper's editor and general manager. In its next issue the *Chronicle* hastened to state that when it had called for prompt police action, it had not meant the use of "undue force or shoot[ing] to kill."[58]

Black merchants on Twelfth Street who saw their stores being looted while the police looked on were "highly critical" of the police and the "unmolested vandalism" that had occurred. The black president of the Twelfth Street Businessmen's Association believed that the police could have restored order with fewer casualties than eventually resulted by the "use of fire power" in a "controlled manner."[59]

The *New York Times* found that anger among blacks for the failure of the police to have cracked down on the rioters at the outset was "widespread." "If they had started shooting the first few hours," a black United Automobile Workers official declared, "it wouldn't have lasted a day. When west side blacks were asked in a postriot survey how the police could have stopped the riot, they gave such answers as, "They should have been stricter at the beginning," "Shoot first and ask questions later," and "If the Police had used firearms and let them know they really meant business they would have stop[ped] and went home or some place."[60]

When the Sindlinger Corporation conducted a telephone poll of Detroiters of both races on July 26, it found that 90 percent of them believed the riot could have been halted had the police been given more authority at its outset. A modified probability sample survey of Twelfth

Street blacks conducted just after the riot revealed that 77 percent of the respondents thought the police had "waited too long" before moving into the riot area. When asked why the police had been unable to control the riot during its early stages, two-thirds of the respondents agreed that the police had not been "allowed to use enough force," and only one-third thought the police had acted as they did because they were "outnumbered by the crowds." In another postriot survey of blacks living in the riot areas of both the west and east side, 68 percent of the respondents thought the police should have "acted more firmly" in dealing with the riot, but only 10 percent of the random probability sample believed that the policy of firmness should have included the shooting of looters.[61]

Although Cavanagh and Girardin called attention to police officers who agreed with the policy of restraint, they were describing a small minority of the police force and of those on duty on Twelfth Street on July 23.[62] Echoing Paul Donley, "inspectors with long tenure" complained "bitterly" that the riot had gotten "out of hand" because the police had not been permitted to "shoot" when looting began. A ranking officer, who said that he had repeatedly but vainly requested permission at police headquarters to "let us do something here," maintained that city officials had "gambled—and lost—that a softer approach would slow down the crowd."[63]

Newsmen reported that the policy of restraint of July 23 had left policemen on Twelfth Street "embarrassed," "disgusted," and "confused." The *Detroit Free Press* received unsolicited phone calls of complaint from police officers. "I watched them loot for four hours straight," one such caller stated, "but I had orders not to interfere. We were told," he claimed, "not to open fire—not even to return fire." This seems to have been a rather general view, a Romney aide declaring that, "without exception," the police with whom he had been in contact were critical of what they believed was a decision not to shoot looters who failed to halt when told to do so. There were similar complaints about restraints on making arrests. "Everybody felt we could have done more," one policeman stated.[64]

Quite apart from its failure as a riot control tactic, the policy of restraint led, as we shall see, to unrestrained police behavior once the policy was abandoned. For policemen trained to act when crimes were committed in their presence, the policy of restraint in the face of so many crimes—more in one day than he had witnessed in his previous two years on the force according to one officer—was "an extraordinarily stressful and humiliating experience." "One cannot expect police officers to be ordered to stand by while looting is going on," Ralph Conant declared in his study of the riots of this era, "and then act with restraint when they are turned loose to stop it." "Go help yourself, you nigger!" the police declare to a looter in *Them*. "Soon as we get the word everyone is going to get mowed down, so help yourself now, get it while the getting is good!" Approximately 90 percent of the white police and 86 percent of the black police in a survey of 286 randomly selected police officers indicated that they had been "bothered" by being compelled "to stand by and watch people loot, watch people smile at TV cameras and so on and not be able to do much to stop it."[65]

For all its planning, the Police Department was simply unprepared to cope with a riot of the magnitude that the city experienced beginning on July 23. The stress in training on riot formations, for example, proved irrelevant to the control of the roving bands of looters and firebombers that replaced the large crowds that had formed during the first half day or so of the riot. Also, although the riot plan recognized that looting, arson, and sniping had become riot tactics, the department was uncertain as to how to react. Like other cities, Detroit was also unprepared for the kind of "team effort" riot control required. Normally, police officers interacted with the public in situations involving individuals or small groups. In enforcing the law in such circumstances, police were trained to exercise their individual discretion, to act autonomously. "A collective behavior situation" like a riot, however, required "disciplined personnel . . . organized and trained to work as members of a team under a highly unified command and control system," with orders promulgated from above regarding the use of "proper force." As the failure of Girardin and the superintendent to issue orders on July 23 on such a critical matter as the use of firearms indicates, the Detroit department found it difficult to shift from the normal model of police behavior to a "collective behavior" model.[66]

From inspectors on down, police personnel complained about the "lack of clear decisions from the top administration" during the riot. The "people upstairs," a black officer on duty on July 23 complained, failed to issue the necessary orders regarding police behavior. "Everyone," he said, "waited for everyone else" to issue an order. Part of the blame for this must certainly rest with the police commissioner. As Damon Keith noted, Girardin was "as nice a human being" as there could be, but he could not "make a decision and would not tackle a problem." Keith, consequently, bypassed the commissioner during the riot and dealt directly with the mayor. Concluding that Girardin "didn't know too much about what was going on," Romney relied on Deputy Superintendent Nichols for his riot briefings.[67]

To compound the problems of command at the riot's outset, there were no ranking officers on the scene to make the critical decisions that the rapidly developing situation required. "A major lesson of the 1967 disorders," the Kerner Commission concluded, was that it required "a seasoned senior officer to make the all-important initial assessments and decisions" to contain a riot. That "seasoned officer" was not present on Twelfth Street on July 23. Nichols and Central District Inspector Anthony Bertoni wanted "to go to the scene," but Girardin insisted that they were needed at headquarters.[68]

The effort of the police to cope with the riot was plagued from the start by insufficient and inadequate equipment and faulty intelligence. Although the 479 shotguns and 137 rifles the Police Department had on hand on July 23 were sufficient for "the ordinary police function," the supply was insufficient for a riot in which more than two thousand police were out on the streets at one time. The shotguns, moreover, proved to be "inaccurate over any distance" and hence useless against snipers, "a piece of junk," one officer said. Short of rifles, the police were forced to borrow hundreds of these weapons from gun stores and pawnshops and to purchase additional ammunition. The police, at the same time, delayed much too long in acting to deny rioters easy access to guns. It was not until 4:40 P.M. on July 23 that the department notified all commanding officers to remove all guns from gun shops in their commands. Hundreds of guns had been stolen by that time.[69]

Since the department had a "severe shortage" of scout cars, it had to borrow unmarked cars without radio equipment from other city departments. It did not have a sufficient supply of army-style helmets designed to protect the wearer against bullets, and it had to turn to private companies to borrow five armored personnel carriers, which proved invaluable as "lead vehicle[s] for tactical formations" and in combating snipers. Lacking airplanes of its own, it had to rent a fixed-wing plane once it discovered that equipment of this sort could serve as an excellent means of observation and as a deterrent against rooftop sniping. As more and more police were assigned to riot duty, the department discovered that it did not have enough walkie-talkies for police officers to communicate with one another. Although its heralded PREP system proved "invaluable" and gave the police, the State Police, and the National Guard "a common communication capability," the battery life of the radios was too short and the noise level too high, and the sets were also large and cumbersome.[70]

Short of equipment, the Police Department, as we have seen, was also short of manpower and included few blacks in its ranks. "Where are the Negro policemen?" was the question on Twelfth Street on July 23, according to the *Michigan Chronicle*. A black neighborhood worker said that he had seen a black sergeant have a calming effect on the crowd that morning, but the *Detroit News* reported that when a black sergeant drove down Twelfth Street that day and told the crowd to disperse, they pelted his car with missiles, smashing the windshield.

As the contrasting reports of the presence of a black sergeant might indicate, there is conflicting evidence regarding the rioters' reaction to black police officers. Cyrus Vance noted that "a sampling of informal opinion" in the riot areas revealed "a strong conviction" that more black policemen and Guardsmen would have made a difference. By contrast, an informal poll by army counterintelligence agents on July 31 indicated that black residents were more fearful of black than of white officers.

The black police officers were "some of the greatest head crackers," the executive director of Wayne County Suburban Legal Services declared. It will be recalled that about 75 percent of Detroit black respondents in the fifteen-city survey did not think that there was much difference in the way black and white police treated them.[71]

Seeming to believe that the presence of black police would make a difference, the Police Department, at 5:30 P.M. on July 23, instructed all precincts to send black officers to the riot scene to replace white officers. A black officer, however, who had been on Twelfth Street on July 24 was then assigned to guard duty, the fate, he recalled, of some other black officers as well. "I think the effort was to keep black officers off the street," he asserted. He assumed that this was because the department feared that black officers would refuse to take action against black rioters.[72] The evidence regarding the reaction of black rioters to black police and the role of black police in the riot is thus conflicting, but it is safe to say that the massively white character of the Detroit police force, a force mistrusted in the black ghetto in any event, did not make it any easier for the police to deal with the July riot.

It was, to be sure, no easy matter to be a black policeman during the riot. "You had to make decisions very carefully," a black police officer noted shortly after the riot. When, for example, he carried a crippled white woman from her burning apartment, a black observing the action asked him what side he was on. The black policeman "started to swing" but caught himself. One black policeman later recalled being shot at by a fellow white officer during the riot. On another occasion, when the same black officer protested the harassment by white officers of an elderly black on his way to work during curfew hours, one of the white officers said to his black colleague, "Whose side are you on anyway?"[73]

Like many police departments, the Detroit department had not been successful in gathering "street" or "tactical" intelligence. At about 6:00 A.M. on July 23 the western district inspector dispatched two young black plainclothesmen to the Twelfth Street area to gather intelligence. Additional intelligence was gathered by the Central Intelligence Bureau of the Police Department and the STF. Cavanagh later noted that some of the intelligence he received was "quite bad," and this appears to have been particularly true during the first day of the riot, when the police effort was hampered by "sketchy and overly rosy" information. Nichols later recalled that he received more useful information during the riot from two black detectives who had once been on his staff than from regular intelligence channels.[74]

Seeking support for his riot control policies after having summoned the State Police and the National Guard, Cavanagh at 5:00 P.M. met at the Tenth Precinct station with about seventy-five black leaders and Twelfth Street representatives. The message that came through "loud and clear" from the group was, "Do everything you have to do, just bring peace and order back to our city." Not only did a large majority approve the use of the State Police and the Guard, but there was also similar support for calling in the army should that prove necessary. Those like Charles Colding who opposed a "militaristic response" to the riot "went unheard." There was also scant support for the suggestions that citizens be assigned to monitor the behavior of the police and the Guard and that "Citizen Peace Patrols" be formed.

The Tenth Precinct community meeting revealed a sharp split between the black leadership and a minority of militant youths. As the leadership saw it, the rioters were "a completely lawless element," "a bunch of no good, lazy hoodlums," or youngsters "getting out of hand," although Robert Potts observed that "the young cats" were "getting support from the other guys." Turning on the leadership, a young black steelworker from Twelfth Street declared, "You leaders have failed the black community. . . . The black leadership brought it [the riot] on the black people." One youth thought that what was happening in the streets was "a form of rebellion," but the militant Colding, who said that he would have supported "a real revolution," thought the disturbance was "ridiculous" and did no one any good.[75]

It was probably after the community meeting and the rejection of the monitoring suggestion that Damon Keith called Arthur Johnson to say, "Art, we've got to have some blacks at police headquarters." Keith thought that he, as cochairman of the state Civil Rights Commission, and Johnson, then its deputy director, should be present to inject a black perspective into the decision making in addition to that provided by Hubert Locke. They remained at police headquarters off and on for the remainder of the riot, even sleeping there for a time, and consulted regularly with Cavanagh, Romney, Girardin, and Nichols.[76]

The rejection of additional peace patrols at the Tenth Precinct meeting did not negate the fact that efforts were underway throughout the day by one party or another to calm the riotous crowd. The MCHRD, at a staff meeting at 9:00 A.M., decided to put a "containment plan" into effect. MCHRD staffers contacted community people, preachers, and officials of civic organizations and block clubs to solicit their assistance. Many clergymen promised in response to make "calming statements" at church services that day. Staff members and community aides went out into the streets to gather intelligence for the STF and to dispel rumors. MCHRD personnel contacted Neighborhood Youth Corps enrollees to urge them not to become involved in the disturbance, counsel that the enrollees heeded.[77]

The MCHRD efforts were supplemented by school community agents, who went out into the disturbance areas seeking to keep school children off the streets, by staff members of the Commission on Community Relations, and, at the request of the mayor, Neighborhood Service Organization personnel. The head of the Urban Youth Program of the YMCA of Metropolitan Detroit and some of his aides were "partially successful" in getting their contacts, youths aged sixteen to twenty-one, to "cool it." The next day the youths with whom YMCA workers were in touch promised that there would be "no more burning" on their part. Radio station WJLB, primarily directed at blacks, canceled its usual Sunday evening programs to permit popular disc jockey Martha Jean to plead for calm in what the *Detroit News* described as "a one-woman peace campaign." The station also made time available to black ministers and politicians for the same purpose. It remained on the air all night broadcasting messages from black leaders. Without all these efforts, so largely ignored in the literature, it is possible that the rioting, bad as it was, would have been even worse. One black minister, the Reverend Albert Cleage, refused to add his voice to those seeking to bring calm to the turbulent streets of Detroit. Asked by a radio station to urge the rioters to desist, he refused, saying that he had been telling whites for years to do something that would have made it possible to "cool" it.[78]

It is unlikely that a temporary news blackout on July 23 deterred very many individuals from going out to Twelfth Street who might otherwise have done so. At 9:00 A.M. Keith phoned the general manager of radio station WJR and asked him to contact other radio and TV stations to request that they, like WJR, keep news of the riot off the air for a few hours or "to be calm and as quiet as possible" in describing what was going on and to refer to it as a "civil disturbance," not a riot. Keith phoned the *Detroit News* and the *Detroit Free Press* with a similar request. Hoping that the riot could be quickly contained, Keith feared that publicity would attract "troublemakers, racists and professional agitators" and, if the news were carried nationally, would draw "nuts" to Detroit from all over the nation. By the time Keith made his first call, Detroit radio stations had routinely reported a disturbance on Twelfth Street, and the ABC radio outlet in the city had transmitted a voice report, at 8:55 A.M., to its network, which aired the story nationally, "the first newsbreak to the nation" about the riot.

The Detroit radio stations observed a moratorium on riot news until late in the afternoon of July 23. The first TV report of the riot was put out by a Windsor, Canada, television station at 2:00 P.M. on July 23, and TV reports became more detailed after that. One TV station that day falsely reported that a policeman had been killed in the riot, and another relayed an anonymous tip that the riot was spreading to the suburbs. Since July 23 was a Sunday, the first newspaper account of the riot did not hit the streets until 8:15 P.M. that day.[79]

Despite efforts to achieve a news blackout, blacks in Detroit learned about the riot through "informal sources of communication" and the "communications chain" in predominantly black areas. By noon, according to a postriot survey, 43 percent of the city's blacks had heard about the riot, and 94 percent knew about it before the day was out. Only 28 percent of blacks in the riot area and only 25.5 percent of black riot arrestees found out about the riot from radio and TV, the remainder depending on interpersonal communication and direct experience.[80]

Although the news blackout may have slightly reduced the flow of potential participants and spectators to the riot area, it also had an opposite effect: some people wandered into the riot zone who would have avoided the area had they been informed of the disturbance. Four women who attended a concert that afternoon were "amazed, shocked and terrified" to discover that they were passing through a riot area on their way home. One of them complained bitterly to Governor Romney that they would have remained at home that day had they not been kept ignorant of the situation.[81]

The question of what news to disseminate about the riot became an issue for the city government itself on July 23 because more than thirty-four thousand persons were attending a doubleheader at Tiger Stadium that afternoon. Shortly before the second game ended, the mayor authorized the police to make a public announcement at the ball park regarding the streets spectators should avoid on their way home but without explaining the reason.[82]

By the time the announcement was made at Tiger Stadium, the riot had spread as far west as Seven Mile and Livernois and east of Woodward as well. During the remaining hours of the evening the riot grew in intensity. Ordered to arrest looters, the police began apprehending them in droves. Dexter, Linwood, and Grand River on the west side were "ablaze"; and according to a local contact of the Community Relation Service of the Department of Justice, there was "mass confusion" among policemen and firemen, and the citizens were in "despair." By midnight the area affected by the riot extended from the Detroit River on the south to Seven Mile on the north and from Livernois on the west side to Connor on the east side. An estimated eleven thousand persons had been out on the streets, about eight thousand of them on the west side.[83]

Typical entries in the police log after 5:00 P.M. were: "Window breaking on Grand River"; "large gangs forming . . . at Grand River and Oakman"; "3,000 people looting at Oakland and Westminister"; "Hamilton and Lawrence, Monterey and Linwood, Fire Dept. in trouble"; "Mack and McClellan, throwing fire bombs in market"; "Fire and looting at Jefferson and Rohns"; and "Livernois and Florence . . . shooting at officers." The first sniper fire, directed at a helicopter, occurred at 9:00 P.M. according to the log, and there were additional reports of sniping and of shooting at firemen later in the evening.[84]

The number of "incidents" reported to the police, an incident being defined as "a distinct riot-related occurrence mentioned in a police radio message," increased from 28 between noon and 1:00 P.M. to a high of 182 between 11:00 P.M. and midnight. Of 960 riot-related messages received between 10:45 A.M. and midnight, 495 were looting reports, 90 were calls to assist police officers and 28 to assist firemen, 45 were sniper and shooting reports, and 22 were "gun carrying reports." In a separate compilation, federal government sources listed 5,270 incidents for the day, the number increasing from 98 between 5:00 and 6:00 A.M. to a high of 626 between 6:00 and 7:00 P.M. The incident rate and the number of riot-related messages provided some indication of the degree of riot activity even though the police radio carried a good many unfounded reports.[85]

Looting was the most conspicuous form of riot activity on July 23, several hundred stores falling prey to looters. "Twelfth Street," a reporter remarked, "became an eight-block long supermarket with no check-out counters." Looters "grabbed everything they could. Anywhere they could." According to an MCHRD worker at the scene and others, the initial looters were "pimps and hustlers—the Cadillac and silk-suit crowd." Then, in the second wave, came teenagers and young adults, but by evening, the looters, some of them having drunk their booty and become intoxicated, comprised a cross section of the community, not just "kids and hoodlums" but also respectable and middle-class adults. Cars full of looters drove through the area, and there were many accounts of cars and pick-up trucks loaded with loot. Youngsters of tender age rode bicycles with loot under their arms or inside their shirts. In the carpet department of one store, looters provided "customer service," cutting carpets to size to accommodate the requests of other looters.[86]

Observing the looting of the Starbrite Market on Twelfth and Atkinson, Arthur Weiseger, a DUL housing assistant, heard such comments as "Help yourself baby, gets what you want, Whitey has had it all but now it's our turn." Once the store had been emptied, someone set it afire, and the blaze consumed the market and a black-owned drugstore. Some looters, Weiseger concluded, were "inexperienced," but some were "pros." The inexperienced, he observed, "suffered glass cuts on legs, arms and hands." The pros wore or carried "leather gloves" and "hard soled shoes" and were the first to depart when the police arrived. At Twelfth and Gladstone, he saw a group of looters "shopping at leisure" in a corner market and "exchanging light banter with friends who asked for specific items."[87]

Although the number of fires the rioters set on July 23 was well below the total for the next day, they presented a formidable problem for the city's smallish Fire Department. Whereas Newark had one thousand fire fighters to cover an area of 16 square miles, Detroit's seventeen hundred firemen had to protect a city of 139 square miles. Once fires became a problem on Twelfth Street, Chief Charles J. Quinlan ordered the city's forty black fire fighters to join fire companies in the riot zone and designated Captain Marcene Taylor, a black, as acting battalion chief for the area. It turned out, however, that the crowd subjected the black firemen to even more verbal abuse than white firemen. "We seem to be their favorite target," Taylor reported. As firemen responded to fires raging up and down Twelfth Street and Linwood, the rioters began to pelt them with missiles. Since the police, despite the riot plan's call for a "rifle-shotgun guard" for fire fighters, were unable to provide needed protection, Quinlan ordered his men to withdraw from the scene if they came under attack. At 4:30 P.M. the firemen were forced to quit a one-hundred block area west of Twelfth Street.[88]

By late evening on July 23 the Fire Department, having committed 153 pieces of equipment to the riot area, had only four engine companies available to combat fires in the rest of the city. Although Detroit did not have a mutual aid fire pact with surrounding communities in the metro-politan area, Quinlan called on neighboring fire departments for assis-tance, and Governor Romney later directed fire departments in the state to dispatch all available equipment to Detroit.[89]

The 209 fire alarms on July 23 were about double the usual number for a July day. Raging out of control for blocks on Twelfth Street, the fires spread from stores to private dwellings and forced some families to spend the night outside their burned homes. "Thick black smoke and cinders rained down," a black *Detroit News* reporter who lived in the area observed, "at times so heavy they blocked out the vision of homes 20 feet away." The smoke created by the fires made it appear that a good part of Detroit was ablaze. Romney told the Kerner Commission that when he flew over the city between 8:30 and 9:00 P.M., it looked to him like the west side "had been bombed." Arriving in Detroit that night, the syndicated columnist Jimmy Breslin found the air "bitter with smoke" and the sky "a red glow." Talking to four black youths outside a burning drugstore, he said, "Bad fire." One youth answered, "Good fire. . . . The toothpaste burnin' now," and the four boys laughed.[90]

The police made 1,030 arrests after 5:00 A.M. on July 23, 653 of them after 8:00 P.M. In their confrontation with the rioters, the police suffered twenty-eight injuries that day, the Guard and the State Police one injury each. Most police injuries were the result of missiles thrown by rioters. Although only thirteen civilian injuries, mostly lacerations from broken glass, were reported to the Homicide Bureau, Detroit hospi-tals stated that they had treated more than two hundred individuals injured in the riot by midnight. Among persons treated in the emergency room of Detroit General Hospital that day, five had sustained gunshot wounds, and sixty, laceration and stab wounds. It is unclear, however, just how many of these injuries were riot-related. Seven newsmen were among the injured.[91]

Two persons injured on July 23 subsequently died, and two others found dead later had died on the riot's first day. When Krikor Messer-lian, a sixty-eight-year-old, white shoe repairman, saw looters removing clothes from the dry cleaning establishment next to his Linwood shop, he attacked them with a saber, cutting one of them. One youth said to his wounded companion, "I'll get the old man for you," and began beating Messerlian with a thirty-inch club. Messerlian, who sustained a skull fracture, a broken right forearm, a broken left hand, facial lacerations, and numerous bruises, died four days later. His assailant, Darryl McCurtis, a twenty-eight-year-old black who had arrived from Alabama only six weeks earlier, was tried for murder and sentenced to life imprisonment.[92]

The day before Messerlian's death, the badly burned bodies of two black men, Willie Hunter and Prince Williams, were found in the basement of a drugstore on Twelfth Street. Caught in the store when it was looted and set afire on July 23, they had died of carbon monoxide asphyxiation. The fourth death resulting from the rioting of July 23 was that of Sheren George, a twenty-eight-year-old white woman. She had been riding in a car with her husband and others on Woodward shortly before midnight when they were apparently blocked by a crowd of blacks beating a white male. A shot rang out that hit Mrs. George. She was rushed to Detroit General Hospital but did not survive. Her assailant was not discovered.[93]

City and state authorities took a series of actions toward the end of July 23 to cope with the escalating disorder. At 7:45 P.M., announcing that the situation was "critical" but "not out of control," Cavanagh proclaimed a 9:00 P.M. to 5:30 A.M. curfew. The mayor followed up the curfew notice at 9:30 P.M. by ordering the closing of all bars and theaters in the city. Following reports that gas stations were selling gasoline in "buckets and bottles," the mayor at 10:25 P.M. ordered the closing of the city's gas stations.[94]

Acting on authority granted by the Michigan Liquor Control Commission, Colonel Davids at 11:58 P.M. suspended the sale of liquor in Detroit and in the Highland Park and Hamtramck enclaves in the city. Finally, at midnight Romney declared a state of emergency applying to these three cities and also to Ecorse and River Rouge. The executive order accompanying the governor's proclamation forbade anyone other than law enforcement personnel to carry firearms, ammunition, explosives, or inflammable materials; closed all places of amusement and all places selling or dispensing alcoholic beverages; forbade the assemblage of more than five persons; and stipulated a 9:00 P.M. to 5:30 A.M. curfew that superseded the one announced by Cavanagh. Violations of the order under a 1945 Michigan law—Michigan, apparently, was the only state having a statute authorizing an emergency proclamation of this sort—constituted a misdemeanor, but the governor neglected to include the violation provision in his original order and consequently had to amend it the next day.[95]

The principal action the Detroit city government took on July 23 to supplement the efforts of its Police Department to quell the riot was, of course, to summon the State Police and National Guard to the city. The

State Police made every effort to bring as many troopers as possible into Detroit as rapidly as possible; by 9:10 P.M. 800 of the state's 1,459 troopers had been assigned to the city. After the troopers arrived in Detroit, some were assigned to Detroit police units, two troopers joining two police officers in a scout car. The troopers also escorted police buses, arrested looters, and tried to protect firemen. Although reasonably well prepared for their riot role, the troopers encountered both equipment and communications problems in carrying out their assignments.[96]

Girardin was highly critical of the slowness with which the Guard was able to deploy its forces on the streets of Detroit. Although the authorized strength of the Guard was approximately 10,000, 1,300 Guardsmen were involved in a six-month army training mission outside Michigan on July 23, and another 430 men were assigned to Nike missile sites. Of the remaining 8,270 Guardsmen, 4,300 were in the midst of a two-week training session at Camp Grayling, more than two hundred miles from Detroit, and the remainder were on inactive status throughout the state. As with other reinforcing Guard divisions, only the Selected Reserve Force (SRF) of the 46th Division, a brigade of 3,600 men, was at full strength in men and equipment. The remainder of the division was at about 50 percent strength. The SRF brigade and the 156th Signal Battalion, which were at their home stations when the riot began and had completed their summer training, were the first Guard units deployed in Detroit.[97]

At 5:00 P.M. 200 Guardsmen were sent to Central High School in the riot area, a designated assembly point in Operation Sundown. By midnight, eight hours after Detroit had asked for the Guard, only 859 soldiers had arrived at the Central High Command Post. Schnipke, however, had stated as part of the planning for Operation Sundown that the Guard would be able to bring 2,000 men to the two Detroit armories by the end of three hours after mobilization and that another 4,000 men could be assembled outside the Detroit metropolitan area by the end of eight hours. The National Guard, Girardin told the Kerner Commission, "threw a couple of generals [Moore and Simmons] down from Grayling" and told Detroit officials how many soldiers were on the way, but, said Girardin, "we could not find them on the streets." He complained that the Guard had "a great technique of holding people in reserve" even though "the town was burning."[98]

Not all of Girardin's criticisms of the Guard were justified. Like the Detroit police, many members of the SRF brigade were away from their homes on July 23. The unit, moreover, was without most of its vehicles, which had been used to move the remainder of the 46th Division to Grayling — the SRF had to rely on public transportation to get to Detroit. The governor did not order the mobilization of the Grayling Guardsmen until 10:50 P.M. When the status of these troops was changed from field training, a federal role, to state duty, they had to leave most of their equipment at Camp Grayling, and 225 men had to be left behind to secure this equipment. An additional 350 soldiers also remained behind to haul supplies to Detroit. Finally, there were more than 1,000 "Army Reserve fillers" assigned to the 46th Division for training who could not be mobilized for state duty. Since it took seven hours for a military convoy to move from Grayling to Detroit, it is hardly surprising that most of the Grayling contingent did not arrive in Detroit until the late morning hours of July 24. Although very critical of the Guard's behavior once it got to Detroit, the deputy commander of the army task force assigned to Detroit for riot duty nevertheless judged that the Guard had "executed a very professional and rapid movement" from Grayling.[99]

There was an additional delay after the Guard began arriving until it could be determined who was authorized to order its deployment. It was finally decided that this was the responsibility of Colonel Davids, who released the Guard for duty once Superintendent Reuter asked him to do so. Because of the deteriorating condition in the streets, Guardsmen were committed piecemeal, without any consideration for unit integrity, as rapidly as they became available. "They sliced us up like baloney," Simmons asserted. The initial pattern was for the police to form " 'integrated' patrols" consisting of fifteen Guardsmen and five or six police officers or state troopers and to dispatch them to where trouble had developed. Sometimes a small group of Guardsmen was sent out with a single policeman as escort. The presence of police officers with the Guard was necessary since the police knew the city, there was a desire to use the police communications system to the extent possible, and the Guard could not legally make arrests. Occasionally, however, Guardsmen operated without a police escort. Girardin knew that it was a "mistake" to use the Guard in this fragmented way but thought that he had no alternative considering "the way the city was going."[100]

As instructed by the governor, General Simmons ordered the Guard to use such force as was required to enforce the laws of Michigan. Guardsmen were instructed to return fire if fired upon and to halt looting by shooting "if necessary." "A tough old soldier," Simmons believed that the way to deal with rioters was to "hit 'em with everything you've got right away. As soon as a guy gets away with something," he said, "he'll do it again." If prospective looters knew they were going to be shot, he thought, they would be less likely to loot. This was Romney's view as well. "Violence and law breaking will not be condoned," he stated in ordering the Guard to Detroit. When he conferred with Cavanagh and Girardin at police headquarters Sunday night, he later told the Kerner Commission, he found them "overly optimistic" regarding what could be done to end the riot "without the application of minimum but necessary force." Unlike Girardin and Cavanagh, he thought that the shooting of fleeing looters and arsonists, but not shooting to kill, was required.[101]

"This thing has been brewing a long time," a National Guard officer asserted after the Guardsmen arrived in Detroit. "It's a shame. But if we have to have it out, let's have it out here. Let's have it out tonight."[102] The Guard, however, did not "have it out" that night, and the next day the governor and mayor concluded that the Detroit police, the State Police, and the Guard could not subdue the rioters without the assistance of the United States Army.

CHAPTER 8

"They Have Lost All Control in Detroit": July 24, 1967

In terms of criminal offenses reported to the Detroit Police Department, the hours between midnight and 5:00 A.M. on July 24 were the most violent of the entire Detroit riot.[1] It was during these hours that Governor George Romney first contacted Washington about the possible use of federal troops. For the remainder of the day the Detroit police, the National Guard, and the State Police sought in vain to quell the escalating disturbance while, behind the scenes, Romney engaged in labyrinthine negotiations with the Johnson administration that led, eventually, to the dispatch of army paratroopers to Detroit and their deployment on the streets of the city.

The temperature soared to 90° in Detroit on July 24, and it was an uncomfortably humid, breezeless day. The police log for the five hours after midnight carried reports of "rioting, looting, . . . burning," and sniping over a wide area of the city both east and west of Woodward. The spread of the riot to the lower east side led the police and the Guard to decide at 1:55 A.M. to set up a second field command post at Southeastern High School, and five minutes later Cavanagh called for a curtailment of business activity downtown that day.[2]

The Police Department's central district inspector reportedly said at 12:30 A.M. that the police were using firearms only to protect their lives and the lives of fire fighters but not to halt looting and firebombing. When Romney and Cavanagh were asked at a 3:00 A.M. press conference if police would fire at looters, Cavanagh hesitated to reply, but Romney responded, "fleeing felons are subject to being shot at." The orders to the Guard at that point were "to shoot to kill if fired upon, and to shoot any person seen looting," but Guardsmen needed permission from General Moore to fire fully automatic weapons. Later in the morning Cavanagh expressed a reluctance "to lay down [a] hard and fast rule" regarding use of firearms, saying that police officers had to use their "professional judgment" in this critical matter. Perhaps it was this that led to "the word that went through the Department," according to a reporter covering the riot, "that it was all right [for the police] to open fire." By evening the police, the Guard, and the State Police were all firing at fleeing looters.[3]

When Inspector James A. Cole arrived at noon to take charge of the Southeastern High command post, he received orders to stop the riot and enforce the law by whatever means necessary. He was not, however, briefed on any specific tactics to follow. He decided to deploy his men four to a car, four cars to a patrol unit, and to use the Guard to protect strategic points. His task was complicated by the fact that the telephones, riot guns, ammunition, helmets, and scout cars available to him were all in short supply, a problem that increasingly affected the riot control efforts of the department as a whole. Because of the shortage of weapons, the department requested police officers to use their own rifles and shotguns.[4]

At 9:28 A.M. the Seventh Precinct station came under sniper fire, and at 12:10 P.M. the police reported the situation as being "out of control" in that precinct and in the Fifth Precinct as well. Looting during the morning was described in police reports as "almost citywide." At 4:17 P.M. air intelligence reported twenty-three fires burning west of Woodward and six east of Woodward. There were rumors that rioters would make well-to-do blacks a target that night, and the Police Department advised the FBI that employers in the predominantly white northwestern part of the city were arming their employees to protect against looting. In the final two or three hours of the day sniping, whose incidence was exaggerated throughout the riot, appeared to be the major riot problem, as the police, Guardsmen, and state troopers were all reportedly pinned down by sniper fire; and two precinct stations, the Southeastern High command post, and at least three fire stations also came under attack. Tanks and armored personnel carriers rumbled through the streets to rescue law enforcement personnel reportedly immobilized by sniper fire. "It looks like Berlin in 1945," the mayor stated. By midnight, according to Hubert Locke, veteran police officers were "convinced that they were engaged in the worst urban guerrilla warfare witnessed in the United States in the twentieth century."[5]

July 24 was a day of confusion for law enforcement personnel. A rookie policeman recalled that the police were "piling in cars and patrolling up and down and up and down and hours of confusion—trained policemen—a bunch of them just doing whatever they wanted to. . . . We stopped lots of cars full of loot. Sometimes we took it away. Other times we arrested people. There was no reasonable approach to anything." Another police officer sent to Twelfth Street recalled that "the whole place was unbelievable. Rioters and looters, what looked like thousands, were running all over the place like they were crazy. . . . There was smoke and fire everywhere—burned out buildings in all directions." When a Romney aide visited police headquarters, he found "confusion throughout the building. The entire administrative apparatus of the Detroit Police Department and the city," he reported, "was in shambles."[6]

The confusion reached its height during the waning hours of July 24. A police source informed the FBI that the police and the Guard were firing at one another due to the darkness and "state of general confusion." Jimmy Breslin reported that one Guardsman was firing up a dumbwaiter shaft while a fellow Guardsman fired down the shaft. A trooper on Linwood fired his weapon at the same time as police officers in the vicinity were screaming for everyone to stop shooting. A law enforcement officer hollered that he had spotted a sniper or snipers on a roof, but a police car radio called on everyone to hold fire since the alleged snipers were State Police troopers. When an automobile came around the corner, Breslin reported, the police aimed their shotguns at it, and a black male staggered from the vehicle claiming he had been shot in the leg. He pulled down his pants to prove the point, and, despite a police order not to move, he started walking around the car, saying "Shoot me!" "The city is an asylum," Breslin concluded.[7]

The Detroit riot on July 24, like other major riots, began to take on the character of a "tandem riot." In this second phase of the riot, "control agents" responded to disorderly behavior in the streets by resorting to "official violence" against the rioters. Reinforced by the Guard and humiliated and frustrated by their "enforced passivity" and the successful challenge to their authority the previous day, the police sought to reestablish their "dominance and control" and "to teach the bastards a lesson." "The worm has turned," the executive director of Wayne County Suburban Legal Services heard a policeman say that night to a black lad riding a new bicycle. In Detroit, as in Watts and Newark, what had begun, to some degree, as a riot of blacks against police became, in some degree, "a riot of police against blacks," illustrating the point that "civil disorder is an emergent process very much dependent on the nature of the interaction between control agents and disturbance participants."[8]

The behavior of the police beginning on July 24 and their excessive use of physical force were the product of more than their desire for revenge. Working twelve-hour shifts, with scant rest between tours of duty, the police were fatigued—two police officers entered a looted furniture store at one point, rested on a sofa there, and then started chasing looters again. The police, furthermore, were "thrown off balance" by the sheer magnitude of the disorder, and they were apprehensive about the personal danger to which they were being exposed. "You're damn right I was scared," one policeman replied when asked in a later interview if he had been frightened during the riot.[9]

The "norms of [police] professionalism" were weakened, if not altogether eroded, by "the fear and rage building in those early riot hours," with the result that the racial attitudes of white police officers were increasingly expressed in behavior that would have been more restrained under normal conditions. He had not realized before, a *Detroit Free Press* reporter who covered the riot remarked, that "there are large numbers of Policemen who do not like Negroes." He heard one police officer say of blacks during the riot, "They are savages." Another *Free Press* reporter heard a policeman assert, "Those black son-of-a bitches. I'm going to get me a couple of them before this is over."[10]

Given their view of blacks as a privileged minority, it is not surprising that a sizable majority of white officers below the rank of inspector, as a survey revealed, did not see the riot as a "protest against unjust conditions" or the product of "social conditions of inequality." Like the white working-class community from which they largely came and like white police officers in other cities, white patrolmen tended to view the riot as caused by "agitators" and "conspiratorial groups," desire to get "something for nothing," "undisciplined self-interest," "lack of respect for law and order," and "temper of the times." Beliefs of this sort probably help to explain police behavior in the riot's second phase.[11]

Looking back on the "bad excesses" of some policemen during the riot, Ray Girardin explained, "Everybody's got a breaking point. . . . They don't resign from the human race when they join the police department. And it's a lousy job and considering their background and their training, they can blow up too. . . . [T]he police aren't supposed to; there [*sic*] not allowed to, but it's understandable that sometimes they do." The riot was surely one of those times — a black policeman, noting the conditions under which the police had been operating, recalled, "I'm black and I wanted to hit on someone by Monday, so how did they [white police] feel by Thursday?"[12]

When asked in the sample survey of 286 police officers after the riot why some police officers had treated "suspects" roughly during the riot, 53 percent of the white inspectors, 44 percent of the whites of other ranks, and 42 percent of the black officers attributed it to "stress, strain; police tense, overwrought." Only 2 percent of the white inspectors and 3 percent of other white officers were willing to admit to "personal prejudice" as the motivating factor, but 19 percent of the black police thought this the cause.[13]

The arrival of the National Guard in Detroit was followed by an escalation of the violence. The Guard's behavior, so much criticized both during and after the riot, resulted from the nature of the organization and its personnel, the lack of significant training for Guardsmen in riot-control tactics, fatigue and fear, and the manner in which the Guard was deployed. The Guardsmen were mainly high school graduates in their middle twenties who held primarily white collar or skilled jobs. A substantial majority had joined the Guard to avoid the draft. Like the National Guard elsewhere in the nation, only about 1 percent of whom were black, the Michigan Guard was essentially lily white — of the more than eight thousand Guard soldiers who served in Detroit, only forty-two were black. Judging by a postriot survey of the Second Battalion of the 182d Artillery, a Detroit unit, white Guardsmen had the same view of blacks as Detroit's white police did. When one of them was asked if the riot had changed his view of blacks, he replied, "Yes, I no longer consider Negroes civilized." Undersecretary of the Army David McGiffert concluded that the experience of the Michigan Guard in the riot confirmed that the National Guard could not "conduct civil disturbance operations in urban Negro communities without creating the impression" that it was a "discriminatory organization."[14]

"They are gutsy guys," a member of Cavanagh's staff said of the Guard during the riot, "but they have no more training for this kind of situation than a good group of Boy Scouts." The United States Army determined the basic riot training program for the Army National Guard, but it did not, as of July 1967, specify the number of hours the Guard had to devote to such training. Of the 280 hours required by the Guard training program, Michigan devoted only 6 hours to riot-control training, which was less than most states required. It appears, moreover, that officers were more likely than other ranks to receive even this minimal training. The riot training, furthermore, was largely devoted to crowd control, which was not particularly relevant to the kind of situation the Guard faced in Detroit.

Among the 405 members of the Second Battalion of the 182d Artillery who served on Twelfth Street, only 11 percent believed themselves well trained, and 31 percent claimed to have received no training at all. Governor Romney stated on July 28 that only 180 of the more than 8,000 Guardsmen then serving in Detroit had received any significant amount of training. The responsibility for this was primarily that of the army, which had been "remarkably indifferent" to the readiness of the Guard to cope with civil disorders and had been slow to react to training requirements that should have been "obvious" after the Watts riot.[15]

The Guardsmen were lacking in discipline and military appearance. When reporter William Serrin visited the Guard at its Grayling training camp just before the riot, he found that a large number of the soldiers were "sloppy in uniform and bearing" and that many were "just plain fat." In Detroit, army commanders, the police, and reporters all were troubled by Guardsmen's disregard for their weapons and their lax discipline. Guardsmen on duty were apt to sit on the sidewalk or lean against store fronts, and saluting by them was "almost nonexistent."[16]

When the Guardsmen arrived in Detroit, many of them were wearing "badly soiled" uniforms, and many needed haircuts and shaves. This was not, however, their fault. The men from Grayling had been in the field for four days and nights before leaving for Detroit, and they had not received advance notice of their new assignment. Some of them had clothes in the laundry, others had not had time to pack their belongings. They were immediately committed upon arrival in Detroit and did not have an opportunity to improve their appearance, to which the army attached so much importance.[17]

The Michigan Guardsmen were not only poorly trained; they were also, in the main, poorly led. Too many Guard officers, in the army's view, were "substandard." In Detroit, Guard commanders at the outset rarely went out into the field to circulate among their men, "staff coordination was poor[,] and staff follow-up almost nonexistent." Some officers did not know where their men were or what they were doing. Only 38 percent of the men in the Second Battalion of the 182d Artillery thought that their officers knew what was going on all the time, and 18 percent believed that their officers never knew what was happening.[18]

The equipment of the Guard left a good deal to be desired. The Guard was particularly short of radio equipment, which often required Guardsmen to position themselves near police officers so as to take advantage of the police communications system. Guardsmen occasionally had to use pay telephones to communicate! Although the Guard had sufficient weapons for each soldier, most were of World War II vintage. The Guard had the capacity to use chemical agents, but most of its training had been with "dispensers" that were effective against crowds rather than the small groups the Guard usually encountered in Detroit. The Guard, finally, did not have enough maps of the same scale for all of its commands.

The quality of the intelligence available to it handicapped the Guard during the early stages of its operation in Detroit. The collection of intelligence by the Guard was slow, and reports were often incomplete and inaccurate. Information gathered by individual Guardsmen and patrols was not reported back to headquarters in many instances, sometimes because of the shortage of radios. The Guard also lacked detailed information on the city of Detroit and the area of the city in which it was operating. Finding it difficult to assess the meaning of patrol reports, Guard headquarters relied on a "situation overlay" showing the degree of hostile action in each area that was updated every two hours during the night and every six hours during the day.[19]

In seeking to carry out their assignments in Detroit, Guardsmen, particularly at the outset of their service, suffered from both fatigue and fear. After having been on the road for most of the night, the large number of Guardsmen arriving on July 24 were almost immediately sent out into the streets, and many went for thirty hours without sleep. Since they were committed piecemeal, it was initially difficult for the Guard command to establish normal shifts of relief and rest, with the result that some Guardsmen received minimal relief from their duties during the first two or three days in Detroit. When separated from their police escorts, some Guardsmen got "lost" and could not be located for a time. A *Detroit News* reporter recalled that while he was hiding under a burned-out truck early one morning, Guardsmen pulled up in an armored personnel carrier, and one of them said, "We're lost! Can you tell us where we are? We're from Grand Rapids."

It is not surprising, furthermore, that most Guardsmen, unfamiliar with Detroit, lacking a "feel of the community," and thrust into the city in piecemeal fashion in the midst of a riot, were "scared shitless," to quote Girardin. "Take these kids out of a small town up in the sticks of Michigan," Girardin told the Kerner Commission, "and bring them into a city, straight to a congested area with all the tension and excitement going on, they did not know how to act." They became jittery and "itchy," started "seeing things," and began firing their weapons at no visible target and without regard for the safety of bystanders.[20]

The principal charge levied against Guardsmen was that they were "trigger happy." "Left in isolated locations with little or no instructions," away from their commissioned and noncommissioned officers, fatigued and frightened, and new to combat, Guardsmen fired their weapons all too frequently and without any real cause. The Department of the Army reported that the 46th Division had fired 155,576 rounds of ammunition by the morning of July 29. Although the figure is suspect, there is no doubt that Guardsmen fired their weapons at a rate that alarmed police and reporters alike. A *Free Press* reporter heard one Guardsman say to another, "I'm going to say halt and then bang, bang, bang." The second Guardsman replied, "No, that's not the way to do it. You say bang, bang, bang, halt."

Arriving in Detroit on July 23, one Guardsman remarked, "I'm gonna shoot anything that moves and that is black." A Guardsman would fire at an alleged sniper or at streetlights to protect against sniping, and other Guardsmen, hearing the shots, would nervously begin firing at "nothing in particular" in response. Sometimes Guardsmen ended up shooting at one another. One night a soldier at a Guard staging point accidentally fired his weapon, and seventy-five other Guardsmen began firing at nearby buildings to defend themselves, one of many examples of "nervous people firing answering shots for the accidental shots." Armored personnel carriers of the Guard moved through the streets spraying bullets at buildings suspected of harboring snipers — the Guard, according to an army general who served in Detroit during the riot, fired ten thousand rounds into a single building. Reporters joked that "the only thing that saved . . . [them] was that the Guard couldn't hit anything." According to the deputy commander of the Army Task Force in Detroit, eight Guardsmen injured themselves or their buddies by aimless firing.[21]

At 4:20 A.M. on July 24 General Noble Moore authorized the Guard to make "straight line patrols on major thoroughfares without [an] accompanying Detroit Police officer." The 46th Division then began assigning some of its men to jeep patrols consisting of two jeeps with four men in each. Other Guardsmen were assigned to "on-call task forces" made up of fifteen soldiers and two police officers that responded to looting and other reports. Still other Guardsmen, 450 of them eventually, were assigned to protect fire fighters, two to three soldiers serving with each piece of equipment responding to a fire. The Guard used tanks and armored personnel carriers in combating alleged snipers. By 7:15 P.M. the Guard was supposedly "committed to independent action" and was no longer available for police use, but the facts appear very much otherwise, no doubt because of Guard communication problems.[22]

The 1,761 riot-oriented mobile radio messages after 11:00 A.M. on July 24 compared with 903 such messages during the same hours on July 23; and the criminal offenses reported to the Police Department increased from 777 on the riot's first day to 1,289 on the second. As in most large-scale riots, the second day of rioting exceeded the first day in its severity.[23]

Looting, reported by 9:40 A.M. to be "almost citywide," continued to be the major form of riot activity on July 24. A *Free Press* reporter viewed the looting as not just a consequence of the riot but as "the chief reason for prolonging it. It was just too sweet, too simple and too stupid not to join in," Barbara Stanton remarked. She noted that thousands of rioters were "grabbing and running in a sometimes senseless, sometimes calculated snatch at the good things of life." "They were having a hell of a time on Twelfth Street" on Monday morning, another reporter noted. The crowd, he observed, was running through the streets "picking and choosing, their faces glistening with sweat and whiskey and sometimes pure joy." "I want my size," one looter said to another in a shoe store. "Who cares what your size is," the second looter responded. "Take everything in the whole mother place." The police arrested many looters, but they could not stem the thievery. "You pick 15 up, and there's 20 more," one officer said.[24]

On July 24 Detroit faced what its fire chief called "probably the worst fire emergency ever faced by an American city in modern times." There were 617 alarms in the riot areas that day compared to the 209 alarms on July 23. Fires were "breaking out all over" on the west side and, increasingly, on the east side, as entire city blocks were damaged by fire. Fires that would normally have been fought by 150 men were now being attended by only 10 or 12 fire fighters. Chief Quinlan thought that the arsonists were employing "a divide-and-conquer-strategy. They set a fire in one area," he declared, "and when the firemen get there the guys who started them are several blocks away starting another." Some calls to the department, Quinlan believed, were "merely traps to lure the Fire Fighters into ambush to be sniped at." Arriving at a fire, firemen were sometimes pelted with rocks, bottles, and cement block and, perhaps, subjected to sniping. Until they received Guard protection, firemen sometimes attempted to defend themselves by using the lids of garbage cans as shields.

By late Monday the nine hundred to one thousand firemen on duty, many having worked for twenty-four straight hours, were approaching exhaustion, and five of them had collapsed from heart attacks or fatigue. Thirty-five fire departments were by that time aiding the Detroit department. In a successful effort to gain control of the situation, the Detroit department decided to establish three command posts on the perimeters of the riot sectors, which enabled fire officials to assign their crews in shifts, one shift resting while the other responded to fire calls.[25]

The racial feelings that white firemen, like white policemen, might have suppressed in normal times were occasionally given expression in the strained conditions of the riot. While Guardsmen frisked two blacks on July 25, firemen observing the action shouted, "Kill the black bastards! Control those coons. Shoot 'em in the nuts!"[26]

The police made 2,931 riot-related arrests on July 24, far above the number on any other day of the disturbance.[27] Seventeen riot-related deaths resulted from the events of the day, again the largest number on any one day of the riot. Police officers shot and killed seven black looters or alleged looters, one of whom was also a suspected arsonist. Two additional black looters were killed as the result of simultaneous firing by policemen and Guardsmen. One death resulting from police action appears to have been entirely accidental—the police officer involved, who had had only five hours of sleep the night before, slipped while chasing a looter, and the officer's weapon discharged with fatal result. The officer fainted when he learned what had happened.

Quite apart from their possible role in two of the deaths already noted, Guardsmen were responsible for two additional deaths on July 24. One was a white male who was incorrectly alleged to have been a sniper and who had not received a command to halt. The other, John Leroy, was a black passenger in a car that allegedly ran a road block. It is more likely that the car stopped on command, that an unknown person then fired, and that this led to aimless firing by Guardsmen that wounded the four passengers in the car, including Leroy, who died on July 28 following abdominal surgery.[28]

Two persons, a black male and a white fireman, were accidentally killed by high tension wires on July 24.[29] White store owners shot two looters, one black and one white. Two other deaths, those of Herman Ector and Nathaniel Edmonds, led the prosecutor's office to seek warrants for murder. Ector, a thirty-year-old black male, was shot by a black private guard who was apparently displeased by something Ector had said about the guard's treatment of some looters he had seized. Although the police told the victim's brother that the unfortunate Ector had been looting, as the private guard claimed, he had done nothing of the sort. A Recorder's Court judge freed the guard following the preliminary examination. Ector's father went berserk after his son's "senseless death," locked his family in the house one day, and held the police at bay for seventeen hours.[30]

Edmonds, a twenty-three-year-old black, was shot on the porch of his aunt's home by Richard Shugar, a white who said Edmonds was a looter and who claimed self-defense. A witness at Shugar's preliminary examination asserted that the assailant had said to Edmonds before firing, "I will paint my picture on you," and had then pulled the trigger, saying "Bam." The state brought Shugar to trial on a first-degree murder charge, a Wayne County assistant prosecutor telling the jury that the accused had gone "on a hunting expedition that ended in an execution." The all-white jury found Shugar guilty of second-degree murder.[31]

Detroit was itself a victim of the large-scale rioting of July 24, as much of the city outside the riot areas took on the character of "a ghost town." The downtown was deserted, stores, banks, and the Detroit Stock Exchange closing their doors in response to the mayor's request to curtail business that day. General Motors and Chrysler Corporation canceled their second and third shifts so that workers could observe the curfew, and there was high absenteeism during the first shift. Kroger closed all its Detroit stores, and A&P closed twenty stores in the riot areas. The public schools canceled their summer classes, and Wayne State University, the University of Detroit, Marygrove College, and Mercy College followed suit. No mail was delivered in Detroit on July 24, garbage collection was suspended, bus transportation was curtailed, and the Detroit Public Library and its branches, the Detroit Institute of Arts, and the zoo were closed. Two airlines canceled flights to Detroit, and the Detroit Tigers shifted their scheduled July 25 home game with Baltimore to that city.[32]

Detroit General Hospital, operating under a disaster plan rehearsed since World War II, looked like a military field hospital on July 24, with State Police and National Guardsmen stationed at every entrance. The number of doctors on duty rose from a normal fifty to seventy-five to two hundred. Seeking to concentrate on the numerous riot-related injuries, the hospital closed its clinics for the duration of the disturbance and moved ambulatory patients to Detroit Memorial Hospital next door.[33]

The escalation of the riot on July 24 "horrified" and "frightened" leaders of Detroit's black community. A meeting of clergymen and community leaders, most of them black, resulted in a "strong statement" condemning the riot and calling for a "strong police crackdown" but "with citizens observers present."[34] Seemingly "confused and surprised" by what was happening on the streets of Detroit, fifty Trade Union Leadership Council leaders issued a public statement that blamed the riot on a "relatively small number of hoodlums and hatemongers" whose actions were hurting "the total [black] community." Although Detroit blacks, the statement asserted, were "far from satisfied" with their conditions, they were well aware of the "substantial progress" that had been achieved. The grievances of blacks, the statement continued, were no excuse for the violence that threatened to "destroy years of effort to build a community" of which both blacks and whites could be "proud."[35]

Most of Detroit's black leaders, the police, and state and city officials concluded during the riot's second day that federal troops were needed to quell the disturbance. Since it was Romney's understanding by late on July 23 that all available law enforcement personnel had been committed to the riot and since there were "strong rumors" that the rioters were planning to invade the suburbs, the governor asked Girardin, Reuter, and Nichols to consider what additional manpower Detroit needed. They concluded that three thousand federal troops were required. "To be on the safe side," Romney upped the figure to five thousand, Cavanagh and Davids concurring according to the governor.[36]

Cavanagh phoned Vice President Hubert Humphrey either just before midnight on July 23 or at 2:00 A.M. on July 24 to say that the situation was "getting out of hand" and to inquire about the possible deployment of federal soldiers in Detroit. A sympathetic Humphrey told Cavanagh, "If it can happen in your town, it can happen anywhere." While the mayor was speaking to the vice president, Romney entered the room. Unaware that Cavanagh was going to phone Humphrey, the governor was suspicious of the mayor's motives. Cavanagh gave Romney the phone, and he too expressed the need for federal troops. Either then or in a return call, Humphrey advised that a request for troops should be transmitted through Attorney General Ramsey Clark.[37]

Despite the recognized need for the army, there was a long delay of almost twenty-four hours before paratroopers actually appeared on the streets of Detroit. The delay was the result of a complex of factors: the uncertainty of Attorney General Clark regarding the legal requirements a state government had to meet before the president could aid it with troops; Romney's vacillation in seeking the troops; Lyndon B. Johnson's mistrust of Romney and the president's desire to make things as difficult for the governor as possible and, at the same time, to deflect any criticism from himself should the army have to be deployed in Detroit; and, finally, the coincidental war in Vietnam. If Clark had been more familiar with the history of previous federal interventions in local civil disorders, especially in Detroit in 1943, had there been a different cast of characters in the key positions in Lansing and Washington, and had there been no ongoing war in Vietnam, army paratroopers would probably have appeared on the streets of Detroit hours before they actually did, and at least some of the deaths and destruction resulting from the riot could have been averted.

There really was no excuse for responsible federal officials not to know what the law required regarding the use of federal troops in civil disorders, particularly in view of the memoranda President Roosevelt had ordered following Detroit's 1943 riot.[38] The Constitution authorized the federal government, on "application" of the legislature or governor of a state, to protect the state against "domestic violence." The applicable federal legislation, dating from 1792, used the word "request" rather than "application" and the phrase "insurrection in any State against its government" rather than "domestic violence." The statute, however, had been invoked in situations that could hardly have been called insurrections. On nineteen occasions before July 1967, the last time in Detroit's 1943 riot, the president had responded affirmatively in whole or in part to state government or District of Columbia requests for armed assistance. Some weeks before the 1967 Detroit riot the Office of Legal Counsel of the Department of Justice began assembling material on the use of federal military force in civil disturbances, but Clark's recollection is that he had not reviewed the matter "in detail." Also, during the Newark riot, which immediately preceded the Detroit riot, the Justice Department had given consideration to the use of federal troops.[39]

Romney phoned Clark at his home at 2:40 A.M. on July 24 to say that five thousand army soldiers "might" be required in Detroit if conditions did not improve. When Romney asked Clark if it was necessary for him to send a telegram asking for troops, the attorney general, who had been roused from his sleep, gave the governor to understand that an oral request for troops would be sufficient and that he was not to "worry about procedures." Romney seemed to believe and later claimed that he had asked for troops in this initial conversation with Clark, but he clearly had not. Although Clark later alleged that he had been referring only to the alerting of troops in telling Romney not to "worry about procedures," it does not appear that this is what he said to the governor. In any event, following his conversation with Romney, the attorney general called the president, who authorized the alerting of army units for possible dispatch to Detroit. Clark passed this word to Secretary of the Army Stanley Resor, who instructed Chief of Staff Harold K. Johnson to initiate the necessary planning. At 4:20 A.M. General Johnson issued "alert orders" to the 82nd Airborne at Fort Bragg, North Carolina, and the 101st Airborne at Fort Campbell, Kentucky. By 7:15 A.M. the headquarters of the XVIII Airborne Corps had developed plans to send one brigade from each division, about five thousand men in all, to Detroit.[40]

Believing, it would appear, that he had requested federal troops, Romney called a press conference following his conversation with the attorney general to announce what he had done. Although troops might not be needed, the governor asserted, the "prudent thing" under the circumstances was to ask for them. He said that he expected the troops to arrive that morning. Cavanagh also indicated at the press conference that Romney and he had made "a formal request" for troops.

In the midst of the press conference Romney was called to the phone by Clark, who now told the governor that he must submit a written request for troops and must state that there was an "insurrection" in

Michigan that he could not suppress. This advice to Romney makes it evident that Clark had been referring to more than just the alerting of troops in their initial conversation. What is likely is that the attorney general, who had gone to the Department of Justice by that time, had either examined the applicable legislation or sought advice about required procedures for sending federal troops and consequently found it necessary to correct what he had originally told the governor. The attorney general, it should also be noted, used the word "insurrection" and not "domestic violence" in speaking to Romney this second time, although he later claimed otherwise. A city official told the press that Romney believed that Clark had broken his word to the governor. "I had the impression," Romney later said of the attorney general, that "he was making more of a political than a legal request everything considered."[41]

By the time Clark phoned Romney, General Johnson had contacted General Simmons and Inspector Arthur C. Sage of the Detroit Police Department, both of whom indicated that they did not believe federal troops were needed. Clark passed these views on to Romney when he called the governor away from his press conference. Returning to the press conference, Romney stated that he would confer with law enforcement officials and would reappraise the situation before making "a final and official request" for troops. Quite apart from the difficulty of predicting the course of the riot and hence the possible need for troops, Romney was undoubtedly reluctant to state categorically that he could not control the disorder, as Clark now insisted he must, lest this reflect adversely on his leadership as a state governor and presidential candidate. His legal advisor, also, informed him that if he declared that Detroit was in a state of insurrection, which it decidedly was not, this might cancel insurance policies in the riot areas.[42]

At 5:50 A.M. Resor asked Clark if he wanted the paratroopers alerted so as to be able to arrive at Selfridge Field, thirty miles from Detroit, by noon or two or three hours later. Clark replied that it was difficult to answer the question because he did not know what Romney would do and he did not want "to press" the governor. If Romney wanted the troops, Clark said, Washington "would hate to delay it very long." After Resor told him that the Associated Press had reported that Romney had withdrawn his request for troops, which overstated what Romney had said on the subject, Clark told the army secretary that he could "probably start letting down" with regard to alerting the paratroop brigades.[43]

When Romney spoke to Clark again, at 6:50 A.M., the governor reported that Simmons, whom Romney had accused of having "countermanded" the request for troops, was unable to provide assurance that the Guard could "control the whole situation." Clark's judgment was that Romney had "really worked him [Simmons] over" to get this response. Simmons, however, later said that he had not been that familiar with the situation in Detroit when he had spoken to General Johnson, which is almost certainly correct. Romney told Clark about the looting and arson in Detroit, said that the police were "picking up shortwave radio talk by a bunch of young hoodlums . . . about keeping the fires going," and claimed that the damage by then was greater than it had been in Watts or any other riot. He asserted, however, that he could not state categorically either that he could control the situation or could not do so. If, however, he said, he waited until the riot was completely out of control, there would be "a much worse situation to deal with." Clark told the governor that he had a maximum of three hours to decide about federal troops if they were to arrive in Detroit before dark. He urged Romney to be "very cautious" about requesting troops because Washington had to think about trouble elsewhere in the nation also. "If we commit too much at one place too early," Clark said, "we just can't play that game."[44]

Following this third conversation with Clark, Romney and Cavanagh toured the riot areas while Romney staff members worked on drafts of a troop request. At 8:55 A.M. Romney read Clark over the phone a lengthy telegram in which the governor and Cavanagh "officially recommend[ed] the immediate deployment of federal troops into Michigan to assist state and local authorities in reestablishing law and order in . . . Detroit." Romney indicated that no more than 5,800 to 6,000 men — 4,000 Guardsmen, 350 to 500 State Police troopers, and 1,500 police — were available at any one time to enforce the law, that they had to "cover" a city of 139 square miles, and that many of them were overworked. He reported, however, that there was "no evidence" that Detroit was in a "state of insurrection."

Stating that Cavanagh and he believed five thousand army soldiers were needed, Romney asserted, as before, that the mayor and he were unable to "state unequivocally" that the situation could not "soon be contained," but, at the same time, they "most emphatically" could not say it would be contained "under existing circumstances." The governor correctly noted that experience had demonstrated that the second night of riots was "usually more violent" than the first and pointedly reminded Washington that the delay in sending troops to Detroit in 1943 had caused "a great deal of unnecessary bloodshed."[45]

Clark told Romney that a "recommendation" of troops was unacceptable, that he would have to "request" the soldiers in order to comply with the law. Furthermore, the attorney general pointed out, the governor had not stated that all the manpower available to the state had been fully committed nor had he categorically asserted that he could not control the disorder. Wanting to place the burden of the decision to commit troops on Washington, Romney, in asking for federal help, had substituted the word "recommend" for "request," which appeared in an earlier version of the telegram but had then been crossed out. He knew, moreover, that the Guard had not yet been fully committed to the streets of

Detroit, and he remained reluctant to state that he was unable to enforce law and order in his state without the aid of the United States government.

Clark claimed a few days later that Romney had not actually asked for troops in the wire but had simply been "running some language" past the attorney general. This assertion strains credulity. Romney, for his part, complained to Cavanagh that Clark was being "unreasonable" and had switched the rules on him, presumably at the direction of the president. As to why the state had delayed its "recommendation" until 8:55 A.M., Romney lamely explained that only one slow typist had been available and had taken "an inordinately long time" to type the wire.[46]

After his conversation with Clark, Romney conferred with Simmons, Davids, Girardin, and Reuter, and all agreed on the need for federal troops. At 9:45 A.M. Romney read Clark a second telegram, addressed to the president, in which the governor and the mayor "officially request[ed] the immediate deployment of federal troops" in Michigan and stated that there was "reasonable doubt" that Cavanagh and he could "suppress the existing looting, arson and sniping" without federal aid. Wanting the troops "before nightfall," Romney stated that time "could be of the essence." Although Romney used neither the words "insurrection" nor "domestic violence," did not assert that the state had committed all its forces, and did not assert categorically that the state could not cope with the riot unaided, Clark, despite all he had earlier told the governor, now raised no objection. A few minutes later Romney sent the wire to the president, whom Clark had already advised of its contents.[47]

It should hardly be a matter of surprise that Lyndon Johnson was keeping in close touch with developments in Detroit. The manner in which he was to respond to Romney's request for troops reflected his concern about race relations at that time of racial turbulence, the mounting criticism directed at him because of the war in Vietnam, and, not least of all, the fact that Romney was a leading contender for the 1968 Republican presidential nomination.[48]

Despite the official request for troops, the president was not immediately certain that he would comply, telling Clark that it was "60–40 for me [Johnson] to go." The president instructed Clark, in the meantime, to get the "best General possible," as well as "level-headed civilian people," for the assignment, to tell Resor "to go full speed ahead," and, if troops were to be dispatched, to use units with "as many Negroes as possible."[49]

Beginning at 10:40 A.M. Johnson met in the cabinet room with advisors and staff to decide how to respond to Romney's request. Those present were Secretary of Defense Robert McNamara; Clark; Roger Wilkins, the head of the Community Relations Service; Warren Christopher, confirmed that day as deputy attorney general; John Doar, head of the Civil Rights Division of the Justice Department; George Christian,

Tom Johnson, and Lawrence Levinson of the White House staff; and Justice Abe Fortas, the president's key advisor on the troops issue. As Wilkins recalled, Johnson was not "very charitable" in dealing with Romney's riot behavior. No doubt reflecting Clark's view that the state of affairs in Detroit was being "substantially exaggerated" by Romney, Johnson described the governor as being "a bit hysterical and substantially uninformed." Johnson assumed that Romney had been reluctant to state flatly that he could not control the situation because to have done so would have been tantamount to an "admission of failure."[50]

Johnson was exceedingly reluctant to send troops to Detroit. He was especially troubled about "the danger [of the] first picture of [a] fed'l soldier shooting [a] negro." He made it clear at the White House meeting that he did not "want hate [transferred] to LBJ and fed'l troops," which he suspected was Romney's motive in asking for the army. Johnson knew, however, that he had to respond in some fashion to the Romney request — concern, indeed, was expressed around the table about the president's delaying action while Detroit "burned." Shortly after 11:00 A.M., consequently, the president told McNamara "to prepare troops for movement," and the secretary of defense then instructed Resor "to load the troops on the aircraft." Their destination was to be Selfridge Field, and, as Johnson had stipulated, the troops were ordered to "hold there." Johnson, furthermore, wanted it understood that, if troops were deployed in Detroit, they were to "assist and support," not "supplant," local forces.[51]

As noted, Johnson was concerned about who would command the federal troops. He did not want a Douglas MacArthur type, a "hero," as the president put it, "riding . . . on [a] white horse." He wanted someone, rather, who would exercise restraint, would have "a high degree of respect for human life," and "would instill great discipline in the troops," someone, in short, Johnson said, who would "know [the] party line." The army had already selected General John L. Throckmorton, commanding general of the XVIII Airborne Corps, and he fit the Johnson prescription. "A thoroughly professional, no-nonsense officer" who had served in World War II, Korea, and Vietnam and who had commanded the 82nd Airborne when it had been sent to Mississippi to protect James Meredith, Throckmorton was a person of "very good judgment" and one possessed of "courage and common sense."[52]

Mistrusting Romney, all Johnson was prepared to do in sending troops to Selfridge was to have them available should a "trusted" presidential emissary on the scene personally decide that they were needed in Detroit, regardless of what Romney said. The president had not displayed the same reluctance regarding troops in dealing with Democratic governors. Through Joseph Califano, the special assistant to the president, Johnson had offered Governor Edmund (Pat) Brown of California "all the assistance in the world" during the Watts riot; and without even waiting for a request for troops from Governor Richard Hughes of New Jersey, with whom Johnson enjoyed a "close relationship," the president had phoned, as Hughes recalled it, to ask the governor if he needed the army to quell a 1966 New Jersey disorder, and the White House, apparently, had also stood ready to provide whatever was needed to aid the state during the Newark riot. Quite apart from Johnson's misgivings about Romney, it probably did not help Michigan's cause in seeking troops that the president and Cavanagh, as already noted, had begun "to fall out somewhat" because of the mayor's opposition to the war in Vietnam and his criticism of federal spending for space exploration.[53]

The man Johnson selected to make the "on-the-spot assessment" before federal troops could actually be deployed in Detroit was Cyrus Vance, who had just resigned as deputy secretary of defense. McNamara suggested Vance for the assignment because he had dealt with racial incidents while in the Department of Defense and had also served as a troubleshooter for the president in the Dominican Republic. Clark initially opposed the choice because he thought the use of a special emissary might make it appear that the president was "trying to disassociate himself" from the trouble, because "the use of hotshots for special missions" reflected adversely on the incumbent bureaucracy, and because he feared that Vance, as a former Defense Department official, might be too inclined to recommend the use of force. Fortas, however, sided with McNamara, and the president, who had "great confidence" in Vance, endorsed the choice.[54]

When McNamara phoned Vance to ask if he would accept the Detroit assignment, he agreed to do so provided his wife could accompany him. Suffering from back trouble, Vance at the time needed assistance in putting on his socks and tying his shoes. When Vance arrived at the White House shortly after agreeing to go to Detroit, he was briefed on the riot and became aware, as he recalled, that "the political aspects" of the situation made matters "a little more difficult" than they might otherwise have been. He was informed that he was to go to Detroit as a special assistant to the secretary of defense to confer with Romney and Cavanagh and to make plans for providing them with troop support if needed. Johnson instructed Vance to take "a very hard look" at the situation before deciding if troops were needed.[55]

At the close of the discussion in the cabinet room, Johnson, in consultation with Clark and McNamara, prepared a telegram for Romney that Fortas then edited. Romney was told that since he had stated that there was "reasonable doubt" that he could "maintain law and order," the president was sending troops to Selfridge Field to be available for "immediate deployment if required" and that Vance had been directed to confer with him and "to make specific plans" for providing the state "with such support and assistance" as might be required. When Clark read the wire to Romney, the governor pronounced it "very helpful," according to the attorney general, but Romney was clearly unaware that the decision actually to deploy troops in Detroit was still open.[56]

The Vance party, which included Christopher, Doar, Wilkins, and Albert Fitt, the army's general counsel and a native Detroiter, left Washington just after noon on July 24. During the flight Vance asked members of the party, on arrival, to secure an estimate of the situation in Detroit from federal agencies in the city so that he would be able to make an informed judgment about the use of troops by early evening. The airlift of the two brigades from Fort Bragg and Fort Campbell began at about 2:00 P.M. Upon their arrival at Selfridge, Vance and Throckmorton decided to place the incoming troops on a thirty-minute alert so that they could be quickly moved into the city if needed. The two men then went to police headquarters to confer with Romney, Cavanagh, and law enforcement personnel, Throckmorton, as instructed, changing into civilian clothes for the trip.[57]

The Vance party found the scene at police headquarters "one of considerable confusion and frantic[,] exhausted men." Cavanagh and Romney seemed to Fitt to be near the "end of their physical tethers." What most "astonished" federal officials was that although about 5,000 Guardsmen had been deployed on the streets, at least 1,900 Guardsmen were being held in reserve, and an additional 956 men were in rear detachments at Grayling or en route to Detroit. The Vance party concluded that the state had failed to take full responsibility for the riot and did not understand the importance of trying "to flood the riot-torn areas with as many law enforcement personnel as possible." "They seemed to feel," Clark recalled, "that somebody else had to take care of the situation." Vance and Throckmorton lost no time in telling Romney and Simmons to "Get them [Guardsmen] out on the streets right now." Romney's defense was that Girardin and he, while awaiting the arrival of the Vance party, had worked out plans for deploying the Guard reserve but had delayed putting the plan into effect because they expected federal authorities to federalize the Guard and then to coordinate its use with that of the army. Wilkins, however, thought that city and state officials "didn't know what to do" and "had no moves planned." "I had never seen as impotent a group of men in my life," he recalled.[58]

In briefing Vance, Cavanagh stressed the number of arrests, the number of fires in the city—"It's a great town if you're a fire buff," Christopher told Clark over the phone—and intelligence reports about likely attacks by rioters that night on the homes of middle-class blacks, who were allegedly arming themselves. When Romney urged immediate deployment of the troops, Vance, according to the governor, asked if he could say that Detroit was in a state of insurrection that he could not control. "They are still pressing me on this insurrection thing," Romney told his legal advisor. Explaining to Vance why insurance considerations prevented him from making the statement the presidential emissary appeared to desire, Romney, at the same time, said that he did not want "semantics" to prevent the entry of the federal paratroopers into the city.[59]

Since Vance insisted that he had to assess the situation and report to the president before he could decide on the use of the paratroopers, Romney and Cavanagh suggested that he tour the city. The touring party, which included Vance, Throckmorton, Doar, Romney, and Cavanagh, departed in a five-car convoy at about 5:15 P.M. and spent about two hours observing the three hardest hit riot areas. Although the party observed a good deal of damage during the tour, they saw no looting or sniping or any "undue amount of surliness," and the fires they witnessed appeared to be being brought under control. "The only incident during our tour," Vance stated, "was a flat tire." Seeking to explain what appeared to be a lull in the riot, Romney, as he recalled it, said to Vance, "Rioters gotta eat too." The Vance party came away from its tour with the distinct impression that the disorder was subsiding. This appeared to be confirmed for Vance and Throckmorton when they received a similar appraisal from federal agencies in Detroit, an appraisal, however, that was "fragmentary" and admittedly "left much to be desired."[60]

To assist Vance in judging the course of the riot, Colonel John Elder of the Vance party began to compile an incident summary based on data from a variety of sources but mainly from the police. This hastily put together document indicated a very sharp decline in incidents on July 24 as compared to July 23, especially during the late afternoon and early evening hours while Vance was trying to assess the need for federal troops. Elder's summary, for example, listed 183 incidents for the two hours of the Vance tour on July 24 as compared to 654 incidents during these same hours the day before. These figures, however, were altogether at variance with those provided in the more carefully compiled statistical report on the riot issued by the Police Department shortly after the disturbance. According to the police report, the 208 riot-related messages the police received during the two hours of the Vance tour, despite the seeming lull in the riot, compared with 132 such messages during the same hours on July 23, and the seventy-one criminal offenses reported to the police during the tour exceeded the sixty-three reported during the same two hours the day before. As a confidential FBI report indicated, the Police Department did not believe that the riot was subsiding during the time of the Vance tour.[61]

John Doar quickly came to realize that the Vance tour left a good deal to be desired as a basis for assessing the state of the riot. Doar thought that the Vance party should have flown over the riot areas or at least observed aerial photographs of the disturbance areas. Also, and more important, he concluded that the party should have visited the "lowest police command post" and questioned its commander. As it was, the Vance party passed within blocks of the Herman Keifer command post without visiting it. Vance later conceded that he probably should have spent more time with the police.[62]

Following the tour, Vance, whom Johnson had asked to call the White House with a status report every thirty minutes, informed the president that the situation appeared to be "under control," primarily because more men were patrolling the streets than on July 23.[63] After reporting to the president, Vance met with a group of black community leaders who wanted to express their views on the troops issue. Accounts of the meeting, which Damon Keith chaired, differ, but it seems certain that a majority of the black leaders—perhaps all but John Conyers and Julian Witherspoon, who feared the army presence would "inflame" the situation—favored immediate deployment of the paratroopers. Later in the evening Keith told the president's emissary that he would be personally to blame if any more deaths resulted from delay in sending in the federal troops.[64]

At a press conference following the community meeting, Vance continued to insist that the paratroopers were not needed in the city. Although he said that he did not want "to appear to be an ungrateful host" to the city's "distinguished guests," Cavanagh expressed disagreement with this judgment. Blundering and seemingly unaware of what he was saying, Romney declared that the situation had become "more hopeful" since the previous day because of the arrival of the paratroopers, the efforts of the police, the Guard, and the community as a whole, and the assistance fire departments from outside Detroit were providing the city. He indicated that it might even be possible to lift the emergency the next day. Inexplicably, Romney later maintained that these remarks "represented no modification" of his request for troops.[65]

Black community leaders were "furious" with Romney, and he was quickly made to realize that he had not expressed himself correctly at the press conference. A few minutes after the session, at about 8:30 P.M., he told Vance that he wanted the troops in the city before dark. At 9:30 he informed Vance and Throckmorton that conditions were worse than the night before. According to his own account, Romney told Vance that he realized that the fact that he, Romney, was requesting the troops was a factor in the federal government's reluctance to commit them. He wished it understood, however, that it was he who was running the "major risks" in making the request, and he wanted the troops committed whatever it might cost him politically. He told Vance, Romney stated, that he was not "going to continue being pushed around the way Clark had been pushing [him] around." The governor informed the press later that he could not say that Detroit was in a state of insurrection that he could not control, which implies that Vance was still pressing him on this point even though Clark had already accepted the governor's request for troops as meeting legal requirements.[66]

Although Vance was unpersuaded by Romney's pleas and allegedly thought that the governor was being "very cagey" about what he was willing to say, the sharply rising incident rate persuaded Vance and Throckmorton at 9:00 P.M. to move three battalions of paratroopers from Selfridge to the State Fairgrounds, close to the east side riot area. As the incident rate continued to mount and after further consultation with Throckmorton, Cavanagh, and Romney, Vance concluded at 11:00 P.M. that local law enforcement personnel could no longer contain the disorder. Reporting this to the president ten minutes later, Vance recommended, at long last, that the paratroopers be committed to the streets of Detroit.[67]

Johnson, who had been meeting in the White House from about 8:30 P.M. with members of the administration, Fortas, and J. Edgar Hoover, was following the reports coming in from Vance, the FBI, and the news media. "The atmosphere," the president recalled in his memoirs, "was heavy with tension and concern." Before the president announced a decision regarding use of the paratroopers, both Walter Reuther and the black Michigan Congressman Charles Diggs, Jr., called the White House to urge the commitment of the soldiers. At the request of Cavanagh, who claimed that Romney was still wavering with regard to troop use, Reuther telephoned Johnson to recommend deployment of the paratroopers. The president's response was that he could not do so "in good conscience" since Romney was still "vacillating." Reuther warned the president that the longer he waited, the worse the situation would be.[68]

According to a White House staffer, the Diggs call came after the president had decided to commit the troops but before he had made the decision known. Although critical of Romney, Diggs allegedly "raised hell on the phone for about ten minutes about the failure to bring in the troops" and said that "the blood was on the Administration's hands." Not trying "to be diplomatic about it," Diggs made it clear that he thought the delay in committing the troops had "some kind of political implication" since it was Romney who had requested the action. The White House thought that Diggs, who made his call public, was himself "playing politics in this to the hilt."[69]

At about the same time as Reuther phoned, Hoover told the president, "They have lost all control in Detroit. Harlem," the FBI director warned at the same time, "will break loose within thirty minutes. They plan to tear it to pieces." Harlem did not "break loose," but Vance, in effect, soon confirmed what Hoover had said about Detroit. Responding to Vance's recommendation that the paratroopers be committed, Johnson cautiously replied, "We will look at it and call you back shortly." When Throckmorton came on the phone once Johnson had decided to deploy the paratroopers, the president expressed concern about "the ground rules of engagement" and the reaction of the soldiers to sniper fire. "Well," Johnson said, "I guess it is just a matter of minutes before federal troops start shooting women and children." Tormented by repeated assertions that he was responsible for the killing of women and children in Vietnam, Johnson was troubled that his critics were "just waiting" to "charge that we cannot kill enough people in Vietnam, so we go out and shoot civilians in Detroit." This led Throckmorton to respond, "Mr. President, we will only shoot under the most severe provocations."[70]

Cautious to the end, Johnson asked Vance if Romney had declared martial law, as the president, referring to back issues of the *New York Times* as his source, incorrectly believed Governor Harry Kelly had done during the 1943 Detroit riot. "This would show," the president declared, that Romney had "taken all the steps which he can take." Before the troops were deployed, Johnson also wanted Vance to consider calling a press conference to plead for law and order, which Vance did just before midnight, and to set up loud speakers in the riot areas to "appeal to the people . . . to cease and desist and obey the law," which Vance could hardly have done. Johnson also wanted Vance to inform Detroit's blacks that the paratroopers being deployed in the city were the very same soldiers who had defended black school-children in Little Rock (101st Airborne) and James Meredith in Mississippi (82nd Airborne).[71]

At 11:20 P.M. President Johnson signed a proclamation ordering all persons engaged in "acts of violence" in Detroit to "cease and desist therefrom and to disperse and retire peaceably forthwith." He also issued an executive order authorizing the secretary of defense to use the armed forces of the United States to disperse the rioters and to federalize Michigan's Army National Guard and Air National Guard for the same purpose. Concerned about the long delay in responding to Romney, the White House sought to make it appear that the president had decided to commit the troops almost one hour before he actually did.[72]

Throckmorton sent reconnaissance patrols into the riot areas at about 11:30 P.M., but the main body of paratroopers did not move into the streets of Detroit until 2:30 A.M. on July 25. This was more than ten hours after the troops had begun arriving at Selfridge and seventeen and one-half hours after Romney had first recommended the action. The looting and burning had escalated in the meantime, and the death toll had mounted. Throckmorton, however, characterized the "timing" for the deployment as "just about perfect," and Vance saw no reason to second-guess his own action.[73]

Just before midnight on July 24, President Johnson, flanked by McNamara, Clark, and Hoover, addressed the nation on television. Declaring that "pillage and looting and arson have nothing to do with civil rights," Johnson asserted that the federal government would not "tolerate lawlessness" or "endure violence." With characteristic Johnson overkill, the president stated a mere six times during his seven-minute speech that he had committed federal troops because Romney could not control the situation. As Cavanagh noted, Johnson "whacked the hell out of Romney."[74]

In his memoirs, presidential aide Harry McPherson, who had prepared a draft of the speech that Johnson did not use, stated that the speech had been written by "a Washington lawyer." Actually, the speech had been written or, at least, rewritten by Justice Fortas, although he denied even having approved the speech in testifying before a Senate committee that was considering confirmation of his appointment to be chief justice of the United States Supreme Court.[75]

Cavanagh and Romney watched the president's speech together. When the address was over, a "visibly shaken" Romney, Cavanagh recalled, "walked around in circles, just mad as hell." "That isn't fair," Romney said to an aide. "Here I've been working all day and he lays it onto me like that." As Cavanagh was aware, Johnson "saw a chance to prod a pretender for the presidency . . . and he did it." According to the mayor, Vance was later startled by Romney's bitter reaction to Johnson, Cavanagh claiming that when Vance mentioned the president to the governor on one occasion, he "just got livid and almost went for Vance's throat."[76]

Although both McPherson and Califano thought the Johnson speech "excessive," they had remained silent when they saw the draft of the address. McPherson thought that this was because they were intimidated by the stature and brains of Fortas. The *Detroit News* remarked that the speech was Johnson "at his worst," and the *Free Press* was critical of the "petty, irrelevant political overtones" of the address. Denying any political motivation, the White House insisted that sensitivity about the requirements of the law and a concern about setting a precedent for federal intervention explained the president's stress on the inability of local authorities to maintain law and order.[77]

Concerned about the negative reaction to Johnson's "tough" speech, Fortas advised the president on July 26 that it would now be appropriate for him to play a different role and to speak to the nation as "a teacher and moral leader, appealing for public order." Fortas suggested an address in which the president would call for "a day of reflection" on the racial crisis and urge the churches to devote themselves to prayer about the subject. Johnson delivered the suggested speech the next day.[78]

In another effort to respond to the criticism both of the president's delay in committing federal troops to Detroit and the political "overkill" of his TV address, the White House fed information to the press that placed the blame for what had happened on Romney's vacillation. A White House–inspired story that appeared in the *New York Times* on July 30 argued that the president had moved "as swiftly as possible but also as prudently as necessary." The *Times* account made the White House seem more responsive to the state's request for troops than it actually had been, ignored the different signals Romney had received from Clark, misrepresented what had transpired at the meeting of black community leaders following the Vance tour of the riot areas, and moved up the time both of Vance's recommendation that the paratroopers be deployed and Johnson's signing of the emergency proclamation. An "obviously angry" Romney struck back in a press conference the next day. Ignoring his own changes in position, Romney incorrectly asserted that, from his first phone call to Clark, he had "never ceased hounding" the attorney general and then Vance for federal troops; and he charged that "the President of the United States played politics in a period of tragedy and riot." If the paratroopers had entered the city at 6:00 or 7:00 P.M. on July 24, the governor stated, "it would have made a difference."[79]

The White House decided to have Ramsey Clark reply to Romney in a press conference on August 1, with Fortas preparing an opening statement to be used by the attorney general. Clark, "a shy person" who had not met with the press since becoming attorney general, was willing to talk to reporters on this occasion because, he recalled, he was troubled by Romney's "effort to have his fiction agreed upon." Denying that the president had asked him to hold the conference, Clark presented an account of his initial phone conversation with Romney that differed from the governor's version, recalled no dispute with Romney about the word "insurrection," and claimed, contrary to the record of his phone calls, that he had used both the words "insurrection" and "domestic violence" when he discussed the troops issue with Romney just after 5:00 A.M. on July 24. He insisted that Romney's "recommend" telegram was not intended as a request for troops, which was not Romney's understanding of the matter.[80]

On the same day as Clark's press conference Charles Bartlett authored an article in the *Washington Star* about the Romney-Johnson controversy that supported the White House version of the matter. The article, which benefited from "a long backgrounder" provided by Vance, was regarded by the White House as "the best indictment of Romney's double-talking" about the troops issue.[81] Also on that same day the White House twice phoned the assistant director of the FBI to inquire if the Bureau could obtain a tape of a Romney statement on radio and TV on the morning of July 24 purportedly showing that the governor had changed his mind about the need for troops. Hoover, who viewed the request as "fraught with political dynamite," thought it foolish to attempt to secure the tape since he assumed that the press would become aware of the action and that this would cause Romney to "pop off again." Despite Hoover's concern, the FBI did seek to secure the reported tape but was unable to do so. If Romney or the Detroit media learned of this failed effort, they made no public mention of it.[82]

Although newsmen were given to understand following the Clark press conference that the White House would have nothing more to say on the Johnson-Romney dispute, Johnson, who found it hard to let go of a subject, "surprised" the press by returning to the controversy during an August 3 press conference. It was the Constitution, the law, and tradition that explained his action, the president said. After Johnson left the room, Vance told the assembled reporters that "there was no politics involved" in the president's actions.[83]

Johnson may have been somewhat reassured about his conflict with Romney when he received advance notice on July 31 of a Gallup presidential preference poll that had the president running five percentage points ahead of the Michigan governor. A Sindlinger poll a week later, however, indicated that 64 percent of the respondents in the nation and 79 percent in Michigan thought the president had waited too long before sending troops to Detroit. In Michigan, 64 percent thought Johnson had played politics in dealing with the troops issue, but only 35 percent of the respondents in the nation held this view.[84]

The administration's continuing concern about Romney's criticism of White House behavior became evident as it awaited the governor's testimony before the Kerner Commission on September 12, 1967. In anticipation of what Romney might say, the White House prepared to release the Vance report on the riot since, as Califano told the president, it contained factual information that the governor had "vacillated and was looking for federal help to get bailed out." When Romney defended himself before the commission, claiming that it was Clark, not he, who had changed his mind about troops and denying, in effect, that any Guardsmen had been held in reserve, the administration, "with almost frantic suddenness," released the Vance report and also had Clark issue a statement to the press rebutting what Califano considered to be the Michigan governor's "grossly distorted account." In his memoirs, the only riot Lyndon Johnson discussed was the Detroit riot. The events of July 24–28, 1967, he wrote, "will forever remain etched in my memory."[85]

Although the charges and countercharges of Romney and the Johnson administration probably contributed more to public confusion than enlightenment, it is likely that Romney gained some advantage in the dispute as the "underdog" and that Johnson came off "second best."[86] Whatever the public reaction, the essential fact is that the misunderstandings, misperceptions, and conflicting ambitions of the public officials involved delayed the deployment of federal troops in Detroit until after the riot's worst day had come to a close.

CHAPTER 9

"Law and Order Have Been Restored to Detroit": July 25–August 2, 1967

I

The Department of the Army's July 24 instructions to General Throckmorton for Operation Garden Plot, the code name for the army's civil disturbance plan, directed him to use "minimum force" in Detroit, but without jeopardizing his mission "to restore or maintain law and order." The army was to apply force, according to the instructions, in the following order of priority: (1) unloaded rifles with bayonets fixed and sheathed; (2) unloaded rifles with bare bayonets fixed; (3) riot control agent CS (gas); and (4) loaded rifles with bare bayonets fixed. Only Throckmorton was authorized to order the use of gas. He was to take advice from the Department of Justice regarding the "political implications" of his assignment and was to be "responsive" to Cyrus Vance's instructions, but he was not to take orders from state and local civil authorities.[1]

To simplify the "command structure" and to keep the two forces entirely separate, Throckmorton and Vance decided to deploy the paratroopers east of Woodward and to concentrate the Guard on the west side of town. The assumption of the two men when they made this decision early on July 25 was that the east side would be the more "active" of the two riot sectors, an assumption based on their understanding of the pattern of incidents during the late hours of July 24. The eastern riot zone, also, was closer to Selfridge Field, the initial staging point of the paratroopers, whereas the Artillery Armory, the major Guard staging point, was closer to the western riot zone.[2]

As Throckmorton later recalled, his decision to use Woodward as the dividing line between the paratroopers and the Guardsmen was spur of the moment. When President Johnson phoned to inquire how he would use the two forces, he had not yet decided the matter; but since he noticed on the city map lying on the table in front of him that Woodward ran through the center of the city, he told the president that he would use that as the boundary line between the two units. "It was just blind luck," Throckmorton recalled.[3]

In accordance with his instructions, Throckmorton ordered all para-troopers and Guardsmen at 4:00 A.M. on July 25 to unload their weapons and not to fire unless ordered to do so by a commissioned officer. The order, as Adjutant General Schnipke reported it, was, "You will unload all weapons. You will put the round[s] in your pocket[s]. You will not fire at looters. You will return fire on snipers only on the command of a commissioned officer." Each paratrooper, but not the Guardsmen, car-ried a card reminding him not to fire unless authorized by an officer or "when required to save my life."[4]

When Throckmorton visited General Simmons on the morning of July 25, he told the commander of the 46th Division that he wanted an officer to take statements and to investigate every shooting incident. "This is not my idea," Throckmorton said, "this comes from the boss — the president." He said that the president called him every thirty or forty minutes and wanted to know what was "going on." The Guard, however, does not appear to have fully complied with Throckmorton's reporting instructions. "We were supposed to fill out those goddam reports after every exchange of fire," one Guardsman declared, but "You can't fight a battle and be filling out forms. We just shot and forgot."[5]

Believing that a loaded gun offered no protection against being shot at in a built-up area and that he was "confronted with a group of trigger-happy, nervous" Guardsmen, Throckmorton sought by his firing order to avoid "too rapid [a] response" by individual Guardsmen as well as paratroopers. The Guard command "disagreed . . . entirely" with Throckmorton on the use of firearms. "How can you tell the soldier[s] to arm their weapons, and to fire, and the next instant you unload them?" Schnipke asked. Were Guardsmen, Guard commanders asked, to remain passive when looting and sniping occurred in their presence if no officer was present to authorize them to load and fire, and how were Guardsmen riding on fire trucks with unloaded weapons to protect themselves and the firemen to whom they had been assigned? When Simmons asked Throckmorton if his weapons order meant looters were to be permitted to escape if they could not be arrested, he replied that it was better to let them escape with a few dollars of merchandise than to shoot them. Simmons remonstrated, saying that "from time immemorial" looters had been shot in a disaster and "this word should get out." Throckmorton's response, according to Simmons, was, "I am not interested in that. You have your orders."[6]

After receiving his instructions from Throckmorton, Simmons "immediately" told his chief of staff and unit commanders that the orders were to be obeyed. When Major General Charles P. Stone, deputy commander of Task Force Detroit, toured the Guard sector on July 27 and 28, he discovered, however, that 90 percent of the Guardsmen whom he encountered still had their weapons loaded. This was partly because of the difficulty in disseminating Throckmorton's order verbally in view of the fragmented character of the Guard's deployment, but it probably also resulted from willful disobedience of an order that Guardsmen found difficult to accept.

Concerned about the quality of "command and control" in the Guard and believing that Guard orders "were not defined precisely, not understood and poorly executed," Stone consequently suggested to the Guard that the orders be placed in writing and distributed to each Guardsman. The Guard command complied on July 28, providing each Michigan soldier with "Special Instructions" not to display ammunition on his person or in vehicles, not to load or fire without specific instructions from a commissioned officer, not to extinguish street lights, and to take cover and await instructions from an officer if fired upon. This, according to Stone, resolved the matter at once.[7]

Seeking to answer the complaint of Task Force Detroit commanders about the appearance and discipline of the Guardsmen, Simmons on July 29 issued an order to his men to avoid "any overt acts" that might be "damaging to the high standards of personal conduct and discipline in the Army." All Guardsmen were instructed to "maintain a clean, well-groomed appearance" and "to conduct themselves in a firm but considerate manner." They were to exercise "extreme restraint . . . to avoid bodily contact with any individual in carrying out necessary duties."[8]

The army decided following the Detroit riot that its orders regarding the use of firearms had been unduly restrictive. The required order from an officer before a soldier could fire was based on the assumption that troops would be deployed in a riot control formation with an officer present, but this did not describe the way law enforcement personnel were deployed in Detroit or in other riot cities in the 1960s. The army concluded that, although individual soldiers had to be taught restraint in the use of firearms, they must have the right when fired upon to return "aimed, single-shot fire" without awaiting an order from an officer.[9]

The army also decided that the order requiring the permission of the senior commander before chemical agents could be used in a civil disorder was too restrictive. On the one occasion on July 25 when paratroopers requested permission to use gas, the situation had changed by the time Throckmorton gave his approval. The general then secured army consent to delegate the authority to order the use of gas to company commanders. Vance, furthermore, concluded that it had been a mistake to place the use of riot control agents third on the priority list for the application of force and therefore recommended that the use of gas be permitted at any time in a disorder at the discretion of the senior commander.[10]

As the assumptions behind its rules for the use of firearms suggest, the plan for the use of regular army troops in civil disorders, which dated from 1963, contemplated disorders quite different from the major riots of the 1960s. The army was so ill-prepared that Task Force Detroit moved into the city without city maps and had to rely on street maps provided by gasoline stations. Maps remained a problem for the army throughout its stay in Detroit, army command posts using "at least two maps of different scales."

Like the police and the Guard, which were able to provide federal troops with "only minimal information" about the area into which the paratroopers were deployed,[11] the army was handicapped by the quality of the intelligence it was able to develop in Detroit. There was, to begin with, inadequate coordination until late in the riot between the intelligence staff of the Task Force and the Detroit field office of the 113th Military Intelligence Group. The Task Force intelligence staff relied initially on the media for its intelligence, only to conclude that this source presented "a highly exaggerated picture" of the disturbance. The staff found it difficult to decide which incidents occurring in the city were actually riot-related. It also found that reporting by subordinate units, if it occurred at all, was often "untimely, incorrect, incomplete."

The Military Intelligence Group initially received intelligence information from the police or from agents who went into the streets in unmarked cars. The quality of the information the Intelligence Group gathered was "poor," and its spot reports were without influence on the army's operation in Detroit. The intelligence the FBI provided was largely derivative, the Detroit office of the FBI simply passing on information provided by one or another police source.[12]

Throckmorton decided after the Detroit riot that the army was lacking in the type of equipment that he believed the Guard had used to good effect. He concluded that tanks and armored personnel carriers had a "protective and psychological influence on a riot situation" and that M-60 machine guns mounted on quarter-ton trucks served to restrain potential rioters. Like Guard commanders, Throckmorton decided that 40-millimeter gas grenades were "urgently needed to assist in rooting out snipers in built-up areas."[13]

When the army first appeared on the streets, an army officer declared that the troops, although "polite," would not "say something twice." The paratroopers were assigned to mobile units that operated either independently or in combined patrols with police officers. By midnight, 2,750 of the paratroopers were bivouacked in five high schools on the east side, and the remainder were being held in reserve at the State Fairgrounds.[14]

The presence of the paratroopers, their frequent patrols, their "saturation" of their area of responsibility, and their professional bearing and manner had a calming effect on the "fear-ridden" inhabitants of the east side. When asked if there was any hostility to the army when it moved into Detroit, Assistant Secretary of Defense Daniel Z. Henkin replied, "My God, they didn't want to leave us go. We had to leave very, very carefully. They wanted us to stay forever."[15]

The fact that 20 to 25 percent of the paratroopers and an even larger percentage of the noncommissioned officers were black may partly explain why the predominantly black residents of Detroit's lower east side accorded the federal soldiers so favorable a reception. The large number of black paratroopers, according to Warren Christopher, made a "tremendous difference on the streets of Detroit." There is no evidence, however, that black paratroopers were anything but firm in their treatment of black rioters. A Romney aide who came across a black paratrooper guarding seven blacks caught looting noted of the soldier, "He was not particularly kind to them."[16]

The army made a determined effort to win "the hearts and minds" of residents in its area of responsibility. Army personnel made it a point to explain to civilians, particularly those residing near army command posts and in the more active areas on the east side, that the army was "on their side." The fact that the paratroopers were largely drawn from outside the state and were a symbol of federal authority made it easier for them than for local forces to persuade residents that they had "no local axe to grind" and would behave in an entirely neutral manner in seeking to restore law and order. In an effort to return the army sector of Detroit to a normal condition, the paratroopers helped to clean the streets and collect the garbage, traced lost persons, and invited youngsters in the area to join soldiers in softball games. In a gesture of good will, the army granted leaves to the twenty-eight black soldiers whose homes were in the area so that they could visit their families. Throckmorton also granted permission to black activists Karl Gregory and Charles Colding to drive around the army sector to urge residents to stay out of trouble.[17]

Army commanders regarded the disciplined use of firearms as especially important in reducing the level of fear on the east side. When Colonel Alexander Bolling, commanding officer of the Third Brigade of the 82d Airborne, arrived at the Southeastern High command post on July 25, he discovered Guardsmen "hiding" in the building to protect themselves against alleged snipers. It turned out that a couple of snipers had fired on the Guardsmen from an apartment building across the street, and the soldiers, in return, had shot out the windows and riddled the building with hundreds of bullets. When the paratroopers replaced the Guardsmen, Bolling, after ordering the lights in the school turned on, the shades pulled up, and the paratroopers to show themselves, promised the frightened apartment residents that there would be no more shooting from the school.

"I'd rather miss 100 snipers than hit a single innocent person," Bolling declared. Another officer commented, "We don't shoot just because something moves or because someone runs." The preferred army tactic in dealing with snipers was to attempt to maneuver them into a position where they could be arrested, and soldiers were instructed not to fire at buildings until they had a human target in sight. As of July 29, the 82d and 101st Airborne, according to the army, had fired only 202 rounds of ammunition as compared to the 155,576 rounds fired by the 46th Guard Division. It should be noted, however, that there were very few sniping incidents on the east side, the 82d Airborne recording only ten such incidents in six days.[18]

Won over by the army's good behavior, east side residents became an important source of intelligence for the paratroopers. Residents also provided the soldiers with food and coffee. When the 82d Airborne was withdrawn to Chandler Park before leaving the city, the paratroopers were besieged by well-wishers.[19]

In part because of the presence of the paratroopers, the expectation of Vance and Throckmorton that the east side would become the more "active" of the two riot sectors turned out to be incorrect. Throckmorton conceded on July 26 that he did not "know of another hot spot in the City like 12th Street." Ranking police officers wanted the paratroopers to be deployed on the west side, where, the police thought, they were "badly needed"; and the police also wondered why some paratroopers were being held in reserve. Congresswoman Martha Griffiths phoned the White House to urge that the paratroopers be assigned to protect the people on the west side, noting, "these are the people who pay the taxes." Vance had stated at the time of the initial army deployment that the decision to place the paratroopers on the east side was only "for the time being," and an army spokesman declared on July 26 that Throckmorton would move the paratroopers to the west side if conditions required that. The general, however, did not do so even though conditions appeared to require just such an action. Vance stated in a later interview that Throckmorton and he had actually considered pulling the Guardsmen from the streets altogether because of concern about their behavior and appearance but had decided against doing so lest such a move destroy the morale of the Guard not only in Michigan but throughout the nation and impair its future usefulness.[20] The decision not to reinforce the Guard on the west side may have stemmed from a similar consideration.

II

The allegedly heavy sniper fire that began shortly before midnight on July 24 continued during the early hours of July 25, Hubert Locke characterizing the hours from 2:30 A.M. to 6:00 A.M. that day as "the most intense period of the riot." Sniper fire was reported on both the west side and the east side, and both police officers and firemen reported themselves under attack. It was "a total state of war," Locke later told a

Kerner Commission interviewer. The sniper fire diminished during the daylight hours, but there were sporadic attacks on Detroit Street Railways buses and Public Lighting Commission and Detroit Edison Company crews.

Darkness brought renewed sniper fire, the *Detroit News* melodramatically declaring that snipers had turned 140 blocks of the west side riot zone into "a bloody battlefield." Forty police officers and Guardsmen were pinned down by gunfire almost on the grounds of Ford Hospital on the west side. At 11:00 P.M., policemen, firemen, and State Police troopers were ordered out of the area between West Grand Boulevard, Clairmount, Woodrow Wilson, and Dexter, and a few minutes later the Guard was told to sweep the affected streets "clean." Tanks then "thundered through the streets and heavy machine guns chattered." A reporter remarked that "it was as though the Viet Cong had infiltrated the riot-blackened streets." For all the reports and concern about sniping, however, police records indicated that a maximum of ten persons were hit by snipers that day, including four policemen, one Guardsman, and one state trooper.[21]

A patrolman later recalled that "a police roll call message" on July 25 instructed the officers that "the rioting and looting had to be squelched 'at all costs.'" Almost every policeman was now armed with a rifle, shotgun, or automatic weapon in addition to sidearms. The weapons were not just for display: the police shot ten civilians that day, but this was less than the nineteen suspected looters and arsonists the officers had shot the previous day.[22]

There were eleven additional riot deaths on July 25, including a fireman and a policeman. The fireman, Carl Smith, had been away from duty because of an appendectomy, but he had nevertheless rejoined his fire company to help in the emergency. Police reports listed him as shot by "person/s unknown while mobilizing fire department vehicles," but he seems to have been caught in a crossfire between police and Guardsmen engaged in a gun battle with a sniper or snipers, and a Guardsman apparently fired the fatal shot. The patrolman, Jerome Olshove, who was scheduled to leave the force on July 27 to take an IBM job, was shot in the abdomen while three other officers and he were arresting three blacks caught looting an A&P market. According to patrolman Roy St. Onge, while he was trying to handcuff twenty-year-old Danny Royster, the young man grabbed St. Onge's gun, and in the ensuing struggle the gun discharged, fatally wounding Olshove. "My god, he's been shot by my gun," St. Onge recalled saying, but he testified that he had not had his finger on the trigger. Royster was later convicted on a second-degree murder charge and sentenced to from five to fifteen years in prison.[23]

Two blacks and possibly a third were shot by Guardsmen on July 25. One victim, Henry Denson, was accused of having run a roadblock and then driving his car at Guardsmen. Two *Newsweek* reporters who witnessed the event disputed that assertion, however. Denson was actually only a passenger in the car, and a jury later found the vehicle's driver innocent after he had been charged with felonious assault with an auto. According to eyewitnesses, Guardsmen shot Roy Banks in cold blood. The police claimed that Banks was seen running from a building and that police and Guardsmen had fired when he refused to halt. If this were so, and the second police report on the incident contradicted the first one, Banks, a deaf mute, did not hear the order. Julius Dorsey, a private guard, was apparently accidentally shot by a Guardsman when, according to the police, he "ran into the line of fire from Military and Police personnel who were firing at escaping looters." *Detroit Free Press* reporters who investigated the fatality concluded, however, that the cause of Dorsey's death was something of a "mystery."[24]

Police officers killed five blacks believed to be looters and one black sniper on July 25. Jack Sydnor, who was drunk, had fired a gun from his apartment window, according to the manager of the building, who summoned the police. When a patrolman entered the apartment, Sydnor fired several shots, wounding the officer in the abdomen. He returned fire, killing Sydnor, the only confirmed sniper known to have met this fate during the riot.[25]

There was a decrease in riot-related incidents on July 25 as compared to July 24. Riot-oriented mobile radio messages dropped from 1,594 to 1,231, and the number of criminal offenses reported to the police, from 1,289 to 398. The incident summary on which Vance and Throckmorton relied reflected a similar drop-off in riot activity, from 2,556 incidents on July 24 to 1,595 the next day. There was a sharp decline, also, in the number of arrests, from 2,931 on July 24 to 732 on July 25.[26]

In an effort to return the city to a more normal condition and, in that way, as Vance hoped, to induce citizens to behave normally, Vance, Romney, and Cavanagh requested at an early morning press conference on July 25 that businesses and industries resume normal operations. City, state, and federal offices in Detroit reopened that day, and immigration officials lifted the ban on travel on the Ambassador Bridge and through the Detroit-Windsor Tunnel, links between the United States and Canada. Romney announced late in the day that gasoline stations could henceforth remain open from 9:00 A.M. to 5:00 P.M., with customers limited to five gallons of gasoline placed in the tanks of their cars. Michigan Consolidated Gas Company crews went into the riot areas under Guard protection to close gas outlets near fires. Public Works Department crews, also under Guard protection, began to remove debris from the Twelfth Street riot area, and the city resumed garbage collection in the riot sectors. Although absenteeism was high, the Big Three auto companies resumed operations in Detroit area plants on July 25. There were other "small signs" that order might be returning to the riot-torn city. There was less smoke, fewer sirens sounded, and more people ventured from their homes. Commenting on the absence of young rioters on Grand River, a store owner bitterly remarked, "They all must be home watching their color television."[27]

The riot had begun without any formal demands by any black organization or group. On July 25, however, the black nationalists Richard Henry and his brother, attorney Milton Henry, sought to use the riot to extract concessions from city officials. Claiming to speak for the Malcolm X Society, the Henrys informed Cavanagh and Romney that they would ask for a cessation of "all hostilities" that day if the governor and mayor accepted as a "basis of discussion" that all troops be withdrawn from the city, prisoners released, amnesty granted all "insurrectionists," district police commissioners appointed, residents given veto power over urban renewal decisions, the Common Council and the school board elected on a district basis rather than at large, funds provided for black business, and "compensatory and compulsory equal employment enforcement" instituted. Although conceding that they had no control over the rioters, which is certainly correct, the Henry brothers claimed that they could stop the riot, which is certainly incorrect. It is hardly surprising that Romney and Cavanagh ignored the Henry wire. When Cavanagh met with black leaders and Twelfth Street representatives that day, they once again condemned the rioters, but they were no more able than the Henrys to bring a halt to the riot.[28]

As during the early morning hours of July 25, there were reports of "fierce sniper attacks" on the police and Guardsmen before dawn on July 26.[29] During these same hours the riot death toll was increased by seven, including the most notorious slayings of the entire disturbance. The victims were a four-year-old black girl, a white woman, a National Guardsman, and four black youths.

As the *Free Press* put it, little Tonia Blanding was "too small to slip the trap of Twelfth Street violence, but not too young to die." A Guard corporal, who saw a flash in the window of an upper-level apartment on the corner of Euclid and Twelfth, reported this to a sergeant commanding a tank in the area. Believing that he was responding to a sniper attack, the sergeant fired a burst from the tank's 50-caliber machine gun at the window. What the sergeant was actually responding to was the lighting of a cigarette by one of the thirteen occupants of the apartment, eight of them children. Neighbors reported that they had screamed to the Guardsmen to stop the shooting since there were children in the apartment, but one neighbor declared, "They just started shooting and shooting." Ninety-two bullet holes were later discovered in the room that the window served.

The Guard hustled the thirteen occupants out of the building and lined them up to be searched even though Tonia had a hole in her right chest—a morgue official reported that she had twenty-seven wounds—and the nearly severed right arm of her aunt, Valerie Hood, was hanging by "just a piece of skin." Either Tonia's mother or father begged the Guard to take the injured child to the hospital, but a Guardsman, according to Tonia's father, said, "Say another word and I'll kill all of you 'mother-f____rs.' " The injured were eventually taken to Ford Hospital, where Tonia was pronounced dead on arrival. The Blandings and Valerie Hood later instituted negligence suits in federal court.

There were several peculiar aspects to the Blanding tragedy. The detective to whom the case was assigned reported that he had found spent 38-caliber shells in the apartment when he searched it on July 28. A private guard who had searched the apartment just after the shooting, however, did not see any spent shells there. William Hood, Jr., one of the thirteen persons in the apartment, owned a 38-caliber gun, but it had not been fired. The detective also found a storehouse of goods in the apartment, including such items as thirty-five pairs of men's pants, women's clothing with pawn shop or cleaners' tags not in the names of the occupants, twenty-three paint brushes, two portable record players, five radios, and a movie camera. The detective understandably assumed that the merchandise had been looted, but the occupants of the apartment insisted that the police had planted it there. Tonia's father pointed out that Guardsmen had searched the apartment just after they removed the occupants and had not called for their arrest, as the searchers would have done had they found loot in the apartment. What was also puzzling was why the three Hoods involved had left their home in a "relatively calm" part of the city to sleep on the floor in the crowded Blanding apartment, located in the very center of the riot area.[30]

In Detroit on a business trip, fifty-year-old Helen Hall, the white woman slain in the early morning of July 26, had checked into the Harlan House Motel on John Lodge across the freeway near Ford Hospital. When she opened the window curtain in her room after hearing gunfire, she was struck and killed by a rifle shot. The chief of the criminal division of the county prosecutor's office thought that a Guardsman had fired the shot, but the police later convinced Hall's daughter that her mother had been killed by a shot from a deer rifle, which was not a Guard weapon.[31]

According to the police report, Sergeant Larry Post of the 182d Artillery of the Guard was shot by an "unknown" person or persons. He had ordered an automobile approaching a Guard checkpoint to halt, the homicide report stated, but when the driver ignored the order, Guardsmen manning the checkpoint with Post fired and disabled the vehicle. The soldiers arrested the three black occupants of the car, one of whom, Post claimed, had shot him. The Guardsmen, however, found no weapons in the car. Post was taken to Ford Hospital, where he died on August 9. The three blacks, who denied receiving an order to halt, were physically assaulted by the police while in their custody and had to be hospitalized. They were later found guilty of curfew violation.[32]

Three black males were found shot to death in the early morning of July 26 in the annex of the Algiers Motel. As we shall see later, the manner in which they met their fate made this affair the cause célèbre of the Detroit riot.[33] The fourth black male shot that morning, nineteen-year-old William Dalton, was found lying in the street suffering gunshot wounds of the chest and abdomen. The police who discovered the body took Dalton to Detroit General Hospital, where he was pronounced dead on arrival. The autopsy report revealed that Dalton had sustained "five shotgun pellet entry wounds to the back."

Discovering that there was no police report of the shooting, as there should have been, the *Detroit News* conducted its own investigation, interviewing numerous eyewitnesses. The *News* turned the information over to the Homicide Bureau, which had begun looking into the death and now made a detailed investigation of the shooting. What appears to have happened is that a fire at a furniture warehouse and a report of arsonists in the area had drawn police and Guardsmen to the scene. They apprehended Dalton in a parking lot and handcuffed him. He "suddenly bolted," according to the initial report of the detective lieutenant investigating the case, Edward Rohn; and when he failed to respond to a command to halt, a policeman or Guardsman fired at him as he climbed over the roof of a parked car and disappeared. Rohn thought that whoever had fired was probably not aware that Dalton had been hit. When asked to submit statements, ten police officers involved all denied having fired.

When Rohn continued his investigation, a patrolman who had failed to report his action now admitted that he had fired at Dalton with a 12-gauge shotgun but stated that he did not believe that he had hit the victim. Several witnesses alleged, however, that Dalton had been ordered to run before being shot, and other witnesses claimed that the only shots fired had been the ones that struck the victim, disputing the police claim that they had left the scene without discovering Dalton's body because of sniper fire in the area.[34]

Three additional riot deaths on July 26 brought the total to forty-two. The victims were two black men slain by Guardsmen and a white male shot by a police officer. The most inexcusable death was that of George Tolbert, a twenty-year-old black. Guardsmen on the afternoon of July 26 had been attempting to divert traffic on the side streets away from Twelfth Street. According to a *Detroit Free Press* reporter, the Guardsmen stood in the middle of the street, shouted obscenities at pedestrians and drivers to get off the street, and then fired over their heads if they did not obey. Tolbert and a companion walked toward two Guardsmen, one of whom opened fire, killing Tolbert and wounding his companion. The soldier claimed that the two men had ignored com-

Blind pig at 9125 Twelfth Street. (Copyright 1967 the *Detroit News*.)

Twelfth Street on the first day of the riot, July 23, 1967. (Copyright 1967 the *Detroit News*.)

ational Guard clears Linwood Avenue of curfew violators on July 23, 1967.
Copyright 1967 the *Detroit News*.)

ly 24, 1967, at Linwood and Hazelwood. (Copyright 1967 the *Detroit News*.)

Federal troops land at Selfridge Air Force Base on July 24, 1967. (Copyright 1967 the *Detroit News*.)

George Romney, Cyrus Vance, and Jerome Cavanagh hold a press conference on July 24, 1967. Copyright 1967 the *Detroit News*.)

Algiers Motel Manor House where three young blacks were slain on July 25. (Copyright 1967 the *Detroit News*.)

Fires at Michigan and Trumbull, across
from the Detroit Tigers Baseball Stadium.
(Copyright 1967 the *Detroit News*.)

ederal paratrooper on guard duty. (Copyright 1967 the *Detroit News*.)

Detroit police look for snipers at Fourteenth and Grand River. (Copyright 1967 the *Detroit News*.)

Twelfth Street and Blaine. (Detroit Police Department Photograph Collection, Bentley Historical Library, University of Michigan.)

Firefighters covered by the National Guard at Twelfth and Hazelwood on July 28, 1967. (Copyright 1967 the *Detroit News*.)

Northwest corner of the John Lodge and Virginia Park West. (Detroit Police Department Photograph Collection, Bentley Historical Library, University of Michigan.)

Detroit police headquarters' gym filled with loot recovered by police. (Copyright 1967 the *Detroit News*.)

Food line at St. Leo's School, Fifteenth Street and Warren on July 27, 1967. (Copyright 1967 the *Detroit News*.)

ree-year-old Thomas Allen stands in the ruins of his home burned down during 67 riots. (Copyright 1967 the *Detroit News*.)

mands to get off the street, which hardly justified what had occurred, but Julian Witherspoon, who witnessed the shooting and gave sworn statements to the police and the FBI, declared that he had not heard any command to halt before the Guardsman fired. When the Department of Justice investigated the slaying, John Doar concluded that the two soldiers had been "scared out of their minds." The Guardsman involved, incidentally, had disobeyed Throckmorton's order not to load and fire except at the command of a commissioned officer.[35]

Albert Robinson, a twenty-eight-year-old black, was the resident of a west side apartment house from which snipers were allegedly firing at Guardsmen. After police were summoned, they and the Guardsmen, returning fire, "knocked the hell" out of the building. Guardsmen then entered the building and brought out Robinson, who, according to a sergeant, tried to grab his weapon. The sergeant then bayoneted Robinson and apparently shot him. A police officer who witnessed what had occurred later recalled that as Robinson hollered for help, an unnamed person, presumably the Guardsman, jabbed him with a bayonet and said something like, "That feel good? You dead yet?" According to the homicide report, however, the medical record specifically stated that Robinson had not sustained any bayonet wounds.[36]

Responding to a report that some men had climbed the fence of an auto parts yard, two police officers discovered Julius Lust, a twenty-six-year-old white, inside the yard. They shouted at him to halt, but, according to their report, after raising his left hand toward them, he began to run. Both officers fired, and one of their shots "took effect." Before he died later that day, Lust claimed that an employee of the firm had given him permission to secure a needed part in the yard, but the employee denied this.[37]

The final riot death, occurring on July 29, was the sole riot fatality attributable to paratrooper action. The shooting resulted from a police raid on an apartment house in search of loot. What officers appear to have discovered was a "teen-age marijuana den." Two men fled the apartment when the police entered, one of whom, the police reported, had a revolver. Stationed outside, a paratrooper sergeant heard a police officer yell, "Watch it, one of the men has a gun." When the man with the alleged weapon pointed it at the paratrooper, he fired, killing not the gunholder but Ernest Roquemore, a nineteen-year-old black who had run into the line of fire. The police shot three other individuals at the scene, one of whom had to have his leg amputated.[38]

The events of July 26 provided mixed signals as to whether the tide had turned in the riot. "Progress is being made," Vance stated in a predawn press conference, "but," he said, "we are not out of the woods yet." Throckmorton reported at the same press session that the east side was "pretty well under control" and that the Guard was gaining the upper hand on the turbulent west side as the result of the assignment of additional troops to the area. During the afternoon, Vance and Throckmorton toured the west side riot area and discovered that the Guard had barricaded Twelfth Street at both ends of the riot sector and was permitting neither vehicles nor pedestrians to pass through the street. Anxious to restore the city as quickly as possible to a more normal condition, Throckmorton ordered the Guard to open up the street at once, and Vance and he then walked down the street for several blocks, urging the people to come out of their homes. Some did, and cars filled with gawkers began to move through Twelfth Street.[39]

Although the *Free Press* reported that downtown business was "nearly back to normal" on July 26, only about half the downtown stores opened that day, and the largest were not among them. Absenteeism in the auto plants, however, was only slightly above normal that day; the Detroit Public Library and the Detroit Institute of Arts reopened; mail was delivered on all but two hundred of the city's 1,550 routes, as compared to 617 routes without mail the previous day; and Detroit Street Railways buses ran on all but two lines. Gross riot statistics also indicated a somewhat improving situation, the number of riot-related police mobile radio messages dropping from 1,594 to 1,231; the number of criminal offenses reported to the police, from 398 to 231; the number of arrests, from 732 to 425; and the police incidents, from 1,595 to 1,433. As far as the Fire Department was concerned, "order from near chaos" started to emerge on July 26. Many fires that day were reignitions of earlier fires that the besieged department had not had time to put out professionally. Before the day was out, the fire fighters, who had been permitted only six hours of rest between tours of duty, were placed on twelve-hour shifts; and the out-of-town fire departments that had been aiding Detroit began to return to their home stations.[40]

Public authorities in Detroit no doubt derived some comfort on July 26 not only from better riot statistics but also from a joint statement by the nation's four most prominent black leaders calling upon the rioters to cease and desist. "Riots," declared Martin Luther King, Jr., Roy Wilkins, Whitney Young, and A. Philip Randolph, "had proved highly ineffective, disruptive and highly damaging to the Negro population, the civil rights cause and to the entire nation." The four maintained that blacks themselves were "the primary victims of the riots" and that riots had "not contributed in any substantial measure to the eradication of . . . the just complaints" of blacks.[41]

The optimism expressed at the beginning of July 26 and the signs that the riot might be ebbing were belied by some of the day's events. The early morning hours were punctuated by sniper fire, reporters claiming that the streets were "filled with shooting and chaos," and Romney asserting that sniper fire was at its worst since the riot's beginning. The Tenth Precinct station came under attack in the afternoon, and sniper fire in the precinct was reported to be so heavy that city and state police once again were ordered out of the area so that the Guard could move in with heavy equipment. Guardsmen raked rooftops and burned-out buildings with machine-gun fire, and helicopters swooped low to frighten snipers.[42]

Increasingly concerned about sniping, both the police and the Guard devised new tactics to meet the problem. Both had engaged in "uncontrolled and unnecessary firing" that not only endangered innocent bystanders but also led to the assumption that sniping was far more widespread than it actually was. On July 26, however, Superintendent Reuter ordered the police not to enter buildings from which sniper fire was coming but rather to take up positions on the periphery, contain the building, and await orders from a ranking officer. Rather than firing from the street, as it had been doing, the Guard, beginning on July 26, used tanks and armored cars to clear sniper nests, and then the soldiers rushed into the affected building. The new tactics appeared to be successful, the *Free Press* reporting the next day that the Guard had "crushed the guerilla warfare."[43]

The Police Department was far from convinced on July 26 that the riot was under control. Advising Girardin that police manpower and firepower were "insufficient to restore order," Deputy Superintendent Nichols urged the reinforcement of the police by an additional 1,500 men. In response to the Police Department's request, Throckmorton that day released two hundred paratroopers to the police to use in non-contact missions. The general also mobilized the 1,300-man Michigan Air National Guard, 659 of whom were then assigned to riot duty, primarily to guard vital installations.[44]

July 27 was described by the *Free Press* as "the first day of real peace" since the beginning of the riot. "I think it's over," Cavanagh declared, his hopes perhaps buoyed by a severe rainstorm in the early morning hours. Agreeing with the mayor, Throckmorton ordered all troops to remove the bayonets from their rifles, unload their weapons, carry the magazines in their pockets, and place all belted ammunition out of sight. At Vance's urging, Romney that morning lifted the curfew and removed all restrictions on the operation of gas stations except for the sale of gasoline in portable containers. Since Vance, despite the opposition of the Guard, wanted the lights on Twelfth Street turned on in the evening, the police asked the Public Lighting Commission to dispatch as many crews to the area as were available.

The State Police began leaving Detroit on July 27, and the army drew up plans to turn over its responsibilities on the east side to the Guard. Most police runs on July 27 were no longer in response to reports of looting or sniping but rather to search for stolen weapons. Romney reimposed the curfew in the evening but only because spectators and photographers had flooded the area and were hampering the restoration of public utility service and the cleaning of the streets and sidewalks.

Business and community leaders had also pleaded with Romney to restore the curfew because of their fear of renewed violence.[45]

A predawn gun battle on Twelfth Street on the morning of July 28, in the midst of a Cavanagh tour of the area, was just about the "only serious incident" that day. The 46th Division began relieving the paratroopers on the east side on the 28th, a process that was completed on July 30. Continuing the process of normalization, Romney on July 29 shortened the curfew to the hours between 11:00 P.M. and 5:30 A.M. The most unusual event of the day was an unsuccessful early morning attack on a Guardsman by a rioter armed with a bow and arrow![46]

The only "riot-connected" problem on July 30, according to the *Free Press,* was sightseeing, as "swarms of people" flocked to Twelfth Street. The army by then was more troubled by friends than foes, finding it necessary to dispatch scout cars to the State Fairgrounds "to 'protect the army boys' " because the girls were "after them." On July 31 Romney shortened the curfew further and authorized the reopening of establishments serving alcoholic beverages; the next day the governor lifted the curfew entirely. The Police Department returned to eight-hour shifts on July 31. On August 1 most Guardsmen were pulled off the streets, and the paratroopers began their return to Forts Bragg and Campbell. "Law and order have been restored to Detroit," Vance declared on August 2, the day the last of the paratroopers left the city, the Guard was defederalized, and the police made their final entry in the riot disorder log. "We believe this mission has been accomplished efficiently and effectively," Vance asserted.[47]

The police removed the perimeter defense around police headquarters on August 3, the Guard left the city on August 6, and Romney that day announced the end of the state of emergency and returned control of law enforcement to the city. Romney also proclaimed August 6 to be a day of mourning in Detroit in memory of those who had lost their lives in the riot and a day of prayer for the success of community rehabilitation efforts.[48]

III

It required a total of about seventeen thousand men drawn from the army, the Michigan National Guard, the State Police, and the Detroit Police Department to quell the Detroit riot. As in other riot cities, coordination among the various control agencies proved difficult once higher-level forces were introduced. The various forces used different maps, their radios transmitted on different frequencies, and their intelligence units worked independently of one another for the most part. Because of the "confusion and inadequate coordination" among the control forces, Throckmorton later recommended that, if legally possible, the army in similar situations in the future should be given command of city and state police forces as well as the Guard.[49]

In a postriot critique session, the Police Department characterized liaison with the State Police in the riot as "excellent." Because the communications systems of the two were incompatible, however, and because they had separate command headquarters, police officers and state troopers were often dispatched to deal with the same incident.[50] Despite Operation Sundown, the liaison between the police and the Guard was less than perfect, and relations between the two were sometimes strained. Unlike the army, the Guard established brigade and battalion headquarters to coincide with police precinct boundaries, but the Guard thought that the police should have had a better understanding of the organizational structure of Guard company- and battalion-size units. Sundown, curiously, had failed to provide for the presence of a high-ranking Guard officer at police headquarters, an oversight that apparently affected the coordination of forces.[51]

The assistant chief of information of Task Force Detroit hailed the "cooperation" between the police and the army as "splendid." John Nichols, however, thought that liaison between the two was "very, very poor" since they had never before operated together. He spent half his time, he recalled, "trying to teach their generals what the hell to do."[52]

The most troublesome relationship among the control forces was between the army and the Guard. Calling for a better system of coordination when federal forces were sent to deal with a civil disorder, Romney complained that during the first twenty-four hours after Throckmorton took command, neither the governor nor local authorities "knew what the heck was going on." The governor told the Kerner Commission that during those hours "the distance between offices on the same floor was often as far as Lansing is from Washington."[53]

There was some tension between the army and the Guard at the command level. Throckmorton thought that Guard commanders "resented him," and the army high command thought poorly of the Guard leadership. "It is a pretty touchy situation when you are dealing with all these non-military types and with the National Guard," Throckmorton recalled. The deputy commander of Task Force Detroit had an especially poor opinion of Guard officers above the rank of major. He characterized all but one brigade commander and three battalion commanders as "below average."[54]

The army and the Guard, as we have seen, had difficulty coordinating their different views regarding the firing of weapons. Trained to operate in darkness and not to reveal themselves at night in confronting the enemy, the Guard, in dealing with snipers or alleged snipers, shot out the street lights. Vance and Throckmorton believed that this led to panic and the unnecessary firing of weapons and that the restoration of illumination had a "calming effect" on both civilians and law enforcement personnel. They therefore issued an order "to light up 12th Street," an order the Guard did not always obey.[55] The army was so concerned about Guard behavior that it ordered the 113th Military Intelligence Group to conduct an undercover surveillance of the 46th Division. Three mobile radio units, each manned by two special agents, conducted the surveillance from July 29 to July 31.[56]

Reporters (many of whom had frightening encounters with Guardsmen), city officials, the black community, and the Kerner Commission all agreed with the army appraisal of the Guard's performance. A Kerner Commission staffer dismissed the enlisted Guardsmen in Detroit as "a joke." None of the twenty-six blacks questioned in the survey conducted by the Military Intelligence Group expressed respect for the Guard. They indicated that they feared for their safety because they lacked confidence in the Guardsmen, and they were "resentful" because of the small number of blacks in the Guard.[57]

The consensus view in Detroit was that the paratroopers were more professional and better disciplined than the Guard. The comparison, however, was an unfair one. The 82d and 101st Airborne were experienced units, nearly all of whose noncommissioned officers and 35–40 percent of whose enlisted men were Vietnam veterans. Most Guardsmen, by contrast, had never before fired a weapon in anger. As Throckmorton noted, troops in combat for the first time are apt to be panicky and to jump "at any shadow." The manner in which the Guard arrived and was then deployed further limited its effectiveness as a riot control force. It must be noted, in addition, that the army had an easy time of it on the east side, whereas the Guard had to cope with the riot's most active sector throughout the disturbance. In a July 26 press conference Throckmorton asserted that the paratroopers would have had as much trouble as the Guard had the army been deployed on the west side. "I don't attribute anything magic to the Federal troops. They are good troops," he said. "But when Federal troops move into an area everybody just doesn't suddenly fall dead." Throckmorton, Vance, and Stone agreed, also, that however poorly the Guard had performed at the outset, it "improved markedly" and was "doing a good job" by the end of the riot.[58] It was the Guardsmen and the police, in the final analysis, who subdued the rioters, not the paratroopers.

The Michigan Guard defended itself against its many critics, characterizing 99 percent of the attacks upon it as uninformed. It pointed out that it was the army that determined the nature of Guard training and that the much-criticized Guard officers had to undergo training at regular army installations and had to attend regular army service schools. It claimed, inaccurately, that Throckmorton's order to unload came after the Guard had already brought the riot under control using loaded weapons. It denied discriminating against blacks, General Simmons asserting that no one was refused enlistment in the Guard who met the qualifications set forth by the Department of the Army. Revealingly, Simmons stated that the Guard did not have a "social mission" and that he was opposed to the lowering of enlistment standards so as to recruit more blacks.[59]

The Guard attributed part of its image problem to the fact that for the first several days after it had been federalized, it could release information only through the army. The public information officer of the National Guard Bureau concluded that the Guard had failed to get the press "under . . . control" before federalization and had then had no opportunity to report its activities accurately or to rebut criticism. In his view, there appeared to have been "a deliberate attempt by the press to show the paratroopers as real soldiers, while Guardsmen were just amateurs." There was, however, more truth to the criticism of the Guard than the public information officer and Guard spokesmen were willing to admit.[60]

Like the army, the State Police largely escaped criticism. A *Detroit Free Press* reporter who covered the riot thought that the state troopers assigned to riot duty handled themselves extremely well. "They are really pros," he remarked. Although there were some allegations of State Police misbehavior,[61] the bulk of the criticism about law enforcement misdeeds was directed at the police and the Guard, and properly so.

Quite apart from fatigue, stress, fear, desire for revenge, and racial bias that, as we have seen, affected police behavior beginning on July 24, the police were influenced in their treatment of rioters by the death of Olshove and the injuries suffered by other police officers. "After Olshove died . . .," one police officer recalled, "everything just went loose. The police officers weren't taking anything from anyone." Although Girardin commented as the riot drew to a close, "Never in any revolution, if this be one, have the rights of those involved been so protected," a minority of police officers were guilty of what Girardin himself later characterized as "bad excesses."[62] They subjected blacks and some whites to verbal and physical abuse, used excessive force in making arrests, mistreated and sometimes brutalized riot prisoners, behaved improperly in conducting searches, and may have engaged in some looting themselves.

There were complaints that the police removed their badges and taped over license plates and squad car numbers so that they could not be identified when they engaged in improper behavior. Actually, the department's riot control plan provided that officers wearing summer uniforms during a disturbance were to "take special safety precautions" by removing their badges, which reflected light, as well as neckties, tie clasps, leather shoulder straps, and metal collar insignia. The west side district inspector went beyond that, authorizing the police on July 23 to remove such identifying insignia as rank stripes and precinct numbers so as to avoid retaliation from rioters. The police apparently took this as authorization to conceal squad car numbers and license plates, allegedly because the numbers on squad cars had been painted with luminous paint and the white license plates made the cars visible at night. Girardin on July 28 ordered the immediate removal of tape that concealed identifying information, and the next day the department ordered police officers to wear their badges and insignia. The riot was subsiding by then, "so," as the head of the Detroit Police Officers Association said, "it didn't make much difference," but he nevertheless viewed Girardin's action as designed to appease the black community.[63]

Instructions to the police regarding the proper way to address blacks were forgotten in the heat of the riot. "Move you black nigger. Move, I said," a reporter heard a white police officer say to a black male while hitting him in the side with a shotgun. A black Guardsman escorting a black nurse to work heard a police officer address her as a "nigger bitch." While being held in the Tenth Precinct station, a black complained that he was called a "Nigger" who looked "like a dog."[64]

Although blacks were subjected to a good deal of verbal abuse, it was physical abuse that aroused their greatest resentment. Some blacks and whites were beaten so badly that they required hospitalization. On July 25 Guardsmen halted a car in which Ronnie Moore and two other blacks were riding. Two police officers arrived on the scene, one saying, "We have some more smart Niggers." One policeman reached into the car to hit Moore, and when he got out of the vehicle, the police hit him in the mouth, blackjacked him, and smashed the car's windshield.[65]

On the same day that Moore was abused, three police officers subjected Edward A. Rosario, the black owner of three gasoline stations, to both verbal and physical abuse at one of his closed stations. When Rosario objected to the action of a policeman in throwing a gasoline pump handle to the ground, another officer, Rosario claimed, hit him on the head with a rifle and directed obscenities at him. The sergeant in charge of the detail refused to give Rosario the offending officer's badge number, and the two patrolmen responded to Rosario's request for this information by pressing their guns against his face. Rosario took his complaint to Michigan's Civil Rights Commission (CRC), which upheld the complaint and recommended disciplinary action against the police officers involved and reimbursement of Rosario for medical costs and out-of-pocket expenses. The city eventually made an out-of-court settlement with Rosario but without conceding guilt.[66]

In another case stemming from police behavior, the CRC formally charged the police with physically abusing Jacob Bailey. Bailey, whose mother was president of the Highland Park chapter of the National Association for the Advancement of Colored People, and another young man were stopped by police on Twelfth and Clairmount as curfew violators while they were driving to Ft. Wayne to take physical examinations prior to their induction in the army. The police insulted and beat Bailey.

"They don't want any niggers in the Army," one officer declared, and another officer said, "run, nigger, so we can shoot you." The police beat Bailey so severely that he required medical attention, and they also damaged his car. Bailey was able to identify three of the officers, and a Guard captain also witnessed the affair.[67]

A United Press International reporter saw a policeman smash a drunk in the face with a rifle butt until the man collapsed. Five witnesses reported seeing the police and the Guard bayonet and shoot two blacks who came out of a west side building with their hands up. Seizing a young black who was observing looters fleeing from the scene as the police arrived, a policeman hit the youth across the face with a rifle and then pummeled him with the butt of the weapon. "They had missed the main event, so they settled for harassment of spectators," wrote a *Newsweek* reporter who had witnessed the episode.[68]

Two prominent blacks had experiences that indicated the physical danger blacks faced when they encountered police officers in the riot zone. After being interviewed on the street by an ABC-TV crew on July 27, Leon Atchison, administrative assistant to Congressman John Conyers, turned a corner and came face to face with a policeman who placed his shotgun against Atchison's forehead and wanted to know what he was doing there. Atchison pushed the gun away, scraping skin from his forehead. The officer cursed the congressional aide and, according to Atchison, was ready to blow his brains out, when the TV crew appeared.[69]

Roger Wilkins was out riding on the west side on the night of July 26 with two black Community Relations Service staff members when a caravan of police cars approached and they heard the order, "Stop that Damn Car." Accusing the three of being curfew violators, the police ordered them to get out of the car with their hands up. As they emerged from the vehicle, they heard the sound of the release of the safety mechanisms of the officers' guns. The three were permitted to leave after they identified themselves as Department of Justice personnel and showed their curfew passes. When Wilkins returned to police headquarters, Throckmorton said to him, "Jesus, Roger, you're lucky to be alive."[70]

The police were often none too gentle in making arrests. When a sample of 233 black male arrestees was questioned after the riot as to how they had been treated during the arrest process, 45 percent of them said that they had been treated "badly." They complained that they had been assaulted with the hand or weapon of the arresting officer, threatened with a weapon, or simply handled roughly. Law enforcement people are "combat oriented," observed Dr. Elliot Luby, who conducted the survey.[71]

Barbara Tinker did not exaggerate in her novel when she stated that the police were "arresting looters and throwing them up against buildings and calling them 'fucking niggers' and 'black bastards' and so forth and so on and hustling them into paddy wagons. More than one head," she noted, "was split open." The police took three blacks suspected of sniping to a precinct station and, according to their attorney, "beat 'the living shit' out of them. 'The police literally stomped them.' " The three suffered broken jaws, deep cuts, and bruises. When one of the three responded affirmatively to the question of whether he wanted a cup of coffee, a policeman threw the coffee in his face. The three were released the next day without being charged. A black woman reported that she had been told by the police who arrested her, "if you give us some pussy we will not arrest you."[72]

One case of abusive arrest during the riot led eventually to a state judicial ruling regarding the culpability of a city for the improper behavior of its police. On July 25 Charles Jackson, a black who worked at the W. J. Maxey Boys Training School in Whitmore Lake, was stopped at a roadblock on Grand River by two police officers. One of them said to Jackson, "You niggers are the reason why we are out here." When Jackson sought to open the trunk of his car to permit a police search, one officer hit him on the arm with a nightstick. The police rifled the trunk, beat the top of the vehicle and shattered its windows with a blackjack, and hit Jackson on the head with a blunt instrument. Left bleeding by the police, Jackson was eventually taken to the hospital by a Guard sergeant. Jackson, who had suffered a concussion, remained in the hospital for three and one-half weeks. Although he was unable to identify either of the two police officers, the state Court of Appeals in 1973 upheld a lower court ruling that the city was liable for the behavior of its police officers if their intentional negligence could be proved even though the complainant could not identify the perpetrators. Jackson was eventually awarded $13,184 in damages.[73]

The prominence of the individual involved drew attention to still another instance of police use of excessive force in making arrests. On July 24 James Del Rio, a black Detroit member of the lower house of Michigan's legislature, saw police abusing a black woman and a black man suspected of looting. According to Del Rio's sworn deposition, one officer jabbed the woman in the stomach with his shotgun and slammed the man across the back. Del Rio stated that he identified himself and asked in vain for the badge numbers of the police. As they placed the two suspects in a wagon, one officer struck a third black, holding a lunch pail, who was watching the proceedings, and also ordered him into the wagon as a suspected looter. He protested his innocence, and when the police, at Del Rio's request, searched the lunch pail, they found that it contained two sandwiches and nothing more. The police decided to let the man go, but a sergeant told Del Rio, "All right, nigger, you take his place." The police took the state representative to the Tenth Precinct station, where he was charged with interfering with an officer and inciting to riot. Del Rio was released without the police pressing charges against him.[74]

The bulk of the police brutality cases involved arrestees confined in one or another place of detention in the city. Arrestees interviewed in the Luby study reported that they had been kicked, beaten, whipped, and even shot by the police. United Press International reporter Justinas Bavarskis, who was twice arrested without being permitted to show his press credentials, saw arrestees systematically beaten, the degree of their punishment apparently varying with the seriousness of the crime with which they were being charged. While Bavarskis was in a room in the Herman Keifer command post, his hands up against the wall, his feet spread apart, a policeman held a rifle to his back while a fellow officer shouted, "Shoot the — — —! Go on, kill him." One police officer, Atchison told the Kerner Commission, carved his initials on a prisoner's back with cigarette burns, knocked out six of the prisoner's teeth, and blackened his eyes. When a handcuffed and bloody black arrestee whom a policeman brought to the emergency room of Detroit General Hospital begged, "Somebody help me, somebody help me," the policeman kicked him in the groin and said, "You should have thought of that before you started this, nigger." Two *Washington Post* reporters witnessed this incident.[75]

A black photographer arrested for alleged curfew violation discovered that practically all the arrestees with whom he was jailed had been beaten, and some were bloody. Another arrestee, who was jailed in the Tenth Precinct station, made a similar discovery. "Nearly everyone that came there in jail," he told an interviewer, "had a cut in their head or something wrong with them, that the police had did to them." He saw the police jab arrestees with guns and beat them with "those sticks." When a drunk attempted to walk out of the police garage where the arrestees were being held, he was shot, and the police then, as others confirmed, entered the garage and began hitting people on the head. When a woman prisoner, according to a falsely arrested female prisoner who was a city employee, asked for a drink, she was given a cup of urine. "You animals shouldn't be fed at all," a policeman said. "They don't consider us human," a black remarked in reflecting on his arrest experience. "We are animals to them. We have to be tamed, our spirits must be broken."[76]

The Tenth Precinct was the principal trouble spot insofar as the physical abuse of riot prisoners was concerned.[77] According to Hubert Locke, about twenty police officers were involved in misbehavior in that precinct. Police officials attributed this to the fact that the commanding officer of the precinct had been reassigned to the Herman Keifer command post, but the more likely explanation is that, because the riot centered in this precinct, the police were under greater strain there than elsewhere. On July 26 Conyers, Atchison, Del Rio, and three other black leaders went to the Tenth Precinct station to offer their services in urging citizens to obey the curfew. While waiting for the police to finish their dinner, the black leaders became eyewitnesses to a good deal of police brutality. They saw a detective in an interrogation room smash the nose of a prisoner who was already covered with blood and saw another officer jab handcuffs into the side of an arrestee on whom the officer had a judo lock. They yelled when they heard a black woman prisoner, stripped to the waist and covered with blood, beg for mercy. The black leaders decided not to go through with the mission that had brought them to the station.[78]

Among the numerous instances of police abuse of prisoners, the Murdock and the Rubin cases drew the most attention. Jackie Lee Murdock was arrested allegedly because there were guns in the apartment she shared with three others, a false charge as it turned out. While searching her in the squad car that was taking her to the Tenth Precinct station, one officer ripped the pajama top that served as her blouse. Inside the station, she was photographed while an officer fondled one of her exposed breasts. She was later ordered to undress, and the officers then made comments about her private parts—"look at that jungle, will you," one of them said. A photograph of the officer fondling Murdock that was thrown in the wastepaper basket ended up in Mayor Cavanagh's office.[79]

Twenty-seven-year-old Robert Rubin, his seventeen-year-old brother Raymond, and nineteen-year-old Albert Hammonds were white. Robert and his wife, an attorney, owned a home in the west side riot area that they had rented to three "hippies" when the Rubins moved to New York. Informed that their tenants, whom they had tried to evict, had abandoned the house a few days before the riot, Robert, Raymond, and Hammonds returned to the city and occupied the house. When the tenants sought to reoccupy the dwelling on July 26, Robert informed them that it had been repossessed. The three threatened to "get even" by telling the Guard that the house was a "snipers' nest." That same evening a Guard detachment with a tank appeared outside the house, the Guard having been informed, apparently by the former tenants, that the people in the house were "going to start shooting." The captain in charge exploded a firecracker device on the front lawn to attract the attention of the occupants and gave them a voice warning—he had no amplifying equipment—to come out of the house by the count of ten. Claiming that he heard a shot coming from inside the house although admitting that he did not see a flash, the officer ordered a machine-gun attack on the house, with perhaps 250 rounds being fired. The Rubins' attorney had advised them to take a gun into the house because they had been threatened by the tenants. The three told the police that one of them had fired a single shot into a pillow to see if the gun was working but denied any additional firing. Bavarskis claimed, however, that Hammonds, while in custody, had told him that Robert had fired a shot at the tank.

When bullets began hitting the house, the three occupants retreated to the third floor, and Robert waved an old bathrobe out the window as a cease-fire signal. The shelling then stopped, and the three men emerged from the house. After the Guardsmen forced them to lie down on the street on their stomachs, an officer ordered the tank to run over them. The tank moved to within three feet of the three before halting. The Guardsmen roughed up their prisoners before taking them to the Tenth Precinct station, where they were charged with assault with intent to commit murder, a charge that was later dismissed at the preliminary examination.

The treatment of the Rubins and Hammonds by the police in the Tenth Precinct once the three had been removed from their cell for interrogation borders on the incredible. Robert was stabbed in the rectum with a bayonet and was kicked so severely in the groin area that his testicles were still black and blue two weeks later. A policeman stepped on Robert's glasses and then rubbed the broken glass into the prisoner's hands. After a police officer hit Raymond on the head with a rifle butt, he collapsed on the floor from loss of blood. An elderly black prisoner "raised such a . . . fuss" over this that the police decided to take Raymond to the hospital, but they beat the black prisoner for protesting their brutality. En route to the hospital, the driver stopped the vehicle in which the police were transporting Raymond, and the police told him to get out and run. When he refused, they threw hot coffee in his face and beat him. It took a number of stitches to close his head wound. The police, finally, beat Hammonds about the face and forehead with a blackjack, causing "a severe conjunctival hemorrhage" in his right eye.

Mug shots proved that the Rubins and Hammonds had sustained their injuries after they had been brought to the police station. The detective assigned to investigate the case described the condition of the three men as "unbelievable" when he saw them three or so days after their victimization. Robert had to be hospitalized later and required psychiatric treatment. Affected by loud noises, he "went into something like a trance" when his two-year-old child shot a toy gun, and he "began choking . . . and tried to kill" his wife. The three were able to identify only one police officer who had assaulted them, the same officer who two days later was the principal guilty party in the abuse of Jackie Lee Murdock. According to the head of the Citizen Complaint Bureau (CCB), the policeman involved was "a good officer" who "went berserk during the riot." He resigned from the department while under police investigation and was subsequently tried and convicted for felonious assault.[80]

Unreasonable police searches and seizures threatened "a new explosion" during the waning days of the riot. By July 26 the police were receiving hundreds of tips about locations where loot was supposedly stored. Since the prosecutor would not sanction warrants for these searches, the police took what was called "direct action" to seize weapons and other loot in the hands of "the wrong people." One woman testified that the police had told her that if she would not let them into her dwelling, they would enter forcibly; and another woman said that the police had told her that she had forfeited her right to refuse a search because she lived in public housing! On August 1 the department ordered precinct commanders to stop all unauthorized searches and to have police seek a search warrant if they could not receive consent for a search. The order followed the initiation of a suit in Wayne County Circuit Court by the Neighborhood Legal Service Centers (NLSC), later joined in by the Metropolitan Detroit Branch of the American Civil Liberties Union (ACLU), to enjoin the police from making searches for stolen property without search warrants and from removing personal property in the process.[81]

Although the police were supposed to obtain the consent of residents before conducting a warrantless search for stolen property, it is questionable how meaningful "consent" given to "heavily armed law enforcement officers operating in a war atmosphere" actually was. Asked if he had given his consent to a search, one person replied, "Sure, what would you do if you opened a door and saw rifles staring you in the face?"[82]

Not only did the police engage in illegal searches, but there were also numerous complaints that, once having entered a dwelling, they confiscated new material for which the residents could not provide a receipt, as well as money and other goods, and sometimes ransacked the premises. A *Free Press* photographer who witnessed the search of the apartment of "a terror-stricken woman of 47" erroneously suspected of being a sniper reported that the police riddled the kitchen door with bullets, blew off the locks, smashed the living room door, shot up the apartment, emptied the bureau drawers, and "dismantled" the bed. "I ought to shoot you right now, you bitch," an officer said to her.[83]

The complaints about illegal searches and seizures by the police did not persuade Circuit Court Judge Carl Weideman to grant the injunction sought by the NLSC. "You're asking me to handcuff the police," he said. "I am not about to do that." The NLSC and ACLU also failed to persuade the state Court of Appeals to grant the injunction they sought. They called off their suit after Cavanagh on August 4 ordered the police to seek search warrants if they could not obtain the *written* permission of residents to conduct a search.[84] That this, in the circumstances of the time, was very much of a change in the direction of legality is doubtful.

Just after the riot, 83 percent of adult blacks in a sample survey of Twelfth Street residents claimed that they had heard that the police took things or burned stores during the disturbance. The "taking things" no doubt referred primarily to police seizure of goods while conducting searches, but Detroit Urban League officials told a Kerner Commission interviewer that the police had "looted" during the riot. A black police officer recalled seeing officers outside the Tenth Precinct station arguing, "pushing and screaming" over fur coats and jewelry seized from looters. Another person claimed that he had witnessed the police filling a paddy wagon with goods taken from a store.[85]

The only notable case of police arson involved Edward Vaughn's bookstore, which specialized in Afro-American literature.[86] Eyewitnesses reported that the police pulled up to the store in three cars in the early hours of July 27 and first vandalized the store and then firebombed it, destroying three-fourths of the books. The police returned the next night, according to Vaughn, removed the boards he had placed over the broken windows, knocked down the books he had put back on the shelves, and left the water in the bathroom running. The next morning Vaughn found books floating in water in the store. A Tenth Precinct sergeant admitted the firebombing but claimed that this was because the police had been informed that there were guns on the premises.[87]

The illegal, sometimes brutal behavior of the police in their effort to suppress the Detroit riot elicited a strong reaction in the black community and in civil rights groups in Detroit and Michigan. After their disturbing visit to the Tenth Precinct station on July 26, Conyers and Del Rio met with Girardin to demand that the police in precinct stations wear their badges and give their names when asked. They also urged the immediate establishment of a nonpartisan committee to visit precinct stations to investigate the treatment of prisoners. At a July 29 press conference Conyers announced the formation of an ad hoc committee to deal with complaints regarding civil rights violations. Grievants were invited to come to Conyers's office, where volunteers made written records of the allegations. A record of seventy-three such complaints survives, some of them pertaining to the same incident, although Atchison claimed that far more than this number were received by the volunteers.[88]

After the riot, Conyers met with John Doar to seek federal prosecution of police guilty of depriving Detroiters during the disturbance of their federally guaranteed civil rights. Although a Detroit attorney thought that the United States attorney in Detroit was "not very interested" in prosecuting such cases, Attorney General Ramsey Clark promised "priority handling." The task was undertaken by the Civil Rights Division of the Justice Department, which looked into forty-two cases of possible violation of federal civil rights laws by the police and Michigan Guard. The division was handicapped in its investigation because the police refused to be interviewed by the FBI except in the presence of their attorneys and a court reporter, conditions unacceptable to the FBI, and because the Michigan Guard insisted that since it had been federalized, the Justice Department had to provide accused Guardsmen with counsel, a condition that troubled Doar.[89] In the end, as we shall see, the federal government instituted legal proceedings in only one case stemming from the riot, the celebrated Algiers Motel affair.

The Michigan CRC intervened during the riot in an effort to protect the rights of arrestees. On July 26 its two Detroit representatives visited the Tenth Precinct station to check on reports concerning mistreatment of prisoners. Although National Guardsmen ushered them out of the station at gunpoint, the two did succeed in arranging for the separate confinement of two women prisoners who had been incarcerated in the same detention area with two hundred men. Two days later Girardin complied with a CRC request to send observers to places where riot arrestees were being held. The CRC then sent observers to nineteen places of detention, including all the precinct stations housing riot arrestees. Although staff members believed the commission's action had been "conducive to the civil treatment" of arrestees, the observers did not begin their visits until the worst of the riot was over.[90]

The CRC was "not too well received" by the police, who complained that the observers were interfering with police work. The head of the Detroit Police Officers Association protested to Romney, "We resent the Civil Rights Commission looking over our shoulders, just waiting for some officer to stub his toe." At one precinct station, a white officer "bitterly abused" a black CRC observer, saying that "all people of his kind should be killed."[91]

On July 26 Detroit Catholic and Protestant clergymen approached Cavanagh and Romney for permission to supply a chaplaincy service to "all points of special need" and to gain access to precinct stations where conditions were reported to be "difficult." On July 29 Girardin authorized the chaplaincy service, and from that day until August 6 chaplaincy teams served the city and county jails. The seventy clergymen who participated in this "ministry of service" provided eyewitness reports of "considerable over-reaction" by the police, especially in dealing with nonwhites in three precincts. A Baptist minister, who found the "hatred" of blacks by the police to be "unbelievable," concluded that it was the police who needed the counseling, not the prisoners. Although they were of some help to the prisoners, the ministers, like the CRC observers, provided a service that was "too little and too late."[92]

The Police Department, of course, had its own agency for dealing with complaints of police misbehavior, the Citizen Complaint Bureau (CCB). As of September 12, 1967, the CCB had received fifty-eight riot-related complaints. Girardin thought this a "remarkably small number" considering that forty-four hundred police officers had been involved in "a week-long semi-war," but not all complaints against the police stemming from the riot were directed to the CCB. According to a CRC official, the total number of complaints submitted to agencies of government and individuals like Conyers was about three hundred. Not much came of the complaints submitted to the CCB, largely because it proved to be "virtually impossible" for complainants to identify offending officers since they had not been wearing identifying insignia. Some officers, however, agreed to resign from the police force or retire on the condition that the complaint against them not be placed in their personnel file.[93]

Residents of the Twelfth Street riot area made their own judgment about police behavior in the riot. In a survey of 270 black adults in the area, about three-quarters of the respondents evaluated the police performance in the riot as "not good" or "poor," and half thought that the force used by the police and the Guard had been "too strong." Almost one-third of the respondents judged that "policemen treated people even worse during the riot than they had previously."[94]

As their actions in the Blanding and Rubin cases reveal, the behavior of Guardsmen paralleled that of the police. If a National Guard major claimed that young Guardsmen simply adopted the brutal practices of the police with whom they were deployed, a veteran police officer complained that Guardsmen were so aggressive that some police officers were afraid to patrol with them.[95] Whatever the reason, blacks made the same kind of complaints about the Guard as about the police.

The epithet "nigger" rolled off the tongues of Guardsmen as readily as off the tongues of police officers. The black photographer who had been improperly incarcerated reported that Guardsmen spoke without inhibition about the "niggers" in their custody and "thought it a great joke to show off 'the Zoo' " to other Guardsmen. In the Tenth Precinct station, Guardsmen sought to frighten prisoners by shooting blanks at them. To add insult to injury, a reporter saw a Guardsman in the station selling cigarettes to arrestees at inflated prices.[96]

Blacks who brought their complaints to Conyers's office told of being pistol-whipped by a Guardsman and of soldiers walking on the hands of two black youths ordered to lie on the grass. One black reported that after a Guardsman had physically assaulted his brother, a Guard sergeant said, "I always wanted to kill me a nigger." While a bus driver was visiting his girlfriend, according to Atchison, Guardsmen began firing into the house. When those inside the dwelling emerged, the soldiers shot both the bus driver and the girl's stepfather. A Guard officer then drove up in a jeep to tell the men that they were attacking the wrong house. The two gunshot victims were taken to the hospital, where they were chained to their beds because the Guardsmen reported them to be arrestees. A reporter saw Guardsmen, joined by State Police troopers, rake a building with gunfire and then invade it, shooting off locks, battering down doors, and ripping up the furniture in a futile search for weapons.[97]

Some Guard actions were simply mean-spirited. A *New York Times* reporter saw a Guardsman halt a black city employee during curfew hours, remove four cases of beer from the trunk of his car, and smash them to pieces. When the driver presented the receipt for the beer, the soldier told him that he was lucky he had not been shot. Seizing some black looters on another occasion, Guardsmen stuck bayonets in the tires of their car. The president of the Parent-Faculty-Student Council of Central High complained to Romney that Guardsmen stationed at the school had helped themselves to a projector, a television receiver, a camera, a typewriter, and microphones. "Who," the president asked, "is going to be charged with policing the National Guard?"[98]

IV

In a manifestation of the so-called "propagation effect," a big riot in one city in the 1960s was apt to trigger racial disturbances in surrounding communities.[99] This is precisely what occurred while the Detroit riot was underway, the disorder spreading in some degree or other to fourteen Michigan communities, especially Highland Park, Pontiac, Grand Rapids, Flint, and Saginaw. These extra-Detroit disturbances were marked by window breaking, the stoning of cars, firebombing, looting, and a very limited amount of sniping. They were free of deaths except in Pontiac, where two blacks were killed, one of them shot by a member of the Michigan legislature whose store the victim had attempted to set on fire. Romney issued emergency proclamations for Grand Rapids and Flint, and his proclamation for Detroit applied to Highland Park as well. The State Police supplemented the efforts of local police officers in nine communities, and some Guardsmen serving in Detroit also helped out in Highland Park.[100]

Colonel Davids thought that the Flint and Grand Rapids disturbances did not escalate because law enforcement forces, unlike in Detroit, used "a little beef" at the outset. Saying that the riot "must be put down immediately by force of men and arms," the State Police high command ordered the squads sent to Grand Rapids "to use necessary force without hesitation." The chief of police of Highland Park told a Kerner Commission interviewer that he got "tough" at once when the disorder spread to his city and that this had been crucial in minimizing the trouble. Whatever the reason, the damage in the Michigan cities that experienced disorders in the last week of July 1967 was miniscule as compared to Detroit.[101]

CHAPTER 10

Rioters and Judges

"It would now appear," George E. Bushnell, Jr., wrote the deputy director of the Lawyers' Committee for Civil Rights and Law on August 3, 1967, "that, for all practical purposes, the United States Constitution was absolutely suspended from sometime during the evening of Sunday, July 23rd, to Tuesday, August 1, 1967." Bushnell was referring to the operation of the criminal justice system as it applied to the thousands of persons arrested during the Detroit riot. In Ray Girardin's view, by contrast, it was the large number of arrests, which, he maintained, was "fully effective in getting people off the streets," that prevented the riot from taking an even uglier turn than it did.[1]

A total of 7,231 individuals were arrested during the riot. This compared with 3,952 arrests during the Watts riot and 1,510 during the Newark riot. Of the Detroit arrestees, 6,528 were adults, 781 of whom (11.9 percent) were white, and 806 of whom (12.3 percent) were women. The 703 juveniles (under seventeen years of age) arrested included 43 whites (6 percent) and 81 females (11.5 percent). The age of the juvenile arrestees ranged from ten to sixteen, most of them being between fourteen and sixteen. The adult arrestees ranged in age from seventeen to eighty, but about half were twenty-five years of age or younger. Including juveniles, Detroit arrestees twenty-five years of age or under constituted 58 percent of the total number of arrestees, very similar to the 60 percent figure for arrestees of these ages in eighteen riots occurring in American cities between June and August 1967. Just about half (48.6 percent) of the Detroit arrestees had criminal records, slightly above the 45 percent with such records among Newark arrestees but well below the 73 percent figure for Watts. It is likely that no more than half of the Detroit arrestees with records had actually been convicted following their arrests.[2]

Of the adult arrests, about 64 percent were for looting, and about 14 percent for curfew violations. Two hundred and ninety persons were arrested while carrying firearms, but only 26 arrestees were charged with sniping. Seven arrestees were charged with homicide, 206 with felonious assault, 34 with arson, and 28 with inciting to riot. Looting appears to

249

have been a more common cause for arrest in Detroit than in most other cities experiencing riots between 1964 and 1967, but relatively fewer Detroiters were arrested for assault or weapons offenses.[3]

Not all those who rioted were arrested, and not all arrestees were rioters. The police, as we have seen, made few arrests at the beginning of the riot, and they appear to have been more reluctant to arrest females than males.[4] Not authorized to make arrests, Michigan National Guardsmen were not always able to summon police in time to apprehend lawbreakers. When police appeared, looters would flee, the police arresting "the poor dumb people who didn't know how to run or where to run." "All we are arresting," declared the chief of the Criminal Division of the Wayne County prosecutor's office, "are the ham-and-egg people." Snipers, insofar as there were snipers, fired and ran, generally escaping arrest, and the police had little success in apprehending the numerous arsonists. The police, on the other hand, often made arrests on a wholesale basis, nonrioters being swept up in police dragnets along with rioters. Seeking to contain the disturbance, the police, in effect, sometimes "spread a huge net over the riot area" and seized everyone caught within it.[5]

The normal procedure in Detroit was for the police to take arrestees to a precinct station, where they were booked, fingerprinted, and interrogated. Those suspected of having committed a felony or a serious misdemeanor were usually held at the station while a detective investigated the case to determine whether to recommend the issuance of a warrant by the prosecutor. If after examining the "write-up" of the arrest, the prosecutor's office decided to recommend that the magistrate issue a warrant, the prisoner's file was sent to the warrant clerk's office in the Recorder's Court, where a complaint and warrant of arrest were prepared. The prisoner was then brought to police headquarters and lodged in one of the thirteen detention cells in the building. He was subsequently arraigned on the warrant before one of the thirteen Recorder's Court judges, who set the prisoner's bond. The prisoner was then turned over to the county sheriff and remained in the county jail until his release.[6]

Neither the Detroit Police Department, the prosecutor, nor the Recorder's Court was prepared for the flood of prisoners during the 1967 riot. The Police Department's riot control plan provided for the use of a departmental bus parked close to the riot zone in which arrestees could be booked, thus permitting a quick return to the streets by the arresting officers. The "mobile jail" concept, however, was implemented to only a limited extent, probably because of the large geographical spread of the disturbance and the sheer number of arrestees. Instead of 3,000 arrestees over a nine-day period that the department had anticipated in the event of a riot, the police had to process 4,784 arrestees during the first three days of the riot alone, the normal load for an entire month. The result was a virtual breakdown in the booking and investigation process. Booking became an "assembly-line" operation, with arresting officers some-times finding it necessary to assist in filling out the arrest cards before they could return to the streets.

Since the Police Department was understandably concerned that arresting officers would not remember the looters they had apprehended and the merchandise the looters had allegedly seized, it followed the Newark practice and provided for the arresting officer and his prisoner, when booked, to be photographed side by side, with the loot included in the photograph. The postbooking investigation by detectives was designed to eliminate weak cases, but the Police Department did not have enough detectives to permit adequate investigation of the thousands of arrests. The result was that the department requested warrants for about 75 percent of the riot arrests as compared to the normal 50 to 60 percent, which was still below the 90 percent of arrests prosecuted in the Watts riot. The Detroit department requested prosecution for most looting and curfew offenses but less than half of the arrests for homicide, aggravated assault, robbery, and arson.[7]

The problem for the prosecutor's office in responding to police requests for warrants was that it had to process about half as many cases in one week during the riot as it had processed in the entire preceding year. It was supposed to make its warrant decisions within seventy-two hours so that there would be "no 'unnecessary delay' between arrest and initial court appearance" of an arrestee. The prosecutor's office, how-ever, had only so many assistant prosecutors to process write-ups and issue warrant recommendations. Not only did forty assistant prosecutors work shifts around the clock to move the files, but it also became neces-sary for them to do some of the clerical work themselves. William L. Cahalan, who became the county prosecutor at the beginning of 1967, recalled that at one point during the riot assistant prosecutors were down on their hands and knees in the prosecutor's offices sorting papers and seeking to match arrest reports and arrest records.[8]

To some degree, the prosecutor's office met the deluge of warrant requests by recommending "about everything that was brought in," to quote an assistant prosecutor. The 4,260 arrestees for whom warrants were issued, 3,230 for felonies and 1,030 for misdemeanors, constituted about 98 percent of the number for whom the police had requested warrants, excluding 514 of the original 4,881, who, it was determined, had been arrested for reasons unrelated to the riot. This 2 percent rejec-tion rate compared with a rate of about 20 percent in normal times.[9]

Normally, the prosecutor's office provided Recorder's Court judges with the arrest and conviction records of arrestees before their arraign-ment. Discovering arrest records in time for a speedy arraignment proved, however, to be a "horrendously large job" in the riot since many arrestees gave the police fictitious names and the Identification Bureau of the Police Department could analyze only about two hundred fingerprints in a twenty-four-hour period. The prosecutor's office consequently arranged on July 25 for the police to fly about one thousand prints to Washington for FBI analysis, a task completed within twenty-four hours. The Alcohol Tax Division sent ten agents to Detroit on July 26 to aid the Police Department in checking fingerprints, and the Windsor Police Department also provided assistance. A high proportion of the arrestees, however, had been arraigned and their bonds set before the prosecutor's office could determine if they had criminal records.[10]

It was the prosecutor's responsibility to decide not only whether an arrestee should be prosecuted but also the offense with which he was to be charged. When Cahalan, after returning to Detroit from out-of-town on the evening of July 23, went out on the roof of the police headquarters building, it looked to him as though the city were "burning down." "I want to warn these people who are stealing and burning and looting," he announced the next day, "that they will be charged with the full criminality of their acts." He warned rioters that they faced up to life imprisonment for "crimes of vandalism and arson."[11]

Because of the sketchy nature of the arrest reports, the result of a much overburdened police force, Cahalan did not have the usual information available to him in deciding on the proper charge for arrestees. Aware that it was easier to lower a charge than to raise it and that "high papering" would lead to the setting of high bonds, which he initially favored, Cahalan opted for a high proportion of felony charges.

The crucial question for the prosecutor regarding charging was how to treat looting. Looters usually could not be charged with "breaking and entering" since proof of actual "breaking" was generally lacking. Cahalan's assistants, even before the prosecutor had returned to the city, consequently decided on the charge of "entering without breaking [EW/OB] with intent to commit a felony or larceny therein." This was a felony punishable by not more than five years imprisonment or a fine of not more than $2,500. Larceny under $100, on the other hand, was a misdemeanor. More than half (54.6 percent) of the prosecution arrests in the riot were for EW/OB.[12]

Cahalan told a Kerner Commission interviewer just after the riot that he was "quite proud" of his staff for having decided on the EW/OB charge. He had second thoughts about the matter, however, recognizing that it was "100 times easier to move [a misdemeanor charge] through the system than a felony." Drawing on his riot experience, he advised the State's Attorney's staff in Chicago in February 1968 to use misdemeanor rather than felony charges whenever possible in a riot situation since the latter charges "cluttered trial dockets and imposed heavy evidentiary burdens on the prosecution."[13]

The Recorder's Court was unprepared for the wholesale arrests resulting from the riot. The court between July 23 and July 31 was "virtually inundated with humanity" — the number of felony defendants added to its caseload during the first five days of the riot was the equivalent of the number the court normally had to deal with in a six-month period. In its annual report for 1967 the court reported that its caseload for the last half of the year was "more explosive" than anything ever before encountered by any metropolitan court in the United States. The flood of cases posed a challenge to "all the established procedures" of the court, and, in adjusting to the situation, the court, according to the executive director of its Psychiatric Clinic, threw all precedents "in the ash can."[14]

Since the Recorder's Court regularly convened on Saturday and Sunday, one judge, Donald Leonard, was on duty on July 23. Judge Vincent Brennan opened a second court that day; and before the day was out, Judge Robert J. Colombo also became available. The court operated throughout the night arraigning prisoners, but there were only two warrant clerks on duty, which caused the court to fall behind in processing cases. On July 24 the court announced that it would remain open around-the-clock until further notice solely to handle arraignments on the warrant in felony and misdemeanor cases.[15]

Like the police and the prosecutor's office, the Recorder's Court was "completely overwhelmed by the paperwork and record keeping" necessitated by so many arrests and by antiquated administrative procedures. The consequent delays in the administration of justice meant that arrestees were kept in jail who might otherwise have been released. The presiding judge of the Wayne County Circuit Court offered clerical assistance from his court on July 24, but the Recorder's Court did not accept the offer until later in the week. A Recorder's Court clerk then sought to instruct county court clerks in the use of Recorder's Court's files, but since they were unfamiliar with Recorder's Court procedures, the instruction ceased "after a day of frustration," and the proffered assistance was rejected as likely to prove "more trouble" than it was "worth." The staff of the clerk's office was, however, augmented during the week by fifty stenographers, typists, and clerks drawn from various city departments. Cahalan arranged for additional clerical assistance by turning to his godmother nun, a member of the Immaculate Heart of Mary, who sent over some of the sisters to serve as typists. The court rejected the suggestion of federal judge Wade H. McCree, Jr., that it use federal probation officers to interview prisoners as a possible basis for their release on their own recognizance and that it deputize volunteer attorneys as special prosecutors to interview prisoners and to recommend the nol-prossing of misdemeanor cases such as curfew violations.[16]

The chief judge of the Wayne County Circuit Court, which had suspended operations because of the riot, offered the Recorder's Court the services of the county court's twenty-six judges on July 25. According to the executive judge of the Recorder's Court, Vincent Brennan, the Recorder's Court rejected this offer as well as the offer of aid from municipal court judges in the Detroit metropolitan area on the ground that the delay in the court's operations was caused by the logjam in the warrant clerk's office, not because of a lack of judges. It is a little difficult, however, to square this assertion with the "assembly line techniques" used by Recorder's Court judges during the week. It is more likely that the court, viewing the Circuit Court's offer as "implied criticism" of Recorder's Court operations, wished to forestall passage of a state bill that would have merged the two courts and eliminated the Recorder's Court as an independent entity.

Justice Theodore T. Souris of the Michigan Supreme Court thought that the Recorder's Court simply "didn't want anyone to observe what was going on. They had a fixed notion of what they were going to do," Souris said, "and didn't want anyone to interfere." Believing that the court was "more or less under the thumb of the police department," Judge George Crockett, a black, maintained that the court's time-consuming processes provided the judges the necessary excuse to keep arrestees in custody. Circuit Court judges, to be sure, were eventually used to replace absent Recorder's Court judges, but this did not add to the available judicial manpower to deal with riot cases.[17]

The arraignment on the warrant of riot prisoners that began on July 23 was designed to inform defendants of the charges against them, advise them of their constitutional rights, fix bail, and set the date for the preliminary examination if the felony defendant desired same. In approaching their duties, most judges, like many in the white community, were simply "scared to death" by what was happening in the city. According to University of Detroit Law School professor Frank Sengstock, a "significant number" of the judges privately conceded that as they watched the fires and smoke in the city through the windows of their courtrooms, they were concerned about "the capacity of the structured society" to combat the riot. "We had no way of knowing," one judge later declared, "whether there was a revolution in progress or whether the city was going to be burned to the ground."[18]

As a result of their fears, the judges saw the court's role as that of an "assistant to the police in enforcing the law instead of a check on police activities." Nowhere was this concern more evident than in the setting of bail by all but Crockett. In setting bail in Michigan, a judge was to consider the seriousness of the offense, the past record of the defendant, and the probability of his appearance in court on the required day. Relying perhaps on Michigan case law that permitted a judge to consider "all the circumstances of the case" in setting bail, Cahalan on the evening of July 23 urged the court to adopt a high bail policy and suggested $10,000 as the proper sum for looters. He justified this high figure because of the "chaos and complete lawlessness" in the streets and the fact that the arrest records of most defendants were not available at that time. A high bond policy of this sort was tantamount to preventive detention, but this was apparently "a normally accepted practice" of the Recorder's Court.[19]

In fixing bail, Recorder's Court judges left no doubt that their purpose was "to stop the rioting." "We will allocate an extraordinary bond," Brennan declared. "We must keep these people off the streets. We will keep them off." When the Reverend Albert Cleage complained about the high bond policy, Brennan attacked him as "a racist who would like nothing better than for us [the judges] to turn loose these thugs and . . . the other extreme take-over-by violence mob he is a part of." Brennan later explained that since arrest records were unavailable, the high bond policy was justified lest serious offenders be released to the streets, thereby harming the morale of law enforcement personnel. The criticism, he said, came from people who did not realize "how tense the situation was."[20]

Like Brennan, Colombo defended a high bail policy as necessary to keep rioters off the streets. "In a way," he said, "we're doing what the police didn't do," by which he was undoubtedly referring to the policy of police restraint at the outset of the riot. Colombo told one defendant, "I can set bonds up to $10 million if I wish," and he said to an accused looter, "You can't get a personal bond in this court. You're nothing but lousy, thieving looters." One judge told a defendant he was arraigning, "It's too bad they didn't shoot you."[21]

When the judges met in Brennan's office on July 24, the executive judge recommended that they set high bonds of $10,000 to $25,000. No vote was taken, and, as Crockett recalled, "there wasn't even much discussion of the constitutionality of high bail." All but Crockett, however, apparently agreed with what he thought was Brennan's "arbitrary . . . decision." On July 24 all the judges but Crockett set bonds at $10,000 or $25,000 or more for most arrestees. Crockett, on the other hand, set bonds as low as $1,000 and released some defendants on personal bonds. For the most part, the judges made little effort to make "individual decisions in individual cases." In one instance, a judge lined up six defendants, told them they had been accused of EW/OB, and set the bonds for all of them at $10,000 without any regard for their individual circumstances. A newsman who observed Judge Colombo in action on July 24 reported that his rulings were "fast, decisive and unyielding" and that not a single defendant was able to make his bond.[22]

Beginning on July 25, as fear for the city's survival lessened, the Recorder's Court judges began to moderate their bail policy somewhat. Most judges, however, continued to set bonds at levels well above what was normal for the court. On July 26 Crockett, who thought the high bond policy was being followed because most defendants were black, sent a letter to Brennan denouncing the bonds as "not only excessive, but prohibitive."[23]

A study that began on July 26 of one thousand riot arrestees incarcerated in the state prison in Jackson indicated that 50 percent had bonds of $10,000 or more. The severity of the crime seemed to have little relationship to the size of the bond. Of those charged with EW/OB, for example, 24 percent had bonds of under $3,000, but 43 percent had bonds ranging from $8,000 to $12,000. Thirty-five percent of the curfew violators had bonds ranging from $8,000 to $12,000, although under Michigan law misdemeanants of this sort could have been released on a $100 bond.

There was also wide disparity in the bond-setting practices of different judges. Two judges, Crockett and Elvin L. Davenport, set bonds of less than $3,000 for more than half of the defendants coming before them, but the percentage of defendants for whom bonds were set at this level ranged from 1 to 41 percent for the other judges. At the other extreme, one judge set bonds of $23,000 to $27,000 for 36 percent of the defendants he arraigned, whereas the highest percentage of bonds at this level set by the remaining judges was 7. It made little difference to most of the judges, furthermore, whether the defendant was employed or unemployed, married or single, or with or without a criminal record. Ronald Reosti of the Neighborhood Legal Service Centers (NLSC) guessed that 90 percent of the bonds the judges set violated constitutional standards.[24]

In Watts and Newark, the judges also initially sought to prevent riot arrestees from returning to the streets by setting high bonds, but the bonds in these two riot cities were well below the Detroit figures. In Watts, the typical bond set ranged from $4,400 to $5,500. In Newark, judges set uniform bonds of $1,000 for curfew violation, $2,500 for breaking and entering and receiving stolen goods, $5,000 for the possession of deadly weapons, and $10,000 for firebombing or the possession of Molotov cocktails.[25]

Although the judges began to set lower bonds beginning on July 25, some were still reluctant to see any riot prisoners released even if they could post their bonds. Early in the week of July 23 Brennan and perhaps some other judges told Sheriff Peter Buback to report back to them before releasing prisoners who had posted bonds, apparently so that a check could be made to see if they had been involved in other riots or their records showed that they were "wanted" or on parole. Crockett claimed that the thinking behind this concern was that anyone who could post bond "must be a riot 'leader.' " Some attorneys reported that there was a sign in the sheriff's office on July 25 or 26 that no bonds would be honored until further notice, and two bondsmen said that they had been unable to get anyone released from the Wayne County jail during the riot's early days. The refusal of the sheriff to release prisoners for whom bonds had been posted produced a heated reaction from judges Frank Schemanske and Crockett in particular and a threat of contempt action by the latter.[26]

As a further indication of their reluctance to see riot prisoners released, Recorder's Court judges virtually suspended the writ of habeas corpus during the disorder by making the relatively few writs filed returnable only after a number of days. On July 24 one judge thus set a hearing for July 31 on four writs brought before her, and writs brought on the same day before another judge were not granted until eight days later. Lawyers claimed that some judges "simply announced and/or put up signs" that they would not entertain any habeas corpus writs.[27]

The NLSC was especially anxious to persuade the court to set more reasonable bonds. The centers' new Bail Bond Program went into effect on July 24, and Brennan, accordingly, authorized NLSC attorneys to gather relevant information for bond-setting purposes from prisoners awaiting arraignment. Crockett availed himself of the information the agency provided, but most judges at the outset would not even permit NLSC attorneys to interview defendants in their courtrooms. Meeting with the judges on July 25, Michigan Supreme Court Justice Thomas Brennan assured them that a majority of the state's Supreme Court justices supported the Recorder's Court bail policy.[28]

Pressure on the Recorder's Court to reconsider its bail policy began to build after the first couple of days of the riot. At a July 25 meeting attended by representatives of the NLSC, the National Lawyers Guild, Wayne County Suburban Legal Services, the Detroit Bar Association, and the Wolverine Bar Association (the association of black Detroit attorneys), NLSC and Lawyers Guild attorneys proposed filing a writ of superintending control with the Michigan Court of Appeals directing the Recorder's Court to fix bail in accordance with constitutional requirements. Arguing that such an action would have no immediate effect and would only "antagonize" the judges, Detroit Bar Association representatives proposed as an alternative direct negotiation with the Recorder's Court and Cahalan, the strategy that the group adopted. Those present at the meeting formed a Policy Committee that met each day during the riot and sought to work with the judges to secure a reduction in the bonds set for arrestees and to consider other legal problems stemming from the riot. When the Policy Committee met with Brennan on the day it was formed, he promised to end the court's "high bond policy," and asked the committee's assistance in doing so. The court did not "end" the high bond policy, but some judges began to moderate their bond policy that day.[29]

Following the July 25 meeting with Brennan, the NLSC and the Detroit Urban Law Program dispatched NLSC attorneys and interns and Urban Law Clinic lawyers and students to interview riot prisoners in Detroit, Milan, and Jackson as a basis for recommending the granting of personal bonds by the judges where appropriate. Two groups of VISTA workers who had gained experience in the bail programs in Philadelphia and Los Angeles aided the NLSC in verifying information provided by arrestees. Ultimately, the NLSC and the Urban Law Clinic sent more than one thousand files to the Recorder's Court for the use of attorneys and to aid the judges in setting or resetting bonds.[30]

The Metropolitan Detroit Branch of the American Civil Liberties Union (ACLU) added its opposition to the court's bail policy on July 26. The day before, Ernest Mazey, the branch's executive director, said of the Recorder's Court, "What is being done maybe is not consistent with the highest ideals of justice, but under the circumstances it's all that can be done." At an extraordinary session the next day, the executive board, whose members, Mazey later stated, had "panicked" at the outset of the riot, called for "the prompt and individual review" of bonds as soon as arrest information became available and urged that any judge who had "engaged in prejudicial conduct" in his official capacity be disqualified from handling riot cases. Judge McCree, prominent representatives of the black community, and the Michigan Civil Rights Commission (CRC) joined in the next few days in criticizing the Recorder's Court's bail policy and what the black leaders characterized as "the flagrant denials" of the civil liberties of arrestees.[31]

The major impetus to a change in the court's bail policy came from the federal government, the prosecutor's office, and Governor Romney. John Doar thought that temporary detention without bail might be justified in an emergency, but he saw "no justification for a policy of arbitrary bail applied to everyone." Cahalan, for his part, was ready for a change in bail policy by July 26 because the jails were filled to overflowing and because of rumors of a prisoner revolt in the Wayne County jail, where conditions were "just terrible." He agreed on that day to assemble and match the arrest reports and arrest records of riot prisoners and to recommend the release on their own recognizance of those without records who had not engaged in "aggravated violence." As of July 28, however, the court had still released relatively few arrestees, partly because it had proved difficult to locate the appropriate court files and because the sheriff still "didn't know where anyone was." As of that date, only 2 percent of the riot arrestees had been released on personal bonds, whereas 26 percent of arrestees had been freed by the court on their own recognizance in 1966.

With concern mounting about a possible uprising at Jackson prison, Governor George Romney and Mayor Jerome Cavanagh sought to add their weight on July 28 to the effort to persuade the court to alter its bail policy. Although believing it would harm the State Fair, Romney, in order to pressure Brennan to act, seems to have threatened the use of the State Fairgrounds as "a large 'concentration camp'" for prisoners. With questionable authority, Cahalan also talked of unilaterally releasing prisoners whose records warranted the action or seeking authority from the governor to do so. At a press conference that afternoon that followed a meeting of Romney, Cavanagh, Cahalan, Vance, Doar, and the judges, the governor announced that the prosecutor's office would supply the court that night with the records of 2,000 prisoners to review; and Brennan stated that now that arrest records were being made available, the judges would begin to set personal bonds for those without arrest records who had not been "a major factor" in the riot. Brennan also agreed that it would not be necessary to match the records provided by the prosecutor with the corresponding court files.

The next day, thanks to the efforts of the prosecutor as well as the information provided by the NLSC and the Urban Law Clinic, Romney was able to announce that 1,400 prisoners had been ordered released, most on their personal recognizance and some after having pled guilty to violating the curfew and being sentenced to the number of days they had already spent in jail. By August 4 only 1,200 riot arrestees remained incarcerated, and the number had dwindled to 350 by August 10. Of those released, only one was rearrested while the riot continued, the cause being curfew violation. Cahalan regarded the prosecutor's role in the affair as "one of the finest things his office did" during the riot. He concluded from the experience, however, that it had been a mistake to arraign arrestees before checking arrest and conviction records and that to have waited for this information would not have violated the requirement that arrestees be brought before a magistrate without delay.[32]

The court's high bond policy placed a crushing burden on the detention facilities in the city and county. Conditions were little better for prisoners waiting arraignment, who were the responsibility of the Police Department, or those already arraigned, who were the responsibility of the Wayne County sheriff. The number of arrestees had also placed an enormous burden on detention facilities in Watts and Newark, but the problem was much more severe in Detroit. Wherever they were, Detroit riot prisoners, to quote a University of Michigan faculty member who had gathered information for the Kerner Commission, were "detained under conditions that were enough to make a vulture puke." By the afternoon of July 24 detention cells in the precinct stations and at police headquarters were overflowing. Once the cell blocks in some precincts filled to three or even five times their capacity, some prisoners were transferred to police headquarters; but when the cell blocks there also filled up, prisoners, if at all possible, were kept in the precincts until they could be brought to Recorder's Court for arraignment. When a policeman in one precinct, according to an apocryphal story that made the rounds, opened a closet door, prisoners fell out. The advice of his superior when the officer asked what he was to do was not to "open any more closet doors."[33]

Conditions were at their worst in the Tenth Precinct, where 1,398 adults were arrested. After the precinct's cells were filled, 150 to 200 arrestees were placed in the filthy precinct garage. There was no toilet in the garage, a greasy pool in the center of the floor, whose drain was stopped up, serving that purpose for a time. One prisoner complained that when he asked permission of a guard to use a toilet, he was hit with a rifle, and when he then used the floor, he suffered the same fate. The prisoners, many of whom had been "beaten badly" by the police, were not allowed to make phone calls.[34]

"The 'cell' became unbearable," the falsely imprisoned black photographer said of the makeshift detention area in which he had been placed with fifty-five others in one precinct. "We were starving, dirty," he remarked. The prisoners begged for food, and fights broke out among them when the guard appeared. "We were not far from becoming the animals our guards believed us to be," the photographer observed. "Everything I had believed about the country just didn't seem real anymore."[35]

Prisoners brought downtown to police headquarters while awaiting arraignment were initially lodged in the thirteen detention cells in the building. Nine hundred prisoners were crowded into cell blocks that were intended for 184 persons, and there was some mixing of the sexes. It was impossible for the prisoners to sleep since there was no room to lie down.[36]

Prisoners who could not be lodged in cell blocks at police headquarters were placed in the building's underground garage or in seven buses parked outside. Conditions in the garage, where as many as one thousand prisoners were confined at one time, were deplorable. The cement floor, on which the arrestees had to relieve themselves, was covered with grease and urine, and the stench was horrible. There was only one source of drinking water, and, as in the Tenth Precinct garage, prisoners went hungry for long periods of time. One prisoner recalled that when the guards passed food in, the prisoners would try to "beat somebody out of a place in line for a second sandwich. . . . I learned to think like an animal and feel like an animal—and was dirty enough to be an animal," he told an interviewer.[37]

The prisoners on the buses were, for the most part, segregated by sex, there being up to 75 persons on a bus. They were brought water in a bucket and served sandwiches—"they gave you a little bit to make you want more." They were initially permitted to leave the bus one at a time to relieve themselves alongside, but then a single portable latrine was made available. Some arrestees remained on the hot buses for more than twenty-four hours. As in the precincts, prisoners at police headquarters were not permitted to make phone calls.[38]

When brought to the Recorder's Court, prisoners were placed in one of the court's bullpens to await arraignment. At one point during the riot week, 750 prisoners were confined in space designed for a maximum of 360 persons. Sometimes they remained in a bullpen overnight, "stuffed in like sardines" and forced to stand. When arraigned, those who could not make bail were supposed to be transferred to the Wayne County jail, but this was easier said than done. The jail was designed for 1,260 prisoners, but there were already 1,099 inmates in the facility the day before the riot began. By July 25, 1,772 prisoners were lodged in the jail. As many as 150 prisoners were crammed into holding tanks with a normal capacity of 50. Since the air-conditioning was not functioning satisfactorily, there was only one sanitary plumbing fixture for each tank, the toilets did not function properly, and there was no toilet paper, the stench as well as the heat became almost unbearable.[39]

In addition to the prisoners in the county jail, about 2,000 prisoners in the precincts, police headquarters, and on the buses were awaiting transfer to the jail, but there was obviously no room for them. This forced local authorities to turn to the state and federal government for assistance. Some prisoners were already lodged in the state's Jackson prison, and the federal government offered additional space in Milan, the state government in Ionia as well as Jackson, and county governments in Monroe, Washtenaw, and Ingham Counties. As of the morning of July 28, 1,805 riot prisoners were being held outside Detroit, 1,186 of them in Jackson prison.[40]

The transfer of prisoners out of Detroit did not entirely solve the prisoner detention problem. Following a "very chaotic" July 27 meeting of Romney, city, county, and court officials, the city's corporation counsel suggested the use of the women's bathhouse on Belle Isle. After Police Department and Department of Street Railways personnel modified the structure to accommodate prisoners, about five hundred arrestees were moved there on July 29. "Belcatraz," as the facility came to be known, "with every cell a showerbath," was used as a detention facility until August 13. There was no hot water for showering or shaving, but the CRC's inspection staff concluded that the sheriff was "doing as good a job as possible" under the circumstances. With the opening of Belcatraz, it became possible to bring some of the prisoners being detained outstate back to Detroit.[41]

Quite apart from the physical abuse and discomfort prisoners suffered, the inability of authorities to provide a master list of arrestees and their inability to communicate with the outside meant that arrestees sometimes could not be located for judicial or release purposes and that their relatives did not know where family members were being held. Prisoners simply "sort of vanished" for a few days, the *Detroit Free Press* referring to one such prisoner as an "invisible man." Six months after the riot, according to one attorney, riot arrestees were still turning up in jail who had been missing since late July. Until the police were able to provide a master list of prisoners, the NLSC served as an information center, answering hundreds of requests to locate missing prisoners. Individual attorneys also performed this role. One of them recalled that when he walked out of the Recorder's Court building, people waiting outside would call out names, and he would go inside to see what he could learn about the location of these individuals.[42]

After "two frantic days" of tracing prisoners dispersed about the state, the Police Department on July 28 opened a prisoner information center in police headquarters. At a meeting that day of a newly created Co-ordinating Committee to Deal with Prisoners that consisted of representatives of the prosecutor's office, the Recorder's Court, the Department of Justice, the Police Department, and the Michigan Supreme Court, Brennan agreed that the preparation of a master list of prisoners was the first priority. Not until August 1, however, were the police able to provide a list of all those being detained.[43]

By the end of July the Recorder's Court had arraigned and set bond for most prisoners. Arraignments were handled on "a mass production basis," one thousand prisoners being arraigned on July 25 alone. As John Emery, head of the Detroit Legal Aid and Defender Association, chairman of the Detroit Bar Association's Criminal Law Committee, and a part-time Birmingham, Michigan, municipal court judge, put it, "They [prisoners] were on the old assembly line, with the Detroit sound, Detroit style, and they were shuffled through awfully fast." "We didn't get any due process of law. We got railroaded," one arrestee said. "While the judge was carrying on the due process of law, he didn't even look at you."[44]

Counsel was not required at the arraignment stage, but some judges failed to advise defendants that they could be represented by counsel, and some went so far as to bar lawyers from their courtroom. One judge told an attorney that defendants in his court would not be permitted to see an attorney because "there isn't time for those niceties." Emery and some bar association attorneys suggested on July 24 that the court appoint attorneys to represent the indigent at the arraignment stage and right up to their trial, but the judges were unwilling to agree to this "continuity of counsel." When a *Detroit News* reporter asked Brennan if a public defender system would have been helpful, he replied, "What are you anyway, a blinking bleeding heart?" Although three judges availed themselves of the offer of volunteer counsel, Emery reported that it turned out to be "a pretty perfunctory service" because of the bond policy the judges were following. He noted that a couple of judges, who, as they admitted, were thinking of appeals, "lined the defendants up, like pigs, . . . 15–20 at a time," and told them that a lawyer or Legal Aid representative was present to advise them of their rights.[45]

The preliminary examinations, whose purpose was to determine whether probable cause existed to believe a particular defendant had committed a crime, began on August 1. The examinations, which continued for about two weeks, were held from 9:00 A.M. to 9:00 P.M., the justices working six-hour shifts to deal with the large number of cases. Michigan law required that defendants who did not waive their right to the preliminary examination be examined within ten days of their arraignment on the warrant. The court neither waived this rule because of the large number of arrestees, nor did it always adhere to it. Philip Colista, head of the Urban Law Program, suggested that defendants be examined in order of the date of their imprisonment, a sensible idea considering the conditions of confinement and the fact that some arrestees were losing their jobs because of their inability to report to work. The court, however, did not adopt the Colista suggestion.[46]

Normally, about two-thirds to three-fourths of the defendants in Recorder's Court waived their right to a preliminary examination, but only 38 percent (1,224 of 3,230) of the riot felony defendants did so. Although assistant prosecutors and the judges placed "unusual pressure" on defendants to waive their right to an examination, attorneys often counseled their clients not to do so in the hope that their case would be dismissed, not an unreasonable expectation given the state of evidence in so many cases, and because of fear that pleas that accompanied waiving might not be honored at a later time. Some defendants, to be sure, did waive their preliminary examination on the promise that their charge would be reduced to a misdemeanor.[47]

Defendants were entitled to counsel for their preliminary examination, and the court was required to provide counsel for the indigent. About 70 percent of the defendants could not afford counsel, which posed a serious problem for the Recorder's Court in terms both of manpower and funding. In 1966 the court had appointed counsel in 2,552 cases at a cost of $328,685. Now it was faced with the necessity of providing counsel in just about as many cases stemming from the riot alone. Detroit, the "last of the major American cities to adopt an organized defender system," had arranged by that time to initiate a private defender system administered by the Legal Aid and Defender Association, but the system was not scheduled to go into effect until the end of the year. Cavanagh and Romney, therefore, joined Brennan on July 28 in requesting the Detroit bar, the state bar, and the Wolverine Bar Association to provide volunteers to defend indigent arrestees. "If we are to advocate justice in normal times," the telegram requesting aid stated, "we must surely practice justice in abnormal times."[48]

Although the Detroit bar enjoyed a reputation of being more committed to the defense of civil rights than most big city bars, the Detroit Bar Association, as such, had done relatively little during the first week of the riot to protect the rights of arrestees. The bar, even including attorneys among the left-leaning National Lawyers Guild, was "paralyzed" by the riot, according to Sengstock. "Everything was burning . . . we were stunned," one attorney declared. The president of the state bar conceded that the Bill of Rights had not been observed in some instances during the riot's first week, but, he asserted on July 31, "there wasn't a constitutional question last week, there was a question of survival." Reacting like lawyers in other riot cities, Detroit attorneys may have been "intimidated" to some degree by the law enforcement personnel who surrounded the Recorder's Court and the soldiers sitting in the courtrooms, "rifles held at the ready."[49]

The plea for legal assistance produced a very favorable reaction among the bar, 703 attorneys volunteering for the role. They ranged from youngsters fresh out of law school to a former justice of the Michigan Supreme Court. About 550 volunteers were actually pressed into service, each generally serving for one six-hour court shift. To acquaint them with the nature of the preliminary examination — few were criminal lawyers — experienced counsel such as Emery gave them a fifteen-minute lecture before they appeared in court. They were also provided with a manual hurriedly prepared by the NLSC and the Urban Law Program that covered in a very frank way criminal defense practices and procedures, providing, it was said, "handy tips for naive lawyers." Some Recorder's Court judges regarded this "riot bible" as "unethical" and as "unduly disrespectful of the judicial machinery." Once they had completed their "instant criminal law" course, the volunteer lawyers were assigned in teams to particular courtrooms, not to particular defendants. NLSC and Wayne County Suburban Legal Services attorneys were not permitted to appear in felony cases, but they served as "trouble shooters" during the period of the preliminary examinations.[50]

The conduct of the preliminary examinations for riot arrestees was often marked by a good deal of confusion. Sometimes the defendant could not be found when his name was called, sometimes his file could not be found, and sometimes it arrived at the wrong courtroom. The nonappearance of defendants led to 262 adjournments, sometimes followed by the decision of an angry judge to set a higher bond for the absent defendant or to impose a bond on a defendant who had been released on a personal bond. Sometimes six to eight defendants were examined at once.

Lawyers complained that they did not have enough time or a proper place to consult with their clients. All too often lawyers spent no more than ten minutes with a set of clients before a case was called, the discussion carried on in a noisy hallway or courtroom or perhaps through the bars of a Recorder's Court bullpen. Judges were reluctant to grant adjournments even though the case might be called before the lawyer knew the charge or had the opportunity to see the police file. Lawyers grumbled also that some judges saw them as "an accommodation to the Court," not as participants in an adversarial process. The judges harassed and interrupted counsel and sometimes restricted their opportunity to cross-examine witnesses.

Some judges showed little concern for the "competency of evidence" in binding defendants over for trial. One judge stated that "no motions to suppress evidence would be entertained in his courtroom." Although the rules of evidence required personal identification, judges sometimes permitted police officers to identify defendants from photographs taken at the precinct stations, photographs that were sometimes less than clear. As we have seen, the photographs of alleged looters also pictured the goods they had supposedly seized, but several defendants claimed that they were given something to hold just before their picture was snapped. In one case, according to an attorney, five persons arrested at the same time were each shown holding the same broom and the same can of aerowax. Although defendants were accorded their right to counsel in the preliminary examinations, many of them were denied the "effective counsel" Michigan law specified.[51]

Of the 1,920 preliminary examinations held, 44 resulted in guilty pleas. Whereas about 20 percent of the preliminary examinations in Recorder's Court normally resulted in dismissal, about 48 percent (919 of 1,920) of the examinations of riot defendants had this result. Although the number of dismissals is a good indication of the weakness of the evidence against many defendants, some cases had to be dismissed for reasons not going to the merits but because of procedural difficulties such as the failure of material witnesses to appear.[52]

For those defendants bound over for trial on the preliminary examination or who waived the examination, the prosecution had to draw up an information formally stating the charge, to which the defendant then pleaded. The arraignments on the information began late in August 1967 and continued until March 1968, by which time arraignments had been held for nearly all the 2,189 defendants bound over for trial. The court used only paid counsel for the indigent at this stage, each appointed attorney receiving $200 a day. The court may have preferred to use appointed counsel not only for "patronage" reasons but also because they were more likely to "cop a plea" than the volunteers. The same "assembly-line justice" that had characterized the judicial process up to this point was also evident during this "relatively late step in the criminal process." The two lawyers assigned to each courtroom generally were able to spend only fifteen to twenty minutes with the defendants whom they were representing.

Forty-one of the arraignment-on-the-information cases were dismissed, thirty-eight on motion by the prosecution, three by the court. The plea bargaining that occurred at this step persuaded 557 (27 percent) of the defendants who were arraigned on the information to plead guilty, just slightly above the 25 percent who normally pleaded guilty at this stage of the proceedings in the Recorder's Court. Most who pleaded guilty agreed to do so because the prosecutor, in a departure from the normal practice occasioned by the large number of defendants, was willing to reduce most looting charges to a misdemeanor, with time already served as the sentence for those pleading guilty who did not have a criminal record. Concern about the future may have partially explained the leniency of this arrangement, one court official declaring, "If we jailed these people with no previous records, we might be in trouble all over again."[53]

Of the 1,653 misdemeanor arrests that were processed, 1,030, nearly all involving curfew violation, came to trial. The misdemeanor trials began on August 1, and they were quickly disposed of by two judges, "without any particular problems." About 20 percent of the defendants were represented by counsel secured by the NLSC and the Urban Law Program, about 20 percent had paid or court-appointed counsel, and 60 percent were not represented. As of January 19, 1968, 642 (62 percent) of those accused of misdemeanors had been convicted, 173 acquitted, the cases of 125 dismissed, and 90 cases were pending final disposition. The conviction rate compared with a conviction rate of 88 percent in 1965, reflecting the evidence problems in the cases of riot arrestees and, possibly, their better representation. Most cases were disposed of by guilty pleas, a few by jury trials, and the remainder by bench trials. The cases proceeded rapidly because defendants were aware that the guilty would be sentenced to nothing more than time served. Only 3–4 percent of the guilty were sentenced to additional time.[54]

In an effort to secure the release of curfew violators, the NLSC sought to have Romney's emergency proclamation declared invalid because of its alleged legal defects—the governor, it will be recalled, had initially omitted the violation provision in the proclamation. It gained the release of seventy defendants on a habeas corpus writ despite the rejection of its motion by Judge Leonard, but its efforts to secure a "definitive ruling" on the subject were rendered "moot" by the misdemeanor trials.[55]

Felony trials began in October 1967, with most cases not disposed of until the following spring. Of the 1,871 cases completed as of August 9, 1968, 1,415 or 75 percent resulted in convictions, almost all of them on guilty pleas to misdemeanor offenses. Pleading guilty to a reduced charge was common in Recorder's Court, but it was unusual for the court to permit defendants accused of felonies to plead guilty to misdemeanors. Nearly all the guilty were sentenced to time already served, received suspended sentences, were placed on probation, or fined less than $100. Only about 3 percent of the guilty received jail sentences extending beyond time served, and fewer still received true felony sentences of one year or more. In 1965, by comparison, 57 percent of convicted felony defendants were jailed.[56]

Of the 6,528 adults arrested during the riot, about one-third had pled guilty or been convicted a year later, with less than 10 percent of the cases still pending. Of the arrestees prosecuted (74.2 percent of the total), about one-half of those accused of felonies and about one-third of those accused of misdemeanors escaped conviction. The relatively small number of convictions was the result of the indiscriminate character of the arrests, the sketchiness of the evidence against many defendants because of the difficulty the police faced in making on-site investigations, and the failure of store owners in particular to show up at preliminary examinations as complaining witnesses.[57]

Since Michigan did not have a statute dealing specifically with sniping, the twenty-six alleged snipers who were prosecuted were charged
with "assault with intent to commit murder." Of the twenty-six, one first
pleaded guilty to felonious assault but then denied guilt, and his case was
subsequently dismissed on motion of the assistant prosecutor; one
pleaded guilty to a lesser charge; and the cases against all the others were
dismissed for one reason or another. Brennan explained that none of the
twenty-six had actually been seen holding or discharging a firearm. They
had been arrested by police officers in "very excited states of mind" who
had heard shots, decided where they had come from, searched the suspected location, and then arrested "suspicious looking" persons there.[58]

The forty-three homicides in the riot led ultimately to only three
convictions. It was up to the prosecutor to decide whether a slaying was
justified or if criminal intent was involved. It is likely that the prosecutor's office was inclined to give law enforcement officers the benefit of
the doubt in deciding whether or not to authorize homicide warrants. In
the George Tolbert death, for example—the result of the precipitous
action by a Guardsman, to say the very least—the chief assistant prosecutor informed the governor's legal advisor that the prosecutor's office
was "not necessarily" charging the Guardsman involved with murder
because of the "tenseness of the situation." In another case, the slaying of
a looter by a Guardsman, an assistant prosecutor ruled the death justifiable homicide even though the police had recommended a homicide
warrant.

The prosecutor, in the end, decided that the homicide was justified
or "accidental" in twenty riot deaths, concluded that there was insufficient evidence to authorize a warrant in seventeen cases, and authorized
warrants in six cases—the Darryl McCurtis slaying of Krikor Messerlian;
the private guard's slaying of Herman Ector; Richard Shugar's slaying of
Nathaniel Edmonds; Danny Royster's slaying of Jerome Olshove; and
the slaying by two police officers of two blacks in the annex of the
Algiers Motel. A Recorder's Court judge dismissed the warrant against
the private guard following the preliminary examination; McCurtis,
Shugar, and Royster, as already noted, were convicted; and the Algiers
Motel slayings led, as we shall see, to a "maze of legal actions" but no
convictions.[59]

The Recorder's Court came under severe attack from law professors, some attorneys, the NLSC, the ACLU, and black spokesmen for its
behavior in the processing of riot arrestees. The general complaint was
that the court responded to the "lawlessness" of the riot by "its own
lawless activity." Frightened by the riot and emphasizing the restoration
of law and order, the court, its many critics charged, became an "arm of
the law enforcement agencies" rather than a protector of the constitutional rights of arrestees. Attorney Henry Cleage told a Kerner Commission interviewer that a group of Detroit lawyers had considered filing a

lawsuit against the Recorder's Court judges for conspiring to deny riot defendants their rights but that John Doar had helped to dissuade them from doing so, a contention Doar many years later denied.[60]

Insofar as the Recorder's Court departed from a position of neutrality in the riot, its behavior was similar to that of criminal courts in other riot cities, which, as Jerome Skolnick pointed out, became "instrument[s] of political needs relatively unrestrained by conditions of legality." In other riot cities, as in Detroit, there were "recurring breakdowns in the mechanism of processing, prosecuting, and protecting arrested persons."[61]

The Recorder's Court was not without defenders. In its annual report for 1967, the court claimed that members of the United States Civil Rights Commission who "virtually lived" with the court for two weeks beginning on July 24 "continually and constantly" praised the way it handled riot cases. The president of the Detroit Bar Association stated on July 28 that the court had been "sympathetic to the needs of the prisoners within the limits of the ability so to do." Insisting hyperbolically that "never in the history of civilization have the constitutional rights of people engaged in civil disorder been so well protected," Cahalan appraised the court's conduct as "very, very good." Seventeen years later he found no reason to alter this judgment, considering the difficult circumstances the court faced at the time of the riot. Critics of the court, Brennan told a Kerner Commission interviewer, "didn't know what the hell was going on." "The thugs, the pimps and the whores," he said, "are not going to be objective about the courts. They'll be objecting and bitching all the time." The interviewer thought that Brennan "exhibited . . . no understanding of why people might be critical of his conduct."[62]

The 703 juveniles arrested during the riot were processed by the Wayne County Juvenile Court, not the Recorder's Court. The Juvenile Court had begun devising plans for its reaction to a possible riot about a year before the 1967 disorder. It had decided to keep all juvenile arrestees in the Wayne County Youth Home until the Juvenile Court decided what to do with them, and it had arranged for their feeding by the Wayne County General Hospital. It had not, however, anticipated the modifications in its administrative and judicial procedures that the riot necessitated.[63]

The bulk of the 703 juveniles apprehended during the riot were charged with looting or curfew violation. Of the 673 juveniles actually brought to the Youth Home, about 500 had not had previous contact with the Juvenile Court, 100 had had such contact, and 80 were "active" with the court at the time of their arrest. Forty-one percent claimed that they had had no previous contact with the police. Since the Youth Home had a capacity of only 160, arrestees had to sleep on the floor in the gymnasium, the auditorium, and other rooms. Juvenile Court Judge James H. Lincoln was concerned about the security of the Home because he had received threats from the Black Panthers and black power groups to blow up the building and to firebomb the surrounding area. The security provided by sheriff's deputies, paratroopers, and Guardsmen proved, however, to be more than adequate.[64]

Like the Recorder's Court judges, Lincoln declared at the outset of the riot that he was not going to release any juvenile arrestees back to the streets to sustain the disorder. Having decided on bonds of between $5,000 and $10,000 for the youthful arrestees, Lincoln proudly informed Governor Romney on July 25 that he had not released "a single juvenile . . . back into the community to feed the riot." The judge later explained that he had initially decided on high bonds because he had expected the arrestees to be "arsonists" or snipers rather than "a bunch of looters and curfew violators out for a good time like on Halloween night." His talk of holding arrestees who could not meet their bonds for two to three months while they prepared for their trials proved to be just talk. "It was like I got all lathered up to shave," he remarked, "and then didn't shave." Lincoln also discovered that many parents, if not rioting themselves, were content to have their children remain safely in custody in the Youth Home while the riot lasted — "they wanted us to be babysitters for them," the judge recalled.[65]

The Juvenile Court began the preliminary hearings of arrestees on July 24, the purpose being to determine if there was sufficient evidence to justify detention and hence bail. The hearings were conducted by three referees, and since parents and guardians were not present, as the law required, it was understood that decisions were subject to review. Although Lincoln thought that "probable cause" existed in almost all cases and that the arrests were justified, evidence to sustain convictions was lacking in all but a few cases.[66]

The Juvenile Court began releasing arrestees on July 27. It expedited the action, unlike the Recorder's Court, by reducing the usual amount of paperwork and by devising a recognizance bond form by which the parent signer acknowledged an indebtedness to the state of $1,000 if the juvenile did not appear in Juvenile Court when required. Although its treatment of juvenile arrestees did not, apparently, entirely conform to the United States Supreme Court's May 15, 1967, decision in *In re Gault*, which specified that juvenile defendants were to be accorded virtually the same rights as adult criminal defendants, the Juvenile Court largely escaped the criticism directed at the Recorder's Court for its treatment of adult arrestees.[67]

The administration of criminal justice during the 1967 riot not only may have helped to sustain the riot but also reinforced black attitudes concerning the nature of law enforcement in Detroit. The riot behavior of the Recorder's Court, according to Professor Sengstock, flashed "a green light to the police" that they need not be overly concerned about the constitutional rights of people on the street in the riot areas. As Cyrus

Vance viewed it, the operation of the criminal justice system during the disorder served "to pump up the people's emotions[,] which in turn tended to keep the momentum of the riot going."[68] The prison and judicial treatment of the predominantly black arrestees, at the same time, embittered the arrestees, their relatives and friends, and many others in the black community. "After I came back," one arrestee declared, "slowly but surely I got madder and madder. . . . You know," he said, "they kept them there so long that everybody just said, 'we're going to do something when we get out of here.' " A Romney aide wrote the governor on August 3 that "reliable informants" in the black community reported that there was "considerable discussion" of a second riot among those released from custody who complained about "brutality and abuse" during their imprisonment.[69]

The belief of so many blacks, as indicated in a postriot survey, that the laws were not "fair to all people" and were not "enforced equally" was doubtlessly influenced by their perception of the manner in which the criminal justice system had operated during and just after the riot.[70] Black concern about the alleged unfairness of the criminal justice system was intensified by the manner in which the courts reacted to the slaying of three young blacks in the annex of the Algiers Motel.

CHAPTER 11

"A Night of Horror
and Murder"

A Vietnam veteran who was staying in the Algiers Motel during the night
of July 25, 1967, stated a week later that he had "lived through a night of
horror and murder in Detroit," worse than anything he had experienced
in Vietnam. What occurred during that "night of horror" and its aftermath came to symbolize for many "the riot, police action, [and] the
administration of justice itself." Three young blacks were shot to death in
the motel in the early morning hours of July 26, and law enforcement
officers beat and terrorized other blacks and whites. It is difficult, however, to recreate precisely what happened because the officers involved
tried to conceal their role in the night's events; and the witnesses to what
had occurred were frightened, their opportunity to observe the killings
was limited, at best, they gave conflicting and often contradictory
accounts of events, and they found it difficult to identify their
assailants.[1]

The Algiers Motel was located on the west side of Woodward Avenue at Virginia Park. A three-story Manor House, a converted residence
with fifteen kitchenette units, served as an annex to the motel. The
annex, which fronted on Virginia Park on the south, could also be
entered at the rear from Euclid Avenue. The motel, whose clientele was
"almost one hundred percent" black, had become notorious as "a haven
for pimps, prostitutes, drug pushers and addicts, gamblers, numbers
operators and other criminal element[s]." The police made arrests at the
motel for narcotics violations on five separate occasions from April 24 to
July 17, 1967. There was also a police raid on the annex in the early
morning hours of July 25 that turned up some weapons, according to one
account, and two truckloads of loot from Twelfth Street, according to
the FBI.[2]

On the night of July 25 the Algiers Motel and the Manor House were
occupied, among others, by six young Detroit blacks, Carl Cooper,
Auburey Pollard, Fred Temple, Michael Clark, Lee Forsythe, and James
Sortor; five members of the "Dramatics," a rock group; Robert Lee

271

Green, a black veteran from Kentucky; and two white girls, Juli Hysell and Karen Malloy, both of whom were convicted for accosting and soliciting in September 1967. Cooper, who "managed to keep fairly steadily in trouble" in his short life, was a seventeen-year-old laid-off spot welder who had spent eighteen months in the Boys' Vocational Training School in Lansing as a juvenile offender and had later served time on a narcotics charge. Pollard, who had been laid off from his Ford Motor Company welding job, had served a fifteen-day prison term for assaulting a rehabilitation specialist teacher. Clark, who was eighteen, had been convicted for carrying a concealed weapon and larceny from a building. Like Pollard, the nineteen-year-old Forsythe and Sortor had served time in the Boys' Training School, Forsythe for car theft, Sortor for breaking and entering. Temple, a Ford worker and high school dropout, had made friends with the Dramatics, who had been performing in Detroit and had moved into the motel because of the riot. It is not clear why the twenty-six-year-old Green was in Detroit. Malloy and Hysell, both eighteen, had come to Detroit from Columbus at the end of 1966 and had moved into the Algiers Motel a few days before July 25. They knew Green, Clark, and Cooper and were reportedly under the protection of the "Pimp in Residence" at the motel. They professed not to know who had secured their rooms, but a black resident of the motel "looked after them and people had to contact them through him."[3]

Reports of sniping in the area brought Detroit police, State Police, Guardsmen, and paratroopers to the motel in the early hours of July 26. Theodore J. Thomas, a National Guard warrant officer, had been assigned with four men on the night of July 25 to guard the Great Lakes Mutual Life Insurance Building on the northwest corner of Woodward and Euclid. A private guard, Melvin Dismukes, a black, was at the same time guarding two buildings across the street from the Great Lakes Building. Thomas, who had had almost no sleep the previous two nights and was not, understandably, "mentally alert," thought he heard "about" three or five shots just before or after midnight coming from the direction of the Manor House. After he phoned this information to the police, his men and Dismukes began firing toward the annex and shooting out streetlights in the vicinity. The report of "Guardsmen under fire" and similar reports of sniping drew to the scene two police task forces of seven officers, a dozen more Guardsmen, a State Police squad, and some paratroopers. No police officer above the rank of patrolman was present at the Algiers Motel. Sergeant Vic Wells had responded to the call for assistance and was on his way to the motel but was "diverted" by other police business. John Nichols years later expressed the view that there would have been "more control" inside the motel had the experienced Wells been on the scene.[4]

Although there may have been some sniping in the vicinity, there is a real question whether any shots were actually fired from the motel or the

Manor House to the outside. As we shall see, a motel guest apparently fired a starter pistol inside the annex, and in his *The Algiers Motel Incident* John Hersey concluded that this probably triggered the sniper reports. Bullets from a starter pistol, however, do not sound like bullets fired from a real gun or like sniper fire. A police ballistics expert later testified that there was no evidence a shot had been fired from the annex toward the street, and no weapon was later found inside the annex. Three witnesses, however, testified seeing a black male fire two shots from a long gun from the rear porch of the motel, and three other witnesses living near the motel claimed that they had heard sniper fire coming from the annex.[5]

Among the law enforcement personnel arriving at the Algiers Motel just after midnight on July 26, three policemen, Ronald August, Robert Paille, and David Senak, played central roles in the nightmarish events that were soon to follow. All were relatively junior police officers, all were fatigued, and all had had disconcerting experiences during the initial days of the riot. The twenty-eight-year-old August, who had joined the police force in 1963, had been on duty from 7:30 A.M. on July 23 to 3:00 A.M. on July 24 without relief or food, had returned to work at noon on July 24, and remained on duty until early morning on July 25. Stationed at Fourteenth and Philadelphia on July 23, he had been taunted by black looters, whose lawbreaking, he claimed, he had been advised to tolerate. He had been shot at on July 24 and forced to take cover under a scout car. The next day, Jerome Olshove, from the same precinct as August, was slain.[6]

Paille, who was thirty-one, had joined the police force in 1965. Although he had received a merit citation for his role in an armed robbery case, his superiors had given him lower service ratings than August and Senak. He had a poor opinion of blacks, telling Hersey, "Basically, I believe they're more immoral than corresponding white people." He had been on duty for twenty straight hours and then fourteen hours at the outset of the riot. He had been provoked by the amount of crime he had witnessed on July 23 that he could not stop because, he asserted, "I didn't have the orders." Like other police officers, he had been frightened by the sniping. "We never knew what to expect next," he said. "They were shooting from dark windows and everything else."[7]

Only twenty-three, David Senak had been a patrolman for two years. As a member of the vice squad, 80 percent of whose work, Senak said, was "colored," he was familiar with the character of the Algiers Motel. He too was incensed at the police restraint of July 23, attributing it to a concern that law enforcement personnel not "agitate these people." A looter tossed a brick through the window of his scout car that day, a day on which he was on duty for more than fourteen hours. While chasing one rioter, Senak was attacked by two blacks but suffered no injury. The next day Senak and another officer shot and killed a fleeing looter who had allegedly refused to halt. On July 28, two days after the Algiers Motel slayings, Senak shot and killed a man who he thought was about to draw a gun, although no gun or other weapon was found on the victim. The county prosecutor ruled the slaying, which was not riot-related, as "justifiable homicide."[8]

The discrepant accounts of the witnesses make it difficult to know precisely what happened in the annex just before law enforcement personnel entered the building shortly after midnight on July 26. Malloy, Hysell, Clark, Forsythe, and Cooper were apparently in Clark's apartment on the third floor and were joined by Sortor and Pollard. According to Malloy and Hysell, Cooper pulled a starter pistol from under the bed and shot two blanks toward Forsythe, who ran out of the room. Sortor and Forsythe denied under oath seeing any guns in the annex that night, but Sortor later told Hersey that Cooper had run down to the first floor and shot a pistol twice to frighten Pollard and him and to imitate the police who had searched them early on July 25.

After Cooper fired his pistol, assuming he did, a shot came through the window in Clark's room, and Cooper, looking out the window, said, "the police are out there." The occupants of Cooper's room fell to the floor and began crawling out of the room. Pollard and Sortor hid in a linen closet in the hallway on the third floor, while Forsythe, Cooper, and the two girls took to the stairs, Cooper apparently running down first. According to Clark, someone downstairs then yelled, "everyone come down." When Pollard, Sortor, and he, obeying the command, reached the second floor, State Police troopers and soldiers, presumably Guardsmen, ordered them to the first floor, where they were told to face the east wall of the lobby with their hands over their heads.

Hysell and Malloy made their way to the second floor and into Green's room as they heard additional shots. A policeman then entered the room and fired one shot through the closet door and another through the wall into the bathroom. Two more patrolmen entered, knocked Green and the girls to the floor, and one struck Hysell on the head with his revolver. The three were ordered downstairs, where they joined the others against the lobby wall. Before he too was ordered to take his place against the wall, Forsythe claimed that he heard someone shout, "Get your black ass down here. I already killed one of them." Two members of the Dramatics group, Roderick Davis and Cleveland Reed, were in their first-floor apartment with Temple when they heard shots that they thought came from the rear of the motel. Three policemen — Davis initially said they were soldiers — entered the apartment, struck the occupants with rifle butts, and ordered them to the lobby wall. Davis and Reed claimed that Temple joined them against the wall, but this is almost certainly incorrect.[9]

By the time the two women and the seven men were placed against the wall, Cooper was already dead, and Temple was probably either dead or dying. Clark, Forsythe, Sortor, Green, and Malloy all stated that when they reached the first floor, they saw Cooper's body in the doorway of the apartment (A-2) just to the right of the lobby (see fig. 1). One witness claimed that he had heard Cooper say, "Man, take me to jail. I don't have any weapon," words that were then allegedly followed by a shot. No one was charged with Cooper's death. John Hersey and the FBI concluded that Cooper had been killed in the "initial assault" on the rear of the Manor House by law enforcement officers, who, according to the FBI, were "probably" Detroit policemen. Prosecutor William Cahalan, however, decided that Cooper's death "was not at all tied in" with the slayings of Pollard and Temple.[10]

Although the FBI concluded that August, Paille, and Senak were the first three law enforcement officers to enter the annex, the point is not beyond dispute. The FBI thought that the police entering the Manor House from the front preceded those entering from the rear, but Paille and Senak entered from the rear before August did from the front. Corporal Hubert C. Rosema, in charge of the State Police squad at the scene, informed his superiors that members of his squad were inside the annex *before* the first shots were fired there, but he did not say that they had preceded the police into the building. John M. Fonger, a young State Police trooper in probationary training, reported, on the other hand, that he followed one trooper and two police officers, almost certainly Senak and Paille, into the annex from the rear.[11]

Senak stated flatly that Cooper was already dead when he, Senak, entered the Manor House with the State Police; and Fonger agreed that he found Cooper dead in A-2, "with blood and other parts of the inside of his body on the floor." Like some others, he reported that Cooper's blood had coagulated by then, which meant that he had been dead for at least five to ten minutes. This has fueled speculation that someone other than a law enforcement officer killed Cooper before the "initial assault" on the annex. Lending a soupçon of support to this hypothesis is Roderick Davis's testimony that he heard a "series of shots" inside the motel, presumably not the shots from Cooper's starter pistol, before the police entered the annex; the aforementioned witnesses who claimed a black male had fired shots from the rear porch of the annex, also before the police arrived; and another witness who claimed she saw three young blacks carrying a rifle get out of a car and walk around the motel shortly before the tragic incident.[12]

More intriguing was the statement by Lawanda J. Schettler, a fifty-year-old white woman, that shortly after midnight on July 26 she saw two black males carrying shotguns or rifles walk up to the front porch of the Manor House, causing two white girls sitting on the porch to get up and step aside as though "frightened." Schettler claimed that after the door of the porch opened, as if it had been kicked in, she heard someone say, "man you held out on us," words that were "immediately" followed

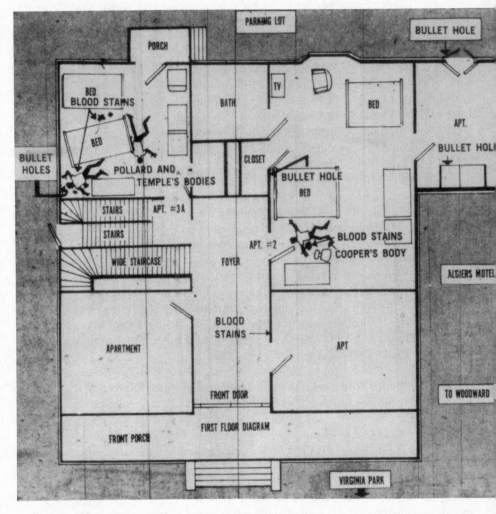

Fig. 1. First-floor layout of the Manor House Annex of the Algiers Motel. (Diagram by Dick Mayer, reprinted with permission of the *Detroit Free Press*.)

by several shots inside the annex. An assistant prosecutor told John Hersey that the pursuit of the Schettler lead, which probably relates to the hypothesis that Cooper was killed in a fight over one of the two girls in the motel, "came to a blah ending."[13] The same might be said regarding all the theories about how Cooper met his death: none of them can be proved beyond a reasonable doubt.

Whether or not Cooper was killed during the initial assault on the annex, it seems certain that Temple met his fate almost immediately after police entered the rear of the annex. After August confessed to killing Pollard, Paille told Lieutenant Gerald Hallmark, "I shot one of the other men," who had to be Temple. When Hallmark asked "what part . . . Senak had in the shooting," Paille replied, "We shot almost simultaneously at the man." The county deputy medical examiner agreed that it was possible that more than one person had fired at Temple, that he had been killed by a shotgun and perhaps another weapon. At a later evidentiary hearing, Paille testified that he had been involved in the shooting almost immediately after arriving in the annex. Michael Clark, not a very reliable witness, to be sure, stated at a mock Algiers Motel trial that he saw Paille standing near Temple, saying "I killed him"; but Paille's attorney, despite his client's confession, enigmatically stated in 1972, "We knew all along that his [Paille's] bullet wasn't the one that killed Fred Temple." The attorney may have been referring to the thesis advanced by Senak's attorney that Temple had been slain by Guardsmen who entered the annex with Senak and fired when Senak yelled, "He's got my gun."

Paille asked to speak to his attorney before the patrolman could amplify his confession to Hallmark, but other available information sheds at least some light on what had occurred. Fonger, who followed Paille and Senak into the rear of the annex, soon heard shots coming from A-3, occupied by Reed, Davis, and Temple, and he then saw a police officer emerge from the room followed by another officer, who was unloading a pistol and saying something like, "That one tried to go for my gun" or "That one had a gun." Fonger at that point saw a black male lying against the bed and breathing with great difficulty. Trooper Archie A. Davies, one of the first troopers to enter the annex from the rear porch, not only saw the deceased Cooper but also saw a black in another room "bleeding badly, but still alive," who could only have been Temple. Trooper Royal K. Caddy and Corporal Rosema appeared to agree regarding the manner and timing of Temple's death. August also made it clear in later testimony that both Cooper and Temple were dead when he entered the annex and while Pollard was still alive.[14]

The night clerk at the motel, Clara Gilmore, was able to provide additional information about what went on in A-3. At about 1:00 A.M. she heard shots coming, she thought, from the annex. Gilmore then received a phone call from Glenda Tucker, who had heard shots during an incompleted phone call to her boyfriend, Reed, and who asked

Gilmore if anyone had been shot. Gilmore picked up the phone to A-3, found the line open, and heard someone yell, "get your hands up." A few seconds later she heard someone shout, "Watch out, he's got the back [butt?] of the gun," or "Watch out, he's going for your gun," and she then heard several shots. Had Paille gone to trial, it can be assumed that he would have maintained that Temple had tried to seize either his or Senak's holstered gun (it was Senak's gun according to his attorney), that one of them had shouted a warning, and that the two had then fired with fatal result.[15]

Despite all the evidence to the contrary, Reed and Davis claimed that Temple was still alive in the lobby when the police permitted those on the line to leave the motel and was thus the last of the three blacks killed in the annex. Hersey accepted this version of events, but the FBI eventually concluded that Temple had been shot immediately after Cooper met his death, which is almost certainly the correct version.[16]

Of the seven men and two women on the line in the annex lobby, only Pollard was killed, but the others were beaten and terrorized in what a federal attorney later described as "a grisly game in which Senak was the quarterback." The scene was one of incredible confusion, as Detroit police officers, State Police troopers, Guardsmen, paratroopers, and private guards moved in and out of the building. The police interrogation of those on the line centered on the questions of "Who was shooting" and "Who had the gun." However exaggerated the reports of sniping in the area, there is no doubt that sniping was a major concern of the police in the motel. One witness heard Senak say, "We've got to find those guns or next they'll be using them on us."[17]

The behavior of the patrolmen in the annex lobby was undoubtedly also affected by their reaction to white prostitutes consorting with black males. As Roy Wilkins, executive secretary of the National Association for the Advancement of Colored People, stated, the police "just could not stomach the idea of these Negro men in the motel with white girls." The women were called "nigger lovers" and "white niggers," Malloy recalling that "all sorts of vulgar things" were said to them. According to Davis, Senak pulled down the dress of one girl, made the other pull hers off, and said, "Why you got to fuck them? What's wrong with us, you nigger lovers?" Forsythe reported one policeman saying, "We're going to get rid of all you pimps and whores."[18]

Beatings accompanied verbal epithets and rough questioning. Since their faces were turned to the wall, those on the line could not really see who was doing what to whom, but Guardsmen, State Police troopers, paratroopers, and August himself testified as to what had occurred and sometimes identified the perpetrators. The principal offenders were alleged to have been Senak and Paille. Thomas testified that the police treated those on the line "pretty rough." A 101st Airborne MP "witnessed several blows to different people with rifles" and what he thought was a blackjack, and another MP saw a policeman stick a shotgun between the legs of one male and threaten "to blow his testicles off." "I was hit so many times I finally stopped counting," Sortor, who emerged with "big knots on his head," recalled. Davis required first aid at a hospital after his beating—someone smashed his fingers with a gun—and Green sustained wounds to his forearm and head and inside his mouth.[19]

The law enforcement officers played a "knife game" with Clark and Pollard. Clark gave varying accounts of who it was that threw a knife down before him and told him to pick it up. When he first refused to do so, fearing the consequences, the law enforcement officer involved beat him, Clark claimed, and threatened to shoot him. "Pick it up so I can blow your goddam head off," Clark had this officer saying. Clark obeyed and then dropped the weapon when told to do so. Another officer played the same game with Pollard.[20]

Fonger, who thought that "the situation was completely out of control" by this time, went outside to find his superior, Corporal Rosema. When Rosema, in turn, witnessed what was happening, he told the State Police troopers to leave the annex since the Detroit police were "in charge."[21]

The State Police troopers left the annex as the police interrogation took a more ominous turn. The police began to remove those against the wall, one by one, for questioning in one of the first floor rooms of the annex. The questioning was accompanied by further beatings and then in some instances by the firing of shots in the interrogation room designed to convince those still on the line that their comrades had been executed for not revealing where the gun or guns were and that they would all be killed if they did not talk. It was during this sequence of events that Pollard became the third black to meet his death in the Algiers Motel.

Forsythe was the first taken from the line. He emerged from the interrogation room with his "head all busted," twelve stitches being required to close the lacerations. The same officer, apparently, then took Sortor from the line, kicked and beat him, and then took him on a vain search of the annex to find the alleged gun or guns before returning him to the line. August apparently selected Malloy, Hysell, and then Green for questioning.[22]

What Hersey called "the death game" began with Davis. Senak took him into a room, told him to lie down on his stomach, shot into the floor, and told Davis he would kill him if he moved or made a sound. It was perhaps then that Hysell heard an officer say, "one down, nine to go." When Senak emerged from the room, he winked to Thomas, who had witnessed what had happened, and asked him if Davis had been killed. Thomas, who thought it "a very good idea" to make those on the line think so, replied in the affirmative. Senak then asked the warrant officer if he also "wanted to shoot a nigger." Thomas then took Clark into one of the rooms, fired into the ceiling, and ordered Clark to "be quiet."

Green claimed that when Thomas returned to the lobby, he said, "that Nigger didn't even kick," a contention Thomas specifically denied. Perhaps it was at this point that Malloy asked the person next to her in line to tell the police about Cooper's starter pistol since he was dead anyhow. A patrolman then reportedly said, "Why didn't you tell us that before we killed the other guy?"[23]

After Thomas returned to the lobby, Senak, according to Thomas, either asked August, who had been the most passive of the three police officers, if he wanted to kill one of the blacks or, as Thomas later told the story, gave August a shotgun and said, "You shoot one." August took Pollard into A-3 — Thomas told him to take Pollard there because "there were too many bodies in A-4," where the fake executions of Davis and Clark had occurred. Thomas was the only witness to what then occurred, although Forsythe and Clark claimed that they heard Pollard say, "don't shoot." How well Thomas could actually have seen what happened is unclear. He said that he could see August's back through "a half-open door," but he stated on other occasions that he was twenty to forty feet from the room and also that he had no clear view of A-3. In any event, he claimed that he saw "a 'flash of clothing,' " heard a shotgun blast, and then heard someone fall "with a thud." He consistently maintained that he had heard no "struggle" before the shooting. Sortor and Clark claimed that it was August, not Thomas, who said after emerging from A-3, "that black nigger didn't even kick" or something similar.[24]

August's version of what took place in A-3 was set forth in his confession five days after the shooting. "Now comes the tragic part," he stated regarding the death of Pollard. Someone on the line, August said, stated that he wanted to talk to an officer. The two went into A-3, where Pollard, according to August, said that he did not know who had shot at the police and pleaded for the officers to permit his friends and him to leave the motel. When Pollard asked if August was going to shoot him, the patrolman claimed he replied, "I never shot a man in all my life and I have no reason to shoot you." Pollard then, according to August, grabbed his shotgun and pushed him onto the bed. August, the patrolman stated in his confession, "screamed 'get back.' We both stood up from the bed and then he let go of the gun and I pulled the trigger. The safety was on and the gun did not fire. I released the safety and he reached for the shotgun again and I pushed him away and fired one shot and struck him. . . . I didn't want to shoot him. I wanted to put him back out there with the rest of them but he just wanted that gun and he wouldn't let go."[25]

Frightened by what he thought he had seen, Thomas said to Senak, "This is strictly police business" or "This is bad business" and that he was "leaving." There was some shooting outside about that time, and some of the law enforcement personnel inside the annex ran outside. An officer now told those on the line that they could leave. Thomas, one of his men, and Dismukes, however, took the two women back to their rooms in the motel proper because they were almost entirely naked.[26]

Although police officers were supposed to file a preliminary complaint report when they fired a weapon, even if no one was shot as a result, none of the officers who had been in the Algiers Motel on July 26 filed a report that day, and none of them reported his own presence or that of any other law enforcement personnel in the building that morning. According to his later testimony, August, once he realized Pollard had died, walked out of the front door of the annex, leaned against a tree, and felt like vomiting, as he did later. When he returned to the station, he claimed, he told Paille and Senak that he intended to make a report on the slaying of Pollard, but one of them advised him to wait until the next day, when he would be feeling better. He discussed the matter with his wife and returned to work at noon that day fully intending to make the required report. By then, he stated, police were talking about the matter, and newsmen were asking to see the police report on what had happened in the Algiers Motel. He feared, he testified, that if he made a report under these circumstances, he would be blamed for all three deaths, and so, "scared" for himself and his family, he decided to remain quiet. Paille later claimed that he had not filed a report because he had seen "police violating the law," and he "didn't want to be held responsible for the action of others."[27]

The first word the Police Department received about the Algiers Motel affair came not from a police officer but from the Wayne County Morgue. At 2:15 A.M. on July 26 a clerk at the morgue or a private guard phoned Detective Joseph Zisler of the Homicide Bureau to report a call from Clara Gilmore that there were three dead bodies in the Manor House.[28] Zisler thereupon dispatched three scout cars to the motel. By that time, as the FBI put it, "guests of the Algiers Motel proper along with private policemen [had] wandered through the Manor House Annex and the bodies were looted." Detective Sergeant Edward Hay and the police dispatched to the Algiers Motel discovered that there was one dead body in A-2 (Cooper) and two in A-3 (Temple and Pollard) and that there were open pocket knives alongside the body in A-2 and one body in A-3. There was no identification on any of the three bodies, and the presence of the knives has never been explained. The police reported in an interoffice memorandum that the three deceased had "apparently" been "shot to death in an exchange of gunfire," but the memorandum noted that no guns were found near the bodies of the three suspected "snipers."[29]

The initial Homicide Bureau investigation of the Algiers Motel left much to be desired. Hay, who got to the motel at about 3:00 A.M., testified that he had made only a cursory examination of the building because it was "too dangerous" to complete the investigation. The Wayne County medical examiner refused to go to the motel for the same reason. Hay stated that he found no expended shotgun shell cases in the annex, but when Pollard's father went to the motel the morning after the slayings, he found two empty shotgun shells, empty rifle cartridge cases, and spent bullets, and the police later found numerous 38-caliber slugs, shotgun shells, and fired cartridge cases. After being challenged by Guardsmen outside the motel who did not think Hay and his party, apparently in plainclothes, were police officers, Hay decided not to photograph the interior of the annex. He simply directed that seals be placed on the doors and that morgue officials remove the bodies. It does not, however, appear that seals were placed on the doors. Detective Charles Schlachter testified that when he arrived at the motel on the morning of July 27, there were no seals on the doors, and maids were cleaning the facility.[30]

The *Detroit Free Press* and, to a lesser extent, the *Detroit News* played a conspicuous role in compelling the police to abandon the thesis that Pollard, Temple, and Cooper were snipers who had met their death in a gun battle with law enforcement personnel. "One strange thing," of course, was that if the victims were snipers, Homicide should have found some weapons in the annex, but an inquiry revealed that this was not so. The story quickly began to spread through the black near west side that the three youths had been killed while unarmed and without provocation by men in uniform. When the *Free Press*'s Barbara Stanton, who had been assigned to the story, went to the motel, she wondered why, if there had been an exchange of gunfire, she saw only six bullet holes in the building, five of them behind a light on the third floor. Stanton's inquiries convinced the *Free Press* to pursue the Algiers story and to engage Dr. Robert Sillery, a pathologist who had worked at the Wayne County Morgue and who was an expert on gunshot wounds, to perform autopsies on the three bodies.

Sillery, who received permission from the families of the victims to examine the three bodies, concluded, as did the deputy medical examiner, that all three youths had been killed by 12-gauge shotguns at close range and that they had been in "non-aggressive postures" when shot. Stanton, on July 29, turned her evidence over to the county prosecutor and the Civil Rights Division of the Department of Justice and told them that the *Free Press* would soon publish a story on the subject. The newspaper saw the matter as "delicate," believing that the responsible officials had not known about "the questionable circumstances" surrounding the three deaths until Stanton gave them her information.[31]

On July 28 family members of the three victims and Sortor, Forsythe, and Clark began telling what they knew about the slayings to John Conyers and civil rights leaders. They gave some of the same information to the police and the *Free Press*. Conyers held a press conference on July 29 at which some of the story was revealed, and he also provided John Doar with information and made witnesses available to Doar's assistant. The next day Doar requested the Detroit office of the FBI to investigate the affair for possible violation of federal civil rights legislation. Within a few days, twenty-eight FBI agents were working on the case.[32]

Additional information about the Algiers Motel affair became available on July 28 or 29 when attorney S. Allen Early, alerted by a pimp client, was able to locate Malloy and Hysell. He took them to the law office of Nathan Conyers, the congressman's brother, where they gave statements about the matter. Early took Hysell to the prosecutor's office, and when that office insisted on talking to both girls, Coleman Young brought Malloy there also. Nathan Conyers telephoned Hubert Locke after talking to the girls to say that if what they had told him was true, "you've got a mess on your hands."[33]

At a meeting on July 30 attended by Cahalan, police officials, Kurt Luedtke of the *Free Press,* and Doar, Cahalan disclosed what the *Free Press* had told him about Sillery's findings and stated that there were "reasonable grounds" to believe a felony had been committed in the Algiers Motel. The next day the *Free Press* reported what it had learned about the case, and the *Detroit News* revealed that it had located a key witness in the case, Robert Green. The *News* had tracked Green to his home in Kentucky and had brought him back to Detroit, where he gave a sworn statement about the affair. Green erroneously held Thomas responsible for two of the slayings but was later unable even to pick him out in a police "show-up."[34]

The police were in the meantime conducting an increasingly intensive investigation of the slayings, one that apparently "did not earn Girardin any points with the troops." Senak, Paille, and August were called into an inspector's office and, when they acknowledged that they had been at the Algiers Motel, were told to file a report about their activities. They decided in doing so, as August put it, "not to involve . . . [themselves] in any shootings." Senak prepared a brief statement that the three signed, August claiming that he had not even read it. The report stated that they had seen three wounded civilians in the motel and had called for a wagon, which did not arrive until after they had been relieved.[35]

At police show-ups that began on July 30, Clark and Sortor identified Paille and Dismukes as having mistreated them, but Malloy, Hysell, Forsythe, Davis, and Green could not pick out a single police officer as having been present in the motel. Thomas identified Senak in one of the lineups and asked for more time before making other identifications. At the urging of Norman Lipnitt, attorney for the Detroit Police Officers Association, who insisted that Thomas had had enough time, the police rejected the warrant officer's request. "Very upset at the way the show up had been conducted," a warrant officer in the Judge Advocate's Office of the Michigan National Guard complained to Cahalan. This led to another show-up the next day with fewer police in the line, and, given more time, Thomas identified August as "the officer who shot a man."

Thomas and Green were both given polygraph tests with "inconclusive results."[36]

On July 31 the seven policemen who had gone to the Algiers Motel just after midnight on July 26 were told to report to the Homicide Bureau. Each was asked to provide a written statement of his part in the affair, Detective Inspector Albert Schwaller saying, "Something is going on, something is wrong here, there's some B——S—— going on." August, who, according to Paille, was "nervous and shaky," wrote out a statement similar to the false report Senak, Paille, and he had filed on July 29. In response to a specific question, he denied firing inside the annex. Paille filed a similarly misleading report in which he reported seeing a body in the motel but said not a word about any beatings, interrogations, or shootings. When a detective sergeant questioned him a bit later, Paille admitted seeing two dead bodies in the motel.[37]

About an hour after he had written his statement, August asked to speak to Lieutenant Gerald Hallmark in private and said, as Hallmark wrote it up, that "he had shot one of the men at the Algiers Motel" and that he wanted his original statement back. August later claimed that what he had said was, "I shot the man in self-defense." In trial testimony, Hallmark supported August on this point, asserting that he had simply failed to include the "self-defense" words when he wrote his report of the conversation three hours later. After making his oral confession, August was advised of his rights and then dictated his confession. August told a fellow officer that he had confessed because "he couldn't live with it."[38]

After August confessed, Paille also approached Hallmark and, before the "tired and negligent" lieutenant could advise him of his rights, made an oral confession that, as already noted, also involved Senak in the shooting of Temple. When a detective tried to question Paille further, he asked to speak to his attorney before answering any questions. Soon after that Senak, the last of the seven police officers to arrive for questioning, was taken to an inspector's office, where he was advised of his constitutional rights and then began to make a statement. He had said nothing to incriminate himself or anyone else when "Lippitt entered and the questioning ceased."[39]

Melvin Dismukes was the first of those involved in the Algiers Motel incident to be tried. He was arraigned on August 3 and charged with felonious assault for beating Clark and Sortor. After a preliminary examination on August 4, in which Sortor, who had made "a positive identification" of the defendant, was the only witness called, Judge Samuel H. Olsen bound Dismukes over for trial. He was acquitted by an all-white jury after thirteen minutes of deliberation in a May 1968 trial. The evidence against him, as Hersey noted, was "somewhat thin."[40]

After the police turned over the results of their in-depth investigation of the affair to Cahalan, the prosecutor on August 7 authorized homicide warrants against August for the slaying of Pollard and against

Paille for the shooting of Temple. Since Cahalan lacked corroborative evidence for Senak's possible role in Temple's death, he limited the homicide warrants to the other two officers. The prosecutor was convinced that no one in uniform had shot Cooper. Both August and Paille, who along with Senak had been suspended on August 1, pleaded innocent and, after spending a night in jail, were released on $5,000 bonds. This occurred despite the objections of the prosecutor's office, which noted that the release on bond of those accused of murder was forbidden under Michigan law if the evidence against them was "heavy" and the presumption of their guilt "great." The bonds set for August and Paille were well below the bonds Recorder's Court judges set for accused looters and even curfew violators during the riot.[41]

The preliminary examination for August and Paille began before Judge Robert DeMascio on August 14. Policemen jammed the courtroom — "It looks more like police headquarters than a courtroom," one observer remarked. Among the witnesses, Senak stated that he had not seen Paille or August fire a weapon in the motel and had not fired one himself. Ruling out Paille's oral confession as inadmissible, DeMascio bound over August for trial and dismissed the charge against Paille. The judge gratuitously remarked regarding the charge against August, "it is totally unlike defendant August."[42]

Displeased with DeMascio's ruling regarding Paille, Cahalan on August 23 authorized the issuance of a complaint and warrant charging Paille, Senak, and Dismukes with violating Michigan law by conspiring "to commit a legal act in an illegal manner." August was named as a coconspirator but not as a defendant. The complaint was that the conspirators had assaulted and beaten Clark, Forsythe, Sortor, Davis, Green, Reed, Malloy, and Hysell with intent of doing "great bodily harm to them . . . less than the crime of murder" by direct threats and "divers other acts of coercion and duress." Three weeks later Cahalan filed a motion to set aside DeMascio's ruling regarding Paille on the ground that only a trial judge, not a judge conducting a preliminary examination, could determine the admissibility of a confession.[43]

Before the preliminary examination was held on the conspiracy charge, Detroit blacks had held a mock Algiers Motel trial. On a visit to Detroit late in August, H. Rap Brown, chairman of the Student Nonviolent Coordinating Committee, had urged his audience at a large rally to hold "a people's tribunal" and, if the police officers were found guilty, to "carry out an execution." By the time Brown spoke, young black radicals in Detroit, notably Dan Aldridge and Lonnie Peek, were preparing the mock Algiers Motel trial. They were disturbed by DeMascio's ruling regarding Paille and had become convinced that the police had executed the three black youths. The trial was originally scheduled for the Dexter Theater but was transferred to Albert Cleage's Central United Church after the theater backed out. According to Aldridge, because the police tried to intimidate the witnesses, the trial's organizers had to hide them away until they testified. Aldridge also alleged that the police tried to kill Peek and himself.[44]

The "People's Tribunal" convened on August 30 before an audience of two thousand according to Cleage, more than seven hundred according to the FBI. Newsmen from Sweden and France covered the "trial." Milton Henry served as prosecuting attorney, attorneys Sol Plafkin and Andrew Perdue served as defense counsel, and Kenneth Cockrell, then fresh out of law school, was the "judge." The jury included Rosa Parks, then on John Conyers's staff, and two whites; the foreman was the author John Killens. The verdict of guilty was based largely on the testimony of Clark, Forsythe, and Sortor. Cockrell ruled that the sentence should be determined and carried out by "the people."[45]

The preliminary examination in the state conspiracy case began on September 27, 1967, and produced 529 pages of testimony. Waiting until December 1 to render his opinion, Judge Frank Schemanske dismissed the prosecutor's warrant on the grounds that the testimony supporting the conspiracy charge was simply not credible. Schemanske noted that it was "scarcely surprising" that there had been violence during the riot, and he criticized the mock trial for adding to the tension in the community and for rehearsing the witnesses for the preliminary examination. He was particularly critical of witnesses Forsythe, Sortor, and Clark, whom he described as "young unemployed Negro school dropouts . . . with no apparent reason for living at the hotel" since they had homes in the city. He said of them and of Hysell, who had also testified, that they were "arrogant to the point of contempt," told "widely different stories" concerning the same incidents "despite evident rehearsing," and provided testimony that was "positively incredible" except where otherwise corroborated. He accused them of attempting to "get the cops" and asserted that "their calculated prevarication to the point of perjury was so blatant as to defeat its object."[46]

Appealing Schemanske's ruling, Cahalan contended that "the *excessive weight*" the judge had *"placed on the credibility* of witnesses completely obscured the primary issue of whether, from the entire record of the proceedings, sufficient facts evidenced commission of the offense charged." Many legal experts and members of the bar were critical of Schemanske's ruling. "He used this case to get how he feels about the riots off his chest," one attorney declared. The decision, one writer noted, was "a thorn in the side" of the black community, which was disposed to believe that "a racist judge" had dismissed the conspiracy charge to protect whites who had abused blacks.[47]

Cahalan was successful neither in his appeal against the DeMascio nor the Schemanske ruling. The prosecutor's motion for a writ of superintending control to reinstate the Paille murder charge with direction to the examining magistrate to hear the excluded confession and to reconsider the dismissal of the charge was granted by the presiding judge of the Recorder's Court and upheld on appeal by the Michigan Court of Appeals. In a 4 to 3 decision on July 11, 1971, however, the Michigan Supreme Court reversed the Court of Appeals and, in "a highly unusual ruling," sent the case to the Wayne County Circuit Court to rule on the prosecutor's motion. The Wayne Court then ordered the Recorder's Court to take additional testimony to determine if Paille's confession was inadmissible under the United States Supreme Court's 1965 *Garrity* decision. An evidentiary hearing was held by a visiting judge, George T. Ryan, who ruled on August 7, 1972, that since Paille had been acting on the "reasonable belief" that he was "under a state of coercion," fearing discharge, suspension, or other adverse administrative action and, also, that he would be held responsible for "other's misconduct," his "damaging admission" was inadmissible under the *Garrity* rule. Saying, "We're almost back to where we were five years ago," Cahalan appealed to the Wayne County Circuit Court, but it denied the appeal, and there the matter rested.[48]

In a second Paille decision, handed down a week after the first one, the Michigan Supreme Court denied the prosecutor's motion to reinstate the state conspiracy charge and upheld the Schemanske ruling, just as the presiding judge of the Recorder's Court and the Court of Appeals had. The Supreme Court held that the examining magistrate "had not only the right but, also, the duty to pass judgment not only on the weight and competency of the evidence but also the credibility of the witnesses."[49]

The August murder trial was initially postponed because of the assassination of Robert Kennedy. Lippitt moved for another postponement in July 1968 because, he argued, publication of John Hersey's *The Algiers Motel Incident* made a fair trial impossible. Judge Robert J. Colombo granted a delay until January 1969, denouncing the Hersey book as "yellow . . . journalism and journalism at its worst." Waiting until Thomas Poindexter, the central figure in opposition to open housing in Detroit before the riot, was presiding judge of the Recorder's Court, Lippitt in December 1968 moved for a change of venue because of the extensive pretrial publicity. Poindexter ordered that the motion be heard by visiting Oakland County Circuit Court Judge William J. Beer, "a man of Poindexter's ideological view" and the judge most frequently reversed by the Michigan Supreme Court during the years 1963–67. Beer granted Lippitt's motion and arranged for the transfer of the trial to Mason, Michigan, where he himself presided. The population of Mason, the town where Malcolm X's father had been murdered, was 99 percent white.[50]

The all-white jury for the August trial consisted of one elderly male machinist and eleven women, seven of them housewives, one a reporter, and the remainder sales and clerical workers. "Even in their wildest imagination," the *Free Press* observed, jurors of this sort could hardly have grasped what Detroit had been like during the riot.[51]

The prosecution in the Mason trial stressed that there had been no sniping around the Algiers Motel, no weapons found there, and no resistance to the police on the part of those in the motel. The only relationship to the riot of what happened in the motel, Wayne County Assistant Prosecutor Avery Weiswasser declared, was that "the color of the skin [of the victims] was the same as some of those who were out there rioting." The witnesses the prosecution put on the stand to prove the case against August left a good deal to be desired once they were subjected to cross-examination. What remained unclear after the prosecution had made its case was whether August could have "defended" himself without killing Pollard.

Claiming self-defense for his client, Lippitt equated the riot with "full scale war" and pictured the police as "soldiers in the battlefield." They had had to work long hours, he argued, and initially had been compelled to "stand by without being permitted to act against looters and arsonists." In a ruling that a criminal law expert regarded as "highly prejudicial," Beer permitted Lippitt to show a twenty-minute, heavily edited color TV film of the riot that showed blacks looting, fires raging, and the police and army on the streets defending the city. Beer overruled Weiswasser's objection that the film was "a blatant appeal to bias and bigotry."[52]

After five weeks of the trial and the testimony of forty-eight witnesses, Judge Beer virtually determined the jurors' verdict by the nature of his instructions. Ruling out the possibility of a verdict of second-degree murder or manslaughter, the judge instructed the jurors that they must rule for August unless they found him guilty of having "killed with malice and premeditation." It took the jury only two hours and thirty-five minutes to render a verdict of innocence. Most legal authorities thought that Beer's "unusual" if not "extraordinary" instructions were "less than correct" but "legal," and a cross section of judges regarded Beer's " 'all or nothing' charge" as "within his discretion." One prominent Detroit criminal lawyer, however, thought that Beer had "kicked the case away deliberately" and was "dead wrong." The judge's instructions, Cahalan later said, "just drove" him "crazy."[53]

Detroit blacks, *Newsweek* reported, were "boiling" over the August verdict. The sentiment of the black people it had interviewed, the *Michigan Chronicle* stated, was that the United States was "not color-blind . . . but actually blinded by color." "I didn't look for them to find him [August] guilty," Pollard's mother bitterly remarked, "because all whites stick together."[54]

Although Cahalan failed to secure a state trial on the conspiracy charge, Schemanske's ruling caused the federal government to reinstitute a suspended investigation of the possible violation of federal law in the affair. On May 3, 1968, a federal grand jury indicted Senak, Paille, August, and Dismukes for conspiracy to injure Pollard, Temple, Clark, Forsythe, Sortor, Reed, Davis, Green, Malloy, and Hysell in "the free exercise and enjoyment of their constitutional rights by inflicting punishment [on them] by injury and death . . . without due process of law." As in the August case, federal judge Steven J. Roth granted a defense motion for a change of venue on the grounds that the defendants could not receive "a fair and impartial trial" in Detroit because of the "prejudice" against them. Roth arranged for the transfer of the trial to Flint, his home town.[55]

As in the August trial, the jury for the federal trial, which began in January 1970, was made up entirely of whites. There were six blacks on the ninety-six member jury panel, but Lippitt used his peremptory challenges to remove the four blacks who might have served as jurors. He doubted, he said after the trial, that blacks could have judged the case fairly, but he did not express similar doubts about whites. Kenneth J. McIntyre, the special assistant United States attorney who conducted the prosecution, sought to challenge for cause two prospective jurors who stated that they did not consider the word "nigger" offensive, but Roth forced McIntyre to use two of his ten peremptory challenges for this purpose.[56]

The only real surprise of the trial was the appearance as witnesses for the prosecution of four paratroopers who had lied to the FBI in August 1967 about what they had witnessed in the Algiers Motel. The defense insisted that there had been no conspiracy in the affair but rather, as Lippitt put it, only "spontaneous action . . . spontaneously conceived." The problem for the prosecution, one that the judge pointedly called to its attention more than once and also stressed in his instructions to the jury, was to prove not that illegal acts had been committed but that there had been a conspiracy among the defendants, some kind of "agreement," to deprive Pollard and the others of their constitutional rights. As in the Mason trial, prosecution witnesses contradicted one another as well as their own earlier testimony. Roth, with this in mind, instructed the jury that witnesses could be discredited by contradictory evidence of their own or of other witnesses or if they had been convicted on a felony charge, as some of the prosecution's witnesses had been. It is hardly surprising that the jury found the defendants innocent of the conspiracy charge. "It's a shame," McIntyre stated, "that such grievous wrongs are going unredeemed."[57]

"If I have anybody to thank for these victories," Lippitt said of both the Mason and Flint trials, "it's John Hersey." He remarked that "it would have been an entirely different matter" trying the cases in Detroit. "I was not too crazy about that idea at all," he stated. The case was "clumsily prosecuted," but Temple's mother blamed Roth for the outcome. "That was the most unfair judge I ever saw," she said. "This latest phase of a step-by-step whitewash of [a] police slaying," Detroit's future mayor, State Senator Coleman Young declared, "demonstrates once again that law and order is a one-way street; there is no law and order where black people are involved, especially when they are involved with the police." Roth, for his part, concluded that the verdict could have gone no other way considering the evidence. "I don't know if I would want this printed or not," he said after the trial, "but I think the findings support Judge Schemanske."[58]

In the end, then, no one was convicted for what had taken place in the Algiers Motel in the early morning hours of July 26. The mothers of Pollard and Temple filed civil damage suits in federal court and Wayne County Circuit Court, but they withdrew the suits after the city of Detroit, in out-of-court settlements, agreed to pay $62,500 to each family. The Temple suit was not settled until 1976.[59]

August and Senak were reinstated in the Police Department on March 15, 1971, both being assigned to the Non-Duty Section. August resigned from the department on July 23, 1977, ten years to the day after the beginning of the 1967 riot. Senak was still a member of the department as late as September 9, 1979. When Paille, however, sought reinstatement in 1973, he was dismissed from the department by the commissioner, effective as of the day of his original suspension, for neglect of duty and making false statements in his Algiers Motel report. After asking for a trial board hearing, Paille changed his mind and accepted the commissioner's decision. Why the Police Department treated Paille differently than August and Senak, who also had violated several departmental regulations, is unclear.[60]

In October 1967 Cahalan filed suit in Wayne County Circuit Court to have the Algiers Motel declared a public nuisance and padlocked. Stating that the motel had been used for purposes of prostitution and that persons had been arrested there for violating the narcotics laws, Cahalan specifically called attention to Hysell's arrest there on September 13 for accosting and soliciting. The motel survived, taking the name Desert Inn until it was torn down in the spring of 1979, as its annex, the scene of the infamous night of horror and murder, already had been. The site was used as the eastern entrance for the integrated residential community planned for the area by the city of Detroit and General Motors. The symbol of the riot, the *Detroit News* observed, thus became "a symbol of reconciliation."[61]

CHAPTER 12

"The Worst Civil Disorder"

The Detroit riot was "the worst civil disorder" experienced by an American city in the twentieth century.[1] The damage caused by the riot took various forms: the numerous stores that were looted or burned; the homes that were damaged or destroyed by fire; the loss of wages for workers and of sales for businesses; the additional costs incurred by city, state, and federal governments; the injuries sustained by civilians and law enforcement personnel; and, above all, the lives that were lost.

The most conspicuous form of riot damage was the looted and/or burned store. According to the American Insurance Association, 2,509 stores were looted, burned, or destroyed by the riot, well above the less than 1,000 buildings suffering a similar fate in the Watts riot. The damaged or destroyed Detroit establishments, nearly all of them looted, included 611 supermarkets, food, and grocery stores; 537 cleaners and laundries; 326 clothing, department, and fur stores; 285 liquor stores, bars, and lounges; 240 drugstores; and 198 furniture stores.[2]

There was considerably more looting on the west side and especially in the Twelfth Street area than on the less densely populated east side. Looters and arsonists victimized almost all the liquor stores, drugstores, and pawnshops on Twelfth Street and the furniture stores on Grand River. An estimated 20 percent of the frontage in the Twelfth Street riot area was destroyed or damaged beyond repair. The destruction tended to be "spotty" rather than "total." An entire block might be destroyed on one side of a business street while the other side remained untouched. The luxury stores, for example, on Livernois and Seven Mile — the Avenue of Fashion — were damaged in a "hit-and-miss" manner, some posh stores being victimized, others not.[3]

Looters tended to seize just about anything. "There was nothing that man has made . . . that wasn't stolen," John Nichols recalled. "You take all you can get and get it while you can," one looter said. Looters seized food, liquor, furniture, TV sets, radios, musical instruments, even flowers. One looter grabbed a twelfth-century English broadsword, another, a section of a circular iron staircase. A Detroit Urban League official saw a woman about seventy-five years of age dragging a nine-by-twelve rug down the street. Five-thousand-dollar coats were taken from a fur store just off West Grand Boulevard, and $100 dresses from Saks Fifth Avenue nearby. TV sets, too heavy to carry, "littered" the streets and sidewalks. The rioters indicated their tastes in looting Grinnell's Music Shop: they removed the electric guitars and jazz records but ignored the classical music records.[4]

Looters appeared to favor items that could be consumed, especially groceries and liquor. Some drank their booty in the liquor stores they looted, and reporters noted dozens of looters staggering in the streets with liquor bottles in their hands. Furniture and appliance stores were also conspicuous targets—a *Free Press* reporter saw looters emerging from the Famous Furniture warehouse "bent under cartons that held end tables, kitchen chairs, lamps and cocktail tables." In the early stages of the riot, some rioters removed chairs from furniture stores and sat in them to observe the proceedings. Rioters broke into five banks but apparently stole no money from them. Although they seized at least twenty safes, they were unable to open most of them. Some homes were looted when fires forced the occupants to leave their dwellings. No schools were looted, one youngster stating that there was "nothing to steal" in a school. "Who wants a book or a desk?" he asked. The police were especially concerned about the 2,498 rifles and shotguns and 35 handguns that were stolen.[5]

A Neighborhood Conservation official saw a mother telling her children what to seize from a furniture store. When they returned with lamps that did not match, she sent them back to select lamps that did. A male looter who brought home a washing machine was berated by his wife for not knowing that it was a dryer they needed; he was arrested pushing the washing machine back to the store. When asked how he liked the TV set he had stolen, a looter replied, "Not so good. The first thing I saw on it was me stealing the damn thing."[6]

Although some black-owned stores with "Soul Brother" signs were conspicuously spared, there is abundant evidence from black and white sources alike that, at least after the early hours of the riot, looters and arsonists did not, for the most part, bypass black-owned or operated establishments. In a fifteen-city study of ghetto merchants and civil disorders that included Detroit, Richard Berk found that other factors were "far more important" than race in determining which businesses would be vandalized. This was probably because ghetto blacks saw white and black merchants as "very much alike . . . in the way they treat[ed] customers." Survey data for Detroit certainly confirm this point. In the Campbell-Schuman postriot survey, although 12 percent of Detroit's black respondents thought that white merchants were more likely than black merchants to overcharge, 14 percent thought the reverse, and 69 percent believed that the race of the merchant made little difference in this regard. About three-fourths of the black respondents thought that black merchants were as likely as white merchants to show disrespect for their customers.[7]

If the rioters wanted something and you had that kind of store, a black store owner declared, "you were going to get looted no matter what color you were." The first store looted, as we have seen, was the black-owned Hardy's Drug Store. The Red Satin Restaurant, the best black restaurant in Detroit, was torched, and the rioters did not spare the very successful black-owned Hawkins Apparel on Dexter. Rioters, interestingly enough, looted a black-owned liquor store on the corner of Fourteenth and McGraw and yet spared the notorious Azzam's Market at the same intersection. Karl Gregory, whose father's store was looted and demolished, thought that there might have been some "discrimination" at the beginning of the riot but that there was "a pattern of increased indiscriminateness as time progressed." The black "rage," the former principal of the Freedom School observed just after the riot, "also rubbed off on Negro-owned stores." Perhaps 27 percent of the stores destroyed were black-owned.

That even more black-owned or operated stores were not vandalized is partly explained by the fact that black owners, living in the riot area, often defended their property against potential attackers, whereas white owners, living in the suburbs and fearful of coming to the riot area, were more likely to leave their stores unprotected. One black recalled that his brother and he protected their father's drugstore on Twelfth Street, threatening to shoot intending looters. "We were protecting our property from other black people who were just out to loot," he asserted.[8]

"Anti-semitic epithets" were heard throughout the riot, and there were press reports that looters were singling out Jewish merchants. "They thought about getting at the white man, at the Jews who own these stores," a young black woman told a reporter. "And they did get at the Jews—they hit them in their pocketbooks," she said. The managing editor of the *Michigan Chronicle* later even went so far as to maintain that Arab money was involved in the attack on Jewish businesses. There is no doubt that the stores of many Jewish merchants were looted or burned— the number of Jewish-owned stores in the Twelfth Street, Dexter, and Linwood neighborhoods dwindled from seventy-eight (about 15 percent of the total) before the riot to thirty-nine (about 9 percent of the total) after the riot, although not all of the abandoned Jewish stores had been vandalized. An intensive study of the matter by the Detroit office of the Anti-Defamation League, however, revealed "no real pattern of damage to Jews as Jews." In his fifteen-city study, Berk, similarly, found that religion had "no predictive value" regarding which merchants would be vandalized in a riot.[9]

The ethnic group suffering the greatest relative damage from looting was not the Jews but Detroit's Chaldean community. Chaldeans owned or operated 192 food stores in the predominantly black areas of the city, ranging from mom-and-pop stores to $300,000 supermarkets, and only three or four of the stores escaped the looters.[10]

Nearly every commercial building set afire had first been looted, but many fewer stores were destroyed or damaged by fire than were looted. The Fire Department responded to 1,617 alarms during the period July 23–29, an average of 231 per day as compared to 119 alarms on a normal day in the preceding months of 1967 and as compared to a total of 250 alarms in the Newark riot. Fires occurred on 132 separate streets, and of the city's 139 square miles, 50 experienced fires. The state's fire marshal estimated that 50 percent of the fires had been set by incendiary devices or such inflammables as Molotov cocktails. Fire boxes in the riot areas became inoperative because of constant use, and other Fire Department circuits ceased to function because the wires had been burned. In combating the fires, the 1,700-man department used 153 pieces of its own equipment, and forty-four communities made an additional 924 men and 88 pieces of equipment available. At one point during the riot, all but three pieces of the available fire equipment had been committed to the streets. Because rioters pelted firemen and fire equipment with missiles and occasionally even shot at them, the fire fighters had to withdraw from the scene of fires on 283 occasions, mostly before the Guard began to provide protection.[11]

Estimates of the number of buildings destroyed or damaged by fire ranged, incredibly, from 316 to 1,087. The lower figure was supplied by the Department of Buildings and Safety Engineering, the higher one by the General Adjustment Bureau, which represented three hundred insurance firms doing business in the Detroit area. In still another compilation, the Fire Department in February 1968 placed the number of fire-affected structures at 690, of which 412 had been totally destroyed. It is impossible at this late date to reconcile these conflicting accounts.[12]

Only in Detroit among twenty-three riot cities studied by the Kerner Commission did riot fires cause "significant damage to residences." This was the result of fires spreading from main streets to side streets or fires set in stores that consumed the apartments above the stores. Among the 552 structures affected by fires according to a Police Department listing, 200 were residences of one sort or another. The Detroit Housing Commission estimated that six hundred persons were rendered homeless by riot fires. Among the commercial establishments set ablaze, grocery and furniture stores appear to have suffered the greatest damage.[13]

The motives of the arsonists can only be guessed at since their identity is largely unknown to us — only thirty-four alleged arsonists were arrested, and only thirteen were prosecuted. Some firebombing, we can nevertheless be sure, was purposive, some purposeless. "Every building that was burned down," Albert Cleage stated, "can be explained," and he later "explained," inaccurately, that the rioters had not been torching their own stores and homes but rather the property of "slum owners," who were being driven from the ghetto. On the other hand, when a reporter asked a black woman who knew some of the rioters what motivated the arsonists, she replied, "They don't know. It was something to do." She understood looting, she asserted, but not burning. The residents of the side streets running perpendicular to Twelfth Street also did not understand burning. They feared that their homes would be set afire, and they were concerned that the stores where they shopped were being destroyed and about the resulting loss of jobs as well.[14]

Charles S. Brown, the black executive director of Wayne County Suburban Legal Services, informed a Kerner Commission interviewer that rioters set fires to retaliate against exploitative merchants, to destroy credit records, or as a "decoy" for looting. There is no question that some firebombing was directed at hated merchants who, the arsonists thought, "deserved it" because of the way they treated their customers. More than half of Twelfth Street's adult blacks in a postriot survey attributed riot fires to this motive. There is also no question that fires were deliberately set to destroy credit records, which partially explains the burning of furniture and appliance stores. "Yes, I burned the damned Jew store down," a black woman said regarding a furniture store she had set ablaze. "That's one bill I will never have to pay." Parents, according to one report, were seen burning credit records they had sent their children to seize from Livernois stores. Brown did not explain what he meant by the setting of fires as a "decoy" for looting, but he was presumably suggesting that fires served to draw law enforcement officers away from looting targets. An arrestee stated that he had heard that arsonists were setting fires to destroy fingerprints that might have revealed the identity of looters.[15]

The head of the Detroit branch of the Anti-Defamation League later claimed that organized crime had taken advantage of the riot to burn dry cleaning establishments and bowling alleys that criminal elements had been unable to gain control of before the riot. Some property owners also burned or arranged for the burning of buildings to collect the insurance.[16]

The losses suffered by commercial establishments as the result of fire, smoke, looting, and the interruption of normal business, plus the losses suffered by homeowners, presented formidable problems for the owners of the affected properties as well as the insurance companies. The city government, authorities on municipal law agreed, was not itself liable for the damage suffered by property owners as the result of the riot.[17]

Securing insurance in the riot areas of Detroit had been a difficult problem for property owners before the riot, as we have seen, and now the uninsured and the inadequately insured faced bankruptcy and ruin, while the insured were threatened with cancellation or nonrenewal of their policies. The 295 insurance companies that wrote policies in the riot areas appeared to have suffered "a tremendous blow." According to David Dykhouse, Michigan's insurance commissioner, the riots in Detroit and elsewhere had "upset the entire international insurance system."[18]

Dun and Bradstreet reported in August 1967 that 86 percent of twelve hundred damaged Detroit businesses that it had been able to contact carried at least some insurance. A different picture, however, emerged from a survey of one hundred randomly selected businesses that had suffered riot damage: only 10 percent had insurance that fully covered their losses, 50 percent had only partial coverage, and 40 percent had no coverage at all.[19]

Concerned about possible cancellations and nonrenewal of policies in the riot areas, the Michigan Insurance Bureau took a series of steps while the riot was underway to protect policyholders. Explaining how policyholders might be taken advantage of by repair and fire construction companies and by public adjusters, the bureau on July 26 urged individuals with damaged property that was insured to contact their agent or insurance company representative before taking any action regarding their insurance. The next day the bureau set up an Insurance Information Center in Detroit to assist the insured in submitting claims and to coordinate segments of the insurance industry involved in adjusting riot losses. The Michigan insurance code permitted insurance companies in the state to cancel policies after giving a five-day notice, but on July 31 Dykhouse appealed to the companies to defer cancellations voluntarily for a ninety-day period.[20]

The Insurance Bureau was anxious that no responsible official in the state refer to the riot as an "insurrection" since policies with extended coverage normally covered the "perils of riot and civil commotion" but excluded losses resulting from insurrections. Although the American Insurance Association and the Mutual Loss Insurance Bureau left the matter to the discretion of individual members, there is no indication that any insurance companies sought to take advantage of the insurrection waiver in Detroit.[21]

There is ample evidence that some insurance companies canceled policies in the riot areas or failed to renew them following the disturbance. This occurred during the moratorium and at an accelerating rate thereafter. In testimony before the Senate Commerce Committee, Arthur Yim, a member of the Cavanagh administration, stated that one company had canceled 411 policies and that an additional 1,300 policyholders had been threatened with cancellation unless they transferred coverage to a nonadmitted company and signed an endorsement excluding losses from riots, civil commotions, and strikes. Yim reported that another company that had written about 700 policies in Michigan had canceled most of them and planned to withdraw from the state. He noted that several large national insurance companies and some foreign corporations were among those canceling policies. Although Yim stated that there had been no "wholesale rate increases" by the companies, the president of the Linwood Organization, representing firms in a major riot area, claimed a few weeks later that the insurance companies had raised rates substantially and that this was hampering rebuilding efforts. A Detroit insurance agent reported at about the same time that 95 percent of those seeking insurance in the riot areas could not obtain it at the standard rate, 75 percent could not obtain insurance at any price, and policies were being canceled "at a tremendous rate."[22]

What the riot meant to those who suffered damage but did not carry insurance or had inadequate coverage can be grasped from the experience of some businesses and individuals. The Esquire Loan Company was insured for $10,000 but lost $200,000 in the riot. Samuel Lipson, owner of a clothing store on Twelfth Street who had been unable to renew his insurance policy when it had expired before the riot, lost $20,000. "They cleaned me out like an army," said Irving Goldstein of the looters who denuded his Twelfth Street store of the cheap rugs and watches that he sold. The warehouse in which Goldstein rented space was burned to the ground; and to add to his woes, rioters or thieves bored through a brick wall to remove his safe, which contained $100,000 in diamonds and cash. Since Goldstein had only $25,000 in the bank, he was able to pay his creditors only 5 percent of what he owed them.[23]

William Henry Stallings, the black owner of Bill's Hardware and Fix It Shop, was one of the more tragic business victims of the riot. Although Stallings thought his store would be spared since everyone in the neighborhood knew he was black, it was looted on July 23 and subsequently burned to the ground. Financially ruined, Stallings began to drink, separated from his wife, and died of a heart attack two years later.[24]

The Fire Department initially estimated the property damage resulting from the riot at $250 million, a highly inflated figure. The Michigan Insurance Bureau at the end of July placed the insured losses resulting from looting, fire, and the interruption of business in the riot areas at $84 million and the uninsured losses at between $50 and $60 million. The insured loss figure approximated the later estimates of $75–80 million by the American Insurance Association and the Mutual Loss Research Bureau and the $80 million estimate by the National Association of Insurance Commissioners. In December 1967, however, Michigan's insurance commissioner drastically reduced the damage figure to between $40 and $45 million.[25]

In the end, $32 million was apparently paid out in insurance claims resulting from the riot. This sum, however, seriously understates the extent of the riot damage. It reveals nothing about the losses of the uninsured, the extent to which the insured were only partially insured, the extent to which the interruption of business in the riot area was covered, and the losses suffered by businesses outside the riot area that had to close as the result of the governor's emergency proclamation or because of a lack of business or staff. Although a rock-bottom figure that conceals more than it reveals, the $32 million constituted about 43 percent of the total insured property loss ($75 million) resulting from the numerous riots in the summer of 1967.[26]

The cited figures of insured and uninsured losses resulting from the riot do not take into account all the financial losses incurred by Detroiters and their city government. Quite apart from the loss of retail sales inside and outside the riot areas, estimated by one source as $8 million, workers throughout the city suffered a loss of wages, which the Greater Detroit Board of Commerce estimated after four days of rioting at the inflated figure of $75 million. Judging from the records of the Michigan Employment Security Commission, at least twelve hundred workers lost their jobs as a result of the riot.

There was a downward trend in business activity in Detroit following the riot that city businessmen attributed to the disturbance. No convention scheduled for the city was actually canceled, but fewer delegates came to these conventions than had been expected—less than half of the four thousand anticipated delegates, for example, appeared for the August convention of the National Association of Counties. Because of a lower occupancy rate, the downtown Pontchartrain Hotel experienced a drop in income of $50,000 in August and September as compared to the same months in 1966. There was, similarly, a 65 percent decline in attendance at Bob-Lo Island between July 23 and Labor Day and a 200,000 fall-off in attendance at Greenfield Village in Dearborn in August. Because of its poor image as a result of the riot, Detroit also suffered a real but difficult-to-calculate loss in the business from conventions that might otherwise have been held in the city.[27]

The city government incurred riot "costs" estimated by officials at $11,625,000. The city administration derived this sum from overtime and shift premium pay (principally for policemen and firemen), damage to equipment, revenue losses, additional operating expenses, and the cost of the demolition of unsafe buildings. The loss in the assessed value of personal and real property came to $11,271,000. The state of Michigan lost an estimated $1.5 million in sales and gasoline taxes, and the deployment of the National Guard in Detroit cost the state just over $500,000. The federal government incurred about $2.5 million in "unprogrammed and unbudgeted costs" because of the riot.[28]

According to the Police Department, 657 persons were injured during the riot. Of this number, 476 were law enforcement officers or fire fighters (167 city police, 16 state troopers, 17 Guardsmen, 3 paratroopers, 273 fire fighters); 109 were persons committing crimes, about half of them looters and 19 allegedly being snipers; and 72 were "citizens," presumably innocent bystanders. Among police suffering injuries, 28 had been stoned, 11 shot, 29 assaulted by prisoners or looters, and 2 bitten, not an "uncommon" type of injury for Detroit police officers. Of the firemen injured, 84 required hospitalization. Ninety-five blacks and 31 whites suffered gunshot wounds. The police were responsible for 30 of these shootings; the Guard for 22; snipers, allegedly, for 36; and unknown persons for 35. One of those shot was thirteen-year-old Albert Wilson, caught inside a store being looted and then shot by the police and left paralyzed for life when he emerged from the store as the police had ordered those inside to do. In 1975 the city awarded Wilson $875,000 in damages.[29]

Judging from hospital records, the police figure of 657 injuries considerably understates the number of persons actually injured. Detroit General Hospital, Ford Hospital, and Metropolitan Hospital reported that they had treated 1,189 riot-related injuries; and since not all of those injured during the riot were treated at hospitals, it is safe to assume that the number injured exceeded one thousand even if the three hospitals overstated the number of riot-related injuries that they treated. The Detroit riot alone accounted for at least 10 percent of all the persons injured in 341 riots in 265 cities from 1963 to 1968.[30]

The 43 deaths in the Detroit riot constituted more than half of the 83 deaths resulting from 164 civil disturbances during the first nine months of 1967 and 20 percent of the 221 deaths in the 341 disturbances between 1963 and 1968. There were persistent reports in Detroit that the official figure of 43 deaths was inaccurate and that the actual number was closer to 100 or even more. According to Garry Wills, even a "police observer" to whom he had spoken claimed that the death toll was above 100, and Wills interviewed a Guardsman who claimed that he had seen at least 6 unreported bodies. Despite the denials of the Wayne County Medical Examiner, there were stories in Detroit about unreported bodies in the morgue, and there were also rumors that city garbage trucks had dumped bodies into the Detroit River. The fact that so many people were missing or at least unaccounted for during the riot helped to sustain the rumors of unreported deaths. There is, however, little reason to dispute the correctness of the official death figure. The *Detroit Free Press,* which made an intensive study of the riot deaths, sent its reporters to the morgue to count bodies and even into the sewer system to check for bodies and concluded that the official figure was accurate.[31]

Among the forty-three dead, thirty were slain by law enforcement personnel. The police accounted for seventeen of these deaths, the Guard for ten (including three probables), the police and/or Guard for two, and the army for one. Store owners killed two persons; rioters, two; a private guard, one; and a white civilian, one. Two deaths were accidental, two looters died of asphyxiation in a looted and burned store, and the assailants of the remaining three victims were not identified. Thirty-three of those who died were black, and ten were white, including two firemen, one police officer, and one

Guardsman. According to police reports, the riot dead included sixteen looters, four snipers, and one arsonist.[32]

After an investigation of each of the deaths by three reporters, the *Free Press* concluded that most could or should have been avoided. The reporters discovered considerable discrepancies between what the police reported and what the reporters learned from more than three hundred interviews and the hundreds of documents they examined. Based on this experience, one of the reporters stated that he would never again "fully believe a Police report." The reporters were particularly critical of trigger-happy Guardsmen and of the police slaying of fleeing looters or alleged looters when the lives of the officers were not in danger.[33]

The police listed four persons killed during the riot as snipers, but only Jack Sydnor fits this description. Although unidentified snipers, according to the police, killed three riot victims, only one death can definitely be attributed to a sniper.[34] Like the deaths as well as the riot injuries attributed to snipers in police reports, the number of sniping incidents in the riot was grossly exaggerated even though there was more sniper fire in Detroit than in all the other 1960s riots combined. The police listed all shootings whose cause could not be determined as sniper fire. Cherry bomb explosions were reported as gunfire, and the same shot was often reported by different sources and treated as separate sniping incidents. Much of the shooting was actually by trigger-happy Guardsmen. Even the sniper fire at police stations was exaggerated. Girardin recalled that on one occasion a police lieutenant in one station was "crawling from under his desk saying he was under fire," but when headquarters dispatched assistance, it turned out that the station was not even under attack.[35]

Of 250 reported sniping incidents between July 26 and August 2, the police were able to confirm only 57. If, similarly, 20 percent of the sniping incidents reported during the first three days of the riot had a basis in fact, the total number of actual sniping incidents for the entire riot was no more than 71. However exaggerated the sniping incidents and however little damage they may have caused, this was the aspect of the riot police feared the most. Finding it difficult to locate and apprehend the assailants, the police were apt to feel themselves surrounded once the shooting began. "This is more than a riot," a police officer declared with sniping in mind. "This is war."[36]

The FBI at one point claimed that there were 251 known snipers in Detroit, but the actual number was almost certainly less than one hundred. Girardin thought that the snipers were of two types, the "casual" and the "determined." The casual sniper, as the commissioner described him, had probably been drinking and fired his weapon without having any real target in mind. The determined sniper shot to kill. If by sniper, however, one means a highly trained marksman with an effective weapon and a telescopic sight, there were very few if any snipers in the disturbance areas during the riot. Indeed, had the snipers been "professionals," the death toll would have been considerably higher than it was.[37]

A self-confessed, teen-aged, black sniper who was certainly not a professional described his behavior to a reporter during the riot. He claimed that his buddy and he had done some looting and thrown some Molotov cocktails but then "got tired" of this. After drinking some of their loot, they "decided to do some shootin." They fired at the police and claimed that they "had them cops so scared . . . they were shooting at one another." They hired a ten-year-old, with whom they communicated by walkie-talkie, to watch out for National Guard patrols while they took to the rooftops. "We controlled the scene," one of them boasted. "We were just like guerrillas — real ones."[38]

The deaths, the injuries, and the looted and burned property in the 1967 riot constituted major tangible losses for the city of Detroit and its inhabitants. The city also suffered an intangible but nevertheless meaningful loss, the death of its well-publicized reputation as a model city in the area of race relations. Detroiters, including himself, said the United Automobile Workers' Douglas Fraser, had been confident — "cocky" is the word he used — that a riot could not occur in their city. "Suddenly," however, the *Michigan Chronicle* observed during the riot, "this great model city of ours became one of chaos and confusion." "Today," said Mayor Cavanagh, reacting to the riot and perhaps to its implications for his own political future, "we stand amidst the ashes of our hopes. We hoped against hope that what we had been doing was enough to prevent a riot. It was not enough." What had occurred, to quote B. J. Widick, was "the death of a dream that Detroit was different." That is why the *Washington Post* characterized the Detroit riot as "the greatest tragedy of all the long succession of Negro ghetto outbursts."[39]

CHAPTER 13

"A Rough Community Division of Labor"

While the riot raged in Detroit, the black and white communities of the city reacted in various ways to the unfolding events. For public officials and voluntary organizations, the problem was how best to deal with the myriad problems the riot produced.

Frustrated by the events that had shattered Detroit's image as a model city in race relations and imperiled his own political future, Mayor Cavanagh concluded that he had been communicating with the wrong blacks. The black leaders on whom he had relied, he blurted out, did not "even know the people in the streets. I've got to talk to different leaders from now on," he asserted. Even though Cavanagh soon denied having said anything like that and stated that he had been talking to the "right people," the black leadership understandably resented the implication that the only "valid reason" for City Hall to be in touch with black leaders was "to keep Negroes from rioting." Robert Tindal, executive secretary of the Detroit branch of the National Association for the Advancement of Colored People (NAACP), thought that the white power structure in Detroit was using the black civil rights organizations and the black middle class as the "scapegoat" for its own failure. Tindal and other black leaders maintained that the blacks being criticized had lobbied for "revolutionary changes in conditions" but that their advice had not been followed.[1]

Throughout the riot, the black civil rights organizations, the black clergy, and black businessmen condemned the rioting in harsh terms. Since they favored working through existing political channels and feared that the rioting was damaging their credibility with the white leadership, the riots in Detroit and elsewhere placed the black middle class in "an extremely difficult position." The rioters were "hoodlums with a total disrespect for law," Damon Keith declared; and Philip Rutledge, head of Detroit's poverty program, informed the Office of Economic Opportunity that the riot was "criminal in direction." Looters and arsonists, the Trade Union Leadership Council's Horace Sheffield commented, "weren't concerned about grievances, they were concerned about looting these stores." In a statement released on July 31, the Detroit NAACP asserted that although it "fully" understood "the frustrations, deprivations and unresolved grievances which so tragically exploded" in the city, it could not "condone looting, arson and sniping or any other form of unlawful conduct." Rioting, the NAACP maintained, would harm, not help, the city's blacks.[2]

The black middle-class view of the riot was captured by a *Michigan Chronicle* reporter who saw "no connection" between the rioting and civil rights. "We must stop cloaking our criminals in civil rights garments," she declared. "Later," she predicted, "sociologists will tell us what caused the riot and how much we need schools, recreation centers and what have you, but the 12th Street crowd has been waiting a long time for a chance to loot the city."[3]

For all of its defensive and understandable reaction to the Cavanagh criticism, the black leadership was aware, as a black attorney put it, that there was "a tremendous breakdown in communication between the Negro middle class and Negro ghetto dweller." No doubt shaken by the hostile reaction to them by the rioters, they realized that a way had to be found to narrow the "wide gulf" between more fortunate and less fortunate blacks and between the leadership and those disposed to riot.[4] Where Cavanagh was in error, if he really believed he was talking to the wrong blacks, was in thinking that there were some blacks, the militants and the black nationalists presumably, who did speak for the ghetto. Men like Albert Cleage and Milton Henry, however, were no more in touch with the rioters than the black leadership was.

Rioters whom newsmen managed to interview during the course of the disturbance spoke in defiant terms. "We'll burn this place down again if we have to," one of them told a *New York Times* reporter. "We'll burn this whole stinking town down." "The brothers aren't playing no more," another rioter declared. When asked whom he thought the rioting hurt, a young black replied, "I don't give a damn who it hurts. I know we don't own the stuff, so you figure out who it hurts."[5] Still another rioter, however, remarked to a Detroit Urban League (DUL) housing assistant about the burning of black homes, "Yeah man, that really is too bad about the cats whose cribs got wasted, no one that was doing the thing tried to get the 'brothers' but the wind was up." The majority of the youngsters contacted during the riot by the Summer Week-End Evening Program justified the riot "because till you do something they [whites] aren't going to change nothing."[6]

If one single reaction most characterized the reaction of the black community as a whole during the riot, it was fear. As the *Detroit Free Press* observed, for every looter, there were thousands of horrified blacks, "prisoners of the new ghetto — bounded on every side by fear." In a sample survey of the black community conducted just after the riot, 67 percent of the respondents admitted that they had been "afraid" during the riot. They expressed their fear, generally, by staying at home or remaining away from work—this was true of 56 percent of the black community according to one survey—but 7 percent of blacks fifteen years of age or older who lived in the riot areas indicated in another survey that they had left their homes for safer locations, such as Windsor, across the Detroit River in Canada. A smaller number armed themselves.

Residents of the west side disturbance area said after the riot that they had feared being burned out or even killed. I was "confused and shocked" and "more afraid" each day, one black declared. Several said that they kept their shades down and lights off and stayed away from doors and windows. "We were sitten in the dark for one whole week," one woman said of her family. "I stayed in my apartment and used can milk for my kids and we eat less," another said. One woman stated that she had "escaped fear by doing housework"; others prayed. A black male said that he had loaded his guns and set up barricades at his house, and a black woman remarked that she had learned how to fire her husband's gun.[7]

The black reporter Sandra West, who lived in the Twelfth Street area, described how blacks in the neighborhood on the riot's first day "cried with fear as burning and looting raged all around them." Two days later she spoke of "the fear that my house would be set afire by flying cinders, the harassment from looters daring me with their stares to order them off my yard, the Guardsmen who glared and pointed their guns at me as they cruised the neighborhood," and all of this "surpassed" by gunshot as snipers and the Guard fired at one another nearby. "It seemed to me," one woman in the riot area said, "the world was coming to an end."[8]

Fear and concern were the characteristic reactions when staff members of the Lafayette Clinic, toward the end of the riot, interviewed 201 individuals who had come to the emergency relief centers for assistance. The interviewees were 91 percent black and 57 percent female. They were mostly in their thirties or forties, poorly educated, and of low socioeconomic status. Almost every one of them had "felt afraid" as the result of the riot. It was "like a 'nightmare,' " one black woman said. "At first I thought it was a useful protest, then I realized it was hooliganism." Interviewees feared a white backlash and the loss of their jobs as the result of the riot. "It only brought harm for the colored person," a twenty-three-year-old male who had lost his job declared. "It's disgraceful, terrible, damaging to the Negro," observed a fifty-year-old man. "Negroes suffered the most and will continue to suffer." Although some younger interviewees defended the rioters, most of the blacks at the relief centers, like the black leadership and the black middle class, were critical of the tactics of the rioters and the use of force to effect change.[9]

Middle-class blacks were tense and anxious during the riot, perhaps more so than whites, the middle-class oriented *Michigan Chronicle* thought, because they were closer to the action. "These people down here," a community organizer on Twelfth Street stated, "don't see any difference between them [middle-class blacks] and white folks." A group of black looters screamed at a well-dressed black, "We're going to get you rich niggers next." Twenty middle-class blacks turned to the Community Relations Service for protection since they had heard rumors that they were to be "burned out" by the rioters. Councilman Nicholas Hood moved his family out of their home on July 24 and 25 after a "menacing. visit" by three young blacks, and we can assume that blacks who fled to Windsor and other places were predominantly middle class.[10]

In one east side, predominantly black neighborhood of 150 blocks adjacent to the riot area in that part of the city, the black residents, working primarily through the ten-thousand-member Positive Neighborhood Action Committee, largely insulated themselves from the nearby rioting. Although the committee identified with the rioters, its members, imbued with "a kind of neighborhood pride," succeeded in keeping their children from joining the rioters and in getting the rioters to "cease and desist" insofar as that neighborhood was concerned.[11]

In a "cursory survey" on July 27 of white reaction to the riot, a Michigan Civil Rights Commission (CRC) staffer concluded that the response depended on where whites lived. In the inner city and black neighborhoods, he judged, whites "tended 'to roll with the punches,' expressed little hostility, and were calmer and less fearful than whites in all-white areas." White merchants in black areas, one suspects, however, were of the view, as one merchant put it, that blacks whom their stores had served and that they were now looting and burning should have been "glad that someone stayed to take care of them." In "changing neighborhoods," some whites expressed understanding of the rioters, and some participated in relief efforts, but the prevalent view appears to have been summed up by the person who said, "We've done so much for them already—what more do they want?" Some whites in areas of this sort talked of moving away as soon as possible. In all-white areas and the suburbs, according to this unscientific survey, "rumors, fear, and hostile reactions" were "thick." There were reports of people arming themselves or, at least, of talking of doing so. Many whites in such areas and, no doubt, elsewhere thought that "the answer" to the riot was, "Machine gun the looters down."[12]

A postriot survey revealed that 64 percent of Detroit's whites reacted to the riot with fear. Nine percent indicated that they had armed themselves, and 5 percent stated that they had left their homes. The principal fear of whites was that the riot would spread to their neighborhoods. "It's a very terrifying experience on all sides," a sensitive white woman wrote her children.[13]

In one white neighborhood, residents not only armed themselves, but one of them stopped cars to ensure that they did not carry rioters. Guns were handed out to the fearful at meetings in other neighborhoods. The white suburbs beefed up police patrols, and store owners who sold guns removed them from their shops. Rumors were rife in white neighborhoods and in the suburbs that they would become the targets of roving bands of rioters. In a foretaste of the role it would play after the riot, Breakthrough, a far-right Detroit organization, issued a poster on July 26 in the form of a purported warrant of arrest and offering a $1,000 reward for the arrest and conviction of either Cavanagh or Romney for "Malfeasance, Misfeasance and Nonfeasance" in their capacities as law enforcement officers.[14]

Whites vented their strong feelings during the riot in letters sent to Cavanagh and Romney. The fear that the riot induced and the virulence of white racism were painfully evident in these letters. Although some writers praised the mayor and the governor for their leadership during the riot, many more were harshly critical. Cavanagh, in particular, was excoriated for his race-relations policies before the riot and for the police restraint at the riot's outset. Unless there was a "drastic" response to the rioting, one writer noted, blacks would "burn America down." "This is no longer America," another correspondent protested, "when hoodlums [sic] can roam the streets destroying while were [sic] shut up in the house like dogs." The letter writers described blacks as "liars" and "crazy animals" and as opposed to law and order. "Laws are not for these animals," one correspondent commented, and another asked, "Why should we white people still go on trying to help those people?"

The mayor's correspondents accused him of being "afraid of the lawless mad-dog negroes" because he was "greedy for their vote." "These niggers have gotten away with murder for years," an irate citizen exclaimed. Cavanagh and, less frequently, Romney, were accused of condoning "the crime committed by black animals swarming our streets and making a hell" of Detroit instead of worrying about "defenseless citizens." Some correspondents wanted the rioters shot "like one would [shoot] a mad dog," and one bloodthirsty individual wanted "2430 corpses" instead of "2430 prisoners."[15]

As the massive proportions of the riot became evident, both public authorities and private organizations grappled with the consequences of the disturbance for the city and its inhabitants. Although there was no formal planning, "a rough community division of labor emerged" as the public and private sectors sought to cope with both the human and the physical devastation that the disorder wrought.[16]

Among the agencies of the city government, the Summer Task Force (STF) came the closest to serving a coordinating role in response to the riot. Although the STF's Neighborhood Reporting System had proved a failure as an "early-warning system," its supervisor concluded that it had been "invaluable" during the riot itself, providing a "clearer picture" of events during the first thirty-six hours of the disorder than was available to the Police Department from law enforcement personnel. Manning the phones on a twenty-four-hour basis, the STF received and logged a host of reports from the field, many of them wildly inaccurate. If the incoming information appeared to be accurate, the STF provided direction for the response of the appropriate city agency; if the information was false, it passed on factual information about the incident to community leaders. The STF sought initially to coordinate efforts to provide emergency food and shelter for riot victims, but, as will become evident, it was a voluntary agency that assumed primary responsibility for that task.[17]

In addition to its vain effort to calm the disturbance at its outset and the important role played regarding arrestees by the Neighborhood Legal Service Centers, one of its agencies, the Mayor's Committee for Human Resources Development (MCHRD) sought to prevent the spread of the riot and to aid its victims. Seeking to divert youngsters from joining the riot and to relieve some of the attendant "tension and anger," the MCHRD instructed the staff of Operation Champ, the agency's summer recreation program, to open fire hydrant sprinklers and to staff playgrounds and recreation facilities in as many locations as possible at the fringes of the riot areas. The riot, however, spread beyond these perimeters before the plan could be put into effect. The committee had its counselor aides contact Neighborhood Youth Corps (NYC) enrollees in what proved to be a highly successful effort to persuade them not to join in the rioting. Some even assisted the hard-pressed police, manning switchboards at headquarters and doing "other jobs" there, and others helped out in the city's hospitals and in other ways. The MCHRD also gathered intelligence for the STF. It surveyed retail food and drug outlets in the riot areas so as to determine which stores were still open, it contacted small businesses to ascertain the effect of the riot on them, and it provided information to city agencies about damaged buildings.

The most conspicuous function of the Community Development Centers and the Neighborhood Service Centers during the riot was the distribution of emergency relief. Food and clothing were made available to the needy, and those requiring shelter were referred to the appropriate agency. When the centers learned of unmet needs, they dispatched a worker to direct those requiring help to a relief station or to provide "on-the-spot service." The centers had served 19,400 persons by July 29.[18]

The Detroit Housing Commission (DHC) and the Wayne County Department of Social Services sought to meet the emergency housing needs of families and individuals displaced by the riot. The DHC secured authority from the federal government's Housing Assistance Administration to use all public housing vacancies for riot victims. It eventually placed ninety families in such housing. The federal government made 159 homes and apartments available to the DHC for riot victims, but it does not appear that any of those displaced by the riot moved into any of these units.[19]

The Wayne County Department of Social Services opened an Emergency Welfare Shelter in the Wolverine Hotel that was accommodating 114 individuals by July 29. They were fed on the premises, a task that enlisted the assistance of Neighborhood Service Organization volunteers and NYC enrollees. Astonished that so few people were taking advantage of its services, the department concluded that persons hurt by the disturbance were "just not moving" from their neighborhoods even when in need.[20]

The concern of the city's Health Department centered about the availability of undamaged food in the riot area, sanitation problems, and the operation of Detroit General Hospital as the principal city facility for treating riot injuries. Inspectors from the department's Food Division began inspecting food establishments on July 25 to determine the extent to which riot damage had affected the availability of food. Although the division condemned more than fifteen hundred pounds of meat, it concluded as of July 26 that untainted food was available to those who could afford it. There were reports that day, however, of price gouging by merchants, which led the Common Council to enact an ordinance forbidding the sale of food products at prices above the average retail price charged for those items before the governor declared the state of emergency. Enforcement of the ordinance was entrusted to the commissioner of health, who found only one violation after inspectors had conducted 125 investigations.

Inspections by the Health Department's Sanitary Division revealed the above-normal presence in the disturbance areas of rats and flies, the result of the accumulation of food in alleys and basements, lack of garbage collection, and basements filled with water. Rats in particular were "on the run throughout the riot areas." Aided by the Wayne County Health Department and VISTA volunteers, the city department distributed more than eight thousand pounds of rat poison for use in 344 city blocks. It borrowed spraying equipment from the Department of Parks and Recreation to spray insecticides in areas with spoiled food. At the request of the commissioner of health, the United States Public Health Service sent two specialists in rat and insect control to Detroit to aid the city and to train city personnel in fly and vector control.[21]

As already noted, Detroit General Hospital put its disaster plan into effect on the riot's first day and made the treatment of riot-related injuries its highest priority. The hospital staff worked twelve-hour shifts, which made it possible for personnel to arrive and leave in daylight, but exhaustion soon became a problem — one resident recalled that he came to the hospital on Sunday, July 23, and remained there until Thursday. Riot victims, some of them police prisoners in leg irons, "filled the rooms and halls in the emergency area" during the riot week. When police and soldiers fired at snipers from one hospital, a black newspaper reported the action under the headline, "Killer Cops Run Hospital."

The Detroit General Hospital and the other hospital disaster plans did not take into account the hostile feelings professional personnel might have for rioters and suspected rioters. Doctors and nurses became concerned about their "feelings of fear, hate, and anxiety under riot conditions." Following the riot, new hospital programs were designed to secure "more equitable patient care" and better employee relations.[22]

The Street Maintenance Division of the Department of Public Works initiated a cleanup operation on July 25, devoting its initial efforts to the removal of heavy rubble, bricks, and other debris that had fallen into the streets from riot-damaged structures. It also removed the damaged part of buildings, making 110 buildings safe by August 4. Sanitation Division crews, aided by personnel from the State Highway Department and the Wayne County Road Department, followed the "heavy cleanup crews" into the riot areas for the final cleanup. This task, which included rubbish and garbage pickup, was largely completed by August 7. One result was that Twelfth Street, a littered, dirty street in normal times, looked "cleaner" by early August than it had "in a long time."[23]

On July 25 the commissioner of public works requested the Common Council to authorize the removal of structures that were beyond repair and had been identified as safety hazards by the Department of Buildings and Safety Engineering and the Fire Marshal's Office. The demolition was financed under the scattered-site demolition program, for which the federal government paid two-thirds of the cost. The council promptly complied with the request and also adopted a companion resolution requiring that a lien be placed against the properties involved equal to the cost of the demolition. The council took this action because it assumed that property owners could afford to pay for the demolition or that insurance would cover all or part of the cost.

Following a survey of 477 structures by its inspectors, the Department of Buildings and Safety Engineering began issuing demolition notices to property owners. The department was constrained by the "time-consuming procedures" of the "dangerous and unsafe structures" ordinance, which entitled the property owner receiving such a notice to a hearing before the department and a second hearing before the Common Council. Delay was also occasioned by the need to wait for the settlement of insurance claims and a shortage of licensed wrecking contractors in Detroit. By the end of 1968, of 316 structures heavily damaged during the riot, 251 had been removed, 90 percent of them by the owners; 55 had been repaired; and the fate of 10 buildings, boarded up against trespass, remained unresolved.[24]

The Department of Streets and Traffic had to replace or repair 125 traffic control signs and to remove or repair 150 damaged parking meters in the riot areas. The Public Lighting Commission (PLC) had to deal with one thousand broken streetlights. At one time during the disturbance three thousand lights in thirty street lighting circuits were out of service. On July 23 the PLC's Construction Division had to be dispatched with police protection to cut burning wires and repair damaged traffic signals in the disturbance areas. The chief riot role of the PLC's Communications Division was to provide emergency telephone communication to police, military, and Fire Department command posts. This service became essential after local phone service to these posts ceased because of fire damage to cables and overload conditions.[25]

In addition to threatening court action under the Fair Neighborhood Practices Ordinance against realty companies that were pressuring whites in neighborhoods in or close to riot areas to sell their homes, the Commission on Community Relations (CCR) performed its basic field functions of "observation, evaluation, and report." Its field staff investigated rumors and received and transmitted reports of "racially inciting behavior," police misconduct, issues troubling the community, and food, clothing, and housing shortages. At a meeting on July 29 the CCR called for "an immediate, radical approach" to the problems that in its view had caused the rioting, and it made specific recommendations with regard to education, jobs, and housing.[26]

On July 28 the mayor's office requested the city's Civil Service Commission (CSC) to deal with the offers of citizens to volunteer their services during the riot. Although about one thousand Detroiters expressed a desire to help, the responses of city departments when canvassed by the CSC regarding the use of volunteer labor were "almost entirely negative." The commission did, however, refer about seventy volunteers to one food distribution agency or another.[27] In addition to their efforts to restore order at the outset of the riot, school community agents helped to man food distribution centers. Closed during the riot, the schools provided encampment space for the army and the Michigan Guard, which occupied twelve school buildings. The Department of Parks and Recreation had the riot responsibility of feeding the police.[28]

The city's Office of Civil Defense (OCD) had played the principal relief role in Detroit's 1943 riot, but it was in the process of being phased out just before the 1967 riot. Seeing a chance to reassert its influence once the July rioting began, the OCD set up five temporary shelters in three Catholic churches and two schools on July 23 and 24. The OCD remained active as a dispenser of relief throughout the riot, but its activities in this area were overshadowed, as we shall see, by the Interfaith Emergency Center.[29]

Quite apart from its efforts to quell the riot by the dispatch of the State Police and the Michigan Guard, the state government sought to cope with one or another problem caused by the disturbance, especially the insurance question. The Michigan Employment Security Commission made "an 'all-out' effort" to deal with riot-caused unemployment by the prompt processing of unemployment claims and by helping to secure jobs or training for those thrown out of work. Industrial agents from the state's Department of Commerce aided Detroit businesses adversely affected by the riot in securing Small Business Administration (SBA) loans.[30]

Like the CCR, the Michigan CRC devoted its efforts in the riot primarily to observation and the gathering of information. It advised Cavanagh, Romney, and Girardin and helped to establish communication between government officials and community leaders. As we have seen, the CRC sent observers to the various places where riot prisoners were being held to check on their treatment. Like the CCR, it stressed that if future riots were to be avoided, it was necessary to "open up society for Negroes" and to alter existing patterns in housing, employment, education, and police-community relations. Governor Romney echoed the CRC in public addresses, but, consistent with his strong belief in voluntary effort, he also called for the personal involvement of individuals in helping to solve the problems of their communities and their "brothers" rather than expecting government "to do it all."[31]

Noting that Congress had "laughed down" a rat-control program for cities just before the riot, Cavanagh speculated that one positive result of the disturbance might be the "awakening" of the nation to the plight of the cities. In a "Meet the Press" appearance on July 30, the mayor complained that Congress was "highly reactionary . . . in the broadest sense of that term" and asserted that this was "reflected, unfortunately, at times, even in the administration." Critical of the nation's priorities, the beleaguered mayor plaintively asked, "What will it profit this country if we put our man on the moon by 1970 and at the same time you can't walk down Woodward Avenue?" Reacting to Cavanagh's remarks, Representative George H. Mahon, chairman of the House Appropriations Committee, referred to Detroit as "one of the most favored cities in the nation" in terms of federal aid and criticized the mayor as an "arrogant man" who was trying to divert attention from the failure of "leadership" in Detroit by an "unprovoked attack" on Congress. Fellow congressmen greeted Mahon's remarks with "heavy applause."[32]

Cavanagh pinned his hopes for immediate help to Detroit on the president rather than Congress. Specifically, the mayor, like Romney, wanted the president to declare riot-scarred Detroit a "disaster area," thus making it eligible for the federal assistance available under the Federal Disaster Act of 1950, as amended by the Disaster Relief Act of 1966. Robert Roselle had advised the mayor that the president had $50 million in discretionary funds to expend under the statute, that most federal agencies had funds earmarked for the same purpose, and that if the act was invoked, the federal government could assign specialists to assist Detroit in recovering from the riot. Writing to Cyrus Vance on

July 28 and going far beyond what could be construed as disaster aid, Cavanagh submitted a request for funds for the recovery of "a grievously wounded city" that totaled $175.8 million. More than $120 million of this sum was for housing purposes. Although the Michigan congressional delegation sought to persuade President Johnson to comply with the Detroit desire to be declared a disaster area, Congresswoman Martha Griffiths informed the White House that the city's request for aid was "greatly exaggerated" and, curiously, that the "underworld" would be the first to seek the low-interest loans that the federal government would make available were the president to make the proposed declaration.[33]

In a communication to the Speaker of the House, President Johnson asserted that one lesson to be learned from the riot was that "public order is the first business of government." He maintained, however, that a second lesson was that riots should not be permitted to serve as "an excuse" for the nation to turn its back on "the forces of poverty and illiteracy and unemployment and despair that are so deeply rooted in our ghettos." It was essential, the president stated, to condemn "aimless violence" but also essential to take steps to prevent it.[34]

Despite these remarks, the president was reluctant to provide Detroit with aid lest it appear that the federal government was rewarding rioting, which is precisely what had happened following the Watts riot.[35] When asked on July 26 what kind of advice to a commission investigating rioting would be useful to the White House, Johnson responded, "No reward for rioters. What else: No reward for rioters. Anything else? No money." When Secretary of Agriculture Orville Freeman wondered if he should visit emergency food centers while in Detroit to make a speech, Joseph Califano told the secretary that the president's instructions were "to get in and out of Detroit as fast as possible—*no* tears." Even the black secretary of Housing and Urban Development, Robert Weaver, was opposed to "anything that would even appear . . . as rewarding rioters."[36]

Despite its reluctance to appear to be "rewarding rioters," the Johnson administration provided Detroit with a fair amount of assistance, but it refused to apply the Federal Disaster Act to the city. As the Office of Legal Counsel advised the president, the major "disasters" Congress had in mind in enacting the disaster statute were natural disasters, defined as "any flood, drought, fire, hurricane, earthquake, storm, or other catastrophe." The law had been invoked more than two hundred times since its enactment but never "in the wake of riot or disorder," and it had not been applied to Watts or Newark. To invoke the statute to aid Detroit, Vance and Warren Christopher advised the president, would be to discriminate against other cities that had experienced riots and would set a dangerous precedent. The advice of Vance and Christopher to the administration was to adopt an "intermediate position," namely, to extend emergency aid to Detroit without invoking the Federal Disaster Act.[37]

Vance insisted that Detroit and Lansing officials did not understand that the "additional" assistance Detroit would have received had the Federal Disaster Act been invoked was actually little more than was already available to the city under other statutes. Vance did not specify what he meant by "additional," but there were actually a variety of kinds of assistance that the federal government could have provided under the Disaster Act that it could not make available under other statutes. These included the repair of streets and roads, cleanup of debris and wreckage, payment of overtime to city employees, repair and replacement of damaged equipment, repair of key public facilities, deferral of the city's contribution to certain federal-city programs, insured loans for disaster victims, special tax deductions for individuals to cover losses, and priority status for city grant or loan applications for public purposes.[38]

On July 21, two days before the riot began, Johnson declared two Michigan counties in the Detroit metropolitan area to be disaster areas because of flooding resulting from heavy rainfall. Cavanagh thought it "absolutely ridiculous" for the federal government to refuse to place a city devastated by a riot in the same category. As Califano put it, however, "most of the steam was taken out of the issue of a disaster declaration" when Vance and Christopher met on August 10 with Richard Strichartz, representing Cavanagh, and the Michigan congressional delegation. Vance appears to have "satisfied" the concerns of those present by specifying what Washington could do to aid Detroit without declaring the city a disaster area.[39]

On July 27 Johnson informed Cavanagh that he had directed members of his cabinet to help meet Detroit's emergency health, food, and safety needs. Two days later the president wired the mayor that he had instructed the SBA to make Detroit eligible for long-term, low-interest loans to homeowners and businessmen whose property had been damaged or destroyed in the riot. Vance and Christopher advised Washington to assign "a small, informal, quiet coordination group" of Budget Bureau officials to the city. The assignment fell to the bureau's William Cannon, the understanding being, as Califano assured Johnson, that the administration would keep "tight control over any new programs."[40]

All in all, the federal government provided Detroit with a variety of forms of assistance to meet emergency needs resulting from the riot. In addition to the aid provided by the Public Health Service and NYC enrollees and the federal contribution to the cost of building demolition, the Department of Agriculture made stockpiles of food worth $100,000 available for distribution to the needy and also eliminated the requirement that Detroit welfare recipients pay $1 to buy $3 worth of food stamps. The federal government dipped into the items stockpiled for emergency disaster hospitals to provide Detroit with six hundred hospital beds that were used mainly for prisoners.[41]

The SBA, which opened two temporary offices in Detroit, had received 497 loan requests by August 10 and had approved 165 of them for a total of about $2 million. The Office of Economic Opportunity (OEO) advanced Detroit $100,000 for low-interest (2 percent) emergency family loans that could not exceed $300 and set aside an additional $300,000 to guarantee small loans by credit unions and similar agencies. On July 28 the OEO dispatched about two hundred VISTA volunteers to Detroit who performed one chore or another at the Community Development and Neighborhood Service Centers, Detroit General Hospital, police headquarters, and the mayor's office, interviewed arrestees, aided in the city's cleanup and rat-control efforts, helped locate missing children, and made door-to-door checks in the riot areas to identify persons needing aid. The National Institute of Mental Health made grants totaling $158,000 to the Lafayette Clinic and the Behavior Research Institute to interview rioters and to appraise their behavior.[42]

Strichartz was "distressed and deeply disturbed" that the Department of Housing and Urban Development appeared unwilling to comply with Detroit's application for funding to construct dwelling units for low-income families. Few of the projects Detroit requested, however, "literally fell in the riot area," and few, in the view of the federal government, would have had any "overt effects in mitigating riot conditions." As Vance correctly noted, Cavanagh's request for housing aid "contained little in the way of justification."[43]

One additional action of the Johnson administration in response to the Detroit riot was the president's establishment on July 27 of the National Advisory Commission on Civil Disorders, the so-called Kerner Commission. Johnson instructed the commission to investigate and make recommendations regarding the origin of the recent civil disorders, including the "influence, if any, of organizations or individuals dedicated to the incitement or encouragement of violence"; "methods and techniques" to avoid or control disorders; and the appropriate role of local, state, and federal governments in dealing with disorders. When Johnson met with his new commission on July 29, he noted that 80 percent of the American people rated racial violence as the nation's number one problem.[44]

According to Michigan's Senator Robert Griffin, the word on Capitol Hill was that Johnson had appointed the Kerner Commission to forestall Congress from looking into the charge that the riots were the result of some conspiracy. Johnson, however, personally subscribed to the conspiracy theory regarding the origin of the riots. It is more likely that many in Congress were concerned that the Kerner Commission would recommend civil rights and welfare legislation as the cure for riots, whereas the prevailing view in Congress was that the proper response was vigorous law enforcement. The Senate, consequently, decided six days after the Kerner Commission had been appointed to have its Permanent Subcommittee on Investigations, whose staff had devoted particular attention to law enforcement, conduct a separate riot probe.[45]

Voluntary organizations, which had helped Detroit gain its reputation as a model city, did not leave it to public authorities alone to deal with the consequences of the riot. Among the voluntary programs to help mitigate the riot's impact on the city's residents, the most important was that undertaken by the Interfaith Emergency Center (IEC).

The decision to create the IEC developed out of earlier efforts of the Detroit clergy to reduce racial tensions in the city by a "Challenge to Conscience." Protestant and Catholic clergy, following the Chicago model, had been holding a Monday morning phone conference since January 1967 to discuss racial and other matters. Members of the "Monday morning hotline," as it came to be known, contacted one another and other clergy on Monday, July 24, and this led to a meeting that afternoon of twenty-five representatives of the Metropolitan Detroit Council of Churches, the Catholic Archdiocese, the Jewish Community Council, and the black Interdenominational Ministerial Alliance at which the decision was taken to set up an information center at the Episcopal Diocesan Center, near the principal riot area. This action, in turn, led to the establishment of the IEC and, as its "governing body," the Interfaith Emergency Council. Calls coming into the center that evening and the next morning made it evident that what was needed was not an information center but rather some means to connect those requiring aid, primarily food, with those offering assistance. Soon the IEC had arranged for twenty-five food collection centers ringing the city and twenty-one distribution centers within the city. Suburban churches volunteered to collect food and clothing, and food companies donated substantial amounts of food. Churches, schools, and the Community Development and Neighborhood Service Centers served as the principal distribution centers within the city.[46]

United Community Services, which made funds available to the IEC to operate the program, the MCHRD, the OCD, the Red Cross, the Detroit school system, and the DUL all cooperated with the IEC. Also, Cavanagh decided on July 25 that the city government should work through the IEC rather than setting up a competing relief organization. Volunteers, many of them social workers, helped to man the center. Individual volunteers made food deliveries to needy individuals who could not get to a distribution center, and volunteer teams visited and assisted persons with special problems.[47]

The IEC distributed food to all comers at the distribution centers without any red tape and without any effort to determine need. This antagonized the OCD, which charged that the IEC was an "illegitimate" organization that was trenching on the civil defense domain. There is no question that the IEC's food distribution system was subject to some abuse. Individuals and families living outside the disturbance areas appeared at the centers to receive food, some who could have afforded to buy food nevertheless sought and obtained free food, and there were some "blatant repeaters" among the food recipients. In a few instances, individuals set up temporary stands to sell the free food they had obtained. A Neighborhood Service Organization worker described the abuse of the food distribution system as a "more sophisticated form of looting."[48]

The IEC began to phase out its food collection and distribution activity on July 30. It was "out of the food business" by August 4, having satisfied itself that the Community Development Centers and other agencies could meet the remaining emergency food needs. The IEC had served 28,610 persons through July 28, a figure that excludes the almost sixty thousand persons served by agencies like the Community Development Centers, whose food distribution the IEC coordinated.[49]

The end of its food distribution activity did not mean the end of the IEC, which continued in existence until succeeded on November 17, 1967, by the Interfaith Action Council. After the riot, the IEC continued to assist families suffering hardship because their homes had been destroyed, damaged, or looted, their means of livelihood had been disrupted, or a family member had been arrested or jailed. These tended to be families with "marginal incomes" that had eschewed seeking welfare assistance. Working through the social service organizations of Detroit's three principal religious faiths, the IEC had aided more than four hundred such families by the end of August. As a result of conditions that became painfully evident during the riot, the Interfaith Action Council sought to reform the bail bond system and also initiated a court-watching program.[50]

The relief efforts of the IEC during the riot were assisted and augmented by a variety of church and lay organizations. The Catholic Archdiocese of Detroit, with the aid of the Red Cross and the OCD, set up three on-site feeding stations in Catholic churches on July 24 before the IEC began to function. The stations were brought under the IEC umbrella on July 25 and changed to food distribution centers the next day. Among the numerous programs of the Archdiocesan Opportunity Program (AOP), the only one that continued to function during the riot was Summer Project Scope, which involved the busing of two hundred youngsters aged twelve to eighteen out of Detroit to Highland, Michigan. Most AOP staff members worked at one or another food distribution center during the riot. The Churches on the East Side for Social Action not only set up food and shelter centers during the riot that became part of the IEC system but also sought to press the view that what was occurring in Detroit was not a "race riot" but "an *economic* riot, a rebellion of the poor."[51]

The Detroit YMCA used its six inner-city branches as temporary housing for riot victims and those unable to return to their homes because of the riot and also as places where Guardsmen and paratroopers could rest. Told by youths in its Urban Youth Program that they wanted to talk to someone about jobs, the YMCA arranged a meeting with Hubert Locke and also contacted Dwight Havens, president of the Greater Detroit Board of Commerce, who promised to take "whatever steps were necessary" to help the youngsters find work. A number of youths in the program not only "stopped their [riot] activity" but volunteered to help in the distribution of food and the cleanup operation and also promised to return what they had looted. As a consequence of its riot experience, the YMCA made the Urban Youth Program its "top priority," regarding this as its contribution to preventing future riots.[52]

The Salvation Army, which expended $100,000 on relief during the riot, opened three emergency relief centers for the needy and operated five canteens for law enforcement personnel. The Salvation Army, Goodwill Industries, Volunteers of America, the Society of St. Vincent De Paul, and Purple Heart all arranged to replace the lost clothing of riot victims. The Salvation Army and Goodwill Industries also provided pickup services for those donating furniture for the riot needy.[53]

At the time of the riot, Red Cross chapters, traditionally committed to dealing with natural disasters, could help out in civil disturbances, but the national organization did not reimburse chapters that did so. The Detroit chapter during the riot serviced five shelters that provided sleeping accommodations for five hundred persons and fed about ten thousand persons. It performed its traditional role of serving the families of military personnel, answering their inquiries regarding the well-being of family members on duty in Detroit. The Red Cross in Detroit normally collected about eighteen hundred pints of blood every five days for use of area hospitals, but it was able to collect five thousand pints during five days of the riot. At its 1968 convention the American Red Cross specifically authorized local chapters to support civil authorities in a civil disturbance.[54]

Like so many other organizations, the West Central Organization (WCO) provided food and clothing for riot victims, serving twenty-nine hundred individuals by July 29. It rushed dry ice to homes where the cutoff of electricity had affected refrigeration. Among the black organizations, the DUL, aided by a $10,000 grant from the United Fund and a private gift of $5,000, played the principal role in providing emergency food, clothing, and shelter. Focusing initially on housing because of the sad condition of those who had been burned out, the DUL received offers to provide shelter for the displaced from more than two hundred Detroit and suburban families only to discover that the displaced generally preferred to double up with relatives and friends. The DUL set up a major food distribution center at Northwestern High and a subcenter on

Twelfth Street that it used after the riot not only to deliver food but to service problem cases and to interview and place job applicants. It had aided an estimated eighteen hundred persons by August 2.[55]

The large number of persons whom family members could not locate during the riot and the smaller number displaced from their homes by fire damage led to the creation of two voluntary programs, Operation Find and Homes by Christmas. Operation Find grew out of a meeting of voluntary agencies convened by United Community Services of Detroit on July 25. Its purpose was to locate missing persons, mostly arrestees. More than one hundred persons manned the operation's phones, answering calls that came in from all over the United States. "It was almost hysterical" during the first two days, the coordinator of the program declared. More than 6,000 persons contacted Operation Find seeking information about 2,090 individuals. It had been able to locate about 1,000 persons by August 2, many of them in police custody or in the hospital, but it had failed to locate 148 persons as of late September 1967, when the project came to an end. The Central Location Registry that Operation Find prepared was used by the Attendance Department of the Detroit Board of Education to help locate the astonishing number of 12,000 school children presumed to be missing because of the riot. Employers used Operation Find's service to locate delivery trucks and drivers missing because of the disturbance.[56]

Homes by Christmas was established on July 30, 1967, by social scientists, members of Human Relations Councils in the Detroit metropolitan area, and persons in church-related organizations. Its goal was to help every family that had lost its home because of the riot to relocate in suitable housing by Christmas. With the discontinuance of emergency relief at the end of July, Homes by Christmas "uncovered *a whole new area of need,*" "desperate" people displaced by the riot but unaccustomed to seeking public assistance and unknown to the relief agencies. Volunteers using school census records found 274 such families, 102 of whom appeared to need assistance.

The families discovered by Homes by Christmas were beset by legal, financial, health, and environmental problems. Once the needs of a family had been determined, a volunteer aided the family in securing dwelling space and in meeting its need for clothing, furniture, and appliances. The emphasis of Homes by Christmas in relocation was on home ownership since the rental property open to blacks was scarce whereas homes were available for purchase at bargain prices because of white flight.

Financed initially by the archdiocese ($15,000) and the IEC ($11,000) and aided by the Salvation Army's Family Welfare Department, New Detroit, and donations of food and clothing, Homes by Christmas received a United Fund grant of $125,000 after the IEC ceased operations. By the end of 1967 Homes by Christmas had aided 120 ghetto families displaced by the riot. Thanks to the purchase money and loans that it provided, many of these families had bought or were in the process of buying homes. The family of the deceased Tonia Blanding was among those enabled to purchase homes.[57]

Believing that the city could not be rebuilt by government effort alone, Mayor Cavanagh and the business community agreed that private industry would have to involve itself actively in reconstruction efforts. In a statement released on July 28, the Greater Detroit Board of Commerce, which represented thirty-eight hundred business, professional, and industrial interests, asserted that since the riot had made it evident that the "basic solution" for "these problems" was jobs, its main response to the disorder would be an effort to cope with unemployment and under-employment in the city's "disadvantaged areas." It promised continued support for the Career Development Center and announced the formation of a Manpower Development Committee among other initiatives.[58]

The most significant response of the private sector to the riot was the establishment of the New Detroit Committee. The initial steps leading to the formation of New Detroit were taken by Cavanagh and Romney, who invited 160 community leaders to attend a meeting on July 27 to consider Detroit's "current and future problems." The governor and the mayor by that time had asked Joseph L. Hudson, Jr., president of the J. L. Hudson Company, which operated Detroit's largest department store, to assume leadership of a new committee that would mobilize and "coordinate the public and private resources necessary to help rebuild" Detroit's "social and physical fabric." Although a wide spectrum of the community was represented at the July 27 meeting, Congressman John Conyers complained that "the voiceless people in the community" were missing. "I didn't hear anyone off of 12th Street," he declared. "Anyone poor or black. And that's what triggered this as I understand it."[59]

What Cavanagh had in mind in proposing the formation of New Detroit was to associate the commanding firms in the private sector with the well-being of the city to a degree that had previously been lacking. This, indeed, was the message the riot conveyed to the heads of the Big Three auto companies whom Cavanagh invited to the July 27 meeting. "We didn't do enough," General Motors's James Roche declared. "An extra effort is needed." Henry Ford II agreed. "I thought I was aware," he stated, "but I guess I wasn't. This terrible thing *has* to wake us up." Conscious of Detroit's model city reputation, Chrysler's Lynn Townsend commented, "We'd *better* make an extra effort. Detroit is the test tube for America. If the concentrated power of industry and government can't solve the problems of the ghetto *here,* God help our country." As Hudson saw it, business leaders in Detroit in the past had left the city's problems to be solved by government and social workers and had absolved their responsibilities by writing a check. Now, he said, they had to involve themselves personally in the rebuilding of Detroit's "social and physical framework."[60]

Following the July 27 meeting, Hudson sought in vain to obtain answers from Romney and Cavanagh regarding the authority and responsibilities of the new committee. Seeking some guidance for the structuring of the committee, Hudson turned to Hugh White and James Campbell, leaders of the Detroit Industrial Mission, "a church related organization involved with the social impact of industrial development." He respected White in particular as someone who had "a pretty good feeling of the racial situation and organization dynamic[s]." Believing that the new organization could "not be the same old blue ribbon committee," White and Campbell were especially concerned that the "militant side of the Negro community" be brought into the committee "with power—and in a way [the militants] consider significant." The two men advised Hudson to consult with leaders of black organizations concerning personnel to serve on the committee, especially "those organizations the established Negro leadership" was "out of touch with," like the Inner City Organizing Committee and the WCO, and with men like Cleage. "The goal of your committee," White and Campbell advised Hudson, "cannot be simply a return to business as usual, but must be nothing less than a model new city."[61]

White and Campbell arranged a meeting on July 30 at which Hudson sought the advice of black militants regarding the operation and membership of the new committee. Milton Henry believed that black nationalists should participate in the reconstruction of Detroit "in a civilized manner," and Cleage pointed to possible areas of cooperation between blacks and the committee. WCO organizer Lorenzo Freeman, however, maintained that the whole idea of an interracial committee was "passé." It was up to the white leadership, he contended, to "unblock" the white community and for the black leadership to "take care" of the black community. Those present at the meeting gave Hudson the names of blacks who might be placed on the committee, and Hudson also sought advice about black members for the committee from Arthur Johnson, Damon Keith, and the office of the mayor.

Hudson decided to include three militants among the nine blacks to be appointed to the thirty-nine member committee: Freeman; Alvin Harrison, then working for Wayne County Suburban Legal Services and awaiting trial for his role in the Kercheval disturbance; and the eighteen-year-old Norvell Harrington, who was associated with the Inner City Organizing Committee, thought that no one over twenty-five years of age could be trusted, and had described democracy as "trash." All three accepted, although Hudson recalled that it had been difficult to get them to associate with "sort of [an] establishment kind of committee."[62]

Hudson rejected the view that New Detroit was responding to "blackmail" and rewarding lawlessness in adding the three militants to the committee. "We are responding to complaints against injustices," he explained. Denying at a much later time that New Detroit was seeking "riot insurance" in embracing the militants, Hudson claimed that his associates and he understood that no one group had caused or controlled the riot or could guarantee that there would not be another disturbance. He had simply concluded, Hudson declared, that the "voices" of the militants had to be heard and hoped that they would "sensitize" the whites on the committee. This is certainly true, but, as Campbell informed Roche, White and he were "extremely sensitive" to the fact that the "ghetto community" had demonstrated its "power to tear Detroit apart" and that New Detroit's recognition of the militants was consequently "an essential prerequisite for building a new Detroit." This suggests that the riot-insurance idea was in the minds of the planners of the new committee, which is hardly surprising.[63]

If Hudson, Campbell, and White were anxious to add black militants to the new committee, they were equally concerned that Detroit's business and labor leaders, especially the former, be personally involved in the committee. Asserting that his goal was "TOTAL PERSONAL INVOLVEMENT," Hudson was willing to permit those individuals who represented "far-flung organizations," like GM or the UAW, to designate a representative from their top management to substitute for them, but the other committee members were not to be permitted that option. The aim, in any event, was "to combine power with the voices of outrage."[64]

On August 1 Hudson, Cavanagh, and Romney announced the membership of what, it was now revealed, was to be known as the New Detroit Committee. The thirty-nine-member committee included the bellwethers of Detroit's business establishment, Walter Reuther, a Teamster vice president, nine blacks, and the principal white community leaders. Cavanagh designated Richard Strichartz, the city's former controller, and Fred J. Romanoff, the mayor's former executive secretary, as his personal representatives on the committee, and Romney selected Charles Orlebecke, his executive assistant, as his representative. Hudson designated Kent Mathewson, president of the Metropolitan Fund, a "powerful" organization concerned with urban affairs in southeastern Michigan, to serve as the coordinator for New Detroit.[65]

On July 27 Hudson sent out a questionnaire to several hundred civic and professional leaders to ascertain their views regarding the subject of "first priority" in the rebuilding of Detroit. The replies placed housing, emergency care for the displaced, and giving neighborhood groups and individuals a voice in making the decisions affecting their neighborhoods well ahead of such important matters as jobs, interracial understanding, education, and the role of the police.[66]

Hudson's goal in selecting the membership of the New Detroit Committee was "a working committee" but one large enough to be able "to mobilize the total resources of the community." Blacks in particular complained about the makeup of the committee, even though, as Hubert Locke said, it was "one of the most representative community efforts ever undertaken in Detroit." The Booker T. Washington Businessmen's Association protested that it was "an affront" to the organization to have been excluded from membership. Claiming to speak for 125 ministers and 150,000 communicants, the Council of Baptist Ministers similarly protested its lack of representation. Several letter writers complained that "grass roots people from the immediate affected community" had been excluded, and the *Michigan Chronicle* asserted that the three militant blacks on the committee did not speak for the "man on the street." Although he had agreed to serve on the committee, Freeman informed Hudson that no one on the committee spoke for the "disenchanted and disillusioned young adults" who, Freeman maintained, were the force behind the "uprising." "Your mistake," he wrote Hudson, "is honest but dangerous." These early complaints about the representativeness of its black membership foretold the difficulties New Detroit was soon to experience in dealing with a black community that was as divided as Detroit's white community.[67]

At the July 27 meeting that led to the formation of New Detroit, Walter Reuther exuberantly pledged the volunteer aid of 600,000 UAW members in "removing the scars" of the Detroit riot. Meeting with the commissioner of public works the next day, Reuther indicated that UAW members would be made available "to turn graded areas into green belt or park facilities." The Reuther offer, however, "turned to smoke," a UAW official stating that the idea was unworkable and that "Walter just got too excited." On September 18, 1967, the Department of Public Works sent the UAW the names and addresses of fifty-eight property owners who had removed the damaged structures on their property and suggested that the union gain their permission to landscape and otherwise improve the property. The matter dragged on until the spring of 1968, with the UAW raising questions about legal clearance before it could proceed and city workers and those concerned about employing ghetto youths objecting to the use of volunteer labor. "It was so complicated that we couldn't follow through, and it simply petered out," a UAW official declared.[68]

Although the Reuther offer of 600,000 workers to help rebuild Detroit came to naught, New Detroit proved to be an enduring Detroit institution. It began its history determined "to find the answers and take the steps necessary to create a 'new' community" in the city where a riot was not supposed to have occurred. Hudson looked to New Detroit to reestablish Detroit's reputation as a model city.[69]

CHAPTER 14

Rioters, Counterrioters, and the Noninvolved

It is difficult, if not impossible, to speak with certainty regarding the identity of the Detroit rioters and the reasons why they behaved as they did. The best evidence is that the riots of the 1960s, including the Detroit riot, were unrelated to the characteristics of particular cities. After examining disturbances in 673 cities between 1961 and 1968, Seymour Spilerman concluded that, controlling for the size of the black population in the cities, neither the occurrence nor severity of the riots outside the South was "contingent upon Negro conditions or their social or economic status in a community." That riots were more likely to occur in cities with large black populations appeared to be explained by the obvious fact that there were simply more potential riot participants and greater resources available to sustain a riot in such cities than in those with smaller black populations.[1]

In their study of the impact of city on racial attitudes, Howard Schuman and Barry Gruenberg found that city of residence had a statistically significant influence on racial attitudes. At the same time, the fact that Detroit, a city in which racial attitudes were certainty not at the "unfavorable extreme," had experienced the worst riot of the 1960s suggested to them, as Spilerman was to demonstrate, that rioting and the character of a city's "social problem indicators" were not necessarily linked. Their cautious conclusion was that "racial tension" in American cities at that time was "so severe" that they were all above a "riot threshold," and thus "the outbreak of rioting in particular cities" was "simply a matter of chance incidents, or variations in police tactics, or other factors that had little to do with basic social, economic, and political differences among cities."[2] The Detroit riot, so much the immediate consequence of chance and police tactics, certainly seems to be a case in point.

Although the riots of the 1960s may have had scant relationship to the characteristics of particular cities, Schuman and Gruenberg argued in another article that blacks in the disorder areas of four cities that experienced major riots in 1967—Cincinnati, Newark, Detroit, and

Milwaukee—were "noticeably more dissatisfied than blacks in the same four cities living outside such tracts." Responses regarding the satisfaction of Detroit blacks with services in the city as a whole in the fifteen-city survey in early 1968 and in the disturbance areas in a *Detroit Free Press* survey conducted between August 31 and September 25, 1968, indicate the validity of this generalization with regard to police protection and merchant behavior. Whereas 44 percent of black respondents in the city as a whole were "generally satisfied" with the police protection they received, this was true of only 33 percent of black respondents in the riot areas. Only about one-quarter of the blacks throughout the city thought that merchants overcharged their customers unfairly, but 55 percent of riot-area blacks were of this opinion.[3] Even if blacks in the riot areas were more dissatisfied than blacks in the rest of the city, that still leaves unanswered the question of why some blacks in these neighborhoods rioted whereas the majority did not.

Ruling out differences among cities as explaining the 1960s riots, Spilerman suggested that the proper approach was to consider the attributes of those individuals who actually rioted.[4] Most social scientists who concerned themselves with the matter adopted this approach and sought to ascertain the attributes and attitudes of self-reported rioters or arrestees. Their studies, the best available to us, have been subjected to strong criticism by the sociologist Clark McPhail. On the basis of ten different efforts to determine individual participation in the Watts, Omaha, Newark, Detroit, and Milwaukee riots, McPhail derived 287 associations between the different independent variables examined in these investigations and five measures of riot participation that they utilized. He concluded that only 2 (0.7 percent) of these associations (age and attitudes about job opportunities) were of high statistical significance and only 17 (6 percent) were of moderate significance. McPhail noted, furthermore, that the 6 associations of moderate significance regarding arrestee opinion of police behavior may have reflected the arrest experience of arrestees rather than their preriot views. The 6 associations of moderate or high significance regarding attitudes toward job and housing opportunities for blacks, voting participation, and the worthiness of fighting for the United States could similarly be explained as the result of the riot experience of those involved or as the product of "*post hoc* rationalizations." McPhail also pointed to a "mounting number of studies" that failed to provide "consistent evidence that an attitude statement . . . is followed . . . by the behavior which the inferred attitude is supposed to produce."

As for the moderate and high associations between riot participation and the attributes of age, sex, ethnicity, educational level, and "social isolation," McPhail noted that these were the attributes of persons with large amounts of "unscheduled or uncommitted time" at their disposal and hence particularly available for riot participation. "There appears to be no way," he concluded, "in which a tendency to behave, inferred from knowledge of an individual's attributes — before or after the event — can be logically connected to the variation in riot participation behaviors of the individual." In their analysis of the Watts riot, David O. Sears and John B. McConahay commented that McPhail had performed a "useful service" in analyzing riot participation on so broad a basis, but they criticized his "rather undiscriminating treatment of all possible attitudinal and demographic measures."[5]

Surveys of both self-reported rioters from the disturbance areas of the city and of arrestees are available for the Detroit riot. Jeffrey M. Paige and Nathan S. Caplan, both program associates of the University of Michigan's Survey Research Center, reanalyzed for the Kerner Commission the results of a survey of a randomly selected sample of 437 blacks fifteen years of age or older in the main riot areas of the city conducted during the two weeks following the riot for a study sponsored by the Detroit Urban League (DUL) and coordinated by the *Detroit Free Press*. The Caplan-Paige analysis was based on 393 of these interviews, all of them conducted by blacks. Of this number, 44 (11.2 percent) identified themselves as "rioters," 62 (15.8 percent) as "counterrioters," and 287 (73 percent) as "noninvolved." Caplan and Paige conducted a survey of Newark for the Kerner Commission about six months after that disorder, and Paige devoted his 1968 doctoral dissertation to a study of the participants in the two riots.[6]

The two principal studies of Detroit riot arrestees were conducted by Dr. Benjamin D. Singer, a specialist in the field of communication and public opinion, and Dr. Elliot Luby, a professor of psychiatry and law and associate director of Detroit's Lafayette Clinic. Singer initiated his study at the University of Western Ontario toward the end of the riot. After developing a questionnaire, he gained permission of the Detroit Police Department to interview arrestees in five places of detention. Under the supervision of Dr. Sheldon Lachman, a Wayne State University psychologist, black interviewers, all at least high school graduates, interviewed 499 black male arrestees from July 31 to August 4 as well as a sample of 499 community residents matched with the arrestees on the basis of sex, race, and residence. The latter interviews were conducted between August 1 and August 15. No guards were present during the interviewing of the prisoners, only about 5 percent of whom refused to be interviewed. Although the 499 prisoners were not selected on the basis of approved sampling methods, the distribution of criminal charges against them corresponded closely to the distribution of such charges among all arrestees. Also, when James Geschwender compared the social characteristics of the 499 arrestees with an unpublished list of the characteristics of all arrestees, another sample of the arrestees, and the Caplan and Paige data for Detroit and Newark, he found "a great similarity in comparable social characteristics in all four data sets."

On August 3 the United States Department of Labor, after an expression of interest by President Johnson, contracted with the Behavior Research Institute of Detroit to add questions to the Singer survey instrument regarding the employment status and indebtedness of the arrestees. The results of the Singer study, which were shared with the Kerner Commission, were first published by the Department of Labor in March 1968, then in a work by Lachman and Singer that the Behavior Research Institute published later in 1968, and, in the fullest form, in a 1970 book authored by Singer, Richard S. Osborn, and Geschwender.[7]

The Luby group's study of arrestees, initially supported by a grant from the National Institute of Mental Health, was based on a 7 percent sample of the 6,528 adult arrestees. The 233 black males aged eighteen and over in this sample became the subject of the study. They were interviewed in their homes in August, September, and October by interviewers of the same race. The arrestee sample compared rather well with the entire group of arrestees in several key variables. There was, however, "a slight overrepresentation" of the age group seventeen to nineteen in the sample and a "slight underrepresentation" of the ages twenty-six to twenty-eight. More than 96 percent of the arrestees contacted agreed to be interviewed. The Luby group understood that the arrestees were not all necessarily rioters.

The Luby group also surveyed a community sample of 451 blacks and 393 whites from Detroit and several small cities within or adjacent to Detroit (Hamtramck, Highland Park, the Grosse Pointes, and Harper Woods). The sample was randomly selected primarily from a directory of addresses, with the riot areas being sampled at triple density. The community sample of blacks included 331 from the riot areas, designated as the riot area supplement sample. The response rate in the community sample, flawed to some degree because transients may not have been included in the directory of addresses, was 79 percent for blacks and 71 percent for whites. The Luby group also set up a control group of 153 black males drawn from the riot area supplement and also, since many arrestees came from outside the riot areas, from the community sample. The group discovered that there were "only small differences" in response frequencies when it compared the interviews of riot-area respondents with interviews from outside the riot areas. In devising its questionnaire, the Luby group secured the cooperation of social scientists who provided Luby with survey instruments already developed and tested for use in other riot surveys, particularly in Watts. Black militants helped the Luby group redraft its questionnaire after it had been pretested with some of the arrestees.

The Luby study led to two largely similar book-length manuscripts, one entitled "Violence in the Model City," the other, "City in Crisis." The chapters in the two manuscripts consisted of summaries of longer research papers prepared by the various members of the Luby team. Although neither manuscript was published, Luby and James Hedegard, a research associate in psychology at the University of Michigan, published a synopsis of some of the group's principal findings, and Joel D. Aberbach and Jack L. Walker used the 1967 data for their book, *Race in the City.*[8]

The results of the Caplan-Paige survey and of the arrestee studies are similar in some respects but at variance with regard to some of the significant attributes of the supposed rioters. Both types of studies were flawed in important respects, and we do not know to what extent the responses in these surveys were affected by the events of the riot itself. The respondents in the Caplan-Paige study were drawn from the riot areas of the city, but if the addresses of 3,304 riot arrestees held by the police are indicative, as many as one-third of the rioters did not live in the disturbance areas. Also, although Caplan and Paige tested for the validity of their distinction between rioters and nonrioters, the respondents in the DUL survey on which the two men relied may not have been telling the truth about their behavior during the riot. They may have been concealing participation for fear of arrest or claiming participation to make themselves appear actors in a great drama. Only 67 percent of the eligible interviewees were actually interviewed, which may have produced "a considerable non-response bias." The Caplan-Paige study included only 44 self-reported Detroit rioters, "too small [a number] for adequate analysis" in many instances, as Paige conceded, although he noted that the self-reported rioters tended to be overrepresented among the younger respondents, the ones most likely to riot. The study's definition of riot participation, furthermore, was rather vague, as we shall see, and, of considerable significance, its data were not age-controlled.[9]

The available arrestee data are superior in one respect to the self-reported rioter data in that they deal, at the very least, with individuals who were out in the streets during the riot. The arrestee data, however, are not without serious shortcomings. Not all rioters, as we have seen, were arrested, and not all arrestees were rioters. Owing to the very special conditions resulting from the riot, only about three-fourths of adult arrestees were prosecuted, and of the arrestees prosecuted, about one-half of those accused of felonies and about one-third of those accused of misdemeanors escaped conviction. Although the Singer study, a product of "instant research," was based on interviews with presumed participants at a time when their memories were "still fresh," the interviews were conducted in the coercive atmosphere of detention facilities, and the questionnaire used was hurriedly put together without any prior testing.[10]

Reports of the preliminary findings of the Luby study drew criticism from social scientists and black spokesmen because of its allegedly "implicit 'sick' definition of the black community." This allegation apparently derived from the fact that the study was financed by the National Institute of Mental Health and also the fact that the psychiatrist director of the study said at one point that he was "becoming weary of social scientists' making white people 'culpable for all of the difficulties which blacks have encountered in this country.' " There was criticism also that the Luby team had failed to establish rapport with the black community and that its research design was "loose and unsophisticated." Criticisms of this sort appear, however, to have been based on news accounts of the study and the preliminary report of its findings rather than on the study in its more-or-less final form.[11]

In their study of the Watts riot, David O. Sears and John B. McConahay not only found that young males were "the most active" in the riot but that "age was the most powerful and consistent demographic factor, other than race, in riot participation." Studies of the Detroit riot, similarly, are in agreement regarding the youthfulness of riot participants. According to the Kerner study, 61 percent of the self-reported rioters were between the ages of fifteen and twenty-four, as compared to 23 percent of the noninvolved. The median age of the arrestees over eighteen in the Luby study was twenty-four, seventeen years younger than the median age of the study's "community riot area sample." Of the arrestees in the Singer sample, 44 percent were between ages fifteen and twenty-four, but only 24.5 percent of those in the study's matched sample were in this age group. The youthful arrestees of the Singer study were, however, charged with only about half as many major offenses as the arrestees aged twenty-five to twenty-nine.[12]

When Mayor Cavanagh showed the Kerner Commission a film of the riot's beginning on July 23, young males were conspicuous among the rioters. A political science professor on the scene that morning reported that he again and again saw young males "yell down or strongly challenge the milder attitudes of their elders," who then "backed down under pressure." "During the first day," he observed, "it was always the young, and they had leadership qualities, for they spoke louder and pushed harder, and made the older ones cooperate through taunts or threats."

Younger blacks were more likely than their elders to have been affected by the civil rights movement of the preceding years. They had a stronger sense of black identification than their elders did, were more likely to be unemployed, and were less subject to the social controls of family and work. They were less patient than older blacks, were largely lacking in "formal representation in government," and were more willing than their elders to employ the tactics of violence. It is possible, also, that riot participation gave the young black male "a degree of self-esteem" and a "feeling of power and manliness generally denied him." The young, furthermore, were more likely than older blacks to be out on the streets with nothing to do.[13]

In the Caplan-Paige sample, 61 percent of the self-reported rioters were male, as compared to 44 percent of the noninvolved. The percentage (39) of women among the self-reported rioters was more than three times as large as the percentage (12) of nonwhite women among the nonwhite arrestees aged fifteen and over in Detroit and five times as large as the percentage of women (8) among the arrestees in forty-one riots between 1964 and 1967. The Detroit arrestees were not only predominantly male (88 percent); they were also predominantly single. Among the Singer sample, for example, 39 percent were married, as compared to 60 percent in the study's matched community sample. The arrestees had a larger proportion of unmarried persons than the community sample at every age level. Like the younger male arrestees, the single arrestees were more apt than married men to have been out on the street, and they were without wives to dissuade them from riot participation.[14]

Unlike self-reported rioters in Watts and Newark, black arrestees in Detroit were more apt to have grown up in one-parent families than the community controls, a difference that held up when the data were age-controlled. In the Luby sample, a father had been present during the first eleven years for 56 percent of the arrestees but for 72 percent of the controls, and a father had never been present for 21.5 percent of the arrestees as compared to 16 percent of the controls. Both parents had been present when 60 percent of the Singer arrestee sample grew up, whereas this condition obtained for 75 percent of the study's matched sample. The arrestees in the Singer sample who grew up in one-parent families or who had never lived with their parents were almost twice as likely to have been charged with serious riot crimes than those who grew up with both parents present or whose parents were separated or divorced.[15]

At a Wayne State University symposium in October 1967, Dr. Luby, according to the *Free Press,* referred to "the breakdown in the Negro family" and the danger this posed because "the Negro youth shows contempt for his elders." In the principal published study of the Luby group's findings, Luby and Hedegard, however, cautiously stated that their data about fatherless families did not represent "value judgments" and that it was "difficult to determine" the significance for arrestees of the disruption of early family life "in the conventional sense." They called attention, nevertheless, to "a number of studies" that described the deleterious effects of parental deprivation upon the personality development of young children in both black and white families. Drawing on the work of Joseph Fischoff, a family case worker, they contended that "a stable male figure in the family provides a sense of security and discipline, and a model for identification." They noted the "intolerable burden" placed on the lower-class black mother in rearing children when the father was absent and the likelihood that the children of such homes would enter school "disadvantaged in several respects" and would be "further handicapped by an inflexible bureaucracy organized around certain assumptions as to the kind of readiness and ability to learn of the lower-class child."

Luby and Hedegard speculated that early experiences at home and in school of a child brought up in a female-headed family, coupled with "repeated exposure to the vocabulary of militancy," might "provide the setting for riot activism." Arguments of this sort were challenged by those who viewed the black female-headed family as the product of unemployment and discrimination and thus as "symptom" rather than as "cause," contended that the extended black family "compensate[d]" for the absence of the father, and claimed that what some whites characterized as the "instability" of the black male growing up in a fatherless family was the failure of blacks to conform to white-determined standards.[16]

The self-reported rioters and the arrestees were clearly not suffering from urban shock. Just about three-quarters of thirty-nine self-reported rioters in the Caplan-Paige study for the Kerner Commission had been brought up in the North, well above the 36 percent of the noninvolved and 47.5 percent of the counterrioters in this category. These figures, however, were not age-controlled. Caplan and Paige also reported that 60 percent of the self-reported rioters but only 34 percent of the noninvolved had been born in Detroit.[17]

Although the Luby study arrestees were more likely than the controls (61 percent as compared to 44 percent) to have been socialized in a large city and more likely to have been born in Detroit or to have migrated there under the age of eleven (59 percent as compared to 36 percent), the difference between the two groups disappeared when the data were age-controlled. The arrestees, indeed, were more likely than the controls to have been born in the South. Singer and associates found that not only arrestees as a whole but arrestees in the crucial fifteen-to-twenty-four age group were far more likely than the matched sample to have lived in Detroit less than one year (9 percent as compared to 4 percent for those fifteen to nineteen years of age, and 16 percent to 5 percent for those in the twenty-to-twenty-four age group). Singer also found that arrestees who had lived in Detroit nine years or less were more likely to have been charged with serious offenses than long-time residents (17 percent as compared to 12 percent). Luby and Hedegard speculated that migration during early childhood between areas that had very different "values and expectations," in this instance the South and the North, predisposed one to militancy.[18]

The Kerner Commission concluded that education was "strongly related" to riot participation. This was not true of Watts, but the data provided by Caplan and Paige supported the generalization for Detroit. According to the two social scientists, whereas 7 percent of the self-reported rioters had only a grade school education or less, 28 percent of the noninvolved and 20 percent of the counterrioters had so limited a formal education. Although in describing the "new ghetto man," Caplan stated that the average rioter was a high school dropout whereas the average noninvolved person was an elementary school dropout, the Caplan-Paige data for Detroit indicated that more than 70 percent (72) of the noninvolved, as compared to 93 percent of the self-reported rioters, had had at least some high school education.[19]

Altogether contrary to the Caplan-Paige study, which did not control for age, the arrestee data gathered by the Singer and Luby groups revealed that when allowances were made for age, the arrestee sample was "significantly less well educated" than the community controls. In the twenty-to-twenty-four age group in the Singer study, for example, 5 percent of the arrestees but only 1.5 percent of the controls had had eight years of education or less; and whereas 67 percent of the controls had graduated from high school or had had some college education, this was true of only 40 percent of the arrestees. "In all age groupings," the Luby group similarly found, "the arrestees had less formal education than the controls." Geschwender and Singer noted, however, that the better-educated arrestees were apt to have been charged with the more serious riot offenses.[20]

Caplan and Paige found no significant difference in the employment rate of the self-reported rioters and the noninvolved, 70 percent of the former and 68.5 percent of the latter listing themselves as employed. The two men did not provide figures on unemployment—not all those without jobs were in the labor force—but Paige concluded that although the *prevalence* of unemployment was not related to riot participation in Detroit, there was "a strong positive relationship between the *incidence* of unemployment and riot participation." Thus, according to the DUL survey of the riot areas, those who had been unemployed for more than a year were more than three times as likely to have rioted as those who had been unemployed for only a month. The Singer study also revealed that the critical factor in inducing riot participation was not the degree of unemployment but its duration. The unemployment rate among the arrestees (13 percent) and among the controls (14 percent) was about the same, but whereas 31 percent of the arrestees had been unemployed for nine or more weeks in the preceding year, only 14 percent of the community sample had been jobless for that length of time. Singer concluded that unemployment was the most important single factor distinguishing the rioter and the nonrioter.[21]

Although there was far more unemployment among the arrestees (16 percent) in the Luby sample than among the riot-area controls (7 percent), when age was controlled, the difference vanished for the thirty-to-forty-nine age group, and the unemployment rate was only slightly higher for arrestees in the twenty-to-twenty-nine age group. Unemployment was particularly high, however, among teenage arrestees. Gerald Wehmer of the Luby team thus found that of the teenage arrestees who had finished school, one of three was without work, and that only half of the teenagers who had not completed their schooling had summer jobs. "That's a lot of young men hanging around the neighborhood," Wehmer concluded, with "no job, no money, nothing much to do, nothing much to hope for, and lots of time to think about all the things they would like to buy but can't."[22]

Arrestees, according to the Singer study, had a lower occupational status than the matched sample, and age standardization increased the gap between the two. This was not because of differences between the two groups in the amount of schooling. Among those with a high school education or better, for example, 26 percent of the community sample but only 14 percent of the arrestees had white-collar jobs. The adult arrestee group as a whole held jobs of lesser skill than the residents of the riot areas. Whereas 29 percent of the arrestees were in semiskilled occupations and 50 percent were unskilled, 41 percent of the disturbance-area residents were classified as semiskilled, and only 27 percent as unskilled.[23]

The self-reported rioters had lower incomes than the noninvolved and the counterrioters (39 percent of the self-reported rioters, 30 percent of the noninvolved, and 21 percent of the counterrioters—all females— had annual incomes of less than $5,000). Although Paige noted that riot participation in Detroit and Newark was "not strongly related to income," he concluded that there was "a general tendency for lower incomes to be associated with more rioters." Singer, indeed, found a close association between low income and arrestee status. Whereas 41 percent of the arrestees in the Singer sample earned less than $100 a week, only 25 percent among the matched sample earned so little. The income difference between the two groups not only increased when ages were standardized, but arrestees earned less than their community counterparts even when the occupational status of the two groups was similar and they had the same amount of schooling. On the other hand, arrestees with the highest income were apt to be charged with the most serious riot offenses. However the income data are interpreted, neither the self-reported rioters nor the arrestees were the poorest of the poor.[24]

Paige thought that the "new element" in the makeup of the rioters was "the increasing sense of racial pride," pride in being black, and Luby agreed. When asked whether blacks were more dependable than whites or about equally dependable, 49 percent of thirty-seven self-reported rioters in the Caplan and Paige survey but only 22 percent of the noninvolved responded that blacks were more dependable. Similarly, 61 percent of the self-reported rioters as compared to 36 percent of the noninvolved thought blacks were "nicer" than whites. When Caplan asked one looter how he had felt during the riot, he replied, "I was feeling proud man, at the fact that I was a Negro. I felt like I was a first-class citizen." Two other looters whom Caplan interviewed also expressed pride in being black, but a fourth black looter said that this was true for him only "sometimes," that "sometimes you get the feeling that you don't want to be a Negro" because "you're envious of something the white people have . . . that you don't."

Although concluding that "the stronger the feeling of racial superiority, the greater the tendency to riot," Paige conceded that postriot expressions of pride could have been the result, not the cause, of rioting. He speculated that if black consciousness was a cause of the riot, Black Muslims should have been overrepresented among the rioters, but, in fact, the Muslims kept their distance from the Detroit disturbance. Also, the data from the DUL survey, on which Caplan and Paige relied, indicated that although there was a "strong tendency" for rioters to see blacks and whites as "unequal," those who considered whites superior to blacks were just about as likely to riot as those who thought the reverse. "Stereotyped thinking, regardless of the direction," the report of the DUL survey concluded, "is the key factor."[25]

As the Kerner Commission saw it, rioters not only took pride in their blackness but appeared to be very hostile to whites. In Detroit, Caplan and Paige found that 36 percent of the self-reported rioters, as compared to 21 percent of the noninvolved, thought that interracial civil rights organizations would "do better without whites." The self-reported rioters were also far more pessimistic than other blacks about the attitudes of whites regarding blacks: only 23 percent of them but 77 percent of the noninvolved thought that these attitudes would improve in the following five years. Paige concluded that pessimism regarding white attitudes was "the best predictor of riot participation."[26]

In seeking to explain the riot, individual rioters sometimes expressed hostility to whites. "I think they riot," a looter told Caplan, "because they're tired of white folks' using them about. And the white folks having everything." She hated whites, the looter said, "because they don't treat me right. They don't treat none of the negroes right." Another looter said about whites, "I can't stand them." "They stink to me," he asserted, and he thought "this country would be alright without the whites." A firebomber explained that he had set a furniture store ablaze because it was owned by "a white man." "He had to do somethin' to the white man," he declared, "because I don't dig um. . . . I don't dig nothin' about um."[27]

The arrestee data, despite some ambiguities, is at variance with the self-reported rioter data concerning the antiwhite character of the riot. When asked why people "bother[ed]" the places that they did during the riot, just under half of the Luby sample of male arrestees, it is true, attributed the choice of targets to "anti-white" causes. Explaining why blacks were rioting, arrestees whom the *Detroit Free Press* interviewed asserted, "They want to 'get back at the white man.' They want to hurt him." On the other hand, when the arrestees in the Luby sample were asked if the riot was "an anti-white event," 91 percent of them answered in the negative. Also, arrestees were just as likely to have white friends as the controls.[28]

The responses of the Luby arrestee sample suggest that blacks may have been trying to distinguish between hatred of "whitey," which they generally downplayed, and hatred of the "white power structure." Their fury was thus directed at the police as the representative and symbol of white authority and at merchants, a majority of them white, as still another symbol of black "oppression." "No one was out to get 'whitey' in the broad sense of the word," a black law student declared, "but 'whitey' in the sense of the power structure. . . . It wasn't racial hatred but the poor revolting against the ghetto." A black secretary on Twelfth Street told an interviewer, "The power structure didn't do anything to serve the people's needs. Black people were sick of being ignored." In Watts, similarly, "grievances against the local white-dominated institutions were among the most powerful instigators of riot participation."[29]

Were rioters, whether or not they were antiwhite, well integrated in the black community? Caplan and Paige answered this question in the affirmative. The self-reported rioters, they found, socialized more frequently with their neighbors and others than the noninvolved and held more organizational memberships. On the other hand, when blacks in the riot area in the DUL survey on which the Caplan and Paige analysis was based were asked if they would tell a bill collector where a former neighbor had moved if they knew the address, the self-reported rioters were twice as likely as the noninvolved to tell. This, the DUL study concluded, was "a significant indicator" that the self-reported rioters, despite their outward sociability, were not well-disposed toward their black neighbors.[30]

Donald I. Warren, in his imaginative study of the social structure of the riot neighborhoods, and Luby and Singer, in their arrestee studies, reached conclusions at considerable variance with Caplan and Paige regarding the social integration of presumed rioters. Warren found a large positive correlation between riot participation and the percentage of persons who had lived less than one year in a riot neighborhood as well as between riot participation and "high neighborhood turnover." He also found that rioting was more apt to occur in neighborhoods where social contacts and social participation were not extensive and where residents neither participated in nor identified with the neighborhood and the local community than in neighborhoods where individuals were "bound to one another by frequent face-to-face contacts and/or extensive membership in formal organizations."[31]

Except for church membership, the Luby team, similarly, found a significantly lower organizational affiliation among arrestees than among riot-area controls. Whereas 27 percent of the controls, for example, belonged to "race groups," only 8 percent of the arrestees reported similar affiliations. A cross-tabulation of age with affiliation revealed that the difference between the two groups was not simply a function of age. Singer and associates also found a statistically significant lower organizational membership among arrestees than among the matched community sample that was independent of age. Since the arrestees in the Singer sample were less likely than the matched community sample to have grown up in a home with at least one parent present, less likely to be married, more likely to be living alone or with friends, more likely to be Detroit newcomers, and less likely to have organizational affiliations, the Singer group concluded that the typical arrestee was "a social isolate, with few community ties or bonds" and hence "less restrained or influenced by larger community norms" and more likely to riot. H. Edward Ransford came to a similar conclusion regarding participants in the Watts riot.[32]

On the basis of Newark data, Caplan and Paige found the self-reported rioters to be more politically sensitive and better informed about politics than the noninvolved. Most arrestees the Luby group interviewed, however, did not come from the "politically sophisticated . . . and militant segment" of Detroit's blacks. They were, for example, less knowledgeable than the controls about black local and national leaders, whether militant or moderate, as well as civil rights and black organizations. The Luby group did not ask any direct questions regarding ideological militancy, but they concluded on the basis of clusters derived from factor analysis and the lack of any significant correlation between arrestee "liking" for militant persons or organizations and riot attitudes that the rioters had not acted because of ideological conviction. It is possibly revealing that, among the Singer arrestees, 48 percent chose Martin Luther King as their favorite or second favorite leader as compared to only 15 percent who selected Stokely Carmichael.[33]

When asked whether the United States was "worth fighting for in a major world war," 39 percent of the self-reported rioters answered in the negative, whereas only 16 percent of the noninvolved and 3 percent of the counterrioters responded in this way. "I don't feel America deserves my patriotism," an articulate looter declared, and a very youthful rioter said that he would not want to be in the army because he "wouldn't want to be saving whites." The Kerner Commission thought that the answer to this question was "perhaps the most revealing and disturbing measure of the rioters' anger at the social and political system."[34]

Although arrestees appraised their existing overall condition somewhat less favorably than the controls did theirs, they were not, on the whole, a despairing lot. When the Luby group asked both samples to place themselves on the Cantril Self-Anchoring Striving Scale as of five years before the survey, at the time of the survey, and five years later, more than half of both groups placed themselves on the three bottom rungs of the ladder for 1962, more than 60 percent on rungs four to seven for 1967, and more than half on the top rungs eight to ten for 1972. A higher percentage of the controls (18 percent) than arrestees (8 percent) placed themselves on rungs eight to ten for 1967, but the reverse was true (64 percent as compared to 52 percent) for 1972. A statistically insignificant higher percentage of Singer's arrestee sample (52 percent) than of the controls (50 percent) thought that their condition had improved in the preceding five years, but more of the former (23.5 percent) than of the latter (18 percent) believed their condition had worsened. Interestingly enough, the arrestees who thought their condition had improved were more likely than the others to have been charged with serious riot offenses. Quite apart from their own condition, the arrestees had a more favorable view than the controls of the condition of Detroit blacks in general.[35]

Arrestees, according to the Singer study, were no more inclined than the community sample to choose violence as the "best way" for blacks to secure civil rights: 19 percent of the former and 21 percent of the latter selected this method. In the DUL survey, by contrast, although 24 percent of the riot-area residents believed blacks had more to gain than lose by violence, 40 percent of the self-reported rioters took this position.[36]

According to the Caplan-Paige study, 71 percent of the self-reported rioters, as compared to 49 percent of the noninvolved, thought "anger with the police" had had "a great deal to do" with causing the riot. "Only the police," one black rioter said to Caplan, "can start a riot. If you want to get a riot started, you have to wait for the police to do something." Smaller percentages of both groups, 43 percent of the self-reported rioters and 20 percent of the noninvolved, thought "anger with politicians" had had "a great deal to do" with causing the disturbance.

The "anger with politicians" question is the closest Caplan and Paige came in their survey to ascertain the degree of black trust in the city's political institutions. If, however, it is argued, as Sears and McConahay have with regard to the Watts riot, that the civil disturbances of the 1960s served as "alternative methods of grievance redress" for blacks who believed that the "normal mechanisms" were "blocked and ineffective for them," the issue of political trust becomes salient. In Newark, among black males aged fifteen to thirty-five in the riot zone, only 2 percent indicated that they trusted their city government "just about always," and 9 percent that they trusted it "most of the time." There was a considerably higher level of trust in Detroit even though the Kerner Commission field team that studied the city thought that inner-city residents had lost faith in "existing grievance channels." Among riot-area blacks in the same age group as those surveyed in Newark, 10 percent responded that they trusted their city government "just about always" and 23 percent, "most of the time." The considerably higher percentages for Detroit regarding political trust undoubtedly reflect the more favorable position of blacks in Detroit than in Newark, but it still means that 67 percent of riot-area blacks in this critical age group trusted the city government only "some of the time" (46 percent) or "none of the time" (21 percent). In a survey of Twelfth Street residents following the riot, furthermore, 78 percent of the respondents were inclined to believe that government leaders before the riot were "just interested in keeping things quiet," as compared to only about 20 percent who believed that the officials "were really interested in solving the problems" blacks faced in the city.[37]

The DUL survey of blacks in the riot areas indicates that 57 percent of them placed police brutality first among the causes having "a great deal" to do with the riot, with "overcrowded living conditions" ranking second (55 percent), and "poor housing" following closely behind (54 percent). Other causes cited were lack of jobs (45 percent), poverty (44 percent), dirty neighborhoods (44 percent), "anger with local business people" (43 percent), "too much drinking" (40 percent), broken political promises (39 percent), and failure of parents to control their children (39 percent).[38]

Although riot-area residents, according to the DUL survey, thought that police behavior was at least as important as any other cause for the riot, a different result emerged from a survey of Twelfth Street blacks conducted just after the disturbance. Asked what were the two or three principal reasons for the riot, 30 percent of the respondents mentioned jobs, as compared to 24 percent who pointed to police practices and about an equal number who mentioned the denial of civil rights. In the Campbell-Schuman survey of Detroit blacks in early 1968, only 5 percent of the respondents, who were presumably thinking of the riot in their city, listed the police as the major cause for the recent riots, as compared to 25 percent who attributed the disturbances mainly to discrimination and 14 percent, to unemployment and lack of job opportunities.[39]

According to the Singer group's data, arrestees, surprisingly, were less likely than the community sample to attribute the riot to "social, economic and political discrimination" (40 percent as compared to 56 percent) and far more likely to see the "immediate triggering event" as the cause (21 percent as against 8 percent). An earlier report of the Singer study that did not include comparable data for the community sample indicated that 46 percent of the arrestees thought police action had caused the riot. On the other hand, when asked what should be done to prevent future riots, only 15 percent of the arrestees and 11 percent of the community sample responded, "end police brutality" and "better police, better training, integrate forces."[40]

When the Luby group asked its arrestee sample, "What are your biggest gripes about living in Detroit?" a surprising 37 percent could not think of anything. Police performance received the most first-place mentions among the specific arrestee "gripes," but this "spontaneously generated hostility toward the police" was voiced by only 13 percent of the arrestees, and by only 19 percent of them even when second and third mentions were included. When the arrestees were directly questioned about police practices, however, they proved to be highly critical. Ninety-four percent of them claimed that the police "beat up people," and 35 percent that this had happened to them; 93 percent responded that the police used "insulting language," and 20 percent that this had happened to them; 94 percent alleged that the police used "unnecessary force," and 35 percent that this had happened to them; and 96 percent asserted that the police searched people without cause, and 82 percent that this had happened to them. Other than the police, job conditions, named by 11 percent of the arrestee sample, were the only "gripe" that received more than 10 percent of arrestee first mentions.[41]

When the Luby group compared arrestees and the community sample, it became evident that, except for their "intense antipathy to police," which may, to some degree, have resulted from their riot experience, the arrestees were no more aggrieved than community blacks. Indeed, although just about equal percentages of arrestees (54) and controls (56) asserted that they had experienced employment discrimination, the controls were more likely than the arrestees to have experienced discrimination by landlords (28 percent vs. 24 percent), in schools (29 percent vs. 16 percent), and in housing (38 percent vs. 21 percent). This was probably because the blacks in the community sample were older, on the average, than the arrestees and hence had had more occasion to experience discrimination. On the basis of cross tabulations, to be sure, the Luby group uncovered a group of thirty-five "highly militant" and "diffusely angry" arrestees, 14 percent of the total, who believed themselves to have been "persistently maltreated" by the police, employers, and merchants and who stressed the retaliatory nature of their looting and burning in the riot.[42]

Despite the abundance of survey data, which point to the police and jobs as the main causes of the riot, one should be cautious about reaching categorical conclusions regarding the precise reasons why individual Detroit blacks took to the streets in July 1967. No demands were voiced by the rioters, and quite different results were obtained in postriot surveys when arrestees were asked to respond to open-ended rather than directed questions about the disturbance's causes. Different reasons no doubt motivated different rioters, and some of the riot participation was undoubtedly unreasoning. That blacks were aggrieved and had every reason to be is easy enough to demonstrate, but that in itself does not explain why a minority of blacks took to the streets when they were no more aggrieved, apparently, than their black neighbors who did not do so.

To sum up, the "typical rioter" portrayed by the Kerner Commission on the basis of the Caplan and Paige analysis was a young, unmarried male, born in Detroit, about as well-off economically as noninvolved blacks, working in a low-status job and often laid off, prideful about his race, better educated than the noninvolved and better informed about politics but distrustful of political leaders and the political system, and more likely than other blacks to have been actively involved in civil rights organizations. This "new ghetto man," to use Caplan's phrase, resembled the riot militants characterized by T. M. Tomlinson on the basis of the Watts riot as "the cream of Negro youth in particular and urban Negro citizens in general."[43]

The typical arrestee, as depicted in the arrestee studies, was similar to the typical self-reported rioter in age, marital status, income, socialization in an urban setting, and pride in race but very different in most other respects. Compared to a matched community sample, the arrestees, controlling for age, were less well educated at every age level, less politically aware, less involved in civil rights activity, more socially isolated, more frequently unemployed and for longer periods of time, held lower-status jobs, earned less at the same educational and occupational level, had lived in Detroit for a shorter period of time, and were more likely to have grown up in a broken home. Except for their reaction to the police, they were not more aggrieved than the community sample although they had a less favorable opinion of their existing condition. They were not the "cream of the crop" or "the so-called average Negro," but neither were they "the dregs of society." As the Luby group put it, they were "well above the bottom of the lower class."[44]

Although about 12 percent of the adult Detroit arrestees were white, the determination of their particular characteristics has attracted scant attention. The Caplan and Paige study of self-reported rioters included women, but separate analyses of women rioters, who made up about 12 percent of the adult arrestees, are similarly rare. The white adult arrestees were even younger on the average than black arrestees; fewer among them, relatively, were married; they were almost twice as likely to have been born in Michigan, but only 87 percent of them, as compared to 97 percent of the black arrestees, lived in Detroit; fewer of them had grown up in fatherless families; a slightly higher proportion were unemployed at the time of the riot; and fewer of them had prior arrest records. They were far less inclined than their black counterparts to have anything favorable to say about the riot or to believe that it would help blacks. They were far more apt than black arrestees to believe that the riot had been planned in advance, to see it as purposeless, and to attribute looting to a desire for material gain.

The motives of whites in joining the riot remain obscure. Some of them, no doubt, shared the resentments of black rioters, but others, judging from their responses to questions about the disturbance, were probably seeking nothing more than personal gain. Whatever the reason for their participation, white rioters appear to have been guilty of a disproportionate number of the major crimes committed during the riot. Although only 12 percent of the arrestees, they accounted for 35 percent of the assault and battery charges, 31 percent of the concealed weapons charges, 27 percent of the arson charges, and 26 percent of the felonious assault charges.[45]

Among female arrestees, 69 percent of the blacks and 42 percent of the whites were unemployed, a jobless rate well above the unemployment rate for male arrestees. In their views concerning the riot and their relationship to it, women arrestees differed little from male arrestees except that women were more inclined than the men to believe that the riot had been planned in advance and that the looters were seeking material gain and less likely to think that the riot had helped the black cause.[46]

A clinical study of the last 70 juvenile arrestees to leave the Youth Home and of a random sample of the remaining 603 juvenile arrestees revealed that the juveniles in school were, on the average, one year behind in grade level. Of the first 448 juveniles arrested, 248 were living with one parent, generally the mother, or in a substitute home. The study found no correlation between the socioeconomic status of the youngsters and their participation in the riot. Generally, they appeared to the authors of the study to be "normal adolescents" who had attained "a higher level of psychological maturation and social adjustment than the average youngster" seen at the Youth Home for delinquency.

Most juvenile arrestees had experienced "some degree of oppression" in their daily lives, and the desire to obtain self-respect and the respect of others was "a dominant striving" among them. Although some juvenile arrestees mouthed black power slogans, Martin Luther King was their most admired leader, they admired Nicholas Hood more than Albert Cleage, and they saw education rather than violence as the way to get ahead. Most had "close" white friends and thought that whites were "like anyone else" but did not understand blacks. Most wanted to conform and to please white authority figures. What they asserted they wanted most in life was "justice for Negroes."

Many juvenile arrestees accused the police of being "brutal" and "unfair." When they were asked what was "most important" about the riot, their most frequent response was "everybody went crazy and followed other people." Judging from the interviews with 300 Youth Service Corps youngsters aged fourteen to sixteen, peer pressure may, indeed, have been a factor in inducing juveniles to join the riot. Of the 300, 180 reported that there had been peer pressure on them to participate, and 120 admitted that they did "go out."[47]

According to Caplan and Paige, roughly 11 percent of blacks aged fifteen and over in the census tracts where the riot centered identified themselves as rioters. On this basis, Robert M. Fogelson and Robert B. Hill speculated that, assuming a population of 149,000 blacks aged ten to fifty-nine in these tracts, sixteen to seventeen thousand blacks participated in the riot. The 11 percent participation rate for Detroit compared with a 15 percent rate for Watts and Newark. Among Detroit blacks as a whole, according to the Campbell-Schuman survey, only 1.5 percent of those aged sixteen to sixty-nine reported themselves as having rioted, which compared with a 4 percent average participation rate in the four cities (Cincinnati, Newark, Detroit, and Milwaukee) that experienced major riots in 1967. The lower participation rate in Detroit may have reflected the somewhat greater satisfaction with their lot of Detroit blacks as compared to blacks in the other cities.[48]

According to the responses of the self-reported rioters in the Caplan and Paige study, 39 percent had "entered stores," 41 percent had simply "picked up goods," which many of them claimed they had found in the street, 14 percent broke windows, 5 percent made firebombs, 5 percent threw firebombs, and 52 percent simply admitted "activity" without further explanation. In the DUL survey from which the Caplan-Paige study was derived, 12 percent of the 437 blacks interviewed admitted riot involvement. Only 2.5 percent, however, responded that they had been "very active," whereas 6.6 percent characterized themselves as "slightly active," and 3 percent as "somewhat active." In the Watts curfew zone, by comparison, 4 percent of the black respondents reported themselves as being "very active," and 18 percent as being "somewhat active," but, as Sears and McConahay noted, "spectators" sometimes "felt they had been active in the riot." In any event, the varying degree of activity of the self-reported rioters lends credence to the speculation of Luby and Hedegard that there were two types of riot participants, "activists . . . rioting for a cause out of a deep sense of social injustice or to change an intolerable social system" and others, the majority, "drawn into the carnival or excitement phase of the riot by social contagion and not necessarily by any revolutionary animus."[49]

It is questionable, actually, whether all those who participated in the rioting should be treated as rioters. Those who broke windows and made and threw firebombs were certainly rioters, but curfew violation, which accounted for 14 percent of the arrests, is hardly a meaningful index of riot participation. Looting was, far and away, the most common form of riot participation, but blacks and some whites looted for a variety of reasons, some because of hostility to particular merchants, merchants in general, or just "whitey," some because they were needy, some because they were greedy, some because of the contagious effect of the disorder, some because opportunity presented itself with modest if any risk, and some because they were criminals. Many, one supposes, joined in the looting out of a mixture of motives.

One rioter explained that looters had been striking at "all the guys who'd been sittin' on us—specially that shopkeeper who charged us 60 cents for a 49-cent half gallon of milk—they got some dues paid."

Another rioter declared regarding the looting of a particular store, "we're just getting back some of what he owes us." A Commission on Community Relations source at the riot scene during the first morning of the disturbance reported that almost everyone was talking about mistreatment by merchants. Arrestees in the Luby sample named grocery stores more frequently than other businesses as places where they had been victimized, and it was grocery stores, food stores, and supermarkets, as we have seen, that were the most frequent target of looters and arsonists. A Wayne State University sociology professor characterized this type of selective looting as "a certain kind of 'street justice.' " Although revenge thus certainly explains some of the looting that occurred, Richard Berk found only "limited support" for the "retaliation model of vandalism" in his fifteen-city study of ghetto retail merchants in civil disorders in the 1960s, including the Detroit riot.[50]

As the riot continued and stores closed, some blacks, leading a "hand to mouth existence" or finding no stores open in the neighborhood, almost had to loot to secure basic necessities. A police officer recalled seeing a black woman climbing through the broken window of a grocery store with only a quart of milk and a loaf of bread. Others, as a black woman in the riot area remarked, looted "to get some of the things they needed and couldn't afford." Greed was a more apt characterization than need for the behavior of other looters, a wish to acquire desired merchandise at no cost. The higher the price in Detroit and other 1967 riot cities the more likely the merchandise was to be looted. She took things she could have bought, an eighteen-year-old looter declared, "but the riot occurred so I looted them. And the reason I did was because the stuff I wanted was a higher price, and so . . . it wasn't worth the price but that's how the white folks had it."[51]

"I wouldn't call it a riot," declared Auburey Pollard's sister Thelma. "When it first started off I'd just call it everybody trying to get something for nothing . . . because everybody was just breaking in and stealing things, trying to get something free." A black woman recalled seeing another black woman in a truck saying, "Oh, everything's great. I've got more furniture than I'll ever use."[52] Observing what appeared to her to be rather brazen looting, the *Free Press*'s Barbara Stanton reported on July 25 that the conviction was growing that the disorder had "less to do with race than with color TV sets, less with Black Power than with something for nothing." A young black girl made the same point but associated it with black resentment against whites. "The point about the riot," she said, "is that people want refrigerators and television sets and all the things which money can buy. In a riot you get whitey, who already has all the things you want."[53]

Blacks in the riot area thought that some people looted simply because they saw everybody else doing it. Ray Girardin agreed. "Craziness just spread," he declared. "The looting was contagious. It went from block to block and section to section." If the impulse to loot became contagious, however, it was at least in part because opportunity presented itself at the outset of the riot with little if any risk. "The police was letting them take it," a looter declared, "so I said it was time for me to get some of these diamonds and watches and rings. It wasn't that I was mad at anyone or angry or trying to get back at the white man. If I saw something that I could get without getting hurt, I got it." A looter earning a good wage as a Chrysler worker declared, "Detroit is the best city in the world to live in if you're colored. Man, there are just no gripes." Why then had he looted? he was asked. "Hell," he replied, "when you see a broken window and stuff laying [sic] all over, anybody will do a little looting." Another looter told a black reporter, "The cops didn't come right away, and everybody was just taking stuff. So I just picked up this radio and a TV. . . . I wouldn't have taken anything, but God, with it all there like that, how you not going to do it?"[54]

The opportunity to acquire goods without risk and the contagious effect of the riot enticed normally law-abiding, respectable, well-dressed, often affluent blacks to join the looting. Some came from better black neighborhoods only to observe but then succumbed to the "looting fever." Hubert Locke was astonished by the "affluent addresses," some in his own neighborhood, at which the police later recovered large quantities of loot.[55] In a later interview, a black woman with a good factory job recalled how she had become a looter during the riot. She had come to the riot area where she observed people looting a supermarket and packing their cars with food. "Wow! Free Food!" She thought, "I'm going to get some too." She realized as she began helping herself to groceries, "I'm not shopping; I'm stealing!" "I knew I was wrong, but I wasn't thinking about Christianity at the time. I just wanted some free food. . . . I didn't have to steal. But I figured, 'What the hell? If I didn't take it, somebody else will. . . .' But I still didn't want my children to think it was alright to steal."[56]

In their discussion of looting under riot conditions, the social scientists E. L. Quarantelli and Russell R. Dynes refer to a second stage of looting "spurred by the involvement of . . . delinquent gangs and theft groups." That professional criminals operated "under cover of the [Detroit] riot" is apparent, but it is doubtful that this occurred only during a "second stage" since, as we have seen, pimps, hustlers, and "professionals" were involved in the looting from the riot's outset. The "really good" looting, in any event, appears to have been done by professionals and criminal gangs who selected large, expensive, easily disposable items and sometimes used trucks to haul their loot away. Locke referred to "well-documented instances" of professionals moving their vehicles behind stores and then breaking in and removing the merchandise.[57]

Blacks in the Luby community sample, 73 percent of whom lived in the riot areas, did not regard the looting as primarily directed against disliked merchants. Only 20 percent of these blacks when asked why people looted gave as their first answer "revenge" (6 percent), characteristics of the businessmen looted (3 percent), or "needs and motives of the looters" (11 percent). This compared with 54 percent who gave as their first answer "opportunity, lack of sanctions" (12 percent) or "saw others doing it or saw chance to get things" (42 percent). On the specific issue of need, 71 percent of blacks in the survey of Twelfth Street residents thought that looters "took anything they could get their hands on" rather than "things they needed but could not afford." The respondents, indeed, thought that 30 percent of the goods looted were for resale rather than personal use. What is perhaps most surprising is that when asked, "Why did people bother the places they did?" only 48 percent of the black male arrestees in the Luby sample, as compared to 64 percent of Watts arrestees, gave antiwhite reasons or "stores cheated people" as their response. Even though one might have expected riot arrestees, most of whom had been apprehended for alleged looting, not to assign selfish motives to looting, 34 percent of the males and about 44 percent of the females attributed the looting to "a desire for material gain."[58]

Quarantelli and Dynes have contended that looting at its height in civil disorders is "undertaken by local people who are selective in their activity and who receive community support" for their action. Looting in civil disorders, the two social scientists claimed, was "a form of group protest about certain aspects of interracial relationships in American society" and involved "a redefinition of property rights." Berk, to be sure, found "a good deal of indirect support" for the "redefinition of property rights" thesis, but this is hardly how matters looked to Detroit blacks in the riot area or even, it would seem, to a majority of riot arrestees. The looting in Detroit was not all that "selective" at its height, and it does not appear to have enjoyed that much support in the black community. Although the poor may not be wedded to "the norms of private property," it would have astonished the many looters who seized goods because they saw a "chance to get things" with little risk that what they were really doing was redefining property rights.[59]

A good deal of the loot in Detroit did not, in the end, remain in the possession of the original looters. A black market in looted goods quickly developed, with popular items being offered at substantially reduced prices. "Makeshift stores" in cellars and rear apartments sold dresses, shirts, TV sets, and radios at prices ranging from fifty cents to ten dollars. The storage, sale, and disposal of looted merchandise resulted in "intense" and often "physical fights" and at least two shootouts involving "formally organized adult professional criminals" and informal teenaged gangs.[60]

An enormous amount of loot ended up in police hands, either

turned over to the department by conscience-stricken looters or seized by the police in legal or, all too often, illegal searches. Individuals who had been unable to resist the temptation to loot but then became ashamed of what they had done began calling the police to say they had been amazed to find in their homes or on their lawns articles like TV sets that did not belong to them. The police accepted the loot held by the contrite without any questions being asked. The police also began to receive hundreds of tips from neighbors of looters or alleged looters and from merchants tipped off by friendly black customers about places where loot was being held, stored, or sold.

All in all, the police recovered about thirty thousand items that had purportedly been looted. Estimated by Locke to constitute about one-fourth of all the looted merchandise, the goods filled the police garage and a substantial portion of the city's main transportation garage as well. About one-third of the items in police hands were returned to their original owners. What was not claimed or could not be traced was disposed of in a series of auction sales. Viewing the variety of goods, which had an estimated value of $200,000, an auctioneer declared, "Some of these guys must have figured they were going into business for themselves."[61]

According to Caplan and Paige, 16 percent of adults in the riot areas were counterrioters, defined by Caplan as "one who engaged in acts which supported agents of social control or who were opposed to the rioters." The self-reported counterrioters were better educated and had higher incomes than the self-reported rioters, were more likely to have been brought up in the South, and were more likely to be living in stable and socially integrated neighborhoods.[62]

The black counterrioters tried to stop the riot, called the Fire Department, helped put out fires, painted Soul Brother signs to deter looting and firebombing, and brought food and beverages to law enforcement personnel and fire fighters. They pleaded with looters to desist, some of them pointed out looters and firebombers to the police, and some reported the location of looted merchandise to the police or to storekeepers.[63]

Assistance to firemen was a conspicuous form of counterrioter activity. "Man, this is crazy," declared one black who was aiding the fire fighters. "We burnin' our own houses up." The Fire Department awarded citations to two young blacks, Earthel Green and Robert Thomas, for the assistance they had rendered firemen. Green, who was twenty-four, had engaged in civil rights demonstrations in his native Georgia, but he "got sick" to his stomach when he saw his first looter during the riot. "I had no sympathy with the rioters," the nineteen-year-old Thomas declared, "they just seemed to be having a good time." Thomas was called an Uncle Tom for his efforts and was hit on the head with a brick.

Longworth Quinn, editor and general manager of the *Michigan Chronicle,* formed a group of block club members in his west side neighborhood into a "core [sic] of riflemen" to escort and protect firemen. In other neighborhoods also, homeowners, and especially block club members, armed with shotguns and fearing that the fires would spread to their dwellings, made it clear that they would shoot to protect the fire fighters. In the Kercheval area on the east side, two young blacks wearing civil defense helmets stood guard to protect their neighborhood. "This has been my neighborhood for 19 years," declared twenty-year-old John Lane. "They're not going to get my block."[64]

Black employees sometimes helped to protect the stores where they worked, the source of their livelihood. A group of juvenile delinquents on the east side protected a liquor store from looters because the owner had provided them with a meeting room and uniforms. The grocery store of one merchant was set afire three times only to have neighborhood people douse the flames in each instance to avoid having to walk ten additional blocks to secure their groceries. A sign on one store that was spared read, "This man helped my family as well as others when we were on welfare."[65]

The city's east side residents, as we have seen, brought food and coffee to the paratroopers and provided them with intelligence. Some shopkeepers invited the soldiers to help themselves to merchandise. Riot-area residents, on occasion, also supplied police, Guardsmen, and firemen with food and beverages. A black owner of a cafe on Twelfth Street kept his establishment open all night and provided Guardsmen with doughnuts and coffee.[66]

Judging from their responses in the DUL's postriot survey and depending how one judges the effort to protect one's property during the riot, the percentage of black counterrioters may have exceeded the 16 percent figure indicated by Caplan and Paige. Asked "which of these things, if any, did you try to do during the riot?" the adult blacks responded as follows: "stop the riot," 4 percent; "call the fire department," 7 percent; "protect own property," 32.5 percent; "help paint 'Soul Brother' signs," 5 percent; "help put out fires," 7 percent; "give sandwiches or coffee to soldiers," 9 percent; and "help people who were lost or homeless," 10 percent.[67] There is no way of knowing how extensive the duplication was in these responses.

Quite apart from the number of rioters and counterrioters, the question remains as to the degree of support accorded the Detroit rioters by the city's blacks who did not themselves riot. Among blacks in the Luby community sample, 81 percent thought that "few" blacks supported the riot, and whereas 25 percent believed that the riot expressed how "most" blacks in the community felt, 72 percent thought it expressed how only a "few" felt. Thirty percent of the Detroit blacks, as well as 30 percent of the blacks in the Watts riot zone, reported that they sympathized with the rioters, which probably meant that they thought the rioters were "expressing their legitimate frustrations." In Newark, where the Caplan-Paige sample was limited to black males between the ages of fifteen and thirty-five, 77 percent of the respondents expressed a general sympathy for the rioters.[68]

The lack of strong support for the riot among members of Detroit's black community is no doubt explained by their view of "why people were rioting." Of the blacks in the Luby community sample, only 5 percent gave as their first answer, "people with reasons or causes— unemployed, frustrated, disillusioned, people who wanted to make things better," and only 11 percent thought people were rioting because they were "culturally and economically deprived." By contrast, 65 percent in their first answers provided what can be construed as disapproving or negative views of the rioters: "undesirables—lazy, greedy, selfish, drunk, irresponsible, sinners, savages, crazy, sick, stupid, scum" (18 percent); "criminal element" (7 percent); "emotional characteristics— angry, hostile, looking for kicks, sheep, people who followed without thinking" (13 percent); "average people . . . caught up in the excitement" (26 percent); and "agitators and organizations" (1 percent).[69]

When asked in the Campbell-Schuman survey what their reaction had been when they first heard of the riot, only 3.5 percent of the black Detroit respondents said that they had been "mostly glad," whereas 82 percent answered that they had been "mostly sorry." Even among adult arrestees in the Luby sample, only 20 percent had a "positive" reaction to the riot, approving of the looting, burning, and sniping; an additional 11 percent reacted in a mixed positive and negative way. What had happened during the riot made Detroit's blacks less willing to be supportive of a future riot than blacks in other large cities. Whereas 54 percent of black respondents in the fifteen-city survey indicated that they would be "sympathetic" to the rioters should another riot occur, only 36 percent of the Detroit respondents expressed this view. Also, whereas 8 percent of the respondents in the fifteen cities said that they would participate if a riot like the one that had occurred in Detroit or Newark occurred in their city, only 2 percent of Detroit blacks were so inclined.[70]

In Los Angeles, 38 percent of the blacks in the riot curfew zone and 54 percent of the arrestees thought that the riot would help the black cause. In Detroit, by comparison, 28 percent of the blacks in the Luby community sample and 46 percent of the male arrestees and 36 percent of the female arrestees in the Luby arrestee sample believed that the gains from the riot would outweigh the losses. In the fifteen-city survey, 37 percent of the males and 30 percent of the women respondents thought the riots would help the black cause, but only 27 percent of the Detroit respondents were of this view. Once again, the severity of the Detroit riot probably explains this result.[71]

Just as there are uncertainties and ambiguities concerning who rioted in Detroit, so doubts remain as to what precisely motivated the rioters to act as they did. Police behavior and unemployment loomed large among their many grievances, but we cannot be sure that they rioted for this reason. Many of those who broke the law, including arrestees and self-reported rioters, can be classified as rioters only by the loosest possible definition of that term. A smaller percentage of Detroit's blacks, in any event, admitted to rioting than did blacks in other cities that suffered through major riots.

CHAPTER 15

The Meaning of Violence

The Detroit riot and the other riots of the 1960s were quite unlike the "communal riots" of an earlier time that were characterized by interracial conflict between blacks and whites. Was it, indeed, a riot at all, or was it, as at least some blacks to this day prefer to label it, a "rebellion"? By a four-to-one margin (48 to 13 percent), Detroit blacks questioned on this point in a survey conducted just after the riot preferred the term "riot." In the Campbell-Schuman survey a few months later, however, the percentages were reversed, 56 percent as compared to 19 percent of Detroit's black respondents choosing to characterize the disturbance as a "rebellion or revolution." It has been suggested in this regard that, at that time in any event, "revolutionary labels" for events like rioting "generally had favorable connotations for blacks." Since, however, those involved in the disturbance in Detroit can hardly be described as having been engaged in "organized armed resistance to an established government," as rebellion is commonly defined, that word hardly fits what took place. Because of the sniping that occurred, some chose to see the disturbance as a form of "urban guerrilla warfare," but this not only grossly exaggerates the amount of sniping but suggests the existence of some kind of organization, a plan of operation, and sanctuaries to which the guerrillas could withdraw, elements lacking in the Detroit disturbance.[1]

Seeking to avoid racial labeling, liberals on the race question dubbed the riots of the 1960s "civil disorders," the term used by the Kerner Commission. Louis H. Masotti and Don R. Bowen have defined "civil violence" as violence directed against the "symbols of the civil order." They characterize riots as a form of civil violence that does not involve an attempt to seize or overthrow "state power" and that is largely "spontaneous, unplanned, and disorganized." The Detroit violence fits this description of riots as a form of civil violence.[2]

The Kerner Commission aptly described the civil disorders of the 1960s as "racial in character" but not "interracial." The Detroit rioters, after all, were mainly although not entirely black, the disturbance occurred in black neighborhoods, and it was policemen and firemen, the overwhelming majority of whom were white, and business establishments, mostly white-owned, that the rioters attacked. A looter thus stated that although there was no "fighting" between blacks and whites, it was "a race riot because the negroes was trying to get the goods from the white folks because the white folks own everything and they [blacks] was just trying to get something so they can own it." There was, as a matter of fact, a very small amount of interracial fighting during the riot, and some rioters were very hostile to whites; but the arrestees, it will be recalled, overwhelmingly rejected the interpretation of the riot as "an anti-white event." Whites in the riot area were sometimes treated with derision, but they were rarely menaced.[3]

Those who wished to play down the racial character of the 1967 riot were able to point to the fact that some whites joined blacks in the rioting. In one disturbance area that included a large number of poor whites, the latter, according to an observer, held out at first but "went out and got into it" when they saw blacks fighting the police. "They don't like the cops either," a resident said of the whites. "This wasn't no Negro riot," a black woman said. "It's an all of 'em riot. They're puttin it on one side, but it's both sides." A reporter saw a white, his arms full of groceries, fleeing a looted store along with a black who had helped the white free a trouser leg caught in a broken window of the store. A black exiting a looted store with four rolls of toilet paper gave two of them to a white woman about to enter the store and said, "Don't bother, honey. That's all that's left." A reporter thought that Detroit had witnessed "the first integrated looting in history," and a black in Barbara Tinker's novel commented, "The riot was about the most integration I have ever seen in Detroit." Twelve percent of the arrestees, it will be recalled, were white.[4]

Some of those who have sought to explain the Detroit riot have stressed what they regard as the class character or, at least, the class component of the disturbance. This interpretation hinges to a limited degree on the participation of poor whites in the disturbance. In a sample survey of Twelfth Street adult blacks conducted just after the riot, more than 75 percent of the respondents thought that black and white rioters had been "fighting on the same side." Among the Elliot Luby group's community sample of blacks, 68 percent, similarly, believed whites and blacks joined in the riot for "the same reasons." It is hard to know precisely what black respondents meant by answers of this sort, but the little information we have about white rioters (insofar as they were included among the riot arrestees) does not suggest that it was class consciousness that brought them out on the streets.[5]

It has been more common for the class interpretation of the riot to be stated in terms of poor blacks rising up against well-to-do blacks as well as whites. Jeffrey Paige thus concluded that "apparently class position as defined purely by economic position is the major determinant of rioting." This, no doubt, is what John Conyers meant when he described the riot at its outset as "a war of the haves against the have nots."

Economic class, indeed, may have been "the major determinant of rioting" in Newark, but it was not so in Watts, and it is, at best, a difficult hypothesis to sustain in explaining the Detroit riot. Many lower-class blacks in Detroit were hostile to middle-class blacks, but, judging from the available arrestee and black community data, there is little reason to think that this provides a major clue to the Detroit rioting.[6]

Social scientists and others seeking to explain the riots of the 1960s have generally related the disturbances to one or another explanatory model for collective behavior. Some, to be sure, have seen the riots as "meaningless outbursts completely devoid of any logic, rationality or justification." This was the view of the McCone Commission, which investigated the Watts riot, and of Edward C. Banfield, who viewed the riots as less a reaction of blacks to whites, slums, and the police than as "outbreaks of the animal spirits" of predominantly youthful slum dwellers who rioted "mainly for fun and profit." The *Detroit Free Press* concluded ten years after the Detroit riot that it had been, after all, "a meaningless event that stimulated nothing, contributed nothing, revealed nothing of any substance or durability." There were, nevertheless, it remarked, "people who felt a substantial stake in interpreting the riot as something more than random law breaking, mob response, carnival."[7] To accept views of this sort, however, one has to assume what cannot be assumed, namely, that blacks had no real grievances that might have induced some of them to riot.

In the view of some who have minimized the purposefulness of the riots, the rioters were "riffraff," either criminals or outcasts or part of an underclass, "a class below the working class" that was uneducated, unemployed, on the welfare rolls, and really "outside of our society." That the rioters in Detroit did not conform to the riffraff model, however, is abundantly evident from both the arrestee and self-reported rioter data. These same surveys demonstrated that the rioters were not recent migrants to the city unable to adjust to urban living and suffering from "culture shock."[8]

Five percent of the blacks and 21 percent of the whites in the Luby community sample attributed the Detroit riot to "agitators" both from inside and outside the city. Although two young blacks outside the blind pig on Twelfth and Clairmount helped to stimulate the spectators to action, there is little reason to accept the agitator theory for the riot that followed. As Senator Philip Hart noted, agitators running up and down the street in fashionable Grosse Pointe urging the residents to riot would have been ignored if not arrested.[9]

Most explanations of the Detroit and other riots of the 1960s have taken the form of one or another variant of the frustration-aggression model. "How," a *Michigan Chronicle* reporter asked, "do you convey the sense of frustration and alienation a rioter feels, the small sense of exhilaration and retribution that comes with a hurled firebomb against whitey, to a person who has never been seriously thwarted in his life?" A black male in the Twelfth Street riot area, seeking on July 24 to explain the riot to a reporter, provided a man-on-the street version of this hypothesis. "Everybody's full of tension right up to the top of their neck," he declared. "It grows and grows and then some damn fool throws a brick and away it goes on a grand scale."[10]

The frustration-aggression hypothesis is a much disputed formulation since frustration does not necessarily lead to aggressive behavior and aggression does not need to be preceded by frustration. Social scientists applying the hypothesis to the riots have commonly phrased it in terms of deprivation. Blacks rioted, these scholars have posited, because they were absolutely or relatively deprived or because their rising expectations were not being satisfied. Bryan T. Downes, an exponent of the absolute deprivation thesis, a thesis that informed the approach of the Kerner Commission, thus contended that a civil disturbance might occur when the social condition in a city reached "a particularly explosive point." Employing regression analysis for an analysis of disturbances in 673 cities between 1961 and 1968, Seymour Spilerman, however, concluded that racial disorders were most likely to occur when the condition of life for blacks was "least oppressive according to objective measures," not most oppressive.[11] Detroit riot arrestees, to be sure, were more deprived in some respects than community blacks, but they were by no means at the bottom of the black community in socioeconomic terms.

Relative deprivation, as applied to black rioters, refers to the discrepancy between their objective condition and an alternative state deemed desirable, specifically a white middle-class income. "The greater the extent of discrepancy that men see between what they seek and what seems to be attainable," Ted Gurr has contended, "the greater their anger and consequent disposition to aggression." Those blacks who were "objectively advantaged" relative to other blacks might nevertheless have felt themselves "subjectively deprived" compared to whites. Irving J. Rubin, director of Detroit's Regional Transportation and Land Use Study, thought that this theory helped to explain why Detroit, where blacks saw themselves as better off than blacks in other cities, nevertheless experienced a major riot and also why the riot did not occur in the city's poorest black neighborhoods.[12]

Although there is a certain plausibility to the relative deprivation explanation of riot participation, it has proved difficult to sustain the thesis empirically with regard to the 1960s riots. In Newark, for example, Nathan S. Caplan and Jeffrey M. Paige found that there was no difference between the self-reported rioters and the noninvolved when asked whether they thought the gap in income between themselves and whites was increasing. Also, in his investigation of the personal attributes and attitudes of rioters and various measures of riot participation, Clark

McPhail found little to support the thesis that either absolute or relative deprivation led individuals to become rioters.[13]

According to the rising expectations theory, a version of the relative deprivation theory, an increase of expectations as the result of some but insufficient actual improvement will increase the level of tension in affected individuals and lead to feelings of frustration. It was easy enough in the 1960s to apply this argument to blacks who had improved their condition somewhat as the result of the civil rights movement and had been led to expect further gains but had not, for the most part, received what they considered their "fair share" and did not enjoy the advantages enjoyed by whites. "We've raised expectations," Cavanagh conceded after the riot, "but we haven't been able to deliver all we should have." It was not surprising, following this kind of reasoning, that Detroit, where blacks had made greater progress than blacks elsewhere but where they had been led to expect still greater advances, experienced the worst riot of all. "Detroit," the *New York Times* editorialized during the July riot, "may be viewed as a victim of its own limited success." "As people get a little help to get off the bottom," the head of Detroit's war on poverty declared in explanation of the city's riot, "they want more from life and they don't want to wait."[14]

The Luby team believed that its arrestee data were consistent with the rising expectations theory. "It's not that things are so bad," Luby and James Grisell asserted in summarizing the perspective of riot arrestees, "it's that things aren't getting better as fast as they are for white people. And that hurts more than believing things can never get better." The difficulty with this speculation, however, is that arrestees in the Luby sample did not, for the most part, differ substantially from the control group of nonrioters in assessing the progress they had made in the preceding five years. In Newark, similarly, Caplan and Paige found no difference in the response of self-reported rioters and the noninvolved when asked if their condition had improved, gotten worse, or remained the same during the preceding few years.[15]

Rejecting the applicability of the various deprivation theories, Caplan and Paige concluded that the "blocked-opportunity" thesis best explained the 1960s riots. According to these two scholars, the riots were the result of "the prolonged exclusion of Negroes from American economic and social life" because of "white discrimination." The blacks who rioted, Caplan and Paige maintained, were more sensitive to racial discrimination and had experienced it more frequently than blacks who did not riot. They pointed out that their Newark data supported this position and that in both Newark and Detroit the self-reported rioters had stronger feelings of racial pride and identity than the noninvolved and hence, presumably, were more sensitive to racial discrimination. There is no question that blacks in Detroit had suffered from discrimination and believed themselves, on the whole, excluded from the larger society.

"They are not a part of what is happening in the city," Councilman Mel Ravitz replied when asked in 1968 why Detroit blacks had rioted. "I work in Detroit [and] live in Detroit but I don't Feel Free," a riot-area black declared just after the disturbance. "There are so many places closed to me." Blacks who felt this way were undoubtedly among the rioters, but the data collected by the Luby team indicated that the riot arrestees, at least, did not believe themselves more victimized by discrimination than blacks in the control group.[16]

In addition to the riffraff and the various frustration-aggression theories, the so-called "contagion theory" has been advanced to help explain the spread of rioting across the nation in the 1960s. One version of this theory stresses "the immediate environmental forces acting upon an individual who by chance happens to be near the action and is caught up in the spirit of the moment as the excitement spreads contagiously through the crowd." Another version is that television, by depicting the tactics of rioters and the "gratifications" they derived from their actions, raised the tension level among some viewers, created a sense of "black solidarity," reduced the viewers' inhibitions to participate in a riot in their own community, and taught them, as it were, how to riot. "All you hear when you turn on the television set," a seventeen-year-old Detroit black girl said, "is riot, riot, riot." Asked why the rioters were looting, a riot-area respondent declared, "it goes with riots," and a Detroit sniper told the FBI that he had learned from Newark that snipers could strike at the police.[17]

Eighty percent of 470 riot arrestees the Singer team interviewed reported that they had viewed riots on television. Television, Singer and associates concluded, raised expectations in Detroit that a riot was likely to occur in the city. "Each time they heard about one [riot] some place else," a riot-area resident declared, "they said Detroit would be next." Another near west side resident remarked that there had been "too much news on riots in Watts and Chicago about shooting and fires so [Detroit rioters] did it too."[18]

Rioters in Detroit, it can be said in defense of the contagion theory, appeared anxious to compare what they were doing with what had happened in other riots. The *Detroit Free Press* reported that riot arrestees it had interviewed "could not divorce themselves from Watts and Newark." "Man, it took them three days in Watts to do as much damage as we did in eight hours," a rioter told a *Newsweek* correspondent. Another rioter asked a United Press correspondent, "Is this as bad as Newark?" Remarks of this sort, however, should not lead one to make too much of the contagion theory. As David O. Sears and John B. McConahay pointed out in their study of the Watts riot, if the theory were valid, "demographic and attitudinal factors" would not be "strongly related" to riot participation, as the former factors, at the very least, appeared to be.[19]

Quite apart from the centrality assigned to television by the contagion theory, some Detroiters with whom John Hersey spoke criticized television as "the *agent provocateur* of the black masses." "The rebellion," Hersey quoted a Wayne State University student as saying, "it was all caused by television. I mean you saw all those things you'd never been able to get—go out and get 'em." Agreeing, the associate director of the Neighborhood Service Organization asserted that mass communications had stimulated dissent by exhorting people to acquire goods that they could not afford to buy. In Watts, to be sure, "scales of exposure" to the media appeared to be unrelated to riot participation, but it is difficult to determine on the basis of the available data whether the same generalization applies to Detroit.[20]

None of the efforts to relate participation in the riots of the 1960s to one or another explanatory model for collective behavior has been fully successful. This, and the widespread character of the racial disturbances, lead one back, in a sense, to the view of Howard Schuman and Barry Gruenberg that so many riots occurred in that decade because all cities with a sizable black population were above a "riot threshold." "What produces riots," T. M. Tomlinson thus stated, "is the shared agreement by most Negro Americans that their lot in life is unacceptable, coupled with the view by a significant minority that riots are a legitimate and productive mode of protest." Cavanagh essentially adopted this line of argument in explaining the Detroit riot, telling the Kerner Commission that the disturbance in his city was but "one flame in . . . a nationwide fire."[21]

Given "the lot in life" of Detroit's blacks and their legitimate grievances regarding education, housing, jobs, and the police, as well as the general state of race relations in the city, there was certainly a good deal of combustible material lying around in Detroit that could be ignited. The hard question is whether it was inevitable that some spark would ignite the tinder, as the raid on the blind pig actually did. We cannot, of course, recreate the Detroit of the second half of the 1960s with the blind pig raid left out and then await the occurrence or nonoccurrence of another triggering event to answer that question. But even if we could, that would still leave unexplained why some blacks rioted and more did not and why some cities experienced major riots, some very minor ones, and some no riots at all. To assume the inevitability of the Detroit riot is to negate the uniqueness of historical events and to ignore the role that chance so often plays in history.

The importance assigned to television in some efforts to explain the 1960s riots raises the question of the role of the media in reporting the Detroit riot. Although Cavanagh told the Kerner Commission that he did not believe the media had contributed to "the extension of the disorder," he reported that Ron Hewitt, a Neighborhood Conservation official who had been on Twelfth Street during the riot's first day, had seen cameramen "sort of incense the people as if they were trying to get certain responses from the crowd," like throwing bottles, "in order to get a certain kind of picture." Hubert Locke maintained that newsmen monitored police calls and, unaware that many of them were inaccurate, ended up reporting incidents that had not occurred. False rumors were also broadcast that added to the fear engendered by blaring headlines about looting, burning, sniping, and alleged guerrilla warfare.[22]

Drawing on 36,608 feet of film compiled by nine newsreel crews that covered the riot on a twenty-four-hour basis, WWJ-TV in Detroit presented a ninety-minute special on July 30 that portrayed the riot as "a chaotic and irrational collection of fires, crime and blind anger." The same station ran pictures of the funerals of two law enforcement officers but none of the funerals of blacks slain in the riot. The *Detroit News* offered rewards on August 2 for information concerning the death of four riot victims, all of them white. Its defense regarding this latter matter was that all the slayings of blacks had been solved by that time![23]

After studying the media treatment of riots in Detroit, Cincinnati, New Haven, Phoenix, and Tampa, Robert E. Smith concluded that the *Detroit Free Press* had provided "the most balanced riot coverage." Its riot coverage won the newspaper a Pulitzer prize in 1968 for "local general reporting."[24]

In the riot areas of Detroit, 49 percent of the black respondents thought that television stations had reported the riot "fairly," as compared to 39 percent who thought the opposite. In the city as a whole, according to the Campbell-Schuman survey, 55 percent of the black respondents agreed that television and the newspapers had reported the riot fairly, whereas 33 percent regarded the coverage as unfair. The principal complaint of blacks who thought the media treatment unfair was the failure to report white participation. Although some Detroit blacks claimed that the media had failed to expose police brutality in the riot, this was a more common complaint of blacks in other riot cities than in Detroit.[25]

Whatever the quality of the riot coverage by the Detroit media, it was more restrained than accounts by the media outside the city, which generally portrayed Detroit as "a city in ashes." Overseas also, the media were inclined to play up the devastation in Detroit. Robert Roselle recalled that an Englishman, persuaded by the BBC that Detroit was burning to the ground, phoned him from London to inquire about the safety of his relatives. Soviet citizens were told that American soldiers were "murdering" blacks on the streets of Detroit.[26]

The available evidence for the riot appears to sustain the view of social scientists and others that the disturbance was "a spontaneous form of protest," a "signaling device" to those in power that concessions must be made. One rioter put the point succinctly: "You wouldn't pay attention to us before; now you will be forced to." At the outset of the riot, militants went through the crowd saying, "Think the man will get the message now." The destruction was terrible in the view of many among the Luby sample of arrestees, but they thought that "it got the message across."[27]

Survey data confirm the view of the riot as protest. Asked directly whether the riot should be seen as "a Negro protest," 60 percent of the Luby arrestee sample responded in the affirmative. Surveys of riot-area residents and of city blacks also indicate their belief that the rioters were protesting unjust conditions and "calling attention to their needs."[28]

One of the "needs" rioters appear to have had in mind was to be treated like human beings by the white community. "They have to stop treating us like things and start treating us like people," declared the public relations director of the West Central Organization. When asked what she wanted from whites, a looter answered, "respect." Another looter told an interviewer that he was seeking "respect as a man, as a first-class citizen."[29]

Some students of the 1960s riots and some members of the Kerner Commission staff thought that the disturbances not only constituted a protest against existing conditions but also "a concerted attempt to achieve political objectives that had not been gained through other means." What the riots entailed, David Boesel thus contended, was "the breaking of white control over black territory and the autonomous exercise of power over that territory by the black masses themselves." The evidence for this was the young black shouting at the police during the riot, "Get off this street, motherfuckers, it belongs to us!" More important, according to Joe Feagin and Harlan Hahn, was the fact that 75 percent of the adult black respondents on Twelfth Street in a postriot survey indicated that they expected to have more say about their neighborhood as the result of the riot and 50 percent thought that they would have more power.[30]

It appears that those who thought the Detroit riot had a political dimension, that it was aimed at restructuring political power since other means had failed, were reading too much into the event. Black radicals, to be sure, seized on the riot to call for self-determination for blacks, and it is possible, although by no means certain, that that is what Twelfth Street blacks meant by having more say over their neighborhoods. When, however, community blacks, three-quarters of whom resided in the disturbance areas, were asked in the Luby survey about the "way to prevent future riots," only 1 percent on the basis of first mentions and 2 percent on the basis of three mentions gave "Negro power" as their answer. In the Campbell-Schuman survey, only 3 percent of the city's black respondents selected "self-determination" as the best way for blacks to gain their rights. What blacks in the riot areas and in Detroit at large said after the riot does not, of course, necessarily tell us what the rioters had in mind in taking to the streets. There is, however, little in the arrestee data to suggest that they intended anything more than to protest the conditions under which they lived, to secure, somehow, a redress of grievances, and to be treated with respect. The rioters, after all, made no demands whatsoever, nor did they seek to negotiate with city officials. It is certainly possible to construe the riot as "the conduct of politics by other means," as an "unruly" means of expressing one's views outside the electoral process, but if so, the politics being conducted was more inarticulate than articulate.[31]

One of the many difficult questions to answer regarding the Detroit riot is whether it was entirely spontaneous in character. Although there is every reason to believe that the disturbance, like the other riots in 1967, was entirely unplanned in its origin,[32] there has been a good deal of speculation that the spread and continuation of the disorder owed something, at least, to organization.

In a series of articles beginning on August 6, 1967, the black journalist Louis Lomax claimed that a "highly organized and well-trained" group of "revolutionaries," largely from outside Detroit, had operated within the city for more than a month before July 23, 1967, laying the groundwork for a riot. According to Lomax, a small number of young blacks, acting as representatives of a New Jersey publishing company, went through black areas offering to sell a range of black magazines to residents. Once admitted to a home, they allegedly preached "Black Power," asked about the community and why it permitted "whitey, particularly the Jews," to run the stores in the neighborhood, and sought to learn who in the neighborhood wanted the stores burned down. The battle plan of "Operation Detroit," as Lomax described it, was to "remain as obscure as possible until the police-ghetto dynamics provided the proper setting for . . . 'the revolution.' "

According to Lomax, after the initial "normal breaking-and-looting scene," "professionals moved in" and directed the riot. They went down Twelfth Street smashing windows with hammers and crowbars and shouting, "Come on baby, help yourself." Another squad of revolutionaries, Lomax claimed, raced down the street several blocks away urging people to go to Twelfth and Clairmount since the police were permitting looting. One of these "professionals," spotting Dewey Shanks, a Detroit poverty-agency worker, said to Shanks that he had not seen the Detroiter since the Newark riot. Shanks had not been in Newark, Lomax noted, but the "professional" obviously had been.

Lomax contended that although some snipers did it for "kicks," "the hard core of sniper activity was organized." The organized snipers, he claimed, were "Detroit's own sons — Black Power advocates . . . trained in guerilla warfare." By Tuesday, according to Lomax, "the professionals had taken over," and Detroit "had fallen." By Wednesday, the professionals had left the city.[33]

One point of the Lomax story can be confirmed: the reported exchange between a rioter and Dewey Shanks did indeed occur. The rest of the Lomax story, however, is suspect. Neither the Police Department, following a thorough investigation of the Lomax account, nor the FBI was able to corroborate the journalist's charges. The FBI discovered that a sales group from the Publishers Marketing Corporation of New Jersey and its Publix Circulation Service had been in Detroit for a couple of weeks before the riot, but the crew manager and company officials in New Jersey denied the Lomax story of the salesmen's behavior, and the FBI found no reason to dispute their denials.[34]

The Lomax articles found little support among well-informed people in Detroit, including the head of the Field Division of the Commission on Community Relations (CCR). The *Detroit Free Press*'s Gene Goltz told a Kerner Commission interviewer that knowledgeable blacks and whites in Detroit thought Lomax was "full of shit." The managing editor of the *Michigan Chronicle* at the time later stated that Lomax had gathered his information from a desk in the offices of the *Chronicle*, had done little investigating on his own, and had invented much of what he reported.[35]

Another version of a riot that was organized was provided to the Kerner Commission by Anthony P. Loccricio and eventually became the core of an NBC documentary. Loccricio had studied at St. John's Seminary in Plymouth, Michigan, been an attorney, school teacher, and social worker, done defense work for ghetto residents, headed up a day-camp project as part of the Archdiocesan Opportunity Program, joined the staff of Mayor Cavanagh toward the end of the riot, and was a consultant for the NBC program of September 15, 1967, "Summer '67: What We Learned." He claimed that he had begun to hear from his contacts with blacks that there would be a "small riot" in Detroit in the summer of 1967 aimed at uniting the diverse elements in the black community and that there would then be a larger riot in the summer of 1968. The blind pig raid, he reported, had not been part of the plan, but shortly thereafter, as he told the story, "organized groups" pulled up in cars at stores in different parts of the Twelfth Street area, broke windows, and said, "Let's get a piece of whitey," which led to further window breaking and also looting. Two hours later the same cars returned, and the same occupants passed the word that the police were on their way and urged that the stores be torched. This pattern, according to Loccricio, was followed in at least three different locations in the disturbance areas.

Loccricio claimed that "key sources" had told him that during the first morning of the riot fifty to seventy-five militants and "extremists" attended a meeting run by a man and a woman—he eventually named them—at which "separate arson teams" were told to set fires in a prescribed pattern along Twelfth Street, Linwood, Livernois, and Grand River, a pattern that corresponded with a graph of riot fires later prepared by the Detroit Fire Department. Those at the meeting, according to Loccricio, were given a Kercheval address where, later that day, two white men and a white woman handed out rifles to rioters, who took to the rooftops and shot to kill. The organizers, according to the NBC program, had not anticipated that the destruction that began on July 23 would "take off like that."[36]

On the basis of information provided by "several informants," one of whom must have been Loccricio, Walter Sheridan of NBC, who had worked in Detroit for a month preparing for the September 15 NBC program, provided John Doar with additional details concerning the alleged organization of the riot. According to Sheridan, an unidentified group of black militants, in preparation for the riot, had rented ten apartments, including one just off Twelfth and Taylor, where they stored gasoline drums, rags, and a few guns. These apartments were supposed to be burned once the riot began — the one on Twelfth Street was. When the disturbance seemed to be lagging following the blind pig arrests, some of the "group," Sheridan reported, broke into two clothing stores and two loan companies, seizing guns in one of the latter that they distributed to rioters. Most of the rest of the Sheridan account appears to have come from Loccricio. Doar relayed the substance of Sheridan's story to the FBI, J. Edgar Hoover later informing the White House that the information was based on "faceless informants and anonymous sources," was not subject to verification, and some of it was certainly false.[37]

Loccricio refused to reveal the names of his sources or to testify under oath. Neither the head of the CCR's Field Division nor Conrad Mallett believed Loccricio's story, and Deputy Superintendent John Nichols later stated that the story was "not accurate." The NBC program, in particular, came under sharp attack in Detroit. Although NBC stated that it had confirmed what the witnesses it presented claimed they had done in Detroit, an ex-convict who had been arrested for looting and who had allegedly been working with Greensleeves and been present at the July 23 meetings described by Loccricio declared that he had lied on camera and had been coached as to what to say. Loccricio and NBC responded that the recanting witness was not, as he had claimed, one of the two principal informants who had been filmed for the program in "protected darkness," whose voices had been distorted, and one of whom had been shot after giving his interview. Cavanagh reported that it had proved impossible on the basis of information available to the police and other sources to corroborate the program's allegations.[38]

The Loccricio story remains uncorroborated, but there are numerous, less elaborate accounts of at least some degree of instigation and organization in the spread of the riot. There were many rumors and reports during the first four days of the riot, for example, about automobiles with out-of-town licenses in the riot areas, cars filled with black passengers and guns on their way to Detroit, and "strangers" and black power representatives from outside the city who "tried to encourage" the riot once it began. The FBI, after checking with fifty-seven different agencies, found nothing to substantiate stories and rumors of this sort, and Girardin and Kerner Commission investigators agreed.[39]

Some observers and many riot-area residents detected what they believed were organization and "patterns" in the looting, burning, and sniping that occurred. "The streets were organized despite official denials," declared a black *Newsweek* reporter. "We're as organized as the Viet Cong, baby," a young rioter declared. A former president of the Catholic Interracial Council, Charles Peck, who was in the west side riot area during the early hours of July 24, thought that the disturbance "seemed to move in phases," from Twelfth Street, to Dexter, to Linwood, to Grand River. "There were certain cars and certain groups," he observed, "who seemed to be initiating the breaking in, stirring up things before the looters arrived, starting the violent action." Peck saw the same cars, moreover, on Twelfth Street and the other locations noted. He thought that "there was a pattern" to all this, but he "lost" the pattern as the rioting continued.[40]

Reporters, city officials, merchants, police officials, riot-area residents, and a Kerner Commission staffer concluded that the looting was directed and organized, at least to some extent. According to a *Detroit News* reporter, youths aged seventeen to nineteen did the window breaking, and after an establishment had been looted, "a special 'match man' " set the store on fire. "And they seemed to know just where to head next," the reporter noted. Locke described an almost identical pattern of window breaking, looting, and burning. Juvenile Court Judge James Lincoln recalled that a Juvenile Court black probation officer saw two black men and a white woman with walkie-talkies directing window breaking on Twelfth Street, heard them say that they would do the same farther out on the same street, and discovered when he drove there that this was not idle talk. Stephen Slingsby, a California political scientist who witnessed the looting, noted that small boys carried lists of goods on which they checked off items as they were looted.[41]

When Councilman Nicholas Hood came down Linwood at about 1:00 P.M. on July 23, he discovered that the street was blocked with railroad ties, apparently placed there to prevent police from driving into the street to check the looting. Since there was no railroad within miles, Hood presumed that this indicated some kind of planning. Proceeding to Twelfth Street, he saw a male with a walkie-talkie "communicating" with some looters. "Little things like that," Hood said later, "made you wonder just what was going on." An 82d Airborne captain reported that looters on the east side operated in small bands, with one member serving as a lookout and using a walkie-talkie to warn the others of the approach of law enforcement officers.[42]

Although police officials saw no pattern in the firebombings, George Romney told the Kerner Commission that the pattern of fires was not "accidental." The Detroit Fire Department, the Michigan State Police, the executive director of Wayne County Suburban Legal Services, and Detroit's former police commissioner, George Edwards, agreed. Edwards thought that the pattern of fires, one-eighth to one-quarter of a mile apart in a straight line down main thoroughfares, the selection of targets, and the fact that it took some premeditation to prepare Molotov cocktails indicated that the firebombing, at least to some degree, was "planned and organized." It was "the pattern of firebombing," Edwards asserted, that "turned a local riot into a city-wide conflagration."

Romney told Attorney General Ramsey Clark on July 24 that the police were picking up on short-wave radio conversation by "a bunch of young hoodlums" about "keeping the fires going" in the city. A black businessman who lived one block away from the main riot area and was listening on his walkie-talkie provided a Senate subcommittee with an affidavit stating that he had overheard walkie-talkie conversation on July 23 and 24 that included a command to burn a drugstore and another business establishment and talk of spreading the disorder to the east side before that had actually occurred. "Some of the burning was planned," Richard Henry told Garry Wills, "in fact, a lot of it was."[43]

After interviewing the prisoners arrested as alleged snipers, the FBI concluded that the sniping was not organized and did not involve either "hate or subversive groups." Since those arrested for sniping, however, were not necessarily snipers and since, in talking to the FBI, they probably would have concealed their organizational affiliation, if any, and their role in the riot had they been snipers, the FBI's evaluation of the matter is hardly persuasive.

In contrast with the FBI, a "top law enforcement officer" with the Detroit Police Department concluded, according to a *Detroit News* report, that the sniping was "very well organized" and was "part of the network of the Black Power movement." "These people have some kind of communication," the source noted, one of several allegations of the use of citizens band or two-way radios to direct sniping. Locke thought that the widely scattered sniping at the same time on July 24 and 25, coupled with reports of a communications system, suggested organization although not necessarily prior planning, and others talked about a "pattern of sniping" or a "very loose" or "informal" organization of snipers that functioned in some instances. Assertions of this sort, however, were based almost entirely on inference rather than real proof and cannot be accepted as fact.[44]

Toward the end of the riot *Detroit Free Press* reporter Gene Goltz met with two young "snipers," Eddie and Frank, who described their role in the riot. Highball in hand, a short-wave radio at his feet on which Frank and he could hear police calls—Girardin confirmed that the police radio system had been monitored during the riot—Eddie claimed that he had been shooting at police and firemen all week. He referred also to a group of six "shooters" who had sniped from rooftops for two and one-half days while consuming twenty-four pints of liquor. The two youths alleged that out-of-towners had brought guns and ammunition into the city for the use of the snipers and that the rioters had secured additional weapons by looting gun shops and pawnshops. The purpose of the riot, Eddie said, was "to burn every Whitey store to the ground," and the role of the snipers was to prevent policemen and firemen from interfering with that goal. At first, Goltz thought that what he had heard was "just bragging and puffing up," but information he later received left him uncertain as to the credibility of Eddie and Frank.[45]

Since Detroit was a major center of black militancy and black nationalism, there has been considerable speculation as to the possible role of black militants and extremists in the riot. George Edwards contended that although black power activists had not planned the riot, they moved in once it had begun and intensified it. An anonymous source wrote June Garner of the *Michigan Chronicle* that once the riot began, "certain groups had very special things to do." According to this source, "Do-Rag Brothers," young nationalists organized into gangs, allegedly led the looting, Revolutionary Action Movement (RAM) members were responsible for the "systematic burning," and the snipers were supposedly RAM members and white "gun-nuts." *Newsweek*'s John Dotson reported that hard-core black nationalists, including RAM members, were among the snipers, and many years later, Edward Vaughn, who was in a position to know, alleged that some of the "brothers" in RAM had joined in the sniping. The Police Department, the Michigan State Police, and the FBI all concluded, however, that there was no RAM participation in the riot. The FBI, indeed, had no information to indicate that any black power group "took over and directed the riot."[46]

On July 25 a black male attempted to buy potassium chlorate in a Flint drugstore. Since the Flint Police, because of the rioting in the state, had requested businesses in the city not to sell inflammable liquids, the druggist refused to make the sale. The customer then sought in vain to purchase ammonium dichromate, another chemical that could be used to make Molotov cocktails. The druggist copied the license number of the Cadillac in which the frustrated purchaser departed, and its owner turned out to be Milton Henry. The State Police placed Henry under surveillance and tried to develop a case against him for "conspiracy to incite [a] riot" or for violating the state's anarchy law. It failed in this effort, nor was any law enforcement agency able to develop a case of this sort against any of Detroit's prominent black militants. The Detroit police, as a matter of fact, had placed most of the known black militants in the city under surveillance immediately after the riot began and discovered that they were not leaders of the disturbance.[47]

Many of Detroit's black militant leaders had attended the Black Power Conference in Newark, which ended on July 22, and did not return to Detroit until July 23. After spending an evening with Kenneth Cockrell and other black power advocates, the journalist Saul Friedman concluded that they had been caught "entirely unprepared" by the riot. "They appeared bewildered and disorganized," Friedman reported, "and were asking themselves where they could have gone wrong, that they were not able to make use of the riot situation." Several black extremists told Friedman during the riot that the leadership in the disturbance had not come from the "brothers" in RAM, Forum 66, the Malcolm X Society, the Northern Student Movement, or the Inner City Organizing Committee but rather from young blacks who hung around the corners, the poolrooms, and the barber shops. Locke agreed, telling the Kerner Commission that the "real leaders" in the riot were inconspicuous individuals who did not emerge as an "active force" until the riot's fourth day.[48]

When asked whether the riot had been "planned in advance," 26 percent of the male and 54 percent of the female arrestees in the Luby sample answered in the affirmative. Among adult blacks on Twelfth Street in another postriot survey, 37 percent thought that "the people who started the trouble were mainly organized," and about one-third thought that the arsonists and snipers "knew each other." In the Campbell-Schuman survey, 60 percent of the Detroit black respondents thought that the riot involved at least some planning.[49]

No law enforcement agency agreed with survey respondents who thought the riot was, at least in some degree, a planned event. President Johnson pressed the FBI to search for a conspiracy that explained the riot's origin, but the Bureau was unable to find any such thing. Although the assistant army chief of staff for intelligence, Major General William Yarbrough, firmly believed that the rioters in Detroit and elsewhere were "tied in with each other," that "they were trained in Havana or Peking or some damned place," army intelligence concluded that there was no "overall direction" of the rioting. Army intelligence, however, as well as the Kerner Commission field team that studied Detroit, the Michigan State Police, the Michigan Commission on Crime, Delinquency, and Criminal Administration, Ray Girardin, and John Nichols all believed that there was some "organized element" in the streets that sustained the riot once it had begun.[50]

Despite widespread agreement that the intensification and prolongation of the riot following the triggering incident were not entirely spontaneous, hard evidence is lacking to support this judgment. If there was any organized effort to spread the riot, it was of a "rudimentary" sort, developed on the street and involving small groups of looters, arsonists, and snipers acting independently of one another or possibly responding to an informal leadership. It is fairly safe to say that there was no mastermind, no "riot central" directing the flow of events as rioters surged through the streets looting and burning and occasionally sniping. As Cleage said, the riot was "a monster without a head."[51]

What emerges from the welter of data concerning the Detroit riot and the Detroit rioters is that, although less aggrieved than blacks in other big cities, Detroit blacks were sufficiently discontented with their lot so that, given the racial climate of the 1960s and what had already occurred in places like Watts and Newark, a particular kind of incident, especially one involving the police, could trigger a riot. The incident that actually led to the riot was the product, to a large degree, of a series of chance factors, which does not exclude the possibility that some other event might have had the same result.

Those who rioted were not riffraff, but neither were they the cream of the crop among blacks in the city. A minority among them were militants and particularly resentful of the treatment they had received from the police, employers, and merchants. Although the rest were drawn into the riot for a variety of reasons, one cannot ignore the opportunity that police restraint presented at the riot's outset or the contagious effect of the rioting once it got underway. No single explanatory model of collective behavior, in any event, accounts for the fact that while some blacks rioted, the overwhelming majority did not.

The riot is best seen as a form of protest designed to call attention to the condition of blacks, but it does not appear to have been aimed at restructuring political power in the city. It enjoyed less support in Detroit's black community than riots did among blacks in other cities that had experienced major civil disorders. Detroit's blacks also appear to have been more pessimistic about what the event portended for their future than blacks in other cities about the consequences of riots in their communities. Some reactions of Detroit blacks may have been the result of a continuing belief that Detroit, for all its faults, was still a better place than most for blacks to live. Some reactions were probably a byproduct of the damaging character of the Detroit riot, the nation's most severe.

CHAPTER 16

The Polarized Community

Whites and blacks in Detroit just after the riot viewed what had happened and its consequences in very different ways. As two University of Michigan political scientists put it, "for the most part it was as if two different events had taken place in the same city, one a calculated act of criminal anarchy, the other a spontaneous protest against mistreatment and injustice."[1]

When asked in the Luby community survey which of three possible interpretations came closest to explaining why the riot had occurred, 69 percent of the blacks but only 28 percent of the whites thought it was because people were "being treated badly." On the other hand, 31 percent of the whites thought that "criminals did it," and 37 percent that the riot had occurred because "people wanted to take things," whereas only 11 percent of the blacks subscribed to the former view, and 18 percent to the latter. In the Campbell-Schuman survey, more than twice as many whites (38 percent) as blacks (18 percent) thought that the riot was "mainly looting."[2]

Thirty-one percent of the blacks in the Luby community sample believed the riot would "help" black-white relations, but only 4 percent of the whites agreed. Three-quarters of the whites, as compared to 38 percent of the blacks, expected that race relations in Detroit would be impaired. Those who believed race relations had been helped thought that the riot had made whites understand that blacks had to be "taken seriously" and had also led to a quest for solutions to the city's racial problems. Those who thought race relations had suffered stressed "white fear, distrust, dislike, anger toward blacks."

In the Campbell-Schuman survey conducted about four months after the Luby survey, a smaller percentage of blacks (27 percent) and a larger percentage of whites (13 percent) believed that the riot had helped black-white relations. Almost 70 percent of the white respondents now thought that blacks were pushing "too fast" for what they wanted, and just over 67 percent believed that blacks in the central city had only themselves to blame for the fact that they had "worse jobs, education, and housing than white people."[3]

Although there was much talk of black separatism following the riot and some scholars asserted that riots like Detroit's had caused blacks to question the goal of integration, support for racial integration was stronger in Detroit's black than in its white community. Whereas only 1 percent of Detroit's blacks in the Luby black community sample favored "total separation" of the races, 17 percent of the whites placed themselves in this camp. More than three times as many blacks as whites (88 percent as compared to 24 percent) favored "integration." The majority of whites (59 percent) preferred a racial relationship somewhere "in between" integration and total separation. Among black respondents in the Campbell-Schuman survey, only 5 percent believed blacks should "shun" whites, as compared to 91 percent who rejected that view. Whereas only 10.5 percent of the black respondents indicated that they preferred to live in an all-black or mostly black neighborhood and 57 percent preferred to live in an integrated neighborhood, 53 percent of the whites conceded that they would mind it "a lot" (21 percent) or at least "a little" (32 percent) even if a black of the same income and education as themselves moved next door to them, and 37 percent believed whites had the right to keep blacks out of their neighborhood entirely.

There was a much greater degree of sympathy for separation among blacks in the Twelfth Street area than among blacks in the city as a whole. As compared to the 1 percent in the Luby community sample who favored total separation, 22 percent of the Twelfth Street adult blacks believed blacks should "try to get along without whites." Blacks favoring separation were more likely than those who did not to have participated in the riot, were more violence-oriented, and more disposed to view the riot as "a direct means of achieving social change."[4]

Blacks and whites following the riot had widely different understandings of the meaning of the words "black power," a slogan that had come into use in 1966 and that had been heard in the streets during the riot. Blacks favorable to the concept in the Luby sample were inclined to interpret it as meaning a "fair share for black people" (25 percent), "racial (black) unity" (17 percent), or "nothing" at all (23 percent), whereas whites were apt to view the words unfavorably as meaning "blacks rule whites" (40 percent) or "trouble, rioting, civil disorder" (12 percent). When the *Detroit Free Press* resurveyed the riot areas of the city in September 1968, it found that black power had become "the dominant idea" among blacks. The meaning of the concept for those favoring it had not, however, changed significantly since the time of the Luby survey.[5]

The polarization between black and white in postriot Detroit was reflected, to some degree, in the assumptions each had about the other. In the Campbell-Schuman survey, for example, almost three-quarters (74 percent) of the white respondents thought that many or almost all blacks disliked whites. Perhaps reflecting their own views, about the same percentage of white respondents (73) believed that "many" or "almost all" whites disliked blacks. Whereas 36 percent of the black respondents thought that whites wanted blacks to get "a better break," 52 percent believed whites wanted "to keep Negroes down" (21 percent) or did not "care one way or the other" (31 percent). Approximately the same percentage of black respondents thought "only a few" whites disliked blacks (46 percent) as thought "almost all" or "many" whites were of this view (47 percent).[6]

The 1960s riots, James A. Geschwender has written, "stimulated a new burst of pride and revived belief that blacks could force changes through united effort." That many blacks derived satisfaction in the riot's aftermath from the fact that blacks had stood up to whites seems evident. "I had a feeling," a black friend told the *Free Press*'s Frank Angelo just after the riot, "that Negroes in Detroit were walking taller" as a result of the disturbance. Judge James Lincoln thought that this was true of even "many . . . law abiding successful blacks" who had probably been horrified while the riot was underway. It is likely, indeed, that the degree of sympathy noninvolved blacks expressed for the rioters in surveys conducted after the event exaggerated the support the rioters enjoyed in the black community during the riot.[7]

Conrad Mallett, the head of the Mayor's Summer Task Force, concluded that the most important consequence of the riot was "a welding together of heretofore fragmented black groups into a cohesive unit."[8] It may have appeared that way for a brief time following the riot, but the divisions within the black community were soon to surface, frustrating efforts of black leaders to speak with a single voice to the white community and New Detroit.

The riot initially enhanced the credibility of black militants and weakened and frightened the moderates. As the Detroit Urban League's (DUL) Francis Kornegay privately informed Henry Ford II on August 3, the moderate black leaders and potential leaders were "scared to death to stand up and be counted." A few weeks later Kornegay stated publicly, "There is no such thing as moderate any more — only militant and more militant."[9] This was simply not so, but it is true that among the militants, some were "more militant" than others.

The militant black community included a small band of Maoists, a few who espoused a black republic carved out of five southern states, and advocates of self-determination. A DUL housing assistant attended a party on Twelfth Street just after the riot at which followers of Malcolm X and field-workers of the Student Nonviolent Coordinating Committee (SNCC) talked of breaking into gun shops to seize weapons so as to increase their ability to deal with the "fire power" of state and local law enforcement personnel. A black attorney told the deputy director of field operations for the Kerner Commission that "the most violent" militants did not think it "immoral" to kill whites.[10]

The most influential spokesman for black militancy and black nationalism in Detroit following the riot was the Reverend Albert Cleage. His "power base" was his own Central United Church of Christ, whose membership increased "at a phenomenal rate" after the disturbance. Renamed the Shrine of the Black Madonna, Cleage's church was reputedly "the only Christian black nationalist church in America." Even the middle-class-oriented *Michigan Chronicle* began to publish a weekly column by Cleage beginning in August 1967.[11]

Whites, Cleage said just after the riot, wanted to keep the community as it was, but blacks would not permit them to do so. "We don't like it the way it was," he remarked, and "we will rebuild it the way we want it, all of us together—or it will be torn down again and again and again. We are determined to control our own community." He asserted that the "white power structure" of Detroit had the "unique opportunity" to "begin the difficult task of transferring meaningful power from the white power structure to the black community." Cleage wanted blacks to control the police, the schools, and the businesses in the black ghetto and to "get the white man out." He favored ward elections that would give blacks political control of the areas where they lived and looked forward to "complete [black] political control of the city government." Rejecting integration as an "issue," Cleage warned that if separation failed, the consequence would be "black warfare."[12]

The young black nationalists who put out the newly founded *Inner City Voice* sought to promote the cause of militancy in Detroit by sponsoring a talk on August 27 by H. Rap Brown, SNCC's national chairman. Brown spoke to a crowd that overflowed the seven-hundred-seat Dexter Theater and then took to the roof of the building to address about twelve hundred listeners gathered outside. In what one newspaper characterized as "a harangue against the white race," Brown claimed that the United States government was readying thirteen concentration camps "to do away" with "a lot of excess niggers." He advised his audience not to go peacefully and to "stop looting," other than for guns, and to "start shooting." Outside the theater, the aroused crowd drove a TV crew from the scene amidst a barrage of rocks and bottles, demolished a press car, kicked and beat a *Detroit Free Press* photographer, and attacked an unmarked police car and injured a detective. Some black nationalists and Brown's entourage restrained the crowd from looting and any further violence lest this result in Brown's arrest.[13]

When Wayne State University arranged a symposium on "New Perspectives on Race and the City" for October 19 and 20, 1967, Cleage urged the scheduled speakers to withdraw. "The day is past," he said, "when any white institution . . . can tell us what our needs are." Militant black students, joined by some whites, called for a boycott of the event since they had not consented to the choice of speakers. Although they withdrew the boycott call, the students picketed the opening session of the symposium. Wayne then granted funds to the university's Association of Black Students to plan a counter conference. Speaking at the October symposium, Milton Henry defiantly stated, "The principal duty of Black men is to make revolution. If it means burning this country to the ground, do it. . . . We are not interested in talking," he said, ". . . revolution is our principal business."[14]

The militants took the initiative in seeking to organize the black community after the riot. At a City Wide Citizens Meeting of Soul Brothers on August 9 that Julian Witherspoon had called, the three hundred blacks assembled decided to launch a new organization that took the name City Wide Citizens Action Committee (CCAC). The meeting hall in the City-County Building rang with the angry, inflated rhetoric so characteristic of the 1960s. "We must control our community or there won't be a community," declared the cultural nationalist Edward Vaughn. "We are going to get half," declared Nadine Brown, a United Automobile Workers (UAW) official, "or there won't be anything for anyone else to have." Robert Tindal of the National Association for the Advancement of Colored People (NAACP) was all but shouted down by the militants when he spoke. "We are [the] new black establishment," Cleage proclaimed, "the Toms are out."

The August 9 meeting approved a resolution calling for the New Detroit Committee to be made advisory to the new black organization. "The Hudson committee will take orders from us," Cleage defiantly stated. "We have power." Shortly after the meeting, Cleage was elected chairman of the CCAC. Glanton Dowdell served as cochairman, Nadine Brown as secretary, and Clyde Cleveland, head of the Detroit chapter of the Congress of Racial Equality (CORE), as secretary. The magazine *City* characterized the CCAC as "possibly the most broadly based Black Power organization in any city."[15]

Following a meeting of his committee on August 10, Joseph L. Hudson announced that New Detroit would "recognize, welcome and cooperate" with the new "Black Establishment Committee." Cleage, after meeting with Hudson, asserted that his organization would cooperate with New Detroit "as long 'as they do what needs to be done' "; and what "needed to be done," he made it clear, was for New Detroit to "transfer the power of the black community to black people."[16]

For the first time in Detroit's history, Cleage claimed in a CCAC report, blacks had created an "informal organization" that could speak for the entire black community. He asserted that the CCAC's method in seeking "to control *everything* that touches the black community" was "confrontation." Warning that the CCAC was "preparing for all kinds of conflict," he advised anyone trying to block the organization to "get out of the way."[17]

The CCAC sought to spread its message by meetings in various sections of Detroit and by the use of motorcades on Saturdays to distribute handbills. One CCAC leaflet called on blacks to struggle against "Police Terror, Uncle Tomism, Retail Exploitation, Slum Lords, Mis-Education of Black Children, [and] False Leaders." A CCAC handbill informed black women that as long as "police terror" against black women and children went unpunished, "the man you're sleeping with is a faggot!"[18]

Although some moderates joined the CCAC, its appeal was to the militants, ranging from those favoring self-determination or separation, the organization's principal thrust, to those advocating "all-out war" if necessary. When a Kerner Commission staffer attended a CCAC meeting in October, he concluded that although there was no talk of violence, it was evident that the organization would not reject violence as a way to solve the problems of the black community. He noted that many of those present wore 50-millimeter machine gun bullets attached to leather thongs as pendants around their necks. According to an assistant general counsel of the Kerner Commission who attended another CCAC meeting, those present spoke approvingly of violence in the schools.[19]

The CCAC received a contribution of $19,000 from the Interfaith Emergency Council in September. Toward the end of 1967 the Interreligious Foundation for Community Organization gave the CCAC a check for $85,000 as "the first black organization in the country" that had displayed "unity and determination" in seeking to "control the community" where blacks were in the majority.

As part of the CCAC's effort to achieve community control, its Black Star Co-op opened a store on Linwood in December 1967, and the CCAC also apparently helped to establish a black-run company to manufacture African-style patterns and dresses. As part of its stress on black nationalism, the CCAC urged the introduction of courses in the public schools dealing with black history and culture and the teaching of African languages.[20]

As survey data reveal, there was little support in the black community for self-determination, separation, or violence as ways to advance the black cause. Asked in the Campbell-Schuman survey about the best means for blacks to secure their rights, only 3 percent of Detroit black respondents, as already noted, chose self-help, which compared with the 15 percent who favored this approach in the fifteen cities as a whole. Whereas 10 percent of the respondents selected violence, more than 80 percent favored "laws and persuasion" (40 percent) and "nonviolent protest" (42 percent) as the best ways for blacks to gain their rights. Only 3.5 percent approved of a separate black nation; only 13 percent thought that black schools should have black principals; only 5 percent believed that teachers in black schools should be black; and only 16 percent thought that stores in black neighborhoods should be black-owned.

There was greater support for violence among Twelfth Street residents than among blacks in the city as a whole. In the survey of Twelfth

Street black residents, about one in six of those interviewed thought that "violence rather than peaceful protests was the 'more effective way for Negroes to get what they want,' " and about one-third thought that violence was the "faster way." When the *Detroit Free Press* resurveyed the riot areas in 1968, it found that 75 percent of the adult blacks ranked rather low on a series of six questions related to black nationalism, but 79 percent of the self-reported rioters ranked high. Although 77 percent of the riot-area blacks had heard of Cleage, only 4 percent of them rated him as "doing the most good" for blacks. Conventional black politicians like Charles Diggs (27 percent), John Conyers (22 percent), and Nicholas Hood (13 percent) received much higher approval ratings. Among the Luby community sample of blacks, 8 percent thought Cleage was "doing well," as compared to 55 percent who thought the NAACP was "doing well" and 42 percent who placed the mainstream UAW in this category. In the Campbell-Schuman survey, 91.5 percent of the Detroit black respondents approved or at least partially approved of Martin Luther King, but only 26 percent were of this view regarding Rap Brown.[21]

If Cavanagh at the time of the riot thought that he had been talking to the wrong blacks, he soon concluded that the militants were not the "right blacks" either. He characterized them as "the unchosen leaders of the potential rioters, the after-the-fact leaders in search of a constituency." The moderates, whom Kornegay had thought feared "to stand up and be counted," decided not to permit the CCAC and the militants to pose as the spokesmen for the black community. As James N. Garrett, the president of the Cotillion Club, stated, "There are a lot of law-abiding citizens in Detroit. Somebody ought to say something in their behalf." The moderates resented the fact that Cleage, whom they regarded as a "Johnnie-come-lately" to the black cause, had been getting so much attention as "Mr. Black Identity."[22]

With the Reverend Roy Allen, president of the Council of Baptist Ministers, taking the lead, the moderates on August 22 established the Detroit Council of Organizations (DCO) as their vehicle. The DCO became "the voice of the 'ins,' " just as the CCAC was "the voice of the 'outs.' " The DCO's appeal was to middle- and upper-class blacks, professional people, black trade union and Democratic party functionaries, and black community leaders. In the next few months, the Cotillion Club, the Wolverine Bar Association, the Trade Union Leadership Council (TULC), and the Detroit NAACP all identified with the DCO. It eventually claimed to speak for twenty-nine organizations and 350,000 Detroit blacks. Cleage, however, charged that it was the creature of the white establishment, City Hall, and the UAW.[23]

Allen stressed at a press conference that the DCO believed the problems of blacks could be solved by "legal and peaceful means." Although he claimed that the DCO was not "out of touch" with the rioters, was not opposed to any black group, and wanted to work with the CCAC, he was

soon attacking some of the CCAC's objectives and methods as "irresponsible." As William T. Patrick, Jr., observed, the militants said to the
whites, "Give us what we want or we'll burn your damn house down,"
whereas the moderates said, "Give . . . us what we want because it is the
morally correct thing to do."[24] Unlike the militants, who were inclined to
be separationists, the DCO espoused integration. Its objectives included
integrated schools, open housing, the building of low-cost homes for
blacks, more blacks on the police force and improved police-community
relations, and increased job opportunities for blacks.[25]

Although the DCO agreed to work with New Detroit, some of the
committee's white establishment figures were more inclined to listen to
the three militant blacks on the committee than to the moderates.
Reflecting this position, Henry Ford declared, "The middle class black is
as far removed from what's happening in the ghetto as we are." The white
establishment leaders on the New Detroit Committee were, in the main,
remarkably naive about blacks and the black community. "They were
really out of it," Arthur Johnson, a moderate black New Detroit member, accurately recalled. "You can shock [the businessmen of New
Detroit]," the militant Norvell Harrington declared, "by telling them
what goes on for one day in a Negro's life." As the *Free Press* observed,
"There was a hypnotic attraction for these middle and upper-class whites
in dealing with the Inner City for the first time."[26]

The New Detroit leadership, Cavanagh maintained, had no understanding of "the nuances, problems and forces extant in the Negro community" and of "the irreconcilable, philosophical differences" in that
community. Those differences manifested themselves at an early date
among the nine blacks on the committee. Whereas all nine met together
initially as a black caucus, the moderates and the militants agreed to
disagree after three such meetings, and the militants thereafter met alone
before and after board meetings. Johnson recalled that he told Lorenzo
Freeman at one meeting that he was "out of touch with reality" after
Freeman had attacked such black establishment leaders as Roy Wilkins
and Whitney Young.[27]

If the white leadership of New Detroit thought that it was buying
riot insurance by including militants on the committee, the militants did
nothing to disabuse them of that notion. "If you fat cats don't give us
what we want," Harrington told them, "it won't be our places that will be
burning next summer; it will be yours." He warned that Ford and General Motors could be set ablaze just "as easily" as rioters had burned
other places in the summer of 1967. And it was the teenaged Harrington
who became the "teacher" of GM's James Roche concerning the nature
of the black community.[28]

If the white business leadership of New Detroit was naive about
blacks, the black militants on the committee had their own misconcep-
tions about the admittedly considerable influence of the white business

establishment. At New Detroit's first meeting, Hudson recalled, the three militants said to the whites, "You guys decide that you're going to change these things and by the first of next year we're going to have it all licked!" As Roche remembered it, a militant said to him, "We regard GM as a great big cow out to pasture that you bring back to milk. That's what we're going to do, milk GM."[29]

New Detroit's views as to who was to be "listened to" in the black community were put to a severe test before 1967 had come to an end. In a second effort to establish a "popular front" type organization that would embrace both militants and moderates, Cleage took the lead in proposing the creation of a "Federation of Black Organizations and Individuals." At a meeting on December 1 the decision was taken to launch the Federation for Self Determination (FSD), with Cleage as chairman and Freeman as one of the two cochairmen. The organization presented itself as a "non-sectarian, non-partisan and non-profit federation devoted to improving the political, social and economic status of black people . . . ; eradicating social prejudice; and . . . develop[ing] self-determination for black people in all areas of community life." It is likely that the FSD had the advance blessing of key New Detroit members, including Hudson himself.[30]

Not only did such organizations as CORE affiliate with the FSD, but even moderates like Tindal, James Garrett, and Longworth Quinn did so. DCO leaders, however, wanted no part of the new organization. Allen claimed he had been told that if he joined, he would "have to do exactly" what the FSD said or he would be "eliminated." When he responded that he was prepared to be "kicked out," he claimed that he was told, "no, not kicked out, 'eliminated.'" In any event, although "a welding of the old and new," it was the "new guard" that was "the driving force" in the FSD.[31]

On December 8 Freeman submitted an FSD proposal to New Detroit that it agreed to consider at its December 14 meeting. The FSD requested $137,000 to create a staff during the succeeding six months and an additional $200,000 during the following two years to set up an urban research center and an organization service center. There appears to have been some preliminary discussion between the FSD and William Patrick, Jr., the vice president of the Metropolitan Fund for New Detroit, before the FSD submitted its proposal to New Detroit.[32]

Before the New Detroit Committee met, the Cotillion Club, the TULC, and other black organizations officially informed the committee that they were not allied with the FSD, as they thought had been implied. While New Detroit was considering the FSD proposal on December 14, a communication arrived from the DCO asserting that an immediate decision to fund the FSD would be "ill advised" since it would preclude consideration of proposals from other organizations. Hudson, however, seconded by Ford, pushed for support of the FSD proposal, but black moderates and some of the whites blocked immediate approval. Although the decision was then taken to defer action for at least three weeks, Hudson, Ford, and some others were sufficiently committed to the FSD to promise to contribute $32,000 of their own money to enable it to get started. Miffed by the decision to defer action on the FSD proposal, Harrington walked out of the meeting, charging that New Detroit had "copped out to the traditional Negro leadership."[33]

Five days after New Detroit's December 14 meeting, the DCO issued a withering attack on the leadership of the committee. In embarking on a program of "buying off" the so-called militants, the DCO statement read, "a few high-placed members" of New Detroit had "completely misinterpreted" the mood of the black community and had "outrageously" insulted "the intelligence of the preponderant majority" of the city's blacks. The DCO warned that it would not tolerate the action of business concerns that profited from black spending but were unwilling to invest in the black community and sought "to destroy the very fabric that binds it together." With the Hudson stores in mind, the DCO threatened to engage in selective buying and other forms of "economic coercion" if necessary to make such firms see the light.[34]

The DCO on December 27 submitted its own proposal to New Detroit, one that called for the committee to help fund three neighborhood centers staffed by residents to assist the poor in obtaining available services; a program centering on inner-city schools that involved the formation of a team of community organizers to serve as "education advocates"; a career development and manpower program aimed at the training and employment of the hard-core unemployed; and two daycare and child development centers. The DCO pledged itself to raise a little more than $240,000 of the expected $600,493 cost of its proposal.[35]

Faced with the rival proposals of the FSD and the DCO, New Detroit, on January 4, 1968, decided to compromise and to provide each organization with $100,000 for one year. Several conditions accompanied the compromise agreement. Each organization was required to match the sum it received dollar for dollar; Patrick was to serve in a coordinating role to ensure that there was no overlap in the services the two organizations provided; provision was to be made for the auditing and evaluation of the programs; and since the money was to be channeled through the tax-exempt Metropolitan Fund, neither organization was to engage in political activities.[36]

The conditions accompanying New Detroit's funding decision led the FSD to withdraw its proposal and to sever "all relations" with New Detroit and also persuaded Freeman and Harrington to resign from the committee. The FSD advised New Detroit that it would accept no money "with strings attached" since "black people must make the decisions affecting their lives just like most white people can do." If it accepted the grant, the FSD stated, it would "set an example nationwide, mortgaging the freedom of black people and playing havoc with their self-respect." Asserting that the FSD was "not for sale," Cleage insisted that the terms of the grant and the appointment of Patrick as "overseer" could not be reconciled with the black quest for self-determination.[37]

Believing that what happened in Detroit might very well set a pattern for the nation, Floyd McKissick, the head of CORE, flew to Detroit to support Cleage. Although New Detroit, McKissick stated, was the first attempt by whites to deal with blacks on a basis of equality, the committee simply did not understand that self-determination was "the first page in the book of black power." He dismissed the $100,000 grant as "just a welfare payment to the black community to keep it happy during the coming summer" and chastised New Detroit for proceeding in the "normal paternalistic manner in dealing with the black community." Accepting the riot-insurance thesis, McKissick said that it did not matter whether the FSD represented the blacks of Detroit since it did represent "the boat rockers," and whites had better understand that "they got to deal with the boat rockers." "The other people," the moderates, he explained, "ain't gonna' throw no rocks, they ain't gonna' throw no Molotov cocktails."[38]

"We can no longer serve as members of the committee and maintain our integrity as representatives of the black peoples of Detroit," Freeman and Harrington informed Hudson in their letter of resignation. They claimed that they had been placed on the committee "merely as showpieces," and Harrington charged that New Detroit was trying "to control 'riots,' " not "to correct wrongs." Their resignations and Alvin Harrison's departure from Detroit at about the same time left New Detroit without any of the three black militants originally appointed to the committee.[39]

Distressed at what had occurred, New Detroit's leadership sought to make it clear that the committee did not oppose black self-determination. New Detroit pressed for "a reconciliation" with the militants, Hudson stating that "nothing" was more important for the committee. Hudson and Patrick explained to the FSD that the limitation on its political activity was required by law, that it could develop its own "evaluative criteria" as a basis for making reports to New Detroit, and that "a liaison and communications bridge" was required since more than one organization was to receive funding. Hudson attempted to meet with FSD representatives to forge "a new relationship," and he sought to persuade Freeman and Harrington to return to the committee, all to no avail.[40]

The DCO accepted the $100,000 New Detroit had offered, but when it was unable to raise the required matching money, it was forced to give up the program it had contemplated and to disband. Well before that had occurred, the FSD had also come to the end of its brief existence. In April 1968 ultramilitants in the organization, disturbed by what they saw as Cleage's increasingly moderate views and his speeches before white audiences, voted to dissolve the FSD.[41]

Neither militants nor moderates saw much reason to be pleased with the manner in which New Detroit had responded to the divisions within Detroit's black community. Dan Aldrich, the leader of SNCC elements in Detroit, commented that since "the white middle class couldn't possibly understand the problems of the disenfranchised black man," the best thing the New Detroit Committee could do was to disband and give its money to the black community. The moderate Hubert Locke thought that New Detroit's "tampering with the delicate balance of black leadership" in the city had been "a disaster." New Detroit, however, did not permit the FSD-DCO fiasco to deter it from continuing to reach out to different elements in the black community.[42]

When Harrington after three months reconsidered his resignation, New Detroit welcomed him back to the committee. On August 8, 1968, the day that it incorporated, New Detroit made a $50,000 grant, this time without any strings attached, to the ultramilitant Frank Ditto and his East Side Voice for Independent Detroit, which, among other things, trained ghetto youths in politics and operated a community youth patrol. After serving as an organizer in Chicago and elsewhere, Ditto had come to Detroit at the beginning of the riot at the invitation of the Churches on the East Side for Social Action to serve as "a catalyst" for their ghetto activities. He was soon calling for "revolution against 'white tyranny' by violent, bloody, or whatever means necessary to 'overthrow the system.'" A New Detroit spokesman understandably described Ditto as "a damn controversial guy who scares the hell out of some people." He was, however, "a real guy," the spokesman said, who could be "useful" to New Detroit. "They know if there aren't some crumbs on the table," Ditto remarked, the militants "might burn down some shit."

Delighted that another militant had approached the committee, New Detroit made Ditto a trustee. In that role, Ditto, who reputedly became New Detroit's "brightest star," receiving about $250,000 in grants from the organization, was "intentionally insulting" to the corporate leaders of the committee. Offended by what they regarded as his foul language, black moderates vainly sought to have Ditto removed from the New Detroit board. One auto executive said he was "getting 'bugged' by [New Detroit] meetings dominated by black-militant harangues," but interviews Helen M. Graves conducted in 1972–73 indicated that there was "an overwhelming consensus" among New Detroit trustees at that time, excluding "senior Black Establishment members," that the militant presence in New Detroit had been "crucial to peacemaking," helped educate the white establishment, and made it "easier" for the moderates to "operate." Ditto resigned from the New Detroit board in December 1974, charging that "vicious back stabbing, murderous madness, hypocrisy and corruption" were rampant in the organization.[43]

At about the same time as the FSD disbanded, two new militant organizations made their appearance in Detroit, the Republic of New Africa (RNA) and the Dodge Revolutionary Union Movement (DRUM). At the end of March 1968 about two hundred blacks gathered at the Shrine of the Black Madonna to form the RNA. Demanding that the United States cede it five southern states to be run by blacks, the RNA declared itself ready to fight for this cession should other tactics prove unavailing. The functional heads of the organization were the Henry brothers, Milton (Brother Gaedi) and Richard (Brother Imari).

General Gordon Baker and the militant blacks who put out the *Inner City Voice*, several of whom had been associated with the Olympics fracas in 1963, the Freedom Now party, UHURU, the Revolutionary Action Movement, and SNCC, played a part in a wildcat strike of about four thousand black and white workers in the Dodge Main plant on May 2, 1968, that led to the establishment of DRUM. Young blacks had been hired in large numbers at the Dodge plant during the expansion of automobile production that began in 1963. Many of them sympathized with the rioters, if they had not been rioters themselves.

In the months following the establishment of DRUM, demonstrations directed principally at the Chrysler Corporation and the UAW led to the formation of additional RUMs. The RUM organizations joined in 1969 under Baker's leadership to form the League of Revolutionary Black Workers, which pledged itself to wage "a relentless struggle against racism, capitalism and imperialism." The League, whose efforts led to a "significant increase" in black foremen and black UAW stewards, collapsed in the early 1970s.[44]

Some blacks who had been active in the FSD involved themselves along with moderates in the Inner City Business Improvement Forum (ICBIF). This was an all-black, nonprofit corporation established in August 1967 to assist in the establishment of black-owned businesses in the inner city by providing them with grants and loans and by aiding them in gaining federal assistance. Hoping "to promote self confidence and dignity" among blacks, the ICBIF has been characterized as "the first well-organized Black effort geared toward improving Black business." Its funding initially came from the Big Three automobile manufacturers and Michigan Bell, which provided $150,000, and the Detroit banks, which made $703,000 available in Small Business Administration (SBA) participation loans. Although willing to accept money from white-owned corporations and banks, the ICBIF, because of the FSD's experience with New Detroit, initially "would not take money" from that organization. In 1969, however, it accepted $350,000 in grant money and $500,000 in loans from the Economic Development Corporation, which New Detroit, as we shall see, had spawned.

By the end of 1969 the ICBIF had invested or loaned funds to eighty-six black businesses and had participated with the SBA and

Detroit banks in loan packages worth $3.7 million. Its largest loan, for $385,000, went to a new black-owned supermarket on Detroit's west side. The ICBIF also contributed to the establishment of a molded plastics company and a large stamping plant, with which GM and others arranged purchasing contracts. Its "top priority" was the establishment of a black-owned bank that could provide working capital and credit to black businesses. A $1.5 million stock-subscription campaign culminated in June 1970 with the opening of the First Independence National Bank, "the first bank predominantly owned by Black investors." Karl Gregory served as the bank's board chairman during its first four years. The bank continues to operate today, as does a successor organization of the ICBIF.[45]

Like the ICBIF, the United Tenants for Collective Action (UTCA) sought to assist blacks to gain a measure of control over their own lives. Founded in July 1967, before the riot, under the leadership of Fred Lyles, the UTCA sought to force landlords to live up to code requirements, which were being indifferently enforced by city officials. When picketing of slumlords yielded no results, the UTCA, which was aided by the West Central Organization and the TULC, turned to legal aid and private attorneys for help and learned that tenants could withhold rent payments from landlords who failed to provide them with habitable dwellings that conformed to code requirements.

In June 1968 the UTCA won a signal victory against the prominent slumlord, Albert Goodman. Goodman had responded to the picketing of some of his apartment buildings and the withholding of rent by tenants by issuing eviction notices. When the UTCA, however, secured an injunction to prevent Goodman from collecting rents in the affected buildings, he became aware of the weakness of his legal position. He agreed, consequently, to turn over to the UTCA the management and control of seventeen of his apartment buildings, most of them in the Twelfth Street area. After the necessary repairs had been made, the arrangement provided that Goodman was to receive 25 percent of the net income from the apartments, and the remainder was to go to the UTCA. The UTCA also acquired an option to purchase the seventeen buildings. About three weeks after the Goodman-UTCA contract had been signed, Lyles was hit by a bullet that came through the window of his Grand River office and left him paralyzed. The assailant remains unknown.

Aided by a Metropolitan Detroit Citizens' Development Authority grant of $30,000 for a down payment, the UTCA's subsidiary, the United Tenants Rehabilitation Company, exercised the option provided by the Goodman contract to purchase nine apartment buildings containing 335 units for $170,000, "the largest land [sic] acquisition ever made in Detroit [to that time] by an all-black group." By the middle of 1970 the Rehabilitation Company had purchased twenty-one apartment buildings, all but two on the near west side, and was rehabilitating them with federal funds, using black-owned firms and black labor to the extent possible. The organization was, however, forced to dissolve a few years later.[46]

The black thrust for self-determination in the housing area was manifested not only by the UTCA but also by Accord. Blacks who had been associated with the FSD, notably Karl Gregory, conceived the idea of buying up apartment buildings in black areas that were owned by absentee landlords, rehabilitating them, organizing the tenants into cooperatives, and then transferring the ownership to them. The labor on the buildings was to be performed by black companies and black workers. To achieve their goals, the proponents in May 1968 organized Accord as a nonprofit corporation, with Gregory as chairman. It was a black-dominated corporation that included men like Cleage, but whites were also associated with Accord, which helped to discredit Cleage in the eyes of black extremists.

Conceived when apartment prices were depressed because of white flight, Accord anticipated using mortgage money from one apartment building turned over to tenants to acquire another building to rehabilitate. Its hopes were dashed when inflation made the acquisition of mortgage money exceedingly difficult and the federal government undertook a similar program under provisions of the Housing Act of 1968. By the time Accord declared bankruptcy late in 1970 or early in 1971, it had rehabilitated two apartment buildings and had done most of the work on a third building. The UTCA wanted Accord to rehabilitate some of the buildings it had acquired, but Accord could not obtain the financing to do so.[47]

As Councilman Mel Ravitz asserted, the Detroit riot "deepened the fears of many whites even as it raised the militancy of many Negroes." If organizations like New Detroit and the Interfaith Action Council spoke for racial integration after the riot, Breakthrough, on the far right, offered Detroiters quite a different formula for race relations. The riot not only widened the gap between the city's two racial communities but also within them.

Whereas Breakthrough had been able to attract only two to three hundred persons to its meetings before the riot, audiences many times larger than that appeared afterward. When interviewed by a Kerner Commission staffer toward the end of 1967, Donald Lobsinger, Breakthrough's chairman, said that the purpose of his organization was "to arm the whites" and to keep them in Detroit because if the city became black, there would be "guerrilla warfare in the suburbs." Breakthrough had to "step in," its vice chairman maintained, because the police had failed to protect the white community.[48]

At meetings in Detroit and the suburbs attended by "enthusiastic and revivalistic whites," many of them middle-aged, many of them of East European extraction, Breakthrough leaders contended that the riot had been a "Communist-inspired insurrection" whose purpose was to "terrorize" blacks to join "the black power movement," after which the "entire Negro community" could "move in on the whites." Breakthrough urged its followers to purchase weapons, told them what supplies to store in preparation for the next "much more terrifying" riot, and suggested that they arrange for safe locations to which they could send their children when the dreaded event occurred. It advised whites to establish a "block-to-block home defense system" for protection against "bands of armed terrorists" invading from the inner city to "murder the men and rape the women." It cautioned its audiences not to allow themselves "to be misled once more by muddle-headed do-gooders and bleeding hearts" who were proposing as measures to forestall race riots the same kinds of "solutions" as had failed in the past.

Breakthrough meetings were sometimes cosponsored by American Legion posts, the Detroit Police and Firemen's Association for Public Safety, and the Chaldean Society for the Preservation of Liberty. The National Rifle Association displayed weapons at the meetings, and TACT (Truth about City Turmoil), a John Birch front, distributed handbills attacking public officials and alleging, as Breakthrough did, that communists had been behind the riots.[49]

Many whites simply fled Detroit in the wake of the riot. White flight was hardly a new phenomenon, but the rate of departure for the suburbs considerably increased in the aftermath of the riot. An average of twenty-two thousand whites had left Detroit each year from 1964 through 1966, but forty-seven thousand departed in 1967 — it is a good guess that three-quarters of them did so after the riot — eighty thousand left in 1968, and forty-six thousand in 1969.[50] Although the *Detroit Free Press* speculated that the whites who left the city, for whatever reason, were probably more progressive and racially tolerant than those who remained, the fear of blacks among whites in the suburbs to which these Detroiters fled was even greater than in the city itself. Suburban communities hired auxiliary police to patrol their streets and spawned a rash of gun clubs. Television enabled viewers around the country to watch white suburbanites in the Detroit metropolitan area as they practiced pistol shooting. In a random sample survey of nine hundred white suburbanites conducted in May 1968, Donald Warren discovered that just about half were very concerned about the likelihood of racial disorders in the coming months and about 30 percent had taken one action or another because of that concern.[51]

Just as whites were preparing for an onslaught by blacks, so the militant black leadership was warning blacks that the police would provoke an incident as an excuse to attack blacks. Cleage advised blacks in March 1968 to store enough food for a month in anticipation of an invasion by armed, racist suburbanites, and the CCAC the next month scheduled a Black Unity Day Rally to inform blacks about defense and survival methods. Echoing Rap Brown, the *Inner City Voice* warned in a headline, "Detroit's Concentration Camps Waiting for Blacks."[52]

Wild rumors circulated in the black and white communities as tension mounted after the riot, particularly during the first several months of the long Detroit daily newspaper strike that began in November 1967 and continued until August 1968. "The hysteria," Ray Girardin declared at the beginning of March 1968, "is awful." Blacks heard rumors that whites would try to provoke a race war and then would invade the inner city to murder blacks, that the police were training suburban whites to shoot, and that the police were anxious for a riot "to get even" with blacks. In the white community it was rumored that blacks would set fire to the expressways by rolling gas drums down the roads or they would mine or block the expressways and shoot whites in their cars. It was also rumored that blacks would shut off the city's water supply and its public utility service. In the suburbs there was talk of black "killer squads" that would come from the inner city to murder children and of black maids dispatched to suburban communities to poison the residents of the households where they served. The castration of young whites by blacks was a common rumor toward the end of February 1968.[53]

The rumors spreading in the black and white communities were accompanied by mounting gun sales. As Cavanagh told an interviewer, there was "literally an arms race inside the city." The number of licenses to purchase handguns rose from 3,177 between August and December 1966 to 5,675 for the same months in 1967. The police registered 10,416 handguns in all of 1967 but 13,145 during the first six months of 1968 alone. According to "reliable sources," sales of rifles, shotguns, and carbines, which did not have to be registered, tripled following the riot, and there were reports that Detroiters were buying handguns in Ohio, whose gun laws were less restrictive than Michigan's. There was so much demand for ammunition that it became difficult to purchase certain calibers of bullets. A black woman said, "If it starts, you gotta shoot someone you don't even know. If you don't get him, he'll get you, so you get him if you can." A white gun shop owner said that his white customers told him, "just gimme a nigger-killin' gun." In March 1968, the *London Evening Free Press* (London, Ontario) described Detroit as "a sick city where fear, rumor, race prejudice and gun-buying have stretched black and white nerves to the verge of snapping."[54]

Cavanagh sought to put a halt to the "arms race" in Detroit by vainly seeking to persuade the Common Council to require the licensing of the sellers and purchasers of long guns as well as the registration of such weapons and also to restrict the sale of ammunition to legitimate gun users. He appeared on television on March 7 to reassure the citizenry that the police were prepared to prevent trouble and to attack the "voices of the right and the left" that were seeking to divide the city. Those who believed the wild rumors sweeping the city, he accurately stated, were "victims of the riot and its aftermath." To guard against harm resulting from false and irresponsible rumors, the mayor announced that he had instructed the Commission on Community Relations (CCR) to establish a Rumor Control Center that would check out rumors and counter false-hood with truth.[55]

The Rumor Control Center, which was established on March 7, had a special phone line to the mayor and another line to the police precincts and bureaus. It received an average of 132 calls per day prior to the assassination of Martin Luther King, Jr., on April 4, 1968, 915 calls the day after the assassination, and one thousand calls a day for the follow-ing three days. Most calls were from whites in the suburbs.[56]

The CCR reported at the time that a rumor control center, an idea endorsed by the Kerner Commission, was "absolutely vital to a commu-nity experiencing heightened racial tension." Richard Marks's retrospec-tive judgment, however, was that the Detroit center, which tied down staff and prevented them from covering street incidents, was not "valid scientifically or any other way," an appraisal that appears closer to the reality than the CCR's contemporaneous judgment. As Terry Knopf pointed out in his study of rumors and riots, rumor control centers like that of Detroit served the white community and did nothing to deal with the discontents of the black community that led to riots. Rumors, Knopf asserted, do not cause riots but are rather "part of the same process that induces collective outburst."[57] It was to that process that the city of Detroit addressed itself in the aftermath of the July riot.

CHAPTER 17

The Law Enforcement Response

In their discussion of the "ghetto revolts" of the 1960s, Joe R. Feagin and Harlan Hahn indicated that the "establishment response" to the riots took three forms: the riot commission, the "law enforcement response," and the adoption of social and economic reforms to allay ghetto grievances. "The most conspicuous governmental reaction," they noted, was the appointment of a riot commission that documented the causes and course of the rioting and proposed remedies to forestall a recurrence.[1]

Following discussions with several urban specialists and the establishment of the National Advisory Commission on Civil Disorders (the Kerner Commission), Mayor Cavanagh decided against the riot-commission approach.[2] The city administration's posture was to "get on with development in the future and forget the mistakes of the past."[3] Cavanagh entrusted the task of charting Detroit's future to the Mayor's Development Team (MDT), which he appointed the day after Cyrus Vance stated that the riot was over. The mayor recalled his former city controller, Richard Strichartz, then Wayne State University's general counsel, to serve as the MDT coordinator. Cavanagh assigned the MDT the short-range responsibility of dealing with the city's postriot emergency needs and taking such actions as were required "to restore public and community services and alleviate hardship." It was also to act in a "liaison capacity" with the New Detroit Committee, and, most important, it was "to coordinate long-range planning by city departments in creating a blueprint for the social and physical rehabilitation" of Detroit.

The mayor instructed department heads to provide the MDT with reports describing their riot activities and their short-range and long-range plans for the city's restoration and development. Cavanagh, who had been anxious before the riot to restructure the city bureaucracy because he thought it "unresponsive to [the] changing demographic characteristics" of Detroit, believed that the riot had exposed the inadequacies of the city government's programs. He looked to the MDT to "produce results" that could help to heal the city's racial divisions.[4]

Operating "under one-hell-of-a-time constraint," the MDT produced a 750-page report in eighty-five days.[5] In transmitting the report to the mayor on October 26, 1967, the MDT observed that although the riot had caused much physical damage, the damage to the spirit of the people was more serious. The report provided "an agonizing reappraisal" of the performance of the departments and agencies of the city government. The authors of the document charged that the city's manpower and training programs did not constitute "an effective manpower system" and criticized the Department of Parks and Recreation as "an ingrown agency" that was "viewed with hostility by large segments of the community." The MDT concluded that Detroit's programs aimed at social renewal had failed to achieve "a comprehensive network of services"; the public housing program had all too often constituted "a blatant effort to contain the ghetto" and the urban renewal program had failed to provide relocatees with decent, low-cost housing; the Commission on Community Relations (CCR) was "not in touch with the community at a neighborhood level"; relations between the community and the Police and Fire departments left a great deal to be desired; and city government agencies were ill-prepared to deal with the necessary postriot "clean-up job." The MDT's appraisal of the city government was at considerable variance with Detroit's preriot model city reputation.

To strengthen the city bureaucracy and to enable it to guide Detroit's physical and social development, the MDT recommended creation of a City Development Agency and a Social Development Agency. The former was to absorb the City Plan Commission and Detroit Housing Commission (DHC) and perhaps other units at a later time. The Social Development Agency, described as a solution for the existing fragmentation of social services, was to serve as an umbrella unit for such agencies as the Mayor's Committee for Human Resources Development and the Commission on Children and Youth. The MDT also recommended the creation in the mayor's office of an agency to evaluate ongoing city government programs.

As Strichartz said of the MDT report, "the thread throughout the whole thing" was the stress on community participation. The MDT recommended immediate creation of Police Neighborhood Communications Units in each precinct to receive complaints against the police. The MDT envisioned the expansion of these units into Police Neighborhood and Referral Centers that would receive and follow up on citizen complaints about city agencies and services in general. The team also urged the establishment of a Citizens Assistance Agency in the mayor's office that would publish citizen and consumer information. In order to improve relations between the Department of Parks and Recreation and the community, the MDT favored the creation of citizens committees, including youth from the area, in every community center as well as a Central Advisory Committee.

Among numerous other recommendations, the MDT called for programs by the city government and New Detroit to further economic development in the inner city, federal and state programs to deal with the problem of insurance in the inner city, enactment by the Common Council of an open housing ordinance, and stepped-up efforts by the Police and Fire departments to recruit more blacks. Characterizing the lack of jobs and job training as "the largest single obstacle to urban tranquillity," the MDT recommended the creation of small neighborhood training centers, a job placement staff in each high school, and a new community college in Detroit.[6]

In addition to its other roles, the MDT helped to develop "a comprehensive plan of operations" for the city government to put into effect in the event of another riot. It prepared the statement Cavanagh presented to the Kerner Commission on August 15, 1967, and the "Report to the People" that he delivered on September 6. It also prepared the city government's requests for aid from the federal and state governments.[7]

The MDT proposals for revamping the city government's bureaucracy, as was predictable, produced "screams of anguish" and "near universal opposition" from the affected departments and agencies. They claimed either that they were already doing what they were being advised to do, that they needed more money to do it, that it was not worth doing, or that it could not be done. Criticizing a major emphasis of the report, the CCR contended that it was not "lack of communication" that led to riots but "hopelessness" and the "frustration" resulting therefrom. The corporation counsel complained that the report ignored the fact that improving the condition of blacks would not make them "one damn bit more acceptable to the intolerant, bigoted white."

The Community Task Force of the New Detroit Committee contended that the MDT report contained "a great many impractical, irrelevant and self-defeating proposals," set no priorities, did not specify how its recommendations were to be implemented, and was too protective of the mayor. Karl Gregory characterized the report as "a quickie effort to appear impressive," and Albert Cleage thought it "shallow." When asked if he had read the document, one city official responded, "No. I'm waiting for the movie to come out."[8]

In contrast to the report's numerous critics, Cavanagh asserted that he could "not think of a more significant document" in the entire history of Detroit. It would serve, he said, as "a partial guidebook" for the city as it sought to write "a happy ending to the tragic events" of the July riot. In their study of riot commissions, Michael Lipsky and David J. Olson concluded that the MDT had done more than any other riot commission both in alleviating hardship and in providing a blueprint for a riot city's social and physical reconstruction. They noted, however, that the team "wholly failed" to secure the implementation of its recommendations.[9]

It is true enough that the major recommendations of the MDT were "ambushed in the jungle of city government bureaucracy." The proposed structural reforms, for example, were torpedoed by the largely autonomous city departments, which enjoyed the support of their client groups, city employees, and the Common Council. The MDT report, however, was not without some effect. As we shall see, the city government established some neighborhood information and referral centers, and it began to develop a resources and project monitoring system; some city planners were transferred to the DHC; the Police Department stepped up its recruitment of blacks and adopted other MDT recommendations as well; the Common Council enacted an open housing ordinance; there was some modest improvement in the Department of Parks and Recreation; and a small amount of low-cost housing was built. Also, New Detroit and the private sector acted on some MDT recommendations even if the city government did not.[10]

Although Detroit eschewed the riot-commission approach, the state government of Michigan appeared eager to undertake the task. After five different committees of the legislature had shown some interest in studying the riot, the lawmakers created the Joint Legislative Committee to Coordinate Studies of Civil Disturbance. In the end, however, the legislature assigned the task of investigation to the already established Michigan Commission on Crime, Delinquency, and Criminal Administration. In its report, issued on January 3, 1968, the commission stressed the role of undefined organized elements in intensifying and prolonging the riot; and it was critical of police intelligence as well as of the initial police response. It called for the improvement of police-community relations and "dramatic and specific programs in employment, education, and housing."[11]

The Kerner Commission devoted special attention to the Detroit riot. Commission members visited the city in two different groups, toured the riot areas, and met with city and federal officials and local black leaders. One of the commission's field teams conducted numerous interviews in Detroit, assembled information on the city, and prepared a three-volume report for the commission on the background of the riot, the riot itself, and its immediate aftermath.

When Cavanagh testified before the Kerner Commission, he brought along Ray Girardin, Norman Drachler, Hubert Locke, Philip Rutledge, other city officials, and some black militants. The commission was much impressed by their testimony, and it also learned a great deal about black grievances, especially black "fear and hatred" of the police, from the members' meetings with blacks in Detroit. "The most striking aspects of the meeting," a memorandum summarizing one of these sessions concluded, "were the graphic illustrations of the frustration and humiliation of day-to-day Negro life, the expressions of bitterness at the complacency of the whites, and the open distrust of the Commission as a mechanism for change." No doubt what the commissioners heard in and from Detroit explained the stress in their report on "white racism" as being "essentially responsible for the explosive mixture . . . accumulating in . . . [American] cities since the end of World War II." Conrad Mallett was "surprised as hell" at this appraisal since he thought that the commissioners, when they visited Detroit, had "demonstrated an awesome ignorance of the problems black people face in America."[12]

In its account of individual riots, the Kerner Commission report devoted the most space to Detroit. Its general profile of rioters, counterrioters, and the noninvolved relied heavily on Detroit survey and arrest data. Like other riot commissions, the Kerner Commission stressed the need for both improved law enforcement and measures of social and economic reform.[13]

In most communities that had experienced riots, "the most welcome response . . . from the perspective of white powerholding groups" was the strengthening of the forces of control. When the Luby community sample of whites was asked what could be done to prevent future riots, 37 percent first mentioned stronger law enforcement, as compared to 31 percent whose first response was "programs to help the Negroes or the poor." Far stronger white support for a law-enforcement response to the riot was evidenced a few months later in the Campbell-Schuman survey, in which 51 percent of the white respondents thought that strengthened police protection was "the most important thing" the city government could do to prevent another riot, as compared to only 16 percent who assigned the top priority to measures of social and economic reform, equal rights for blacks, and improved police treatment of blacks. Although the Cavanagh administration placed greater stress on the ameliorative than on the law-enforcement approach to riot prevention, the mayor asserted in his initial report to the people of Detroit following the riot, "We must start with law and order."[14]

The center of attention in postriot law enforcement in Detroit was the Department of Police, but the Fire Department also came under city government scrutiny. Although only 2.25 percent of the fire fighters were black at the time of the riot, Chief Charles J. Quinlan attributed this to the civil service requirements that determined departmental hiring standards. The department sought to ease these standards after the riot, but with little success in terms of recruiting more blacks. As of December 1969, when the department adopted a new recruitment program to improve its racial balance, only 45 of the department's 1,704 fire fighters (2.6 percent) were black. The department also sought to improve its relations with the community by sending command officers to block club meetings to acquaint members with departmental problems and concerns.[15]

Seeking to apply the lessons it had learned in the riot, the Fire Department revised its procedures and practices so as to be better prepared should another riot occur. Since it concluded that it had been "critically short" of fire-fighting apparatus and "front line heavy equipment," the department sought and received approval to acquire twenty-eight pieces of additional equipment with bullet-proof windshields. It prepared a new Civil Disturbance Manual and instituted a new training program for fire-fighting personnel that stressed "field operational tactics" in fighting the kind of large fires that might occur in a riot. It equipped all ladder-truck tillermen with high-impact plastic helmets and face shields for protection against thrown objects, and it investigated the use of flak vests, armored vests, and protective goggles. It met with city police, State Police, and the National Guard to devise security measures for fire installations and to arrange for the armed escort of each piece of fire equipment in a riot, and it inventoried strategic locations requiring protection. It launched a program in November 1967 to recruit citizens for a Fire Fighter Auxiliary Force to serve as a reserve in event of a disorder or disaster.

To augment its forces further should another riot occur, the Fire Department reversed preriot policy and negotiated a Selective, Mutual, Emergency Fire Aid Pact with forty-seven communities in the Detroit metropolitan area. "The big plus factor" of the pact, Quinlan informed the Common Council, was that it gave Detroit "back-up reserve fire protection" of at least 50 percent in manpower and equipment.[16]

Poor police-community relations during the postriot period heightened racial tensions in the city. Police departments across the country viewed the 1960s riots as "the conspiratorial product of authoritarian agitators" and as "illegitimate misbehavior" rather than a "legitimate dissent against policies and practices that might be wrong." White police officers in Detroit, as we have seen, were very much of this mind.[17] As the deputy director of field operations for the Kerner Commission observed, the Detroit police, embittered by the riot, were driven even further to the right. To some extent, the police transferred their animosity toward rioters to blacks in general, and police-community relations, a sore point in black-white relations before the riot, became even "worse" afterwards. Blacks complained that their community was actually being "terrorized" by the police. When the *Detroit Free Press* resurveyed riot-area blacks between August 31 and September 25, 1968, a higher percentage of them than just after the riot indicated that the police treated blacks disrespectfully in their neighborhood (57 percent as compared to 41 percent) and used unnecessary force in making arrests (53 percent as compared to 33 percent). Paradoxically, however, 22 percent of the sample thought that police treated people in the neighborhood "better" since the riot, whereas only 15 percent thought the police treatment was "worse."[18]

According to the head of the Police Department's medical division and its director of personnel, an increasing number of police officers suffered emotional disturbances as the result of the riot. The department by early November 1969 had found it necessary to transfer twenty-three police officers to lighter duties because they feared to walk their beats. Other police claimed they were ignoring minor violations lest they become involved in "something bigger." Some, remembering the riot, refused to act on traffic violations when they saw a crowd congregating.[19]

Detroit police officers derived at least one benefit from the riot: because of what he characterized as the "excellent response" of the department during the riot, Cavanagh, following Commissioner Girardin's recommendation, dropped all charges against police officers who had been suspended during the blue flu episode. The police also won the higher pay for which they had been "striking" before the riot. The city agreed to the fact-finders' recommendation that, effective as of July 1, 1968, police salaries were to begin at $7,500 and rise to $10,300 after four years of service. This made the Detroit police the highest paid in the nation.[20]

A conspicuous police riot casualty was the police commissioner himself, Ray Girardin. The riot, the commissioner's wife recalled, broke her husband's heart. "You've got to bleed some, in a job like this," Girardin told Garry Wills. "But my God, I've been gushing." Three days before his sixty-fifth birthday on October 5, 1967, Girardin requested retirement. Despite the trauma of the riot, 52 percent of the black respondents and 58 percent of the white respondents in the Luby community survey thought that Girardin had been performing at least "fairly well." Many blacks regretted the commissioner's decision to retire, the managing editor of the *Michigan Chronicle* appraising Girardin as "the best commissioner" Detroit had ever had. Some of the mayor's aides, however, had reportedly been urging Cavanagh to appoint a new commissioner because they believed Girardin was "too soft an administrator," had handled the blue flu episode poorly, and had reacted too slowly to the beginning of the riot. By the time Girardin made his decision to retire, the Police Department had also lost the services of Hubert Locke, who had intended to return in June 1967 to the Wayne State University post from which he was on leave but had been persuaded by Girardin to defer action until the end of July.[21]

Although Girardin agreed to stay on as commissioner until the mayor could find a successor, he retired as of April 1, 1968. It was not until the end of June, after nine others had turned down the position, that Johannes Spreen agreed to become commissioner. The German-born Spreen had served as chief of operations of the New York City Police Department before leaving that post to teach at the State University of New York. He was sworn in as Detroit's police commissioner on July 22, 1968.[22]

The principal lessons the police high command derived from the July riot were that the department needed additional equipment and a new riot plan. The department requested the city government to provide it with four hundred additional PREP radios; scrambling equipment to prevent the monitoring of the police radio system, which had occurred during the riot; four frequency receivers to permit the "more flexible deployment of task force units in various parts of the city"; seven hundred shotguns, one thousand carbines, and one hundred Stoner rifles, described by an armaments expert as "one of the most brutal weapons in gun history," for use against snipers; twelve hundred gas masks, four thousand gas grenades, two thousand gas projectiles, five thousand Mace gas dispensers, and twenty-five gas guns; 500,000 rounds of ammunition; fifteen hundred flak vests; fifty scout cars; four mobile support vans to provide logistical support for street forces; eight armored personnel carriers that could serve as lead vehicles for tactical formations and provide protection for police from gunfire; an airplane and helicopter for surveillance; two prisoner buses equipped with radios; and prisoner processing equipment. The equipment request totaled $2,131,225.[23]

Cavanagh included the equipment request in a $9.1 million emergency bond package that he submitted to the Common Council in October 1967 that also contained funds for Fire Department equipment and riot overtime pay for policemen, firemen, and other city employees. A Kerner Commission staffer thought that the police were asking for enough weaponry "to wage a moderate-size war," and the *Detroit Free Press*, which judged the request to be "wild and wasteful," agreed. Cleage, who mistakenly thought that the entire $9.1 million was for weapons, said that blacks had to arm themselves to prevent "wholesale killings" since the police were preparing to commit "genocide."[24]

After the Common Council's reduction of the mayor's request had induced a Cavanagh veto, the two compromised toward the end of October on a figure of $7.135 million that reduced the number of weapons the police sought and eliminated the scout cars, armored personnel carriers, and the two aircraft. Although the council at first approved the Stoner rifle request, it killed that controversial item in the end. In addition to the sum the council approved, the Police Department apparently received $100,000 from the federal government for "riot weaponry."[25]

Without waiting for the department's request for arms to go through proper channels, individual police officers began applying for membership in the National Rifle Association (NRA) so as to be able to purchase government surplus rifles at bargain prices. Although those joining the NRA had to certify that they intended to use the rifles they obtained only for target practice, the police officers, reacting to the shortage of weapons during the riot, wanted the weapons to combat snipers. "We need these rifles to fight riots," Carl Parsell, the Detroit Police Officers Association (DPOA) head, candidly declared. The army "reluctantly" agreed to permit the sale of the rifles to the police, about three hundred of whom had taken advantage of the opportunity by early November 1967.[26]

In an effort to determine what changes in its training and riot control procedures were required to deal with possible future riots, the Police Department reviewed every step it had taken in the July riot and also undertook a "methodical and meticulous in-depth study" of all of its existing riot procedures. At a critique session on September 8, twenty-four department officials considered such matters as intelligence, deployment of personnel, command posts, equipment issuance and security, liaison with other units, and the handling of prisoners.[27]

Aware of the mobilization problems that had occurred in the July riot, the Police Department revised its mobilization plan so as to make more men available more quickly. Recalling the small number of police on duty on the morning of July 23, 1967, the department redeployed its manpower to assure that adequate force would be available to respond to a disturbance at any hour. Before the riot only the Big Four cruisers, one per precinct, were equipped with shotguns and tear gas, but after the riot all sergeants' cars carried this equipment.[28]

The department's new riot plan sought to ensure more effective use of the command post system. Manuals were prepared detailing the operation of sector command posts, and the department "pre-installed" detailed instructions, communication equipment, maps, and clerical supplies in each sector post. Unlike what had happened in the July riot, the central and the sector command posts were to have joint staffs made up of representatives of the Police Department, the State Police, and the Guard. Plans were also developed for the joint deployment, control, and direction of the three law enforcement units.

Arrangements were made in the postriot planning for the Police Department to establish close liaison with other city departments and with the public utilities in the event of a disorder. A City of Detroit Master Alert and Mobilization Manual was prepared that applied to all city government agencies. Shaken by efforts in Philadelphia to poison the police, the city government took precautions to ensure that the police received poison-free food in an emergency situation. To relieve police officers from support duties in a riot, the Police Department made a "substantial" effort to recruit and train an Emergency Police Reserve. The reservists, who numbered six hundred by February 1968, were to be used only until "professional auxiliary forces" arrived. Employees of public utility firms and similar businesses were also recruited to serve on the premises of their employer in an emergency.[29]

The revised police riot control plan called for new training programs for administrative, supervisory, and patrol personnel. The specialized training, again with the July riot in mind, included instruction on when weapons were to be used. Lieutenants and sergeants received "command school training" designed to define their responsibilities as ranking officers on the street, while the training of administrative personnel aimed at preparing them for the role of sector commanders. A few officers as well as designated "reaction forces" were specifically trained to cope with snipers.[30]

The revised riot control plan provided for the likelihood of mass arrests in a disturbance. Once a riot developed, a senior staff officer was to take charge of a Prisoner Control Section. Representatives of the prosecutor's office were to report to the precinct stations and the command posts to determine the proper charge for arrestees and to advise regarding the release of arrestees against whom charges could not be sustained. Arresting officers were to be provided with a checklist for writing up arrests designed to speed up the arresting process. The department also made plans to increase personnel in its Identification Bureau so that it could process one thousand fingerprints per day rather than the usual two hundred. A computerized prisoner information center was to be used in a riot to provide a central source of information regarding the location and status of prisoners. Plans were also formulated for the effective utilization of the department's detention facilities and the use, if needed, of other prison locations, a list of which the sheriff prepared. These various arrangements for dealing with prisoners were an obvious response to the severe prisoner problems that had developed during the 1967 disturbance.[31]

Concerned about media attention and rumors in a riot, Cavanagh in March 1968 set up a hot line designed to provide close contact between the city government and the news media in an emergency. As we have seen, the city government in that same month also established a Rumor Control Center. In still another riot control action, the Common Council enacted an ordinance authorizing the mayor to declare a state of emergency in the event of a civil disorder.[32]

The prosecutor's office devised a "riot emergency plan" that called for a "riot executive committee" of senior prosecutors to coordinate prosecutorial activities. There was to be "a constant check" of identifications in an emergency, arrest reports and complaints and warrants were to be combined into a standard form for "high volume charges" such as EW/OB and curfew, and felony charges were to be reduced to misdemeanors "in proper cases." Eventually, the prosecutor devised "a method of preparing all of the pleadings with automated equipment."[33]

The Recorder's Court after the riot transferred its warrant drafting function to the prosecutor's office, thus eliminating what had been a major bottleneck in the court's operations during the riot. The court cooperated with the city's new defender program in planning to supplement its customary method of assigning counsel, and it agreed to work with the Neighborhood Legal Service Centers in employing a pretrial release program rather than resorting to commercial bail-bondsmen. Supplementing the actions of the Recorder's Court, the Legal Aid and

Defender Association developed a comprehensive plan for the participation of volunteer attorneys at every stage of the criminal justice process.[34]

Judge James H. Lincoln spelled out in detail the procedures to be followed by Juvenile Court in the event of a riot with regard to intake, administrative problems, space needs, security, Youth Home management, and the handling of judicial problems. The Michigan Supreme Court in the summer of 1968 adopted "a resolution of policy" regarding the treatment of persons accused of crime and disorder that called for the chief justice or a judicial officer he designated to "direct and coordinate the work of all affected courts" for the duration of the disorder and to do what was necessary "to assure the orderly and efficient administration of justice." The court administrator and his staff were empowered to assign and transfer judges of any court in the state to "emergency judicial duties" and were to employ such legal assistance and clerical help as necessary.[35]

Cavanagh established the Mayor's Committee on the Administration of Justice during Civil Disorders to coordinate the riot plans of the police, the prosecutor, the courts, the bar, and the Legal Aid and Defender Association. The committee was concerned, very much as the Kerner Commission had recommended, with such matters as providing information about arrestees; community relations; mobilization of legal manpower; arrests, booking, and screening procedures; bail procedures (such as releasing misdemeanants at the precincts on interim personal bonds); detention and transportation of large numbers of prisoners; clarification of existing legislation applicable to civil disorders; and court administration and policy.[36]

The Detroit riot not only stimulated the city to revise its riot control procedures; it also served as "a catalyst for a greatly expanded Department of the Army program of preparing for future disturbances." "We got a good deal better geared up" after Detroit, Warren Christopher recalled. On July 27, 1967, President Johnson directed Secretary of Defense Robert McNamara to provide National Guard units with new instructions regarding training for riot control, a subject that Attorney General Ramsey Clark stated at an August 2 cabinet meeting deserved the "highest priority."[37]

By the time of the August 2 meeting, the Continental Army Command had sent Guard units a preliminary list of lessons learned from the Detroit and other riots that they were to take into account in weekend drills. On August 9 the army chief of staff sent all state adjutant generals a 136-page revised schedule for an "intensive training program" that specified thirty-two hours of Guard unit training and an additional sixteen hours of command and staff officer training to be completed by September 30. Eight of the hours, supposedly reflecting lessons learned from the recent disturbances, were to be devoted to such matters as night operations, barricades, measures to protect against looting, arson, and sniping, protection of fire fighters, security of vital installations, and operations in residential and downtown areas. The emphasis in the training was to be on the use of minimum force, using tear gas, for example, before resorting to firearms and surrounding a house before entering it rather than firing volleys at suspected snipers. Eighteen of the thirty-two hours, however, were still devoted to the relatively useless subject of riot control formations.[38]

The continued emphasis on riot control formations in the new Guard training schedule puzzled some adjutant generals, who also complained that the prescribed tactics for dealing with snipers and firebombers consisted of "glittering generalities." Although seen by some as simply a " 'quick fix' measure," the new training program did deal with problems in riot control pinpointed by Cyrus Vance and Major General Charles P. Stone as the result of their appraisal of the tactics used by control forces in seeking to contain the Detroit riot.

The army issued a revised and updated training circular in February 1968 that devoted more attention to such matters as sniping. It also required that all state combat support units assigned to civil disturbance missions receive a minimum of sixteen hours of refresher training and that other combat support units receive at least eight more hours of such training. Michigan's adjutant general regarded the new training circular as a "great improvement" over previous training documents. Possibly because of the new training requirements, the National Guard "behaved with extreme circumspection" in the twenty-two communities to which its units were assigned following the assassination of Martin Luther King, Jr., on April 4, 1968.[39]

On the basis of his Detroit experience, Vance had recommended not only that the riot control training of the Guard be "improved and expanded" but also that federal and state officials review the qualifications of Guard officers, steps be taken by the Guard to recruit more blacks, and "low-priority" Guard units be eliminated and all units be manned at not less than 90 percent of full strength. In accordance with these recommendations, the army appointed a board to study black participation in the Guard and army reserve and another board to review Guard promotion procedures and to make a "general assessment of the qualifications and performance of Reserve Component officers." It also provided for the reorganization of the Guard so that all units would be manned at at least 90 percent of full strength. In addition, the army on August 10 instructed Guard commands to develop "formal riot control plans," and it then initiated liaison and coordination visits to each state by army planning teams.[40]

The army was concerned not only about enhancing the capability of the Guard to control civil disturbances but also about its own readiness for that role. It consequently established a Civil Disturbance Task Group on August 4 to study the recent riots and to evaluate the role of the army and its reserve components in civil disturbances. The Task Group report, completed in December, contained many recommendations concerning "doctrine, planning and operational capabilities." The Task Group was succeeded by the Army Civil Disturbance Committee, which was to be the planning agency for prospective and actual civil disturbances.[41]

The army published a new training circular in January 1968 that stressed planning, coordination, and tactics by army units in dealing with looting, arson, and sniping in built-up areas. Two months later the army issued a revised version of its standard field manual dealing with civil disturbances and disasters that was heavily influenced by the experience of the army and the Guard in Detroit. A new army civil disturbance plan was issued in February that provided for the organization of six brigades that were to be ready to respond to civil disorders within twenty-four hours. Army intelligence was given the responsibility of devising planning packets for 127 cities classified into four priority categories, which met the recommendation in the Vance report on the Detroit riot for "city-by-city planning." Army training teams then visited the cities to aid civil authorities in riot control planning. In February 1968 the army also initiated a five-day Senior Officers' Civil Disturbance Orientation Course at Fort Gordon, Georgia, for army and selected National Guard officers as well as state and local law enforcement officials. Members of the Michigan Guard and the Michigan State Police were among the first to enroll in the course.[42]

The Detroit riot proved to be "a significant turning point" as regards civil disturbance planning for the Department of Justice as well as the Department of Defense. Reacting to the differences he had had with Governor Romney, Ramsey Clark wrote a letter to state governors on August 7, 1967, setting forth the legal prerequisites for the use of federal troops and stating that the governors should address these elements in a written communication to the president but noting that "in case of extreme emergency" an oral request from a governor could lead to the selection of the troops that the president might later dispatch. Romney regarded the letter as a vindication of his position in the dispute with the Johnson administration. Romney could also take some comfort from the recommendation of the Kerner Commission that the word "insurrection" in the federal legislation providing for the use of federal troops in civil disorders be changed to "domestic violence."[43]

Working with the International Association of Chiefs of Police, the Department of Justice beginning in January 1968 invited mayors and chiefs of police to sessions at Airlie House to discuss the prevention and control of civil disorders. The emphasis in these sessions was on community relations, command supervision, and the necessity for a strong initial response to a disorder. Believing that the procedure had been effective in the Detroit riot, the Justice Department also arranged for teams of its officials representing the various units of the department to accompany federal troops dispatched to help quell a disturbance.[44]

Following the recommendation of the Kerner Commission, the Justice Department established the Interdivisional Information Center as "a national center and clearinghouse to develop, evaluate, and disseminate riot prevention and control data." In September 1967 Clark authorized the FBI to develop intelligence regarding the possibility of a conspiracy to initiate or intensify "riot activity." FBI director J. Edgar Hoover's response was to establish the Ghetto Informant Program, a network of racial informants who supplied the FBI with information about developments in black communities across the nation. Shortly before the FBI set up the informant program, Hoover, in another response to the riots, approved a COINTELPRO (counterintelligence program) designed to disrupt and discredit "black nationalist, hate-type organizations." Finally, the Omnibus Crime Control and Safe Streets Act of 1968, whose provisions Hoover had helped to shape, specified that the Law Enforcement Assistance Administration of the Department of Justice was to pay special attention to local projects pertaining to the training of law enforcement personnel to deal with "the prevention, detection, and control of riots and other violent civil disorders."[45]

Like the city of Detroit and the federal government, the state of Michigan following the Detroit riot sought to enhance its ability to cope with civil disorders. Although the Department of the Army before the riot had proposed a 717-man reduction in the size of the Michigan Guard, Secretary of Defense McNamara, responding to the Detroit riot and a plea from Governor Romney, increased the size of the Guard after the disturbance by 510 men. The Guard was subsequently reorganized to bring all units up to 93 percent of full strength.[46]

The Michigan Guard conducted its required thirty-two hour riot training exercise in three separate periods so that the bulk of the soldiers would be available for an emergency at all times. The final eight hours were devoted to a field training exercise in an area of vacant buildings to provide a "realistic environment." The Guard turned aside a Cavanagh request just after the July riot that a Detroit Guard battalion, which would be available to the city in the event of trouble, begin immediate training in antiriot procedures and that the Detroit police and the Guard carry out "a simultaneous test of mobilization, deployment and organizational command as a precautionary measure."[47]

A reporter who drilled in September with a National Guard unit that had served in Detroit found these riot veterans "sullen and feel[ing] sorry for themselves." Many of them fell asleep during classroom sessions of the required training exercise. Irked by General Throckmorton's criticism of the Guard's behavior in Detroit, they drafted a mock letter of apology to him that began, "I am a nervous trigger-happy National Guardsman," and expressed sorrow that they had had to serve under the general. "It was a terrible experience for both of us," the letter concluded.[48]

Following the riot, commanders of the staffs of all Guard units stationed in Detroit during the riot met to review actions taken during the disturbance, examine provisions of Operation Sundown, and revise and update the plan in the light of the Detroit experience. Representatives of the Detroit Police and Fire departments and the State Police joined in the discussion. The revised riot plan provided that in the future the Guard would not necessarily wait for a request from Detroit's mayor to move into the city but would do so on the basis of State Police intelligence reports, again an obvious reaction to what had happened on July 23, 1967.[49]

Reacting to Washington's view that the Detroit riot experience had indicated "strongly" that the Guard must recruit more blacks, Schnipke informed Governor Romney in February 1968 that since there was a freeze on new Guard enlistments at that time and since army policy required the Guard to enlist non-prior service personnel on its waiting list in the order in which they had applied for enlistment, the Michigan Guard had not been seeking to recruit blacks. He noted, however, that the Michigan Guard had secured a list of about twenty-five hundred Detroit blacks with prior military experience whom it would invite as guests to Guard social functions so that they could become acquainted with Guardsmen. This effort was coordinated with the Michigan Civil Rights Commission.[50]

Following the riot, the Michigan state legislature authorized the State Police to add 225 troopers to the force and to enlarge its intelligence section. Reacting to the arson problem during the riot, the Department of State Police added an arson squad to its fire marshal's division. At the conclusion of the Detroit riot, Colonel Davids directed all State Police command officers to submit a critique of their activities during the riot. They were then brought to East Lansing to meet with staff officers and to review operational plans and procedures, training needs, and equipment and communications requirements. As a result of these discussions, the State Police Department devised a new disturbance plan. It also revised its recruit and in-service training "to cover the new dimensions such as sniping, looting and arson" and paid special attention to the use of tear gas in riot situations. State Police officers were dispatched to various locations outside the state to participate in one or another civil disorder training program, and 213 officers took part in several training programs for local law enforcement officers in Michigan.

Before the riot the State Police had not had an independent intelligence operation in Detroit. "We didn't get accurate reporting on what was going on," Romney declared after the riot, "and we're not going to be caught in that position [again]." What this came to mean in practice was that the State Police worked "hand in hand" with the Detroit Police

Department after the riot "to develop the best type of civil disorder intelligence," with the State Police, in Colonel Davids's words, serving as "the central intelligence file."[51]

Like the Detroit Police and Fire departments, the State Police following the riot began to recruit an emergency reserve to man State Police posts in quiet areas when the troopers were dispatched to trouble spots. An all-white force at the time of the Detroit riot, the State Police on August 18, 1967, swore in the first black trooper in the fifty-year history of the organization. Summarizing what the State Police had done to prepare for future civil disorders, Davids wrote Romney, "I do feel we have some good plans and the department is in much better position to respond [to a disorder] than we were in Detroit."[52]

Like the legislatures of many other states that had experienced riots, the Michigan state legislature enacted several new laws following the Detroit riot whose need, the lawmakers believed, that event had made evident. The measures provided a statutory definition of rioting for the first time in Michigan history; made it illegal to possess a Molotov cocktail, block a public thoroughfare without authority, or forge an application to purchase a pistol; and made it a felony to interfere with fire fighters in the performance of their duties.[53]

The effect of riot planning by Detroit, the state of Michigan, and the federal government following the Detroit riot became evident when blacks in Detroit, like blacks in so many other cities, reacted with violence to the assassination of Martin Luther King, Jr., on April 4, 1968. When the Police Department, at 8:13 P.M., learned of the assassination, the commissioner, the superintendent, and the deputy superintendent promptly reported to police headquarters, established liaison with the State Police, the Michigan Guard, and concerned city government agencies, and sent black plainclothes officers into black areas to gather intelligence. The State Police and the Guard put their alert plans into effect and also ordered intelligence officers into the streets. The first "incident" occurred just after 10:30 P.M., when a fire truck rushing to a false alarm was pelted. The Police Department promptly ordered a tactical alert on Twelfth Street, and the afternoon shift, which was to go off duty at midnight, was held over to increase the available manpower. The first firebombing occurred shortly before midnight. Between midnight and 2:00 A.M. on April 5, someone fired at a scout car, wounding two police officers. Within minutes, the police arrested a suspect, who was indicted on a charge of assault with intent to commit murder.[54]

The principal trouble in Detroit following the King assassination occurred on April 5. At 9:40 A.M. black students walked out of Cooley High, where there were fights between black and white students and at least one white student was beaten. Before long more than twenty schools, in several of which there had been some vandalism, had been closed, either because students staged "memorial walkouts" or because school principals ordered the closing. Gangs of thirty to two hundred youngsters roamed the streets, breaking windows, stoning cars, and engaging in sporadic looting. Students also blockaded fire equipment arriving at two east side schools. About two hundred students staged a sit-in in the lobby of the City-County Building, where Dan Aldrich spoke to them and Conrad Mallett gave them bus tickets to return to their homes. Crowds milled about on the west side, and there were reports of looting and fires on Twelfth Street, Dexter, and Linwood. Black workers walked out of Chrysler's East Jefferson plant, forcing it to close.[55]

The response of law enforcement officers to the disorderly conduct of April 5 was both prompt and effective. The Tactical Mobile Unit (TMU) was dispatched to Cooley High at 9:50 A.M., followed quickly by the precinct support unit. Shortly after noon Governor Romney alerted nine thousand Guardsmen in the Lower Peninsula, and they began reporting to their designated armories. At 1:00 P.M. the Police Department ordered "a complete on and off duty mobilization," which was completed in about two hours. At 1:10 P.M. Cavanagh requested National Guard assistance. The Police Department at about the same time set up two sector command posts, and task force groups moved into the affected areas. At 1:30 P.M. the mayor put the city's alert and mobilization plan into effect, ordering departmental liaison personnel to their assigned stations.[56]

At 1:35 P.M. a special United States Army intelligence agent arrived at the police headquarters command post. In contrast to July 1967, Acting Attorney General Warren Christopher advised Romney that the president wished him to know that if the state needed help, the federal government stood "ready to render every appropriate assistance to restore and maintain law and order."[57]

At 2:15 P.M. the Police Department dispatched the Emergency Police Reserve to guard public utilities. Stating that he had learned from the 1967 riot that "prompt and effective action" was critical in responding to a disturbance, Cavanagh declared a state of emergency at 3:15 P.M., imposing a curfew from 8:00 P.M. to 5:00 A.M. and placing restrictions on the possession and carrying of firearms and inflammable materials, the sale of alcoholic beverages, and large assemblages. Later in the afternoon Romney issued an emergency proclamation for Wayne County that paralleled the mayor's proclamation.[58]

The police sealed off Twelfth Street at 3:00 P.M., and a task force of the TMU, the Mounted Bureau, and the Motor Traffic Bureau swept the street and kept it clear by saturation patrolling. The police shot three looters fleeing after "breaking and entering," one of them near Twelfth and Clairmount and one of whom died the next day. The Guard and the State Police took the field around 5:00 P.M., and by the next day four thousand Guardsmen and four hundred troopers were on duty in Detroit. The Fire Department, which promptly put its civil disturbance plan into effect, responded to 480 alarms on April 5 and 6, little above the daily average for the month; but the fire fighters had to deal with more than twice as many incendiary fires as on an average April day.[59]

Romney, who stated on April 5, "We have learned that action in time can prevent trouble," accurately reported at a press conference on April 6 that the situation was "in very good control." Schnipke let it be known that Guardsmen, unlike during the July riot, would fire only if fired upon and only if they knew who had shot at them. As it was, the Guard fired not a single shot that day. Although the forces of law and order were in firm control, the curfew continued in effect for three more days. Blacks complained that the curfew was unequally enforced against them and that suburban law enforcement officers subjected blacks going to their jobs to unreasonable searches and seizures and "unprecedented verbal abuse." Detroit police on April 9 arrested three prominent blacks who had returned to the city from Dr. King's funeral during curfew hours. They were held for seven hours without being permitted to post bond, the officers, who allegedly abused them verbally, refusing to acknowledge the reason for their violation of the curfew. Judge George Crockett called for the suspension of the police inspector who had refused to obey his order to release the men. "I'm convinced," Crockett said, "that the Detroit Police department is the sickest, most dangerous agency in this city."[60]

Of the 2,074 arrests the police made from April 5 through April 11, 517 were white, 199 were women, and 189 were juveniles. It is uncertain, however, how many of the arrests were actually riot-related. Although 40 percent of the arrests, for example, were for breaking and entering or larceny, the official Police Department report of the riot lists only sixty-eight instances of looting. The police were shot at only twice during the disturbance, the Guard only once. Seven civilians were shot, one of them, as we have seen, fatally.[61]

Although such cities as Washington, D.C., Baltimore, Chicago, and Kansas City experienced a great deal of violence following the assassination of Martin Luther King, Detroit was able to quell its disturbance with only one death, injuries to twenty-two persons, fifty-five incendiary fires, a minimum of looting, and property damage of only a little more than $80,000. There were several reasons why the April 1968 disturbance in Detroit ended with so little damage and anguish as compared to the riot of July 1967. As John Nichols noted, the time of day at which the trouble began was in the department's favor, and it also had the advantage of "preliminary warning signals." Of greater importance though, as Girardin observed, the police, the Guard, and the State Police had "profited" from their "costly experiences" in the July riot. This was the first test of the Police Department's revised riot control plan, and as Nichols recalled, it became "a model for much of the country" as the result of its successful application.

The entire law enforcement operation in April was conducted in "an efficient, orderly professional" manner, reflecting the intense riot planning and the improved training of the police, the Guard, and the State Police that had followed the July riot. The effect of the training was especially apparent in the "efficiency, appearance and restraint" of the Michigan Guard, some of whose least qualified officers had been weeded out or left the organization since July 1967. The early "saturation" of the disturbance areas by law enforcement personnel prevented the formation of mobs and the initiation of violence, and the early shooting by the police of fleeing looters may very well have discouraged the large-scale looting that police restraint appears to have encouraged at the outset of the 1967 riot. The Fire Department, for its part, had also learned from its 1967 experience that the "quick and positive suppression of fires," especially those of an incendiary nature, helped to dampen "mob readiness" since large fires attract a crowd.[62]

It was not only improved riot control tactics that account for the failure of the April disturbance to escalate into a major riot. The city's blacks, having so recently experienced a major riot, were hardly of a mind to become involved in another such event. The black leadership as well as grass-roots people made a determined effort to preserve the peace. Teams of blacks used the phones to urge parents to keep their youngsters off the streets. "There's a new sophistication here," declared Robert Tindal. "Negroes saw it was black people who died in riots." Cleage put it differently: "Black people," he said, "are just too busy for rioting, for throwing molotov cocktails." Whatever the reason for Detroit's success in coping with the reaction to the King assassination, Cavanagh thought it was an important "turning point" for the city. "You can't smell insurrection in the air any more," he was quoted as saying.[63]

Although the Cavanagh administration could hardly have predicted the assassination that triggered the disorder of April 1968, it had been concerned from the beginning of 1968 about devising programs to prevent any recurrence in the summer of 1968 of the events of late July 1967. The Youth Opportunity Council (YOC) that Cavanagh had created just before the 1967 riot advised the mayor's office in January that it was essential both to provide summer jobs for young people and to involve them in the planning for a summer program. This, the YOC believed, would make the youngsters feel as though they "belong[ed]" and had a future in Detroit and would also serve as a riot preventive. Before the month was out, the mayor had appointed Robert L. Potts, the executive director of the Citizens Committee for Equal Opportunity (CCEO) and chairman of the Virginia Park Rehabilitation Committee, to coordinate a summer program involving employment, education, and recreation for inner-city youths.[64]

"Detroit Is Happening," as the summer program came to be known, was financed by the United Fund, United Community Services, New

Detroit, the federal government, and private individuals and companies, more than $1 million being raised from these sources. Young people were "directly involved" in planning the program, and Potts and his staff also sought the advice of a variety of public and private agencies. The program encompassed "the largest variety and quantity of special vacation projects" in Detroit's history. Finding summer jobs, particularly for inner-city youths, ranked at or near the top of the objectives of the summer program. A Job Central that the YOC established served as an employment agency, and both the National Alliance of Businessmen (NAB)[65] and the Neighborhood Youth Corps aided the effort. Despite the shortcomings of the NAB's contribution, the employment drive produced thirty thousand jobs, well above the number earlier summer programs had been able to generate.

As part of Detroit Is Happening, thirty thousand young men and women enrolled in summer school classes, and an additional seventy thousand received remedial education of one sort or another. The Department of Parks and Recreation, as its contribution, mounted the "most ambitious" and "best staffed" recreational program in its history. In addition to its playgrounds, gyms, play locations, swimming pools, and street showers and its program of individual and team sports, the department used mobile units "to bring the advantages of a park right into the inner-city," and its playmobiles transported portable play equipment to inner-city locations. The recreation program also included a camping experience for more than fifty thousand inner-city youngsters.

Detroit Is Happening included a heavy emphasis on cultural programs. Black Arts and Culture Workshops and Teen Drop Inn Centers were established at which city youths studied black history and culture and where cultural events were staged. In addition to "a full range of concerts, shows and other cultural events," young people were taken on trips to cultural centers.

As part of Detroit Is Happening, the YOC enlisted two thousand young people in community beautification efforts, and another fifty thousand youths participated in what was characterized as "the largest inner-city clean-up drive in Detroit's history." The YOC also formed neighborhood youth patrols whose activities included mediating gang fights and escorting women to bus stops in unsafe neighborhoods.[66]

Although the authors of a report on Detroit Is Happening appraised the program, despite all that it had accomplished, as only "moderately successful," they noted that it had achieved its goal of providing opportunity for inner-city youngsters. If Detroit Is Happening is to be seen, at least to some degree, as a riot preventive, it can be said that Detroit was riot-free during the summer of 1968, the police nipping in the bud a disturbance allegedly planned for July 24.[67]

The Police Department understood that, although it was essential to have a riot control plan, the department could do its part to avoid racial trouble by improving police-community relations. Police-community relations were a major concern not just of the Police Department but of New Detroit and the MDT as well. New Detroit's Community Services Subcommittee thought it necessary to take "a new look at the entire police department" because the prevalence of police brutality indicated "absence of professionalism from the top down." The "Detroit Police Department[,] as is true of every metropolitan law enforcement agency," New Detroit asserted, "is the personification of all that is deficient, intolerable or 'sick' in 'the system' with which the Negro feels he must cope." New Detroit assumed that the nation was watching Detroit as the city where "it couldn't happen" and that whatever actions it took regarding the police would set the pattern for the nation.[68]

Acting on a Cavanagh suggestion, New Detroit began a search for a professional police investigator, to be hired jointly by New Detroit and the city, to examine the Police Department and make recommendations for its improvement. The assignment was entrusted to Arthur F. Brandstatter, director of the Michigan State University School of Police Administration and Public Safety, who agreed to complete the study in three years. On January 3, 1968, however, Cavanagh announced the abrupt end of the study, allegedly because of the expected appointment of a new police commissioner, a reorganization of the department then underway, and the intended length and cost of the study. The real reason for the termination decision, however, appears to have been "bureaucratic resistance." Brandstatter could do little more than issue a preliminary report in which he noted that the planning function of the department was "geared almost entirely to 'crisis' or short-term planning" and that citizen complaints were not being adequately processed.[69]

The MDT thought that the establishment of the precinct Neighborhood Communication Units that it had recommended would "humanize" the Police Department in the eyes of the citizenry. Cavanagh recommended the establishment of twelve Police Neighborhood Information and Referral Centers, as he named them, but the Common Council refused approval. The council also rejected a Police Department proposal of January 1968 to use three storefront offices as Neighborhood Information Centers. Before Cavanagh left office, however, the department had opened storefront offices in four precincts, funded by neighborhood business and civic groups and, since the council had forbidden the use of police in such offices, staffed by community service aides trained by the New Careers Division of the Mayor's Committee for Human Resources Development.[70]

In November 1967 the Police Department inaugurated a human relations program for six hundred officers designed to educate police regarding their role in a changing society. One point stressed in the program was that riots could be prevented by the reform of social conditions. In August 1968 the Police Department announced that newly appointed sergeants would henceforth receive training that included not only command responsibilities but community relations and a "refresher course in law and procedures."[71] Neither the new training for sergeants, the human relations program for patrolmen, nor the precinct storefront offices, however, contributed in any significant way to an improvement in police-community relations during the remainder of the Cavanagh administration.

The manner in which the Police Department processed citizen complaints was a key determinant of the state of its relations with the black community. As a member of the Citizen Complaint Bureau (CCB) wrote its commanding officer, citizens were less concerned about the inevitable mistakes police officers made than about efforts to cover up those mistakes.[72] In the main, blacks could derive scant satisfaction from the way the CCB functioned following the July riot.

According to the head of the CCB, Girardin immediately following the riot did not want complaints against the department investigated too strenuously since he feared that this would detract from his efforts to restore departmental morale, which had been shaken by the riot. Mallett informed the mayor's office in December 1967 that, since the riot, the CCB, in the opinion of its staff members, had been "ignored, its recommendations unheeded, and its operations downgraded." Brandstatter characterized the CCB at the beginning of 1968 as "in 'limbo[,]' with no action being taken on complaints."[73]

The immobilization of the CCB aroused the strong concern of the Michigan Civil Rights Commission (CRC), leading it to demand a meeting with Cavanagh in February 1968. The CRC's executive director, Burton Gordin, informed Girardin that same month that the Police Department had failed in sixteen cases to implement conciliation agreements arrived at between the CRC and the CCB. Police officers, in violation of the agreement between the Police Department and the CRC, were refusing to be interviewed by the CRC, and Girardin had failed to take the disciplinary action against these officers that the agreement specified. Gordin informed the CRC executive staff that the cases the CRC had filed against the Police Department proved that police officers abused their authority and that their supervisors and peers "all too often" either condoned or did not interfere with the misbehavior.[74]

The Police Department issued new "Guidelines for the Successful Handling of Citizen Complaints" on February 1, 1968, noting that the glossing over of the "truth" regarding complaints was a "major source of problems" in the area of police-community relations. The new procedures, however, were without discernible effect. Although the investigation of complaints was "comprehensive and complete," the problem, as the Detroit branch of the National Association for the Advancement of Colored People (NAACP) asserted, was that "prompt, effective and public action" did not follow. Cavanagh blamed the ineffectiveness of the CCB, at least in part, on the "extremely active role" the DPOA played in the Police Department.[75]

Of 213 citizen complaints processed by the CCB in 1968, twenty-six were sustained, and thirty-three, partially sustained. About 90 percent of the complaints involved allegations of the use of "excessive force" by the police.[76] At the end of July 1969 Commissioner Spreen issued new rules for the handling of citizen complaints. A new advisory panel comprised of a representative of the commissioner, the head of the CCB, and the civilian administrative assistant to the commissioner was to study the case reports and make recommendations to the commissioner; additional supervisory personnel were assigned to investigations; teams of investigators were to deal with large-scale investigations; new complaints were to be processed within ninety days; and there was to be a monthly public disclosure of the status of cases without names being mentioned.[77]

When he announced his new complaint rules, Spreen reported that of the 274 cases pending when he had taken office twelve months earlier or filed since then, 233 had been resolved by June 1, 1969. Of these, 31 had been sustained and 34 partially sustained. Once again, however, new rules appeared to make little difference in the responsiveness of the Police Department to complaints. A committee studying police-community relations reported in December 1969 that the complaint procedure was "out of hand." Official conclusions in cases, the committee reported, were often not prepared, notices of reprimand were not placed in the personnel files of the officers involved, follow-up was lacking, and there were "investigatory breakdowns." In the committee's judgment, the CCB was "a mystery to most policemen."[78]

In September 1969 the Police Department revised its "archaic" trial board procedures. Attorneys for civilian complainants and witnesses were thereafter to be permitted to attend full proceedings of the board, and the Commission on Community Relations (CCR) and the CRC could send observers. Attorneys for both sides were to have equal access to investigative reports submitted in evidence. The Michigan state bar was asked to establish a roster of volunteer attorneys to serve as nonvoting legal advisors to the board. As with the CCB, however, the Police Department had improved its established procedures, but the results did nothing to allay black concerns about the fairness of the process.[79]

Disenchantment with the processing of complaints by the Police Department led to black demands for a civilian review board. In August 1969 state Senator Coleman Young proposed the creation of a civilian board made up of one elected representative from each precinct that would have full disciplinary powers in responding to civilian complaints. The proposal attracted the support of the Detroit NAACP, the Human Relations Council of the Detroit Archdiocese, the Metropolitan Detroit Branch of the American Civil Liberties Union (ACLU), the National Lawyers Guild, and the Association of Black Students of Wayne State

University. Proponents of the measure failed, however, in the effort to have their proposal submitted to a referendum of the voters in the 1969 election.[80]

The small number of blacks in the Police Department, like the reaction of the department to citizen complaints, was a source of tension between the police and the black community or, to put it more accurately, between the police and the black leadership. As the Luby and Campbell-Schuman postriot surveys indicated, blacks in the city as a whole were far less concerned about the race of police officers than about their behavior. It is true, however, that in the riot areas, according to a *Detroit Free Press* survey of the late summer of 1968, 49 percent of the respondents thought that "things" would have been "better" in their part of town had more police officers been black.[81]

About 5 percent of the Detroit police force (237 of 4,326 officers) were black at the time of the riot, and blacks were even less well represented in the ranks of sergeant and above.[82] For 1967 as a whole, the Police Department hired 71 blacks, as compared to 38 in 1966 and as compared to the 112 it would have hired according to an expert's analysis of the relevant labor market had there been no discrimination. Blacks constituted 47 percent of the applicants for positions in the department but only 22 percent of those hired, indicating that the increase in the percentage of black officers at that time depended less on the willingness of blacks to make police work a career than on their ability to satisfy the department's hiring requirements. In October 1967 the department appointed its first black district inspector, and it designated another black to be second deputy commissioner, the number three position in the department.[83]

The year 1968 witnessed a stepped-up effort to add blacks to the Police Department. The mayor's office, the CCR, New Detroit, the CCEO, the Interfaith Action Council, and the Coordinating Council on Human Relations all lent their weight to this effort. Following a meeting of the mayor with the CCEO, Girardin in April 1968 requested a team that included five psychologists and was headed by Lawrence Vickery, on loan from General Motors to New Detroit, to review the Police Department's recruitment procedures. In its report of May 22, 1968, the Vickery committee recommended changes in the age, physical, and educational requirements for police hiring since it concluded that the existing standards were not related to job performance. It also recommended that "a brief standardized test of 'problem solving ability' " administered by an outside agency in a location outside the department replace the two-and-a-half-hour written examination then being used and that the committee contended had no bearing on police performance. The committee favored the establishment of a permanent oral review board of trained interviewers that included one black and recommended that the marital status of applicants be ignored, a record of juvenile offenses and misdemeanors not automatically disqualify an applicant, traffic and felony records be subject to review for mitigating circumstances, more blacks be assigned to investigate the background of applicants, and the time interval between approval of an applicant and the actual hiring be substantially reduced.

Cavanagh ordered the implementation of the Vickery recommendations, and the Police Department had put most of them into effect by early July. Fearing that the police "system" was being used to "frustrate" the implementation of the recommendations, Vickery did not regard the new twelve-minute written test the department had introduced as being bias-free (blacks failed the test at three times the white rate); and he was dissatisfied that the examination continued to be administered inside the department. Also, white applicants continued to be favored over black applicants in the preliminary screening, and the oral boards continued to make "anti-black judgments."[84]

Cavanagh took two additional steps in May 1968 to spur police recruitment of blacks. He appointed a Special Task Force on Police Recruitment and Hiring that was cochaired by Ross Corbit of the Greater Detroit Board of Commerce and Robert Tindal, executive secretary of the Detroit NAACP, and included such prominent blacks as Roy Allen, Coleman Young, Frank Ditto, and Inspector George Harge. At the suggestion of the committee, Cavanagh also arranged for the Police Department to put together a team of sixteen black and four white officers, headed by the black Lieutenant Avery Jackson, to devote full time for six weeks to an extensive recruitment campaign. The Jackson group was able during that time to compile a "reservoir" of more than nine hundred blacks who appeared to be eligible to take the examination for the Police Department, but more than half of these individuals failed to appear for either the required physical or mental examination.[85]

The Special Task Force endorsed and monitored the Vickery recommendations. It reported in August that community service officers were contacting all the unsuccessful black applicants of that year to inform them of the new standards for police personnel, to encourage their reapplication, and also to let them know that the Detroit Urban League had begun to counsel unsuccessful applicants in an effort to help them meet whatever requirements they had failed to satisfy. The Task Force recommended that twenty-five hundred additional police officers, fifteen hundred of them black, be added to the department.[86]

Between January 1 and June 22, 1968, the Police Department hired 154 whites but only 38 blacks. Also, of a class of 36 in the Police Academy on July 1, only 5 were black, "a dramatic reversal of past trends," according to the mayor's executive secretary. Since the department was only 350 officers short of its authorized complement at that time, the mayor's aide believed department officials were "pushing those white applicants in the pipeline ahead" as fast as they could so that the full strength of the department could be reached without altering its racial balance.

Seeking to increase the proportion of blacks in the department to 10 percent, Cavanagh responded to the information his executive secretary had provided by instructing the police commissioner to arrange for quotas of blacks and whites in academy classes beginning on July 8. When the mayor discovered that his instructions were being "subverted" by the department, he secretly ordered the commissioner on August 9 to fill the remaining 202 vacancies in the department in the ratio of four blacks to one white.[87]

Despite his order, Cavanagh learned in the middle of October that only about one-third of the members of the academy class of 60 that was to begin on October 21 were black. Spreen, who was opposed to "any form of quota hiring" and complained, as did other police officials, about the alleged lowering of standards, privately indicated that he could not adhere to the mayor's August 9 directive. Also, someone in the department leaked the four-to-one order to one of the mayor's political enemies on the council after Cavanagh had denied issuing such an order. Despite foot-dragging by police officials, however, the department added 180 blacks to the force in 1968, which constituted about 35 percent of the number hired that year and exceeded the total number of blacks recruited from 1962 through 1967. The recruitment of blacks slackened in 1969 to 23 percent of those hired. Had there been no discrimination, the department, according to the aforementioned expert analysis of the relevant labor market, would have hired 239 black police officers in 1968 and 241 in 1969. Cavanagh, nevertheless, could take some comfort from the fact that during the years 1962–69, the years of his mayoralty, the percentage of blacks in the Police Department had increased more than fourfold, from 2 to 9.[88]

The slowly increasing percentage of blacks on the Detroit police force did not alter the fact, as Tindal put it, that "every confrontation" between the police and blacks became "a racial confrontation" because of the largely white complexion of the Police Department. In February 1968 Gordin told the CRC and, apparently, Cavanagh that the police and the city's blacks seemed to be on "a direct collision course" and that "dramatic remedial action" of a kind no city had ever before undertaken was required. On April 11 the Michigan State Advisory Committee to the United States Civil Rights Commission informed Governor Romney that "the greatest threat to racial peace" in the state was the manner in which law enforcement officers operated in and serviced the black community.[89]

On May 13, 1968, after the first contingent of the Midwest Caravan of the Southern Christian Leadership Conference's Poor People's Campaign had arrived in Detroit, the first in a series of confrontations between the Detroit police and blacks occurred that exacerbated police-community relations until the end of the Cavanagh administration. A police escort, which had picked up the marchers in Toledo, escorted them to the Blessed Sacrament Cathedral in Detroit, where Cavanagh welcomed them to the city. While the marchers were meeting in Cobo Hall, the city's large convention center, Sergeant Fred Wright told the driver of a caravan car—it was apparently the command car—that was stalled in the service drive in front of the hall, away from traffic, to move the vehicle. The driver responded that the car's battery was dead, but he was apparently reluctant to permit the vehicle to be towed away, as the sergeant insisted. Answering the driver's call for assistance, about forty caravan members quickly surrounded the car and climbed upon it, singing and clapping their hands. Although Lieutenant Ted Sikora and an unidentified officer apparently decided that the car could remain where it was since it was not obstructing traffic, Sergeant Wright signaled for a tow truck to move forward.[90]

Reacting to the crowd that had moved around and onto the stalled vehicle, Sikora called for the assistance of the Mounted Bureau. What happened then was witnessed by three CCR observers, four CCB members, and two officials of the Community Relations Service (CRS) of the Department of Justice and also became the subject of a comprehensive CCB investigation. Within a few minutes of Sikora's call for help and while caravan marshals were trying to get the crowd outside to return to Cobo Hall, fifteen to twenty mounted police charged into the marchers "swinging billy clubs indiscriminately and trampling men, women, and children." The police drove the fleeing marchers into the hall, where they were met by "baton wielding" foot patrolmen who attempted to push them out of the building. "This," according to a CCR observer, "led to the chasing and trampling of the blacks indiscriminately in the vestibule area and up and down the main hallway!" This same observer noted at least four instances of groups of police officers beating blacks who had fallen to the ground. Additional police, including a group of TMU officers, arrived on the scene, and some of them joined in the assault, beating "many persons maliciously to the ground." Although they had PREP radios, there was "a total lack of communication" between the mounted police outside and the foot patrolmen inside the hall.

Worse trouble threatened when an officer removed a carbine from a squad car trunk. Told to put the weapon back by a black CCR observer, the officer responded that the police did not "take orders from no NIGGERS"; but he returned the weapon to the trunk when one of the CRS observers told him his action was "unnecessary and inflammatory." After about an hour the two CRS observers were able to persuade the lieutenant commanding the mounted unit to remove his men. The same officer had earlier responded to a similar request by one of the CRS observers, who had identified himself, by having his horse step on the foot of the official. The police claimed that only four persons had suffered injuries in the melee, but others placed the injury toll at twenty-six. The CCR, CCB, and CRS observers all agreed that the police attack on the marchers both inside and outside Cobo Hall was "completely unwarranted and unprovoked."[91]

Some leaders of the Poor People's Campaign and more than one hundred marchers carried their protest about the police action directly to Cavanagh and demanded the suspension of three officers identified by their badge numbers. Andrew Young told the mayor that the police had "brutalized" the marchers, and Hosea Williams asserted, "Either there is a conspiracy here in Detroit or someone is guilty of gross negligence." An interracial group that included John Conyers, Ernest Mazey, Coleman Young, and Father James Sheehan denounced the police behavior in a letter to Cavanagh as "a demonstration of callous racism" and warned, with 1967 in mind, "This is the stuff of which riots are made."[92]

Cavanagh promptly ordered an investigation of the Cobo Hall affair, entrusting the task to Conrad Mallett. The principal investigation, however, was by a six-man CCB team. After about two weeks the department announced the suspension of Wright for "conduct unbecoming an officer" and Sikora for "neglect of duty," but the trial board subsequently cleared both officers. Dissatisfied that officers whom citizens had identified as beating marchers had not been suspended and alleging that they could not obtain any information from the department, a newly formed Ad Hoc Action Group vented its displeasure by picketing police headquarters. Made up primarily of white middle-class individuals and coordinated by Sheila Murphy, a *Catholic Worker* employee, the Ad Hoc Action Group was essentially a "cop watching" organization.[93]

The CCB, as the result of its investigation, was able to identify the officer who had removed the carbine and another officer who had engaged in a physical altercation with a black. Carl Heffernan, the head of the CCB, softened the agency's report, however, by claiming that evidence from many sources indicated that marchers had "taunted and harassed" the police during their march. Whether or not this was true of the caravan before it arrived in Detroit, there is no evidence that there was any provocation in front of Cobo Hall preceding the police attack.[94]

Although Cavanagh concluded that command officers on the scene at Cobo Hall had been guilty of "some extremely bad judgment, to put it mildly, both of omission and commission," he thought that the trial board's acquittal of the two officers closed the case. The case was reopened, however, when Sheila Murphy released copies of the eyewitness reports of the two CRS observers. This action led to an unsuccessful lawsuit filed in federal court against the individuals named in the two reports by a group that included Lonnie Peek. Also, Spreen, who had been silent about the matter, finally issued a statement in November alleging that there had been "errors" on both sides and reporting that the two officers the CCB had named had been suspended. The officer who had wielded his nightstick "with great force" against a bystander was subsequently ordered to forfeit fifteen leave days, the one who had removed the carbine, three days.[95]

By the time the May 13 episode had finally been resolved, other events had served to keep police-community relations in a state of high tension. Shortly after the Cobo Hall incident, dozens of police officers stormed out of a Common Council hearing shouting racial epithets at Robert Tindal, who had been arguing against permitting Detroit police officers to live outside the city. In July 1968 the Common Council passed and the mayor approved a stop-and-frisk ordinance that the black community saw as directed at it.

The enactment of the stop-and-frisk ordinance reflected a mounting concern about crime in Detroit that followed the riot. Detroit had averaged about 130 homicides per year during Cavanagh's first term, but there were 214 murders in the city in 1966, 281 in 1967, and 389 in 1968. The *Detroit American*, published while the regular city dailies were on strike, played up crime news and implied that blacks were the major cause. The Common Council late in February 1968 tabled a stop-and-frisk ordinance, but the result was different in July. The ordinance authorized the police to stop and make a "limited search" of individuals if there was "reasonable cause" to believe their behavior warranted investigation for "criminal activity" or if there was "reasonable cause" to believe the officer or someone else was in danger. In signing the measure, Cavanagh stated that he would not "tolerate" its abuse, and he instructed the Police Department and the corporation counsel to draw up "strict guidelines" for the ordinance's enforcement.[96]

The mayor's approval of the stop-and-frisk ordinance produced a heated response from the black members of the Special Task Force on Police Recruitment and Hiring and their eventual resignation. They denounced the mayor's action as "a clear and final capitulation to the get tough 'take the handcuffs off the police' demands of . . . certain police organizations and the bigots" and "a slap in the face" of the Task Force. They demanded that Cavanagh act on three demands they had previously made, namely, the appointment of a civilian review board, appointment of blacks to head the five predominantly black precincts, and issuance of an order dealing with police "racism." They warned that the "largely lily-white Racist Police force" was capable of "provoking new rebellions" in the ghetto, the constant refrain when police-community relations took a turn for the worse in the riot's aftermath. Cavanagh responded that the voters would have to approve the creation of a civilian review board and that the scheme had not proved effective where it was employed; that two of the department's three black inspectors headed precincts; and that Spreen, who had been sworn in only a few days earlier, had agreed with the mayor to issue a departmental order on racism.[97]

Following a strong reminder by the mayor, Spreen on August 2 issued the promised directive. Stating that "racism or abusive treatment of citizens, whether physical or verbal," would not "be tolerated," the order admonished police officers to treat all citizens with every "possible courtesy and consideration" and not to resort to "derogatory racial designations" no matter how "severe" the circumstances. Spreen on that same day also issued guidelines for police enforcement of the stop-and-frisk ordinance, which went into effect on August 8. The police were reminded that the Fourth Amendment was "applicable to all persons at all times" and that police officers had to be prepared to account for their actions. They were justified in making a search, the guidelines stated, only if they believed the suspect was armed and dangerous. A search that went beyond the "patting down" of the suspect, the police were instructed, could be conducted only after "formal arrest on probable cause."[98]

A second Cobo Hall incident on October 29, 1968, followed on November 1 by still another police-black confrontation, further embittered police-community relations. Cobo Hall II, as it came to be known, resulted from a George Wallace rally in the hall. While Wallace supporters and hecklers battled one another with fists and chairs inside Cobo Hall, a crowd of several thousand milled around outside, heckling the police and Wallace supporters and setting fire to a Wallace pennant and picket sign. After the crowd apparently failed to heed an order to disperse, the police decided to clear the area. As they moved forward, their nightsticks at chest level, a TMU officer fell to his knees, having been blinded by Mace thrown by someone in the crowd. There may also have been interference by some in the crowd with a police effort to make an arrest. In any event, a CCR observer heard an officer say, "Let's get em, let's get em," and the police began flailing away at the crowd. Sheila Murphy claimed that two officers sandwiched her and that one of them said, "We'd kill you if we thought we could get away with it." The attitude of the police, according to a CCR observer, was, "Hit as many people as possible and they won't do that again." There were second and third attacks on the wounded, some officers removing their badges once the action became "hot."

Chased by the police, several hundred demonstrators ran toward the nearby Pontchartrain Hotel. Some anti-Wallaceites stood on the fifteen-foot-high patio outside the hotel, threw stones at the police, and shouted insults at them. The officers charged, swinging their clubs. Some demonstrators jumped to the sidewalk below, others ran through the hotel. Police and sheriff's deputies chased them down Washington Boulevard, a main downtown thoroughfare, clashing with them and jabbing them in the back and chest with nightsticks.[99]

The police action in the Cobo Hall II incident led to renewed picketing of police headquarters by the Ad Hoc Action Group. Criticizing the police behavior as "deliberate" and as having proceeded "according to a pernicious plan," the Detroit ACLU complained to Cavanagh that the failure of the Police Department and the mayor's office to take effective action against police misbehavior in the Cobo Hall I affair had encouraged a repeat performance. Spreen complied with demands for an investigation, but his report of the affair, which was not released until early March 1969 and which blamed anti-Wallace demonstrators for what had occurred, cleared the sheriff's deputies and the police involved despite photographs in *Detroit Scope* showing police officers clubbing civilians.[100]

Cobo Hall II was soon overshadowed as a source of police-community discord by an ugly episode that occurred outside Veterans Memorial Hall on the night and early morning of November 1–2, 1968. The Ebenezer AME Church was sponsoring a high school dance on the hall's sixth floor that was attended by a black audience, while on the first floor at the same time off-duty police officers were at a dance arranged by wives of DPOA members. Derrick Tabor, the seventeen-year-old son of the Reverend Willis Tabor, pastor of the Drayton Avenue United Presbyterian Church of Ferndale, and James Evans III, the seventeen-year-old son of the director of the Fisher YMCA, alleged that they had been the object of racial slurs when they had first entered the building, but the real trouble developed when the youths left the hall after the sixth-floor dance had come to an end just after midnight. Tabor stated that he had been halted at gunpoint just outside the building and beaten by six or eight men, some of whom had been drinking and none of whom identified himself as a police officer. Evans charged that he had been chased from the hall and beaten into unconsciousness by a group of policemen, one of whom had fired at least one shot. According to their mother, Grady and Bruce Stallworth were choked in the hall's parking lot by a group of whites. When they locked themselves in the family car in self-defense, their assailants kicked in the car's fenders and dented the roof. When the Reverend Tabor visited the building at about 2:00 A.M., he reported that he saw several policemen in plainclothes "staggering around drunk," one with a pistol in his hand.[101]

The blatant behavior of the police and the prominence of the families of the youthful victims led a variety of community groups, black and white, to demand a complete investigation of the Veterans Memorial Hall incident. On November 4 more than four hundred persons meeting in the Central Methodist Church organized the Detroit Task Force for Justice, a biracial organization aimed at curbing "police power" and one that called for the dissolution of the DPOA and civilian control of the Police Department. In a front-page editorial, the *Free Press* asked, "Who's the Boss of Detroit Police?" and asserted that Detroit faced "a growing crisis over control of its police department and policemen." The CCR staff feared that "the polarization of the community" was occurring "at an increasing tempo."[102]

The Police Department immediately began an "intense investigation" of the Veterans Memorial Hall affair. Asserting that the traditional "blue curtain" was hampering the investigation, Cavanagh warned that if the department did not conduct "a fair and impartial investigation," some "outside agency" would do so. On November 13 Spreen revealed that the department had suspended two sergeants and seven patrolmen on open charges of conduct unbecoming an officer and that the department was seeking the prosecution of seven officers. Two days later the chief assistant Wayne County prosecutor, James Brickley, recommended that one patrolman be charged with felonious assault for beating Evans with a gun and that a second patrolman be charged with assault and battery for beating Grady Stallworth. Brickley stated that the police assault on the young blacks had been unprovoked, that some officers had been "under the influence of alcohol," and that others had participated in criminal action but could not be prosecuted because their victims could not make the required identifications.[103]

Trial board hearings of the suspended officers who had not been charged by the prosecutor resulted in the dismissal of one officer, the demotion of two from sergeant to patrolman, and the forfeiture by a fourth officer of $5,000 in pay and benefits. Cavanagh later reversed one of the demotions on the grounds that the evidence did not sustain it. The Common Council by that time had agreed to pay for the damaged Stallworth car. One of the two officers against whom criminal charges had been brought was later acquitted.[104]

The DPOA was outraged by the Police Department's reaction to the Veterans Memorial episode and the criticism of police behavior in the two Cobo Hall incidents. Carl Parsell maintained that whereas the situation had been allowed to get "out of hand" in the 1967 riot, the officers had restored order in the two Cobo Hall incidents because they had used "proper force." The DPOA portrayed the police as "victims of uncourageous political leaders" and charged that allegations of police brutality were, to quote Parsell, "part of a nefarious plot by those who would like our form of government overthrown." The head of the Detectives Association characterized police morale early in 1969 as "lower than whale shit," and white officers complained that Cavanagh was prepared to "sacrifice them to appease the Negro community."[105]

The most serious of the postriot confrontations between the police and the black community began on March 29, 1969, with the killing of one police officer and the wounding of another outside the New Bethel Baptist Church on Linwood, in the 1967 riot area. Two to three hundred members of the Republic of New Africa (RNA) were meeting inside the church on March 29 to celebrate the first anniversary of the founding of the RNA. The gathering was breaking up shortly before midnight when patrolmen Michael Czapski and Richard Worobec, who were cruising in the area, encountered about a dozen RNA members outside the church, some armed and all wearing military fatigues with leopard-skin epaulets.

When the two officers stopped to question the men—there is no evidence that their approach was "threatening or improper"—shots were fired at them, killing Czapski and wounding Worobec in the thigh. Worobec was able to drag himself to his scout car and to summon help. About fifty police officers converged on the scene within twenty minutes.

What happened after police reinforcements arrived outside the New Bethel Church soon became the subject of intense controversy. The police claimed that some of the assailants of Czapski and Worobec fled back into the church. According to the police, a ranking officer who knocked on the church door demanding entry was answered by gunfire. The police further alleged that when they broke into the darkened church, a rifleman from the center of the altar and a sniper from the loft fired at them, leading them to return fire. The Field Division of the CCR, however, reported that the available witnesses did not see any armed RNA members run back into the church, and the Field Division, a CRC official, those inside the church, and a church janitor all agreed that the police allegation of being fired on from inside the church was inaccurate. Women and children in the church, the janitor reported, were "screaming and completely hysterical trying to get away from the shots" as the police shot their way in.[106]

The police, who discovered 142 people inside the church, confiscated nine rifles, three pistols, and some ammunition. They lined the occupants up along the walls of the church and, according to some RNA members and the janitor, hit some of them with gun butts, hurled "racially derogatory epithets at them," engaged in "open and unrestricted searching of females," and refused the occupants toilet privileges.[107]

A ranking officer ordered the arrest of all those inside the church, an action the police justified on the grounds that one officer had been killed and another wounded, the police had allegedly been fired upon from inside the church, the occupants were wearing military uniforms, and some had weapons. Both the Detroit ACLU and the CRC, however, maintained that the police had no constitutional right to arrest all those in the church since there was no probable cause to believe that they had participated in the commission of a common crime. The ACLU also noted that the police had failed both in the church and later to inform their prisoners of their right to remain silent and to avail themselves of counsel. The police conveyed their prisoners in police buses to the garage in police headquarters downtown (First Precinct). They then administered nitrate tests to the prisoners to detect possible traces of gunpowder, fingerprinted them, and registered them for arrest.[108]

Judge George Crockett, scheduled for duty on the Recorder's Court on March 30, was awakened at 5:00 A.M. by Representative James Del Rio and the Reverend C. L. Franklin, whose New Bethel Church the RNA had rented, and told that prisoners apprehended in the church were being held incommunicado in the First Precinct station. Learning that the police did not have a list of their prisoners, Crockett contacted Commissioner Spreen, who promised to provide a list and agreed to Crockett's holding court in police headquarters, where the judge ordered the prisoners brought before him. Crockett, who began holding court at 6:00 A.M., heard the cases of thirty-nine prisoners, releasing sixteen on personal bonds of $100 with instructions to reappear at noon in the Recorder's Court, discharging one with the consent of the assistant prosecutor, and remanding the other twenty-two to police custody until the noon court hearing.

When Prosecutor William Cahalan arrived at police headquarters, he protested Crockett's actions. Cahalan contended that the police needed more time to process and fingerprint their prisoners and administer nitrate tests, and he complained that Crockett had released ten prisoners who were prime suspects, including two with positive nitrate tests and a third with specks of nitrate on one hand. Crockett responded that the police had had several hours by then to check out their prisoners and had run nitrate tests without permission of the prisoners and without their having the benefit of counsel, which violated their constitutional rights; and he warned Cahalan not to interfere with the release of prisoners. When Cahalan then instructed the police to rearrest one person whom Crockett had released and not to process additional prisoners, the judge ordered the prosecutor to appear in court later that day to show why he should not be cited for contempt. Crockett charged that Cahalan's behavior was "not only a personal affront, but it also had racial overtones." He certified the Cahalan case to the presiding judge of the Recorder's Court but later decided not to press the charge.[109]

Responding that there were no "racial overtones" to his action, Cahalan contended that Crockett's blanket order to the police to produce all their prisoners was "not a proper writ" since, the prosecutor claimed, a Recorder's Court judge could not issue such a writ on his own motion and, in any event, it was not on the record and had never actually been served. As Crockett remembered it, he had not signed a habeas corpus writ until after the morning session in police headquarters. He conceded that he had not really been sure of the applicable law when he had ordered the prisoners brought before him but that when he looked up the law after leaving police headquarters, he discovered that he had acted properly. "It just seemed to be it should be the law," he remarked.[110]

By the time Crockett resumed holding court at 12:30 P.M., the police, following Cahalan's instructions, had released about one hundred additional Bethel prisoners because of lack of probable cause, leaving only twelve prisoners still to be taken before the judge. Crockett ordered two prisoners against whom there were outstanding warrants held without bail, set a bond of $1,000 for a third, and released the others even though the assistant prosecutor wanted seven of them held because tests indicated that they had gunpowder on their hands. Three of the original arrestees were later tried for the murder of Czapski and the wounding of Worobec, but they were all acquitted following jury trials.[111]

The New Bethel incident and, above all, the conduct of Judge Crockett unleashed strong emotions in Detroit and revealed both how polarized the community had become and the extent to which police-black confrontations tended to be appraised in the light of the 1967 riot. Cavanagh stated that the police had responded "in the only appropriate way" in charging into the New Bethel Church and that there otherwise would have been a "full-scale riot." The media and the *Detroit News* in particular saw Crockett as the villain in the affair. The *News*, which quoted an unnamed Recorder's Court judge as saying that Crockett was so prejudiced against the police that he did not belong on the court, asked in an editorial, "Have law enforcement and justice taken another beating from . . . George Crockett, Jr.? It looks that way." In an April 16 editorial, the *Free Press* stated that the media, including the *Free Press*, had inaccurately reported the facts regarding the New Bethel affair, and it expressed "regret" for its own reporting. The Ad Hoc Action Group subjected the unrepentant *News* to picketing and threatened a boycott of the newspaper.[112]

At a well-attended meeting on April 16, Breakthrough charged that Crockett, if not a communist, was acting like one. The most vociferous and determined attack on the judge was mounted by the DPOA, which portrayed its old enemy as being "an advocate" rather than "an impartial administrator of justice." Off-duty police officers and their wives picketed the Tenth Precinct to protest Crockett's actions, and the DPOA placed a full-page ad in the *Detroit News* blasting the judge's conduct; the *Free Press* refused to print the ad, regarding it as "inflammatory." The DPOA's goal was to have Crockett removed from the bench through action by the governor, impeachment, or as the result of an inquiry by the state's Judicial Tenure Commission. The grounds for Crockett's removal, as the DPOA saw it, were "gross misconduct," "persistent failure to perform his duties," and "conduct clearly prejudicial to the administration of justice." Late in May the DPOA presented Governor William Milliken with petitions bearing 200,000 signatures calling for Crockett's impeachment. The governor, as a matter of fact, had requested a probe of Crockett by the Judicial Tenure Commission within a few days of the New Bethel affair, and the state senate, by a vote of 25 to 0, had agreed. The commission quietly undertook the requested inquiry but abandoned it in November by a 5 to 4 vote.[113]

Defending himself, Crockett declared that the best way to avoid a riot like that of July 1967 was "prompt judicial action with strict observance of constitutional rights." He asserted in response to specific criticisms of his conduct that the Recorder's Court was in session wherever one of its judges sat, that he would have been guilty of malfeasance had he not issued a writ of habeas corpus, and that it was the prosecutor and the police, not he, who had released most of the arrestees. Asserting that "a black judge's views in Detroit will be obeyed as long as he has the power to act," Crockett asked in a press conference, "Can any of you imagine the Detroit Police invading an all-white church and rounding up everyone in sight to be bussed to a wholesale lockup in a police garage?" He asserted that black judges had "an obligation" to search the law "to find new remedies for the ailments of their people."[114]

There was almost universal support for Crockett in Detroit's black community, more than five hundred blacks representing every shade of organizational opinion joining together to form the Black United Front. In cooperation with the Guardians, the organization of black police officers, the Black United Front demonstrated in Crockett's behalf and picketed the Recorder's Court until halted by a court injunction. The Wolverine Bar Association expressed support; William T. Patrick, Jr., called Crockett "an authentic hero of these trying times"; and Albert Cleage declared, "Now, at last, Judge Crockett has brought law and order to the Recorder's Court and Detroit . . . , the most important thing that has happened in Detroit in more than a century." The word among "the younger 'more militant' blacks" was, "If Crockett goes, Detroit goes."[115]

Both the ACLU and the CCR came to Crockett's defense. The Executive Board of the Detroit ACLU released a statement defending Crockett's behavior on every disputed point and criticizing the misrepresentation of the facts in the news media as well as the "campaign of vituperation" by the DPOA and the *Detroit News*. Richard Marks analyzed what had happened as "part of the inheritance" of the 1967 riot. He attacked the DPOA for "usurping in a way which no responsible leadership would permit, the logical role of orderly government." It had to be "frankly stated," he declared, that the Detroit community had failed to achieve "racial or community change in substance" since the riot.[116]

Fearing that the city was "just about at a point of exploding," New Detroit sought to defuse the New Bethel controversy. At a press conference just after the event, New Detroit's chairman, Max M. Fisher, cautioned, "We can't go back to 1967," and stated that Crockett had used "very good common sense" in dealing with the arrestees. New Detroit solicited funds to repair the damaged New Bethel Church and offered a reward of $7,500 for information leading to the apprehension of Czapski's killer. Fisher met with radio, television and press officials as well as with black and white community leaders to gain their cooperation in resolving the controversy, and he made several calming statements on TV and radio. The Law Committee of New Detroit concluded in a report unanimously approved by the organization's board of trustees that there was "more than merely a justifiable basis for [Crockett's] conduct and exercise of judicial discretion." Criminal law instructors at the law schools in Ann Arbor and Detroit all agreed with this judgment. Fisher said for the New Detroit board, "We can take hope from the fact that this highly provocative set of circumstances did not erupt in a repetition of July 23, 1967," the point of reference throughout the New Bethel affair. New Detroit's defense of Crockett, the author of the major study of the organization concluded, "turned the situation around." It "helped," as Joseph L. Hudson later maintained "to keep a lid on something that was extremely emotional."[117]

Although the New Bethel episode did not erupt into the riot so many feared, the perception of the affair by blacks and whites provided strong evidence of the "dramatic polarization" of the races and the "conflict climate" in postriot Detroit. A survey based on neighborhood clusters conducted by Donald Warren among 507 blacks and 603 whites revealed that whereas 52.5 percent of the whites described the attack on Czapski as an "ambush," only 15 percent of the blacks did so. More than half the blacks but only one in four whites thought Crockett's actions were consistent with legal requirements, and whereas only 14 percent of the blacks thought the police had been right in entering the church, 84 percent of the white respondents defended the police entry.[118]

The distressing state of police-community relations, which it regarded as "the single most critical barrier to progress in race relations" in the city, led New Detroit to continue to press for a study of the Police Department following the abrupt termination of the Brandstatter effort. On March 11, 1969, New Detroit announced the initiation of two studies of the department, a police-community relations study and a police management study. New Detroit had actually expected the studies to get underway in December 1968, but the initial resistance of Cavanagh and the determined opposition of Commissioner Spreen led to delay.

Spreen was particularly concerned about the community relations inquiry, fearing its impact on what he characterized as the "4700 good men in the Department" since its primary focus, he assumed, would be "the racist nature" of the department. A high-ranking police officer remarked regarding the studies, "The big guys are on the niggers' side." Eventually, Spreen appointed eight police officers to join the sixteen other committee members selected by Cavanagh and New Detroit to undertake the police-community relations study. Perhaps it was the pending study that persuaded the commissioner to launch a new program aimed at improving police relations with the black community that included a so-called "love-in," which involved opening police gyms to ghetto youths and more personal contacts between the police and the community.[119]

The police management study, completed in 1970, was concerned with "the nuts-and-bolts operation of the department." Two professional firms worked with the department to implement the study's recommendations and to update the department's management. In addition to the overall police-management study, New Detroit in 1969 engaged the International Association of Chiefs of Police to examine the headquarters operation of the Detroit department. The report of the association's Field Operations Division, delivered in September 1969, recommended more central control and monitoring of complaints investigations. It noted that many police still bore "the psychological scars" of the 1967 riot, that line personnel were determined not to permit any future disorder "to get out of control," and that for some supervisors the "primary function of the department" had become the suppression of civil disorders. The 1967 riot had clearly left its mark on the department.[120]

The Police-Community Relations Committee released its report on July 15, 1970, one committee member describing it as "more an exhausted consensus than anything else." The report called for the recruitment of police from college campuses, more education for police officers, a much longer probationary period for new officers, a review of policies regarding the use of firearms and deadly force, and the concealment of long guns from the view of people on the street. It criticized police who removed their badges and other means of identification during civil disturbances but recommended awards and recognition for police who behaved coolly when confronted by an angry mob. It called for greater protection of the civil rights of police officers, especially in trial board proceedings. Because it concluded that civilian review boards had been ineffective in other jurisdictions, it opposed the adoption of this mechanism for Detroit, preferring the strengthening of the CCB and its firm support by the department.[121]

Of seventy-three administrative changes recommended by the Police-Community Relations Committee, the Police Department had implemented sixty-eight within two years, including all the priority items. It had recruited more blacks, who made up 14 percent of the department by the end of July 1972. Scout cars by then had locking devices that kept long guns secured and out of sight of viewers, and the department had resolved ambiguities regarding the use of deadly force. Not only had the department increased in-service training, especially for supervisors, but about 18 percent of the police officers by July 1972 were enrolled in college courses. New programs of police-community relations were in effect by that time, and police officers accused of wrongdoing enjoyed greater legal protection than they had before the riot.

Although New Detroit judged what had occurred to be only "a qualified success," police-community relations were in a far less troubled state as of July 1972 than they had been during the final seventeen months of the Cavanagh administration that followed the July 1967 riot. "At least on the institutional level," the *Detroit Free Press* judged at the end of July 1972, "the Detroit Police Department has conducted more serious post-riot self-reform than any other agency in the city."[122] Far more important changes in the department were soon to occur.

CHAPTER 18

The Ameliorative Response

"In addition to being the scene of the nation's worst Negro riot of this period, Detroit," the *Detroit Free Press*'s Philip Meyer judged in November 1968, "may be remembered as the city that tried the hardest to do the most for racial peace" in response to a riot. Five years later J. David Greenstone and Paul Peterson concluded that Detroit's Mayor Cavanagh "responded in a more ameliorative, less punitive fashion to the 1967 race riots than did the mayor of any other large city."[1] The same generalization can also be made regarding the riot response of Detroit's private sector. If the Detroit riot is best seen as a form of protest designed to call attention to black grievances and the black community, the rioters succeeded at least in part in attaining their objective.

"Detroit," the head of the Mayor's Development Team (MDT) observed a few days after the riot, "faces a great challenge in rebuilding itself as a social and physical community—in creating a livable city." The principal responsibility of creating this "livable city" rested with the city government, but it recognized that it could not hope to accomplish the task without substantial assistance from the state and federal governments and the private sector as well. "It's too big for any city to handle," Ray Girardin remarked with regard to the crisis of the cities just after the riot. "It will take [the] combined brains and effort of the nation."[2]

In responding to the 1967 riot, Detroit was handicapped by the racial polarization the riot had magnified and the city's deteriorating fiscal condition. Two major strikes—by Ford Motor Company workers from September 6 to October 25, 1967, and by the city's two daily newspapers from November 16, 1967, to August 9, 1968—further hampered the city's efforts to deal with its racial problems.[3]

After incurring a deficit of $11 million in the fiscal year 1966–67, Detroit anticipated even more serious budget shortfalls in the years to come because of the diminished yield from the local property tax, the city's chief source of revenue. In seeking to fill the gap between the city's income and its needs, Cavanagh not only had to deal with a Common Council that was reluctant to raise taxes, but he was also disappointed in the degree of assistance Detroit received from the state of Michigan and the federal government.[4]

Testifying before the Kerner Commission on August 15, 1967, Cavanagh warned that it was a delusion to think that the remedy for riots was "sterner measures of force and repression" rather than a frontal assault on the underlying causes of the disorders. He spoke in a similar way to the people of Detroit in his initial postriot report on September 6. While seeking to assure his constituents that law and order would be maintained, he told them that the way to prevent riots was to "convert social liabilities into community assets" and to eliminate the second-class status of Detroit's black citizens. It was essential, he said, to make the Twelfth Street area a safe and dynamic neighborhood, improve housing, provide jobs and job training, reduce the welfare rolls, and improve ghetto schools.[5]

The effort to rehabilitate Twelfth Street and the Virginia Park area, it will be recalled, had been initiated before the riot with the establishment of the Virginia Park Services Corporation. Following the riot, the Service Corporation hired Wayne State University sociologist James E. Boyce as a planner for the rehabilitation project and as an "advocate" of the community's needs with city departments. This was the first use in the United States of the advocate-planner concept. By the end of 1967 the Services Corporation had prepared a blueprint for the rehabilitation of the Virginia Park area and had gained Common Council approval. The plan, which embodied the wishes of the people living in the area, called for a 120-foot-wide boulevard on Twelfth Street, with three lanes on each side of a central parkway extending the mile from West Grand Boulevard to Clairmount. A shopping area and a community center on the west side of the street were to replace the 175 stores built in the decade following World War I. New low-cost housing was to be constructed along the boulevard. In January 1968 the Services Corporation submitted a grant application to the Department of Housing and Urban Development (HUD) for funds to widen and landscape Twelfth Street, but the money was not immediately forthcoming.[6]

As of October 1968, virtually nothing had been done to rehabilitate Twelfth Street. The burned-out buildings had been demolished and replaced by block-long patches of weeds and broken bottles. A new style of architecture, derisively dubbed "riot renaissance," was conspicuous in the area—storefronts whose plate-glass windows had been replaced by concrete blocks, "the cheapest, drabbest and ugliest method available." In October the federal government provided Detroit with a loan of slightly more than $6 million to remove 154 structures from Twelfth Street and to begin its planned development. Progress continued at a snail's pace, however, and when Cavanagh left office at the end of 1969, the process of acquiring land to widen Twelfth Street had just begun.[7]

The failure of the federal and city governments to provide needed funds continued to delay the rehabilitation of Twelfth Street and the Virginia Park neighborhood. Most buildings on both sides of Twelfth Street had been removed by the fifth anniversary of the riot, and fifteen apartment buildings had been rehabilitated, but there had been no new construction. Victim of a lack of public concern and "an almost total lack of imaginative leadership" in the city, the Twelfth Street neighborhood remained an area of decreasing population, high crime, high unemployment, and poor health. As the structures on Twelfth Street were removed and the land cleared, some of the area's blight simply moved with the departing population to Fourteenth Street, Linwood, Dexter, and Grand River.[8]

Renamed Rosa Parks Boulevard by the riot's tenth anniversary, Twelfth Street was described at that time as "a smooth scar of vacant lots, new pavement and a few remaining buildings." Ground, however, was broken that month for a large townhouse complex on Seward, two blocks from the boulevard. By late 1981 the Virginia Park area, whose population had dwindled since the riot from forty thousand to sixteen thousand, had "risen from the ashes," as 351 housing units had been completed at a cost of $16 million and an additional 900 units had been rehabilitated. A new community center had been erected, and a seven-store shopping center was completed the next year. Owned and operated by the residents, the shopping center was "the only community-owned, non-profit shopping center in the country." North Entrance Park now occupied the space on the corner of Twelfth and Clairmount where the blind pig had been located. Little had been done, however, to rehabilitate other areas of the city scarred by the riot.[9]

In one of his mea culpa statements after the riot, Cavanagh told the National Commission on Urban Problems that if he had to point to one area where the city had failed to do enough to prevent a riot, it was housing. Although the basic problem was the "totally inadequate" supply of low-income housing, relatively little was done during the remainder of the Cavanagh administration to alleviate the problem. The housing market at the end of the riot was exceedingly tight—the vacancy rate was only 2.5 percent—and the problem was compounded by relocation forced by urban renewal, decline of the housing stock as more homes were demolished than were built, deterioration of the existing housing stock, rising cost of construction, lack of mortgage money for housing in the inner city, and, perhaps most important of all, a shortage of vacant land.[10]

As of August 1967, Detroit had gained federal approval for the construction of 1,500 units of public housing, earmarked by the Detroit Housing Commission (DHC) for senior citizens and large families. Only 70 units, apparently, had been completed by September 1969, although 700 more were under construction. As authorized by the Housing Assistance Administration, the DHC entered into agreements with private developers to rehabilitate existing structures, after which the commission took possession. The DHC used this method to make 660 low-rent units available to senior citizens. In a postriot interview, Robert Knox, the DHC's director-secretary, conceded that Detroit's public housing effort was "a nibble on the edge of a massive problem." The same judgment could have been rendered when Cavanagh left office.[11]

In June 1968 the cochairmen of the Michigan Civil Rights Commission (CRC), noting that only one of the sites the DHC had proposed for housing construction that year was outside the city's black areas, requested Robert Weaver, the secretary of HUD, to review the pattern of site selection to determine if public funds were being used to "perpetuate racial segregation." This, indeed, was the opinion of the CRC as well as the Commission on Community Relations (CCR). After Weaver had agreed to the CRC request, the Housing Assistance Administration in 1969 approved a DHC proposal to purchase one hundred homes at scattered sites to be made available for public housing tenants.[12]

The bulk of Detroit's housing tenants, of course, lived in private, not public housing. Supplementing the efforts of the United Tenants for Collective Action, the state legislature following the riot sought to provide tenants with a measure of protection against abusive landlords. In July 1968 the legislature enacted five tenants' rights laws drafted by the University of Detroit's Urban Law Program, laws for which it had mobilized support even before the riot. The laws, "the strongest set" of such measures in the United States, required landlords to provide tenants with a lease specifying that the premises were in fit repair and would be kept that way. If a landlord failed to receive a certificate of compliance or if such a certificate was suspended as a result of the required periodic code inspections, the tenant was to pay his rent not to the landlord but to the enforcement agency, which could obtain a court order requiring the landlord to make the needed repairs or could appoint a receiver to undertake the task. Tenants could sue to enforce code requirements, and they were protected against retaliatory evictions. Public housing authorities, the legislation provided, could evict tenants only for "just cause." Finally, one of the laws called for the creation of a sixteen-member board of tenant affairs, half to be appointed by the mayor and the remainder to be elected, with public housing tenants represented on a proportional basis.[13]

In the first major application of the tenants' rights legislation, New Detroit in the spring of 1969 loaned $10,000 to Woodward East Project, Inc., a community group named as the receiver of a blighted twenty-nine-unit apartment building. New Detroit regarded the loan as having "historical and nationwide implications," but the building went up in flames soon after the loan had been extended.[14]

In an effort to protect residents against hazards associated with urban renewal, the Michigan legislature in June 1968 not only required the creation of citizen district councils in urban renewal areas but also specified that no action taken under the statute could have the effect of "promoting or perpetuating racial segregation in housing." In response to the law, the Common Council enacted an ordinance requiring the establishment of fourteen district councils, each with fifteen members elected by area residents and ten appointed by the mayor. The councils were empowered to advise the city on redevelopment plans for their districts.[15]

That Detroit needed the stricter code enforcement called for by the tenants' rights legislation had been made evident in a CCR report issued just after the riot. In September 1968 Cavanagh appointed the Mayor's Special Task Force on Code Enforcement to make a study of the subject. In its report at the beginning of 1969, the task force contended that the lack of a "systematic and periodic inspection and effective code enforcement program" for both single homes and multiple family dwellings was "the major factor in the deterioration of inner city housing." Recommending stricter enforcement and heavier fines for both housing and environmental violations, the task force attributed the "mood of despair" among inner-city residents to their belief that the city government lacked "a sense of concern and obligation about their living conditions."

Following the recommendations of the task force, Cavanagh not only ordered some bureaucratic reshuffling to tighten enforcement but also set up a City Hall Central that a citizen could call for information or service regarding code matters. Code enforcement, however, still left something to be desired, partly because the principal official involved, according to a Cavanagh aide, was "hung up on his professionalism, at the expense of better ways of enforcing living codes."[16]

Like the passage of the tenants' rights and urban renewal legislation and the increased concern for code enforcement in Detroit, the enactment of a city open housing ordinance in November 1967 was a direct consequence of the 1967 riot. Open housing was not a subject with particular appeal to militants like Albert Cleage, who believed that it would "only panic white people." A sizable minority of blacks, however, indicated that integrated housing was more important to them than better housing where they already lived. This was the position of 44 percent of adult blacks in the riot areas, judging from a *Detroit Free Press* survey of August–September 1968, and of 37 percent of the adult blacks in the city as a whole, according to a University of Michigan Survey Research Center survey of September 1970–April 1971.[17]

In August 1967 Michigan's attorney general ruled that the CRC's jurisdiction over discrimination in housing was limited to civil procedures and that local open occupancy ordinances enforced by criminal procedures were not in conflict with state authority. The Detroit Council of Organizations, following the recommendation of the MDT, drafted an open housing ordinance that Councilman Nicholas Hood introduced.

Although the Common Council had rejected an open housing measure in 1963, it now approved such an ordinance. The ordinance, to be enforced by the CCR, outlawed discrimination on the basis of race, color, religion, or national origin in the selling or rental of property by owners, realtors, advertisers, salesmen, and financial institutions. It exempted rental units in which rooms were rented to no more than three people.

The open housing ordinance was to have gone into effect on December 31, 1967, but petitions with signatures in excess of one hundred thousand, fifty-four thousand more than required, were filed with the city clerk before that date referring the ordinance to the voters. In August 1968, however, United States District Court Judge Talbot Smith, asserting, "The status quo cannot be restored. Too much has happened," ruled that the matter was no longer one for a public vote in view of federal and state laws and court decisions. Seen by the Detroit Urban League (DUL) as "little more than a moral victory" for blacks, the ordinance, because of white flight, lack of affordable homes for blacks to purchase, and, according to the CCR, a real estate industry that constituted "a gigantic conspiracy" to maintain segregated housing patterns, did not make Detroit an integrated city. By the end of 1969 the CCR had received thirty complaints of violation, several of which were resolved in favor of the complainants.[18]

The Detroit Fair Housing Ordinance did not, of course, apply to the white suburbs of metropolitan Detroit. "Absolutely frustrated" by the real estate industry in seeking to persuade suburban communities to make homes available to people of all races, the Detroit Archdiocese and New Detroit concluded that the enactment of a state open housing law was essential. Told by Professor Robert Harris of the University of Michigan Law School that open occupancy was the key to desegregation and to combating the black sense of exclusion, New Detroit sought to persuade Governor Romney to place fair housing on the agenda for the special session of the legislature called by the governor after the riot. Romney favored open housing legislation, but he had promised state legislators not to seek such a measure during the special session. On October 13, 1967, while the special session was in progress, Romney recommended the enactment of a "statewide open occupancy law."[19]

In an effort to persuade the special session to follow the governor's recommendation, a large delegation of New Detroit members, other influential Detroit citizens, and Mayor Cavanagh, in an unprecedented action, flew to Lansing on November 14 to indicate by their "presence" their "personal conviction and willingness" to support an open housing law. "This bill is as big as anything [the legislators] have faced in their public lives," declared Joseph L. Hudson. The legislature adjourned on November 17, however, without taking action on the housing bill. This was a "severe setback" for New Detroit, but it had lost a battle, not the war.

When the lawmakers returned to Lansing in January 1968 for the regular session of the legislature, Romney told them that they would be encouraging "armed insurrection" unless they enacted a fair housing law and the aforementioned tenants' rights measures. The legislature responded in May by enacting what was characterized as the strictest fair housing law in the nation. The law was without immediate effect, however, the percentage of blacks living in the Detroit suburbs being slightly lower in 1970 than in 1960 (3.8 percent in 1960 compared to 3.6 percent in 1970).[20]

Since Detroit's war on poverty had failed to save the city from a riot, it is hardly surprising that critics of the program like Julian Witherspoon asserted that the disturbance would not have occurred had there been more "effective" citizen participation and that, in any event, "new approaches" were required to do the job that had "not been done . . . in Detroit."[21] There was a "new approach" here and there, as, for example, in the consumer area,[22] but Detroit's war on poverty, so much praised in the past, was on the defensive during the postriot period of the Cavanagh administration. The federal government substantially reduced its funding for the antipoverty effort, and the enthusiasm of officials running the program waned. In reports in 1968 a committee of the Michigan House of Representatives headed by James Del Rio subjected the program to severe criticism. The criticism was then echoed in a series of editorials on a Detroit television station. The Mayor's Committee for Human Resources Development (MCHRD), as already noted, was able to rebut most of the charges, which were, in the main, inaccurate or misleading, but the damage had been done.[23]

More serious than the politically inspired Michigan legislative investigation was a full-scale appraisal of the Detroit program at the end of 1968 by a federal interagency regional council composed of representatives of the departments of Health, Education, and Welfare, HUD, and Labor and the Office of Economic Opportunity. The council concluded that the MCHRD's lack of a central management function and information system "seriously impaired" its ability to manage its programs and to monitor their performance or that of its delegate agencies. The council pointed to gaps in the services offered by the Community Development Centers, complained about insufficient citizen participation, drew attention to the limited possibility for career advancement for the MCHRD's nonprofessional employees, and criticized the lack of comprehensive health-care planning. The report was not made public, but it could hardly have improved the morale of Detroit's beleaguered poverty officials.[24]

Although the bloom was off Detroit's antipoverty program following the riot, Cavanagh told the MCHRD's Policy Advisory Committee when his service as mayor drew to a close that none of the achievements of his administration made him prouder than Detroit's community action program. He knew, he said, that the war on poverty had "scarcely been able to touch the lives of many of the poor," but he contended that Detroit had not only pioneered in the development of the programs that made up the national war on poverty but had also proved that the effort was worthwhile.[25]

Detroit had played a major role in the development of the nation's Model Cities program, but it could hardly have taken much comfort from the way the program got underway in the city. Torn by conflict, the Citizens Governing Board for the program was unable to devise an application for the first year's action grant, with the result that federal officials had to put together the application just before the 1968 deadline. Funds for the first year were not forthcoming until the beginning of the fiscal year 1969–70, by which time, as Robert Conot has written, the new administration in Washington and the Cavanagh administration in Detroit had resigned themselves to the program's failure.[26]

The MDT, as already noted, had stressed the lack of jobs as the major obstacle to racial peace in Detroit following the riot. The principal responsibility for meeting this problem rested, of course, with the private sector. In his September 1967 report to the people, however, Cavanagh announced what he called the "Detroit Plan," which involved, among other things, the creation of a Job Advancement Committee to seek the promotion of blacks to positions commensurate with their abilities, a Talent Bank that would compile a job roster of unemployed blacks with superior qualifications, and a Committee on Job Exploitation to assist workers with job grievances in the absence of established grievance machinery. Although it does not appear that anything of importance was done to implement this phase of the Detroit Plan, the city government did establish a central job-finding and referral service for unemployed youths aged sixteen to twenty-one. In its role of ensuring that city contractors pursued nondiscriminatory employment policies, the CCR succeeded in opening up some jobs for blacks, especially in the construction trades, where the number of black journeymen rose from 4 percent of the total in 1967 to 16 percent in 1969 (11,314 of 66,881).[27]

Federal funds aided Detroit to some extent in seeking to find employment for jobless blacks. A Department of Transportation grant of $300,000 enabled the city government to establish a busing system in cooperation with Southeastern Metro-Transport authorities to transport inner-city residents to jobs in the outer city and the suburbs. As of February 1968, forty-five hundred Detroiters were enrolled in the three surviving federal manpower programs, the Neighborhood Youth Corps, On-the-Job Training, and the Concentrated Employment Program.[28]

The city of Detroit following the riot sought to deal with the long-standing problem of lack of recreational services in the inner city. It used HUD funds to begin construction of five playgrounds in the riot area and a 1968–69 Urban Beautification Program grant to provide landscaping and playground equipment for ten vest pocket parks in the inner city. It planned to undertake a variety of additional recreational and improvement projects, 59 percent of them in the riot areas, with a similar grant for 1969–70. Since the Department of Parks and Recreation was slow to respond to the mayor's call for the development of the vest pocket parks, regarding the proposal as "a knee-jerk response to the riot," the program was pushed by the Deprived Areas Recreation Team (DART), a coalition of the United Automobile Workers and church groups that had been organized in March 1967, and Detroit's Youth Opportunity Council, which spoke for sixty inner-city groups. Ten vest pocket parks were eventually constructed, but they were too small to include enough equipment to attract different age groups in the riot areas or to warrant the assignment of play supervisors by the Department of Parks and Recreation.[29]

Detroit public school administrators and city government officials saw the riot as pointing up the need for an improved educational system if Detroit were to be made a more livable city. To meet immediate needs allegedly stemming from the riot and to prevent a recurrence, Superintendent of Schools Norman Drachler asked the state government for $5.3 million in additional funding. The sum was for 250 additional teachers to help reduce class size in some schools to thirty students; for one hundred mobile classrooms to accommodate about thirty-five hundred students displaced by the riot and having to enter overcrowded schools elsewhere; to help provide free textbooks for each child in grades one to eight – the school system at the time was providing only one textbook for every two children in these grades – and for students in grades eleven and twelve (students in grades nine and ten already received free textbooks); and to keep school facilities open on Saturday and Sunday for tutoring purposes and community use. Drachler reported that when the schools reopened in the riot areas, the students were "dazed. They came in with stone faces," he said. More counselors, he advised, were needed not just for vocational purposes but "to restore some hope and confidence" in the students. The school system at the same time launched a massive orientation program for staff members to help them adjust to postriot conditions.[30]

New Detroit joined the city government in urging Lansing to provide the additional funds the school system was seeking. Romney was reluctant to ask the legislature to act at the postriot special session because the requested sum was not entirely for needs stemming from the riot and because state aid for education had not previously been made available for capital expenditures. The governor, however, did request the legislature to appropriate an additional $5 million for disadvantaged students in the state, $2.3 million of the sum for Detroit. The legislature refused to act during the special session, but when Romney renewed the request during the 1968 regular session, the lawmakers agreed to provide some additional funding for poverty-area schools.[31]

The slightly increased state aid for Detroit public schools after the riot was supplemented by federal aid and assistance from New Detroit. In addition to the Elementary and Secondary Education Act assistance it was already providing, the federal government, shortly after the riot, awarded the city $2 million for each of three years, the largest such grant in the nation, to raise the educational achievement levels of six thousand students in five schools in areas adversely affected by the riot by providing them a full range of educational, vocational, health, and remedial services. New Detroit granted the public schools $400,000 for the summer of 1968 for scholarships for indigent students and a junior high school work-training program and an additional $100,000 for textbooks for sixth-grade students in the inner city.[32]

Despite outside aid, the public schools had incurred a $4 million deficit by December 1968, and larger deficits loomed as the result of the shrinking property valuation in the school district. Faced with increasing budgetary problems and the high cost of educating children from disadvantaged backgrounds, the Detroit school board in January 1968 joined three black children and their parents and three white children and their parents in filing a suit against the state of Michigan for failing "to discharge its constitutional obligation to provide equal educational opportunity for all children" attending public schools in the state. The school system not only failed to win the suit but suffered a defeat at the polls in November 1968, when the voters, this time including voters in the inner city, resoundingly rejected a ten-mill increase in the school tax that the school system claimed it needed to finance the recommendations of the High School Study Commission, a building program, and remedial education. Unable to secure the funds it sought, the school system spent less on its pupils than the school systems of other big cities: Detroit's expenditure of $575 per pupil in 1968 compared with $1,031 in New York, $655 in Boston, $636 in Los Angeles, and $630 in Cleveland. Although sixth among the states in personal income as of 1968, Michigan ranked twenty-eighth in its support for public elementary and secondary education.[33]

Despite the overwhelming desire of Detroit's blacks for integrated schools, the city's schools after the riot became increasingly segregated as the city itself became increasingly black. The percentage of blacks in the public schools between 1967 and 1970 increased from 56.7 to 63.8, and the percentage of blacks attending predominantly white schools decreased from 9 to 5.8. In 1968 the effort that had begun in 1965 to preserve racial integration in three high school constellations by using additional state funding to enrich the curriculum and provide additional educational services for the fifty thousand students involved collapsed as population shifts in the school neighborhoods substantially reduced the white student enrollment.[34]

As the black student population increased in the public schools, so too did the black instructional and administrative staff. The percentage of black faculty rose from 31.7 in October 1966 to 38 in November 1968, and 50 percent of the new faculty hires by that time were black. In an effort to place more blacks in administrative positions at a time when so many black teachers lacked very much seniority, the school administration reduced the amount of experience required for promotion. This contributed to an increase in the number of black school principals from 6 percent of the total in February 1967 to 12 percent by October 1968 and an increase in the number of positions above the rank of teacher held by blacks from 192 in October 1966 to 271 in February 1968.[35]

The quality of education in predominantly black schools continued to raise grave concerns in the black community following the riot. In the Iowa Test of Basic Skills in 1968, the average performance of fourth, sixth, and eighth grade students was below class level in every school in Detroit with a majority black enrollment. What was even more distressing was that the performance in Great Cities schools was no better than in other schools. While achievement scores fell, the dropout rate rose — there were three thousand more dropouts in 1968 than in 1965. The schools "[are] worse off than they were before," remarked Charles Colding, a leader of the 1966 Northern High boycott. An aide to Cavanagh warned the mayor in September 1969 that the schools were "deteriorating dangerously."[36]

The "lousy" quality of black schools, the sense among black students that the education that they were receiving was "irrelevant," the pressure of elements in the black community for black control of black schools, overcrowding and underfinancing, and "a complete break-down in communication between the public school system and the black community" made the schools "a hotbed of racial friction" following the riot. The lesson many black students appeared to have derived from the riot was that peaceful protests were useless and that direct action was the way to produce educational change. "We will not secure quality education for black children in our schools," Cleage declared, "until we create enough conflict to force basic changes in the administration of these schools." There were "skirmishes" between black and white students, small fires in school buildings, student boycotts of classes, sometimes for such "inconsequential reasons" as changed locker assignments, and attacks on and intimidation of white teachers and administrators.[37]

Seeking the replacement of a white principal by a black, students at Knudsen Junior High went on a rampage in October 1967 and vandalized the school. In March 1968 a more serious incident occurred at Post Junior High, where black students thought that the white assistant principal was unsympathetic to them. Someone, probably a student, pulled the fire alarm, bringing the Fire Department to the scene. As the fire trucks were leaving, students threw snowballs at them. A fireman jumped from one of the trucks and began "beating on the students." Police arrived and "roughed up" some students and bystanders and were "extremely abusive." Widespread protests in the black community and among black parents followed the incident. Drachler ordered an investigation, and the word was soon out that the assistant principal would be transferred.[38]

There were additional confrontations between students and school authorities in October 1968. After walking out of an assembly called by the principal of McKenzie High to discuss student grievances, black students remained away from classes for two days. The next week Cooley High students marched eight miles to the Schools Center Building to confront Drachler and Arthur Johnson with their demands. Student leaders of at least ten senior and junior high schools enlisted the aid of an adult advisory board in seeking to "force" the Detroit Board of Education to resolve student grievances about the quality of their education. At a board meeting in March 1969, "screaming teenagers" demanded that an intermediate school be named the "Malcolm X School." When the board met again that night at the Butzel School, where a teacher had been stabbed a short time earlier, black separatists seized the microphone, shouted "genocide," and demanded black control of black schools. Responding to Drachler's statement that the separatists did not represent the black majority, a black girl yelled, "Shut up, you honkie." Two policemen guarded the meeting, the first time police had ever done so, and they made five arrests.[39]

The turbulence in the schools and the "atmosphere of intimidation" took its toll on white principals in particular and made it difficult for the school system to hire teachers to work in the inner city. "We were beginning to feel more and more like a punching bag," an able white principal who headed an increasingly black high school recalled. The *New York Times* reported in March 1969 that fifteen inner-city white principals had been transferred, had become ill from the pressure, or had resigned during the preceding year. A black elementary school principal who left for the suburbs explained, "There was the pressure, the social revolution, the changes, the money shortage, the crowded conditions." Drachler told a United States Senate subcommittee in May 1968 that of 1,300 teachers hired during the previous summer, 330 had quit rather than accept an inner-city assignment. The white suburb of Livonia, which hired 36 former Detroit school teachers in the two years following the riot, claimed in the fall of 1970 that it had received close to one thousand applications for teaching positions from Detroit teachers, some of them with as much as twenty-five years of experience.[40]

Judging from survey data, a large majority of Detroit black adults did not support the demand of the militants for black teachers and black principals in predominantly black schools. Asked in the Campbell-Schuman survey of early 1968 about the desired race of teachers in black schools, a mere 5 percent of the black respondents, as we have seen, preferred blacks, whereas 34 percent preferred white teachers, and 59 percent favored a "half and half" distribution. Only 13 percent of the black respondents in the same survey thought that the principals of predominantly black schools should be black. When the University of Michigan's Detroit Area Study asked blacks in an April 1968 survey whether they agreed or disagreed with the statement that predominantly black schools should have black principals because blacks "should have the most say in running inner city schools," 43 percent of the respondents answered in the affirmative, but 57 percent did not.[41]

In 1969 advocates of community control of the Detroit schools won a major victory when the state legislature enacted a measure requiring decentralization of the Detroit school system. In the voting that followed, however, blacks won a majority in only two of the eight districts into which the school system had been divided. When the Commission on the Cities of the Urban Coalition visited Detroit in 1971, it found the school system "reeling from an insufficiently prepared and explained redistricting plan." There was a sense in Detroit in the years that followed that whatever gains the city might have made since the riot, public education was not among them and that the school system was "a disaster."[42]

In a message to Governor Romney of August 23, 1967, Cavanagh pointed out that Detroit's problems were compounded by its fiscal condition and that tax limitations Lansing imposed on the city were partly responsible. The mayor urged the state to provide a tax abatement or reimbursement plan for property owners whose property had been damaged in the riot, to increase the state gas and weight tax and revise the distribution formula so as to return more of the money to Detroit, and to authorize local government to levy excise taxes. Believing that the availability of insurance was essential to the "survival" of the inner city, Cavanagh also called on the state to adopt a risk insurance plan to cover persons who could not otherwise obtain coverage.[43]

Although the state did not enact the tax measures Cavanagh proposed, it did authorize Detroit to increase the local income tax on residents from 1 to 2 percent. This was in line with Cavanagh's desire, but the state did not permit Detroit to increase to 1 percent the 0.5 percent income tax levied on the 320,000 nonresidents who worked in the city. Responding to the mayor's insurance request, the legislature in the 1968 regular session enacted the Basic Property Insurance Act, which required licensed insurers in the state to contribute to an insurance pool that was to provide insurance to any businessman or homeowner who could not obtain insurance from two insurance companies.[44]

Joe R. Feagin and Harlan Hahn have described the response of most state governments to the civil disorders of the 1960s as one of "inaction" insofar as ameliorative measures are concerned.[45] This generalization, however, is not entirely applicable to Michigan's state government.

Although the Michigan legislature was readier to adopt punitive than ameliorative measures, it did respond to the riots by enacting legislation of substance regarding tenants' rights, open housing, urban renewal, and insurance, increasing state aid to education somewhat, and authorizing Detroit to increase its income tax.

Although looking to Lansing for some postriot assistance, it was primarily to Washington that Cavanagh appealed for government aid. "The offending party," he declared after the riot, "is the nation, and the injured party is the Negro population." Appearing before the Kerner Commission on August 15, 1967, Cavanagh asserted that the federal government must adopt "a new principle" on which to base federal programs, "the principle of reparation for long-standing injustices," reparations for the "great discrimination" against blacks and the denial of equal opportunity.

Reparations, Cavanagh advised, should take the form of "very special work training programs and special educational programs, special community construction and reconstruction programs involving and including both housing and business." He wanted the federal government to place a higher priority on urban needs than it had in the past and "to write . . . a new textbook for the two Americas" with which every city had to deal. He favored a program of tax incentives and tax credits to encourage private enterprise to create jobs in the ghetto, as well as the provision of insurance and reinsurance for those willing to invest in such areas, and he wanted the federal government to be the employer of last resort. He recommended a Reconstruction and Urban Public Works Act that would combine training and employment and would emphasize the employment of ghetto residents to rebuild blighted areas and areas that had been devastated. He also urged the creation of an urban development corporation and an urban development fund to encourage investment in low-cost housing and slum-based industries. "The future of this Nation and the balance of the twentieth century," Cavanagh warned the commission, "hangs in the balance."[46]

The Kerner Commission's report recommended a substantial program of social and economic reform. Appalled at the cost of these recommendations, which, he claimed, the Bureau of the Budget estimated at $30 billion, President Johnson received the report with "loud official silence." He had said, after all, that the federal government should not reward rioting, but this proved to be "more rhetoric than reality." After the riot, Detroit received some additional federal funding for job training, education, Model Cities, and improvement projects in areas affected by the riot; and it was the presumed beneficiary of an expensive housing program designed to rehabilitate inner-city structures that proved, unfortunately, to be "a dismal failure." Cavanagh, however, did not win administration support for the large federal programs he believed were required to make Detroit a "livable city."[47]

Whatever official Detroit may have thought, blacks in Detroit believed that the federal government was trying at least "as hard" as the city government and harder than the state government to solve Detroit's problems. In the Campbell-Schuman survey, 44 percent of the black respondents thought that Cavanagh was trying as hard as he could to solve the city's problems, slightly below the 45 percent who had this view of the federal government but well above the 28 percent who believed the same of the state government. The comparable percentages in the *Free Press* survey of the riot areas in 1968 were 42, 48, and 35.[48]

In his September 6 report to the people of Detroit, Cavanagh implied that the New Detroit Committee would play a large role in the reconstruction of the city. By the time New Detroit held its first full committee meeting on August 10, 1967, Joseph L. Hudson had decided that there should be two restrictions on its activities: it was to "look forward; not backward," leaving the task of discovering the riot's causes to others; and it was not to be a fund-raising organization but rather a body that evaluated and documented needs and recommended priorities. Overly optimistic about what New Detroit could accomplish, Hudson saw the committee as finishing its job "within a fairly short space of time" and then leaving "long-range completion" to agencies capable of implementing the committee's recommendations. With the self-assurance that came from being associated with what was then the world's largest manufacturing complex, Detroit's industrial leaders thought that they could come up with answers to the city's problems in a matter of months, "give Detroit's legitimate institutions a push in the right direction," and then let them complete the job.[49]

At New Detroit's August 10 meeting, Hudson told the committee members that there were two aspects to their role, "material reconstruction and building human relationships," and he thought the latter the more "urgent and delicate task." Maintaining that one thing that had been learned from the riot was "how little real listening" there had been among "some important groups" in the city, he urged committee members to listen to and to try to understand "the long-unheard needs and frustrations of the inner-city inhabitants."[50]

New Detroit initially operated through five subcommittees respectively concerned with communications, community services, education and employment, law and finance, and redevelopment. It had a staff of forty "loaners," who were supplied to New Detroit on a temporary basis by private corporations and public agencies and who were organized into task forces to engage in "research and brainstorming" for the subcommittees. Becoming increasingly aware of the intractability of Detroit's problems, Hudson and New Detroit's business leadership had concluded by the time of the committee's October 12 meeting that the committee's "activity and thrust" should be made permanent. Before the year was out, the committee had decided to become a permanent organization as the New Detroit Division of the Metropolitan Fund, to replace the loaners with a permanent staff, and to appoint William T. Patrick, Jr., as vice president of the Metropolitan Fund for New Detroit.[51]

Before accepting his new position, Patrick on November 24 addressed a private and confidential memorandum to Hudson that he titled "Life or Death of New Detroit." He remarked that his wife, aware of his "growing frustration" that New Detroit did not have the funds or the financial commitment "even [to] begin to approach the overwhelming responsibility of its mission," had said, "Why, Bill, they are trying to handle their nigger problem out of their petty cash fund!" New Detroit, Patrick maintained, was "trying to fight packs of lions and tigers with a fly-swatter." He believed that it was essential to convince the business community of the urgency of the "immediate and unequivocal commit- ment of large funds and resources" to New Detroit. He pointed out that the inner city was seeking to develop "*new* institutions," and he urged that New Detroit help this process, which he considered "one of the most important sagas in American history," by providing needed grants and loans.

If he were to accept his new post, Patrick stated, he wanted the business community to provide the committee with at least $1 million by December 1 and more millions later so that New Detroit could win some needed "victories" to counter "the pervasive spirit of despair and hope- lessness" that he believed had gripped "large parts of the city." The city with "the biggest civil disorder," Patrick wrote, "needs the biggest input of money and capital." New Detroit, as Patrick had urged, was soon to become a funding agency, but it is unclear if the business community had actually committed $1 million to the organization by December 1.[52]

The restructuring of New Detroit as a permanent organization took place in January 1968. A new permanent staff of one hundred, which included fifteen blacks, replaced the loaners, but it was a staff that was largely unaware of ghetto problems. On April 1, 1968, New Detroit decided to raise $10 million, and four months later, on August 15, 1968, it incorporated as New Detroit, Inc., with Max D. Fisher as chairman and Patrick as president. Leaving his leadership position, Hudson declared that running New Detroit had been "the most moving experi- ence" of his life, but he conceded that "the major challenges" the com- mittee faced remained "unanswered." By August 1969 New Detroit had exceeded its fund-raising goal.[53]

Although Cavanagh had helped to launch New Detroit, the rela- tionship between the mayor and New Detroit was an uneasy one from the start. New Detroit, as Hudson recalled, held the city bureaucracy "partially responsible" for the riot and believed that the city administra- tion was insufficiently sensitive to Detroit's racial problems. Privately, at least, Hudson complained that the city government did not give the committee "complete support" and used it as "a convenient buffer" to deflect criticism from itself. Cavanagh, for his part, responded that many New Detroit members had just "discovered" that there were "Negroes and slums" in Detroit. He criticized New Detroit for "a tendency to stand aloof from the problems of City government" and, on the other hand, for not making the "distinction between the responsibilities of city government and the role of business." New Detroit staffers thought that Cavanagh felt himself "threatened" by the committee, and he may, indeed, have viewed New Detroit as "a rival power center."[54]

New Detroit and the private sector received more publicity initially for the jobs they provided than for any other of their riot-related activities. "Nowhere else in the nation," the *New York Times* declared on November 19, 1967, "is a more concerted drive underway by business and industry to eradicate slum joblessness." The Detroit unemployment rate was 3.2 percent at that time, but the jobless rate in the black ghetto may have been five times higher than that. New Detroit judged that 80 percent of the hard-core unemployed were being excluded from jobs by unrealistic and irrelevant job qualifications.[55]

In August 1967 the Manpower Development Committee of the Greater Detroit Board of Commerce (GDBC) launched a campaign in which New Detroit joined to find jobs within two months for ten thousand unemployed and "previously unemployable" persons. As part of the campaign, employers agreed to reexamine their job application forms and hiring standards for entry-level jobs and to create or expand training programs for marginal workers. Volunteers were to assist new hires to adjust to their jobs by "a glorified buddy system." The GDBC contacted all Detroit employers who had fifty or more employees to seek their support, and it encouraged employers to establish employment offices in neighborhoods where potential workers lived. The GDBC and New Detroit helped to organize temporary job recruitment centers in the inner city in cooperation with the Congress of Racial Equality (CORE), the National Association for the Advancement of Colored People, and the Franklin-Wright Settlement.[56]

William M. Day, president of Michigan Bell and chairman of the Manpower Development Committee, informed New Detroit on October 12 that Detroit firms had hired ten thousand workers, half of them black, since the campaign had begun. In the next several weeks various figures were reported in the press regarding the numbers hired, ranging, bewilderingly, from 2,000 to 31,766, about half of whom, it was regularly stated, were black.[57]

The Big Three auto manufacturers actively participated in the campaign to provide jobs for the unskilled and the hard core. This was at least in part because the riot, during which looting had occurred near General Motors and Chrysler headquarters, had had a "profound effect" on the auto manufacturers. The Ford Motor Company made the most substantial effort of the three companies to hire from the inner city. On

October 26, following a forty-nine-day strike of its employees, Ford announced that it would open two job recruitment centers in MCHRD facilities in the inner city to fill sixty-five hundred positions. Only persons living in the inner city and registered with an antipoverty agency were to be eligible for the jobs. This was the first time Ford had hired away from its own premises, and, in another innovative action, it eliminated the usual written examination for its job applicants. "If they want jobs we will give them jobs," Henry Ford II grandly declared, and Arjay Miller, the company's president, proclaimed the company's purpose as nothing less than to "eliminate hard-core unemployment in the inner city."[58]

"A small army" stormed the two Ford job centers, which were altogether unprepared for the onslaught, when they opened on October 27. Specialized Training and Employment Placement Service soon began to cooperate with Ford by sending letters to the hard-core unemployed on its list advising them of the job opportunities, and it sought to help newly hired employees to adjust to their jobs. The MCHRD also aided Ford by identifying and screening qualified workers. By the end of October 1968 Ford had hired about five thousand of the hard-core unemployed.[59]

GM claimed that it had hired 12,000 Detroit workers, 5,300 of them black, by the middle of November. How many were hard core or employees it would have hired in any circumstances it did not say. In early 1968, however, GM and the DUL put Operation Opportunity into effect in Detroit, a program in which the DUL screened and referred the hard core to GM for orientation and then employment at Chevrolet Gear and Axle. The DUL helped these workers, 282 of whom were hired in 1968, to develop acceptable work habits. Chrysler reported that it had hired 13,000 workers by November 12, 1967, 60 to 70 percent of them black. Three hundred had been hired through a CORE job drive on Twelfth Street, and another 100 were youth gang members referred to Chrysler by the YMCA. Chrysler did some of its hiring at the job centers the GDBC and New Detroit had set up in the riot areas. When it turned out that some of these employees could not read, Chrysler hired fifty high school teachers to tutor them, and it supplied alarm clocks to workers who appeared to need them to get to work on time.[60]

The automobile companies were not the only Detroit employers to develop programs to hire or train the hard-core unemployed. The J. L. Hudson Company agreed in November 1967 to hire and train five hundred potential high school dropouts, half of whom were to receive full-time jobs, half, part-time. The next month the National Bank of Detroit arranged for the DUL to screen and refer individuals qualified for employment at the bank, leading to the hiring of twenty-eight such persons by January 1968. In October 1967 Michigan Bell "adopted" Northern High, apparently the first such partnership in the nation. It arranged to finance a twelve-week course to acquaint students with job application forms, employment tests, and the importance of deportment and grooming, and it purchased special equipment and met the cost of Saturday classes that provided training in basic electricity, switchboards, and secretarial work. It agreed to hire qualified Northern graduates and also contributed $1,500 annually to a college fund for the school's graduates. Chrysler made a similar arrangement with Northwestern High, establishing an auto mechanics course and shop in the school, placing some students in a preapprenticeship training class, hiring some Northwestern graduates, and retraining others.

Detroit Edison helped to finance the Twelfth Street Academy that the DUL set up in 1968 to tutor unemployed high school dropouts for the General Education Development Test, the satisfactory completion of which was the equivalent of a high school diploma. New Detroit, GM, Ford, and Michigan Bell all contributed to the Volunteer Placement Corps, founded by Carole Williams and consisting of two hundred volunteers who worked with inner-city students to help them find jobs or to matriculate in a college or to provide them with training. The corps assisted five thousand inner-city high school students during the 1968–69 school year.[61]

Convinced of the success of the Ford Motor Company's hiring program in the inner city, Henry Ford suggested to President Johnson that the federal government join hands with the private sector to mount similar programs across the nation. Preferring programs of this sort to public-service employment, Johnson early in 1968 announced the establishment of the Job Opportunities in the Business Sector (JOBS) program to be run by a newly created National Alliance of Businessmen (NAB), with Henry Ford serving as chairman. The government under this program provided subsidies to employers to train and employ the hard-core unemployed, the goal being the employment of one hundred thousand such individuals within two years.[62]

On February 1, 1968, Chrysler received the first grant under the new program to provide jobs for 750 hard-core unemployed and to enroll an additional 1,295 underemployed persons in a "skill-improvement program" that involved job training, counseling, and remedial education for up to twenty-three weeks preparatory to regular employment. Later in the year the GDBC received a $3.4 million JOBS grant, the largest sum awarded under the program to that time, to train and find jobs for 970 hard-core unemployed. The GDBC acted as the contractor for thirty-one companies, thus enabling smaller companies to participate in the JOBS program. The grant reportedly led to 2,000 permanent jobs for the unemployed in 1968–69.[63]

Quite apart from the Chrysler and GDBC grants, the NAB provided 17,000 summer jobs in Detroit in 1968. In addition, Detroit area employers pledged themselves to supply jobs for 18,000 hard-core unemployed by July 1, 1969, far above the 4,000 jobs goal the NAB had set for

Detroit. The employers claimed that they had hired 35,000 of the hard core between April 1968 and August 1969 and that 17,773 of them remained on the job. How many new jobs the NAB actually provided in Detroit is, however, a matter of some doubt since JOBS turned out to be more a "job-redistribution program" than a job-creation program.[64]

As with the JOBS program, it is difficult to know how many new jobs were created as a result of the efforts of the GDBC, New Detroit, and private employers following the July riot. The principal employers in the city were the Big Three automobile manufacturers, and Walter Reuther said of them in 1968, "They've done a terrific job of hiring and training in the ghetto." What this meant precisely in terms of new hires is another matter, however. When Hudson announced in March 1968 that 28,400 more persons were working than in the previous year at the same time, the Michigan Employment Security Commission countered that new entrants in the labor force had increased the number of the unemployed by 1,000. Much of the new hiring simply reflected the good times of 1968 and employment of persons who would have found jobs without the efforts then underway to employ the hard core. Also, insofar as the hard core were among those hired, they had a high turnover rate in at least some companies and, because of low seniority, were the first to be laid off when economic conditions took a turn for the worse in Detroit. The city's unemployment rate was higher in 1969 (8.5 percent) than in 1968 (7.3 percent), and it continued to climb in the next two years (11.9 percent in 1970, 14.1 percent in 1971).[65]

The one certain gain in employment stemming from the riot was the widespread change in hiring standards for entry-level jobs. Responding to the urging of New Detroit and the GDBC, employers simplified job application forms, abandoned testing for entry-level unskilled jobs, adopted more liberal policies regarding dress and deportment, and paid less attention than they had been doing to previous work experience, references, and police records for minor offenses. "Equal employment opportunity for at least entry level jobs has surely become a reality in Detroit," New Detroit proclaimed in September 1968. "For over 75 years," a Michigan Bell employment supervisor declared, "business tried to screen people out. Now we are trying to find reasons to screen them in." Discrimination against blacks and women had not suddenly come to an end in Detroit, but the riot did lead to at least some improvement in the hiring criteria for entry-level jobs. In the *Free Press* survey of the riot areas in the late summer of 1968, 39 percent of the respondents thought that business had become "more fair" since the riot, as compared to 14 percent who thought it had become "less fair" and 47 percent who saw no change.[66]

As New Detroit noted in its report to the people in April 1968, the organization had directed "a major portion of its attention and resources to the subject of housing." Its primary housing concern was to provide dwellings for blacks of low or modest income. Of the city's 700,000 dwelling units, New Detroit estimated in October 1967 that 75,000, mostly occupied by blacks, were substandard. It believed that it was necessary to supply about 20,000 new units in the next two years, three-fourths of them for low- and middle-income persons.[67]

To achieve its housing goals, New Detroit relied primarily on the Metropolitan Detroit Citizens Development Authority (MDCDA), a nonprofit corporation organized in 1966 by Walter Reuther and Walker Cisler to assist community groups in building and rehabilitating needed housing by providing seed money and technical assistance. The MDCDA characterized itself as a "servant organization" that believed the community groups it assisted should select the planners, architects, and contractors for their housing projects. It was sensitive, at least in theory, to the black demand for self-determination. Between January 1, 1968, and December 31, 1972, New Detroit invested $3,449,700 in the MDCDA.[68]

The MDCDA's principal project was Elmwood II on the east side, where it sought to assist the Ralph Bunche Community Council in the construction of some of the 352 units for moderate- and low-income families that the council was projecting. Interested in developing new construction techniques, the MDCDA joined with H. F. Campbell Company in sponsoring the demonstration of a new low-cost construction method in the building of 24 units on one site, and it also sponsored a competition in low-cost building techniques that resulted in the award of a contract to the winner to build 800 units and to the runner-up to construct 200 units. It cooperated with the Virginia Park Rehabilitation Committee in the rehabilitation of 188 apartment units, and it provided the $30,000 down payment that enabled the United Tenants for Collective Action to purchase the nine Goodman apartments.[69]

Although the MDCDA talked of building 25,000 units for low-income families over a five-year period, in the end it built or rehabilitated only 2,713 units before conceding failure. When it started its first project in June 1968, an MDCDA spokesman said, "All we've been able to do is scratch the surface—literally," and that described the overall record of the MDCDA, figuratively. One source of difficulty was its often tense relations with black community groups. "Many black people," the MDCDA's executive director declared, "are more concerned over the whole matter of self-determination than they are about having holes dug and bricks placed upon bricks." The MDCDA's failure, however, is explained by more fundamental matters than its relations with community groups. Its program was "overly ambitious," its management was poor, it dissipated its funds among too many small groups that then failed, the unions objected to the new building techniques it encouraged, and one of its major contractors had to declare bankruptcy. Its failure to accomplish more was New Detroit's "largest fiasco" during the first several years of its existence.[70]

In a minor but rather unusual way of encouraging blacks to rehabilitate their own dwellings, the Chevrolet Division of GM, Detroit Edison, and the Fruehauf Trailer Corporation initiated Project Handyman. They equipped a huge trailer truck with building equipment, dispatched it to the ghetto manned by young blacks who were receiving instruction in the building trades from a black contractor, and offered residents the opportunity to have their homes repaired at the cost of the materials.[71]

A vigorous supporter of the postriot request of the Detroit public schools for $5.3 million in additional state aid, New Detroit made grants in 1968 and 1969 to the public schools, two high schools not part of the Detroit system, and Oakland Community College so that inner-city youngsters could attend summer school. It came to the assistance of the newly created Wayne County Community College, the first community college to be established in the inner city, with grants of $150,000 in 1969 and $175,000 in 1970. It encouraged the interest of blacks in their heritage by a grant to the Detroit public schools to support an Afro-American Workshop Program in the summer of 1968 and by a $300,000 grant in 1969 to a new Afro-American Development Foundation, a coalition of black artists and cultural leaders. Adopting a suggestion of the youthful Norvell Harrington, New Detroit established a Special Task Force on Youth Involvement designed especially to stimulate teenagers to help solve the problems "spotlighted" by the riot and to aid them in "translating their ideas into action." New Detroit's grants to the East Side Voice for Independent Detroit and its Political Education Project, a mock junior government to train the young in politics, followed logically from this same concern.[72]

It was its interest in youth that led New Detroit to pay a good deal of attention to the recreational needs of the inner city. Early in 1968 New Detroit formed a Youth, Recreation and Cultural Affairs Subcommittee, and a Cavanagh aide informed the mayor that it seemed as though New Detroit had become more interested in recreation than in any other subject. Taking note of the "sad state of recreational facilities and programs" in the inner city, New Detroit sought to energize the Department of Parks and Recreation and to induce United Community Services to move off "dead center" and to understand that recreation was its prime mission. In December 1967 New Detroit played a key role in the organization of the Joint Recreation Committee, made up of representatives of the numerous organizations concerned about recreation. It provided grants in July 1968 for three inner-city projects to provide more recreational and guidance facilities for teenagers and seniors, and it supported DART's efforts to spur the building of vest pocket parks in the black ghetto.[73]

New Detroit sought to promote the development of black-owned business in the inner city. After creating an Economic Development Subcommittee early in 1968 with this purpose in view, New Detroit in October 1968 spawned the Economic Development Corporation (EDC), a nonprofit corporation that included Detroit's top business leadership and to which New Detroit allocated $1.45 million. The EDC, "an effort to put white capitalism to work to promote black capitalism," was designed to aid blacks in starting their own businesses and to provide them with management training, technical assistance, and market support. Sensitive like the MDCDA to black demands for self-determination, it sought "not to dominate but support." In its first year, as already noted, it aided the Inner City Business Improvement Forum (ICBIF) with $850,000 in grants and loans, and it made $100,000 available to the Metropolitan Contractors Credit Corporation, an organization that provided financial and managerial support to minority group contractors. Like the ICBIF, the EDC joined with the Small Business Administration in arranging bank loans for black businesses. Between 1968 and 1973 the EDC aided 273 black businesses. In January 1975 EDC and ICBIF merged. By that time, many of Detroit's major corporations had become "apathetic about the whole effort." As one executive conceded, "you lose interest if people aren't creating trouble for you."[74]

Despite their efforts, the ICBIF and the EDC achieved only modest success in the long run. "You'd have a hell of a hard time making a cost effective case" for what the two had accomplished, Hudson said in 1984, but he thought that what had occurred was an important learning experience for those involved. In a far harsher appraisal, Nicholas Hood remarked in 1982 that the money spent for black economic development "went nowhere, went right down the drain." Small business was on the decline in the postriot years, and because of the small market usually available to them, black-owned businesses in black areas faced special difficulties. Some ICBIF ventures were ill-advised and entered into without adequate planning because, as its president explained in 1972, blacks felt themselves under pressure after the riot to show that they "could do something" for themselves if they received "the necessary financial aid." Blacks owned about 10 percent of Detroit's businesses in 1972 as compared to 7 percent in 1967, but more than half of the businesses the ICBIF had funded were no longer in existence by then. Still, a black poverty official declared in 1972, "Black businesses are doing better in Detroit than in any other city in the North."[75]

Initially, New Detroit appeared to think that "building human relationships," a task whose urgency Hudson had stressed, meant convincing inner-city blacks of the white establishment's goodwill and of New Detroit's willingness to listen to what blacks had to say. With this in mind, New Detroit committee members and staff established contacts with inner-city residents and organizations and sought to learn their needs. After William Day had met with a group of black ADC mothers, he said that he had "learned a few things that he had never before known." Believing that informal contacts of this sort had had a "favorable impact" on the black community and had resulted in the development of "new, meaningful associations," New Detroit officially adopted a "community contact program" involving sixteen committee members who met informally with selected black individuals and groups for an exchange of views. New Detroit officials thought that this "continuing dialogue" with inner-city residents, which continued until March 1968, was the organization's "most significant . . . accomplishment" during the first several months of its existence.[76]

Increasingly, New Detroit became concerned about the polarization of the black and white communities and the consequent need not only to communicate with blacks but to educate whites and to deal with white racism. In espousing open housing and similar measures, New Detroit discovered that it had "outrun [white] community attitudes," and, as Hudson noted, opposition to the organization was "quick to form and quick to speak out." Some angry whites went so far as to close their Hudson accounts and to picket the firm's downtown store. Disturbed by what it believed was "a serious lack" of personal concern about racial problems in "many sectors of the white community," New Detroit, as the president of the Metropolitan Fund declared, decided to become "a burr on the conscience" of its "white neighbors."[77]

New Detroit supported a variety of programs to combat white racism in the city and its suburbs. Acting on behalf of New Detroit, the Metropolitan Fund's Citizen Information Division implemented a Comprehensive Suburban Communications Project to involve suburbanites in activities designed to alter their racial attitudes. New Detroit helped to fund the Interfaith Action Council's Suburban Action Centers program, which involved the projected establishment of eleven centers to devise programs with local organizations to improve racial attitudes. Through the Metropolitan Fund, New Detroit funded a color film, "The Black Eye," written and produced entirely by blacks and used in suburban communities to give whites some understanding of the black community.

New Detroit also served as a clearinghouse for television programs dealing with urban and racial problems. The most important of these, produced by the Interfaith Action Council and funded by it and New Detroit, was to have been shown in five parts during prime time on WWJ-TV beginning in May 1968 and was coupled with organized living-room meetings and discussion of the issues raised by each program. After the second program, which dealt with the way the media treated racial issues, the station manager canceled the showing of the remainder of the series because the programs allegedly lacked "proper balance." The final three programs were then shown on an educational television station.[78]

When Marketing Strategy, Inc., in June and July 1968 interviewed a sample of 635 whites and 565 blacks drawn from the inner city, the outer city, and the suburbs, it found that 42 percent of the black respondents and 44 percent of the white respondents thought that the black and white communities had come "closer together" since the riot, whereas 30 percent of the blacks and 29 percent of the whites believed they had drawn further apart. It is possible that New Detroit deserved some of the credit for the improved racial feeling the survey seemed to indicate, but the committee itself let it be known in the month before the survey was conducted that the racial conflict, "if anything," was "in a more advanced state" than it had been at the time of the riot. Many blacks and whites involved with New Detroit became personally aware of the depth of racial feeling in the city. In a summary of New Detroit activities released in November 1969, Patrick revealed that some of the organization's black trustees had lost face in the black community as "tools of the white establishment" and that when some white staffers returned to their middle-management positions, they encountered "recrimination and isolation from their peers."[79]

New Detroit at its outset and for a short time thereafter enjoyed "a remarkable image" as "the hope of Detroit." Its luster as "a race relations laboratory for the country" began to dim, however, once it became evident that the organization, for all the power of the business establishment, could not work wonders in the city. Increasingly, New Detroit was criticized for "coming up with a lot of talk . . . but little action." This, indeed, was Cavanagh's judgment when he appraised the organization in 1971, after he had left office: "It's a lot of puffery really," he said. "I don't think it has lived up to its press notices." Quite in contrast to its naive view at the outset as to what the private sector could accomplish in a short time, New Detroit had come to recognize that the city's problems were beyond its capacity to solve. Although private aid was a must, only the federal government, Patrick said in 1970, could rebuild the city. "I have become really impressed with the inability to do anything on a local basis," Hudson asserted two years later.[80]

When Detroit's business and industrial elite, led by Henry Ford II, launched Detroit Renaissance in November 1970 in an effort to arrest the flight of business from the city by building a $600 million hotel, office, and retail complex on the riverfront, Lorenzo Freeman said it marked "a clear shift in emphasis away from New Detroit and people to the brick and mortar development of downtown." New Detroit insisted that the two were "complementary," but as Richard Child Hill commented, the creation of the Detroit Renaissance partnership, "the largest private investment group ever assembled in the United States for an urban real estate project," reflected the conclusion of the city's top business leadership that New Detroit was "a poor substitute for the massive economic transformation Detroit needed." But for all their concern about rebuilding the city, the city's corporate leaders had not hesitated to remove their own businesses from Detroit to the suburbs or to other states.[81]

Despite the criticism to which it came to be subjected, New Detroit was not without important accomplishments. Quite apart from such specific matters as the enactment of state open housing legislation and the changes in hiring practices for entry-level jobs, New Detroit was successful in "getting the Detroit business community off its comfortable cushioned seat" and causing it to focus attention on the city's racial problems. Detroit, the *Detroit News* remarked, was seen around the country as "the home ground of big business paying attention to the problems of the city." New Detroit, moreover, provided both moderate and militant blacks with direct access to the city's white establishment and served as a forum where "those with power and influence" could "begin to listen and learn from those without power." According to Arthur Johnson, New Detroit's "strongest impact" was in the realm of public policy. Although reluctant to modify their own "institutional behavior" to any great degree, the corporate leaders of New Detroit, he observed, were willing "to put their weight forward" when it came to public-policy matters involving the city.[82]

In the riot's aftermath, New Detroit served as the model urban coalition for the nation—there were forty-two such coalitions by December 1968—and it was nationally recognized as "unique among big city attempts to strike at a root cause" of the riots. A national urban coalition, Urban America, Inc., in whose organization Detroiters played a prominent role, was established on August 24, 1967, in response to the Detroit and other riots. When two advance men from Urban America visited Detroit in October, they said that they had "not seen the likes of New Detroit anywhere in the country"; and, as Hudson recalled, Urban America spent its first few years "sort of picking [New Detroit's] brains[,] figuring out what we were doing."[83]

New Detroit, over the years, certainly did as much if not more than any other private organization in responding to Detroit's racial problems, and it deserves at least some of the credit for helping to maintain the city's racial peace. The Citizens Committee for Equal Opportunity, which had been founded when there was "no visible, coordinated effort on the part of top civic leadership" to promote the cause of equal opportunity in the city, no longer saw the need for its existence once New Detroit had been established. After limping along following the riot, the committee ceased to function at the end of 1969.[84]

How Detroiters viewed New Detroit and its big business members was revealed in surveys conducted in the first few years following the riot. Although New Detroit appeared to think that it was having more trouble reaching whites than blacks, 23 percent of the white respondents in the 1968 Marketing Strategy survey, as compared to 13 percent of the blacks, placed New Detroit first on the list of organizations that had contributed the most since the riot to improving racial conditions in the city. Both whites (39 percent) and blacks (19 percent) gave "big companies" the most credit, a choice that can be equated, to some degree, with New Detroit. In the riot areas, according to the 1968 *Free Press* survey, 52 percent of the respondents thought that private businesses in Detroit were "trying as hard" as they could to solve the city's problems, above the percentage having a similar opinion of federal, state, and city governments.[85]

In a survey concerning New Detroit's "image" that Market Opinion Research conducted in the Detroit metropolitan area in 1972, it turned out that New Detroit was better known among whites (58 percent) than among blacks (41 percent). Only 1.5 percent of the blacks, as compared to 13 percent of the whites, indicated that "better race relations" was what came to mind when they thought of New Detroit. "Rebuilding Detroit" was the most common reaction to this question among both blacks (23 percent) and whites (19 percent). "Redevelopment of the inner city," by contrast, was the response of only 8 percent of the blacks and 5.5 percent of the whites. Asked to register the extent of their agreement or disagreement (the range was from strong agreement to strong disagreement) with the statement that New Detroit was helping to improve race relations, establish minority business, find jobs for people, and promote black cultural organizations, both whites and blacks placed themselves between "neutral" and "agree."[86]

The 1972 Market Opinion Research survey reflected the modest success of the ameliorative approach followed by New Detroit from its inception. Although the Detroit city government had made a more determined effort than virtually all other riot cities to deal with the basic social and economic causes of racial discord that appear to have led to the 1960s riots, "modest success" may be even too generous an appraisal of what the Cavanagh administration had been able to accomplish. If, as the dean of the University of Detroit Law School thought, "outsiders" viewed Detroit after the 1967 riot as "an advance test, a stalking horse for the solution of urban problems," the nation had little reason for optimism about the future of its great cities.[87]

CHAPTER 19

"God Help Our City"

As the city that had been viewed as the nation's model in race relations but had nevertheless experienced the nation's worst riot, Detroit continued to attract a great deal of attention after July 1967. Periodically, especially at the time of the great riot's anniversary date, newsmen and others took the city's pulse to test the health of the patient and its reaction to the terrible shock its system had experienced.

During the first year after the riot the qualitative judgment about conditions in Detroit tended to be quite pessimistic. "The long standing problems are still problems," Father James Sheehan wrote on October 16, 1967. "The commitment to move on these problems is still minimal, although the riots did give some impetus to movement." In a headline of February 26, 1968, the *Michigan Chronicle* rendered its judgment: " 'Containment,' Not Prevention," the journal stated, "Is Now City's Only Concern." Complaining that the Detroit community failed to recognize the need for "radical changes" despite the riot, the chairman of the Commission on Community Relations wrote Mayor Cavanagh at about the same time that Detroit had "failed to provide adequate jobs, housing, education, health and recreation" for all of the city's inhabitants and that blacks remained "the most disadvantaged members" of the community.[1]

"Who Cares about Rebuilding the City?" the fine newsman William Serrin asked in a *New Republic* piece of May 1968. He thought that Cavanagh had shown "little zest" for the task, pronounced Detroit's war on poverty and its urban renewal program to be failures, minimized what New Detroit had accomplished, and castigated "the hands-off attitude of the state legislature over the years" as bordering on "the criminal." He concluded that "Detroit, whose automobiles changed the face of the world," was "not changing itself." On the riot's first anniversary, the *New York Times*'s Jerry Flint, although calling attention to some hopeful signs in the city, noted the lack of progress in rebuilding areas devastated by the riot, the lack of new low-income public housing, the dwindling enthusiasm for the war on poverty, and the crimes with racial overtones. *Newsweek* cited Ray Girardin and Joseph L. Hudson as conceding that the problems that had caused the riot remained uncorrected. "Blacks and whites are further apart than ever," Girardin remarked.[2]

Survey data gathered about a year or so following the riot are, on the whole, at variance with the negative qualitative evaluations of the city's condition. Asked their opinion regarding the degree of progress the city had made in "eliminating problems" that had caused the riot, 44 percent of the black respondents and 36 percent of the whites in the Marketing Strategy survey of June–July 1968 thought that there had been a "great deal of progress" or that things were "beginning to improve," as compared to 23 percent of the blacks and 18 percent of the whites who believed that there had been "a lot of talk, little progress." Blacks and whites agreed that there had been improvement in job opportunities in particular but also in terms of the "greater involvement" of inner-city residents in "solving city problems" and in "overall understanding and communication between whites and blacks." Half the black respondents, however, believed that middle-class Detroit whites preferred to "keep things" as they were.[3]

In an effort to ascertain black attitudes a year after the riot, the *Detroit Free Press* in the late summer of 1968 conducted a follow-up survey in the same riot areas in east and west Detroit that it had had surveyed just after the riot. When it asked the 452 blacks in its probability sample about a list of possible riot causes, it found that they had pretty much the same opinions as blacks had expressed on this point in the 1967 survey. Indeed, anywhere from 7 to 16 percent more black respondents in 1968 than in the 1967 survey complained about police brutality, poor housing, lack of jobs, and poverty, possibly because they now expected their complaints to "lead to action."

There were, nevertheless, several indications in the 1968 *Free Press* survey that riot-area blacks were less alienated than they had been just after the disturbance. Whereas 24 percent of the respondents in the 1967 survey thought that blacks had more to gain than lose by resorting to violence, the percentage agreeing to this dropped somewhat to 20 in 1968. In 1967, 67 percent of those surveyed thought the United States "worth fighting for in a big war," but in 1968, 77 percent took this position. Just over 58 percent of the 1967 respondents believed that they would receive the same pay as whites if employed to do the same work; one year later 67 percent of the sample were of this opinion. When asked to place themselves on Cantril's Self-Anchoring Striving Scale, riot-area blacks averaged 4.9 on the ten-step ladder for the summer of 1967 but 5.7 at the time of the 1968 survey and 7.7 for five years later, indicating that they believed their condition had improved since the riot and was likely to improve still more in the future. Riot-area blacks in 1968 were also more committed to integration than their 1967 counterparts: 75 percent of the 1968 blacks as compared to 61 percent of the 1967 sample expressed a preference for living in mixed black-white neighborhoods.[4]

Just after the riot, 50 percent of the blacks in the Luby team's survey of the black community indicated that they believed the city's whites had become more sympathetic to blacks as a result of the riot. In its survey of the black community conducted between April 24 and July 31, 1968, the University of Michigan's Detroit Area Study found that 58 percent of the city's blacks thought that more of the city's whites favored equal rights as the result of the riot. Neither the samples in the two surveys nor the questions asked were identical, but, along with the Marketing Strategy survey and the answers to at least some questions in the *Detroit Free Press* survey of the riot areas, they do nothing to weaken the impression that Detroit blacks were more inclined to view developments in the city during the first year after the riot in optimistic rather than pessimistic terms.[5]

The qualitative evaluations of Detroit continued to be pessimistic during the second year after the riot. Detroit, Serrin judged late in October 1968, was "unable to effect even the beginnings of meaningful reconstruction." He portrayed Cavanagh as "still dazed" by what had happened, as being "sullen and defensive, unwilling to grasp the levers of government." The mayor of whom it had once been said that he could see the White House on a clear day was now, according to Serrin, even unable to "see" the nearby Ambassador Bridge. "Detroit," the *Michigan Chronicle* proclaimed on March 22, 1969, "is a city of confused people, frightened and angry, misunderstanding and misunderstood. Fear has taken its toll of the city's vitality," the *Chronicle* asserted, "far faster than education and progress could build it up again. We are a city divided not only between its black and white citizenry but within them as well."[6]

"God Help Our City" was the title of another gloomy Serrin appraisal of Detroit in March 1969. He pointed this time to the "abysmal police-Negro relations" as "a symbol" of all that he saw "wrong with the city: a teetering war on poverty, shoddy schools, an inhuman urban-renewal program, polluted air and water, an archaic tax structure, and, for the most part, its unconcerned politicians, business leaders, and citizenry." Detroiters appeared to agree with this harsh, probably excessively harsh, assessment. In a Market Opinion Research survey conducted in May 1969, 57 percent of the sample thought that Detroit was worse off than it had been five years earlier; only 11 percent believed that conditions had improved. Crime, racial problems, and the condition of the public schools appear to have explained the survey's results. In twenty-four months, Hubert Locke asserted in his book on the 1967 riot, "the city of hope" had become "the city in crisis."[7]

His electoral support slipping, as the polls indicated, and beset by personal problems, Cavanagh announced in June 1969 that he would not be a candidate for reelection that year.[8] "It was our riot-producing, hatred-producing social system," declared the *Michigan Chronicle*, "that unseated the liberal Prince Charming from the white charger on which he rode into the fray in 1961." He had known, Cavanagh said just after the riot, that "the golden days just couldn't last," and how right he was. The events of late July 1967 had shaken the mayor to the core. "I was sure of myself, got praised, and now I can't guarantee anything," he said in reacting to the calamity that had befallen him and his city.[9]

In the Detroit primary election in 1969, the two winners were Richard Austin, the black Wayne County auditor, and Roman Gribbs, the white sheriff of Wayne County. A "racial moderate" who had appointed blacks to important positions in his department, Gribbs had nevertheless alienated blacks by seeking as sheriff to use Mace in combating crime. Given the racially polarized character of the Detroit community and the state of police-community relations following the New Bethel incident, it is hardly surprising that race was the decisive issue in the primary.

In the final election, Gribbs made crime in the streets, "for many whites a nagging, deep fear," his principal issue. Austin stressed open housing and claimed that a black mayor would have a better chance than a white mayor of unifying the racially divided city. Possibly aided by the fact that homicides in Detroit hit an all-time high in October 1969, Gribbs narrowly defeated Austin by a little more than six thousand votes in a total vote of just over 511,000. Austin received about 15 percent of the white vote, while Gribbs received only an estimated 4 percent of the black vote. Of the nine councilmen elected, three were black.[10]

The cutback in auto production in the winter of 1969–70 and the decline in the Detroit economy that set in then added to Detroit's woes. As the decade of the 1960s ended, the city, in B. J. Widick's words, was "floundering in economic insecurity and social instability." "Riot Trauma Lingers in Detroit," the *New York Times* declared on the riot's fourth anniversary.[11]

Judging from survey data compiled in 1971 by the Detroit Area Study and the political scientists Joel D. Aberbach and Jack L. Walker,[12] Detroit blacks were far more pessimistic about the state of race relations at that time than they had been during the first year following the riot. They were less inclined to believe that there had been "a lot of progress in getting rid of racial discrimination" in the preceding fifteen years, less optimistic about the future of race relations in the city, more distrustful of whites and of the city government, less supportive of integration, and more willing to believe violence was "the best way" for blacks to attain their goals. But at the same time as Detroit blacks were becoming more distrustful of whites, Detroit whites — judging from responses to questions concerning school and neighborhood integration, play between black and white children, and racial intermarriage — had become somewhat more liberal in their view of blacks since the riot although "still far from [a position of] complete racial tolerance."[13]

Gribbs has been described as a "transitional" mayor, preparing Detroit for black rule. "The black man has the feeling he is about to take power in the city," Hudson observed on the riot's fifth anniversary, "but," said Hudson with the condition of the Detroit economy in mind, "he is going to be left with an empty bag." As the *Detroit Free Press* saw it, he was also going to be left with a city which, "challenged by the worst riot in history," had "responded at best in piecemeal ways, at worst hardly at all." The city's former mayor agreed. "If you objectively try to measure where the city was after the riot," Cavanagh said, "you have to conclude we're far worse off today, the city and the people that live in it." The magazine *Black Enterprise* nevertheless thought that Detroit, despite all that had happened, was still "probably better than most cities in handling its race problems." It quoted a black Chevrolet dealer as wryly remarking that if hard times brought soup lines in the nation's cities, Detroit would have "the best soup."

In the 1973 Detroit mayoral race, the militant black, Coleman Young, defeated the white police commissioner, John Nichols, by a margin of fourteen thousand votes. The campaign centered on police behavior and the STRESS (Stop Robberies, Enjoy Safe Streets) unit that Nichols had created and that began to function in January 1971. Composed of about one hundred, mostly white, police officers and serving in high crime, predominantly black areas, STRESS engaged in surveillance and, of far greater importance, decoy operations. Since it was responsible during the three years that it functioned for the slaying of twenty-two citizens, most of them black, STRESS came to be viewed in the black community as "a killer squad."

Young received fewer white votes in 1973 than Austin had, but he was carried to victory by the black electorate. For blacks, the election had both substantive and symbolic significance: their votes had not only elected Detroit's first black mayor, but they had also provided the votes to enable a long-time critic of the city's largely white police force to defeat the white police commissioner who had been deputy superintendent during the riot and was the originator of the STRESS unit. Also, as a result of the new city charter approved by the voters in the election, oversight of the Police Department was henceforth to be vested in a five-person civilian Board of Police Commissioners appointed by the mayor with the approval of the Common Council. The position of police commissioner was abolished, and the administration of the department was vested in a chief of police appointed by the mayor. The Board of Police Commissioners was not only to be the policy-making body for the department, but it could also investigate citizen complaints against the police.[14]

Young, who had gained an "inside" view of the Police Department while serving on Mayor Cavanagh's Special Task Force on Police Recruitment and Hiring, made reform of the department a major objective of his administration. He abolished the STRESS unit, oversaw the reorganization of the department, and initiated an affirmative action program involving the hiring, assignment, and promotion of officers that was designed to integrate the department fully and make the force 50 percent black, a goal that was just about attained in thirteen years. In 1976 the mayor appointed a black career officer to serve as chief of police. Police-community relations, which had inflamed race relations before, during, and after the riot, took a decided turn for the better as the result of Young's election and the substantial changes in the Police Department that ensued.[15]

The early years of the long Young mayoralty not only led to improved police-community relations but also to a greater sense of black self-confidence. Judging by their responses to six of the same questions the Detroit Area Study had asked in 1968, blacks in Detroit in 1976 viewed their condition and the state of race relations in the city much as they had in 1968 rather than in the pessimistic vein of 1971. Whatever Detroit's problems, and they were enormous, blacks, in control of the city, no longer had that "desolate feeling of estrangement, of being on the outside looking in" that they had had before 1967. "Blacks look on this as our city now," declared the black vice president of Detroit Renaissance in 1978, by which time the mayor, the chief of police, the superintendent of schools, five of the nine council members, and eight of the thirteen members of the Detroit Board of Education were black. The riot, by speeding up the white exodus from Detroit that was already underway, had shortened the time leading to black political control of the city, but economic power continued to be in white hands.[16]

As the riot reached its twentieth anniversary, Detroit was a city beset with problems. Although political power was securely lodged in the hands of blacks, the city government, as Hudson had indicated, was "left" holding "an empty bag." Despite "a renaissance on the riverfront and new hope and excitement for downtown and the Woodward corridor," Detroit's economy was in far worse shape than in 1967. This was largely due to the declining fortunes of the American automobile industry, which "devastated the city in ways that mere looters and arsonists never could." As compared to a 5 percent unemployment rate in 1967, the jobless rate in Detroit in 1987 was over 11 percent and four to five times that among teenagers. Between 1967 and 1982 Detroit lost about 45 percent of all the jobs in the city. Of the 195,000 jobs that disappeared between 1967 and 1985, more than half were in manufacturing. Less than 10 percent of the jobs in 1987 were manufacturing jobs, and the decent-paying entry-level jobs for those with low skills were vanishing. More than one-half of Detroit's manufacturing, retail, and wholesale establishments had disappeared in the twenty years since the riot. In 1960, 45.6 percent of the tax base of Wayne, Oakland, and Macomb Counties was in Detroit, but only 12.6 percent of the tax base remained in the city by 1987. In the year of the riot, 8.5 percent of Detroit's population was on the welfare rolls; twenty years later, 34 percent of the city's inhabitants were receiving public assistance of one sort or another.[17]

The declining economy had its effect on the quality of life in the city, which two of three Detroiters in 1987 believed had deteriorated in the preceding ten years. Detroit as of 1987 had the second highest infant mortality rate in the nation, about 65 percent of its families were single-parent households, and the teenage pregnancy rate stood at about 20 percent. Violent crime was of special concern to Detroiters, the per capita homicide rate being three times higher in 1987 than in 1967 and higher than that of any other city by a fairly substantial margin. There were just about as many slayings of youths under seventeen in 1986 as there had been deaths in the 1967 riot.[18]

Detroiters were more dissatisfied with their schools in 1987 than they had been just after the 1967 riot. In the Campbell-Schuman survey of early 1968, 36 percent of the black respondents and 22 of the white were "somewhat" or "very dissatisfied" with the city's schools; but according to a survey conducted for the *Detroit News* in April 1987 by the Gordon S. Black Company,[19] which, admittedly, used a quite different sample, 45 percent of the city's respondents were "somewhat" or "very dissatisfied" with the schools. As a result of the white exodus, the school system, despite a busing plan that went into operation in January 1976, was more segregated than it had been at the time of the riot, the percentage of white students in the public schools having declined from 41 in 1967 to 9 in 1986.

Chronic budget deficits made it impossible for the school system to implement many of the principal recommendations of the High School Study Commission of 1968. In the 1966–67 school year Detroit ranked 44th among the state's 585 school districts in expenditures per pupil, but it had fallen to 93d place in the 1985–86 school year. Average teacher salaries in Detroit suffered a similar fate, plunging from 12th to 104th among the state's school districts during the same period. Violence and the fear of violence, reflecting what was happening in the city outside the schools, became an in-school problem, as "the weapons culture," to quote the president of the Detroit Federation of Teachers (DFT), "invaded" the school buildings.

One positive educational note was the slow rise in student performance on standard achievement tests that began in 1976, even though Detroit scores were still below the state average. Also, although a dropout rate of 41 percent was distressingly high, it was still below the 50 to 62.5 percent dropout rates in predominantly black schools at the time of the riot. The president of the DFT found some additional cause for encouragement in the fact that there was "far more community involvement" with the schools in 1987 than in 1967.[20]

The quality of life and the sad state of the public schools accelerated the flight of Detroiters to the suburbs. In the twenty years following the riot, Detroit lost about one-third of its population. Middle-class blacks joined whites in fleeing to the suburbs, as the substantial increase of the number of blacks in Detroit suburbs like Southfield and Oak Park indicates.[21]

If Detroiters were more dissatisfied with their schools in 1987 than in 1967, blacks, at least, had a considerably better opinion of the Police Department than they did at the time of the 1967 riot. The change in the composition and behavior of the police force was one area where black control of the city had had a decisive impact, and it removed what was perhaps the major black grievance leading to the 1967 riot. As Mayor Young stated in 1987, the "change in the black community's perception of the police" was "the single big difference" in Detroit since the riot. In the 1971 Aberbach-Walker survey of the Detroit community, 82 percent of the black respondents thought that the police were more likely ("definitely" or "probably") to mistreat blacks than whites, but only 20 percent of the blacks in the 1987 Black Company survey thought the police treated blacks worse than whites. "As a black person, I can tell you," a retired Detroit Board of Education employee said in 1987, "we're treated with a lot more respect and consideration now than we were in 1967."[22]

Detroit remained a racially polarized community twenty years after the great riot. The riot had made blacks considerably more visible to the white community and had gained the attention of the city's white leadership, but "the dialogue between black and white" that ensued, as the *Detroit Free Press* observed in 1987, was "mostly at the top, in a thin layer of civic, cultural and political activities," among the black and white members, for example, of New Detroit. Most whites, it is clear, continued to prefer to live alongside other whites and were disinclined to send their children to predominantly black schools. "Detroit is the most racially polarized city in the nation," said Arthur Johnson in 1987, speaking as president of the Detroit branch of the National Association for the Advancement of Colored People. No mainstream black leader in Detroit would have said anything like that in 1967.[23]

It is difficult to determine from the available survey data whether Detroiters thought race relations had improved, deteriorated, or remained the same in the twenty years following the 1967 riot. The problem is compounded by the fact that the available surveys used quite different samples. In the Marketing Strategy survey of June 1968, 42 percent of the black respondents and 44 percent of the white thought the two races had drawn "closer together" since the riot. Nineteen years later, in a Market Opinion Research survey of blacks and whites in Detroit and its suburbs who had been at least fifteen years of age when the riot occurred, 59 percent of the blacks and 47 percent of the whites believed the two races were "closer together" than they had been in 1967, indicating, possibly, that blacks, at least, believed there had been an improvement in race relations since the riot. A higher percentage of blacks in 1987 than in 1968 thought blacks had as good an opportunity as whites to obtain "good housing," in part the result of the open occupancy ordinance the Common Council had approved following the riot; but about two-thirds of the blacks surveyed in 1987 as in 1968 thought that blacks lost out on good jobs because of their race even though equally qualified with white job applicants.

The most dramatic evidence of the perceived degree of racial polarization in Detroit in 1987 as compared to 1968 was the response of blacks to the question of whether they thought most whites wanted "to keep blacks down." When this question was asked in the Campbell-Schuman survey in 1968, only 21 percent of the black respondents thought this was so, but in the Gordon Black survey in 1987, 59 percent of the blacks agreed with the statement, as did even 39 percent of the whites. Both blacks and whites, however, were more inclined in 1987 than in 1968 to think that the 1967 riot had helped rather than hurt the cause of civil rights. In the Campbell-Schuman survey, 27 percent of the blacks and 13 percent of the whites thought the riot had helped "the Negro cause." In the 1987 Black survey, however, 46 percent of the blacks and 33 percent of the whites were of this opinion.[24]

Detroit's "image problem" in the nation dates from the 1967 riot, and the perception of the city continued to suffer as a result of its high homicide rate, its well-publicized social ills, and even the violence that briefly flared after the Detroit Tigers won the 1984 World Series. In a survey of one thousand black and white adults outside Detroit conducted in November 1984 by RMH Research for the *Detroit Free Press*, the model city of 1967 was rated as the "worst" of seventeen major American cities. Among those viewing Detroit so unfavorably, 52 percent cited "social problems"; 35 percent, crime; and 21.5 percent, "urban decay." Only 7 percent, by contrast, specifically mentioned "racial problems," and only 30 percent, racial violence. Racial attitudes, nevertheless, influenced the judgment of respondents, about 40 percent of whom thought that the fact Detroit was then about two-thirds black contributed to its negative image. About 55 percent of those interviewed remembered the 1967 riot, a high figure for a citizenry so unfamiliar with the American past.[25]

Were the Detroit of the late 1980s to return to the conditions prevailing in the city in 1967 with regard to the state of the economy, the level of unemployment, the percentage of inhabitants living in poverty and on the welfare rolls, the quality of the public schools and of housing, the degree of violent crime, and the general quality of life, it would undoubtedly be hailed as a remarkable and happy achievement. And yet it was in 1967, not 1987, that Detroit experienced its great riot. How is one to explain this seeming anomaly?

On the positive side, it is evident that blacks in Detroit in 1987, unlike twenty years earlier, no longer felt themselves excluded from the city government and the larger society. It was, after all, their city, governed by a black leadership with which they could readily identify. Also, Detroit blacks in 1987 had an entirely different view of their integrated police force than black Detroiters in 1967 had of their largely white police force. The police in the 1960s had become for blacks the very symbol of their grievances against the white community, and it was possible, in certain circumstances, for a routine police action – like a raid on a blind pig in a black neighborhood, followed by questionable police tactics and a delay in the city's bringing in higher levels of force – to trigger a racially related riot.

The differences in the historical context of the two times are also relevant to an understanding of why there was a riot in 1967 but not in 1987. The young black males who were so conspicuous among the rioters in 1967 had been strongly affected by the civil rights movement of the preceding two decades, had a strong sense of black identity, and took great pride in their race. Like other blacks in the city, and with good reason, they complained about police brutality, the incidence of unemployment, the quality of their schools and housing, and the treatment accorded them by ghetto merchants. They did not, however, think that there was anything inevitable about this state of affairs. Since they did not believe that the existing political system was responsive to their needs, they turned to rioting, then very much in the air, as their means of protest, as a way of signaling to those in power that they must pay attention to the black ghetto and its problems. In this sense, the rioting of 1967 was born of hope, not of despair, the hope that improvement would follow the disorder in the streets.

It would be foolish, of course, to predict that a riot could no longer occur in Detroit because conditions had changed so much since 1967. A speculation of this sort, after all, brings to mind what the city leadership, bemused by Detroit's model city image, believed on the eve of the 1967 riot. As the Miami riot of 1980 demonstrated, a particular juxtaposition of events could produce a riot with racial overtones in any large city, today as in the 1960s. Having said this, however, one has to recognize the difference in outlook of Detroit blacks in 1987 as compared to 1967. Their mood, it would seem, was now one of despair rather than hope. Their material conditions having deteriorated during the preceding twenty years and with the civil rights movement a fading memory for them, they may very well have sensed that although rioting might possibly serve as an outlet for frustration, it was unlikely to lead to an improvement in their circumstances.

The matter was put differently by reporter Barbara Stanton, a lifelong Detroit resident who had covered the 1967 riot for the *Detroit Free Press*. The "inescapable reality," she remarked, was that there was "far more destruction and violence in Detroit in 1987 than in 1967. . . . It is," she wrote, "as if the riot had never ended, but goes on in slow motion. Instead of a single, stupendous explosion, there is steady, relentless corrosion." To the question, "Could it happen again?" her sad answer was, "It is happening right now, a riot without end, a tragedy still without resolution."[26]

Abbreviations

ALHUA	Archives of Labor History and Urban Affairs, Walter P. Reuther Library, Detroit, Michigan
A-W Riot Studies	Institute of Public Policy Studies, Aberbach-Walker Riot Studies, Michigan Historical Collections, Bentley Library, Ann Arbor, Michigan
CCR Papers	Detroit Commission on Community Relations Papers, Archives of Labor History and Urban Affairs
DFP	*Detroit Free Press*
DN	*Detroit News*
DPD	Detroit Police Department
DNAACP Papers	Papers of the Detroit Branch of the National Association for the Advancement of Colored People, Archives of Labor History and Urban Affairs
DRSB	Detroit Riot Scrapbook, Michigan Historical Collections
DUL Papers	Detroit Urban League Papers, Michigan Historical Collections
FBI	Federal Bureau of Investigation
FOIA	Freedom of Information Act
GPO	United States Government Printing Office
GR Papers	George Romney Papers, Michigan Historical Collections
JPC Papers	Jerome P. Cavanagh Papers, Archives of Labor History and Urban Affairs
LBJ Library	Lyndon Baines Johnson Presidential Library, Austin, Texas
MC	*Michigan Chronicle*
MHC	Michigan Historical Collections, Bentley Library, Ann Arbor, Michigan
NACCD Records	Records of the National Advisory Commission on Civil Disorders, Johnson Library
NARA	National Archives and Records Administration, Washington, D.C.
ND Papers	New Detroit Papers, Archives of Labor History and Urban Affairs
NEA	National Education Association
NYT	*New York Times*
ORA Papers	Wayne State University, Office of Religious Administration Papers, Archives of Labor History and Urban Affairs
RG	Record Group
WHCF	White House Central Files, Lyndon Baines Johnson Presidential Library

Notes

Chapter 1

1. *Washington Post*, July 25, 1967.

2. *DN*, Mar. 1, 1966; *Los Angeles Times*, Feb. 6, 1966, DRSB No. 1; Stanley H. Brown, "Detroit: Slow Healing of a City," *Fortune* 7 (June 1965): 144.

3. For the 1943 riot and its background, see Dominic J. Capeci, Jr., *Race Relations in Wartime Detroit: The Sojourner Truth Controversy* (Philadelphia: Temple University Press, 1984); Robert Shogan and Tom Craig, *The Detroit Riot* (Philadelphia: Chilton Books, 1964); Alfred McClung Lee and Norman Raymond Humphrey, *Race Riot* (New York: Dryden Press, 1943); Alan Clive, *State of War: Michigan in World War II* (Ann Arbor: University of Michigan Press, 1979), pp. 136–37, 141–42, 144–50, 156–62; Harvard Sitkoff, "The Detroit Race Riot of 1943," *Michigan History* 53 (Fall 1969): 183–206; Robert Conot, *American Odyssey* (New York: William Morrow and Co., 1974), pp. 376–86; B. J. Widick, *Detroit: City of Race and Class Violence* (Chicago: Quadrangle Books, 1972), pp. 93–111; and Baker et al. and Bratton et al. vs. City of Detroit et al. . . . Civil Nos. 5–71837 and 5–72264, U.S. District Court, Eastern District of Michigan, Southern Division, 1979, pp. 10–11, copy of manuscript opinion in my possession (hereafter cited as Keith opinion).

4. *DN*, June 30, 1943; Shogan and Craig, *Detroit Riot*, pp. 67, 70–71, 75–76, 79–82, 116–17, 149–50, 153–59; Lee and Humphrey, *Race Riot*, pp. 42–43, 61, 75; Sitkoff, "Race Riot," pp. 190–91, 193–96, 205.

5. *DN*, June 30, 1943.

6. Tyrone Tillery, "The Conscience of a City: A Commemorative History of the Detroit Human Rights Department, 1943–1983" [1983]; *Los Angeles Times*, Feb. 6, 1966, DRSB No. 1; United States Commission on Civil Rights, *Hearings, Detroit, Michigan, 1960* (Washington: GPO, 1961), pp. 26–27; Shogan and Craig, *Detroit Riot*, pp. 123–24.

7. Civil Rights Commission, *Hearings*, pp. 18, 197–98; CCR, "Annual Report, 1961," pp. 6–8.

8. Research Division, City Plan Commission, "An Economic Base Study of the Detroit Metropolitan Area," Dec. 1961, Box 535, JPC Papers; Widick, *Detroit*, pp. 137–39; Conot, *Odyssey*, pp. 452–55; Steve Babson, *Working Detroit: The Making of a Union Town* (New York: Adama Books, 1984), pp. 161–62; United States Department of Commerce, Bureau of the Census, Census

of Population and Housing, 1960, *Final Report Series, Census Tracts, Detroit, Michigan* (Washington: GPO, 1961), pp. 200, 262; Executive Director's Report, 1961, Box 12, DUL Papers; CCR, *Employment and Income by Age, Sex, Color and Residence*, May 1963, p. 12, Box 9, Francis A. Kornegay Papers, MHC; Civil Rights Commission, *Hearings*, p. 86.

9. Research Division, CCR, *The Detroit Area Setting* . . . , June 1962, pp. 1, 4, Box 22, DUL Papers; Research Department, DUL, *A Profile of the Detroit Negro, 1959–1967*, Dec. 1967, pp. 3–4, Box 45, ibid.

10. Stanley B. Greenberg, *Politics and Poverty* (New York: John Wiley and Sons, 1974), pp. 35–36; *DFP*, Mar. 9, 1969; Hubert G. Locke, *The Detroit Riot of 1967* (Detroit: Wayne State University Press, 1969), p. 53; Detroit Housing Commission, *Quarterly Report to the Commissioners, Second Quarter, 1971*, p. 5; Harold Bellamy to Richard Strichartz, Aug. 14, 1967, Box 393, JPC Papers; Harold Black and James Wiley, "Dissecting a Riot Neighborhood," *Nation's Cities* 6 (Sept. 1968): 20; Survey to Determine Attitude of Residents . . . , Oct. 8, 1959, Box 51, DUL Papers; "Twelfth Street Study" [1961], Box A-8, ibid.; CCR Minutes, July 16, 1962, Series IV, Box 4, CCR Papers.

11. Black and Wiley, "Riot Neighborhood," p. 20; George Henderson, "Twelfth Street . . . ," *Phylon* 25 (Spring 1964): 91; *Michigan Catholic*, Aug. 3, 1967; Bellamy to Strichartz, Aug. 14, 1967, Box 393, JPC Papers; "Community Data," n.d., Box 77, NACCD Records; Conot, *Odyssey*, pp. 435–36; National Commission on Urban Problems, *Hearings*, 5 vols. (Washington: GPO, 1968), 5:10.

12. *DFP*, July 24, 1967; *DN*, July 24, 1967; Van Gordon Sauter and Burleigh Hines, *Nightmare in Detroit* (Chicago: Henry Regnery Co., 1968), pp. 1–2; National Commission on Urban Problems, *Hearings*, 5:10; *Michigan Catholic*, Aug. 3, 1967; J. Anthony Lukas, "Postscript on Detroit: 'Whitey Hasn't Got the Message,'" *NYT Magazine*, Aug. 27, 1967; Capture and Record of Civil Disorder, July 23–28, 1967, Box 345, GR Papers; Detroit Housing Commission, *Quarterly Report, Second Quarter 1971*, pp. 5–6.

13. *DN*, July 24, 1967; Black and Wiley, "Riot Neighborhood," p. 20; William Walter Scott III, *Hurt, Baby, Hurt* (Ann Arbor: New Ghetto Press, 1970), pp. 88–89.

14. Survey of Residents, Oct. 1959, Box 51, DUL Papers; "Twelfth Street Study," Box A-8, ibid.; Henderson, "Twelfth Street," pp. 93–95; *Michigan Catholic*, Aug. 3, 1967; Maurice Kelman and Ed Batchelor interview with Ray Girardin, Oct. 29, 1971, p. 431, transcript in my possession; CCR Minutes, Aug. 15, Sept. 19, 1960, Series IV, Box 3, CCR Papers; CCR, "Annual Report, 1960," p. 6, ibid.; Highlights of the Commission Meeting, Sept. 1960, Box 9, Kornegay Papers; Robert E. Smith to Robert D. Knox, May 14, 1965, Box 211, JPC Papers.

15. CCR, *Employment and Income*, p. 6, Box 9, Kornegay Papers. In the *Report of the National Advisory Commission on Civil Disorders* (Washington: GPO, 1968), p. 351, the median family income figures for 1960 for whites and nonwhites are given as $6,776 and $4,366 respectively. The median nonwhite family income in census tracts surrounding Twelfth Street ranged from $3,086 to $5,514. Bureau of the Census, *Census Tracts, Detroit, Mich.*, pp. 268, 271. Since nearly all nonwhites in Detroit at the time were black, I have not always distinguished between the two.

16. DUL, *The Detroit Low-Income Negro Family*, Apr. 1966, pp. 7, 24, Box 45, DUL Papers; Research Department, DUL, *Detroit Negro*, pp. 11, 24, ibid.

17. On this point, see *DN*, Oct. 15, 1962, and J. David Greenstone, "A Report on the Politics of Detroit" (Cambridge, Mass.: Joint Center for Urban Studies, 1961), p. 35.

18. *DN*, Oct. 16, 1962, June 25, 1963; Greenstone, "Politics of Detroit," pp. 32-34.

19. Greenstone, "Politics of Detroit," pp. 36-37; *DN*, Oct. 16, 17, 1962, June 25, 1963; Haywood L. Perry to Milan C. Miskovsky, Dec. 27, 1967, John K. Scales Memorandum to Miskovsky (interview with James A. Bush), Jan. 17, 1968, Series No. 4, Box 22, NACCD Records; Robert Sinclair and Bryan Thompson, *Metropolitan Detroit* (Cambridge, Mass.: Ballinger Publishing Co., 1977), p. 31.

20. J. David Greenstone, *Labor in American Politics* (New York: Alfred A. Knopf, 1969), pp. 256-57; Bernard Dobranski Memorandum to Herman Wilson (interview with William T. Patrick, Jr.), Oct. 13, 1967, Series 59, Box 2, NACCD Records; *DN*, Oct. 17, 1962; Locke, *Detroit Riot*, p. 56.

21. Widick, *Detroit*, pp. 149-50; Babson, *Working Detroit*, pp. 165-66; *DN*, Oct. 15, 1962; [F.] Ray Marshall, *The Negro and Organized Labor* (New York: John Wiley and Sons, 1965), pp. 68-70; Civil Rights Commission, *Hearings*, pp. 84-85.

22. CCR, *Employment and Income*, p. 4, Box 9, Kornegay Papers.

23. Civil Rights Commission, *Hearings*, pp. 53-54, 57, 63-65.

24. Ibid., pp. 36, 106; Herbert R. Northrup, *The Negro in the Automobile Industry* (Philadelphia: Wharton School of Finance and Commerce, 1968), pp. 37, 53, 55.

25. Civil Rights Commission, *Hearings*, pp. 124-25, 128-29, 168.

26. Marilyn Gittell and T. Edward Hollander, *Six Urban School Districts* (New York: Frederick A. Praeger, 1968), pp. 143-46; Conot, *Odyssey*, p. 440; Civil Rights Commission, *Hearings*, pp. 152, 186-87.

27. National Commission on Professional Rights and Responsibilities of the National Education Association of the United States, *Detroit, Michigan: A Study of Barriers to Equal Educational Opportunity in a Large City* (Washington, 1967), p. 27, Box 334, JPC Papers; Intergroup Relations Department, Division of School Community Relations, Racial Distribution of Students as of Oct. 19, 1967, Box 48, DUL Papers.

28. Civil Rights Commission, *Hearings*, pp. 131-34, 154-55, 159-60, 165, 168; Greenstone, "Politics of Detroit," p. 45; CCR Minutes, May 18, 1959, Series IV, Box 3, CCR Papers; *Conscience of a Community* [1959], Box A-13, DUL Papers; *DN*, Oct. 11, 1960; NEA, *Detroit*, pp. 30-31, Box 334, JPC Papers.

29. Interview with Arthur Johnson, July 23, 1984, pp. 9-10, transcript in MHC; Interview with George Crockett, Aug. 7, 1984, p. 32, ibid.; Conot, *Odyssey*, pp. 438-39; Board of Education and Administrative Actions on Integration and Non-Discrimination, 1945-1970, Box 1 (unprocessed), Detroit Public Schools, Division of Community Relations Papers, ALHUA; Civil Rights Commission, *Hearings*, pp. 161, 168; Gittell and Hollander, *School Districts*, p. 146; NEA, *Detroit*, pp. 26-27, Box 334, JPC Papers; Samuel M. Brownell, *Pursuing Excellence in Education: The Superintendent's Ten-Year Report, 1956-1966* (Detroit: Board of Education, 1966), pp. 14, 15, Part 2, Series II, Box 13,

NAACP Papers; Minutes, Pupil Placement Subcommittee, Citizens Concerned with Equal Educational Opportunities, Nov. 4, 1965, Part 2, Series I, Box 2, ibid; *Bradley* v. *Milliken*, 338 F. Supp. 582, 587–88 (1971); *MC*, Oct. 29, Nov. 5, 1960; CCR, "Annual Report, 1961," p. 2.

30. Brownell, *Pursuing Excellence*, pp. 16–17.

31. Gittell and Hollander, *School Districts*, pp. 13–14; Civil Rights Commission, *Hearings*, pp. 170–78; Brownell, *Pursuing Excellence*, pp. 15–16; Conot, *Odyssey*, pp. 440, 443, 575; *Examination of the War on Poverty, Staff and Consultant Reports*, prepared for the Subcommittee on Employment, Manpower, and Poverty of the Senate Committee on Labor and Public Welfare, 90th Cong., 1st sess., Committee Print, 8 vols. (Washington: GPO, 1967), 6:1765–70.

32. Civil Rights Commission, *Hearings*, pp. 192, 193, 228–29, 235–36; DUL, *Detroit Negro*, p. 4, Box 45, DUL Papers.

33. Civil Rights Commission, *Hearings*, p. 193; Albert J. Mayer, "Public Housing, Urban Renewal and Racial Segregation in Detroit," June 1962, Box 183, JPC Papers; Mayer and Thomas F. Hoult, "Race and Residence in Detroit," in Leonard Gordon, ed., *A City in Racial Crisis: The Case of Detroit . . .* ([Dubuque, Iowa]: Wm. C. Brown Co., 1971), pp. 3, 5–9; Taeuber and Taeuber, *Negroes in Cities: Residential Segregation and Neighborhood Change* (Chicago: Aldine Publishing Co., 1966), pp. 32–34.

34. Dobranski Memorandum to Wilson (interview with Robert Knox), Oct. 19, 1967, Series 59, Box 2, NACCD Records; Civil Rights Commission, *Hearings*, pp. 36, 260–63; Greenstone, "Politics of Detroit," p. 41; Research Division, CCR, *Detroit Area*, pp. 1–2, Box 22, DUL Papers; Richard Cross to Louis C. Miriani, Oct. 6, 1961, Series IV, Box 3, CCR Papers; CCR, "Annual Report, 1961," pp. 8–9.

35. *NACCD Report*, pp. 257–58, 351; DUL, *Detroit Negro*, pp. 4–5, Box 45, DUL Papers; Research Division, CCR, *Detroit Area*, p. 15, Box 22, ibid. The comparable figures are slightly different in the *NACCD Report* and *Detroit Area*.

36. Locke, *Detroit Riot*, p. 54; Conot, *Odyssey*, p. 386; Arthur Kornhauser, *Detroit as the People See It* (Detroit: Wayne State University Press, 1952), pp. 120–21.

37. DUL, The Detroit Police Department's Policy and Practice in the Recruitment and Assignment of Police Officers, Dec. 1958, Box A-19, DUL Papers; Civil Rights Commission, *Hearings*, pp. 335, 340–41, 497; Conot, *Odyssey*, p. 414; Keith opinion, pp. 12–13.

38. [Herbert W. Hart] to CCR, July 18, 1960, Series IV, Box 3, CCR Papers; Civil Rights Commission, *Hearings*, pp. 358–60.

39. Marks to Police-Community Relations Subcommittee, CCR, Feb. 29, 1968, Box A-19, DUL Papers.

40. CCR Minutes, Dec. 19, 1960, Series 4, Box 3, CCR Papers; CCR, "Annual Report, 1961," p. 3; Research Division, CCR, A Study of Detroit Police Department Personnel Selection Practices, Jan. 15, 1962, p. 7, Box 29, JPC Papers; Strichartz to Cavanagh, Jan. 8, 1962, Joseph B. Sullivan to Cavanagh, n.d., Box 27, ibid.; [Hart] to Miriani, Apr. 18, 1960, and enclosure, Series IV, Box 3, CCR Papers.

41. Civil Rights Commission, *Hearings*, pp. 365-67; DUL, Policy and Practice, Box A-19, DUL Papers; [Hart] to Miriani, Apr. 18, 1960, and enclosure, Series IV, Box 3, CCR Papers; Conot, *Odyssey*, p. 414.

42. Civil Rights Commission, *Hearings*, pp. 304, 321-24, 330-34; Keith opinion, p. 97.

43. Civil Rights Commission, *Hearings*, pp. 370-71, 374, 497-98.

44. Ibid., pp. 305, 314, 390; [Hart] to Miriani, Apr. 18, 1960, and enclosure, Series IV, Box 3, CCR Papers; Burton Levy, "Cops in the Ghetto . . . ," in Louis H. Masotti and Don R. Bowen, eds., *Riots and Rebellion* (Beverly Hills: Sage Publications, 1968), p. 350.

45. Civil Rights Commission, *Hearings*, pp. 390-92.

46. Ibid., pp. 194, 344, 351.

47. Ibid., pp. 312, 335-36, 341, 364, 396; *DN*, Oct. 15, 1962; *MC*, Dec. 17, 1960.

48. CCR Minutes, July 20, 1959, Series IV, Box 3, CCR Papers; [Hart] to Miriani, Apr. 18, 1960, and enclosure, ibid.

49. Civil Rights Commission, *Hearings*, pp. 363, 497; CCR Minutes, July 18, 1960, and enclosure, Series IV, Box 3, CCR Papers; [Hart] to Miriani, Apr. 18, 1960, and enclosure, ibid.

50. Civil Rights Commission, *Hearings*, pp. 344-46, 351-68; [Hart] to Miriani, Apr. 18, 1960, and enclosure, Series IV, Box 3, CCR Papers; *DFP*, Mar. 18, 1961.

51. Civil Rights Commission, *Hearings*, pp. 315, 348; *DN*, Dec. 19, 1960.

52. *DN*, Dec. 19, 1960; *DFP*, Dec. 28, 1960; CCR Minutes, Jan. 16, 1961, Series IV, Box 3, CCR Papers.

53. *DFP*, Dec. 28, 29, 31, 1960, July 9, 1962; *DN*, Oct. 15, 1962; Hubert Locke to Sidney Fine, Jan. 4, 1984; Tom Nicholson, "Detroit's Surprising Mayor," *Harper's* 227 (Dec. 1963): 77; Babson, *Working Detroit*, p. 166; Widick, *Detroit*, pp. 151-52; Civil Rights Commission, *Hearings*, pp. 507-8.

54. *DFP*, Jan. 1, Feb. 10, 1961; *DN*, Oct. 15, 1962; CCR Minutes, Jan. 16, 1961, Series IV, Box 3, CCR Papers.

55. Nicholson, "Surprising Mayor," pp. 76-77; *DFP*, Sept. 3, 1967; DeWitt S. Dykes, "Jerome Patrick Cavanagh," in Melvin Holli and Peter d'A. Jones, eds., *Biographical Dictionary of American Mayors, 1820-1920* (Westport: Greenwood Press, 1981), p. 58; Conot, *Odyssey*, p. 447.

56. Nicholson, "Surprising Mayor," p. 77; Johnson interview, p. 5; Crockett interview, p. 35; Herman J. Glass to Members Citizens Committee on Police Relations, Jan. 22, 1965, and enclosed letter to Cavanagh, n.d., Part 2, Series I, Box 24, NAACP Papers; Widick, *Detroit*, p. 155; *DN*, Oct. 16, 1962; Conot, *Odyssey*, p. 449; Edward C. Banfield, *Big City Politics* (New York: Random House, 1965), p. 57.

57. In the primary, Miriani received 80,645 votes, Cavanagh, 35,897. Conot, *Odyssey*, p. 448.

58. Ibid., p. 449; Dudley W. Buffa, *Union Power and American Democracy: The UAW and the Democratic Party, 1935-1972* (Ann Arbor: University of Michigan Press, 1984), p. 140; Banfield, *Big City Politics*, p. 58; Locke, *Detroit Riot*, p. 57; *DN*, Oct. 14, 1962; Glass to Citizens Committee, Jan. 22, 1965, and enclosure, Part 2, Series I, Box 24, DNAACP Papers.

Chapter 2

1. *Time* 78 (Oct. 26, 1961): 27; *Look*, Sept. 21, 1965, copy in Box 212, JPC Papers.

2. Edward C. Banfield and James Q. Wilson, *City Politics* (New York: Random House, Vintage Books, 1966), pp. 37, 263.

3. *NYT*, Jan. 3, 1962; *MC*, Jan. 6, 1982.

4. *NYT*, Apr. 25, 1962; J. Anthony Lukas, "Postscript on Detroit: 'Whitey Hasn't Got the Message,' " *NYT Magazine*, Aug. 27, 1967; William Serrin, "How One Big City Defeated Its Mayor," ibid., Oct. 27, 1968; Fred Powledge, "The Flight from City Hall," *Harper's* 239 (Nov. 1969): 84–85; Robert Conot, *American Odyssey* (New York: William Morrow and Co., 1974), p. 451; National Commission on Urban Problems, *Hearings*, 5 vols. (Washington: GPO, 1968), 5:3; Appearance of the City of Detroit . . . , Aug. 15, 1967, Box 378, JPC Papers; *Cleveland Plain Dealer*, Jan. 3, 1965, clipping in Box 212, ibid.

5. Herbert R. Northrup, *The Negro in the Automobile Industry* (Philadelphia: Wharton School of Finance and Commerce, 1968), p. 35; Lukas, "Whitey"; Subcommittee of the Senate Committee on Public Works, *Accelerated Public Works Program, Hearings*, 88th Cong., 1st sess., 1963, 2:113–14, 116; *DFP*, Mar. 24, Sept. 3, 1967; *DN*, Nov. 16, 1962; Release, July 17, 1963, Box 81, JPC Papers; Survey of Detroit's Urban Renewal Program [1968], Box 505, ibid.; National Commission on Urban Problems, *Hearings*, 5:15; Tom Nicholson, "Detroit's Surprising Mayor," *Harper's* 227 (Dec. 1963): 78–79, 82; Serrin, "One Big City."

6. Conot, *Odyssey*, pp. 341–42, 374, 384, 386, 402, 403–5, 450–51; Nicholson, "Surprising Mayor," p. 78; Hubert G. Locke, *The Detroit Riot of 1967* (Detroit: Wayne State University Press, 1969), pp. 57–58; B. J. Widick, *Detroit: City of Race and Class* (Chicago: Quadrangle Books, 1972), pp. 155–56; Powledge, "City Hall," p. 86; Interview with Arthur Johnson, July 23, 1984, pp. 5–6, transcript in MHC.

7. Highlights of Commission Meeting, Feb. 1962, Box 9, Francis A. Kornegay Papers, MHC; CCR Minutes, May 21, 1962, ibid.; Cavanagh to Civil Service Commission and CCR, Oct. 22, 1962, ibid.; Richard Marks Memorandum to Cavanagh, June 6, 1963, Box 112, JPC Papers.

8. *MC*, Dec. 11, 1965, Apr. 2, 1966; Supplementary Analysis of City of Detroit . . . Racial Census, Mar. 29, 1966, Box 47, DUL Papers; Marks and Charles A. Meyer to Cavanagh, Mar. 24, 1966, Box 302, JPC Papers. The estimated Detroit population for individual years in the 1960s is given in Baker et al. and Bratton et al. vs. City of Detroit et al. . . . , United States District Court for Eastern District of Michigan, Southern Division, Civil Nos. 5-77937 and 5-72264, 1979, pp. 42–43, copy of manuscript opinion in my possession.

9. Cavanagh to CCR, Oct. 11, 1962, Box 9, Kornegay Papers; CCR, "Annual Report, 1962," p. 6; CCR, "Annual Report, 1963," p. 8; CCR, "Annual Report, 1964," p. 4; CCR Minutes, Dec. 16, 1963 (and enclosed Contract Compliance Division Report, Dec. 16, 1963), Sept. 22, 29, 1966, Series IV, Box 4, CCR Papers; CCR to Cavanagh, Mar. 17, 1965, Box 241, JPC Papers; Background Statement of Ad Hoc Committee of Clergymen, Mar. 15, 1965, ibid.; Mayor's Inspection Team to Cavanagh, July 29, 1967, Box 567, ibid.; *DFP*, Sept. 28, 1966.

10. CCR Minutes, Feb. 19, 1962, Box 39, JPC Papers; Mayor's Inspection Team to Cavanagh, July 13, 1967, Box 339, ibid.; Mayor's Inspection Team to Cavanagh, July 27, 1967, Box 567, ibid.; Interview with Richard Marks, pp. 3–4, transcript in MHC.

11. *Los Angeles Times*, Feb. 6, 1966, DRSB No. 1; Richard Strichartz to Cavanagh, Oct. 26, 1967, and enclosed MDT Report, Box 534, JPC Papers; Mayor's Inspection Team to Cavanagh, July 13, 1967, Box 339, ibid.; Burton Levy Memorandum to Arthur Johnson, Sept. 3, 1965, Records of the CRC, RG 83-55, unprocessed, State Archives, Lansing, Michigan; James Boudouris, "The Kercheval-Pennsylvania Incident, August, 1966," Mar. 1967, Series IV, Box 4, CCR Papers.

12. Article V, Section 29, Michigan Constitution of 1964; *Los Angeles Times*, Feb. 6, 1966, DRSB No. 1; *NYT*, Jan. 5, 1964; *MC*, Feb. 27, 1965, Apr. 8, 1967; Mayor's Inspection Team to Cavanagh, July 27, 1967, Box 567, JPC Papers; Tom Popp Memorandum to Herman Wilson, Oct. 26, 1967, Series 4, Box 22, NACCD Records; Johnson interview, p. 66.

13. Reuther to Lawrence V. Britt et al., June 17, 1963, Reuther to Edward Turner, June 25, 1963, Reuther to Emrich, July 3, 1963, Mildred Jeffrey to Reuther, Sept. 20, Dec. 2, 1963, Box 475, Walter Reuther Papers, ALHUA; "Report of Evaluation Committee," Apr. 22, 1966, Box 2, Horace W. Gilmore Papers, ibid.; Declaration of Purposes, Sept. 5, 1963, ibid.; CCEO letterhead, Box 17, Kornegay Papers; Locke to Emrich, Jan. 22, 1964, Box 21, ORA Papers; Stanley H. Brown, "Detroit: Slow Healing of a City," *Fortune* 71 (Jan. 1965): 144; *Los Angeles Times*, Feb. 6, 1966, DRSB No. 1.

14. Locke to Clarence Hilberry, Mar. 23, 1964, Emrich to Edward Cushman, June 12, 1964, Box 476, Reuther Papers; Summary Report, CCEO . . . , Oct. 1963–Sept. 1964 [Sept. 14, 1964], ibid.; Emrich to Charles H. Hewitt, May 25, 1964, Locke to . . . Executive Committee, CCEO, May 27, 1964, Box 21, ORA Papers; "Meeting with Mass Media," Jan. 22, 1965, Box 1, Gilmore Papers; Special Committee on Police-Community Relations, Jan. 14, 1965, ibid.; Special Report on Activities of the Committee on Police-Community Relations [May 6, 1967], ibid.; Emrich to Frank Foucault, June 1, 1965, ibid.; "Report of Evaluation Committee," Apr. 22, 1966, Box 2, ibid.

15. Robert L. Potts, "Program for Affirmative Action . . ." [May 8, 1967], Box 476, Reuther Papers; Summary Report, CCEO, Oct. 1963–Sept. 1964, ibid.; Locke to All Members, Mar. 4, 1965, Jeffrey to Reuther, Sept. 30, 1965, ibid.; A Report from the Special Sub-Committee on Police Community Relations, Feb. 16, 1965, ibid.; CCEO Report to Community—Summer 1967 [June 6, 1967], ibid.; A Report . . . on Housing, Feb. 1967, ibid.; Potts to Churches . . . , May 5, 1967, Box 18, ORA Papers; News Releases, May 23, 1967, ibid.; "Mr. Kaler called," June 9, 1967, ibid.; *MC*, Feb. 5, 1966; *Equal Employment Seminar* [1964], Box 2, Gilmore Papers; "Report of Evaluation Committee," Apr. 22, 1966, ibid.

16. Locke, "Race Relations . . . Summer 1965," Sept. 29, 1965, Box 37, ORA Papers.

17. Jeffrey to Reuther, Sept. 30, 1965, Box 476, Reuther Papers; Locke, *Detroit Riot*, p. 63; James A. Geschwender, *Class, Race, and Worker Insurgency* (London: Cambridge University Press, 1977), p. 71; Denise J. Lewis, "Black Consciousness and the Voting Behavior of Blacks in Detroit, 1961–1968" (M.A. thesis, Wayne State University, 1969), pp. 88–89.

18. CCEO Release, Oct. 11, 1965, Box 17, Kornegay Papers; Emrich et al. to All Clergy of Detroit [Oct. 1965], ibid.; Jeffrey to Reuther, Sept. 30, Oct. 4, 1965, Irving Bluestone to Reuther, Oct. 11, 1965, Box 476, Reuther Papers; "Committee Actions during Month of October" [Oct. 1965], Box 18, ORA Papers; Emrich to James Schiavone, Oct. 7, 1965, Locke to Frank Angelo, Nov. 24, 1965, ibid.; Xavier Nicholas interview with Albert J. Dunmore [1982], copy of tape in my possession.

19. "The Nov. 2 election," n.d., Box 17, Kornegay Papers; *DFP*, Nov. 4, 1965; Locke to Angelo, Nov. 24, 1965, Box 18, ORA Papers.

20. Joseph Ross speech, with Ross to Locke, Nov. 18, 1965, Box 37, ORA Papers; Locke to Members Committee on Evaluation and Emrich [1968], Box 22, ibid.; Memo Prepared by . . . Cavanagh . . . , Apr. 15, 1965, Box 16, Hobart Taylor Papers, MHC; "Report of Evaluation Committee," Apr. 22, 1966, Box 2, Gilmore Papers.

21. *Los Angeles Times*, Feb. 6, 1966, DRSB No. 1; Sheehan to Harvey McIntyre, Aug. 1, 1966, Sheehan to Wilma Ray, Mar. 22, 1967, Sheehan to Harvey G. Bowen, Mar. 28, 1967, Sheehan to Bishop Schoenherr, Oct. 7, 1968, Father Sheehan Correspondence, 1962–69 (unprocessed), Archives of the Archdiocese of Detroit, Detroit, Michigan; *DN*, Dec. 25, 1968.

22. Grady Williams to CCR, May 17, 1965, Series IV, Box 4, CCR Papers; Sheehan to Bowen, Mar. 28, 1967, Sheehan to Schoenherr, Oct. 7, 1968, Sheehan Correspondence; CCR, "Annual Report, 1964," p. 4; Background Statement of Ad Hoc Committee . . . , Mar. 15, 1965, Box 241, JPC Papers; *DN*, June 21, July 22, 1965, Dec. 25, 1968.

23. Sheehan to Bowen, Mar. 28, 1967, Sheehan Correspondence; Leonard Gordon, "Attempts to Bridge the Racial Gap . . . ," in Gordon, ed., *A City in Racial Crisis: The Case of Detroit* . . . ([Dubuque, Iowa]: Wm. C. Brown Co., 1971), pp. 21–23; Metropolitan Conference on Open Occupancy . . . , Jan. 2–3, 1963, enclosed with CCR Minutes, Jan. 21, 1963, Box 9, Kornegay Papers; CCR, "Annual Report, 1962," p. 5.

24. From Locke, Mar. 26, 1964, Box 18, ORA Papers.

25. David Paul Boesel, "The Ghetto Riots 1964–1968" (Ph.D. diss., Cornell University, 1972), pp. 7–11, 19, 26, 36–41, 45–54; Bill Sudomier to Lee Hills et al., May 21 [1963], Box 11, Frank Angelo Papers, MHC; David Paul Boesel and Peter H. Rossi, *Cities under Siege: The Anatomy of Ghetto Riots, 1964–1968* (New York: Basic Books, 1971), pp. 13–14; *MC*, Nov. 16, 1963, Mar. 13, 1965; Dunmore interview; Locke, "Race Relations in Detroit: Problems and Prospects," Apr. 27, 1964, Box 21, ORA Papers.

26. Wilson Memorandum to Charles E. Nelson (interview with Karl Gregory), n.d., Series 59, Box 2, NACCD Records; Deposition of Stanley Webb, Jan. 11, 1968, Series 32, Box 2, ibid.; Lukas, "Whitey"; Report by Rene Freeman [Aug. 3, 1967], Series III, Box 3, CCR Papers; [Nathan Caplan] interview with Owner of Blind Pig, n.d., p. 1, transcript in my possession.

27. Walter Dukes Memorandum to Wilson (interview with Arthur Johnson), n.d., Peter Rossi File, in my possession; E. S. Evans, "Ghetto Revolts and City Politics," in Louis H. Masotti and Don R. Bowen, eds., *Riots and Rebellion* (Beverly Hills: Sage Publications, 1968), pp. 392–93; J. R. Brown to Romney [Aug. 3, 1967], Box 343, GR Papers.

28. James Raschard to Wilson, n.d., Series 59, Box 2, NACCD Records;

Harry McPherson, *A Political Education* (Boston: Little, Brown and Co., 1972), p. 344; Locke to Sidney Fine, Jan. 4, 1984; Evans, "Ghetto Revolts," pp. 391, 398; George Henderson, "The Block Club Movement within the Detroit Tenth Police Precinct," May 1962, Box 36, DUL Papers; Charles E. West, "The Role of Block Clubs in the Detroit Civil Disorder of July, 1967" (M.A. thesis, Wayne State University, 1970), pp. 44, 72; *DFP*, Aug. 6, 1967; Nicholas interview with Lorenzo Freeman [1982], copy of tape in my possession; Interview with George Crockett, Aug. 7, 1984, p. 39, transcript in MHC; Charlotte Darrow and Paul Lowinger, "The Detroit Uprising: A Psychological Study," in Jules Masserman, ed., *The Dynamics of Dissent* (New York: Greene and Stratton, 1968), p. 126.

29. *DN*, Oct. 14, 18, 1962; Conot, *Odyssey*, p. 527; John K. Scales Memorandum to Milan C. Miskovsky (interview with James Bush), Jan. 17, 1968, Series 4, Box 22, NACCD Records; Wilson Memorandum to Nelson (interview with Hubert Locke), Oct. 17, 19, 1967, ibid.

30. *DN*, Oct. 16, 18, 1962, July 22, 1963, Sept. 23, 25, 1967; Laurence Niblett, "An Illustration of Provocative News," Box 5, Remus G. Robinson Papers, ALHUA; *MC*, June 20, Oct. 3, 1964; *Illustrated News*, Apr. 2, 1962, Sept. 2, Dec. 9, 1963, Feb. 3, 1964; Nicholas interview with Albert Cleage [1982], copy of tape in my possession; James C. Gaither for the President, May 9, 1967, Box 29, WE9, WHCF.

31. "The Black Madonna" [Mar. 1967], Joseph A. Labadie Collection, University of Michigan, Ann Arbor, Michigan; *DFP*, Mar. 25, 1967; *DN*, Sept. 10, 1967; John Hersey, *The Algiers Motel Incident* (New York: Alfred A. Knopf, 1968), pp. 346–47.

32. Louis Goldberg, "Ghetto Riots and Others: The Faces of Civil Disorder in 1967," in Boesel and Rossi, eds., *Cities*, p. 169; Result of Robert Conot Interview with Saul Friedman, n.d., Box 81, NACCD Records; Reconnaissance Survey Field Research Reports, Detroit, Michigan, 1:65, Series 10, Box 46, ibid.; *DN*, Sept. 10, 1967; *DFP*, July 27, 1967; Locke, "Race Relations," Box 21, ORA Papers; Freeman Report [Aug. 3, 1967], Series III, Box 3, CCR Papers; Gaither for President, May 9, 1967, Box 29, WE9, WHCF; Lukas, "Whitey."

33. *DFP*, July 31, 1966; *MC*, Aug. 6, 1966; *DN*, June 20, July 31, Sept. 8, 1966; Permanent Subcommittee on Investigations of the Senate Committee on Government Operations, *Riots, Civil and Criminal Disorders, Hearings*, 90th Cong., 2nd sess., 1968, pt. 6:1443. Carmichael spoke in Detroit on Sept. 27, 1966, to a crowd of more than 1,000 in Cleage's church. *DFP*, Sept. 28, 1966; *DN*, Sept. 28, 1966.

34. *Riots, Civil and Criminal Disorders*, pt. 6:1414–15, 1430; *MC*, Feb. 3, 1962, July 13, 27, Aug. 3, Sept. 28, Oct. 25, 1963, Jan. 18, July 4, 1964, July 31, 1965; *Illustrated News*, Sept. 2, 1963; Exhibit No. 92, Case No. 55-15-X, Records of the United States Senate, RG 46, NARA; CCR Minutes, Nov. 18, 1963, Series IV, Box 4, CCR Papers; Haywood L. Perry to Miskovsky, Dec. 27, 1967, Series 4, Box 22, NACCD Records; Henry to Cavanagh, Sept. 25, 1963, Box 112, JPC Papers; Conot, *Odyssey*, p. 533.

35. *Riots, Civil and Criminal Disorders*, pt. 6:1402–11; Harvard Sitkoff, *The Struggle for Black Equality* (New York: Hill and Wang, 1981), p. 152; Revolutionary Action Movement Manifesto, n.d., Exhibit No. 82, Case No. 55-15-X, RG 46; W. L. Sullivan to C. D. DeLoach, July 31, 1967, enclosed with "Racial Disturbances 1967," FBI-FOIA.

36. James Boggs, *Racism and the Class Struggle* (New York: Monthly Review Press, 1970), pp. 41, 45–48; *Riots, Civil and Criminal Disorders*, pt. 6:1440.

37. *Riots, Civil and Criminal Disorders*, pt. 6:1398–1402, 1460–64; *MC*, Oct. 19, 1963; *DN*, Aug. 2, Oct. 15, 16, 1963; *DFP*, Oct. 12, 15, 1963, Feb. 24, 1966; "Open Protest to Mayor Cavanagh" [Aug. 1, 1963], Exhibit No. 78, Case No. 55-15-X, RG 46.

38. *MC*, May 25, 1963; *DN*, June 8, 1963; *DFP*, June 25, 1963.

39. *MC*, June 8, 15, 1963; *DN*, June 8, 25, 1963; Johnson interview, pp. 11–13, MHC.

40. *DFP*, June 24, 25, 1963; *MC*, June 29, July 6, Nov. 2, 1963; *DN*, June 25, 1963; *Illustrated News*, July 8, 1963; ". . . Conversations in Detroit between James Boggs and Xavier Nicholas, Spring 1973, Labadie Collection.

41. *DN*, Nov. 10, 11, 1963; *Illustrated News*, Oct. 14, 28, Nov. 25, 1963; Grace Boggs, "New Northern Negro Organization Launched," n.d., Labadie Collection; Boggs-Nicholas Conversations, Spring 1973, ibid.

42. *Illustrated News*, Oct. 28, 1963, Feb. 3, Mar. 9, 1964; *DFP*, Oct. 12, 1963; *MC*, Feb. 15, 1964; *Michigan Manual, 1965–1966* [Lansing, 1966], p. 455.

43. *MC*, Aug. 8, 1964, July 24, 31, 1965, Aug. 20, 1966; *DFP*, Apr. 23, 1966; *DN*, Apr. 14, 1964, Aug. 21, 1966; *Riots, Civil and Criminal Disorders*, pt. 6:1437; Field Division Memorandum to CCR, Aug. 25, 1966, Series IV, Box 4, CCR Papers; Boudouris, "Kercheval-Pennsylvania Incident," ibid.; Memorandum to Files, Meeting Held June 14 [1966], Box 319, GR Papers; Scales Memorandum to Miskovsky (Bush interview), Jan. 17, 1968, Series 4, Box 22, NACCD Records; Webb to Emrich, Mar. 31, 1966, Box 22, ORA Papers.

44. Harold Black to Cavanagh, Sept. 8, 1966, Box 271, JPC Papers; *MC*, July 30, 1966, Apr. 8, 1967; CCR Field Division Case Reports, July 28, 1966, Series IV, Box 4, CCR Papers.

45. *MC*, Aug. 8, Dec. 5, 1964, July 9, 1966; *DN*, June 21, 1965, Oct. 28, 1966; Committee on Race and Cultural Relations, Minutes, June 1, Sept. 14, 1965, Part II, Series II, Box 4, Metropolitan Detroit Council of Churches Papers, ALHUA; Northern Student Movement, Detroit Project, "Confidential: Rough Draft," n.d., Box 25, ORA Papers; Memorandum to Files, Meeting Held June 14 [1966], Box 319, GR Papers; Field Division Memorandum to CCR, Aug. 25, 1966, Series IV, Box 4, CCR Papers.

46. "Forum 66 . . . and the Black Arts Confederation of Unity . . . 1967," Exhibit No. 94, Case No. 55-15-X, RG 46; Nicholas interview with Edward Vaughn, Summer 1982, pp. 25–26, in Nicholas's possession; *Riots, Civil and Criminal Disorders*, pt. 6:1431–32.

47. "The Black Arts Confederation of Unity," n.d., Exhibit No. 95, Case No. 55-15-X, RG 46; Vaughn interview, pp. 25–26; *MC*, July 2, 1966.

48. *Riots, Civil and Criminal Disorders*, pt. 6:1415–19, 1464–67; Professional Staff Person to Kornegay, July 6, 1967, Box 12, DUL Papers; *MC*, July 1, 1967; *Report of the National Advisory Commission on Civil Disorders* (Washington: GPO, 1968), pp. 2–8; Racial Disturbance, Chicago and Detroit, July 4, 1967, FBI-FOIA; Conot, *Odyssey*, p. 529.

49. "West Central Organization," June 1966, Box 26, ORA Papers; Perry to Miskovsky, Dec. 27, 1967, Series 4, Box 22, NACCD Records; Wilson Memorandum to Nelson (interview with Mary Valentine), n.d., Series 59, Box 2, ibid.;

DFP, Aug. 15, 1965; *DN*, Aug. 15, Sept. 24, 1965, Mar. 6, 1966; *MC*, Mar. 12, 1966.

50. *Examination of the War on Poverty, Staff and Consultant Reports*, prepared for Subcommittee on Employment, Manpower, and Poverty of the Senate Committee on Labor and Public Welfare, 90th Cong., 1st sess., Committee Print, 8 vols. (Washington: GPO, 1967), 6:1835; Black to Cavanagh, Sept. 8, 1966, Box 241, JPC Papers; Charles Maynard to Commanding Officer, CIB, Apr. 24, 1967, Box 11, Ray Girardin Papers, Burton Historical Collection, Detroit Public Library; *DN*, Mar. 6, 1966.

51. Scales Memorandum to Miskovsky (Bush interview), Jan. 17, 1968, Series 4, Box 22, NACCD Records; *MC*, July 20, 1963, June 6, 27, 1964, Nov. 6, 1965; CCR Minutes, May 17, 1965, Series III, Box 4, CCR Papers; Field Division to CCR, June 21, 1965, ibid.; August Meier and Elliott Rudwick, *CORE* (New York: Oxford University Press, 1973), p. 359.

52. Locke, "Race Relations," Apr. 27, 1964, Box 21, ORA Papers; *DN*, June 8, 25, July 7, Oct. 15, 1963, Sept. 8, 1966; *MC*, Nov. 16, 1963; *DFP*, June 25, 26, Oct. 5, 1963, Jan. 21, 1965; Nicholas interview with Cleage, copy of tape in my possession.

53. *DN*, Oct. 16, 1962, Sept. 8, 1966; *DFP*, June 28, 1963.

54. *DN*, Oct. 16, 1962, July 7, 1963; *MC*, Nov. 21, 1964; *Examination of War on Poverty*, 6:1739–41, 1838; Widick, *Detroit*, p. 160; J. David Greenstone, *Labor and American Politics* (New York: Alfred A. Knopf, 1969), pp. 259–60; Wilson Memorandum to Nelson (interview with Nadine Brown), n.d., Series 59, Box 2, NACCD Records; Northrup, *Automobile Industry*, pp. 53, 55.

55. *NYT*, July 25, 1967; Northrup, *Automobile Industry*, p. 35; *Wall Street Journal*, Aug. 12, 1964; *MC*, Jan. 8, 1966; *Los Angeles Times*, Feb. 2, 1966, DRSB No. 1; Van Gordon Sauter and Burleigh Hines, *Nightmare in Detroit: A Rebellion and Its Victims* (Chicago: Henry Regnery Co., 1968), p. 220; Lukas, "Whitey"; *Washington Post*, July 25, 1967; Brown, "Detroit," p. 144; *DN*, Mar. 1, 1966; Cavanagh, "Civil Rights: The Next Frontier," July 8, 1966, Box 301, JPC Papers.

56. *Wall Street Journal*, Aug. 12, 1964; Sauter and Hines, *Nightmare*, p. 220; Gaither for President, May 9, 1967, Box 29, WE9, WHCF; Lukas, "Whitey"; Karl E. and Alma F. Taeuber, *Negroes in Cities: Residential Segregation and Neighborhood Change* (Chicago: Aldine Publishing Co., 1966), pp. 32, 37; *DN*, Apr. 30, May 28, 1967; *Washington Post*, July 25, 1967; Ross Speech, enclosed with Ross to Locke, Nov. 18, 1965, Box 37, ORA Papers; Locke, *Detroit Riot*, p. 65.

57. *Wall Street Journal*, Aug. 12, 1964; Brown, "Detroit," p. 144; *MC*, Apr. 23, 1966; *Los Angeles Times*, Feb. 6, 1966, DRSB No. 1; *Look*, Sept. 21, 1965, copy in Box 212, JPC Papers; *Newsweek* 69 (Mar. 13, 1967): 43.

58. Gilmore to Editor, *DN*, July 15, 1965; Box 1, Gilmore Papers; *MC*, Jan. 8, 1966; *DN*, May 13, 1967.

59. *DFP*, May 18, June 27, 1967; Locke to Fine, Jan. 4, 1984. See chap. 6.

60. Locke, *Detroit Riot*, p. 65; Locke to Fine, Jan. 4, 1984; Brown, "Detroit," pp. 142–45ff; *Newsweek* 69 (Mar. 13, 1967): 42–43; *U.S. News and World Report*, May 23, 1966, p. 37; CCEO, "Race Relations in Detroit–Summer 1965," n.d., Box 18, ORA Papers; *Los Angeles Times*, Feb. 6, 1966, DRSB No. 1; Nicholson, "Surprising Mayor," pp. 76–82; *Look*, Sept. 21, 1965, copy in Box

212, JPC Papers; *Cleveland Plain Dealer*, Jan. 3, 1965, in ibid.; *Wall Street Journal*, Aug. 12, 1964; *NYT*, Apr. 4, 1965; Lukas, "Whitey"; *DFP*, Mar. 24, 1967; Reconnaissance Survey Field Research Reports, Detroit, Michigan, 1:3, Box 46, NACCD Records.

61. Serrin, "One Big City"; Nicholson, "Surprising Mayor," p. 76; Brown, "Detroit," pp. 144, 256, 262; *Cleveland Plain Dealer*, Jan. 3, 1965, in Box 212, JPC Papers; *Look*, Sept. 21, 1965, copy in ibid.

62. *DFP*, Aug. 3, 4, 1966, Sept. 3, 1967; Nicholas interview with Bernard Klein [1982], copy of tape in my possession; Johnson interview, p. 49; Serrin, "One Big City"; Gordon, "Racial Gap," p. 25; Cavanagh Oral History Interview, Mar. 22, 1971, pp. 18, 36–38, LBJ Library; Marvin Watson to Bill Moyers, Box 9, Watson Office Files, LBJ Library; Widick, *Detroit*, pp. 163–64; *DN*, Aug. 18, 1968.

63. Cavanagh interview, p. 40; *DFP*, June 13, July 19, 20, Sept. 3, 1967; Locke, *Detroit Riot*, pp. 66–67; transcripts of Gordon broadcasts, Box 353, JPC Papers; Pearson column, May 14 [1967], typed copy in Box 339, ibid.; Cavanagh to Benjamin Bradlee, May 12, 1967, Cavanagh to Celestin J. Steiner, July 18, 1967, ibid.; Serrin, "One Big City"; Gordon, "Racial Gap," p. 25; *NYT*, July 25, 1967; Nicholas interview with Patricia Knox [1982], copy of tape in my possession; *DN*, May 14, July 20, 1967, Aug. 18, 1968. After six weeks of effort, Beck was able to gather only 42,000 of the 114,118 signatures required for an election to recall the mayor. *DFP*, June 13, 1967.

64. *DN*, May 14, June 11, 19, 1967; *Newsweek* 69 (Mar. 13, 1967): 38; *Washington Post*, July 25, 1967; *NYT*, July 25, 1967.

65. See *DN*, Feb. 3, 1965, and White File, No. 262, Inter-University Consortium for Political and Social Research, Detroit data for Angus Campbell and Howard Schuman, "Racial Attitudes in Fifteen American Cities," in *Supplemental Studies for the National Advisory Commission on Civil Disorders* (Washington: GPO, 1968).

66. Raschard Memorandum to Wilson (interview with Michael Ward), n.d., Series 4, Box 22, NACCD Records; Tom Popp Memorandum to Wilson, Oct. 26, 1967, ibid.; John Ursu Memorandum to Wilson (interview with John Feikens), n.d., ibid.; Black to Cavanagh, Sept. 8, 1966, Box 271, JPC Papers; National Commission on Urban Problems, *Hearings*, 5:3; Potts Speech, June 8, 1967, Box 24, ORA Papers; *Los Angeles Times*, July 30, 1967, DRSB No. 1.

67. Remarks by Cavanagh . . . , Sept. 26, 1967, Box 386, JPC Papers; Girardin to Jeanelle L. Baker, Aug. 11, 1967, Box 3, Girardin Papers; *MC*, Mar. 19, Apr. 23, 1966; *DN*, Oct. 10, 1967; *NACCD Report*, p. 149.

68. Bernard Dobranski Memorandum to Wilson (interview with Patrick), Oct. 13, 1967, Series 59, Box 2, NACCD Records; *DN*, May 28, July 31, 1967; Gaither for President, May 9, 1967, Box 29, WE9, WHCF; Serrin, "One Big City."

69. Howard Schuman and Barry Gruenberg, "Dissatisfaction with City Services . . . ," in Harlan Hahn, ed., *People and Politics in Urban Society* (Beverly Hills: Sage Publications, 1972), p. 374; Campbell and Schuman, "Racial Attitudes," pp. 22, 41; Black File, Nos. 183–87, 193, Detroit data for ibid.; *The People Beyond 12th Street: A Survey of Attitudes of Detroit Negroes after 1967* (Detroit: Detroit Urban League, 1967).

70. *MC*, July 24, 1982; Joel D. Aberbach and Jack L. Walker, *Race in the City* (Boston: Little, Brown and Co., 1973), p. 35.

71. *DN*, July 31, 1967.

72. Archie Perry to Cavanagh, May 10, 1967, Box 368, JPC Papers.

Chapter 3

1. Herman Wilson Memorandum to Charles E. Nelson, Part IV, n.d., Peter Rossi File, in my possession.

2. Ralph V. Smith, "Behind the Lines," *American Educator* 3 (Nov. 1967): 3–4.

3. Hubert Locke to Executive Board, CCEO, Mar. 19, 1964, Series III, Box 2, CCR Papers; Richard S. Emrich to CCEO, Feb. 16, 1965, Box 11, Frank Angelo Papers, MHC; Summary Report, CCEO, Oct. 1963–Sept. 1964, Box 476, Walter Reuther Papers, ALHUA; Subcommittee on Public Accommodations, A Report to the People of Detroit . . . , June 15, 1965, Box 26, ORA Papers; Stella P. Fizazi to Various, Oct. 3, 1966, Box 22, ibid.

4. CCR, "Annual Report, 1961," p. 10; CCR, "Annual Report, 1963," pp. 1, 10; CCR, "Annual Report, 1966," p. 5; CRC, Report on Detroit Area Hospitals, Feb. 1967, Part 2, Series I, Box 19, DNAACP Papers; *MC*, June 15, Sept. 21, Oct. 12, 1963, June 30, 1966; *DN*, Oct. 9, 1963.

5. Permanent Subcommittee on Investigations of the Senate Committee on Government Operations, *Riots, Civil and Criminal Disorders, Hearings*, 90th Cong., 2d sess., 1968, pt. 5:1340; Richard Fermoile to Francis A. Kornegay, Sept. 18, 1968, Box 46, DUL Papers; Harold Bellamy to Richard Strichartz, Aug. 14, 1967, Box 393, JPC Papers; TAP, Social Data Bank . . . 1965, Box 530, ibid.

6. Inter-University Consortium for Political and Social Research, Black File, Nos. 184, 185, White File, Nos. 184, 185, Detroit data for Angus Campbell and Howard Schuman, "Racial Attitudes in Fifteen American Cities," in *Supplemental Studies for the National Advisory Commission on Civil Disorders* (Washington: GPO, 1968); Greenleigh Associates, "Study of Services to Deal with Poverty in Detroit, Michigan" (1965), p. 35; James Boudouris to Richard Marks, Sept. 8, 1966, Box 301, JPC Papers; Mayor's Development Team (MDT) Report, with Strichartz to Cavanagh, Oct. 26, 1967, Box 534, ibid.; Tom Popp Memorandum to Wilson (interview with Maryann Mahaffey), Oct. 13, 1967, Series 59, Box 2, NACCD Records; CCR Minutes, Oct. 27, 1966, Series IV, Box 4, CCR Papers; Interview with John M. May [1967 or 1968], Box 16, A-W Riot Studies.

7. *MC*, Sept. 21, Dec. 28, 1963, May 23, 1964, Mar. 12, Nov. 5, 1966, Aug. 5, 1967; *DFP*, Aug. 7, 1967; Richard Alan Berk, "The Role of Ghetto Retail Merchants in Civil Disorders" (Ph.D. diss., Johns Hopkins University, 1970), p. 124; Jerome P. Madin to George Romney, July 31, 1967, Box 344, GR Papers; Wilson Memorandum to Nelson, Part IV, n.d., Peter Rossi File, in my possession; John L. Cooley to Cavanagh, Sept. 8, 1967, Box 394, JPC Papers; Questionnaires Nos. 5061, 6001, 6022, 6050, 6105, Boxes 10, 11, A-W Riot Studies.

8. Black File, Nos. 225–227, Detroit data for "Racial Attitudes"; *Return to 12th Street: A Follow-Up Survey of Attitudes of Detroit Negroes, October 1968* [Detroit: Detroit Free Press, 1968], p. 16.

9. *DFP*, July 16–18, Aug. 7, 1967, Sept. 5, 1968; Agenda, New Detroit, Inc., Sept. 5, 1968, Box 372, JPC Papers; "Food Stores and the Poor," Nov. 15, 1965, Box 10, Francis A. Kornegay Papers, MHC; Mary C. Sengstock, "The Corporation and the Ghetto . . . ," in Richard A. Chikota and Michael C. Moran, eds., *Riots in the Cities* (Rutherford, N.J.: Farleigh Dickinson University Press, 1970), p. 185.

10. Sengstock, "Corporation and Ghetto," pp. 203–12; Peter Rossi et al., *The Roots of Urban Discontent* (New York: John Wiley and Sons, 1974), pp. 204–61; *Riots, Civil and Criminal Disorders*, pt. 7:1524, 1526; *DFP*, July 17, Aug. 7, 1967, Sept. 5, 1968.

11. Report of Bernard Dobranski to Robert Conot, n.d., Box 77, NACCD Records; Wilson Memorandum to Nelson (interview with Fred Lyles), n.d., Series 59, Box 2, ibid.; Berk, "Ghetto Retail Merchants," pp. 127–28; B. J. Widick, *Detroit: City of Race and Class* (Chicago: Quadrangle Books, 1972), p. 195; Leonard Milstone, "Jewish Merchants in Detroit's Prime Riot Affected Areas" [Jan. 1968], pp. 2–5 and table, Burton Historical Collection, Detroit Public Library.

12. National Commission on Professional Rights and Responsibilities of the National Education Association of the United States, *Detroit, Michigan: A Study of Barriers to Equal Educational Opportunity in a Large City* (Washington, Mar. 1967), pp. 16–17; Subcommittee of the Senate Committee on Labor and Public Welfare, *Education Legislation, 1967, Hearings*, 90th Cong., 1st sess., Aug. 7, 1967, pt. 4:1466; Baker et al. and Bratton et al. vs. City of Detroit et al. . . . , United States District Court for the Eastern District of Michigan, Southern Division, Civil Nos. 5–77937 and 5–72264 (1979), p. 43, copy of manuscript opinion in my possession; Intergroup Relations Department, Division of School-Community Relations, Racial Distribution of Students and Personnel . . . , Oct. 19, 1967, Box 48, DUL Papers.

13. Marilyn Gittell and T. Edward Hollander, *Six Urban School Districts* (New York: Frederick A. Praeger, 1968), pp. 98, 208, 215; *Riots, Civil and Criminal Disorders*, pt. 7:1536; NEA, *Detroit*, pp. 18–19; Report of Finance Subcommittee of Detroit High School Study Commission, Working Draft, June 7, 1968, Box 22, DUL Papers; "Report of Detroit High School Study Commission," June 1968, p. 319; Official Transcript of Proceedings before the National Advisory Commission on Civil Disorders, Aug. 15, 1967, pp. 447–48, Series 1, Box 2, NACCD Records; Wilson Memorandum to Nelson (interview with Karl Gregory), n.d., (interview with Albert Boer), n.d., Series 59, Box 2, ibid.; Smith, "Behind the Riots," p. 31; Karl Gregory, "The Walkout . . . ," *New University Thought* 5 (Spring 1967): 35.

14. Finance Subcommittee Report, Box 22, DUL Papers; Gittell and Hollander, *Six Districts*, p. 208; "Report of High School Study Commission," p. 320; *Report of National Advisory Commission on Civil Disorders* (Washington: GPO, 1968), p. 341. Cf. Information Requested by Governor's Office . . . , Aug. 2, 1967, Box 327, GR Papers.

15. Grants to Selected School Districts . . . , Aug. 3, 1967, Box 345, GR Papers; *NACCD Report*, p. 341; Finance Subcommittee Report, Box 22, DUL Papers.

16. Reconnaissance Survey Field Research Reports, Detroit, Michigan, 1:79, Series 10, Box 46, NACCD Records; Wilson Memorandum to Nelson (Boer

interview), n.d., Series 59, Box 2, ibid.; Official Proceedings, Aug. 15, 1967, p. 456, Series 1, Box 2, ibid.; Gittell and Hollander, *Six Districts*, pp. 219–20, 222–23.

17. *Findings and Recommendations of the Citizens Advisory Committee on Equal Educational Opportunities*, abr. ed., Mar. 1962, pp. viii–x, 61, 76, p 1–2, 4; *DFP*, Mar. 11, 1962; *NYT*, Mar. 11, 1962; Gittell and Hollander, *Six Districts*, p. 146.

18. *Findings and Recommendations*, CG-1; Report of Progress . . . , Sept. 28, 1965, Box 17, Kornegay Papers; *DFP*, Mar. 14, 1962; *DN*, Mar. 12, Apr. 11, 1962.

19. Official Transcript, Aug. 15, 1967, p. 447, Series 1, Box 2, NACCD Records; CCR Field Division Case Reports, June 23, 1966, Series IV, Box 4, CCR Papers.

20. Executive Secretary's Report, Jan. 14, 1963, Part 1, Box 21, DNAACP Papers; *DN*, Dec. 5, 1962, May 21, Oct. 2, Sept. 28, 1963, Apr. 22, June 29, 1964, June 23, 1965; *MC*, Feb. 24, 1962, Aug. 31, Sept. 7, 21, 1963, June 13, 1964; *NYT*, June 2, 1963; CCR, "Annual Report, 1963," p. 11.

21. *DN*, Apr. 3, May 26, 1965; NEA, *Detroit*, p. 49; CCR, "Annual Report, 1964," p. 3; CCR Minutes, Feb. 15, June 21, 1965, Series IV, Box 4, CCR Papers; Ardrey Memorandum to Members, Apr. 20, 1965, Part 2, Series II, Box 28, DNAACP Papers; Minutes Ad Hoc Committee . . . , Mar. 8, 1965, Part 2, Series I, Box 1, ibid.; *MC*, Apr. 17, May 22, 29, 1965.

22. Lawrence Niblett, "An Illustration of Provocative News," Mar. 1, 1963, Box 5, Remus G. Robinson Papers, ALHUA; *Illustrated News*, Jan. 14, Sept. 2, 30, 1963; *MC*, Sept. 21, 1963, Jan. 18, 1964; CCR Minutes, Nov. 18, 1963, Series IV, Box 4, CCR Papers.

23. William R. Grant, "Community Control vs School Integration — The Case of Detroit," *Public Interest* no. 24 (Summer 1971): 66–67; Vivian Pope Memorandum to Burton Levy, May 16, 1967, Box 28, Records of the Michigan Civil Rights Commission, RG 74-90, State Archives, Lansing, Michigan; Inner City Parents Council, Inner City Parents Present Program . . . , June 13, 1967, Box 54, ND Papers; *DN*, June 14, 1967.

24. *Illustrated News*, Feb. 12, 19, 1962; *DFP*, Sept. 27, 28, 1966; *MC*, Mar. 12, May 28, 1966; CCR Field Division Case Reports, June 23, 1966, Series IV, Box 4, CCR Papers.

25. [Nathan Caplan] interview with First Looter, Nov. 7, 1967, p. 1, transcript in my possession; *MC*, Apr. 8, 1967; *NACCD Report*, p. 242; John J. Ursu Summation of Interview with Ed Simpkins, n.d., Series 59, Box 2, NACCD Records; Nelson Memorandum to Wilson (interview with Richard . Simmons), n.d., (interview with Stewart House and Norvel [*sic*] Harington), n.d., ibid.; Popp Memorandum to Wilson (interview with Father)'Hara and Valerie Childs), Oct. 12 [1967], ibid.; Wilson Memorandum to Nelson, Part IV, n.d., Rossi File.

26. "Report of High School Study Commission," p. 189; Richard Dresher to enior High School Principals, Dec. 1, 1966, Series 45, Box 12, NACCD ecords; Detroit Public Schools Guidance and Counseling Department, Senior ligh School Withdrawal Study, 1965–1966, ibid.; Education and Youth Incenves Department, DUL, Comparison Study of Six Detroit High Schools . . . , pr. 1967, Box 47, DUL Papers; Minutes of Board of Directors Meeting, DUL,

Apr. 9, 1967, Box 42, ibid.; Wilson Memorandum to Nelson (Boer interview), n.d., Series 59, Box 2, ibid.; Ursu Summation, n.d., ibid.

27. Report of Recommendations of Task Force on Quality Integrated Education in Detroit Schools, Sept. 13, 1967, Box 6, Detroit Public Schools, Division of Community Relations Papers (hereafter DPS-DCR), ALHUA; *MC*, May 28, 1966; DUL, Quarterly Report, Apr.–June 1966, Box 43, DUL Papers; Gregory, "Walkout," pp. 30–33; Inner City Parents Council Program, June 13, 1967, Box 64, ND Papers. Primary and secondary schools in Detroit were classified according to the high school area in which they were located.

28. Inner City Parents Council, Program, June 13, 1967, Box 64, ND Papers; *DN*, June 14, 1967.

29. *DN*, Jan. 21, 23, 1962; *DFP*, Aug. 15, 1962; *Illustrated News*, Feb. 26, 1962; *MC*, Jan. 27, Feb. 3, June 12, July 7, Aug. 18, 1962, May 25, 1963, May 9, 1964.

30. *MC*, Sept. 26, 1964, Mar. 6, May 1, 1965, July 16, 1966; *DFP*, Apr. 21, 1965; *DN*, June 21, Nov. 25, 1964, Apr. 13, 21, 22, 1965; Civil Action No. 22092, Sept. 18, 1964, Box 139, JPC Papers; A Progress Report . . . [Feb. 23, 1965], Box 10, Frank Angelo Papers, MHC; Ardrey Memorandum to Members, Apr. 20, 1965, Part 2, Series II, Box 28, DNAACP Papers; Grant, "Community Control," p. 65; Interview with George Crockett, Aug. 7, 1984, pp. 29–32, transcript in MHC; William R. Grant, "Community Control vs School Integration in Detroit," *Public Interest* no. 24 (Summer 1971): 63.

31. DUL, Information Re: De Facto Segregation in Schools [1963?], Box 46, DUL Papers; Intergroup Relations Department, Racial Distribution . . . , Oct. 19, 1967, Box 48, ibid.; *DN*, June 10, 1966; NEA, *Detroit*, pp. 29–32.

32. Progress Report, Box 10, Angelo Papers; Minutes of Pupil Placement Subcommittee . . . , Nov. 4, 1965, Part 2, Series I, Box 2, DNAACP Papers; Pupil Placement Subcommittee Chronology, ibid.; *DN*, June 22, 1962, Apr. 21, 1965, July 13, 1966; Gittell and Hollander, *Six Districts*, pp. 146–47; NEA, *Detroit*, pp. 29–31; *Bradley* vs. *Milliken*, 338 F.Supp. 582, 588, 592–93 (1971).

33. Norman Drachler, Testimony on H.R. 17846, June 30, 1970, Box 10, Angelo Papers; Grant, "Community Control," p. 65; 338 F.Supp. 588.

34. Board of Education and Administrative Actions on Integration, 1945–1970, Box 2, DPS-DCR Papers; NEA, *Detroit*, pp. 48–50; Information Re: De Facto Segregation [1963?], Box 46, DUL Papers; Roy L. Stephens to Ardrey, June 23, 1965, Part 1, Series II, Box 28, DNAACP Papers; Employment Division Memo to CCR, Sept. 20, 1965, Series IV, Box 4, CCR Papers; Ruffin Memorandum to CCR, Jan. 26, 1967, ibid.; CRC Newsletters, May, Sept. 1965; CCR, "Annual Report, 1966", pp. 14–15; CCR, "Annual Report, 1967"; CCR Release, July 25, 1967, Box 370, JPC Papers; Official Transcript, Aug. 15, 1967, p. 451, Series 1, Box 2, NACCD Records; *DN*, Sept. 24, 25, 1963, Jan. 23, 1967; *MC*, Sept. 28, 1963, July 22, 1967.

35. Minutes of Executive Board of Coordinating Council on Human Relations, Sept. 5, 1962, Series II, Box 6, CCR Papers; Brownell, *Pursuing Excellence in Education: The Superintendent's Ten Year Report, 1956–1966* (Detroit: Detroit Board of Education, 1966), pp. 14–15; Gittell and Hollander, *Six Districts*, p. 146; Marks Memorandum to CCR, Aug. 22, 1963, Box 12, JPC Papers; CCR Minutes, July 15, 1965, Series IV, Box 4, CCR Papers; Marks Memoran-

dum to CCR, Nov. 15, 1965, ibid.; *MC*, Apr. 28, Sept. 1, 1962, Aug. 31, Sept. 14, 1963, May 1, 1965; *DN*, June 9, 1965.

36. *DFP*, June 26, 1963; Notes for Subcommittee on Education Meeting, Jan. 15, 1964, Box 21, ORA Papers; Teacher Placement in Detroit Schools . . . , June 1, 1965, Box 7, Robinson Papers; CCR Minutes, June 21, 1965, Series IV, Box 4, CCR Papers; *DN*, June 9, 1965.

37. Racial Distribution . . . in Detroit Public Schools, Oct. 1966, in Reconnaissance Survey, Detroit, 1: Exhibit 3, Series 10, Box 46, NACCD Records; Marks Memorandum to CCR, Nov. 15, 1965, Series IV, Box 4, CCR Papers; CCR, "Annual Report, 1965," p. 8; DUL Education and Youth Incentives Department, Comparison Study, Apr. 1967, Box 47, DUL Papers; Gittell and Hollander, *Six Districts*, p. 146; "Report of High School Study Commission," pp. 59–60; United States Commission on Civil Rights, *Racial Isolation in Public Schools*, 2 vols. (Washington: GPO, 1967), 2:10; *DN*, Nov. 16, 1965; NEA, *Detroit*, p. 36.

38. Grant, "Community Control," pp. 64–65; CCR Minutes, Sept. 21, 1964, Series IV, Box 4, CCR Papers; *MC*, June 24, 1965, Feb. 19, 1966; Interview with Arthur Johnson, July 23, 1984, p. 19, transcript in MHC; Robert Conot, *American Odyssey* (New York: William Morrow and Co., 1974), pp. 574–75.

39. John J. Ursu and Bernard Dobranski, Interview with Arthur Johnson and Dr. Wattenberg, n.d., Series 59, Box 2, NACCD Records; CRC Newsletter, Sept. 1966; Johnson interview, pp. 3–4, 17.

40. Progress Report, Box 10, Angelo Papers; Intergroup Relations Department, Racial Distribution, Oct. 19, 1967, Box 48, DUL Papers; *MC*, Mar. 30, 1963, Feb. 12, 1966; *DN*, Feb. 8, 1967; Inner City Parents Council, Program, June 13, 1967, Box 64, ND Papers; Ursu notes of interview with A. L. Zwerdling, n.d., Series 59, Box 2, NACCD Records; Official Transcript, Aug. 15, 1967, p. 449, Series 1, Box 2, ibid.

41. Progress Report, Box 10, Angelo Papers; Stephens to Ardrey, June 23, 1965, Part 1, Box 28, DNAACP Papers; Board of Education . . . 1945–1970, Box 2, DPS-DCR Papers; Official Transcript, Aug. 15, 1967, p. 450, Series 1, Box 2, NACCD Records.

42. Ursu and Dobranski, Interview with Johnson and Wattenberg, n.d., Series 59, Box 2, NACCD Records; Official Transcript, Aug. 15, 1967, p. 450, Series 1, Box 2, ibid.; Board of Education . . . 1945–1970, Box 2, DPS-DCR Papers; Information Re: De Facto Segregation [1963], Box 46, DUL Papers; Progress Report, Box 10, Angelo Papers; Drachler Testimony, June 30, 1970, ibid.; *MC*, June 16, July 7, 1962, May 4, 1963, Oct. 8, 1966; *Wall Street Journal*, Aug. 12, 1964.

43. *Examination of the War on Poverty, Staff and Consultant Reports*, prepared for Subcommittee on Employment, Manpower, and Poverty of the Senate Committee on Labor and Public Welfare, 90th Cong., 1st sess., 1967, Committee Print, 8 vols. (Washington: GPO, 1967), 6:1765–69; Greenleigh Associates, "Services," pp. 83–85; Brownell, *Pursuing Excellence*, pp. 16–17.

44. NEA, *Detroit*, pp. 69–70; Progress Report, Box 10, Angelo Papers; "Detroit Program for an Integrated School System," Oct. 5, 1964, Box 21, ORA Papers; Information Requested by Governor's Office . . . , Aug. 2, 1967, Box 327, GR Papers; Brownell, *Pursuing Excellence*, pp. 18–19; Minutes, Pupil Placement Subcommittee, CCEO, Nov. 4, 1965, Part 2, Series I, Box 3,

DNAACP Papers; Report B, Pupil Integration in Detroit Public Schools, Box 7, Robinson Papers; *MC*, Feb. 19, 1966, Aug. 26, 1967; *NYT*, Apr. 15, 1968.

45. City of Detroit, Elementary and Secondary Education Act of 1965, Box 327, GR Papers; Brownell, *Pursuing Excellence*, pp. 17-18; *DN*, Nov. 28, 1965; TAP Program Status, June 1966, Box 304, JPC Papers; *Examination of War on Poverty*, 6:1770-72, 1782-84.

46. NEA, *Detroit*, pp. 70, 85; *MC*, Apr. 8, 1967.

47. F. Jansen Memorandum to E. Mazey, Apr. 11 [1966], Box 1, ACLU-Metropolitan Detroit Branch Papers (1971), ALHUA; NEA, *Detroit*, pp. 73-74; David Gracie, "The Walkout at Northern High," *New University Thought* 5 (Spring 1967): 13; Gregory, "Walkout," pp. 30-31; *MC*, Apr. 16, 1966; *DFP*, Apr. 19, 20, 1966; William Walter Scott III, *Hurt, Baby, Hurt* (Ann Arbor: New Ghetto Press, 1970), p. 42.

48. Result of Robert Conot's Discussion with Stanley Webb, n.d., Box 81, NACCD Records; *DFP*, Apr. 19, 20, 1966; NEA, *Detroit*, pp. 76-77, 80-81; Gracie, "Walkout," pp. 13, 26; CCR Field Division Case Reports, Apr. 21, 1966, Series IV, Box 4, CCR Papers; Conot, *Odyssey*, p. 515; Mary Ellen Riordan to Robinson, Apr. 17, 1966, Box 7, Robinson Papers.

49. *DFP*, Apr. 8, 20, 1966; NEA, *Detroit*, pp. 74-76.

50. NEA, *Detroit*, p. 76; Jansen Memorandum to Mazey, Apr. 11, 1966, Box 1, ACLU Papers (1971); *DFP*, Apr. 18-20, 1966; Gracie, "Walkout," p. 15.

51. *DFP*, Apr. 8, 20, 1966; *MC*, Apr. 16, 1966; Gracie, "Walkout," pp. 15-16; NEA, *Detroit*, pp. 76-77; list of demands adopted, Apr. 7, 1966, Part 2, Series I, Box 12, DNAACP Papers; Walker, Batchelor, and Colding to Brownell, Apr. 15, 1966, Box 16, Robinson Papers; "Background—Northern High School," May 3, 1966, ibid.; Report from School Community Relations Committee, Northern High School to Board of Education, n.d., Box 7, ibid.; Jansen Memorandum to Mazey, Apr. 11 [1966], Box 1, ACLU Papers (1971).

52. *DFP*, Apr. 13, 16, 1966; Gracie, "Walkout," pp. 16-18, 26; NEA, *Detroit*, pp. 77-78; Report from Community Relations Committee to Board, n.d., Box 7, Robinson Papers.

53. Brownell to Walker et al., Apr. 15, 1966, Box 16, Robinson Papers; Colding to Robinson, Apr. 18, 1966, Box 7, ibid.

54. "Background—Northern High School," May 3, 1966, Box 16, ibid.; NEA, *Detroit*, p. 78; Gracie, "Walkout," pp. 18-20; *DFP*, Apr. 21-23, 1966; *MC*, Apr. 30, 1966; CCR Field Division Case Reports, Apr. 21, 1966, Series IV, Box 4, CCR Papers; Interview with Karl D. Gregory, July 12, 1984, pp. 8-9, transcript in MHC.

55. *MC*, July 2, 1966; *DFP*, Apr. 27, 1966; Gracie, "Walkout," p. 20.

56. *DFP*, Apr. 21, 22, 25, 1966; Brownell to Parents . . . , Apr. 22, 1966, Box 7, Robinson Papers; NAACP Educational Committee Meeting, Apr. 20, 1966, Part 2, Series I, Box 14, DNAACP Papers; Gracie, "Walkout," pp. 21-23; Robert F. Revitte, "Northern High School Problem," with Community Relations Department Meeting, Apr. 27, 1966, Father Sheehan Correspondence, 1962-1969, Archives of the Archdiocese of Detroit, Detroit, Michigan.

57. *DFP*, Apr. 27-30, 1966, July 21, 1966; *MC*, Apr. 30, 1966; Gracie, "Walkout," p. 27; Release, Apr. 29, 1966, Box 16, Robinson Papers; "Background—Northern High School," May 3, 1966, ibid.; Superintendent of Schools to Members, Board of Education, May 3, 1966, ibid.; Interim Report of Northern High

School Study Committee, June 1966, Box 428, Reuther Papers. In April 1967 Dr. Leonard F. Sain, a black, replaced Donaldson. *DFP*, Apr. 17, 1967; Gracie, "Walkout," pp. 24, 26–27.

58. Webb to Roger Wilkins, n.d., and enclosed report, Detroit Riot File, Section I, Community Relations Service (CRS), FOIA; NEA, *Detroit*, p. 79; Herman M. Smathers to Robinson, May 13, 1966, Martin Kalish to Robinson, Apr. 19, 1966, Box 1, Robinson Papers; *DFP*, Apr. 28, 30, 1966; *MC*, May 14, 1966.

59. James R. Hurst and James N. Garrett to NAACP, May 5, 1967, Part 2, Series I, Box 7, DNAACP Papers; *MC*, May 28, June 18, 1966, Apr. 15, 1967; *DN*, May 12, 1967; Webb, "Race Relations in Detroit–Summer 1966," June 9, 1966, Box 17, Kornegay Papers; Webb to Wilkins, n.d., Detroit Riot File, CRS, FOIA.

60. Central High School Study Commission Final Report, July 1967, Series 45, Box 12, NACCD Records; Interim Report of the Northwestern High School Study Group, Oct. 1966, Part 2, Series 1, Box 12, DNAACP Papers; "Report of High School Study Commission," p. 6 and passim; *Newsweek* 72 (July 8, 1968): 46–47.

61. Wilson Memorandum for Nelson (interview with Kornegay et al.), n.d., Series 59, Box 2, NACCD Records; Official Transcript, Aug. 15, 1967, Series 1, Box 2, ibid.; Black File, No. 183, White File, No. 183, Detroit data for "Racial Attitudes."

62. *DFP*, Apr. 27, 1966, Apr. 28, 1967; *MC*, Oct. 1, 1966, Jan. 21, 28, 1967; Johnson interview, pp. 21–22; Albert Zack to Sidney Fine, Apr. 20, 1984; Gracie, "Walkout," p. 28. Eighty students walked out of Southeastern High on Apr. 27, 1966, claiming, "They just don't learn us nothing." *DFP*, Apr. 28, 1966. For changes at Northern, see *MC*, Jan. 21, 1967.

63. *MC*, July 21, 1962, May 29, 1965, Jan. 8, 1966, Feb. 25, 1967; Research Department, DUL, *A Profile of the Detroit Negro, 1959–1967* (Dec. 1967), p. 4, Box 45, DUL Papers; Opening Statement of Richard S. Emrich, June 25, 1964, Box 476, Reuther Papers; Locke, "Race Relations in Detroit–Fall 1966," Oct. 5, 1966, Box 21, ORA Papers; National Commission on Urban Problems, *Hearings*, 5 vols. (Washington: GPO, 1968), 5:9.

64. Dobranski Memorandum to Wilson (interview with Robert D. Knox), Oct. 19, 1967, Series 59, Box 2, NACCD Records; *Riots, Civil and Criminal Disorders*, pt. 5:1341; Mayor's Committee for Community Renewal, Population and Housing Study, Technical Report 11, Aug. 1965, p. 29, Box 346, GR Papers; *DN*, Mar. 22, 1964.

65. *Riots, Civil and Criminal Disorders*, pt. 5:1340; *NACCD Report*, p. 342; undated document in 1969 folder, Box 514, Reuther Papers; Dobranski and Popp Memorandum for Wilson (interview with Malcolm Dade), Oct. 11, 1967, Series 59, Box 2, NACCD Records; Dobranski Memorandum to Wilson (Knox interview), Oct. 18, 1967, ibid.; Roy Levy Williams to Kornegay et al., Jan. 11, 1967, Box 45, DUL Papers; Earl Nathaniel M. Gooding, "Urban Race Riots and Social Change: An Analysis of Two Cities" (Ph.D. diss., Vanderbilt University, 1977), p. 69.

66. DUL, Quarterly Report, Jan.–Mar. 1966, Box 43, DUL Papers; "City of Detroit Totals," enclosed with Susan Jokelson to Anne A. Lewis, Aug. 29, 1968, Box 45, ibid.; Gooding, "Race Riots," p. 139; *DN*, June 2, Oct. 27, 1967.

67. Minutes, Detroit Committee for Neighborhood Conservation and Improved Housing (DCNCIH), June 29, 1967, Part 2, Series I, DNAACP Papers; Chicago Regional Council, *The Detroit Survey*, Mar. 1969, p. 31, Box 508, JPC Papers; National Commission on Urban Problems, *Hearings*, 5:9; *DN*, Aug. 5, 1967; Popp Memorandum to Wilson, Oct. 26, 1967, Rossi File; James C. Gaither for the President, May 9, 1967, Box 29, WE9, WHCF.

68. Albert J. Mayer, "Public Housing, Urban Renewal and Racial Segregation in Detroit," June 1962, p. 11, Box 83, JPC Papers; Sub-Committee on Housing, CCEO, "A Report to the People of Detroit on Housing in the City of Detroit," Part I, Feb. 1967, Box 336, ibid.; Julian A. Cook and John Dempsey to Robert C. Weaver, June 13, 1968, Box 564, ibid.; Fred J. Romanoff to Cavanagh, Feb. 18, 1966, Box 271, ibid.; MDT Report, Box 534, ibid.; CCR Field Division Case Reports, June 23, 1966, Series 4, Box 4, CCR Papers; DHC, *Report to the Commissioners, Third Quarter, 1966*, p. 4, *First Quarter, 1967*, p. 9; *MC*, Nov. 12, 1966; Chicago Regional Council, *Detroit Survey*, p. 33, Box 509, JPC Papers.

69. CCR, "A Report on Population Movement and Neighborhood Stabilization," July 16, 1962, Box 9, Kornegay Papers; Locke Memorandum, Apr. 27, 1965, Box 17, ibid.; CCR Minutes, July 16, 1962, Series IV, Box 4, CCR Papers; Marks to Common Council, July 9, 1963, Box 112, JPC Papers; Urban Renewal Subcommittee Memorandum to CCR, Jan. 19, 1967, Box 370, ibid.; Locke to All Members, May 27, 1964, To Members of the Sub-Committee on Housing, Oct. 28, 1964, Box 21, ORA Papers; Fizazi to George E. Bushnell, Feb. 25, 1966, Box 22, ibid.; Joseph Ross speech, with Ross to Locke, Apr. 27, 1965, Box 37, ibid.; Summary Report, CCEO, Oct. 1963–Sept. 1964, Box 476, Reuther Papers; *MC*, July 21, 1962, July 20, 1963, Aug. 29, 1964, June 11, 1966, Feb. 25, 1967; *DN*, June 6, 1962, Apr. 27, 1965.

70. *MC*, Oct. 13, 1962, Jan. 26, 1963; CCR Field Division Case Reports, June 23, July 28, 1966, Series IV, Box 4, CCR Papers; Marks Memoranda to CCR, Oct. 4, 11, 1962, Box 59, JPC Papers; CCR, "Report on Population Movement," July 16, 1962, Box 9, Kornegay Papers; Thomas Ford Hoult, "About Detroit . . . ," *Crisis* 74 (Oct. 1967): 407–8; Black File, Nos. 271, 272, Detroit data for "Racial Attitudes."

71. *Detroit: The New City* [Detroit, 1967], p. 73; Mayor's Committee for Community Renewal, Technical Report 11, p. 31, Box 346, GR Papers; Marks to Common Council, Sept. 26, 1962, Box 59, JPC Papers; CCR Minutes, Dec. 16, 1963, Series IV, Box 4, CCR Papers; Housing Division to CCR, July 28, 1966, July 7, 1967, ibid.; Minutes, Coordinating Committee on Human Relations, Jan. 5, 1966, Series II, Box 6, ibid.; CCR, "Annual Report, 1963," pp. 3–4; CCR, "Annual Report, 1965," pp. 2–3; CCR, "Annual Report, 1966," pp. 9–10; Housing Committee Memorandum to CCR, Apr. 21, 1966, Part 2, Series I, Box 4, DNAACP Papers; DUL, Quarterly Report, Jan.–Mar. 1966, Box 43, DUL Papers; *MC*, Sept. 22, Dec. 1, 1962, Mar. 5, 1966.

72. *DN*, July 31, 1966; CCR, "Annual Report, 1966," p. 11; MDT Report, Box 534, JPC Papers.

73. CCR, "Annual Report, 1963," p. 6; Marks Memorandum to CCR, July 5, 1963, Box 112, JPC Papers; *DN*, June 8, July 2, 6, 12, Aug. 12, 23, 1963; *MC*, Aug. 31, 1963.

74. *DFP*, Sept. 19, 1963; *DN*, Sept. 18, 1963.

75. *DN*, Oct. 3, 1963; *MC*, Oct. 5, 12, 1963.

76. *MC*, Sept. 14, 1963, Feb. 8, Sept. 12, Nov. 28, 1964; Locke to Members CCEO, Nov. 10, 1964, Box 476, Reuther Papers; *DN*, Feb. 3, May 6, 1964, July 3, 1966; *DFP*, Oct. 9, 1963, Feb. 4, 1964, Nov. 4, 1965; *Detroit Daily Press*, Sept. 2, 3, Nov. 4, 1964; Bruce A. Miller to Robert Tindal, Dec. 30, 1966, Part 2, Series I, Box 9, DNAACP Papers.

77. *DN*, Oct. 12, 1962, Nov. 14, 1965; *Detroit*, p. 11.

78. Joe Darden et al., *Detroit, Race and Uneven Development* (Philadelphia: Temple University Press, 1987), pp. 156–58; *Detroit*, pp. 13–14; Conot, *Odyssey*, pp. 400–403, 408–9, 445–46; Robert J. Mowitz and Deil S. Wright, *Profile of a Metropolis* (Detroit: Wayne State University Press, 1962), pp. 13–17; Lawrence M. Friedman, *Government and Slum Housing* (Chicago: Rand McNally and Co., 1968), pp. 148–50; *DN*, Dec. 22, 1963.

79. Friedman, *Slum Housing*, pp. 150–51, 156, 158, 162, 164; Mark I. Gelfand, *A Nation of Cities: The Federal Government and Urban America, 1933–1965* (New York: Oxford University Press, 1975), pp. 172–73; Summary of Detroit's Urban Renewal Program [1968], Box 508, JPC Papers; United States Commission on Civil Rights, *Hearings Held in Detroit, Michigan*, Dec. 14, 15, 1960 (Washington: GPO, 1961), p. 230.

80. Civil Rights Commission, *Hearings*, pp. 230–37; Knox to C. R. Anderson, July 23, 1962, Box 26, JPC Papers; Strichartz to Cavanagh, Sept. 16, 1962, ibid.; Cavanagh to Pat Lieberson, Nov. 25, 1969, Box 511, ibid.; *Detroit*, p. 4.

81. *Detroit*, pp. 8, 10, 49–50; CCR, "A Look at the Changing Face of Detroit," Mar. 8, 1963, Box 112, JPC Papers; Summary of Detroit's Urban Renewal Program [1968], Box 508, ibid.; *DN*, Oct. 12, 1962. Detroit's urban renewal projects are described in *Detroit*, pp. 11–23.

82. "What's Wrong with Urban Renewal in Detroit?" Nov. 30, 1965, Box 316, GR Papers; National Commission on Urban Problems, *Hearings*, 5:31–33; Agenda, New Detroit Committee, Oct. 26, 1967, Box 372, JPC Papers; Charles R. Blessing to Cavanagh, Nov. 22, 1967, and enclosed "Detailed Analysis . . . ," Box 535, ibid.; Steve Babson, *Working Detroit* (New York: Adama Books, 1984), p. 158. For delays between announcement of an urban renewal project and the taking of property, see Harold Black, "Urban Renewal: A Program Involving a Multiplicity of Participants" (Ph.D. diss., University of Michigan, 1973), p. 106.

83. Friedman, *Slum Housing*, pp. 159–60, 166, 169–71; William Serrin, "How One Big City Defeated Its Mayor," *NYT Magazine*, Oct. 27, 1968; *Detroit*, p. 13; Mayer, "Public Housing," pp. 28–29; DHC, *Gratiot Redevelopment Project: Final Project Report*, June 30, 1964; Knox to Gary W. Krause, Oct. 15, 1962, Box 27, JPC Papers; Chicago Regional Council, *Detroit Survey*, pp. 31, 32, 33, 35, Box 508, ibid.; Agenda, New Detroit Committee, Oct. 26, 1967, Box 372, ibid.; Wilson Memorandum to Nelson (Boer interview), n.d., Series 59, Box 2, NACCD Records; DUL, Quarterly Report, Jan.–Mar. 1966, Box 43, DUL Papers; Questionnaire Nos. 5061, 6028, Boxes 10, 11, A-W Riot Studies; *DN*, Oct. 19, 1962; *DFP*, Apr. 24, 1965; *MC*, Aug. 3, 1963. In the Lafayette Park Subdivision of the Gratiot Project, 801 nonwhite dwellings and 60 white dwellings were replaced by 35 nonwhite and 348 white dwellings. Mayer, "Public Housing," p. 28. See also Mowitz and Wright, *Profile*, pp. 73–78.

84. *Detroit*, pp. 21–22; Robert Sinclair and Bryan Thompson, *Metropolitan*

Detroit (Cambridge, Mass.: Ballinger Publishing Co., 1977), p. 37; Re Romney WCO letter, n.d., Box 240, JPC Papers; Al Applegate to Romney, Nov. 26, Dec. 13, 1965, WCO Statement to Governor Romney, draft copy, Dec. 1965, Box 331, GR Papers; WCO release, Dec. 21, 1965, ibid.; "What's Wrong with Urban Renewal in Detroit?" n.d., Box 316, ibid.; West Central Organization, June 1966, Box 50, DUL Papers; Wilson Memorandum to Nelson (interview with Mary Valentine), n.d., Series 59, Box 2, NACCD Records; *DN*, Dec. 17, 1965; *DFP*, Dec. 22, 1965; *MC*, Dec. 11, 18, 25, 1965, Apr. 2, 1966; *NYT*, Nov. 23, 1965.

85. Henry Rubin to Ken Ichiura, Sept. 18, 1962, Box 27, JPC Papers; [DHC] Statement of Charges by WCO . . . [Dec. 1965], Box 240, ibid.; Knox to Common Council, Oct. 10, 1966, Box 366, ibid.; DHC, Urban Relocation Statement, Apr. 23, 1965, Box 50, DUL Papers; *Detroit*, p. 80; DHC, *Report to the Commissioners, Second Quarter, 1965*, p. 5, *First Quarter, 1967*, p. 5.

86. Cavanagh to Committee for Community Renewal, Feb. 1, 1966, Box 271, JPC Papers; RS and JR to JPS [*sic*], n.d., ibid.; Cavanagh to James H. Quello, Oct. 12, 1967, Box 366, ibid.; Robert Roselle to MDT, Dec. 15, 1967, Box 339, ibid.; James Bush Memorandum to CCR, Sept. 29, 1966, Series IV, Box 4, CCR Papers; Dobranski Memorandum to Wilson (Knox interview), Oct. 19, 1967, Series 59, Box 2, NACCD Papers; *West Central Action News*, Nov. 24, 1966, Box 50, DUL Papers; DHC, *Report to the Commissioners, First Quarter, 1966*, pp. 3–4, *Third Quarter, 1966*, p. 8, *First Quarter, 1967*, p. 6; *DFP*, Feb. 16, 23, Sept. 27, Oct. 6, 7, 1966, Mar. 24, 30, 1967; *MC*, Mar. 12, 19, Oct. 1, Nov. 12, 1966; *DN*, Aug. 17, 1965, June 21, 23, Mar. 6, 1966.

87. *DN*, Nov. 14, 1965; Roselle to MDT, Dec. 15, 1967, Box 339, JPC Papers; Dobranski Memorandum to Wilson (Knox interview), Oct. 19, 1967, Series 59, Box 2, NACCD Records.

88. Eleanor Paperno Wolf and Charles N. Lebeaux, *Change and Renewal in an Urban Community: Five Case Studies of Detroit* (New York: Frederick A. Praeger, 1969), pp. 385–437, 443–57.

89. Ibid., pp. 175–78, 270–76; Black File, No. 157, Detroit data for "Racial Attitudes."

90. DCNCIH, A Report on Neighborhood Blight . . . , Mar. 29, 1962, Box A5, DUL Papers; Friedman, *Slum Housing*, pp. 161–62; DHC, *Report to the Commissioners, Fourth Quarter, 1962*, p. 4.

91. DCNCIH, Statement of Purpose . . . , July 1963, Box A5, DUL Papers; DCNCIH, *Neighborhood Conservation in Detroit, Annual Report, 1965*, Box 50, ibid.; Hugh G. Blanding to Theodore Morgan, May 21, 1962, Box 62, JPC Papers; Cavanagh to Whitney Young, Aug. 24, 1964, Box 184, ibid.; DHC, *Report to the Commissioners, Second Quarter, 1964*, pp. 2–4; Charles E. West, "The Role of Block Clubs in the Detroit Civil Disorder of July 1967" (M.A. thesis, Wayne State University, 1970), p. 18.

92. *Detroit*, pp. 24–27; Summary of Detroit's Urban Renewal Program [1968], Box 508, JPC Papers; Mayer, "Public Housing," p. 25.

93. Summary of Detroit's Urban Renewal Program [1968], Box 508, JPC Papers; Robert E. Smith to Knox, May 14, 1965, Box 211, ibid.; CCR, "A Look at the Changing Face of Detroit," Mar. 8, 1963, Box 112, ibid.; *Detroit*, pp. 27–29; Community Relations Service, U.S. Conference of Mayors, Community

Planning and Civil Disturbance, Experience Report No. 8, in Reconnaissance Survey, Detroit, 1: Exhibit 1, Series 10, Box 46, NACCD Records.

94. West, "Block Clubs," pp. 44, 72, 84; Research Department, DUL, *Profile of Detroit Negro*, p. 5, Box 45, DUL Papers; George Henderson, "The Block Club Movement within the Detroit Tenth Police Precinct," May 1962, pp. 7, 11, Box 46, DUL Papers; Williams to Kornegay, May 17, 1967, ibid.; *DN*, Oct. 19, 1962; William Kelly to New Detroit Committee, Aug. 8, 1967, Box 84, ND Papers; DHC, *Report to the Commissioners, Fourth Quarter, 1967*, p. 12; *DFP*, Mar. 24, 1967; Knox to Common Council, Dec. 6, 1963, Box 84, JPC Papers; Harold Black to Cavanagh, Sept. 8, 1966, Box 271, ibid.

95. *DN*, June 6, Oct. 19, 1962, July 30, 1967; *MC*, Jan. 15, 29, 1966; DHC, *Report to the Commissioners, Second Quarter, 1971*, pp. 5–7; Bellamy to Strichartz, Aug. 14, 1967, Box 393, JPC Papers.

96. *DN*, June 2, 1963; *MC*, Dec. 18, 1965; Knox to Common Council, Mar. 5, 1964, Box 141, JPC Papers; Statement of Arthur Yim . . . , Aug. 29, 1967, Box 531, ibid.

97. New Detroit Committee, *Progress Report, April, 1968* [Detroit: n.p., 1968], p. 41; Chicago Regional Council, *Detroit Survey*, p. 35, Box 509, JPC Papers; *Detroit*, pp. 29–32; Dobranski Memorandum to Wilson (Knox interview), Oct. 19, 1967, Series 59, Box 2, NACCD Records; Wilson Memorandum to Nelson, Part IV, n.d., Rossi File; Issues Committee Minutes, Series II, Box 11, CCR Papers; *DN*, Oct. 14, 1965.

98. Chicago Regional Council, *Detroit Survey*, p. 35, Box 509, JPC Papers; Richard L. Sanderson to Cavanagh, Jan. 13, 1967, and enclosed, "Detroit Area Code Enforcement," Box 379, ibid.; CCR, Enforcement of Health, Building, and Safety Codes . . . , Aug. 1967, Box 567, ibid.; Smith to Knox, May 14, 1965, Box 211, ibid.; Urban Housing Council, "A Study of Housing Code Enforcement in Detroit," 1966, Box 50, DUL Papers; Minutes, Coordinating Council on Human Relations, Dec. 1, 1966, Series II, Box 11, CCR Papers.

99. Urban Housing Council, "Code Enforcement," Box 50, DUL Papers; George D. King, "Report on . . . Code Enforcement," Jan. 26, 1967, Box 42, ibid.; Field Division Memorandum to CCR . . . , Oct. 21, 1966, Series IV, Box 4, CCR Papers; *MC*, Oct. 27, 1962, Jan. 7, 1967; *Examination of War on Poverty*, :1744–45.

100. "New Detroit Committee Report on Open Occupancy, Tenants' Rights, Housing Code Enforcements," Oct. 12, 1967, Box 2, Horace W. Gilmore Papers, ALHUA; Urban Renewal Subcommittee Memorandum to CCR, Jan. 19, 1967, Box 370, JPC Papers; Field Division to CCR, June 21, 1965, Series IV, Box 4, CCR Papers; CCR Minutes, May 17, June 21, 1965, ibid.; Williams to Kornegay, Feb. 3, 1967, Box 45, DUL Papers; *Examination of War on Poverty*, 6:1745; DHC, *Report to the Commissioners, First Quarter, 1967*, p. 10; *MC*, June 15, 1963, Jan. 2, 1965, Jan. 22, 1966; *DN*, Nov. 14, 1965; August Meier and Elliott Rudwick, *CORE* (New York: Oxford University Press, 1973), p. 368.

101. *MC*, Sept. 24, Dec. 24, 1966, Apr. 8, 1967; Meier and Rudwick, *CORE*, . 368.

102. [Caplan] interview with Second Looter, Nov. 7, 1967, p. 14, transcript in y possession; Elliot D. Luby and James Grisell, "Grievances of Detroit Negro rrestees" [1968], p. 17, Detroit Public Library, Detroit, Michigan; *NACCD eport*, p. 48; John S. Adams, "The Geography of Riots and Civil Disorders in

the 1960s," *Economic Geography* 48 (Jan. 1972): 35, 38; Wilson Memorandum to Nelson, Part IV, n.d., Rossi File.

Chapter 4

1. Permanent Subcommittee on Investigations of the Senate Committee on Government Operations, *Riots, Civil and Criminal Disorders, Hearings*, 90th Cong., 2d sess., 1968, pt. 5:1336-37, 1341; Transportation and Land Use (TALUS) Tables, Table 5, Box 393, JPC Papers; *Wall Street Journal*, Aug. 12, 1964.

2. MCHRD, "Developing Human Resources in the City of Detroit" [Mar. 1967], Box 379, JPC Papers; TAP, A Proposed Community Action Program for Detroit [1964], Box 178, ibid.; TALUS Tables, Table 6, Box 393, ibid.; CCR, Employment and Income by Age, Sex, Color and Residence, May 1963, Box 9, Francis A. Kornegay Papers, MHC.

3. Ralph V. Smith, "Behind the Riots," *American Educator* 3 (Nov. 1967): 4; James Hedegard, "Racial Attitudes and Responses to the Riot in the Community" [1968], p. 4, Detroit Public Library, Detroit, Michigan; Inter-University Consortium for Political and Social Research, Black File, No. 260, Detroit data for Angus Campbell and Howard Schuman, "Racial Attitudes in Fifteen American Cities," in *Supplemental Studies for the National Advisory Commission on Civil Disorders* (Washington: GPO, 1968); ibid., p. 23; Tom Popp Memorandum to Herman Wilson (interview with Nelson Jack Edwards), Oct. 12, 1967, Series 59, Box 2, NACCD Records; Kyran McGrath Memorandum, Aug. 17, 1967, Series 4, Box 22, ibid.

4. *MC*, July 6, 13, 20, Aug. 3, 10, 17, Sept. 14, Oct. 25, Dec. 21, 1963, Apr. 18, May 2, 9, June 27, 1964; *DN*, July 22, 1963; August Meier and Elliott Rudwick, *CORE* (New York: Oxford University Press, 1973), pp. 361, 369.

5. Subcommittee on the War on Poverty Program of the House Committee on Education and Labor, *Economic Opportunity Act of 1964, Hearings*, 88th Cong., 2d sess., 1964, pt. 2:776, 778; *Examination of the War on Poverty, Staff and Consultant Reports*, prepared for Subcommittee on Employment, Manpower, and Poverty of the Senate Committee on Education and Labor, 90th Cong., 1st sess., Committee Print, 8 vols. (Washington: GPO, 1967), 6:1713; *DN*, Apr. 15, 17, 1964; Oral History Interview of Jerome P. Cavanagh, Mar. 22, 1971, p. 7, LBJ Library.

6. MCHRD, "Human Resources," pp. 2-3, Box 379, JPC Papers; Cavanagh to Common Council, Sept. 25, 1962, Box 66, ibid.; CADY, A Request for a Planning Grant . . . , Aug. 1, 1962, Box 63, ibid.; Richard Strichartz and Robert Roselle to Cavanagh, n.d., Box 142, ibid.; *DN*, May 27, 1962, Apr. 15, June 12, 1964; *MC*, Sept. 14, 1963; Robert Conot, *American Odyssey* (New York: William Morrow and Co., 1974), p. 473.

7. Cavanagh to Sargent Shriver, Feb. 18, 1964, Box 165, JPC Papers; Cavanagh to Common Council, June 23, 1964, Box 178, ibid.; Philip Rutledge to Robert E. Toohey, Jan. 16, 1966, Box 304, ibid.; Toohey to Ray Girardin, Apr. 5, 1965, Box 215, ibid.; MCHRD, Project Summaries, June 1, 1967, Box 379, ibid.; *Examination of Poverty*, 6:1716; *Economic Opportunity Act*, p. 776; *MC*, Sept. 14, 1963; *DN*, Dec. 22, 1963, June 12, 1964.

8. *DN*, Mar. 17, Apr. 15, 17, 1964; *DFP*, Jan. 19, 21, Apr. 14, 1964; Releases, Jan. 19, 20, 1964, Box 165, JPC Papers; MCHRD, "Human Resources," pp. 3–4, Box 379, ibid.; Cavanagh to Shriver, Feb. 18, 1964, Box 165, ibid.; Roselle to Cavanagh, through Strichartz, n.d., Box 179, ibid.; TAP, Proposed Community Action Program, Box 178, ibid.; Minutes, Mayor's Committee for Community Renewal, Mar. 27, 1964, ibid.; *Examination of Poverty*, 6:1716–17; *Economic Opportunity Act*, p. 777; Greenleigh Associates, "Home Interview Study of Low-Income Households in Detroit, Michigan" (New York, 1965), ii.

9. TAP, Proposed Community Action Program, Box 178, JPC Papers; MCHRD, "Human Resources," pp. 3–4, Box 379, ibid.; TAP, Social Data Bank, Box 530, ibid.; Comptroller General of the United States, *Review of Community Action Program in Detroit . . .* , Apr. 10, 1965, p. 5; National Commission on Professional Rights and Responsibilities of the National Education Association of the United States, *Detroit, Michigan: A Study of Barriers to Equal Education Opportunity in a Large City* (Washington, Mar. 1967), p. 58.

10. MCHRD, "Human Resources," p. 5, Box 379, JPC Papers; Greenleigh Associates, "Home Interview Study," passim.

11. Greenleigh Associates, "Study of Services to Deal with Poverty in Detroit" (New York, 1965), passim; Remarks by . . . Cavanagh, Sept. 9, 1966, Box 298, JPC Papers; Subcommittee on Employment, Manpower, and Poverty of Senate Committee on Labor and Public Welfare, *Examination of the War on Poverty, Hearings*, 90th Cong., 1st sess., 1967, pt. 1:20. For a service agency response to the Greenleigh Associates report, see *DN*, Mar. 31, 1965.

12. *Examination of Poverty*, 6:1713, 1717; Cavanagh to Common Council, June 23, 1964, Box 178, JPC Papers; Ravitz to Cavanagh, Aug. 7, 1964, and enclosed Summary Report of Poverty Meetings, Box 179, ibid.; Remarks by Cavanagh, Sept. 9, 1966, Box 298, ibid.; Common Council Proceedings, July 14, 1964, in Michigan Legislature, House of Representatives, Special Committee to Investigate Irregularities in the Total Action against Poverty Program in . . . Detroit, "Examination of the War on Poverty," 74th Legislature, Regular Session of 1968; *DN*, June 16, 1964.

13. Cavanagh interview, p.5, LBJ Library; *Economic Opportunity Act*, pp. 780–81; MCHRD, "Human Resources," p. 4, Box 379, JPC Papers; Strichartz and Roselle to Cavanagh, n.d., Box 142, ibid.; Roselle to Cavanagh, through Strichartz, n.d., ibid.; Stephen M. David, "Leadership of the Poor in Poverty Programs," *Proceedings of the Academy of Political Science* 29 (1968): 90; *Examination of Poverty*, pt. 6:1717.

14. MCHRD, "Human Resources," p. 4, Box 379, JPC Papers; Richard Simmons to Cavanagh, Apr. 24, 1968, Box 341, GR Papers; *DN*, Nov. 25, Dec. 15, 1964, July 30, Sept. 2, 1967; *DFP*, Nov. 5, 1967; Conot, *Odyssey*, p. 487. OEO grants required a matching contribution of 10 percent from the local government unit.

15. *Examination of Poverty*, 6:1713–14, 1718–19, 1720; MCHRD, "Human Resources," pp. 4–5, 12–13, 26–27, Box 379, JPC Papers; Cavanagh to Common Council, Mar. 8, 1967, ibid.; Cavanagh to Committee Members, Mar. 8, 1967, Box 52, Richard Austin Papers, ALHUA; *DN*, June 10, 1966, Mar. 11, 1967. TAP delegated a few of its programs to United Community Services, Visiting Nurses Association, and other agencies. Evaluation of a Community Action

Agency (CAA), Detroit, Michigan, Apr. 1967, Series 6, Box 32, NACCD Records.

16. Robert B. Plotnick and Felicity Skidmore, *Progress against Poverty: A Review of the 1964-1974 Decade* (New York: Academic Press, 1975), pp. 23-24; Daniel P. Moynihan, *Maximum Feasible Misunderstanding* (New York: Free Press, 1969), p. 131; Allen J. Matusow, *The Unraveling of America: A History of Liberalism in the 1960s* (New York: Harper and Row, 1984), pp. 124, 244.

17. David, "Leadership of Poor," p. 98; Extracts from PAC Minutes, Aug. 12, 1964, July 13, 1965, in Michigan "Examination of War on Poverty"; Response of MCHRD to the Interim Documentation Report on TAP, n.d., Box 434, JPC Papers; *NYT*, June 29, 1965.

18. *DN*, July 8, 14, 23, Aug. 6, 17, 1965, June 24, 1966; Extracts from PAC Minutes, July 13, 1965, Michigan "Examination of War on Poverty"; PAC Minutes, Aug. 6, 1965, Part II, Series 1, Box 26, DNAACP Papers.

19. *DN*, Aug. 9, 17, 1965, Jan. 12, 24, 1966; PAC Minutes, Aug. 6, 1965, Part II, Series 1, Box 26, DNAACP Papers; Rutledge to Toohey, Jan. 21, 1965, Toohey to Cavanagh, Jan. 22, 1965, Box 304, JCP Papers; MCHRD, "Human Resources," pp. 4-5, Box 379, ibid.

20. Evaluation of a CAA, Apr. 1967, Series 6, Box 32, NACCD Records; *Examination of Poverty*, 6:1720; J. David Greenstone and Paul E. Peterson, *Race and Authority in Urban Politics: Community Participation and the War on Poverty* (New York: Russell Sage Foundation, 1973), p. 36; Interview with Robert Roselle, Aug. 30, 1984, pp. 14-15, transcript in MHC.

21. *DN*, Oct. 14, 1965; Testimony of . . . Austin . . . , July 27, 1965, Box 52, Austin Papers; Roselle Memo to Cavanagh, Jan. 18, 1968, Box 406, JPC Papers; *Examination of Poverty Hearings*, pt. 1:106-7; David, "Leadership of Poor," pp. 91-98; Matusow, *Unraveling*, pp. 269-70.

22. Extracts from PAC Minutes, Feb. 1, 1965, Michigan "Examination of War on Poverty"; Minutes, Citizen Participation Sub-Committee, Jan. 26, 1967, Box 67, Austin Papers; Austin Testimony, July 27, 1965, Box 52, ibid.; *Examination of Poverty*, 6:1715-16, 1728-32, 1826-27; Greenstone and Peterson, *Urban Politics*, pp. 174-75; *DN*, Dec. 15, 1965; Conot, *Odyssey*, p. 505.

23. *Examination of Poverty*, 6:1727, 1732, 1823; MCHRD, Administrative Staff Meeting, Apr. 28, 1967, Box 544, JPC Papers; *DN*, Nov. 28, Dec. 15, 1965, Jan. 24, 1966.

24. MCHRD, Administrative Staff Meeting, Apr. 28, 1967, Box 544, JPC Papers; Roselle interview, p. 5; *Examination of Poverty*, 6:1721-22, 1833; Extracts from PAC Minutes, Dec. 19, 1966, Jan. 16, Mar. 23, 1967, Michigan "Examination of War on Poverty"; PAC Minutes, Oct. 18, 1967, Box 16, Kornegay Papers; CAP81, C.A.A., "Community Action Agency, Plans and Priorities, Fiscal Year 1970," May 1969, ibid.; Evaluation of a CAA, Apr. 1967, Series 6, Box 32, NACCD Records; *DFP*, Oct. 26, 1967; Conot, *Odyssey*, p. 506.

25. *Examination of Poverty*, 6:1826-31.

26. Ibid., pp. 1724-28; Roselle interview, p. 5; Greenstone and Peterson, *Urban Politics*, pp. 183-84. See, for example, *Examination of Poverty*, 6:1724-25.

27. *Examination of Poverty*, 6:1720-21, 1820-23, 1832; HRD Project Summaries, June 1, 1967, Box 379, JPC Papers; TAP (Program Status: June, 1966), Box 304, ibid.; PAC Minutes, Oct. 5, 1965, Box 16, Kornegay Papers; Materials

Prepared for the Hearings . . . Committee on Federal Relations, July 27, 1965, Box 17, ibid.; Simmons to Cavanagh, Box 341, GR Papers; Evaluation of a CAA, Apr. 1967, Series 6, Box 32, NACCD Records; *DN*, Aug. 28, 1966.

28. Roselle to Cavanagh, Aug. 14, 1964, Box 179, JPC Papers; PAC Minutes, Nov. 2, 1964, ibid.; Joint Statement for Immediate Release [Jan. 1965], Box 275, ibid.; Extracts from PAC Minutes, May 4, 1965, Apr. 5, 1966, Mar. 23, 1967, Michigan "Examination of War on Poverty"; *Examination of Poverty*, 6:1746-47; Greenstone and Peterson, *Urban Politics*, pp. 212-14; Evaluation of a CAA, Apr. 1967, Series 6, Box 32, NACCD Records; *DN*, July 28, 1965; *MC*, Jan. 23, 1965; *DFP*, Dec. 29, 1966.

29. *Journal of the House of Representatives of the State of Michigan*, 1968 Regular Session, pp. 41, 43-44; Michigan "Examination of War on Poverty," pp. 1, 3; Extracts from PAC Minutes, Mar. 23, Apr. 5, 1966, ibid.; Kildee Report, ibid.; *Examination of Poverty*, 6:1746-50; MCHRD, "Human Resources," pp. 30-31, Box 379, JPC Papers; HRD Project Summaries, June 1, 1967, ibid.; TAP (Program Status: June, 1966), Box 304, ibid.; Chicago Regional Council, *The Detroit Survey: An Interagency Review of Federal Assistance to Detroit*, Mar. 1969, pp. 10, 26, Box 508, ibid.; Malcolm R. Lovell to Romney, Jan. 6, 1965, Box 335, GR Papers; Waymon Howard to New Detroit Committee, Sept. 13, 1967, Box 84, ND Papers; Evaluation of a CAA, Apr. 1967, Series 6, Box 32, NACCD Records; Greenstone and Peterson, *Urban Politics*, pp. 213-14; *DN*, Dec. 15, 1964, Oct. 14, 1965; *MC*, Jan. 6, 1968.

30. PAC Minutes, June 7, 1966, Box 16, Kornegay Papers; TAP (Program Status: June, 1966), Box 304, JPC Papers; Public Hearing for Redesignation of Detroit as a CAA, June 20, 1968, pp. 60-61, Box 433, ibid.; Interview with Karl Gregory, July 12, 1984, pp. 4-5, transcript in MHC; *Examination of Poverty*, 6:1728-30, 1748-49; Evaluation of a CAA, Apr. 1967, Series 6, Box 32, NACCD Records; Greenstone and Peterson, *Urban Politics*, p. 39; *DFP*, Oct. 26, 1967. Cf. Chicago Regional Council, *Detroit Survey*, p. 7, Box 508, JPC Papers; and H. C. McKinney, Jr., Memorandum to Romney et al., Aug. 2, 1967, Box 186, GR Papers.

31. Plotnick and Skidmore, *Progress against Poverty*, p. 23; *Examination of Poverty*, 6:1756; TAP (Program Status: June, 1966), Box 304, JPC Papers; MCHRD, "Human Resources," pp. 26-27, Box 379, ibid.; *Examination of Poverty Hearings*, pt. 1:87-88, 91; Matusow, *Unraveling*, p. 244.

32. Materials Prepared for Committee on Federal Relations, July 27, 1965, Box 17, Kornegay Papers; PAC Minutes, Feb. 1, 1965, Box 16, ibid.; HRD Project Index, June 1967, Box 379, JPC Papers; MCHRD, "Human Resources," pp. 27, 28-29, ibid.; HRD Project Summaries, June 1, 1967, ibid.; TAP (Program Status: June, 1966), Box 304, ibid.; *Examination of Poverty*, 6:1719, 1756-57, 1813-14; *DN*, Dec. 24, 1964, Nov. 28, 1965; Evaluation of a CAA, Apr. 1967, Series 6, Box 32, NACCD Records.

33. MCHRD, "Human Resources," pp. 26-28, Box 379, JPC Papers; Chicago Regional Council, *Detroit Survey*, p. 28, Box 508, ibid.; TAP Project Summaries, June 1966, Box 16, Kornegay Papers; Evaluation of a CAA, Apr. 1967, Series 6, Box 32, NACCD Records; *Examination of Poverty*, 6:1813-14; New Detroit Committee, *Progress Report, April, 1968* [Detroit: n.p., 1968], pp. 91-92; *DN*, Dec. 10, 1965, Jan. 14, 23, 1966; *DFP*, June 30, Nov. 6, 1967; *MC*, Mar. 12, 1966.

34. MCHRD, "Human Resources," p. 24, Box 379, JPC Papers.

35. New Detroit, *Progress Report*, pp. 59, 61; *Examination of Poverty*, 6:1810–12; Chicago Regional Council, *Detroit Survey*, p. 14, Box 508, JPC Papers; MCHRD, "Human Resources," p. 27, Box 379, ibid.; Greenleigh Associates, "Services," pp. 23, 62–64; [Nathan Caplan] interview with First Looter, Nov. 7, 1967, pp. 35–36, transcript in my possession.

36. Greenleigh Associates, "Services," p. 66; New Detroit, *Progress Report*, pp. 65–66; *DN*, May 28, 1967; *MC*, Dec. 17, 1966, Jan. 13, 1968; Kornegay to James N. Garrett, Dec. 30, 1966, Box 12, Kornegay Papers.

37. *MC*, Feb. 25, 1967; Walter R. Greene to Burton I. Gordin, May 10, 1967, Box 19, Records of the Michigan Civil Rights Commission, RG 74–90, Michigan State Archives, Lansing, Michigan; "DUL Economic Development and Employment Department," n.d., Box 12, Kornegay Papers; Bill Davidson, "If We Can't Solve the Problems of the Ghetto Here . . . ," *Saturday Evening Post* 241 (Oct. 5, 1968): 82.

38. *Examination of Poverty*, 6:1801–4; TAP (Program Status: June, 1966), Box 304, JPC Papers; HRD Project Summaries, June 1, 1967, Box 379, ibid.; HRD Project Index, June 1967, ibid.; MCHRD, "Human Resources," pp. 19, 20–22, Box 379, ibid.; Evaluation of a CAA, Apr. 19, 1967, Series 6, Box 32, NACCD Records.

39. *Examination of Poverty*, 6:1796–97; TAP (Program Status: June, 1966), Box 304, JPC Papers; MCHRD, "Human Resources," pp. 19–20, 22–23, Box 379, ibid.; Materials Prepared for Committee on Federal Relations, July 27, 1965, Box 17, Kornegay Papers; Errol Miller Memorandum to Robert Nelson and Jacques Feuillan, Mar. 1, 1967, Series 10, Box 46, NACCD Records; *Examination of Poverty Hearings*, pt. 1:88, 108–9; *DN*, Nov. 28, 1965, Jan. 25, 1966.

40. Memo Prepared by Cavanagh, Apr. 15, 1965, Box 16, Hobart Taylor Papers, MHC; *Examination of Poverty*, 6:1798–99; *Examination of Poverty Hearings*, pt. 1:88; HRD Project Summaries, June 1, 1967, Box 379, JPC Papers; MCHRD, "Human Resources," pp. 20, 23–25, ibid.

41. HRD Project Summaries, June 1, 1967, Box 379, JPC Papers; HRD Project Index, June 1967, ibid.; MCHRD, "Human Resources," pp. 20, 25–26, ibid.; *DN*, Oct. 8, 1966; *Examination of Poverty*, 6:1806–12; Evaluation of a CAA, Apr. 1967, Series 6, Box 32, NACCD Records; *DN*, Oct. 8, 1966.

42. HRD Project Index, June 1967, Box 379, JPC Papers; Urban Areas Employment Program Fact Sheet, n.d., Box 52, Austin Papers; *Examination of Poverty*, 6:1813; *DN*, June 22, July 30, 1967.

43. HRD Project Index, June 1967, Box 379, JPC Papers; MCHRD, "Human Resources," p. 27, ibid.; Strichartz to Cavanagh, Sept. 15, 1966, and enclosure, Box 271, ibid.; Chicago Regional Council, *Detroit Survey*, p. 23, Box 508, ibid.; *DFP*, Dec. 29, 1966; *DN*, Mar. 14, 1966, May 28, 1967; *MC*, Jan. 13, 1968; Evaluation of a CAA, Apr. 1967, Series 6, Box 32 NACCD Records; R. J. Hillery et al., "Unemployment in an Inner-Core City Area," Oct. 15, 1967, p. 10, Series 45, Box 14, ibid.; *Report of the National Advisory Commission on Civil Disorders* (Washington: GPO, 1968), pp. 79, 340.

44. MCHRD, "Human Resources," pp. 21–26, Box 379, JPC Papers; Roselle interview, pp. 10–11; *Examination of Poverty Hearings*, pt. 1:88, 96, 124–25; Evaluation of a CAA, Apr. 1967, Series 6, Box 32, NACCD Records.

45. Chicago Regional Council, *Detroit Survey*, pp. 12, 14–15, Box 508, JPC Papers; CCR Release, June 13, 1967, Box 370, ibid.; MDT Report, with

Strichartz to Cavanagh, Oct. 26, 1967, Box 534, ibid.; Minutes, Manpower Development Committee, Greater Detroit Board of Commerce, Aug. 21, 1967, Box 64, ND Papers; Evaluation of a CAA, Apr. 1967, Series 6, Box 32, NACCD Records.

46. AOP Report . . . , Nov. 29, 1965, Father Sheehan Correspondence, 962-1969, Archives of the Archdiocese of Detroit, Detroit, Michigan.

47. *DN*, Nov. 28, 1965, Apr. 5, 1966; TAP (Program Status: June, 1966), Box 304, JPC Papers; MCHRD, "Human Resources," pp. 20, 26, Box 379, ibid.; HRD Project Summaries, June 1, 1967, ibid.; *Examination of Poverty*, 6:1792-93; Mary Ann Beattie Memorandum to John Forsythe and Frederick Hansen, Jan. 2, 1968, Human Relations-Community Affairs, Archives of the Archdiocese; PAC Minutes, Apr. 5, 1966, Box 16, Kornegay Papers; "NLS Centers," Nov. 3, 1967, Box 15, ND Papers; Evaluation of a CAA, Apr. 1967, Series 6, Box 32, NACCD Records.

48. Evaluation of a CAA, Apr. 1967, Series 6, Box 32, NACCD Records.

49. Ibid.; *Examination of Poverty*, 6:1765, 1770-72; *DN*, Nov. 28, 1965; TAP (Program Status: June, 1966), Box 304, JPC Papers; MCHRD, "Human Resources," pp. 29-30, Box 379, ibid.; HRD Project Index, June 1966, ibid.

50. Simmons to Cavanagh, Apr. 22, 1968, Box 341, GR Papers; "Economic Opportunity Act 1964, AOP . . . ," Dec. 9, 1964, Box 77, ibid.; *Examination of Poverty*, 6:1774, 1776.

51. "Archdiocesan Opportunity Program," June 1967, Box 52, DUL Papers; TAP (Program Status: June, 1966), Box 379, JPC Papers; HRD Project Index, June 1967, ibid.; MCHRD, "Human Resources," p. 30, ibid.; *Examination of Poverty*, 6:1774-84, 1786; *DN*, Nov. 28, 1965.

52. Chicago Regional Council, *Detroit Survey*, p. 25, Box 508, JPC Papers; *Examination of Poverty*, 6:1779, 1785-88; James C. Gaither for the President, Box 29, WE9, WHCF, LBJ Library; *MC*, Aug. 19, 1967; *DFP*, Aug. 17, 1967.

53. Anthony Ripley to Cavanagh, Nov. 10, 1965, Cavanagh to Johnson, Sept. 7, 1965, Box 213, JPC Papers; Cavanagh, "The Unfinished City," Jan. 31, 1966, Box 281, ibid.; Statement of Cavanagh before Subcommittee on Executive Reorganization . . . , Aug. 23, 1966, Box 530, ibid.; Cavanagh interview, pp. 3-24; Subcommittee on Housing of the House Committee on Banking and Currency, *Demonstration Cities* . . . , 89th Cong., 2d sess., 1966, pp. 194-98; *Examination of Poverty Hearings*, pt. 1:389; *DN*, Nov. 11, 1965, Jan. 21, 1966, Nov. 15, 1967.

54. Cavanagh interview, p. 31; Plotnick and Skidmore, *Progress against Poverty*, p. 26; Conot, *Odyssey*, p. 500.

55. Summary of Proposal for Progress, Detroit's Model Neighborhood Planning Program Grant Application . . . , Mar. 1967, Series 38, Box 3, NACCD Records; *DFP*, Nov. 17, 1967, Dec. 22, 1968; *DN*, July 29, 1966, Mar. 29, Apr. , Oct. 18, 1967; Robert B. Smock, "Inner City Problems: The View from the Inside in Detroit" (Center for Urban Studies, University of Michigan, Dearborn, 1968), pp. 1-3, 17-20; "Statement on the Needs of the City," n.d., Box 398, JPC Papers.

56. Roselle Memorandum to Cavanagh, Mar. 7, 1968, Box 406, JPC Papers; *Examination of Poverty*, 6:1837; Joint Conference Grass Roots Organizations, Jan. 7, 1967, Box 23, ORA Papers; GROW's Statement of Purpose [Jan. 1967], Box 50, DUL Papers; George D. King, "Congress of Grass Roots People Meeting," Jan. 26, 1967, Box A-17, ibid.; *DFP*, Nov. 17, 1967.

57. Roselle Memorandum to Cavanagh, Mar. 7, 1968, Box 406, JPC Papers; Conot, *Odyssey*, pp. 500-507, 569-73.

58. *DFP*, Dec. 29, 1966, Nov. 5, 8, 1967; MCHRD Administrative Staff Meeting, Apr. 28, 1967, Box 544, JPC Papers.

59. *Examination of Poverty Hearings*, pt. 1:86-87, 100, 389; Cavanagh to Johnson, Sept. 17, 1965, Box 281, JPC Papers; Cavanagh to Shriver, Mar. 23, 1966, ibid.; Remarks by Cavanagh, Sept. 9, 1966, Box 298, ibid.; Cavanagh interview, pp. 18, 39.

60. Evaluation of a CAA, Apr. 1967, Series 6, Box 32, NACCD Records; CAP81 C.A.A., "Community Action Agency, Plans and Priorities Fiscal Year 1970," May 1969, Box 16, Kornegay Papers; *DFP*, July 25, Nov. 5, 9, 1967.

61. Evaluation of a CAA, Apr. 1967, Series 6, Box 32, NACCD Records; *DN*, Dec. 10, 1965, Jan. 23, 24, 26, Feb. 7, 1966; *DFP*, July 25, 1967; Shriver to Cavanagh, n.d., Box 434, JPC Papers; *MC*, Feb. 5, 1966.

62. MCHRD, "Human Resources," pp. 19-27 passim, Box 379, JPC Papers; TAP (Program Status: June, 1966), Box 304, ibid.; HRD Project Summaries, June 1, 1967, Box 379, ibid.; Remarks by Cavanagh . . . , Dec. 19, 1969, Box 583, ibid.; *DN*, Dec. 9, 1965; *DFP*, July 13, 1967.

63. *DN*, Nov. 28, 1965; *Examination of Poverty Hearings*, pt. 1:113-14.

64. *DN*, Dec. 10, 1965, Jan. 14, 26, July 10, 1966; Comptroller General, *Review of Community Action Program*, p. 29; *Examination of Poverty*, 6:1840-41; *Examination of Poverty Hearings*, pt. 1:116; MCHRD, "Human Resources," pp. 9, 10, Box 379, JPC Papers; Chicago Regional Council, *Detroit Survey*, p. 19, Box 508, ibid.; Evaluation of a CAA, Apr. 1967, Series 6, Box 32, NACCD Records; Plotnick and Skidmore, *Progress against Poverty*, p. 24; Matusow, *Unraveling*, p. 265.

65. *Journal of the House . . . Michigan*, 1968 Regular Session, p. 44; Alan A. Beals for Georgia Brown, Apr. 11, 1968, Simmons to Cavanagh, Apr. 22, 1968, James Del Rio et al. to Johnson et al., n.d., Box 341, GR Papers; *Muskegon Chronicle*, Apr. 10, 1968, clipping in ibid.; Release, Apr. 24, 1968, ibid.; City of Detroit, TAP Program Report No. 1 [Aug. 1, 1965], Box 16, Kornegay Papers; Materials Prepared for Committee on Federal Relations, July 27, 1965, Box 17, ibid.; *DN*, July 28, 1965, Jan. 23, 1966; TAP (Program Status: June, 1966), Box 304, JPC Papers; MCHRD, "Human Resources," p. 8, Box 379, ibid.

66. Black File, No. 200, Detroit data for "Racial Attitudes"; *The People Beyond 12th Street: A Survey of Attitudes of Detroit Negroes after the Riot of 1967* (Detroit: Detroit Urban League, 1967); Evaluation of a CAA, Apr. 1967, Series 6, Box 32, NACCD Records. See also *NACCD Report*, p. 80.

67. Popp Memorandum to Wilson, Oct. 26, 1967, Peter Rossi File, in my possession; Extracts from PAC Minutes, Dec. 19, 1966, Michigan "Examination of Poverty"; *DN*, Jan. 14, 23, 1966; *MC*, Feb. 5, 1966.

68. *DN*, Nov. 28, 1965, July 10, Sept. 13, 1966; *DFP*, July 13, Sept. 2, 1967; *Examination of Poverty Hearings*, pt. 1:95; Statement by Cavanagh . . . , Aug. 23, 1966, Box 530, JPC Papers; Remarks by Cavanagh, Dec. 19, 1969, Box 583, ibid.

69. "Model Neighborhood: Characteristics," Series 45, Box 10, NACCD Records; Fact Sheet Prepared by GB, Aug. 30, 1967, Box 263, GR Papers; Simmons to Cavanagh, Apr. 22, 1968, Box 341, ibid.; TALUS Tables, Table 5, Box 393, JPC Papers; U.S. Bureau of the Census, *Current Population Reports*,

eries p-60, No. 68, "Poverty in the United States: 1959 to 1968" (Washington: GPO, 1969), p. 24.

70. MESC, *Annual Report for Fiscal Year Ended July 30, 1967*, p. ii; ibid., uly 30, 1968, ii; MESC, *Manpower Review* 22 (July 1967): 22; *DFP*, July 25, Aug. 10, 1967; "Labor Force and Employment Estimates, Detroit, 1967," Series 15, Box 14, NACCD Records; Deposition of Carolyn Williams, Jan. 11, 1968, eries 32, Box 2, ibid.; Popp Memorandum for Wilson (interview with Father)'Hara), Oct. 19 [1967], Series 59, Box 2, ibid.; Wilson Memorandum to Charles E. Nelson, Part IV, n.d., Peter Rossi file, in my possession; Civil Rights Commission Newsletter, Apr. 1967; *NACCD Report*, p. 126; DUL, Quarterly Report, uly-Sept. 1967, Box 43, DUL Papers; Stanley Webb to Roger Wilkins, n.d., Detroit Riot File, Community Relations Service, Department of Justice, FOIA; ames Bush and Charles Rouls to Richard Marks, May 10, 1967, Series III, Box •, CCR Papers; Harold Bellamy to Strichartz, Aug. 14, 1967, Box 393, JPC Papers; [Caplan] interview with First Looter, p. 1, transcript in my possession.

71. Black File, No. 198, Detroit data for "Racial Attitudes"; ibid., p. 41; Harlan Hahn, "Ghetto Sentiments on Violence," *Science and Society* 33 (Spring 969): 206-7; McKinney Memorandum to Romney et al., Aug. 2, 1967, Box 186, GR Papers; Joe R. Feagin and Harlan Hahn, *Ghetto Revolts* (New York: Macmillan Co., 1973), p. 288; Popp Memorandum to Wilson, Oct. 26, 1967, Rossi ile. See also John J. Ursu Summation of Interview with Ed Simpkins, n.d., eries 59, Box 2, NACCD Records.

72. Conrad Mallett to B. L. Coyne, Sept. 5, 1967, Box 394, JPC Papers; *DN*, une 16, 1964, Feb. 1, 1966; Greenstone and Peterson, *Urban Politics*, p. 38; Gregory interview, pp. 4-5; Interview with Harold Johnson, Aug. 14, 1984, pp. -3, transcript in MHC; Roselle interview, p. 5; *Examination of Poverty*, :1751-54. For the reaction of some of the war on poverty's satisfied clients, see 'AP (Program Status: June, 1966), Box 304, JPC Papers; and Public Hearing . . , June 20, 1968, Box 433, ibid.

73. *Examination of Poverty Hearings*, pt. 1:99; *MC*, Apr. 23, 1966; Official Transcript of Proceedings before the National Advisory Commission on Civil Disorders, Aug. 15, 1967, pp. 544-46, Series 1, Box 2, NACCD Records; Mallett o Coyne, Sept. 5, 1967, Box 394, JPC Papers; *DFP*, Aug. 11, 1967. See also "Negro Youths and Civil Disorders," n.d., Series 7, Box 1, NACCD Records.

Chapter 5

1. Hahn and Feagin, "Riot Precipitating Police Practices . . . ," *Phylon* 31 Summer 1970): 183; *MC*, Sept. 19, 1964.

2. Levy, "Cops in the Ghetto," in Louis H. Masotti and Don R. Bowen, eds., *Riots and Rebellion* (Beverly Hills: Sage Publications, 1968), pp. 347-48, 353-54; Ralph W. Conant, *The Prospects for Revolution: A Study of Riots . . .* (New York: Harper's Magazine Press Book, 1971), pp. 177-78; Albert J. Reiss, "How Much 'Police Brutality' Is There?" in Edward S. Greenberg et al., eds., *Black Politics* (New York: Holt, Rinehart and Winston, 1971), p. 185.

3. Robert Fogelson, "From Resentment to Confrontation: The Police, the Negroes, and the Outbreak of the Nineteen-Sixties Riots," *Political Science Quarterly* 83 (June 1968): 232, 243-46; George Edwards, *The Police on the Urban Frontier* (New York: Institute of Human Relations, 1968), p. 17; Hubert

Locke, "Beyond the Algiers Motel Incident," Apr. 13, 1969, Box 48, Richard Austin Papers, ALHUA; "Working Papers for Mayor's Conference . . . ," Mar. 10–11, 1967, Box 351, JPC Papers; Burton I. Gordin to Executive Staff, Mar. 22, 1968, and enclosed, "The Civil Rights Commission and Police-Community Relations," n.d., Box 4, Records of the Civil Rights Commission-Detroit Office, RG 80–17, State Archives, Lansing, Michigan.

4. James Q. Wilson, *Varieties of Police Behavior* (Cambridge: Harvard University Press, 1968), p. 233; National Center on Police and Community Relations, "A National Survey of Police and Community Relations," Jan. 1967, p. 29; William Serrin, "God Help Our City," *Atlantic Monthly* 223 (Mar. 1969): 116; Background Material for the Ad Hoc Committee on Police-Community Relations, Jan. 1, 1965, Box 476, Walter Reuther Papers, ALHUA; Bernard Dobranski and John Ursu, Memorandum to Herman Wilson (interview with Ernest Goodman), Oct. 11, 1967, Series 59, Box 2, NACCD Records; Wilson Memoranda to Charles E. Nelson (interview with Richard Simmons), n.d., (interview with Leon Atchison), n.d., ibid.; Staff Memorandum to CRC, Aug. 6, 1964, Box 26, Records of the Civil Rights Commission, RG 74-90, State Archives.

5. Interview with John Nichols, Aug. 13, 1984, pp. 28–29, transcript in MHC; Maurice Kelman and Ed Batchelor interview with Ray Girardin, Oct. 29, 1971, pp. 410–11, transcript in my possession; Richard McGhee to Burton Levy, Box 16, Richard McGhee Papers, ALHUA.

6. Robert A. Mendelsohn, "The Police Interpretation of the Detroit Riot of 1967" [1968], pp. 38, 46–47, 58–59, 61, 65–66, Box 30, ORA Papers; idem, "Inside the Detroit Policeman," in Elliot D. Luby, "Violence in the Model City" [1969], p. 1, Box 378, JPC Papers.

7. James M. Raschard Memorandum to Wilson (interview with Mel Ravitz), Oct. 9, 1967, Series 45, Box 10, NACCD Records; Serrin, "Our City," p. 115; Levy Memorandum to Gordin, Aug. 31, 1965, Box 15, McGhee Papers; Fred Romanoff to Cavanagh, Sept. 21, 1964, Box 213, JPC Papers; Xavier Nicholas interview with Albert J. Dunmore [1982], transcript of tape in my possession; Peter H. Rossi et al., "Between White and Black: The Faces of American Institutions in the Ghetto," in *Supplemental Studies for the National Advisory Commission on Civil Disorders* (Washington: GPO, 1968), p. 109; Robert Conot, *American Odyssey* (New York: William Morrow and Co., 1974), p. 521.

8. Luby, "Summary," in "Violence in Model City," p. 13, Box 378, JPC Papers; David H. Bayley and Harold Mendelsohn, *Minorities and the Police* (New York: Free Press, 1969), p. 107; *DFP*, Jan. 11, 1965.

9. "Working Papers," Mar. 10–11, 1967, Box 351, JPC Papers; Greater Detroit Board of Commerce, Police Report, May 12, 1967, Box 342, ibid.; A Report from the Special Sub-Committee on Police Community Relations, with Richard S. Emrich to CCEO, Feb. 16, 1965, Box 11, Frank Angelo Papers, MHC; Harlan Hahn, "A Profile of Urban Police Work," *Law and Contemporary Problems* 36 (Autumn 1971): 452; Patrick James Ashton, "Race, Class and Black Politics: The Implications of the Election of a Black Mayor for the Police and Policing in Detroit" (Ph.D. diss., Michigan State University, 1981), pp. 22–23.

10. Riot Questionnaire, n.d., Series 22, Box 1, NACCD Records; Mendelsohn, "Police Interpretation," pp. 40–42, Box 30, ORA Papers; Mendelsohn, "Inside," pp. 11–12; Harlan Hahn, "Local Variations in Urban Law Enforcement," in Peter Orleans and Walter Russell Ellis, eds., *Race, Change, and Urban Society*

(Beverly Hills: Sage Publications, 1971), pp. 380–81; Edwards, *Urban Frontier*, pp. 34–35, 72.

11. Police Report, May 12, 1967, Box 342, JPC Papers; Working Papers, Mar. 10–11, 1967, Box 351, ibid.; *DFP*, June 22, 1967; Presidential Commission on Law Enforcement and Administration of Justice, *Task Force Report: The Police* (Washington: GPO, 1967), p. 134; Girardin interview, p. 402.

12. *DN*, Nov. 6, 1963; *DFP*, June 22, 1967, Apr. 20, 1969; Police Report, May 12, 1967, Box 342, JPC Papers.

13. Staff Memorandum to CRC, Aug. 6, 1964, Box 26, RG 74-90; *Report of the National Advisory Commission on Civil Disorders* (Washington: GPO, 1968), p. 157; Dobranski and Ursu Memorandum to Wilson (Goodman interview), Oct. 11, 1967, Series 59, Box 2, NACCD Records; Dobranski Memorandum to Wilson (interview with William T. Patrick, Jr.), Oct. 13, 1967, ibid.; Joe R. Feagin and Harlan Hahn, *Ghetto Riots* (New York: Macmillan Co., 1973), p. 157; Edwards, *Urban Frontier*, p. 25; Anthony Oberschall, "The Los Angeles Riot of 1965," in David Boesel and Peter Rossi, eds., *Cities under Siege: An Anatomy of Ghetto Riots, 1964–1968* (New York: Basic Books, 1971), p. 89.

14. *DFP*, Jan. 10, 1965; Reiss, "Police Brutality," p. 177.

15. Reiss, "Police Brutality," p. 177; Fogelson, "Confrontation," p. 230; Questionnaires Nos. 3009, 4011, 4046, 5016, 6021, 6073, 6098, Boxes 7–9, 11, 12, A–W Riot Studies; Wilson Memorandum to Nelson (interview with Karl Gregory), n.d., Series 59, Box 2, NACCD Records; Inter-University Consortium for Political and Social Research, Black File, Nos. 210, 211, Detroit data for Angus Campbell and Howard Schuman, "Racial Attitudes in Fifteen American Cities," in *Supplementary Studies for the National Advisory Commission on Civil Disorders* (Washington: GPO, 1968); ibid., p. 42.

16. *MC*, Aug. 15, 1964, July 24, 1982; Walter Dukes Memorandum to Nelson, n.d., Peter Rossi File, in my possession; Questionnaires Nos. 3018, 4002, 4050, 6049, 6141, Boxes 7, 8, 11, 12, A–W Riot Studies; Black File, Nos. 214, 215, Detroit data for "Racial Attitudes"; ibid., p. 43.

17. *MC*, Aug. 8, 1964; Questionnaires Nos. 5017, 6077, Boxes 9, 11, A–W Riot Studies; Reiss, "Brutality," pp. 177–78.

18. Reiss, "Brutality," pp. 178–79, 182, 184–85, 187–88; Dobranski and Ursu Memorandum to Wilson (Goodman interview), Oct. 11, 1967, Series 59, Box 2, NACCD Records; Mildred Jeffrey to Irving Bluestone, July 30, 1965, Box 54, Reuther Papers; Fogelson, "Confrontation," pp. 224–26; Bayley and Mendelsohn, *Minorities*, p. 164; Hahn, "Local Variations," p. 382; *DN*, Dec. 29, 1964; Elliot Luby and James Grissel, "Grievances of Detroit Negro Arrestees" [1968], p. 2, Detroit Public Library, Detroit, Michigan.

19. Interview with Arthur Johnson, July 23, 1984, pp. 7–8, transcript in MHC; *MC*, Aug. 15, 1964; Romanoff to Cavanagh, Aug. 30, 1965, Box 213, JPC Papers; Hubert Locke to Executive Board, Mar. 19, 1964, Series III, Box 2, CCR Papers; [Citizens Committee on Police-Community Relations] to Cavanagh [Jan. 1965], Box A-19, DUL Papers; Black File, Nos. 218, 219, White File, Nos. 219, 220, 222, 223, 226, 227, Detroit data for "Racial Attitudes"; ibid., p. 43; David O. Sears and John B. McConahay, *The Politics of Violence: The New Urban Blacks and the Watts Riot* (Boston: Houghton Mifflin Co., 1973), p. 56.

20. *DFP*, Dec. 29, 1964; *DN*, Dec. 29, 1964; *MC*, July 24, 1982; Eleanor Paperno Wolf and Charles N. Lebeaux, *Change and Renewal in an Urban Com-

munity: Five Case Studies of Detroit (New York: Frederick A. Praeger, 1969), p. 337; James Boudouris, "The Kercheval-Pennsylvania Incident, Aug. 1966" (Mar. 1967), Series IV, Box 4, CCR Papers.

21. Fogelson, "Confrontation," p. 233; Feagin and Hahn, *Ghetto Revolts*, pp. 153–55; Vivian Pope Memorandum to Levy, May 23, 1967, Box 19, RG 74-90; NAACP Proposals . . . , n.d., Box 351, JPC Papers; Daniel Schechter to Cavanagh, Aug. 25, 1966, Box 271, ibid.; Errol Miller Memorandum to Robert Nelson, Feb. 3, 1967, Series 10, Box 46, NACCD Records; Wilson Memorandum to Nelson (interview with Richard Simmons), n.d., Series 59, Box 2, ibid.; Wolf and Lebeaux, *Change and Renewal*, p. 337; Edwards, *Urban Frontier*, p. 331; Baker et al. and Bratton et al. vs. City of Detroit et al. . . . , United States District Court for Eastern District of Michigan, Southern Division, Civil Nos. 5-77937 and 5-72264 (1979), xxvii, copy of manuscript opinion in my possession (hereafter cited as Keith opinion); Questionnaires Nos. 6043, 6051, 6081, 6128, Boxes 11, 12, A-W Riot Studies; Black File, Nos. 206, 207, White File, Nos. 214, 215, Detroit data for "Racial Attitudes."

22. Miller Memorandum to Nelson, Feb. 7, 1967, Series 10, Box 46, NACCD Records; Dobranski and Ursu Memorandum to Wilson (interview with Philip Colista), Oct. 12, 1967, Series 59, Box 2, ibid.; Report of Dobranski to Robert Conot, Box 77, ibid.; Hahn and Feagin, "Riot Precipitating Practices," p. 185; Edwards, *Urban Frontier*, pp. 31–32, 57; Wolf and Lebeaux, *Change and Renewal*, p. 336; [Nathan Caplan] interview with Fourth Looter, Nov. 7, 1967, p. 38, transcript in my possession.

23. Minutes of a Meeting with . . . Kerner Commission, Aug. 21, 1967, Box 394, JPC Papers; *MC*, Feb. 23, Mar. 9, Aug. 10, 1963, Jan. 15, 1966; *DFP*, Jan. 11, 1965; Miller Memorandum to Nelson, Feb. 7, 1967, Series 10, Box 46, NACCD Records; Detroit Information: Aaron, n.d., Box 81, ibid.; Sub-Committee on Police-Community Relations, "The Police, Law Enforcement and the Detroit Community—Summer 1965," Aug. 29, 1965, Box 51, DUL Papers; Eugene Carey to George Romney, July 31, 1967, Box 344, GR Papers; Hubert Locke, *The Detroit Riot of 1967* (Detroit: Wayne State University Press, 1969), pp. 24–25.

24. Questionnaire No. 4001, Box 8, A-W Riot Studies; *DN*, Feb. 3, 1965; Harlan Hahn, "Cops and Rioters . . . ," *American Behavioral Scientist* 13 (Aug. 1970): 765, 767.

25. Hahn, "Cops and Rioters," p. 765; Report, with Emrich to CCEO, Feb. 16, 1965, Box 11, Angelo Papers; Background Material, Jan. 1, 1965, Box 476, Reuther Papers; CRC Weekly Report, July 30, 1965, Box 92, GR Papers; Dobranski and Ursu Memorandum for Wilson (Colista interview), Oct. 12, 1967, Series 59, Box 2, NACCD Records; Miller Memorandum to Nelson and Jacques Feuillan, Mar. 1, 1967, Series 10, Box 46, ibid.

26. *DFP*, May 2, 1965, May 7, Oct. 15, 1967; Report, with Emrich to CCEO, Feb. 16, 1965, Box 11, Angelo Papers; Dobranski and Ursu Memorandum to Wilson (Colista interview), Oct. 12, 1967, Series 59, Box 2, NACCD Records; Dobranski Report to Conot, n.d., Box 77, ibid.; Background Material, Jan. 1, 1965, Box 476, Reuther Papers; [Citizens Committee] to Cavanagh [Jan. 1965], Box A-19, DUL Papers; *MC*, Jan. 5, 1965, June 25, 1966; Minutes of Meeting with Kerner Commission, Aug. 21, 1967, Box 394; Black File, No. 224, Detroit

data for "Racial Attitudes." For criticism of the task force report by some Recorder's Court judges, see *DN*, May 7, 1967.

27. *DN*, May 15, 1962, Jan. 15, 1963; *MC*, Feb. 24, 1962; George Edwards, 'Law Enforcement, 1965: The Police and Race Relations," May 30, 1965, Box 15, McGhee Papers; Edwards to Cavanagh, Jan. 11, 1963, Box 87, JPC Papers; Edwards to Royce Howes, Apr. 11, 1963, Box 68, George Edwards Papers, ALHUA; Edwards, "Order and Civil Liberties: A Complex Role for the Police," *Michigan Law Review* 64 (Nov. 1965): 56; Dobranski Report to Conot, n.d., Box 77, NACCD Records; *Wall Street Journal*, Aug. 12, 1964.

28. Steve Babson, *Working Detroit* (New York: Adama Books, 1984), p. 166; Robert Shogan and Tom Craig, *The Detroit Riot* (Philadelphia: Chilton Books, 1964), p. 132; Edwards to William O. Douglas, Feb. 23, 1962, Box 64, Edwards Papers; Edwards to Cavanagh, Jan. 11, 1963, Box 87, JPC Papers; *DN*, Dec. 17, 22, 1963; *MC*, June 23, 1962, Aug. 31, 1963; *NYT*, Dec. 7, 1965; Tom Nicholson, "Detroit's Surprising Mayor," *Harper's* 227 (Dec. 1963): 78.

29. D. T. Burton to Cavanagh, Mar. 19, 1962, Box 29, JPC Papers; Marc Stepp et al. to Cavanagh, Jan. 26, 1965, Box 215, ibid.; Dobranski and Ursu Memoranda to Wilson (Colista interview), Oct. 12, 1967, (Goodman interview), Oct. 11, 1967, Series 59, Box 2, NACCD Records; Dobranski Report to Conot, n.d., Box 77, ibid.; Miller Memorandum to Nelson, Feb. 7, 1967, Series 10, Box 46, ibid.; A. F. Brandstatter to Edwards, Nov. 26, 1962, Box 66, Edwards Papers; *DFP*, Jan. 21, Dec. 29, 1964, Jan. 11, 1965; *DN*, Jan. 29, 30, 1965; *Wall Street Journal*, Aug. 12, 1964; Interview with James Bannon, Mar. 12, 1985, pp. 4–6, transcript in MHC; Nichols interview, p. 3; Conference, Mar. 2, 1964, Box A-19, DUL Papers; Notes for Conference with Police . . . , June 8, 1964, ibid.; Minutes for Police Community Task Force Meeting, Jan. 26, 1965, Box 1, Horace W. Gilmore Papers, ALHUA. Cf. Minutes of Conference with Girardin, Aug. 28, 1964, Box A-19, DUL Papers.

30. Nicholson, "Surprising Mayor," p. 78; Shogan and Craig, *Detroit Riot*, p. 132; *DN*, May 15, Aug. 7, 1962, Jan. 15, Dec. 17, 1963; *DFP*, July 8, 1962; Edwards to Cavanagh, Jan. 11, 1963, Box 87, JPC Papers; *Wall Street Journal*, Aug. 12, 1964; *U.S. News and World Report* 52 (May 21, 1962): 66, 67; *MC*, Aug. 25, 1962, Apr. 20, 27, 1963.

31. CCR Minutes, Feb. 26, Mar. 19, 1962, Series IV, Box 3, CCR Papers; Edwards to CCR, Feb. 26, 1962, ibid.; *DN*, Feb. 27, Mar. 20, 1962. For the CCR report on police recruitment, see chap. 1.

32. *DN*, Mar. 20, 1962, Jan. 21, June 21, 1964; *DFP*, Jan. 21, 1964; *MC*, Jan. 11, 18, 1964; Edwards to Cavanagh, Jan. 11, 1963, Box 87, JPC Papers; DUL, Revised Report on Employment Practices of Detroit Police Department, Oct. 1963, Box 17, Francis A. Kornegay Papers, MHC; Keith opinion, p. 43.

33. DUL, Revised Report, Oct. 1963, Box 17, Kornegay Papers; Marks Memorandum to CCR, Jan. 20, 1964, Series IV, Box 4, CCR Papers; *MC*, May 19, 1962, Jan. 18, 25, 1964; *DN*, May 16, 1962, June 21, 1964.

34. Dobranski Report to Conot, n.d., Box 77, NACCD Records.

35. *U.S. News and World Report* 52 (May 21, 1962): 67; Robert Conot, *American Odyssey* (New York: William Morrow and Co., 1974), pp. 466–67; Minutes of Tenth Precinct's . . . Committee, May 21, 1963, Box A-8, DUL Papers; Marks Memorandum to CCR, Jan. 20, 1964, Series IV, Box 4, CCR

Papers; Dobranski Report to Conot, n.d., Box 77, NACCD Records; *DN*, Jan. 21, 1964.

36. Dobranski Report to Conot, n.d., Box 77, NACCD Records; Edwards to Cavanagh, Jan. 11, 1963, Box 87, JPC Papers.

37. Dobranski Report to Conot, n.d., Box 77, NACCD Records; J. Anthony Lukas, "Postscript on Detroit: 'Whitey Hasn't Got the Message,' " *NYT Magazine*, Aug. 27, 1967; Charles Schlachter and Harry Hill to CO, Homicide Bureau, July 10, 1963, Box 87, JPC Papers; *DFP*, July 6, Aug. 8, 1963; *MC*, July 13, Aug. 3, 1963; *Illustrated News*, July 22, 1963; Dunmore interview.

38. Olsen Release, July 8, 1963, Box 87, JPC Papers; Dobranski and Ursu Memorandum to Wilson (Colista interview), Oct. 12, 1967, Series 59, Box 2, NACCD Records; *DFP*, July 9, 14, Aug. 1, 2, 8, 1963; *DN*, July 14, Aug. 2, 10, 1963; *MC*, July 13, 20, 27, Aug. 3, 1963; Permanent Subcommittee on Investigations of the Senate Committee on Government Operations, *Riots, Civil and Criminal Disorders, Hearings*, 90th Cong., 2d sess., 1968, pt. 6:1398-1401; Diggs to Cavanagh, July 23, 1963, Box 87, JPC Papers; Tinker, *When the Fire Reaches Us* (New York: William Morrow and Co., 1970), p. 142.

39. *MC*, Aug. 3, 17, 1963; *DFP*, Aug. 8, 1963; Dobranski Report to Conot, n.d., Box 77, NACCD Records; Executive Secretary's Report, Sept. 9, 1963, Part 1, Box 21, DNAACP Papers.

40. *DFP*, Aug. 8, 1963.

41. Bannon interview, pp. 1-2; Bill Sudomier to Lee Hills, May 21 [1963], Box 11, Angelo Papers; Dobranski and Ursu Memorandum to Nelson (Goodman interview), Oct. 11, 1967, Series 59, Box 2, NACCD Records; *DFP*, July 9, 10, 12, 1962; *DN*, Dec. 17, 22, 1963; *MC*, Apr. 20, 27, Dec. 28, 1963; Edwards to Howes, Apr. 11, 1963, Box 68, Edwards Papers; Interview with Richard Marks, Aug. 6, 1964, p. 11, transcript in MHC.

42. Statement by James N. Garrett, June 24, 1963, Box 68, Edwards Papers; King to Edwards, June 27, 1963, Marks to Edwards, June 25, 1963, Box 112, JPC Papers.

43. *DN*, Oct. 4, 1967, Jan. 29, 1968; Nicholas interview with Mrs. Girardin [1982], copy of tape in my possession; Bannon interview, pp. 2-3; Locke, *Detroit Riot*, pp. 58-59; *NYT*, July 28, 1967; Garry Wills, *The Second Civil War* (New York: New American Library, 1968), pp. 48-49.

44. Wilson Memoranda to Nelson (interview with Charles Brown), n.d., (Simmons interview), n.d., (interview with Leon Atchison), Series 59, Box 2, NACCD Records; (Ursu) Memorandum to Wilson (interview with Ray Girardin), n.d., ibid.; Interview with Damon Keith, June 21, 1985, p. 27, transcript in MHC; Johnson interview, p. 15; *DN*, Jan. 29, 1965, Aug. 24, 1967; Minutes from Police Community Task Force Meeting, Jan. 26, 1965, Box 1, Gilmore Papers; Stepp et al. to Cavanagh, Jan. 26, 1965, Box 215, JPC Papers; Police Report, May 12, 1967, Box 342, ibid.; Locke, *Detroit Riot*, p. 59.

45. Locke, *Detroit Riot*, p. 60; *MC*, Jan. 18, 1964; Minutes of Conference with Girardin, Jan. 20, 1964, Box 17, Kornegay Papers; *DFP*, Jan. 9, 21, 1964; *DN*, Oct. 14, 1965; Conference, Mar. 2, 1964, Box A-19, DUL Papers; Keith opinion, p. 43.

46. Locke to Fine, Jan. 4, 1984; Girardin to Kornegay, Jan. 9, 1964, Box 17, Kornegay Papers; Robert Tindal to Issues Committee, Sept. 22, 1966, Box A-19, DUL Papers; Conrad Mallett to Robert Potts, Nov. 21, 1966, Box

302, JPC Papers; Working Papers, Mar. 10–11, 1967, Box 351, ibid.; Locke to Cavanagh, Oct. 6, 1966, Box 273, ibid.; Anthony Ripley to Cavanagh, May 4, 1967, Box 583, ibid.; *MC*, Apr. 1, 1967; CRC Newsletter, Oct. 1966; Minutes, Subcommittee on Police Community Relations, Aug. 24, 1966, Box 10, ORA Papers; Riot Questionnaire, Series 32, Box 1, NACCD Records; Reconnaissance Survey Field Research Reports, Detroit, Michigan, 1:49, 53, Series 10, Box 46, ibid.; Keith opinion, p. 43; *NACCD Report*, pp. 165, 169; For Judge Gilmore . . . , Oct. 24, 1966, Box 1, Gilmore Papers. I have used the figures cited in the Keith opinion for new hires.

47. *DFP*, Jan. 21, 1964, Jan. 11, 1965, July 23, 1972; *DN*, Jan. 21, 1964; Wilson Memorandum to Nelson (Simmons interview), n.d., (Atchison interview), n.d., Series 59, Box 2, NACCD Records; Dobranski and Ursu Memorandum to Wilson (Goodman interview), Oct. 11, 1967, ibid.; Reconnaissance Survey Reports, Detroit, 1:53, Series 10, Box 46, ibid.; Riot Questionnaire, Series 22, Box 1, ibid.; Dunmore interview.

48. *DN*, Apr. 30, 1967; Louis Radelet to Police Executives, Apr. 20, 1966, and enclosed questionnaire, Box 2, ORA Papers; Minutes of Sub-Committee on Police Community Relations, Aug. 24, 1966, Box 10, ibid.; Wilson Memorandum to Nelson (interview with Carl Heffernan et al.), n.d., Series 59, Box 2, NACCD Records; Dunmore interview. See also *NACCD Report*, p. 169, and Benjamin D. Singer et al., *Black Rioters* (Lexington, Mass.: D.C. Heath and Co., 1970), p. 26.

49. Girardin to Kornegay, Apr. 8, 1964, Box A-19, DUL Papers; Conferences with Girardin, Aug. 28, 1964, June 14, 1965, ibid.; CCR Minutes, Feb. 17, Oct. 19, 1964, Box 153, JPC Papers; [William Owen] to Robert Roselle, Aug. 22, 1967, Box 342, ibid.; CCR, "Annual Report, 1965," p. 6; Report, with Emrich to CCEO, Feb. 16, 1965, Box 11, Angelo Papers; Radelet to Police Executives, Apr. 20, 1966, and enclosed questionnaire, Box 2, ORA Papers; *DN*, Jan. 21, Feb. 8, 1964, Jan. 15, 19, Feb. 5, 1965; *MC*, Jan. 23, 1965.

50. *MC*, Mar. 26, Apr. 9, 1966; *DN*, Mar. 23, 1966; McGhee to Levy, Mar. 28, 1967, Box 16, McGhee Papers; Miller Memorandum to Feuillan et al., Apr. 14, 1967, Series 10, Box 46, NACCD Records; Dobranski and Ursu Memorandum to Wilson (Colista interview), Oct. 12, 1967, Series 59, Box 2, ibid.; Marks interview, pp. 16–18.

51. Miller Memorandum to Nelson, Feb. 7, 1967, Series 10, Box 46, NACCD Records; Carey to Romney, July 31, 1967, Box 344, GR Papers; Reiss, "Brutality," pp. 185–86; Notes for Meeting of Mar. 22, 1965, Box 1, Gilmore Papers; *NACCD Report*, p. 169; Hahn, "Urban Police," pp. 458–59; Ashton, "Race, Class and Black Politics," p. 254; Keith opinion, p. 43.

52. President's Commission on Law Enforcement and Administration of Justice, *The Challenge of Crime in a Free Society* (Washington: GPO, 1967), p. 99; idem, *Task Force Report: Police*, p. 193.

53. Girardin to Cavanagh, Aug. 26, 1966, Box 273, JPC Papers; Working Papers, Mar. 11–12, 1967, Box 351, ibid.; Radelet to Police Executives, Apr. 20, 1966, and enclosed questionnaire, Box 2, ORA Papers; Heffernan to Girardin, Dec. 15, 1965, Box 26, RG 74-90; Miller Memorandum to Nelson, Feb. 7, 1967, Series 10, Box 46, NACCD Records; Miller Memorandum to Feuillan et al., Apr. 14, 1967, ibid.; Dobranski Report to Conot, n.d., Box 77, ibid.; *DN*, Apr. 30, 1967; President's Commission, *Task Force Report: Police*, pp. 36–37; CCEO

Interim Staff Report on Police Officers Training . . . [1965], Box 4, Gilmore Papers.

54. Miller Memorandum to Nelson and Feuillan, Mar. 1, 1967, Series 10, Box 46, NACCD Records; L. Mazei, "Preliminary Proposal . . . ," Aug. 18, 1967, in my possession; *DFP*, July 23, 1972.

55. Greenleigh Associates, "Study of Services to Deal with Poverty in Detroit, Michigan" (New York, 1965), p. 124; National Center on Police and Community Relations, "National Survey," pp. 315-19; *DN*, June 22, July 30, 1965; CCR Minutes, May 17, 1965, Series IV, Box 4, CCR Papers; CRC Newsletter, June, Nov. 1965; Materials Presented for Hearing . . . , July 27, 1965, Box 17, Kornegay Papers; Boudouris Memorandum to Marks, Box 20, ORA Papers; *MC*, Aug. 7, Sept. 4, 11, 1965; "A Summer Police In-Service Training Program . . ." [1965], Box 14, Gilmore Papers.

56. CCR Minutes, Aug. 23, Nov. 15, 1965, Series IV, Box 4, CCR Papers; *MC*, Aug. 7, 1965; Miller Memorandum to Feuillan et al., Apr. 14, 1967, Series 10, Box 46, NACCD Records; Jeffrey to Bluestone, July 30, 1965, Box 54, Reuther Papers.

57. Boudouris Memorandum to Marks, Sept. 6, 1966, Box 20, ORA Papers; Marks Memorandum to CCR, June 30, 1967, Box 24, ibid.; James R. McGowan Memorandum to CCR, Jan. 26, 1967, Series IV, Box 4, CCR Papers; Nichols interview, pp. 58-59; National Center on Police and Community Relations, "National Survey," pp. 318-19; Ripley to Cavanagh, May 4, 1967, Box 338, JPC Papers.

58. Tenth Precinct's Minutes, May 21, 1963, Box A-8, DUL Papers; "Excerpts from a . . . Study of the Fifth Precinct . . . Committee . . . ," July 20, 1967, Box A-19, ibid.; "Police Community Relations Program," Reconnaissance Survey Reports, Detroit, 1: Exhibit 2, Series 10, Box 46, NACCD Records; Dobranski Report to Conot, Box 77, ibid.; Fifth Precinct Citizen-Police Committee [1966], Box 17, McGhee Papers; *DFP*, Dec. 1, 1965; *DN*, Aug. 21, 1966, May 24, 1967.

59. "Police Community Relations Program," Series 10, Box 46, NACCD Records; Owen to Girardin, Apr. 5, 1966, Series 45, Box 14, ibid.; CCB Information . . . , n.d., Box 20, ORA Papers.

60. "Police Community Relations Program," Series 10, Box 46, NACCD Records; Dobranski Report to Conot, n.d., Box 77, ibid.; Riot Questionnaire, n.d., Series 22, Box 1, ibid.; Official Transcript of Proceedings before the NACCD, Aug. 15, 1967, p. 469, Series 1, Box 2, ibid.; Miller Memorandum to Nelson, Feb. 7, 1967, Series 10, Box 46, ibid.; Miller Memorandum to Nelson and Feuillan, Mar. 1, 1967, ibid.; Miller Memorandum to Feuillan et al., Apr. 4, 1967, ibid.; (Ursu) and Dobranski Memorandum to Wilson (Heffernan et al. interview), n.d., Series 59, Box 2, ibid.; "Excerpts . . . Fifth Precinct . . . , Committee," July 20, 1967, Box A-19, DUL Papers; Minutes of Ad Hoc Committee on Community Peace, Aug. 15, 1966, Part 2, Series I, Box 1, DNAACP Papers; Bannon interview, p. 4; Wolf and Lebeaux, *Change and Renewal*, pp. 337-38; From Jean Washington [June 30, 1967], Commissioner's File, DPD; Notes from Police-Community Relations Breakfast Meeting, Mar. 30, 1966, Box 1, Gilmore Papers; President's Commission, *Task Force Report: Police*, pp. 150-51; *NACCD Report*, p. 167; Ashton, "Race, Class and Black Politics," p. 46.

61. Edwards, *Urban Frontier*, pp. 82-83; Cavanagh to Chester Arrington,

June 11, 1965, Box 246, JPC Papers; Robert E. Toohey to Girardin, Apr. 5, 1965, Box 215, ibid.; ACT, Inc. Evaluation Report, n.d., Box 22, ORA Papers; *MC*, Oct. 9, 1965, Aug. 13, 1966; *DN*, Dec. 9, 1965.

62. Emeric Kurtagh to CCEO [Oct. 1965], Box 17, Kornegay Papers; "Crime in the Streets . . . Summer 1967," Draft No. 3, Box 9, ibid.; Robert Potts, "Neighborhood Service Organization . . . 1967," Box 16, ibid.; Potts, ". . . YSC Program Summary" [1967], ibid.; Sub-Committee on Police-Community Relations, CCEO, "Police . . . Summer 1965," Aug. 29, 1965, Box 51, DUL Papers; YSC, A Report and Recommendations . . . , Dec. 1, 1966, Box 19, ORA Papers; McGhee to Levy, Mar. 28, 1967, Box 16, McGhee Papers; *DN*, Jan. 22, 1967; Ripley to Cavanagh, May 4, 1967, Box 338, JPC Papers; Philip Rutledge to Cavanagh, July 10, 1967, Box 373, ibid.

63. DUL Release, Dec. 30, 1964, Box A-19, DUL Papers; Conference, Mar. 2, 1964, ibid.; Kornegay to Burton, Jan. 5, 1965, Box 65, ibid.; *DFP*, Dec. 29, 1964, Jan. 11, 26, 1965; *DN*, Dec. 28, 29, 1964; *MC*, Sept. 19, 1964, Jan. 2, 1965; Johnson Memorandum to Gordin, Dec. 29, 1964, Box 26, RG 74-90; Committee on Police Community Relations Memorandum to CCR, Mar. 4, 1965, Box 241, JPC Papers; Minutes, Roundtable Police-Community Relations Conference, Nov. 17, 1964, Part 1, Box 28, DNAACP Papers; Edwards, *Urban Frontier*, pp. 67–72; Girardin interview, pp. 408–9, 410.

64. *MC*, Jan. 18, 1964; Dunmore interview; Johnson to Marks, Feb. 18, 1964, Series III, Box 2, CCR Papers; Gordin Memorandum to John Feikens and Keith, June 8, 1964, Box 26, RG 74-90; Dobranski Report to Conot, n.d., Box 77, NACCD Records; Ashton, "Race, Class and Black Politics," p. 33.

65. Conference, Mar. 2, 1964, Box A-19, DUL Papers; Gordin Memorandum to Feikens and Keith, June 8, 1964, Box 26, RG 74-90.

66. CCR Release, Sept. 21, 1964, Box 50, DUL Papers; Gordin to Girardin, Dec. 14, 1964, Jan. 12, 1965, Series III, Box 2, CCR Papers; Procedures of the Michigan CRC . . . [Oct. 1964], Box 165, JPC Papers; CCR News Release, Apr. 27 [1965], Box 17, Kornegay Papers.

67. *MC*, Sept. 19, 1964, Jan. 23, 1965; *DN*, Jan. 19, 1965, June 28, 1966; John Joy to Romanoff, Sept. 22, 1964, Box 177, JPC Papers; Detroit Police Department Notation No. 1410, Jan. 14, 1965, Box A-19, DUL Papers; Gordin to Girardin, Jan. 12, 1965, Series III, Box 2, CCR Papers; CCR Minutes, Feb. 24, 1966, Series IV, Box 4, ibid.

68. Wilson Memorandum to Nelson (Heffernan et al. interview), n.d., Series 59, Box 2, NACCD Records; Official Transcript, Aug. 15, 1967, p. 491, Series 1, Box 2, ibid.; Radelet to Police Executives, Apr. 20, 1966, and enclosed questionnaire, Box 2, ORA Papers; Mayor's Development Team Report, with Richard Strichartz to Cavanagh, Oct. 26, 1967, Box 534, JPC Papers.

69. Heffernan to Research Development Bureau, Sept. 12, 1967, Series 45, Box 40, NACCD Records; Official Transcript, Aug. 15, 1967, p. 492, Series 1, Box 2, ibid.; (Ursu) Memorandum to Wilson (Girardin interview), n.d., Series 59, Box 2, ibid.; Wilson Memorandum to Nelson (Heffernan et al. interview), n.d., ibid.; *Los Angeles Times*, Feb. 6, 1966, DRSB No. 1; *DFP*, Jan. 11, 1965; *DN*, June 28, 1966.

70. Owen to Locke, Aug. 22, 1967, Box 342, JPC Papers; Heffernan to Research Development Bureau, Sept. 12, 1967, Series 45, Box 14, NACCD Records; CRC, "Report on Investigations of . . . Claims . . . against . . . Detroit

Police Department," June 24, 1966, Box A-19, DUL Papers; CRC, Claims Filed
against Detroit Police Department, Jan. 1–Apr. 27, 1967, Box 28, ORA Papers;
J. R. McGowan to James Bush, Aug. 16, 1966, Part 2, Series I, Box 10,
DNAACP Papers; Serrin, "God Help Our City," p. 120; Fogelson, "Confronta-
tion," pp. 224, 238–39. The official police record erroneously lists only four trial
board cases.
   71. Report, with Emrich to CCEO, Feb. 16, 1965, Box 11, Angelo Papers;
DFP, Jan. 11, Feb. 1, 1965, May 18, 1967; *MC*, Mar. 19, 1966; *DN*, Feb. 1, 1965;
Romanoff to Cavanagh, Aug. 30, 1965, Box 213, JPC Papers; NAACP Pro-
posals . . . [Mar. 18, 1966], Box 476, Reuther Papers; Heffernan to Girardin,
Dec. 15, 1965, Box 26, RG 74-90; CRC, "Report on Claims," July 30, 1966, Box
A-19, DUL Papers; CRC Weekly Report, Dec. 17, 1965, Box 92, GR Papers;
Radelet to Police Executives, and enclosed questionnaire, Box 2, ORA Papers;
Ursu Memoranda to Wilson (interview with Feikens), n.d., (interview with Janet
Cooper), n.d., Series 59, Box 2, NACCD Records; Johnson interview, p. 14;
Detroit Police . . . Consensus Statement of League of Women Voters of Detroit,
Feb. 1967, Part 1, Series I, Box 24, DNAACP Papers.
   72. Girardin interview, pp. 410, 412–13; *DN*, June 28, 1966; (Ursu) and
Dobranski Memorandum to Wilson (Heffernan et al. interview), n.d., Series 59,
Box 2, NACCD Records; Miller Memorandum to Feuillan, et al., Apr. 14, 1967,
Series 10, Box 46, ibid.; Dobranski Report to Conot, n.d., Box 77, ibid.; Minutes
of Meeting with Girardin, Aug. 28, 1964, Box A-19, DUL Papers; CRC, "Report
on Claims," July 30, 1966, ibid.; CRC Weekly Report, June 17, 1966, Box 135,
GR Papers; CCR Minutes, Series IV, Box 4, CCR Papers; Henry J. Syzmanski
Memorandum to CCR, Dec. 20, 1965, Series IV, Box 5, ibid.; Michigan Civil
Rights Commission, *Case Digest, 1964–1975* (Detroit, n.d.), p. 25.
   73. *MC*, Sept. 12, Dec. 19, 1964; *DFP*, Jan. 11, 1965; *DN*, Apr. 30, 1965;
Gordin to Girardin, Jan. 12, 1965, Series III, Box 2, CCR Papers; CRC News
Release, Apr. 27 [1965], Box 17, Kornegay Papers.
   74. Roy Allen Memorandum to CCR, Dec. 22, 1966, Series IV, Box 4, CCR
Papers; CCR Field Division Case Reports, July 28, 1966, ibid.; CCR Minutes,
Jan. 26, 1967, ibid.; Wilson Memorandum to Nelson (interview with Mary Val-
entine), n.d., Series 59, Box 2, NACCD Records; Mallett to Cavanagh, Mar. 2,
1967, Box 338, JPC Papers; Locke to Cavanagh, Oct. 6, 1966, Box 273, ibid.;
DN, July 19, 1966; *DFP*, Sept. 27, 1966, Aug. 24, 1968; *MC*, July 30, 1966, Mar.
23, 1968; CRC, *Case Digest, 1964–1975*, pp. 24–25.
   75. CRC News Release, Apr. 27 [1965], Box 17, Kornegay Papers; *MC*, May 1,
Sept. 11, 1965; CRC, "Report on Claims," June 24, 1966, Box A-19, DUL
Papers; Detroit Police Department News Bulletin, May 24, 1966, ibid.; Background Statement on Police-Community Relations [Feb. 1965], Series III, Box 2,
CCR Papers.
   76. Report, with Emrich to CCEO, Feb. 16, 1965, Box 11, Angelo Papers;
Sub-Committee on Police-Community Relations, CCEO, "Police—Summer
1965," Box 51, DUL Papers; *DN*, Feb. 21, Aug. 29, 1965; Reconnaissance Survey Reports, Detroit, 1:25, Series 10, Box 46, NACCD Records.
   77. *DFP*, May 18, July 13, 1967; Albert Callewaert and Arthur Yim, "The
Detroit Police Department and the Detroit Civil Disorder," Dec. 1967, unpagi-
nated table, Box 407, JPC Papers.
   78. Girardin to Toohey, Mar. 27, 1965, Box 217, JPC Papers; Romanoff et al.

Memorandum to Cavanagh, Apr. 11, 1965, Box 215, ibid.; Release, Apr. 14, 1965, ibid.; Robert Lothian to Commissioner, Aug. 17, 1965, ibid.; Ripley to Cavanagh, May 4, 1967, Box 338, ibid.; Girardin to Douglas Rowe, Mar. 14, 1966, Box 272, Records of the President's Commission on Law Enforcement and Administration of Justice, LBJ Library; Wilson Memorandum to Nelson (Simmons interview), n.d., Series 59, Box 2, NACCD Records; *DFP*, Aug. 21, 1965, May 18, 1967.

79. *DN*, Apr. 19, 1965; *MC*, Nov. 27, 1965, Feb. 5, Apr. 2, 1966; James Trainor to Cavanagh, Nov. 19, 1965, Horace Sheffield to Cavanagh, Nov. 24, 1965, Cavanagh to Nicholas Katzenbach, Nov. 27, 1965, Box 217, JPC Papers; Press Release, Nov. 20, 1965, ibid.; NAACP Proposals . . . [Mar. 18, 1965], Box 476, Reuther Papers; Levy, "Law Enforcement and Civil Rights" [Apr. 1966], Box 17, Kornegay Papers; Notes from Police-Community Relations Breakfast Meetings, Mar. 30, 31, 1966, Box 1, Gilmore Papers.

80. *DFP*, Mar. 11, 12, 1967; *DN*, Mar. 11, 12, 1967; Stanley Winkelman to Richard Marks, Mar. 14, 1967, Box 1, Gilmore Papers.

81. Beck to Cavanagh, Apr. 14, 1967, Box 362, JPC Papers; *NYT*, May 7, 1967; *MC*, May 6, 1967; *DN*, May 14, 1967; *DFP*, May 18, 1967; Hahn, "Cops and Rioters," pp. 767–78.

82. *DFP*, May 18, 1967; *DN*, June 11, 1967; "Crime in the Streets . . . Summer 1967," Draft No. 3, Box 9, Kornegay Papers.

83. *DN*, Jan. 22, 23, 1966, May 14, 1967; *DFP*, Aug. 28, 1966, Sept. 1, 2, 1967, Nov. 11, 1969; Serrin, "How One Big City Defeated Its Mayor," *NYT Magazine*, Oct. 27, 1968; Detroit Police Department Board of Inquiry, Summary of Findings and Summary Report [Dec. 1966], Box 273, JPC Papers; Cavanagh to Benjamin Bradlee, May 14, 1967, Box 339, ibid.; Dobranski Report to Conot, n.d., Box 77, NACCD Records.

84. Locke to Fine, Jan. 4, 1984; Bannon interview, pp. 6–8; Inquiry Board Report [Dec. 1966], Box 273, JPC Papers; [Caplan] interview with Fourth Looter, p. 38.

85. *DFP*, May 18, June 16, 21, 22, 1967; Nichols interview, p. 7; Bannon interview, pp. 8–9; Chronological Record of Events – Labor Relations Difficulties [1967], Box 570, JPC Papers; Girardin to Cavanagh, Nov. 15, 1967, ibid.

86. *DFP*, May 25, June 13, 15–20, 1967; Girardin to Cavanagh, Nov. 15, 1967, Box 570, JPC Papers; Chronological Record [1967], ibid.; *NYT*, June 17–21, 1967, Oct. 27, 1968; Serrin, "One Big City." For police opposition to striking, see Police Report, May 12, 1967, Box 341, JPC Papers.

87. [CCEO], "Special Meeting," June 20, 1967, Box 22, ORA Papers; *DFP*, June 21, 22, 1967.

88. *DFP*, June 23, 28–30, July 12, 14, 1967. The charges against the suspended police were dropped after the riot. *DN*, Aug. 3, 1967.

89. Girardin interview, pp. 411–12; *Washington Post*, Dec. 15, 1968; Nichols interview, pp. 6–7; Oral History Interview of Jerome P. Cavanagh, Mar. 22, 1971, p. 41, LBJ Library; Interview with Arthur P. Howison, July 24, 1984, p. 45, transcript in MHC; John Hersey, *The Algiers Motel Incident* (New York: Alfred A. Knopf, 1968), p. 153.

90. Locke, *Detroit Riot*, p. 75.

91. *DFP*, Oct. 25, 1967; "The Detroit 'Riot': A Challenge to Society and the

Legal Profession," Oct. 11, 1967, University of Michigan Law Library, Ann Arbor, Michigan.

92. *MC*, Aug. 13, Sept. 3, Nov. 19, 1966, Apr. 1, 1967; *DN*, Jan. 22, Apr. 30, 1967. Cf. McGhee to Levy, Mar. 28, 1967, Box 16, McGhee Papers.

93. Police Report, May 12, 1967, Box 342, JPC Papers; *DFP*, Mar. 11, 1967; *DN*, Apr. 30, 1967.

94. *DFP*, Mar. 11, 1967; *DN*, Apr. 30, 1967. See also *Wall Street Journal*, Aug. 12, 1964; Locke, *Detroit Riot*, p. 65; *DN*, May 28, 1967; and *Washington Post*, July 25, 1967. See chap. 6 for the Kercheval disturbance.

95. Marks to Cavanagh, Sept. 15, 1964 (draft of letter that became Nicholas Hood et al. to CCR), Series III, Box 2, CCR Papers.

Chapter 6

1. Girardin address, Mar. 9, 1967, Box 1, ORA Papers; Maurice Kelman and Ed Batchelor interview with Girardin, Oct. 29, 1971, pp. 406–8, transcript in my possession; Girardin to Douglas Rowe, Mar. 14, 1966, Box 272, Records of the President's Commission on Law Enforcement and Administration of Justice, LBJ Library; Permanent Subcommittee on Investigations of the Senate Committee on Government Operations, *Riots, Civil and Criminal Disorders, Hearings*, 90th Cong., 2d sess., 1968, pt. 6:1363.

2. Girardin to Cavanagh, Aug. 26, 1966, Box 273, JPC Papers; *Riots, Civil and Criminal Disorders*, pt. 6:1363; *NYT*, July 28, 1967; Recommendations of Committee on Means of Handling Civil Disturbances, Aug. 17, 1965, Commissioner's File, DPD; Interview with John Nichols, Aug. 13, 1984, pp. 8–9, transcript in MHC.

3. My treatment of the Detroit riot control plan and the thinking behind it is based on the following: ["Riot and Mob Control Manual"], July 1, 1966, DPD; Recommendations of Committee, Aug. 17, 1965, Commissioner's File, ibid.; Procedures for Handling Emergency Incidents of Civil Disobedience, Aug. 21, 1965, ibid.; Nichols to Girardin, Aug. 31, 1965, ibid.; Girardin to Rowe, Mar. 14, 1966, Box 272, Records of President's Commission on . . . Justice; *Riots, Civil and Criminal Disorders*, pt. 6:1362, 1363; and Nichols interview, p. 8.

4. President's Commission on Law Enforcement and Administration of Justice, *The Challenge of Crime in a Free Society* (Washington: GPO, 1967), pp. 118–19. See, for example, first Draft of a Proposed Guide for Police . . . , May 4, 1966, Box 271, Records of President's Commission on . . . Justice.

5. For Girardin's statement, see *NYT*, July 28, 1967.

6. Nichols to Robert A. Lothian, Aug. 24, 1965, Nichols to Girardin, Aug. 31, 1965, Commissioner's File; Girardin to Common Council, Sept. 22, 1967, Box 342, JPC Papers; Nichols interview, pp. 17–18.

7. ["Riot and Mob Control Manual"], July 1, 1966, DPD; Recommendations of Committee, Aug. 17, 1965, Commissioner's File; Riot Questionnaire, n.d., Series 22, Box 1, NACCD Records; *DN*, Sept. 26, 1967; Hubert Locke, *The Detroit Riot of 1967* (Detroit: Wayne State University Press, 1969), pp. 63–64; Nichols interview, pp. 19–20.

8. Girardin to Common Council, Oct. 18, 1967, Box 570, JPC Papers; Girardin, "After the Riots . . . ," *Saturday Evening Post* 240 (Sept. 3, 1967): 10; *DN*, Aug. 25, 1961, Sept. 26, 1967; Locke, *Detroit Riot*, p. 74; Locke, "Riot

Response: The Police and the Courts," in Richard A. Chikota and Michael C. Moran, eds., *Riot in the Cities* (Rutherford, New Jersey: Farleigh Dickinson University Press, 1970), p. 323; ["Riot and Mob Control Manual"], July 1, 1966, DPD.

9. Surveillance of ———, Oct. 25, 26, 1966, Box 343, JPC Papers; Charles Maynard to Commanding Officer, Criminal Intelligence Bureau, Apr. 24, 1967, Box 11, Ray Girardin Papers, Detroit Public Library, Detroit, Michigan; CCR Minutes, May 7, 1965, May 5, 1967, Series IV, Box 4, CCR Papers; Interview with James Bannon, Mar. 12, 1985, p. 43, transcript in MHC; Nichols interview, p. 3; Girardin interview, pp. 412, 415-16.

10. Girardin to Rowe, Mar. 14, 1966, Box 273, Records of President's Commission on . . . Justice; Remarks prepared for . . . Romney . . . , Sept. 12, 1967, Box 346, GR Papers; Glenn W. Dafoe to Melvin G. Kaufman, Aug. 23, 1965, Walter DeVries et al., to Romney et al., Aug. 24, 1965, Richard Graham to Frederick E. Davids, May 4, 1967, Richard H. Davis to Noble D. Moore, May 22, 1967, Box 319, ibid.; Winston Wessels Field Notes, July 26, 1967, Winston Wessels Papers, copy in my possession; C. C. Simmons to Moore, Aug. 23, 1965, Commissioner's File; Clarence C. Schnipke to Richard Russell, Aug. 3, 1967, Box 29, Philip A. Hart Papers, MHC; Howard Dryden, "National Guard Association of Michigan," n.d., Box 7, Records of the Department of Military Affairs–Division of Public Information, RG 77-45, State Archives, Lansing, Michigan; *DN*, Aug. 24, 1967. Cf. Billy Dansby, "Operation Sundown," *National Guardsman* 21 (Sept. 1967): 6-7, and Dryden, "National Guard Association" regarding the contemplated use of the Guard.

11. MS [July 1967], Box 3, Girardin Papers; Vincent W. Piersante to Girardin, Aug. 27, 1965, Commissioner's File; Recommendations of Committee, Aug. 17, 1965, ibid.

12. Bill Sudomier to Lee Hills et al. [May 21, 1965], Box 11, Frank Angelo Papers, MHC.

13. Locke, "Race Relations in Detroit: Problems and Prospects," Apr. 27, 1964, Box 21, ORA Papers.

14. CCR, "Annual Report, 1964," p. 7; Locke to Members CCEO [Summer 1964], Box 17, Francis A. Kornegay Papers, MHC; CCR Minutes, Oct. 19, 1964, Series IV, Box 4, CCR Papers; *Wall Street Journal*, Aug. 12, 1964; *MC*, Aug. 15, 1964.

15. *DFP*, Apr. 8, 15, 17, 1965; *MC*, June 5, 1965; Locke to Executive Committee, CCEO, Apr. 15, 1965, Box 21, ORA Papers; Arthur Ford to CCR, Apr. 19, 1965, James A. Bush to CCR, Apr. 19, 1965, Series IV, Box 4, CCR Papers; Field Division Memorandum to CCR, Aug. 23, 1965, ibid.; ACLU Release, Apr. 8, 1965, Box 6, American Civil Liberties Union–Metropolitan Detroit Branch Papers (General Office), ALHUA; Statement of Louis and Emily Azzam [Apr. 13, 1965], ibid.

16. James A. Bush to CCR, Apr. 19, 1965, Series IV, Box 4, CCR Papers; Field Division Memorandum to CCR, Aug. 23, 1965, ibid.; Memorandum to Files, June 14 [1965], Box 319, GR Papers; *DN*, Apr. 20, 1965; *DFP*, May 2, 1965.

17. CCR Minutes, Apr. 19, 1965, Series IV, Box 4, CCR Papers; Bush Memorandum to CCR, n.d., ibid.; Locke, "Race Relations . . . Summer 1965," Sept. 29, 1965, Box 37, ORA Papers; *MC*, May 15, 1965.

18. SWEEP-1965, Report by Alex Stein, Oct. 26, 1965, Box 4, United Community Services Papers (hereafter UCS Papers), ALHUA; 1967 SWEEP Report by United Community Services of Metropolitan Detroit, n.d., ibid.

19. United Community Services of Detroit, May 24, 1965, Part II, Series II, Box 4, Metropolitan Detroit Council of Churches Papers, ALHUA; CCEO, "A Special Report to the Mass Media . . . Summer 1965," Box 18, ORA Papers.

20. Field Division Memorandum to CCR, Aug. 23, 1965, Series IV, Box 4, CCR Papers; Locke, "Race Relations," Sept. 29, 1965, Box 37, ORA Papers; *MC*, Aug. 21, 1965; *DFP*, Aug. 16, 1965.

21. *DFP*, Dec. 2, 1965. The conference was designed to commemorate the tenth anniversary of the Montgomery bus boycott.

22. *MC*, Jan. 8, Apr. 23, 1966; *U.S. News and World Report* 60 (May 23, 1966): 37.

23. James R. McGowan to Bush, Mar. 24, 1966, Stein to Marks, Mar. 4, 1966, Bush and McGowan to Marks, Apr. 4, 1966, Marks to Stein, Mar. 31, 1966, Series III, Box 3, CCR Papers; McGowan to Bush, Proposal for Summer Tension Control Program, Jan. 20, 1967, ibid.; CCR Field Division Case Reports, June 23, 1966, Series IV, Box 4, ibid.; Bush Memorandum to Marks, Apr. 7, 1967, ibid.

24. 1966 SWEEP, A Report by United Community Services of Metropolitan Detroit, Dec. 27, 1967, Series III, Box 3, CCR Papers; UCS, SWEEP, n.d., Box 4, UCS Papers.

25. Joseph H. Kyles and John B. Forsyth, "The Churches' Summer Opportunities Action," May 10, 1967, Part II, Series II, Box 4, Council of Churches Papers; Detroit Area 1966 Summer Program for Youth, n.d., Series III, Box 3, CCR Papers; "TAP," n.d., ibid.; Philip Rutledge to Cavanagh, Apr. 11, 1967, Box 373, JPC Papers; *MC*, July 2, 1966; *DFP*, May 4, 1967; Evaluation of a Community Action Agency, Apr. 1967, Series 6, Box 32, NACCD Records.

26. CCR Field Division Case Reports, July 28, 1966, Series IV, Box 4, CCR Papers; Stella Fizazi to Richard Emrich, Aug. 2, 1966, Box 23, ORA Papers; *MC*, July 9, 1966.

27. Locke, "Race Relations in Detroit-Fall 1966," Oct. 5, 1966, Box 21, ORA Papers; Stanley Webb to Emrich, Mar. 31, 1966, Box 23, ibid.; Bush and McGowan to Marks, Apr. 4, 1966, Series III, Box 3, CCR Papers; United States Department of Commerce, Bureau of the Census, Census of Population and Housing, 1960, *Final Report Series, Census Tracts, Detroit, Mich.* (Washington: GPO, 1961), pp. 262, 277; *DFP*, Aug. 14, 1966; *DN*, Aug. 21, 1966; *MC*, Aug. 20, 1966; *Riots, Civil and Criminal Disorders*, pt. 6:1374; James Boudouris, "The Kercheval-Pennsylvania Incident," Aug. 1966, pp. 5–8, 10–12, DPD.

28. Field Division Memorandum to CCR, Aug. 25, 1966, Series IV, Box 4, CCR Papers; *DFP*, Aug. 14, 1966; *DN*, Aug. 12, 21, 1966; *MC*, Aug. 20, 1966; Boudouris, "Kercheval," pp. 9, 17–18, DPD.

29. See chap. 2.

30. *MC*, Dec. 5, 1964. See also Field Division Memorandum to CCR, Aug. 25, 1966, Series IV, Box 4, CCR Papers.

31. Commission on Race and Cultural Relations, Minutes, Sept. 14, 1965, Part II, Series II, Box 4, Council of Churches Papers; "CORCR-Incidents-ACME-1965," Box 9, ibid.; Thomas A. Bailey to Paul Sheridan, June 22, 1965, Girardin

to Robert Hoppe, June 22, 1965, ibid.; CRC Weekly News Report, July 30, 1965, Box 92, GR Papers; *DN*, June 2, 1965; *MC*, July 9, 23, 1966.

32. *DFP*, Aug. 14, 1966; *DN*, Aug. 14, 1966; Stenographic Report of Conversation between John Kent Scales and Anthony P. Locricchio, Feb. 16, 1968, Series 4, Box 22, NACCD Records; *Riots, Civil and Criminal Disorders*, pt. 6:1394-95.

33. CCR Field Division Case Reports, July 28, 1966, Series IV, Box 4, CCR Papers; *DFP*, July 31, Aug. 14, 1966; *MC*, July 30, Aug. 14, 1966; *DN*, Aug. 14, 1966; *Riots, Civil and Criminal Disorders*, pt. 6:1395; Boudouris, "Kercheval," pp. 2, 15, 24, DPD; Locke, "Race Relations . . . Fall 1966," Oct. 5, 1966, Box 21, ORA Papers; Locke to Emrich and Horace W. Gilmore, Aug. 17, 1966, Box 1, Horace W. Gilmore Papers, ALHUA. See chap. 2 for Harrison and the Carmichael talk.

34. *DFP*, Aug. 25, 26, 1966.

35. William R. McCoy to Chief of Detectives, Aug. 9, 1966, Box 12, ORA Papers; Girardin to Cavanagh, Aug. 26, 1966, Box 273, JPC Papers; Field Division Memorandum to CCR, Aug. 25, 1966, Series IV, Box 4, CCR Papers; *Riots, Civil and Criminal Disorders*, pt. 6:1386-87; People of State of Michigan vs. Albert Harrison and Moses Wedlow, A131586, Box 12, ACLU-Metropolitan Detroit Branch Papers (July 23, 1971); *DFP*, Aug. 14, 1966; Boudouris, "Kercheval," pp. 2-3, DPD; *DFP*, Aug. 14, 1966. Girardin's account of the event differs somewhat from the police report.

36. Girardin to Cavanagh, Aug. 26, 1966, Box 273, JPC Papers; Boudouris, "Kercheval," p. 24, DPD; *DN*, Aug. 21, 1966, May 17, 1987; Deposition of John Nichols, Jan. 10, 1968, Series 32, Box 2, NACCD Records.

37. Community Relations Service, United States Conference of Mayors, Community Planning for Civil Disturbance, Experience Report 108, Reconnaissance Field Survey Research Reports, Detroit, Michigan, 1: Exhibit 2, Series 10, Box 46, NACCD Records; Girardin to Cavanagh, Aug. 26, 1966, Box 273, JPC Papers; Marks Memorandum to CCR, Aug. 24, 1966, Box 301, ibid.; Notes of Meeting . . . , Aug. 13, 1966, Box 301, ibid.; CCR, "Annual Report, 1966," pp. 2-3; Fizazi to Emrich, Aug. 26, 1966, Box 23, ORA Papers; Boudouris, "Kercheval," pp. 15, 24, DPD; *DFP*, Aug. 10, 1966; *DN*, Aug. 10, 21, 1966.

38. *DFP*, Aug. 10, 11, 1966; *DN*, Aug. 10, 21, 1966; *NYT*, Aug. 10, 1966; Field Division Memorandum to CCR, Aug. 25, 1966, Series IV, Box 4, CCR Papers; Girardin to Cavanagh, Aug. 26, 1966, Box 273, JPC Papers; Experience Report 108, Series 10, Box 46, NACCD Records; Boudouris, "Kercheval," p. 3, DPD.

39. Complaint Form, Aug. 10, 1966, Box 12, ORA Papers; *Riots, Civil and Criminal Disorders*, pt. 6:1389-1403; *DFP*, Aug. 11, 24, 1966; Girardin to Cavanagh, Aug. 26, 1966, Box 273, JPC Papers.

40. Girardin to Cavanagh, Aug. 26, 1966, Box 273, JPC Papers; Marks Memorandum to CCR, Aug. 24, 1966, Box 301, ibid.; Experience Report 108, Series 10, Box 46, NACCD Records; Sheehan to Dear Father, Aug. 10, 1966, Father Sheehan Correspondence, 1962-1969, Archives of the Archdiocese of Detroit, Detroit, Michigan.

41. Girardin to Cavanagh, Aug. 26, 1966, Box 273, JPC Papers; Field Division Memorandum to CCR, Aug. 25, 1966, Series IV, Box 4, CCR Papers; Experience

Report 108, Series 10, Box 46, NACCD Records; *DFP*, Aug. 11, 12, 14, 1966; *DN*, Aug. 11, 14, 21, 1966, Aug. 25, 1967.

42. Experience Report 108, Series 10, Box 46, NACCD Records; Girardin to Cavanagh, Aug. 26, 1966, Box 273, JPC Papers; Marks Memorandum to CCR, Aug. 24, 1966, Box 301, ibid.; Field Division Memorandum to CCR, Aug. 25, 1966, Series IV, Box 4, CCR Papers; *Riots, Civil and Criminal Disorders*, pt. 6:1393–94, 1395; *DN*, Aug. 12, 21, 1966, Aug. 5, 1967; *MC*, Aug. 20, 1966; *DFP*, Aug. 13, 1966.

43. *DFP*, Aug. 13, 1966; *DN*, Aug. 13, 21, 1966; *MC*, Aug. 20, 1966; Field Division Memorandum to CCR, Aug. 25, 1966, Series IV, Box 4, CCR Papers; Marks Memorandum to CCR, Aug. 24, 1966, Box 301, JPC Papers; Girardin to Cavanagh, Aug. 26, 1966, Box 273, ibid.; Boudouris, "Kercheval," pp. 3–4, 24, DPD.

44. Isaac D. Balbus, *The Dialectics of Legal Repression: Black Radicals before the American Criminal Courts* (New York: Russell Sage Foundation, 1973), pp. 107–13; *Riots, Civil and Criminal Disorders*, pt. 5:1306–7, 6:1390; *MC*, Oct. 15, 1966, Apr. 8, 1967; *DFP*, Aug. 24, Sept. 7, 1966, Mar. 7, 28, 1967; *DN*, Apr. 7, 28, 1967.

45. Minutes of Ad Hoc Committee on Community Peace, Aug. 15, 1966, Part 2, Series I, Box 1, DNAACP Papers; Roger Barney to Friend, Aug. 15, 1966, Box 5, ibid.; Executive Secretary's Report, Sept. 1966, Box 9, ibid.; *MC*, Aug. 20, 27, Sept. 3, 1966; *DFP*, Aug. 13, 1966.

46. Minutes of Ad Hoc Committee, Aug. 15, 1966, Part 2, Series I, Box 1, DNAACP Papers; CCR Minutes, Aug. 25, 1966, Series IV, Box 4, CCR Papers; *DN*, Aug. 21, 1966.

47. Notes of Meeting . . . , Aug. 13, 1966, Box 301, JPC Papers; *DFP*, Aug. 16, 1966.

48. Minutes of Ad Hoc Committee, Aug. 24, 1966, Part 2, Series I, Box 1, DNAACP Papers; Executive Secretary's Report, Sept. 1966, Box 9, ibid.; Marks Memorandum to CCR, Aug. 24, 1966, Series IV, Box 4, CCR Papers; *MC*, Aug. 20, 1966.

49. Girardin to Cavanagh, Aug. 26, 1966, Box 273, JPC Papers; Bush to Marks, Aug. 25, 1966, ibid.; *Riots, Civil and Criminal Disorders*, pt. 6:1364; Minutes of Ad Hoc Committee, Aug. 15, 1966, Part 2, Series I, Box 1, DNAACP Papers; Herman Wilson Memorandum to Charles E. Nelson (interview with Hubert Locke), Oct. 17, 19, 1967, Peter Rossi File, in my possession; Official Transcript of Proceedings before the National Advisory Commission on Civil Disorders, Aug. 15, 1967, p. 471, Series 1, Box 2, NACCD Records; Nichols Deposition, Jan. 10, 1968, Series 32, Box 2, ibid.; Locke, "Race Relations . . . Fall 1966," Box 21, ORA Papers; Girardin interview, p. 403; *DFP*, Aug. 14, 1966; *MC*, Aug. 20, 27, 1966; Locke, *Detroit Riot*, pp. 65–66.

50. J. Anthony Lukas, "Postscript on Detroit: 'Whitey Hasn't Got the Message,' " *NYT Magazine*, Aug. 27, 1967; Interview with Damon Keith, June 21, 1985, p. 2, transcript in MHC; Locke, "Race Relations . . . Fall 1966," Box 21, ORA Papers; Black to Cavanagh, Sept. 7, 1966, Box 271, JPC Papers; Oral History Interview of Jerome P. Cavanagh, Mar. 22, 1971, p. 54, LBJ Library.

51. Experience Report 108, Series 10, Box 46, NACCD Records.

52. "The Picture This Summer," Apr. 3, 1967, enclosed with Francis Kornegay to Horace Gilmore, Apr. 5, 1967, Box 4, Kornegay Papers; Conrad

Mallett to Cavanagh, May 1, 1967, Box 340, JPC Papers; CCEO handwritten notes, Apr. 3, 1967, Box 5, Gilmore Papers; Marks Memorandum to CCR, Apr. 17, 1967, Box 370, JPC Papers; Statement from the CCR: The Summer Outlook, May 5, 1967, Series IV, Box 4, CCR Papers; John F. Russell to Special Group on "Summer Problems," Apr. 27, 1967, Series III, Box 3, ibid.; Subcommittee on Employment, Manpower, and Poverty of the Senate Committee on Labor and Public Welfare, *Examination of the War on Poverty, Hearings*, 90th Cong., 1st sess., 1967, pt. 1:113–14, 115; *DFP*, May 3, 4, 1967; *DN*, May 2, 6, 1967; *MC*, May 13, 20, 1967; *NYT*, Mar. 4, May 7, 1967; James Gaither for the President, May 9, 1967, Box 29, WE9, WHCF; Cavanagh interview, pp. 39–40.

53. Gaither for President, May 9, 1967, Box 29, WE9, WHCF; *DFP*, May 3, June 27, 1967; *DN*, May 2, 1967; *NYT*, May 7, 1967.

54. Statement from CCR, May 5, 1967, Series IV, Box 4, CCR Papers; *DFP*, May 4, 1967; *DN*, May 6, 1967; *MC*, May 13, 1967.

55. Gaither for President, May 9, 1967, Box 29, WE9, WHCF; *DN*, May 3, 6, 1967; *NYT*, May 7, 1967.

56. Mallett to Cavanagh, May 1, 1967, Box 340, JPC Papers; Gilmore to Religious Leadership, May 3, 1967, Emrich to Leonard Sznewajs, Mar. 15, 1967, Box 18, ORA Papers; Special Report on Activities of Committee on Police-Community Relations, May 6, 1967, ibid. See chap. 2 for the Jobs Now Conference.

57. Statement from CCR, May 5, 1967, Series IV, Box 4, CCR Papers; CCR Minutes, Apr. 7, 1967, ibid.; McGowan to Bush, Apr. 5, 1967, ibid.; Marks Memorandum to CCR, May 26, 1967, Series III, Box 3, ibid.

58. City of Detroit Commission on Children and Youth, Summary of Planning . . . , Apr. 14, 1967, Series III, Box 3, ibid.; Minutes of Ad Hoc Committee, June 14, 1967, ibid.; 1967 SWEEP Report, Box 4, UCS Papers.

59. G. Merrill Lenox, "After Due Reflection . . . ," *Christian Century* 84 (Oct. 11, 1967): 1300; Cavanagh to Lenox, Apr. 11, 1967, Russell to Carl Bielby, July 10, 1967, David H. Evans to Bielby, July 10, 1967, Part II, Series II, Box 4, Council of Churches Papers; "Churches Summer Opportunity Action Program, July 3, 1967 to Sept. 4, 1967," ibid.; Kyles and Forsyth, "Churches Summer Opportunities Action for 1967," May 10, 1967, ibid.; Russell Memoranda to Bielby, June 29, July 7, 10, 1967, Part II, Series VII, Box 14, ibid.

60. *Examination of Poverty, Hearings*, pt. 1:110; *DN*, June 4, 1967; *DFP*, May 18, June 4, 1967; MCHRD, General Summary, Summer Program 1967, Part II, Series VII, Box 14, Council of Churches Papers; Rutledge to Cavanagh, July 10, 1967, Box 373, JPC Papers; Official Transcript, Aug. 15, 1967, p. 405, Series 1, Box 2, NACCD Records; *Business Week*, July 29, 1967, p. 23.

61. *Riots, Civil and Criminal Disorders*, pt. 7:1536; *DFP*, June 26, 1967; Mallett to Cavanagh, May 1, 1967, Box 340, JPC Papers; Malcolm G. Dade, Jr., Memo to Mallett, Sept 8, 1967, ibid.; Cavanagh to Mildred Jeffrey, June 23, 1967, Box 375, ibid.; Jeffrey to Irving Bluestone, Jan. 23, 1968, Box 54, Walter Reuther Papers, ALHUA.

62. McGowan to Bush, Proposal . . . , Jan. 20, 1967, Series III, Box 3, CCR Papers; Bush Memorandum to Marks, Apr. 7, 1967, ibid.; McGowan to Charles Rouls, Apr. 26, 1967, John W. McCrary to Rouls, Apr. 28, May 8, 1967, Bush and Rouls to Marks, May 10, 1967, Marks to Mallett, May 23, 1967, ibid.; Marks

Memorandum to CCR, Apr. 17, 1967, Box 370, JPC Papers; Interview with Richard Marks, Aug. 6, 1984, p. 23, transcript in MHC; *NYT*, June 11, 1967.

63. Interview with Robert P. Roselle, Aug. 30, 1984, pp. 28–29, transcript in MHC; Mayor's Inspection Team to Cavanagh, July 13, 1967, Box 339, JPC Papers; Mallett to Cavanagh, May 1, 1967, Box 340, ibid.; Detroit Housing Commission, *Report to the Commissioners, Fourth Quarter 1968*, p. 6; Marks Memorandum to CCR, May 26, 1967, Series III, Box 3, CCR Papers.

64. Mallett to Cavanagh, May 1, 1967, Box 340, JPC Papers; Dade Memo to Mallett, Sept. 8, 1967, ibid.; Cavanagh to All Department Heads . . . , June 14, July 18, 1967, Box 338, ibid.; Rouls to Marks, May 31, 1967, Series III, Box 3, CCR Papers; Minutes of Ad Hoc Committee, June 14, 1967, ibid.; CRC to Mayors et al., May 26, 1967, ibid.; Cavanagh to Detroit Urban League, June 19, 1967, Box 4, Kornegay Papers; *DN*, June 4, 1967; *DFP*, July 20, 27, 1967. Cf. Harold Black to Richard Strichartz, Aug. 8, 1967, Box 398, JPC Papers.

65. Mallett to Cavanagh, May 1, 1967, Box 340, JPC Papers.

66. Juliet Sabit to Mallett, June 28, 1967, Series III, Box 3, CCR Papers; "Contact with Summer Task Force," 1967, ibid.; Dade Memo to Mallett, Sept. 8, 1967, Box 370, JPC Papers; Responses to the Recent Civil Disorders in Detroit by the MCHRD, n.d., Box 570, ibid.

67. Dade Memo to Mallett, Sept. 8, 1967, Box 370, JPC Papers; Floyd W. Radike to Cavanagh, Nov. 21, 1967, Box 535, ibid.

68. *DN*, Aug. 10, 1967, May 17, 1987; Official Transcript, Aug. 15, 1967, p. 404, Series 1, Box 2, NACCD Records. Mallett, many years later, recalled that he had placed the incident at Woodrow Wilson and Glendale or at Glendale and Twelfth Street, a few blocks from Twelfth and Clairmount. He also recalled that the departments concerned claimed they could handle the situation he had projected. Fine phone conversation with Mallett, July 13, 1984; Xavier Nicholas interview with Mallett [1982], copy of tape in my possession.

69. Mallett interview.

70. Handwritten sheets, July 13, 17, 1967, Box 1, ORA Papers; Disorder Log, July 21, 1967, Box 4, Girardin Papers; CCR Minutes, May 5, 1967, Series IV, Box 4, CCR Papers; *Detroit Daily Press*, Jan. 4, 1968; Nichols interview, p. 24; Locke, *Detroit Riot*, p. 125. See chap. 2 for the Second Black Arts Convention.

71. *DFP*, July 12, 1967; Locke to Fine, Jan. 4, 1984.

72. *DFP*, June 13, 16, 1967; *MC*, June 24, 1967.

73. Deposition of Albert J. Dunmore, Jan. 9, 1968, Series 32, Box 2, NACCD Records; Haywood L. Perry to Milan C. Miskovsky, Jan. 2, 1968, Series 4, Box 22, ibid.; Bernard Dobranski and Tom Popp Memorandum to Wilson (interview with Malcolm Dade), Oct. 11, 1967, Series 59, Box 2, ibid.; *MC*, July 1, 1967; *DFP*, July 26, 27, 1967. The accounts of what went on in Rouge Park differ in detail but not in their general substance.

74. Barbara Wilson Tinker, *When the Fire Reaches Us* (New York: William Morrow and Co., 1970), pp. 170–72; Dade Memo to Mallett, Sept. 8, 1967, Box 340, JPC Papers; Sabit to Mallett, June 28, 1967, Series III, Box 3, CCR Papers; CCR Field Division Case Reports, July 7, 1967, Series IV, Box 4, ibid.

75. *Report of the National Advisory Commission on Civil Disorders* (Washington: GPO, 1968), p. 48; Dobranski and Popp Memorandum to Wilson (Dade interview), Series 59, Box 2, NACCD Records; Report of Dobranski to Robert Conot, n.d., Box 77, ibid.; Dunmore Deposition, Jan. 9, 1968, Series 32, Box 2,

ibid.; CCR Field Division Case Reports, July 7, 1967, Series IV, Box 4, CCR Papers; Girardin interview, pp. 428–29; *DFP*, Dec. 31, 1968.

76. Dunmore Deposition, Jan. 9, 1968, Series 32, Box 2, NACCD Records; Dobranski and Popp Memorandum to Wilson (Dade interview), Oct. 11, 1967, Series 59, Box 2, ibid.; NACCD, News Media Seminar, Newspapers, Nov. 11, 1967, pp. 53–58, Series 12, Box 1, ibid.; *DFP*, June 26, 1967; *DN*, June 26, 1967.

77. *MC*, July 15, 1967; *DN*, Aug. 10, 1967; *DFP*, Aug. 10, 1967; Perry to Miskovsky, Jan. 2, 1968, Series 4, Box 22, NACCD Records; Dunmore Deposition, Jan. 9, 1968, Series 32, Box 2, ibid.; Dobranski Report to Conot, n.d., Box 77, ibid.; Elliot Luby and James Grisell, "Grievances of Detroit Negro Arrestees" [1968], p. 2, Detroit Public Library; Tinker, *Fire*, p. 170. For a somewhat different version of the story, see handwritten sheets, June [1967], July 1 [1967], Box 1, ORA Papers.

78. *DFP*, July 24, 1967; [John Ursu] Memorandum to Wilson (interview with Girardin), n.d., Series 59, Box 2, NACCD Records; Locke, *Detroit Riot*, p. 26.

79. Transportation and Land Use Study (TALUS) Tables 2, 4, 5, Box 393, JPC Papers.

80. Ernest Harburg et al., "A Family Set Method for Estimating Heredity and Stress – I," *Journal of Chronic Diseases* 23 (1970): 70, 72, 77; TALUS Tables 2, 5, 6, Box 393, JPC Papers. Cf. "Community Data," n.d., Box 77, NACCD Records, and TALUS Table 5, Box 393, JPC Papers.

81. Harburg, "Set Method," pp. 70–71, 76–77.

82. Lukas, "Postscript on Detroit"; *NACCD Report*, p. 49; Lee Rainwater, "Open Letter on White Justice in the Riots," *Trans-Action* 4 (Sept. 1967): 30; Van Gordon Sauter and Burleigh Hines, *Nightmare in Detroit* (Chicago: Henry Regnery Co., 1968), p. 231.

83. See chap. 4 for unemployment data.

84. Downes, "Social and Political Characteristics of Riot Cities: A Comparative Study," in James A. Geschwender, ed., *The Black Revolt* (Englewood Cliffs, N.J.: Prentice-Hall, 1971), p. 336; *NACCD Report*, p. 6; Locke, *Detroit Riot*, p. 23.

Chapter 7

1. Hubert G. Locke, *The Detroit Riot of 1967* (Detroit: Wayne State University Press, 1969), p. 26n; Miller Memorandum to Jacques Feuillan et al., Apr. 14, 1967, Series 10, Box 46, NACCD Records. See also Capture and Record of Civil Disorder in Detroit, July 23–July 28, 1967, Box 345, GR Papers.

2. Xavier Nicholas interview with Anthony Fiermonti, n.d., pp. 1–2, transcript in Nicholas's possession; *Report of the National Advisory Commission on Civil Disorders* (Washington: GPO, 1968), p. 47.

3. *DFP*, July 24, Aug. 6, 1967; *DN*, Aug. 3, 1967; William Walter Scott III, *Hurt, Baby, Hurt* (Ann Arbor: New Ghetto Press, 1970), pp. 98–102; Ray Girardin to Cavanagh, Oct. 20, 1967, Commissioner's File, DPD; Summary Report of Arthur Howison, July 23, 1967, Box 398, JPC Papers; Albert Callewaert and Arthur Yim, "The Detroit Police Department and the Civil Disorder," Dec. 1967, pp. 17–18, Box 407, ibid.; Howison draft report, n.d., Maurice Kelman Papers, copy in my possession; [Nathan Caplan] interview with Owner of Blind Pig [Nov.

1967], pp. 4–5, transcript in my possession; Deposition of James Del Rio, Jan. 9, 1968, Series 32, Box 2, NACCD Records; Report of Bernard Dobranski to Robert Conot, n.d., Box 77, ibid.

4. Girardin to Cavanagh, Oct. 20, 1967, Commissioner's File; [DPD] *Statistical Report on the Civil Disorder Occurring in the City of Detroit, July 1967*, p. ii; Callewaert and Yim, "Police Department," Box 407, JPC Papers; transcript of Howison debriefing by Girardin, n.d., Kelman Papers, copy in my possession; Permanent Subcommittee on Investigations of the Senate Committee on Government Operations, *Riots, Civil and Criminal Disorders, Hearings*, 90th Cong., 2d sess., 1968, pt. 6:1350–52; Interview with Arthur Howison, July 24, 1984, pp. 6–7, 8–9, transcript in MHC; *DFP*, Aug. 6, 1967.

5. Fiermonti interview, p. 3; Howison Report, Box 398, JPC Papers; Interview with John Nichols, Aug. 13, 1984, pp. 27–28, transcript in MHC; Howison interview, pp. 11–12, 14–15; Interview with James Bannon, Mar. 12, 1985, pp. 10–12, ibid.; Maurice Kelman and Ed Batchelor interview with Girardin, Oct. 29, 1971, p. 386, transcript in my possession; Benjamin D. Singer et al., *Black Rioters* (Lexington, Mass.: D. C. Heath and Co., 1970), p. 100; *DFP*, Aug. 6, 1967; Howison debriefing, Kelman Papers.

6. *DN*, July 24, 30, Aug. 3, 1967; Howison Report, Box 398, JPC Papers; Howison interview, p. 14; Howison debriefing, Kelman Papers; "Re Rioting Beginning July 23, 1967," Aug. 9, 1967, FBI-FOIA.

7. Callewaert and Yim, "Police Department," p. 21, Box 407, JPC Papers; Howison Report, Box 398, ibid.; Howison debriefing, Kelman Papers; Howison interview, pp. 17–19; *DFP*, Aug. 6, 1967.

8. *DN*, July 24, 1967, May 17, 1987; Scott, *Hurt*, p. 119; Howison interview, p. 18; Nichols interview, p. 29; Official Transcript of Proceedings before the National Advisory Commission on Civil Disorders, Aug. 15, 1967, p. 470, Series 1, Box 2, NACCD Records; *Detroit Scene* 1, no. 5 (1967): 13; Singer et al., *Black Rioters*, p. 39; Clark McPhail, "Civil Disorder Participation: A Critical Examination of Recent Research," *American Sociological Review* 36 (Dec. 1971): 1070–71; [DPD] *Statistical Report*, p. 51.

9. David Boesel, "The Ghetto Riots 1964–1968" (Ph.D. diss., Cornell University, 1972), p. 115; Girardin to Cavanagh, Oct. 20, 1967, Commissioner's File; Callewaert and Yim, "Police Department," p. 20, Box 407, JPC Papers; Howison Report, Box 398, ibid.; George Edwards, *The Police on the Urban Frontier* (New York: Institute of Human Relations, 1968), p. 61; *DFP*, Aug. 15, 1967.

10. "Field Notes: The Geography of the Children of Detroit" [1971], Map Room, University of Michigan Library, Ann Arbor, Michigan; "Incidents Reported at the time of the Detroit riot . . . , n.d., Joseph A. Labadie Collection, ibid.; [Caplan] interview with First Looter, Nov. 7, 1967, pp. 5–6, with Fourth Looter, Nov. 7, 1967, p. 39, transcripts in my possession; Scott, *Hurt*, pp. 121–24; *MC*, July 29, 1967; *DFP*, July 24, 30, 1967; *DN*, July 24, 1967; J. Anthony Lukas, "Postscript on Detroit: 'Whitey Hasn't Got the Message,'" *NYT Magazine*, Aug. 27, 1967; Interview of John Conyers by Robert Conot, n.d., Box 81, NACCD Records.

11. Official Transcript, Aug. 15, 1967, pp. 401–2, Series 1, Box 2, NACCD Records; *Riots, Civil and Criminal Disorders*, pt. 6:1419; Howison debriefing, Kelman Papers; Howison draft report, ibid.; Howison Report, Box 398, JPC Papers; Howison interview, p. 17; *DFP*, July 24, 1967; *DN*, July 24, 1967.

12. People of Michigan vs. Michael Lewis, A 139845–139847, Examination, Aug. 24, 1967, pp. 46–47, 54–55, Detroit Recorder's Court, Detroit, Michigan; *Riots, Civil and Criminal Disorders*, pt. 6:1352, 1364; Fiermonti interview, p. 4; *DN*, Aug. 3, 1967; *DFP*, July 30, Aug. 15, 1967; Reconnaissance Survey Field Research Reports, Detroit, Michigan, 2:2–3, 5, Series 10, Box 46, NACCD Records.

13. Scott, *Hurt*, pp. 120–26; [Caplan] interview with person who broke first window [Nov. 1967], pp. 1–4, transcript in my possession; *DFP*, July 29, 1967; Nichols to Girardin, Aug. 1, 1967, Commissioner's File.

14. Lieutenant Raymond Good claims he gave the order, but it appears to have been given before he arrived on the scene. *DN*, July 23, 1972.

15. Nichols to Girardin, Aug. 1, 1967, Commissioner's File; Source: Inspector Ware, n.d., ibid.; Callewaert and Yim, "Police Department," p. 20, Box 407, JPC Papers; Howison interview, pp. 19–20; Nichols interview, p. 38; *Riots, Civil and Criminal Disorders*, pt. 7:1563; *DFP*, July 24, 1967; Scott, *Hurt*, p. 126; Carl C. Turner, "Planning and Training for Civil Disorder," *Police Chief* 35 (May 1968): 28; *NACCD Report*, pp. 23–24; *Newsweek* 70 (Aug. 7, 1967): 19; *Time* 90 (Aug. 4, 1967): 16.

16. *DN*, Aug. 3, 1967; *DFP*, Aug. 6, 1967; *Riots, Civil and Criminal Disorders*, pt. 7:1482–83, 1491, 1493; Girardin interview, p. 385; Howison debriefing, Kelman Papers.

17. *DFP*, Aug. 15, 1967; *DN*, July 23, 1972, July 18, 1982; Nicholas interview with Raymond Good [1982], copy of tape in my possession; Nichols to Girardin, Aug. 1, 1967, Commissioner's File; Michigan vs. Lewis, Examination, Aug. 24, 1967, pp. 74–83, Recorder's Court; Callewaert and Yim, "Police Department," pp. 20, 24, Box 407, JPC Papers; [DPD] *Statistical Report*, p. iii.

18. Michigan vs. Lewis, Examination, Aug. 24, 1967, pp. 57–58, 69–70, 84, 92, 97, 100–103, and warrant sheet, Recorder's Court; *DFP*, Aug. 15, 1967, July 24, 1977; *MC*, Sept. 23, 1967, Mar. 9, 1968; Scott, *Hurt*, pp. 147–50.

19. Sheldon Levy, "Communication Processes in the Detroit Riot" [1968], pp. 20–21, Detroit Public Library, Detroit, Michigan; Questionnaires Nos. 3033, 4034, 4052, 5016, 5017, 5055, 5056, 5059, 5060, Boxes 8–10, A-W Riot Studies; Boesel, "Ghetto Riots," pp. 101–15; James R. Hundley, "The Dynamics of Recent Ghetto Riots," in Richard A. Chikota and Michael C. Moran, eds., *Riot in the Cities* (Rutherford, N.J.: Farleigh Dickinson University Press, 1970), pp. 141–43; Ralph W. Conant, *The Prospects for Revolution: A Study of Riots, Civil Disobedience and Insurrection in Contemporary America* (New York: Harper's Magazine Book Co., 1971), pp. 32–35; Report by Rene Freeman [Aug. 1967], Series III, Box 3, CCR Papers; Joe R. Feagin and Harlan Hahn, *Ghetto Riots* (New York: Macmillan Co., 1973), pp. 144–46, 149–50, 159, 163–64; *NACCD Report*, p. 64; Herbert J. Gans, "The Ghetto Rebellions and Urban Class Conflict," *Proceedings of the Academy of Political Science* 29 (1968): 43; Neil J. Smelser, *Theory of Collective Behavior* (New York: Free Press, 1962), p. 249.

20. *Riots, Civil and Criminal Disorders*, pt. 6:1375–76; Girardin to Cavanagh, Oct. 20, 1967, Commissioner's File; Girardin interview, pp. 386, 401.

21. Callewaert and Yim, "Police Department," p. 34, app. A, Box 407, JPC Papers; Nichols to All Precincts, July 23, 1967, Nichols to All Members, July 23, 1967, Nichols to Girardin, Aug. 1, 1967, Girardin to Cavanagh, Oct. 20, 1967,

Commissioner's File; Nichols interview, pp. 16–17; Girardin interview, p. 399; *DFP*, Aug. 27, 1967, Aug. 11, 1968; *DN*, Sept. 21, 27, 1967.

22. Callewaert and Yim, "Police Department," pp. 32–33, app. A, Box 407, JPC Papers; Locke, *Detroit Riot*, pp. 28–29; *DFP*, July 24, 1967.

23. Callewaert and Yim, "Police Department," p. 37, Box 407, JPC Papers; Scott, *Hurt*, p. 129; *MC*, July 29, 1967.

24. Lukas, "Postscript"; Interview with Robert Potts, June 4, 1985, pp. 6–7, transcript in MHC; Tom Parmenter, "Breakdown of Law and Order," *Trans-Action* 4 (Sept. 1967): 15; Deposition of Stanley Webb, Jan. 11, 1968, Series 32, Box 2, NACCD Records; Boesel, "Ghetto Riots," pp. 131–32; Louis Goldberg, "Ghetto Riots and Others," in David Boesel and Peter H. Rossi, eds., *Cities under Siege: An Anatomy of Ghetto Riots, 1964–1968* (New York: Basic Books, 1971), p. 139; *NACCD Report*, p. 50; Joyce Carol Oates, *Them* (New York: Vanguard Press, 1969), p. 486; *DFP*, Sept. 3, 1967; Senate Committee on the Judiciary, *Antiriot Bill 1967*, 90th Cong., 1st sess., 1967, p. 784.

25. *NACCD Report*, pp. 48, 72; ["Riot and Mob Control Manual"], July 1, 1966, p. 32, DPD; Callewaert and Yim, "Police Department," pp. 34, 36, 38, Box 407, JPC Papers; Girardin to Cavanagh, Oct. 20, 1967, Commissioner's File; Interview with Robert Roselle, Aug. 30, 1984, p. 31, transcript in MHC; Herman Wilson Memorandum to John Ursu (interview with John Nichols), n.d., Series 59, Box 2, NACCD Records; Webb Deposition, Jan. 11, 1968, Series 32, Box 2, ibid.; Robert Conot, *Rivers of Blood, Years of Darkness* (New York: Bantam Books, 1967), p. 192; Locke to Sidney Fine, Jan. 4, 1984, Aug. 23, 1985; *DN*, July 24, 30, Aug. 4, 1967; James S. Campbell et al., *Law and Order Reconsidered* (Washington: GPO, [1968]), p. 310; Leonard Berkowitz, "The Study of Urban Violence," in Louis H. Masotti and Don R. Bowen, eds., *Riots and Rebellion* (Beverly Hills: Sage Publications, 1968), p. 48. Although the sweep is consistently treated as a commando operation, only seventeen commandos were on duty at the time, and more than that number of police conducted the sweep.

26. Callewaert and Yim, "Police Department," p. 34, Box 407, JPC Papers; Detroit Incident . . . Col. Davids, Box 319, GR Papers; *DN*, July 24, 1977; Locke to Fine, Jan. 4, 1984; Roselle interview, p. 34; Nichols interview, p. 3.

27. *NACCD Report*, p. 72; Callewaert and Yim, "Police Department," app. A, Box 407, JPC Papers; *DFP*, July 30, 1967; Roselle interview, pp. 31–32; Mutual Loss Research Bureau, "The Detroit Report" [Sept. 1967], Series 4, Box 22, NACCD Records; *DN*, Aug. 11, 1967. For another version of how the fire began, see Scott, *Hurt*, pp. 172–73.

28. *DFP*, July 24, 1967; *DN*, July 24, 1967; Nicholas interview with Colding [1982], copy of tape in my possession; N. C. Rayford to Milan C. Miskovsky, Jan. 2, 1968, Series 4, Box 22, NACCD Records; Wilson Memorandum to Charles E. Nelson (interview with Karl Gregory), n.d., (interview with Stewart House and Norvel [sic] Harrington), n.d., Series 59, Box 2, ibid.; Gregory to Fine, July 29, 1985; *Los Angeles Times*, July 24, 1967, DRSB No. 1; *MC*, Aug. 12, 1967; Howison debriefing, Kelman Papers; [Caplan] interview with window breaker, p. 6; *NACCD Report*, p. 50; Tinker, *When the Fire Reaches Us* (New York: William Morrow and Co., 1970), pp. 192–93.

29. *NACCD Report*, p. 173; Robert Shogan and Tom Craig, *The Detroit Race Riot* (Philadelphia: Chilton Books, 1964), pp. 42–43.

30. Edwards, *Urban Frontier*, p. 62; *DN*, Aug. 1, 3, 4, 17, 1967; Wilson

Memorandum to Nelson (Gregory interview), n.d., Series 59, Box 2, NACCD Records; *NACCD Report*, pp. 50, 267.

31. *DN*, July 24, 1967; *DFP*, Aug. 6, 1967; Official Transcript, Aug. 15, 1967, p. 540, Series 1, Box 2, NACCD Records.

32. *DN*, July 24, Aug. 1, 4, 1967; *DFP*, Aug. 6, 1967; Potts interview, pp. 9-10; Interview with Damon Keith, June 2, 1985, pp. 4-5, transcript in MHC; Locke, *Detroit Riot*, pp. 29-30; Freeman Report, Series III, Box 3, CCR Papers; ["Riot and Mob Control Manual"], July 1, 1966, DPD; Girardin interview, p. 405; Frank Angelo to Executive Committee, Aug. 2, 1967, Box 12, Frank Angelo Papers, MHC; Callewaert and Yim, "Police Department," pp. 29, 30, app. A, Box 407, JPC Papers. For Harlem, see Fred C. Shapiro and James W. Sullivan, *Race Riots: New York 1964* (New York: Thomas Y. Crowell Co., 1964), pp. 76, 80. For Philadelphia, see Leona Berson, *Case Study of a Riot: The Philadelphia Story* (New York: Institute of Human Relations, 1966), p. 80. For Watts, see Conot, *Rivers of Blood*, p. 193, and David O. Sears and John B. McConahay, *The Politics of Violence: The New Urban Blacks and the Watts Riot* (Boston: Houghton Mifflin Co., 1973), pp. 152-53. For Newark, see *NACCD Report*, pp. 33, 34.

33. *DN*, July 24, Aug. 1, 1967; *DFP*, July 24, Aug. 6, 1967; Freeman Report, Series III, Box 3, CCR Papers; *NACCD Report*, p. 50; Locke, *Detroit Riot*, pp. 30-31; Interview with Arthur Johnson, June 23, 1984, pp. 27-29, transcript in MHC; Girardin interview, p. 405; Conot interview with Conyers, n.d., Box 81, NACCD Records.

34. Locke, *Detroit Riot*, p. 31; Locke to Fine, Jan. 4, 1984; Johnson interview, p. 29; Fine phone conversation with Reuter, May 30, 1985; Nichols interview, pp. 22-23; Girardin interview, p. 406; Disorder Log, July 23, 1967, Box 4, Ray Girardin Papers, Burton Historical Collection, Detroit, Michigan; Edwards, *Urban Frontier*, p. 65; Reconnaissance Survey Reports, Detroit, 2:20, Series 10, Box 46, NACCD Records. Cavanagh claimed that Donley told Girardin that he was not referring to Detroit "politicians" but to the "whole national climate." *DN*, Aug. 4, 1967.

35. Locke, *Detroit Riot*, p. 31; Callewaert and Yim, "Police Department," app. A, Box 407, JPC Papers; Girardin to Cavanagh, Oct. 20, 1967, Commissioner's File; Detroit Disturbance, Chronology of Significant Events, July 23, 1967, Box 319, GR Papers; Complaint 20-762-67, Captain's Log, July 23, 1967, ibid.; Detroit Incident, ibid.; Official Transcript, Aug. 15, 1967, p. 419, Series 1, Box 2, NACCD Records.

36. Disturbance Chronology, July 23, 1967, Box 319, GR Papers; Detroit Incident, ibid.; Official Transcript, Sept. 12, 1967, p. 911, Series 1, Box 2, NACCD Records; *DN*, Sept. 28, 1967; *Riots, Civil and Criminal Disorders*, pt. 5:1217-18.

37. Callewaert and Yim, "Police Department," p. 34, app. A, Box 407, JPC Papers; Headquarters Command Post Activity Log, July 23, 1967, Box 4, Girardin Papers; Disturbance Chronology, July 23, 1967, Box 319, GR Papers; Chronological Sequence of Events, Detroit Civil Disturbance, July 23, 1967, ibid.; Transcript of [Romney] Press Conference, July 31, 1967, ibid.; Nichols interview, p. 36.

38. Gary T. Marx, "Civil Disorder and Agents of Social Control," *Journal of Social Issues* 26 (Winter 1970): 46; Roselle interview, p. 38; phone conversation

with George Edwards, June 19, 1985. For Watts, see Sears and McConahay, _Politics of Violence_, pp. 149-50; for Newark, see Governor's Select Commission on Civil Disorder . . . , _Report for Action_ (n.p., 1968), p. 143.

39. Nicholas interview with Roselle [1982], copy of tape in my possession; Oral History Interview of Jerome P. Cavanagh, Mar. 22, 1971, pp. 44-45, 49, LBJ Library; Interview with George Romney, July 24, 1984, pp. 1, 4, 31, transcript in MHC; Tom Nicholson, "Detroit's Surprising Mayor," _Harper's_ 227 (Dec. 1963): 82; Keith interview, p. 17.

40. _DN_, Aug. 27, Sept. 17, 22, Dec. 17, 1965; Cavanagh interview, p. 51; Interview with Cyrus Vance, Mar. 14, 1985, p. 28, transcript in MHC.

41. Nichols interview, pp. 21-22, 44; Girardin interview, p. 418; Garry Wills, _The Second Civil War_ (New York: New American Library, 1968), p. 50; _DFP_, July 24, 1967; Wilson Memorandum to Nelson (interview with Hubert Locke), Oct. 17, 19, 1967, Peter Rossi File, in my possession.

42. _DN_, July 24, 1967; _DFP_, Aug. 11, 1968; Van Gordon Sauter and Burleigh Hines, _Nightmare in Detroit_ (Chicago: Henry Regnery Co., 1968), p. 224; Bannon interview, pp. 16-18; Locke Statement [Sept. 22, 23, 1967], Box 28, ORA Papers; Official Transcript, Aug. 15, 1967, p. 467, Series 1, Box 2, NACCD Records; Anthony Ripley to Francis G. Little, Aug. 7, 1967, Box 394, JPC Papers.

43. On this point, see especially Marx, "Civil Disorder," pp. 37-38, 43-44.

44. Smelser, _Collective Behavior_, p. 262; Conant, _Prospects for Revolution_, pp. 37-38; _DFP_, July 30, 1967; _Time_ 90 (Aug. 4, 1967): 16; Boesel, "Ghetto Riots," p. 128. Cf. Feagin and Hahn, _Ghetto Revolts_, pp. 188-91.

45. Callewaert and Yim, "Police Department," app. A, Box 407, JPC Papers; Bannon interview, pp. 17-18; Interview with Richard Marks, Aug. 6, 1984, p. 27, transcript in MHC.

46. Girardin interview, p. 418; _Riots, Civil and Criminal Disorders_, pt. 6:1371, 1383; _DN_, Sept. 28, 1967; Jack Vandenberg to Romney, Aug. 29, 1967, Box 345, GR Papers; Schnipke to Richard Russell, Aug. 3, 1967, Box 29, Philip Hart Papers, MHC.

47. Nicholas interview with Mrs. Girardin [1982], copy of tape in my possession; Nichols interview, pp. 4-5; Marks interview, p. 21.

48. _DFP_, July 29, 30, 1967; _Newsweek_ 70 (Aug. 7, 1967): 19; _Police Manual_, 1962, chap. 14, sec. 25; Callewaert and Yim, "Police Department," p. 35, app. A, Box 407, JPC Papers; unidentified draft, n.d., Commissioner's File; Headquarters Command Post Activity Log, July 23, 1967, Box 4, Girardin Papers.

49. _DN_, July 26, Aug. 4, 1967, July 18, 1982; _DFP_, July 30, 1967; Del Rio Deposition, Series 32, Box 2, NACCD Records; Official Transcript, Aug. 15, 1967, pp. 469, 482, Series 1, Box 2, ibid.; Ursu Memorandum to Wilson (interview with Girardin), n.d., Series 59, Box 2, ibid.; Girardin to Cavanagh, Oct. 20, 1967, Commissioner's File; _Meet the Press_ 11 (July 30, 1967): 3; John Hersey, _The Algiers Motel Incident_ (New York: Alfred A. Knopf, 1968), p. 66; Locke, _Detroit Riot_, p. 71.

50. _DFP_, July 24, Aug. 11, 1967; James H. Lincoln, _The Anatomy of a Riot_ (New York: McGraw-Hill Book Co., 1968), pp. 14-15; _Newsweek_ 70 (Aug. 7, 1967): 19; Howison interview, p. 24; Deposition of Gene Goltz and William Serrin, Jan. 8, 1968, Series 32, Box 2, NACCD Records; Deposition of Carl Parsell, Jan. 10, 1968, ibid.; Wilson Memorandum to Nelson (interview with

Leon Atchison), n.d., Series 59, Box 2, ibid.; Reconnaissance Survey Reports, Detroit, 2:14, Series 10, Box 46, ibid.; Report of Bernard Dobranski to Robert Conot, n.d., Box 77, ibid.; Conot, *Rivers of Blood*, p. 242; Governor's Select Commission, *Report for Action*, p. 133.

51. *MC*, July 24, 1982; Nicholas interview with Ron Hewitt [1982], copy of tape in my possession; James Trainor tape, July 23, [1967], Box 393, JPC Papers; Cavanagh Press Conference [July 23, 1967], Box 398, ibid.; *Meet the Press* 11 (July 30, 1967): 2-3; Girardin to Cavanagh, Oct. 20, 1967, Commissioner's File; Girardin interview, pp. 404-5; Girardin, "After the Riots . . . ," *Saturday Evening Post* 240 (Sept. 3, 1967): 10; *DN*, Aug. 4, Sept. 21, 1967, Dec. 25, 1968; *DFP*, Aug. 11, 1968; Official Transcript, Aug. 15, 1967, pp. 467-68, 472-73, Series 1, Box 2, NACCD Records; Locke to Fine, Aug. 23, 1985; Minutes, Police and Public Safety Committee, Michigan Commission on Crime . . . , Aug. 16, 1967, Box 12, ORA Papers.

52. *NACCD Report*, pp. 176, 271; Turner, "Planning and Training," p. 28.

53. Disorder Log, July 23, 1967, Box 4, Girardin Papers; [DPD] *Statistical Report*, pp. 51-52; Callewaert and Yim, "Police Department," app. A, Box 407, JPC Papers; Girardin to Cavanagh, Oct. 20, 1967, Commissioner's File; Nichols interview, p. 14.

54. Girardin to Cavanagh, Oct. 20, 1967, Commissioner's File; Girardin interview, pp. 403-4; Nichols interview, pp. 14-15; *DFP*, Nov. 1, 1967; *DN*, Aug. 29, 1967; Locke to Fine, Aug. 23, 1985.

55. Bannon interview, pp. 20-23; Special Subcommittee of the House Committee on Armed Services to Inquire into the Capability of the National Guard to Cope with Civil Disturbances, *Hearings*, 90th Cong., 1st sess., 1967, p. 6077 (hereafter *Capability Hearings*); "Final Report of Cyrus R. Vance Concerning the Detroit Riots, July 23 through Aug. 2, 1967," p. 57, with Vance Oral History, Nov. 3, 1969, LBJ Library; Detroit Information: Grant Friley, n.d., Box 81, NACCD Records. See also Callewaert and Yim, "Police Department," p. 13, Box 407, JPC Papers; and *Riots, Civil and Criminal Disorders*, pt. 7:1511.

56. Arrests-Tenth Precinct-July 23, 1967, Commissioner's File; [DPD] *Statistical Report*, p. 11; *Riots, Civil and Criminal Disorders*, pt. 6:1383; Wilson Memorandum to Nelson (Locke interview), Oct. 17, 19, 1967, Rossi File; *DN*, July 24, 1967; *MC*, July 29, 1967.

57. *NYT*, July 25, 26, 28, 30, 1967; Parmenter, "Breakdown," p. 15; Deposition of Rita Griffin, Jan. 9, 1968, Series 32, Box 3, NACCD Records; Goltz and Serrin Deposition, Series 32, Box 2, ibid.; Del Rio Deposition, ibid.; Wilson Memoranda to Nelson (interview with Richard L. Simmons), n.d., (interview with Albert Boer), n.d., Series 59, Box 2, ibid.; Robert Shellow et al., "The Harvest of Racism," 1967, pp. 9-10, Series 7, Box 1, ibid.; [Caplan] interview with Arrestee, [Nov. 1967], p. 8, transcript in my possession; Lukas, "Postscript"; *Newsweek* 70 (Aug. 7, 1967): 26; *Time* 90 (Aug. 4, 1967): 14; *DN*, July 22, 1977; Boesel, "Ghetto Riots," p. 131; Charles Tilly, *From Mobilization to Revolution* (Reading, Mass.: Addison-Wesley Publishing Co., 1978), p. 100.

58. Nichols interview, pp. 36-37; Marks interview, pp. 26-27; Girardin interview, p. 414; *DFP*, July 24, Sept. 21, 1967; Coordinating Council on Human Relations, Executive Board Minutes, July 27, 1967, Series II, Box 6, CCR Papers; James Raschard and Tom Popp Memorandum to Wilson (interview with

Nicholas Hood), Oct. 12, 1967, Series 59, Box 2, NACCD Records; *MC*, July 29, Aug. 5, 1967.

59. *Christian Science Monitor*, July 26, 1967, DRSB No. 1; *NYT*, July 28, 1967; *DFP*, July 30, 1967; Raschard Memoranda to Wilson (interview with J. Thompson), n.d., (interview with Michael Ward), n.d., Rossi File; Wilson Memorandum to Nelson (Simmons interview), n.d., Series 59, Box 2, NACCD Records.

60. *NYT*, July 26, 1967; Questionnaires Nos. 6027, 6043, 6135, 6195, Boxes 11, 12, 13, A-W Riot Studies.

61. *DFP*, July 28, 1967; Harlan Hahn, "Cops and Rioters . . . ," *American Behavioral Scientist* 13 (May–Aug. 1970): 769; *The People Beyond 12th Street: A Survey of Attitudes of Detroit Negroes after the Riot of 1967* (Detroit: Detroit Urban League, 1967).

62. See, for example, *DN*, Aug. 4, 1967; and Trainor tape, July 27 [1967], Box 393, JPC Papers.

63. Capture and Record, Box 345, GR Papers; *DN*, Aug. 4, 1967.

64. *DFP*, July 28, 30, 1967; *DN*, Aug. 4, 1967; Goltz and Serrin Deposition, Series 32, Box 2, NACCD Records; Parsell Deposition, ibid.; Deposition of Justinas Bavarskis, Jan. 10, 1968, ibid.; Dobranski Report to Conot, n.d., Box 77, ibid.; Howison interview, pp. 46–47; Robert A. Mendelsohn, "The Police Interpretation of the Detroit Riot of 1967" [1968], p. 34, Box 30, ORA Papers; Ted Blizzard Riot Notes, undated, Box 345, GR Papers; Hersey, *Algiers Motel*, p. 63; *National Observer*, July 30, 1967, DRSB No. 1.

65. Hersey, *Algiers Motel*, pp. 73–75; Elliot D. Luby, Summary, in "Violence in the Model City" [1969], pp. 13–14, Box 378, JPC Papers; Conant, *Prospects for Revolution*, p. 36; Boesel, "Ghetto Riots," p. 142; Marx, "Civil Disorder," p. 49; Mendelsohn, "Police Interpretation," p. 34, Box 30, ORA Papers; Oates, *Them*, p. 489; Turner, "Planning and Training," pp. 24, 27.

66. Wilson Memorandum to Nelson, Part IV, undated, Rossi File; *Tuebor*, Sept. 1967, p. 16; Hersey, *Algiers Motel*, p. 69; Minutes of Police and Public Safety Committee, Aug. 16, 1967, Box 12, ORA Papers; Locke Statement [Sept. 22, 23, 1967], Box 28, ibid.; Campbell et al., *Law and Order Reconsidered*, pp. 310, 312; Dennis Wenger, "The Reluctant Army: The Functioning of Police Departments in Civil Disturbances," *American Behavioral Scientist* 16 (Jan.-Feb. 1973): 328–29, 338–40.

67. Capture and Record, Box 345, GR Papers; Detroit Information: Friley, n.d., Box 81, NACCD Records; Keith interview, p. 27; Romney interview, pp. 32–33.

68. Edwards, *Urban Frontier*, pp. 62, 65; *NACCD Report*, p. 267; Nichols interview, p. 45; *DN*, Sept. 13, 1967.

69. Callewaert and Yim, "Police Department," p. 13, Exhibit 11, app. A, Box 407, JPC Papers; Girardin to Common Council, Oct. 18, 1967, Box 570, ibid.; Girardin to Chester Loomis, Sept. 28, 1967, Commissioner's File; *DFP*, July 24, Sept. 15, Nov. 2, 1967, July 23, 1972; Wilson Memorandum to Nelson (Nichols interview), n.d., Series 59, Box 2, NACCD Records; Deposition of John Nichols, Jan. 10, 1968, Series 32, Box 2, ibid.; Sequence of Events, July 25, 1967, Box 345, GR Papers.

70. Girardin to Common Council, Sept. 22, 1967, Box 342, JPC Papers; Girardin to Common Council, Oct. 18, 1967, Box 570, ibid.; Callewaert and

Yim, "Police Department," Exhibit A, Box 407, ibid.; Girardin to Robert Griffin, Aug. 8, 1967, Commissioner's File; Girardin, "After the Riots," p. 10; *DFP*, Sept. 12, 1967.

71. *MC*, July 29, 1967; Hewitt interview; *DN*, July 24, 1967; "Vance Report," p. 52; Tracy L. Clark to Commanding General, July 31, 1967, Box 1, [Paul J. Scheips] Civil Disturbance File, Task Force Detroit, Center of Military History, Washington, D.C.; Wilson Memorandum to Nelson (interview with Charles Brown), n.d., Series 59, Box 2, NACCD Records; Frank H. Joyce, "American Dream Plagues Detroit," *National Guardian* 19 (Aug. 5, 1967): 5. See chap. 5 for the black reaction to black police.

72. Callewaert and Yim, "Police Department," app. A, Box 407, JPC Papers; *DFP*, July 23, 1972.

73. Detroit Information: Friley, Box 81, NACCD Records; "Black Cop," *Metropolitan Detroit* (Aug. 1987): 60, 61.

74. Campbell et al., *Law and Order Reconsidered*, p. 312; Callewaert and Yim, "Police Department," p. 59, app. A, Box 407, JPC Papers; Official Transcript, Aug. 15, 1967, pp. 548–49, Series 1, Box 2, NACCD Records; *Newsweek* 70 (Aug. 7, 1967): 19; *Riots, Civil and Criminal Disorders*, pt. 7:1568; Minutes, Police and Public Safety Committee, Oct. 18, 1967, Box 12, ORA Papers; Nichols interview, pp. 24–25.

75. *DFP*, July 24, 1967; *DN*, July 24, 1967; *MC*, July 29, 1967; Stanley Webb to George Roberts, July 24, 1967, Series 4, Box 22, NACCD Records; Webb Deposition, Jan. 11, 1968, Series 32, Box 2, ibid.; Conot interview of Conyers, n.d., Box 81, ibid.; Webb to Roger Wilkins, n.d., Detroit Riot File, Community Relations Service, Department of Justice, FOIA; Cavanagh Press Conference [July 23, 1967], Box 398, JPC Papers; Colding interview; Nicholas interview with Susan Watson [1982], p. 16, transcript in Nicholas's possession; Conrad Komrowski, "The Detroit Ghetto Uprising," *Political Affairs* 46 (Sept. 1967): 15–16; Robert Conot, *American Odyssey* (New York: William Morrow and Co., 1974), p. 535.

76. Keith interview, pp. 11–13; Johnson interview, pp. 32–33.

77. Philip J. Rutledge to Richard Strichartz, Aug. 8, 1967, Box 533, JPC Papers; Responses to the Recent Civil Disorders in Detroit by the MCHRD, n.d., Center for Urban Studies Papers (unprocessed), ALHUA; Official Transcript, Aug. 15, 1967, pp. 545–46, Series 1, Box 2, NACCD Papers.

78. Subcommittee on Education of the Senate Committee on Education and Public Welfare, *Hearings*, 90th Cong., 1st sess., 1967, pt. 4:1453; Special Meeting of NSO Board of Directors, Aug. 14, 1967, Box 532, JPC Papers; *MC*, July 23, 1977; YMCA of Metropolitan Detroit, "Urban Youth Program at Work," Aug. 2, 1967, Box 64, Richard Austin Papers, ALHUA; *DN*, July 24, 25, 1967; Robert E. Smith, "How the News Media Covered the Negro Rioting and Why," Oct. 1967, Series II, Box 6, NACCD Records; Albert B. Cleage, Jr., *The Black Messiah* (New York: Sheed and Ward, 1968), p. 121; Wills, *Civil War*, p. 118.

79. Keith interview, p. 3; *DN*, July 24, 1967; Bill Axtell, *Seven Days in July, July 23–29, 1967* (Detroit, 1968), Box 394, JPC Papers; Singer et al., *Black Rioters*, pp. 41–42; Angelo to Executive Committee, Aug. 2, 1967, Box 12, Angelo Papers; Angelo, "The Detroit Experience—I," *Seminar* (Sept. 1968): 10, Box 11, ibid.; American Newspaper Publishers Association, *Reporting the Detroit Riot* (New York [1968]), pp. 3, 4.

80. Levy, "Communication Processes," pp. 3-5; *MC*, July 29, 1967; News Media Seminar, Television, Nov. 11, 1967, Series 12, Box 1, NACCD Records; *People Beyond 12th Street.*

81. Mrs. Lawrence Terbrueggen to Romney, Aug. 2, 1967, Box 344, GR Papers.

82. Callewaert and Yim, "Police Department," app. A, Box 407, JPC Papers; Girardin interview, pp. 417-18; *MC*, July 24, 1982.

83. *DFP*, July 24, 1967; *NYT*, July 24, 1967; Webb to Wilkins, Detroit Riot File, Community Relations Service, FOIA; Sauter and Hines, *Nightmare*, p. 32; Locke, *Detroit Riot*, pp. 33-34.

84. Headquarters Command Post Activity Log, July 23, 1967, Box 4, Girardin Papers; Callewaert and Yim, "Police Department," app. A, Box 407, JPC Papers.

85. Callewaert and Yim, "Police Department," p. 27, Box 407, JPC Papers; "Vance Report," app. C.

86. *DFP*, July 24, Aug. 6, 1967; *DN*, July 24, 30, 1967; To Director from Detroit, July 23, 1967, 6:30 P.M., FBI-FOIA; FBI Confidential Report, July 24, 1967, Box 32, NACCD Records; *Christian Science Monitor*, July 26, 1967, DRSB No. 1; Disorder Log, July 23, 1967, Box 4, Girardin Papers; Freeman Report, Series III, Box 3, CCR Papers; Sauter and Hines, *Nightmare*, pp. 6-7; Henry Slayton, "The Voice of the 'Grass Roots,' Message from the Ghetto," in Detroit Riot File, Community Relations Service, FOIA.

87. Weiseger Memorandum to Francis Kornegay, Aug. 7, 1967, Box 12, DUL Papers. See also Locke, *Detroit Riot*, p. 127.

88. *NACCD Report*, pp. 51-52; Quinlan to Mayor's Development Team, Aug. 11, 1967, Box 533, JPC Papers; *Riots, Civil and Criminal Disorders*, pt. 7:1493; *DN*, Aug. 11, 1967.

89. Quinlan to Mayor's Development Team, Aug. 11, 1967, Box 533, JPC Papers.

90. *DN*, July 24, 1967; *DFP*, July 24, 1967; Josephine Gomon to Kids, July 25, 1967, Box 8, Josephine Gomon Papers, MHC; Detroit Fire Department, Civil Disturbance, A Partial Report [Feb. 1968], Box 5, Girardin Papers; *NACCD Report*, p. 52.

91. [DPD] *Statistical Report*, p. 12; Chronological Index, Civil Disturbance, July 1967, Reported to the Homicide Bureau, Box 79, NACCD Records; *DFP*, July 24, 1967; Alexander J. Walt et al., "The Anatomy of a Civil Disturbance," *JAMA* 202 (Oct. 30, 1967): 395.

92. Sauter and Hines, *Nightmare*, pp. 15-21; *NACCD Report*, p. 53; *DFP*, Aug. 17, 1967; People of Michigan vs. Darryl McCurtis, No. 139885, Detroit Recorder's Court; Homicide File No. 7186, Aug. 16, 1967, Box 79, NACCD Records.

93. Sauter and Hines, *Nightmare*, pp. 22-26, 29-32; Albert J. Schwaller to Chief of Detectives, Oct. 26, 1967, Exhibit 67, Case No. 55-15-X, Records of the United States Senate, RG 46, NARA.

94. Trainor tape, July 23 [1967], Box 393, JPC Papers; Callewaert and Yim, "Police Department," app. A, Box 407, ibid.; Quinlan to Mayor's Development Team, Aug. 11, 1967, Box 583, ibid.; Locke, *Detroit Riot*, p. 33.

95. Complaint 20-762-67, Captain's Log, July 23, 1967, Box 319, GR Papers; Detroit Incident, ibid.; Executive Order No. 1967-3, Amended, July 24, 1967,

Box 281, ibid.; *DFP*, July 24, 1967; *DN*, Nov. 5, 1967; Locke, *Detroit Riot*, p. 34.

96. Complaint 20-762-67, Captain's Log, July 23, 1967, Box 319, GR Papers; Detroit Incident, ibid.; Davids to Romney, Mar. 12, 1968, ibid.; Additional Complaint Report, July 23, 1967, SP 20-762-67, State Police Records, Department of State Police, Lansing, Michigan; Complaint Report, Aug. 1, 1967, Dennis H. Payne, ibid.

97. Remarks Prepared by . . . Romney, Sept. 12, 1967, Box 346, GR Papers; *Riots, Civil and Criminal Disorders*, pt. 7:1503-4; John K. Mahon, *History of the Militia and the National Guard* (New York: Macmillan Co., 1983), p. 234.

98. Chronological Sequence, July 23, 1967, Box 319, GR Papers; Walt DeVries to Romney et al., Aug. 24, 1965, ibid.; Official Transcript, Aug. 15, 1967, pp. 473-74, Series 1, Box 2, NACCD Records; Wills, *Civil War*, p. 51.

99. Schnipke to Russell, Aug. 3, 1967, Box 29, Hart Papers; *Capability Hearings*, p. 5687.

100. Complaint 20-762-67, Captain's Log, July 23, 1967, Box 319, GR Papers; Chronological Sequence, July 23, 1967, ibid.; Winston Wessels Field Notes, July 23, 1967, Winston Wessels Papers (copy in my possession); Locke, *Detroit Riot*, p. 32; Callewaert and Yim, "Police Department," pp. 38-39, Box 407, JPC Papers; Girardin to Common Council, Sept. 22, 1967, Box 342, ibid.; Wills, *Civil War*, pp. 52-53; Howard Dryden, "National Guard Association of Michigan," n.d., Box 7, Records of the Michigan Department of Military Affairs— Public Information, RG 77-45, State Archives, Lansing, Michigan; Official Transcript, Sept. 12, 1967, pp. 909-10, Series 1, Box 2, NACCD Records; *Riots, Civil and Criminal Disorders*, pt. 7:1504; Girardin interview, p. 419; *Capability Hearings*, p. 6035.

101. Simmons Memorandum for Governor, Aug. 3, 1967, Box 319, GR Papers; Statement by . . . Romney, July 23, 1967, Box 232, ibid.; *Capability Hearings*, p. 5805; Popp Memorandum to Wilson (interview with Cecil Simmons), n.d., Series 59, Box 2, NACCD Records; Official Transcript, Sept. 12, 1967, pp. 913-14, Series 1, Box 2, ibid.

102. *DFP*, July 24, 1967; *DN*, July 24, 1967; Callewaert and Yim, "Police Department," app. A, Box 407, JPC Papers.

Chapter 8

1. [DPD] *Statistical Report on the Disorder Occurring in the City of Detroit, July 1967*, p. 32.

2. Ibid., p. 51; *NYT*, July 25, 1967; Albert Callewaert and Arthur Yim, "The Detroit Police Department and the Detroit Civil Disorder," Dec. 1967, app. A, Box 407, JPC Papers; Robert Conot, *American Odyssey* (New York: William Morrow and Co., 1974), p. 536; Hubert G. Locke, *The Detroit Riot of 1967* (Detroit: Wayne State University Press, 1969), p. 35; Detroit Incident, Col. Davids, GR Papers, Box 319; Sequence of Events, July 24, 1967, Box 345, ibid.

3. To Director from Detroit, July 24, 1967, 1:13 A.M., 9:48 P.M., FBI-FOIA; Robert C. Cassibry Memorandum for the Record, July 24, 1967, Box 4, Office Files of James Gaither, LBJ Library; For General [Harold K.] Johnson from [Lawrence] Levinson, July 24, 1967, Box 26, HU2/ST22, ibid.; Headquarters Command Post Activity Log, Box 4, Ray Girardin Papers, Burton Historical

Collection, Detroit, Michigan; *DFP*, July 25, 1967; *DN*, July 24, 1967; James Trainor tape, July 24 [1967], Box 393, JPC Papers; Callewaert and Yim, "Police Department," app. A, Box 407, ibid.; Deposition of Gene Goltz and William Serrin, Jan. 8, 1968, Series 32, Box 2, NACCD Records.

4. Callewaert and Yim, "Police Department," app. A, Box 407, JPC Papers; To Director from Detroit, July 24, 1967, 1:37 P.M., FBI-FOIA; *DFP*, July 25, 1967; Capture and Record of Civil Disorder in Detroit, July 23–July 28, 1967, Box 345, GR Papers.

5. Callewaert and Yim, "Police Department," app. A, Box 407, JPC Papers; To Director from Detroit, July 24, 1967, 9:20 P.M., 11:34 P.M., FBI-FOIA; *DFP*, July 25, 1967; *DN*, July 25, 1967; *NYT*, July 25, 1967; Sequence of Events, July 24, 1967, Box 345, GR Papers; Locke, *Detroit Riot*, pp. 40–41. The higher Locke figures for the number of police and fire facilities under attack involved some duplication.

6. *DFP*, July 23, 1972; *DN*, July 22, 1977; Capture and Record, Box 345, GR Papers.

7. To Director from Detroit, July 24, 1967, 11:34 P.M., FBI-FOIA; FBI Confidential Report, July 25, 1967, Box 32, NACCD Records; *DN*, July 25, 1967.

8. David Paul Boesel, "The Ghetto Riots 1964–1968" (Ph.D. diss., Cornell University, 1972), pp. 141–42, 145–47; Louis Goldberg, "Ghetto Riots and Others," in David Boesel and Peter H. Rossi, eds., *Cities under Siege: An Anatomy of Ghetto Riots, 1964–1968* (New York: Basic Books, 1971), p. 137; Joe R. Feagin and Harlan Hahn, *Ghetto Revolts* (New York: Macmillan Co., 1973), pp. 178–79, 191–92; Elliot D. Luby, Summary, in "Violence in the Model City: A Social Psychological Study of the Detroit Riot of 1967" [1969], pp. 13–14, Box 378, JPC Papers; Robert A. Mendelsohn, "The Police Interpretation of the Detroit Riot of 1967" [1968], pp. 34, 72, Box 30, ORA Papers; Herman Wilson memorandum to Charles E. Nelson (interview with Charles Brown), n.d., Series 59, Box 2, NACCD Records; Gary T. Marx, "Civil Disorder and the Agents of Social Control," *Journal of Social Issues* 26 (Winter 1970): 31, 42, 49, 51–52; Marx, "Two Cheers for the Riot Commission Report," *Harvard Review* 4 (Second Quarter 1968): 5.

9. *NYT*, July 25, 1967; *DFP*, July 24, 1977; Stanley Webb to Roger Wilkins, n.d., and enclosed report, Detroit Riot File, Community Relations Service, Department of Justice, FOIA; Robert Shellow et al., "The Harvest of American Racism," Nov. 1967, pp. 13–14, Series 7, Box 1, NACCD Records; Mendelsohn, "Police Interpretation," pp. 73, 81, Box 30, ORA Papers; Marx, "Civil Disorder," p. 49; Interview with Arthur Howison, July 24, 1984, p. 28, transcript in MHC.

10. Mendelsohn, "Police Interpretation," pp. 71–78, Box 30, ORA Papers; Luby, "Police and Jail Treatment of Detroit Negro Riot Arrestees" [1968], Box 427, JPC Papers; Goltz and Serrin Deposition, Series 32, Box 2, NACCD Records; *Ann Arbor News*, July 29, 1967.

11. Mendelsohn, "Police Interpretation," pp. 9, 11, 13, 19–20, 62, 65–66, Box 30, ORA Papers; Peter H. Rossi et al., "Between White and Black: The Faces of American Institutions in the Ghetto," in *Supplemental Studies for the National Advisory Commission on Civil Disorders* (Washington: GPO, 1968), p. 111.

12. Maurice Kelman and Ed Batchelor interview with Ray Girardin, Oct. 29,

1971, pp. 414–15, transcript in my possession; Detroit Information: Grant Friley, n.d., Box 81, NACCD Records.

13. Mendelsohn, "Police Interpretation," p. 80, Box 30, ORA Papers.

14. Paul Lowinger and Frida Huige, "The National Guard in the 1967 Detroit Uprisings" [1969], pp. 7, 10–11, 13, University of Michigan Law School Library, Ann Arbor, Michigan; *NYT*, Aug. 11, 1967; *DFP*, July 23, Aug. 11, 1967; *DN*, Aug. 22, 1967; Van Gordon Sauter and Burleigh Hines, *Nightmare in Detroit* (Chicago: Henry Regnery Co., 1968), p. 229. See also Goltz and Serrin Deposition, Series 32, Box 2, NACCD Records; and Special Subcommittee of the House Committee on Armed Services to Inquire into the Capability of the National Guard to Cope with Civil Disturbances, *Hearings*, 90th Cong., 1st sess., 1967, p. 5870 (hereafter *Capability Hearings*).

15. *DFP*, July 28, 30, 31, 1967; Address by Ralph E. Haines, Sept. 19, 1967, (Paul J. Scheips) Civil Disturbance File, Task Force Detroit, Center of Military History, Washington, D.C.; NACCD, Transcript of Proceedings, Aug. 11, 1967, pp. 248–56, Series 1, Box 1, NACCD Records; *Capability Hearings*, p. 5968, app. 2, p. 6287; Permanent Subcommittee on Investigations of the Senate Committee on Government Operations, *Riots, Civil and Criminal Disorders, Hearings*, 90th Cong., 2d sess., 1968, pt. 7:1505; House Committee on Armed Services, Special Subcommittee to Inquire into the Capability of the National Guard . . . , *Report*, 90th Cong., 1st sess., no. 36, 1967, p. 5655; James Richard Gardner, "The Civil Disturbance Mission of the Department of the Army, 1963–1973 . . ." (Ph.D. diss., Princeton University, 1977), p. 86; James F. Cantwell to Stanley R. Resor, July 28, 1967, Box 77, Accession 71A3073, Records of the Office of the Secretary of the Army, RG 335, Adjutant General's Office, Alexandria, Virginia; Richard Davis to Commanding General, XVIII Airborne Corps, Aug. 7, 1967, in "After Action Report," Task Force Detroit, 24 July–2 August 1967, D-3, Box 1, Records of the Michigan Department of Military Affairs, Adjutant General Division, RG 78-125, State Archives, Lansing, Michigan; Sauter and Hines, *Nightmare*, pp. 59, 226; Lowinger and Huige, "National Guard," p. 8; Conot, *Odyssey*, p. 538.

16. *DFP*, July 23, 1967; Sauter and Hines, *Nightmare*, pp. 227, 228; *Capability Hearings*, pp. 5915, 5970, 6129–31.

17. *Capability Hearings*, pp. 5915, 5965, 5967, 5971–72, 6031, 6044; Winston Wessels Field Notes, July 30, 1967, Winston Wessels Papers (copy in my possession); Davis to Commanding General, Aug. 7, 1967, in "After Action Report," D-5, Box 1, RG 78-125.

18. Sauter and Hines, *Nightmare*, pp. 225, 228; *Capability Hearings*, pp. 5970, 6122–24; Lowinger and Huige, "National Guard," p. 9.

19. *Capability Hearings*, pp. 5969, 5917–18, 5920, 6051, 6077; *DN*, Aug. 19, 1967; Davis to Commanding General, Aug. 7, 1967, D-3, 4, 5, Box 1, RG 78-125; Sauter and Hines, *Nightmare*, p. 225; Lowinger and Huige, "National Guard," p. 9; John Alfred Berendt, "From the Wonderful Men Who Gave You Kent State," *Esquire* 75 (Apr. 1971): 46; [Doar] "Lessons Learned," Box 15, Warren Christopher Papers, LBJ Library.

20. *Report of the National Advisory Commission on Civil Disorders* (Washington: GPO, 1968), p. 54; *Capability Hearings*, pp. 6031, 6041; Official Transcript of Proceedings before the NACCD, Aug. 15, 1967, pp. 474, 550, Sept. 12, 1967, pp. 909, 927, Series 1, Box 2, NACCD Records; Tom Popp Memorandum

for Wilson (interview with Cecil Simmons), n.d., Series 59, Box 2, ibid.; Howard M. Dryden, "National Guard Association of Michigan," n.d., Box 3, Records of Michigan Department of Military Affairs—Public Information, RG 77-45, State Archives; Conot, *Odyssey*, p. 538; Xavier Nicholas interview with Jon Lowell, 1982, pp. 13–14, transcript in Nicholas's possession; *Christian Science Monitor*, July 27, 1967, DRSB No. 1; Garry Wills, *The Second Civil War* (New York: New American Library, 1968), p. 50; John Hersey, *The Algiers Motel Incident* (New York: Alfred A. Knopf, 1968), p. 159; Tracy L. Clark to Commanding General, July 31, 1967, Civil Disturbance File, Task Force Detroit; *Riots, Civil and Criminal Disorders*, pt. 7:1504–5; Roger Wilkins, *A Man's Life* (New York: Simon and Schuster, 1982), p. 198.

21. *DN*, Aug. 24, 1967; Dryden, "National Guard," Box 3, RG 77-45; DA to JCS, July 29, 1967, Civil Disturbance File, Task Force Detroit; *DFP*, July 30, 1967; *Newsweek* 70 (Aug. 7, 1967): 20; Wills, *Civil War*, p. 52; Goltz and Serrin Deposition, Series 32, Box 2, NACCD Records; Deposition of Saul Friedman, Jan. 19, 1968, ibid.; Official Transcript, Aug. 15, 1967, pp. 474, 552, Series 1, Box 2, ibid.; Lowell interview, p. 15; *Christian Science Monitor*, July 27, 1967, clipping in Box 345, GR Papers; *Time* 90 (Aug. 4, 1967): 16; Oral History Interview of Jerome P. Cavanagh, Mar. 22, 1971, p. 51, LBJ Library; Frank Angelo, "Riot Coverage," n.d., Box 12, Frank Angelo Papers, MHC; *Capability Hearings*, pp. 5877, 5970; Conot, *Odyssey*, pp. 538–39; Bob Clark, "Nightmare Journey," *Ebony* 22 (Oct. 1967): 124; To Director from Detroit, July 24, 1967, 12:55 A.M.–11:31 P.M., FBI-FOIA; Paul J. Scheips phone conversation with Alexander Bolling, Apr. 30, 1967, Civil Disturbance File, Task Force Detroit; Scheips phone conversation with Charles P. Stone, May 1, 1979, ibid. Cf. Scheips phone conversation with John Throckmorton, Aug. 27, 1979, ibid.

22. Headquarters Command Post Activity Log, July 24, 1967, Box 4, Girardin Papers; Sequence of Events, July 24, 1967, Box 345, GR Papers; Levinson for Johnson, July [24], 1967, Box 26, HU2/ST22; DA/Sit Rep 1/25/0600, Box 4, Accession 71A1, RG 335; Cassibry Memorandum, July 24, 1967, Box 44, Gaither Files; Callewaert and Yim, "Police Department," app. A, Box 407, JPC Papers; Charles J. Quinlan to Mayor's Development Team (MDT), Aug. 11, 1967, Box 533, ibid.; Davis to Commanding General, Aug. 7, 1967, in "After Action Report," D-5, Box 1, RG 78-125; *Capability Hearings*, p. 5960; *DN*, July 25, 1967; Official Transcript, Aug. 15, 1967, p. 536, Series 1, Box 2, NACCD Records.

23. [DPD] *Statistical Report*, pp. 22, 23, 32, 53; *DFP*, July 30, 1967.

24. Callewaert and Yim, "Police Department," app. A, Box 407, JPC Papers; *DN*, July 25, 1967; *DFP*, July 25, 1967; *NYT*, July 25, 1967; Sequence of Events, July 24, 1967, Box 345, GR Papers.

25. Official Transcript, Aug. 15, 1967, pp. 532–35, Series 1, Box 2, NACCD Records; *DN*, July 25, 1967; *DFP*, July 25, 1967; *Riots, Civil and Criminal Disorders*, pt. 5:1262–64; Sauter and Hines, *Nightmare*, p. 59; Daniel C. Myre to Frederick Davids, Aug. 7, 1967, SP 20-762-67, State Police Records, Department of State Police, Lansing, Michigan; Quinlan to MDT, Aug. 11, 1967, Box 533, JPC Papers; Joe Lapointe, "Six Days in July," *Detroit Monthly*, July 1987, p. 65; Detroit Fire Department, Civil Disturbance, July 1967, A Partial Report, Feb. 1968, Box 5, Girardin Papers.

26. Clark, "Nightmare Journey," p. 24.

27. [DPD] *Statistical Report*, p. 13.

28. Sauter and Hines, *Nightmare*, pp. 47–52, 73–94, 104–12, 182–84; Albert Schwaller to Chief of Detectives, Oct. 26, 1967, Exhibit No. 67, Case No. 55-15-X, Records of the United States Senate, RG 46, NARA; Chronological Index, Civil Disorder, July 1967, Box 79, NACCD Records; Homicide File No. 7187, Aug. 3, 1967, ibid.; *DFP*, Aug. 25, 1967, July 24, 1977; John Doar Memorandum for Attorney General, Sept. 28, 1967, Box 29, Ramsey Clark Papers, LBJ Library. There are discrepancies in the various accounts of riot-related deaths.

29. Sauter and Hines, *Nightmare*, pp. 35–40, 52–58, 65–73; Schwaller to Chief of Detectives, Oct. 26, 1967, Case No. 55-15-X, RG 46.

30. Norton Cohen to William Cahalan, Aug. 14, 1967, Box 12, American Civil Liberties Union–Metropolitan Detroit Branch Papers (July 23, 1971), ALHUA; Bernard Dobranski Memorandum to Wilson (interview with William Cahalan), Oct. 12, 1967, Series 59, Box 2, NACCD Records; Homicide File No. 7153, Aug. 3, 1967, Box 79, ibid.

31. Sauter and Hines, *Nightmare*, pp. 94–98; Homicide File No. 7170, July 31, 1967, Box 79, NACCD Records; People of Michigan vs. Richard Paul Shugar, A139609, Preliminary Examination, Aug. 29, 1967, Detroit Recorder's Court, Detroit, Michigan; *DN*, Jan. 29, 1969.

32. *DFP*, July 25, 1967; *DN*, July 25, 1967.

33. *DFP*, July 25, 1967.

34. Ibid.; *DN*, July 25, 1967; Webb to Wilkins, n.d., and enclosed report, Detroit Riot File, Community Relations Service, FOIA; Charles S. Brown to ———, n.d., Series 45, Box 15, NACCD Records.

35. *DN*, July 25, 1967; text of statement [July 24, 1967], Box 393, JPC Papers.

36. "Detroit Riot – July 23, 1967," Box 232, GR Papers; Transcript of [Romney] Press Conference, July 31, 1967, Box 319, ibid.; Official Transcript, Sept. 12, 1967, pp. 914–15, Series 1, Box 2, NACCD Records.

37. Detroit Disturbance, Chronology of Significant Events, July 24, 1967, Box 319, GR Papers; Transcript of Press Conference, July 31, 1967, ibid.; Cavanagh interview, p. 46; Interview of George Romney, July 24, 1984, pp. 1–2, 12, transcript in MHC; Sauter and Hines, *Nightmare*, p. 35; Memo for the Record from the Vice President, July 24, 1967, Box 15, Christopher Papers; Ramsey Clark Statement, Sept. 12, 1967, Box 11, Office Files of Joseph Califano, ibid.

38. See chap. 1.

39. "Riot Control and the Use of Federal Troops," *Harvard Law Review* 81 (Jan. 1982): 638–46; Robert Griffin, "The Role of the President in Civil Disorder," Aug. 4, 1967, Box 232, GR Papers; Attorney General to Romney, Aug. 5, 1967, Box 346, ibid.; *Capability Hearings*, p. 5813; Statement of Martin F. Richman, Aug. 15, 1967, Office of Legal Counsel, Department of Justice, FOIA; Richman to Sol Lindenbaum [Aug. 8, 1967], ibid.; Oral History Interview of Warren Christopher, Oct. 31, 1968, pp. 1–2, LBJ Library; Interview with Ramsey Clark, Mar. 4, 1984, p. 1, transcript in MHC.

40. Telephone Calls of Attorney General, July 24 [1967], Box 58, Califano Files; The Detroit Riots Chronology, Box 43, Gaither Files, ibid.; Press Conference of Ramsey Clark, Aug. 1, 1967, Box 44, ibid.; Oral History Interview of Ramsey Clark, Apr. 16, 1969, pp. 7–8, ibid.; Clark interview (1984), pp. 5–6; Disturbance Chronology, July 24, 1967, Box 319, GR Papers; Transcript of Press

Conference, July 31, 1967, ibid.; Trainor tape, July 24 [1967], Box 393, JPC Papers; *DN*, Aug. 4, 1967; "After Action Report," p. 2, Box 1, RG 78-125.

41. Disturbance Chronology, July 24, 1967, Box 319, GR Papers; transcript of Romney-Cavanagh press conference, July 24, 1967, ibid.; Transcript of Press Conference, July 31, 1967, ibid.; Trainor tape, July 24 [1967], Box 393, JPC Papers; Attorney General Calls, July 24 [1967], Box 58, Califano Files; *DFP*, July 30, 1967; *DN*, Aug. 4, 1967; Clark interview (1984), p. 6; Cavanagh interview, p. 46.

42. Resor-Clark telephone transcripts, July 24, 1967, Box 58, Califano Files; Attorney General Calls, July 24 [1967], ibid.; Information Brief No. 1, Army Operations Center, July 24, 1967 (0930), Box 44, Gaither Files; Clark Press Conference, Aug. 1, 1967, ibid.; Trainor tape, July 24 [1967], Box 393, JPC Papers; transcript of press conference, July 24, 1967, Box 346, GR Papers; Transcript of Press Conference, July 31, 1967, Box 319, ibid.; Robert Danhof Log, July 24, 1967, ibid.; *NYT*, July 30, 1967; *DFP*, July 30, 1967.

43. Resor-Clark transcripts, July 24, 1967, Box 58, Califano Files; Attorney General Calls, July 24 [1967], ibid.; Trainor tape, July 24 [1967], Box 393, JPC Papers; Sequence of Events, July 24, 1967, Box 345, GR Papers.

44. Attorney General Calls, July 24 [1967], Box 58, Califano Files; Resor-Clark transcripts, ibid.; *Capability Hearings*, p. 6076; Official Transcript, Sept. 12, 1967, pp. 918-19, Series 1, Box 2, NACCD Records; Transcript of Press Conference, July 31, 1967, Box 319, GR Papers.

45. Danhof Log, July 24, 1967, Box 319, GR Papers; Transcript of Press Conference, July 31, 1967, ibid.; Romney to Clark, July 24, 1967, with Remarks . . . , Sept. 12, 1967, ibid.

46. Attorney General Calls, July 24 [1967], Box 58, Califano Files; Clark Press Conference, Aug. 1, 1967, Box 44, Gaither Files; draft of telegram [July 24, 1967], Box 232, GR Papers; Transcript of Press Conference, July 31, 1967, Box 319, ibid.; Sauter and Hines, *Nightmare*, p. 60; Conot, *Odyssey*, p. 537.

47. Disturbance Chronology, July 24, 1967, Box 319, GR Papers; Romney to Johnson, July 24, 1967, with Remarks . . . , Sept. 12, 1967, ibid.; Transcript of Press Conference, July 31, 1967, ibid.; Trainor tape, July 24 [1967], Box 393, JPC Papers; Detroit Riots Chronology, Box 43, Gaither Files; Attorney General Calls, July 24 [1967], Box 58, Califano Files.

48. See the polling data in White House Name File—Romney, Box 256, LBJ Library.

49. Attorney General Calls, July 24 [1967], Box 58, Califano Files.

50. Detroit Riots Chronology, Box 43, Gaither Files; handwritten notes [July 24, 1967], Box 44, ibid.; Clark Memorandum for President, July 24, 1967, Box 71, Appointment File [Diary Backup], LBJ Library; Wilkins, *Man's Life*, p. 195.

51. Handwritten notes [July 24, 1967], Box 44, Gaither Files; Detroit Riots Chronology, Box 43, ibid.; George Christian Memorandum for President, July 24, 1967, Box 71, Appointment File [Diary Backup], LBJ Library; Lyndon Baines Johnson Diary, July 24, 1967, microfilm copy in University of Michigan Library, Ann Arbor, Michigan; Wilkins, *Man's Life*, pp. 195-96; *Washington Post*, July 30, 1967; [Brooke E. Kleber] Chronology, Detroit Civil Disturbance, July 23-Aug. 2, 1967, Civil Disturbance File, Task Force Detroit.

52. Handwritten notes [July 24, 1967], Box 44, Gaither Files; [Kleber] Chro-

nology, Civil Disturbance File, Task Force Detroit; Christopher interview, p. 10; *DFP*, July 26, 1967; *NYT*, July 26, 1967; Sauter and Hines, *Nightmare*, p. 86; Interview with Cyrus Vance, Mar. 14, 1985, p. 4, transcript in MHC.

53. Lyndon Baines Johnson, *The Vantage Point: Perspectives on the Presidency, 1963-1969* (New York: Holt, Rinehart and Winston, 1971), p. 169; Oral History Interview of Edmund Gerald (Pat) Brown, Feb. 20, 1969, Aug. 19, 1970, p. 18, LBJ Library; Oral History Interview of Governor and Mrs. Richard Hughes, Aug. 6, 1969, p. 83, ibid.; Oral History Interview of Harry McPherson, Apr. 9, 1969, p. 19, ibid.; Paul J. Scheips and M. Warner Stark, "Use of Troops in Civil Disturbances since World War II," Supplement II (1967), p. 78. Johnson had also offered help to Acting Mayor Paul Screvane in the 1964 Harlem riot. Fred C. Shapiro and James W. Sullivan, *Race Riots: New York 1964* (New York: Thomas Y. Crowell Co., 1964), p. 182.

54. Detroit Riots Chronology, Box 43, Gaither Files; Tom Johnson Memorandum for President, July 24, 1967, Box 71, Appointment File [Diary Backup]; Christian Memorandum for President, July 24, 1967, ibid.; LBJ Diary, July 24, 1967; Johnson, *Vantage Point*, p. 169; *DFP*, July 30, 1967; Oral History Interview of Albert Fitt, Oct. 25, 29, 1968, p. 24, LBJ Library; McPherson interview, p. 20; Clark interview (1984), pp. 13-15.

55. Oral History Interview of Cyrus Vance, Nov. 3, 1969, pp. 30-31, LBJ Library; "Final Report of Cyrus Vance . . . Concerning the Detroit Riots, July 23 through August 2, 1967," pp. 7-8, with ibid.; Vance interview (1985), pp. 1-4; Christopher interview, p. 10; Johnson Diary, July 24, 1967.

56. Johnson to Romney, July 24, 1967, Box 232, GR Papers; Detroit Riots Chronology, Box 43, Gaither Files; handwritten notes [July 24, 1967], Box 44, ibid.; Attorney General Calls, July 24 [1967], Box 58, Califano Files.

57. "Vance Report," pp. 8-9; Vance interview (1969), p. 33; Detroit Riots Chronology, Box 43, Gaither Files; Attorney General Calls, July 24 [1967], Box 58, Califano Files; Chronology of Events, July 24, 1200 Hours to July 25, 0900 Hours, Box 15, Christopher Papers; DA/SITREP/1/25 0600, Civil Disturbance File, Task Force Detroit.

58. Fitt interview, p. 25; July 24, 1967, card, Box 345, GR Papers; Transcript of Press Conference, July 31, 1967, Box 319, ibid.; Disturbance Chronology, July 24, 1967, ibid.; "Vance Report," pp. 10, 14; Vance interview (1969), pp. 33-34; Throckmorton, "After Action Report," p. 3, Box 1, RG 78-125; Johnson Memorandum for President, July 29, 1967, Box 72, Appointment File [Diary Backup]; Califano to President, Sept. 12, 1967, and enclosed Clark Statement, Box 11, Califano Files; Christopher interview, p. 12; Clark interview (1969), p. 13; Detroit Riots Chronology, Box 43, Gaither Files; Official Transcript, Aug. 15, 1967, pp. 555-56, Sept. 12, 1967, pp. 883-84, 925-26, Series 1, Box 2, NACCD Records; Department of the Army, Office of the Adjutant General, Operations Report, Lessons Learned Report 5-67, Civil Disorder Task Force Detroit, Sept. 28, 1967, p. 4, microfiche copy in my possession; Wilkins, *Man's Life*, p. 196. The estimates of the number of Guardsmen in reserve range from 1,900 to 3,000. Cf. "Vance Report," pp. 13-14, and Cassibry Memorandum for the Record, July 24, 1967 (21:30), Box 44, Gaither Files.

59. "Vance Report," pp. 9-10; Transcript of Press Conference, July 31, 1967, Box 319, GR Papers; Throckmorton, "After Action Report," p. 3, Box 1, RG 78-

125; Chronology of Events, Box 15, Christopher Papers. Vance maintained that he used the words "insurrection or domestic violence." "Vance Report," p. 10.

60. "Vance Report," pp. 11–12; Throckmorton, "After Action Report," pp. 3, 4, Box 1, RG 78-125; Reconnaissance Survey Field Research Reports, Detroit, Michigan, 2:84, Series 10, Box 46, NACCD Records; Official Transcript, Sept. 12, 1967, p. 949, Series 1, Box 2, ibid.; Sequence of Events, July 24, 1967, Box 345, GR Papers; Transcript of Press Conference, July 31, 1967, Box 319, ibid.; Detroit Riots Chronology, Box 43, Gaither Files; Lessons Learned Report 5-67, p. 7; Sauter and Hines, *Nightmare*, p. 102; *DN*, May 18, 1967.

61. "Vance Report," p. 12, app. C; [DPD] *Statistical Report*, pp. 32, 53; John Nichols to Sidney Fine, Mar. 28, 1986; *DFP*, July 25, 1967; FBI Confidential Report, July 25, 1967, Box 32, NACCD Records.

62. [Doar] "Lessons Learned," n.d., Box 15, Christopher Papers; Vance interview (1985), p. 31.

63. J. Edgar Hoover to Clyde Tolson et al., July 25, 1967, FBI-FOIA; Detroit Riots Chronology, Box 43, Gaither Files.

64. "Vance Report," pp. 12–13; Vance et al., Press Conference transcript, July 29, 1967, Box 43, Gaither Files; Detroit Riots Chronology, ibid.; Locke, *Detroit Riot*, pp. 37–38; Disturbance Chronology, July 24, 1967, Box 319, GR Papers; Transcript of Press Conference, July 31, 1967, ibid.; Chronology of Events, Box 15, Christopher Papers; *DFP*, July 26, 1967; Sauter and Hines, *Nightmare*, pp. 103, 112–13; Vance to Keith, Aug. 4, 1967, Box 11, Records of the Michigan Civil Rights Commission, RG 74-90, State Archives.

65. "Vance Report," pp. 15–16; Disturbance Chronology, July 24, 1967, Box 319, GR Papers; Transcript of Press Conference, July 31, 1967, ibid.; Detroit Riots Chronology, Box 43, Gaither Files; *DN*, July 25, Aug. 4, 1967; Cavanagh interview, pp. 48–49.

66. Sauter and Hines, *Nightmare*, pp. 103–4; "Vance Report," p. 16; Trainor tape, July 25 [1967], Box 393, JPC Papers; Transcript of Press Conference, July 31, 1967, Box 319, GR Papers; Romney interview, pp. 20–21; Vance interview (1985), pp. 10–11.

67. "Vance Report," pp. 16–18; Vance interview (1969), pp. 35–37; Throckmorton, "After Action Report," p. 5, Box 1, RG 78-125; *NYT*, July 30, 1967. The number of incidents, according to the Police Incident Summary, rose from 108 between 7:00 and 8:00 P.M. to 147 between 8:00 and 9:00 P.M., 194 between 9:00 and 10:00 P.M., and 231 between 10:00 and 11:00 P.M. "Vance Report," app. C. The White House chronology placed Vance's call recommending deployment at "around 10:20 P.M." Detroit Riots Chronology, Box 43, Gaither Files.

68. Detroit Riots Chronology, Box 43, Gaither Files; Marvin [Watson] Memorandum for President, July 24, 1967, LG/D, LBJ Library; WPR [Reuther] Note, July 31, 1967, Box 369, Walter Reuther Papers, ALHUA; Johnson Memorandum for President, July 25, 1967, Box 71, Appointment File [Diary Backup]; Johnson Diary, July 24, 1967; Johnson, *Vantage Point*, p. 170.

69. Barefoot Sanders Memo for Watson, July 26, 1967, Box 26, HU2/ST22, LBJ Library; Oral History Interview of Clarence Diggs, Jr., Mar. 13, 1969, pp. 8–9, ibid.; *DN*, July 25, 1967.

70. Johnson Memorandum for President, July 25, 1967, Box 71, Appointment File [Diary Backup]; WPR Note, July 31, 1967, Box 369, Reuther Papers; Johnson, *Vantage Point*, p. 170; Hoover to Tolson et al., July 25, 1967, FBI-FOIA.

71. WPR Note, July 31, 1967, Box 369, Reuther Papers; Johnson Memorandum for President, July 25, 1967, Box 71, Appointment File [Diary Backup]; *NYT*, July 30, 1967; "Vance Report," p. 18; Detroit Riots Chronology, Box 43, Gaither Files; Johnson, *Vantage Point*, pp. 170–71.

72. Law and Order in the State of Michigan, July 24, 1967, Box 319, GR Papers; Executive Order, July 24, 1967, ibid.; "Vance Report," p. 18; Throckmorton, "After Action Report," p. 5, Box 1, RG 78-125; Johnson Memorandum for President, July 25, 1967, Box 71, Appointment File [Diary Backup]. The chronology the White House supplied the *NYT* had Vance making his recommendation at 10:30 P.M. and the president signing his proclamation at 10:31 P.M. *NYT*, July 30, 1967. See also Detroit Riots Chronology, Box 43, Gaither Files.

73. Detroit Riots Chronology, Box 43, Gaither Files; *Capability Hearings*, app. 2, pp. 6258, 6264.

74. Detroit Riots Chronology, Box 43, Gaither Files; Johnson Memorandum for President, July 25, 1967, Box 71, Appointment File [Diary Backup]; Johnson Diary, July 24, 1967; Cavanagh interview, p. 50. The text of the Johnson address is in *DN*, July 25, 1967.

75. Harry McPherson, *A Political Education* (Boston: Little, Brown and Co., 1972), p. 359; McPherson Memorandum for the President, July 24, 1967, Box 32, Office Files of Harry McPherson, LBJ Library; McPherson interview, p. 21; *NYT*, July 13, 1968; Senate Committee of the Judiciary, *Nomination of Abe Fortas and Homer Thornberry*, 90th Cong., 2d sess., 1968, pp. 104–5. President Johnson told the Kerner Commission that the speech had been written by "a man who has no political background and a man who thoroughly understands constitutional law." Johnson Memorandum for President, July 29, 1967, Box 72, Appointment File [Diary Backup].

76. Cavanagh interview, pp. 50–51; *DN*, July 25, 1967; *Newsweek* 70 (Aug. 7, 1967): 20; Cavanagh to Johnson, July 25, 1967, Box 232, GR Papers; Sauter and Hines, *Nightmare*, p. 118.

77. McPherson interview, pp. 21–22; McPherson, *Political Education*, p. 360; *DN*, July 26, 1967; *DFP*, July 27, 1967; *NYT*, July 25, 27, 30, 1967; Johnson Memorandum for President, July 29, 1967, Box 72, Appointment File [Diary Backup].

78. McPherson Memorandum for President, July 26, 1967, and LBJ note on same, Box 32, McPherson Files; Douglas Cater for President, July 27, 1967, Box 29, Ramsey Clark Papers, LBJ Library; *DFP*, July 28, 1967.

79. *NYT*, July 30, Aug. 11, 1967; transcript of news conference . . . , July 25, 1967, Box 346, GR Papers; Romney's Report to the People, July 30, 1967, Box 319, ibid.; Transcript of Press Conference, July 31, 1967, ibid.; *Capability Hearings*, app. 2, pp. 6272–74.

80. Johnson Diary, July 31, Aug. 1, 1967; Califano for President, Aug. 2, 1967, and enclosed "Response to Romney," Box 26, HU2/ST22; Clark interview (1984), pp. 18–19; Clark Press Conference of Aug. 1, 1967, Box 44, Gaither Files; *DN*, Aug. 2, 1967; *DFP*, Aug. 2, 1967.

81. Release, Aug. 2, 1967, Box 26, HU2/ST22; Cater to Johnson, Aug. 2, 1967, ibid.

82. Hoover Memorandum to Tolson and William Sullivan, Aug. 2, 1967, Cartha D. DeLoach to Tolson, Aug. 3, 1967, FBI-FOIA.

83. *NYT*, Aug. 4, 1967.

84. Panzer Memorandum to President, July 31, 1967, Box 256, White House Name File—Romney; *DFP*, Aug. 8, 1967.

85. Levinson for President, Sept. 5, 1967, Box 256, White House Name File—Romney; Official Transcript, Sept. 12, 1967, pp. 883-85, 922, 925-26, 932-33, 949, Series 1, Box 2, NACCD Records; Califano for President, Sept. 11, 12, 1967, and enclosed Clark Statement, Box 11, Califano Files; *DFP*, Sept. 13, 1967; *NYT*, Sept. 13, 1967; Johnson, *Vantage Point*, pp. 107-8.

86. *DFP*, Aug. 5, 1967; *NYT*, Aug. 23, 1967; Cavanagh interview, p. 50. Cf. *NYT*, Aug. 6, 1967.

Chapter 9

1. Department of the Army to Commander, July 24, 1967, CF HU2, LBJ Library.

2. *DN*, July 26, 1967; "After Action Report, Task Force Detroit, 24 July-2 August 1967," pp. 7-8, Box 1, Records of the Michigan Department of Military Affairs, Adjutant General Division, RG 78-125, State Archives, Lansing, Michigan; "Final Report of Cyrus R. Vance . . . Concerning the Detroit Riots, July 23 through August 2, 1967," with Oral History Interview of Cyrus Vance, Nov. 3, 1969, LBJ Library; *Report of the National Advisory Commission on Civil Disorders* (Washington: GPO, 1968), p. 55. There was some speculation that the army was placed on the east side to protect fashionable Grosse Pointe and also because there was supposedly a greater danger of race war there than on the west side because of the presence of so many whites of eastern European descent. See B. J. Widick, *Detroit: City of Race and Class Violence* (Chicago: Quadrangle Books, 1972), p. 176; and Herman Wilson Memorandum to Charles E. Nelson (interview with Karl Gregory), n.d., Series 59, Box 2, NACCD Records.

3. Debriefing Conversation with General John L. Throckmorton . . . , Mar. 14, 1978, pp. 35-36, copy in Center of Military History, Washington, D.C.; CG CONARC to DA, Aug. 5, 1967, (Paul J. Scheips) Civil Disturbance File, Task Force Detroit, ibid. See also Special Subcommittee of the House Committee on Armed Services to Inquire into the Capability of the National Guard to Cope with Civil Disturbances, *Hearings*, 90th Cong., 1st sess., 1967, pp. 5684, 5967 (hereafter *Capability Hearings*); "Lessons Learned—Detroit" [1967], Box 1, Accession 69A632, Records of United States Army Commands, RG 338, Office of the Adjutant General, Alexandria, Virginia.

4. Throckmorton order, July 25, 1967, Box 32, NACCD Records; C. L. Simmons Memorandum for the Governor, Aug. 3, 1967, Box 319, GR Papers; *Capability Hearings*, p. 5805; Permanent Subcommittee on Investigations of the Senate Committee on Government Operations, *Riots, Civil and Criminal Disorders, Hearings*, 90th Cong., 2d sess., 1968, pt. 7:1518. Some accounts—for example, Detroit Disturbance, Chronology of Significant Events, July 25, 1967 (Box 319, GR Papers)—place the order at 1:00 A.M.

5. Winston Wessels Field Notes, July 25, 1967, Winston Wessels Papers (copy in my possession); Garry Wills, *The Second Civil War* (New York: New American Library), p. 56.

6. *Capability Hearings*, pp. 5805-6, 5877, 5881, 5925-26, 6066; Wessels Field Notes, July 28, 1967, Wessels Papers; Simmons Memorandum to Romney, Aug.

3, 1967, Box 319, GR Papers; Richard H. Davis to Commanding General, XVIII Airborne Corps, Aug. 7, 1967, D-4, 8, in "After Action Report," Box 1, RG 78-125; *NYT*, Aug. 19, 1967.

7. *Capability Hearings*, pp. 5686-87, 5688, 5881, 5892, 5896-97, 5912, 5970-71, 6066-68; Paul J. Scheips and Karl E. Cocke, *Army Operational and Intelligence Activities in Civil Disturbances since 1957*, rev. ed., 1971, OCMH Study 73, p. 67; *DN*, Aug. 29, 1967; Simmons Memorandum to Romney, Aug. 3, 1967, Box 319, GR Papers; Paul Lowinger and Frida Huige, "The National Guard in the 1967 Detroit Uprisings" [1969], p. 9, University of Michigan Law Library, Ann Arbor, Michigan.

8. *Capability Hearings*, p. 5974; "Michigan Minute Man," July 29, 31, 1967, Wessels Papers.

9. "Lessons Learned," Box 1, Accession 69A632, RG 338; "Control of Civil Disorders: Guidelines for Small Unit Commanders and Troops" [1967], p. 18, ibid.; "Vance Report," p. 56.

10. "After Action Report," Box 1, RG 78-125, pp. 9-10; H. J. Trum Memorandum for the Record, July 26, 1967, Box 44, Office Files of James Gaither, LBJ Library; "Vance Report," p. 55; *Capability Hearings*, pp. 5883-84; To Director from Detroit, July 28, 1967, 5:38, FBI-FOIA.

11. On the map problem and the information the Guard received, see James Richard Gardner, "The Civil Disturbance Mission of the Department of the Army, 1963-1973 . . ." (Ph.D. diss., Princeton University, 1973), pp. 23-24, 55, 66; Department of the Army, *Field Manual, 19-15: Civil Disturbances and Disasters* (Dec. 1964), pp. 19-49; "After Action Report," p. 17, Box 1, RG 78-125; *State Journal*, July 25, 1967, DRSB No. 1; James H. Shotwell to CG, Aug. 18, 1967, Box 1, Accession 69A632, RG 338; "Lessons Learned—Detroit," ibid.; and Christopher Howard Pyle, "Military Surveillance of Civilian Politics, 1964-1970" (Ph.D. diss., Columbia University, 1974), pp. 36, 40, 44.

12. D. G. Wood to US CONARC, Sept. 22, 1967, Box 1, Accession 69A632, RG 338; Pyle, "Military Surveillance," pp. 41-47; Scheips and Cocke, *Operational and Intelligence Activities*, pp. 72-75. Cf. Gardner, "Civil Disturbance Mission," p. 100. I have based my conclusion about FBI intelligence on FBI documents on the riot that I obtained under the Freedom of Information Act.

13. "After Action Report," pp. 16, 21, Box 1, RG 78-125; CG USCONARC to DA, Aug. 5, 1967, Civil Disturbance File, Task Force Detroit.

14. *DN*, July 25, 1967; Van Gordon Sauter and Burleigh Hines, *Nightmare in Detroit* (Chicago: Henry Regnery Co., 1968), pp. 19, 147; *DFP*, July 26, 1967; "After Action Report," pp. 7-8; *Capability Hearings*, app. 1, p. 6528; Sequence of Events, July 25, 1967, Box 345, GR Papers; John Nichols to Commanding Officer, Control Center, July 25, 1967, ibid.; FBI Confidential Report, Aug. 9, 1967, FBI-FOIA.

15. *Capability Hearings*, app. 1, p. 6263; Drew Horgan to Robert Conot, n.d., Box 77, NACCD Records; "Control of Civil Disorders," p. 9, Box 1, Accession 69A632, RG 338; Tracy L. Clark to Commanding General, July 31, 1967, Shotwell to Commanding General, Aug. 18, 1967, ibid.; *DFP*, July 26, 1967; *DN*, July 26, 1967; Paul J. Scheips, "The Army and Civil Disobedience in Oxford and Detroit" [1982], p. 15, in my possession; Adam Yarmolinsky, *The Military Establishment* (New York: Harper and Row, 1971), p. 171.

16. NACCD Transcript of Proceedings, Aug. 11, 1967, Series 1, Box 1, NACCD Records; *NACCD Report*, p. 56; *Washington Post*, July 30, 1967; Xavier Nicholas interview with Willie Toone [1982], copy of tape in my possession; Capture and Record of Civil Disorder in Detroit, July 23–July 28, 1967, Box 345, GR Papers.

17. *DN*, July 26, 1967; Shotwell to Commanding General, Aug. 18, 1967, Box 1, Accession 69A632, RG 338; Horgan to Conot, n.d., Box 77, NACCD Records; NACCD Transcript, Aug. 11, 1967, p. 238, Series 1, Box 1, ibid.; *NACCD Report*, p. 56; *National Observer*, July 31, 1967, DRSB No. 1; Scheips phone conversation with Alexander Bolling, Civil Disturbance File, Task Force Detroit; Nicholas interview with Charles Colding [1982], copy of tape in my possession.

18. Horgan to Conot, n.d., Box 77, NACCD Records; *DFP*, July 26, 1967; *DN*, July 26, 1967; Sauter and Hines, *Nightmare*, pp. 185–86; *National Observer*, July 31, 1967, DRSB No. 1; DA to JCS, July 29, 1967, Civil Disturbance File, Task Force Detroit; "Control of Civil Disorders," p. 13, Box 1, Accession 69A632, RG 338.

19. *National Observer*, July 31, 1967, DRSB No. 1; *Los Angeles Times*, July 27, 1967, ibid.; Shotwell to Commanding General, Aug. 18, 1967, Box 1, Accession 69A632, RG 338.

20. *Capability Hearings*, app. 1, p. 6276; *DN*, July 26, 1967; *DFP*, July 27, 1967; *NYT*, July 27, 1967; Barefoot Sanders for President, July 27, 1967, Box 58, Office Files of Joseph Califano, LBJ Library; *Los Angeles Times*, July 27, 1967, DRSB No. 1; Interview with Cyrus Vance, Mar. 14, 1985, pp. 18–19, transcript in MHC. See also *DFP*, Aug. 6, 1967.

21. Albert Callewaert and Arthur Yim, "The Detroit Police Department and the Detroit Civil Disorder," Dec. 1967, app. A, Box 407, JPC Papers; Locke, *Detroit Riot*, pp. 41, 42–43; Sequence of Events, July 25, 1967, Box 345, GR Papers; Disorder Log, July 25, 1967, Box 4, Ray Girardin Papers, Burton Historical Collection, Detroit, Michigan; To Director from Detroit, July 25, 1967, 3:02 A.M., 7:30 A.M., 1:31 P.M., July 26, 1967, 6:32 A.M., FBI-FOIA; Selected Racial Developments and Disturbances, July 26, 1967, ibid.; Wilson Memorandum to Nelson (interview with Hubert Locke), Oct. 17, 19, 1967, Peter Rossi File, in my possession; *DFP*, July 26, 1967; *DN*, July 26, 1967; Chronological Index, Civil Disorder, July 1967, Reported to the Homicide Bureau, Box 79, NACCD Records.

22. *DN*, Feb. 4, 1970; Capture and Record, Box 345, GR Papers; Wilson Memorandum to Nelson (Locke interview), Oct. 17, 19, 1967, Rossi File; Numerical Index of Injured and Fatal Victims, July 1967 . . . , n.d., Detroit Recorder's Court, Detroit, Michigan.

23. Albert P. Schwaller to Chief of Detectives, Oct. 26, 1967, Case No. 55-15-X, Records of the United States Senate, RG 46, NARA; Sauter and Hines, *Nightmare*, pp. 130–33; John Hersey, *The Algiers Motel Incident* (New York: Alfred A. Knopf, 1968), p. 130; People of Michigan vs. Danny Royster and Charles L. Latimer, No. A139736, Examination, Aug. 15, 1967, Recorder's Court; Order of Conviction, A139736, ibid.

24. Schwaller to Chief of Detectives, Oct. 26, 1967, Case No. 55-15-X, RG 46; Sauter and Hines, *Nightmare*, pp. 119–21, 134–38; John Doar Memorandum for Attorney General, Sept. 28, 1967, Box 29, Ramsey Clark Papers, LBJ Library;

Deposition of Gene Goltz and William Serrin, Jan. 8, 1968, Series 32, Box 2, NACCD Records; *MC*, July 13, 1968.

25. Schwaller to Chief of Detectives, Oct. 26, 1967, Case No. 55-15-X, RG 46; *NACCD Report*, p. 57; Sauter and Hines, *Nightmare*, pp. 122–30, 142–46, 148–50; *DFP*, July 27, 1967.

26. [DPD] *Statistical Report on the Civil Disorder Occurring in the City of Detroit, July 1967*, pp. 11, 32, 53; "Vance Report," app. C.

27. *DFP*, July 26, 30, 1967; *DN*, July 29, 1967; *Capability Hearings*, app. 1, pp. 6260–61; "Vance Report," p. 20; Executive Order No. 1967-3, Amended, July 25, 1967, Box 281, GR Papers; Sauter and Hines, *Nightmare*, pp. 139–40.

28. Milton Henry to Cavanagh, July 25, 1967, Box 393, JPC Papers; Sauter and Hines, *Nightmare*, pp. 139–40; *DFP*, July 26, 1967; *DN*, July 26, 1967; Hubert Locke, *The Detroit Riot of 1967* (Detroit: Wayne State University Press, 1969), pp. 111–12.

29. Sauter and Hines, *Nightmare*, p. 155.

30. For the Blanding slaying, see *DFP*, July 26, 1967, July 23, 1972; Ralph O. Wilbur Memorandum for Commanding General, Aug. 3, 1967, Box 345, GR Papers; Capture and Record, ibid.; Sauter and Hines, *Nightmare*, pp. 150–54; Schwaller to Chief of Detectives, Oct. 26, 1967, Case No. 55-15-X, RG 46; *DN*, Aug. 19, 1968; *MC*, Aug. 19, 1967, May 4, 1968; E. W. Morris to Vice Chief of Staff, Aug. 9, 1967, Civil Disturbance File, Task Force Detroit; and Homicide File No. 7178, July 30, 1967, Box 79, NACCD Records.

31. Sauter and Hines, *Nightmare*, pp. 169–72; Joe A. Lapointe, "Six Days in July," *Detroit Monthly*, July 1987, p. 66.

32. Homicide File No. 7201, Aug. 6, 1967, Box 79, NACCD Records; Sauter and Hines, *Nightmare*, pp. 172–76. Adjutant General Schnipke maintained that the Guard could not have been responsible for Post's death since he was killed by a 22-caliber bullet, which the Guard did not use. *Capability Hearings*, pp. 5807–8.

33. See chap. 11.

34. Schwaller to Chief of Detectives, Oct. 26, 1967, Case No. 55-15-X, RG 46; Homicide File No. 7179, Aug. 23, 1967, Box 82, NACCD Records; Deposition of John O'Brien et al., Jan. 9, 1968, Series 32, Box 2, ibid.; *DN*, Aug. 9, 1967; Sauter and Hines, *Nightmare*, pp. 200–204.

35. Sauter and Hines, *Nightmare*, pp. 177–81; Homicide File No. 7192, Aug. 25, 1967, Box 82, NACCD Records; Robert C. Danhof to File, Oct. 10, 1967, Box 319, GR Papers; *MC*, Sept. 16, 1967; Doar Memorandum for Attorney General, Sept. 28, 1967, Box 29, Clark Papers.

36. Bernard Dobranski Report to Robert Conot, n.d., Box 77, NACCD Records; Homicide File No. 7194, Aug. 23, 1967, Box 79, ibid.; Sauter and Hines, *Nightmare*, pp. 192–96; *DN*, July 22, 1977.

37. Homicide File No. 7185, Aug. 2, 1967, Box 79, NACCD Records; Sauter and Hines, *Nightmare*, pp. 187–90.

38. Homicide File No. 7190, July 31, 1967, Box 82, NACCD Records; Sauter and Hines, *Nightmare*, pp. 211–18; Doar Memorandum for Attorney General, Sept. 28, 1967, Box 29, Clark Papers.

39. *Capability Hearings*, app. 1, pp. 6268–69, 6275, 6276; "After Action Report," pp. 9–10, Box 1, RG 78-125; Wessels Field Notes, July 26, 1967, Wessels Papers; Operations Report, Lessons Report 5-67, Sept. 28, 1967, Civil Dis-

turbance File, Task Force Detroit; *DFP*, July 27, 1967; *Riots, Civil and Criminal Disorders*, pt. 7:1510.

40. *DFP*, July 27, 1967; Sequence of Events, July 26, 1967, Box 345, GR Papers; To Director from Detroit, July 27, 1967, 5:52 A.M.., FBI-FOIA; [DPD] *Statistical Report*, pp. 11, 32, 53; "Vance Report," Appendix C; Charles J. Quinlan to Mayor's Development Team, Aug. 11, 1967, Box 533, JPC Papers.

41. *NYT*, July 27, 1967. King, David Garrow tells us, did not have an opportunity to review the statement before it was issued. *Bearing the Cross* (New York: William Morrow and Co., 1986), p. 571.

42. *DFP*, July 27, 1967; Sauter and Hines, *Nightmare*, p. 177; Callewaert and Yim, "Police Department," app. A, Box 407, JPC Papers; Disorder Log, July 26, 1967, Box 4, Girardin Papers; To Director from Detroit, July 26, 1967, 3:18 A.M., 5:48 P.M., 8:59 P.M., FBI-FOIA; Selected Racial Disturbances and Developments, July 27, 1967, ibid.; *NYT*, July 27, 1967; Locke, *Detroit Riot*, pp. 43–44, 47–48; *NACCD Report*, p. 59.

43. [Henry H. Gerecke] report, n.d., Box 77, NACCD Records; Headquarters Command Post Activity Log, July 26, 1967, Box 4, Girardin Papers; *DFP*, July 27, 28, 30, 1967; *NYT*, July 27, 1967.

44. Nichols to Girardin, July 26, 27, 1967, Throckmorton to Girardin, July 27, 1967, Commissioner's File, DPD; Sequence of Events, July 26, 1967, Box 345, GR Papers; [Air National Guard] "History," ibid.; *Capability Hearings*, pp. 5687–88, 5972; "After Action Report," p. 10, F-3, 12–14, 17.

45. *DFP*, July 28, 1967; *DN*, July 27, 28, 1967; *NACCD Report*, p. 61; Headquarters Command Post Activity Log, July 27, 1967, Box 4, Girardin Papers; Sequence of Events, July 27, 1967, Box 345, GR Papers; Thomas Turkaly to Nichols, July 27, 1967, ibid.; Romney Press Release, July 27, 1967, Box 346, ibid.; *Capability Hearings*, app. 1, pp. 6278, 6280, 6283–85; Harold K. Johnson to Throckmorton, July 25, 1967, Civil Disturbance File, Task Force Detroit; "After Action Report," pp. 10–11, Box 1, RG 78-125; To Director from Detroit, July 27, 1967, 9:12 P.M., FBI-FOIA; Locke, *Detroit Riot*, p. 48.

46. *DFP*, July 29–31, 1967; *DN*, July 28, 1967; Sauter and Hines, *Nightmare*, p. 205; "After Action Report," pp. 11–12, Box 1, RG 78-125; "Vance Report," pp. 22–23; To Director from Detroit, July 28, 1967, 1:22 A.M., July 29, 1967, 1:47 P.M., FBI-FOIA; Locke, *Detroit Riot*, pp. 49–50; *Capability Hearings*, app. 1, pp. 6286, 6297; "Michigan Minute Man," Aug. 2, 1967, Wessels Papers.

47. *DN*, July 31, 1967; *DFP*, July 31, Aug. 1–3, 1967; Locke, *Detroit Riot*, p. 51; Executive Order No. 1967-3, Amended, July 31, Aug. 1, 1967, Box 281, GR Papers; Sequence of Events, July 31, Aug. 1, 2, 1967, Box 345, ibid.; *Capability Hearings*, app. 1, pp. 6308, 6318, 6319; Disorder Log, Aug. 2, 1967, Box 4, Girardin Papers; "After Action Report," p. 13; "Vance Report," p. 26.

48. Callewaert and Yim, "Police Department," app. A, Box 407, JPC Papers; Proclamations, Aug. 3, 6, 1967, Box 281, GR Papers; *DFP*, Aug. 7, 1967.

49. Gary T. Marx, "Civil Disorder and Agents of Social Control," *Journal of Social Issues* 26 (Winter 1970): 46; Pyle, "Military Surveillance," p. 45; Paul J. Scheips and M. Warner Stark, "Use of Troops in Civil Disturbances since World War II, Supplement II (1967)" (Apr. 1969), p. 92; "After Action Report," pp. 15–16, Box 1, RG 78-125; CG USCONARC to DA, Aug. 5, 1967, Civil Disturbance File, Task Force Detroit.

50. Callewaert and Yim, "Police Department," Exhibit A, Box 407, JPC

Papers; "Vance Report," p. 53; NACCD Transcript, Aug. 11, 1967, p. 43, Series 1, Box 1, NACCD Records. Cf. Interview with James Bannon, Mar. 12, 1985, p. 29, transcript in MHC.

51. Davis to Commanding General, XVIII Airborne Corps, Aug. 7, 1967, D-5, Box 1, RG 178-25; Callewaert and Yim, "Police Department," p. 60, Box 407, JPC Papers.

52. *DN*, July 27, 1967; Interview with John Nichols, Aug. 13, 1984, p. 19, transcript in MHC.

53. *DN*, Aug. 30, 1967; Remarks Prepared for . . . Romney, Sept. 12, 1967, Box 346, GR Papers.

54. Vance interview (1969), pp. 38–39; Wessels Field Notes, July 28, 1967, Wessels Papers; Lowinger and Huige, "National Guard," p. 9; Throckmorton Debriefing Conversation, Mar. 14, 1978, pp. 34–35; Results of Civil Disturbance Task Group Review of Report of Deputy Commander, TF Detroit [Sept. 1967], pp. 36–39, in my possession.

55. *Michigan Daily*, Aug. 31, 1967, DSRB No. 2; Headquarters Command Post Activity Log, July 27, 1967, Box 4, Girardin Papers; *Riots, Civil and Criminal Disorders*, pt. 7:1512; "Vance Report," p. 56; Turkaly to Nichols, July 27, 1967, Box 345, GR Papers; Official Transcript of Proceedings before the NACCD, Aug. 15, 1967, p. 552, Series 1, Box 2, NACCD Records; *Capability Hearings*, app. 1, pp. 6287, 6289; Maurice Kelman and Ed Batchelor interview with Ray Girardin, Oct. 29, 1971, p. 397, transcript in my possession.

56. Norman E. Rolle to CO, HQ, XVIII Airborne Corps, July 31, 1967, Box 1, Accession 69A632, RG 338.

57. Official Transcript, Aug. 15, 1967, pp. 474–75, 525, 550, Series 1, Box 2, NACCD Records; Goltz and Serrin Deposition, Series 32, Box 2, ibid.; American Newspaper Publishers Association (ANPA), *Reporting the Detroit Riot* [New York, 1968], pp. 16–17; Sauter and Hines, *Nightmare*, pp. 225–28; Memo from Wilson to Nelson, n.d., Rossi File; *DN*, Aug. 15, 1967; "Riot Coverage," n.d., Box 12, Angelo Papers; Clark to Commanding General, July 31, 1967, Box 1, Accession 69A632, RG 338.

58. Oral History Interview of Jerome P. Cavanagh, Mar. 22, 1971, pp. 52–53, LBJ Library; Nicholas interview with Jon Lowell [1982], p. 15, transcript in Nicholas's possession; NACCD Transcript, Aug. 1, 1967, p. 238, Series 1, Box 1, NACCD Records; Results of [Robert Conot] interview with Saul Friedman, n.d., Box 87, ibid.; *Capability Hearings*, pp. 5756, 5877–78, 5910–11, 5965, 5970, app. 1, pp. 6277, 6287; *DN*, Aug. 11, 1967; "Vance Report," p. 51; "Michigan Minute Man," No. 6, Aug. 1, 1967, Wessels Papers.

59. Information from General Simmons, n.d., Box 345, GR Papers; Billy Dansby to *DFP*, Sept. 7, 1967, Jack Vandenberg to Romney, Aug. 29, 1967, ibid.; undated press conference, Box 7, Records of Department of Military Affairs, Division of Public Information, RG 77-45, State Archives; Howard M. Dryden, "National Guard Association of Michigan," n.d., ibid.; *Capability Hearings*, pp. 5957, 6031–32, 6044–47, 6065, 6072–73; Official Transcript, Sept. 12, 1967, pp. 906–11, Series 1, Box 2, NACCD Records; *Riots, Civil and Criminal Disorders*, pt. 5:1267–68; Wessels Field Notes, Aug. 3, 1967, Wessels Papers; *DFP*, Aug. 25, 26, 1967; C. C. Schnipke to Richard Russell, Aug. 3, 1967, Box 129, Philip Hart Papers, MHC.

60. Wessels Field Notes, July 25, 28, 31, 1967, Wessels Papers; *Capability*

Hearings, pp. 5956–57; James C. Elliott Memorandum to Chief, National Guard Bureau, Box 4, Accession 71A1, RG 335. Cf. *Capability Hearings*, p. 5913.

61. Goltz and Serrin Deposition, Series 32, Box 2, NACCD Records. For allegations of State Police misbehavior, see Official Transcript, Nov. 9, 1967, p. 3833, Series 1, Box 6, NACCD Records; Elliot D. Luby, "Police and Jail Treatment of Detroit Negro Arrestees" [1968], p. 3, Box 427, JPC Papers; Incidents reported at the time of the Detroit riot to . . . John Conyers . . . , n.d., Joseph A. Labadie Collection, University of Michigan Library, Ann Arbor, Michigan; and William Walter Scott III, *Hurt, Baby, Hurt* (Ann Arbor: New Ghetto Press, 1970), p. 60.

62. Hersey, *Algiers Motel*, p. 155; *DFP*, July 30, 1967; *NYT*, July 30, 1967; Detroit Information: Grant Friley, n.d., Box 81, NACCD Records; Girardin interview, p. 414.

63. ["Riot and Mob Control Manual"], July 1, 1966, p. 52, DPD; Wilson Memorandum to Nelson (Locke interview), Oct. 17, 19, 1967, Rossi File; Nichols to Commissioner, July 28, 1967, Turkaly to All Precincts and Bureaus, July 29, 1967, Commissioner's File; Deposition of John Nichols, Jan. 10, 1968, Series 32, Box 2, NACCD Records; Dobranski Report to Conot, n.d., Box 77, ibid.

64. *Washington Post*, July 25, 1967; Lowinger and Huige, "National Guard," p. 13; *DFP*, July 30, 1967; Incidents reported, Labadie Collection.

65. Ernest Mazey to Girardin, Aug. 18, 1967, Carl Heffernan to Girardin, Dec. 28, 1967, Box 12, ACLU–Metropolitan Detroit Branch Papers (July 23, 1971), ALHUA; Incidents reported, Labadie Collection.

66. Edward A. Rosario vs. City of Detroit . . . , Apr. 25, 1968, Box 6, Records of the Michigan Civil Rights Commission-Administration, RG 74-90, State Archives; Michigan Civil Rights Commission, *Case Digest, 1964–1975* (Detroit, n.d.), p. 26; *MC*, May 11, Aug. 10, 1968; *DFP*, Nov. 5, Dec. 3, 1968; Interview with Arthur Howison, July 24, 1984, pp. 31–32, transcript in MHC.

67. Frederick M. Carpenter, Complaint Report, SP 20-762-67, State Police Records, Department of State Police, Lansing, Michigan; Jacob Bailey vs. City of Detroit . . . , Apr. 25, 1968, Box 6, RG 74-90; *MC*, May 11, July 27, Aug. 10, 1968.

68. *DFP*, Aug. 4, 1967; *Grand Rapids Press* [July 26, 1967], DRSB No. 1; *Newsweek* 70 (Aug. 7, 1967): 26.

69. Official Transcript, Nov. 9, 1967, pp. 3821–22, Series 1, Box 6, NACCD Records; Wilson Memorandum to Nelson (interview with Leon Atchison), n.d., Series 59, Box 2, ibid.

70. Deposition of Stanley Webb, Jan. 11, 1968, Series 32, Box 2, NACCD Records; Roger Wilkins, *A Man's Life* (New York: Simon and Schuster, 1982), p. 199; Webb to Wilkins, n.d., and enclosed report, Detroit Riot File, Section I, Community Relations Service, Department of Justice, FOIA.

71. Luby, "Treatment of Arrestees," pp. 6–8, 14–16, Box 427, JPC Papers.

72. Barbara Wilson Tinker, *When the Fire Reaches Us* (New York: William Morrow and Co., 1970), p. 208; Capture and Record, Box 345, GR Papers; Dobranski and John Ursu Memorandum to Wilson (interview with Ernest Goodman), Oct. 11, 1967, Series 59, Box 2, NACCD Records; Wilson Memorandum to Nelson (interview with Henry Cleage), n.d., ibid.; Dobranski Report to Conot, n.d., Box 77, ibid.; Incidents reported, Labadie Collection.

73. Nicholas interviews with Charles E. Jackson, Jan. 22, 1981, with Elliot

Hall [1982], copy of tapes in my possession; Incidents reported, Labadie Collection.

74. Deposition of James Del Rio, Jan. 9, 1968, Series 32, Box 2, NACCD Records; "The Administration of Justice in the Wake of the Detroit Civil Disorder of July 1967," *Michigan Law Review* 66 (May 1968): 1616n; *DFP*, July 26, 1967; Donald F. Pohl, "Arrest of Del Rio," July 24, 1967, Commissioner's File.

75. Luby, "Treatment of Arrestees," pp. 16–17, Box 427, JPC Papers; ANPA, *Detroit Riot*, p. 13; John T. Scales Memorandum to Milan C. Miskovsky (interview with Justinas Bavarskis), Dec. 30, 1967, Series 4, Box 22, NACCD Records; Deposition of Bavarskis, Jan. 10, 1968, Series 32, Box 2, ibid.; *DFP*, July 27, 1967; *Washington Post*, July 30, 1967.

76. Bob Clark, "Nightmare Journey," *Ebony* 22 (Oct. 1967): 126–28; [Nathan Caplan] interview with person who broke first window [Nov. 4, 1967], pp. 8, 10, 11, transcript in my possession; Official Transcript, Nov. 9, 1967, p. 3823, Series 1, Box 6, NACCD Records; Dobranski Report to Conot, n.d., Box 77, ibid.; Scott, *Hurt*, pp. 153–54, 159. See also *DN*, Aug. 3, 1967; *MC*, Aug. 5, 1967; and Deposition of Loretta Smith, Jan. 10, 1968, Series 32, Box 2, NACCD Records.

77. When police began to get "rambunctious" in the Thirteenth Precinct, the precinct commander told them that they would be held responsible for any prisoner who was physically abused in the interrogation rooms. Dobranski Report to Conot, n.d., Box 77, NACCD Records.

78. Ibid.; Official Transcript, Nov. 9, 1967, pp. 3819–21, Series 1, Box 6, NACCD Records; Del Rio Deposition, Series 32, Box 2, ibid.; Wilson Memorandum to Nelson (Atchison interview), n.d., Series 59, Box 2, ibid.; Anthony Ripley to Cavanagh, July 26, 1967, Box 398, JPC Papers; *NACCD Report*, pp. 58–59; Hersey, *Algiers Motel*, pp. 38–40; *DFP*, July 27, 1967.

79. Incidents reported, Labadie Collection; Dobranski Report to Conot, n.d., Box 77, NACCD Records; Nichols Deposition, Series 32, Box 2, ibid.; Smith Deposition, ibid.; "Administration of Justice," p. 1630.

80. For the Rubin case, see Official Transcript, Nov. 9, 1967, pp. 3823–31, Series 1, Box 6, NACCD Records; Deposition of Vivian Rubin, Jan. 11, 1968, Series 32, Box 2, ibid.; Deposition of Robert Rubin et al., Jan. 11, 1968, ibid.; Bavarskis Deposition, Jan. 10, 1968, ibid.; Dobranski Report to Conot, n.d., Box 77, ibid.; Kenneth J. Hodson to Chief of Staff, Aug. 31, 1967, and enclosed V. Rubin to Philip Hart, Aug. 21, 1967, Civil Disturbance File, Task Force Detroit; DPD, Report on Case Investigated for Warrant Recommendation, July 27, 1967, Recorder's Court; People of Michigan vs. Robert Leroy Rubin . . . , A139458, Examination, Aug. 7, 1967, Box 78, NACCD Records; *NACCD Report*, pp. 57–58; and *MC*, July 24, 1982.

81. Ernest Mazey, "The Lessons of the Detroit Riots," n.d., Box 12, ACLU–Metropolitan Detroit Branch Papers; Irving Low et al. vs. City of Detroit et al. . . . , Complaint for Injunctive Relief, July 31, 1967, ibid.; Petition for Leave to Intervene . . . ACLU of Michigan, Aug. 3, 1967, ibid.; handwritten notes, "Court of Appeals," Aug. 6, 1967, ibid.; To Director from Detroit, July 26, 1967, 1:15 P.M., 8:36 P.M., 9:12 P.M., July 27, 1967, 12:33 P.M., FBI-FOIA; Selected Racial Disturbances and Developments, July 27, 28, 1967, ibid.; "Re Rioting Beginning July 23, 1967," Aug. 9, 1967, ibid.; DA to JCS, July 30, 1967, Civil Disturbance File, Task Force Detroit; Headquarters Command Post Activity

Log, Aug. 1, 1967, Box 4, Girardin Papers; *DFP*, July 29, 30, Aug. 4, 5, 1967; *MC*, Aug. 12, 1967; *NACCD Report*, p. 59.

82. Yale Kamisar, "Some Salient Features of the Administration of Criminal Justice during and after the July 23-28, 1967 Detroit 'Riot,' " Oct. 5, 1967, p. 2, Series 4, Box 22, NACCD Records; "Footnote to Introduction," n.d., Series 34, Box 2, ibid.

83. *DFP*, July 27, 29, 30, Aug. 4, 6, 12, 1967; *MC*, Sept. 2, 1967; Incidents reported, Labadie Collection; Norton J. Cohen to Girardin, Aug. 9, 1967, and enclosed Memorandum, Box 12, ACLU-Metropolitan Detroit Branch Papers; Typical Loot Searching Incident, July 31, 1967, Series III, Box 3, CCR Papers; Official Transcript, Nov. 9, 1967, p. 3834, Series 1, Box 6, NACCD Records.

84. *DN*, Aug. 4, 5, 1967; *DFP*, Aug. 1, 6, 8, 1967; *MC*, Aug. 12, Sept. 2, 1967; Cavanagh to Common Council, Aug. 4, 1968, Box 398, JPC Papers; NLSC Newsletter 1 (July-Aug. 1967), Box 360, ibid.; Kamisar, "Salient Features," pp. 2-3, Series 4, Box 22, NACCD Records.

85. Harlan Hahn, "Cops and Rioters: Ghetto Perceptions of Social Conflict and Control," *American Behavioral Scientist* 13 (May-Aug. 1970): 774; Incidents reported, Labadie Collections; Wilson Memorandum to Nelson (interview with Francis Kornegay et al.), n.d., Series 59, Box 2, NACCD Records; "Black Cop," *Metropolitan Detroit*, July 1987, p. 80.

86. See chap. 2 for Vaughn and his store.

87. *DN*, July 31, 1967; *MC*, Aug. 5, 1967; *Detroit Journal*, Aug. 11, 1967; "White Power in the Ghetto" [Aug. 24, 1967], Box 12, ACLU-Metropolitan Detroit Branch Papers; Nicholas interview with Edward Vaughn, Summer 1982, pp. 23-24, transcript in Nicholas's possession.

88. Ripley to Cavanagh, July 26, 1967, Box 398, JPC Papers; *DFP*, July 30, 1967; *DN*, July 30, 1967; *MC*, Aug. 5, Sept. 12, 1967; Hersey, *Algiers Motel*, pp. 41-42, 46; Incidents reported, Labadie Collection; Wilson Memorandum to Nelson (Atchison interview), n.d., Series 59, Box 2, NACCD Records.

89. *DN*, Aug. 3, 19, 23, 1967; *DFP*, Aug. 23, 1967; Mazey, "Lessons," ACLU-Metropolitan Detroit Branch Papers; Cohen to John Doar, Jan. 9, 1968, ibid.; Dobranski and Ursu Memorandum to Wilson (Goodman interview), Oct. 11, 1967, Series 59, Box 2, NACCD Records; To Director from Detroit, July 31, 1967, Algiers Motel File, FBI-FOIA; Doar Memorandum for Attorney General, Sept. 28, 1967, Box 29, Clark Papers.

90. Thomas L. Johnson to Walter R. Greene, Aug. 16, 1967, Records of the Michigan Civil Rights Commission, RG 83-55 (unprocessed), State Archives; Ruth Rasmussen to Burton I. Gordin, July 31, 1967, Box 11, RG 74-90; Headquarters Command Post Activity Log, July 28, 1967, Box 4, Girardin Papers; Damon Keith to Lyndon Baines Johnson et al., July 28, 1967, Recorder's Court; *DN*, July 29, 30, 1967; *DFP*, July 30, 1967; Ursu Memorandum to Wilson (interview with Burton Levy), n.d., Series 59, Box 2, NACCD Records; Sequence of Events, July 28, 1967, Box 393, JPC Papers.

91. "The Detroit 'Riot': A Challenge to Society and the Legal Profession," Oct. 11, 1967, University of Michigan Law Library; Rasmussen Memorandum to Gordin, July 31, 1967, Box 11, RG 74-90; *DFP*, July 30, 1967; *DN*, July 30, 1967. The police officer who abused the black CRC observer was reportedly suspended as a result.

92. J. Russell to Carl Bielby et al., Aug. 29, 1967, Father Sheehan Correspon-

dence, 1962–1969, Archives of the Archdiocese of Detroit, Detroit, Michigan; Headquarters Command Post Activity Log, July 29, 1967, Box 4, Girardin Papers; Callewaert and Yim, "Police Department," app. A, Box 407, JPC Papers; *NYT*, July 30, 1967; *DFP*, Aug. 14, 1967; Locke, *Detroit Riot*, pp. 92–93.

93. Heffernan to Research and Development Bureau, Sept. 12, 1967, Series 45, Box 14, NACCD Records; Official Transcript, Aug. 15, 1967, p. 484, Series 1, Box 2, ibid.; Wilson Memorandum to Nelson (interview with Stanley Webb), n.d., Series 59, Box 2, ibid.; Bannon interview, pp. 34–35. Cf. *DFP*, Aug. 4, 1967; and Josephine Gomon to Bill and Olga, Box 8, Josephine Gomon Papers, MHC.

94. Joe R. Feagin and Harlan Hahn, *Ghetto Riots* (New York: Macmillan Co., 1973), p. 284.

95. Wessels Field Notes, July 31, 1967, Wessels Papers; *Capability Hearings*, p. 5971; Goltz and Serrin Deposition, Series 32, Box 2, NACCD Records; Bavarskis Deposition, ibid.; Scales Memorandum to Miskovsky (Bavarskis interview), Dec. 30, 1967, Series 4, Box 22, ibid.; *Los Angeles Times*, July 27, 1967, DRSB No. 1.

96. Clark, "Nightmare Journey," pp. 123–24, 127–28; Luby, "Treatment of Arrestees," p. 15, Box 427, JPC Papers; *DN*, July 27, 1967; *DFP*, July 29, 1967.

97. Incidents reported, Labadie Collection; Official Transcript, Nov. 6, 1967, pp. 3831–32, Series 1, Box 6, NACCD Records; Charles Estus to Locke, Aug. 8, 1967, Locke to Estus, Aug. 18, 1967, Box 1, ORA Papers; *Los Angeles Times*, July 27, 1967, DRSB No. 1.

98. *NYT*, July 27, 1967; Luby, "Treatment of Arrestees," p. 15, Box 427, JPC Papers; Raymond Clemons to Romney, May 20, 1968, Box 402, ibid. I omitted the italics in the Clemons letter. The federal government eventually paid the Detroit school system $6,159 for items missing or damaged as the result of the federal presence in Detroit during the 1967 riot. *DN*, Jan. 26, 1970.

99. Louis Goldberg, "Ghetto Riots and Others . . . ," in David Boesel and Peter H. Rossi, eds., *Cities under Siege: An Anatomy of Ghetto Riots, 1964–1968* (New York: Basic Books, 1971), pp. 146–48.

100. Detroit Incident, July 23, 1967, Box 319, GR Papers; Detroit Disturbance Chronology, July 23–26, 1967, ibid.; [Ted] Blizzard Notes, July 25, 1967, Box 345, ibid.; "Program Development," July 25, 26, 1967, ibid.; Executive Office, July 25, 1967, Box 186, ibid.; C. H. Sonneveldt to Romney, July 31, 1967, ibid.; Remarks Prepared, Sept. 12, 1967, Box 346, ibid.; Wilson Agar to Davids, July 23, 25–29, 1967, Jack P. Foster to Davids, July 27, 1967, Jack L. Bouck to Davids, July 23, 25, 26, 1967, Glenn Foster to Davids, July 25–28, 1967, Box 319, ibid.; To Director from Detroit, July 25–28, 1967, FBI-FOIA; From Detroit to Director, July 24–27, 1967, ibid.; "Racial Developments, 1967," Aug. 1, 1967, ibid.; Selected Racial Developments and Disturbances, July 26–28, 1967, ibid.; *DFP*, July 25–28, 1967; *NYT*, July 26, 1967; Dobranski Report to Conot, n.d., Box 77, NACCD Records; *Riots, Civil and Criminal Disorders*, pt. 7:1478–83; Permanent Subcommittee on Investigations of the Senate Committee on Government Operations, *Staff Study of Major Riots and Civil Disorders—1965 through July 31, 1968*, 90th Cong., 2d sess., 1968, pp. 8–10.

101. Minutes, Public Safety Committee, Michigan Commission on Crime . . . , Aug. 16, 1967, Box 12, ORA Papers; Sonneveldt to Hart, Aug. 7, 1967, Box 129,

Hart Papers; Dobranski Report to Conot, n.d., Box 77, NACCD Records. See also James W. Rutherford to Davids, July 31, 1967, Box 319, GR Papers.

Chapter 10

1. Bushnell, Jr., to Jacques Feuillan, Aug. 3, 1967, Box 1, ORA Papers; John Ursu Memorandum to Herman Wilson (interview with Ray Girardin), n.d., Series 59, Box 2, NACCD Records.

2. [DPD] *Statistical Report on the Civil Disorder Occurring in the City of Detroit, July 1967*, pp. 1–3; Robert Conot, *Rivers of Blood, Years of Darkness* (New York: Bantam Books, 1967), pp. 379, 381; *Report of the National Advisory Commission on Civil Disorders* (Washington: GPO, 1968), pp. 20, 184n; "Negro Youths and Civil Disorders," Series 7, Box 2, NACCD Records; Isaac Balbus, *The Dialectics of Legal Repression: Black Rebels before the Criminal Courts* (New York: Russell Sage Foundation, 1973), p. 141; Bryan T. Downes, "A Critical Reexamination of the Social and Political Characteristics of Riot Cities," *Social Science Quarterly* 51 (Sept. 1970): 351–52; Robert M. Fogelson and Robert B. Hill, "Who Riots: A Study of Participation in the 1967 Riots," in *Supplemental Studies for the National Advisory Commission on Civil Disorders* (Washington: GPO, 1968), pp. 236–37. Under Michigan law, an arrest, in theory but not necessarily in practice, was to be expunged from an arrestee's record if not followed by a conviction. B. E. Ponder to Trotter, July 26, 1967, FBI-FOIA.

3. [DPD] *Statistical Report*, p. 4; *NACCD Report*, pp. 189n, 190n; Robert B. Hill and Robert M. Fogelson, "A Study of Arrest Patterns in the 1960s Riots" (Final Progress Report, Dec. 1969), p. 66.

4. Elliot D. Luby, "A Comparison between Detroit Negro Riot Arrestees and a Riot Area Control Sample" (1968), p. 3; Fogelson and Hill, "Who Riots," p. 234.

5. Hubert Locke statement [Sept. 22–23, 1967], Box 28, ORA Papers; *DFP*, Sept. 3, 1967; Arthur Weiseger to Francis Kornegay, Aug. 7, 1967, Box 12, DUL Papers; William Cahalan, "The Detroit Riot," *Prosecutor* 3 (Nov.–Dec. 1967): 431; *DN*, July 26, 1967; Balbus, *Legal Repression*, pp. 114–15, 116; Yale Kamisar, "Some Salient Features of the Administration of Criminal Justice during and after the July 23–28, 1967 Detroit 'Riot,' " Oct. 5, 1967, pp. 1–2, Series 4, Box 22, NACCD Records; "Footnote to Introduction," n.d., Series 45, Box 17, ibid.; Xavier Nicholas interview with Claudia Morcum and Myron Wahls, Aug. 6, 1981, copy of tape in my possession; *NACCD Report*, p. 187n.

6. "Final Report of Cyrus Vance Concerning the Detroit Riots, July 23 through Aug. 2, 1967," pp. 41–42, with Oral History Interview of Cyrus Vance, Nov. 3, 1969, LBJ Library; "The Administration of Justice in the Wake of the Detroit Civil Disorder of July 1967," *Michigan Law Review* 66 (May 1968): 1545–47; Cahalan, "Riot," pp. 431–32.

7. ["Riot and Mob Control Manual"], July 1, 1966, p. 46, DPD; Cahalan, "Riot," pp. 430, 433; Balbus, *Legal Repression*, pp. 113–14, 115–16; *NACCD Report*, pp. 184, 193n; Governor's Select Commission, State of New Jersey, *Report for Action* (n.p., 1968), p. 132; John Hersey, *The Algiers Motel Incident* (New York: Alfred A. Knopf, 1968), p. 120; [DPD] *Statistical Report*, pp. 3–4; Balbus, *Legal Repression*, p. 51.

8. Cahalan, "Riot," p. 430; Balbus, *Legal Repression*, p. 117; *DN*, July 28, 1967; Interview with William Cahalan, July 23, 1984, pp. 7–8, 49, transcript in MHC.

9. Balbus, *Legal Repression*, pp. 115, 117–18; Kalliope K. Resh, "Total Cases Processed . . . ," Aug. 4, 1967, Commissioner's File, DPD.

10. Cahalan, "Riot," p. 431; "Administration of Justice," p. 1552n; *DFP*, July 26, 1967; *DN*, July 26, 1967; Balbus, *Legal Repression*, p. 126; N. E. McDaniel to Trotter, July 25, 1967, FBI-FOIA; Albert Callewaert and Arthur Yim, "The Detroit Police Department and the Detroit Civil Disorder," Dec. 1967, pp. 113–14, app. A, Box 407, JPC Papers.

11. Cahalan interview, p. 15; *DFP*, July 25, 1967; *DN*, July 25, 1967.

12. James S. Campbell et al., *Law and Order Reconsidered* (Washington: GPO, 1969), p. 536; Balbus, *Legal Repression*, pp. 118–19; Cahalan, "Riot," p. 431; [DPD] *Statistical Report*, p. 3.

13. Dobranski Memorandum to Herman Wilson (interview with William Cahalan), Oct. 12, 1967, Series 59, Box 2, NACCD Records; Cahalan interview (1984), pp. 12–13; "Criminal Justice *in Extremis* . . . ," *University of Chicago Law Review* 36 (Spring 1969): 484–85.

14. Balbus, *Legal Repression*, p. 113; Interview with George Crockett, Aug. 7, 1984, p. 4, transcript in MHC; *Annual Report of the Recorder's Court of the City of Detroit, Michigan, 1967* (n.p., n.d.), pp. 3, 4; Notes of Meeting . . . July 31, 1967, Box 345, GR Papers.

15. *DN*, July 24, 1967; *DFP*, July 25, 1967; Dobranski and Ursu Memorandum to Wilson (interview with Vincent Brennan), Oct. 13, 1967, Series 59, Box 2, NACCD Records; Wilson Memorandum to Nelson (interview with George Crockett), n.d., ibid.; Recorder's Court Notice, July 24, 1967, Commissioner's File.

16. Official Transcript of Proceedings before the National Advisory Commission on Civil Disorders, Nov. 9, 1967, pp. 3796–97, 3802, Series 1, Box 6, NACCD Records; Frank Sengstock address, Dec. 29, 1967, Series 45, Box 15, ibid.; Kamisar, "Salient Features," pp. 6–7, Series 4, Box 22, ibid.; *DFP*, Sept. 23, 1967; *DN*, July 28, 1967; "Administration of Justice," p. 1602; Cahalan interview (1984), p. 8; Balbus, *Legal Repression*, p. 122.

17. *DFP*, July 26, 1967; Dobranski and Ursu Memorandum to Wilson (Brennan interview), Oct. 13, 1967, Series 59, Box 2, NACCD Records; Cahalan interview (1984), p. 50; Crockett interview (1984), p. 21; "Administration of Justice," pp. 1558, 1602; Balbus, *Legal Repression*, pp. 122, 132–33; George W. Crockett, "Recorder's Court and the 1967 Civil Disturbance," in Richard A. Chikota and Michael C. Moran, eds., *Riot in the Cities* (Rutherford, N.J.: Farleigh Dickinson University Press, 1970), p. 352; "The Detroit 'Riot': A Challenge to Society and the Legal Profession," Oct. 11, 1967, p. 20, University of Michigan Law Library, Ann Arbor, Michigan. Circuit Court judges eventually took over the regular docket of Recorder's Court felony cases.

18. "Administration of Justice," p. 1548; Dobranski and Ursu Memorandum to Wilson (interview with Ernest Goodman), Oct. 11, 1967, Series 59, Box 2, NACCD Records; Kamisar, "Salient Features," p. 3, Series 4, Box 22, ibid.; Sengstock address, Series 45, Box 15, ibid.; *DFP*, Oct. 15, 1967.

19. Sengstock address, Series 45, Box 15, NACCD Records; Dobranski Memorandum to Wilson (Cahalan interview), Oct. 12, 1967, Series 59, Box 2, ibid.; *DFP*, July 26, 1967; "Administration of Justice," pp. 1546–47; Cahalan, "Riot,"

pp. 431–32; Balbus, *Legal Repression*, p. 119. Cahalan was referring specifically to *People* vs. *McDonald*, 223 Mich. 98, 106 (1925).

20. *DFP*, July 24, 25, 1967; *DN*, July 26, 1967; Special Subcommittee of the House Committee on Armed Services to Inquire into the Capability of the National Guard to Cope with Civil Disturbances, *Hearings* (hereafter cited as *Capability Hearings*), 90th Cong., 1st sess., app. 2, p. 6291; *NYT*, Sept. 22, 1968; Dobranski and Ursu Memorandum to Wilson (Brennan interview), Oct. 13, 1967, Series 59, Box 2, NACCD Records; Sengstock address, Series 45, Box 15, ibid.; "Administration of Justice," pp. 1562–63, 1566–67; "Detroit 'Riot': A Challenge," p. 19.

21. *DN*, July 25, 26, 1967; *DFP*, July 25, 1967; Van Gordon Sauter and Burleigh Hines, *Nightmare in Detroit* (Chicago: Henry Regnery Co., 1968), p. 91.

22. *DFP*, July 25, Oct. 15, 1967; Balbus, *Legal Repression*, pp. 119–20, 158n; Sengstock address, Series 45, Box 15, NACCD Records; Wilson Memorandum to Nelson (Crockett interview), n.d., Series 59, Box 2, ibid.; Official Transcript, Nov. 9, 1967, pp. 3801–2, Series 1, Box 6, ibid.; Crockett interview (1984), p. 7; *NACCD Report*, p. 185; F. Philip Colista and Michael Domonkos, "Bail and Civil Disorder," in Chikota and Moran, eds., *Riot*, pp. 326–27, 343, 345; "Administration of Justice," p. 1549.

23. *DFP*, July 26, 1967; Wilson Memorandum to Nelson (Crockett interview), n.d., Series 59, Box 2, NACCD Records; Sengstock address, Series 45, Box 15, ibid.; Crockett, "Recorder's Court," pp. 352–53.

24. Colista and Domonkos, "Bail," pp. 326–29, 341–49; Deposition of Philip Colista, Jan. 9, 1968, Series 32, Box 3, NACCD Records; Balbus, *Legal Repression*, pp. 120–21; Jerome H. Skolnick, *The Politics of Protest* (n.p. [1969]), pp. 228–29; Jonathan Rose notes on interview with Ronald Reosti, n.d., in Jonathan Rose's possession.

25. For Watts, see Balbus, *Legal Repression*, pp. 154–55. For Newark, see Governor's Select Commission, *Report for Action*, p. 132; and Tom Hayden, *Rebellion in Newark* (New York: Random House, 1967), p. 35. See also Skolnick, *Protest*, pp. 229–33.

26. "Administration of Justice," pp. 1550–51; Balbus, *Legal Repression*, pp. 122, 159; Kamisar, "Salient Features," pp. 3–4, Series 4, Box 22, NACCD Records; Sengstock address, Series 45, Box 15, ibid.; Wilson Memorandum to Nelson (Crockett interview), n.d., Series 59, Box 2, ibid.; Colista Deposition, Series 32, Box 3, ibid.; Crockett, "Recorder's Court," p. 356; *DFP*, Sept. 23, 1967.

27. Official Transcript, Nov. 9, 1967, pp. 3803–4, Series 1, Box 6, NACCD Records; Kamisar, "Salient Features," p. 8, Series 4, Box 22, ibid.; Sengstock address, Series 45, Box 15, ibid.; "Administration of Justice" [Aug. 1967], Box 15, Warren Christopher Papers, LBJ Library; "Administration of Justice," pp. 1577–78, 1580–81.

28. NLSC Newsletter 1 (July–Aug. 1967), Box 360, JPC Papers; Responses to the Recent Civil Disorders in Detroit by the Mayor's Committee for Human Resources Development (hereafter MCHRD), Center for Urban Studies Papers, unprocessed, ALHUA; Wilson Memorandum to Nelson (Crockett interview), n.d., ibid.; *DN*, Nov. 28, 1965; Colista and Domonkos, "Bail," p. 326n; "Administration of Justice," pp. 1555–56; Balbus, *Legal Repression*, p. 121.

29. MCHRD Responses, Center for Urban Studies Papers; Charles S. Brown

Summary, n.d., Series 45, Box 15, NACCD Records; Balbus, *Legal Repression*, pp. 124-25; *DFP*, July 27, 1967.

30. *DN*, July 30, 1967; Colista and Domonkos, "Bail," p. 326n; NLSC Newsletter, Box 360, JPC Papers; *In Brief* 45 (Oct. 16, 1967).

31. *DFP*, July 26, 1967; *DN*, July 27, 1967; Balbus, *Legal Repression*, pp. 126-27; ACLU-Metropolitan Detroit Branch Release, July 27, 1967, Box 12, ACLU-Metropolitan Detroit Branch Papers (July 23, 1971), ALHUA; Crockett, "Recorder's Court," p. 356; Damon J. Keith et al. to Lyndon Baines Johnson et al., July 28, 1967, Commissioner's File.

32. [Doar] "Lessons Learned," n.d., Box 15, Christopher Papers; "Vance Report," pp. 43-44, 45, 47, LBJ Library; Balbus, *Legal Repression*, pp. 122-23, 127-31; *NACCD Report*, p. 185n; Capture and Record of Civil Disorder in Detroit, July 23-July 28, 1967, Box 345, GR Papers; Minutes of First Meeting of Co-ordinating Committee to Deal with Riot Prisoners [July 28, 1967], ibid.; Wilson Memorandum to Nelson (Crockett interview), n.d., Series 59, Box 2, NACCD Records; Dobranski and Ursu Memorandum to Wilson (Cahalan interview), Oct. 12, 1967, ibid.; Cahalan, "Riot," pp. 433-34; Crockett, "Recorder's Court," p. 356; *Capability Hearings*, app. 2, pp. 6291-97; *DFP*, July 29, 30, 1967; "Administration of Justice," p. 1551; MCHRD Responses, Center for Urban Studies Papers.

33. Conot, *Rivers of Blood*, p. 321; Governor's Select Commission, *Report for Action*, p. 132; "Administration of Justice," pp. 1572-73; "Detroit 'Riot,' " p. 39; To Director from Detroit, July 24, 1967, 11:37 P.M., FBI-FOIA; Balbus, *Legal Repression*, pp. 128, 159; Sauter and Hines, *Nightmare*, pp. 146-47; Callewaert and Yim, "Police Department," app. A, Box 407, JPC Papers; *NACCD Report*, p. 185; Cahalan interview (1984), p. 9.

34. [DPD], *Statistical Report*, p. 9; *DFP*, July 29, 1967; *DN*, July 30, 1967; Hersey, *Algiers Motel*, pp. 113-14; Deposition of Robert Rubin et al., Jan. 11, 1968, Series 32, Box 3, NACCD Records; John Nelson Casey to Romney, July 29, 1967, Box 186, GR Papers; [Nathan Caplan] interview with person who broke first window [Nov. 4, 1967], pp. 6-11, transcript in my possession; William Walter Scott III, *Hurt, Baby, Hurt* (Ann Arbor: New Ghetto Press, 1970), pp. 154, 160.

35. Bob Clark, "Nightmare Journey," *Ebony* 22 (Oct. 1967): 128-29.

36. Cahalan, "Riot," p. 431; *DFP*, July 26, 1967; [Caplan] interview with window breaker, p. 17; Balbus, *Legal Repression*, p. 116.

37. *NACCD Report*, p. 185; *DFP*, July 25, 29, 1967; Scott, *Hurt*, pp. 165-69, 174-77; [Caplan] interview with window breaker, pp. 15-16; [Caplan] interview with arrestee [Nov. 9, 1967], p. 2, transcript in my possession; Capture and Record, Box 345, GR Papers.

38. *DN*, July 26, 29, 1967; "Administration of Justice," pp. 1576-77n; *NACCD Report*, pp. 60, 185; Wilson Memorandum to Nelson (Crockett interview), n.d., Series 59, Box 2, NACCD Records; Rubin et al. Deposition, Series 32, Box 3, ibid.; [Caplan] interview with window breaker, pp. 13-14, 19-20; [Caplan] interview with arrestee, p. 2; Locke, *Detroit Riot*, p. 50.

39. Balbus, *Legal Repression*, pp. 123, 159; "Detroit 'Riot,' " p. 17; Cahalan, "Riot," p. 430; *DFP*, July 26, 1967; J. W. McGinnis to R. A. Miller, Oct. 16, 1967, Series 45, Box 17, NACCD Records; *DN*, May 18, 1987.

40. McGinnis to Miller, July 27, 28, Oct. 16, 1967, Series 45, Box 17, NACCD

Records; Official Transcript, Nov. 9, 1967, p. 3795, Series 1, Box 6, ibid.; Callewaert and Yim, "Police Department," p. 44, Box 407, JPC Papers; Hubert G. Locke, "Riot Response: The Police and the Courts," in Chikota and Moran, eds., *Riot*, p. 321; Prisoner Population—Morning of July 28, 1967, Box 345, GR Papers.

41. Capture and Record, Box 345, GR Papers; Locke, *Detroit Riot*, pp. 50–51; Cahalan interview (1984), pp. 9–10; Fred J. Romanoff et al. to Cavanagh, July 31, 1967, Box 398, JPC Papers; Callewaert and Yim, "Police Department," app. A, Box 407, ibid.; Civil Disturbance, Detroit, Health Department Activities, July 23–Aug. 1, 1967, Box 533, ibid.; Hersey, *Algiers Motel*, p. 54; Interview with Damon Keith, June 21, 1985, p. 23, transcript in MHC; Walter R. Greene to Burton I. Gordin, Aug. 8, 1967, Box 11, Records of the Michigan Civil Rights Commission-Administration, RG 74-90, State Archives, Lansing, Michigan; Scott, *Hurt*, p. 196; *DFP*, July 30, 1967.

42. "Administration of Justice" [Aug. 1967], Box 15, Christopher Papers; *NACCD Report*, pp. 60, 184; *DFP*, July 29, 1967; *DN*, Oct. 15, 1967; Wilson Memorandum to Nelson (interview with Henry Cleage), n.d., Series 59, Box 2, NACCD Records; Nicholas interview with Morcum and Wahls; Nicholas interview with Elliot Hall, n.d., copy of tape in my possession; NLSC Newsletter, Box 360, JPC Papers.

43. *DFP*, July 29, 1967; Locke, *Detroit Riot*, p. 50; Henry S. Sedmark to John Nichols, Aug. 9, 1967, Detroit Recorder's Court, Detroit, Michigan; Callewaert and Yim, "Police Department," app. A, Box 407, JPC Papers; SAC Detroit to Director, FBI, Aug. 1, 1967, FBI-FOIA; Minutes First Meeting Co-ordinating Committee [July 28, 1967], Box 345, GR Papers.

44. "Detroit 'Riot,' " pp. 15–16; *DFP*, July 26, 31, Oct. 15, 1967; "Administration of Justice," pp. 1547–48, 1554–55, 1557; *NACCD Report*, p. 185; *Grand Rapids Press*, n.d., DRSB No. 1; Scott, *Hurt*, p. 185.

45. Sengstock address, Series 45, Box 15, NACCD Records; Official Transcript, Nov. 9, 1967, pp. 3804–5, Series 1, Box 6, ibid.; "Detroit 'Riot,' " pp. 12–14; Balbus, *Legal Repression*, pp. 121, 124–25; *DFP*, July 26, 1967; *DN*, July 31, 1967; Frank Joyce, "American Dream Plagues Detroit," *National Guardian* 19 (Aug. 5, 1967): 5; Crockett interview (1984), pp. 10–11; "Administration of Justice," pp. 1553–54, 1556.

46. Balbus, *Legal Repression*, pp. 132–33; "Administration of Justice," pp. 1594–1601.

47. Balbus, *Legal Repression*, pp. 135–36; Official Transcript, Nov. 9, 1967, pp. 3809–10, Series 1, Box 6, NACCD Records; Cahalan, "Riot," pp. 432–33; *Annual Report of Recorder's Court, 1967*, p. 4.

48. "Administration of Justice," pp. 1595n, 1603–4; *DFP*, July 20, 1967; Cavanagh et al. to Thomas L. Munson, July 28, 1967, Box 186, GR Papers; Balbus, *Legal Repression*, pp. 133–34.

49. Balbus, *Legal Repression*, pp. 35–36, 127, 160; Sengstock address, Series 45, Box 15, NACCD Records; Official Transcript, Nov. 9, 1967, p. 3811, Series 1, Box 6, ibid.; Wilson Memorandum to Nelson (interview with Charles Brown), n.d., Series 45, Box 17, ibid.; "Detroit 'Riot,' " p. 16; *DFP*, Aug. 1, 1967; Skolnick, *Protest*, p. 226; NLSC Newsletter, Box 360, JPC Papers.

50. "Footnote to Introduction," n.d., Series 45, Box 17, NACCD Records; Official Transcript, Nov. 9, 1967, p. 3809, Series 1, Box 6, ibid.; Kamisar,

"Salient Features," p. 9, Series 4, Box 22, ibid.; Brown Summary, Series 45, Box 15, ibid.; NLSC Newsletter, Box 360, JPC Papers; *In Brief* 45 (Oct. 16, 1967); Balbus, *Legal Repression*, pp. 134-35; "Administration of Justice," pp. 1604-5; *DN*, Aug. 5, 1967; Cahalan, "Riot," p. 433.

51. For the conduct of the preliminary examinations, see *DFP*, Aug. 2, 5, 8, 1967; *DN*, Aug. 4, 1967; William Whitbeck to Michael Levin, Aug. 9, 1967, Box 345, GR Papers; "Footnote to Introduction," Series 45, Box 17, NACCD Records; Sengstock address, Series 45, Box 15, ibid.; Kamisar, "Salient Features," p. 10, Series 4, Box 22, ibid.; *NACCD Report*, p. 186; "Administration of Justice," pp. 1602, 1605-20; and Balbus, *Legal Repression*, p. 135.

52. Permanent Subcommittee on Investigations of the Senate Committee on Government Operations, *Riots, Civil and Criminal Disorders, Hearings*, 90th Cong., 2d sess., 1968, pt. 7:1585; Balbus, *Legal Repression*, pp. 136-37; Cahalan to James Brickley, Aug. 14, 1967, Commissioner's File; Dobranski and Ursu Memorandum to Wilson (Brennan interview), Oct. 13, 1967, Series 59, Box 2, NACCD Records; "Footnote to Introduction," n.d., Series 45, Box 17, ibid.

53. Cahalan, "Riot," p. 433; *Annual Report of Recorder's Court, 1967*, p. 4; "Administration of Justice," pp. 1622-27; *Riots, Civil and Criminal Disorders*, pt. 7:1584-85; Balbus, *Legal Repression*, pp. 140-41; Kamisar, "Salient Features," pp. 10-12, Series 4, Box 22, NACCD Records; Dobranski Memorandum to Wilson (Cahalan interview), Oct. 12, 1967, Series 59, Box 2, ibid.; Official Transcript, Nov. 9, 1967, p. 3810, Series 1, Box 6, ibid.; "Detroit 'Riot,' " pp. 22-23; *DFP*, Oct. 15, 1967.

54. Cahalan, "Riot," pp. 432-33; *Riots, Civil and Criminal Disorders*, pt. 5:1346; *DFP*, Aug. 7, 1967; Balbus, *Legal Repression*, pp. 119, 130, 138-39. About 75 percent of the misdemeanants were found guilty in the Watts riot. Conot, *Rivers of Blood*, p. 381.

55. *DN*, July 28, 1967; *MC*, May 11, 1968; Crockett, "Recorder's Court," p. 352; NLSC Newsletter, Box 360, JPC Papers; MCHRD Responses, Center for Urban Studies Papers; Brown Summary, n.d., Series 45, Box 15, NACCD Records.

56. *Riots, Civil and Criminal Disorders*, pt. 5:1346, pt. 7:1585-86; Campbell et al., *Law and Order Reconsidered*, p. 544; *MC*, May 11, 1968; Balbus, *Legal Repression*, pp. 142-44. The conviction rate in felony cases in the Watts riot was about 50 percent. Conot, *Rivers of Blood*, p. 381.

57. *NACCD Report*, p. 184; Notes of Meeting . . . July 31, 1967, Box 345, GR Papers; Crockett interview (1984), pp. 16-17.

58. Resh to E. Burke Montgomery, Feb. 12, 1968, Detroit Recorder's Court; People vs. Clovie Smith, A 139339, ibid.; People vs. Walter Ronald Thompson, A 139528, ibid.; L. C. Guinot to Milan C. Miskovsky, Feb. 16, 1968, Box 22, NACCD Records; Exhibit No. 70, Case No. 55-15-X, Records of the United States Senate, RG 46, NARA.

59. Robert Danhof to File, Oct. 10, 1967, Box 319, GR Papers; Report of Dobranski to Robert Conot, n.d., Box 77, NACCD Records; Dobranski Memorandum to Wilson (Cahalan interview), Oct. 12, 1967, Series 59, Box 2, ibid.; Albert P. Schwaller to Chief of Detectives, Oct. 26, 1967, Series 4, Box 22, ibid.; Hersey, *Algiers Motel*, p. 390.

60. Official Transcript, Nov. 9, 1967, p. 3804, Series 1, Box 6, NACCD Records; Sengstock address, Series 45, Box 15, ibid.; Wilson Memoranda to

Nelson (Cleage interview), n.d., (Brown interview), n.d., Series 59, Box 2, ibid.; "Detroit 'Riot,' " p. 17; Locke, "Riot Response," p. 323; *DFP*, July 30, Aug. 5, 8, Sept. 23, 1967; *DN*, Aug. 5, 1967; Balbus, *Legal Repression*, p. 121; Ernest Mazey, Summary of Detroit Riot Developments . . . , Sept. 23, 1967, Box 12, ACLU-Metropolitan Detroit Branch Papers; ACLU-Metropolitan Detroit Branch Release, July 27, 1967, ibid.; Paul Harbrecht statement [Sept. 22-23, 1967], Box 28, ORA Papers; Doar to Fine, July 16, 1985.

61. Skolnick, *Protest*, p. 239; *NACCD Report*, pp. 183-84. See also David Paul Boesel, "The Ghetto Riots 1964 to 1968" (Ph.D. diss., Cornell University, 1972), p. 160.

62. *Annual Report of Recorder's Court, 1967*, p. 4; *Capability Hearings*, app. 2, pp. 6291, 6292; *DFP*, Oct. 15, 1967; Dobranski Memoranda to Wilson (Cahalan interview), Oct. 12, 1967, (Brennan interview), Oct. 13, 1967, Series 59, Box 2, NACCD Records; Cahalan interview (1984), pp. 38-39. Cf. *NYT*, Sept. 22, 1968.

63. James Gaither for President, May 9, 1967, Box 29, WE 9, WHCF; James H. Lincoln, *The Anatomy of a Riot* (New York: McGraw-Hill Book Co., 1968), p. 21; Capture and Record, Box 345, GR Papers; Interview with James H. Lincoln, June 14, 1984, pp. 15-17, transcript in MHC.

64. Richard Komisaruk and Carol Pierson, "Children of the Ghetto," in Chikota and Moran, eds., *Riot*, p. 121; Lincoln, *Anatomy*, pp. 15-16, 29-32, 45, 131; *DFP*, July 26, 1967; Lincoln to Romney, July 25, 1967, Box 345, GR Papers; Lincoln interview, pp. 32-35.

65. *DFP*, July 25, 26, 1967; *DN*, July 25, 1967; Lincoln to Romney, July 25, 1967, Box 345, GR Papers; Lincoln interview, pp. 19-23; Lincoln, *Anatomy*, p. 17.

66. *DFP*, July 26, 1967; Capture and Record, Box 345, GR Papers; Lincoln, *Anatomy*, pp. 127, 131-34, 138.

67. Lincoln interview, pp. 17-19, 21; Lincoln, *Anatomy*, pp. 149, 154-56; Rose notes on Reosti interview, n.d.; 387 U.S. 1 (1967).

68. Sengstock address, Series 45, Box 15, NACCD Records; Colista Deposition, Series 32, Box 3, ibid.; Interview with Cyrus Vance, Mar. 14, 1985, p. 24, transcript in MHC.

69. Crockett, "Recorder's Court," p. 359; "Administration of Justice," pp. 1573-74, 1628-30; "Detroit 'Riot,' " pp. 40-41; *MC*, Mar. 11, 1968; [Caplan interview] with window breaker, pp. 25-26; Harlan Hahn, "Cops and Rioters: Ghetto Perceptions of Social Conflict and Control," *American Behavioral Scientist* 13 (Mar.-Aug. 1970): 765; H. C. McKinney Memorandum to Romney, Aug. 3, 1967, Box 319, GR Papers.

70. Hahn, "Cops and Rioters," p. 765.

Chapter 11

1. *DN*, Aug. 2, 1967; *DFP*, July 26, 1972; John Doar Memorandum for Attorney General, Sept. 28, 1967, Box 29, Ramsey Clark Papers, LBJ Library; *NYT*, Mar. 1, 1970.

2. Floor plan of the Manor House, in Warrant Request, Death of: Fred Temple, Algiers Motel File (hereafter AM File), DPD; Ray Glinski to Chief of Detectives, July 26, 1967, ibid.; State of Michigan, ex rel, William L. Cahalan vs. Algiers Motel, Sept. 26, 27, 1967, ibid.; People of Michigan vs. Robert Paille,

David Senak, Melvin Dismukes, No. A-140012 (hereafter No. A-140012), Opinion and Order . . . , Dec. 1, 1967, ibid.; Report of SA, Aug. 16, Oct. 10, 1967, FBI-FOIA; Hersey, *The Algiers Motel Incident* (New York: Alfred A Knopf, 1968), pp. 14–16, 131–33; *DN*, July 31, 1969.

3. Hersey, *Algiers Motel*, pp. 19–21, 72, 75–78, 174–81, 188, 191–92, 354–55; Van Gordon Sauter and Burleigh Hines, *Nightmare in Detroit* (Chicago: Henry Regnery Co., 1968), pp. 162–63, 166–67; *DFP*, July 31, 1967; *DN*, June 5, 6, 1969; Report of Bernard Dobranski from Detroit, Dec. 11–13 [1967], Box 77, NACCD Records; No. A-140012, Examination, Sept. 28, 1967, p. 23, Sept. 29, 1967, pp. 112–13, 157–65, AM File; No. A-140012, Opinion and Order, Dec. 1, 1967, ibid.; Michigan, ex rel, Cahalan vs. Algiers Motel, Sept. 26, 1967, ibid.

4. Synopsis of statements taken from Theodore Thomas, Melvin Dismukes, David Senak, Gerald Kiss, Paul Rehn, Edward Riley, Hubert C. Rosema, and William Jones, Homicide File 7182, AM File; Thomas statement, July 31, 1967, ibid.; No. A-140012, Examination, Sept. 28, 1967, p. 190, ibid.; *DN*, July 26, 1967; *DFP*, May 23, 1969; *NYT*, May 23, 1969; Hubert Locke, *The Detroit Riot of 1967* (Detroit: Wayne State University Press, 1969), pp. 45–46; Hersey, *Algiers Motel*, pp. 157–64, 244–45; Report of SA, Jan. 4, 1968, FBI-FOIA; Interview with John Nichols, Aug. 13, 1984, pp. 56–57, transcript in MHC.

5. Hersey, *Algiers Motel*, p. 226; *NYT*, May 21, 28, 1969; *DN*, May 15, 1969, Feb. 19, 22, 24, 1970; *DFP*, July 31, 1967, Feb. 19, 25, 1970; Synopsis of statements taken from Willie Harris, Frank Amermon, Minnie Moore, Homicide File 7182, AM File.

6. *DFP*, Aug. 8, 1967, June 4, 1969; *DN*, May 5, 1969, July 22, 1977; Hersey, *Algiers Motel*, pp. 68–70, 117.

7. *DFP*, Aug. 8, 1967; service ratings of August, Paille, and Senak, in AM File; Notes on Evidentiary Hearing: Robert N. Paille, Feb. 14, 1972, ibid.; Hersey, *Algiers Motel*, pp. 73–74, 119, 126.

8. *DFP*, Feb. 8, 1970; Hersey, *Algiers Motel*, pp. 63–66, 69; Homicide File No. 7155, Aug. 8, 1967, No. 7188, July 31, 1967, Box 79, NACCD Records.

9. Synopsis of Malloy, Hysell, Forsythe, Green, Davis, Reed statements, and report by Albert Schwaller, Homicide File 7182, AM File; *DFP*, Aug. 1, 1967, May 17, 1969, Feb. 7, 11, 1970; *NYT*, May 7, 1969; *DN*, July 31, Aug. 8, 1967; Hersey, *Algiers Motel*, pp. 13, 222–25, 239–41.

10. Schwaller report, Synopsis of Sortor, Forsythe, Green, Malloy, Hysell statements, Homicide File 7182, AM File; To Director from Detroit, Aug. 2, 4, 1967, FBI-FOIA; Report of Dobranski to Robert Conot, n.d., Box 77, NACCD Records; Hersey, *Algiers Motel*, pp. 246, 297.

11. Report of SA, Jan. 4, 1968, FBI-FOIA; Rosema Complaint Report, SP File 20-762-67, Department of State Police, Lansing, Michigan; Fonger Complaint Report, Aug. 1, 1967, Warrant Request: Temple, AM File; Hersey, *Algiers Motel*, pp. 246–47.

12. Senak statement [July 31, 1967], AM File; Fonger Complaint Report, Aug. 1, 1967, Warrant Request: Temple, ibid.; No. A-140012, Opinion and Order, Dec. 1, 1967, ibid.; Royal K. Caddy Complaint Report, Aug. 1, 1967, SP File 20-762-67; *NYT*, May 24, 1969; *DN*, May 21, 1969, Feb. 12, 19, 24, 1970; *DFP*, Feb. 11, 15, 25, 1970; Locke, *Detroit Riot*, p. 46.

13. Synopsis of Lawanda J. Schettler statement, Homicide File 7182, AM File; Hersey, *Algiers Motel*, pp. 291–93; *DFP*, Feb. 11, 1970.

14. Statement by Hallmark [July 31, 1967], AM File; People vs. Ronald August, No. 139718, People vs. Robert Paille, No. 139719 (hereafter Nos. 139718, 139719), Examination, Aug. 14, 1967, pp. 125–29, Aug. 16, p. 400, AM File; Fonger Complaint Report, Aug. 1, 1967, Warrant Request: Temple, ibid.; Synopsis of Archie Davis statement, Homicide File 7182, ibid.; Caddy Complaint Report, Aug. 1, 1967, SP File 20-762-67; *Fifth Estate*, Sept. 15–30 [1967], Case 55-15-X, Records of the United States Senate, RG 46, NARA; *DFP*, May 24, June 4, 1969, Jan. 29, Feb. 12, 1970, Aug. 8, 1972; *DN*, Jan. 31, 1970.

15. Synopsis of Gilmore and Tucker statements, Homicide File 7182, AM File; *DN*, Aug. 3, 1967; *DFP*, June 3, 1969, Jan. 30, 1970.

16. Synopsis of Reed and Davis statements, Homicide File 7182, AM File; To Director from Detroit, Aug. 2, 12, 1967, FBI-FOIA; Hersey, *Algiers Motel*, pp. 283–84, 297–99.

17. *DFP*, Jan. 29, Feb. 15, 1970; Schwaller report, Homicide File 7182, AM File.

18. Official Proceedings before the National Advisory Commission on Civil Disorders, Aug. 15, 1967, p. 483, Series 1, Box 2, NACCD Records; Hersey, *Algiers Motel*, pp. 254, 271–72; *DN*, July 31, 1967, Feb. 6, 1970; *DFP*, May 17, 1969; Tom Parmenter, "The Breakdown of Law and Order," *Trans-Action* 4 (Sept. 1967): 8.

19. No. A-140012, Sept. 27, 1967, pp. 8, 11, 84, Sept. 28, 1967, pp. 11, 142, 195–96, 202, Sept. 29, 1967, pp. 94–96, 107–8, 142, AM File; Schwaller report, Synopsis of Thomas, Forsythe, Davis, Sortor, Malloy, and Hysell statements, Homicide File 7182, ibid.; Thomas statements, July 31, Aug. 2, 1967, ibid.; Incidents reported to . . . John Conyers . . . , n.d., Joseph A. Labadie Collection, University of Michigan Library, Ann Arbor, Michigan; *DFP*, Aug. 1, 1967, May 20, 23, 24, June 4, 1969, Feb. 6, 11, 1970; *DN*, July 31, 1967, May 23, 1969, Feb. 6, 7, 11, 12, 1970, July 23, 1977; Hersey, *Algiers Motel*, pp. 254–56, 261–62.

20. Schwaller report, Synopsis of Malloy and Davis statements, Homicide File 7182, AM File; Nos. 139718, 139719, Aug. 14, 1967, pp. 53–54, ibid.; *DN*, July 31, 1967, May 20, 21, 1969; *DFP*, July 31, Aug. 1, 1967; Hersey, *Algiers Motel*, pp. 269–70.

21. Fonger Complaint Report, Aug. 1, 1967, Warrant Request: Temple, AM File; Confidential Report, Aug. 1, 1967, ibid.; *NYT*, May 24, 1969; *DFP*, May 24, 1969; Hersey, *Algiers Motel*, pp. 249–50.

22. Schwaller report, Synopsis of Forsythe, Sortor, Green, and August statements, Homicide File 7182, AM File; No. A-140012, Sept. 29, 1967, p. 109, ibid.; *DFP*, Aug. 1, 1967, May 20, 21, 1969, Feb. 11, 1970; *DN*, July 31, 1967, May 27, 1969, Feb. 11, 1970; Hersey, *Algiers Motel*, pp. 264–68.

23. Synopsis of Davis, Reed, Green, Malloy, and Hysell statements, Schwaller report, Homicide File 7182, AM File; Thomas statement, July 31, 1967, ibid.; No. A-140012, Sept. 28, 1967, pp. 197–98, Sept. 29, 1967, p. 23; George H. Bays Complaint Report, Aug. 8, 1967, SP File 20-762-67; *DN*, July 31, 1967, Feb. 11, 1970; *DFP*, May 23, 1969, Feb. 7, Aug. 1, 1970; Hersey, *Algiers Motel*, pp. 273–76, 279.

24. Synopsis of Forsythe and Thomas statements, Schwaller report, Homicide File 7182, AM File; Thomas statement, July 31, 1967, ibid.; Nos. 139718, 139719, Aug. 15, 1967, pp. 191, 193, ibid.; No. A-140012, Sept. 27, 1967, pp.

12–13; *DFP*, May 20, 23, June 4, 1969; *NYT*, Aug. 18, 1967, May 21, 23, 1969; *DN*, May 21, 23, 1969, July 23, 1977.

25. Synopsis of August statement, July 31, 1967, Homicide File 7182, AM File. There is a copy of the August confession in Hersey, *Algiers Motel*, pp. 213–14.

26. Synopsis of Thomas, Sortor, Dismukes, Hysell, and Wayne Henson statements, Homicide File 7182, AM File; *DFP*, May 23, 1969; *NYT*, May 23, 1969; Hersey, *Algiers Motel*, p. 282.

27. *DFP*, July 31, 1967, May 27, June 4, 1969; *DN*, June 4, 1969, Feb. 17, 1972, July 23, 1977; *NYT*, June 4, 1969.

28. A bleeding Green had told Gilmore about the three bodies, and Fletcher Williams of the Hendrix Patrol Service and other Hendrix guards went to the Manor House to check. Synopsis of Williams statement, Homicide File 7182, AM File; "July 31, 1967 – Zisler," ibid.; *DFP*, July 31, 1967.

29. Synopsis of Gilmore and Williams statements, Homicide File 7182, AM File; Glinski to Chief of Detectives, July 26, 1967, Edward Hay and Lyle Thayer to Commanding Officer, July 30, 1967, ibid.; Case No. 5677 Reported from Garden, July 26, 1967, ibid.; Report of SA, Aug. 16, 1967, FBI-FOIA; Chronological Index, Civil Disorder, July 1967, Reported to Homicide Bureau, Series 4, Box 22, NACCD Records; DRK, July 26, 1967, Box 345, GR Papers; *DN*, July 26, 1967; *DFP*, July 31, 1967.

30. *NYT*, May 24, 1969; *DFP*, July 31, 1967, May 24, 27, 28, 1969; *DN*, May 27, 1969; "Evidence," in Warrant Request: Temple, AM File.

31. *DFP*, July 31, 1967; American Newspaper Publishers Association, *Reporting the Detroit Riot* [New York, 1968], pp. 30–32; Nos. 139718, 139719, Aug. 14, 1967, pp. 17, 23, AM File.

32. Hersey, *Algiers Motel*, pp. 41–43, 45–46; *DN*, July 30, 1967; *DFP*, July 31, 1967; To Director from Detroit, July 31, Aug. 2, 1967, C. R. McGowan to A. Rosen, FBI-FOIA; Report of SA, Aug. 16, 1967, ibid.

33. *DFP*, July 31, 1967; Hersey, *Algiers Motel*, pp. 49, 54–55; Xavier Nicholas interviews with S. Allen Early and Elliot Hall [Jan. 1981], copy of tapes in my possession; Report of SA, Aug. 16, 1967, FBI-FOIA; Interview with William Cahalan, July 23, 1984, pp. 20–21, transcript in MHC; Hubert Locke to Fine, Jan. 4, 1984.

34. Minutes of Meeting Held . . . July 30, 1967, AM File; *DFP*, July 31, 1967; *DN*, July 31, Aug. 1, 1967; Bays Complaint Report, Aug. 5, 1967, SP File 20-762-67.

35. Locke to Fine, Jan. 4, 1984; *DFP*, May 17, June 4, 1969; *DN*, July 22, 1977; Evidentiary Hearing Notes, Feb. 14, 1972, AM File; Senak Report, July 26, [29], 1967, ibid. The Senak report carries a July 26 date, but it was submitted on July 29.

36. "Show-Ups," Warrant Request: Temple, AM File; Polygraph tests, Thomas and Green, Aug. 3, 1967, ibid.; Bays Complaint Report, Aug. 5, 1967, SP File 20-762-67; Hersey, *Algiers Motel*, pp. 288–89, 296–97.

37. Hallmark statement [July 31, 1967], AM File; August report, July 31, 1967, Warrant Request: Temple, ibid.; Synopsis of Paille statement, Homicide File 7182, ibid.; Evidentiary Hearing Notes, Feb. 14, 1972, AM File; People vs. Robert Paille, Nos. 139718, 139719, Opinion of George T. Ryan [Aug. 7, 1972], ibid.

38. Hallmark statement [July 31, 1967], AM File; Synopsis of August state-

ment, ibid.; Hersey, *Algiers Motel*, p. 215; *DFP*, May 17, 27, June 4, 1969; *NYT*, May 27, 1969.

39. Hallmark statement [July 31, 1967], AM File; Paille statement, ibid.; Senak statement, July 31, 1967, ibid.; Evidentiary Hearing Notes, Feb. 14, 1972, ibid.; Ryan Opinion, ibid.; Hersey, *Algiers Motel*, pp. 212, 215–16.

40. *DN*, Aug. 1, 1967; *DFP*, Aug. 1, 5, 1967; People vs. Melvin Dismukes, No. 139613, Examination, Aug. 4, 1967, AM File; *NYT*, Mar. 1, 1970; Hersey, *Algiers Motel*, pp. 302–3, 390–91.

41. *DN*, Aug. 3, 8, 1967; *DFP*, Aug. 5, 8, 9, 1967; Bays Complaint Report, Aug. 8, 1967, SP File 20-762-67; Hersey, *Algiers Motel*, pp. 299, 301.

42. Nos. 139718, 139719, Aug. 15, 1967, pp. 274–76, Aug. 17, 1967, pp. 408–16, AM File; *DFP*, Aug. 16, 1967; *MC*, Aug. 19, 1967; Hersey, *Algiers Motel*, pp. 315, 316.

43. *DFP*, Aug. 24, Sept. 16, 1967; SA Reports, Aug. 25 (and enclosed complaint), Sept. 21, 1967, FBI-FOIA.

44. *DN*, Aug. 28, 1967; Hersey, *Algiers Motel*, pp. 344–49; *MC*, Aug. 26, Sept. 2, 1967; "Hear-Ye," handbill in Detroit Riot File, Community Relations Service, Department of Justice, FBI-FOIA; Albert B. Cleage, Jr., "The Death of Fear," *Negro Digest* 17 (Nov. 1967): 29–30; "The People's Tribunal . . . Aug. 30, 1967," Aug. 31, 1967, FBI-FOIA. Nicholas interview with Dan Aldridge [1982], copy of tape in my possession; Interview with Kenneth Cockrell, Aug. 26, 1985, p. 41, transcript in MHC. Cleage later claimed that the trial had been held in his church because of fear that the police would have blown up any other place. Nicholas interview with Jerimaje [1982], copy of tape in my possession.

45. "The People's Tribunal," Aug. 31, 1967, FBI-FOIA; *MC*, Sept. 16, 1967; Cockrell interview, pp. 1, 39–41; *Fifth Estate*, Sept. 15–30, 1967, Case 55-15-X, RG 46; Hersey, *Algiers Motel*, pp. 349–51. The Detroit Bar Association considered the possible disbarment of the attorneys who participated in the trial. *DN*, Sept. 20, 1967; *MC*, Sept. 9, 1967.

46. No. A-140012, Sept. 27–29, 1967, AM File; ibid., Opinion and Order, Dec. 1, 1967, ibid.

47. *People vs. Paille* no. 2, 383 Mich. 621, 626 (1970); *Detroit Daily Press*, Dec. 6, 1967; John C. Emery to John Feikens, n.d., Box 15, ND Papers; John Pittoni, "Perspectives and Prospects on Law," May 1, 1968, ibid.

48. *MC*, Mar. 23, 1968; *People* vs. *Paille* no. 1, 383 Mich. 605 (1970); Evidentiary Hearing, Feb. 14, 1972, AM File; Ryan Opinion [Aug. 7, 1972], ibid.; *Garrity* vs. *New Jersey*, 385 U.S. 493 (1965); *DFP*, July 26, Aug. 8, 1972; FBI Document, Aug. 5, 1971, FBI-FOIA; FBI Reports, Nov. 10, 1972, Mar. 20, 1973, ibid.; *DN*, Aug. 4, 1971, Sept. 16, 1972; Hersey, *Algiers Motel*, pp. 388–89.

49. 383 Mich. 621; *DFP*, Nov. 6, 1968; *DN*, July 18, 1971.

50. SA Report, July 16, 1968, FBI-FOIA; Opinion and Order, Dec. 8, 1968, AM File; *DFP*, Dec. 20, 1968, Jan. 30, 1969, July 23, 1972; *MC*, June 28, 1969; *NYT*, June 28, July 9, 1968, Jan. 30, June 15, 1969; Cahalan interview, p. 26.

51. *DFP*, May 14, 18, 1969; *NYT*, May 14, 1969.

52. *DFP*, May 12, 14, 16–June 9, 1969, passim, July 26, 1972; *DN*, May 13–June 9, 1969, passim; *NYT*, May 13–June 9, 1969, passim, Mar. 1, 1970.

53. *DFP*, June 10, 11, 15, 1969; *DN*, June 12, 1969; *NYT*, June 10, 11, 1969, Mar. 1, 1970; Cahalan interview, p. 28.

54. *Newsweek* 73 (June 2, 1969): 32; *MC*, June 21, 28, 1969; *DN*, June 11, 1969; *DFP*, June 11, 1969. Beer informed the court that Mrs. Pollard and Carl Cooper's mother told him that it had been a fair trial. *NYT*, June 11, 1969.

55. *NYT*, May 4, 1968; *DFP*, Jan. 18, 21, 29, 1970, July 26, 1972; Doar Memorandum for Attorney General, Sept. 28, 1967, Box 29, Clark Papers; Doar to Director, July 31, 1967, From Director to SAC Detroit, Dec. 19, 1967, To Director from Detroit, May 3, 1968, To Director from SAC Detroit, Sept. 23, 1969, FBI-FOIA; U.S.A. vs. August et al., 43459, Motion by Lippitt and Konrad Kohl, Aug. 15, 1968, ibid.; *NYT*, Jan. 1970.

56. *DFP*, Jan. 23, 24, 28, Mar. 1, 1970; *NYT*, Jan. 28, 1970.

57. For the Flint trial, see *DFP*, Jan. 29–Feb. 26, 1970, passim, July 26, 1972; *DN*, Jan. 31–Feb. 27, 1970, passim; and *NYT*, Feb. 1–26, 1970, passim.

58. *NYT*, Mar. 1, 1970; *DFP*, Mar. 1, July 26, 1970; *DN*, Feb. 26, 1971.

59. *DFP*, June 20, 1969, July 26, Aug. 8, Nov. 7, 1972; *DN*, Feb. 12, 1976.

60. Teletype, Jan. 16, 1968, FBI-FOIA; *DFP*, Feb. 26, 27, 1970; To Delore Richard, Apr. 11, 1972, Lippitt to John Nichols, June 27, 1973, James Bannon to Anthony Bertoni, July 3, 1973, Paille to Philip G. Tannian, Feb. 19, 1974, James Jackson to George Bennett, Sept. 23, 1975, AM File; Order of Tannian, Feb. 21, 1974, ibid.; Paille statement, May 1, 1974, ibid.; August and Senak personnel files, ibid.; *DN*, Sept. 9, 1979.

61. Michigan, ex rel, Cahalan vs. Algiers Motel, Sept. 26, 1967, AM File; SA Report, Oct. 10, 1967, FBI-FOIA; Hersey, *Algiers Motel*, pp. 368, 387; *NYT*, May 4, 1968; *DFP*, July 23, 1972; *DN*, May 2, 1979.

Chapter 12

1. Hubert G. Locke, *The Detroit Riot of 1967* (Detroit: Wayne State University Press, 1969), p. 23.

2. Elliot D. Luby and James Grisell, "Grievances of Detroit Negro Arrestees" [1968], pp. 15–16, Detroit Public Library, Detroit, Michigan; David O. Sears and John B. McConahay, *The Politics of Violence: The New Urban Blacks and the Watts Riot* (Boston: Houghton Mifflin Co., 1973), p. 9. For other estimates of the number of Detroit stores looted, see Mutual Loss Research Bureau, "The Detroit Report" [Sept. 1967], Series 4, Box 22, NACCD Records; *DN*, Aug. 11, 1967, July 18, 1982; *DFP*, Aug. 12, 1967; Leonard A. Proctor to Richard Strichartz, Aug. 14, 1967, Box 393, JPC Papers; and E. L. Quarantelli and Russell Dynes, "Looting in Civil Disorders: An Index of Social Change," in Louis H. Masotti and Don R. Bowen, eds., *Riots and Rebellion* (Beverly Hills: Sage Publications, 1968), p. 131.

3. [David] Chambers Memorandum, Aug. 24, 1967, Series 4, Box 22, NACCD Records; *NYT*, July 28, Dec. 10, 1967; *Detroit Jewish News*, July 28, 1967.

4. *DFP*, July 24, 1967; *NYT*, July 25, 1967; Herman Wilson Memorandum to Charles E. Nelson (interview with Francis Kornegay et al.), n.d., Series 59, Box 2, NACCD Records; Interview with John Nichols, Aug. 13, 1984, pp. 71, 76, transcript in MHC; American Newspaper Publishers Association (ANPA), *Reporting the Detroit Riot* [New York, 1968], pp. 13–14.

5. N. C. Rayford to Milan C. Miskovsky, Dec. 27, 1967, Series 4, Box 22, NACCD Records; *NYT*, July 25, 1967; *DFP*, July 24, 26, Aug. 3, 1967; Quarantelli and Dynes, "Looting," p. 134; Edward C. Banfield, *The Unheavenly City*

(Boston: Little, Brown and Co., 1970), p. 197; Interfaith Emergency Center, Progress Report, Aug. 30, 1967, Human Relations, 1966–1970, Archives of the Archdiocese of Detroit, Detroit, Michigan; Detroit to Director, Sept. 18, 1967, 1:58 P.M., FBI-FOIA; [DPD] *Statistical Report on the Civil Disorder Occurring in the City of Detroit, July 1967*, p. 44; Edward L. Sash [sic], Commissioner's File, DPD.

6. Xavier Nicholas interviews with Ron Hewitt [1982] and Bernard Klein [1982], copy of tapes in my possession; Nichols interview, p. 76.

7. Richard Alan Berk, "The Role of Ghetto Retail Merchants in Civil Disorders" (Ph.D. diss., Johns Hopkins University, 1970), pp. 48, 163, 179; Inter-University Consortium for Political and Social Research, Black File, Nos. 229–30, Detroit data for Angus Campbell and Howard Schuman, "Racial Attitudes in Fifteen American Cities," in *Supplemental Studies for the National Advisory Commission on Civil Disorders* (Washington: GPO, 1968).

8. Barbara Wilson Tinker, *When the Fire Reaches Us* (New York: William Morrow and Co., 1970), p. 197; Deposition of Stanley Webb, Jan. 11, 1968, Series 32, Box 2, NACCD Records; Detroit to Director, Sept. 18, 1967, 1:58 P.M., FBI-FOIA; *Report of the National Advisory Commission on Civil Disorders* (Washington: GPO, 1968), p. 49; *MC*, July 29, Aug. 5, 12, 1967; *DFP*, July 24, 25, 28, 30, Aug. 7, 1967; *DN*, July 26, 1967, July 18, 1982; Interview with Karl Gregory, July 12, 1984, pp. 22–23, transcript in MHC; John M. Koval to Nicholas P. Thomas, Aug. 22, 1967, Box 346, GR Papers; Joe Lapointe, "Six Days in July," *Detroit Monthly*, July 1987, p. 67.

9. *Detroit Jewish News*, July 28, 1967; *Los Angeles Times*, July 27, 1967, DRSB No. 1; Nicholas interview with Albert J. Dunmore [1982], copy of tape in my possession; Leonard Milstein, "Jewish Merchants in Detroit's Prime Affected Areas" [Jan. 4, 1968], p. 5, Burton Historical Collection, Detroit, Michigan; Richard Lobenthal to Benjamin Epstein, Aug. 7, 1967, Box 6, Leonard Moss Papers, ALHUA; Berk, "Ghetto Retail Merchants," p. 179.

10. *DFP*, July 26, 1967. Luby and Grisell, "Grievances," pp. 14–15, places the number of Chaldean stores at 96 and states that 90 had been burned.

11. John Ursu Memorandum on Detroit interviews, n.d., Box 82, NACCD Records; Detroit Fire Department, Civil Disturbance July 1967, A Preliminary Report, Feb. 1968, Box 5, Ray Girardin Papers, Burton Historical Collection; Charles J. Quinlan to Mayor's Development Team, Aug. 11, 1967, Box 533, JPC Papers; Chronological Order of Events at Detroit Fire Department . . . , July 23, 1967 to Aug. 6, 1967, Box 564, ibid.; Official Transcript of Proceedings before the National Advisory Commission on Civil Disorders, Aug. 15, 1967, pp. 533–36, Series 1, Box 2, NACCD Records; Permanent Subcommittee on Investigations of the Senate Committee on Government Operations, *Riots, Civil and Criminal Disorders, Hearings*, 90th Cong., 2d sess., 1968, pt. 7:1493–98, 1499; Senate Committee on the Judiciary, *Antiriot Bill 1967, Hearings*, 90th Cong., 1st sess., 1967, pt. 2:836; "Re Rioting Beginning July 23, 1967," Aug. 9, 1967, FBI-FOIA; Capture and Record of Civil Disorder, July 23–July 28, 1967, Box 345, GR Papers; Statistical Data, Detroit Civil Disorder, ibid.; *NACCD Report*, p. 38; *DFP*, Aug. 2, 1967.

12. James A. Wiley to Cavanagh, n.d., and enclosures, Box 565, JPC Papers; American Retail Federation, "The Crisis in American Cities: A Report on Civil Disorders in 1967," Sept. 6, 1967, Series 45, Box 15, NACCD Records; *DN*, Aug.

5, 1967; *DFP*, Aug. 12, 1967; Detroit Fire Department, Civil Disturbance, Box 5, Girardin Papers; *NACCD Report*, p. 325.

13. *NACCD Report*, p. 67; Capture and Record, Box 345, GR Papers; [DPD], *Statistical Report*, p. 45; *DFP*, Aug. 6, 1967; Van Gordon Sauter and Burleigh Hines, *Nightmare in Detroit* (Chicago: Henry Regnery Co., 1968), p. 210; Burt Bradley to Conrad Mallett, Aug. 7, 1967, Box 532, JPC Papers; Statement of Arthur Yim . . . , Aug. 29, 1967, Box 531, ibid.

14. [DPD] *Statistical Report*, p. 4; Albert B. Cleage, Jr., *The Black Messiah* (New York: Sheed and Ward, 1968), p. 140; Garry Wills, *The Second Civil War* (New York: New American Library, 1968), p. 119; *Los Angeles Times*, July 27, 1967, DRSB No. 1; *DFP*, July 24, 1967.

15. Wilson Memorandum to Nelson (interview with Charles Brown), n.d., Series 59, Box 2, NACCD Records; Re Rioting, Detroit . . . July 23, 1967, Aug. 17, 1967, FBI-FOIA; Joe R. Feagin and Harlan Hahn, *Ghetto Revolts* (New York: Macmillan Co., 1973), p. 178; Capture and Record, Box 345, GR Papers; *DFP*, Aug. 2, 1967; *DN*, Aug. 7, 1967; "Detroit Fires of 1967," *Firemen* 34 (Oct. 1967): 14; Frank Truesdale et al., Everybody was Eating Back Then, in "Field Notes . . . Discussion Paper No. 3: The Geography of the Children of Detroit," University of Michigan Library, Ann Arbor, Michigan.

16. Nicholas interviews with Richard Lobenthal [1982] and Ernest Wilsoy [1982], copy of tapes in my possession; *Newsweek* 70 (Aug. 7, 1967): 19; Minutes of the Third Meeting of the Ad Hoc Committee . . . , Nov. 11, 1967, Box 345, GR Papers; Locke statement [Sept. 22-23, 1967], Box 28, ORA Papers; Charlotte Darrow and Paul Lowinger, "The Detroit Uprising . . . ," in Jules H. Masserman, ed., *The Dynamics of Protest* (New York: Grune and Stratton, 1968), p. 126.

17. John E. Gross to Robert McClear, Aug. 9, 1967, Box 532, JPC Papers.

18. Yim statement, Aug. 29, 1967, Box 531, ibid.; Dykhouse to Romney, Box 319, GR Papers. See chap. 3.

19. *DFP*, Aug. 11, 1967; Yim statement, Aug. 29, 1967, Box 531, JPC Papers.

20. Releases, July 26, 27, 1967, Box 346, GR Papers; Dykhouse to Romney, July 31, 1967, Box 319, ibid.; Strichartz to Cavanagh, Oct. 26, 1967, Box 534, JPC Papers.

21. Dykhouse to Romney, July 31, 1967, Box 319, GR Papers; Mutual Loss Research Bureau, "Detroit Report," Series 4, Box 22, NACCD Records; John Wrench to Sarah Carey, Dec. 18, 1967, and enclosed John Denenberg to Thomas E. Crowley, Aug. 17, 1967, ibid.; *DFP*, Aug. 12, 1967.

22. Yim statement, Aug. 29, 1967, Box 531, JPC Papers; Mayor's Development Team report, with Strichartz to Cavanagh, Oct. 26, 1967, Box 534, ibid.; Cavanagh testimony, Apr. 30, 1968, Box 465, ibid.; Cavanagh to Stanford G. Ross, Nov. 6, 1967, Box 358, ibid.; *NYT*, Aug. 30, 1967; Charles Young to Philip Hart, Oct. 23, 1967, Box 129, Philip Hart Papers, MHC; John Pittoni to Joseph Hudson, Aug. 5, 1968, Box 15, ND Papers; *DFP*, Aug. 30, 1967; *NACCD Report*, pp. 307-8.

23. *MC*, July 29, 1967; *DFP*, July 28, 1967, July 23, 1972.

24. Abe H. Cherow to Hart, Oct. 17, 1967, Box 129, Hart Papers; *DN*, July 18, 1982.

25. *NYT*, July 29, 1967; *DFP*, Aug. 5, 12, 1967; *DN*, Aug. 11, Nov. 3, 9, 1967; Detroit Fire Department, Civil Disturbance, Box 5, Girardin Papers; Dykhouse

to Romney, July 31, 1967, Box 319, GR Papers; Mutual Loss Research Bureau, "Detroit Report," Series 22, Box 4, NACCD Records; *NACCD Report*, p. 326.

26. *NACCD Report*, pp. 61, 306; Willard A. Heaps, *Riots, U.S.A., 1765-1970*, rev. ed. (New York: Seabury Press, 1970), pp. 153-54; Mutual Loss Research Bureau, "Detroit Report," Series 22, Box 14, NACCD Records.

27. Minutes of Third Meeting of Ad Hoc Committee, Nov. 11, 1967, Box 345, GR Papers; Koval to Thomas, Aug. 22, 1967, and enclosure, Box 346, ibid.; *DFP*, July 27, 30, 1967; *DN*, Nov. 3, 1967; ANPA, *Detroit Riot*, p. 14.

28. "City Costs of Civil Disturbance," Aug. 14, 1967, Box 393, JPC Papers; "Statistics on Detroit Riot July 1967," ibid.; Proctor to Strichartz, Aug. 14, Sept. 11, 1967, ibid.; Harold W. Pearson to Mayor's Development Team, Aug. 7, 1967, Box 533, ibid.; Koval to Charles Orlebeke and Thomas, Aug. 17, 1967, Box 346, GR Papers; Minutes of Third Meeting of Ad Hoc Committee, Nov. 11, 1967, Box 345, ibid.; *NACCD Report*, p. 326; John M. Taylor to Glenn S. Allen, Jr., Sept. 15, 1967, Box 1, Records of the Michigan Department of Military Affairs, Adjutant General's Division, RG 78-125, State Archives, Lansing, Michigan; David E. McGiffert to James O. Eastland, Sept. 23, 1967, Box 4, Accession 71A1, Records of the Office of the Secretary of the Army, RG 335, Office of the Adjutant General, Alexandria, Virginia.

29. [DPD] *Statistical Report*, pp. 46, 48, 49; *Riots, Civil and Criminal Disorders*, pt. 7:1495; Albert P. Schwaller, "Total Injured by Gunfire . . . , July, 1967," Commissioner's File, DPD; Numerical Index of Injured and Fatal Victims, July 1967, ibid.; Ursu Memorandum on Detroit interviews, n.d., Box 82, NACCD Records; *DFP*, July 19, 1987.

30. Alexander J. Walt et al., "The Anatomy of a Civil Disturbance," *JAMA* 202 (Oct. 30, 1967): 394-95; Louis Graff, "A New Kind of Hospital Disaster," *Michigan Hospitals* 3 (Aug. 1967): 24-25, 26; Emil Mazey to Officers . . . , Aug. 14, 1967, Box 638, Walter Reuther Papers, ALHUA; Civil Disturbance Detroit . . . Health Department Activities, July 23-Aug. 1, 1967, Box 533, JPC Papers; Bryan T. Downes, "A Critical Reexamination of the Social and Political Characteristics of Riot Cities," *Social Science Quarterly* 5 (Sept. 1970): 351-52. Cf. Robert Roselle to John L. McClellan, Jan. 11, 1968, Box 426, JPC Papers.

31. *NACCD Report*, p. 66; Bernard Rosenberg, "Detroit . . . ," *Dissent* 14 (Nov.-Dec. 1967): 677; *DFP*, July 27, 1967; *DN*, Aug. 3, 1967; Wills, *Civil War*, pp. 55-56; Sauter and Hines, *Nightmare*, pp. 55-56; Lobenthal interview; ANPA, *Detroit Riot*, p. 11; Locke to Sidney Fine, Jan. 4, 1984; Downes, "Critical Reexamination," pp. 351-52.

32. [DPD] *Statistical Report*, p. 46; Detroit Riot Injuries and Fatalities folder, Box 5, Girardin Papers. My summary of the responsibility for riot deaths is based on the deaths described in previous chapters. For a somewhat different breakdown, see *DFP*, Sept. 3, 1967, and *NACCD Report*, pp. 60-61.

33. ANPA, *Detroit Riot*, pp. 11, 35, 40; *DFP*, Sept. 3, 1967; Sauter and Hines, *Nightmare*, p. 219; Deposition of William Serrin and Gene Goltz, Jan. 8, 1968, Series 32, Box 2, NACCD Records.

34. Detroit Riot Injuries and Fatalities folder, Box 5, Girardin Papers; miscellaneous statistics in Box 82, NACCD Records; *DFP*, Sept. 3, 1967.

35. *NACCD Report*, pp. 55-56; *DFP*, Sept. 3, 1967; S. D. Romero and N. C. Rayford to Miskovsky, Dec. 18, 1967, Series 4, Box 22, NACCD Records; Nicholas interview with Jon Lowell [1982], copy of tape in my possession;

Maurice Kelman and Ed Batchelor interview with Ray Girardin, Oct. 29, 1971, pp. 420–22, transcript in my possession.

36. Headquarters Command Post Sniper Log, July 26–Aug. 2, 1967, Box 82, NACCD Records; Sniper Reports, July 23–29, 1967, Commissioner's File; *DFP*, July 25, 27, 31, 1967; Charles J. Quinlan to Mayor's Development Team, Aug. 11, 1967, Box 533, JPC Papers; Morris Janowitz, *Social Control of Escalated Riots* (Chicago: University of Chicago Center for Policy Study [1968]), p. 15; Robert M. Fogelson, *Violence as Protest: A Study of Riots and Ghettos* (Garden City, N.Y.: Doubleday and Co., 1971), p. 79.

37. To Director from Detroit, July 29, 1967, 3:39 P.M., 3:53 P.M., FBI-FOIA; *NYT*, July 27, 1967; *Detroit Scene* 1, no. 5 (1967): 13, Box 429, Reuther Papers; Girardin interview, pp. 421–22; Special Subcommittee of the House Committee on Armed Services to Inquire into the Capability of the National Guard to Cope with Civil Disturbances, *Hearings*, 90th Cong., 1st sess., 1967, pp. 5685, 5968; *DFP*, July 31, 1967.

38. *DN*, July 29, 1967; Richard Hofstadter and Michael Wallace, eds., *American Violence: A Documentary History* (New York: Alfred A. Knopf, 1970), pp. 268–69.

39. Strichartz to Cavanagh, Oct. 26, 1967, Box 534, JPC Papers; *MC*, July 29, Aug. 5, 1967; *DFP*, Oct. 26, 1967; *NYT*, Aug. 28, 1967; Hal DeLong, "Detroit Remembers July 1967 . . . ," *Police* 12 (May–June 1968): 7–8; Widick, "Motown Blues," *Nation* 205 (Aug. 14, 1967): 103; *Washington Post*, July 25, 1967.

Chapter 13

1. *DN*, July 28, 1967; *MC*, Aug. 12, 1967; *DFP*, Aug. 23, 1967; CCR Minutes, Aug. 17, 1967, Series IV, Box 4, CCR Papers; Interview with Arthur Johnson, July 23, 1984, pp. 6–7, transcript in MHC; Interview with Damon Keith, June 21, 1985, p. 30, ibid.

2. Robert M. Fogelson, *Violence as Protest: A Study of Riots and Ghettos* (Garden City, N.Y.: Doubleday and Co., 1971), pp. 129–31; *DFP*, July 25, 26, 1967; *DN*, July 25, 26, 1967; NAACP Release, July 31, 1967, Part 1, Series I, Box 24, DNAACP Papers; Tom Popp Memorandum to Herman Wilson (interview with William T. Patrick, Jr.), Oct. 13, 1967, Series 59, Box 2, NACCD Records.

3. *MC*, July 29, 1967.

4. Ibid.; *DN*, July 28, 1967; *MC*, Aug. 5, 1967; J. Anthony Lukas, "Postscript on Detroit: 'Whitey Hasn't Got the Message,' " *NYT Magazine*, Aug. 27, 1967; David Paul Boesel, "The Ghetto Riots 1964–1968" (Ph.D. diss., Cornell University, 1972), p. 98.

5. *NYT*, July 28, 1967.

6. Arthur Weiseger Memorandum to Francis Kornegay, Aug. 7, 1967, Box 12, DUL Papers; Neighborhood Service Organization Summer Week End Program, July–Aug. 1967, Box 21, United Community Services Papers, ALHUA.

7. *DFP*, July 25, 1967; Sheldon Levy, "Communication Processes in the Detroit Riot" [1968], pp. 11–15, Detroit Public Library; *The People Beyond 12th Street: A Survey of Attitudes of Detroit Negroes after the Riot of 1967* (Detroit: Detroit Urban League, 1967); *DN*, July 26, 1967; *DFP*, July 27, 1967; Questionnaires nos. 4001–67 passim, 6001–22 passim, Boxes 8–11, A-W Riot Studies;

David O. Sears and John B. McConahay, *The Politics of Violence: The New Urban Blacks and the Watts Riot* (Boston: Houghton Mifflin Co., 1973), p. 166.

8. *Grand Rapids Press*, July 24, 1967, DRSB No. 1; *DN*, July 24, 26, 1967; *DFP*, July 25, 1967.

9. [Jacqueline Giering, "The Innocent Victims," 1968], pp. 1-16, Edward Lurie Papers, in my possession; Paul Lowinger et al., "Case Study of the Detroit Uprising . . . ," *Archives of General Psychiatry* 21 (July 1969): 35.

10. *MC*, Aug. 5, 1967; *NYT*, July 28, 1967; *Time* 90 (Aug. 4, 1967): 14; Stanley Webb to Roger Wilkins, n.d., Detroit Riot File, Section I, Community Relations Service (CRS), Department of Justice, FBI-FOIA; *DFP*, July 24-27, Sept. 16, 1967.

11. Detroit Information: PNAC . . . , n.d., Box 79, NACCD Records; Deposition of Annie M. Watkins and George L. Kelley, Jan. 9, 1968, Series 32, Box 2, ibid.; Institute of Urban Dynamics, Urban Dynamics Proposal, n.d., Box 70, ND Papers.

12. Bill Dwyer to Burton Levy, July 28, 1967, Records of the Michigan Civil Rights Commission, RG 83-55 (unprocessed), State Archives, Lansing, Michigan; *MC*, July 29, 1967.

13. Levy, "Communication Processes," pp. 11-15; Josephine Gomon to Kids, July 25, 1967, Box 8, Josephine Gomon Papers, MHC.

14. CCR Minutes, Aug. 4, 1967, Series IV, Box 4, CCR Papers; *DN*, July 24, 26, 1967; Xavier Nicholas interview with Richard Lobenthal [1982], copy of tape in my possession; *DN*, July 24, 26, 1967. There is a copy of the Breakthrough poster in Box 232, GR Papers.

15. The letters sent to Cavanagh are in Boxes 394, 396, 397, JPC Papers, the letters to Romney, in Boxes 343, 344, GR Papers.

16. Richard V. Marks Memorandum to Richard Strichartz, Aug. 8, 1967, Box 533, JPC Papers.

17. "Summer Task Force and Post-Riot Emergency Needs" (hereafter "STF . . . Needs"), n.d., Box 534, JPC Papers; Malcolm G. Dade Memorandum to Conrad Mallett, Sept. 8, 1967, Box 340, ibid.; Burt Bradley to Mallett, Aug. 7, 1967, Box 532, ibid.; Testimony by . . . Cavanagh, Apr. 30, 1968, Box 465, ibid.; Sequence of Events, July 24, 26, 1967, Box 345, GR Papers; Romney-Cavanagh Press Conference, July 24, 1967, Box 244, ibid.; *DFP*, July 27, 1967.

18. For the role of the MCHRD, see Responses to the Recent Civil Disorders of the MCHRD, Center for Urban Studies Papers (unprocessed), ALHUA; Vivian Hogan and Luther Holt, ". . . Champ Summary Report," n.d., Box 16, Francis A. Kornegay Papers, MHC; Philip J. Rutledge to Strichartz, Aug. 8, 1967, Box 533, JPC Papers; Bradley to Mallett, Aug. 2, 1967, Box 398, ibid.; "STF . . . Needs," Box 534, ibid.; Willard Wirtz to Lyndon Johnson, Aug. 1, 1967, Box 6, EX HU2, WHCF; Report on Riot Cities, Detroit . . . , July 26, 1967, Box 43, Office Files of James Gaither, LBJ Library; and *DFP*, Aug. 22, 1967.

19. Robert D. Knox to Cavanagh, July 28, 1967, Box 398, JPC Papers; Knox to Mayor's Development Team (MDT), Aug. 7, 1967, Box 533, ibid.; "STF . . . Needs," Box 534, ibid.; "Status of Emergency Housing" [Aug. 2, 1967], Box 398, ibid.; Detroit Housing Commission, *Report to the Commissioners, Third Quarter, 1967*, pp. 5-6; *DFP*, Aug. 6, 1967.

20. *DFP*, July 25, 1967; Paul G. Conlan to R. Bernard Houston, July 29, 1967, Box 345, GR Papers.

21. For Health Department activities during the riot, see Civil Disturbance, Detroit, Michigan, Health Department, July 23-Aug. 1, 1967, Box 533, JPC Papers; Robert Willson to Roselle, July 26, 1967 (two letters), Box 398, ibid.; "STF . . . Needs," Box 534, ibid.; Sequence of Events, July 26, 1967, Box 345, GR Papers; Gaither to Joseph Califano, July 31, 1967, Box 43, Gaither File; *DFP*, July 27, 28, 1967; and Van Gordon Sauter and Burleigh Hines, *Nightmare in Detroit* (Chicago: Henry Regnery Co., 1968), p. 199.

22. Health Department Activities, July 23-Aug. 1, 1967, Box 533, JPC Papers; E. P. Henry to George Moriarty, Aug. 10, 1967, Commissioner's File, DPD; Larry Berkower, "Emergency Room Psychiatry during the Detroit Riot," *New Physician* 16 (Oct. 1967): 283; Alexander J. Walt et al., "The Anatomy of a Civil Disturbance," *JAMA* 202 (Oct. 30, 1967): 394-97; Louis Graff, "A New Kind of Hospital Disaster," *Michigan Hospitals* 3 (Aug. 1967): 24-27; Maria Phaneuf and Paul Lowinger, "Healers in a Sick Society," *American Journal of Nursing* 68 (June 1968): 1283; *DN*, July 24, Oct. 31, 1967; *DFP*, July 25, 1967; Joe Lapointe, "Six Days in July," *Detroit Monthly*, July 1987, p. 67.

23. Commissioner's Report, Department of Public Works, Re Recent Civil Disorder, Aug. 7, 1967, Box 533, JPC Papers; Meeting Re Riot-Damaged Buildings, Aug. 1, 1967, Box 532, ibid.; *DN*, July 26, 1967; *DFP*, July 26, 28, 1967.

24. For the demolition problem, see Commissioner's Report, Department of Public Works, Box 533, JPC Papers; R. F. Goddard to W. J. Robinson, Aug. 7, 1967, ibid.; Meeting Re Riot-Damaged Buildings, Aug. 1, 1967, Box 532, ibid.; "Building Demolition" [Oct. 16, 1967], ibid.; Alfred Berarducci Memo to File, Aug. 9, 1967, ibid.; MDT Report, with Strichartz to Cavanagh, Oct. 26, 1967, Box 534, ibid.; Robert W. Kearns to Cavanagh, Nov. 27, 1967, Goddard to Kearns, Nov. 24, 1967, Box 535, ibid.; Testimony by Cavanagh, Apr. 30, 1968, Box 465, ibid.; and James Wiley to Cavanagh, n.d., and enclosures, Box 565, ibid.

25. A. F. Malo to MDT, Aug. 8, 1967, Harold W. Pearson to MDT, Aug. 7, 1967, Pearson to Roselle, July 28, 1967, John Milko to Pearson, Aug. 7, 1967, Robert Forrest to Pearson, Aug. 8, 1967, Box 533, ibid.

26. *DFP*, July 28, 1967; Marks Memorandum to Strichartz, Aug. 8, 1967, Box 533, JPC Papers; Testimony by Cavanagh, Apr. 30, 1968, Box 465, ibid.

27. Charles A. Meyer to Cavanagh, Aug. 9, 1967, Box 398, JPC Papers.

28. Official Transcript of Proceedings before the National Advisory Commission on Civil Disorders, Aug. 15, 1967, p. 453, Series I, Box 2, NACCD Records; MCHRD Responses, Center for Urban Studies Papers; Permanent Subcommittee on Investigations of the Senate Committee on Government Operations, *Riots, Civil and Criminal Disorders, Hearings*, 90th Cong., 2d sess., 1968, pt. 7:1536-37; Interview with John M. May [1967], Box 16, A-W Riot Studies.

29. Alfred McClung Lee and Norman Raymond Humphrey, *Race Riot* (New York: Dryden Press, 1943), p. 48; Thomas R. Forrest, "Emergent Communal Response," in Leonard Gordon, ed., *A City in Crisis: The Case of Detroit* . . . ([Dubuque, Iowa]: Wm. C. Brown Co., 1971), pp. 94-95; Bradley to Mallett, Aug. 2, 1967, Box 398, JPC Papers; *DN*, July 26, 1967; *MC*, Feb. 10, 1968.

30. Michigan Employment Security Commission News Release, July 28, 1967, Box 244, GR Papers; Armond D. Bove to Glenn Allen et al., July 28, 1967, Box 319, ibid.

31. Thomas R. Johnson to Walter R. Greene, Aug. 16, 1967 (two letters),

James L. Rose Memorandum to Burton I. Gordin, July 26, 27, 28, 1967, RG 83-85; Governor Romney Report to the People, July 31, 1967, Box 346, GR Papers; Address by Romney, July 31, 1967, ibid.

32. *DN*, July 26, Aug. 1, 1967; *DFP*, July 31, 1967; *Meet the Press* 11 (July 30, 1967): 5-6; *NYT*, July 31, 1967; *Congressional Record*, 90th Cong., 1st sess., 1967, vol. 113, pt. 15:20596-97.

33. Romney and Cavanagh to Johnson, July 27, 1967, in "Final Report of Cyrus R. Vance Concerning the Detroit Riots, July 23 through August 2, 1967," app. 1, with Oral History of Cyrus Vance, Nov. 3, 1969, LBJ Library; Roselle to Cavanagh, n.d., Box 398, JPC Papers; Cavanagh to Vance, July 28, 1967, Philip Hart et al. to Johnson [July 27, 1967], Hart to Cavanagh, July 27, 1967, Box 393, ibid.; John Dingell to Romney, July 26, 1967, Box 345, GR Papers.

34. "For the Speaker," n.d., Box 58, Office Files of Joseph Califano, LBJ Library.

35. On this point, see James W. Button, *Black Violence: Political Impact of the 1960s Riots* (Princeton: Princeton University Press, 1978), pp. 31, 64.

36. Donald Lee Scruggs, "Lyndon Baines Johnson and the National Advisory Commission on Civil Disorders . . ." (Ph.D. diss., University of Oklahoma, 1980), p. 195; Note from Califano to Gaither on Gaither to Califano, July 31, 1967, Box 36, Gaither Files; Gaither for Califano, July 27, 1967, ibid.

37. Draft for President of letter to Romney, July 26, 1967, Office of Legal Counsel, Department of Justice, FOIA; Christopher to David Ginsburg [Nov. 22, 1967], and enclosed Memorandum, ibid.; Recommendations of Vance and Christopher . . . , July 27 [1967], Box 44, Gaither Files; Oral History Interview of Warren Christopher, Nov. 18, 1968, p. 3, LBJ Library.

38. "Vance Report," pp. 33-34; Farris Bryant Memorandum to Califano, July 27, 1967, Box 58, Califano Files; Matthew Nimetz to Califano, Aug. 9, 1967, Box 43, Gaither Files; Christopher to Ginsburg [Nov. 27, 1967], and enclosed Memorandum, Office of Legal Counsel, FOIA.

39. *DFP*, July 22, 26, 1967; Califano for President, Aug. 10, 1967, Box 58, Califano Files; Christopher to Robert E. Waldron, Aug. 16, 1967, Box 129, Philip Hart Papers, MHC.

40. Johnson to Cavanagh, July 27, 29, 1967, Box 395, JPC Papers; "Vance Report," pp. 34-35, 36-37; Califano for President, July 28, 1967, Box 58, Califano Files; Califano to President, Aug. 1, 2, 1967, Nimetz to Califano, Aug. 9, 1967, Box 43, Gaither Files; Gaither to Califano, Aug. 1, 1967, Box 36, ibid.

41. *DFP*, July 28, 1967; Christopher to Waldron, Aug. 16, 1967, Box 129, Hart Papers; "Vance Report," app. K; John Schnittker Memorandum to Christopher, Aug. 10, 1967, Box 15, Warren Christopher Papers, LBJ Library; Nimetz to Califano, Aug. 9, 1967, Box 43, Gaither Files; Testimony by Cavanagh, Apr. 30, 1968, Box 465, JPC Papers.

42. Testimony by Cavanagh, Apr. 30, 1968, Box 465, JPC Papers; Cavanagh to William Crook, Aug. 24, 1967, Box 394, ibid.; "Vance Report," pp. 36-37, app. K; Pat Kennedy to Vance, Aug. 2, 1967, Box 15, Christopher Papers; Notes on Meeting Held by Christopher, Aug. 9, 1967, ibid.

43. Strichartz to Christopher, Aug. 18, 1967, Box 15, Christopher Papers; Notes of Meeting, Aug. 9, 1967, ibid.; "Vance Report," pp. 38-40.

44. *DFP*, July 28, 1967; *Report of the National Advisory Commission on Civil*

Disorders (Washington: GPO, 1968), pp. 295-96; Special Advisory Commission on Civil Disorders, Minutes, July 29, 1967, Series 1, Box 1, NACCD Records.

45. *DN*, Aug. 2, 1967; Michael Lipsky and David J. Olson, *Commission Politics and the Processing of Racial Crises in America* (New Brunswick: Transaction Books, 1977), pp. 109-10. For Johnson's views regarding the riots and conspiracy, see Minutes and Documents of the Cabinet Meetings of President Johnson, 1963-1969, Aug. 2, 1967, Reel 3, University of Michigan Library; Richard Gid Powers, *Secrecy and Power: The Life of J. Edgar Hoover* (New York: The Free Press, 1987), pp. 422-23; and Fred R. Harris, *Potomac Fever* (New York: W. W. Norton and Co., 1977), p. 111.

46. Leonard Gordon, "Attempts to Bridge the Racial Gap: The Religious Establishment," in Gordon, ed., *City in Racial Crisis*, pp. 21-26; Forrest, "Communal Response," pp. 88-92; MCHRD Responses, Center for Urban Studies Papers; Paul G. Conlan to R. Bernard Houston, July 29, 1967, Box 345, GR Papers; IEC Release, July 26, 1967, Human Relations—Community Affairs, Archives of the Archdiocese of Detroit, Detroit, Michigan; United Community Services of Detroit (UCS) Newsletter, Aug. 8, 1967, Part II, Series II, Box 4, Metropolitan Detroit Council of Churches Papers, ALHUA; *DFP*, July 25, 1967.

47. MCHRD Responses, Center for Urban Studies Papers; *DFP*, July 27, 1967; Forrest, "Communal Response," pp. 95-98, 101; IEC Release, July 26, 1967, Human Relations—Community Affairs, Archives of Archdiocese; UCS Newsletter, Aug. 8, 1967, Part II, Series II, Box 4, Council of Churches Papers.

48. Forrest, "Communal Response," pp. 93, 95; CESSA Summaries, I, No. 6, n.d., Human Relations, 1966-1970, Archives of Archdiocese; Barefoot Sanders Memo for Califano, July 28, 1967, Box 58, Califano Files; MCHRD Responses, Center for Urban Studies Papers; Bradley to Mallett, Aug. 7, 1967, Box 532, JPC Papers; Harold Johnson statement [Aug. 16, 1967], ibid.

49. Forrest, "Communal Response," pp. 92, 95, 102-3; Roselle to Mallett, July 28, 1967, Bradley to Mallett, Aug. 2, 1967, Box 398, JPC Papers.

50. Forrest, "Communal Response," p. 103n; Inter-Faith Emergency Center, Progress Report, Aug. 30, 1967, Human Relations, 1966-1970, Archives of Archdiocese; CESSA, Sept. 12, 1967, ibid.; "Interfaith Emergency Program," n.d., Box 530, JPC Papers; S. Sidney Newhouse to Clay Howell, Nov. 27, 1967, Box 3, United Community Services of Detroit Papers (Feb. 2, 1976), ALHUA; *DN*, Sept. 20, 1967.

51. Conlan to Houston, July 29, 1967, Box 345, GR Papers; *DFP*, July 25, 1967; MCHRD Responses, Center for Urban Studies Papers; "A Reaction to the Detroit Riot of 1967," Human Relations-Community Affairs, Archives of Archdiocese; James Sheehan to Jack P. Sisson, Aug. 1, 1967, ibid.; Sheehan to Robert A. Hoppe, Aug. 1, 1967, Sheehan Correspondence, 1962-1969, ibid.; CESSA Summaries, I, No. 6, n.d., Human Relations, 1966-1970, ibid.; Statement by the CESSA Churches, n.d., ibid.; MCHRD Responses, Center for Urban Studies Papers; Roselle to Mallett, July 28, 1967, Bradley to Mallett, Aug. 2, 1967, Box 398, JPC Papers.

52. YMCA of Metropolitan Detroit, "Urban Youth Program at Work," July 27, 1967, Box 64, Richard Austin Papers, ALHUA; idem, "Report of Experience" [Sept. 1967], ibid.

53. *DFP*, July 25, 1967; *DN*, Aug. 1, 1967; Paul J. Carlson to Romney, July

26, 1967, Box 186, GR Papers; UCS Newsletter, Aug. 8, 1967, Part II, Series II, Box 4, Council of Churches Papers; Testimony by Cavanagh, Apr. 30, 1968, Box 465, JPC Papers.

54. Forrest, "Communal Response," pp. 93–94; Statement of Red Cross during Detroit Civil Disturbance, July 31, 1967, Box 348, JPC Papers; UCS Newsletter, Aug. 8, 1967, Part II, Series II, Box 4, Council of Churches Papers; "Michigan Minute Man," Special Edition, No. 1, July 27, 1967, Winston Wessels Papers (copy in my possession).

55. Report by Rene Freeman, n.d., Series III, Box 3, CCR Papers; Bradley to Mallett, Aug. 2, 1967, Box 398, JPC Papers; Minutes of the Extraordinary Session of the Board of Directors of the DUL, July 26, 1967, Box 41, DUL Papers; DUL Quarterly Report, July–Sept. 1967, Box 43, ibid.; DUL Release, July 26, 1967, Box 345, GR Papers; Lobenthal interview.

56. UCS, "A Report on 'Operation Find,' " Dec. 1967, Box 212, GR Papers; Sequence of Events, July 26, 1967, Box 345, ibid.; *DN*, Aug. 2, 1967; Testimony by Cavanagh, Apr. 30, 1968, Box 465, JPC Papers.

57. For Homes by Christmas, see Wilson Memorandum to Nelson (interview with Sally Cassidy), n.d., Series 59, Box 2, NACCD Records; Memorandum on Homes by Christmas, Sept. 15, 1967, Box 3, UCS Papers; Newhouse to Howell, Nov. 27, 1967, Raymond T. Huetteman, Jr., to Joseph S. Iannucci, Oct. 24, 1967, H. Frederick Brown to Richard F. Huegli, Oct. 4, Nov. 7, 1967, Emeric Kurtagh to Huegli, Oct. 3, 1967, ibid.; Memorandum of Understanding, Dec. 2, 1967, ibid.; Special Meeting of NSO Board of Directors, Aug. 14, 1967, Box 532, JPC Papers; *DFP*, Sept. 13, 1967; *City* 2 (Jan. 1968): 6; Joseph L. Hudson, "In the Aftermath of the Long, Hot Summer of 1967," *Michigan Courthouse Review* 17 (Dec. 1967): 17; and UCS Newsletter, Aug. 8, 1967, Part II, Series II, Box 4, Council of Churches Papers.

58. Anthony Ripley to Cavanagh, July 26, 1967, Box 398, JPC Papers; Statement of the . . . Detroit Board of Commerce, July 28, 1967, Box 319, GR Papers.

59. Romney and Cavanagh to ――――, July 27, 1967, Box 393, JPC Papers; "Aug. 8, 1967" (draft of Hudson remarks), Box 533, ibid.; New Detroit Committee, *Progress Report, April, 1968* [Detroit, 1968], pp. 21–22; *DN*, July 28, 1967; *DFP*, July 28, 1967.

60. Testimony by Cavanagh, Apr. 30, 1968, Box 465, JPC Papers; "Aug. 8, 1967," Box 533, ibid.; Bill Davidson, "If We Can't Solve the Problems of the Ghetto Here . . . ," *Saturday Evening Post* 241 (Oct. 5, 1968): 30.

61. Helen M. Graves, "New Detroit Committee/New Detroit, Incorporated: A Case Study of an Urban Coalition" (Ph.D. diss., Wayne State University, 1975), pp. 722–23; Interview with Joseph L. Hudson, Oct. 2, 1984, p. 4, transcript in MHC; [White and Campbell to Hudson], n.d., Joseph L. Hudson Papers, MHC; White and Campbell to Hudson, July 28, 1967 (two letters), ibid.

62. Campbell to Lena Bivens, Aug. 3, 1967, and enclosed "Meeting between . . . Hudson and Militant Negro Leadership . . . ," July 30, 1967, Hudson Papers; Hudson to Freeman [July 30 or 31, 1967], ibid.; Graves, "New Detroit," pp. 43–44; *NYT*, Aug. 13, 1967; Hudson interview, pp. 4–6; ―――― to Cavanagh, n.d., Box 372, JPC Papers.

63. Hudson, "In the Aftermath," p. 12; Hudson interview, pp. 6–7; Campbell to Roche, Aug. 3, 1967, Hudson Papers.

64. Kent Mathewson, "The Message . . . ," Feb. 23, 1968, Hudson Papers; [Hudson report, Aug. 10, 1967], ibid.; "Aug. 8, 1967," Box 533, JPC Papers.

65. New Detroit, *Progress Report*, pp. 22–23, 152–54; Graves, "New Detroit," pp. 760–62; *DFP*, Aug. 2, 1967; "Aug. 8, 1967," Box 533, JPC Papers; [Hudson report, Aug. 10, 1967], Hudson Papers; Lynda Ann Ewen, *Corporate Power and Urban Crises in Detroit* (Princeton: Princeton University Press, 1978), pp. 202, 210; *DFP*, Aug. 2, 1967; New Detroit, *Progress Report*, pp. 25–26, 152–54. Hudson was at the time chairman of the board of trustees of the Metropolitan Fund.

66. Hudson to Dear Friend, July 31, 1967, Box 533, JPC Papers; Notebook dated Oct. 11–23, 1967, Tag No. 21, ND Papers; Mildred Jeffrey to Reuther, July 28, 1967, Box 476, Walter Reuther Papers, ALHUA; Special Committee of the CCEO to Hudson, July 29, 1967, ibid.

67. "Aug. 8, 1967," Box 533, JPC Papers; Hudson interview, p. 8; Hubert Locke, *The Detroit Riot of 1967* (Detroit: Wayne State University Press, 1969), p. 103; Edgar Brazelton to Romney, Aug. 3, 1967, Roy Allen to Hudson, Aug. 14, 1967, Concerned Citizens for Action to Hudson, Aug. 8, 1967, Citizens–West Side Disaster Area to Hudson, Aug. 4, 1967, Jean Washington to Hudson, Aug. 4, 1967, Rolland E. Fisher to Cavanagh, Aug. 3, 1967, Freeman to Hudson, Aug. 9, 1967, Hudson Papers; Sidney Rosen to Hudson, Aug. 10, 1967, Robert Mejia to Hudson, Aug. 4, 1967, Box 533, JPC Papers; Brewster-Douglas Inter-Agency Association to Hudson, Aug. 4, 1967, Box 187, GR Papers; *MC*, Aug. 12, 1967.

68. *DFP*, July 28, Nov. 6, 1967, July 24, 1972; Meeting with Walter Reuther, July 28, 1967, Box 532, JPC Papers; Meeting Re Riot-Damaged Buildings, Aug. 1, 1967, ibid.; MDT Report, with Strichartz to Cavanagh, Oct. 26, 1967, Box 534, ibid.; Robert E. Toohey to Larry Gettlinger, Jan. 25, 1968, Gettlinger to Toohey, Mar. 8, 1968, Toohey to Reuther, Mar. 20, 1968, James Ogden to William T. Gossett, Apr. 21, 1968, Box 512, Reuther Papers; Jeffrey to Irving Bluestone, Aug. 1, 1967, Box 54, ibid.; *DN*, Aug. 2, 1967; *NYT*, Aug. 28, 1967.

69. Hudson to Orlando Wilson, Sept. 15, 1967, Box 533, JPC Papers.

Chapter 14

1. Seymour Spilerman, "The Causes of Racial Disturbances: A Comparison of Alternative Explanations," *American Sociological Review* 35 (Aug. 1970): 630, 645–46; idem, "The Causes of Racial Disturbances: Tests of an Explanation," *American Sociological Review* 36 (June 1971): 430, 446; idem, "Structural Characteristics of Cities and the Severity of Racial Disorders," *American Sociological Review* 41 (Oct. 1976): 789; Peter H. Rossi, "Urban Revolts and the Future of American Cities," in David Boesel and Rossi, eds., *Cities under Siege: An Anatomy of Ghetto Revolts, 1964-1968* (New York: Basic Books, 1971), p. 415; William Freithalter Ford and John H. Moore, "Additional Evidence on the Social Characteristics of Riot Cities," *Social Science Quarterly* 51 (Sept. 1970): 339–48; Joe R. Feagin and Harlan Hahn, *Ghetto Revolts* (New York: Macmillan Co., 1973), pp. 116–27. Cf. Bryan T. Downes, "Social and Political Characteristics of Riot Cities: A Comparative Study," *Social Science Quarterly* 49 (Dec. 1968): 521–33; idem, "A Critical Re-examination of Social and Political Characteristics of Riot Cities," *Social Science Quarterly* 51 (Sept. 1970): 349–60; William R. Morgan and Terry Nicholas Clark, "The Causes of Racial Disorders:

A Grievance Level Explanation," *American Sociological Review* 38 (Oct. 1973): 622–23; and Jules J. Wanderer, "An Index of Riot Severity and Some Social Correlates," *American Journal of Sociology* 74 (Mar. 1969): 500–505.

2. Schuman and Gruenberg, "The Impact of City on Racial Attitudes," *American Journal of Sociology* 76 (Sept. 1970): 214 and passim.

3. Schuman and Gruenberg, "Dissatisfaction with City Services: Is Race an Important Factor?" in Harlan Hahn, ed., *People and Politics in Urban Society* (Beverly Hills: Sage Publications, 1972), pp. 387–88; *DFP*, Feb. 4, 1969; *Return to 12th Street: A Follow-up Survey of Attitudes of Detroit Negroes, October 1968* [Detroit, 1968], p. 16; Inter-University Consortium for Political and Social Research, Black File, Nos. 183–87, Detroit data for Angus Campbell and Howard Schuman, "Racial Attitudes in Fifteen American Cities," in *Supplemental Studies for the National Advisory Commission on Civil Disorders* (Washington: GPO, 1968). The figures cited include only those surveyed who answered the questions. The differences between the riot areas in Detroit and the rest of the city were slight with regard to the degree of general satisfaction expressed regarding the public schools and recreational facilities.

4. Spilerman, "Comparison," p. 645.

5. McPhail, "Civil Disorder Participation: A Critical Examination of Recent Research," *American Sociological Review* 36 (Dec. 1971): 1059–71; Sears and McConahay, *The Politics of Violence: The New Urban Blacks and the Watts Riot* (Boston: Houghton Mifflin Co., 1973), 91n.

6. *Report of the National Advisory Commission on Civil Disorders* (Washington: GPO, 1968), pp. 330–31; Paige, "Collective Violence and the Culture of Subordination: A Study of Participants in the July 1967 Riots in Newark . . . and Detroit . . ." (Ph.D. diss., University of Michigan, 1968).

7. *DFP*, Aug. 23, 1970; *The Detroit Riot: A Profile of 500 Prisoners* (Mar. 1968); Lachman and Singer, *The Detroit Riot of 1967* (Detroit: Behavioral Research Institute, 1968), pp. 5, 8; Singer et al., *Black Rioters: A Study of Social Factors and Communication in the Detroit Riot* (Lexington, Mass.: D. C. Heath and Co., 1970), pp. 2–5; Geschwender, *Class, Race, and Worker Insurgency: The League of Revolutionary Black Workers* (London: Cambridge University Press, 1977), p. 236; Donald Lee Scruggs, "Lyndon Baines Johnson and the National Advisory Commission on Civil Disorders . . ." (Ph.D. diss., University of Oklahoma, 1980), p. 436.

8. "City in Crisis" [1969], app., Detroit Public Library; "Violence in the Model City" [1969], chap. 1, Box 378, JPC Papers; Luby et al., "A Preliminary Report on Two Populations Involved in Detroit's Civil Disturbance" [1967], Edward Lurie Papers, in my possession; Luby and Hedegard, "A Study of Civil Disorder in Detroit," *William and Mary Law Review* 10 (1969): 592–95; Aberbach and Walker, *Race in the City* (Boston: Little, Brown and Co., 1970), pp. 246–49, 250.

9. United Community Services . . . , A Report on "Operation Find" (Dec. 1967), Box 212, GR Papers; Deposition of James Del Rio, Jan. 9, 1968, Series 32, Box 2, NACCD Records; Caplan and Paige, "A Study of Ghetto Riots," *Scientific American* 219 (Aug. 1968): 16; David Paul Boesel, "The Ghetto Riots 1964–1968" (Ph.D. diss., Cornell University, 1972), p. 86; Paige, "Collective Violence," p. 16; Robert B. Hill and Robert M. Fogelson, "A Study of Arrest Patterns in the 1960's Riots," Final Progress Report, Dec. 1969, pp. 7–9.

10. Fogelson, *Violence as Protest: A Study of Riots and Ghettos* (Garden City: Doubleday and Co., 1971), pp. 33–34; Singer et al., *Black Rioters*, pp. 2–3, 53–54; Hill and Fogelson, "Arrest Patterns," pp. 9–11; Luby and Hedegard, "Civil Disorder," p. 593. See chap. 10.

11. Donald I. Warren, "Some Observations on Post-Riot Detroit: The Role of the Social Researcher in Contemporary Social Conflict," *Phylon* 34 (June 1973): 175–77; *DFP*, Oct. 21, 1967; *Ann Arbor News*, Mar. 11, 1968.

12. Sears and McConahay, *Politics of Violence*, pp. 26–27; *NACCD Report*, p. 331; Luby and Hedegard, "Civil Disorder," p. 596; Singer et al., *Black Rioters*, pp. 55–56.

13. Official Transcript of Proceedings before the National Advisory Commission on Civil Disorders, Aug. 15, 1967, pp. 412–13, Series 1, Box 2, NACCD Records; "Negro Youths and Civil Disorders," n.d., Series 7, Box 2, ibid.; Tom Popp Memorandum to Herman Wilson (interview with Father O'Hara), Oct. 12 [1967], Series 59, Box 2, ibid.; *DFP*, Sept. 3, 1967; Boesel, "Ghetto Riots," pp. 36–52, 95–96; Sears and McConahay, *Politics of Violence*, pp. 44–47; Cavanagh to Philip Rutledge, July 28, 1967, Box 398, JPC Papers; Fogelson, *Violence as Protest*, p. 147; Charlotte Darrow and Paul Lowinger, "The Detroit Uprising: A Psychological Study," in Jules H. Masserman, ed., *The Dynamics of Dissent* (New York: Greene and Stratton, 1968), pp. 128–29; "City in Crisis," chap. 8, p. 11; Harold Johnson to Neighborhood Service Organization (NSO) Board of Directors, Aug. 17, 1967, and enclosed report, July 31, 1967, Box 532, JPC Papers.

14. *NACCD Report*, p. 331; [DPD] *Statistical Report on the Civil Disorder Occurring in the City of Detroit, July 1967*, pp. 1–3; Hill and Fogelson, "Arrest Patterns," p. 60; Singer et al., *Black Rioters*, pp.71–72; Luby and Hedegard, "Civil Disorder," p. 596; Luby, "A Comparison between Detroit Arrestees and a Riot Area Sample Control" (1968), p. 17.

15. Luby and Hedegard, "Civil Disorder," pp. 601–2; Singer et al., *Black Rioters*, pp. 69–71. Caplan and Paige provided figures or percentages only for Newark, where the self-reported rioters differed hardly at all from the noninvolved. Sears and McConahay came to a similar conclusion for Watts. *NACCD Report*, p. 332; *Politics of Violence*, p. 26.

16. *DFP*, Oct. 21, 1967; Luby and Hedegard, "Civil Disorder," pp. 625–26; "Violence in the Model City," chap. 9. For criticism of the assessment regarding the damaging effects of the female-headed family, see Lee Rainwater and William Yancey, *The Moynihan Report and the Politics of Controversy* (Cambridge: MIT Press, 1967), pp. 451, 475, and passim; and James Hedegard, "Detroit Race Attitudes and Responses to the Riot" [1968], pp. 27–28, Lurie Papers.

17. *NACCD Report*, p. 332; Caplan and Paige, "Ghetto Rioters," p. 18; Paige, "Collective Violence," pp. 77–78; Sears and McConahay, *Politics of Violence*, p. 29.

18. Luby and Hedegard, "Civil Disorder," pp. 597–99; Singer et al., *Black Rioters*, pp. 76–77.

19. *NACCD Report*, pp. 75, 332; Sears and McConahay, *Politics of Violence*, p. 24; Caplan and Paige, "Ghetto Rioters," p. 17.

20. Luby and Hedegard, "Civil Disorder," p. 599; Singer et al., *Black Rioters*, pp. 58–61; Geschwender and Singer, "Deprivation and the Detroit Riot," *Social Problems* 17 (Spring 1970): 460–61.

21. *NACCD Report*, p. 332; Paige, "Collective Violence," pp. 48-51; Singer et al., *Black Rioters*, pp. 62, 64, 66; Lachman and Singer, *Detroit Riot*, p. 56; Sears and McConahay, *Politics of Violence*, p. 24; *The People Beyond 12th Street: A Survey of Attitudes of Detroit Negroes After the Riot of 1967* (Detroit: Detroit Urban League, 1967); Fogelson and Hill, "Who Riots? A Study of Participation in the 1967 Riots," in *Supplemental Studies*, p. 236. My italics.

22. Luby and Hedegard, "Civil Disorder," pp. 596-97; "City in Crisis," chap. 3, pp. 4-5. Hill and Fogelson place the unemployment rate among 3,214 Detroit male arrestees at 23.6 percent, but it is possible that this figure includes students not in the labor force. "Arrest Patterns," p. 64.

23. Geschwender and Singer, "Deprivation," p. 461; Singer et al., *Black Rioters*, pp. 61-64; Fogelson and Hill, "Who Riots?" p. 236; Fogelson, *Violence as Protest*, p. 41.

24. *NACCD Report*, pp. 75, 332; Paige, "Collective Violence," pp. 45-46; Singer et al., *Black Rioters*, pp. 65-68; Geschwender and Singer, "Deprivation," pp. 461-62. The mean weekly income of the arrestees in the Singer sample was $109.67, approximately $10 below the figure for the community sample. *Black Rioters*, p. 64.

25. Paige, "Collective Violence," pp. 73-74, 140; Luby and Hedegard, "Civil Disorder," pp. 624-25; *NACCD Report*, pp. 76, 333; Luby, "The Detroit Riot," *Sinai Hospital Bulletin* 16 (Oct. 1968): 138; *DFP*, Oct. 21, 1967; *Ann Arbor News*, Mar. 11, 1968; Caplan and Paige, "Ghetto Rioters," p. 21; [Caplan] interviews with First Looter, p. 7, Second Looter, p. 12, Third Looter, p. 22, Fourth Looter, p. 33, Nov. 7, 1967, transcripts in my possession; *People Beyond*, FBI Confidential Report, Aug. 9, 1967, FBI-FOIA.

26. *NACCD Report*, pp. 76, 334; *People Beyond*; Paige, "Collective Violence," p. 75. In Watts, the "greatest riot participation" occurred among blacks "high" in hostility toward whites. Sears and McConahay, *Politics of Violence*, pp. 92-94.

27. [Caplan] interviews with Second Looter, pp. 17, 20, with Third Looter, pp. 22, 30, 31, with Fourth Looter, p. 45; [Caplan] interview with Fire Bomber [Nov. 1967], p. 2, transcript in my possession.

28. [Robert Mendelsohn, "Arrestee Interpretation of the Riot," 1968], pp. 6-7, Lurie Papers; *DFP*, July 30, 1967; Luby and Hedegard, "Civil Disorder," p. 602.

29. Johnson to NSO Board of Directors, Aug. 17, 1967, and enclosed report, July 31, 1967, Box 532, JPC Papers; Hahn, "The Political Objectives of Ghetto Violence," Sept. 1969, p. 5, in my possession; idem, "The Aftermath of a Riot," *Discourse* 12 (Autumn 1969): 550; *Washington Post*, July 30, 1967; Darrow and Lowinger, "Detroit Uprising," p. 127; "Riots," *Journal of Housing* 24 (Aug. 1967): 375; Boesel, "Ghetto Revolts," pp. 97-98; Sears and McConahay, *Politics of Violence*, p. 127.

30. Caplan, "The New Ghetto Man: A Review of Recent Empirical Studies," *Journal of Social Issues* 26 (Winter 1970): 64; Caplan and Paige, "Ghetto Rioters," p. 19; *People Beyond*.

31. Warren, "Neighborhood Structure and Riot Behavior in Detroit: Some Exploratory Findings," *Social Problems* 16 (Spring 1969): 467-68, 473, 475, 483.

32. Luby and Hedegard, "Civil Disorder," pp. 600, 624-25; Singer et al., *Black Rioters*, pp. 69, 78-79, 83-84; Ransford, "Isolation and Participation in Vio-

lence: A Study of Attitudes and Participation in the Watts Riot," *American Journal of Sociology* 73 (Mar. 1968): 581-91.

33. Caplan, "New Ghetto Man," p. 69; Paige, "Political Orientation and Riot Participation," *American Sociological Review* 36 (Oct. 1971): 819; *NACCD Report*, pp. 76-77, 334; "City in Crisis," chap. 8, pp. 6-7; Luby and Hedegard, "Civil Disorder," pp. 602-3; Lachman and Singer, *Detroit Riot*, p. 27.

34. *NACCD Report*, pp. 77, 335; Caplan and Paige, "Ghetto Rioters," p. 21.

35. Luby and Hedegard, "Civil Disorder," pp. 603-4; Singer et al., *Black Rioters*, pp. 85-89.

36. Singer et al., *Black Rioters*, p. 90; *People Beyond*. In Watts, only 12 percent of the curfew zone residents chose "violent protest" as "the most effective method" for blacks to use. Sears and McConahay, *Politics of Violence*, p. 63.

37. *NACCD Report*, p. 335; Sears and McConahay, *Politics of Violence*, pp. 52-54, 103; Aberbach and Walker, *Race in the City*, p. 183; Reconnaissance Survey Field Research Reports, Detroit, Michigan, 3:86-87, Series 10, Box 46, NACCD Records; Feagin and Hahn, *Ghetto Revolts*, p. 290.

38. *People Beyond; DFP*, Oct. 25, 1967.

39. Harlan Hahn, "Cops and Rioters: Ghetto Perceptions of Social Conflict and Control," *American Behavioral Scientist* 13 (May-Aug. 1970): 766; Black File, No. 234, Detroit data for "Racial Attitudes"; ibid., p. 48. For the causes of the Watts riot as seen by arrestees and curfew zone residents, see Sears and McConahay, *Politics of Violence*, p. 160.

40. Singer et al., *Black Rioters*, p. 94; Lachman and Singer, *Detroit Riot*, p. 48.

41. Luby and James Grisell, "Grievances of Detroit Negro Arrestees" [1968], pp. 5-11, Detroit Public Library; Luby, "Police and Jail Treatment of Detroit Negro Riot Arrestees" [1967], pp. 10-13, Box 427, JPC Papers.

42. Luby and Hedegard, "Civil Disorder," pp. 600-601, 606; "City in Crisis," chap. 8, pp. 7-8; Luby and Grisell, "Grievances," pp. 25-26.

43. Caplan, "New Ghetto Man," p. 60; Tomlinson, "The Development of a Riot Ideology among Urban Negroes," *American Behavioral Scientist* 11 (Mar.-Apr. 1968): 28. Donald Warren similarly contended on the basis of his study of neighborhoods that it was the individual above his neighbors in "typical (modal) socioeconomic levels" who was most apt to riot. "Neighborhood Status Modality and Riot Behavior: An Analysis of the Detroit Disorders of 1967," *Sociological Quarterly* 12 (Summer 1971): 350-68. The *NACCD Report* defines the typical 1967 rioter on pp. 93-94.

44. Singer et al., *Black Rioters*, p. 68; *DFP*, Aug. 23, 1970; "City in Crisis," chap. 6, p. 8; "Violence in the Model City," chap. 5, p. 6. Cf. Fogelson and Hill, "Who Riots?" p. 243, for a composite portrait of arrestees derived from arrestee data for nineteen riot cities.

45. Hill and Fogelson, "Arrest Patterns," pp. 59, 61, 62, 64; Luby, "Detroit Riot," pp. 137-38; [Mendelsohn, "Arrestee Interpretation"], pp. 41-48; S. D. Romero and N. C. Rayford to Milan C. Miskovsky, Dec. 18, 1967, Series 4, Box 22, NACCD Records; Robert Shellow et al., "The Harvest of American Racism: The Political Meaning of Violence in the Summer of 1967," Nov. 1967, p. 91, Series 7, Box 1, ibid.

46. [Mendelsohn, "Arrestee Interpretation"], pp. 3-15.

47.Richard Komisaruk and Carol E. Pearson, "Children of the Detroit Riots," in Richard A. Chikota and Michael C. Moran, eds., *Riot in the Cities* (Rutherford, N.J.: Farleigh Dickinson University Press, 1970), pp. 109–18, 129, 130–35; James H. Lincoln, *The Anatomy of a Riot* (New York: McGraw-Hill Book Co., 1968), pp. 5–6, 10, 113, 117–18, 121–24; Minutes, Police and Public Safety Committee, Michigan Commission on Crime . . . , Sept. 20, 1967, Box 31, ORA Papers.

48. *NACCD Report*, p. 331; Hill and Fogelson, "Arrest Patterns," pp. 230–31; Sears and McConahay, *Politics of Violence*, pp. 9–12; Black File, No. 289, Detroit data for "Racial Attitudes"; ibid., p. 54.

49. Paige, "Collective Violence," pp. 18–20; *People Beyond*; Sears and McConahay, *Politics of Violence*, pp. 11–12; "City in Crisis," chap. 8, p. 8.

50. J. Anthony Lukas, "Postscript on Detroit: 'Whitey Hasn't Got the Message,' " *NYT Magazine*, Aug. 27, 1967; *Ann Arbor News*, July 31, 1967; John K. Scales Memorandum to Miskovsky (interview with James A. Bush), Jan. 17, 1968, Series 4, Box 22, NACCD Records; Popp Memorandum to Wilson (interview with Maryann Mahaffey), Oct. 31, 1967, Series 59, Box 2, ibid.; Luby and Grisell, "Grievances," pp. 14–16; Questionnaires Nos. 4029, 6027, 6121, 6134, 6139, 6191, Boxes 8, 11, 12, 13, A-W Riot Studies; Sheldon Levy, "Communication Processes in the Detroit Riot" [1968], p. 35, Detroit Public Library; Hahn, "Ghetto Sentiments on Violence," *Science and Society* 33 (Spring 1969): 205; Richard Alan Berk, "The Role of Ghetto Retail Merchants in Civil Disorders" (Ph.D. diss., Johns Hopkins University, 1970), pp. 173, 178–79.

51. Questionnaire No. 6008, Box 10, A-W Riot Studies; Berk, "Ghetto Retail Merchants," pp. 163, 165–66; [Caplan] interview with Second Looter, pp. 16–17; Shellow et al., "Harvest of Racism," p. 6, Series 7, Box 1, NACCD Records; Joe Lapointe, "Six Days in July," *Detroit Monthly*, July 1987, p. 66.

52. John Hersey, *The Algiers Motel Incident* (New York: Alfred A. Knopf, 1968), p. 71; [Caplan] interview with Fire Bomber, pp. 6–7; Hahn, "Ghetto Sentiments," p. 205; Joe Lapointe, "Six Days in July," *Detroit Monthly*, July 1987, p. 66. See also Questionnaires Nos. 5056, 6137, 6205, Boxes 10, 12, 13, A-W Riot Studies.

53. [Caplan] interview with First Looter, pp. 7–8; *DFP*, July 25, 1967; Popp Memorandum to Nelson (O'Hara interview), Oct. 12, [1967], Series 59, Box 2, NACCD Records.

54. Van Gordon Sauter and Burleigh Hines, *Nightmare in Detroit* (Chicago: Henry Regnery Co., 1968), pp. 27–28; *DN*, July 28, 30, 1967, May 22, 1980; Detroit to Director, Sept. 18, 1967, FBI-FOIA; Questionnaires Nos. 3017, 4001, 4015, 4038, 4060, 6046, 6091, 6096, 6097, 6134, 6146, Boxes 7, 8, 9, 11, 12, A-W Riot Studies; E. S. Evans, "Ghetto Rioters," in Louis H. Masotti and Don R. Bowen, eds., *Riots and Rebellion* (Beverly Hills: Sage Publications, 1968), p. 402; Tom Parmenter, "Breakdown of Law and Order," *Trans-Action* 4 (Sept. 1967): 15; *NYT*, July 29, 1967; *Newsweek* 70 (Aug. 7, 1967): 19, 26; "The Detroit 'Riot': A Challenge to Society and the Legal Profession," Oct. 11, 1967, pp. 45–46, University of Michigan Law Library, Ann Arbor, Michigan; Hubert G. Locke, *The Detroit Riot of 1967* (Detroit: Wayne State University Press, 1969), pp. 96–97.

55. *NYT*, July 28, 1967; *DFP*, Aug. 2, 6, 1967; *DN*, July 28, 1967; Maurice Kelman and Ed Batchelor interview with Ray Girardin, Oct. 29, 1971, pp. 395–96, transcript in my possession; Xavier Nicholas interviews with Mrs. Girardin [1982], with Richard Lobenthal [1982], copy of tapes in my possession; Locke statement [Sept. 22–23, 1967], Box 28, ORA Papers; Lincoln, *Anatomy*, p. 8; Lukas,

"Whitey"; Official Transcript, Aug. 15, 1967, p. 414, Series 1, Box 2, NACCD Records.

56. *MC*, July 24, 1982.

57. Quarantelli and Dynes, "Looting and Civil Disorders: An Index of Social Change," in Masotti and Bowen, eds., *Riots and Rebellion*, p. 136; Rayford to Miskovsky, Dec. 27, 1967, Series 4, Box 22, NACCD Records; Scales Memorandum to Miskovsky (Bush interview), Jan. 17, 1968, ibid.; Robert Conot's Discussion with Stanley Webb, n.d., ibid.; Wilson Memoranda to Nelson (interview with Charles Brown), n.d., (interview with Leon Atchison), n.d., Series 59, Box 2, ibid.; *Christian Science Monitor*, July 26, 1967, DRSB No. 1; Arthur Weiseger to Francis Kornegay, Aug. 7, 1967, Box 12, DUL Papers; Oral History Interview of Jerome P. Cavanagh, Mar. 22, 1971, p. 53, LBJ Library; Barefoot Sanders Memo for Joseph Califano, July 28, 1967, Box 58, Office Files of Joseph Califano, ibid.; D. L. Ransom to Area Administrator, July 27, 1967, Box 373, JPC Papers; Summary of Informal Discussion . . . , Aug. 25, 1967, Lurie Papers; "Detroit 'Riot,' " p. 34; Interview with Harold Johnson, Aug. 14, 1984, p. 9, transcript in MHC; *NACCD Report*, p. 51; Locke statement [Sept. 22–23, 1967], Box 28, ORA Papers; Locke to Fine, Jan. 4, 1984.

58. Levy, "Communication Processes," pp. 32–34; Hahn, "Ghetto Sentiments," p. 205; *People Beyond*; "City in Crisis," chap. 6, p. 3; Sears and McConahay, *Politics of Violence*, p. 159.

59. Quarantelli and Dynes, "Property Norms and Looting: Their Patterns in Community Crises," in James A. Geschwender, ed., *The Black Revolt* (Englewood Cliffs, N.J.: Prentice-Hall, 1971), pp. 285–99; Anthony Oberschall, "The Los Angeles Riot of 1965," in ibid., pp. 96–97; Berk, "Ghetto Retail Merchants," pp. 96–97; Feagin and Hahn, *Ghetto Revolts*, p. 176.

60. *DFP*, July 25, 28, 1967; *DN*, July 26, 1967; To Director from Detroit, July 25, 1967, 12:32 P.M., July 26, 1967, 1:15 P.M., FBI-FOIA; Ransom to Administrator, July 27, 1967, Box 373, JPC Papers; *Newsweek* 70 (Aug. 7, 1967): 27.

61. *DN*, July 28, 1967; *DFP*, July 29, 1967; *NYT*, July 28, 29, 1967, Feb. 28, 1968; *MC*, Dec. 23, 1967; Locke, *Detroit Riot*, pp. 94–95; Mrs. Girardin interview; *Nation* 206 (Mar. 11, 1968): 326; Mutual Loss Research Bureau, "The Detroit Report" [Sept. 1967], Series 4, Box 22, NACCD Records; Frank I. Lewis, Jr., to Member Companies . . . , Aug. 12, 1967, Commissioner's File, DPD.

62. *NACCD Report*, pp. 331–32; Paige, "Collective Violence," p. 20; Warren, "Neighborhood Structure," pp. 473–76.

63. Paige, "Collective Violence," p. 20; *DFP*, July 25, 29, 1967; *NYT*, July 29, 1967; Girardin interview, p. 399.

64. *Newsweek* 70 (Aug. 7, 1967): 27; "Detroit Fires of 1967," *Firemen* 34 (Oct. 1967): 14; Detroit Information: Earthel Green, n.d., ibid.: Robert Thomas, n.d., ibid.; Longworth Quinn, n.d., Box 78, NACCD Records; Popp Memorandum to Wilson (interview with Charles Quinlan), Oct. 31, 1967, Series 59, Box 2, ibid.; Official Transcript, Sept. 15, 1967, p. 1736, Series 1, Box 3, ibid.; News Media Seminar, Television, Nov. 11, 1967, Series 12, Box 1, ibid.; *MC*, July 29, 1967; *Detroit Courier*, Aug. 5, 19, 1967; *DFP*, July 25, Sept. 3, 1967; Capture and Record of Civil Disorder in Detroit, July 23–July 28, 1967, Box 345, GR Papers; Sauter and Hines, *Nightmare*, p. 21; Lukas, "Whitey."

65. Argie White Post, *The Rape of Detroit* (Hicksville, N.Y.: Exposition Press, 1975), p. 16; Popp Memorandum to Wilson (O'Hara interview), Oct. 12

[1967], Series 59, Box 2, NACCD Records; Wilson Memorandum to Nelson (interview with Stanley Webb), n.d., ibid.; *DN*, July 27, 1967; *DFP*, July 23, 1972.

66. *Los Angeles Times*, July 27, 1967, DRSB No. 1; *Control of Civil Disorders: Guidelines for Small Unit Commanders and Troops* [1967], p. 16, Box 1, Accession 69A632, Records of the United States Army Commands, RG 338, Office of the Adjutant General, Alexandria, Virginia; Special Subcommittee of the House Committee on Armed Services to Inquire into the Capability of the National Guard to Cope with Civil Disturbances, *Hearings*, 90th Cong., 1st sess., 1967, pp. 5940–41; Nicholas interview with John Farnsworth, 1982, p. 24, transcript in Nicholas's possession. See chap. 9.

67. *People Beyond.*

68. Boesel, "Ghetto Riots," pp. 135–36; *NACCD Report*, p. 331; Levy, "Communication Processes," pp. 40, 42–43, 45; Sears and McConahay, *Politics of Violence*, p. 163.

69. Levy, "Communication Processes," pp. 31–32.

70. Black File, Nos. 236, 246, 253, Detroit data for "Racial Attitudes"; ibid., pp. 52, 55.

71. Sears and McConahay, *Politics of Violence*, p. 161; Fogelson, *Violence as Protest*, p. 45; Levy, "Communication Processes," pp. 45–46; [Mendelsohn, "Arrestee Interpretation"], p. 12; Black File, No. 241, Detroit data for "Racial Attitudes"; ibid., p. 49.

Chapter 15

1. Morris Janowitz, "Patterns of Collective Racial Violence," in Hugh Davis Graham and Ted Robert Gurr, eds., *Violence in America* (New York: Bantam Books, 1969), pp. 421, 423; Joel D. Aberbach and Jack L. Walker, *Race in the City* (Boston: Little, Brown and Co., 1973), p. 58; Inter-University Consortium for Political and Social Research, Black File, No. 232, Detroit data for Angus Campbell and Howard Schuman, "Racial Attitudes in Fifteen American Cities," in *Supplemental Studies for the National Advisory Commission on Civil Disorders* (Washington: GPO, 1968).

2. Allen D. Grimshaw, "Three Views of Urban Violence . . . ," in Louis H. Masotti and Don R. Bowen, eds., *Civil Violence in the Urban Community* (Beverly Hills: Sage Publications, 1968), pp. 110–11; Bowen and Masotti, "Civil Violence . . . ," in ibid., pp. 11–18.

3. *Report of the National Advisory Commission on Civil Disorders* (Washington: GPO, 1968), p. 64; Interview with Richard Marks, Aug. 6, 1984, p. 54, transcript in MHC; [Nathan Caplan] interview with Second Looter, Nov. 7, 1967, pp. 18–19, transcript in my possession; *DN*, July 24, 1967; *DFP*, July 25, 1967; *NYT*, July 25, 1967; *Los Angeles Times*, July 24, 1967, DRSB No. 1; Herman Wilson Memorandum to Charles E. Nelson (interview with Albert Boer), n.d., Series 59, Box 2, NACCD Records; Disorder Log, July 23, 1967, Box 4, Ray Girardin Papers, Burton Historical Collection, Detroit, Michigan; Sequence of Events, July 24, 1967, Box 345, GR Papers; [Robert Mendelsohn, "Arrestee Interpretation of the Riot," 1968], p. 6, Edward Lurie Papers, in my possession. See chap. 14.

4. J. Anthony Lukas, "Postscript on Detroit: 'Whitey Hasn't Got the Message,'" *NYT Magazine*, Aug. 27, 1967; Report by Rene Freeman, n.d., Series III, Box 3, CCR Papers; Bill Dwyer to Burton Levy, July 28, 1967, Records of the Michigan Civil Rights Commission, RG 83-55 (unprocessed), State Archives, Lansing, Michigan; William McCord et al., *Life Styles in the Black Ghetto* (New York: W. W. Norton and Co., 1969), p. 273; *Grand Rapids Press*, July 25, 1967, DRSB No. 1; *DFP*, July 25, 1967; *DN*, July 27, 30, 1967; Xavier Nicholas interview with Richard Lobenthal [1982], copy of tape in my possession; Barbara Wilson Tinker, *When the Fire Reaches Us* (New York: William Morrow and Co., 1970), p. 191.

5. McCord et al., *Life Styles*, p. 273; Joe R. Feagin and Harlan Hahn, *Ghetto Revolts* (New York: Macmillan Co., 1973), p. 286; Sheldon Levy, "Communication Processes in the Detroit Riot" [1968], p. 36, Detroit Public Library, Detroit, Michigan. See chap. 14.

6. Jeffrey Mayland Paige, "Collective Violence and the Culture of Subordination: A Study of Participants in the July 1967 Riots in Newark . . . and Detroit . . ." (Ph.D. diss., University of Michigan, 1968), pp. 33, 47-48; *DFP*, July 24, 30, 1967; *Detroit Journal*, Aug. 11, 1967; David Cason, "Some Probable Causes of the Recent Civil Disturbance," Sept. 26, 1967, Box 393, JPC Papers; *NACCD Report*, p. 76; David O. Sears and John B. McConahay, *The Politics of Violence: The New Urban Blacks and the Watts Riot* (Boston: Houghton Mifflin Co., 1973), pp. 123-24.

7. David John Olson, "Racial Violence and City Politics: The Political Response to Civil Disorders in Three American Cities" (Ph.D. diss., University of Wisconsin, 1972), p. 31; Robert B. Fogelson, *Violence as Protest: A Study of Riots and Ghettos* (Garden City: Doubleday and Co., 1971), pp. 28-29; Banfield, *The Unheavenly City* (Boston: Little, Brown and Co., 1970), pp. 185, 197-98; *DFP*, July 24, 1977.

8. Sears and McConahay, *Politics of Violence*, pp. 20-25; Fogelson, *Violence as Protest*, pp. 28-31; Feagin and Hahn, *Ghetto Revolts*, pp. 8-9; *Meet the Press* 11 (July 30, 1967): 2, 7, Box 242, GR Papers; Notes of Meeting Held . . . , July 31, 1967, Box 345, ibid.; *DFP*, Aug. 6, 1967; Nathan S. Caplan and Jeffrey M. Paige, "A Study of Ghetto Rioters," *Scientific American* 219 (Aug. 1968): 17-19; Peter Lupsha, "On Theories of Urban Violence," *Urban Affairs Quarterly* 4 (Mar. 1969): 281-82.

9. Levy, "Communication Processes," p. 25; Lupsha, "Theories," p. 279; Feagin and Hahn, *Ghetto Revolts*, pp. 7-8; Senate Committee on the Judiciary, *Antiriot Bill—1967, Hearings*, 90th Cong., 1st sess., 1967, pt. 1:12.

10. H. L. Nieburg, *Political Violence; the Behavioral Process* (New York: St. Martin's Press, 1969), p. 40; *MC*, July 29, 1967; *DFP*, July 25, 1967; Feagin and Hahn, *Ghetto Revolts*, p. 17; Lupsha, "Theories," p. 288.

11. Feagin and Hahn, *Ghetto Revolts*, pp. 19, 22, 114; Downes, "Social and Political Characteristics of Riot Cities: A Comparative Study," *Social Science Quarterly* 49 (Dec. 1968): 521-33; Seymour Spilerman, "The Causes of Racial Disorders: A Comparison of Alternative Explanations," *American Sociological Review* 35 (Aug. 1970): 642-43.

12. Gurr, "Urban Disorder Perspectives . . . ," in Masotti and Bowen, eds., *Civil Violence*, pp. 52-53; idem, *Why Men Rebel* (Princeton: Princeton University Press, 1970), pp. 24, 54, 68, 343-44; Philip Meyer, "Telling It Like It Is,"

Seminar, no. 9 (Sept. 1968): 16–17; Box 11, Frank Angelo Papers, MHC; Rubin to Richard Strichartz, Aug. 14, 1967, Box 393, JPC Papers; Rubin, "Analyzing Detroit's Riot . . . ," *Reporter* 38 (Feb. 22, 1968): 34–35.

13. Caplan and Paige, "Ghetto Rioters," p. 20; McPhail, "Civil Disorder Participation: A Critical Examination of Recent Research," *American Sociological Review* 36 (Dec. 1971): 1063–64; Paige, "Collective Violence," pp. 39–43; Feagin and Hahn, *Ghetto Revolts*, pp. 22–23. Sears and McConahay contend that the subjective deprivation thesis applies to the "new urban blacks" in general. *Politics of Violence*, pp. 88–89.

14. Robert A. Mendelsohn, "Profile of the Riot Causes and Participants," in Leonard Gordon, ed., *A City in Racial Crisis: The Case of Detroit . . .* ([Dubuque, Iowa]: Wm. C. Brown Co., 1971), pp. 76–77; Robert Fogelson, "Violence and Grievances: Reflections on the 1960's Riots," *Journal of Social Issues* 26 (Winter 1970): 160; *NYT*, July 27, 1967; *DFP*, July 25, 1967; Lukas, "Whitey"; Bernard Dobranski Memorandum to Wilson (interview with William T. Patrick, Jr.), Oct. 13, 1967, Series 59, Box 2, NACCD Records; [Caplan] interview with First Looter, p. 9, Nov. 7, 1967, transcript in my possession; Lupsha, "Theories," pp. 283–85, 289–90; "City in Crisis" [1969], chap. 8, p. 11, Detroit Public Library.

15. [Mendelsohn, "Arrestee Interpretation"], pp. 50–51; "Violence in the Model City" [1969], chap. 5, p. 7, Box 378, JPC Papers; Caplan and Paige, "Ghetto Rioters," p. 20. See chap. 14.

16. Caplan and Paige, "Ghetto Rioters," pp. 15, 20–21; Interview with Mel Ravitz, May 8, 1968, Box 16, A-W Riot Studies; Questionnaire No. 6040, Box 11, ibid. For additional support of the blocked-opportunity thesis, although it is based on a very small sample, see John R. Forward and Jay R. Williams, "Internal-External Control of Black Militancy," *Journal of Social Issues* 26 (Winter 1970): 75–92.

17. Sears and McConahay, *Politics of Violence*, p. 18; Janowitz, "Patterns," pp. 440–41; *NACCD Report*, p. 203; Herbert J. Gans, "The Ghetto Dwellers and Urban Class Conflict," *Proceedings of the Academy of Political Science* 29 (1968): 44; Cason, "Possible Causes," Box 393, JPC Papers; Peter R. Clark to Cavanagh, Aug. 15, 1967, Box 531, ibid.; Spilerman, "Structural Characteristics of Cities and the Severity of Racial Disorders," *American Sociological Review* 41 (Oct. 1970): 790; Wilson Memorandum to Nelson (Patrick interview), Oct. 13, 1967, Series 59, Box 2, NACCD Records; Tom Popp Memorandum to Wilson (interview with Father O'Hara), Oct. 12 [1967], ibid.; Banfield, *Unheavenly City*, pp. 198–99; Questionnaire No. 5068, Box 10, A-W Riot Studies; "Re Rioting Detroit . . . July 23, 1967," Aug. 17, 1967, FBI-FOIA; Benjamin D. Singer et al., *Black Rioters: A Study of Social Factors and Communication in the Detroit Riot* (Lexington, Mass.: D. C. Heath and Co., 1970), p. 12.

18. *The Detroit Riot: A Profile of 500 Prisoners* (Mar. 1968), p. 21; Singer, "Mass Media and Communication Processes in the Detroit Riot of 1967," *Public Opinion Quarterly* 34 (Summer 1970): 239, 244–45; Questionnaires Nos. 5061, 6019, Boxes 9, 11, A-W Riot Studies; Louis C. Goldberg, "Ghetto Riots and Others . . . ," in David Boesel and Peter H. Rossi, eds., *Cities under Siege: An Anatomy of Ghetto Riots, 1964–1968* (New York: Basic Books, 1971), p. 148.

19. *DFP*, July 30, 1967; *Newsweek* 70 (Aug. 7, 1967): 27; Deposition of Justinas Bavarskis, Jan. 10, 1968, Series 32, Box 2, NACCD Records; Sears and

McConahay, *Politics of Violence*, pp. 109, 201. See also Questionnaire No. 6050, Box 11, A-W Riot Studies; and John K. Scales Memorandum to Milan C. Miskovsky, Dec. 30, 1967, Series 4, Box 22, NACCD Records.

20. John Hersey, *The Algiers Motel Incident* (New York: Alfred A. Knopf, 1968), p. 71; Harold Johnson to Neighborhood Service Organization Board of Directors, Aug. 17, 1967, and enclosed report, July 31, 1967, Box 532, JPC Papers.

21. Tomlinson, "Riot Ideology and Urban Negroes," in Masotti and Bowen, eds., *Riots and Rebellion*, p. 422; Official Transcript of Proceedings before the National Advisory Commission on Civil Disorders, Aug. 15, 1967, pp. 398–99, Series 1, Box 2, NACCD Records; *DFP*, July 26, 1967.

22. Official Transcript, Aug. 15, 1967, p. 530, Series 1, Box 2, NACCD Records; *Newsweek* 70 (Aug. 14, 1967): 78; Singer, "Mass Media," pp. 240, 245; Nicholas interview with Ron Hewitt [1982], copy of tape in my possession; Hubert G. Locke, *The Detroit Riot of 1967* (Detroit: Wayne State University Press, 1969), pp. 82, 84–86, 89; *DFP*, July 27, 1967; B. J. Widick, *Detroit: City of Race and Class Violence* (Chicago: Quadrangle Books, 1972), pp. 173–74; Sears and McConahay, *Politics of Violence*, p. 110.

23. Robert E. Smith, "How the News Media Covered the Negro Rioting and Why," Oct. 1967, Series 11, Box 1, NACCD Records; Permanent Subcommittee on Investigations of the Senate Committee on Government Operations, *Riots, Civil and Criminal Disorders, Hearings*, 90th Cong., 2d sess., 1968, pt. 5:1208; *DN*, July 28, Aug. 2, 1967; Singer, "Mass Media," p. 240.

24. Smith, "News Media," Series 11, Box 1, NACCD Records; American Newspaper Publishers Association, *Reporting the Detroit Riot* [New York, 1968], introductory note, pp. 6–7.

25. *Return to 12th Street: A Follow-up Survey of Attitudes of Detroit Negroes, October 1968* [Detroit: Detroit Free Press, 1968], p. 17; Black File, No. 243, Detroit data for "Racial Attitudes"; *NACCD Report*, p. 207. For additional criticism of TV reporting, see News Media Seminar, Television . . . , Nov. 11, 1967, pp. 8–9, 32, 34, Series 12, Box 1, NACCD Records.

26. Frank Beckman to Cavanagh, Sept. 18, 1967, Box 339, JPC Papers; James Trainor to Cavanagh, Sept. 17, 1968, Box 507, ibid.; *DFP*, July 26, 1967; Nicholas interview with Robert Roselle [1982], copy of tape in my possession.

27. Ralph W. Conant, *The Prospects for Revolution: A Study of Riots . . .* (New York: Harper's Magazine Press Book, 1971), pp. 21, 40–41; James H. Skolnick, *The Politics of Protest* (n.p. [1969]), p. 259; Peter Goldman, *Report from Black America* (New York: Simon and Schuster, 1970), p. 115; Popp Memorandum to Wilson (interview with Maryann Mahaffey), Oct. 13, 1967, Series 59, Box 2, NACCD Records; James Raschard to Wilson, Oct. 29, 1967, ibid.; *Life* 63 (Aug. 4, 1967): 24; *DN*, July 25, 1967; *DFP*, Aug. 6, Sept. 23, 1967; Summer Week-End Evening Program, July–Aug. 1967, Box 21, United Community Services Papers, ALHUA; "City in Crisis," chap. 6, p. 4.

28. [Mendelsohn, "Arrestee Interpretation"], pp. 3–4; Hahn, "The Political Objectives of Ghetto Violence" (Sept. 1969), p. 10; Black File, No. 235, Detroit data for "Racial Attitudes." In Watts, 62 percent of the blacks in the curfew zone saw the Watts riot as "a Negro protest." Sears and McConahay, *Politics of Violence*, p. 159.

29. Wilson Memorandum to Nelson (interview with Mary Valentine), n.d., Series 59, Box 2, NACCD Records; [Caplan] interviews with First Looter, p. 10, with Second Looter, p. 20; *MC*, Aug. 5, 1967; Questionnaire No. 6022, Box 11, A-W Riot Studies.

30. Robert Shellow et al., "The Harvest of American Racism: The Political Meaning of Violence in the Summer of 1967," Nov. 22, 1967, p. 4, Series 7, Box 1, NACCD Records; Feagin and Hahn, *Ghetto Revolts*, pp. 27, 43-48, 291-92; Hahn, "Political Objectives," pp. 5, 12, 15, 20, 23, 26; *MC*, July 29, 1967; David Paul Boesel, "The Ghetto Riots 1964-1968" (Ph.D. diss., Cornell University, 1972), pp. 3-7, 165-69, 195-97; *DFP*, Nov. 13, 1967; Charlotte Darrow and Paul Lowinger, "The Detroit Uprising: A Psychological Study," in Jules H. Masserman, ed., *The Dynamics of Dissent* (New York: Greene and Stratton, 1968), pp. 127-28; Paige, "Collective Violence," pp. 111, 134; Rossi, "Urban Riots and the Future of American Cities," in Boesel and Rossi, eds., *Cities under Siege*, pp. 413, 419-20.

31. Levy, "Communication Processes," p. 55; Black File, No. 274, Detroit data for "Racial Attitudes"; [Mendelsohn, "Arrestee Interpretation"], p. 4; Boesel, "Ghetto Riots," p. 4.

32. *NACCD Report*, p. 89.

33. *DN*, Aug. 6-10, 1967.

34. Albert Callewaert and Arthur Yim, "The Detroit Police Department and the Detroit Civil Disorder," Dec. 1967, p. 30, Box 407, JPC Papers; "Re Rioting, Detroit . . . Beginning July 23, 1967," Aug. 10, 19, 1967, FBI-FOIA; Director to Fred M. Vinson, Jr., Sept. 5, 1967, ibid.

35. Scales Memorandum to Miskovsky (interview with James A. Bush), Jan. 17, 1968, Series No. 4, Box 22, NACCD Records; Report of Bernard Dobranski to Robert Conot, n.d., Box 77, ibid.; Nicholas interview with Albert J. Dunmore [1982], copy of tape in my possession.

36. Scales Memorandum to Miskovsky, Jan. 12, 1968, Series 4, Box 22, NACCD Records; Stenographic Account of Conversation between Scales and Loccricio, Feb. 16, Mar. 4, 1968, ibid.; "Summer '67: What We Learned," Sept. 15, 1967, ibid.; John Doar Memorandum for the File, Sept. 14, 1967, Box 10, Warren Christopher Papers, LBJ Library; Anthony Ripley and Loccricio, "The Situation" [Aug. 1967], Box 531, JPC Papers; *DN*, Nov. 24, 1977.

37. Doar Memorandum for File, Sept. 14, 1967, Box 10, Christopher Papers; [J. Edgar Hoover] to Mildred Stegall, Sept. 26, 1967, FBI-FOIA.

38. Scales Memoranda to Miskovsky, Jan. 12, 17, 1968 (Bush interview), Series 4, Box 22, NACCD Records; Phone Conversation with Conrad Mallett, July 13, 1984; Interview with John Nichols, Aug. 13, 1984, pp. 32-33, transcript in MHC; [Hoover] to Stegall, Sept. 26, 1967, Detroit to Director, Sept. 28, 1967, FBI-FOIA; *DN*, Sept. 28, 29, 1967; *DFP*, Sept. 29, 1967; *NYT*, Sept. 16, 1967; *MC*, Sept. 23, 1967.

39. Detroit Incident, Col. Davids, July 23, 1967, Box 319, GR Papers; *DN*, July 24-26, 1967; *DFP*, July 27, 30, 1967; *Lansing State Journal*, July 26, 1967, DRSB No. 1; *NYT*, July 27, 1967; To Director from Detroit, July 24, 1967, 8:13 P.M., July 25, 1967, 9:46 P.M., July 30, 1967, Aug. 15, 1967, FBI-FOIA; W. L. Sullivan to C. D. DeLoach, July 31, 1967, and enclosed "Racial Disturbances 1967," ibid.; NACCD Transcript of Proceedings, Aug. 1, 1967, p. 80, Series 1, Box 1, NACCD Records; Official Transcript, Sept. 12, 1967, p. 984, Series 1,

Box 2, ibid.; S. A. Romero and N. C. Rayford to Miskovsky, Dec. 18, 1967, Series 4, Box 22, ibid.; *Riots, Civil and Criminal Disorders*, pt. 5:1299; Maurice Kelman and Ed Batchelor interview with Ray Girardin, Oct. 29, 1971, p. 386, transcript in my possession; Interview with Damon Keith, June 21, 1985, pp. 13–14, transcript in MHC.

40. *Newsweek* 70 (Aug. 7, 1967): 27; *Michigan Catholic*, July 27, 1967.

41. "The Detroit 'Riot': A Challenge to Society and the Legal Profession," Oct. 11, 1967, pp. 31–32, University of Michigan Law Library, Ann Arbor, Michigan; Rayford to Miskovsky, Dec. 27, 1967, Series 4, Box 22, NACCD Records; Shellow et al., "Harvest of Racism," Series 7, Box 1, ibid.; Wilson Memorandum to Nelson (interview with Hubert Locke), Oct. 17, 19, 1967, Peter Rossi File, in my possession; Disorder Log, July 23, 1967, Box 4, Girardin Papers; *Riots, Civil and Criminal Disorders*, pt. 7:1530; *DN*, July 26, Aug. 15, 1967; *MC*, July 29, 1967; *Detroit Courier*, Aug. 5, 1967; Lukas, "Whitey"; Summary of Informal Discussion . . . , Aug. 25, 1967, Lurie Papers; Locke, *Detroit Riot*, p. 127; Minutes, Police and Public Safety Committee, Michigan Commission on Crime . . . , Aug. 16, 1967, Box 12, ORA Papers; James H. Lincoln, *The Anatomy of a Riot* (New York: McGraw-Hill Book Co., 1968), pp. 4–5; Interview with James H. Lincoln, June 14, 1984, pp. 3–6, transcript in MHC; *Christian Science Monitor*, July 26, 1967, DRSB No. 1; *DFP*, July 28, 1967.

42. Nicholas interview with Nicholas Hood [1982], copy of tape in my possession; James H. Shotwell to Commanding General, Aug. 18, 1967, Box 1, Accession 69A632, Records of the United States Army Commands, RG 338, Office of the Adjutant General, Alexandria, Virginia; Freeman Report, Series III, Box 3, CCR Papers. Cf. Interview with James Bannon, Mar. 12, 1985, pp. 41–42, transcript in MHC.

43. Romero and Rayford to Miskovsky, Dec. 18, 1967, Series 4, Box 22, NACCD Records; Wilson Memorandum to Nelson (interview with Charles S. Brown), n.d., Series 59, Box 2, ibid.; Official Transcript, Sept. 12, 1967, p. 936, Series 1, Box 2, ibid.; *Riots, Civil and Criminal Disorders*, pt. 5:1263, 7:1532–33, 1580–82; Tom Parmenter, "Breakdown of Law and Order," *Trans-Action* 4 (Sept. 1967): 15; Edwards, *The Police on the Urban Frontier* (New York: Institute of Human Relations, 1968), pp. 21–22, 66; phone conversation with Edwards, June 19, 1985; *Detroit Courier*, Aug. 19, 1967; Stanley Resor–Ramsey Clark Conversations, July 24, 1967, Box 58, Office Files of Joseph Califano, LBJ Library; Disorder Log, July 24, 1967, Box 4, Girardin Papers; Locke, *Detroit Riot*, p. 126; Garry Wills, *The Second Civil War* (New York: New American Library, 1968), pp. 125–29.

44. Special Subcommittee of House Committee on Armed Services to Inquire into the Capability of the National Guard to Cope with Civil Disturbances, *Hearings*, 90th Cong., 1st sess., 1967, p. 6287; To Director from Detroit, July 26, 1967, 7:12 P.M., FBI-FOIA; "Re Rioting, Detroit . . . , July 23, 1967," Aug. 17, 1967, ibid.; Detroit to Director, Sept. 18, 1967, 1:58 P.M., ibid.; *DN*, July 28, 30, Aug. 1, 1967; Locke, *Detroit Riot*, pp. 127–28; DA SITREP No. 3/26/0600, No. 4/26/1800, (Paul J. Scheips) Civil Disturbance File, Task Force Detroit, Center of Military History, Washington, D.C.; Ripley and Loccricio, "Situation," Box 531, JPC Papers; Charles J. Quinlan to Mayor's Development Team, Aug. 11, 1967, Box 533, ibid.; Romero and Rayford to Miskovsky, Dec. 18, 1967, Series 4, Box 22, NACCD Records.

45. *DFP*, July 31, 1967; Dobranski Report to Conot, n.d., Box 77, NACCD Records.

46. Edwards, *Police*, p. 66; *MC*, July 29, Aug. 5, 1967; *Newsweek* 70 (Aug. 7, 1967): 27; Betty DeRamus, "Black Power, Black Rebellion," *Negro Digest* 17 (Nov. 1967): 26; *Michigan Catholic*, July 27, 1967; Stanley Webb to Roger Wilkins, n.d., and enclosed report, Detroit Riot File, Community Relations Service, Department of Justice, FBI-FOIA; NACCD transcript, Aug. 1, 1967, p. 76, Series 1, Box 1, NACCD Records; [FBI] to David Ginsburg, Aug. 22, 1967, Series 4, Box 22, ibid.; Scales Memorandum to Miskovsky (Bush interview), Jan. 17, 1968, ibid.; Nicholas interview with Edward Vaughn, pp. 2, 9, transcript in Nicholas's possession; Sullivan to DeLoach, July 31, 1967, and enclosed "Racial Disturbances 1967," FBI-FOIA; FBI Confidential Report, Aug. 9, 1967, ibid.; To Director from Detroit, July 30, Aug. 15, 1967, ibid.

47. *Riots, Civil and Criminal Disorders*, pt. 7:1533–34, 1582–84; Wilson Memorandum to Nelson (Locke interview), Oct. 17, 19, 1967, Rossi File.

48. "Mattie Mays," n.d., Box 12, ORA Papers; Conot, Result of My Interview with Saul Friedman, n.d., Box 81, NACCD Records; Wilson Memorandum to Nelson (Locke interview), Oct. 17, 19, 1967, Rossi File; Locke, *Detroit Riot*, pp. 125–26. See also Ripley and Loccricio, "Situation," Box 531, JPC Papers; FBI to Ginsburg, Aug. 22, 1967, FBI-FOIA; and Freeman Report, Series III, Box 3, CCR Papers.

49. [Mendelsohn, "Arrestee Interpretation"], p. 5; Hahn, "Ghetto Sentiments," p. 204; Black File, No. 237, Detroit data for "Racial Attitudes."

50. Sullivan to DeLoach, July 31, 1967, and enclosed "Racial Disturbance 1967," To Director from Detroit, Aug. 15, 1967, 6:59 P.M., Detroit to Director, Sept. 18, 1967, 1:58 P.M., FBI-FOIA; NACCD transcript, Aug. 1, 1967, p. 84, Series 1, Box 1, NACCD Records; Romero and Rayford to Miskovsky, Dec. 18, 1967, Series 4, Box 22, NACCD Records; John T. Elliff, *Crime, Dissent, and the Attorney General: The Justice Department and the 1960s* (Beverly Hills: Sage Publications, 1971), p. 102; *DN*, Sept. 15, Oct. 26, 1967, Aug. 8, 1978; Richard Gid Powers, *Secrecy and Power: The Life of J. Edgar Hoover* (New York: Free Press, 1987), pp. 422–23; Christopher Howard Pyle, "Military Surveillance of Civilian Politics, 1967–1970" (Ph.D. diss., Columbia University, 1974), p. 47; D. G. Wood to U.S. Continental Army Command, Sept. 27, 1967, Box 1, Accession 69A632, RG 338; *Riots, Civil and Criminal Disorders*, pt. 5:1283, 1299; Official Transcript, Sept. 12, 1967, pp. 970–71, 983–84, Series 1, Box 2, NACCD Records; Michigan Commission on Crime . . . , Analysis by Police and Public Safety Committee, Nov. 8, 1967, Box 12, ORA Papers; Minutes, Michigan Commission on Crime . . . , Dec. 15–16, 1967, Box 31, ibid.; Report of Commission on Crime . . . , [Jan. 3, 1968], p. 2, Box 327, GR Papers; *Detroit Daily Press*, Jan. 4, 1968; *Detroit Scene* 1, no. 5 [1967]: 13, Box 429, Walter Reuther Papers, ALHUA; Girardin interview, pp. 386–87, 416–17; Nichols interview, p. 33.

51. On this point, see *DFP*, July 30, 1967; Freeman Report, Series III, Box 3, CCR Papers; Boesel, "Ghetto Riots," p. 37; James R. Hundley, Jr., "The Dynamics of Recent Ghetto Riots," in Richard A. Chikota and Michael C. Moran, eds., *Riot in the Cities* (Rutherford, N.J.: Farleigh Dickinson University Press, 1970), p. 43; Locke to Fine, Jan. 4, 1984; and Nicholas interview with Jerimaji (Cleage) [1982], copy of tape in my possession.

Chapter 16

1. Joel D. Aberbach and Jack L. Walker, *Race in the City* (Boston: Little, Brown and Co., 1973), p. 56.

2. Ibid., pp. 57–58; Sheldon Levy, "Communication Processes in the Detroit Riot" [1968], pp. 35, 49, Detroit Public Library, Detroit, Michigan; Inter-University Consortium for Political and Social Research, Black File, No. 235, White File, No. 237, Detroit data for Angus Campbell and Howard Schuman, "Racial Attitudes in Fifteen American Cities," in *Supplemental Studies for the National Advisory Commission on Civil Disorders* (Washington: GPO, 1968).

3. Aberbach and Walker, *Race*, p. 59; James Hedegard, "Detroit Race Attitudes and Responses to the Riot" [1968], p. 15, Edward Lurie Papers, copy in my possession; Levy, "Communication Processes," pp. 52, 54, 57; Black File, No. 244, White File, Nos. 244, 257, 262, Detroit data for "Racial Attitudes."

4. Joe R. Feagin and Harlan Hahn, *Ghetto Revolts* (New York: Macmillan Co., 1973), p. 302; Hedegard, "Race Attitudes," pp. 1–2; Aberbach and Walker, *Race*, 64; Black File, Nos. 294, 304, White File, Nos. 262, 270, 274, Detroit data for "Racial Attitudes"; Hahn, "Black Separatists: Attitudes and Objectives in a Riot-Torn Ghetto," *Journal of Black Studies* 1 (Sept. 1970): 39–50.

5. Aberbach and Walker, *Race*, p. 109; *Return to 12th Street: A Follow-up Survey of Attitudes of Detroit Negroes, October, 1968* [Detroit: Detroit Free Press, 1968], p. 10.

6. White File, Nos. 287, 288, Black File, Nos. 316, 317, Detroit data for "Racial Attitudes."

7. Geschwender, *Class, Race, and Worker Insurgency: The League of Revolutionary Black Workers* (London: Cambridge University Press, 1977), p. 82; *DFP*, Aug. 6, 1967; Interview with James H. Lincoln, June 14, 1984, p. 42, transcript in MHC; Feagin and Hahn, *Ghetto Revolts*, pp. 301–4; Tom Popp Memorandum for Herman Wilson, Oct. 26, 1967, Peter Rossi File, in my possession.

8. James Raschard Memorandum to Wilson (interview with Conrad Mallett), n.d., Rossi File.

9. Wilson Memoranda to Charles E. Nelson (interview with Henry Cleage), n.d., (interview with Nadine Brown), n.d., Series 59, Box 2, NACCD Records; Sarah L. Carey Memorandum to Milan C. Miskovsky, Dec. 22, 1967, Series 4, Box 22, ibid.; Popp Memorandum to Wilson, Oct. 26, 1967, Rossi File; Conference Notes Between Henry Ford and Francis Kornegay, Aug. 3, 1967, Francis A. Kornegay Papers (unprocessed portion); *DFP*, Oct. 1, 1967.

10. *DFP*, Aug. 20, 1967; *DN*, Sept. 10, 25, 1967; Walter Dukes Memorandum to Wilson (interview with John Watson), n.d., Series 59, Box 2, NACCD Records; Wilson Memoranda to Nelson (Cleage interview), n.d., (interview with Charles Brown), n.d., ibid.; Popp Memorandum to Wilson, Oct. 26, 1967, Rossi File; John Doar Memorandum for File, Sept. 14, 1967, Box 10, Warren Christopher Papers, LBJ Library; Arthur Weiseger to Kornegay, Aug. 14, 1967, Box 12, DUL Papers.

11. Wilson Memoranda to Nelson, n.d., (interview with Stewart House and Norvel [*sic*] Harrington), n.d., Series 59, Box 2, NACCD Records; *DN*, Sept. 10, 29, 1967.

12. *MC*, Aug. 12, 19, Sept. 23, 1967; *DFP*, Aug. 19, Oct. 1, 1967; *DN*, Sept.

25, 1967; John K. Scales Memorandum to Miskovsky (interview with Albert Cleage), Jan. 17, 1967 [1968], Series 4, Box 22, NACCD Records; Cleage, "Transfer of Power," *Center Magazine* 1 (Mar. 1968): 47-48; William Serrin, "Cleage's Alternative," *Reporter* 38 (May 30, 1968): 29-30.

13. Hubert Locke, *The Detroit Riot of 1967* (Detroit: Wayne State University Press, 1969), pp. 98-101; Detroit to Director, Sept. 18, 1967, FBI-FOIA; *DFP*, Aug. 28, 1967; *DN*, Aug. 28, 1967; *MC*, Sept. 2, 1967.

14. Donald I. Warren, "Some Observations from Post-Riot Detroit: The Role of Social Researchers in Contemporary Racial Conflict," *Phylon* 34 (June 1973): 174-75; *DN*, Oct. 20, 1967; *MC*, Oct. 21, 28, Nov. 4, 1967; Permanent Subcommittee on Investigations of the Senate Committee on Government Operations, *Riots, Civil and Criminal Disorders, Hearings*, 90th Cong., 2d sess., 1968, pt. 6:1429.

15. *DFP*, Aug. 10, 1967; *DN*, Aug. 10, 19, 1967; *MC*, Aug. 19, 26, 1967; *NYT*, Aug. 13, 1967; Locke, *Detroit Riot*, pp. 113-14; Stanley Webb to Roger Wilkins, n.d., and enclosed report, Detroit Riot File, Community Relations Service, Department of Justice, FBI-FOIA; *Riots, Civil and Criminal Disorders*, pt. 6:1467-68; *City* 2 (Jan. 1968): 6.

16. *DFP*, Aug. 11, 18, 19, 1967; *DN*, Aug. 19, 1967; *MC*, Aug. 26, 1967; Helen M. Graves, "New Detroit Committee/New Detroit Incorporated . . ." (Ph.D. diss., Wayne State University, 1975), p. 62.

17. CCAC, "What CCAC Membership Means . . . ," Sept. 27, 1967, Series 45, Box 10, NACCD Records; Wilson Memorandum to Nelson (A. Cleage interview), Series 59, Box 2, ibid.; *DFP*, Oct. 1, 1967; *MC*, Sept. 16, 30, Oct. 7, 1967.

18. Wilson Memorandum to Nelson, Oct. 12, 1967, Series 59, Box 2, NACCD Records; Reconnaissance Survey Reports, Detroit, 3:61, Series 10, Box 46, ibid.; Cleage and Brown to Dear Member, Nov. 4, 1967, and enclosed handbill, Box 3, Part 2, Series I, DNAACP Papers; CCAC handbill, Nov. 6, 1967, Exhibit No. 98, Case 55-15-X, Records of the United States Senate, RG 46, NARA.

19. *DFP*, Oct. 1, 1967; Wilson Memoranda to Nelson, Oct. 12, 1967, (A. Cleage interview), n.d., Series 59, Box 2, NACCD Records; Nathaniel R. Jones Memorandum to Merle C. McCurdy, Oct. 18, 1967, Series 4, Box 22, ibid.

20. *MC*, Sept. 23, 30, Dec. 9, 23, 30, 1967; *DN*, Sept. 20, 1967; Haywood L. Perry to Director of Investigations, Dec. 21, 1967, Series 4, Box 22, NACCD Records; *City* 2 (Jan. 1968): 7; Serrin, "Cleage's Alternative," p. 30.

21. Black File, Nos. 246, 274, 276, 312, 314, 315, Detroit data for "Racial Attitudes"; ibid., p. 52; *Return to 12th Street*, pp. 12-14, 17; Feagin and Hahn, *Ghetto Revolts*, pp. 275-76; Hedegard, "Race Attitudes," p. 3.

22. *Riots, Civil and Criminal Disorders*, pt. 7:1568; *DFP*, Aug. 25, 1967; Interview with Robert Potts, June 4, 1985, pp. 15-16, transcript in MHC.

23. DCO Release, Aug. 22, 1967, Joseph L. Hudson Papers, MHC; *DFP*, Aug. 24, Oct. 1, 1967; *MC*, Aug. 26, Sept. 16, Oct. 28, 1967; Robert Battle III and Horace Sheffield to Hudson, Dec. 11, 1967, Allen to Hudson, Dec. 27, 1967, and enclosed document, Garrett to Hudson, Box 579, JPC Papers; Sheffield to . . . TULC Education Foundation, Dec. 12, 1967, Box 53, Richard Austin Papers, ALHUA; *City* 2 (Jan. 1968): 7; *Business Week*, Feb. 3, 1968, p. 124; Locke, *Detroit Riot*, p. 117.

24. *DFP*, Aug. 24, Oct. 1, 1967; Bernard Dobranski Memorandum to Wilson

(interview with William T. Patrick, Jr.), Oct. 13, 1967, Series 59, Box 2, NACCD Records; *Business Week*, Nov. 25, 1967, p. 83.

25. *DFP*, Aug. 25, Oct. 1, 1967; *MC*, Oct. 7, Nov. 25, 1967; *Business Week*, Feb. 3, 1968, p. 124.

26. Bill Davidson, "If We Can't Solve the Problems of the Ghetto Here . . . ," *Saturday Evening Post* 24 (Oct. 25, 1968): 30; Earl L. Selby, "Detroit's Realistic Response to Riot," *Reader's Digest* 93 (Dec. 1968): 189; Interview with Arthur Johnson, July 23, 1984, p. 37, transcript in MHC; Wilson Memorandum to Nelson (interview with Francis Kornegay et al.), n.d., Series 59, Box 2, NACCD Records; *Business Week*, Nov. 25, 1967, p. 84; *DFP*, Aug. 11, 1968.

27. Cavanagh to Henry Ford II, Dec. 28, 1967, Box 340, JPC Papers; Graves, "New Detroit," p. 215; Johnson interview, pp. 38-39.

28. *Business Week*, Nov. 25, 1967, p. 83; *Newsweek* 71 (Jan. 1, 1968): 48; Selby, "Detroit's Response," p. 189.

29. Interview with Joseph L. Hudson, Oct. 2, 1984, pp. 21-22, transcript in MHC; *DN*, Oct. 18, 1967, May 19, 1987.

30. *City* 2 (Jan. 1968): 7; *NYT*, Dec. 3, 1967; *MC*, Dec. 9, 1967; Freeman to Patrick, Dec. 8, 1967, and enclosed Three Phase Proposal . . . , Box 579, JPC Papers; W. H. Schoen Memorandum to Hudson, n.d., Hudson Papers; *Business Week*, Feb. 3, 1968, p. 120.

31. *NYT*, Dec. 3, 1967; *London Evening Free Press*, Mar. 14, 1968, clipping in Hudson Papers; Interview with Karl Gregory, July 12, 1984, p. 34, transcript in MHC.

32. Freeman to Patrick, Dec. 8, 1967, and enclosed Three Phase Proposal . . . , Box 579, JPC Papers; New Detroit Committee, *Progress Report, April, 1968* [Detroit: n.p., 1968], pp. 68-69; *NYT*, Dec. 3, 1967; Graves, "New Detroit," pp. 64-65; *MC*, Jan. 9, 1968; Gregory interview, pp. 30, 33.

33. Graves, "New Detroit," pp. 66-68; Battle and Sheffield to Hudson, Dec. 11, 1967, Franklin Brown to Hudson, Dec. 11, 1967, Nelson Jack Edwards and Rudolph H. McCulloch to Hudson, Dec. 11, 1967, Executive Board, DCO, to Patrick, Dec. 14, 1967, Box 579, JPC Papers; [Hudson] "History of Federation-DCO-Etc.," n.d., Hudson Papers; Hudson interview, p. 21; Johnson interview, pp. 39-41; Interview with Damon Keith, Jan. 21, 1985, pp. 30-32, transcript in MHC; Coalition of Black Trade Unionists . . . , "New Detroit and the (Negro) People, 1967-1977" [1977], pp. 9-10, Box 17, Kornegay Papers; *NYT*, Dec. 15, 1967.

34. Text of statement . . . , Dec. 19, 1967, Box 84, ND Papers; *NYT*, Dec. 20, 1967; *Detroit Daily Press*, Dec. 20, 21, 1967; Graves, "New Detroit," pp. 68-69.

35. Allen to Hudson, Dec. 27, 1967, and enclosed document, Box 579, JPC Papers; New Detroit, *Progress Report*, p. 67; Graves, "New Detroit," pp. 70-71.

36. [Hudson] "History of Federation," Hudson Papers; *MC*, Jan. 13, 1968; Graves, "New Detroit," pp. 71-72.

37. Cleage to Hudson, Jan. 5, 1968, Allen Dreyfuss to Hudson, Jan. 25, 1968, Hudson Papers; FSD Release, Jan. 5, 1968, ibid.; *Business Week*, Feb. 3, 1968, p. 121; Graves, "New Detroit," pp. 72-73.

38. Excerpts from McKissick Press Conference, Jan. 8, 1968, Hudson Papers; FSD Release, Jan. 7, 1968, ibid.; *Detroit Daily Press*, Jan. 9, 1968.

39. Freeman and Harrington to Hudson, Jan. 5, 1968, Harrison to Hudson, Jan. 23, 1968, Hudson Papers; *Detroit Daily Press*, Jan. 9, 1968; *MC*, Jan. 13, 1968; *NYT*, Jan. 9, 1968; "Community Dissensus," in Leonard Gordon, ed., *A*

City in Racial Crisis: The Case of Detroit . . . ([Dubuque, Iowa]: Wm. C. Brown Co., 1971), pp. 111-12.

40. ND Release, Jan. 8, 1968, Hudson Papers; Hudson to Harrison, Jan. 26, 1968, Hudson and Patrick to Karl Gregory, Jan. 19, 1968, and enclosed document, Hudson to Cleage, Jan. 29, 1968, Hudson Papers; Summary of Task Force Leaders Meeting, Jan. 11, 1968, Box 15, ND Papers; Graves, "New Detroit," pp. 76-77; "Community Dissensus," pp. 76-77.

41. DCO Release, Jan. 24, 1968, Hudson Papers; *MC*, Feb. 3, Apr. 27, May 11, 1968; Coalition of Black Trade Unionists, "New Detroit," p. 17; John Sheehan to John F. Dearden, May 25, 1968, Father Sheehan Correspondence, 1962-1969, Archives of the Archdiocese of Detroit, Detroit, Michigan; Jim Ingram, "The Black Power Split . . . ," *Detroit Scope* 1 (Nov. 30, 1968): 6-8; Graves, "New Detroit," pp. 77-79.

42. "Community Dissensus," p. 116; Locke to George Edwards, Oct. 23, 1969, Box 20, ORA Papers.

43. Graves, "New Detroit," pp. 86-89, 128-30, 337, 658; Curtis E. Rodgers to Fred J. Romanoff, Oct. 25, 1968, Box 406, JPC Papers; *MC*, Aug. 31, 1968; *DFP*, May 4, 1969; *DN*, Nov. 19, 1967, May 3, 1970, Nov. 12, Dec. 13, 1974; *Newsweek* 73 (June 2, 1969): 62; Coalition of Black Trade Unionists, "New Detroit," pp. 13, 21-22; Johnson interview, pp. 43-44.

44. *MC*, Apr. 6, 1968; Dan Georgakas and Marvin Surkin, *Detroit: I Do Mind Dying* (New York: St. Martin's Press, 1975), pp. 23-24, 44, 83-84; Ingram and Wesley Hills, "Is Detroit the Capital of the Black Revolution?" *Detroit Scope* 2 (July 19, 1969): 6-7; Steve Babson, *Working Detroit* (New York: Adama Books, 1984), pp. 173-74; Steve Jefferys, *Management and Managed: Fifty Years of Crisis at Chrysler* (Cambridge: Cambridge University Press, 1986), pp. 162, 169, 177, 181, 183, 261; Geschwender, *Class*, p. 185 and passim.

45. Graves, "New Detroit," pp. 144-47, 150; Ann Scott, "Report from Detroit," *Fortune* 81 (Feb. 1970): 71-72; Alex Kroker, "Why There Was No Riot . . . ," *Detroit Scope* 1 (Sept. 20, 1968): 11; Economic Development Corporation to New Detroit, Sept. 4, 1969, Box 516, Walter Reuther Papers, ALHUA; *NYT*, June 9, 1968; *MC*, Apr. 20, June 15, Dec. 28, 1968, Jan. 18, Mar. 29, May 24, 1969; Gregory interview, pp. 36-39.

46. Wilson Memorandum to Nelson (interview with Fred Lyles), n.d., Series 59, Box 2, NACCD Records; To Archdiocese Development Fund: Re UTCA Funding Proposal, n.d., Sheehan Correspondence, Archives of Archdiocese; *NYT*, June 29, July 23, 1968; *DFP*, Dec. 19, 1968; *DN*, July 15, Aug. 25, Nov. 27, 1968, Aug. 10, 1970, Jan. 19, 1981.

47. *NYT*, May 20, 1968; Gregory interview, pp. 40-43; Ingram, "Black Power Split," pp. 6-7; Gregory to Fine, May 12, 1987.

48. *MC*, Sept. 23, 1967; *DFP*, Sept. 28, 1967; Scales Memorandum to Miskovsky, Dec. 27, 1967, Series 4, Box 22, NACCD Records; Robert Conot, *American Odyssey* (New York: William Morrow and Co., 1974), p. 577.

49. "Re Meeting to Discuss 'The Detroit Riot . . . , Aug. 22, 1967,' " Aug. 23, 1967, FBI-FOIA; Dukes Memorandum to Nelson (interview with Donald Lobsinger), n.d., Series 59, Box 2, NACCD Records; Wilson Memorandum to Nelson (interview with Karl Gregory), n.d., ibid.; Dobranski Report to Robert Conot, n.d., Box 77, ibid.; Popp Memorandum to Wilson, Oct. 26, 1967, Rossi File; *DN*, Aug. 7, 1967; *MC*, Sept. 23, Dec. 2, 1967; *DFP*, Sept. 28, 1967.

50. Leonard Gordon, "A Limited View . . .," in Albert J. Mayer and Leonard Gordon, eds., *Urban Life and the Struggle To Be Human* (Dubuque, Iowa: Kendall/Hunt Publishing Co., 1979), p. 141.

51. *DN*, Oct. 8, 1967; *NYT*, Mar. 3, 8, 1968; *MC*, Mar. 9, 1968; B. J. Widick, *Detroit: City of Race and Class Violence* (Chicago: Quadrangle Books, 1972), p. 189; Warren, "Community Dissensus: Panic in Suburbia," in Gordon, ed., *City*, pp. 124–29, 141; Warren, "Suburban Isolation and Race Tension: The Detroit Case," *Social Problems* 17 (Winter 1970): 333–34; Marilyn Rosenthal, "When Rumor Raged," *Trans-Action* 8 (Feb. 1971): 41.

52. *MC*, Mar. 9, Apr. 20, 1968; Rosenthal, "Rumor," pp. 40, 42.

53. *Riots, Civil and Criminal Disorders*, pt. 6:1377–78; Paul Borman to Cavanagh, Feb. 26, 1968, Box 406, JPC Papers; Rosenthal, "Rumor," pp. 35–37. In the *DFP* survey of August–September 1968, by which time the rumor hysteria had subsided, 17 percent of the black respondents indicated that they had heard stories about "whites planning to attack Negro neighborhoods," but only 7 percent of the respondents believed the stories. *Return to 12th Street*, p. 20.

54. Oral History Interview of Jerome P. Cavanagh, Mar. 22, 1971, pp. 59–60, LBJ Library; Vivian Pope Memorandum to Burton I. Gordin, Feb. 19, 1968, Box 26, Records of the Michigan Civil Rights Commission, RG 74-90, State Archives, Lansing, Michigan; *Newsweek* 70 (July 29, 1968): 13; Official Transcript of Proceedings before the National Advisory Commission on Civil Disorders, Nov. 1, 1967, p. 3840, Series 1, Box 6, NACCD Records; *Riots, Civil and Criminal Disorders*, pt. 6:1378–80; Fred Powledge, "The Flight from City Hall," *Harper's* 239 (Nov. 1969): 118; *London Evening Free Press*, Mar. 11, 12, 1968, clippings in Hudson Papers; *NYT*, Mar. 8, 1968.

55. Cavanagh to Common Council, June 2, 1969, Box 481, JPC Papers; Borman to Cavanagh, Feb. 26, 1968, Box 406, ibid.; Release, Mar. 6, 1968, Box 562, ibid.; *NYT*, Mar. 8, 1968.

56. Borman to Robert Roselle, Mar. 20, 1968, Box 453, JPC Papers; CCR Release, July 10, 1968, ibid.; CCR to Mayor's Offices, n.d., Series III, Box 3, CCR Papers.

57. *Report of the National Advisory Commission on Civil Disorders* (Washington: GPO, 1968), p. 173; CCR to Mayor's Offices, n.d., Series III, Box 3, CCR Papers; Interview with Richard Marks, Aug. 6, 1984, p. 45, transcript in MHC; Knopf, *Rumors, Race, and Riots* (New Brunswick, N.J.: Transaction Books, 1975), pp. 305, 308–10, 313.

Chapter 17

1. Feagin and Hahn, *Ghetto Revolts* (New York: Macmillan Co., 1973), pp. 199–202.

2. Cavanagh spoke to Daniel Patrick Moynihan, director of the Harvard-MIT Joint Center for Urban Studies, Julius Edelstein, director of Urban Studies at the City University of New York, and Adam Yarmolinsky of the Harvard Law School. *Detroit Daily Express*, Dec. 10, 1967.

3. David J. Olson, "Racial Violence and City Politics" (Ph.D. diss., University of Wisconsin, 1971), p. 147; Michael Lipsky and David J. Olson, *Commission Politics* (New Brunswick, N.J.: Transaction Books, 1977), pp. 398–99.

4. Cavanagh to Department Heads, Aug. 3, 1967, Box 393, JPC Papers; Strichartz to Cavanagh, Oct. 26, 1967, Box 534, ibid.; Testimony by . . . Cavanagh . . . , April 30, 1968, pp. 7–8, Box 465, ibid.; *City* 2 (Jan. 1968): 7; Olson, "Racial Violence," p. 147; Hubert G. Locke, *The Detroit Riot of 1967* (Detroit: Wayne State University Press, 1969), p. 102; Interview with Robert Roselle, Aug. 30, 1984, p. 43, transcript in MHC.

5. Olson, "Racial Violence," pp. 147–56; *City* 2 (Jan. 1968): 7.

6. MDT report, enclosed with Strichartz to Cavanagh, Oct. 26, 1967, Box 534, JPC Papers; Olson, "Racial Violence," pp. 158–59, 354n.

7. MDT report, Box 534, JPC Papers; Olson, "Racial Violence," pp. 156–58.

8. *Detroit Daily Express*, Dec. 10, 1967; Olson, "Racial Violence," p. 243; *City* 2 (Jan. 1968): 7; Richard Marks Memorandum to Cavanagh, Nov. 28, 1967, Box 339, JPC Papers; Robert Reese to Cavanagh, Nov. 27, 1967, Box 535, ibid.; Community Services Task Force . . . Memorandum, Nov. 30, 1967, Box 55, ND Papers; *DFP*, Jan. 26, 1969. The responses of the departments to the MDT report are in Box 535, JPC Papers.

9. *DFP*, Oct. 27, 1967, Jan. 26, 1969; Lipsky and Olson, *Commission Politics*, p. 328; Interview with Mel Ravitz, May 8, 1968, Box 16, A-W Riot Studies.

10. MDT Report [1969], Box 582, JPC Papers; Lipsky and Olson, *Commission Politics*, pp. 400–410; *DFP*, Jan. 26, 1969.

11. *DFP*, Aug. 3, 1967; *DN*, Aug. 19, 1967; General Departmental Communication No. 22, Aug. 14, 1967, Box 186, GR Papers; Romney to All Department Heads, Aug. 14, 1967, Box 232, ibid.; Report of the Commission on Crime . . . , [Jan. 3, 1968], Box 323, ibid.; *Detroit Daily Press*, Jan. 4, 1968.

12. Donald Lee Scruggs, "Lyndon Baines Johnson and the National Advisory Commission on Civil Disorders . . ." (Ph.D. diss., University of Oklahoma, 1980), pp. 292–93, 323; Minutes of Meeting . . . , Aug. 21, 1967, Box 394, JPC Papers; Mallett Thoughts on the Kerner Report, Box 427, ibid.; [David] Chambers Memorandum, Aug. 24, 1967, Series 4, Box 22, NACCD Records; Kyran McGrath Memorandum, Aug. 17, 1967, ibid.; *Report of the National Advisory Commission on Civil Disorders* (Washington: GPO, 1968), pp. 91, 319–21; Oral History Interview of Jerome P. Cavanagh, Mar. 22, 1971, pp. 63–64, LBJ Library; *DN*, Aug. 17, 22, 1967. The Records of the NACCD, including the Reconnaissance Survey Field Research Report for Detroit, are in the LBJ Library. For the Detroit testimony, see Official Transcript of Proceedings before the NACCD, Aug. 15, 1967, pp. 390–562, Series 1, Box 2.

13. *NACCD Report*, pp. 47–61, 73–77, 321 and passim; Feagin and Hahn, *Ghetto Revolts*, p. 219.

14. Feagin and Hahn, *Ghetto Revolts*, p. 261; Sheldon Levy, "Communication Processes in the Detroit Riot" [1968], pp. 55–56, Detroit Public Library, Detroit, Michigan; White File, No. 247, Black File, No. 254, Inter-University Consortium for Political and Social Research, Detroit data for Angus Campbell and Howard Schuman, "Racial Attitudes in Fifteen American Cities," in *Supplemental Studies for the National Advisory Commission on Civil Disorders* (Washington: GPO, 1968).

15. MDT report, Box 534, JPC Papers; Quinlan to MDT, Aug. 15, 1967, and enclosure, Box 529, ibid.; Quinlan to Cavanagh, Nov. 22, 1967, Box 535, ibid.; Quinlan and John Nichols to Common Council, Feb. 6, 1968, Quinlan to Common Council, Feb. 6, 1968, Box 403, ibid.; Minutes of Executive Committee,

MDT, Dec. 15, 1967, Box 339, ibid.; MDT Report [1969], Box 582, ibid.; CCR, "Annual Report, 1969," p. 3.

16. Quinlan to MDT, Aug. 15, 1967, Box 529, JPC Papers; Quinlan and Nichols to Common Council, Feb. 6, 1968, Quinlan to Common Council, Feb. 6, 1968, Robert E. Tighe to Cavanagh, Jan. 17, June 28, 1968, Box 403, ibid.; Minutes of Executive Committee, MDT, Dec. 15, 1967, Box 339, ibid.; *DFP*, Aug. 11, Oct. 21, 1967; National Commission on Urban Problems, *Hearings*, 5 vols. (Washington: GPO, 1968), 5:22; Permanent Subcommittee on Investigations of the Senate Committee on Government Operations, *Riots, Civil and Criminal Disorders, Hearings*, 1968, pt. 7:1500–1501.

17. Jerome H. Skolnick, *The Politics of Protest* (n.p., [1969]), p. 197. See chap. 8.

18. Herman Wilson Memorandum to Charles E. Nelson, undated, Peter Rossi File, in my possession; Sarah L. Carey Memorandum to Milan C. Miskovsky, Dec. 27, 1967, Series 4, Box 22, NACCD Records; Minutes of Meeting with Members of Kerner Commission, Aug. 21, 1967, Box 396, JPC Papers; *NYT*, Aug. 28, 1967; *Ann Arbor News*, Jan. 4, 1968; *DFP*, Aug. 31, 1967; *The People Beyond 12th Street: A Survey of Attitudes of Detroit Negroes after the Riot of 1967* (Detroit: Detroit Urban League, 1967); *Return to 12th Street: A Follow-up Survey of Attitudes of Detroit Negroes, October 1968* [Detroit: Detroit Free Press, 1968], p. 20.

19. *DN*, Nov. 9, 12, 1967; *Ann Arbor News*, Jan. 4, 1968.

20. Cavanagh to D. C. Harms, Oct. 3, 1967, Box 342, JPC Papers; Statement by . . . Cavanagh on the Progress . . . since July 23, 1967, Box 426, ibid.; *NYT*, Feb. 28, Mar. 21, 1968; William Serrin, "God Help Our City," *Atlantic Monthly* 223 (Mar. 1969): 116, 119.

21. Xavier Nicholas interview with Mrs. Ray Girardin [1982], copy of tape in my possession; Garry Wills, *The Second Civil War* (New York: New American Library, 1968), p. 48; *DN*, Aug. 10, 24, Oct. 4, 1967; James Hedegard, "Race Attitudes and Responses to the Riot in the Community" [1968], p. 4, Edward Lurie Papers, in my possession; Locke to Fine, May 7, 1987.

22. *NYT*, Jan. 22, 1968; Serrin, "God Help Our City," p. 117; Minutes of Meeting with Cavanagh, Mar. 22, 1968, Box A-19, DUL Papers.

23. Girardin to Common Council, Oct. 18, 1967, Box 570, JPC Papers.

24. *DFP*, Oct. 19, 1967; *DN*, Oct. 18, 20, 1967; Bernard Dobranski Memorandum to Wilson (interview with Walter J. Stecher), Oct. 18, 1967, Series 59, Box 2, NACCD Records; John Diamond to Members, Dec. 4, 1967, Box 187, GR Papers; James L. Trainor to Cavanagh, Oct. 25, 1967, Box 339, JPC Papers; Wills, *Second Crusade*, p. 117; *Ann Arbor News*, Jan. 4, 1968.

25. Cavanagh to Common Council, Oct. 20, 1967, Box 531, JPC Papers; Girardin to Common Council [Feb. 1968], Box 409, ibid.; *DFP*, Oct. 21, 24, 27, Nov. 2, 1967; *DN*, Oct. 20, 27, 1967; Interview with John Nichols, Aug. 13, 1984, pp. 67–69, transcript in MHC; Serrin, "Who Cares About Rebuilding the City?" *New Republic* 158 (May 4, 1968): 10; Hudson . . . meeting with Task Force Leaders, Oct. 13, 1967, Tag No. 21, ND Papers. Cf. Hal De Long, "Detroit Remembers July 1967 . . . ," *Police* 12 (May–June 1968): 6.

26. *DFP*, Sept. 15, Nov. 2, 9, 1967; *Detroit Journal*, Sept. 29, 1967.

27. Agenda, Special Meeting, Aug. 8, 1967, Box 398, JPC Papers; Albert Callewaert and Arthur Yim, "The Detroit Police Department and the Detroit

Civil Disorder," Dec. 1967, pp. 54-60, Box 407, ibid.; *Riots, Civil and Criminal Disorders*, pt. 5:1365; To John F. Nichols, Aug. 10, Oct. 25, 1967, Commissioner's File, DPD; *DFP*, Oct. 13, 1967; *DN*, Oct. 24, 1967.

28. *Riots, Civil and Criminal Disorders*, pt. 5:1365, 1366; Girardin to Common Council [Feb. 1968], Box 409, JPC Papers; *DFP*, Aug. 27, 1967.

29. *Riots, Civil and Criminal Disorders*, pt. 5:1365, 1366-67; Roselle Memorandum to Cavanagh, Feb. 23, 1968, Box 406, JPC Papers; Girardin to Common Council [Feb. 1968], Box 409, ibid.; Cavanagh Statement, Box 426, ibid.; Peter C. McGillwray to Strichartz, Oct. 11, 1967, Box 529, ibid.; Trainor to Frank Judge, Dec. 19, 1967, Box 372, ibid.; Callewaert and Yim, "Police Department," p. 60, Box 407, ibid.; Detroit Fire Department, Report of Civil Disturbance Alert, Apr. 5, 1968 [May 14, 1968], Exhibit No. 122, Case No. 55-15-X, Records of the United States Senate, RG 46, NARA; "Detroit Civil Disturbance Support Plan," June 14, 1968, Series III, Box 1, CCR Papers.

30. Girardin to Common Council [Feb. 1968], Box 409, JPC Papers; Minutes of Meeting with Cavanagh, Mar. 22, 1968, Box A-19, DUL Papers; *DN*, Oct. 4, 1967; *DFP*, Oct. 4, 1967; *Riots, Civil and Criminal Disorders*, pt. 5:1365-66.

31. Mayor's Committee on the Administration of Justice during Civil Disorders, Subcommittee on Arrest, Booking and Screening, Aug. 20 [1968], Box 510, JPC Papers; Girardin to Common Council [Feb. 1968], ibid.; *DN*, Oct. 15, 1967; Isaac D. Balbus, *The Dialectics of Legal Repression: Black Rebels before the American Criminal Courts* (New York: Russell Sage Foundation, 1973), p. 148.

32. Cavanagh Statement, Box 426, JPC Papers; Subcommittee on Arrest, Booking and Screening, Aug. 20 [1968], Box 510, ibid.; *Riots, Civil and Criminal Disorders*, pt. 5:1366.

33. Balbus, *Legal Repression*, pp. 148-49; Interview with William Cahalan, July 23, 1984, pp. 35-36, transcript in MHC; Cahalan to Fine, June 30, 1986.

34. *Annual Report of the Recorder's Court for the City of Detroit, Michigan, 1968*, p. 2; *DN*, Oct. 15, 1967; Cavanagh to Judges . . . , Oct. 24, 1967, Box 346, JPC Papers; Balbus, *Legal Repression*, p. 150.

35. James H. Lincoln, *The Anatomy of a Riot* (New York: McGraw-Hill Book Co., 1968), pp. 21-47; *Michigan State Bar Journal* 47 (Aug. 1968): 31.

36. Cavanagh to Louis F. Simmons, June 18, 1968, and enclosed "Rough Draft," Box 427, JPC Papers; Remarks by Mayor Cavanagh to initial meeting . . . , June 24, 1968, Box 465, ibid.; Outline of Mayor's remarks for second meeting, July 22, 1968, Maurice Kelman Papers, in Kelman's possession; Remarks for third meeting, Aug. 20, 1968, ibid.; Remarks at the 4th meeting, June 27, 1969, ibid.; Kelman to Cavanagh, Aug. 19, 1968, May 26, 1969, ibid.; Cavanagh to T. E. Brennan, May 27, 1969, ibid.; Kelman to Fine, June 24, 1986; Balbus, *Legal Repression*, pp. 152-54; *NACCD Report*, pp. 194-95.

37. Jean R. Moenk, *USCONARC Participation in Suppression of Civil Disorders, April 1968* (Fort Monroe, VA.: Historical Branch, U.S. Continental Army Command, 1968), p. 14; James Richard Gardner, "The Civil Disturbance Mission of the Department of the Army, 1963-1973 . . ." (Ph.D. diss., Princeton University, 1977), p. 112; Oral History Interview of Warren Christopher, Oct. 31, 1968 (tape no. 1), pp. 19-20, LBJ Library; Address by Ralph E. Haines, Sept. 19, 1967, (Paul J. Scheips) Civil Disturbance File, Task Force Detroit, Center of Military History, Washington, D.C.; John K. Mahon, *History of the Militia and the National Guard* (New York: Macmillan Co., 1983), p. 241; Minutes and

Documents of the Cabinet Meetings of President Johnson, 1963–1969, Aug. 2, 1967, microfilm copy in the University of Michigan Library, Ann Arbor, Michigan.

38. David E. McGiffert to Deputy Secretary of Defense, Aug. 1, 1967, in "Results of the Civil Disturbance Task Group Review of the Deputy Commander TF Detroit [1967]," in my possession; James S. Campbell et al., *Law and Order Reconsidered: Report of the Task Force on Law Enforcement* . . . (Washington: GPO, 1969), pp. 319–20; Robert McNamara Memorandum to Vice-President, Aug. 16, 1967, Civil Disturbance File, Task Force Detroit; Gardner, "Civil Disturbance Mission," pp. 87–88; Special Subcommittee of the House Committee on Armed Services to Inquire into the Capability of the National Guard to Cope with Civil Disturbances, *Hearings*, 90th Cong., 1st sess., 1967, pp. 5683–5749 (hereafter *Capability Hearings*).

39. Special Subcommittee of the House Committee on Armed Services to Inquire into the Capability of the National Guard to Cope with Civil Disturbances, 90th Cong., 1st sess., *Report No. 36*, 1967, pp. 5656–57; Gardner, "Civil Disturbance Mission," pp. 89–90; Wills, *Second Civil War*, p. 65; John H. Berendt, "From the Wonderful Men Who Gave You Kent State," *Esquire* 75 (Apr. 1971): 50; R. N. Kugler to HQ Fifth Army . . . , Feb. 26, 1968, Clarence Schnipke to Romney, Feb. 14, 1968, Box 319, GR Papers; *Challenge: Compendium of Army Accomplishments: A Report by the Chief of Staff* (Washington, D.C., 1964–68), pp. 83–84, Civil Disturbance File, Task Force Detroit; *Riots, Civil and Criminal Disorders*, app., pt. 6:1577–78; Adam Yarmolinsky, *The Military Establishment* (New York: Harper and Row, 1971), p. 189.

40. "Final Report of Cyrus R. Vance Concerning the Detroit Riots, July 23 through August 2, 1967," pp. 51–53, with Oral History of Cyrus R. Vance, Nov. 3, 1969, LBJ Library; Transcript of Proceedings, NACCD, Aug. 9, 1967, pp. 175–82, 201, Series 1, Box 1, NACCD Records; Elias C. Townsend Memorandum for Heads of Army Staff Agencies, Aug. 31, 1967, in "Results of Civil Disturbance Review"; Campbell et al., *Law and Order Reconsidered*, p. 320; Berendt, "Those Wonderful Men," pp. 58, 62; Paul J. Scheips and Karl E. Cocke, *Army Operational and Intelligence Activities in Civil Disturbances since 1957*, rev. ed., 1971, Office of the Chief of Military History Study 73, pp. 71–72; Gardner, "Civil Disturbance Mission," p. 91.

41. Moenk, *CONARC Participation*, pp. 19–21; Campbell et al., *Law and Order Reconsidered*, pp. 316–17; Gardner, "Civil Disturbance Mission," pp. 91–94; *Challenge*, pp. 83–84.

42. Haines Memorandum for the Undersecretary of the Army, Apr. 30, 1968, and enclosure, Box 2, Accession 71A3100, Records of the Army Staff, RG 319, Office of the Adjutant General, Alexandria, Virginia; Scheips and Cocke, *Operational and Intelligence Activities*, p. 71; *Riots, Civil and Criminal Disorders*, app., pt. 6:1577–78; Gardner, "Civil Disturbance Mission," pp. 97–99, 106–8; Campbell et al., *Law and Order Reconsidered*, p. 320; *Challenge*, pp. 83–84; Christopher Howard Pyle, "Military Surveillance of Civilian Politics, 1967–1970" (Ph.D. diss., Columbia University, 1974), pp. 76–77, 81–83; Schnipke to Romney, Feb. 14, 1968, Box 319, GR Papers. See also DA to CG CONARC, Oct. 4, 1967, Box 4, Accession 71A1, Records of the Office of the Secretary of the Army, RG 335, Office of the Adjutant General; and *Control of Civil Disorders: Guide Lines for Small-Unit Commanders and Troops*, n.d., Box

1, Accession 69A632, Records of the United States Army Commands, RG 338, ibid.

43. James W. Button, *Black Violence: Political Impact of the 1960s Riots* (Princeton: Princeton University Press, 1978), p. 121; Clark to Dear Governor, Aug. 5, 1967, Office of Legal Counsel, Department of Justice, FOIA; *Capability Hearings*, pp. 5758–59; *NACCD Report*, pp. 287–88; Robert E. Jordan III Memorandum for Undersecretary of the Army, Jan. 10, 1968, Box 17, Accession 71A3078, RG 338.

44. Christopher interview, pp. 20–21; Jordan Memorandum for Undersecretary of Army, Jan. 10, 1968, Box 17, Accession 71A3078, RG 338; Campbell et al., *Law and Order*, p. 316; Urban America and the Urban Coalition, *One Year Later* (New York: Frederick A. Praeger, 1969), pp. 67–68; Button, *Black Violence*, pp. 122–24.

45. John T. Elliff, *Dissent and the Attorney General: The Justice Department in the 1960s* (Beverly Hills: Sage Publications, 1971), p. 105; Jordan Memorandum for Undersecretary of Army, Jan. 10, 1968, Box 17, Accession 71A3078, RG 338; Pyle, "Military Surveillance," p. 51; Button, *Black Violence*, pp. 124, 127; Feagin and Hahn, *Ghetto Revolts*, pp. 231–32; Richard Gid Powers, *Secrecy and Power: The Life of J. Edgar Hoover* (New York: Free Press, 1987), pp. 424–25; Kenneth O'Reilly, "The FBI and the Politics of Riots," *Journal of American History* 75 (June 1988): 113.

46. Winston P. Wilson to Romney, Aug. 9, 1967, Romney to Wilson, Aug. 22, 1967, Box 181, GR Papers; Schnipke to Romney, Feb. 14, 1968, Box 319, ibid.; *Riots, Civil and Criminal Disorders*, pt. 5:1220; *DN*, Aug. 23, Nov. 6, 1967; *NYT*, Aug. 23, 1967; *DFP*, Nov. 8, 1967; Berendt, "Those Wonderful People," p. 47.

47. *Riots, Civil and Criminal Disorders*, pt. 5:1220; *DFP*, Aug. 22, 1967; Schnipke Memo ARNG 45-3-3, Feb. 20, 1968, with Schnipke to Robert Danhof, Mar. 5, 1968, Box 319, GR Papers; Cavanagh to Romney, Aug. 21, 1967, Box 181, ibid.; Charles E. Harmon to Romney, Aug. 16, 1967, Box 186, ibid.; Romney to Cavanagh, Aug. 21, 1967, Box 181, ibid.; Wills, *Second Crusade*, p. 61; *DN*, Sept. 1, 1967.

48. William A. McWhirter, "Favorite Haven for the Comic Soldier," *Life* 63 (Oct. 27, 1967): 94–95.

49. McNamara Memorandum to Vice-President, Aug. 16, 1967, Civil Disturbance File, Task Force Detroit; Floyd W. Radike to FBI, Aug. 30, 1967, SAC Detroit to Director, Sept. 15, 1967, FBI-FOIA; Schnipke to Romney, Feb. 14, 1968, Frederick E. Davids to Romney, Mar. 12, 1968, Box 319, GR Papers; *DN*, Sept. 1, 1967; *Riots, Civil and Criminal Disorders*, pt. 5:1217.

50. Schnipke to Romney, Feb. 14, 1968, Box 319, GR Papers.

51. Davids to Romney, Mar. 12, 1968, ibid.; *DFP*, Oct. 14, 1967.

52. Romney Special Message, Oct. 10, 1967, Box 263, GR Papers; Davids to Romney, Mar. 12, 1968, Box 319, ibid.; *DFP*, Aug. 19, 1967, Aug. 11, 1968; *DN*, Oct. 13, 1967.

53. Feagin and Hahn, *Ghetto Revolts*, pp. 234–35; *Public and Local Acts of the Legislature of the State of Michigan Passed at the Regular Session of 1968* (Lansing: Department of Administration, n.d.), pp. 214, 512–13, 597; *Riots, Civil and Criminal Disorders*, pt. 5:1220; *DFP*, Aug. 11, 1968.

54. DPD, *Report on Civil Emergency, April 5th–April 11th, 1968*, p. i, DPD;

Death of Martin Luther King and events thereafter, n.d., Box 319, GR Papers; *Riots, Civil and Criminal Disorders*, pt. 7:1472-73.

55. [Martin Luther King Assassination] Log, Apr. 5, 1968, Box 407, JPC Papers; DPD, *Civil Emergency*, pp. i-viii, DPD; *NYT*, Apr. 6, 7, 1968; *MC*, Apr. 13, 1968; *Riots, Civil and Criminal Disorders*, pt. 7:1473, 1565-66.

56. King Log, Apr. 5, 1968, Box 407, JPC Papers; *DPD, Civil Emergency*, p. i, DPD; King Death, Box 319, GR Papers; *Riots, Civil and Criminal Disorders*, pt. 7:1473, 1474, 1476.

57. Trainor Log, Apr. 5, 1968, Box 583, JPC Papers; Headquarters Command Post Activity Log, Apr. 6, 1968, ibid.; King Log, Apr. 5, 1968, Box 407, ibid.; Christopher to Romney [Apr. 5, 1968], Box 319, GR Papers.

58. King Log, Apr. 5, 1968, Box 407, JPC Papers; *NYT*, Apr. 6, 1968; Executive Order No. 1968-1, Apr. 5, 1968, Box 319, GR Papers; *Riots, Civil and Criminal Disorders*, pt. 6:1506.

59. Department Report and Information Committee, Fact Sheet, Apr. 6 [1968], Box 583, JPC Papers; Detroit Fire Department, Report of Civil Disturbance Alert, Apr. 5, 1968 [May 14, 1968], Exhibit No. 122, Case No. 55-15-X, RG 46.

60. "Press Conference on Michigan Situation" [Apr. 5, 1968], Box 346, GR Papers; Text of News Conference, Apr. 6, 1968, ibid.; King Log, Apr. 6, 1968, Box 407, JPC Papers; Minutes of Task Force on Police Recruitment and Hiring, July 15, 1968, Box 585, ibid.; *NYT*, Apr. 7-10, 1968; *MC*, Apr. 20, 1968.

61. DPD, *Civil Emergency*, pp. 1-3, 13-14, 20, 21, DPD; *Riots, Civil and Criminal Disorders*, pt. 7:1476-77.

62. *Riots, Civil and Criminal Disorders*, pt. 7:1472, 1474, 1500-1501; Ralph C. Phillips to Chief, National Guard Bureau, May 1, 1968, Box 17, Records of the Michigan Department of Military Affairs, Adjutant General's Division, RG 78-125, State Archives, Lansing, Michigan; Girardin to Schnipke, Apr. 18, 1968, Box 319, GR Papers; Release, Apr. 5, 1968, Box 346, ibid.; Text of News Conference, Apr. 6, 1968, ibid.; Cavanagh to Theodore R. Mosch, Mar. 11, 1969, Box 481, JPC Papers; Cavanagh interview, pp. 66-67; Detroit Fire Department, Civil Disturbance Alert [May 14, 1968], Exhibit No. 122, Case No. 55-15-X, RG 46; *NYT*, Apr. 7, 1968; *DN*, May 19, 1987.

63. *Riots, Civil and Criminal Disorders*, pt. 7:1424; Cavanagh to Mosch, Mar. 11, 1969, Box 481, JPC Papers; *MC*, Apr. 20, 1968; Marilynn Rosenthal, "While Rumors Raged," *Trans-Action* 8 (Feb. 1971): 43; Urban America and the Urban Coalition, *One Year Later*, pp. 102, 105; Bill Davidson, "If We Can't Solve the Problems of the Ghetto Here . . . ," *Saturday Evening Post* 241 (Oct. 5, 1968): 82.

64. Joseph Vilino, Jr., to David Nelson, Jan. 22, 1968, Box 406, JPC Papers; Cavanagh Statement, Box 426, ibid.; *MC*, Feb. 3, 1968.

65. See chap. 18.

66. "Detroit Is Happening—1968," Aug. 29, 1968, Box 428, JPC Papers; "Detroit Is Happening Report: Summer 1968," ibid.

67. "Detroit Is Happening Report," Box 428, ibid.; *NYT*, July 25, 26, 1968; Interview with Robert Potts, June 4, 1985, pp. 20-21, transcript in MHC.

68. Girardin to Common Council [Feb. 1968], Box 409, JPC Papers; Agenda,

New Detroit Committee, Sept. 14, 1967, Box 532, ibid.; Joseph L. Hudson to Orlando Wilson, Sept. 15, 1967, Box 533, ibid.; *DFP*, Sept. 15, 27, 1967.

69. Hudson to Wilson, Sept. 15, 1967, Box 533, JPC Papers; School of Police Administration . . . , "A Report on Preliminary Work Completed . . . ," Jan. 3, 1968, Box 456, ibid.; Release, Jan. 3, 1968, Box 583, ibid.; *DFP*, Sept. 15, 27, 1967, Aug. 11, 1968; Special Meeting of Task Force Leaders with Hudson, Oct. 20, 1967, Tag 21, ND Papers; Release . . . Mayor and New Detroit, Dec. 18, 1967, Joseph L. Hudson Papers, MHC; Helen M. Graves, "New Detroit Committee/New Detroit Incorporated . . ." (Ph.D. diss., Wayne State University, 1975), p. 115; Interview with Joseph L. Hudson, Oct. 2, 1984, pp. 18–19, transcript in MHC; *MC*, Jan. 13, 1968.

70. MDT Report [1969], Box 582, JPC Papers; Eugene Reuter to Common Council, Jan. 8, 1968, Box 401, ibid.; Trainor to Cavanagh, Apr. 8, 1968, Box 410, ibid.; Cavanagh Statement, Box 426, ibid.; Statement of . . . Spreen, Apr. 13, 1969, Box 481, ibid.; *MC*, May 11, Aug. 3, 1968; *DFP*, July 24, 1972.

71. *DN*, Nov. 15, 1967; *MC*, Jan. 13, Aug. 3, 1968; Girardin to Common Council [Feb. 1968], Box 409, JPC Papers; Cavanagh Statement, Box 426, ibid.; Minutes of Meeting with Cavanagh, Mar. 22, 1968, Box A-19, DUL Papers; DUL Release, Aug. 2, 1968, ibid.

72. _____ to Commanding Officer, CCB, Feb. 1, 1968, Records of the Michigan Civil Rights Commission, RG 83-55 (unprocessed), State Archives.

73. Reconnaissance Survey Field Research Reports, Detroit, Michigan, 3:23–24, Series 10, Box 46, NACCD Records; *DN*, Aug. 15, 1967; Mallett to Roselle, Dec. 14, 1967, Box 583, JPC Papers; Mallett to Cavanagh, Jan. 19, 1968, Box 406, ibid.; School of Police Administration, "Report," Jan. 3, 1968, Box 456, ibid.

74. Gordin to Girardin, Feb. 13, 1968, Box 26, Records of the Civil Rights Commission-Administration, RG 74-90, State Archives; Recommendations to the Mayor by the CRC, Feb. 21, 1968, Box 6, ibid.; Gordin Memorandum to Commission, Feb. 23, 1968, ibid.; Gordin Memorandum to Commission, Feb. 16, 1968, and enclosed, "Police Community Relations in Detroit," Box 4, Records of the Michigan Civil Rights Commission, Detroit Office, RG 80-17, ibid.; Gordin to Executive Staff, Mar. 22, 1968, and enclosure, ibid.; Roselle Memos to Cavanagh, Feb. 20, 21, 1968, Box 406, JPC Papers.

75. _____ to Commanding Officer, CCB, Feb. 1, 1968, RG 83-55; Vivian Pope Memorandum to Gordin, Feb. 19, 1968, Box 26, RG 74-90; Minutes of Special Task Force . . . , Box 412, JPC Papers; Trainor to Cavanagh, Sept. 5, 1968, Box 410, ibid.; Trainor to Cavanagh, Feb. 6, 7, 1969, Box 477, ibid.; Trainor to Spreen, July 26, 1968, Box 481, ibid.; [CCR] Field Division Report to Aug. 21, 1968, Series IV, Box 4, CCR Papers.

76. DPD News Release, Sept. 4, 1969, Box 482, JPC Papers; Field Operations Division . . . , An Inspection Report of the DPD, Sept. 1969, Box 478, ibid.; *MC*, Sept. 20, 1969.

77. Trainor to Cavanagh, Feb. 6, 7, 1969, Box 477, JPC Papers; DPD Public Information Center News Release, July 31, 1969, Box 522, ibid.

78. DPD Public Information Center News Release, July 31, 1969, Box 522, ibid.; Interim Committee, Nov. 21, 1969, Box 583, ibid.; Management Study and Police-Community Relations Project, A Review, Dec. 17, 1969, Box 482, ibid.; *NYT*, Aug. 3, 1969; *MC*, Sept. 27, 1969.

79. Serrin, "God Help Our City," p. 115; Cavanagh to Tom Turner, Sept. 18, 1969, Box 481, JPC Papers; CCR, "Annual Report, 1969," p. 9.

80. *MC*, July 12, 19, 1969; *DFP*, Feb. 2, Aug. 3, 1969; *NYT*, Aug. 3, 1969; Frank Ditto et al. [to Cavanagh, July 22, 1968], Box 412, JPC Papers.

81. Joel D. Aberbach and Jack L. Walker, *Race in the City* (Boston: Little, Brown and Co., 1973), p. 66; Black File, No. 222, Detroit data for "Racial Attitudes"; *Return to 12th Street*, p. 18.

82. MDT report, Box 534, JPC Papers; MDT and Police Department Meeting, Sept. 21, 1967, Box 532, ibid.; Girardin to Cavanagh, Nov. 21, 1967, Box 535, ibid.; *MC*, Sept. 16, 1967; *NACCD Report*, p. 169; Baker et al. and Bratton et al. vs. City of Detroit et al. . . . , U.S. District Court for Eastern District of Michigan, Southern Division, Civil Nos. 5–77937 and 5–72264 (1979), p. 43, copy of manuscript opinion in my possession (hereafter cited as Keith opinion).

83. Special Task Force Report, Aug. 14, 1968, Box 412, JPC Papers; Trainor to Cavanagh, Sept. 27, 1968, Box 406, ibid.; *DFP*, Oct. 12, 14, 1967; Summary of Meeting with . . . Girardin, May 31, 1968, Box 1, Horace W. Gilmore Papers, ALHUA.

84. Minutes of Meeting with Cavanagh, Mar. 22, 1968, Box A-19, DUL Papers; Remarks by Cavanagh, May 27, 1968, ibid.; Paul Borman to Cavanagh, Mar. 15, 1968, Trainor to Roselle, Apr. 18, 1968, Ernest C. Browne to Roselle, May 28, 1968, To Staff from Roselle, May 28, 1968, Box 406, JPC Papers; Review and Recommendations Concerning the DPD's Recruiting Procedure, May 22, 1968, Box 412, ibid.; Release, July 13, 1968, ibid.; Vickery to Cavanagh, Oct. 10, 1968, ibid.; Cavanagh to Girardin, May 23, 1968, Cavanagh to Spreen, Oct. 16, 1968, Box 410, ibid.; Trainor to Cavanagh, July 3, 1968, Robert Quaid to Girardin, July 23, 1968, Box 585, ibid.; DPD Inter-Office Memorandum, July 3, 1968, ibid.; Minutes Police-Community Relations Subcommittee, Dec. 5, 1968, Mar. 6, 1969, Box 511, ibid.; Memo to CCR from Subcommittee on Police-Community Relations, July 14, 1969, Box 586, ibid.; Trainor to Cavanagh, Mar. 11, 1969, Box 477, ibid.; CCR, "Annual Report, 1968," p. 9; New Detroit, "Beyond the Difference," Aug. 28, 1969 (draft), pp. 16–17, Box 516, Walter Reuther Papers, ALHUA; CCR Minutes, July 15, 1968, Series IV, Box 4, CCR Papers; *NYT*, May 28, 29, 1968; Keith opinion, p. 25.

85. Trainor to Girardin, May 3, 1968, Cavanagh to Tindal and Corbit, July 26, 1968, Box 412, JPC Papers; Release, May 27, 1968, ibid.; DPD Inter-Office Memorandum, July 3, 1968, Box 585, ibid.; *MC*, June 1, 1968.

86. Special Task Force Report, Aug. 14, 1968, Box 412, JPC Papers; Cavanagh to Tindal and Corbit, July 26, 1968, ibid.

87. Trainor to Cavanagh, July 1, 1968, Box 458, ibid.; DPD Inter-Office Memorandum, July 3, 1968, Box 585, ibid.; Cavanagh to Spreen, Aug. 9, Oct. 16, 1968, Box 410, ibid.; Field Division Report to Aug. 21, 1968, Series IV, Box 4, CCR Papers; *MC*, Nov. 9, 1968; *NYT*, Nov. 10, 1968; Minutes, Police-Community Relations Subcommittee, Aug. 19, 1968, Box 1, Gilmore Papers.

88. Trainor to Cavanagh, Sept. 5, 1968, Box 406, JPC Papers; Cavanagh to Spreen, Oct. 16, 1968, Box 410, ibid.; Trainor to Cavanagh, Mar. 3, 1969, Box 477, ibid.; Memo to CCR from Subcommittee on Police-Community Relations, July 14, 1969, Box 586, ibid.; *MC*, Nov. 9, 1968; Serrin, "God Help Our City," p. 120; Keith opinion, pp. 26, 43.

89. Coordinating Council on Human Relations, Executive Board Minutes,

Apr. 3, 1968, Series II, Box 6, CCR Papers; Field Division Memorandum to Richard Marks, Feb. 1, 1968, Series IV, Box 4, ibid.; Pope Memorandum to Gordin, Feb. 19, 1968, Box 26, RG 74-90; Recommendations to the Mayor . . . , Feb. 21, 1968, Box 5, ibid.; Gordin Memorandum to the Commission, Feb. 16, 1968, and enclosed "Police-Community Relations in Detroit," Box 4, RG 80-17; *MC*, Feb. 3, 10, 1968; Borman to Cavanagh, Feb. 26, Mar. 15, 1968, Box 406, JPC Papers; Statement to Governor by Michigan State Advisory Committee . . . , Apr. 1, 1968, Box 321, GR Papers. A survey of 522 police in Detroit and twelve other cities revealed that the perception of hostility of blacks toward the police was highest among Detroit's police. W. Eugene Groves and Peter H. Rossi, "Police Perceptions of a Hostile Ghetto," in Harlan Hahn, ed., *Police in Urban Society* (Beverly Hills: Sage Publications, 1971), p. 180.

90. *MC*, May 25, 1968; Marks Memorandum to CCR [May 14, 1968], Box 419, JPC Papers; Roselle Memo to Cavanagh, June 2, 1968, Box 406, ibid.; Statement of Philip H. Mason, June 11, 1968, Box 567, JPC Papers; Statement of Sam J. Dennis, June 13, 1968, ibid.; CCB Investigation and Final Report of Cobo Hall Incident . . . , July 11, 1968, Box 561, ibid.; Longworth D. Quinn, Jr., Report . . . , May 14, 1968, Series IV, Box 4, CCR Papers; Fred Linsell to Marks, May 14, 1968, ibid.

91. Linsell to Marks, May 14, 1968, A. Nicholas Memorandum to Marks, May 14, 1968, Series IV, Box 4, CCR Papers; Quinn Report, May 14, 1968, ibid.; Dennis Statement, June 13, 1968, Box 567, JPC Papers; CCB Report, July 11, 1968, Box 561, ibid.; Heffernan to Spreen, July 25, 1968, ibid.; Interview of Leon Atchison, May 29, 1968, ibid.; Highlights of Commission Meeting, May 1968, Box 50, DUL Papers; *MC*, May 18, 1968.

92. *MC*, May 25, 1968; Ditto et al. [to Cavanagh, June 22, 1968], Box 412, JPC Papers; Highlights of Commission Meeting, May 1968, Box 50, DUL Papers; Coordinating Council on Human Relations, Executive Board Minutes, May 29, 1968, Series II, Box 6, CCR Papers.

93. *MC*, May 25, June 18, Aug. 17, 31, 1968; Cavanagh to Ralph D. Abernathy, n.d., Roselle Memos to Cavanagh, May 21, June 2, 1968, Box 442, JPC Papers; CCB Report, June 11, 1968, Box 561, ibid.; Mazey to Mallett, May 27, 1968, Box 1, Records of the ACLU–Metropolitan Detroit Branch (Aug. 27, 1974), ALHUA; CCR Minutes, July 1, 15, 1968, Series IV, Box 4, CCR Papers; *DFP*, Oct. 30, Nov. 27, 1968.

94. CCB Report, July 11, 1968, Box 561, JPC Papers; Heffernan to Spreen, July 25, 1968, ibid.

95. *DFP*, Nov. 8, 9, 14, 20, 23, 29, 1968; Roy Allen to Spreen, Nov. 13, 1968, Box 567, JPC Papers; Statement of Police Commissioner relative to Poor People's March . . . , n.d., ibid.; CCR Minutes, Nov. 20, 1968, Box 419, JPC Papers; CCB Report, July 11, 1968, Box 561, ibid.; *MC*, Aug. 17, Dec. 7, 1968.

96. Statement before Detroit Common Council, Feb. 28, 1968, Box 26, RG 74-90; *MC*, Mar. 9, May 25, July 13, 1968; Serrin, "God Help Our City," pp. 117, 119; "Summer 1968 in Detroit: A Survey of Attitudes toward Inner-City Unrest," p. 30, Box 456, JPC Papers; Releases, July 9, Aug. 2, 1968, Box 412, ibid.; Cavanagh to Tindal and Corbit, July 26, 1968, ibid.; Annual Report of the Executive Board, Coordinating Council on Human Relations, 1967–68, Box 51, DUL Papers; *DN*, Nov. 7, 12, 1967; *NYT*, July 23, 1968; Peter K. Eisinger, *The Politics of Displacement* (New York: Academic Press, 1980), p. 63.

97. *MC*, Aug. 3, 10, 1968; Ditto et al. [to Cavanagh, July 22, 1968], Cavanagh to Tindal and Corbit, July 26, 1968, Box 412, JPC Papers; Minutes of Meetings of Mayor's Task Force, July 15, 29, 1968, Box 585, ibid.

98. Cavanagh to Spreen, July 28, 1968, Spreen to All Members, Aug. 2, 1968, Box 410, JPC Papers; Guidelines for Police Personnel . . . [Aug. 2, 1968], ibid.; Field Division Report to Aug. 21, 1968, Series IV, Box 4, CCR Papers.

99. Spreen to Common Council, Nov. 7, 1968, Box 582, JPC Papers; Lee Williams to Marks, Oct. 30, 1968, James Herman Memorandum to Marks and Lonnie Saunders, Nov. 8, 1968, Box 567, ibid.; David Klein to Cavanagh, Oct. 30, 1968, Robert Gittleman to Cavanagh, Oct. 31, 1968, Box 413, ibid.; *DN*, Oct. 30, 1968; *DFP*, Oct. 30, 31, Nov. 20, 1968; *MC*, Aug. 30, 1969.

100. *DFP*, Oct. 31, Nov. 27, 1968, Mar. 7, 1969; *MC*, Nov. 9, 16, 1968.

101. *MC*, Nov. 9, 1968; *DFP*, Nov. 3, 1968; *DN*, Nov. 3, 1968; *NYT*, Nov. 10, 1968.

102. *DFP*, Nov. 3, 5, 7, 8, 10, 1968; *MC*, Nov. 9, 16, 1968; *DN*, Nov. 16, 1968; Marks Memorandum to CCR, Nov. 14, 1968, Box 567, JPC Papers.

103. Cavanagh to Coleman Young, Nov. 4, 1968, Box 413, JPC Papers; Cavanagh to William H. Daniels, Dec. 3, 1968, Box 411, ibid.; *DFP*, Nov. 5, 6, 9, 10, 14, 16, 1968; *DN*, Nov. 16, 1968; Serrin, "God Help Our City," pp. 118–19.

104. Trainor to Cavanagh, Mar. 3, 1969, Box 477, JPC Papers; *MC*, Mar. 15, Aug. 2, Sept. 13, 1969; *DFP*, Nov. 19, 1968; *DN*, Nov. 16, 1968; Graves, "New Detroit," p. 137.

105. *Tuebor* 29 (Nov. 1968): 23, 26; *Tuebor* 30 (Mar. 1969): 1; *DFP*, Nov. 15, 21, 22, 1968; Serrin, "God Help Our City," p. 115.

106. *DFP*, Mar. 30, 31, Apr. 2, 9, 1969; *DN*, Mar. 31, Apr. 6, 8, 15, 1969; *NYT*, Mar. 31, Apr. 1–3, 1969; *MC*, Apr. 5, 1969; Marks Memorandum to Commission, Apr. 16, 1969, Box 483, JPC Papers; Saunders to Marks, Apr. 30, 1969, Marks Memorandum to Common Council, May 1, 1969, enclosing Field Division Case Report, Box 567, ibid.; Pope Memorandum to Wilma Ray, Apr. 1, 1969, RG 83-55; *Tuebor* 30 (Apr. 1969): 5.

107. *DFP*, Mar. 31, 1969; *DN*, Apr. 6, 8, 15, 1969; *MC*, Apr. 5, 12, June 7, July 26, 1969; Saunders to Marks, Apr. 30, 1969, Marks Memorandum to Common Council, May 1, 1969, enclosing Field Division Case Report, Box 567, JPC Papers; Pope Memorandum to Ray, Apr. 1, 1969, RG 83-55.

108. *Tuebor* 30 (Apr. 1969): 5; *DN*, Apr. 15, 1969; *DFP*, Mar. 31, 1969; ACLU Release, Apr. 9, 1969, Box 483, JPC Papers; Saunders to Marks, Apr. 30, 1969, Box 567, ibid.

109. Saunders to Marks, Apr. 30, 1969, Marks Memorandum to Common Council, May 1, 1969, enclosing Field Division Case Report, Box 567, JPC Papers; Statement by George C. Crockett, Apr. 3, 1969, Box 483, ibid.; Marks Memorandum to Commission, Apr. 16, 1969, ibid.; *DFP*, Mar. 31, Apr. 2–4, 1969; *DN*, Apr. 15, 1969; *NYT*, Mar. 31, 1969; *MC*, Apr. 12, 1969; *Tuebor* 30 (Apr. 1969): 48.

110. *DFP*, Mar. 31, Apr. 1, 3, 1969; Cahalan interview, p. 41; Interview with George Crockett, Aug. 7, 1984, pp. 24–25, 27–28, transcript in MHC.

111. Saunders to Marks, Apr. 30, 1969, Box 567, JPC Papers; Crockett Statement, Apr. 3, 1969, Box 483, ibid.; Marks Memorandum to Commission, Apr. 16, 1969, ibid.; *DFP*, Mar. 31, Apr. 3, 7, 12, 16, 19, 20, May 10, 22, June 21, 22,

1969, Apr. 15, June 17, 18, 1970; *NYT*, Apr. 4, 11, 19, 1969; Crockett interview, pp. 26-27.

112. *DFP*, Apr. 1, 2, 16, 1969; *DN*, Apr. 1, 2, 6, 1969; *MC*, Apr. 19, 26, May 3, 1969; Marks Memorandum to Commission, Apr. 16, 1969, Box 483, JPC Papers; Donald Warren, "Mass Media and Racial Crisis: A Study of the New Bethel Incident in Detroit," *Journal of Social Issues* 28 (1972): 113-17, 125; CRC Weekly Report, Apr. 18, 1965, RG 83-55.

113. CRC Weekly Report, Apr. 18, 1969, RG 83-55; *DFP*, Apr. 1-3, 15, 24, 26, May 20, Nov. 29, 1969; *MC*, Apr. 12, May 3, June 7, Dec. 6, 1969; CCEO, "A Report to the People of Detroit," Sept. 1969, Box 477, Reuther Papers; *DN*, Apr. 15, 1969; *NYT*, Apr. 2, 1969.

114. Crockett Statement, Apr. 3, 1969, Box 483, JPC Papers; *DFP*, Apr. 4, 1969; *MC*, Apr. 12, 1969; *DN*, Apr. 6, 1969; *NYT*, Apr. 4, 1969.

115. *DFP*, Apr. 3-6, 9, 15, 1969; *MC*, Apr. 12, 1969; Dan Georgakas and Marvin Surkin, *Detroit: I Do Mind Dying* (New York: St. Martin's Press, 1978), pp. 68-70; Abraham Ulmer Memorandum to Burton Levy, Apr. 3, 1969, RG 83-55; *Tuebor* 30 (May 1969): 4.

116. ACLU Release, Apr. 9, 1969, Box 483, JPC Papers; Marks Memorandum to Commission, Apr. 16, 1969, ibid.; Saunders to Marks, Apr. 30, 1969, Box 567, ibid.; *MC*, Apr. 19, 26, 1969; *DFP*, Apr. 17, 19, May 21, 1969.

117. New Detroit Press Conference, Apr. 3, 1969, Hudson Papers; Fisher to Hudson, Apr. 12, 1969, ibid.; New Detroit Summary of Minutes of Board of Trustees Meeting, Apr. 3, 1969, Box 515, Reuther Papers; Law Committee, "The Law on Trial," Apr. 1969, ibid.; Summary of Minutes . . . , May 2, 1969, Box 516, ibid.; *MC*, Apr. 19, May 3, 17, 1969; *DFP*, Apr. 4, 8, 24, 26, May 3, 1969; Hudson interview, pp. 35-36; Graves, "New Detroit," pp. 139-41.

118. Warren, "Mass Media," pp. 117-31.

119. New Detroit Release (draft), Mar. 4, 1969, Box 501, JPC Papers; New Detroit Release, Mar. 20, 1969, Box 583, ibid.; Trainor to Cavanagh, Feb. 4, 1969, Cavanagh to Spreen, Feb. 5, 1969, Box 481, ibid.; Statement of . . . Spreen, Apr. 3, 1969, ibid.; Trainor to Cavanagh, Feb. 6, 1969, Box 477, ibid.; Cavanagh to Roy Allen, Mar. 4, 1969, Box 482, ibid.; Joint Statement by Max Fisher and William T. Patrick, enclosed with Fisher to New Detroit, Mar. 11, 1969, Box 515, Reuther Papers; *DFP*, Dec. 13, 1968, Jan. 14, 1969; Serrin, "God Help Our City," p. 119; *Business Week*, Aug. 2, 1969, p. 103.

120. Police Management Study . . . A Review, Dec. 17, 1969, Box 482, JPC Papers; Field Operations Division . . . , Inspection Report, Sept. 1969, Box 478, ibid.; New Detroit Resolution . . . , Aug. 6, 1970, Box 40, Richard Austin Papers, ALHUA; New Detroit, "Beyond the Difference," p. 16, Box 516, Reuther Papers; *DFP*, July 28, 1972.

121. Police Management Study and the Community Relations Project, Dec. 17, 1969, Box 478, JPC Papers; *DFP*, July 16, 1970; *DN*, July 16, 1970.

122. *DFP*, July 28, 1972.

Chapter 18

1. *DFP*, Nov. 1, 1968; Greenstone and Peterson, *Race and Authority in Urban Politics: Community Participation and the War on Poverty* (New York: Russell Sage Foundation, 1973), p. 153.

2. Richard Strichartz to James L. Trainor, Aug. 8, 1967, Box 339, JPC Papers; Girardin to Jeanelle L. Baker, Aug. 11, 1967, Box 3, Ray Girardin Papers, Burton Historical Collection, Detroit, Michigan; William Serrin, "How One Big City Defeated Its Mayor," *NYT Magazine*, Oct. 27, 1968.

3. *DN*, Oct. 15, 1967; New Detroit Committee, *Progress Report, April, 1968* [Detroit: n.p., 1968], p. 29.

4. New Detroit, *Progress Report*, p. 130; *MC*, May 25, 1968; *Business Week*, Aug. 2, 1969, p. 103; Maurice Kelman to Cavanagh, Sept. 10, 1969, Box 507, JPC Papers.

5. Official Transcript of Proceedings before the National Advisory Commission on Civil Disorders, Aug. 15, 1967, p. 416, Series 1, Box 2, NACCD Records; "Cavanagh Reports to the People," Sept. 6, 1967, Box 531, JPC Papers; *DFP*, Sept. 6, 1967.

6. *DFP*, Aug. 6, 13, 15, 22, 25, Sept. 1, 17, 22, Oct. 27, Nov. 16, 1967; National Commission on Urban Problems, *Hearings*, 5 vols. (Washington: GPO, 1968), 5:14; Detroit Housing Commission (DHC), *Quarterly Report to the Commissioners, Third Quarter, 1967*, p. 5, *Third Quarter, 1969*, p. 3; New Detroit Notes on Mass Meeting, Aug. 18, 1967, Box 70, ND Papers; New Detroit, *Progress Report*, pp. 70-71; *Metropolitan Fund Report*, Feb. 1968, Joseph L. Hudson Papers, MHC; *NYT*, Dec. 10, 1967; *DN*, Aug. 18, 1968.

7. *DFP*, Aug. 13, 1967; *NYT*, July 23, 1968; *DN*, Aug. 18, 1968; *MC*, Oct. 12, 1968, Dec. 20, 1969; James D. Wiley to Cavanagh [1969], and enclosures, Box 507, JPC Papers; Serrin, "One Big City"; DHC, *Quarterly Report to the Commissioners, Fourth Quarter, 1969*, p. 3; Citizens Committee for Equal Opportunity (CCEO), "A Report to the People of Detroit . . . ," Sept. 1969, Box 477, Walter Reuther Papers, ALHUA.

8. *DN*, June 7, 1971, July 23, 1972; *DFP*, July 25, 27, 1972; *NYT*, July 23, 1971.

9. *DFP*, July 24, 1977, July 24, 1984, July 19, 1987; *DN*, Apr. 15, 1978, Oct. 21, 1982, May 19, 1987; New Detroit, *1982: Fifteen Years of Progress*, p. 2, Hudson Papers; Alex Poinsett, "Motor City Makes a Comeback," *Ebony* 33 (Apr. 1978): 37.

10. National Commission on Urban Problems, *Hearings*, 5:9; MDT report, with Strichartz to Cavanagh, Oct. 26, 1967, Box 534, JPC Papers; *MC*, Nov. 25, 1967, Aug. 10, 1968; *DFP*, July 23, 1972; New Detroit, *Progress Report*, p. 33.

11. National Commission on Urban Problems, *Hearings*, 5:9-10, 16-17; *DFP*, Oct. 21, 1967; *DN*, Nov. 7, 1967; *NYT*, Jan. 29, 1968; *MC*, May 25, June 13, 1968; MDT report, Box 534, JPC Papers; MDT Report [1969], Box 582, ibid.; Wiley to Cavanagh [1969], and enclosures, Box 507, ibid.; Statement by . . . Cavanagh on . . . Progress . . . , n.d., Box 426, ibid.; "Housing for Detroit in 1968: Annual Report of the DHC," pp. 4, 8, Box 404, ibid.; undated document in [Jan. 1969] folder, Box 514, Reuther Papers; CCEO, "Report to People," Sept. 1969, Box 477, ibid.; DHC, *Quarterly Report to the Commissioners, Fourth Quarter, 1967*, pp. 9-10, *Second Quarter, 1969*, pp. 8-9; Bernard Dobranski Memorandum to Herman Wilson (interview with Robert Knox), Oct. 19, 1967, Series 59, Box 2, NACCD Records.

12. James L. Rose to Burton I. Gordin, Feb. 20, 1968, Box 12, Records of the Civil Rights Commission, RG 74-90, State Archives, Lansing, Michigan; Julian Cook and John Dempsey to Robert C. Weaver, June 13, 1968, Box 3, Records of

the Civil Rights Commission, Detroit Office, RG 80-17, ibid.; CRC Newsletter, July 1968; Paul Borman to Robert Roselle, Mar. 20, 1968, Box 453, JPC Papers; *NYT*, June 29, 1968; *MC*, July 6, 1968; DHC, *Quarterly Report to the Commissioners, Second Quarter, 1969*, pp. 8–9.

13. Mary Ann Beattie Memorandum to John Forsythe and Frederick Jansen, Jan. 2, 1968, Human Relations–Community Affairs, Archives of the Archdiocese of Detroit, Detroit, Michigan (unprocessed); F. Philip Colista to Cavanagh, July 8, 1968, Box 450, JPC Papers; "Housing for Detroit in 1968," pp. 1–2, 3, Box 404, ibid.; *Public and Local Acts of the Legislature of the State of Michigan Passed at the Regular Session of 1968* (Lansing: Department of Administration, n.d.), pp. 499–503, 664–67; *NYT*, July 28, 1968; *MC*, July 27, Dec. 14, 1968; *DFP*, Aug. 11, 1968; DHC, *Quarterly Report to the Commissioners, Third Quarter, 1968*, pp. 6, 8, *Fourth Quarter, 1968*, p. 10, *First Quarter, 1969*, p. 10; New Detroit, *Progress Report*, pp. 11, 44.

14. New Detroit, "Beyond the Difference" (draft), Aug. 28, 1969, p. 20, Box 516, Reuther Papers.

15. *Public and Local Acts . . . 1968*, pp. 281–84; DHC, *Quarterly Report to the Commissioners, Third Quarter, 1968*, pp. 7, 10–11; "Housing of Detroit in 1968," p. 11, Box 404, JPC Papers.

16. CCR, Enforcement of . . . Codes . . . Housing–Urban Renewal Report No. 2, Aug. 1967, Box 567, JPC Papers; Warren D. Couger to Cavanagh, Jan. 6, 1969, Box 564, ibid.; MDT Report [1969], Box 582, ibid.; Daniel Carlson to Cavanagh, June 3, 1969, Cavanagh to All Department Heads, July 23, 1969, Box 477, ibid.; unidentified report in folder 10, Box 569, ibid.; CCR, "Annual Report, 1968," p. 8; CCEO, "Report to People," Sept. 1969, Box 477, Reuther Papers.

17. Wilson Memorandum to Charles E. Nelson (interview with Albert Cleage), n.d., Peter Rossi File, in my possession; Minutes of the Board of Directors of the Detroit Urban League, Jan. 11, 1968, Box 42, DUL Papers; *Business Week*, Feb. 3, 1968, p. 123; Hubert G. Locke, *The Detroit Riot of 1967* (Detroit: Wayne State University Press, 1969), p. 104; *Return to 12th Street: A Follow-up Survey of Attitudes of Detroit Negroes, October, 1968* [Detroit: Detroit Free Press, 1968], p. 17; Joel D. Aberbach and Jack L. Walker, *Race in the City* (Boston: Little, Brown and Co., 1973), p. 66.

18. MDT report, Box 534, JPC Papers; *DN*, Oct. 29, 1967; *MC*, Nov. 25, Dec. 2, 1967, July 6, Aug. 31, 1968; *NYT*, Nov. 29, Dec. 30, 1967, Aug. 17, 1968; *DFP*, Aug. 17, 1968; Borman to Cavanagh, Jan. 4, 1968, Box 406, JPC Papers; Minutes of DUL Board of Directors, Jan. 11, 1968, Box 42, DUL Papers; CCR, "Annual Report, 1968," p. 6; CCR, "Annual Report, 1969," p. 4.

19. James J. Sheehan to Romney, Sept. 7, 1967, Box 214, GR Papers; Romney Special Message, Oct. 10, 1967, Box 263, ibid.; Romney Special Message on Open Occupancy . . . , Oct. 13, 1967, Box 321, ibid.; New Detroit Committee Report on Open Occupancy . . . , Oct. 12, 1967, Box 323, ibid.; Minutes of Meeting of Legal and Finance Subcommittee, Aug. 7, 1967, Box 15, ND Papers; New Detroit Full Meeting, Oct. 12, 1967, Tag No. 21, ibid.; *DFP*, Aug. 21, Sept. 29, Oct. 3, 11–14, 1967; *NYT*, Nov. 18, 1967.

20. Hudson to New Detroit Committee Members, Nov. 10, 1967, Box 187, GR Papers; Release, Jan. 11, 1968, Box 319, ibid.; New Detroit Full Meeting, Oct. 12, 1967, Tag No. 21, ND Papers; *DFP*, Nov. 11, 14, 15, 1967, Aug. 11, 1968,

July 24, 1972; *NYT*, Nov. 18, Dec. 22, 1967, Jan. 12, Apr. 5, May 18, 1968; Helen M. Graves, "New Detroit Committee/New Detroit, Incorporated . . ." (Ph.D. diss., Wayne State University, 1975), pp. 105, 107–9; *Public and Local Acts . . . 1968*, pp. 112–25.

21. Minutes of Mayor's Committee for Human Resources Development (MCHRD) Policy Advisory Committee, Aug. 23, Oct. 18, 1967, Box 16, Francis A. Kornegay Papers, MHC.

22. The MCHRD set up a Community Consumers Cooperative in Target Area 2, aided 150 buying clubs in the four target areas, and developed a financial counseling service in the Community Development Centers. *MC*, Oct. 19, 1968.

23. "MCHRD" [1968], Box 393, JPC Papers; Response of the MCHRD to the Interim . . . Report, n.d., Box 434, ibid.; Cavanagh Release, Apr. 24, 1968, Box 406, ibid.; Kelman to Cavanagh, Sept. 16, 1969, ibid.; Michigan Legislature, House of Representatives, Special Committee . . . , "Examination of War on Poverty," 74th Legislature, Regular Session of 1968; Del Rio et al. to Lyndon Baines Johnson et al., n.d., enclosing report of John T. Lynch Investigating Agency, Box 322, GR Papers; Georgia A. Brown to Alan Beals, Apr. 11, 1968, ibid.; *Muskegon Chronicle*, Apr. 10, 1968, copy in ibid.; Richard Simmons to Cavanagh, Apr. 22, 1968, Box 341, ibid.; *MC*, Jan. 6, Dec. 7, 1968; *DN*, Sept. 2, 1967; *DFP*, Sept. 2, 1967; Serrin, "One Big City"; Interview with Robert Roselle, Aug. 30, 1984, pp. 13–14, transcript in MHC.

24. Chicago Regional Council, *Detroit Survey*, pp. 10, 12, 14, 19, 23–25, Box 508, JPC Papers.

25. Remarks by Cavanagh, Dec. 17, 1969, Box 583, ibid.; William Serrin, "God Help Our City," *Atlantic Monthly* 223 (Mar. 1969): 115; Serrin, "One Big City."

26. Wiley to Cavanagh [1969], and enclosures, Box 507, JPC Papers; Trainor to Cavanagh, Apr. 17, 1969, Box 477, ibid.; Remarks by Cavanagh, Dec. 17, 1969, Box 583, ibid.; *MC*, May 25, 1968; Robert Conot, *American Odyssey* (New York: William Morrow and Co., 1974), pp. 570–71.

27. H. C. McKinney, Jr., Memorandum to Romney et al., Aug. 2, 1967, Box 186, GR Papers; MDT report, Box 534, JPC Papers; "Cavanagh Reports," Sept. 6, 1967, Box 531, ibid.; *DFP*, Sept. 7, 1967; *MC*, Oct. 12, 1968, Feb. 1, 1969; CCR, "Annual Report, 1968," pp. 2–3; CCR, "Annual Report, 1969," p. 3.

28. Earl Nathaniel Gooding, "Urban Race Riots and Social Change: An Analysis of Two Cities" (Ph.D. diss., Vanderbilt University, 1977), p. 116; David B. Nelson to Cavanagh, Feb. 26, 1968, Box 406, JPC Papers; *MC*, Feb. 24, Aug. 3, 1968; New Detroit, *Progress Report*, pp. 65–66.

29. Wiley to Cavanagh [1969], and enclosures, Box 507, JPC Papers; "Detroit Is Happening Report: Summer 1968," Box 428, ibid.; Charles A. Blessing, "America's Riot-Torn Cities," in American Society of Planning Officials, *Planning, 1968* (Chicago: American Society of Planning Officials, 1968), p. 26; Youth, Recreation and Cultural Affairs Committee, New Detroit, Evaluation Report of DART, Oct. 1969, Box 516, Reuther Papers; *MC*, Feb. 24, 1968, July 19, 1969; *Newsweek* 73 (June 2, 1969): 62; *DFP*, July 25, 1972.

30. Official Transcript, Aug. 15, 1967, pp. 452–57, Series 1, Box 2, NACCD Records; Drachler, *A Report on Immediate Needs of Public Schools . . .* , Sept. 19, 1967, Part 2, Series I, Box 29, DNAACP Papers; New Detroit Full Meeting, Oct. 12, 1967, Tag No. 21, ND Papers; Permanent Subcommittee on Investiga-

tions of the Senate Committee on Government Operations, *Riots, Civil and Criminal Disorders, Hearings*, 1968, pt. 7:1537.

31. *DFP*, Aug. 25, Nov. 6, 1967, Aug. 11, 1968; Hudson to Romney, Aug. 24, 1967, Emil Lockwood to Romney, Aug. 31, 1967, Box 187, GR Papers; Executive Office, Sept. 11, 1967, ibid.; draft of Romney to Hudson, n.d., Box 327, ibid.; Romney Special Message, Oct. 10, 1967, Box 263, ibid.; Romney to Hudson, Sept. 10, 1967, Box 84, ND Papers; New Detroit Full Meeting, Oct. 12, 1967, Tag No. 21, ibid.; Agenda, New Detroit Committee, Oct. 26, 1967, Box 372, JPC Papers; *Riots, Civil and Criminal Disorders*, pt. 7:1536; New Detroit, *Progress Report*, pp. 46–47.

32. Ted Blizzard to Robert Winger, July 25, 1967, Box 327, JPC Papers; *Regional Report*, May 1968, Box 456, ibid.; *DN*, Oct. 12, 1967; *MC*, May 4, 1968; New Detroit, *Progress Report*, pp. 51–54; CCEO, "Report to People," Sept. 1969, Box 477, Reuther Papers; *Riots, Civil and Criminal Disorders*, pt. 7:1538, 1558–59.

33. Chicago Regional Council, *Detroit Survey*, pp. 8–9, Box 508, JPC Papers; *MC*, Feb. 3, 1968; *DFP*, Nov. 6, 1968; *NYT*, Feb. 3, Dec. 5, 1968; Commission on the Cities . . . , *The State of the Cities* (New York: Frederick A. Praeger, 1972), p. 51; *Riots, Civil and Criminal Disorders*, pt. 7:1559.

34. Commission on the Cities, *State of Cities*, p. 56; *NYT*, Apr. 15, 1968. See chap. 3.

35. Staff to Drachler, Nov. 30, 1967, Part 2, Series I, Box 29, DNAACP Papers; *MC*, Nov. 11, 1967, Mar. 30, Aug. 31, Nov. 9, 1968; *NYT*, Oct. 20, 1968, Mar. 23, 1969; *Riots, Civil and Criminal Disorders*, pt. 7:1539–40.

36. Report of Recommendations of the Task Force on Quality Integrated Education in Detroit Schools, Sept. 13, 1967, Box 6, Detroit Public Schools, Division of Community Relations Papers (unprocessed), ALHUA; CCEO, "Report to People," Sept. 1969, Box 477, Reuther Papers; *MC*, May 24, June 28, 1969; Kelman to Cavanagh, Sept. 16, 1969, Box 507, JPC Papers.

37. CCR Minutes, Aug. 25, 1967, Series IV, Box 4, CCR Papers; Cleage to Remus G. Robinson, Mar. 17, 1968, Box 1, Remus G. Robinson Papers, ALHUA; Wilson Memoranda to Nelson (interview with Karl Gregory), n.d., (interview with Francis Kornegay et al.), n.d., Series 59, Box 2, NACCD Records; Nelson Memorandum to Wilson (Cleage interview), n.d., Rossi File; Albert B. Cleage, Jr., *The Black Messiah* (New York: Sheed and Ward, 1968), pp. 222–23; William Serrin, "Cleage's Alternative," *Reporter* 38 (May 30, 1968): 30; CCEO, "Report to People," Sept. 1969, Box 477, Reuther Papers; B. J. Widick, *Detroit: City of Race and Class Violence* (Chicago: Quadrangle Books, 1972), p. 215; *MC*, Feb. 3, 10, Mar. 9, 23, May 24, 1968; *NYT*, Mar. 20, 23, 1969; Albert Zack to Freeman Flynn, Feb. 26, 1968, in my possession; Zack to Sidney Fine, Sept. 20, 1984.

38. New Detroit Full Meeting, Oct. 12, 1967, Tag No. 21, ND Papers; Reconnaissance Survey Field Research Reports, Detroit, Michigan, 3:66, Series 10, Box 46, NACCD Records; John J. Ursu and Dobranski interview with Arthur Johnson and Dr. Wattenberg, n.d., Series 59, Box 2, ibid.; Wilson Memorandum to Nelson (interview with Gregory), n.d., ibid.; *MC*, Feb. 8, Mar. 23, 30, Apr. 15, June 1, 1968; unidentified pages [Mar. 15, 1968], Box 410, JPC Papers; Borman to Roselle, Mar. 20, 1968, Box 453, ibid.; CCR Minutes, Mar. 20, 1968, Series

IV, Box 4, CCR Papers; Minutes of Meeting with Cavanagh, Mar. 22, 1968, Box A-19, DUL Papers.

39. To New Detroit Subcommittees [Oct. 1968], Box 64, ND Papers; *MC*, Feb. 8, 1969; *NYT*, Mar. 23, 1969; CCR, "Annual Report, 1969," p. 6.

40. Zack to Fine, Sept. 20, 1964; *NYT*, Mar. 23, 1969; Employment and Education Subcommittee Meeting Minutes, Oct. 13, 1967, Box 64, ND Papers; *Riots, Civil and Criminal Disorders*, pt. 7:1554–55; [*Livonia Observer*, Fall 1970], clipping in my possession.

41. Inter-University Consortium for Political and Social Research, Black File, Nos. 183, 312, 314, White File, No. 183, Detroit data for Angus Campbell and Howard Schuman, "Racial Attitudes in Fifteen Cities," in *Supplemental Studies for the National Advisory Commission on Civil Disorders* (Washington: GPO, 1968); Howard Schuman and Shirley Hatchett, *Black Racial Attitudes* (Ann Arbor: Institute for Social Research, University of Michigan, 1974), p. 8.

42. William R. Grant, "Community Control vs School Integration—the Case of Detroit," *Public Interest* no. 24 (Summer 1971): 63–64, 68–78; "Detroit—Some Post Riot Progress . . . ," *Black Enterprise* 2 (Mar. 1972): 77–78; Commission on the Cities, *State of Cities*, p. 18; Widick, *Detroit*, p. 215; *DFP*, July 24, 1972; *MC*, July 23, 1977.

43. Cavanagh to Romney, Aug. 23, 1967, Box 232, GR Papers; Testimony of . . . Cavanagh . . . , Apr. 30, 1968, Box 465, JPC Papers.

44. Romney to Cavanagh, Sept. 8, 1967, Box 346, GR Papers; *Release*, Jan. 11, 1968, Box 319, ibid.; Serrin, "One Big City"; Graves, "New Detroit," p. 109; Cavanagh testimony, Apr. 30, 1968, Box 465, JPC Papers; *Public and Local Acts . . . 1968*, pp. 451–56.

45. Feagin and Hahn, *Ghetto Revolts* (New York: Macmillan Co., 1973), pp. 248–49.

46. Official Transcript, Aug. 15, 1967, pp. 416, 433–43, Series 1, Box 2, NACCD Records; Cavanagh to Dear Congressman or Senator, Sept. 12, 1967, Box 531, JPC Papers; *DFP*, Sept. 3, 1967.

47. *Report of the National Advisory Commission on Civil Disorders* (Washington: GPO, 1968), pp. 229–63; Johnson, *The Vantage Point* (New York: Holt, Rinehart and Winston, 1971), pp. 172–73; Donald Lee Scruggs, "Lyndon Baines Johnson and the National Advisory Commission on Civil Disorders . . ." (Ph.D. diss., University of Oklahoma, 1980), p. 473; David B. Nelson to Cavanagh, Mar. 2, 1968, Box 407, JPC Papers; Statement by Cavanagh, Mar. 8, 1968, Box 426, ibid.; Wiley to Cavanagh [1969], and enclosures, Box 507, ibid.; Cavanagh testimony, Apr. 30, 1968, Box 465, ibid.; *DFP*, Aug. 20, 1967; *MC*, July 19, 1969, July 23, 1977; *Riots, Civil and Criminal Disorders*, pt. 7:1537–38; James W. Button, *Black Violence: The Political Impact of the 1960s Riots* (Princeton: Princeton University Press, 1978), pp. 80, 92; Allen J. Matusow, *The Unraveling of America: A History of Liberalism in the 1960s* (New York: Harper and Row, 1984), pp. 232–37; Urban America and the Urban Coalition, *One Year Later* (New York: Frederick A. Praeger, 1969), p. 21.

48. Black File, Nos. 193–195, Detroit data for "Racial Attitudes"; *Return to 12th Street*, p. 16.

49. "Cavanagh Reports," Sept. 6, 1967, Box 531, JPC Papers; "Aug. 8, 1967," Box 533, ibid.; [Hudson report, Aug. 10, 1967], Hudson Papers; *DFP*, Aug. 11,

1968; John J. Ursu interview with Hudson and Joseph Bianco, n.d., Series 59, Box 2, NACCD Records.

50. [Hudson report, Aug. 10, 1967], Hudson Papers; New Detroit, *Progress Report*, pp. 24–25.

51. New Detroit, *Progress Report*, pp. 26–27, 30; *DFP*, Oct. 27, Nov. 6, 1967, Aug. 11, 1968; Bianco to Lawrence H. Martin, Nov. 3, 1967, Box 187, GR Papers; Hudson to Ralph T. McElvenney, Dec. 15, 1967, Hudson Papers; Hudson to Robert Potts, Dec. 12, 1967, Box 30, ORA Papers; Graves, "New Detroit," pp. 89–90; Interview with Joseph L. Hudson, Oct. 2, 1984, p. 14, transcript in MHC.

52. Patrick Memorandum to Hudson, Nov. 24, 1967, Hudson Papers.

53. Kent Mathewson, "The Message . . . ," Feb. 23, 1968, ibid.; JLH notes for Press Conference, Apr. 18, 1968, ibid.; *Regional Report*, Sept.–Oct. 1968, ibid.; Patrick Memo to Members of Board of Trustees, Nov. 1, 1968, and enclosures, ibid.; New Detroit, Inc., "Statement of Principles and Objectives," Jan. 24, 1969, ibid.; "The New Detroit Committee . . . ," *Detroit Scope*, May 11, 1968, pp. 8–9, in ibid.; Graves, "New Detroit," pp. 90, 96–100, 126, 275–77; *DFP*, Aug. 11, 1968; New Detroit Release, Aug. 15, 1968, Box 456, JPC Papers; Hudson to Cavanagh, Sept. 10, 1968, ibid.; New Detroit, "Beyond the Difference," pp. 27, 47, Box 516, Reuther Papers.

54. Special Meeting of Task Force Leaders with Hudson, Oct. 20, 1967, Tag No. 21, ND Papers; Graves, "New Detroit," pp. 118–19, 417, 436, 443–45; Cavanagh testimony, Apr. 30, 1968, Box 465, JPC Papers; Review and Commentary for . . . Press Conference, Apr. 18, 1968, Box 456, ibid.; *Business Week*, Feb. 3, 1968, p. 121; Serrin, "One Big City"; *DFP*, Aug. 11, 1968; Hudson interview, p. 16; Interview with Harold Johnson, Aug. 14, 1984, p. 16, transcript in MHC; Hudson, "In the Aftermath of the Long Hot Summer of 1967," *Michigan Courthouse Review* 17 (Dec. 1967): 10; David John Olson, "Racial Violence and City Politics: The Political Response to Civil Disorders in Three American Cities" (Ph.D. diss., University of Wisconsin, 1971), pp. 165–66.

55. *NYT*, Nov. 19, 1967; Department of Civil Rights to Romney, May 3, 1968, Box 199, GR Papers; Gertrude Samuels, "Help Wanted: The Hard Core Unemployed," *NYT Magazine*, Jan. 26, 1968; *Regional Report*, May 1968, Box 456, JPC Papers; Chicago Regional Council, *Detroit Survey*, pp. 10, 12, Box 508, JPC Papers.

56. Manpower Development Committee Minutes, GDBC, Aug. 21, 1967, Box 64, ND Papers; Employment and Education Subcommittee Meeting Minutes, Oct. 27, 1967, ibid.; *DFP*, Aug. 22, 1967; Third Meeting of Ad Hoc Committee . . . , Nov. 11, 1967, Box 345, GR Papers; *Metropolitan Fund Reports*, Feb. 1968, Hudson Papers; New Detroit, *Progress Report*, pp. 55–56.

57. New Detroit Full Meeting, Oct. 12, 1967, Tag No. 21, ND Papers; Employment and Education Subcommittee Meeting Minutes, Oct. 6, 13, Nov. 1, 1967, Box 64, ibid.; Statement of Hudson . . . , Oct. 26, 1967, Hudson Papers; *DFP*, Oct. 25, 27, 31, Nov. 13, 1967; *DN*, Oct. 16, 1967; *MC*, Oct. 28, 1967.

58. Herbert W. Northrup, *The Negro and the Automobile Industry* (Philadelphia: Wharton School, 1968), p. 62; *DFP*, Oct. 27, 1967; *NYT*, Oct. 29, 1967.

59. *DFP*, Oct. 28, Nov. 6, 10, 1967; *DN*, Oct. 30, 31, 1967; *NYT*, Oct. 31, 1968; *MC*, Feb. 24, June 8, 1968; New Detroit, *Progress Report*, pp. 56–57; Samuels, "Help Wanted"; Trainor Memorandum to Cavanagh, Jan. 1968,

Box 406, JPC Papers; Simmons to James O. Cole, Jan. 30, 1969, Box 498, ibid.; *Regional Report*, Apr. 1968, Box 456, ibid.; Minutes of DUL Board of Directors, May 9, 1968, Box 42, DUL Papers; Northrup, *Automobile Industry*, p. 64.

60. *DFP*, Oct. 25, Nov. 8, 10, 13, 1967; *DN*, Nov. 7, 9, 10, 1967; *NYT*, Oct. 29, Nov. 12, 1967; *MC*, Jan. 27, Mar. 5, 1968; Agenda, New Detroit, Sept. 5, 1968, Box 456, JPC Papers; DUL Annual Report, 1968, Box 43, DUL Papers; Frederick H. Pryor to Kornegay, May 9, 1968, Box 49, ibid.; National Bank of Detroit–DUL Recruiting Project, Jan. 29, 1968, Box A-20, ibid.; New Detroit, *Progress Report*, pp. 49, 56; Northrup, *Automobile Industry*, pp. 63–64; Bill Davidson, "If We Can't Solve the Problems of the Ghetto Here . . . ," *Saturday Evening Post* 241 (Oct. 5, 1968): 31–32.

61. *NYT*, Oct. 29, 1967; *DFP*, Aug. 11, 1968; *MC*, May 18, Aug. 17, 1968; Minutes of DUL Board of Directors, Sept. 12, 1968, Box 42, DUL Papers; Alan Kroker, "Why There Was No Riot in Detroit . . . ," *Detroit Scope* 1 (Sept. 1968): 10; New Detroit, *Progress Report*, pp. 62–63, 65–66; *Regional Report*, May 1968, Box 456, JPC Papers; New Detroit Release, Sept. 5, 1968, ibid.; *Metropolitan Fund Reports*, Feb. 1968, Hudson Papers; New Detroit Committee Chronology, May 9, 1968, Box 81, ND Papers.

62. Conot, *American Odyssey*, p. 601; Sar A. Levitan and Robert Taggart, *The Promise of Greatness* (Cambridge: Harvard University Press, 1976), p. 135.

63. U.S. Department of Labor Release, Feb. 1, 1968, Hudson Papers; *MC*, Feb. 10, Dec. 21, 1968; GDBC, A Proposal for a NAB Consortium, May 14, 1968, Box 14, Kornegay Papers; Gooding, "Urban Race Riots," pp. 170–71; *NYT*, Aug. 11, 1968.

64. Hubert Locke Memorandum, June 3, 1969, Box 20, ORA Papers; *NYT*, July 23, 1968; *MC*, Dec. 28, 1968; New Detroit, "Beyond the Difference," p. 28, Box 516, Reuther Papers; Conot, *American Odyssey*, p. 601.

65. Davidson, "If We Can't Solve," p. 82; *MC*, Mar. 16, 1968; Olson, "Racial Violence," pp. 261–62; Michael Lipsky and David Olson, *Commission Politics* (New Brunswick, N.J.: Transaction Books, 1977), p. 349; Trainor Memorandum to Cavanagh, Jan. 1968, Box 406, JPC Papers; *DFP*, July 24, 1972; Widick, *Detroit*, p. 193.

66. *NYT*, Oct. 29, 1967; Frank L. Gavan to William M. Day, Aug. 9, 1968, and enclosed "Follow-Up Review of Detroit Area Hiring Standards," Aug. 5, 1968, Box 456, JPC Papers; *Return to 12th Street*, p. 16.

67. Agenda, New Detroit, Oct. 26, 1967, Box 372, JPC Papers; New Detroit, *Progress Report*, p. 33.

68. Graves, "New Detroit," pp. 55, 117, 151; *NYT*, June 9, 1968; MDCDA Chairman's Report to Board of Directors, Nov. 22, 1967, Metropolitan Detroit Citizens Development Authority Papers, MHC; Text of Presentation . . . by Edward J. Robinson, Aug. 8, 1968, ibid.; New Detroit, *Progress Report*, p. 33; National Commission on Urban Problems, *Hearings*, 5:13, 39; *Inside New Detroit, Progress Report, 1973*; New Detroit, "Beyond the Difference," p. 45, Box 516, Reuther Papers; Gooding, "Urban Race Riots," pp. 131–33.

69. MDT report [1969], Box 582, JPC Papers; Wiley to Cavanagh [1969], and enclosures, Box 507, ibid.; Summary of Minutes of New Detroit Board of Trustees Meeting, Apr. 3, 1969, Box 515, Reuther Papers; ibid., May 2, 1969, Box 516, ibid.; New Detroit, "Beyond the Difference," p. 27, ibid.; *DFP*, Dec. 19, 1968;

New Detroit, *Progress Report*, pp. 34-35; Gooding, "Urban Race Riots," p. 137; Stanley B. Greenberg, *Politics and Poverty* (New York: John Wiley and Sons, 1974), p. 5; DHC, *Quarterly Report to the Commissioners, First Quarter, 1968*, p. 3, *Third Quarter, 1968*, p. 2.

70. *NYT*, June 9, Oct. 27, 1968, July 23, 1970; Robinson Presentation, Aug. 8, 1968, MDCDA Papers; *DN*, July 23, 1972; *DFP*, Feb. 14, 1971, July 24, 1972; New Detroit, *A Decade of Progress, 1967-1977* (reprint, New York: New York Times, 1977), p. 22; undated document (Jan. 1969 folder), Box 569, JPC Papers; Graves, "New Detroit," pp. 152-53.

71. Davidson, "If We Can't Solve," p. 82. Beginning about 1970, the Michigan Housing Development Authority began rehabilitating apartments in Detroit on a rather large scale. *DFP*, July 24, 1972.

72. New Detroit, *Progress Report*, pp. 50-51; New Detroit, *Decade of Progress*, p. 11; New Detroit, "Beyond the Difference," pp. 28-29, 46, Box 516, Reuther Papers; Detroit Public Schools Programs Funded by New Detroit, Inc., 1968, Box 515, ibid.; Graves, "New Detroit," pp. 175-77; New Detroit Release, Nov. 9 [1967], Box 372, JPC Papers; *Regional Report*, May 1968, Sept.-Oct. 1968, Box 456, ibid.; Statement by Cavanagh on . . . Progress . . . , n.d., Box 426, ibid.; Jerry Sullivan Memorandum to Hudson, Nov. 8, 1967, and enclosed release, Hudson Papers; New Detroit Committee Chronology, Apr. 18, 1968, Box 81, New Detroit Papers; *MC*, Nov. 25, 1967, May 4, June 15, July 19, 1968; *DFP*, Mar. 9, 1969.

73. Trainor to Cavanagh, Jan. 2, 1968, Box 406, JPC Papers; New Detroit Release, Dec. 13, 1967, Hudson Papers; Youth, Recreation and Cultural Affairs Committee, Study and Evaluation Report of DART, Oct. 1969, Box 516, Reuther Papers; New Detroit, *Progress Report*, pp. 77-79; *MC*, July 27, Nov. 16, 1968.

74. *MC*, Dec. 21, 1968, Sept. 13, 1969; *DFP*, Nov. 12, 1969; *NYT*, Nov. 10, 1969; New Detroit, "Beyond the Difference," p. 44, Box 516, Reuther Papers; Gooding, "Urban Race Riots," pp. 192-94; Graves, "New Detroit," pp. 141-51; Minutes of Board of Trustees Meeting, Jan. 14, 1969, Box 519, JPC Papers; New Detroit, *Decade of Progress*, p. 16; Ann Scott, "Report from Detroit," *Fortune* 81 (Feb. 1970): 71-72; *Newsweek* 73 (June 2, 1969): 62; Richard Child Hill, "At the Crossroads: The Political Economy of Postwar Detroit," *Urbanism Past and Present* 6 (Summer 1978): 13-14.

75. Hudson interview, p. 33; Xavier Nicholas interview with Nicholas Hood [1982], copy of tape in my possession; *MC*, Mar. 29, 1969, July 23, 1977; Scott, "Report from Detroit," p. 72; "Detroit: Some Post-Riot Progress," p. 83; Widick, *Detroit*, p. 195; *DFP*, July 24, 1972.

76. Strichartz to Trainor, Aug. 8, 1967, Box 339, JPC Papers; Agenda, New Detroit Committee, Sept. 28, 1967, Box 532, ibid.; [Hudson report, Aug. 10, 1967], Hudson Papers; Mathewson, "Message," ibid.; Hudson statement, Oct. 26, 1967, ibid.; Hudson address [Oct. 17, 1967], ibid.; New Detroit Full Meeting, Oct. 12, 1967, Tag No. 21, ND Papers; Graves, "New Detroit," pp. 55, 58; New Detroit, *Progress Report*, pp. 119-20; *DFP*, Aug. 11, 1968.

77. Hudson address [Oct. 17, 1967], Hudson Papers; Hudson to Roy R. Lichta, Dec. 13, 1967, Hudson to Dear _____, n.d., ibid.; Mathewson, "Message," Feb. 23, 1968, ibid.; New Detroit Full Meeting, Oct. 12, 1967, Tag No. 21,

ND Papers; *DFP*, Sept. 22, Oct. 22, Nov. 6, 1967, Aug. 11, 1968; *MC*, Dec. 2, 1967, Jan. 25, 1968.

78. Graves, "New Detroit," pp. 115–16, 118–19; Press Release, June 10, 1968, Box 431, JPC Papers; New Detroit Release, Sept. 5, 1968, Box 456, ibid.; *DFP*, Nov. 6, 1967, Aug. 11, 1968; *NYT*, June 9, Aug. 7, 1968; *MC*, July 27, 1968; New Detroit, *Progress Report*, pp. 103–4, 122; New Detroit, "Beyond the Difference," p. 21, Box 516, Reuther Papers; New Detroit Committee Chronology, Apr. 4, 1968, Box 81, ND Papers.

79. "Summer 1968 in Detroit: A Survey of Attitudes toward Inner City Unrest," Box 456, JPC Papers; "New Detroit Committee," clipping in Hudson Papers; "Beyond the Difference," p. 53, Box 516, Reuther Papers.

80. *DFP*, Nov. 6, 1967, Aug. 11, 1968, Feb. 14, 1971; *NYT*, Jan. 16, 1968, July 23, 1970; New Detroit, *Progress Report*, pp. 128–29, 148; Review and Commentary . . . , Apr. 18, 1968, Hudson Papers; Judd Arnett column [May 23, 1968], ibid.; Serrin, "One Big City"; Davidson, "If We Can't Solve," p. 82; *Newsweek* 73 (June 2, 1969): 62; *Detroit Tribune*, Apr. 21, 1968; *DN*, July 23, 1972.

81. Graves, "New Detroit," pp. 186–87; Gooding, "Urban Race Riots," pp. 204–5; *DFP*, Feb. 14, 1971; Hill, "At the Crossroads," pp. 14–15; Conot, *American Odyssey*, pp. 604, 607–8; Steve Babson, *Working Detroit* (New York: Adama Books, 1984), p. 172; Hudson interview, pp. 34–35; *Ann Arbor News*, Apr. 12, 1987; Joe T. Darden et al., *Detroit, Race and Uneven Development* (Philadelphia: Temple University Press, 1987), pp. 46–49.

82. *DFP*, Nov. 6, 1967; *Business Week*, Feb. 3, 1968, p. 120, Aug. 2, 1969, p. 103; Graves, "New Detroit," pp. 620, 623–24, 627–35; Ursu interview with Hudson and Bianco, n.d., Series 59, Box 2, NACCD Records; Interview with Robert Potts, June 4, 1985, pp. 14–15, transcript in MHC; Interview with Arthur Johnson, July 23, 1984, pp. 44–48, ibid.; Mathewson, "Message," Hudson Papers; *DN*, Aug. 25, 1968; *MC*, July 23, 1977.

83. *DFP*, Aug. 25, Sept. 7, 1967; *Business Week*, Feb. 3, 1968, p. 128; *Newsweek* 71 (Jan. 1, 1968): 48, 50; *NYT*, Jan. 16, 1968; Task Force Leaders Meeting, Oct. 17 [1967], Tag No. 21, ND Papers; Graves, "New Detroit," pp. 593, 597–605; Hudson interview, p. 15; Conot, *American Odyssey*, pp. 541–42.

84. Locke, "The Detroit Primary . . . ," Sept. 20, 1969, Box 51, DUL Papers; Irving Bluestone to Walter Reuther, June 20, 1968, Locke to Reuther, June 30, 1969, Box 477, Reuther Papers; *DN*, Feb. 14, 1971.

85. "Summer 1968 in Detroit," Box 456, JPC Papers; *Return to 12th Street*, p. 16.

86. Marketing Opinion Research, "Image Study for New Detroit, Inc. (Analysis Report)," Apr. 1972, Box 11, Frank Angelo Papers, MHC. Marketing Opinion Research interviewed 500 adults over 18 years of age in the Detroit metropolitan area, only 19 percent of whom were black.

87. *DN*, Aug. 25, 1968. Cf. Feagin and Hahn, *Ghetto Revolts*, p. 254.

Chapter 19

1. Sheehan to Leonard Gordon, Oct. 16, 1967, Father Sheehan Correspondence, 1962–1969, Archives of the Archdiocese of Detroit, Detroit, Michigan; Edward L. Cushman to Cavanagh, Feb. 21, 1968, Box 453, JPC Papers.

2. Serrin, "Who Cares About Rebuilding the City?" *New Republic* 158 (May 4, 1968): 10–11; *NYT*, July 23, 1968; *Newsweek* 72 (July 29, 1968): 13.

3. "Summer 1968 in Detroit: A Survey of Attitudes toward Inner City Unrest," pp. 8, 9, 26, 28, Box 456, JPC Papers.

4. *The People Beyond 12th Street: A Survey of Attitudes of Detroit Negroes After the Riot of 1967* (Detroit: Detroit Urban League, 1967); *Return to 12th Street: A Follow-up Survey of Attitudes of Detroit Negroes, October 1968* [Detroit: Detroit Free Press, 1968], pp. 5, 8, 16–20.

5. Joel D. Aberbach and Jack L. Walker, *Race in the City* (Boston: Little, Brown and Co., 1973), p. 59; Howard Schuman and Shirley Hatchett, *Black Racial Attitudes* (Ann Arbor: University of Michigan Press, 1974), p. 9.

6. Serrin, "How One Big City Defeated Its Mayor," *NYT Magazine*, Oct. 27, 1968; *MC*, Mar. 22, 1969.

7. Serrin, "God Help Our City," *Atlantic Monthly* 223 (Mar. 1969): 115; Citizens Committee for Equal Opportunity (CCEO), "A Report to the People of Detroit . . . ," Sept. 1969, Box 477, Walter Reuther Papers, ALHUA; Locke, *The Detroit Riot of 1967* (Detroit: Wayne State University Press, 1969), p. 146.

8. The divorce for which Cavanagh's first wife had sued on July 18, 1967, became final in July 1968. The mayor had also had to endure a "humiliating" but unsuccessful lawsuit in which his sister-in-law charged him with assault. Cavanagh, additionally, had to contend with press allegations of Mafia connections. *DFP*, July 20, 1967, June 25, 1969; *Business Week*, Aug. 2, 1967, p. 103; Wesley Hills, "Mayor Cavanagh's Links to the Mafia," *Detroit Scope* 2 (June 7, 1969): 10–12, 20.

9. *DFP*, June 25, 1969; *NYT*, June 25, 1969; *MC*, July 5, 1969; *Life* 67 (Aug. 11, 1967): 60.

10. *DFP*, Nov. 5, 1969; *NYT*, Nov. 9, 19, 1969; B. J. Widick, *Detroit: City of Race and Class Violence* (Chicago: Quadrangle Books, 1972), pp. 206–8; Locke, "The Detroit Primary and the City's Racial Climate . . . ," Sept. 20, 1969, Box 477, Reuther Papers; CCEO, "Report to People," Sept. 1969, ibid.; Joe T. Darden et al., *Detroit, Race and Urban Development* (Philadelphia: Temple University Press, 1987), pp. 209–13.

11. Widick, *Detroit*, p. 208; *NYT*, July 23, 1971.

12. The Detroit Area Study put thirteen of the same questions to a sample of 619 blacks interviewed between April 24 and July 31, 1968, and a sample of 405 blacks surveyed between April 15 and September 20, 1971. Those interviewed were heads of households and wives of heads aged 21–69. Schuman and Hatchett, *Racial Attitudes*, pp. 2–3, 10. Aberbach and Walker derived their 1967 data from the Luby survey. Their 1971 sample of 348 whites and 170 blacks was similarly drawn from the Detroit directory. *Race in the City*, pp. 248–52.

13. Aberbach and Walker, *Race in the City*, pp. 46–49, 64; Schuman and Hatchett, *Black Racial Attitudes*, pp. 6–9; Otis Dudley Duncan et al., *Social Change in a Metropolitan Community* (New York: Russell Sage Foundation, 1973), pp. 98–103, 105.

14. *DFP*, July 23, 27, 1972, Nov. 7, 1973; Peter K. Eisinger, *The Politics of Displacement: Racial and Ethnic Transition in Three American Cities* (New York: Academic Press, 1980), pp. 64, 68; "Detroit: Some Post-Riot Progress . . . ," *Black Enterprise* 2 (Mar. 1972): 77, 83; Patrick James Ashton, "Race, Class and Black Politics: The Implications of the Election of a Black Mayor for the

Police and Policing in Detroit" (Ph.D. diss., Michigan State University, 1981), pp. 270–82, 320, 421; Darden et al., *Detroit*, p. 75.

15. *DFP*, Nov. 7, 1973; *NYT*, Dec. 5, 1983; Earl Nathaniel Gooding, "Urban Race Riots and Social Change: An Analysis of Two Cities" (Ph.D. diss., Vanderbilt University, 1977), p. 142; *DN*, June 28, 1987; Ashton, "Race, Class and Black Politics," pp. 301, 329–30, 333–38, 342–59, 366–71.

16. *USA Today* 107 (Oct. 1978): 2–3; *MC*, July 23, 1977; Alex Poinsett, "Motor City Makes a Comeback," *Ebony* 33 (Apr. 1978): 34, 36.

17. *DN*, May 20, June 28, 30, 1987; *DFP*, July 19, 1987; *Report of the Detroit Strategic Planning Project, November 1987*, preproduction ed. [Detroit: n.p., 1987], p. 57; Darden et al., *Detroit*, pp. 22–23, 54–62, 186–95.

18. *DN*, June 28, 29, 1987; *DFP*, July 19, 1987.

19. The Black Company, a Rochester firm, interviewed 1,200 randomly selected residents of the Detroit metropolitan area. Of these, 410 were black, and their responses were weighted to reflect the proportion of blacks in the area. The standard margin of sampling error was plus or minus 3 percent. *DN*, June 29, 1987.

20. Inter-University Consortium for Political and Social Research, Black File, No. 183, White File, No. 183, Detroit data for Angus Campbell and Howard Schuman, "Racial Attitudes in Fifteen American Cities," in *Supplemental Studies for the National Advisory Commission on Civil Disorders* (Washington: GPO, 1968); *DFP*, July 19, 1987; *DN*, May 20, June 7, 28–30, July 22, 1987. See chap. 3 for preriot dropout rates.

21. *DN*, May 18, June 28, 1987; *DFP*, July 19, 1987.

22. Aberbach and Walker, *Race in the City*, p. 54; *DN*, June 28, July 20, 1987; *DFP*, July 19, 1987.

23. *DN*, July 30, 1987; *DFP*, July 19, 1987.

24. "Summer 1968 in Detroit," p. 8, Box 456, JPC Papers; Black File, Nos. 241, 259, 272, 316, White File, No. 244, Detroit data for "Racial Attitudes."

25. *DFP*, Nov. 27, 1984. The sampling error in this survey was plus or minus three percent.

26. *DFP*, July 19, 1987.

Bibliography

Although I have listed virtually all the manuscript collections that I examined in the research for this book, I have made no attempt in the pages that follow to include all the published and unpublished items cited in the notes. I have confined myself primarily to material of particular value or interest for this study.

Manuscript Collections

Archives of Labor History and Urban Affairs, Detroit, Michigan. The single most important manuscript collection for the study of the Detroit riot and race relations in Detroit from 1962 to 1969 is the Jerome P. Cavanagh Papers. It is, in every respect, a splendid urban history collection. The Detroit Commission on Community Relations Papers contain a good deal of information on race relations in Detroit during the Cavanagh mayoralty. The minutes of the commission and its Field Division case reports are especially important. The Papers of the Detroit branch of the National Association for the Advancement of Colored People are valuable for the background and consequences of the riot, less so for the riot itself.

The George Edwards Papers and the Richard McGhee Papers contain a few items on the Detroit Police Department while Edwards was police commissioner. There is material in both the Remus G. Robinson Papers and the Detroit Public Schools, Division of Community Relations Papers bearing on public education issues in the 1960s. The Robinson Papers are an especially good source for the Northern High boycott. The Richard Austin Papers contain material on Detroit's war on poverty.

Some Hubert G. Locke files ended up in the Wayne State University, Office of Religious Administration Papers. The collection contains a good deal of information on the Citizens Committee for Equal Opportunity (CCEO) and the police and some items on the riot as well. There is additional material on the CCEO and on the police in the Horace W. Gilmore Papers. More CCEO data and a substantial amount of New Detroit documentation are included in the large collection of Walter Reuther Papers. The New Detroit Papers are valuable for every aspect of New Detroit activity in the 1960s but are thin on the committee's origins. The Papers of the United Community Services, the Metropolitan Detroit Council of Churches, and the American Civil Liberties Union–Metropolitan Detroit Branch all contain items relative to one or another aspect of the riot, its background, and its consequences.

Other Collections in Detroit. The Ray Girardin Papers in the Burton Historical Collection in the Detroit Public Library include, among other things, the Headquarters Activity Log and the Disorder Log compiled by the Police Department during the riot. There are one or two relevant items in the Records of the Detroit City Plan Commission, also in the Burton Historical Collection. Two important riot files survive in the Museums and Archives Unit of the Detroit Police Department, a large Algiers Motel File and a Commissioner's File. There are court files on the key legal cases arising from the riot in the Frank Murphy Hall of Justice of the Detroit Recorder's Court. Copies of many of these files are in my possession. The manuscripts in the unprocessed Archives of the Archdiocese of Detroit help to illuminate the role of the Catholic church in seeking to improve race relations and combat poverty in Detroit.

Michigan Historical Collections, Ann Arbor, Michigan. The George Romney Papers are indispensable for the study of the background of the Detroit riot, the riot itself, and the riot's aftermath. The collection sheds a good deal of light on the role of the State Police and the Michigan Guard in the riot. The Detroit Urban League Papers and the interrelated Francis A. Kornegay Papers contain a treasure trove of documents on racial matters during the Cavanagh mayoralty. The principal item in the Institute of Public Policy Studies, Aberbach-Walker Riot Studies is the completed questionnaires used in the Elliot Luby postriot survey. The remarks of interviewees on the questionnaires are of special interest. The Joseph L. Hudson Papers are a small but valuable supplement to the New Detroit Papers in the Archives of Labor History and Urban Affairs and are of critical importance for the beginnings of New Detroit. There is scattered information pertaining to the riot and Detroit in the 1960s in the Frank Angelo Papers, the Philip Hart Papers, the Josephine Gomon Papers, the Hobart Taylor Papers, and the Metropolitan Detroit Citizens Development Authority Papers.

Michigan History Division, State Archives, Lansing, Michigan. The Records of the Michigan Civil Rights Commission as they pertain to the Detroit riot are in three separate record groups: RG 74-90 (Civil Rights Commission—Administration); RG 80-17 (Civil Rights Commission—Detroit Office); and RG 83-55 (Civil Rights Commission—unprocessed). RG 77-45 (Records of the Michigan Department of Military Affairs—Public Information) and RG 78-125 (Military Affairs—Adjutant General Divison) contain material on the role of the Michigan Guard in the riot.

Lyndon Baines Johnson Library, Austin, Texas. The Subject Files, the Confidential File, the Aides Files (especially the Office Files of James Gaither and Joseph Califano), and the Name File of the White House Central Files all contain material relevant to the Detroit riot. The Appointment File, which is the "backup" for President Johnson's diary, includes some important riot documents. There is additional riot material in the Warren Christopher Papers and the Ramsey Clark Papers.

The Records of the National Advisory Commission on Civil Disorders (NACCD) include a mine of material on the Detroit riot. The summaries of interviews conducted by the Detroit field team, the witness depositions, transcripts of commission hearings, the three-volume Reconnaissance Survey Field Research Report on Detroit and the accompanying exhibits, and the Detroit Police Department and the relevant FBI files in the collection are all essential for an understanding of the Detroit riot.

Washington, D.C., Area Collections. The role of the United States Army in the Detroit riot is touched upon in one or another accession of the Records of the United States Army Commands (RG 338), the Records of the Office of the Secretary of the Army (RG 335), and the Records of the Army Staff (RG 319) in the Office of the Adjutant General, Department of the Army, Alexandria, Virginia. Paul J. Scheips collected a file of manuscripts pertaining to Task Force Detroit in the Center of Military History in Washington, D.C., that he permitted me to examine. The unpublished exhibits accompanying Permanent Subcommittee on Investigations of the Senate Committee on Government Operations, *Riots, Civil and Criminal Disorders, Hearings*, 90th Cong., 2d sess., 1968, are included in Records of the United States Senate (RG 46), in the National Archives and Records Administration.

Miscellaneous Manuscript Collections. The principal document of value regarding the riot in the Joseph A. Labadie Collection, University of Michigan Library, Ann Arbor, Michigan, is "Incidents of alleged police and Guard brutality reported at the time of the Detroit riot to Congressman John Conyers and the Detroit branch of the NAACP." There are also some miscellaneous items in the collection on black radicalism in Detroit. There are microfilm copies in the University of Michigan Library of the Daily Diary of President Johnson, 1963–1969, Minutes and Documents of the Cabinet Meetings of President Johnson, 1963–1969, and Civil Rights during the Johnson Administration, 1963–1969. File 20-762-67, the principal Michigan State Police file resulting from the Detroit riot, is available on film in State Police Headquarters in Lansing, Michigan.

The Winston Wessels Papers, copies of which are in my possession, are concerned with the role of the National Guard in the Detroit riot. There are a variety of documents pertaining to the riot in the Edward Lurie Papers, now in my possession. The Jonathan Rose Papers, in Mr. Rose's possession, relate to legal issues arising from the riot. The Maurice Kelman Papers, in Professor Kelman's possession, include a transcript of Ray Girardin's debriefing of Arthur Howison following the raid on the blind pig on Twelfth and Clairmount and some of the documents stemming from the work of the Mayor's Committee on the Administration of Justice during Civil Disorders. There are copies of these documents in my possession.

The Federal Bureau of Investigation, the Community Relations Service of the Department of Justice, and the Office of Legal Counsel of the same department provided me with numerous documents in response to Freedom of Information Act requests. The voluminous FBI files help to illuminate a point here and there, and there are a few important items among the Community Relations Service documents.

Interviews

The NACCD Records include summaries of interviews with more than sixty Detroiters. There are a few additional summaries of NACCD interviews in the Peter Rossi File, in my possession. The NACCD Records also include the depositions of fifteen Detroit witnesses. Conducted or sworn to shortly after the riot, the NACCD interviews and depositions are indispensable for an understanding of the Detroit riot. The Lyndon Baines Johnson Library Oral History Collection includes transcripts of interviews with Jerome P. Cavanagh, Warren Christopher,

Ramsey Clark, Charles C. Diggs, Jr., Harry McPherson, Cyrus Vance, and Roger Wilkins. There is a transcript of a Debriefing Conversation in March 1978 between General John L. Throckmorton and two army officers in the Center of Military History in Washington, D.C.

Nathan Caplan provided me with the transcripts of invaluable postriot interviews with four looters, a firebomber, the person who allegedly broke the first window in the riot, a riot arrestee, and one of the owners of the blind pig on Twelfth and Clairmount. Dr. Philip Mason supplied me with the transcript of a revealing 1971 interview of Ray Girardin conducted by Maurice Kelman and Ed Batchelor. Dr. Xavier Nicholas permitted me to copy the tapes or examine the transcripts of twenty-five riot interviews that he conducted in 1981 and 1982.

In addition to the above, I conducted interviews with James Bannon, William Cahalan, Ramsey Clark, Kenneth Cockrell, George Crockett, Jr., Karl Gregory, Arthur Howison, Joseph L. Hudson, Jr., Arthur Johnson, Henry Johnson, Damon Keith, James Lincoln, Richard Marks, John Nichols, Robert Potts, Mel Ravitz, George Romney, Robert Roselle, and Cyrus Vance. Transcripts of all these interviews have been deposited in the Michigan Historical Collections. Hubert Locke was good enough to provide written answers to a long list of my questions. General John Throckmorton responded to one of my questions by letter. George Edwards, Conrad Mallett, and Eugene Reuter answered some of my questions by telephone.

Newspapers

The *Detroit Free Press*, the *Detroit News*, the *New York Times*, and the *Michigan Chronicle*, Detroit's black weekly newspaper, are chock-full of information on race relations in Detroit in the 1960s and, especially, on the Detroit riot. Copies of the *Detroit Daily Press* and the *Detroit Daily Dispatch* for November 1967 to January 1968, a time when the two Detroit daily papers were on strike, are in the Burton Historical Collection. *Tuebor*, the publication of the Detroit Police Officers Association, the *Michigan Catholic*, and the *Detroit Jewish News* are also available in the Burton. There are copies of some issues of the *Illustrated News* in the Labadie Collection and the Remus G. Robinson Papers. A variety of newspapers are represented in two Detroit riot scrapbooks in the Michigan Historical Collections.

Government Documents

United States government. United States Department of Commerce, Bureau of the Census, *Census of Population and Housing, 1960, Final Report Series, Census Tracts, Detroit, Mich.* (Washington: GPO, 1961), contains vital demographic information on both riot-area and non-riot-area census tracts. There is a revealing picture of race relations in Detroit as of December 1960 in United States Civil Rights Commission, *Hearings, Detroit, Michigan*, December 14, 15, 1960 (Washington: GPO, 1961).

There is a good deal of information on Detroit's war against poverty in the following: Subcommittee on the War on Poverty Program of the House Committee on Education and Labor, *Economic Opportunity Act, Hearings*, 88th Cong., 2d sess., 1964, pt. 2; Subcommittee on Employment, Manpower, and Poverty of the Senate Committee on Labor and Public Welfare, *Examination of the War on Poverty, Hearings,* 90th Cong., 1st sess., 1967, pt. 1; and *Examination of the War on Poverty, Staff and Consultant Reports* Prepared for the Subcommittee on Employment, Manpower and Poverty of the Senate Committee on Education and Labor, 90th Cong., 1st sess., Committee Print, Sept. 1967, vol. 6. The latter contains a detailed appraisal of Detroit's war on poverty by the Center for Urban Studies of the University of Chicago. Poverty rate figures for Detroit are given in United States Bureau of the Census, *Current Population Report,* Series P-60, No. 18, "Poverty in the United States: 1959 to 1968" (Washington: GPO, 1969). Mayor Cavanagh provided information on housing in Detroit in volume 5 of the National Commission on Urban Problems, *Hearings,* 5 vols. (Washington: GPO, 1968).

Special Subcommittee of the House Committee on Armed Services to Inquire into the Capability of the National Guard to Cope with Civil Disturbances, *Hearings,* 90th Cong., 1st sess., 1967, is a major source for the operation of the National Guard in the Detroit riot. There is abundant information on Detroit before, during, and after the riot in Permanent Subcommittee on Investigations of the Senate Committee on Government Operations, *Riots, Civil and Criminal Disorders, Hearings,* 90th Cong., 2d sess., 1968, pts. 5–7.

The *Report of the National Advisory Commission on Civil Disorders* (Washington: GPO, 1968), contains, among other things, an account of the Detroit riot and a statistical profile of the self-reported Detroit rioters prepared for the commission by Nathan S. Caplan and Jeffrey M. Paige. The three *Supplementary Studies for the National Advisory Commission on Civil Disorders* (Washington: GPO, 1968): Angus Campbell and Howard Schuman, "Racial Attitudes in Fifteen American Cities"; Peter H. Rossi et al., "Between White and Black: The Faces of American Institutions in the Ghetto"; and Robert M. Fogelson and Robert B. Hill, "Who Riots: A Study of Participation in the 1967 Riots," make it possible to see the Detroit riot in a comparative sense. Data on Detroit available at the Inter-University Consortium for Political and Social Research in Ann Arbor, Michigan, enable one to compare racial attitudes in Detroit and in the other fourteen cities surveyed by Campbell and Schuman. The Fogelson and Hill study was based on arrestee data from seventeen riot cities; more than two-thirds of the arrests were in Detroit. United States Department of Labor, *The Detroit Riot: A Profile of 500 Prisoners,* March 1968, has additional information on Detroit riot arrestees.

Jerome H. Skolnick, *The Politics of Protest* (n.p. [1969]), a report of the Task Force on Violent Aspects of Protest and Confrontation to the National Commission on Causes and Prevention of Violence, has some pertinent observations on the response of the police and the courts to protest actions. James S. Campbell et al., *Law and Order Reconsidered* (Washington: GPO, 1969), a report to the same commission by the Task Force on Law Enforcement, includes information on legal problems stemming from the riot and the impact of the Detroit and other riots on United States Army preparations to cope with future civil disorders. There is a chapter on Detroit in Paul J. Scheips and Karl E. Cocke, *Army Operational and Intelligence Activities in Civil Disturbances since 1957,* rev. ed., 1971, Office of the Chief of Military History Study 73. The opinion of Federal District Court Judge Damon Keith in Baker et al. and Bratton et al. vs. City of Detroit et al. . . . . , United States District Court for the Eastern

District of Michigan, Southern Division, Civil Nos. 5–77937 and 5–72264, a manuscript copy of which is in my possession, is an invaluable source for Detroit Police Department recruitment policies both before and after the riot.

State of Michigan documents. House Special Committee to Investigate Irregularities in the Total Action against Poverty Program in the City of Detroit, "Examination of the War on Poverty," 74th Legislature, Regular Session of 1968, Committee Print, January 1968, contains a mass of information on Detroit's war on poverty. Michigan Civil Rights Commission, *Case Digest, 1964–1973*, includes several Detroit Police brutality cases. Report of the Michigan Commission on Crime, Delinquency and Criminal Administration [Jan. 3, 1968], a copy of which is in Box 327 of the Romney Papers, attributes the spread of the riot to organized effort. The measures enacted by the Michigan legislature in response to the Detroit riot are included in *Public and Local Acts of the Legislature of the State of Michigan Passed at the Regular Session of 1968* (Lansing: Department of Administration, n.d.).

City of Detroit documents. Findings and Recommendations of the Citizens Advisory Committee on Equal Educational Opportunities, abridged edition, Mar. 1962; "Report of the High School Study Commission," June 1968; and Samuel M. Brownell, *Pursuing Excellence in Education: The Superintendent's Ten Year Report, 1956–1966* (Detroit: Board of Education, 1966), provide essential information on public education matters in Detroit during the Cavanagh mayoralty. Mayor's Committee for Human Resources Development, "Developing Human Resources in the City of Detroit," March 1967, is a good general history of Detroit's war on poverty up to the time of the riot.

Mayor's Committee for Community Renewal, *Detroit: The New City* [Detroit, 1966], provides a picture of the state of housing in Detroit as of October 1966. Housing developments in Detroit during the Cavanagh years are reported in the quarterly reports of the Detroit Housing Commission, *Report to the Commissioners*. The annual reports of the Detroit Commission on Community Relations chart the course of civil rights and race relations in the city from 1962 to 1969. [Detroit Police Department] *Statistical Report on the Civil Disorder Occurring in the City of Detroit, July 1967*, which is the Police Department's report on the riot, is especially useful for the statistical information it contains. The *Annual Report of the Recorder's Court of the City of Detroit, Michigan, 1967*, and the similar report for 1968 reveal something of the impact of the Detroit riot on the city's criminal court.

Doctoral Dissertations

David Paul Boesel, "The Ghetto Riots 1964–1968" (Ph.D. diss., Cornell University, 1972), is an intelligent analysis of the 1960s riots, including the Detroit riot. Jeffrey Mayland Paige, "Collective Violence and the Culture of Subordination: A Study of Participants in the July 1967 Riots in Newark, New Jersey, and Detroit, Michigan" (Ph.D. diss., University of Michigan, 1968), analyzes the reasons for riot participation in the two cities that experienced the biggest riots in 1967. Natalie Motise Davis, "Blacks in Miami and Detroit: Communities in Contrast" (Ph.D. diss., University of North Carolina at Chapel Hill, 1976), compares Miami and Detroit in an effort to test the importance of community in the formation of black attitudes. Richard Alan Berk, "The Role of Ghetto Retail

Merchants in Civil Disorders" (Ph.D. diss., Johns Hopkins University, 1970), relies heavily on statistical data in appraising the treatment accorded ghetto merchants in ten riot cities, including Detroit, among the fifteen cities the author examines.

Patrick James Ashton, "Race, Class and Black Politics: The Implications of the Election of a Black Mayor for the Police and Policing in Detroit" (Ph.D. diss., Michigan State University, 1981), is especially valuable for the information that it provides on the reorganization of the Detroit Police Department once Coleman Young became Detroit's mayor. Harold Black, "Urban Renewal: A Program Involving a Multiplicity of Participants" (Ph.D. diss., University of Michigan, 1973), is critical of the administrative structure of Detroit's urban renewal program.

There is much undigested information concerning Detroit in Earl Nathaniel M. Gooding, "Urban Race Riots and Social Change: An Analysis of Two Cities" (Ph.D. diss., Vanderbilt University, 1977); Washington, D.C., is the other city Gooding examines. David John Olson, "Racial Violence and City Politics: The Political Response to Civil Disorders in Three American Cities" (Ph.D. diss., University of Wisconsin, 1971), provides a fine account of the Mayor's Development Team that Cavanagh appointed following the Detroit riot. Helen M. Graves, "New Detroit Committee/New Detroit, Incorporated: A Case Study of an Urban Coalition" (Ph.D. diss., Wayne State University, 1975), is the major study of the principal private-sector response to the Detroit riot.

Donald Lee Scruggs, "Lyndon Johnson and the National Advisory Commission on Civil Disorders: A Study of the Johnson Domestic Policy Making System" (Ph.D. diss., University of Oklahoma, 1980), explains how the Kerner Commission functioned. United States Army planning to deal with civil disturbances is described and appraised in James Richard Gardner, "The Civil Disturbance Mission of the Department of the Army: An Analysis of Perceptions, Policies, and Programs" (Ph.D. diss., Princeton University, 1977). Christopher Howland Pyle, "Military Surveillance of Civilian Politics, 1967–1970" (Ph.D. diss., Columbia University, 1974), points up the shortcomings of army intelligence during the Detroit riot.

Other Unpublished Material

There is an excellent analysis of politics in Detroit at the time Jerome P. Cavanagh became mayor in J. David Greenstone, "A Report on the Politics of Detroit" (1961). Tyrone Tillery provides a history of the Detroit Commission on Community Relations and its predecessor and successor organizations in "The Conscience of a City: A Commemorative History of the Detroit Human Rights Department, 1943–1983" [1983]. Charles West concludes that block clubs were not a riot deterrent in "The Role of Block Clubs in the Detroit Civil Disorder of July, 1967" (M.A. thesis, Wayne State University, 1970). The results of a survey of families in the model city neighborhood are presented in Robert B. Smock, "Inner-City Problems: The View from the Inside in Detroit in 1968" (1968). Leonard Milstein, "Jewish Merchants in Detroit's Prime Riot Affected Areas" [1968], available in the Burton Historical Collection, provides statistical information on the number of Jewish merchants in the major riot areas at the time of the riot and the number that survived the riot. Robert E. Smith, "How the News

Media Covered the Negro Rioting and Why," Oct. 1967, a copy of which is in Series 11, Box 1, of the NACCD Records, is the best general summary of the manner in which the Detroit media covered the riot.

"Final Report of Cyrus Vance Concerning the Detroit Riots, July 23 through August 2, 1967," includes a narrative of events regarding the army's role in helping to combat the Detroit riot, details the assistance the federal government provided Detroit, and comments on the administration of justice during the riot. There is a copy of the report in the Johnson Library. "After Action Report, Task Force Detroit, 24 July–2 August 1967," is a full account of army operations in Detroit during the riot. There is a copy of the document in the Records of the Michigan Department of Military Affairs, RG 78-125, State Archives Lansing, Michigan. "Results of Civil Disturbance Task Group Review of Report of Deputy Commander TF Detroit" [Sept. 1967], contains an elaborate analysis of the report of Major General Charles P. Stone on the performance of the Michigan Guard and the army in the riot and includes additional material on riot control training. The Center of Military History provided me with a copy of the document. Paul J. Scheips, "The Army and Civil Disturbances: Oxford and Detroit" [1982], a copy of which is in my possession, notes the similarities and differences between the use of federal forces in Oxford in 1962 and Detroit in 1967.

Paul Lowinger and Frida Huige, "The National Guard in the 1967 Detroit Uprisings" [1969], is based on a survey of the 182d Artillery, a unit that served in Detroit during the riot. Some of the legal issues resulting from riot arrests are among the topics considered in "The Detroit 'Riot': A Challenge to Society and the Legal Profession," the product of an October 11, 1967, discussion at the University of Michigan Law School by a panel comprised of Nathan S. Caplan, Judge John C. Emery, and Assistant State Attorney General William F. Bledsoe. There is a copy of the item in the University of Michigan Law Library. Robert B. Hill and Robert M. Fogelson extended their study of riot arrestees to include pre-1967 arrest data in "A Study of Arrest Patterns in the 1960s Riots," Final Progress Report, December 1969.

"Violence in the Model City" [1969], a copy of which is in Box 378 of the Cavanagh Papers, and "City in Crisis: The People and Their Riot" [1969], a copy of which is in the Detroit Public Library, are major studies of various aspects of the Detroit riot prepared under the direction of Dr. Elliot D. Luby. Longer versions are available of several of the chapters that make up the two works: James Hedegard, "Race Attitudes and Responses to the Riot in the Community" (in the Detroit Public Library); Sheldon D. Levy, "Communication Processes in the Detroit Riot" (in the Detroit Public Library); Luby and James Grisell, "Grievances of Detroit Negro Arrestees" (in the Detroit Public Library); Luby, "A Comparison between Detroit Negro Arrestees and a Riot Area Control Sample" (in the University of Michigan Library); Robert A. Mendelsohn, "The Police Interpretation of the Detroit Riot of 1967" (in Box 30 of the Wayne State University, Office of Religious Administration Papers), an especially valuable study; Luby, "Police and Jail Treatment of Detroit Negro Riot Arrestees" (in Box 427 of the Cavanagh Papers); [Mendelsohn, "Arrestee Interpretation of the Riot"] (in the Edward Lurie Papers, in my possession); and [Jacqueline Giering, "The Innocent Victims"] (in the Lurie Papers).

Published Sources

Federal policy. Allen J. Matusow, *The Unraveling of America: A History of Liberalism in the 1960s* (New York: Harper and Row, 1984), is a good introduction to federal policies in the 1960s that had their impact on Detroit. The shortcomings of the urban renewal program in the nation are explained in Lawrence M. Friedman, *Government and Slum Housing: A Century of Frustration* (Chicago: Rand McNally Co., 1968). The national context for Detroit's war on poverty can be gleaned from the following: Stephen M. David, "Leadership of the Poor in Poverty Programs," *Proceedings of the Academy of Political Science* 29 (1968): 91–98; J. David Greenstone and Paul E. Peterson, *Race and Authority in Urban Politics: Community Participation and the War on Poverty* (New York: Russell Sage Foundation, 1973); and Robert D. Plotnick and Felicity Skidmore, *Progress against Poverty: A Review of the 1964–1974 Decade* (New York: Academic Press, 1975).

Riots: General. There is a substantial social science literature on the riots of the 1960s. Some of the better periodical articles have been anthologized in the following: Louis H. Masotti and Don R. Bowen, eds., *Riots and Rebellion* (Beverly Hills: Sage Publications, 1968); James A. Geschwender, ed., *The Black Revolt* (Englewood Cliffs, N.J.: Prentice-Hall, 1971); David Boesel and Peter H. Rossi, eds., *Cities under Siege: An Anatomy of the Ghetto Riots, 1964–1968* (New York: Basic Books, 1971); and Harlan Hahn, ed., *People and Politics in Urban Society* (Beverly Hills: Sage Publications, 1974).

Three book-length studies that help to place the Detroit riot in its proper setting are Robert M. Fogelson, *Violence as Protest: A Study of Riots and Ghettos* (Garden City, N.Y.: Doubleday and Co., 1971); Ralph W. Conant, *The Prospects for Revolution: A Study of Riots, Civil Disobedience, and Insurrection in Contemporary America* (New York: Harper's Magazine Press Book, 1971); and, especially, Joe R. Feagin and Harlan Hahn, *Ghetto Revolts* (New York: Macmillan Co., 1973). Among the individual riot pieces, the following deserve special mention: Bryan T. Downes, "Social and Political Characteristics of Riot Cities: A Comparative Study," *Social Science Quarterly* 49 (Dec. 1968): 521–33; Downes, "A Critical Re-examination of Social and Political Characteristics of Riot Cities," *Social Science Quarterly* 51 (Sept. 1970): 349–60; Seymour Spilerman, "The Causes of Racial Disturbances: A Comparison of Alternative Explanations," *American Sociological Review* 35 (Aug. 1970): 627–49, which rebuts Downes; Spilerman, "The Causes of Racial Disturbances: Tests of an Explanation," *American Sociological Review* 36 (June 1971): 424–42; Spilerman, "Structural Characteristics of Cities and the Severity of Racial Disorders," *American Sociological Review* 41 (Oct. 1976): 771–93; Clark McPhail, "Civil Disorder Participation: A Critical Examination of Recent Research," *American Sociological Review* 36 (Dec. 1971): 1058–73, which challenges the deprivation-frustration-aggression interpretation of riot participation and much of the research as to why riots occurred; Morris Janowitz, "Patterns of Collective Racial Violence," in Hugh Davis Graham and Ted Robert Gurr, eds., *Violence in America: Historical and Comparative Perspectives* (New York: Bantam Books, 1969), pp. 412–44, which distinguishes between the "communal riots" during World War I and its aftermath and the "commodity riots" of the 1960s; and Peter

A. Lupsha, "On Theories of Urban Violence," *Urban Affairs Quarterly* 4 (Mar. 1969): 273-96, a critical summary of the principal riot theories.

Among the analyses of the forces of law and order in riot situations, one of the best is Gary T. Marx, "Civil Disorder and the Agents of Social Control," *Journal of Social Issues* 26 (Winter 1970): 19-57. Morris Janowitz deals with the same subject in *Social Control of Escalated Riots* (Chicago: University of Chicago Center for Policy Study [1968]), as does Carl C. Turner in "Planning and Training for Civil Disorders," *Police Chief* 35 (May 1968): 22-28. The confrontation between the police and the black ghettos is a central concern of the insightful, brief work by George Edwards, *The Police on the Urban Frontier* (New York: Institute of Human Relations, 1968). Robert M. Fogelson, "From Resentment to Confrontation: The Police, the Negroes, and the Outbreak of the Nineteen-Sixties Riots," *Political Science Quarterly* 83 (June 1968): 217-47; and Dennis Wenger, "The Reluctant Army: The Functioning of Police Departments in Civil Disturbances," *American Behavioral Scientist* 16 (Jan.-Feb. 1973): 326-42, are first-rate appraisals of the role of the police in coping with the civil disorders of the 1960s. Albert Bergesen is concerned with police misbehavior in "Race Riots of 1967: An Analysis of Police Violence in Detroit and Newark," *Journal of Black Studies* 12 (Mar. 1982): 261-74.

Other Riots. Detroit's 1943 riot is treated in the following: Alfred McClung Lee and Norman Raymond Humphrey, *Race Riot* (New York: Dryden Press, 1943); Robert Shogan and Tom Craig, *The Detroit Riot* (Philadelphia: Chilton Books, 1964); Harvard Sitkoff, "The Detroit Race Riot of 1943," *Michigan History* 53 (Fall 1969): 183-206; and Alan Clive, *State of War: Michigan in World War II* (Ann Arbor: University of Michigan Press, 1979). Lenora E. Berson, *Case Study of a Riot: The Philadelphia Story* (New York: Human Relations Press, 1966), deals with the Philadelphia riot of 1964, and Fred C. Shapiro and James W. Sullivan, *Race Riots: New York 1964* (New York: Thomas Y. Crowell Co., 1964), is concerned with the Harlem and Bedford-Stuyvesant riots of the same year. The major Watts riot of 1965 is treated in narrative form in Robert Conot, *Rivers of Blood, Years of Darkness* (New York: Bantam Books, 1967), and analytically in the excellent David O. Sears and John B. McConahay, *The Politics of Violence: The New Urban Blacks and the Watts Riot* (Boston: Houghton Mifflin Co., 1973). Nathan Cohen, ed., *The Los Angeles Riots: A Socio-Psychological Study* (New York: Praeger Publishers, 1970), summarizes the findings of the various members of the research team that studied the Watts riot. The principal studies of the Newark riot that immediately preceded the Detroit riot are Tom Hayden, *Rebellion in Newark* (New York: Random House, 1967), and Governor's Select Commission on Civil Disorder, *Report for Action* (n.p., Feb. 1968).

Detroit: General. The best general histories of Detroit for the 1960s are Robert Conot, *American Odyssey* (New York: William Morrow and Co., 1974); and B. J. Widick, *Detroit: City of Race and Class Violence* (Chicago: Quadrangle Books, 1972). There is a chapter on politics in Detroit in J. David Greenstone, *Labor in American Politics* (New York: Alfred A. Knopf, 1969). Steve Babson, *Working Detroit: The Making of a Union Town* (New York: Adama Books, 1984), deals with Detroit's blue-collar workers. There is a miscellany of information on racial, political, and urban development issues from 1940 to 1980 in Joe T. Darden et al., *Detroit, Race and Urban Development* (Philadelphia: Temple

University Press, 1987). Richard Child Hill, "At the Cross Roads: The Political Economy of Postwar Detroit," *Urbanism Past and Present* no. 6 (Summer 1978): 1-21, provides a brief overview of Detroit's economy in the three decades after World War II.

Detroit before the Riot. Tom Nicholson, "Detroit's Surprising Mayor," *Harper's* 227 (Dec. 1963): 76-82, is a laudatory piece on Jerome P. Cavanagh. Cavanagh comments on some of his successes in Fred Powledge, "The Flight from City Hall," *Harper's* 239 (Nov. 1969): 83-86. Stanley H. Brown, "Detroit: Slow Healing of a City," *Fortune* 71 (June 1965), views developments in Detroit under Cavanagh's leadership in favorable terms. The degree of residential segregation in Detroit in the 1960s is made evident in Albert J. Mayer and Thomas F. Hoult, "Race and Residence in Detroit," in Leonard Gordon, ed., *A City in Racial Crisis: The Case of Detroit Pre- and Post- the 1967 Riot* ([Dubuque, Iowa]: Wm. C. Brown Co., 1971), pp. 3-14; and T. F. Hoult, "About Detroit . . . We Told You So," *Crisis* 74 (Oct. 1967): 407-10. The thrust of Ralph V. Smith, "Behind the Riot," *American Education* 3 (Nov. 1967), is that social segregation accompanied residential segregation. Eleanor Paperno Wolf and Charles N. Lebeaux, *Change and Renewal in an Urban Community: Five Case Studies of Detroit* (New York: Frederick A. Praeger, 1969), is a study of urban renewal in Detroit and the reaction of relocatees.

Greenleigh Associates, "Home Interview Study of Low-Income Households in Detroit, Michigan" (New York, 1965), and Greenleigh Associates, "Study of Services to Deal with Poverty in Detroit, Michigan" (New York, 1965), provided background information about conditions in Detroit that influenced the character of Detroit's war on poverty. Detroit is one of the school districts examined in Marilyn Gittell and T. Edward Hollander, *Six Urban School Districts: A Comparative Study of Institutional Response* (New York: Frederick A. Praeger, 1968). National Commission on Rights and Responsibilities of the National Education Association of the United States, *Detroit, Michigan: A Study of Barriers to Equal Educational Opportunity in a Large City* (Washington, 1967), a copy of which is in Box 334 of the Cavanagh Papers, provides the essential facts about the interrelationship of public education policies and race in Detroit before the riot. Karl D. Gregory, the principal of the 1966 Freedom School, deals with the conditions that led to the Northern High boycott in "The Walkout: Symptom of Dying Inner City Schools," *New University Thought* 5 (Spring 1967): 29-54. The boycott itself is described and appraised in David Gracie, "The Walkout at Northern High," *New University Thought* 5 (Spring 1967): 13-28.

The Detroit Riot. The character of the principal riot area is examined in George Henderson, "Twelfth Street: An Analysis of a Changed Neighborhood," *Phylon* 25 (Spring 1964): 91-96; Harold Black and James D. Wiley, "Dissecting a Riot Neighborhood," *Nation's Cities* 6 (Sept. 1968): 18-20; and Ernest Harburg et al., "A Family Set Method for Estimating Heredity and Stress-I," *Journal of Chronic Diseases* 23 (1970): 69-81.

The principal general study of the riot is Hubert G. Locke, *The Detroit Riot of 1967* (Detroit: Wayne State University Press, 1969). This is, to some degree, an insider's history since Locke was the administrative assistant to the police commissioner at the time of the disturbance. Van Gordon Sauter and Burleigh Hines, *Nightmare in Detroit: A Rebellion and Its Victims* (Chicago: Henry Regnery Co., 1968), focuses on the forty-three individuals who were slain during the riot. The riot's cause célèbre is the subject of John Hersey, *The Algiers Motel Incident* (New York: Alfred A. Knopf, 1968), a poorly integrated work that nevertheless includes a good deal of valuable information. It was published before the legal proceedings stemming from the event had been completed. William Walter Scott III, the son of one of the owners of the blind pig at Twelfth and Clairmount and a riot participant, tells his story in *Hurt, Baby, Hurt* (Ann Arbor: New Ghetto Press, 1970). The rather frightening experience of a black photographer following his unjustified riot arrest is reported in Bob Clark, "Nightmare Journey," *Ebony* 22 (Oct. 1967): 121–30. Sidney Fine, "Chance and History: Some Aspects of the Detroit Riot of 1967," *Michigan Quarterly Review* 25 (Spring 1986): 403–23, was the initial statement of the results of some of my research on the riot.

The principal focus of the various contributors to Richard A. Chikota and Michael C. Moran, eds., *Riot in the Cities* (Rutherford, N.J.: Farleigh Dickinson University Press, 1970), is the legal issues surrounding the riot. The already noted Gordon, ed., *A City in Racial Crisis*, includes some useful pieces on the riot and racial issues in Detroit in the 1960s.

Isaac Balbus, *The Dialectics of Legal Repression: Black Rebels before the American Criminal Courts* (New York: Russell Sage Foundation, 1973), and "The Administration of Justice in the Wake of the Detroit Civil Disorder of July 1967," *Michigan Law Review* 66 (May 1968): 1544–1630, are indispensable sources for the various problems associated with the administration of criminal justice during and after the riot. Sidney Fine, "Rioters and Judges: The Response of the Criminal Justice System to the Detroit Riot of 1967," *Wayne Law Review* 33, no. 5 (1987): 1723–63, deals with the same general subject. William Cahalan, "The Detroit Riot," *Prosecutor* 3 (Nov.–Dec. 1967): 430–45, reports on the activities of the Wayne County prosecutor during the riot, and James H. Lincoln, *The Anatomy of a Riot: A Detroit Judge's Report* (New York: McGraw-Hill Book Co., 1968), does the same for the Juvenile Court.

The manner in which Detroit hospitals and particularly Detroit General Hospital responded to the riot is considered in the following articles: Alexander J. Walt et al., "The Anatomy of a Civil Disturbance," *JAMA* 202 (Oct. 30, 1967): 394–97; Larry Berkower, "Emergency Room Psychiatry during the Detroit Riot," *New Physician* 16 (Oct. 1967): 283–84; Louis Graff, "A New Kind of Hospital Disaster," *Michigan Hospitals* 3 (Aug. 1967): 24–27; and Maria C. Phaneuf and Paul Lowinger, "Healers in a Sick Society," *American Journal of Nursing* 68 (June 1968): 1283–84. Benjamin D. Singer, "Mass Media and Communication Processes in the Detroit Riot of 1967," *Public Opinion Quarterly* 34 (Summer 1970): 236–45, is concerned with the impact of the media on riot arrestees. American Newspaper Publishers Association, *Reporting the Detroit Riot* [New York, 1968], describes the *Detroit Free Press*'s coverage of the riot, and Bill Axtell does the same for radio station WXYZ in *Seven Days in July* (1968).

J. A. Lukas, "Postscript on Detroit: 'Whitey Hasn't Got the Message,' " *New York Times Magazine*, Aug. 27, 1967, is a superior journalistic account of some aspects of the riot. There are some revealing comments about the riot by the rioters themselves in Tom Parmenter, "Breakdown of Law and Order," *Trans-Action* 4 (Sept. 1967): 13–22. Garry Wills, *The Second Civil War* (New York: New American Library, 1968), includes information based on interviews on the performance of the Michigan Guard and the police during the riot. There are many discerning observations about the riot and its background in Barbara Wilson Tinker's novel, *When the Fire Reaches Us* (New York: William Morrow and Co., 1970). The riot also provides some of the context for the Joyce Carol Oates novel *Them* (New York: Vanguard Press, 1969). Joe Lapointe, "Six Days in July," *Detroit Monthly*, July 1987, is composed of reminiscences about the riot by various Detroiters.

There are two interesting chapters on the Detroit police in Harlan Hahn, ed., *Police in Urban Society* (Beverly Hills: Sage Publications, 1971). Police Commissioner Ray Girardin comments on the riot in "After the Riots: Force Won't Settle Anything," *Saturday Evening Post* 240 (Sept. 23, 1967): 10, 12. The reminiscences of a black police officer twenty years after the event are provided in "Black Cop," *Metropolitan Detroit*, July 1987. Billy Dansby, "Operation Sundown: Devastation in Detroit," *National Guardsman* 21 (Sept. 1967), defends the performance of the Guard in the riot. A quite different view of the Guard is presented in John Berendt, "From Those Wonderful People Who Gave You Kent State," *Esquire* 75 (Apr. 1971). David W. Jordan, "Civil Disturbance, A Case Study of Task Force Detroit, 1967," *Perspectives in Defense Management* (Aug. 1968): 21–36, although concerned primarily with the army, has some things to say about the performance of the police and the Guard in the riot. The problem of riot fires is considered in "Detroit Fires of 1967," *Firemen* 34 (Oct. 1967): 13–14.

There is a substantial amount of survey data on the purported rioters in addition to what has already been cited. Nathan S. Caplan and Jeffrey M. Paige, "A Study of Ghetto Rioters," *Scientific American* 219 (Aug. 1968): 15–21, is a good succinct account of survey data from Detroit and elsewhere to support the blocked-opportunity thesis. Caplan's "A New Ghetto Man: A Review of Recent Empirical Studies," *Journal of Social Issues* 26 (Winter 1970): 59–73, is based on similar data. The Detroit data drawn on by Caplan and Paige were derived from a survey of the riot areas just after the riot sponsored by the Detroit Urban League and published as *The People Beyond 12th Street: A Survey of Attitudes of Detroit Negroes after the Riot of 1967* (Detroit: Detroit Urban League, 1970). In "The Impact of City on Racial Attitudes," *American Journal of Sociology* 76 (Sept. 1970): 213–62, Howard Schuman and Barry Gruenberg base their conclusions on the Campbell-Schuman survey noted above.

The results of the Singer team's study of riot arrestees are published in their fullest form in Benjamin D. Singer et al., *Black Rioters: A Study of Social Factors and Communication in the Detroit Riot* (Lexington, Mass.: D.C. Heath and Co., 1970). *Black Rioters* supersedes Sheldon J. Lachman and Singer, *The Detroit Riot of 1967: A Psychological, Social and Economic Profile of 500 Arrestees* (Detroit: Behavior Research Institute, 1968). Some of the conclusions of the Singer team are nicely summed up in James A. Geschwender and Singer, "Deprivation and the Detroit Riot," *Social Problems* 17 (Spring 1970): 457–63.

Elliot D. Luby and James Hedegard, "A Study of Civil Disorder in Detroit," *William and Mary Law Review* 10 (1969): 586–630, is the principal published version of the Luby team's study of Detroit arrestees. Joel D. Aberbach and Jack L. Walker draw on the Luby sample for the 1967 data in their *Race in the City* (Boston: Little, Brown and Co., 1973).

Harlan Hahn is the author of several articles based on a modified probability sample survey of 270 Twelfth Street black adults following the riot. Among these, "Cops and Rioters: Ghetto Perceptions of Social Conflict and Control,"

American Behavioral Scientist 13 (May–Aug. 1970): 761–99, an especially important piece, deals with Twelfth Street reactions to the police before and after the riot. "Black Separatists: Attitudes and Objectives in a Riot-Torn Ghetto," *Journal of Black Studies* 1 (Sept. 1970): 30–53, concludes that blacks living in a riot area were more likely than other blacks to favor separation rather than integration. "Ghetto Sentiments on Violence," *Science and Society* 33 (Spring 1969): 197–208, compares Twelfth Street survey results with the Campbell-Schuman data.

Charlotte Darrow and Paul Lowinger, "The Detroit Uprising: A Psychological Study," in Jules H. Masserman, ed., *The Dynamics of Dissent* (New York: Greene and Stratton, 1968), pp. 120–33, is based on a study of 222 militants, most of whom were out on the streets during the riot. Irving J. Rubin relates the Detroit riot to the rising expectations thesis in "Analyzing the Detroit Riot: The Causes and Responses," *Reporter* 38 (Feb. 22, 1968): 34–35. The results of Donald I. Warren's study of neighborhoods and rioting are set forth in "Neighborhood Structure and Riot Behavior in Detroit: Some Exploratory Findings," *Social Problems* 16 (Spring 1969): 464–84; and "Neighborhood Status Modality and Riot Behavior: An Analysis of the Detroit Disorders of 1967," *Sociological Quarterly* 12 (Summer 1971): 350–68.

Lyndon Johnson singles out the Detroit riot for comment in his memoirs, *The Vantage Point: Perspectives on the Presidency, 1963–1969* (New York: Holt, Rinehart and Winston, 1971). Roger Wilkins, who came to Detroit during the riot as head of the Community Relations Service, recalls the disturbance in his autobiography, *A Man's Life* (New York: Simon and Schuster, 1982). In his memoirs, *A Political Education* (Boston: Little, Brown and Co., 1972), Harry McPherson comments on Abe Fortas's part in the Johnson speech belaboring George Romney. The impact of the Detroit and other riots on federal policymaking is assayed in James W. Button, *Black Violence: Political Impact of the 1960s Riots* (Princeton: Princeton University Press, 1978); John T. Elliff, *Crime, Dissent, and the Attorney General: The Justice Department in the 1960s* (Beverly Hills: Sage Publications, 1971); and Kenneth O'Reilly, "The FBI and the Politics of Riots, 1964–1968," *Journal of American History* 75 (June 1988): 91–114.

Postriot Detroit. Albert Cleage's views are set forth in *The Black Messiah* (New York: Sheed and Ward, 1968); "Transfer of Power," *Center Magazine* 1 (Mar. 1968): 44–46; and William Serrin, "Cleage's Alternative," *Reporter* 38 (May 30, 1968): 29–30. Hal DeLong, "Detroit Remembers July 1967 . . . ," *Police* 12 (May–June 1968): 6–12, is concerned with postriot police preparations for a possible future disturbance. The Mayor's Development Team is one of the commissions examined in Michael Lipsky and David J. Olson, *Commission Politics: The Processing of Racial Crisis in America* (New Brunswick, N.J.: Transaction Books, 1977), which draws on Olson's thesis. William Serrin has contributed three discerning, critical pieces on postriot Detroit: "Who Cares about Rebuilding the City?" *New Republic* 158 (May 4, 1968): 10–11; "How One Big City Defeated Its Mayor," *New York Times Magazine*, Oct. 27, 1968; and "God Help Our City," *Atlantic* 223 (Mar. 1969): 115–21. There are several articles in the magazine *Detroit Scope* bearing on postriot developments in the city.

New Detroit's efforts to bring racial peace to Detroit are recounted in Joseph L. Hudson, "In the Aftermath of the Long, Hot Summer of 1967," *Michigan Courthouse Review* 17 (Dec. 1967); New Detroit, *Progress Report, April, 1968*

[Detroit: n.p., 1968]; Earl Selby, "Detroit's Realistic Response to Riot," *Reader's Digest* 93 (Dec. 1968): 189–96; New Detroit, "Beyond the Difference" (Nov. 1969), a copy of which is included with the *Michigan Chronicle* of Nov. 29, 1969; and *New Detroit, A Decade of Progress, 1967–1977* (reprint; New York: New York Times, 1977). Gertrude Samuel, "Help Wanted: The Hard Core Unemployed," *New York Times Magazine*, Jan. 28, 1968, deals with the efforts of New Detroit and Detroit employers to hire the unemployed, and Herbert R. Northrup, *The Negro in the Automobile Industry* (Philadelphia: Wharton School of Finance and Commerce, 1968), indicates what the automobile manufacturers did in this regard. Bill Davidson, "If We Can't Solve the Problems of the Ghetto Here . . . ," *Saturday Evening Post* 24 (Oct. 5, 1968): 29–33, indicates the various ways the automobile companies sought to help alleviate ghetto problems after the riot. The efforts of New Detroit to promote black business are described in Ann Scott, "Report from Detroit," *Fortune* 81 (Feb. 1970): 71–72.

Marilynn Rosenthal summarizes the rumors that spread in Detroit in the winter of 1967–68 and led to the creation of the city's Rumor Control Center in "When Rumor Raged," *Trans-Action* 8 (Feb. 1971): 34–43. The Police Department's response to the disturbance in Detroit following the assassination of Martin Luther King is set forth in Detroit Police Department, *Report on Civil Emergency, April 5th–April 11th, 1968* [1968], a copy of which is available at police headquarters. Donald I. Warren deals with the inflamed media response to the New Bethel incident in "Mass Media and Racial Crisis: A Study of the New Bethel Church Incident in Detroit," *Journal of Social Issues* 28 (1972): 111–31. The decision to decentralize the Detroit public schools is considered in William R. Grant, "Community Control vs. School Integration—the Case of Detroit," *Public Interest* no. 24 (Summer 1971): 62–79. Detroit is one of the six cities examined in Commission on the Cities in the 1970s, *The State of the Cities* (New York: Praeger Publishers, 1972).

Return to 12th Street: A Follow-up Survey of Attitudes of Detroit Negroes, October 1968 [Detroit: Detroit Free Press, 1968]; surveys the response of the riot areas to developments in Detroit a little more than a year after the riot. A comparison between racial attitudes in Detroit in 1967 and 1971 is drawn in Aberbach and Walker, *Race in the City*, and between 1968 and 1971 in Howard Schuman and Shirley Hatchett, *Black Racial Attitudes* (Ann Arbor: Survey Research Center, 1974).

Index

A&P, 72, 202
ABC, 184, 238
Aberbach, Joel, 329, 456, 460
Accelerated Public Works Act, 18
Accord, 383
Active Community Teams, 113
Ad Hoc Action Group, 414, 416, 421
Ad Hoc Committee of Clergymen
  Concerned with the Elimination of
  Discrimination in Employment, 23
Ad Hoc Committee Concerned with
  Equal Educational Opportunities, 44
Ad Hoc Committee on Community
  Peace, 141-42
Adult and Youth Employment Program,
  82-83, 84, 91
Adult Community Movement for
  Equality, 29, 30, 133; and police, 29,
  136-37
Afro-American Development
  Foundation, 446
Afro-American Unity Movement, 136;
  and Kercheval miniriot, 137, 139,
  140-41
Afro-American Workshop Program,
  440
Afro-American Youth Movement, 136,
  137; and Kercheval miniriot, 139-40,
  140-41
Alcohol Tax Division, 252
Aldridge, Dan, 285-86, 380, 403
Algiers Motel incident, 229, 245, 267,
  270, 271, 553 n. 28; and motel
  occupants, 271-72; and sniping
  reports, 271-72, 272-73, 274-75, 279,
  282; and Hersey book, 272, 287; and
  entry of law enforcement personnel,
  273-74, 275; and Cooper death,

275-77; and Temple death, 277-78;
  and Paille confession, 277, 285,
  286-87; and beatings, 278-79; and
  knife game, 279; and mock
  executions, 279-80; and Pollard
  death, 280; and police failure to
  report, 281; and Homicide
  investigation, 281-82, 283-84; and
  role of press, 282-83; and Dismukes
  trial, 284; and homicide warrants,
  284-85; and August and Paille
  preliminary examination, 285; and
  state conspiracy charge, 285, 287, 288;
  and mock trial, 285-86, 554 nn. 44,
  45; and Michigan Supreme Court
  cases, 287; and August trial, 287-88,
  289, 555 n. 54; and federal conspiracy
  trial, 288-90; and civil damage suit,
  290; and reinstatement of August and
  Senak, 290; and fate of motel, 290
Alinsky, Saul, 30
Allen, Roy, 141, 375, 377, 411
Ambassador Bridge, 226
American Civil Liberties Union,
  Metropolitan Detroit Branch, 15, 106,
  243, 258, 267, 409-10, 416-17, 419,
  422
American Institute of Architects, 34
American Insurance Association, 291,
  296, 297
American Legion, 384
American Motors, 7
American Red Cross, 318
Angelo, Frank, 371
Anti-Defamation League, 293, 295
Apprentices, 7, 44, 47, 48-49
Archbishop's Committee on Human
  Relations, 22-23, 26

623